# Introduction to AutoCAD® 2009
## A Modern Perspective

**Paul Richard**

*Clackamas Community College*

**Jim Fitzgerald**

*Octavian Scientific Corporation*

PEARSON

Prentice
Hall

Upper Saddle River, New Jersey
Columbus, Ohio

Library of Congress Control Number: 2008 921114

**Editor in Chief:** Vernon R. Anthony
**Acquisitions Editor:** Jill Jones-Renger
**Editorial Assistant:** Doug Greive
**Production Coordination:** Lisa S. Garboski, bookworks publishing services
**Project Manager:** Louise Sette
**AV Project Manager:** Janet Portisch
**Operations Specialist:** Deidra Schwartz
**Art Director:** Diane Ernsberger
**Cover Designer:** Jason Moore
**Cover Image:** Super Stock
**Director of Marketing:** David Gesell
**Senior Marketing Coordinator:** Alicia Dysert
**Copyeditor:** Terry Andrews

This book was set by Aptara, Inc. It was printed and bound by Bind-Rite Graphics. The cover was printed by Coral Graphic Services, Inc.

Certain images and materials contained in this publication were reproduced with the permission of Autodesk, Inc. © 2008. All rights reserved. Autodesk and AutoCAD are registered trademarks of Autodesk, Inc., in the U.S.A. and certain other countries.

**Disclaimer:**
The publication is designed to provide tutorial information about AutoCAD® and/or other Autodesk computer programs. Every effort has been made to make this publication complete and as accurate as possible. The reader is expressly cautioned to use any and all precautions necessary, and to take appropriate steps to avoid hazards, when engaging in the activities described herein.

Neither the author nor the publisher makes any representations or warranties of any kind, with respect to the materials set forth in this publication, express or implied, including without limitation any warranties of fitness for a particular purpose or merchantability. Nor shall the author or the publisher be liable for any special, consequential, or exemplary damages resulting, in whole or in part, directly or indirectly, from the reader's use of, or reliance upon, this material or subsequent revisions of this material.

Pearson Education Ltd., London
Pearson Education Singapore, Pte. Ltd
Pearson Education Canada, Inc.
Pearson Education–Japan

Pearson Education Australia Pty, Limited
Pearson Education North Asia Ltd., Hong Kong
Pearson Educación de Mexico, S.A. de C.V.
Pearson Education Malaysia, Pte. Ltd.

10 9 8 7 6 5 4 3 2 1
ISBN-13: 978-0-13-603454-4
ISBN-10:     0-13-603454-3

# THE NEW AUTODESK DESIGN INSTITUTE PRESS SERIES

Pearson/Prentice Hall has formed an alliance with Autodesk® to develop textbooks and other course materials that address the skills, methodology, and learning pedagogy for the industries that are supported by the Autodesk® Design Institute (ADI) software products. The Autodesk Design Institute is a comprehensive software program that assists educators in teaching technological design.

## Features of the Autodesk Design Institute Press Series

**JOB SKILLS**—Coverage of computer-aided job skills, compiled through research of industry associations, job websites, college course descriptions, and the Occupational Information Network database, has been integrated throughout the ADI Press books.

**PROFESSIONAL** and **INDUSTRY ASSOCIATIONS INVOLVEMENT**—These books are written in consultation with and reviewed by professional associations to ensure they meet the needs of industry employers.

**AUTODESK LEARNING LICENSES AVAILABLE**—Many students ask how they can get a copy of the AutoCAD® software for their home computer. Through a recent agreement with Autodesk®, Prentice Hall now offers the option of purchasing textbooks with either a 180-day or a 1-year student software license agreement for AutoCAD. This provides adequate time for a student to complete all the activities in the book. The software is functionally identical to the professional license, but is intended for student personal use only. It is not for professional use.

Learning licenses may only purchased by ordering a special textbook package ISBN. Instructors should contact their local Pearson Professional and Career sales representative. For the name and number of your sales representative please contact Pearson Faculty Services at 1-800-526-0485.

This text presents a modern approach to using AutoCAD. That is, it addresses advances in technology and software evolution and introduces commands and procedures that reflect a modern, efficient use of AutoCAD 2009. Features include:

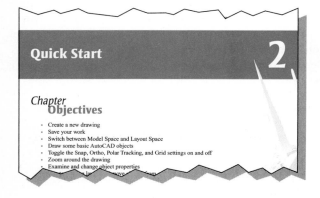

A "Quick Start" chapter at the beginning of the book allows users to get up to speed in no time to create and even plot AutoCAD drawings. Quick Start topics and concepts are linked to corresponding chapters later in the book, providing a motivational preview and allowing the user to delve into detailed topics of instruction as they choose, at their own pace.

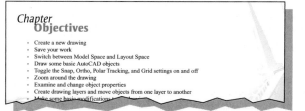

Chapter Objectives, a bulleted list of learning objectives for each chapter, provide users with a roadmap of important concepts and practices that will be introduced in the chapter.

Key Terms are boldfaced and italicized within the running text, briefly defined in the margin, and defined in more detail in the Glossary at the end of the book to help students understand and use the language of the computer-aided drafting world.

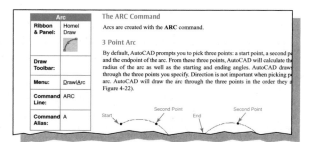

Command Grids appear in the margin, alongside the discussion of the command. These grids provide a visual of the action options using the Standard Toolbar, Menu, Command Line, or Command Alias, ensuring that the student is in the right place at the right time and correctly following the authors' direction.

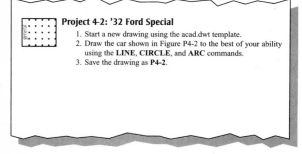

Discipline Icons are placed in the margin alongside each project and identify the discipline to which each project applies: General, Mechanical, Architectural, Electrical, Plumbing/HVAC, or Civil. These icons allow instructors to quickly identify homework assignments that will appeal to the varying interests of their students and allow students to work on projects that have the most interest and relevance depending on their course of study.

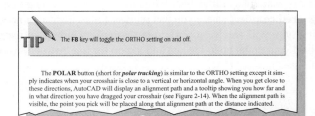

### The AutoCAD User Interface

Because AutoCAD is a program for drawing, the focal poi
dow. This is where you create your drawing. Everything els
you accomplish this task. Figure 1-14 shows the major fea

A New to AutoCAD 2009 icon flags features that are new to the 2009 version of the AutoCAD software, creating a quick "study guide" for instructors who need to familiarize themselves with the newest features of the software to prepare for teaching the course. Additional details about these new features can be found in the Online Instructor's Manual.

**TIP** The **F8** key will toggle the ORTHO setting on and off.

The **POLAR** button (short for *polar tracking*) is similar to the ORTHO setting except it simply indicates when your crosshair is close to a vertical or horizontal angle. When you get close to these directions, AutoCAD will display an alignment path and a tooltip showing you how far and in what direction you have dragged your crosshair (see Figure 2-14). When the alignment path is visible, the point you pick will be placed along that alignment path at the distance indicated.

TIP, NOTE, and FOR MORE DETAILS boxes highlight additional helpful information for the student.

### SUMMARY

You have now walked through a typical AutoCAD drawing session. Although your drawing sessions will no doubt be different and most likely involve a variety of more complex tasks, the exercises in this chapter give you an idea of what is

involved in working with AutoCAD. The tasks y
in this chapter will be built on and expanded in t
text. You should now feel fairly comfortable n
AutoCAD workspace and drawing some basic o

### CHAPTER TEST QUESTIONS

**Multiple Choice**
1. Model space is:
   a. Only for three-dimensional objects.
   b. Limited in size so you must scale your model appro-

   c. Pan the drawing up and down.
   d. Zoom the drawing in and out.
6. Which of the following is NOT a property o

End-of-Chapter material, easily located by shading on page edges, provides:

- Summaries
- Test Questions
- Projects

to help students check their own understanding of important chapter concepts.

### Exercise 2-25: Adjusting Dimensions

1. Change the **Viewport Scale** back to 1:1 on the Status Bar. T
   scale of 1:1, and the dimension features are scaled down by ha
2. Choose the **Undo** tool to set the scale back to 1:2.
3. Click on the icon with the lightning bolt to the right of the **V**
   shown in Figure 2-54. Turn it on so that all scale representatio
   are shown when it is selected and grips are turned on.
4. Use grips to relocate the dimensions so that they no longer overl
5. Double-click outside the viewport to close the viewport and sv
6. Save your drawing as **EX2-25**.

Exercises throughout the chapters provide step-by-step walk-through activities for the student, allowing immediate practice and reinforcement of newly learned skills.

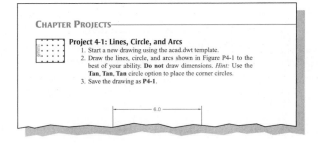

### CHAPTER PROJECTS

**Project 4-1: Lines, Circle, and Arcs**
1. Start a new drawing using the acad.dwt template.
2. Draw the lines, circle, and arcs shown in Figure P4-1 to the best of your ability. **Do not** draw dimensions. *Hint:* Use the **Tan, Tan, Tan** circle option to place the corner circles.
3. Save the drawing as **P4-1**.

Projects are organized by discipline to allow for application of skills to various fields, and numbered consistently among the chapters for easy back-and-forth reference. The 12 end-of-chapter projects require students to use all the commands and skills they have learned cumulatively. Project types include:

- Mechanical B-Size Title Borders/Annotation symbols
- Architectural D-Size Title Borders/Annotation symbols
- Electrical schematics
- Plumbing/HVAC schematics
- Architectural plans
- Architectural details
- Mechanical—English
- Mechanical—Metric
- Civil plans
- Civil details

A CD, bound into the textbook, contains student data files.

## INSTRUCTOR RESOURCES

The Online Instructor's Manual provides answers to chapter exercises and tests and solutions to end-of-chapter problems; drawing files to get users started; and lecture-supporting PowerPoint slides.

To access supplementary materials online, instructors need to request an instructor access code. Go to **www.pearsonhighered.com/irc,** where you can register for an instructor access code. Within 48 hours after registering, you will receive a confirming e-mail including an instructor access code. Once you have received your code, go to the site and log on for full instructions on downloading the materials you wish to use.

## STUDENT RESOURCES

Companion Website—A Companion Website at **www.prenhall.com/richard** for student access includes an interactive study guide.

# Preface

We live in digital world where the trend in technology is to duplicate reality as much as possible. As time goes on, more and more industries and fields require the use of AutoCAD drafting and design software. AutoCAD has long been, and will remain, the industry standard for generating top-of-the-line CAD drawings in the least amount of time possible.

*Introduction to AutoCAD® 2009: A Modern Perspective* offers a complete guide for students and professionals who want to enter the interesting world of computer-aided drafting using AutoCAD. This book covers all aspects of the AutoCAD program's 2D tools, from the basic concepts to the most powerful tools used in design and engineering.

In this book, readers will find an interesting combination of theory and many complex projects and exercises, as well as many clear and descriptive illustrations. Real design problems starting from scratch will be solved throughout the projects. In addition, many other short exercise sections are included to ensure full comprehension of the commands.

Concepts are explained clearly in easy-to-understand language and are accompanied by descriptive illustrations, which will help the reader to understand each topic and to speed up the learning process. By following the steps in each project, readers will see results immediately and will understand the development process as they go along, rather than just entering instructions.

After using this book, readers will realize that AutoCAD is the premier software for generating 2D drawings. Its ease of use, combined with its ability to create complex drawings, makes it the first choice among many design and drafting professionals.

## About This Book

This book can serve as a reference for designers, draftspersons, or anyone with a basic knowledge of technical drawing who wants to learn how to use the AutoCAD program to create their work. The projects and the exercise sections are designed to enhance and help the reader retain the content learned in each chapter.

You do not need to be an expert draftsperson to use this book, but you should have some drafting background. This book focuses more on using AutoCAD as a tool for creating 2D CAD drawings. Occasionally, industry standards are referenced as they relate to a topic. Unfortunately, it is impossible to address standards thoroughly because each industry and discipline is different.

It is also assumed that you have some knowledge of computers and basic file management. Because some of the topics in the later chapters are rather technically advanced, having some computer background is helpful. A basic technical background is required because AutoCAD has many Internet and network-enabled features that facilitate the sharing of electronic information.

In addition to learning the basic AutoCAD tools, you will also learn to recognize and use these tools to achieve specific goals. A number of challenging end-of-chapter projects from varying disciplines progress through multiple chapters so you can see how a drawing is put together from beginning until end. Brief definitions of the commands involved, as well as notes containing tips and warnings, will give you extra help in understanding the commands.

## Chapter Organization

The book is organized into seven parts that advance in complexity as you go through each chapter. Each subsequent chapter is meant to build on the preceding chapters so you can see the steps typically taken to create a set of drawings from start to finish.

### PART ONE – An Introduction to AutoCAD

*Chapter 1: Introduction to AutoCAD* introduces you to fundamental CAD concepts and the AutoCAD interface.

*Chapter 2: Quick Start* allows you to hit the ground running so that you learn the basics necessary to start a new drawing, create and modify some objects, add annotation features, and print out your work. All topics are then explained in detail in the subsequent chapters.

## PART TWO – Drafting Skills: Drawing with AutoCAD

*Chapter 3: Controlling the Drawing Display* shows you how to move around in a drawing by panning and zooming. It also introduces some different display performance settings.

*Chapter 4: Basic Drawing Commands* provides an overview of the basic drawing commands such as **LINE** and **CIRCLE** so you can create a simple drawing.

*Chapter 5: Drawing Tools and Drafting Settings* explains the different drawing tools and settings available to help you create and modify your work.

*Chapter 6: Managing Object Properties* shows how to set up and apply different layer systems and manage other object properties.

## PART THREE – Understanding Editing Techniques: Basics Through Advanced

*Chapter 7: Basic Editing Techniques* explains how to select groups of AutoCAD objects that can be modified as a single unit. Grips are introduced to teach you how to modify objects directly by simply selecting them in your drawing.

*Chapter 8: Advanced Editing Techniques* introduces some of the more advanced modify commands that allow you to perform complex operations.

## PART FOUR – Working with Complex Objects

*Chapter 9: Drawing and Editing Complex Objects* looks at creating and editing complex polyline-based objects with multiple line segments.

*Chapter 10: Pattern Fills and Hatching* provides information about incorporating different predefined pattern fills and hatch patterns into your drawings to create filled areas.

## PART FIVE – Annotating Drawings

*Chapter 11: Adding Text* shows the different ways to manage and create text in a drawing.

*Chapter 12: Working with Tables* explains how to insert and modify different types of tables in a drawing, including those linked to Microsoft Excel spreadsheets and those extracted from object information in a drawing.

*Chapter 13: Dimensioning Drawings* outlines the different dimensioning tools and shows how to manage their appearance using dimension styles.

## PART SIX – Outputting Your Work

*Chapter 14: Managing Paper Space Layouts* shows you step by step how to set up paper space layouts for plotting using industry standard techniques, including multiple layouts and multiple scaled viewports.

*Chapter 15: Plotting and Publishing* provides an overview of the different plotting tools and settings, including how to batch plot a group of drawings using the **PUBLISH** command.

## PART SEVEN – Advanced Drawing and Construction Methods

*Chapter 16: Blocks and Block Attributes* explains how to create complex named symbols that can be inserted anywhere in a drawing or drawings. Dynamic block attribute text examples are explained to show how to update individual blocks quickly, as well as extract alphanumeric information to a table or external file.

*Chapter 17: Working with External References* shows you how to reference external files (drawings, images, DWF, and DGN files) into your current drawing so that you can coordinate and communicate work without having to open the referenced file.

*Chapter 18: File Management Tools and Object Linking and Embedding* provides an overview of AutoCAD's Drawing Utilities for fixing and/or restoring drawings. Object linking and embedding is explained so that you can share information with other Windows programs.

## Acknowledgments

We would like to thank the following individuals, who reviewed this book:

*Reviewers*

Dr. Beverly K. Jaeger
Northeastern University College of Engineering

Randal Reid
Chattahoochee Technical College

Howard M. Fulmer
Villanova University

Scott Anthony Boudreau
Joliet Junior College

Charles Kimball
City College of San Francisco, CA

Dennis Hughes
CS Mott Community College, MI

Dr. Robert Cobb, Jr.
North Carolina A&T State University

Dr. Tony E. Graham
North Carolina A&T State University

Gene Fosheim
Lake Washington Technical College, WA

Harold S. Lamm
San Antonio College, TX

James Freygang
Ivy Tech Community College, IN

John Knapp
Metro Community College, NE

John L. Irwin, EdD
Michigan Technological University

Jon Bridges
Lane Community College, OR

Leland Scott
Baker College of Owosso, MI

Lloyd W. Lunde
Southeast Technical Institute

Marsha Walton
Finger Lakes Community College, NY

Mary Tolle
South Dakota State University, SD

Michael B. Daniels
Western Piedmont Community College, NC

Paul Clarke
MiraCosta College, CA

Richard Garthe
Kalamazoo Valley Community College, MI

Tony Thomas
Amarillo College

*Content Contributors*

**Appendix A**
Dr. Gerald L. Bacza
Coordinator and Professor: Drafting/Design/CAD Engineering Technology
Fairmont State Community and Technical College

**Appendices B through E**
Marsha Walton
Finger Lakes Community College, NY

**Chapter 17: Working with External References**
Craig Stinchcomb
Terra Community College, OH

**Chapter 18: File Management and Object Linking and Embedding**
Kelly Keala
Clackamas Community College, OR

**Drawings and Drawing Expertise**
Hennebery Eddy Architects, Inc.

Kimi Barham
Student, Clackamas Community College, OR

Jason Lee Strother
Student, Clackamas Community College, OR

*Supplements*

**Companion Website**
Brian Maitland
Pittsburgh Technical Institute

**PowerPoint Presentation**
Craig Stinchcomb
Terra Community College, OH

**Transition Guides**
Jon Bridges
Lane Community College, OR

Kelly Keala
Clackamas Community College, OR

Craig Stinchcomb
Terra Community College, OH

| Text Element | Example |
|---|---|
| **Key terms—Boldface** and *italic* on first mention (first letter lowercase, as it appears in the body of the text). Brief definition in margin alongside first mention. Full definition in Glossary at back of book. | Views are created by placing *viewport* objects in the paper space layout. |
| **AutoCAD commands**—Bold and uppercase. | Start the **LINE** command. |
| **Ribbon and panel names, palette names, Toolbar names, menu items, and dialog box names**—Bold and follow capitalization convention in AutoCAD toolbar or pull-down menu (generally first letter cap). | The **Layer Properties Manager** palette<br><br>The **File** menu |
| **Panel tools, Toolbar buttons and dialog box controls/buttons/input items**—Bold and follow the name of the item or the name shown in the AutoCAD tooltip. | Choose the **Line** tool from the **Draw** panel.<br><br>Choose the **Symbols and Arrows** tab in the **Modify Dimension Style** dialog box.<br><br>Choose the **New Layer** button in the **Layer Properties Manager** palette.<br><br>In the **Lines and Arrows** tab, set the **Arrow size:** to **.125**. |
| **AutoCAD prompts**—Dynamic input prompts are italic. Command window prompts use a different font (Courier New) and are not italicized. This makes them look like the text in the command window. Prompts follow capitalization convention in AutoCAD prompt (generally first letter cap). | AutoCAD prompts you to *Specify first point:*<br><br>AutoCAD prompts you to *Specify next point or* ↓.<br><br>Specify center point for circle or [3P/2P/Ttr (tan tan radius)]: |
| **Keyboard input**—Bold with special keys in brackets. | Type **3.5 <Enter ↵>** |

# Contents

## Chapter 12    Working with Tables

## Chapter 13    Dimensioning Drawings

# PART SIX    *Outputting Your Work*

## Chapter 14    Managing Paper Space Layouts

## Chapter 15    Plotting and Publishing

## Part Seven    *Advanced Drawing and Construction Methods*

## Chapter 16    Blocks and Block Attributes

## Chapter 17    Working with External References

Chapter 18        File Management Tools and Object
                        Linking and Embedding

## Appendix A

## Appendix B

## Appendix C

## Appendix D

## Appendix E

# Introduction to AutoCAD

**1**

## Chapter Objectives

- Explore CAD's uses and benefits
- Understand fundamental CAD concepts
- Start AutoCAD
- Tour the AutoCAD user interface
- Explore the different AutoCAD data input methods
- Display and manipulate multiple AutoCAD drawings simultaneously
- Maximize AutoCAD's online Help System and InfoCenter features

## INTRODUCTION

This textbook is designed to allow you to "hit the ground running" using AutoCAD so that you can quickly start creating accurate technical drawings using accepted industry drafting standards. The next chapter (Chapter 2, Quick Start) shows you the minimum you need to know in order to create and plot an AutoCAD drawing starting from scratch. These introductory concepts and techniques are then linked to detailed information about each topic so you can explore them at your own pace.

Before you can do any of that though, we need to cover some basics. This chapter introduces you to some fundamental CAD concepts and the AutoCAD ***user interface*** so you are prepared to hit the ground running in Chapter 2.

**user interface:** The commands and mechanisms the user interacts with to control a program's operation and input data.

## WHAT IS CAD?

In a little over a generation's time the methods used to create technical drawings have fundamentally changed from using pencil and paper to the use of Computer Aided Drafting, better known as CAD. The analog world of drafting boards, T squares, triangles, and even the romantic french curve (see Figure 1-1) has given way to the brave new digital world of computers. No longer must you refill your mechanical pencil when you run out of lead, find your eraser when you make a mistake, or walk across the room to share a design with another person.

Using CAD, you can draw something once and copy it hundreds, or even thousands, of times. Changing a design can be as simple as pushing a button. Drawings can be shared instantaneously across the room or even around the world over a computer network. These and the other benefits of CAD include the following:

- Increased productivity
  - Drawing content can be continuously reused.
  - Text and dimensions can be created and updated automatically.
  - Hatch and pattern fills can be placed with a single pick of the mouse.
  - Revising and editing drawings can be done quickly with minimum effort.

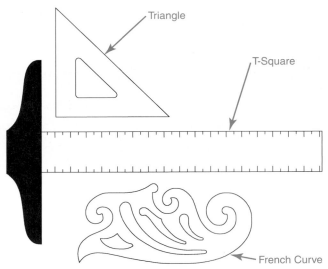

Figure 1-1     A T square, a triangle, and a french curve

- Improved precision
  - Digital information is accurate to 14 decimal places.
  - Geometry is precisely located using the Cartesian coordinate system.
  - It is possible to snap to control points and features on existing drawing geometry to accurately locate drawing information.
  - Polar and object tracking features can be utilized for precise angular measurements.
- Better collaboration
  - Drawings can be shared across a network (locally and globally).
  - Drawings can be referenced and updated in real time with notification.
  - Revisions and markups can be managed electronically via email and Internet-based document management systems.
- 3D visualization and analysis (see Figure 1-2.)

Figure 1-2     Sample 3D rendering created in AutoCAD

- 3D animations and walk-throughs can be easily generated to allow you and potential clients to visualize a design before it is constructed.
- Interference checking can be done to ensure that parts do not run into each other before they are created.
- Engineering calculations such as Finite Element Analysis (FEA) and other structural calculations can be performed automatically.
- Computer prototypes can be created and tested, eliminating the time and materials needed to manufacture a real-world prototype.

All these benefits are explored in this textbook, except for 3D visualization and analysis, which is beyond the scope of this text. The following chapters explain how to utilize the tools provided in AutoCAD to create and share the most accurate technical drawings in the quickest and most efficient manner. Using AutoCAD you will learn how to do the following:

- Set up and lay out different types of AutoCAD 2D drawings using AutoCAD model space and paper space techniques.
- Quickly create accurate 2D drawing information using AutoCAD's precision drafting aids.
- Edit and modify 2D drawing information in a productive fashion.
- Annotate and dimension drawings using AutoCAD's automated annotation and dimensioning features.
- Create section views utilizing AutoCAD's predefined and custom hatch and pattern fills.
- Utilize and manage CAD standards including:
    - Layers
    - Linetypes
    - Text styles
    - Dimension styles
- Coordinate drawing information with other team members using external reference files.
- Create and manage symbol libraries using AutoCAD's DesignCenter and Tool Palettes.
- Output your drawings to different plotting devices with specific colors and lineweights.
- Share information with other Windows Office applications using Object Linking and Embedding (OLE).

## FUNDAMENTAL CAD CONCEPTS

Because CAD-based drafting is a digital pursuit, some of the concepts that apply to its analog "on the board" cousin are a bit different. It is important that you are aware of and understand these concepts before we begin any drawing.

### Drawing Actual Size

Board drafting requires that you select a scale before you begin a drawing. This is to ensure that whatever it is that you are drawing fits properly on the selected paper, or **sheet size**.

Large objects are scaled down so that you can see the complete design on the sheet while smaller objects are scaled up so that you can clearly discern finer details.

Unlike drawing on the board, CAD-based drafting does not require design information to be scaled as it is drawn. Everything is drawn actual size as it exists in the real world. This means that the layout of a floor plan that is $100'\text{-}0'' \times 50'\text{-}0''$ is actually drawn $100'\text{-}0''$ long $\times$ $50'\text{-}0''$ wide in AutoCAD. The scaling process occurs when the drawing is being set up to be printed or plotted to ensure that your drawing fits properly on the desired sheet size.

**sheet size:** The size of the paper on which a drawing is printed or plotted.

**FOR MORE DETAILS**    See Appendix A for detailed information about standard sheet sizes.

Using CAD, you have a theoretically infinite amount of space within your CAD drawing file to create your design. A drawing can be as large as our entire solar system or small enough to fit on the head of a pin. To help navigate within this infinite drawing space, AutoCAD provides a number of display tools that allow you to zoom and pan around a drawing similar to the zoom and pan functions found on a camera. This allows you to zoom up close to your drawing for detailed work or zoom out so that you can view the complete drawing.

**Note:**

Annotation features like text and dimensions have their own unique scaling issues. You must typically scale annotation features so that they appear at the correct size in relation to the actual size drawing you are creating. For instance, 1/8"-high text appears as a tiny speck next to a 100'-0"-long wall. AutoCAD now has an **Annotation Scale** feature that helps automate the process. This feature is explained later in the "Annotation Scale" section.

| **FOR MORE DETAILS** | AutoCAD's display tools are described in detail in Chapter 3. |
|---|---|

## The Cartesian Coordinate System

The primary means of locating information in an AutoCAD drawing is the Cartesian coordinate system. The Cartesian coordinate system is a grid-based system where points are represented by their $X$ and $Y$ coordinate values separated by a comma as follows:

$X,Y$

For example, a point located at $X = 4$ and $Y = 2$ is represented as follows:

4,2,

There is also a $Z$ coordinate, but we'll talk about that later. For now, think of your computer screen as a 2D sheet of paper where the origin of the coordinate system (0,0) is in the lower left-hand corner of your screen as shown in Figure 1-3.

Positive $X$ and $Y$ coordinate values are represented in the upper right quadrant of the grid. Because it is easiest to work with positive coordinates exclusively, this is where most of your drawings will be created.

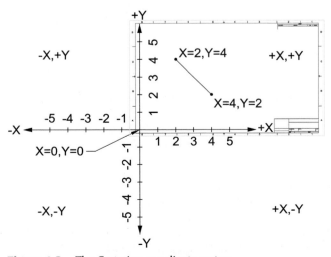

Figure 1-3    The Cartesian coordinate system

## Right-Hand Rule

As alluded to earlier, the Cartesian coordinate system also has a $Z$ coordinate that is used to locate points in 3D space. The $Z$-axis runs perpendicular to the $XY$ plane shown in Figure 1-3.

The easiest way to represent this concept is to rely on what is known as the ***right-hand rule***—it's as easy as 1-2-3.

To start, clench your right hand into a fist with your palm facing towards you.

1. Extend your thumb to the right.
2. Uncurl your pointer finger so that it points straight up.
3. Uncurl your middle finger so that it points towards you.

Your hand should now look similar to the one shown in Figure 1-4. Using the right-hand rule, your thumb represents the positive $X$-axis, your pointer finger represents the positive $Y$-axis, and your middle finger represents the positive $Z$-axis.

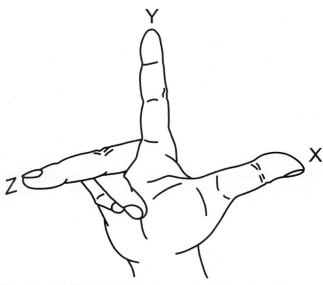

**Figure 1-4**    The right-hand rule

Your palm, and by extension, your computer screen, represents the 2D $XY$ plane where $Z=0$. Using this analogy, positive $Z$ values are towards you, or above the screen, while negative $Z$ values are away from you, or into the screen.

By default, the $Z$ coordinate value is set to 0. Because of this, there is no need to specify a $Z$ coordinate value when you locate 2D points. If the $Z$ coordinate is omitted, it is interpreted as 0. For instance, to locate a 2D point where $X = 4$ and $Y = 2$, you can enter either of the following:

4,2,0    or    4,2

Of course, it makes sense to type the least amount as possible, so all examples in this book rely on the shorthand version.

 **TIP**    In AutoCAD, the default Cartesian coordinate system explained in this section is referred to as the ***World Coordinate System***, or ***WCS***. It is possible to change the origin and orientation of the X, Y, and Z axes for high-level drawing operations by creating your own temporary ***User Coordinate System***, or ***UCS***. Creating and modifying User Coordinate Systems are beyond the scope of this book. For more information, please consult the AutoCAD help.

**right-hand rule:** Easy-to-understand reference that can be used to determine the positive and negative direction of the *X*, *Y*, and *Z* axes.

**World Coordinate System (WCS):** The default coordinate system in AutoCAD upon which all objects and user coordinate systems are based.

**User Coordinate System (UCS):** A user-defined variation of the World Coordinate System.

## Grid Units

In AutoCAD, one unit on the Cartesian coordinate grid system can represent whatever you want it to represent. A unit can be 1 inch, 1 foot, 1 millimeter, 1 meter, 1 nautical league, or even 1 **parsec**.

parsec: A unit of astronomical length.

Fortunately for us, the majority of the drafting and design world works in either inches (Imperial) or millimeters (Metric) where the following applies:

**Imperial:**

1 grid unit = 1 inch

**Metric:**

1 grid unit = 1 millimeter

There are of course exceptions to this unwritten rule, most notably the civil design field. Because civil engineers work with drawings that cover large areas (parcel plans, highway plans, etc.), it is common for them to work in decimal feet or decimal meters where the following applies:

**Imperial:**

1 grid unit = 1 foot

**Metric:**

1 grid unit = 1 meter

Unless otherwise noted, most of the examples and drawing problems in this book will rely on 1 unit = 1 inch for Imperial type drawings and 1 unit = 1 millimeter for Metric type drawings.

The default drawing setup in AutoCAD is an Imperial-type drawing where 1 grid unit = 1 inch. Setting a drawing up for the Metric system where 1 grid unit = 1 millimeter is described in Chapter 4.

## Angle Measurement

By default, angles in AutoCAD are measured counterclockwise from 0°, which is due east, or right, on the positive *X*-axis as shown in Figure 1-5. Using this system of angle measurement, 90° is north, 180° is west, and 270° is south. It is possible to change the default 0° base angle to any

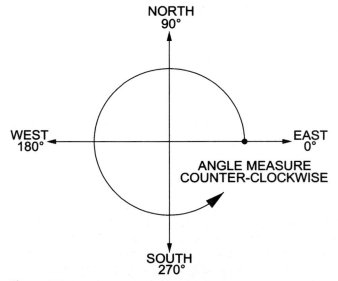

**Figure 1-5**    AutoCAD base angle and direction

of the other three compass directions, or a custom angle, as well as change the default angle measurement direction from counterclockwise to clockwise.

AutoCAD provides five different types of angle unit settings so you can enter angles in a format that applies to the type of work you are doing. Most architects and engineers prefer angles in decimal units (i.e., 45.00°), or degrees, minutes, and seconds (i.e., 45°00′00″), while those in the civil engineering world rely on surveyor units (i.e., N45°0′0″E).

---

**FOR MORE DETAILS**   Setting different angle unit settings as well as setting a different base angle and angle direction is described in Chapter 4.

---

**TIP**   You can also enter negative angle measurements when working in AutoCAD to input an angle that is measured in the clockwise direction. For example, an angle of 315° can also be entered as −45°.

---

## Exercise 1-1: Using Cartesian Coordinates

1. Using pencil and paper, lay out a Cartesian coordinate grid system similar to the one shown in Figure 1-3.
2. Draw a line from the coordinate point (2,1) to the coordinate point (4,5).
3. Draw a line from the origin (0,0) at an approximate angle of 135° to the edge of the grid.
4. Draw a line from the coordinate point (−2,−1) to the origin (0,0).
5. Draw a line from the origin at an approximate angle of −30° to the edge of the grid.

## Annotation Scale

As mentioned earlier in the section "Drawing Actual Size," the lines, circles, and other geometry that represent your design are drawn to their exact "real-world" specifications; the scaling occurs when you set your drawing up to plot on the desired sheet size.

To accommodate this scaling process, the size of annotation features such as text and dimensions must be adjusted accordingly when they are added to your drawing. This ensures that they print out at the correct size after they are scaled up or scaled down. Most organizations rely on drafting standards that define specific text heights, arrowhead sizes, and other annotation specifications so that drawings maintain a consistent appearance. The proper scaling of annotation features is very important so that drafting standards are always maintained.

As an example, annotation features on a drawing that is going to be scaled to 1/2 of its original size when it is printed must be scaled up by the reciprocal of 1/2, or 2 times, when they are created. With this in mind, if your drafting standards require that text print out 1/8″ high, you must apply the following formula:

1/8″ × 2 = 1/4″ high text

When the drawing is then plotted, the 1/4″-high text is scaled by 1/2 and prints out at the correct standard text height of 1/8″. See Figure 1-6. In this example, 2 is considered the scale factor. The *scale factor* is the reciprocal of the plotted scale. Calculating the scale factor in the preceding example is easy because the plotted scale is a simple ratio of 1:2. It's obvious that the reciprocal of 1:2 is 2.

**scale factor:** Multiplier that determines the size of annotation features when a drawing is plotted or printed.

---

**FOR MORE DETAILS**   See Appendix A for more information about standard annotation specifications and the steps necessary to calculate other scale factors, based on standard drawing scales. Appendix A also contains a list of the most common standard drawing scales, their corresponding scale factor, and even suggested text sizes and dimension scales.

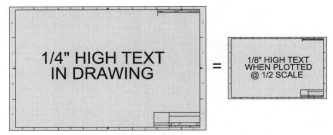

**Figure 1-6**    1/4″ text scaled to 1/8″ at plot time

Calculating, *and applying,* scale factors for all the different annotation-type objects can be a tedious, time-consuming process. Fortunately, it is possible to automate the process using the AutoCAD **Annotation Scale** feature. Annotation objects such as text and dimensions have an **Annotative** property that, when enabled, automatically scales the objects according to the scale selected. The **Annotation Scale** is controlled via an easily accessible list of the same standard drawing scales found in Appendix A. Annotation objects can even have more than one **Annotation Scale** so that they are displayed at the correct size on multiple different scale drawings!

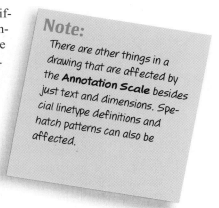

**Note:**
There are other things in a drawing that are affected by the **Annotation Scale** besides just text and dimensions. Special linetype definitions and hatch patterns can also be affected.

| FOR MORE DETAILS | See Chapter 6 for details regarding scaling linetype definitions. See Chapter 10 for more information about scaling hatch patterns. See Chapter 11 for more information about the **Annotation Scale** feature. |
|---|---|

## Object Properties

In AutoCAD, the lines, circles, text, dimensions, and just about everything else that make up a drawing are commonly referred to as *objects.* All these drawing objects have properties associated with them that control their appearance and behavior. Some properties are unique to a particular type of object, especially properties that relate to an object's geometry. For example, a circle object has a radius, whereas text has a height. Other object properties are shared by all the objects in a drawing. These general object properties are introduced in the following sections.

*Layers.*    Before the advent of CAD, drafters and designers coordinated their drawings by physically overlaying them on top of each other. The paper, known as *vellum,* was translucent so that as you layered each drawing on top of the previous one, the drawing(s) underneath were still visible. This allowed the drafters and designers to compare the work on each individual drawing and coordinate them as a complete system. See Figure 1-7.

Flash forward to the digital world of the twenty-first century. Using CAD, this concept of physically "layering" multiple drawings one on top of another has morphed into the ability to separate distinct drawing information using named layers. Typically, the name of the layer reflects the type of information that resides on it. For instance, a layer named **WALL** might contain drawing information that relates to the walls of a floor plan, while a layer named **DOOR** might contain the lines and arcs that represent the doors. In fact, numerous standard layer-naming conventions and guidelines have been created that allow people to share CAD drawings and understand what type of drawing information resides on each layer.

CAD-based layers provide much more functionality and control than their analog vellum-based cousins. Layers in CAD can be turned off and on so that you can create multiple views of

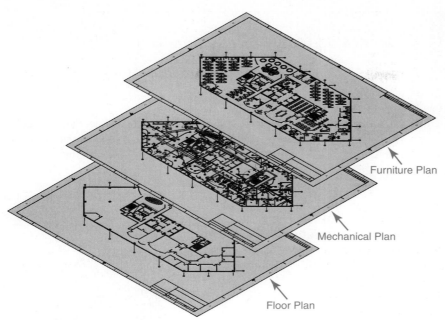

Furniture Plan

Mechanical Plan

Floor Plan

**Figure 1-7**    Overlay drafting

your drawing information. For instance, text and dimensions can be put on their own unique layers so that they can be turned off when you want to concentrate on your design. Similar drawing information can be grouped on specific layers so that you can coordinate between different disciplines. The electrical wiring might be located on a layer named **ELEC** while the mechanical heating ductwork might be located on a layer named **HVAC**. Basically, layers give your drawings a level of intelligence that allows you to indicate what objects in a CAD drawing represent in the real world.

Besides controlling the visibility of drawing information, layers also can be used to control the color, linetype, and lineweight of an object. You can even use layers to determine whether an object is plotted or not.

**FOR MORE DETAILS**    Layer property management is discussed in greater detail in Chapter 6.

## Colors

Colors serve two purposes in an AutoCAD drawing:

1. They separate drawing information so that it is easily identifiable on the computer screen.
2. They allow printing and plotting with specific line thicknesses.

The first use of colors is fairly obvious. One of the easiest ways to differentiate between different drawing information on the computer screen is by using color. You might set up your drawing so that all the walls are green, the doors are blue, and the text is yellow. This color coding makes your drawing easier to comprehend and work with.

The second use of colors might seem a bit obscure to many new AutoCAD users—to control line thicknesses when plotting. This use of colors was introduced very early on in AutoCAD's life as one of the only means of plotting a drawing with varying line thicknesses, a necessity for most organizations. This color-based approach to controlling lineweights is still in use today because of the time and effort necessary to update legacy systems. For this reason, it is a good idea to at least have a basic understanding of how the color-based approach works.

> **FOR MORE DETAILS**  See Appendix A for detailed information about standard line thicknesses.

Without getting into too much detail, color-based plotting is based on the fact that each color in AutoCAD is associated with an integer value. This relationship is referred to as the *AutoCAD Color Index,* or *ACI.* The ACI consists of 255 colors numbered from 1 to 255, with the first seven colors represented as follows:

1 = Red

2 = Yellow

3 = Green

4 = Cyan

5 = Blue

6 = Magenta

7 = White

**plot style:** A collection of property settings that is applied when the drawing is plotted to control the appearance of the drawing objects on the printed drawing.

> **Note:**
> There is another approach to controlling line thicknesses on a plot using **plot styles**. It is possible to assign a unique plot style directly to an object that will control the object's appearance on the printed page.

In the early days, plotting was done on pen plotters using numbered ink pens with varying pen tip sizes that created different line thicknesses. The numbered plotter pens were associated with the information in the drawing via the object's color. For example, red drawing objects plot with pen #1 because the color red = 1 in AutoCAD's Color Index. This color–to–plot pen relationship is referred to as a plotter's "pen mapping." Thankfully, this antiquated approach to controlling plotter pens is quickly being heaped on the trash bin of history as the much simpler approach of using AutoCAD's lineweight property becomes more popular.

> **FOR MORE DETAILS**  Plotting with lineweights and plot styles is discussed in detail in Chapter 15.

## Linetypes

Manually drawing objects with different linetypes on the board is a very tedious process, if not an art form. A mechanical pencil and a scale must be utilized so that you can accurately measure out the dashes, dots, and/or gaps over the distance of a line.

> **FOR MORE DETAILS**  See Appendix A for a detailed description of different linetype standards.

Fortunately, AutoCAD provides more than 40 different predefined linetypes that can be applied directly to your line work with a click of a button. Figure 1-8 shows examples of linetypes that come with AutoCAD.

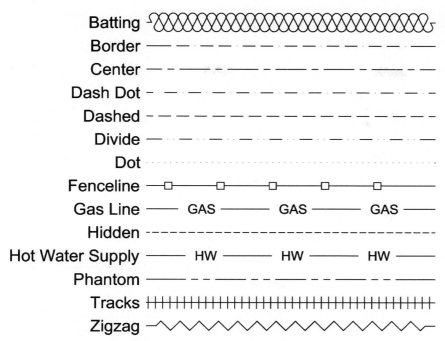

**Figure 1-8**    Examples of default AutoCAD linetypes

The dashes, dots, and gaps that make up a linetype definition are also affected by the scale factor described earlier. Their size must be adjusted to accommodate the plot scale in the same fashion as the other annotation features in order for them to print out at the right size.

**FOR MORE DETAILS**    Linetypes and linetype scaling is explained in detail in Chapter 6.

## Lineweights

In AutoCAD, the term *lineweight* is used to refer to a line's thickness. Different drafting standards dictate how line thicknesses should be applied in technical drawings.

Drawing different line thicknesses on the board requires that you use different pencils with different lead thicknesses. AutoCAD provides graphical lineweights that you can assign to your line work, which allows you to see different line thicknesses on the screen *before* you plot your drawing. There are more than 20 different lineweights available in both Imperial (inches) and Metric (millimeters) format.

**FOR MORE DETAILS**    See Appendix A for detailed information regarding line thickness drafting standards. AutoCAD lineweights are discussed in detail in Chapter 6.

*Controlling Object Properties.*    The common approach to controlling the general object properties discussed in the previous sections is to set the desired object property active, or current, before drawing an object. An object assumes the current object properties when it is drawn. This does not mean you cannot change an object's properties after it is drawn. In fact, there is a multitude of tools in AutoCAD to help you accomplish this.

| FOR MORE DETAILS | Controlling AutoCAD object properties is discussed in detail in Chapter 6. |
| --- | --- |

### Exercise 1-2: Researching CAD Layer Guidelines

1. Using the Internet, search for Websites with information about the "AIA layer guidelines." *(Note: AIA is the abbreviation for the American Institute of Architects.)*
2. Describe the AIA layer-naming scheme and how it is organized.
3. Find an example of at least one other layer standard or guideline.

## Model Space and Paper Space

AutoCAD has two distinct drawing environments: model space and paper space. Model space is the 3D drawing environment described in the "Cartesian Coordinate System" section earlier that is used for the drawing *model*, or 3D representation of your design. Model space contains most of the line work, text, and dimensions that make up a drawing.

**model:** The geometry (lines, circles, etc.) created in a drawing that defines the object or objects drawn.

Paper space is the 2D environment used for laying out different views of the model space information on a standard sheet size and scale for plotting purposes. This 2D page setup is known as a layout in AutoCAD and typically consists of one or more views of your drawing along with a border and title block.

Metaphorically speaking, an AutoCAD paper space layout can be thought of as a 2D sheet of paper that hovers over your 3D model space drawing. Scaled views are created by cutting holes in the paper so you can see the 3D drawing model below. See Figure 1-9.

**layout:** 2D page setups created in paper space that represents the paper size and what the drawing will look like when it is printed.

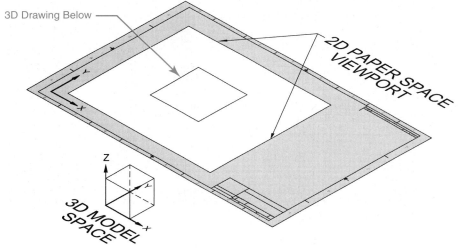

**Figure 1-9**   Model space and paper space

It is possible to have multiple layouts in an AutoCAD drawing. Each layout can be a different sheet size and can also contain multiple scaled views.

| FOR MORE DETAILS | Layouts and views are discussed in detail in Chapter 14. |
| --- | --- |

# A FIRST LOOK AT AUTOCAD

Now that we have the preliminaries out of the way, it's time to start AutoCAD so we can take the grand tour. AutoCAD is one of the more complex Windows programs. There are a myriad of commands, menus, toolbars, palettes, and dialog boxes. The following sections explain all these features and how they work so you can get the most out of the AutoCAD user interface.

## Starting AutoCAD

Like most Windows programs, there are multiple ways to start AutoCAD. The three most popular methods are explained next.

*Using the Start Menu.*    The traditional method of starting a Windows program is to rely on the **Start** menu.

To start AutoCAD via the **Start** menu, select the **Start** button on the Windows task bar and select **All Programs** so that all the programs installed on your computer are displayed. Open the Autodesk folder to see all your installed Autodesk programs and then select the **AutoCAD 2009** icon as shown in Figure 1-10 in the **AutoCAD 2009** folder.

**Figure 1-10**    Starting AutoCAD via the Start menu

*Using the AutoCAD Program Icon.*    One of the quickest and most convenient ways to start AutoCAD, or most Windows programs for that matter, is to click on a program icon on your Windows desktop. Typically, when you install a program it will create a program icon on your desktop as well as add it to the **Start** menu. The standard **AutoCAD 2009** icon is shown in Figure 1-11.

TIP

If you do not have an **AutoCAD** program icon on your desktop, you can easily create one from the **Start** menu by right-clicking on the **AutoCAD** icon shown in Figure 1-10 and dragging and dropping it on your desktop. When you release the right mouse button, the shortcut menu shown in Figure 1-12 is displayed. Make sure you select **Copy Here** or **Create Shortcuts Here** from the shortcut menu; otherwise, the original program shortcut will be removed from the AutoCAD folder and put on your desktop.

Double-click on
AutoCAD Program Icon

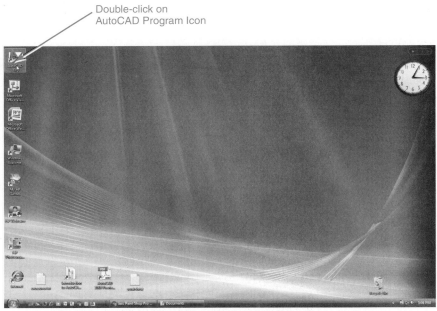

Figure 1-11      Starting AutoCAD via its program icon

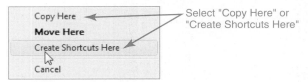

Select "Copy Here" or
"Create Shortcuts Here"

Figure 1-12      Shortcut menu

***Double-Clicking on a Drawing File.***     When you install a new program, Windows associates the program's three-letter file extension (i.e., .DWG) with the program so that you can double-click on a file in Windows Explorer and the program will automatically start and open the file.

Double-clicking on a .DWG file in Explorer will start AutoCAD and open the drawing. Double-clicking on a .DOC file starts Microsoft Word, while double-clicking on a file with an .XLS extension starts Excel. There are literally thousands of different file extensions and associations. You can typically discern what program is associated with a file by looking at the Type column in Windows Explorer when files are displayed using the detailed view as shown in Figure 1-13.

***AutoCAD File Types.***     By default, a drawing in AutoCAD is saved as a file with a .DWG file extension. For example, a floor plan drawing might be saved with the file name:

**Floor Plan.dwg**

A file name can be up to 256 characters long and can include most of the alphanumeric characters, including spaces ( ), dashes (-), and underscores (_). A file name **CANNOT** include any of the following special characters:

**\ / | : " * ? > <**

Windows is not case sensitive, so you can mix uppercase and lowercase letters when naming a file and Windows will not distinguish between them. For instance, the file name in the example above:

**Floor Plan.dwg**

is the same as

**FLOOR PLAN.DWG**

Double-click Drawing File
to Start AutoCAD

Type Column Indicates
Program Association

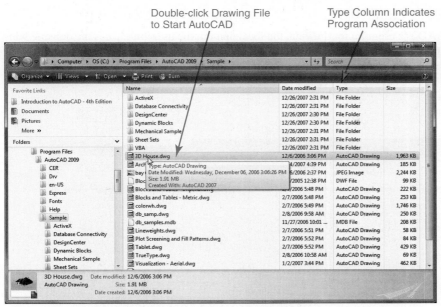

**Figure 1-13**    Starting AutoCAD by double-clicking on a file

Proper file naming, and by extension, proper file management, is one of the most important aspects of using CAD effectively.

**TIP**    By default, every time you save a drawing in AutoCAD, a backup file with the .BAK file extension is created. The backup file is the last saved version of the .DWG drawing file. This allows you to always have the last saved version of your drawing to "roll back" to if something happens to the current .DWG file.

Some of the other common file types and extensions used by AutoCAD are listed in the following table.

| AutoCAD File Types | |
|---|---|
| **File Extension** | **Description** |
| AC$ | Temporary AutoCAD file. Created automatically by AutoCAD |
| BAK | AutoCAD drawing backup file. Created automatically when a drawing is saved |
| DWG | AutoCAD drawing file |
| DWF | AutoCAD Design Web Format file |
| DWL | AutoCAD drawing lock file. Created automatically by AutoCAD |
| DWS | AutoCAD Drawing Standards file |
| DWT | AutoCAD drawing template |
| DXB | Binary AutoCAD drawing exchange format file |
| DXF | ASCII AutoCAD drawing exchange format file |
| PLT | AutoCAD plot file |
| SV$ | AutoCAD automatic save file |

If you are unsure of a file type, consult the Windows Help and Support Center.

## The AutoCAD User Interface

Because AutoCAD is a program for drawing, the focal point of the user interface is the drawing window. This is where you create your drawing. Everything else surrounding the drawing window helps you accomplish this task. Figure 1-14 shows the major features of the AutoCAD user interface.

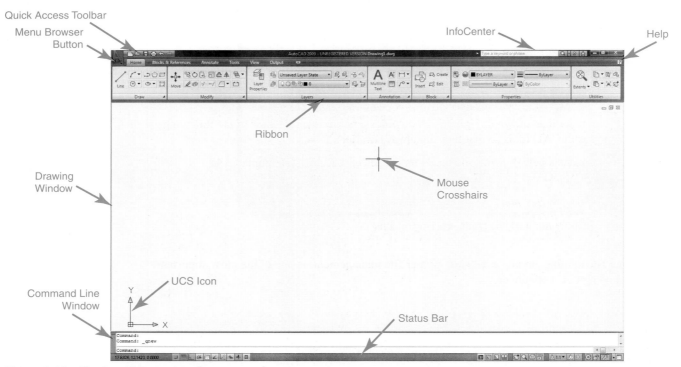

**Figure 1-14**    The AutoCAD user interface

- **Quick Access** toolbar    Provides easy access to all the most commonly used tools such as **New, Open, Save, Plot, Undo,** and **Redo**

- **Menu Browser**    Clicking on the Menu Browser button displays a vertical list of menus that in earlier releases of AutoCAD were displayed horizontally across the top of the AutoCAD window; as well, it provides quick access to other drawings that are currently open, recently opened drawings and a list of recently used commands

- **Ribbon**    Provides easy access to most of the AutoCAD tools via task specific tabs and panels. Each tab has multiple panels containing related tools. Panels with a black arrow in the bottom right corner can be expanded to access additional tools

- **Drawing Window**    The theoretically infinite space where you create the lines, circles, text, and so on that make up your drawing using the Cartesian coordinate system explained earlier

- **Mouse Crosshairs**    Used for locating points and selecting objects when working in a drawing. The crosshairs switch back to a pointer when the mouse is outside of the drawing window

- **UCS Icon**    Represents the current User Coordinate System (UCS); by default, this is set to the World Coordinate System (WCS) explained earlier in this chapter where the $X$-axis is aligned horizontally and the $Y$-axis is aligned vertically

- **Command Line Window**    Provides access to the AutoCAD command line where it is possible to enter commands and their options by typing them at the keyboard. The **Command Line Window** is also where AutoCAD displays many default command settings and other important messages

- **Status Bar**    Mini-dashboard for AutoCAD that does many things, including interactively displaying the current mouse crosshair coordinate location, toggling different drawing tools on and off, switching between model space and paper space layouts, panning and zooming the display, setting the scale factor, managing workspaces, and more

Figure 1-15    The Quick Access toolbar

Figure 1-16    The Quick Access toolbar right-click shortcut menu

- **InfoCenter**  Allows you to search for useful information about a topic by entering key words or phrases, provides access to the Internet-enabled Communication Center for product updates and announcements, and displays a list of Favorites so you can access saved topics

## Quick Access Toolbar

The **Quick Access** toolbar shown in Figure 1-15 provides quick and easy access to the following commonly used AutoCAD tools so that they are always available:

- **New**  Creates a new drawing file based on the selected AutoCAD template file
- **Open**  Opens an existing AutoCAD drawing or template file
- **Save**  Saves the drawing in its current location if it has been saved previously. Otherwise, it performs a "Save As" the first time so that the drawing file name and location can be specified
- **Plot**  Prints a drawing to the specified printing device or file type with the settings specified
- **Undo**  Allows you to undo the most recent commands one step at a time
- **Redo**  Allows you to reverse the effect of the last undo command

You can quickly add and remove tools from the **Quick Access** toolbar by right-clicking on the toolbar and using the shortcut menu shown in Figure 1-16.

This menu can also be used to turn on the old-style pull-down menus located across the top of the AutoCAD window, as well as turn on and off the different AutoCAD toolbar menus discussed later in this chapter.

## Menu Browser

The Menu Browser allows you to browse through a list of menus that contain the majority of commands and tools found in AutoCAD via a list of menus that are displayed when you click on the big "A" Menu Browser button on the top left of the AutoCAD window as shown in Figure 1-17.

**TIP**    The menus displayed vertically in the Menu Browser are the same menus that were displayed horizontally across the top of the AutoCAD window in earlier releases that were commonly referred to as pull-down menus. In fact, it is still possible to turn on the old pull-down menus by right-clicking on the **Quick Access** toolbar menu and selecting the **Show Menu** bar from the shortcut menu shown earlier in Figure 1-16.

The menu is split into a left pane and a right pane so that placing your mouse pointer over a menu item on the left automatically displays a submenu list of related tools on the right as shown in Figure 1-18. If the submenu list is longer than can be displayed, you must use the scroll bar on the right side to scroll down so that you see the desired menu item.

Submenu items that have an arrow icon on the left side indicate that there is a submenu for that item with additional options and commands that can be expanded by clicking on it as shown in Figure 1-19. Selecting the menu item again collapses the submenu so it is no longer displayed.

The search tool on the top right of the Menu Browser allows you to search through all of the AutoCAD tools and menus by specifying key terms. For example, if you start typing L-I-N-E in the search field, AutoCAD dynamically displays all the tools and features that include the word LINE (Line, Command Line, Linetype, Lineweight, etc.) as shown in Figure 1-20. Click on an item in the list to initiate the associated AutoCAD tool or feature.

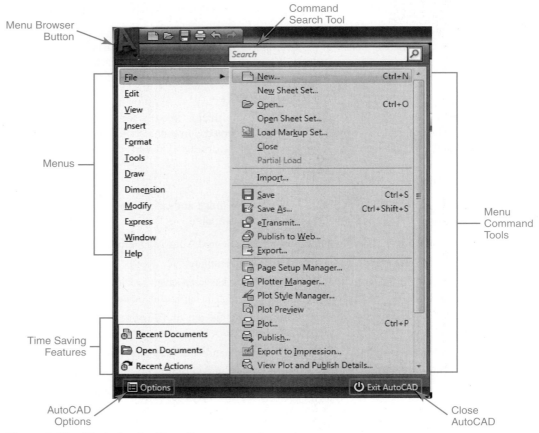

**Figure 1-17**    Displaying the Menu Browser menu

**Figure 1-18**    Browsing the Draw submenu

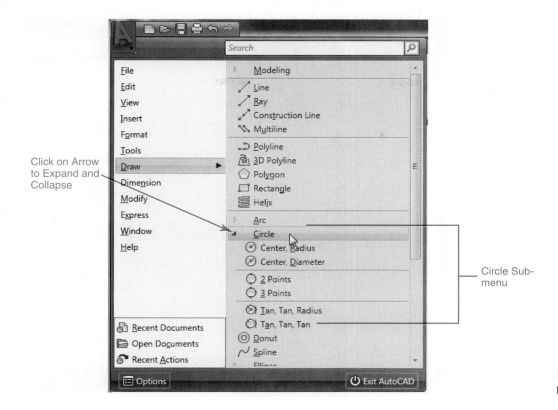

Click on Arrow to Expand and Collapse

Circle Sub-menu

**Figure 1-19**   The Circle tool options submenu

Enter Key Term to Search

**Figure 1-20**   Using the Menu Browser search tool

***Additional Timesaving Menu Browser Features.***   In addition to browsing through menus, it is also possible to view and access recently opened drawings, drawings that are currently open in other windows, and recent actions at the bottom of the Menu Browser. A list of recently opened drawings is shown in Figure 1-21.

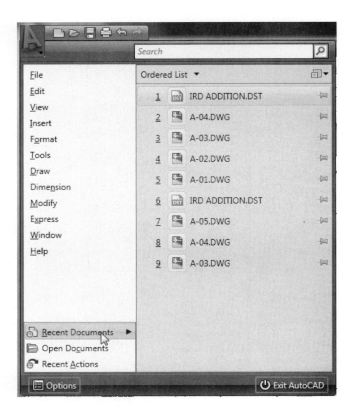

**Figure 1-21** Viewing recently opened drawings

By default, recent drawings are displayed in an ordered list of when they were last accessed. It is also possible to group drawings by date or file type via the **Ordered List** drop-down menu on the top left.

The view icon button on the top right allows you to change the display from icons to small, medium, or large preview images. Additionally, hovering the cursor over the drawing name displays a preview image and other important file information as shown in Figure 1-22.

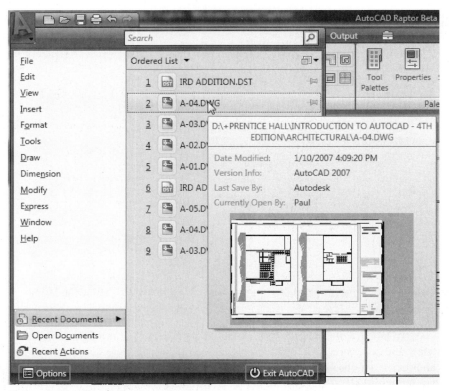

**Figure 1-22** Displaying a preview image

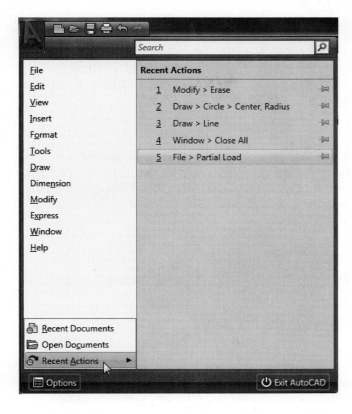

**Figure 1-23**   Recent Actions list

Selecting Recent Actions at the bottom at the Menu Browser displays a list of the actions and commands you have recently performed, as shown Figure 1-23, so that you can quickly repeat them.

Both the Recent Documents and Recent Actions lists include right-click menus that offer additional controls, including the ability to pin a recent document or action so that it will not disappear from the list, as well as the ability to clear the lists when needed.

*AutoCAD Options.*   The **Options** button at the very bottom of the Menu Browser displays the AutoCAD **Options** dialog box shown in Figure 1-24. The **Options** dialog box is your one-stop

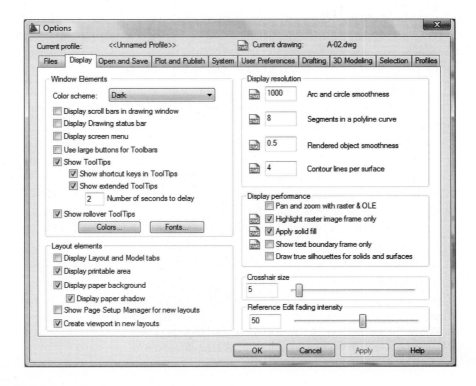

**Figure 1-24**   The Auto-CAD Options dialog box

shop for controlling and maintaining most AutoCAD features and settings such as the color of different window elements, size of the cursor crosshairs, default print settings, and so on. Because it is accessed so often, it is located on the Menu Browser for easy access. It can also be found at the bottom of most AutoCAD right-click shortcut menus discussed later in the chapter. You'll want to remember this, because accessing and using the **Options** dialog box is discussed often throughout the rest of the textbook.

### Ribbon

The ribbon at the top of the AutoCAD window shown in Figure 1-25 provides quick and easy access to the most used AutoCAD tools and features via a variety of task specific tabs and panels. Each task-specific tab has multiple panels that, in turn, contain related tools. In addition, panels with a black arrow in the bottom right corner can be expanded to access additional tools as shown in Figure 1-26.

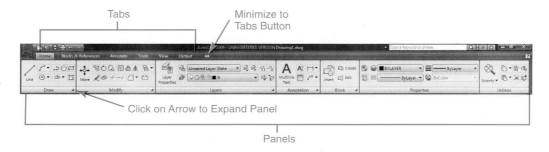

**Figure 1-25**    Ribbon

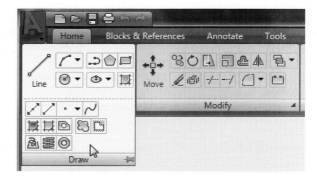

**Figure 1-26**    The Draw ribbon panel with additional tools displayed

The default tab is the **Home** tab shown in Figure 1-25, which provides access to the most commonly used AutoCAD tools and features. The other tabs and their associated ribbons are as follows:

- **Blocks & References**    Tools for working with blocks and block attributes, external references, importing different file formats, and managing drawing data
- **Annotate**    Tools for creating and modifying text and dimensions, creating leader notes and tables, marking up and revising drawings, and managing Annotation Scaling features
- **Tools**    Tools for recording and playing command macros, inquiring about different drawing information, animating 3D drawings, managing and fixing drawings, customizing the AutoCAD interface, loading and running custom programs, and managing CAD standards
- **View**    Tools for managing the User Coordinate System (UCS), managing viewports, turning different palettes on and off, viewing and switching multiple open drawings, and controlling the display of different AutoCAD interface features
- **Output**    Tools for plotting and publishing drawings, transmitting drawings to other people, and changing a drawing so that it looks hand-drawn

Clicking on another tab swaps the current ribbon displayed with the ribbon selected so that a minimum amount of space is required for the tools you need and the drawing space is always maximized. In Figure 1-27 the **Annotation** tab has been selected so that the Ribbon for adding text, dimensions, and other annotation features is now displayed.

**Figure 1-27**    Annotation ribbon

**Figure 1-28**    The Ribbon right-click menu

*Controlling the Ribbon Display.*    You can control the majority of the ribbon display options via the right-click shortcut menu shown in Figure 1-28.

Using the right-click menu, you can turn various ribbon tabs and panels on and off by selecting them from their corresponding submenu. You can also further maximize the drawing window by turning off the panel titles at the bottom of the ribbon by deselecting the **Show Panel Titles** option.

The **Minimize to Panel Titles** button on the far right of the ribbon (see Figure 1-25) allows you to maximize your drawing display window even further by collapsing all the panels on the ribbon so that only the panel titles are visible as shown in Figure 1-29.

**Figure 1-29**    Minimized Ribbon display

Placing your mouse pointer over a panel title temporarily displays the panel so that you can select the desired tool as shown in Figure 1-30. The panel then collapses back to the title only display when you move your mouse pointer back over the drawing window.

**CAUTION:** Be aware that you can reorganize ribbon tabs, or panels within individual tabs, by simply dragging and dropping them to a different location using your mouse. It is even possible to drag panels completely off the ribbon and create separate, individual panels.

Note:
You can completely turn off the ribbon by typing in the **RIBBONCLOSE** command. The **RIBBON** command turns the ribbon back on.

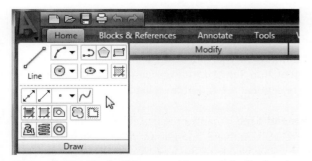

**Figure 1-30**    Single ribbon panel temporarily displayed

**TIP** The ribbon is actually an AutoCAD palette, so it has a number of special properties and features. For instance, palettes can be attached to either side of the AutoCAD window (docked) by dragging them with your mouse. Even better, they can be made to disappear when your mouse is not over them using a nifty feature called **Auto-hide** so that you can maximize the drawing area even more. All the properties and features of palettes are described in detail later in this chapter.

### Tooltips

You may have already noticed that information about a tool automatically appears directly at your mouse pointer if you hover the pointer over a tool for a short period of time. This useful feature is commonly referred to as a Tooltip. The Tooltip for the **Line** tool is shown in Figure 1-31.

Figure 1-31    Line Tooltip

The best part is that if you hover the mouse pointer for a split second more without moving, the Tooltip expands to display additional information if it is available, sometimes even including helpful graphics as shown in Figure 1-32.

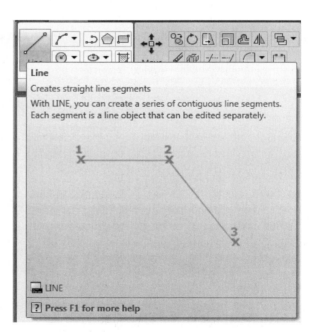

Figure 1-32    Line tooltip with additional information displayed

In addition, pressing the <**F1**> function key on your keyboard will display the complete AutoCAD online help topic for the current tool for even more detailed information. The AutoCAD online help system is discussed in detail at the end of this chapter.

*The Command Line Window.*    The **Command Line** window provides access to the AutoCAD command line. See Figure 1-33. The AutoCAD command line allows you to enter AutoCAD commands by typing them on the keyboard. It is also one of the ways AutoCAD communicates with you via command prompts and messages.

← Command Line Grab Bar

**Figure 1-33**  The Command Line window

***Entering Commands via the Keyboard.***    AutoCAD commands can also be entered by typing them at the keyboard. For instance, the command to draw a line can be entered by typing **Line<Enter ↵>** at the command line as follows:

Command: **Line<Enter ↵>**

AutoCAD commands are not case sensitive so you can enter any combination of uppercase and lowercase characters with the same result.

AutoCAD also provides a feature called AutoComplete that allows you to begin typing a command and then press the **<Tab>** key to cycle through all the commands and *system variables* that start with the letters you typed.

For example, type **DIM<Tab>** at the command prompt to cycle through all the commands and system variables related to dimensioning.

Most commands can also be abbreviated to speed up their entry. The abbreviated version of a command is known as a ***command alias.***

Typically, the command alias is the first one or two letters of the full command. The abbreviation for the line command is **L:**

Command: **L<Enter ↵>**

> **system variable:** A named setting maintained by AutoCAD that controls an aspect of a drawing or the drawing environment.

> **command alias:** An abbreviated definition of a command name that enables you to enter commands faster at the keyboard by typing the first one or two letters of the command.

| **FOR MORE DETAILS** | A complete list of command aliases is provided in Appendix C. |
|---|---|

**TIP**

Hitting the **<Enter ↵>** key when no command has been typed will reenter the last command. This is a timesaving device that allows you to enter the same command repeatedly. For this reason, the most productive way to work in AutoCAD is to group like operations together. This allows you to "stay in the command" without losing focus jumping around to other menus, toolbars, and commands. Always try to focus on one operation.

***Entering Command Options at the Command Line.***    Many commands have options that the user can select by entering a designated response using the keyboard. Options are always displayed as a list in square brackets with each option separated with a forward slash. The **ZOOM** command prompts you with the following options at the command line:

```
Specify corner of window, enter a scale factor (nX or nXP),
or [All/Center/Dynamic/Extents/Previous/Scale/Window/Object] <real
time>:
```

Options can be entered by typing in the complete option keyword, or more simply, by typing in whatever letter is capitalized in the option keyword. For example, to use the **ZOOM** command with the **Window** option, you can enter either **Window** or **W** in response to the **Zoom** command prompt. The **Previous** option can be entered as **P,** the **Extents** option is **E,** and so on. Obviously, typing a shortened abbreviation is faster than typing the complete word so their liberal use is suggested.

***Default Command Options.***    Sometimes a command will display a default option indicated with the option displayed between angle brackets. The default can be selected by simply hitting the **<Enter ↵>** key. For instance, the default option for the **ZOOM** command is always **<real time>**. This means if you simply

> **Note:**
> The space bar at the bottom of the keyboard works exactly the same as the **<Enter↵>** key in AutoCAD. Because it is larger, some people prefer using it over the **<Enter↵>** key because it is easier and faster to get to. The space bar is especially helpful when used as described in the preceding **TIP** to repeat commands!

hit the **<Enter ⏎>** key in response to the **ZOOM** options prompt, you will be automatically placed in the **Zoom Realtime** mode.

AutoCAD remembers some command options so you don't have to type them the next time you use the command. For example, the default radius for a circle always reflects the radius you entered the last time you created a circle. The following is a **CIRCLE** command prompt with the default set to 2.0000 units.

```
Specify radius of circle or [Diameter] <2.0000>: <Enter ⏎>
```

If you are creating another circle with a radius of 2.0000 units, hit the **<Enter ⏎>** key, and voilà!

***Canceling a Command with the <Esc> Key.***   The **<Esc>** key at the top left of the keyboard cancels, or aborts, an active command. It is probably the most used keyboard key in AutoCAD! When you hit the **<Esc>** key, the current command is immediately aborted, and the word *Cancel* is displayed at the command line as follows:

```
Command: *Cancel*
```

Hitting the **<Esc>** key will also "unselect" any objects that are currently selected in the drawing window.

---

**FOR MORE DETAILS**   How to select objects in the drawing window is explained in detail in Chapter 7.

---

***The Command History.***   AutoCAD remembers every command entered in an AutoCAD session from the time you start AutoCAD up until the very last command you enter. This is known as the command history. You can scroll backward and forward through the command history using the arrow keys on your keyboard. The up arrow scrolls backward through the command history, while the down arrow scrolls forward. You can scroll backward or forward to any command in the history and run it again by hitting the **<Enter⏎>** key.

***Resizing and Moving the Command Line Window.***   The command line window can be re-sized, moved, and even made to float. To resize the command line window so you can see more lines of text, place your mouse pointer over the horizontal lines that separate the command line window from the drawing window so that the pointer switches into a double arrow. Hold down your left mouse button and drag up or down, and the window size changes accordingly.

To move the command line window, place your mouse point over the grab bar on the far left, then pick and drag the window out into the drawing window. See Figure 1-34. The command line

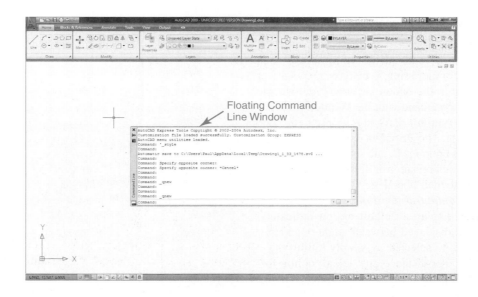

**Figure 1-34**   Floating command line window

window can also be docked on any of the four sides of the drawing window. It is typical to dock it at either the top or the bottom of the drawing window.

*Turning the Command Line Window Off.*    The **Command Line Window** can be turned off and on via the **Tools** menu or the **<Ctrl>+9** keyboard combination. When the **Command Line Window** is turned off, commands can still be entered with the keyboard using **Dynamic Input** explained in the next section.

*The Full Text Window.*    It is possible to switch to a larger separate command line window known as the **Text** window by hitting the **<F2>** function key at the top of your keyboard. All the function key toggles are explained later in this chapter. Hitting **<F2>** once will display the **Text** window as shown in Figure 1-35. The **Text** window can be minimized, maximized, and resized using standard Windows techniques. Hitting the **<F2>** key again toggles the window off.

You'll notice that there is an **Edit** pull-down menu in the **Text** window. Selecting it displays the menu shown in Figure 1-36.

This menu gives you even more command line options. You can run recent commands, select old commands and paste them to the command line to repeat them, and even copy the complete command history.

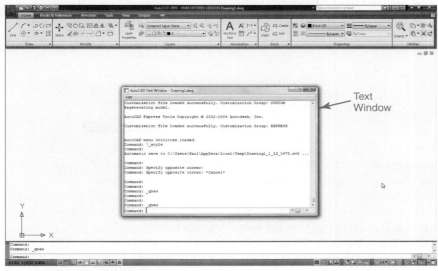

**Figure 1-35**    The Text window

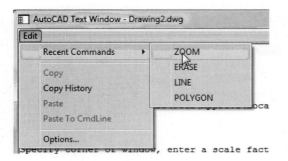

**Figure 1-36**    Text window menu

*Dynamic Input.*    **Dynamic Input** is a set of related input display features that allows you to enter information near the mouse cursor so you can focus on your drawing instead of constantly switching focus to the command line.

***Viewing and Entering Data Near the Mouse Cursor.***    When **Dynamic Input** is on, data input occurs at the cursor by toggling between different input fields. Figure 1-37 shows the **Pointer Input** feature, which allows you to enter $X$ and $Y$ coordinate values right at the cursor. Coordinates are entered by typing the $X$ coordinate value and the $Y$ coordinate value separated by a comma. When you enter the comma, the $X$ value is locked, and input changes to the $Y$ value. You can also use the **<Tab>** key to switch between the $X$ and $Y$ values. Hitting **<Enter ↵>** accepts both values.

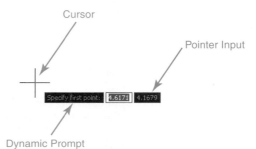

**Figure 1-37**    Viewing and entering data near the mouse cursor

**parametric:** Automated creation of a drawing based on a given set of dimensions referred to as parameters.

**Dynamic Input** also provides a **Dimension Input** feature that displays temporary dimensions as you draw that you can dynamically update to create objects ***parametrically***. The values that you enter in the Dimension Input fields are the values used to create the object. See Figure 1-38.

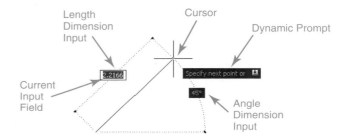

**Figure 1-38**    Using dynamic dimensions to create a line

The **<Tab>** key allows you to toggle between the different input fields. For instance, pressing the **<Tab>** key in the example shown in Figure 1-38 switches the input field from the dynamic length dimension to the dynamic angle dimension as shown in Figure 1-39.

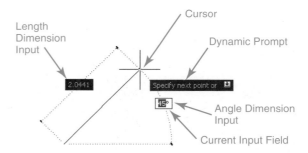

**Figure 1-39**    Using the **<Tab>** key to toggle through input fields

***Selecting Command Options Near the Mouse Cursor.***    Earlier we saw that command options can be specified by typing all or part of them at the AutoCAD command line. Using the **Dynamic Prompt** feature you can select command options using your mouse! If you press the down arrow key on your keyboard, a list of the valid command options is displayed near the cursor as shown in Figure 1-40. You can either use your mouse to select the desired option or navigate up and down the list using the arrow keys on your keyboard. Using this method, you must press **<Enter ↵>** when the desired option is indicated.

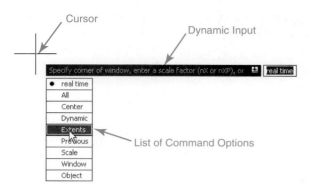

Cursor

Dynamic Input

List of Command Options

**Figure 1-40**   Selecting ZOOM command options using Dynamic Input

> **FOR MORE DETAILS**   See Chapter 6 for more information about **Dynamic Input** features and settings.

*Right-Click Shortcut Menus.*   AutoCAD is chock-full of right-click shortcut menus. They're everywhere. If you're ever in doubt, right-click with your mouse, and you are bound to find something useful. Some of the more prominent right-click menus are introduced below.

If you right-click with your mouse over the drawing window when no drawing objects are selected, the **Default** shortcut menu shown in Figure 1-41 is displayed.

**Figure 1-41**   Default shortcut menu

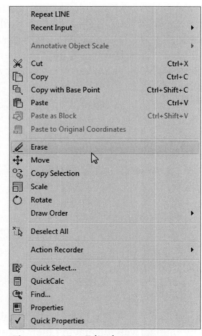

**Figure 1-42**   Edit shortcut menu

**Figure 1-43**  Command shortcut menu

If you right-click when objects are selected in the drawing window, the **Edit** shortcut menu shown in Figure 1-42 is displayed so that you can modify the selected object(s).

If you right-click when a command is active, the **Command** shortcut menu shown in Figure 1-43 is displayed, providing access to different command options, etc.

*Accessing Recent Input.*   It is possible to access recent command input using the keyboard up and down arrow keys or the right-click shortcut menu shown in Figure 1-44.

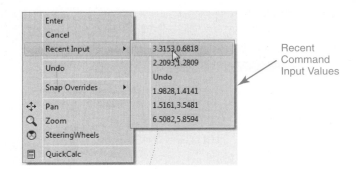

Figure 1-44    Accessing recent input

Using the **Recent Input** feature is a timesaving feature that allows you to recall recently entered data values so you don't have to type them again regardless if the values were entered via the keyboard in the first place. AutoCAD remembers all the input values from all the input methods.

> If you use the right-click menu to list the recent input when no command is active, AutoCAD will display a list of recently used commands.

## Status Bars

There are two different status bars in AutoCAD; the Drawing Status Bar, which is at the bottom of every individual drawing window, and the Application Status Bar, which is located at the very bottom of the AutoCAD window shown earlier in Figure 1-14.

The Drawing Status Bar is used primarily for controlling the Annotation and Viewport scale in each drawing and is explained in detail in Chapter 14. It is turned off by default.

The Application Status Bar, on the other hand, is always on because it controls so many different things. It is like a mini-dashboard for AutoCAD. See Figure 1-45.

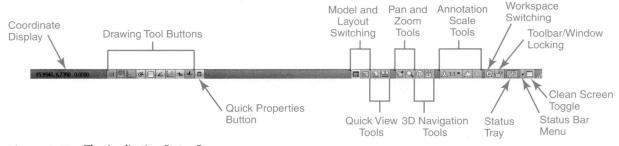

Figure 1-45    The Application Status Bar

Like your car's dashboard, the Application Status Bar provides a myriad of different features and functionality:

*Coordinate Display.*    The Coordinate display keeps track of where your mouse crosshairs are located by interactively displaying their coordinates as you move your mouse.

You can disable the Coordinate display by double-clicking on it with your mouse. Right-clicking on the Coordinate display button displays a shortcut menu that allows you to switch between relative, absolute, and geographic coordinate display. The difference between absolute and relative coordinates is explained in Chapter 4.

*Drawing Tool Buttons.*    The **Drawing Tool** buttons allow you to toggle different drawing tools on and off interactively as you work in your drawing. The majority of the tools are explained in detail in Chapter 5.

Each **Drawing Tool** button has its own unique right-click menu that allows you to control that tool's specific settings and features. In addition, each tool's right-click menu has a **Display** submenu that allows you to remove any of the **Drawing Tool** buttons from the Status Bar, as well

**Figure 1-46**    Drawing Tool buttons in text-only mode

as switch from the icon-type buttons that have pictures back to the traditional text-only style shown in Figure 1-46 that was used in earlier releases of AutoCAD.

*Quick Properties Button.*    The **Quick Properties** button toggles on and off the **Quick Properties** feature that allows you to quickly view and modify object properties directly where the objects are located on your screen via a trimmed down **Properties** palette like the one shown in Figure 1-47.

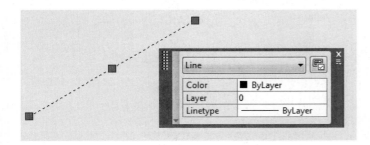

**Figure 1-47**    The Quick Properties palette for a line object

When **Quick Properties** is on, the **Properties** palette is automatically displayed near your mouse pointer whenever you select one or more objects in your drawing, saving both time and valuable screen real estate! The **Quick Properties** feature and the **Properties** palette are explained in detail in Chapter 6.

*Model and Layout Switching.*    The **Model** and **Layout** buttons allow you to quickly switch between the model space and paper space environments introduced earlier in this chapter. The **Model** button switches the drawing environment to model space, the 3D environment where most of your drawing is created. The **Layout** button will switch the drawing environment to whatever paper space layout was last current. The **Layout Quick View** tool explained next is the best way to switch to any other layouts. Paper space layouts are explained in detail in Chapter 14.

*Quick View Drawings and Layouts Tools.*    The **Quick View Drawings** and **Quick View Layouts** tools allow you to visually switch between open drawings or layouts via a horizontal row of preview images. The **Quick View Drawings** tool is explained later in this chapter. See Chapter 14 for more information about the **Quick View Layouts** tool.

*Pan and Zoom Tools.*    The **Pan** and **Zoom** tools allow you to navigate the drawing display window so that you can view all the information in your drawing at the scale necessary to do your work.

Clicking on the **Pan** tool changes your mouse pointer to a hand icon that indicates that you can click and hold you left mouse button down to drag your drawing around the drawing display. You can hit <**Enter**> or <**Esc**> to close the **Pan** tool. Right-clicking will display a handy shortcut menu that also allows you to exit, or switch to a few useful **Zoom** tools.

The **Zoom** tool allows you to zoom in on your drawing by picking two points to define a rectangular window that is zoomed in to fill the drawing display. Pressing the <**Enter**> key instead of picking a point changes your mouse pointer to a small magnifying glass icon that indicates that you are in the interactive **Zoom** "realtime" mode. If you click and hold your left mouse button down and drag the icon up the screen you will zoom in on the drawing. Dragging the mouse down will zoom out on the drawing. The **Pan** and **Zoom** tools are explained in detail in Chapter 3.

*SteeringWheel and Show Motion 3D Navigation Tools.*    The **SteeringWheel** and **Show Motion** navigation tools are primarily for navigating around in a 3D drawing. The **SteeringWheel** combines a variety of display navigation tools like **Pan** and **Zoom** with other complex view manipulation features into one centralized tool. The **Show Motion** tool allows you to easily create 3D animations and walk-throughs. Both tools are beyond the scope of this textbook. For further information about either tool, consult the AutoCAD online help discussed at the end of the chapter.

*Annotation Scale Tools.*    As mentioned earlier in the "Fundamental CAD Concepts" section, it is now possible to automate the process of creating annotation objects such as text and dimensions at the correct size for the final plotted drawing scale using the **Annotation Scale** feature

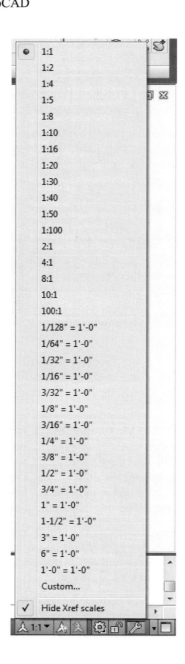

**Figure 1-48** The Annotation Scale menu

located on the right side of the Status Bar. See Figure 1-45. Clicking on the **Annotation Scale** button displays a menu with a list of predefined scales as shown in Figure 1-48.

When annotation objects that have their **Annotative** property enabled are added to the drawing they will automatically scale up or down by the current **Annotation Scale** so that you do not have to scale them manually.

The two buttons to the right of the **Annotation Scale** allow you to add and view annotation objects at multiple scales so that it is possible to reduce redundant annotation information in your drawings.

In the past, drawings that had multiple scales had to have separate copies of all the annotation objects like text and dimensions at different scales to account for each drawing scale factor. Typically, different scale representations of the annotation objects were located on separate layers so that they could be turned on and off for each scale as needed. It was a very complex process, and because it required redundant information, it was prone to errors and omissions.

Chapters 11 through 14 discuss in detail how to utilize the AutoCAD **Annotation Scale** features to add and manage different annotation objects.

*Workspace Switching Button.*  The **Workspace Switching** button allows you to switch between AutoCAD's default workspaces, save a custom workspace, control workspace settings, and customize workspaces.

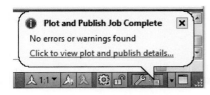

**Note:**
The **2D Drafting & Annotation** workspace is the default workspace for working in the 2D AutoCAD environment. The **AutoCAD Classic** workspace turns off the ribbon feature and turns on the traditional pull-down menus and toolbars found in earlier releases of AutoCAD. As you might have guessed, the **3D Modeling** workspace turns off most of the 2D AutoCAD tools and replaces them with AutoCAD's 3D tools and features.

Workspaces allow you to save and restore the on/off status and positions of the ribbon, palettes, pull-down menus, and toolbars so that you can setup different work environments for different tasks. For instance, you might set up a dimensioning environment that has all the AutoCAD dimension tools turned on while most of the other AutoCAD tools are turned off so that you can focus strictly on the task of dimensioning.

To save your own custom workspace, you first set up the AutoCAD environment in the way you wish to save it by turning on and off the features you want and positioning them accordingly. Click on the **Workspace Switching** button and select **Save Current As...** from the menu and then enter a workspace name.

To restore a saved workspace, click on the **Workspace Switching** button and select it from the list.

The **Workplace Settings...** menu item allows you to control which workspaces are displayed, the menu order, and whether workspace changes are automatically saved when switching workspaces.

The **Customize...** menu item displays the AutoCAD Customize User Interface (CUI) for more high-level-type customization tasks.

*Toolbar/Window Locking.*  The **Toolbar/Window Locking** tool allows you to lock toolbars, palettes, and other AutoCAD features so you do not accidently move them. Locking the various AutoCAD user interface features is discussed later in this chapter after most of the different interface features have been covered.

*Status Tray.*  On the far right of the Status Bar is the Status Tray. The Status Tray dynamically updates with different icons that are used for notification features and different task-specific settings depending on what you're doing. For instance, after a plot is complete a notification balloon is displayed in the Status Tray with information about whether the plot was successful as shown in Figure 1-49.

**Figure 1-49**    Plot status notification balloon

*Clean Screen Toggle.*  The **Clean Screen** toggle temporarily turns off most of AutoCAD's graphical interface features like the ribbon, palettes, and toolbars and maximizes your drawing area so that you have more room to draw. Clicking on the **Clean Screen** toggle again turns everything back on again. The **Clean Screen** toggle is explained in detail in Chapter 3.

**TIP**    It is possible to turn the Application Status Bar features on and off as well as manage the Status Tray settings by clicking on the arrow on the far right of the Application Status Bar to display the Status Bar menu shown in Figure 1-50.

**Figure 1-50**    The Status Bar menu

*Dialog Boxes.* *Dialog box* is the term used to describe any of the graphical windows displayed in response to a command that allows you to select and specify various command options. Auto-CAD has many different dialog boxes. Selecting the **Open** tool from the **Quick Access** toolbar displays the **Select File** dialog box shown in Figure 1-51. This dialog box is common to many file-related commands. The common file dialog boxes work very similarly to Windows Explorer as explained earlier.

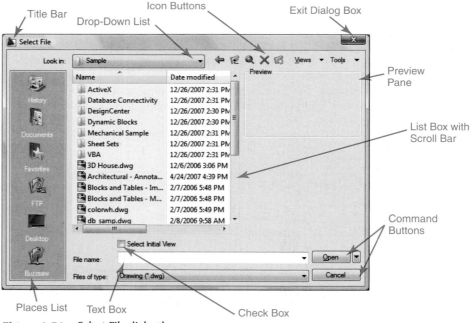

**Figure 1-51**    Select File dialog box

The common file dialog boxes contain a right-click shortcut menu that provides the same commands and options found in Windows Explorer so that you can perform different file operations without leaving AutoCAD.

*Palettes.*    Palettes are separate windows that provide additional AutoCAD functionality. The cool thing is that palettes can be continuously displayed so that you can work between the palette and your drawing, like an artist creating a painting. Because of this capability, palettes have a special feature called *Auto-hide* that can be set to automatically hide a palette when you are not using it, freeing up your drawing window for actual drawing.

The easiest way to turn palettes on and off is via the **Palettes** panel on the **View** ribbon shown in Figure 1-52.

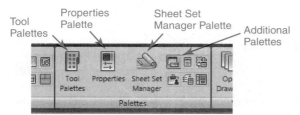

**Figure 1-52**    Palette toolbar buttons

***Tool Palettes.***    **Tool** palettes provide easy access to commands, hatch patterns, and blocks via a series of tabbed palettes as shown in Figure 1-53. To switch to a palette, select the corresponding tab. You can select a **Tool** palette item either by clicking on its icon or by dragging an icon into your drawing window.

**Tool** palettes are meant to be customized, allowing you to add and organize your own commands, blocks, and hatch patterns. The default content is provided as a sample of what you can do. Creating custom **Tool** palettes with your own blocks, hatch patterns, and commands is discussed later in the book.

***Properties Palette.***    The **Properties** palette is your one-stop shop for managing the drawing object properties explained earlier. In Figure 1-54, the properties of a line are displayed in the **Properties** palette.

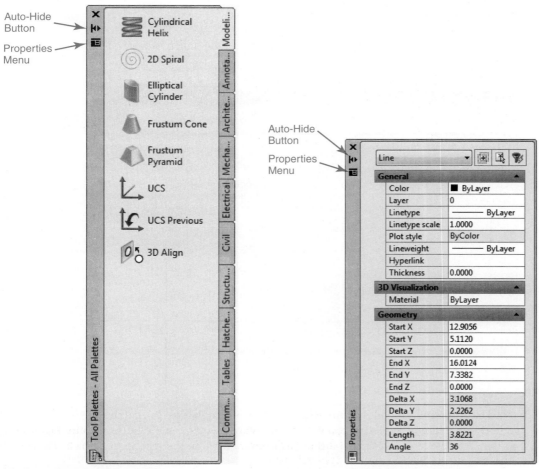

**Figure 1-53**    The Tool palette                    **Figure 1-54**    The Properties palette

**sheet set:** An organized and named collection of sheets created from multiple AutoCAD drawing files.

***Sheet Set Manager and Markup Set Manager Palettes.*** The **Sheet Set Manager** is used to create and manage AutoCAD *sheet sets*. For further information about the **Sheet Set Manager**, please consult AutoCAD Help.

---

**FOR MORE DETAILS**      Using the **Properties** palette is thoroughly detailed in Chapter 6.

---

***Auto-hide Feature.*** As mentioned, it is possible to "hide" a palette using the **Auto-hide** feature. When Auto-hide is on, the palette collapses so only the title bar is visible when your mouse is not over the palette. When you move your mouse back over the palette's title bar, the palette expands so it is completely visible again.

The easiest way to turn the **Auto-hide** feature on and off is by clicking on the **Auto-hide** arrow icon on the palette's title bar. Auto-hide can also be turned on and off using the palette **Properties** shortcut menu explained in the next section.

***Palette Properties.*** Each of the palettes introduced above have similar properties that are controlled by clicking on the **Properties** icon on the palette's title bar. Selecting the **Properties** icon on any palette displays a **Properties** shortcut menu similar to the one shown in Figure 1-55. Using the **Properties** menu, you can turn the **Auto-hide** feature on and off and indicate whether a palette can be docked or not. A palette can be docked on either the left or right side of your drawing window. The **Properties** palette is shown docked on the right side of the screen in Figure 1-56.

Figure 1-55   Palette Properties menu

> **Note:**
> The **Auto-hide** feature can be used when a palette is docked by selecting the "–" button on the right side of the title bar.

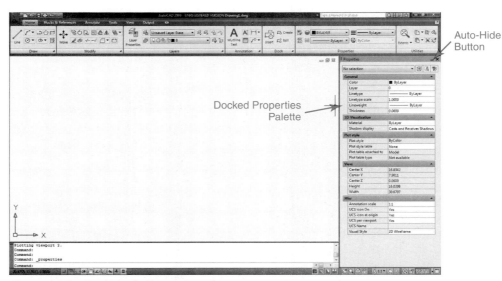

Figure 1-56   Docking the Properties palette

The **Anchor Left** and **Anchor Right** options on the **Palette Properties** menu allows you to dock a palette on the left or right of the AutoCAD window with the **Auto-hide** feature on so that the palette is reduced to a thin strip represented by the palette title bar as shown in Figure 1-57.

**Figure 1-57**    Properties palette anchored on the right

Placing your mouse pointer over the title bar displays the palette temporarily so that you can make any changes or updates. Turning the **Auto-hide** feature off when a palette is anchored will change it back to the docked mode shown earlier.

*Transparency.*    It is possible to make palettes transparent so that you can see the drawing under, or through, the palette. The **Transparency...** menu item on the **Palette Properties** menu displays the **Transparency** dialog box shown in Figure 1-58.

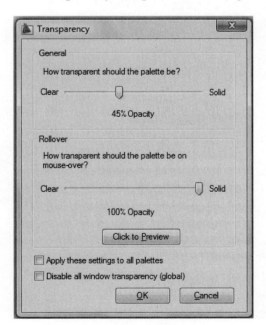

**Figure 1-58**    The Transparency dialog box

The slider bar at the top in the **General** area controls the overall transparency of palettes. By default, palettes are set to 100% opacity so that you cannot see through them. Sliding the bar to the left makes the palettes more transparent.

By default, palettes that are transparent will change back to 100% opacity when your mouse pointer is above them so that you can see them. The slider bar on the bottom in the **Rollover** area allows you to change it so the palette will stay transparent.

It is possible to apply any changes to all the palettes in AutoCAD by selecting the **Apply these settings to all palettes** checkbox at the bottom of the dialog box. To make all palettes 100% opaque and turn off transparency throughout AutoCAD, select the **Disable all window transparency (global)** checkbox.

*Pull-Down Menus.*   The pull-down menus across the top of the AutoCAD window provide access to most of the AutoCAD commands. You'll notice that the menus are organized in the same order from left to right as other Windows programs like Word and Excel. The **File** menu is on the far left and the **Help** menu is on the far right, with many of the same menus in between (**Edit, View, Insert, Format, Tools,** and **Window**). Most of these menus contain similar commands and behavior.

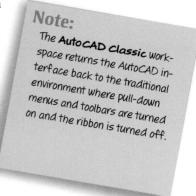

**Note:**
The **AutoCAD Classic** workspace returns the AutoCAD interface back to the traditional environment where pull-down menus and toolbars are turned on and the ribbon is turned off.

**TIP**   Remember that the quickest way to switch workspaces is on the right-hand side of the Application Status Bar via the *Workspace Switching* button. See Figure 1-45.

Putting your mouse pointer over a pull-down menu heading and clicking the mouse will display the pull-down menu. The **File** pull-down menu is shown in Figure 1-59. To select a menu item on a pull-down menu, position your mouse over the desired menu item so it is highlighted and then click with your mouse.

**Figure 1-59**   The File pull-down menu

> It is also possible to select a menu item via the keyboard by selecting the <**Alt**> key on your keyboard in combination with the underlined character on the pull-down menu. For instance, the **File** pull-down menu can be displayed by holding down the <**Alt**> key in combination with the **F** key on your keyboard. You can then select the desired menu item by hitting the key for the underlined letter in the menu label. Hitting the **N** key while the **File** pull-down menu is displayed selects the **New...** menu item.

*Cascading Menus.*    Menu items with an arrow on the right indicate a cascading submenu. Simply placing your cursor over a menu item with an arrow will display the cascade menu. The **Drawing Utilities** cascade menu from the **File** pull-down menu is shown in Figure 1-60. The three dots, or ellipses, next to a menu item indicate that a dialog box is displayed when that menu item is selected. Dialog boxes are explained in the next section.

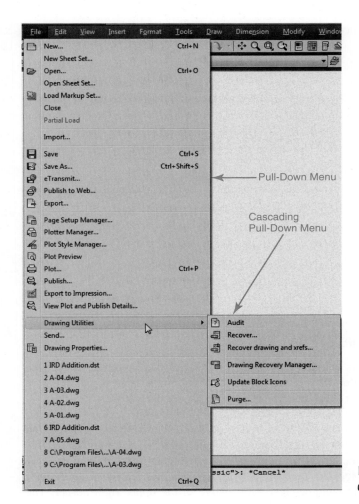

**Figure 1-60**    Cascading pull-down menu

*Toolbars.*    They say a picture is worth a thousand words. Toolbars provide an easy-to-use graphical interface to most of the AutoCAD commands by using pictures called *toolbar icons* to represent different commands. The Standard toolbar is shown in Figure 1-61. You will probably recognize some of the icons from other Windows programs. Toolbar buttons provide quick access to a command because they only require one click of the mouse.

**Figure 1-61**    The Standard toolbar

***Toolbar Flyouts.*** A toolbar button with a small arrow indicates that it is a toolbar flyout. A toolbar flyout button displays a subtoolbar with additional buttons when it is selected. It is the toolbar equivalent of a cascading menu. Figure 1-62 shows the **Zoom** toolbar flyout.

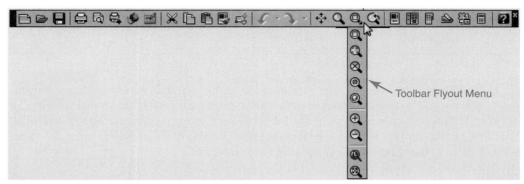

**Figure 1-62**     Zoom toolbar flyout menu

**TIP**     The last toolbar button selected on a toolbar flyout menu will become the button shown on the main toolbar after it is selected. This means that the next time you need the command you don't have to display the flyout menu; you can select it from the main toolbar.

***Turning Toolbars On and Off.*** AutoCAD has over thirty toolbars that can be turned on and off as needed. By default, the **AutoCAD Classic** workspace has the following toolbars turned on:

- **Standard** toolbar    Contains standard commands
- **Layers** toolbar    Used to manage layers in a drawing
- **Properties** toolbar    Used to manage object properties
- **Styles** toolbar    Used to manage styles in a drawing
- **Draw** toolbar    Contains drawing commands
- **Modify** toolbar    Contains modify commands
- **Draw order** toolbar    Controls stacking order of objects

The easiest way to turn toolbars on and off is to simply right-click with your mouse when the mouse pointer is over a toolbar button. This displays the **Toolbar** shortcut menu shown in Figure 1-63 that lists all the toolbars with a check mark next to those that are currently on.

Selecting a toolbar that is not currently checked will turn it on and place it on the screen wherever it was located when it was last displayed. You can then move it and place it where you want using the techniques explained in the next section.

***Moving and Placing Toolbars.*** Toolbars can exist in two states—floating and docked. Floating means that the toolbar is located somewhere (floating) over your drawing window with the title shown at the top and the window-close "X" visible in the upper right corner. The **Dimension** toolbar is shown floating in Figure 1-64. When a toolbar is floating, you can move it by placing your mouse pointer over the title bar on top, clicking with your left mouse button, and dragging the toolbar where you want it.

You can dock a toolbar by dragging it to any side of the drawing window. In Figure 1-64 the **Draw** and **Modify** toolbars are docked. To dock a toolbar, simply drag it to any of the four sides of the drawing window until the shadow line changes shape, indicating it is ready to be docked, and then release the mouse button. In Figure 1-65 the **Dimension** toolbar has been docked on the left side of the screen. To float a toolbar that has been docked, select the grab bars (Figure 1-65) at the top or left side of the toolbar with your mouse pointer and drag the toolbar into the drawing window to the desired location.

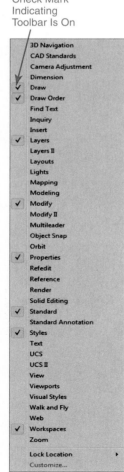

Check Mark
Indicating
Toolbar Is On

**Figure 1-63**    Turning toolbars on and off

Toolbar
Grab
Bars

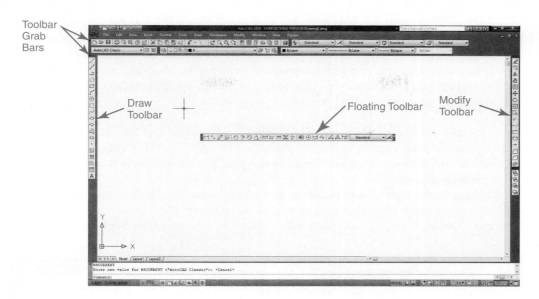

Draw
Toolbar

Floating Toolbar

Modify
Toolbar

**Figure 1-64**   Floating
toolbar

Toolbar
Grab
Bars

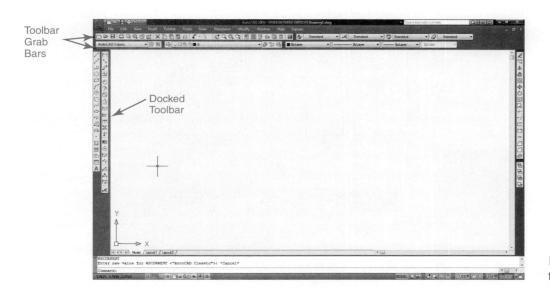

Docked
Toolbar

**Figure 1-65**   Docking a
toolbar

**Figure 1-66**   The Lock
shortcut menu

*Locking Toolbars and Windows.*    As you can see, manipulating toolbars and windows is
easy—almost too easy. To eliminate any accidental changes, AutoCAD provides the ability to
lock them.

The **Lock** icon on the far right of the status bar indicates the current lock status. Select it with
your mouse to display the **Lock** shortcut menu shown in Figure 1-66.

Click on the desired menu item to lock that feature. Once any feature is locked, the **Lock**
icon changes to the locked status on the Status Bar.

You can also lock toolbars and windows via the **Locking** tool located on the **Windows Elements** panel on the **View** ribbon.

You can override toolbar and palette locking by holding down the <**Ctrl**> key while you
select the toolbar or palette with your mouse.

*Multiple Drawing Interface.*    AutoCAD has what is known as a *Multiple Drawing Interface,* or *MDI.* This just means you can open more than one drawing at a time. This allows you to do things like compare multiple related drawings simultaneously so you can coordinate your work, and even better, copy drawing information between drawings using *drag and drop* techniques. In order to facilitate these features, you must be able to quickly switch between open drawings as well as organize your open drawing windows on your screen.

*Switching Between Open Drawings.*    The **Quick View Drawings** tool located on the right side of the Status Bar shown earlier in Figure 1-45 is the best way to switch between open drawings because it provides preview images of the drawings; plus, you can also preview and switch to any layout within a drawing.

Clicking on the **Quick View Drawings** tool on the Status Bar displays a horizontal row of drawing preview images at the bottom of the AutoCAD window of all drawings that are currently open and a toolbar displayed underneath with a few tools, explained later. See Figure 1-67.

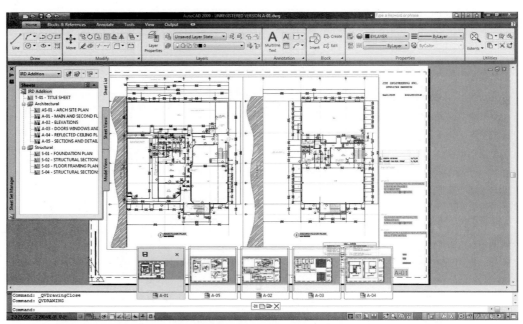

**Figure 1-67**    The Quick View Drawings tool

 **TIP**    You can move the mouse past the edge of the image strip to view drawing images that extend beyond the screen. You can increase or decrease the size of the drawing preview images by pressing the **<Ctrl>** key while rolling the mouse wheel up or down.

When you move your mouse pointer over a **Quick View Drawing** preview, preview images of all the layouts in that drawing, including model space, display above the **Drawing** preview images as a separate image bar as shown in Figure 1-68.

Clicking a preview image will switch AutoCAD's focus to that drawing. It is also possible to save or close a drawing via its preview image by clicking on the corresponding **Save** and **Close** icons in the upper corners of the preview window.

To see a larger view of the layouts, simply move your mouse pointer over a layout preview image. AutoCAD enlarges the size of all the layout images and reduces the size of the drawing images. **Plot** and **Publish** icons are also displayed in the upper corners of the current **Layout** preview making it possible to print directly from the preview. See Figure 1-69.

Moving the cursor back over a drawing preview reverses the process and returns the drawing preview images back to their larger size and the layout preview images back to their smaller size.

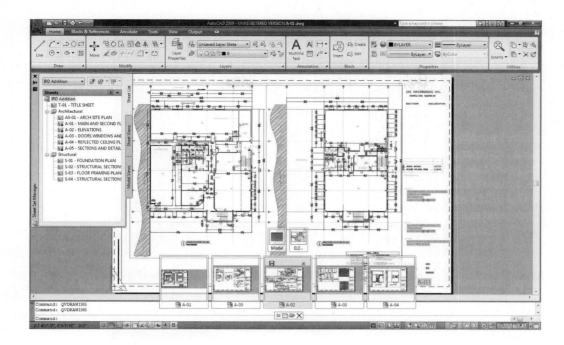

**Figure 1-68**    The Quick View Drawings tool with a drawing selected

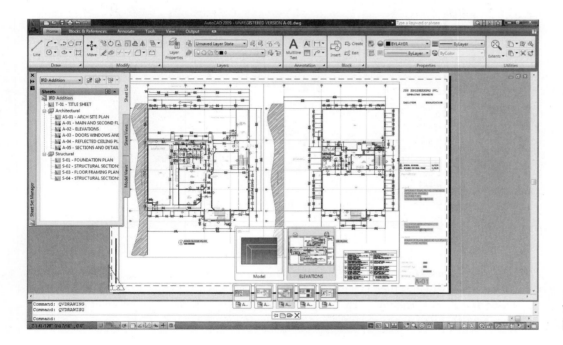

**Figure 1-69**    The Quick View Drawings tool with a layout selected

Additional tools are provided via the **Quick View Drawings** toolbar, which is automatically displayed below the **Quick View Drawing** preview images as shown in Figure 1-67. Using these tools you can pin **Quick View Drawings** open so that it remains visible while you work in the drawing editor. You can use the **Close** tool to turn off **Quick View Drawings** when you no longer want it displayed. The **New** button creates a new drawing and displays the preview at the end of the **Quick View** bar. You can easily open existing drawings using the **Open** tool.

*The Window Panel on the View Ribbon.*    The **Window** panel on the **View** ribbon also allows you to quickly switch between open drawings and provides a number of window display options for viewing multiple drawings.

*Cascading Windows.*    The **Cascade** option displays all open drawings stacked in a tiered fashion so that you can see all open drawings one on top of another as shown in Figure 1-70. You can then switch to another drawing by simply clicking on the desired drawing's title bar.

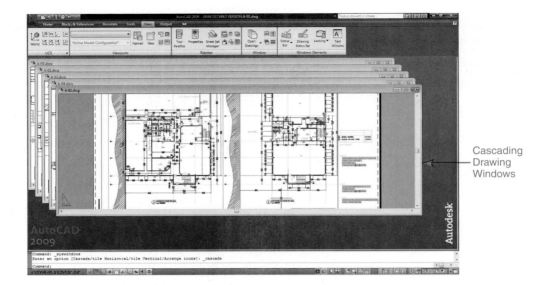

**Figure 1-70**  Cascading drawing windows

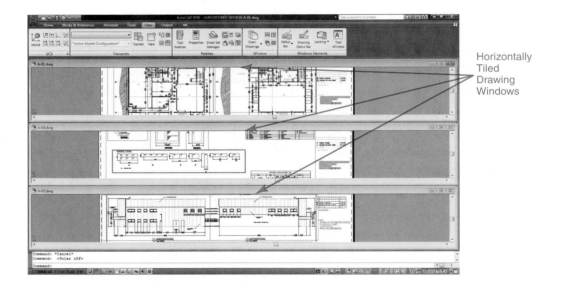

**Figure 1-71**  Tiling windows horizontally

*Tiling Windows Horizontally.*    The **Tile Horizontally** option fills the drawing window with all the open drawings tiled in a horizontal fashion as shown in Figure 1-71.

*Tiling Windows Vertically.*    The **Tile Vertically** option fills the drawing window with all the open drawings tiled in a vertical fashion as shown in Figure 1-72.

**TIP**    Tiling the open drawings either horizontally or vertically is best when you need to share information between drawings. With the drawings tiled, you can use drag and drop techniques to copy information from one drawing to another!

**FOR MORE DETAILS**    Copying information between drawings is discussed in Chapter 7.

Vertically Tiled Drawing Windows

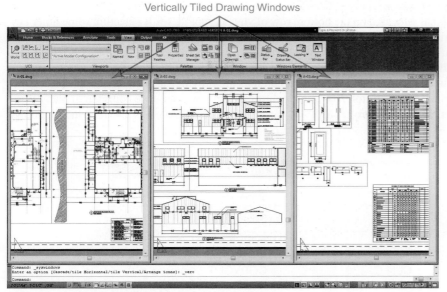

**Figure 1-72**    Tiling windows vertically

*Keyboard Commands.*    AutoCAD has a number of other keyboard commands besides the **<Esc>** key that cancels a command in progress and the **<F2>** function key that displays the **Text** window. Keyboard commands provide quick access to a number of commands and options already available on a pull-down menu, toolbar, or the status bar.

   *Function Keys.*    Function keys are the keys at the top of most keyboards that are labeled **<F1>** through **<F12>**. The most famous function key is **<F1>**, which is used to display the **Help** window in almost every Windows program. We have already seen the **<F2>** key, which toggles the AutoCAD **Text** window on and off. The other function keys also work as toggles, mostly as alternates for the drafting aids found on the AutoCAD Status Bar. A complete list of function keys and their associated functions is provided in the following table.

| AutoCAD Function Keys | |
|---|---|
| **Function Key** | **Description** |
| F1 | AutoCAD online Help system |
| F2 | Text screen toggle |
| F3 | Object snap toggle |
| F4 | Tablet mode toggle |
| F5 | Isoplane toggle |
| F6 | Dynamic UCS toggle |
| F7 | Grid mode toggle |
| F8 | Ortho mode toggle |
| F9 | Snap mode toggle |
| F10 | Polar mode toggle |
| F11 | Object snap tracking toggle |
| F12 | Dynamic Input toggle |

*Control Key Combinations.*    Control key combinations are created by holding down the <Ctrl> key, typically located on the bottom row of your keyboard, while selecting some other key on the keyboard. For example, holding down the <Ctrl> key and selecting the **C** key at the same time copies information to the Windows clipboard. A control key combination is typically expressed as **<Ctrl>+Key.** The copy example above is expressed as **<Ctrl>+C.**

Like the function keys, control key combinations are provided as a quick alternative to commands found elsewhere in AutoCAD. Some control key combinations are common to many Windows programs, while some are exclusive to AutoCAD. A complete list is provided in the following table.

| AutoCAD Control Key Combinations | |
|---|---|
| **Combination** | **Description** |
| Ctrl+A | Select all |
| Ctrl+B | Snap mode toggle |
| Ctrl+C | COPYCLIP command |
| Ctrl+D | Dynamic UCS command |
| Ctrl+E | Isoplane toggle |
| Ctrl+F | Osnap toggle |
| Ctrl+G | Grid mode toggle |
| Ctrl+H | Pickstyle toggle |
| Ctrl+I | Coordinate display toggle |
| Ctrl+J | Repeats last command |
| Ctrl+K | HYPERLINK command |
| Ctrl+L | Ortho mode toggle |
| Ctrl+M | Repeats last command |
| Ctrl+N | NEW command |
| Ctrl+O | OPEN command |
| Ctrl+P | PLOT command |
| Ctrl+Q | QUIT command |
| Ctrl+R | Viewport toggle |
| Ctrl+S | SAVE command |
| Ctrl+T | Tablet mode toggle |
| Ctrl+U | Polar mode toggle |
| Ctrl+V | PASTECLIP command |
| Ctrl+W | Object snap tracking toggle |
| Ctrl+X | CUTCLIP command |
| Ctrl+Y | REDO command |
| Ctrl+Z | UNDO command |

| Ctrl+0 | Clean Screen toggle |
|--------|---------------------|
| Ctrl+1 | Properties Manager toggle |
| Ctrl+2 | DesignCenter toggle |
| Ctrl+3 | Tool Palette toggle |
| Ctrl+4 | Sheet Set Manager toggle |
| Ctrl+5 | Not Used |
| Ctrl+6 | dbConnect Manager toggle |
| Ctrl+7 | Markup Set Manager |
| Ctrl+8 | Quick Calculator |
| Ctrl+9 | Command Line toggle |

**TIP**

The **<Ctrl+Alt>** keyboard combination allows you to cycle through all your open drawings so that you can quickly switch the active drawing window.

## The Online Help System

AutoCAD provides substantial online help via the standard Windows Help system. You are probably familiar with the standard Windows Help system from using other Microsoft Windows programs. Most Windows programs share the same Help interface to make it easier to find help when you need it most.

As mentioned in the "Keyboard Commands" section, the quickest way to activate the Windows Help system is by hitting the **<F1>** function key. You can also access Windows Help via the **Help** menu, clicking on the **Question Mark** on the top right of the AutoCAD window, or by entering a question mark **<?>** at the keyboard. Using any of these methods displays the dialog box shown in Figure 1-73.

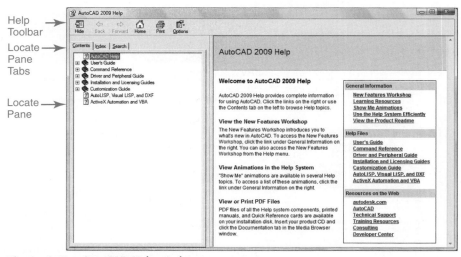

**Figure 1-73**    AutoCAD Help window

The **Help** dialog box is split into two panes. The left side of the dialog box is used to locate different help topics, and the right side of the dialog box displays information about the current topic.

The toolbar at the top of the dialog box provides the following features:

- **Hide**   Toggles the locate pane on the left on and off so you have more space to display the current topic on the right
- **Back Arrow**   Works like the Back button in your Internet browser so that you can display topic information that you previously viewed
- **Forward Arrow**   Works like the Forward button in your Internet browser to allow you to move forward again after using the Back Arrow button
- **Home**   Immediately displays the Help welcome page that is always displayed when you first start the Help system
- **Print**   Allows you to print the topic displayed in the contents pane on the right or the topic selected on the left including all its subtopics
- **Options**   Provides most of the same functionality of the other buttons on the toolbar, including Hide, Back, Forward, Home, and Print. Additional Internet browserlike functionality includes the ability to stop the contents pane from loading, refresh the contents pane, and bring up the **Internet Options** dialog box. You can also turn search text highlighting on and off.

*Locating Information on a Help Topic.*   The tabs at the top of the **Locate** pane on the left allow you to locate information about a topic using a variety of different techniques. How the different tabs are utilized is explained in the following sections.

*Utilizing the Contents Tab.*   The **Contents** tab organizes help information such as topics, guides, and reference manuals using a Windows Explorer–type interface. Topics are represented with an icon that looks like a sheet of paper with a question mark; guides and references are represented with icons that look like books. See Figure 1-73.

Similar to Windows Explorer, if you click on the (+) symbol to the left of a book icon, a tree is expanded to display the chapters and topics in the book in hierarchical format. Using this method, you locate information about a topic in the same manner you locate information in a book. Decide which guide or reference manual contains the info you need, then *drill down* through the chapters and their associated topics until you find what you're looking for.

For example, information about how to draw lines is found in the User's Guide by navigating to the "Draw Lines" topic in the chapter titled "Create and Modify Objects" as shown in Figure 1-74.

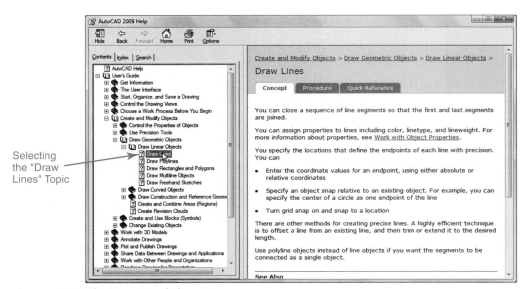

**Figure 1-74**   The Draw Lines help topic

AutoCAD provides the following top-level topics, guides, and reference manuals:

- **AutoCAD Help**    The default Help topic. Provides help on using the Help system with links to General Information topics, other Help files, and resources on the Web

- **User's Guide**    The online AutoCAD user's guide with information organized in chapter and topic form

- **Command Reference**    Reference guide that includes all the AutoCAD commands and system variables listed in alphabetical format. Also includes information about command modifiers and various AutoCAD utilities

- **Driver and Peripheral Guide**    Guide to attaching and setting up various hardware devices such as digitizer tablets, printers, and plotters

- **Installation and Licensing Guide**    Information about installing and licensing AutoCAD in a stand-alone or network environment

- **Customization Guide**    Guide for experienced users that provides information about customizing AutoCAD

- **AutoLISP, VisualLISP, and DXF**    Documentation for AutoCAD's AutoLISP and VisualLISP programming languages along with the DXF file format reference guide

- **ActiveX Automation and VBA**    ActiveX and VBA developer's guide and reference

*Utilizing the Index Tab.*    The **Index** tab allows you to locate information by typing in a keyword. For instance, to find information about drawing lines you could type "line" in the "Type in the keyword to find:" text edit box on the **Index** tab as shown in Figure 1-75.

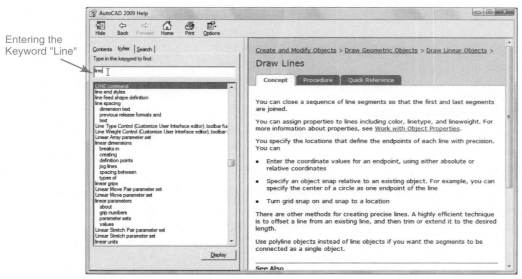

**Figure 1-75**    The Index tab

As you type, every topic that starts with the keyword "line" is displayed in the list box below the keyword. Selecting a topic from the list will usually display information in the **Contents** pane on the right unless multiple rated topics are found. If this is the case, then a **Topics Found** dialog box is displayed so you can further refine your selection.

*Utilizing the Search Tab.*    The **Search** tab allows you to Search Help system for information by asking a question in normal human terms. All you have to do is enter your question or phrase in the "Type in a question and press Enter" text edit box as shown in Figure 1-76.

Selecting the **ask** button returns a list of topics that should answer your question. Select the desired topic to display it in the **Contents** pane on the right.

*Displaying Information about a Help Topic.*    When the information you need is located using one of the tabbed methods provided, it is always displayed in the **Contents** pane, regardless of the technique you used to locate the topic.

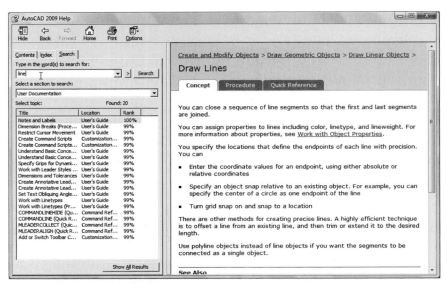

**Figure 1-76**   The Search tab

***The Concepts Tab.***   The **Concepts** tab provides detailed information about the selected topic in conceptual format. In Figure 1-77, detailed information about drawing lines in AutoCAD is displayed, including an explanation of what a line is and how it is drawn. Text that is underlined is a hyperlink to related information that when clicked on will take you to that topic.

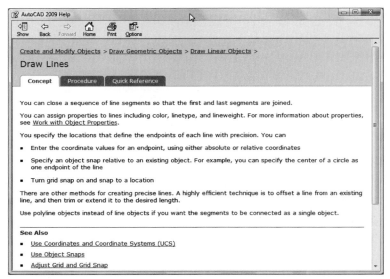

**Figure 1-77**   The Concepts tab

***The Procedures Tab.***   The **Procedures** tab provides step-by-step instructions, or procedures, related to the current topic. In Figure 1-78, the steps necessary to create a line are shown. If there are no procedures related to the current topic, the **Procedures** tab will be disabled so it cannot be selected.

***The Quick Reference Tab.***   The **Quick Reference** tab lists any AutoCAD commands and AutoCAD system variables related to the current topic. In Figure 1-79, the commands used to draw different linear objects are shown along with a brief description.

Because it is hyperlinked, you can click on the command name to go to the topic page for that command.

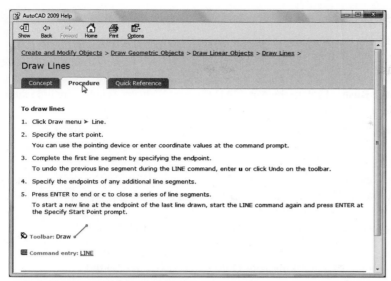

Figure 1-78    The Procedures tab

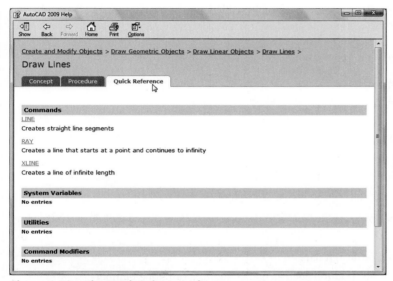

Figure 1-79    The Quick Reference tab

**TIP** If you are not familiar with the standard Windows Help system, the Help welcome page provides detailed information about how to use help by clicking on the "Using the Help System Efficiently" link in the "General Information" section.

## The New Features Workshop

The New Features Workshop is a multimedia presentation that provides a series of animated demonstrations, tutorials, and new feature overviews so that you can quickly get up to speed with all the latest and greatest features in the most recent version of AutoCAD. By default, the New Features Workshop is automatically displayed the first time you start AutoCAD. To start the New Features Workshop manually, you must select it from the **Help** menu.

## Utilizing Online Resources

AutoCAD provides direct links to a number of helpful Internet Websites on the **Additional Resources** cascading submenu located on the **Help** pull-down menu. Selecting any of the menu items on this menu will start your Internet browser and display one of the following Web pages:

- **Support Knowledge Base**   Link to the AutoCAD Support Website. Features include the ability to search the vast Support Knowledge Base and links to Hot Issues
- **Online Training Resources**   Link to the AutoCAD Training Website. Features include links to information about instructor-led training, self-paced training, how-to articles, and various AutoCAD tips
- **Online Developer Center**   Link to the AutoCAD Developer Center that provides information about customizing AutoCAD using the various programming tools provided in AutoCAD
- **Autodesk User's Group International**   Link to the AUGI Website

The beauty of utilizing the Online Resources is that it provides you with real-time information. You will want to make a habit of checking your Online Resources frequently!

## Customer Involvement Program

The Customer Involvement Program is an Internet-enabled feature that automatically sends Autodesk information about the commands and features you use most, any errors or problems that you encounter, and other information helpful to the future development of AutoCAD.

Some types of information that are automatically sent to Autodesk include the following:

- Name and version of AutoCAD
- AutoCAD commands used and frequency of use
- Errors encountered
- File formats imported or exported
- Operating system name and version
- System configuration information such as processor, memory, and graphics card
- IP address

In order to protect your privacy, the Customer Involvement Program cannot do any of the following:

- Collect any drawing or design data
- Collect any identity information such as name, address, or phone number
- Send you email or contact you in any other way

The Customer Involvement Program is a useful feature because it involves you directly in informing Autodesk about the following:

- The commands and features on which Autodesk should focus
- Rarely used commands and features
- The most common types of errors
- The computer hardware typically used with AutoCAD

You can start or stop your participation in the Customer Involvement Program at any time via the **Help** menu.

### Exercise 1-3: Exploring the AutoCAD User Interface

1. Start AutoCAD using one of the three different methods explained in this chapter.
2. Click on the **Menu Browser** button (big "A") on the upper left of the AutoCAD window to display the list of AutoCAD menus.
3. Select each menu to display its contents.

4. Select the **Draw** menu to display its contents.
5. Click on the **Circle** submenu to display the different **Circle** tool options.
6. Pause your mouse pointer over the **Center, Radius** option long enough to see an expanded tooltip with instructions including graphics on how to create a circle.
7. Click on the **Center, Radius** tool to start the **CIRCLE** command.
8. Hit the <**Esc**> key to cancel.
9. Select the **Home** tab on top of the AutoCAD window to display the **Home** ribbon.
10. Click on the black arrow on the far right of Draw panel title to display the expanded panel and all the **Draw** tools.
11. Click on the black arrow on the right of the **Circle** tool to display the **Circle** subpanel with all the **Circle** options.
12. Click on the **3-Point Circle** tool to start the **CIRCLE** command.
13. Hit the <**Esc**> key to cancel.
14. Notice that the **3-Point Circle** tool is now the default **Circle** tool option displayed on the **Draw** panel.
15. Right-click with your mouse on any ribbon panel to display the panel shortcut menu and click on the **Show Panel Titles** option to unselect it (unchecked) so all panel titles are turned off.
16. Right-click with your mouse on any ribbon panel to display the panel shortcut menu and click on the **Show Panel Titles** option again to select it (checked) so all panel titles are turned back on.
17. Click on the **Minimize to Panels Titles** button to right of the **Output** tab on the top right to turn off the panels and display only the panel titles.
18. Put your mouse pointer over the Modify panel title to display the full Modify panel.
19. Click on what is now the **Minimize to Tabs** button to right of the **Output** tab on the top right to turn off the panel titles and display only the tabs.
20. Click on the **Annotate** tab to display the **Annotate** ribbon.
21. Click on what is now the **Show Full Ribbon** button to the right of the **Output** tab on the top right to turn the ribbon back on again.
22. Resize the command line window so it displays six lines.
23. Hit the <**F1**> function key to display the **AutoCAD 2009 Help** window.
24. Locate the "Draw Lines" topic using any of the methods explained in this chapter.
25. Switch between the **Concepts, Procedures** and **Reference** tabs in the **Contents** pane on the right side of the **Help** window.
26. Exit AutoCAD.

## InfoCenter

**InfoCenter** is located on the far right of the menu bar at the top of the AutoCAD window (see Figure 1-80) and provides easy access to different types of useful information. InfoCenter consists of three main features:

- A question box that allows you to enter an AutoCAD question and return a list of results from multiple resources that includes AutoCAD documentation and documentation that you can specify

- The Communication Center panel that displays up-to-date product updates, announcements, and RSS feeds via the Internet

- The Favorites panel that allows you to save links to your favorite topics so that they can be displayed later

**Figure 1-80**   InfoCenter

*Asking an AutoCAD Question.*   When you type a question in the question box and either press <**Enter ↵**> or click on the **Search** button, the search results are displayed as links on a drop-down panel as shown in Figure 1-81.

The results are categorized by the AutoCAD resource where the topic was found. Click on a link to display the topic. The **Display More Results** and **Display Previous Results** arrow

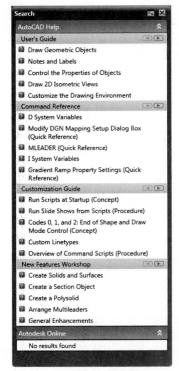

**Figure 1-81**   Search results drop-down panel

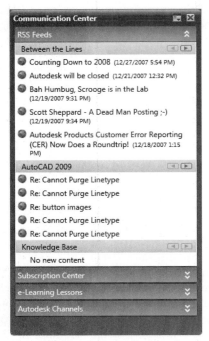

**Figure 1-82**   Communications Center

buttons on the right of the title bar of each category allow you to navigate back and forth between topics.

Clicking on the white star icon to the right of a topic adds the topic to your list of favorites and changes the white star to a gold star so that you can display the topic later via the **InfoCenter Favorites** button.

You can control which locations are searched either by selecting the **Settings** button from the bottom of the search results drop-down panel or by selecting **Search Settings** from the drop-down menu to the right of the **Search** button. This is also where you can specify the number of results to display at one time.

You can send comments to Autodesk via the **Send Feedback** button at the bottom of the search results drop-down panel. Clicking on **Send Feedback** starts your Internet browser and takes you to the Contact Us page on the Autodesk Website.

*Communication Center.*   Selecting the **Communication Center** icon displays a drop-down panel like the one shown in Figure 1-82 with Internet links to product updates, announcements, and RSS feeds. Depending on how it is configured, it may also include links to **Subscription Center** and **CAD Manager** specified files.

Clicking on the white star icon to the right of a link adds the link to your list of favorites and changes the white star to a gold star so that you can access the link later via the **InfoCenter Favorites** button.

*Favorites.*   Selecting the **Favorites** button displays a drop-down panel of topics and links locations saved via the Question Box search results list or **Communication Center**. Select a topic or link to display it. You can use the **Next** and **Previous** buttons to browse search results. It is also possible to click and drag categories or groups and rearrange them. To remove a favorite topic or link, select the "X" icon on the right side of the panel.

*InfoCenter Settings.*   The **InfoCenter Settings** button located on the top right next to the **Close** button of all three **InfoCenter** panels allows you to manage different **InfoCenter** settings via the **InfoCenter Settings** dialog box shown in Figure 1-83.

Figure 1-83 The InfoCenter Settings dialog box

The different **InfoCenter** settings include:

- **General** Your current geographic location, how often to check for new online content, and whether to use animated transition effects for panels.

- **Search Locations** Locations to search for information and the number of results to display for each. You can also add or remove search locations.

- **Communication Center** The maximum age of articles displayed on the **Communication Center** panel and the location and name of the **CAD Manager Channel** if any.

- **Autodesk Channels** Channels to display in the **Communication Center** panel.

- **Balloon Notification** Control notifications for software updates, product support announcements, CAD Manager channel, RSS feeds, and Did You Know messages. You can also control the display time of balloons as well as increase or decrease balloon transparency.

- **RSS Feeds** RSS feed subscriptions. Several default RSS feeds are automatically subscribed to when you install the program. You can also add or remove RSS feeds.

# SUMMARY

The information and concepts explained in this chapter form the basis for the rest of this textbook. Now that you know the basics of AutoCAD you're ready to begin. The next chapter will get you up and running by showing you everything you need to quickly get started. The rest of the textbook delves into these topics in glorious detail so that you will be an AutoCAD expert by time you're finished. Good luck and have fun on your journey!

# CHAPTER TEST QUESTIONS

## Multiple Choice

1. The main benefit of using CAD is:
   a. Increased productivity
   b. Improved precision
   c. Better collaboration
   d. All of the above

2. When you create a drawing using AutoCAD, most of the information that makes up your design should be drawn at what scale?
   a. 1:1
   b. Half scale
   c. Plot scale
   d. None of the above

3. What is the Cartesian coordinate system?
   a. A grid-based system with an $X$- and $Y$-axis
   b. A grid-based system with an $X$-, $Y$-, and $Z$-axis
   c. A system for coordinating your work
   d. None of the above

4. The default units in AutoCAD are:
   a. Millimeters
   b. Inches
   c. Feet
   d. Meters

5. By default, angles in AutoCAD are measured:

   a. Clockwise
   b. Counterclockwise
   c. Using radians
   d. Using a protractor

6. How high should text be if it needs to plot at 1/8″ high on a drawing that is plotted at a scale ratio of 2:1?

   a. 1/4″
   b. 1/2″
   c. 1/16″
   d. 12″

7. Layers in AutoCAD are used for the following:

   a. Controlling object colors
   b. Organizing drawing information
   c. Controlling an object's visibility
   d. All of the above

8. The AutoCAD Color Index consists of how many colors?

   a. 7
   b. 256
   c. 255
   d. None of the above

9. Paper space is primarily used for:

   a. Creating 3D models for visualization
   b. Laying out multiple 2D sheets for plotting purposes
   c. Storing extra copy paper
   d. All of the above

10. AutoCAD can be started by:

    a. Using the **Start** button to navigate to and start AutoCAD
    b. Double-clicking on the **AutoCAD** program icon
    c. Double-clicking on an AutoCAD drawing file
    d. All of the above

11. The default three-letter file extension for AutoCAD is:

    a. DWL
    b. DWT
    c. DWG
    d. BAK

12. The large window in AutoCAD where you do most of your drawing is known as the:

    a. Graphics display
    b. Drawing window
    c. Command window
    d. Layout

13. To turn off the tool ribbon at the top of the AutoCAD window so that only the panel titles are displayed, you should:

    a. Right-click with your mouse while it is over any ribbon panel
    b. Click on the arrow on the right side of a panel title
    c. Click on the button to the right of the **Output** tab near the top of the AutoCAD window
    d. None of the above

14. The abbreviated version of a command is referred to as a:

    a. Command accelerator
    b. Command shortcut
    c. Command control
    d. Command alias

15. What keyboard key cancels any active command?

    a. **<Tab>** key
    b. **<F1>** key
    c. **<F2>** key
    d. **<Esc>** key

16. What keyboard key toggles the full text command window on and off?

    a. **<F1>** key
    b. **<Esc>** key
    c. **<F2>** key
    d. **<Tab>** key

17. What keyboard key toggles between input fields when using the **Dynamic Input** feature?

    a. **<F2>** key
    b. **<F1>** key
    c. **<Tab>** key
    d. **<Esc>** key

## Matching

**Column A**

a. Cartesian coordinate system

b. Right-hand rule

c. Scale factor

d. Layer

e. Model space

f. Paper space

g. Drawing window

**Column B**

1. 3D drawing environment where most of a drawing's linework and text reside

2. Main window in AutoCAD where you create and modify drawing object

3. Grid-based system where points are represented by their $X$ and $Y$ coordinate values

4. 2D environment used to layout a drawing for plotting

5. Technique for visualizing the $X$, $Y$, and $Z$ axes

6. Multiplier applied to annotation features like text and dimensions

7. Window that provides access to the AutoCAD command line

h. Command window

i. Dynamic Input

j. Status Bar

8. Feature that allows you to enter input information near the mouse cursor

9. AutoCAD mini-dashboard at the bottom of the AutoCAD window

10. Object property used to organize drawing information

## True or False

1. True or False: Using CAD requires that you scale your drawing as you create it so everything will fit on the printed paper size.

2. True or False: You must always specify a $Z$ coordinate when locating 2D points in CAD, even if $Z = 0$.

3. True or False: A grid unit always equals 1 inch.

4. True or False: Angles in AutoCAD are always measured counterclockwise.

5. True or False: Annotation features such as text and dimensions must usually be scaled by the reciprocal of the drawing's plotted scale to appear the correct size.

6. True or False: All objects in an AutoCAD drawing have a Layer property.

7. True or False: The Color property of objects can be used to determine the object's line thickness when it is plotted.

8. True or False: Model space is where you create most of the line work and text that represents your design.

9. True or False: AutoCAD creates a backup file with a BAK extension each time you save a drawing.

10. True or False: The main focus of the AutoCAD user interface is the drawing window.

11. True or False: The command line window can be moved and resized.

12. True or False: It is possible to lock toolbars and palettes so they are not accidentally moved.

# Quick Start

# 2

## Chapter Objectives

- Create a new drawing
- Save your work
- Switch between Model Space and Layout Space
- Draw some basic AutoCAD objects
- Toggle the Snap, Ortho, Polar Tracking, and Grid settings on and off
- Zoom around the drawing
- Examine and change object properties
- Create drawing layers and move objects from one layer to another
- Make some basic modifications to the drawing
- Add basic dimensions and annotation to your drawing
- Plot your drawing

## INTRODUCTION

This chapter will give you an overview of a typical AutoCAD drawing session. You will examine some of the basic operations you will do on a day-to-day basis when using AutoCAD, including starting an AutoCAD session, drawing and modifying some objects, and saving and plotting your drawing. All the topics touched on in this chapter will be explained in greater detail in the following chapters. Let's start by creating a new drawing.

## CREATING A NEW DRAWING

When AutoCAD starts, it places you in a blank drawing by default. This blank drawing is based on a number of default AutoCAD settings, which are stored in a ***drawing template***. In addition to this default template, AutoCAD gives you other templates to choose from, which can save you time setting up your drawing.

**drawing template:** A drawing used as a starting point when creating a new drawing. Drawing templates can contain page layouts, borders, title blocks, layer settings, and any other settings or drawing objects you use on a regular basis.

### Using a Template

AutoCAD provides a number of predefined templates with default settings for various drawing disciplines. These drawing templates typically have title blocks in them and predefined settings for text, dimensioning, and plotting. You can also create your own templates or save any drawing as a template.

You can create a new drawing by selecting **New...** from the **Quick Access** toolbar. This displays the **Select template** dialog box (see Figure 2-1), which allows you to select one of these predefined templates as a starting point.

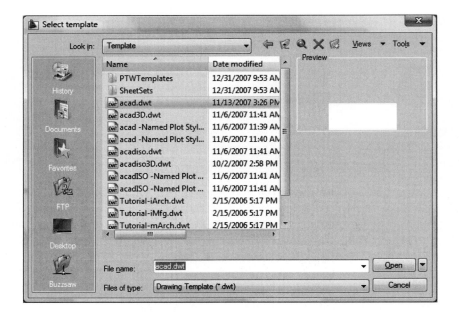

**Figure 2-1** The Select Template dialog box

## Saving Your Work

When you create a new drawing using a template, it is initially named "Drawing" followed by an incremental number (Drawing1.dwg, Drawing2.dwg, Drawing3.dwg, etc.) indicating its place in the series when it was created. The drawing does not exist as a file on your computer or network until you save it at least once using the **QSAVE** command.

The **QSAVE** command is short for "Quick Save," although it is not so quick the first time you use it. The first time you use **QSAVE,** the standard Windows **Save Drawing As** file dialog box shown in Figure 2-2 is displayed so that you can give the drawing a file name and folder location to store the file on your computer or network. Subsequent use of the **QSAVE** command simply updates the file in its specified location, hence the "Quick" part.

**Note:**
The template files that contain "ISO" in the file name are set up for metric units. In fact, the acadiso.dwt template is the default metric template.

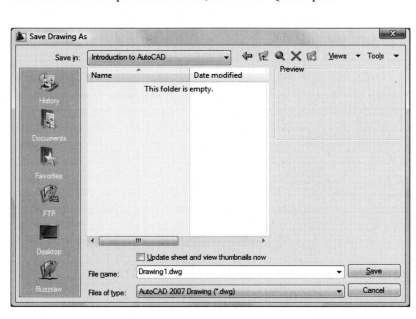

**Figure 2-2** The Save Drawing As file dialog box

Select the drive or device where you want to save the file by selecting it from the **Save in:** drop-down list at the top and navigate to the desired folder using the Explorer-type interface in the middle. Enter the drawing name in the **File name:** list box or select a previous name from the drop-down list. Select the **Save** button to save the drawing in the specified folder and close the dialog box.

> **TIP**
>
> You can use the **SAVEAS** command to save your drawing to a new location or to change the file name. You can access the **SAVEAS** command by choosing **File, Save As...** from the Menu Browser (the big red A). In addition to changing the location and name of your file, the **SAVEAS** command allows you to save your drawing to a previous version of Auto-CAD or to convert it to a DXF (Drawing eXchange Format) file. This allows you share your drawing data with earlier versions of AutoCAD or with other CAD packages. You can also use the **SAVEAS** command to save your drawing as a drawing template. See Chapter 18 for more on file formats and exchanging drawing data.

> **FOR MORE DETAILS**
>
> See Chapter 1 for more information about naming drawing files and the other AutoCAD file types.

Now that the drawing is named, each time you use the **QSAVE** command from now on, AutoCAD will update the file in the specified location and overwrite the last saved version. You should save your drawing often using the **QSAVE** command to ensure that you don't lose too much work if an unexpected and/or catastrophic failure occurs. A good rule of thumb is to save your drawing every 10 to 15 minutes. Get in the habit of choosing **Save** from the **Quick Access** toolbar or by using the **<Ctrl>+S** keyboard combination.

> **Note:**
> By default, the current file name and path is always displayed in the blue title bar at the top of the AutoCAD window. Keeping your eye on the title bar after a drawing is saved is a good way to keep track of the file you're currently working on.

## File Safety Precautions

After you save a drawing once, every time you use the **QSAVE** command thereafter, a backup of the previous saved version of the drawing is saved in the same location with the same name as the drawing, except with a .BAK file extension. This feature allows you to recover drawing information up until the last time you saved if for some reason this is necessary. In order to open the backup file you must either rename the .BAK extension to .DWG or use the **Drawing Recovery Manager.**

As double insurance, AutoCAD automatically saves your drawing at preset intervals to the Windows Temporary folder using a file name that consists of the drawing name followed by six numbers generated by AutoCAD and the file extension .SV$. The default interval between saves is 10 minutes. In order to restore an automatically saved file with the .SV$ extension, you must either rename the extension to .DWG or use the **Drawing Recovery Manager.**

> **Note:**
> The automatic save feature is meant to be used as a failsafe so that you can recover drawing information when things go wrong. It should not be relied on as a primary means of saving your work. In fact, because the automatic save files (.SV$) are saved to the Windows Temporary folder, their lifespan is unpredictable, and they may be deleted at any time.

TIP     The **Options** command is your one-stop shop for controlling most of the user settings that affect the AutoCAD environment. You can access the **Options** command by selecting **Tools, Options** from the **Menu Browser**, or by right-clicking anywhere in the drawing area and choosing **Options** from the right-click menu. You can also type **OPTIONS** or **OP** at the AutoCAD command line.

### Exercise 2-1: Setting Up a Drawing

1. Choose **New...** from the **Quick Access** toolbar to display the **Select Template** dialog box shown in Figure 2-1. The **Select Template** dialog box opens in the default AutoCAD **Template** folder.
2. Select your CD drive in the **Look in:** list at the top of the dialog box, and open the **Chapter 2** folder on the student CD.
3. Select the **ANSI-A.dwt** template file and select the **Open** button to start a new drawing with the predefined **ANSI-A** title block shown in Figure 2-3.
4. Choose the **Save** button from the **Quick Access** toolbar, and save your drawing as **EX2-1** using the **Save Drawing As** file dialog box shown in Figure 2-2.

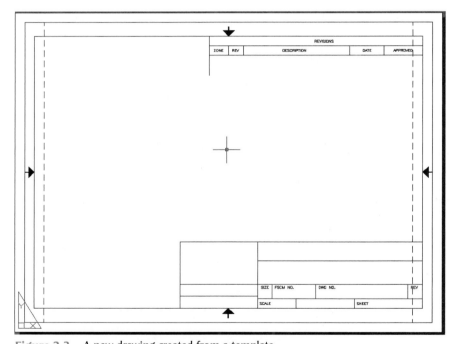

**Figure 2-3**     A new drawing created from a template

## MODEL SPACE AND LAYOUT SPACE

Chapter 1 discussed AutoCAD's two distinct drawing environments, model space and layout space. Generally speaking, model space is used for creating the geometry of your drawing. Objects that exist in the physical world (walls, doors, mechanical parts, etc.) are generally drawn in model space. Objects that exist only on a piece of paper (annotation, dimensions, notes, title blocks, etc.) are generally placed in layout space. Each drawing has only one model space but can have multiple layout spaces, each with their own name.

Model Space        Layout Space

Figure 2-4   The Model Space and
Layout buttons on the Status Bar

The drawing template used in this chapter has one layout named "ANSI A Title Block." You can switch between model space and layout by selecting the respective button on the Status Bar (see Figure 2-4).

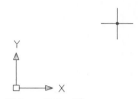

Figure 2-5   The
AutoCAD model space
UCS icon.

### Exercise 2-2: Switching Between Model and Layout Space

1. Click on the **Model** button on the Status Bar. AutoCAD switches to model space (see Figure 2-5).
2. Click on the **ANSI A Title Block** button. AutoCAD switches back to layout space.
3. Save your drawing as **EX2-2.**

AutoCAD's model space looks distinctively different from layout space. There is no "edge" to the space as there is in layout space. The **XY** icon (called the **UCS** icon) looks different as well. In contrast, layout space looks like a piece of paper. The space has edges (and the appearance of a shadow along the edges), and the **UCS** icon looks like a page corner. See Figure 2-6.

### Viewports

An AutoCAD layout can be thought of as a sheet of paper with scaled views or pictures of the Au- toCAD model placed on it. These views are created by placing *viewport* objects in the paper space layout. Viewports are holes or windows in the paper that look into the model space environ- ment. You can open the viewports and make changes directly to the model space environment through the viewport.

The **ANSI A Title Block** layout contains a single viewport. In the following exercise, you'll examine this viewport.

viewport: A window in the paper space environment that shows the view of the model space environment.

### Exercise 2-3: Activating a Viewport

1. Double-click with your mouse near the center of the drawing within the border outline. AutoCAD outlines the viewport (see Figure 2-7).
2. Drag your mouse around the screen. Notice that the crosshair appears only inside the viewport. When you drag the cursor outside the viewport, the crosshair turns into a pointer.
3. Double-click outside the viewport to close the viewport and return to layout space.
4. Save your drawing as **EX2-3.**

The drawing template used in this chapter contains a single viewport; however, you can create multiple viewports in each layout.

| **FOR MORE DETAILS** | Chapter 14 gives detailed information about model space, paper space, layouts, and how to create and control viewports. |

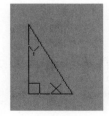

Figure 2-6    The AutoCAD paper
space UCS icon

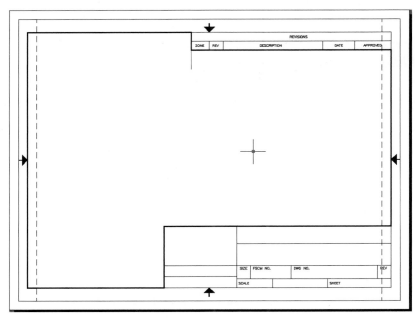

Figure 2-7    The active model space viewport

## COMMUNICATING WITH AUTOCAD

objects: Graphical drawing
elements, such as lines, arcs,
circles, polylines, and text.

When you create a drawing, you are placing AutoCAD **objects** in the drawing. There are differ-ent types of objects (lines, arcs, circles, text, etc.). Each type of object has a unique set of prop-erties. When you create an object, AutoCAD will ask you to specify the various aspects of that object. This is done primarily through prompts. AutoCAD will prompt you for information at both the cursor and the Command: line area.

### The Command Line

The command line window is docked at the bottom of the drawing area by default (see Figure 2-8). This is one place where AutoCAD communicates with you. When you select a tool, AutoCAD will display the command name in the command line window and then prompt you for more informa-tion. The command line window can be undocked and moved or can be turned off completely.

Figure 2-8    The command line window

| FOR MORE DETAILS | Chapter 1 gives detailed information about the command line window and how to move it, dock and undock it, and turn it on and off. |
| --- | --- |

### Dynamic Input

Dynamic Input (see Figure 2-9) uses a floating command prompt that moves with your cursor and provides instant, dynamic feedback as you move around the drawing. Dynamic Input provides you with active, heads-up feedback that allows you to read and respond to AutoCAD's prompts without changing focus away from your drawing. Dynamic Input can be turned on and off by tog-gling the **Dynamic Input** button on the Status Bar.

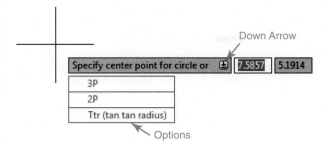

**Figure 2-9**   Dynamic Input

Whether using Dynamic Input, the command window, or both, the general process you'll follow when creating drawing objects is:

1. Start a command.
2. Read AutoCAD's prompt.
3. Pick points and/or respond to prompts.
4. Press **<Enter ↵>** or **<Esc>** to end the command.

Sometimes the AutoCAD prompts can be difficult to decipher. There are some general conventions that AutoCAD uses.

> **FOR MORE DETAILS**   See Chapter 4 for more on coordinate entry methods.

- AutoCAD will ask you to *specify* a placement point (for example, the start point of a line or arc or the center point of a circle). You can specify a placement point by picking a point on the screen, typing in a coordinate, or using an object snap.
- When there are multiple ways to create an object, AutoCAD will display a down arrow next to the Dynamic Input prompt (see Figure 2-9). Press the down arrow key to see the list of command options.
- In the command window, options are enclosed in square brackets [] and are separated by a slash mark (/). You specify an option by typing in the capital letter(s) shown for that option. For example, when drawing a circle, AutoCAD gives you the following prompt and options:

```
Specify center point for circle or [3P/2P/Ttr (tan tan radius)].
```

In this example, AutoCAD is asking you either to specify the center point of the circle or to select one of three options (3P, 2P, or TTR). To specify the TTR option, you would type **T** and press **<Enter ↵>.**

> **FOR MORE DETAILS**   See Chapter 4 for all the specifics on the **CIRCLE** command and its options.

Keep in mind that when you specify a point or select an option, AutoCAD will continue to ask you for more information until it has everything it needs to create that object.

## Exercise 2-4: Draw a Line

1. Select the **Model** button from the Status Bar to switch to model space.
2. Choose the **Line** tool from the **Draw** panel (see Figure 2-10). AutoCAD prompts you to *Specify first point:*.

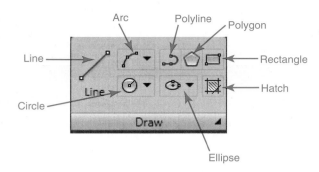

**Figure 2-10**    The Line tool on the Draw panel

3. Look in the command window. AutoCAD shows the following:

   `Command: _line Specify first point:`

   **_line** is the command you started when you chose the **Line** tool. AutoCAD is asking where you want to start the line.

**rubber band:** A live preview of a drawing object as it is being drawn. The rubber-band preview allows you to see objects as they are being created.

4. Pick anywhere on the screen to start the line. You should now have a ***rubber-band*** line extending from the first point you specified along with dynamic information about the length and direction of the rubber-band line (see Figure 2-11).
5. AutoCAD prompts you to *Specify next point or ↓*. The down arrow indicates that a command option is available. Press the down arrow key, and you'll see the **Undo** option appear (see Figure 2-12).

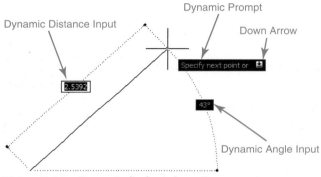

**Figure 2-11**    Dynamic display information

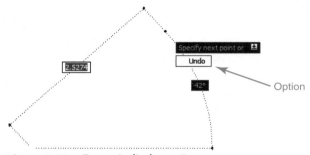

**Figure 2-12**    Dynamic display options

6. Look again at the command window. It says:

   `Specify next point or [Undo]:`

   You can now either specify the next point on the line, choose the **Undo** option from the dynamic display, or type **U<Enter ↵>** to undo that point.
7. Pick another point anywhere on the screen. AutoCAD will draw a single line segment and automatically start drawing another line segment. AutoCAD again prompts you to *Specify next point or ↓*.
8. Press the down arrow and select **Undo** from the option list. The second point you specified is "undone," and the rubber-band line is now extending from the first point you selected.
9. AutoCAD again prompts you to *Specify next point or ↓*. Pick another point on the screen. AutoCAD draws that line segment and repeats the prompt.
10. Press **<Esc>** to end the **LINE** command.
11. Save your drawing as **EX2-4.**

Your drawing may look different from Figure 2-13 since you specified different points, but it should be similar. The Dynamic Input at the cursor should disappear and the you should now see the **Command:** prompt in the command window. This is AutoCAD's way of letting you know that it is idle and ready for the next command.

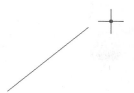

**Figure 2-13** Drawing some lines

**TIP** You can repeat the last command you used by pressing either **<Enter ↵>** or **<Space>** at the command prompt. In most cases, AutoCAD interprets pressing **<Space>** the same as pressing **<Enter ↵>**. The exception to this is when you are typing in a line of text where spaces are expected.

## OBJECT SNAPS, ORTHO, AND POLAR TRACKING

Because precision is important, AutoCAD can look for key points on objects and select those points automatically. These key points are known as *object snaps* or *osnaps*.

object snaps/osnaps: Geometric points on objects such as the endpoints or midpoint of a line or the center of an arc or circle.

**FOR MORE DETAILS** See Chapter 5 for a complete list of object snaps and how to use them.

By default, AutoCAD will look for the endpoints of lines and arcs and the center points of circles. You can turn object snapping on and off by pressing the **Object Snap** button on the Status Bar.

**TIP** Right-click on the **Object Snap** toggle in the status bar and choose **Settings...** to change the default object snap setting.

AutoCAD can help you draw perfectly vertical or horizontal lines. AutoCAD does this with both the **Ortho Mode** and **Polar Tracking** buttons (see Figure 2-6). When turned on, the **Ortho Mode** (which stands for *orthographic*) button will restrict the crosshair movement to either horizontal or vertical movement. The **Ortho Mode** setting only takes effect when you are specifying a point relative to another point (when specifying the second point of a line, for example).

orthographic:  90° increments.

**TIP** The **F8** key will toggle the **Ortho Mode** setting on and off.

polar tracking: A process where AutoCAD will lock the cursor movement to predefined angles.

The **Polar Tracking** button is similar to the **Ortho Mode** setting except it simply indicates when your crosshair is close to a vertical or horizontal angle. When you get close to these directions, AutoCAD will display an alignment path and a tooltip showing you how far and in what direction you have dragged your crosshair (see Figure 2-14). When the alignment path is visible, the point you pick will be placed along that alignment path at the distance indicated.

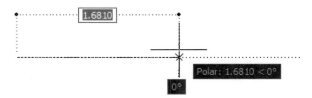

**Figure 2-14**    Polar tracking

By default, polar tracking is set to select angles in increments of 90°. Right-click on the **Polar Tracking** button in the Status Bar and choose **Settings...** to change the default increment angle and to detect specific angles to track.

**FOR MORE DETAILS**        See Chapter 5 for more on using the **Ortho Mode** and **Polar Tracking** buttons.

**Exercise 2-5:** Object Snaps, Ortho, and Polar Tracking

1. Toggle the **Object Snap** setting on.
2. Select the **Line** tool from the **Draw** panel.
3. Move your crosshair close to the start of the first line and let it sit there for a moment. A square will appear at the end of the line along with a tooltip that says *Endpoint* (see Figure 2-15).

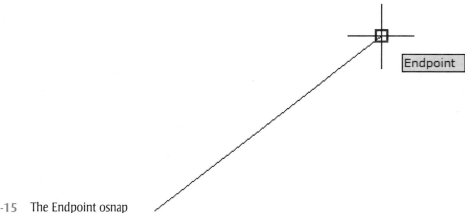

**Figure 2-15**    The Endpoint osnap

4. Pick near the end of the line. AutoCAD will automatically select the endpoint of that line.
5. Toggle the **Polar Tracking** button to the **ON** position.
6. Drag your crosshair straight up until the polar tracking appears. Notice the polar tracking shows a distance and direction (90°).
7. Pick a point approximately 1 < 90° above the end of the line.

8. Toggle the **Polar Tracking** setting **OFF** and the **Ortho Mode** setting **ON**.
9. Drag your crosshair around the screen. The crosshair is now restricted to horizontal and vertical movement only.
10. Drag the cursor to the right and type **3<Enter ↵>.** AutoCAD draws a line, 3 units long to the right.
11. Press **<Esc>** to end the **LINE** command.
12. Save your drawing as **EX2-5.**

**Note:**
The last line you drew was done using a method called *direct distance entry*. This is a combination of cursor movement and keyboard input in which you drag your cursor to indicate direction and use the keyboard to type in the distance. Direct distance input can be used anytime you need to specify a coordinate location. Used with the **Ortho Mode** and **Polar Tracking** controls, it can greatly simplify coordinate entry. See Chapter 5 for more on various coordinate entry methods.

direct distance entry: The process of specifying a point by dragging the AutoCAD cursor to specify direction and typing in a distance.

## UNDO/REDO

AutoCAD keeps a running history of all the commands you've issued within a single drawing session. This allows you to back up to any point in the drawing session. The **UNDO** command will take you back through your drawing session, one command at a time, all the way back to the start of your drawing session. If you go back too far, the **REDO** command will move you forward, one command at a time, until you've restored everything.

### Exercise 2-6: Undo/Redo

1. From the **Quick Access** toolbar, choose **Undo** (or press **<Ctrl> + Z**). The lines created with the previous **LINE** command will disappear. Look at the Command: prompt and see that the lines were undone. The **Redo** button is now active in the **Quick Access** toolbar.
2. Choose the **Redo** tool. The lines will reappear.
3. Choose the **Undo** tool until all the lines are gone (model space is empty). If you go back too far (for example, back into paper space), use the **Redo** tool to get back to an empty model space.
4. Save your drawing as **EX2-6.**

**Note:**
The **REDO** command can only be used immediately after using the **UNDO** command. Once you use **REDO** and resume drawing, you cannot use the **REDO** command again until you use the **UNDO** tool.

## GRID AND SNAP

In addition to polar tracking and object snaps, you can also control the crosshair movement by turning on the **Snap Mode** setting. The **Snap Mode** setting simply locks your crosshair movement to a predefined increment.

Along with the **Snap Mode** setting, you can also display a visual grid of dots on the screen. The **Grid Display** button toggles the display grid on and off. The grid is simply a visual display; it does not print and does not control the cursor movement. The grid and snap settings are not the same thing and are set separately.

**TIP**  The F7 key toggles **Grid Display** ON and OFF. F9 toggles **Snap Mode** ON and OFF.

### Exercise 2-7: Using **Grid Display** and **Snap Mode**

1. Toggle the **Grid Display** button **OFF** and toggle the **Snap Mode** button **ON.**
2. Move the cursor around and notice how it jumps from one point to another. The coordinate readout is locked into .5 unit increments (see Figure 2-16).

**Figure 2-16**    Coordinate readout

3. Toggle the **Grid Mode** button **ON** and toggle the **Snap Mode** button **OFF.** Now move your cursor around the screen and look at the coordinate readout on the cursor. Notice that the cursor is no longer jumping from point to point and the coordinate readout is no longer locked to .5 unit increments.
4. Toggle the **Snap Mode** setting **ON** and pick the **Line** tool from the **Draw** panel.
5. Move your cursor to the coordinate 4,2 and pick that point. Continue picking to draw the outline shown in Figure 2-17.
6. Choose the down arrow to display the options list and choose the **Close** option. AutoCAD will close the figure and end the **LINE** command.
7. Save your drawing as **EX2-7.**

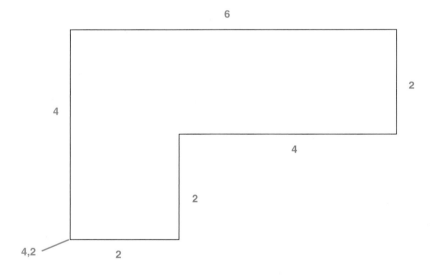

**Figure 2-17**    Drawing with Snap

## DRAW A CIRCLE

Let's add a hole to our drawing. To do that, we'll place a circle on the drawing using the **CIRCLE** command.

### Exercise 2-8: Drawing a Circle

1. Toggle the **Grid Mode** and **Snap Mode** settings **OFF.**
2. Choose the **Center, Radius** tool from the **Draw** panel. AutoCAD prompts you: *Specify center point for circle or* ↧. AutoCAD is asking you to specify either a center point location or choose an option.

3. Type **9,5<Enter ↵>.** AutoCAD places the center of the circle at the coordinate 9,5 and starts dragging a preview of the circle.
4. AutoCAD prompts you to *Specify radius of circle or [Diameter]:.* It is asking you to either specify the radius of the circle or choose an option.
5. Type **3/8<Enter ↵>** to specify a radius of 3/8″. The circle is drawn, and AutoCAD ends the **CIRCLE** command.
6. Save your drawing as **EX2-8.** Your drawing should now resemble Figure 2-18.

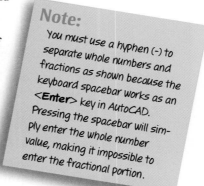

**Note:**
You must use a hyphen (-) to separate whole numbers and fractions as shown because the keyboard spacebar works as an **<Enter>** key in AutoCAD. Pressing the spacebar will simply enter the whole number value, making it impossible to enter the fractional portion.

In the previous exercise, there were a couple of things to notice. First, when you specified the center point of the circle, you typed the coordinate instead of picking it on the screen. This is an example of ***absolute coordinate entry***.

The second thing to note is that when you specified the radius of the circle you typed in a fraction (3/8) instead of the decimal number (.375). AutoCAD will accept fractions and mixed numbers (for example, 1-3/8) as well as decimal numbers.

**absolute coordinate entry:** The process of specifying a point by typing in a coordinate. The coordinate is measured from the origin or 0,0 point in the drawing.

**FOR MORE DETAILS**   See Chapter 4 to learn more about coordinate input methods.

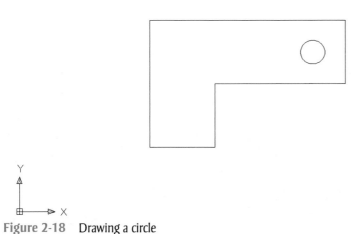

**Figure 2-18**   Drawing a circle

## ZOOMING AROUND THE DRAWING

Object snaps along with the ortho, polar tracking, and snap settings give you a high level of control when selecting points. However, there are times when you need to get a close-up view of an object to see what's going on. AutoCAD calls this ***zooming***. You *zoom in* to get a closer view and *zoom out* to move farther away from your drawing. Like most things in AutoCAD, there are a number of ways to zoom around the drawing. The zoom tools are located on the **Utilities** panel (see Figure 2-19).

**zooming:** The process of moving around the drawing.

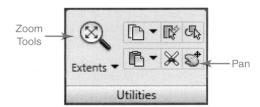

Zoom
Tools

Extents

Pan

Utilities

**Figure 2-19**    The Zoom tools

Some of the commonly used zoom tools are:

- **Zoom Window**    The **Zoom Window** tool allows you to drag a box around an area of your drawing. AutoCAD will then zoom into that area.
- **Zoom Previous**    AutoCAD keeps track of the last 10 zooms and allows you to back up through your zoom history. This is similar to the **Undo** command, but applies only to zoom commands. Think of **Zoom Previous** as a **Zoom Undo.**
- **Zoom Extents**    This displays everything visible in your drawing. It can be easy to get lost or lose track of where you are; a **Zoom Extents** will fit everything visible in your drawing into the viewing area.
- **Zoom Realtime**    This allows you to zoom in and out dynamically by dragging the mouse up and down. Dragging up zooms you in; dragging down zooms you out.
- **Pan**    **Pan** allows you to pan around the drawing by dragging your mouse. You can right-click to bring up a menu that allows you to switch between **Zoom** and **Pan.**

## Exercise 2-9: Zooming Around

1. Choose the **Zoom Window** tool from the **Utilities** panel. AutoCAD prompts you to *Specify first corner:*.
2. Pick a point slightly below and to the left of the circle. AutoCAD now prompts you to *Specify opposite corner:*.
3. Pick a point slightly above and to the right of the circle. AutoCAD will now zoom into the area you selected.
4. Choose the **Zoom Previous** tool. AutoCAD switches back to previous view.
5. Choose the **Zoom Extents** tool. AutoCAD fills the display with the drawing.
6. Choose the **Zoom Previous** tool to return to the original display.
7. Choose the **Zoom Realtime** tool. Notice that there is no prompt, but the status bar displays the message *Press pick button and drag vertically to zoom* (see Figure 2-20).

**Figure 2-20**    The Zoom Realtime prompt

Press pick button and drag vertically to zoom.

8. Hold down the pick button and drag your mouse up and down. AutoCAD will zoom in and out accordingly. Press **<Esc>** to exit the command.
9. Choose the **Pan** tool. Again, there is no prompt but the Status Bar shows the message *Press pick button and drag to pan.*
10. Pick somewhere on the drawing and hold down the pick button. Now drag the mouse, and AutoCAD will drag the drawing around the screen.
11. Press **<Esc>** to end the **Pan** command.
12. Using the **Zoom** and **Pan** tools, zoom and pan your drawing as needed so it resembles Figure 2-21.
13. Save your drawing as **EX2-9.**

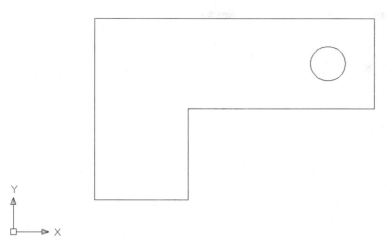

Figure 2-21    The zoomed drawing

## Zooming with a Wheel Mouse

If you use a wheel mouse with your computer, AutoCAD will make use of the scroll wheel. When you scroll the wheel up and down, AutoCAD will zoom in and out, respectively. The zoom will be centered about the location of the cursor.

Pressing and holding down the scroll wheel allows you to dynamically pan around the drawing.

**TIP**    Using the scroll wheel is a system behavior and not technically a command. Because of this, you can use the dynamic zoom and pan of the scroll wheel at any time during the drawing process, even while in the middle of a command.

## OBJECT PROPERTIES

As mentioned earlier in this chapter, when you create a drawing, you are placing AutoCAD objects in the drawing. When you create an object, AutoCAD will ask you to specify the various aspects or *properties* of that object. Chapter 1 described how some properties are common to all objects (for example, layer, color, etc.) and other properties are unique to a given type of object (for example, the radius of a circle or the height of text).

When you select an object, AutoCAD displays the **Quick Properties** panel. This panel displays the layer, color, and linetype of the selected object. It also displays other object properties depending on the type of object selected. Figure 2-22 shows the **Quick Properties** panel for a line segment. If more than one object is selected, AutoCAD will show only common properties of all the selected objects. You can change the properties of any selected object by changing its value in the **Quick Properties** panel.

properties: The settings that control how and where a drawing object is shown in the drawing.

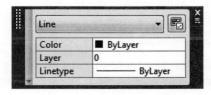

Figure 2-22    The Quick Properties Panel

Exercise 2-10: The Quick Properties
_____

1. Drag your cursor over the circle in the drawing. The circle will highlight when the cursor hovers over it.
2. Select the circle in your drawing. The circle will change to a dashed line to indicate that it has been selected. Blue boxes will also appear on the circle. The **Quick Properties** panel will display the object properties for that circle.
3. Move you cursor over the blue bar on the left of the **Quick Properties** panel to expand the list of properties. Select the **Diameter** box and type **1<Enter↵>.** The circle will immediately change its size. Notice that the values for radius, circumference, and area update as well.
4. Change the **Center X** value to **5.**
5. Change the **Center Y** value to **3.**
6. Press **<Esc>** to deselect the circle.
7. Select the line on the far right of the drawing. The **Quick Properties** panel now shows the properties for that object.
8. While the line is still selected, select the circle. AutoCAD now shows only the properties that are common to those two objects.
9. Press **<Esc>** to clear the selection. Your drawing should resemble Figure 2-23.
10. Save your drawing as **EX2-10.**

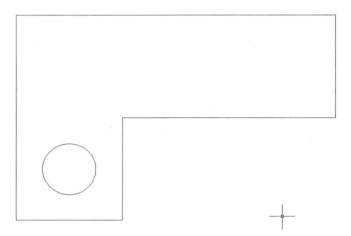

Figure 2-23    The modified circle

# LAYERS

As you saw in the previous exercise, some properties are common to all objects. These include color, linetype, lineweight, and layer. Color is fairly obvious; it is the display color of the object on the screen. Linetype refers to how the line is displayed—for example, a dashed line, dotted line, continuous line, etc. Lineweight is the plotted width of the object (think of it as pen width).

You can assign a color, linetype, and lineweight to each object individually; however, when your drawing grows in complexity, you can quickly find it difficult to manage each object individually. This is where layers come to the rescue.

| FOR MORE DETAILS | Chapter 1 gives a brief description of how layering is used in CAD. Chapter 6 provides a complete description of layers and other object properties. |
|---|---|

Layers give you a way to group objects together logically. The objects are still separate but share common properties and can be manipulated as a group.

Each layer consists of a name, color, linetype, lineweight, and a number of on/off settings. When you draw an object, the properties of the current layer are applied to that object. The **Layer** pull-down list allows you to set the current drawing layer. The **Layer Properties** palette allows you to create and manage drawing layers.

### Exercise 2-11: Create New Layers

1. Choose the **Layer Properties** tool from the **Layers** panel. The **Layer Properties Manager** palette appears (see Figure 2-24). There are three layers currently defined. Layer **0** is the default layer included in every drawing. The Title and Viewport layers came from the drawing template.
2. Choose the **New Layer** button at the top of the palette (see Figure 2-24). Type **Dim<Enter ↵>** for the name.
3. Press **<Enter ↵>** again. AutoCAD will create another new layer. Type **Object <Enter ↵>** for the name.
4. Choose the color setting for the **Object** layer you just created. This will display the **Select Color** dialog box (see Figure 2-25). Choose the color red (Index color 1) and choose **OK** to close the dialog box.
5. Choose the **New Layer** button and create a layer named **Center.**
6. Select the color setting for the **Center** layer. Set the color to blue (Index color 5) and choose **OK** to close the **Select Color** dialog box.

New Layer
New Layer VP Frozen in All Viewports
Delete Layer
Set Current

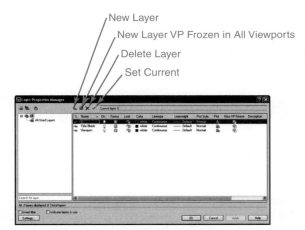

Figure 2-24    The Layer Properties Manager palette

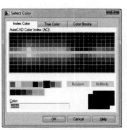

Figure 2-25    The Select Color dialog box

7. Choose the linetype setting for the **Center** layer. This displays the **Select Linetype** dialog box (see Figure 2-26).
8. Choose the **Load** button. This displays the **Load or Reload Linetypes** dialog box (see Figure 2-27).

Figure 2-26    The Select Linetype dialog box

Figure 2-27    Load or Reload Linetypes dialog box

9. Scroll down through the list to see the available linetypes. Next to each line is a text representation of what the linetype looks like. Select the CENTER2 linetype and choose **OK.** This loads this linetype definition into the drawing and returns you to the **Select Linetype** dialog box.

10. In the **Select Linetype** dialog box, select the CENTER2 linetype you just loaded and choose **OK.** This assigns the linetype you just loaded to the layer and returns you to the **Layers Properties Manager** palette.

11. Choose the **Layer Properties** button to close the **Layer Properties Manager** palette.

12. Save your drawing as **EX2-11.**

So far, the appearance of your drawing hasn't changed. All you have done at this point is to define some new layers.

### Exercise 2-12: Drawing on a Layer

1. From the **Layer** panel, choose **Center** from the **Layer Control** drop-down list (see Figure 2-28). This sets the layer **Center** as the current drawing layer.

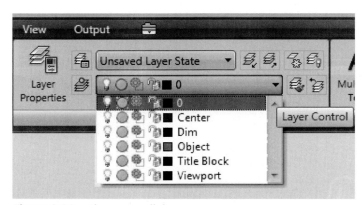

**Figure 2-28**    The Layer pull-down menu

2. Toggle the **Ortho Mode** setting to **ON** and choose the **Line** tool. Type **4.25,3<Enter ↵>** to specify the starting point.

3. Drag your cursor to the right and type **1.5<Enter ↵>** to specify the length and direction of the line segment.

4. Press **<Esc>** to end the **LINE** command.

5. Press **<Space>** to restart the **LINE** command. Type **5,2.25<Enter ↵>** to specify the starting point.

6. Drag the cursor up and type **1.5<Enter ↵>** to specify the length and direction of the line segment.

7. Press **<Esc>** to end the **LINE** command. Your drawing should now resemble Figure 2-29.

8. Save your drawing as **EX2-12.**

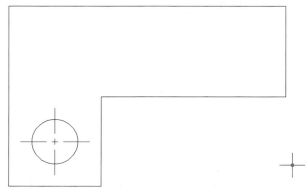

**Figure 2-29**    Adding centerlines to the drawing

The new lines have the color and linetype of the **Center** layer. The rest of the drawing was created on layer **0.** In the next exercise, you'll move those objects from layer **0** to the **Object** layer.

### Exercise 2-13: Moving Objects to Another Layer

1. In the drawing area, pick a point below and to the left of your figure. AutoCAD prompts you to *Specify opposite corner:*. A blue selection window will drag from the point you picked.
2. Pick a point above and to the right of your figure. This will select all the objects inside the box you just specified. The **Quick Properties** panel appears.
3. Hold down the **<Shift>** key and pick the two centerlines you just drew. This removes those lines from the selection.
4. Select the **Layer** property from the **Quick Properties** panel and select **Object** from the drop-down list. The objects "move" to the **Object** layer and take on the properties of that layer.
5. Press **<Esc>** to clear the selection.
6. Save your drawing as **EX2-13.**

Of course, the objects didn't actually move. Their layer property was simply changed from 0 to Object. However, you can think of this as the objects "floating" from one layer to another or (in the pin-board drafting world) moving the objects from one overlay sheet to another.

## Freeze and Thaw a Layer

Your drawing objects are now organized into a few logical layers. Next we'll look at some methods of manipulating layers in your drawing.

### Exercise 2-14: Freezing and Thawing Layers

1. Select layer **0** from the **Layer Control** pull-down menu. This sets layer **0** as the current layer.
2. From the **Layer Control** pull-down menu, click on the sun icon next to layer **Center** (see Figure 2-30). The sun icon will change to a snowflake. Now pick anywhere in your drawing to close the **Layer** pull-down list. This *freezes* the **Center** layer and hides it from view.
3. From the **Layer Control** pull-down menu, click on the snowflake icon next to layer **Center.** The snowflake now turns back to a sun. Pick anywhere in the drawing area to close the **Layer** pull-down list. This *thaws* the **Center** layer, making it visible again.
4. Save your drawing as **EX2-14.**

**freeze/thaw:** Hiding or displaying the contents of a drawing layer. Objects on a frozen layer are ignored by AutoCAD, are not shown in the drawing, and cannot be edited.

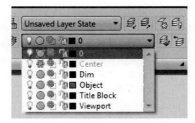

Figure 2-30    The Layer Control pull-down menu

When layers are frozen, AutoCAD acts as if the objects on those layers don't exist. Objects on frozen layers are hidden from view and cannot be changed while the layer is frozen. The current drawing layer cannot be frozen.

AutoCAD also has an ON/OFF setting for layers (represented by the light bulb in the **Layer** pull-down list). While turning layers off will hide them from view, objects on those layers can still be modified (i.e., erased). For this reason, freezing and thawing layers is generally preferred to turning layers on and off.

## Lock and Unlock a Layer

While the **Freeze** option will prevent objects from being modified, it also hides them from view. The Lock/Unlock setting allows you to prevent objects from being modified while still keeping them displayed on screen.

### Exercise 2-15: Locking and Unlocking Layers

1. From the **Layer Control** pull-down menu, click on the **Open lock** icon next to layer **Object** (see Figure 2-31). The **Open lock** icon will change to a closed lock. Pick anywhere in your drawing to close the **Layer Control** pull-down list.

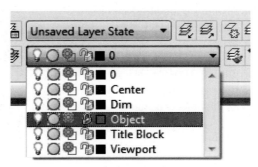

Figure 2-31    Locking the Object layer

Figure 2-32    The AutoCAD alert box

2. Select the circle. The **Quick Properties** panel opens.
3. Change the Radius property of the circle to **1.** AutoCAD responds with an alert box stating: *1 locked object not updated and removed from the selection set* (see Figure 2-32). The circle is now deselected, and the **Quick Properties** panel is hidden.
4. Choose **OK** to close the alert box.
5. From the **Layer Control** pull-down menu, click on the **Lock** icon next to layer **Object** and pick anywhere in the drawing to close the **Layer Control** pull-down list. The **Object** layer is now unlocked.
6. Save your drawing as **EX2-15.**

This section has touched on only a few key elements of layering and AutoCAD's layer management tools. Layer management is a crucial element of using AutoCAD effectively.

> **FOR MORE DETAILS**    Chapter 6 explains how to use AutoCAD's layer management tools and describes some of the issues involved in layer management.

## DIMENSION STYLES

*dimension style:* A collection of dimension settings that control how dimension objects act and are displayed.

Now that you have created a basic drawing, it's time to dimension it. Before we start dimensioning, we need to set up the appearance of the dimensions to reflect industry standards. The look and behavior of dimensions are controlled through ***dimension styles***. A dimension style is simply a collection of dimension settings saved with a certain name. A dimension object takes on the look and behavior of its dimension style. AutoCAD uses a dimension style called *Standard* as a default, but you can modify the Standard dimension style or create new ones as needed. In the following exercise, you'll take a quick tour through all the various dimension style settings.

> **FOR MORE DETAILS**    There are a lot of settings, and the following exercise goes through them quickly: don't get overwhelmed. Chapter 13 gives a detailed description of dimensioning and dimension style settings.

### Exercise 2-16: Changing Dimension Styles

1. Choose the **Dimension Style** tool from the **Dimension** panel in the **Annotate** menu to start the **DIMSTYLE** command. The **Dimension Style Manager** dialog box appears (see Figure 2-33).
2. Choose the **Modify** button to modify the **Standard** dimension style. The **Modify Dimension Style** dialog box appears (see Figure 2-34).
3. Choose the **Symbols and Arrows** tab and change the **Arrow Size** value to **.125.** In the **Center Marks** area, change the **Type** to **None** (see Figure 2-35).
4. Choose the **Text** tab and change the **Text height** value to **.125** (see Figure 2-36).

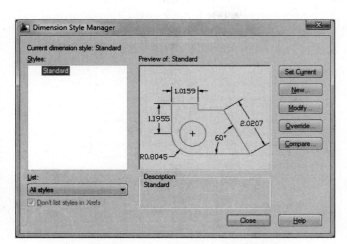

Figure 2-33    The Dimension Style Manager dialog box

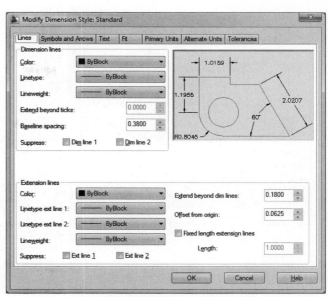

Figure 2-34    The Modify Dimension Style dialog box

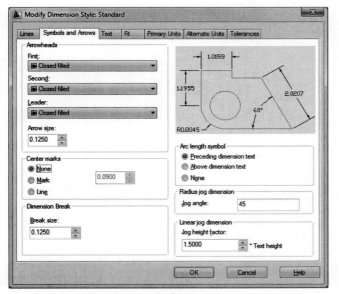

Figure 2-35    The Symbols and Arrows tab

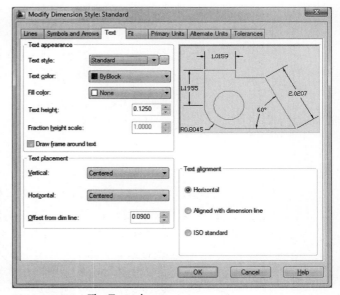

Figure 2-36    The Text tab

5. Click on the down arrow to the right of the **Text Style** drop-down list and select the **Roman** text style (see Figure 2-37).
6. Choose the **Fit** tab and turn on the **Annotative** option (see Figure 2-38).
7. Choose the **Primary Units** tab and select **0.00** from the **Precision** pull-down list (see Figure 2-39).
8. Choose **OK** to close the **Modify Dimension Style** dialog box.
9. Choose **Close** to close the **Dimension Style Manager** dialog box.
10. Save your drawing as **EX2-16**.

Due to the sheer number of options, modifying and managing dimension styles can be one of the more challenging aspects of AutoCAD. Like layers, managing dimensions and dimension styles is a crucial element of using AutoCAD effectively.

**Figure 2-37** The Text Style drop-down list

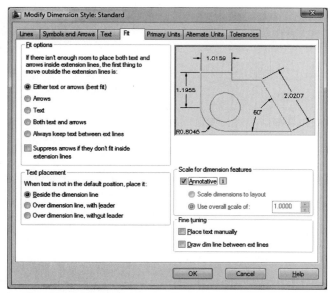

**Figure 2-38** The Fit tab

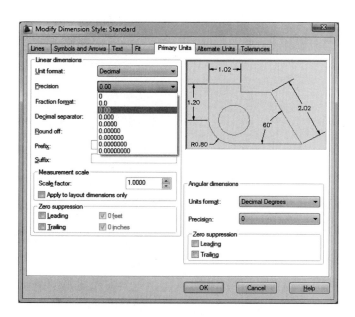

**Figure 2-39** The Primary Units tab

**Figure 2-40** The Dimensions panel

## DIMENSIONING

AutoCAD's dimensioning tools can easily measure distances and place dimensions on your drawing. You tell AutoCAD what type of dimension you want to place and what object or points you wish to dimension, and AutoCAD will measure and place the dimension on the drawing. You can access the dimension tools from the **Dimensions** panel on the **Annotate** ribbon shown in Figure 2-40.

**Exercise 2-17:** Placing Dimensions

1. In the **Layer Control** pull-down menu, set the **Dim** layer current.
2. Choose the **Linear** tool from the **Dimension** panel in the **Annotate** menu to start the **DIMLINEAR** command. AutoCAD prompts you to *Specify first extension line origin or <select object>:*.
3. Press **<Enter ↵>** to select an object. AutoCAD prompts you to *Select object to dimension:*.

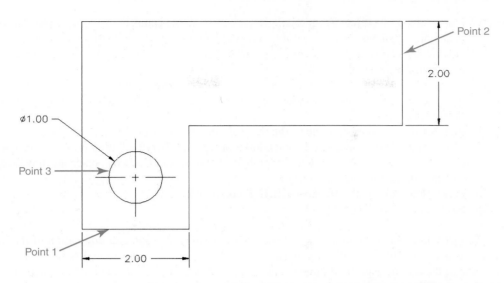

**Figure 2-41**    Adding
dimensions

4. Pick the line at the bottom of the drawing (point 1 in Figure 2-41). AutoCAD starts dragging a dimension from that line and prompts you *Specify dimension line location or ↓*.
5. Pick a point below the line. The dimension is placed, and the **DIMLINEAR** command ends.
6. Press **<Enter ↵>** to restart the **DIMLINEAR** command.
7. Press **<Enter ↵>** to select an object and pick the line at the right side of the drawing (point 2 in Figure 2-41).
8. Drag the dimension to the right and pick a point to place it. The **DIMLINEAR** command ends.
9. From the **Dimension** panel, choose **Diameter** to start the **DIMDIAMETER** command. AutoCAD prompts you to *Select arc or circle:*.
10. Select the circle and pick a point above and to the left of the circle (point 3 in Figure 2-41). The **DIMDIAMETER** command ends.
11. Choose the **Baseline** tool to start the **DIMBASELINE** command. AutoCAD starts dragging a dimension from the end of the last linear dimension. AutoCAD prompts you to *Specify a second extension line origin or ↓*.
12. Press the down arrow and choose the **Select** option from the menu. AutoCAD prompts you to *Select base dimension:*.
13. Pick the left dimension line of the first dimension you created (point 1 in Figure 2-42). A dimension line rubber-bands from the dimension you selected.

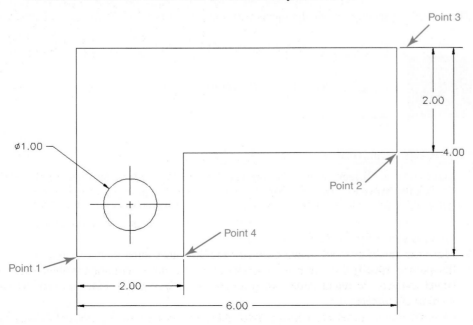

**Figure 2-42**    Adding
baseline dimensions

14. Make sure your **Object Snap** toggle is turned **ON** in the status bar and move your cursor near point 2 shown in Figure 2-42. When the Endpoint object snap appears, pick that point to select the endpoint of that line. AutoCAD will place the dimension and start dragging a new dimension.
15. AutoCAD again prompts you to *Specify a second extension line origin or* ↓. Press the down arrow and choose the **Select** option from the menu. AutoCAD prompts you to *Select base dimension:*.
16. Pick the upper dimension line of the vertical dimension (point 3 in Figure 2-42).
17. Move your cursor near point 4 shown in Figure 2-42. When the Endpoint object snap appears, pick that point to select the endpoint of that line. AutoCAD will place the dimension and start dragging a new dimension.
18. Press **<Esc>** to end the **DIMBASELINE** command.
19. Save your drawing as **EX2-17**.

You now have some basic dimensions on your drawing. The look and orientation of the dimensions is controlled by the dimension style.

One of the unique aspects of dimensions is their ability to update automatically as the drawing changes. This feature is called ***associativity,*** which means that dimensions are associated with the geometry and will automatically update when the geometry changes. In the next section, we'll look at some ways to modify your drawing and see how the associative dimensions follow along.

**associativity:** A link between drawing objects and dimension objects. Associative dimensions will update and follow the drawing objects to which they are linked.

## MODIFYING DRAWING OBJECTS

So far, we've looked at modifying object properties through the **Quick Properties** panel. One of the most powerful benefits of CAD systems is their unique ability to make changes to your drawing. This section introduces you to some of the basic tools used to modify your drawing.

### Selection Sets

As with the drawing tools, AutoCAD has a general process for modifying objects, which is to:

1. Select an editing tool.
2. Specify which object(s) you want to modify.
3. Read the prompt.
4. Specify points and answer prompts.
5. Press **<Enter ↵>** or **<Esc>** to end the command.

The process of specifying which objects you want to edit is called ***building a selection set***.

**building a selection set:** The process of specifying the objects you wish to edit.

**FOR MORE DETAILS** See Chapter 7 for more on building selection sets.

### Exercise 2-18: Moving Objects

1. Make sure the **Object Snap** and **Polar Tracking** toggles in the status bar are turned **ON.**
2. Choose the **Move** tool from the **Modify** panel. AutoCAD prompts you to *Select objects:*.
3. Select the circle. AutoCAD again prompts you to *Select objects:*.
4. Select the two centerlines and press **<Enter ↵>** to stop the selection process. AutoCAD prompts you to *Specify base point or* ↓.
5. Move the cursor near the edge of the circle. When the Center object snap appears, pick that point to specify the center of the circle. AutoCAD starts dragging the objects from the center of the circle and prompts you to *Specify second point of displacement or <use first point as displacement>:*.

6. Drag the object straight up until the polar tracking appears (see Figure 2-43). Once it appears, type **2<Enter ↵>.** The circle, lines, and dimensions move up 2″.
7. Save your drawing as **EX2-18**.

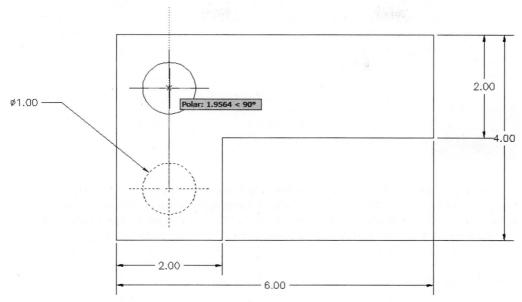

Polar: 1.9564 < 90°

Ø1.00

2.00

4.00

2.00

6.00

**Figure 2-43**    Moving objects

When you started the **MOVE** command, AutoCAD needed to know which objects you wanted to move. The *Select objects:* prompt repeated until you pressed **<Enter ↵>,** telling Auto-CAD you had finished selecting objects. Once you finished selecting objects, AutoCAD then went on to complete the command. It asked you to specify where you wanted to move the objects from (the base point) and where you wanted to drag the objects (the second point).

Notice that even though you didn't select the dimension, it moved as well. This is because of the associativity of the dimension with the circle.

It is possible to preselect the objects you want to modify. If any objects are selected prior to starting a command, AutoCAD will use these objects as the selection set and will skip the *Select objects:* prompt.

**Exercise 2-19:** Select First

1. Pick a point on the screen above and to the right of the circle (point 1 in Figure 2-44). AutoCAD will prompt you: *Specify opposite corner:.*

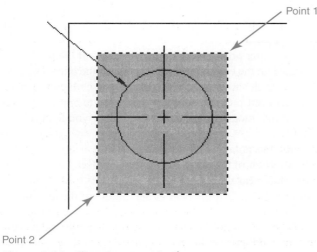

Point 1

Point 2

**Figure 2-44**    Dragging a crossing box

crossing box: A method of selecting objects in a selection set by specifying a rectangular area. Anything that touches the crossing box area is selected.

2. Drag the cursor down and to the left of the circle. AutoCAD will drag a dotted rectangle from the first point you picked (see Figure 2-44). This is called a ***crossing box***.
3. Pick a point below and to the left of the circle (point 2 in Figure 2-44). AutoCAD will select all the objects that are inside or touch the edge of the crossing box you picked.
4. Choose the **Erase** tool from the **Modify** panel. AutoCAD immediately erases the selected objects.
5. Choose the **Undo** tool from the **Quick Access** toolbar to bring the objects back.
6. Save your drawing as **EX2-19**.

> **FOR MORE DETAILS**    The crossing box is one of a number of ways to select objects. Chapter 7 discusses crossing boxes and other ways to select objects.

Notice that AutoCAD did not prompt you to select objects. Because you selected the objects before you started the command, AutoCAD assumed that those were the objects you wanted to erase. AutoCAD doesn't care whether you select the objects before or after you start the command. If no objects are selected, AutoCAD will simply ask you to select them before it continues with the command.

## GRIP EDITING

grips: Editing points that appear at key locations on drawing objects.

You may have noticed in previous exercises that when you preselect objects, the objects highlight and little squares show up on them. These squares are known as ***grips***. Grips appear when you select objects when there is no active command. Grips are located at strategic points on an object. For example, on a circle, grips appear at the center and the four quadrants of the circle. On lines, grips appear at the end and midpoints of the line. On dimensions, they appear on the dimension text and the ends of the dimension lines and arrows.

Grips give you a quick way to modify objects by giving you access to commonly used editing commands and commonly used object points. There are five grip editing modes: stretch, move, rotate, scale, and mirror. When you select a grip, AutoCAD starts the grip editing command and places you in stretch mode. You can toggle between the different editing modes by pressing **<Enter ↵>**. Like other commands, the grip editing modes have prompts and options.

> **FOR MORE DETAILS**    See Chapter 7 for more on grip editing.

### Exercise 2-20: Editing with Grips

1. Select the circle. Grips appear at the center point and the four quadrants of the circle.
2. Select the two centerlines. Grips appear at the endpoints and midpoint of the lines. The grip at the center of the circle coincides with the midpoints of the two lines (see Figure 2-45).
3. Click on the center grip. The grip turns red, and AutoCAD prompts you to *Specify stretch point or* ↓. AutoCAD is now in Stretch mode. AutoCAD is prompting you to specify a stretch point.
4. Move your cursor to the right until the polar tracking appears. Once it appears, type **3.5<Enter ↵>**. AutoCAD moves the center of the circle 3.5″ to the right (see Figure 2-46).
5. Press **<Esc>** to exit grip edit mode and clear the selection set.
6. Select the diameter dimension on the circle. Grips appear at the middle of the text and at two points on the circle.
7. Pick the text grip and drag the text above and to the right of the circle. Pick a point outside of the drawing to place the text (see Figure 2-47).
8. Press **<Esc>** to exit grip edit mode and clear the selection set.
9. Save your drawing as **EX2-20**.

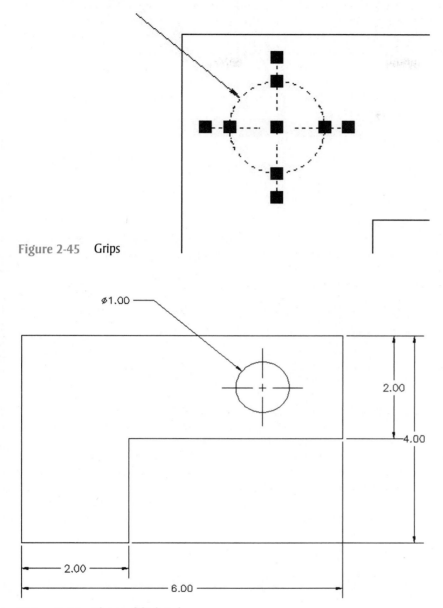

Figure 2-45    Grips

Figure 2-46    The modified circle

Notice that when you *stretched* the center and midpoints of the objects, the end result was that the objects moved. It's a subtle distinction but worth noting. AutoCAD defines circles by a center point (the center grip) and a radius (the quadrant grips). Since you only stretched the center point, only the location of the circle changed, not its size. The same thing applies to the line; because you stretched just the midpoint of the line, the size and direction of the line didn't change, only its location.

In the previous example, once you selected a grip, AutoCAD immediately switched to grip edit mode. It is possible to select multiple grips and modify them as a group. To do this, you simply hold down the **<Shift>** key while selecting the grips. Once you're finished selecting grips, release the **<Shift>** key and then pick one of the grips to start the editing process.

### Exercise 2-21: Editing with Multiple Grips

1. Press **<Esc>** to cancel any active commands and clear any selections.
2. Select the three lines on the right side of the drawing (see Figure 2-48). Select the top line first.
3. Hold down the **<Shift>** key and select the two grips at the corners of the selected lines (see Figure 2-48). The two grips highlight, but grip editing has not started.

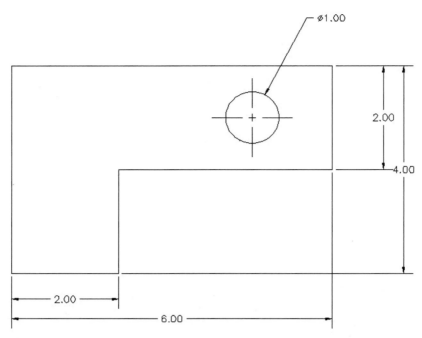

**Figure 2-47**    The modified dimension

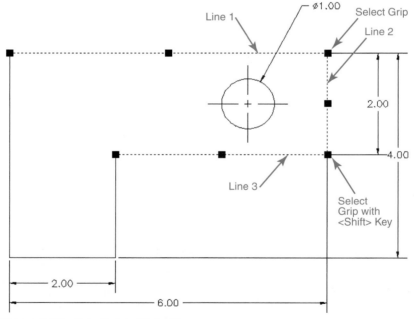

**Figure 2-48**    Selecting multiple grips

4. Release the **<Shift>** key and select either one of the highlighted grips. AutoCAD now enters Grip Edit mode.
5. Drag the grip to the left until the polar tracking appears. Once the polar tracking appears, type **.5<Enter ↵>** into the **Dynamic Input** box (see Figure 2-49).
6. AutoCAD stretches the longest line to a length of 5.5 (see Figure 2-50).
7. Press **<Esc>** to exit grip edit mode and clear the selection set.
8. Save your drawing as **EX2-21**.

The order in which you select the lines is important. The first line you selected determined which dimension would appear in the dynamic input box. You should have also seen the associative dimensions in action again. The dimensions updated to follow the changes in the geometry.

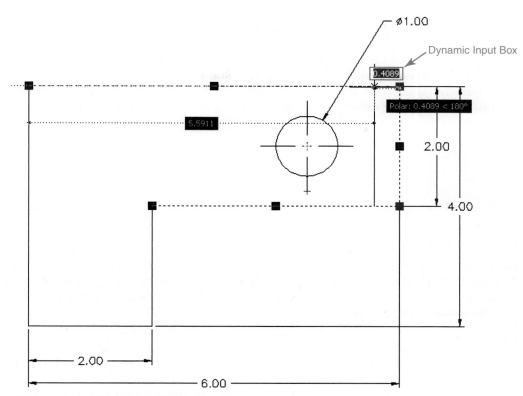

Figure 2-49    Grips and dynamic input

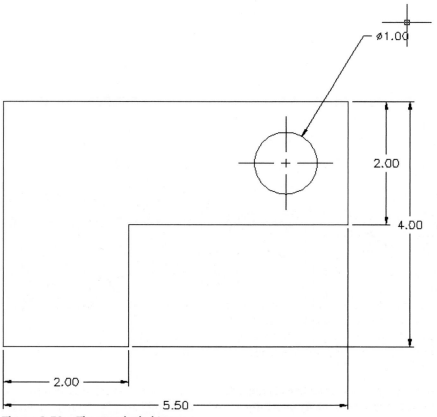

Figure 2-50    The stretched objects

## INTRODUCTION TO ADVANCED EDITING TECHNIQUES

A few of the advanced editing techniques are indispensable in AutoCAD. In fact, these commands and techniques are used extensively when creating AutoCAD drawings, which may seem counterintuitive. Using CAD, it is not uncommon to create a drawing by drawing more than you need and then editing and refining information to make the final product. This section introduces you to a few of these techniques.

> **FOR MORE DETAILS**  See Chapter 8 for more information regarding different advanced editing techniques.

### Making Parallel Copies

Sometimes it is necessary to make an exact copy of a line or circle that is a specific distance from the original. This is referred to as an *offset* in AutoCAD. It is possible to offset a specific distance or even through a point that you specify while maintaining a copy of the original object. It is even possible to make multiple copies.

### Exercise 2-22: Offsetting Objects

1. Choose the **Offset** tool from the **Modify** panel. AutoCAD prompts you to *Specify offset distance or ↓?*
2. Type **.125<Enter ↵>**. AutoCAD prompts you to *Select object to offset or ↓*.
3. Pick the horizontal line at the top of the drawing (point 1 in Figure 2-50). AutoCAD prompts you to *Specify point on side to offset or ↓*.
4. Pick a point below that line (point 2 in Figure 2-51). AutoCAD places a copy of the line .125″ below the original. AutoCAD prompts you again to *Select object to offset or ↓*.

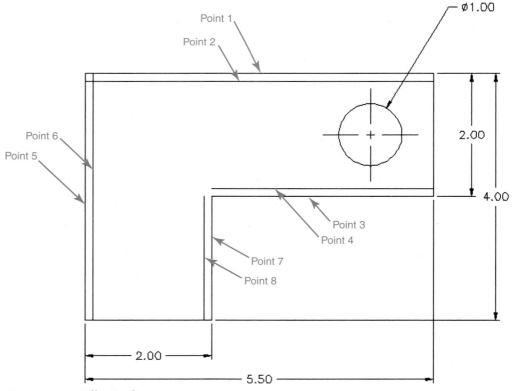

**Figure 2-51**    Offsetting lines

5. Pick the next horizontal line down from the top of the drawing (point 3 in Figure 2-51). AutoCAD prompts you to *Specify point on side to offset or* ↓.
6. Pick a point above that line (point 4 in Figure 2-51). AutoCAD places a copy of the line .125″ above the original. AutoCAD prompts you again to *Select object to offset or* ↓.
7. Pick the vertical line on the left side of the drawing (point 5 in Figure 2-50). AutoCAD prompts you to *Specify point on side to offset or* ↓.
8. Pick a point to the right of that line (point 6 in Figure 2-51). AutoCAD places a copy of the line .125″ to right of the original and prompts you again to *Select object to offset or* ↓.
9. Pick the next vertical line to the right of the drawing (point 7 in Figure 2-51). AutoCAD prompts you to *Specify point on side to offset or* ↓.
10. Pick a point to the left of that line (point 8 in Figure 2-51). AutoCAD places a copy of the line .125″ to the left of the original and prompts you again to *Select object to offset or* ↓.
11. Save your drawing as **EX2-22**.

## Fixing Overlapping Lines and Closing Gaps

Often it is necessary to "clean up" lines that overlap and/or do not meet exactly so that there is a gap. Remember that the key to using AutoCAD effectively is to draw everything as precisely as possible. There is no room for even the tiniest overlap or gap. These small errors can propagate larger errors when dimensions are added or parts are mated together. AutoCAD provides a number of methods for cleaning up your drawings quickly.

### Exercise 2-23: Trimming and Extending Objects

1. Choose the **Trim** tool from the **Modify** panel. The current command settings are displayed in the command window, and AutoCAD prompts you:

```
Current settings: Projection=UCS, Edge=None
Select cutting edges ...
Select objects or <select all>:
```

2. Select lines 1–4 shown in Figure 2-52 and press **<Enter ↵>**. AutoCAD prompts you to *Select object to trim or shift-select to extend or* ↓.

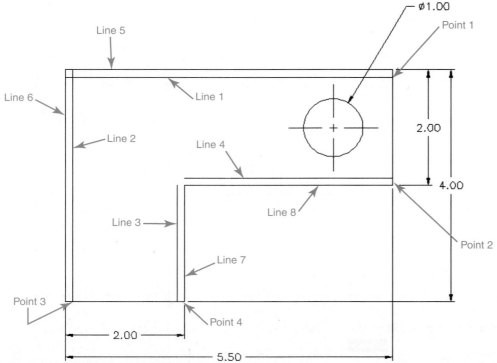

**Figure 2-52**   Trimming and extending lines

3. Pick a point on the short line segment shown at point 1 in Figure 2-52. The vertical line is trimmed, and AutoCAD prompts you again to *Select object to trim or shift-select to extend or* ↓.
4. Pick the line segments shown at points 2, 3, and 4 in Figure 2-52. The lines are trimmed.
5. Press **<Enter ↵>** to exit the **Trim** tool. Notice that the dimensions automatically update to reflect the new sizes.
6. Choose the **Extend** tool from the **Modify** panel. The current command settings are displayed in the command window, and AutoCAD prompts you:

```
Current settings: Projection=UCS, Edge=None
Select boundary edges ...
Select objects or <select all>:
```

7. Select lines 3 and 4 in Figure 2-52 and press **<Enter ↵>**. AutoCAD prompts you to *Select object to extend or shift-select to trim or* ↓.
8. Press the down arrow on your keyboard or type **E<Enter ↵>** and select the **Extend** option.
9. Pick a point on line 3 in Figure 2-52. The vertical line is extended, and AutoCAD prompts you again to *Select object to extend or shift-select to trim or* ↓.
10. Pick a point on line 4 in Figure 2-52. The line is extended.
11. Press **<Enter ↵>** to exit the **Extend** tool.
12. Choose the **Fillet** tool from the **Modify** panel. The current command settings are displayed in the command window, and AutoCAD prompts you:

```
Current settings: Mode = TRIM, Radius = 0.0000
Select first object or ↓.
```

13. Select lines 1 and 2 in Figure 2-52. Both lines are trimmed to form a closed corner by creating a fillet with a radius of 0.0″.
14. Choose the **Erase** tool from the **Modify** toolbar and erase lines 5, 6, 7, and 8 lines (see Figure 2-51).
15. Your drawing should now look like Figure 2-53. Use grips to select the dimension extension line origin as shown and attach it back to the corner of the drawing using an **Endpoint** object snap. Make sure the **Object Snap** button is on.
16. Save your drawing as **EX2-23**.

**Figure 2-53**   The updated drawing

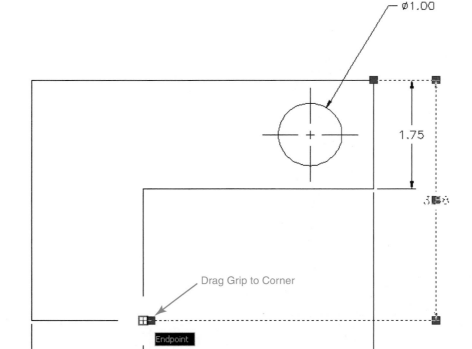

# CLEANING UP LAYOUT SPACE

Now that we have some basic dimensions on the drawing, let's go back to the layout space and make some adjustments to the viewport and the title block.

## Setting the Viewport Scale

Remember that in layout space (paper space), viewports are simply holes or windows into the model space environment. You can open up that viewport to zoom and pan around model space and can even make changes to your model. You can also assign a viewport scale to each viewport. By setting this viewport scale, you are telling AutoCAD to display the model at a certain scale (full-scale, half-scale, 1/8″ = 1′-0″, etc.) within that viewport. The viewport in the **ANSI A Title Block** layout was part of the template file used to create the drawing. In the next exercise, you'll set the scale of the viewport and adjust the position of the model within the title block.

### Exercise 2-24: Setting the Viewport Scale

1. Choose the **ANSI A Title Block** button at the bottom of the drawing to switch to layout space. The geometry from model space will show up in the viewport.
2. Choose the **Zoom Extents** tool from the zoom tools on the **Utilities** panel. This will fill the drawing area with your layout sheet.
3. Double-click inside the viewport to activate it. The viewport will highlight, and the crosshair will appear only inside the viewport.
4. Click on the **Automatically Add Scales** icon with the lightning bolt on the far right of the **Viewport Scale** on the Status Bar shown in Figure 2-54, and turn it on so that the dimensions automatically scale in the next step.

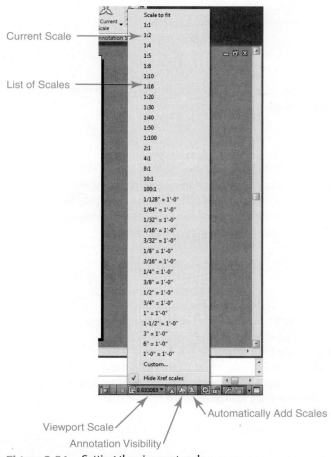

Current Scale

List of Scales

Viewport Scale

Annotation Visibility

Automatically Add Scales

**Figure 2-54**    Setting the viewport scale

5. Click on the down arrow to the right of the **Viewport Scale** on the Status Bar shown in Figure 2-54 and choose **1:2.** Your drawing will zoom so that your model is half-scale (1:2) on your layout (paper).
6. Choose **Pan** from the **Utilites** panel and pan your drawing so that it looks like Figure 2-55.
7. Save your drawing as **EX2-24**.

Notice that the dimension features are now twice as large as they were before you set the vewport scale. This is because the dimension style was set up earlier with the **Annotative** feature turned on (see Figure 2-38). When combined with turning on the feature that automatically scales annotative objects as done in step 4 of Exercise 2-24, this setting actually creates another set of

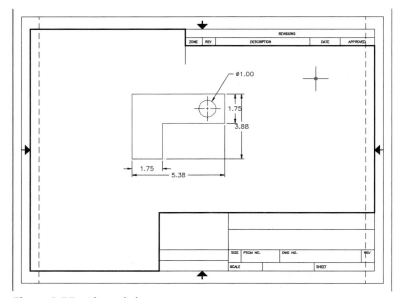

**Figure 2-55**    The scaled viewport

dimensions for the new viewport/annotation scale so that you can view your drawing at different scales and have all the annotation objects display at the correct size.

It is possible to display all of an annotation object's scale representations when you select it so that each size is visible. You can grip edit the current scale's representation without affecting any of the other scale representations. For instance, by using grips, you can relocate one scale representation while leaving the others in their current locations.

**Exercise 2-25:** Adjusting Dimensions

1. Change the **Scale** back to 1:1 on the Status Bar. The view is zoomed in at a scale of 1:1, and the dimension features are scaled down by half.
2. Choose the **Undo** tool to set the scale back to 1:2.
3. Click on the icon with the lightning bolt to the right of the **VP Scale** on the Status Bar shown in Figure 2-54. Turn it on so that all scale representations of an annotation object are shown when it is selected and grips are turned on.
4. Use grips to relocate the dimensions so that they no longer overlap as shown in Figure 2-56.
5. Double-click outside the viewport to close the viewport and switch to paper space.
6. Save your drawing as **EX2-25**.

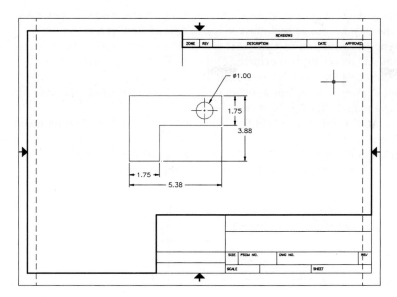

Figure 2-56    The adjusted dimensions

## Text

Let's update the title block and place some text. When placing text in a drawing, AutoCAD will ask you to define a box in which to place the text. Once that text box is defined, a miniature text editor appears where you specified, and you can start typing your text. The text editor has a number of formatting features found in many text editors (fonts, bold, justification, etc.). You can insert predefined text fields (like the file name, date, plot scale, etc.) and can also import text from an external text file.

| **FOR MORE DETAILS** | Chapter 11 describes the various options for placing and formatting text. |
| --- | --- |

## Exercise 2-26: Placing Text

1. Set the **Title Block** layer current by selecting it from the **Layer** drop-down list.
2. Choose **Zoom Window** from the zoom tools on the **Utilities** panel. Drag a box around the lower right corner of the title block as shown in Figure 2-57.

Figure 2-57    Defining a text box

3. Choose the **Multiline Text** tool from the **Annotation** panel. AutoCAD prompts you to *Specify first corner:*.
4. Pick the endpoints at point 1 and point 2 shown in Figure 2-57. The **Multiline Text** ribbon will appear. A flashing text cursor will appear at the upper left corner of the text box. This indicates where the text will appear when you type.
5. In the **Style** panel, set the text height to .125 and the style to Roman.

6. Choose the **Justification** button in the **Paragraph** panel and choose **Middle Center MC** from the menu. The flashing cursor will move to the middle of the text box.
7. In the text box, type **Introduction to AutoCAD** and choose **Close Text Editor** from the **Close** panel. AutoCAD places the text centered in the text box you specified.
8. Press **<Enter ↵>** to repeat the **MTEXT** command.
9. Pick the endpoints at point 1 and point 2 shown in Figure 2-58. The **Multiline Text** ribbon reappears along with the flashing text cursor.
10. Set the text height to **.250** and choose **Middle Center MC** from the **Justification** menu. Set the style to Roman.
11. Type **Angle Bracket** in the text box and then choose **OK** to end the command.
12. Save your drawing as **EX2-26**. **Close Text Editor** to end the command.

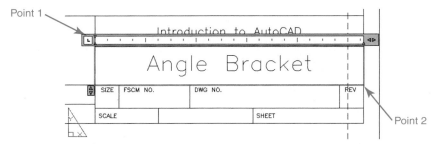

**Figure 2-58**   Placing more text

So far, you've simply typed in the text you want to display. You may want to place text that is specific to the drawing (like the drawing file name) or that is dynamic (for example, the plot time or date the drawing was last revised). AutoCAD provides you with a number of predefined text fields that will display various drawing or system information. In the following exercise, you'll use a text field to create the text.

**Exercise 2-27:** Using a Text Field

1. Choose the **Multiline Text** tool from the **Annotation** panel and select the endpoints at point 1 and point 2 shown in Figure 2-59.

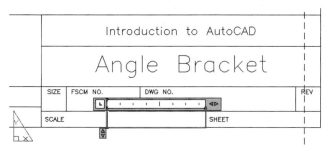

**Figure 2-59**   Placing a text field

2. Set the text height to **.125,** the style to Roman, and the justification to **Middle Center.**
3. Choose **Insert Field** from the **Insert** Panel. This displays the **Field** dialog box (see Figure 2-60).
4. From the **Field names** list, choose **Filename.**
5. In the **Format** area, choose **Uppercase.**
6. Select the **Filename only** option and put a check in the box on the **Display file extension** setting (see Figure 2-60).
7. Choose **OK** to insert the field into the drawing. The **Field** dialog box will close.
8. Choose Close Text Editor to end the command. The drawing file name **EX2-26** appears in the title block (see Figure 2-61). The field text is highlighted to indicate that it is field value.

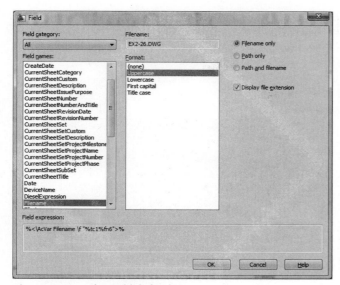

**Figure 2-60**    The Field dialog box

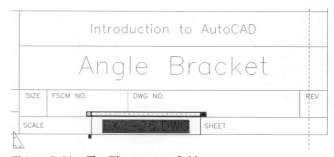

**Figure 2-61**    The Filename text field

9. Choose **Zoom Extents** from the **Utilities** panel.
10. Save your drawing as **EX2-27**.

As you can see from the **Field** dialog box (see Figure 2-60), there are a number of predefined fields. Using field names is a great timesaver. Because the field is updated every time you regenerate, any changes to the drawing file information (such as the file name) will automatically update the text.

> **FOR MORE DETAILS**    Chapter 11 covers text fields and how to use them.

## PLOTTING AND PAGE SETUPS

When you plot a drawing, AutoCAD needs to know a number of different settings (printer, paper size, orientation, margins, color settings, plot scale, etc.). You can specify these settings each time you plot, but for consistency, AutoCAD allows you to save all these settings to a ***page setup***. A page setup is simply a group of plot settings saved to a user-specified name. In the following exercise, you will make changes to the page setup associated with the **ANSI A Title Block** layout.

**page setup:** A collection of plot settings that are applied to a drawing layout.

### Exercise 2-28: Page Setup

1. Choose **Page Setup Manager** from the **Plot** panel on the **Output** panel. This displays the **Page Setup Manager** dialog box shown in Figure 2-62.
2. Choose **New** to display the **New Page Setup** dialog box (see Figure 2-63).
3. Enter **ANSI A Title Block—Windows System Printer** as the new page setup name and choose **OK.** This displays the **Page Setup** dialog box (see Figure 2-64).
4. From the **Printer/plotter** list, select **Default Windows System Printer.pc3.** This is your default Windows printer.
5. From the **Paper size** list, choose **Letter.**
6. Choose **Extents** from the **What to plot:** list. This tells AutoCAD to plot everything currently shown in the drawing.
7. Check the **Center the plot** option in the **Plot offset** area.
8. If checked, clear the check from the **Fit to paper** box.
9. Choose **1:1** from the **Scale** drop-down list.

Figure 2-62   The Page Setup Manager dialog box

Figure 2-63   The New Page Setup dialog box

Figure 2-64   The Page
Setup dialog box

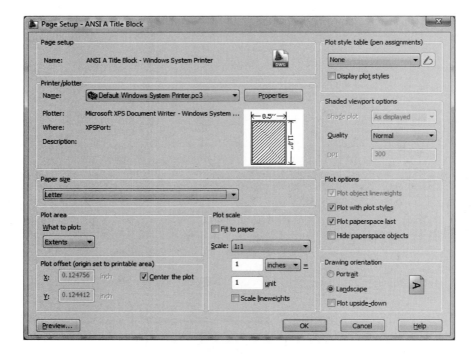

10. Choose **Landscape** in the **Drawing orientation** area. Your selections should be the same as those shown in Figure 2-64.

11. Choose **Preview** to see how your drawing will look when it is printed. AutoCAD will switch to a print preview view (see Figure 2-65). The buttons at the top of the print preview window allow you to pan and zoom around the preview.

12. Choose the **Close Preview Window** button to close the preview window.

13. Choose **OK** to save the page setup. The **Page Setup Manager** dialog box returns with the new page setup listed.

14. Select the page setup you just created and then choose **Set Current.** This applies the page setup settings to the current layout.

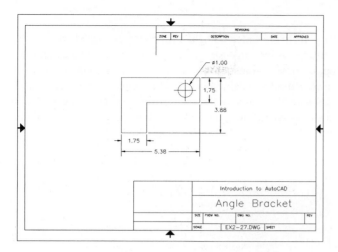

Figure 2-65    The print preview window

15. Choose **Close** to close the **Page Setup Manager** dialog box.
16. Save your drawing as **EX2-28**.

Notice the dashed line that appears around the edge of the layout (see Figure 2-66). This dashed line represents the printable area on your drawing. It's not an actual drawing object (you can't select it), only a visual indication of what part of your drawing will be printed. If any part of your drawing extends outside this dashed line, those parts will be clipped from the final print. To fix this, you can adjust the plot scale of your drawing, move or adjust the geometry within your drawing, or adjust the margins of your printer.

**Note:**

Many times a page setup has the same name as the layout space; however, they are not the same thing. Be careful not to confuse the page setup with the drawing layout. The layout is a drawing space where your drawing objects (title blocks, viewports, etc.) reside. The page setup is a collection of plot settings that are applied to the layout when you plot the drawing.

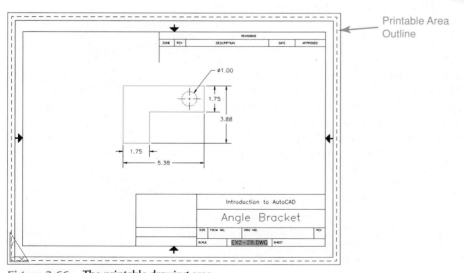

Printable Area Outline

Figure 2-66    The printable drawing area

**FOR MORE DETAILS**    See Chapter 14 for more on page setups.

## Plotting

When you plot a drawing in AutoCAD, you are presented with the **Plot** dialog box (see Figure 2-67). The **Plot** dialog box has all the same settings as the **Page Setup** dialog box (in fact, you can use the **PLOT** command to create page setups). These options allow you to make last-minute changes to your page setup or temporarily override settings contained in the page setup. For example, your page setup may be defined for a C- or D-size plot, but you may want to create a quick check plot on an A-size sheet. The **PLOT** command allows you to change your plot setting without going through the process of creating a new page setup.

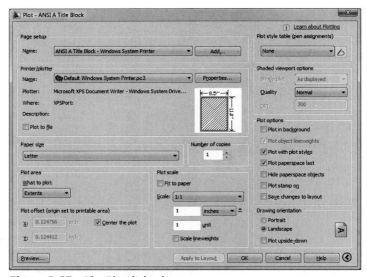

**Figure 2-67**    The Plot dialog box

In the following exercise, you'll do a plot using the page setup you just created.

### Exercise 2-29: Plotting

1. Choose the **Plot** tool from the **Plot** panel in the **Output** ribbon. The **Plot** dialog box appears (see Figure 2-67). If your dialog box looks different, choose the arrow next to the **Help** button to expand the dialog box and see all options.
2. From the **Page setup** list, choose **ANSI A Title Block – Windows System Printer.**
3. Verify that all the settings are correct and choose **Preview.** The plot preview displays.
4. Choose the **Plot** button to plot your drawing to your default Windows system printer. A plot progress bar will appear briefly, and AutoCAD will return to the command prompt when the plot is complete.
5. Save your drawing as **EX2-29**.

> **Note:**
> In the following exercise, your printer features and settings may differ from those shown here.

Once the plot is complete, AutoCAD will display a balloon in the lower right corner of the Status Bar (see Figure 2-68). This indicates the results of the **PLOT** command and reports any errors that may have occurred. To view the plot results, click on the indicated link to display the **Plot and Publish** details box. Here you can view the results of all plots submitted during the current AutoCAD session.

**Figure 2-68**    The Plot and Publish balloon

# SUMMARY

You have now walked through a typical AutoCAD drawing session. Although your drawing sessions will no doubt be different and most likely involve a variety of more complex tasks, the exercises in this chapter give you an idea of what is involved in working with AutoCAD. The tasks you completed in this chapter will be built on and expanded in the rest of the text. You should now feel fairly comfortable navigating the AutoCAD workspace and drawing some basic objects.

# CHAPTER TEST QUESTIONS

## Multiple Choice

1. Model space is:
   a. Only for three-dimensional objects.
   b. Limited in size so you must scale your model appropriately.
   c. Generally used to draw objects that exist in the real world.
   d. Generally used to draw objects that exist only on paper.

2. In the following command window prompt, what would you type to use the TTR option?

   `Specify center point for circle or [3P/2P/Ttr (tan tan radius)]:`

   a. 3P<Enter ⏎>
   b. (tan tan radius)<Enter ⏎>
   c. 2P<Enter ⏎>
   d. T<Enter ⏎>

3. Which of the following settings do NOT allow you to control point specifications?
   a. Grid
   b. Snap
   c. Ortho
   d. Polar

4. The command window:
   a. Cannot be moved.
   b. Can be turned off.
   c. Is the only way to communicate with AutoCAD.
   d. Cannot be undocked.

5. Scrolling the wheel of a wheel mouse will:
   a. Scroll the text in the command window.
   b. Do nothing.
   c. Pan the drawing up and down.
   d. Zoom the drawing in and out.

6. Which of the following is NOT a property common to all objects?
   a. Length
   b. Layer
   c. Color
   d. Lineweight

7. Dimensions:
   a. Can be placed only in model space.
   b. Can be placed only in paper space.
   c. Must be erased and redrawn if the model changes.
   d. Are controlled by their associated dimension style.

8. Grips appear:
   a. At key points on drawing objects.
   b. On a separate layer.
   c. Every time you click on the screen.
   d. Only in model space.

9. A page setup:
   a. Is the same thing as a paper space layout.
   b. Can only be defined in a drawing template.
   c. Is a collection of plot settings.
   d. Must have the same name as a paper space layout.

10. The dashed line that appears around the edge of a layout:
    a. Can be erased if needed.
    b. Is on its own layer and can be turned off if desired.
    c. Shows a visual indication of the area that will be printed.
    d. Shows up on the printed drawing.

## Matching

**Column A**

a. Drawing template

b. Objects

c. Dimension style

d. Page setup

e. Grips

**Column B**

1. The process of moving around the drawing.

2. The settings that control how and where a drawing object is shown in the drawing.

3. A link between drawing objects and dimension objects.

4. The process of specifying the objects you wish to edit.

5. A collection of plot settings that are applied to a drawing layout.

**Column A**

f. Object Snap

g. Object properties

h. Zooming

i. Associativity

j. Building a selection set

**Column B**

6. A drawing file used as a starting point when creating new drawings

7. Editing points that appear at key locations on drawing objects.

8. Graphical drawing elements, such as lines, arcs, circles, polylines, and text.

9. Geometric points on objects such as the endpoints or midpoint of a line or the center of an arc or circle.

10. A collection of dimension settings which control how dimension objects act and are displayed.

## True or False

1. True or False: There is only one layout allowed in a drawing file.

2. True or False: A layout can have only one viewport.

3. True or False: There is only one model space allowed in a drawing file.

4. True or False: Polar tracking can be set to detect any angle.

5. True or False: You can only use the **REDO** command immediately after using the **UNDO** command.

6. True or False: Objects on a layer that is frozen can be seen but not modified.

7. True or False: Objects on a layer that is turned off can still be modified.

8. True or False: To move an object, you must always select the object first and then start the **MOVE** command.

9. True or False: You can override page setup settings when you plot.

10. True or False: Dimensions can update to follow changes to your geometry.

# Controlling the Drawing Display

# 3

## Chapter Objectives

- Zoom in and out of a drawing
- Pan around a drawing
- Create and restore named views
- Split the drawing display into multiple viewports
- Refresh the drawing display
- Toggle all the toolbars and palettes off and on
- Make arcs and circles appear smoother
- Increase drawing display regeneration speed by turning off text and solid fill areas

## INTRODUCTION

The AutoCAD drawing display window is one of the most important features of the AutoCAD user interface. It is here where you do most of your work creating and modifying the objects that make up your drawing. AutoCAD provides a number of tools and settings that allow you to control how and what drawing information is displayed in the drawing display window. The drawing display tools and their settings are explained in detail in this chapter.

## ZOOMING IN AND OUT OF A DRAWING

The AutoCAD drawing display window is like a camera lens. You control what's displayed in your drawing by zooming in to get a closer look and by zooming out to see the big picture, similar to a camera.

Unlike most cameras, AutoCAD provides a number of different ways to control the zooming process. Because they are used so often, the most popular **Zoom** tools are located on the **Home** ribbon on the **Utilities** panel as shown in Figure 3-1.

In fact, all the **Zoom** tools can be accessed on the **Utilities** panel by selecting the **Zoom Extents** tool to display the **Zoom** flyout menu shown in Figure 3-2. As you can see, there are many different **Zoom** tools available. The following sections explain how you can zoom in and out of your drawing.

 **TIP** The **Zoom** tool on the right side of the Status Bar introduced in Chapter 1 defaults to the **Zoom Window** tool. The **Zoom Window** tool is explained in detail later in this chapter.

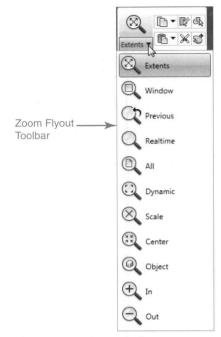

Zoom Flyout Toolbar

Figure 3-1    The Utilities panel Zoom tools

Figure 3-2    The Zoom flyout menu

## Frequently Used Zoom Tools

The following **Zoom** tools are the easiest to use and provide the most "bang for the buck" when you need to zoom in and out of your drawing quickly. You will likely find yourself using the **Zoom** tools explained in this section most often out of the many different **Zoom** tools provided by AutoCAD.

*Zoom Extents.*    The **Zoom Extents** tool is very useful because it allows you to view everything in your drawing on your screen quickly. AutoCAD calculates the extents of the outermost objects in your drawing that are not on a frozen layer and then zooms out so that everything is visible. This is especially helpful when you are zoomed in to a small area of your drawing and you draw an object that goes off the screen. Using **Zoom Extents** allows you to see the complete object.

**TIP**    Sometimes when you use the **Zoom Extents** tool, it might appear that there is nothing in your drawing—don't panic. Usually this means that there is some rogue object out in the nether regions of your drawing. If you zoom out just a little, you can usually find the object and determine its identity so that it might be moved or deleted.

### Exercise 3-1: Using the Zoom Extents Tool

1. Open the drawing **Willhome** located on the student CD.
2. Select the **Model** button on the right side of the Status Bar so that model space is active.
3. Select the **Zoom Extents** tool on the **Utilities** panel and zoom to the extents of the drawing.
4. Zoom in on an area of the drawing using your mouse wheel or any of the techniques introduced in Chapter 2.
5. Select the **Zoom Extents** tool again.
6. All the drawing information is now displayed in the drawing display window.

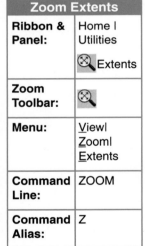

| Zoom Extents | |
|---|---|
| **Ribbon & Panel:** | Home \| Utilities Extents |
| **Zoom Toolbar:** | |
| **Menu:** | <u>V</u>iew\| <u>Z</u>oom\| <u>E</u>xtents |
| **Command Line:** | ZOOM |
| **Command Alias:** | Z |

Student Files

**Note:**
If there are no objects in your drawing or everything is on layers that are currently frozen. The **Zoom Extents** tool will zoom to the limits of your drawing. See Chapter 4 for more information about controlling drawing limits.

Zoom Window
Pick Points

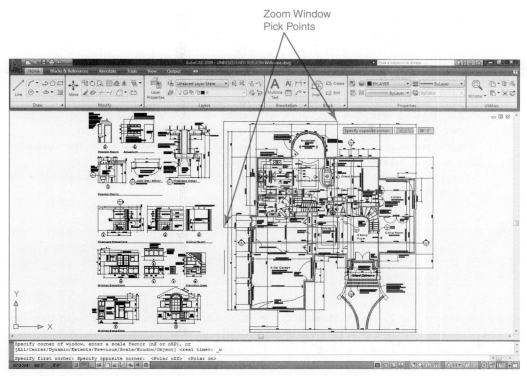

**Figure 3-3**    Defining the Zoom Window area

*Zoom Window.*    The **Zoom Window** tool allows you to define a rectangular area, or window, using two mouse pick points so that you can quickly zoom in on a specific area of your drawing. The windowed area is zoomed *and* centered at a scale that fills your drawing display area.

After selecting the **Zoom Window** tool, you are prompted to select the two corner points of the window. Select two points in your drawing to define the rectangular area you wish to zoom as shown in Figure 3-3.

The display is zoomed immediately after selecting the second corner point as shown in Figure 3-4.

| Zoom Window | |
|---|---|
| **Ribbon & Panel:** | Home \| Utilities |
| | 🔍 Window |
| **Zoom Toolbar:** | 🔍 |
| **Menu:** | View\| Zoom\| Window |
| **Command Line:** | ZOOM |
| **Command Alias:** | Z |

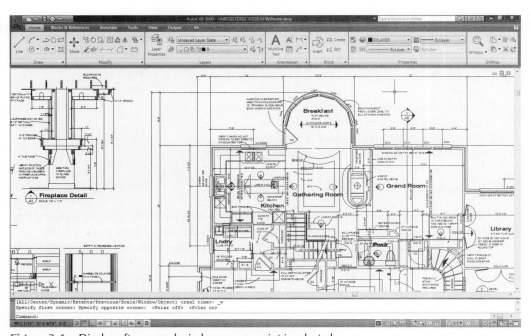

**Figure 3-4**    Display after second window corner point is selected

**Exercise 3-2:** Using the Zoom Window Tool

1. Open the drawing **Willhome** located on the student CD.
2. Select the **Model** button on the right side of the Status Bar so that model space is active.
3. Select the **Zoom Extents** tool on the **Utilities** panel and zoom to the extents of the drawing.
4. Select the **Zoom Window** tool on the **Zoom** flyout menu on the **Utilities** panel. AutoCAD prompts you to *Specify first corner:*.
5. Pick a point in your drawing. AutoCAD places the first point and drags a rectangular rubber-band line from that point and prompts you to *Specify opposite corner:*.
6. Size the rectangle so that the information you want to zoom in on is within the windowed area and pick another point in your drawing (see Figure 3-3).
7. After picking the second point, the windowed area is zoomed to fill the drawing display window (see Figure 3-4).

| Zoom Previous | |
|---|---|
| **Ribbon & Panel:** | Home \| Utilities ⟳Previous |
| **Standard Toolbar:** | ⟳ |
| **Menu:** | View\| Zoom\| Previous |
| **Command Line:** | ZOOM |
| **Command Alias:** | Z |

**TIP** It is also possible to zoom using a window by selecting the **Zoom** button on the right side of the Status Bar introducd in Chapter 1.

*Zoom Previous.*     The **Zoom Previous** tool is probably the most popular of the zoom tools because it allows you to restore the previous drawing display. In fact, you can restore up to ten previous views, so that you can step back in time. This capability allows you to zoom in on an area of your drawing to get close to your work (see Figure 3-4) and then quickly return to the previous overall view (see Figure 3-3). From there you can zoom in on other areas and then zoom back out again. The combination of the **Zoom Window** tool and the **Zoom Previous** tool provides one of the easiest, most efficient ways to navigate around your drawing.

AutoCAD stores up to 10 previous views. The following message is displayed at the command line if there is no previous view to display:

```
Command: No previous view saved.
```

**Exercise 3-3:** Using the Zoom Previous Tool

1. Open the drawing **Willhome** located on the student CD.
2. Select the **Model** button on the right side of the Status Bar so that model space is active.
3. Select the **Zoom Extents** tool and zoom to the extents of the drawing.
4. Follow the steps shown in Exercise 3-2 and zoom in on an area of the drawing so that the drawing display looks similar to Figure 3-4.
5. Select the **Zoom Previous** tool on the **Utilities** panel.
6. The drawing information displayed in the drawing display window returns to the previous view.
7. Continue selecting the **Zoom Previous** tool until AutoCAD displays the following prompt at the command line:

```
No previous view saved.
```

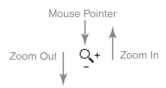

**Note:**
The **Zoom Previous** tool does not undo any drawing or editing commands and affects the display only.

*Zoom Realtime.*     Zooming in "realtime" simply means that the zooming process is interactive. As you zoom in, objects grow larger on the screen; as you zoom out, objects grow smaller.

Selecting the **Zoom Realtime** tool causes the mouse pointer to change to the magnifying glass icon shown in Figure 3-5.

| Zoom Realtime | |
|---|---|
| **Ribbon & Panel:** | Home \| Utilities 🔍 Realtime |
| **Standard Toolbar:** | 🔍 |
| **Menu:** | View\| Zoom\| Realtime |
| **Command Line:** | ZOOM |
| **Command Alias:** | Z |

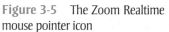

Mouse Pointer

Zoom Out        Zoom In

**Figure 3-5**     The Zoom Realtime mouse pointer icon

Notice that there is a plus sign at the top right of the magnifying glass and a minus sign at the bottom left. Holding your mouse button down and moving the magnifying glass towards the top of the screen zooms in and increases the display magnification (+). See Figures 3-6A and B. Holding the button down and moving the magnifying glass towards the bottom of the screen zooms out and decreases the display magnification (−).

If you run out of mouse pad during the process of moving your mouse up or down the screen, just pick up your mouse, reposition it, and repeat the process. When you are finished zooming and the drawing display appears at the desired magnification factor, press **<Enter ↵>** or **<Esc>** to complete the zoom process.

**TIP**  If you reach a point in zooming in or out when the display will not zoom any farther and appears stuck, don't worry. This just means that you need to regenerate your display using the **REGEN** command. The **REGEN** and **REGENALL** commands are discussed in detail later in the section "Cleaning Up the Drawing Display."

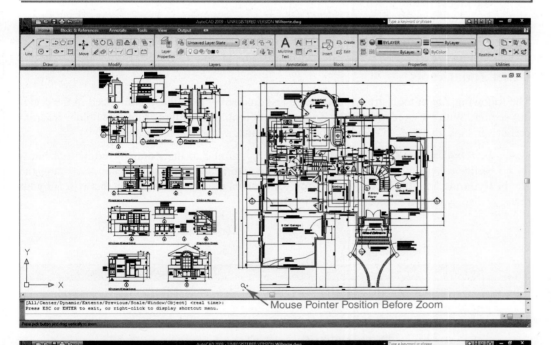

**Figure 3-6A**  Original Zoom Realtime mouse pointer position (bottom of screen)

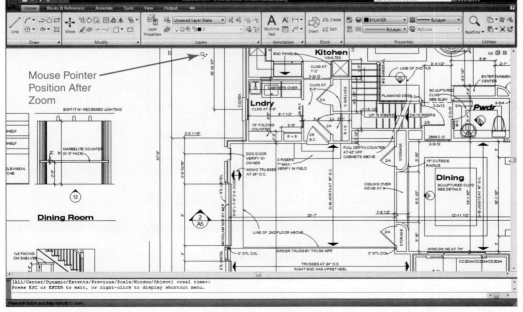

**Figure 3-6B**  New Zoom Realtime mouse pointer position (top of screen)

**Exercise 3-4:** Using the Zoom Realtime Tool

1.  Open the drawing **Willhome** located on the student CD.
2.  Select the **Model** button on the right side of the Status Bar so that model space is active.
3.  Select the **Zoom Extents** tool on the **Utilities** panel.
4.  Select the **Zoom Realtime** tool on the **Utilities** panel.
5.  Notice that your mouse pointer changes to a magnifying glass (see Figure 3-5).
6.  Click with your mouse at the bottom of the drawing display window and hold the mouse button down (see Figure 3-6A).
7.  Drag your mouse to the top of the drawing display window while continuing to hold the mouse button down.
8.  Release the mouse button when the mouse pointer reaches the top of the drawing display window (see Figure 3-6B).
9.  Click with your mouse at the top of the drawing display window and hold the mouse button down.
10. Drag your mouse to the bottom of the drawing display window while continuing to hold the mouse button down.
11. Release the mouse button when the mouse pointer reaches the bottom of the drawing display window.
12. Press **<Enter ↵>** or **<Esc>** to complete the zoom process.

## Other Zoom Tools

The following **Zoom** tools are typically used less frequently than those introduced in the previous section. With the exception of the **Zoom Object** tool, most of these tools are holdovers from earlier versions of AutoCAD when display performance was much more limited.

*Zoom Dynamic.*   The **Zoom Dynamic** tool is very similar to the **Zoom Window** tool introduced earlier except it takes a couple of extra steps to achieve the same result. Selecting the **Zoom Dynamic** tool displays a view box on your screen representing the area that will fill your drawing display once it is accepted. See Figure 3-7.

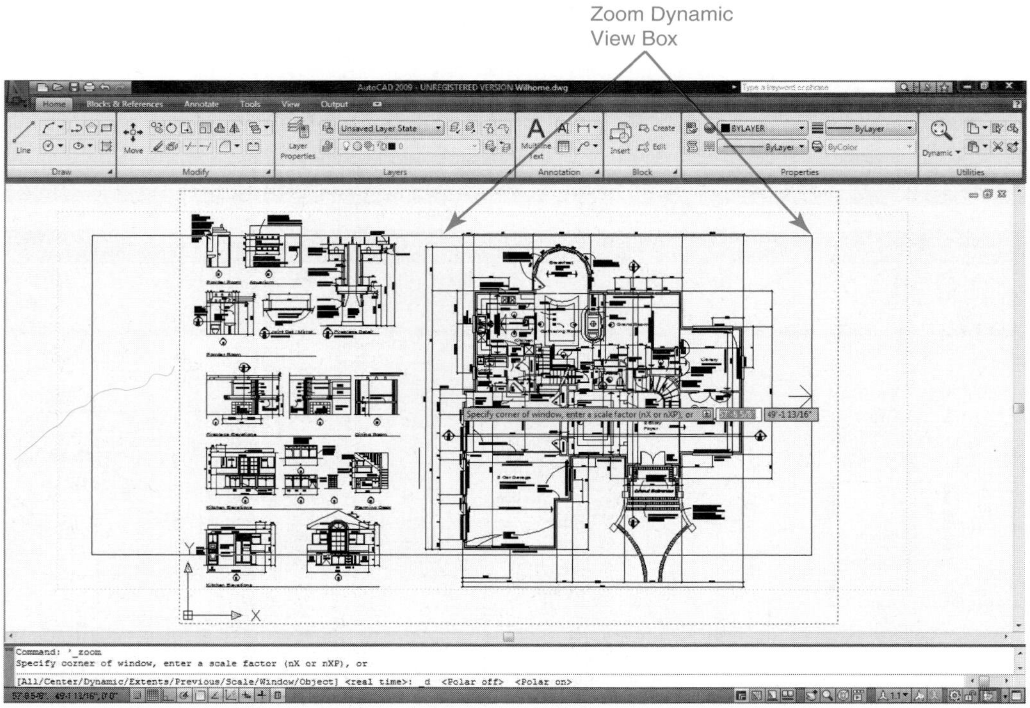

| Zoom Dynamic | |
|---|---|
| **Ribbon & Panel:** | Home I Utilities 🔍Dynamic |
| **Zoom Toolbar:** | 🔍 |
| **Menu:** | Viewl Zoom I Dynamic |
| **Command Line:** | ZOOM |
| **Command Alias:** | Z |

Zoom Dynamic
View Box

**Figure 3-7**   The Zoom Dynamic view box

Clicking with your mouse when the **Zoom Dynamic** box is displayed toggles the view box so that it can be resized. If you click again, the view box switches back so that you can move it to a different location on your screen. You can toggle between these two modes until the drawing information you want to display is within the view box and press **<Enter.↵>** to zoom the display.

**Exercise 3-5:** Using the Zoom Dynamic Tool

1. Open the drawing **Willhome** located on the student CD.
2. Select the **Model** button on the right side of the Status Bar so that model space is active.
3. Select the **Zoom Extents** tool and zoom to the extents of the drawing.
4. Select the **Zoom Dynamic** tool on the **Utilities** panel. AutoCAD displays a view box on your screen representing the area that will fill your drawing display once the view is accepted (see Figure 3-7). The "X" in the middle of the view box indicates you are in pan mode.
5. Move your cursor back and forth on the screen to move the view box.
6. Pick a point in your drawing. The "X" at the center of the view box turns into an arrow on the right side of the view box. You are now in resize mode.
7. Size the rectangle so that the information you want to zoom in on is within the windowed area and pick another point in your drawing. The arrow changes back to an "X," placing you back in pan mode.
8. Move the view box to another area of the drawing.
9. Pick another point in your drawing and press **<Enter.↵>**.
10. The windowed area is zoomed to fill the drawing display.

*Zoom Scale.*    The **Zoom Scale** tool allows you to magnify your drawing display by a specific scale factor so that you can zoom in or zoom out. Specifying a scale factor larger than 1 increases the display magnification (zoom in) while a fractional value less than 1 decreases the display magnification (zoom out).

After you select the **Zoom Scale** tool, AutoCAD prompts you to *Enter a scale factor (nX or nXP):.*

The **X** and **XP** options indicate the different scale options between model space and paper space. The **X** option is used in model space to represent a scale multiplier. For instance, entering a value of **2X** (or **2x**) zooms in by magnifying your drawing display two times the current display scale factor. Entering a value of **1/2x** (or **.5x**) zooms out of your drawing at one-half the current display scale factor.

Figure 3-8 shows what the drawing display looks like after using the **Zoom Scale** tool to zoom the overall floor plan drawing shown in Figure 3-7 by a scale factor of **2X**.

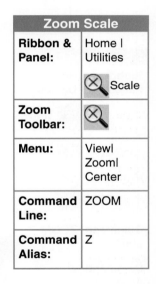

| Zoom Scale | |
|---|---|
| **Ribbon & Panel:** | Home \| Utilities |
| | ⊗ Scale |
| **Zoom Toolbar:** | ⊗ |
| **Menu:** | View\| Zoom\| Center |
| **Command Line:** | ZOOM |
| **Command Alias:** | Z |

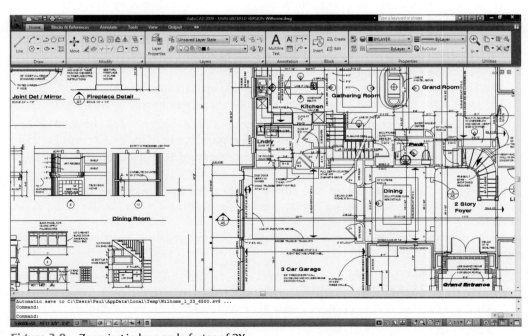

**Figure 3-8**    Zooming in by a scale factor of 2X

| Zoom In | |
|---|---|
| **Ribbon & Panel:** | Home \| Utilities ⊕ In |
| **Zoom Toolbar:** | ⊕ |
| **Menu:** | <u>V</u>iew\| <u>Z</u>oom\| <u>I</u>n |
| **Command Line:** | ZOOM |
| **Command Alias:** | Z |

| Zoom Out | |
|---|---|
| **Ribbon & Panel:** | Home \| Utilities ⊖ Out |
| **Zoom Toolbar:** | ⊖ |
| **Menu:** | <u>V</u>iew\| <u>Z</u>oom\| <u>O</u>ut |
| **Command Line:** | ZOOM |
| **Command Alias:** | Z |

| Zoom Center | |
|---|---|
| **Ribbon & Panel:** | Home \| Utilities ⊕ Center |
| **Zoom Toolbar:** | ⊕ |
| **Menu:** | <u>V</u>iew\| <u>Z</u>oom\| <u>C</u>enter |
| **Command Line:** | ZOOM |
| **Command Alias:** | Z |

The **Zoom Scale** tool's **XP** option is used strictly in paper space to set a viewport scale factor, hence the inclusion of the **P** for paper space.

> **FOR MORE DETAILS**   Utilizing paper space viewport scale factors is explained in detail in Chapter 14.

*Zoom In.*  The **Zoom In** tool allows you to zoom in to your drawing by a scale factor of 2 quickly. AutoCAD simply automates the zoom scale process shown earlier by specifying a scale factor of **2X** with the **Zoom Scale** tool.

*Zoom Out.*  The **Zoom Out** tool allows you to zoom out of your drawing by a scale factor of 1/2 quickly. AutoCAD simply automates the zoom scale process shown earlier by specifying a scale factor of **.5X** with the **Zoom Scale** tool.

**Exercise 3-6:** Using the Zoom Scale Tools

1. Open the drawing **Willhome** located on the student CD.
2. Select the **Model** button on the right side of the Status Bar so that model space is active.
3. Select the **Zoom Extents** tool and zoom to the extents of the drawing.
4. Select the **Zoom Scale** tool on the **Utilities** panel. AutoCAD prompts you to *Enter a scale factor (nX or nXP):*.
5. Type **2x<Enter ↵>**.
6. The drawing display is zoomed in by a scale factor of 2 (see Figure 3-8).
7. Select the **Zoom Scale** tool again. AutoCAD prompts you to *Enter a scale factor (nX or nXP):*.
8. Type **.5x<Enter ↵>**.
9. The drawing display is zoomed out by a scale factor of 1/2 so that the original view is displayed (see Figure 3-7).
10. Select the **Zoom In** tool on the **Utilities** panel.
11. The drawing display is zoomed in so everything appears larger.
12. Look at the **Command Line** window and notice what was entered by AutoCAD:

    ```
    Specify corner of window, enter a scale factor (nX or nXP), or
    [All/Center/Dynamic/Extents/Previous/Scale/Window/Object]: 2x
    ```
13. The drawing display was zoomed in by a scale factor of 2 (see Figure 3-8).
14. Select the **Zoom Out** tool on the **Utilities** panel.
15. The drawing display is zoomed out so everything appears smaller.
16. Look at the **Command Line** window and notice what was entered by AutoCAD:

    ```
    Specify corner of window, enter a scale factor (nX or nXP), or
    [All/Center/Dynamic/Extents/Previous/Scale/Window/Object]: .5x
    ```
17. The drawing display was zoomed out by a scale factor of 1/2 back to the original view.

*Zoom Center.*  The **Zoom Center** tool allows you to zoom *and* center your drawing on the screen by specifying a new drawing display center point and scale factor similar to the **Zoom Scale** tool.

After selecting the **Zoom Center** tool, AutoCAD prompts you for a center point and a magnification factor:

```
Specify center point:
Enter magnification or height <60.7511>:
```

Select the point in your drawing you want to be centered in the drawing display and a scale factor followed by an **X** using the same format as the **Zoom Scale** tool. For instance, entering **2X** zooms in by a factor of 2; entering a scale factor of **.5X** zooms out by 1/2.

## Exercise 3-7: Using the Zoom Center Tool

1. Open the drawing **Willhome** located on the student CD.
2. Select the **Model** button on the right side of the Status Bar so that model space is active.
3. Select the **Zoom Extents** tool and zoom to the extents of the drawing.
4. Select the **Zoom Center** tool on the **Utilities** panel. AutoCAD prompts you *Specify center point:*.
5. Pick a point in your drawing. AutoCAD prompts you to *Enter magnification or height <137'-11 85/128">:*.
6. Type **2x<Enter ↵>**.
7. The drawing display is zoomed in by a scale factor of 2 about the point you picked in the drawing so that the point is now located at the center of the display window.

*Zoom Object.*   The **Zoom Object** tool allows you to zoom up on a selected object, or objects, so that it fills the entire drawing display area.

After selecting the **Zoom Object** tool, AutoCAD prompts you to select the object to zoom in on. Select the objects you want to zoom in on and press **<Enter↵>** to accept the selection. AutoCAD then zooms up on the object to fill the display as shown in Figure 3-9.

This **Zoom Object** tool is especially useful for updating text in a drawing. In this example, the section cut bubble was selected in the windowed view shown in Figure 3-3. You can now update the text and then select the **Zoom Previous** tool to return to the previous view.

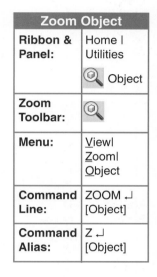

| Zoom Object | |
|---|---|
| **Ribbon & Panel:** | Home \| Utilities |
| | Object |
| **Zoom Toolbar:** | |
| **Menu:** | View\| Zoom\| Object |
| **Command Line:** | ZOOM ↵ [Object] |
| **Command Alias:** | Z ↵ [Object] |

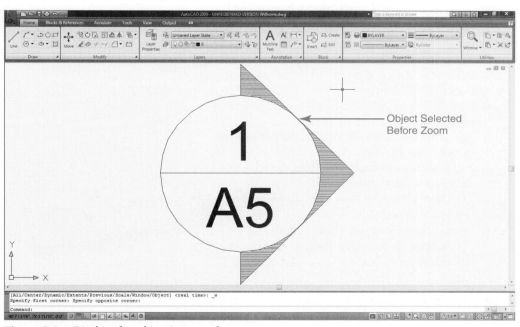

**Figure 3-9**   Display after object is zoomed

## Exercise 3-8: Using the Zoom Object Tool

1. Open the drawing **Willhome** located on the student CD.
2. Select the **Model** button on the right side of the Status Bar so that model space is active.
3. Select the **Zoom Extents** tool and zoom to the extents of the drawing.
4. Follow the steps shown in Exercise 3-2 and zoom in on an area of the drawing so that the drawing display looks similar to Figure 3-3.
5. Select the **Zoom Object** tool on the **Utilities** panel. AutoCAD prompts you to *Select objects:*.
6. Select the section cut bubble labeled "1/A5" and press **<Enter↵>**.
7. The section cut bubble is zoomed so that it fills the whole drawing display (see Figure 3-9).
8. Double-click with your cursor on the "1/A5" text to display the **Enhanced Attribute Editor** dialog box.

9. Type **2** in the **Value:** text box and then select **OK** at the bottom of the dialog box.
10. Select the **Zoom Previous** tool so that the drawing display returns to the view shown in Figure 3-4.

### Using the Mouse Wheel

If you have a wheel mouse, you can use the wheel to zoom in and out. Rolling the wheel towards the computer (away from you) zooms in to your drawing. Rolling the wheel away from the computer (towards you) will zoom out of your drawing.

Each click of the mouse wheel zooms in or out by 10 percent. You can change this zoom scale factor via the **ZOOMFACTOR** system variable. The **ZOOMFACTOR** default value is 60 and can be set to a value of between 3 and 100.

**TIP**    The mouse wheel also acts as a mouse button. In fact, it can be used to either pan your drawing display or display the **Object Snap** shortcut menu (see the next section, "Panning Around a Drawing"). It's also a little-known fact that double-clicking the wheel button will zoom to the extents of your drawing just like the **Zoom Extents** tool!

**Exercise 3-9:** Using the Mouse Wheel to Zoom In and Out

1. Open the drawing **Willhome** located on the student CD.
2. Select the **Model** button on the right side of the Status Bar so that model space is active.
3. Select the **Zoom Extents** tool and zoom to the extents of the drawing.
4. Roll the mouse wheel forward toward your computer screen.
5. The drawing display zooms in as you roll the mouse wheel forward.
6. Roll the mouse wheel away from the computer screen or toward yourself.
7. The drawing display zooms out as you roll the mouse wheel backward.
8. Double-click the mouse wheel button.
9. The drawing display is zoomed to the extents of the drawing.

**Note:**
In order to do this exercise, you must have a mouse with a thumb wheel.

## PANNING AROUND A DRAWING

When you move a camera from side to side to change the subject matter displayed in the camera lens, it is referred to as *panning*. Borrowing yet another term from the world of photography, AutoCAD uses the term ***pan*** to describe the process of moving your drawing from side to side in the drawing display window.

pan: The process of moving your drawing from side to side in the display window so the location of the view changes without affecting the zoom scale

Just as the subject matter doesn't move when you pan a camera, your drawing doesn't actually move, just what's shown in the display window so that you can view another area.

The different methods used to pan around your drawing are explained in the following sections.

### The Pan Tool

The **Pan** tool allows you to pan your drawing so that you can recenter it in the drawing display without affecting the current zoom display scale factor. This allows you to view drawing information quickly that might not be visible because it is off the side of the drawing display.

After you select the **Pan** tool, your mouse pointer changes to the hand icon shown in Figure 3-10.

← Mouse Pointer

**Figure 3-10**   The Pan mouse pointer icon

Using the **Pan** tool, you simply grab on to the drawing with your "hand" by clicking with your mouse and then drag the drawing across the drawing display window by holding the mouse button down. See Figures 3-11A and B.

Like the **Zoom Realtime** tool, if you run out of mouse pad during the process of moving your mouse across the screen, just pick up your mouse, reposition it, and repeat the process. When you are finished panning and the drawing display contains the desired drawing information, press **<Enter ↵>** or **<Esc>** to complete the panning process.

| Pan | |
|---|---|
| **Ribbon & Panel:** | Home \| Utilities 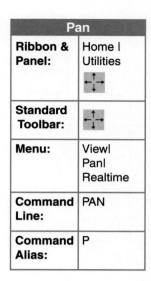 |
| **Standard Toolbar:** | |
| **Menu:** | View\| Pan\| Realtime |
| **Command Line:** | PAN |
| **Command Alias:** | P |

You can quickly switch between the **Pan** tool and the **Zoom Realtime** tool by right-clicking to display the shortcut menu shown in Figure 3-12.

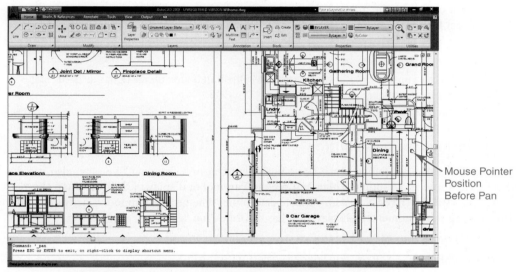

Mouse Pointer Position Before Pan

**Figure 3-11A**    Original Pan mouse pointer position (right side of screen)

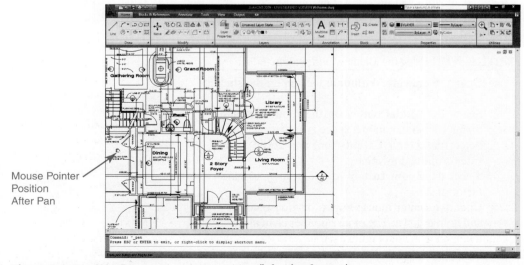

Mouse Pointer Position After Pan

**Figure 3-11B**    New Pan mouse pointer position (left side of screen)

### Exercise 3-10: Using the Pan Tool

1. Open the drawing **Willhome** located on the student CD.
2. Select the **Model** button on the right side of the Status Bar that model space is active.
3. Select the **Zoom Extents** tool and zoom to the extents of the drawing.
4. Select the **Zoom In** tool to zoom in by a scale factor of 2.
5. Select the **Pan** tool on the **Utilities** panel.
6. The mouse pointer changes to a hand icon (see Figure 3-10), and AutoCAD prompts you at the command line:

   `Press ESC or ENTER to exit, or right-click to display shortcut menu.`

7. Place your mouse pointer at the right edge of the drawing display window (see Figure 3-11A).
8. Click with your mouse and drag the drawing display to the left by holding down the mouse button (see Figure 3-11B).
9. Release the left mouse button and then click the right mouse button to display the **Pan and Zoom** shortcut menu (see Figure 3-12).
10. Select **Zoom** from the menu to switch to the **Zoom Realtime** tool.
11. Zoom in and out of the drawing a few times using the **Zoom Realtime** tool.
12. Right-click with the mouse to display the **Pan and Zoom** shortcut menu again.
13. Select **Exit** from the menu to end the command.

**Figure 3-12** Pan/Zoom Realtime shortcut menu

It is also possible to select the **Pan** tool via the **Pan** button on the right side of the Status Bar introduced in Chapter 1.

## Using the Middle Mouse Button

As alluded to earlier in the section "Zooming In and Out of a Drawing," you can also use the wheel on a mouse as a button to either activate the **Pan** tool or display the **Object Snap** shortcut menu. The **MBUTTONPAN** system variable determines whether the **Pan** tool is activated or the **Object Snap** shortcut menu is displayed. It has the following settings:

    **MBUTTONPAN = 0: `Object Snap`** shortcut menu displayed
    **MBUTTONPAN = 1: `Pan`** tool activated (Default)

**Figure 3-13** Pan tool in "joystick" mode

Holding down the <**Ctrl**> key when you use the middle button of your mouse to activate the **Pan** tool will put you in "joystick" mode (see Figure 3-13) so that the mouse pointer acts like a game joystick.

### Exercise 3-11: Using the Middle Mouse Button to Pan

1. Open the drawing **Willhome** located on the student CD.
2. Select the **Model** button on the right side of the Status Bar so that model space is active.
3. Select the **Zoom Extents** tool and zoom to the extents of the drawing.
4. Select the **Zoom In** tool to zoom in by a scale factor of 2.
5. Click the center mouse button or mouse wheel and hold it down. The mouse pointer changes to the hand icon (see Figure 3-10).
6. Hold the button down and pan back and forth in your drawing.

**Note:**
In order to do this exercise you must have a mouse with a center button or a thumb wheel, and the **MBUTTONPAN** system variable must be set to 1.

7.  Release the button.
8.  Hold down the **<Ctrl>** key on your keyboard.
9.  Click the center mouse button or mouse wheel and hold it down. The mouse pointer changes to the joystick icon (see Figure 3-13).
10. Hold the button down and pan around in your drawing.

## PANNING AND ZOOMING TRANSPARENTLY

One of best things about the **Pan** and **Zoom** display tools is that you can use them *transparently*. Select the **Zoom Window** tool and check out the **Command Line** window (see Figure 3-14).

Notice that the **ZOOM** command is preceded by an apostrophe ('). The apostrophe is the flag that indicates that the **ZOOM** command can be run while another command is still active, hence the term *transparent*.

transparent command: A command that can be used without interrupting the currently active command.

Apostrophe Before Command

**Figure 3-14**    A transparent Zoom command

This ability allows you to pan and zoom in the middle of drawing or editing. For instance, you can begin drawing a line by selecting the first point in an overall view (see Figure 3-15A), use the **Zoom Window** tool to zoom closer to your work, and select the endpoint (see Figure 3-15B).

Check out the command line window in Figure 3-15B. When you are prompted for the corner points to define the window area, both prompts are preceded with double arrows (>>) to indicate the command is transparent. After the zoom process is complete and control passes back to the **LINE** command, AutoCAD displays the following prompt at the command line:

`Resuming the LINE command.`

The transparent display commands can be used in conjunction with almost every draw or modify command and can substantially increase both your precision and productivity.

Line Start Point          Cursor

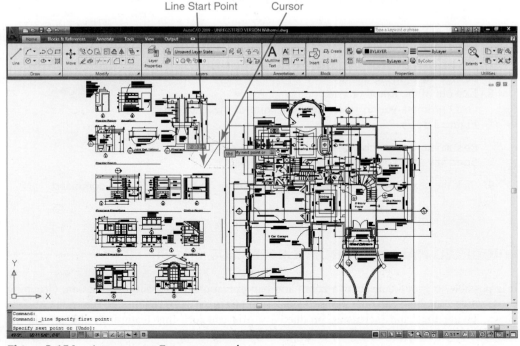

**Figure 3-15A**    A transparent Zoom command

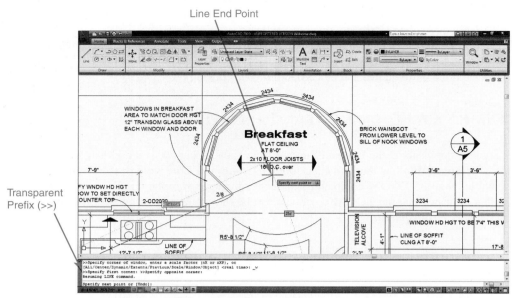

Line End Point

Transparent
Prefix (>>)

**Figure 3-15B**    A transparent Zoom command (continued)

**Exercise 3-12:** Panning and Zooming Transparently

1. Open the drawing **Willhome** located on the student CD.
2. Select the **Model** button on the right side of the Status Bar so that model space is active.
3. Select the **Zoom Extents** tool and zoom to the extents of the drawing.
4. Select the **Line** tool from the **Draw** panel. AutoCAD prompts you:

   ```
   Specify first point:
   ```

5. Pick a point in your drawing to begin the line (see Figure 3-15A).
6. Select any of the **Zoom** or **Pan** tools explained so far in this chapter.
7. Zoom and pan around your drawing and change the drawing display.
8. Exit out of the **Zoom** or **Pan** command. AutoCAD prompts you to select the next point of the line (see Figure 3-15B):

   ```
   Resuming LINE command.
   Specify next point or [Undo]:
   ```

9. Pick the next point for the line and press **<Enter ↵>** to end the **LINE** command.

> **Note:**
> The wheel mouse **Pan** and **Zoom Realtime** tools described earlier also work transparently, although there is no feedback at the command line in the form of an apostrophe.

## GROUPING PAN AND ZOOM COMMANDS TOGETHER

It is possible to group consecutive zoom and pan operations into a single operation. Grouping consecutive zoom and pan operations together minimizes the steps required to return to previous views, saving time and increasing productivity. You can turn this feature on and off via the **Combine zoom and pan commands** check box in the **Undo/Redo** area on the bottom right of the **User Preferences** tab in the **Options** dialog box. It is on by default.

# SPLITTING YOUR SCREEN INTO TILED VIEWPORTS

There are two distinctly different types of viewports in AutoCAD: *floating* and *tiled*. Floating viewports exist *only* in paper space and were first introduced in Chapter 2. Tiled viewports exist *only* in model space and are discussed next. Why the two different types, you might ask? The answer requires a little AutoCAD history lesson.

Before the paper space environment was introduced, all that existed in AutoCAD was the 3D model space environment. Multiple viewports were provided primarily to make it possible to view and work on different views of a 3D model simultaneously. See Figure 3-16.

The screen in Figure 3-16 has been split into four tiled viewports: a front view, a top view, a right-side view, and even an *isometric* view.

Each viewport can be panned and zoomed separately. Using tiled viewports, it is possible to work in any viewport and update all of the other viewports simultaneously. It is even possible to work between multiple viewports so that you can start a line in one viewport and end it in another. You can even move and copy selected objects between viewports.

The term *tiled* is used because model space viewports must abut each other with no space between them and no overlapping edges. These limitations stand in stark contrast to paper space floating viewports, which do not have to adhere to any of these requirements. Paper space viewports can be any shape or size, have space between them, and even overlap if necessary. Paper space viewports can also be edited using standard AutoCAD modify commands so that they can be moved and resized.

**floating viewport:** Paper space viewport created in a drawing layout tab that can have almost any size and shape and can also be modified using standard AutoCAD commands

**tiled viewport:** Rectangular model space viewport

**isometric view:** A pseudo-3D pictorial drawing in which three axes represent accurate measurements of the drawing model in order to show three sides of an object.

---

**FOR MORE DETAILS**   Floating paper space viewports are discussed in detail in Chapter 14.

---

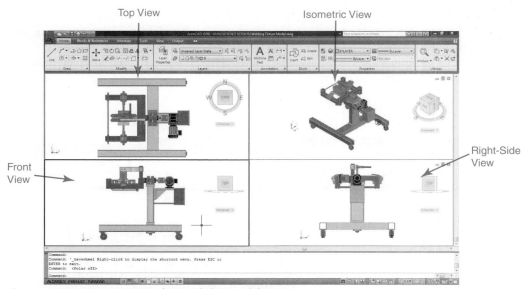

**Figure 3-16**    Four viewports shown tiled in model space

| Viewports | | |
|---|---|---|
| **Ribbon & Panel:** | View \| Viewports New | |
| **Viewports Toolbar:** | | |
| **Menu:** | View\| Viewports\| New Viewports... or View\| Viewports\| Named Viewports... | |
| **Command Line:** | VPORTS | |
| **Command Alias:** | None | |

## Creating Viewports in Model Space

Both model space and paper space viewports are created using the same tool. The type of viewport(s) created depends on your current drawing environment. If you are in model space, tiled viewports are created. If you are in paper space, floating viewports are created.

To split your drawing display screen up into multiple tiled viewports, switch to model space and select the **Viewports** tool.

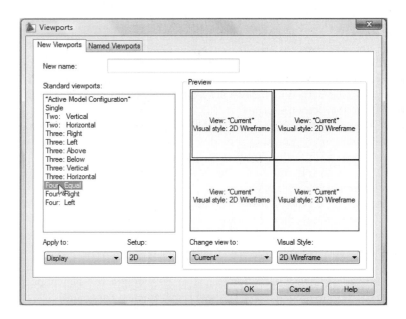

**Figure 3-17**   The Viewports dialog box

Selecting the **Viewports** tool displays the **Viewports** dialog box shown in Figure 3-17.

The **Viewports** dialog box provides a number of different viewports configurations that vary between one and four total viewports. Selecting a configuration on the left previews it in the **Preview** pane on the right.

You can apply the configuration to the current display screen, which is the default, or to the current viewport via the **Apply to:** list.

The **Setup:** list allows you to set up standard viewport configurations for 2D or 3D drawings.

After selecting the desired settings, select **OK** to display the viewports configuration on your screen.

Tiled viewports aren't just for working in 3D; they can also be utilized when creating 2D drawings. For example, you might have one viewport with an overall view of drawing along with a few other viewports that are zoomed in on specific areas as shown in Figure 3-18.

The viewport setup shown in Figure 3-18 allows you to coordinate four different areas of a drawing at the same time.

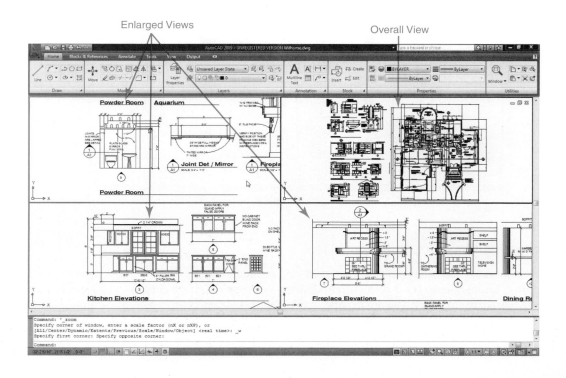

**Figure 3-18**   2D application of tiled viewports

## Saving and Restoring a Viewport Configuration

It is possible to save a tiled viewport configuration with a user-defined name so that it can be recalled later.

Saving a viewport configuration requires that you type in a name when you create the viewports in the **Viewports** dialog box as shown in Figure 3-19 and then select **OK**.

The **Named Viewports** tab of the **Viewports** dialog box allows you to restore a saved viewport configuration. See Figure 3-20. Highlight the configuration you want to restore and select **OK** to restore the viewport configuration on your screen.

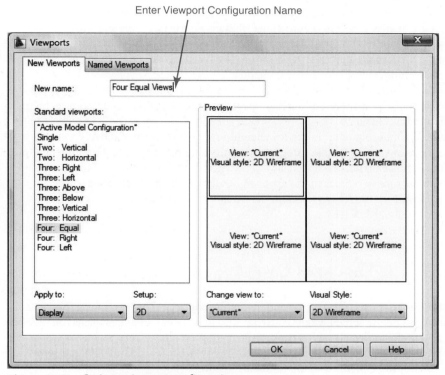

**Figure 3-19**    Saving a viewport configuration

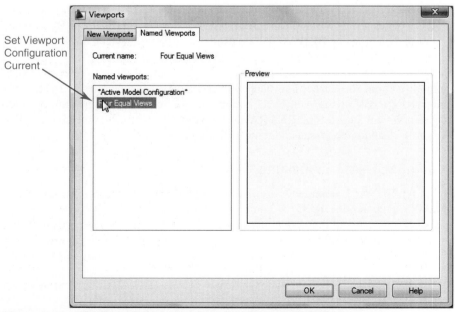

**Figure 3-20**    The Named Viewports tab on the Viewports dialog box

### Exercise 3-13: Working with Tiled Viewports

1. Open the drawing **Willhome** located on the student CD.
2. Select the **Model** button on the right side of the Status Bar so that model space is active.
3. Select the **Zoom Extents** tool and zoom to the extents of the drawing.
4. Select the **New** tool from the **Viewports** panel on the **View** ribbon to display the **Viewports** dialog box (see Figure 3-17).
5. Select the **Four: Equal** viewport configuration from the **Standard viewports:** list box.
6. Type **Four Equal** in the **New name:** text box.
7. Select **OK** to close the **Viewports** dialog box and return to the drawing.
8. The drawing display changes to four equal tiled viewports (see Figure 3-18).
9. Click with the mouse pointer in the upper left viewport to make it active.
10. Change the view in the upper left viewport to the Powder Room elevations using the pan and zoom techniques explained in this chapter.
11. Click with the mouse pointer in the lower left viewport to make it active.
12. Change the view to display the Kitchen elevations using the pan and zoom techniques explained in this chapter.
13. Click with the mouse pointer in the lower right viewport to make it active.
14. Change the view to display the Fireplace elevations using the pan and zoom techniques explained in this chapter.
15. Click with the mouse pointer in the upper right viewport to make it active.
16. Use the **Zoom Extents** tool to zoom to the extents of the drawing.
17. Save the drawing as *EX3-13*.

## CLEANING UP THE DRAWING DISPLAY

Occasionally it is necessary to "clean up" the drawing display area. This can range from removing the blip marks left on the screen when the **BLIPMODE** system variable is turned on (see below) to recalculating the entire display because information on a layer that was frozen does not redisplay when it is thawed (see Chapter 6). AutoCAD provides a few commands that serve this cleanup purpose. They are explained in the following sections.

### The REDRAW Command

The **REDRAW** command is primarily used to remove the small crosses, known as *blips,* that appear on your screen when the system variable **BLIPMODE** has been turned on. By default, **BLIPMODE** is turned off. Turning **BLIPMODE** on displays the blips shown on the screen every time you pick a point in your drawing (see Figure 3-21).

Blips appear for any action that requires a pick point, from drawing lines to selecting existing objects for modification. You can see how quickly your drawing can get cluttered. To clean up the screen, enter **REDRAW** at the AutoCAD command line, or even easier, simply enter **R<Enter ↵>**, the command alias for the **REDRAW** command. Entering either the command or its alias will instantly clean up the screen and remove all the blips.

### The REGEN and REGENALL Commands

The **REGEN** and **REGENALL** commands are like the **REDRAW** command on steroids. Unlike the **REDRAW** command, the **REGEN** commands completely recalculate, or regenerate, your drawing display, updating all drawing objects. So not only are blips cleaned up, but information that is on layers that did not reappear after a layer was thawed is redisplayed and all curved objects such as circles, arcs, and splines are recalculated so that they appear much smoother.

Figure 3-22 shows what occasionally happens when you zoom in on a circle after being zoomed out in a drawing.

Blips

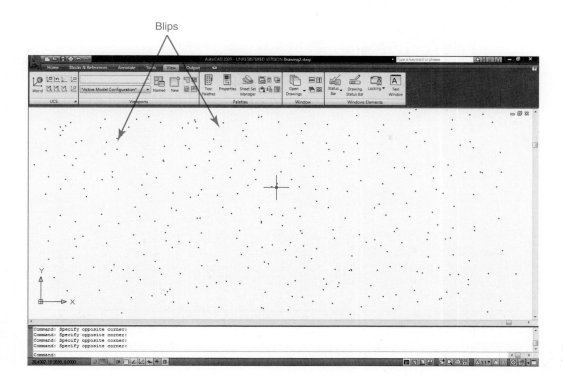

**Figure 3-21**    Blips created when BLIPMODE system variable is turned on

Jagged Straight
Chord Segments

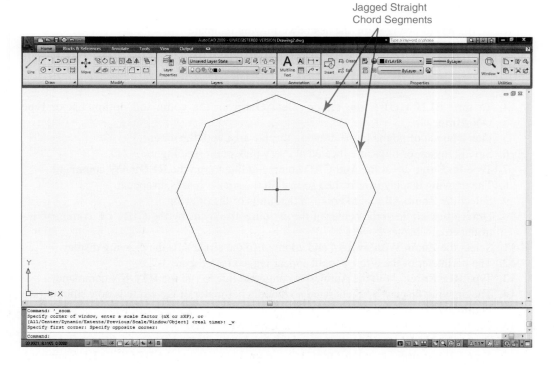

**Figure 3-22**    Zoomed circle before the REGEN command is used

AutoCAD approximates the curve using straight chord segments. This approximation is done primarily to accelerate display performance. To smooth out the curve, you can enter **REGEN<Enter ↵>**, or **RE<Enter ↵>**, at the AutoCAD command line. Entering either will totally recalculate the display so that the curve is smoothed out as shown in Figure 3-23.

The **REGENALL** command allows you to regenerate multiple viewports at the same time if you have split up your display using the techniques shown in the previous section, "Splitting Your Screen into Tiled Viewports." The command alias for the **REGENALL** command is **REA**. The **REGENALL** command works for both tiled viewports (model space) and floating viewports (paper space).

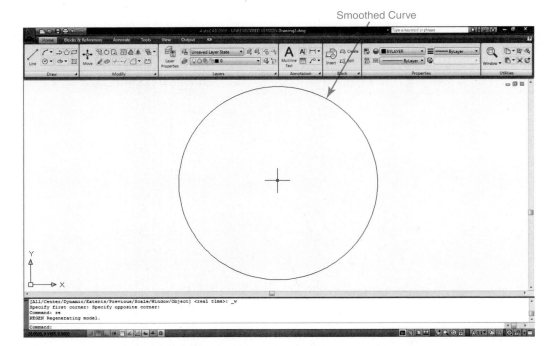

Smoothed Curve

**Figure 3-23** Zoomed circle after the REGEN command is used

## Exercise 3-14: Regenerating the Drawing Display

1. Start a new drawing using the acad.dwt drawing template.
2. Type **BLIPMODE<Enter ↵>**.
3. AutoCAD prompts you to turn the **BLIPMODE** system variable on or off:

   ```
   Enter mode [ON/OFF] <OFF>:
   ```

4. To turn **BLIPMODE** on, either select **On** from the command option list or type **ON<Enter ↵>**.
5. Pick a bunch of points in the drawing display area with the mouse.
6. Small crosses, or blips, are located at every pick point (see Figure 3-21).
7. Type **R<Enter ↵>** at the AutoCAD command line to run the **REDRAW** command.
8. The drawing display is refreshed so that all the small crosses disappear.
9. Select the **Zoom All** tool to zoom to the limits of the drawing.
10. Draw a tiny circle at the center of the drawing display using the **CIRCLE** command introduced in Chapter 2.
11. Select the **Zoom Window** tool and zoom in so the circle fills the drawing display.
12. The perimeter of the circle should appear jagged (see Figure 3-22).
13. Type **RE<Enter ↵>** at the AutoCAD command line to run the **REGEN** command.
14. The drawing display is regenerated so that the perimeter of the circle is now smooth (see Figure 3-23).
15. Open the drawing **EX3-13.DWG** if it is not open already.
16. Select the **Model** tab at the bottom of the display window so that model space is active.
17. Type **REA<Enter ↵>** at the AutoCAD command line to run the **REGENALL** command.
18. All four viewports are regenerated.
19. Turn **BLIPMODE** off by typing **BLIPMODE <Enter↵>** and typing or selecting **Off**.

## The Clean Screen Toggle

The **Clean Screen** toggle temporarily turns off the ribbon and any toolbars toolbars and palettes so that you have more room to draw, because sometimes the screen can get a bit cluttered. See Figure 3-24.

Figure 3-24 is an extreme example of what your screen might look like if you turned on every AutoCAD toolbar and palette. Fortunately, AutoCAD provides a way out of this mess.

Drawing Window

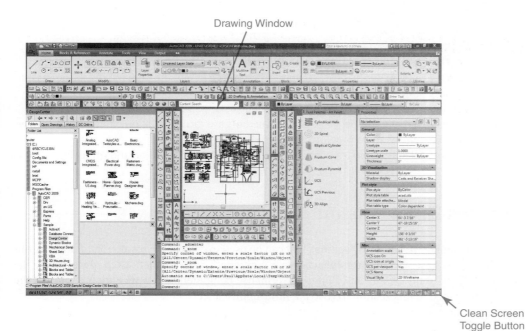

Clean Screen
Toggle Button

**Figure 3-24**    Where's my drawing?

The **CLEANSCREENON** command turns the ribbon, toolbars, and palettes off while the **CLEANSCREENOFF** command turns them back on. You can toggle **Clean Screen** on and off by clicking on the button on the right of the Status Bar as shown in Figure 3-24.

Selecting **Clean Screen** will turn off the ribbon, toolbars, and palettes and maximize your drawing area as shown in Figure 3-25.

When **Clean Screen** is turned on, your drawing display is maximized to completely fill your Windows desktop so that the Windows taskbar is no longer available. You must turn **Clean Screen** off in order to access the Windows taskbar again.

**TIP**    You can also use the **<Ctrl>+0** keyboard combination to toggle **Clean Screen** on and off.

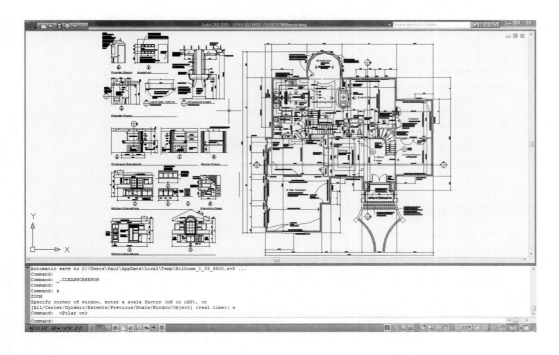

**Figure 3-25**    Drawing display with Clean Screen turned on

<u>Exercise 3-15:</u> Toggling Clean Screen On and Off

1. Start a new drawing using the acad.dwt drawing template.
2. Select the **Clean Screen** button from the right side of the Status Bar.
3. The ribbon and any toolbars are temporarily turned off, and the drawing display area is increased.
4. Select the **Clean Screen** button from the Status Bar again.
5. The ribbon and any toolbars that were turned off are turned back on again, and the drawing display returns to its previous size.
6. Use the **<Ctrl>+0** keyboard combination to turn **Clean Screen** on and off again.

## DRAWING DISPLAY RESOLUTION AND PERFORMANCE

There are a number of AutoCAD settings that can be used to control the resolution of drawing objects on your screen, and in turn, enhance your computer's performance when regenerating the drawing display. With the advent of high-performance computers and workstations, some of the settings described in this section have lost a little significance.

All the display settings can be managed on the **Display** tab in the **Options** dialog box. See Figure 3-26.

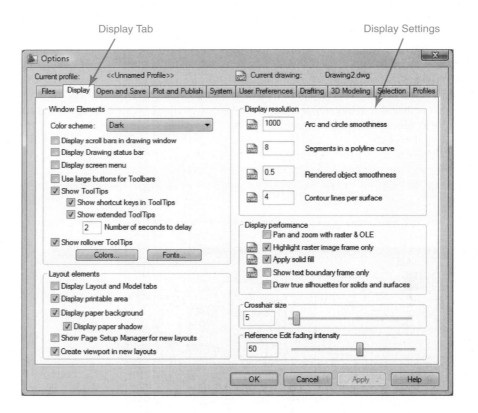

**Figure 3-26** Display tab in Options dialog box

### Controlling Arc and Circle Smoothness

AutoCAD uses short vectors, or chords, to represent radial geometry such as arcs, circles, ellipses, and splines on the drawing display. These chords are not typically noticeable until you zoom in on a curved surface like a circle without regenerating your drawing (see Figure 3-22).

The number of chords used to represent a curve and determine its smoothness is controlled via the **Arc and circle smoothness** setting in the **Display** tab in the **Options** dialog box shown in Figure 3-26. Settings can range from 1 to 20,000. The default setting is 1000. Setting this number higher makes curved surfaces appear smoother by increasing the number of vectors used to represent each curve. This increased resolution does come at a cost in performance, however. The higher the number, the longer it takes to regenerate your drawing.

Exercise 3-16: Controlling Arc and Circle Smoothness

1. Start a new drawing using the acad.dwt drawing template.
2. Select the **Options** button from the bottom of the **Menu Browser** list to display the **Options** dialog box.
3. Select the **Display** tab.
4. Increase the **Arc and circle smoothness** setting in the **Display resolution** area at the top right of the dialog box from the default value of **1000** to **10,000**.
5. Select **OK** to close the **Options** dialog box and return to the drawing.
6. Select the **Zoom Extents** tool to zoom to the limits of the drawing.
7. Draw a tiny circle at the center of the drawing display using the **CIRCLE** command introduced in Chapter 2.
8. Select the **Zoom Window** tool and zoom in so the circle fills the drawing display (see Figure 3-22).
9. The perimeter of the circle should appear smooth (see Figure 3-23).

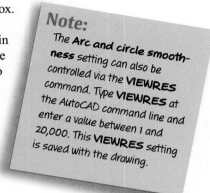

**Note:**
The **Arc and circle smoothness** setting can also be controlled via the **VIEWRES** command. Type **VIEWRES** at the AutoCAD command line and enter a value between 1 and 20,000. This **VIEWRES** setting is saved with the drawing.

## Turning Text Display On and Off

Text is one of the most resource-intensive object types in an AutoCAD drawing because of its detail. If you have a large drawing with lots of text (see Figure 3-27A), regenerating a drawing can become a time-consuming task. To help, AutoCAD provides a way to turn text off in a drawing so that only a boundary frame outline of the text is visible (see Figure 3-27B).

This allows you to still locate each text object in a drawing but not have to regenerate it in finite detail. To turn off text display in a drawing, select the **Show text boundary frame only** check box on the **Display** tab in the **Options** dialog box shown in Figure 3-26. After turning the text display off, you must regenerate the drawing in order to see the results.

Text Boundary Frames Off

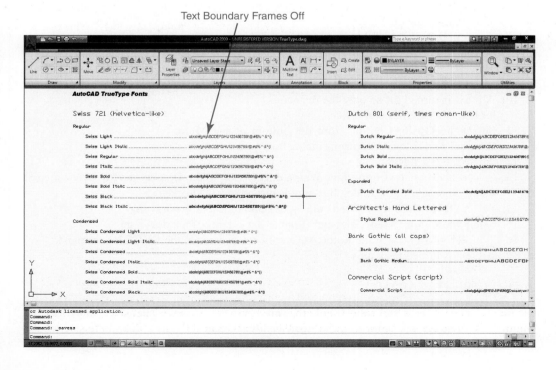

**Figure 3-27A**    Text display on

Text Boundary Frames On

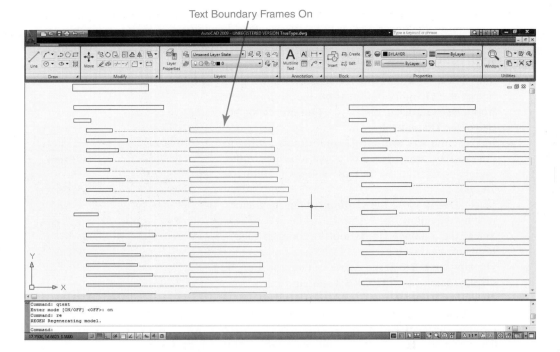

**Figure 3-27B**   Text display off

## Exercise 3-17: Turning Text Display On and Off

1. Open the drawing **Willhome** located on the student CD.
2. Select the **Model** button on the right side of the Status Bar so that model space is active.
3. Select the **Zoom Extents** tool and zoom to the extents of the drawing.
4. Select the Options button from the bottom of the **Menu Browser** to display the **Options** dialog box.
5. Select the **Display** tab.
6. Select the **Show text boundary frame only** option in the **Display performance** area at the middle right of the dialog box so it is turned on (checked).
7. Select **OK** to close the **Options** dialog box and return to the drawing.
8. Zoom in on an area of the drawing that contains text.
9. Type **RE<Enter ⏎>** to run the **REGEN** command.
10. All text is turned off so only the rectangular boundary frames are visible.
11. Select the **Options** button from the bottom of the **Menu Browser** to display the **Options** dialog box.
12. Select the **Display** tab.
13. Select the **Show text boundary frame only** option in the **Display performance** area at the middle right of the dialog box so it is turned off (unchecked).
14. Select **OK** to close the **Options** dialog box and return to the drawing.
15. Select the **Zoom Extents** tool and zoom to the extents of the drawing.
16. Type **RE<Enter ⏎>** at the AutoCAD command line to run the **REGEN** command.
17. All text is turned back on so it is visible.

**Note:**
The **Show text boundary frame only:** setting can also be controlled via the **QTEXTMODE** system variable. Setting **QTEXTMODE** = 1 turns off text display and turns on text boundary frames. Setting **QTEXTMODE** = 0 will turn text back on in a drawing. This **QTEXTMODE** setting is saved with the drawing.

## Turning Fills On and Off

Like text, hatch patterns and solid filled areas are also very resource-intensive. Many hatched and/or solid filled areas in a drawing can significantly increase the time it takes to regenerate the drawing display. Fortunately, you can turn off hatch patterns and solid fills by deselecting (unchecking) the **Apply solid fill** check box on the **Display** tab in the **Options** dialog box shown in Figure 3-26. After turning solid fill areas off you must regenerate the drawing in order to see the results.

### Exercise 3-18: Turning Fill Areas On and Off

1. Open the drawing **Plot Screening and Fill Areas** located on the student CD.
2. Select the **Model** button on the right side of the Status Bar so that model space is active.
3. Select the **Zoom Extents** tool and zoom to the extents of the drawing.
4. Select the **Option** button from the bottom of the **Menu Browser** to display the **Options** dialog box.
5. Select the **Display** tab.
6. Select the **Apply solid fill** option in the **Display performance** area at middle right of the dialog box so that it is turned off (unchecked).
7. Select **OK** to close the **Options** dialog box and return to the drawing.
8. Type **RE<Enter ↵>** at the AutoCAD command line to run the **REGEN** command.
9. All filled areas are now turned off.
10. Select the **Options** button from the bottom of the **Menu Browser** again to display the **Options** dialog box.
11. Select the **Display** tab.
12. Select the **Apply solid fill** option in the **Display performance** area at the middle right of the dialog box so that it is turned on (checked).
13. Select **OK** to close the **Options** dialog box and return to the drawing.
14. Type **RE<Enter ↵>** at the AutoCAD command line to run the **REGEN** command.
15. All filled areas are now turned back on.

> **Note:**
> The **Apply solid fill** setting can also be controlled via the **FILLMODE** system variable. Setting **FILLMODE** = 0 turns off hatching, solid fills, gradient fills, and wide polylines. Setting **FILLMODE** = 1 turns hatching, solid fills, gradient fills, and wide polylines back on in a drawing. This **FILLMODE** setting is saved with the drawing.

## SUMMARY

Mastering the drawing display tools and settings explained in this chapter will help to make you a more productive and a precise drafter. Because there is not one display tool that provides all the ideal functionality, practice using a combination of tools to navigate around your drawing as you are working. Experiment with the different display settings and see how they affect your drawing display and performance. Eventually, you will settle on the tools and settings with which you are most comfortable.

## CHAPTER TEST QUESTIONS

### Multiple Choice

1. The AutoCAD drawing display is similar to a:
   a. Telescope
   b. TV screen
   c. Mirror
   d. Camera lens

2. To make drawing objects appear larger on the screen, you should:
   a. Zoom out
   b. Zoom in
   c. Get a bigger computer monitor
   d. Pan

3. Almost all the **Zoom** tools are available on what ribbon?
   a. View
   b. Tools
   c. Output
   d. Home

4. The **Zoom Realtime** tool allows you to:
   a. Zoom in and zoom out
   b. Zoom interactively
   c. Draw faster
   d. All of the above

5. The **Zoom Window** tool zooms in your drawing when you:

   a. Choose a view
   b. Pick two points
   c. Pick one point
   d. Specify a scale factor

6. The **Zoom Object** tool will zoom in on:

   a. Text
   b. Circles
   c. Lines
   d. All of the above

7. To make the objects in the drawing display appear half the size they are currently displayed, you should enter the following zoom scale factor:

   a. .5
   b. 2X
   c. 1X
   d. .5X

8. To move the drawing display area back and forth without changing the drawing's zoom scale factor, you should use:

   a. **Pan** tool
   b. Middle mouse button
   c. Scroll bars
   d. All of the above

9. The system variable that controls whether the middle mouse button activates the **Pan** tool is:

   a. **MOUSEPANBUTTON**
   b. **MIDDLEBUTTONPAN**
   c. **MBUTTONPAN**
   d. **MPAN**

10. Entering a command transparently allows you to:

    a. Not see the command at the command line window
    b. Use the command while another command is already active
    c. Temporarily turn off the drawing display
    d. All of the above

11. Double-clicking the mouse wheel will:

    a. Display the **Object Snap** shortcut menu
    b. Put the mouse in joystick mode
    c. Pan the display
    d. Zoom Extents

12. Viewports that are created in model space are referred to as:

    a. Floating viewports
    b. Stacked viewports
    c. Cascading viewports
    d. Tiled viewports

13. Which command will clean up and refresh the drawing display?

    a. **REDRAW**
    b. **REGEN**
    c. **REGENALL**
    d. All of the above

14. The **Clean Screen** toggle allows you to:

    a. Clean up blips created when **BLIPMODE** is turned on
    b. Turn off the ribbon, toolbars, and palettes
    c. Erase all objects displayed on the screen
    d. Clear smudge marks off your screen

## Matching

**Column A**

a. **Zoom Realtime** tool
b. **Zoom Window** tool
c. **Zoom Previous** tool
d. **Zoom Extents** tool
e. **ZOOMFACTOR** system variale
f. **Zoom Object** tool
g. **Zoom Scale** tool
h. **Pan** tool
i. **VIEWRES** system variable
j. Tiled viewport

**Column B**

1. Zooms to the outermost visible drawing objects
2. Returns to the previously zoomed view
3. Zooms in on an object or objects
4. Zooms in or out a particular magnification scale factor
5. Zooms interactively
6. Controls mouse thumbwheel zoom increment
7. Control arc and circle smoothness
8. Viewport created in model space
9. Pans interactively
10. Zooms to a user-defined rectangular area

## True or False

1. True or False: The mouse pointer changes from an arrow to a microscope when the **Zoom Realtime** tool is selected.
2. True or False: If you zoom in as far as you can using the **Zoom Realtime** tool and you cannot zoom any farther, you should use the **REGEN** command to recalculate your display.
3. True or False: The **Zoom Previous** tool will also undo the last command.
4. True or False: The mouse wheel button always activates the **Pan** tool.

5. True or False: It is possible to select multiple objects when using the **Zoom Object** tool.
6. True or False: The "P" in the **Zoom Scale** tool's "XP" option stands for Paper space.
7. True or False: When zooming using the mouse wheel, each click of the wheel zooms in or out by 10 percent.

8. True or False: The mouse pointer changes from an arrow to a hand when the **Pan** tool is selected.
9. True or False: Any command can be used transparently when another command is active.
10. True or False: Tiled viewports can only exist in model space.

## CHAPTER PROJECTS

### Project 3-1: Using the Zoom Tools

1. Open the drawing **Willhome** located on the student CD.
2. Select the **Model** tab at the bottom of the display window so that model space is active.
3. Select the **Zoom Extents** tool on the **Zoom** toolbar and zoom to the extents of the drawing.
4. Use the **Zoom Object** tool to zoom in on the "Breakfast" room label text at the top of the floor plan.
5. Double-click on the text and change it to "Breakfast Nook" using the **Edit Text** dialog box.
6. Zoom to the extents of the drawing.
7. Save the drawing as **P3-1**.

### Project 3-2: Creating Tiled Viewports

1. Open drawing **P3-1**.
2. Create the four tiled model space viewports using the **Four: Left** standard viewport option.
3. Use the **Zoom** and **Pan** tools to set up each viewport so that the drawing areas listed in the following table are displayed in the corresponding viewport:

| Viewport | View Area |
|---|---|
| Top Left | Kitchen Area |
| Middle Left | Breakfast Area |
| Bottom Left | Laundry Area |
| Right | Floor Plan |

4. Save the drawing as **P3-2**.

### Project 3-3: Changing Display Resolution and Performance Settings

1. Open drawing **P3-2**.
2. Turn off the text display so only the text boundary boxes are visible.
3. Regenerate all the viewports.

4. Turn off all solid fill areas.
5. Regenerate all the viewports.
6. Increase the arc and circle smoothness factor to 10000.
7. Regenerate all the viewports.
8. Change the drawing display from four viewports to a default single viewport.
9. Save the drawing as **P3-3**.

# Basic Drawing Commands

# 4

## Chapter Objectives

- Create a new drawing
- Establish the drawing units
- Set the drawing limits
- Create lines, circles, and arcs
- Create ellipses and elliptical arcs
- Create point objects and control their size and appearance
- Divide and measure using point objects

## INTRODUCTION

The vast majority of drawings are comprised of three basic drawing elements: lines, circles, and arcs. The size, location, color, line width, and linetype may vary. They may even be combined or joined together to create more complex objects. But most drawings can be broken down to these three basic elements. Even text can be broken down into a series of lines, circles, and arcs. Chapter 2 gave you a quick introduction to these basic drawing objects. In this chapter, we'll take a closer look at these basic drawing commands as well as ellipses and points. We'll also examine some ways to control precisely the placement of AutoCAD objects and take a closer look at the various ways to create new drawings.

## DRAWING SETUP

AutoCAD provides a number of ways to get started in a drawing. In Chapter 2, you used a drawing template to get quickly into a drawing with a number of preconfigured settings.

### Templates

Drawing templates are simply drawings that have been set up and saved as templates. Drawing templates have the file extension *dwt*. AutoCAD comes with a number of predefined templates for various page sizes and industry standards. They typically have specific unit settings, title blocks, layer definitions, page layouts, dimensions styles, and so on. The template acad.dwt is the default template. When you start a new session of AutoCAD, the blank drawing you see is created from the acad.dwt drawing template.

Any drawing can be saved as a template. To save a drawing as a template, choose **File, Save as...** from the Menu browser and choose **AutoCAD Drawing Template (*.dwt)** from the **Files of type**: drop-down list (see Figure 4-1).

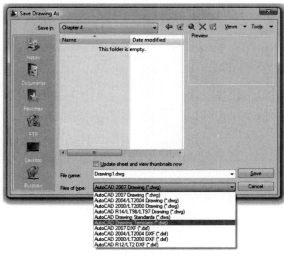

Figure 4-1     Creating a drawing template

Figure 4-2     The Drawing Units dialog box

| Units | |
|---|---|
| **Ribbon & Panel:** | Tools\| Drawing Utilities  `0.0` |
| **Toolbar:** | None |
| **Menu:** | F*o*rmat\| *U*nits... |
| **Command Line:** | UNITS |
| **Command Alias:** | UN |

By default, drawing templates are stored in a specific folder but can be stored and accessed from anywhere on your computer. To use a template, select the template from the file list and choose **OK** to create a new drawing.

## Units

The first step in setting up your drawing is to set the drawing units. Chapter 1 discussed the fact that AutoCAD is, for the most part, a unitless environment. One unit in AutoCAD can represent any measurement you want (1 inch, 1 foot, 1 millimeter, 1 meter, 1 nautical league, or even 1 parsec). The **UNITS** command allows you to control how AutoCAD displays units.

The **UNITS** command displays the **Drawing Units** dialog box (see Figure 4-2).

The **Drawing Units** dialog box allows you to set how both linear and angular measurements are displayed.

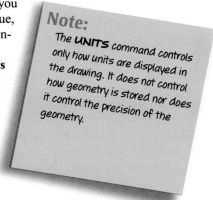

*Note:*
The **UNITS** command controls only how units are displayed in the drawing. It does not control how geometry is stored nor does it control the precision of the geometry.

*Linear Units.*     The **Length** settings control how linear units are displayed. You can choose between five different linear unit display options: **Decimal**, **Engineering**, **Architectural**, **Fractional**, and **Scientific**. They are described in the following table.

| | |
|---|---|
| **Decimal** | This is the default format for displaying units. The decimal setting is unitless in that decimal units can represent any unit of measurement. In general, you should note on your drawing which drawing units you are using. |
| **Engineering** | Engineering units are based on Imperial feet-inch units. 1 unit is 1″ and 12 units are 1′. Inches are displayed in decimal units. For example, 15½″ would be displayed as 1′-3.5″. |
| **Architectural** | Architectural units are similar to engineering units except inches are displayed as fractions. For example, 15½″ would be displayed as 1′-3½″. |
| **Fractional** | Fractional units are similar to decimal units except that numbers are represented as fractions. For example, 15.5 units would display as 15½. Like the decimal setting, the fractional setting is unitless. |
| **Scientific** | Scientific unit display uses exponential notation. For example, 15.5 would display as 1.5500E+01 ($1.55 \times 10^1$). Like the decimal and fractional unit display, scientific unit display is unitless. |

There is also a **Precision** drop-down list that allows you to set the round-off setting for each unit type. The precision setting controls how precisely the number is displayed. The units are rounded off to the specified level of precision. It is important to note that this affects only how units are displayed on the screen. AutoCAD still stores numbers accurately; the numbers are simply rounded off when displayed on screen.

*Angular Units.*     The **Angular** area controls how angles are input and displayed.

> **Note:**
> You can enter feet (') and inches (") only when drawing units are set to either **Architectural** or **Engineering**. If you try to enter either unit designation when drawing units are set to anything else, AutoCAD will reject the entry and display the following ambiguous message at the command line: Point or option keyword required. If you are using Dynamic Input, a bright red border is displayed around the distance input box and you are forced to reenter a valid input value.

| | |
|---|---|
| **Decimal Degrees** | This is the default format for displaying angular measurements. 1 unit equals 1 degree. |
| **Deg/Min/Sec** | Degrees Minutes and Seconds. With this format, there are 360 degrees in a full circle, 60 minutes in 1 degree, and 60 seconds in 1 minute. A 30-degree angle would display as 30d0'0" where d denotes degrees, ' denotes minutes, and " denotes seconds. Latitude and Longitude are typically displayed using Deg/Min/Sec. |
| **Grads** | 400 grads = 360 degrees. 1 grad is roughly 0.9 degree. |
| **Radians** | Radians are measured as multiples of pi (Π). 2pi radians (~6.28r) equals 360 degrees. Pi radians (3.14r) is 180 degrees. |
| **Surveyor Units** | Surveyor's units show angles as bearings, using N or S for north or south, degrees/minutes/seconds to denote how far east or west the angle is from direct north or south, and E or W for east or west. For example, N 45d0'0" E represents 45 degrees from North in the East direction (45 degrees in decimal units). |
| | Angles are always less than 90 degrees and are displayed in the Deg/Min/Sec format. You can simply use E, N, W, and S to represent 0, 90, 180, and 270 degrees, respectively. |

The **Precision** pull-down list works the same for angular units as it does for linear units. The **Clockwise** check box allows you to change the direction that angles are measured. By default, angles are measured in a counterclockwise direction (see Figure 4-3).

Putting a check in the Clockwise box changes the direction of angular measurement so that 90 degrees is south, and 270 degrees is north.

### Exercise 4-1: Setting the Drawing Units

1. Start a new drawing using the acad.dwt drawing template.
2. On the **Tools** ribbon, choose **Units** from the **Drawing Utilities** panel. The **Drawing Units** dialog box is displayed.
3. In the **Length** area, choose **Decimal** from the **Type** drop-down list and set the **Precision** to **0.00** (2 decimal places).
4. In the **Angle** area, choose **Decimal Degrees** from the **Type** drop-down list and set the **Precision** to 0.0 (1 decimal place).

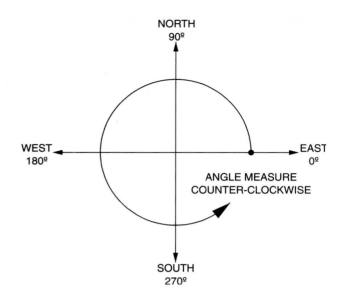

Figure 4-3    Angular measurements

5. Make sure there is no check in the **Clockwise** box and the **Drag-and-drop scale** is set to **Inches**. Choose **OK** to close the dialog box.
6. Save your drawing as **EX4-1**.

## Setting the Drawing Area

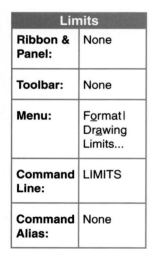

| Limits | |
|---|---|
| **Ribbon & Panel:** | None |
| **Toolbar:** | None |
| **Menu:** | Format \| Drawing Limits... |
| **Command Line:** | LIMITS |
| **Command Alias:** | None |

AutoCAD provides an unlimited space for you to create your drawing. Chapter 1 discussed the concept of drawing objects their actual size. You'll want to set up a large drawing area to draw large objects and a small drawing area to draw small ones. In model space, the drawing area is not critical and can be changed at any time. In layout (paper) space, the drawing area determines the paper size. The drawing area is set up using the **LIMITS** command in model space.

When you start the **LIMITS** command, AutoCAD will ask you to specify two points: the lower left corner and the upper right corner. These two corners determine the drawing area.

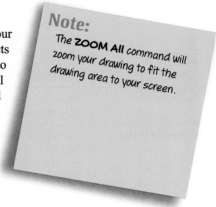

Note:
The **ZOOM All** command will zoom your drawing to fit the drawing area to your screen.

## Exercise 4-2: Setting the Drawing Limits

1. Continue from Exercise 4-1.
2. Choose **Format**, **Drawing Limits** from the Menu browser. AutoCAD prompts you to *Specify lower left corner or ↓*.
3. Press **<Enter ↵>** to accept the default setting of 0,0. AutoCAD then prompts you to *Specify upper right corner <12.00,9.00>:*.
4. Type **11,8.5<Enter ↵>** to set the upper right corner. You now have an 11×8.5 drawing area.
5. Save your drawing as **EX4-2**.

## DRAWING LINES

In Chapter 2, we used the **LINE** command to create some simple geometric shapes. Lines are one of the fundamental drawing objects in AutoCAD. As you've seen, when you start the **LINE** command, AutoCAD prompts you for the first (or start) point and then prompts you for the next point. AutoCAD then simply draws a straight line segment between those two points. AutoCAD will continue to prompt you for the next point and continue to draw line segments until you either press **<Enter ↵>** or cancel the command by pressing **<Esc>**.

While drawing line segments, you have two options available: **Undo** and **Close**. The **Undo** option will delete the last line segment and resume drawing from the end of the previous line segment.

The **Close** option will draw a line segment from the last specified point to the point specified at the start of the line command. For example, in Figure 4-4, if you draw line segments from point A to B to C and to D, selecting the **Close** option would draw a line segment from point D to A. The **Close** option is available only after three points are specified.

| Line | |
|---|---|
| **Ribbon & Panel:** | Homel Draw |
| **Draw Toolbar:** | |
| **Menu:** | Draw|Line |
| **Command Line:** | LINE |
| **Command Alias:** | L |

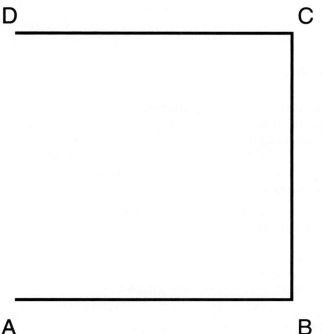

D                 C

A                 B

**Figure 4-4**    Using the Close Option

## Exercise 4-3: Drawing Lines

1. Continue from Exercise 4-2. Toggle the **Dynamic Input** setting off in the Status Bar.
2. Start the **LINE** command. AutoCAD prompts you to:

   `Specify first point:`

3. Type **2,2<Enter ↵>**. AutoCAD places the first point and drags a rubber-band line from that point. AutoCAD then prompts you to:

   `Specify next point or [Undo]:`

4. Type **10,2<Enter ↵>**. AutoCAD places the second point and draws a line segment from the first point to the second. AutoCAD then drags a rubber-band line from the second point and prompts you to:

   `Specify next point or [Undo]:`

5. Type **16,3<Enter ↵>**. AutoCAD places the third point and prompts you to:

   `Specify next point or [Close/Undo]:`

   Since you have specified three points, the **Close** option is now available.

6. Type **U<Enter ↵>** to undo the third point. AutoCAD now drags a rubber-band line from the second point and prompts you to:

   `Specify next point or [Undo]:`

   Since you have now specified only two points, the **Close** option is no longer available.

7. Type **6,10<Enter ↵>**. AutoCAD places the new third point and prompts you to:

   `Specify next point or [Close/Undo]:`

   Since you have specified three points, the **Close** option is available again.

8. Type **C<Enter ↵>** to close the shape. AutoCAD draws a line from the third point back to the first point and ends the **LINE** command. Your drawing should now resemble Figure 4-5.

9. Save your drawing as **EX4-3**.

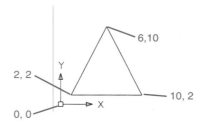

**Figure 4-5**    Drawing lines

## COORDINATE ENTRY METHODS

As you've seen, to place objects in AutoCAD, you need to specify where in the drawing you want to place them. For example, when drawing a line, AutoCAD prompts you to *Specify first point* and to *Specify next point*. This process of specifying point locations is called ***coordinate entry***. AutoCAD uses two basic types of coordinate systems: Cartesian coordinates and polar coordinates.

**coordinate entry:** The process of specifying point locations.

### Cartesian Coordinates

In Chapter 1, we discussed the Cartesian coordinate system, where 0,0 is the origin and a point location is described as an *X* and *Y* coordinate (see Figure 4-6).

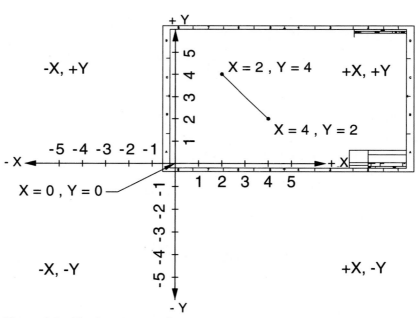

**Figure 4-6**    The Cartesian coordinate system

Using this system, it's possible to describe accurately any position on a two-dimensional plane. However, while it is possible to use basic Cartesian coordinates all the time, it is not always practical or efficient to do so. For example, let's look at a 2 × 2 square with its lower left corner located at the coordinate 3,2. To describe this square using Cartesian coordinates, you would need to calculate the location of each corner by taking the starting coordinate (3,2) and adding the dimensions to the respective *X* and *Y* coordinates (see Figure 4-7).

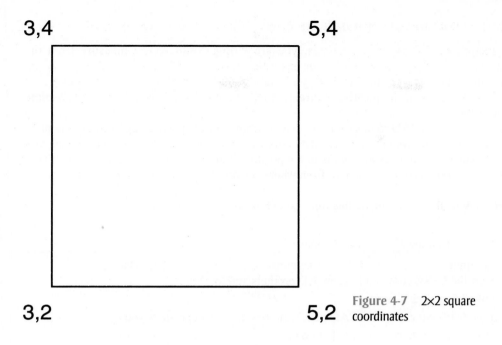

**3,4**                              **5,4**

**3,2**                    **5,2**    Figure 4-7    2×2 square
                                     coordinates

**Exercise 4-4:** Drawing with Cartesian Coordinates

1. Open the drawing **EX4-2**. Toggle the **Dynamic Input** setting off.
2. Start the **LINE** command. AutoCAD prompts you to:
   `Specify first point:`
3. Type **3,2<Enter ↵>**. AutoCAD places the first point and prompts you to:
   `Specify next point or [Undo]:`
4. Type **5,2<Enter ↵>**. AutoCAD places the second point and prompts you to:
   `Specify next point or [Undo]:`
5. Type **5,4<Enter ↵>**. AutoCAD places the third point and prompts you to:
   `Specify next point or [Close/Undo]:`
6. Type **3,4<Enter ↵>**. AutoCAD places the fourth point and prompts you to:
   `Specify next point or [Close/Undo]:`
7. Type **C<Enter ↵>** to close the square and end the **LINE** command. Your drawing should now resemble Figure 4-8.
8. Save your drawing as **EX4-4**.

Y

X

Figure 4-8    Drawing with
Cartesian coordinates

Although drawing using only Cartesian coordinates is possible, it's not an efficient way to draw. The coordinates in the previous exercise are fairly simple, but the problem is made more difficult if the square is rotated or the points do not lie on easily determined coordinates.

To address these issues, AutoCAD gives you some additional ways of specifying coordinates.

### Absolute Versus Relative Coordinate Entry

When specifying Cartesian coordinates, you are telling AutoCAD to measure from the absolute origin of the drawing (0,0). For example, if you specified the point 4,2, you are telling AutoCAD to start at the origin and go to the point measured 4 units in the positive $X$ direction and 2 units in the positive $Y$ direction (see Figure 4-6). This is known as *absolute coordinate entry*.

You can tell AutoCAD to measure coordinates from the last specified point by simply placing the @ character in front of the coordinate—for example, @4,2. By using the @ symbol, you are telling AutoCAD to measure 4 units in the positive $X$ direction and 2 units in the positive $Y$ direction from your current position, or from where you are. This is known as *relative coordinate entry*.

Let's redraw the 2 × 2 square, this time using relative coordinate entry.

### Exercise 4-5: Drawing with Relative Coordinates

1. Continue from Exercise 4-4. Turn **Dynamic Input** on in the Status Bar.
2. Start the **LINE** command. AutoCAD prompts you to:

   `Specify first point:`

3. Type **6,2<Enter ⏎>**. AutoCAD places the first point and prompts you to:

   `Specify next point or [Undo]:`

4. Type **@2,0<Enter ⏎>**. AutoCAD places a point 2 units to the right of the first point and prompts you to:

   `Specify next point or [Undo]:`

5. Type **@0,2<Enter ⏎>**. AutoCAD places a point 2 units above the second point and prompts you to:

   `Specify next point or [Close/Undo]:`

6. Type **@-2,0<Enter ⏎>**. AutoCAD places a point 2 units to the left of the third point and prompts you to:

   `Specify next point or [Close/Undo]:`

7. Type **C<Enter ⏎>** to close the square and end the **LINE** command. Your drawing should now resemble Figure 4-9.
8. Save your drawing as **EX-4-5**.

**Figure 4-9**   Drawing with relative coordinates

You used absolute coordinate entry to place the first point (6,2), but each subsequent point was measured from the last placed point—i.e., from where you were.

### Polar Coordinates

Cartesian coordinates work well when drawing objects with right angles or when coordinates lie on a well-defined grid. However, when drawing objects that have angles other than 90°, calculating coordinate locations is quite a bit more difficult. Let's take our 2 × 2 square and rotate it 45° (see Figure 4-10).

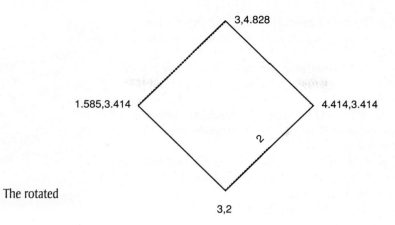

**Figure 4-10**    The rotated 2×2 square

To calculate the location of these coordinates, you'll either need to use the Pythagorean theorem ($x^2 + y^2 = z^2$) or use AutoCAD's polar coordinates.

Polar coordinates use distance and direction to specify locations. For example, if you specify a location of 2<0, 2 is the distance, < is the angle indicator, and 0 is the direction in degrees. The coordinate 2<0 tells AutoCAD to measure 2 units in the 0° direction from the origin (0,0). Remember from Chapter 1 that in AutoCAD, angles are measured counterclockwise from 0°, which is East, or to the right, of the origin along the positive $X$-axis.

Like Cartesian coordinates, polar coordinates can be either absolute (measured from 0,0) or relative (measured from the last specified point). Also, angles can be positive (counterclockwise) or negative (clockwise). Figure 4-11 shows some examples of polar coordinate entry and the resulting point locations.

Let's draw the rotated 2×2 square using polar coordinate entry.

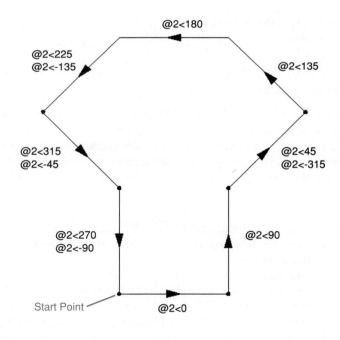

**Figure 4-11**    The polar coordinate examples

**Exercise 4-6:** Drawing with Polar Coordinates

1. Continue from Exercise 4-5.
2. Start the **LINE** command. Type **4,5<Enter ↵>** to specify the first point. AutoCAD starts drawing the line and prompts you for the second point.

3. Type **@2<45<Enter ↵>**. AutoCAD draws a line segment 2 units long at an angle of 45° from the first point.
4. Type **@2<135<Enter ↵>**. AutoCAD draws a line segment 2 units long at an angle of 135° from the second point.
5. Type **@2< −135<Enter ↵>**. AutoCAD draws a line segment 2 units long at an angle of −135° from the third point.
6. Type **C<Enter ↵>** to close the square and end the **LINE** command. Your drawing should now resemble Figure 4-12.
7. Save your drawing as **EX4-6**.

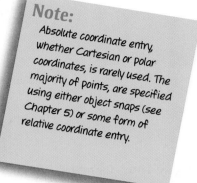

**Note:** Absolute coordinate entry, whether Cartesian or polar coordinates, is rarely used. The majority of points, are specified using either object snaps (see Chapter 5) or some form of relative coordinate entry.

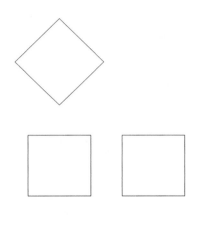

**Figure 4-12**    Drawing with polar coordinates

## Dynamic Input

As you saw in Chapter 2, AutoCAD's dynamic floating prompt moves with your cursor and provides instant feedback as you move around the drawing. One of the advantages of **Dynamic Input** is the immediate coordinate and dimensional information it provides while drawing. Using **Dynamic Input,** you can use the cursor location to determine the angle and dimensions of the objects as they are being drawn. This is best explained with an example.

**Exercise 4-7:** Drawing with Dynamic Input

1. Continue from Exercise 4-6. In the Status Bar, turn on both the **Ortho Mode** and **Dynamic Input** settings.
2. Start the **LINE** command and type **6,5<Enter ↵>** to specify the first point.
3. Drag the cursor to the right. The **Ortho Mode** setting will lock the cursor movement to the 0° direction.
4. Type **2<Enter ↵>**. AutoCAD draws a line 2 units to the right (angle of 0°).
5. Drag the cursor up (90°) and type **2<Enter ↵>**. AutoCAD draws a line 2 units up (angle of 90°).
6. Drag the cursor to the left (180°) and type **2<Enter ↵>**. AutoCAD draws a line 2 units to the left (angle of 180°).
7. Press the down arrow and choose **Close** from the list of options. AutoCAD closes the square and ends the **LINE** command. Your drawing should now resemble Figure 4-13.
8. Save your drawing as **EX4-7**.

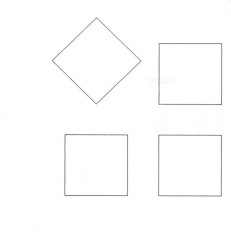

**Figure 4-13**    Drawing with dynamic input

**Dynamic Input** automates the process of specifying relative coordinates. When **Dynamic Input** is turned on, all dimensions and coordinates you type are measured from the last specified point. **Dynamic Input** also allows you to see the length and direction visually without having to calculate the direction angles. You simply point the way and tell AutoCAD how far to go.

| FOR MORE DETAILS | Chapter 5 covers more ways of specifying coordinate locations and demonstrates how to combine Cartesian, polar, and direct distance coordinate entry methods with object snaps and polar tracking. |
| --- | --- |

We've seen that AutoCAD remembers the last specified coordinate. When inputting relative coordinates, AutoCAD will measure coordinates from the last specified point. The **LINE** command can also make use of the last point. When you start the **LINE** command, AutoCAD prompts you to specify the first point. If you simply press **<Enter ↵>**, AutoCAD will start the line from the last specified point.

# DRAWING CIRCLES

| Circle | |
| --- | --- |
| **Ribbon & Panel:** | Homel Draw |
| **Draw Toolbar:** | |
| **Menu:** | Drawl Circle |
| **Command Line:** | CIRCLE |
| **Command Alias:** | C |

A circle is another basic AutoCAD drawing object. By default, AutoCAD asks for a center coordinate and a radius distance. However, there are a number of other ways to draw a circle. When you start the **CIRCLE** command, AutoCAD prompts you to *Specify center point for circle or ↓*. If you choose the down arrow, you'll see that you have three other options for drawing a circle.

Altogether, there are five different options for creating a circle: **Center Radius**, **Center Diameter**, **2 Point**, **3 Point**, or **Tangent Tangent Radius**.

## Center Radius

This is AutoCAD's default method for creating a circle. You can specify the center point using any of the coordinate entry methods. Once you have the center point placed, AutoCAD will then display a rubber-band line and drag a circle from the center point. You can specify the radius by either picking a point on the screen or by typing in a radius value.

## Exercise 4-8: Drawing a Circle

1. Continue from Exercise 4-7. Toggle the **Ortho Mode** setting **off**.
2. Start the **CIRCLE** command, AutoCAD prompts you to *Specify center point for circle or ↓*.
3. Type **1,3<Enter ↵>**. AutoCAD places the center of the circle and starts dragging the radius. A preview image of the circle appears (see Figure 4-14). AutoCAD prompts you to *Specify radius of circle or ↓*.

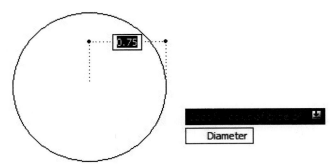

**Figure 4-14**　The preview image of the circle

4. Type **1<Enter ↵>** to specify a radius of 1. AutoCAD creates the circle and ends the **CIRCLE** command. Your drawing should now look like Figure 4-15.
5. Save your drawing as **EX4-8**.

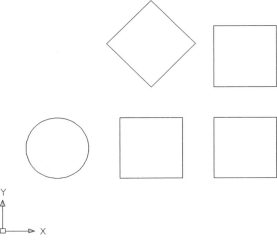

**Figure 4-15**　Drawing a circle

## Center Diameter

This is similar to the **Center Radius** option. Once you specify a center point, AutoCAD prompts you to *Specify radius of circle or ↓*.

You can then type **D<Enter ↵>** or press the down arrow and choose **Diameter**. AutoCAD will then prompt you for the diameter or the circle. The rubber-band line will now stretch out twice the radius of the circle, and the dynamic input will be located at the center of the circle. You can specify the diameter by picking a point on the screen or typing in a diameter.

### Exercise 4-9: Drawing a Circle Using Center Diameter

1. Continue from Exercise 4-8.
2. Start the **CIRCLE** command. AutoCAD prompts you to *Specify center point for circle or ↓*.
3. Type **4,3<Enter ↵>**. AutoCAD places the center of the circle and starts dragging the radius. AutoCAD prompts you to *Specify radius of circle or ↓*.
4. Choose **Diameter** from the options list. AutoCAD prompts you to *Specify diameter of circle:*. Notice that the default value is the diameter of the last circle drawn (2.00).
5. Press **<Enter ↵>** to accept the default diameter value. AutoCAD places the circle and ends the **CIRCLE** command. Your drawing should resemble Figure 4-16.
6. Save your drawing as **EX4-9**.

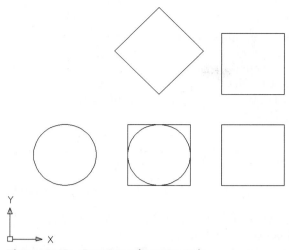

Figure 4-16    Drawing a diameter circle

## 2 Point Circle

A 2 point circle is defined by specifying two points on the diameter of the circle. To use this option, start the **CIRCLE** command and either type **2P<Enter ↵>** at the prompt or choose **2P** from the options list. AutoCAD then asks you to specify the first point of the circle's diameter and the second point and will draw a circle whose diameter passes through the two points.

### Exercise 4-10: Drawing a 2 Point Circle

1. Continue from Exercise 4-9. Toggle the **Ortho Mode** setting on.
2. Start the **CIRCLE** command. AutoCAD prompts you to *Specify center point for circle or ↓*.
3. Select **2P** from the options list. AutoCAD prompts you to *Specify first end point of circle's diameter:*.
4. Type **7,2<Enter ↵>** to specify the first point on the circle's diameter. AutoCAD prompts you to *Specify second end point of circle's diameter:*.
5. Drag the cursor up and type **2<Enter ↵>** to place the second point on the circle's diameter. AutoCAD draws the circle and ends the **CIRCLE** command.
6. Save your drawing as **EX4-10**. Your drawing should resemble Figure 4-17.

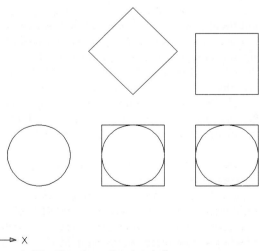

Figure 4-17    Drawing a 2 point circle

## 3 Point Circle

A 3 point circle is defined by specifying three points on the circle's circumference. To use this option, start the **CIRCLE** command and type **3P<Enter ↵>** or choose **3P** from the options list. AutoCAD asks you to specify the first point on the circle, then the second point. Once you specify the second point, AutoCAD will prompt you for the third and will drag a circle that passes through the first two points. AutoCAD will not display the preview circle until the first two points are specified.

### Exercise 4-11: Drawing a 3 Point Circle

1. Continue from Exercise 4-10.
2. Start the **CIRCLE** command. AutoCAD prompts you to *Specify center point for circle or ↓*.
3. Select **3P** from the options list. AutoCAD prompts you to *Specify first point on circle:*.
4. Type **7,5<Enter ↵>** to specify the first point on the circle.
5. Type **1,1<Enter ↵>** to specify the second point on the circle. The dynamic input places the point at the middle of the right side of the square. AutoCAD now displays the preview circle. AutoCAD prompts you to *Specify third point on circle:*.
6. Drag your cursor to the left and type **2<Enter ↵>** to place the last point on the circle. AutoCAD creates the circle and ends the **CIRCLE** command.
7. Save your drawing as **EX4-11**. Your drawing should resemble Figure 4-18.

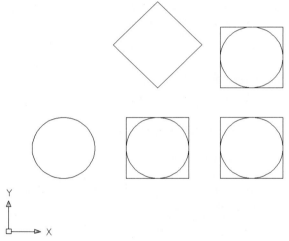

**Figure 4-18**     Drawing a 3 point circle

*Tangent Tangent Radius.*     A tangent tangent radius, or TTR, circle is defined by two points of tangency on existing objects and a radius value. This method of creating a circle is a bit different from the other methods. First, the points of tangency must be on existing objects. AutoCAD uses the tangent object snap to get the points of tangency. Second, the exact points of tangency are determined only after you specify the radius. Because of this, you can't drag and pick the radius of the circle. Lastly, it is possible to specify a combination of tangent points and a radius that cannot be created. In this case, AutoCAD will simply tell you: `Circle does not exist`.

### Exercise 4-12: Drawing a TTR Circle

1. Continue from Exercise 4-11.
2. Start the **CIRCLE** command. AutoCAD prompts you to *Specify center point for circle or ↓*.
3. Select **Ttr** from the options list. AutoCAD prompts you to *Specify point on object for first tangent of circle:*.

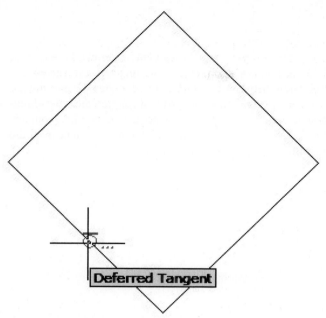

**Figure 4-19**    The Deferred Tangent object snap

4. Drag your cursor over the lower left side of the rotated box (see Figure 4-19). AutoCAD will display the Deferred Tangent object snap.
5. Pick anywhere along the line to select the first tangent point. AutoCAD prompts you to *Specify point on object for second tangent of circle:*.
6. Pick anywhere along the lower right line to select the second tangent point. AutoCAD prompts you to *Specify radius of circle <1.00>:*.
7. Press **<Enter ↵>** to accept the default circle radius (1.00). AutoCAD creates the circle and ends the **CIRCLE** command.
8. Save your drawing as **EX4-12**. Your drawing should resemble Figure 4-20.

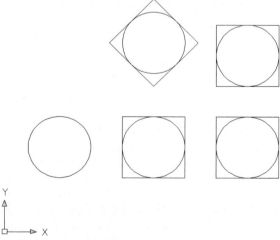

**Figure 4-20**    Drawing a TTR circle

*Tan, Tan, Tan.*    When choosing the **CIRCLE** command from the **Draw** panel, you'll notice that there is yet another option listed: **Tan, Tan, Tan**. This is technically *not* an option of the **CIRCLE** command. It is simply a method of constructing a circle using the **3P** option of the **CIRCLE** command along with AutoCAD's tangent object snap.

## DRAWING ARCS

Arcs are another type of basic drawing object. An arc is simply a segment of a circle. Like circles, arcs are defined by a center point and radius, but they also include a starting angle and an ending angle (see Figure 4-21). The part of the circle between the start and end angles defines the arc segment. Keep in mind that, by default, AutoCAD measures angles in a counterclockwise direction, with 0 along the positive portion of the *X*-axis. Likewise, arcs are also drawn in a counterclockwise direction. This means that by default, AutoCAD will draw the arc segment from the starting angle in a counterclockwise direction towards the ending angle.

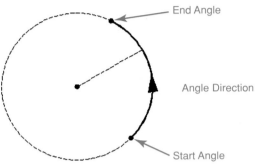

**Figure 4-21**   How arcs are defined

| Arc | |
|---|---|
| **Ribbon & Panel:** | Home\|Draw <br> 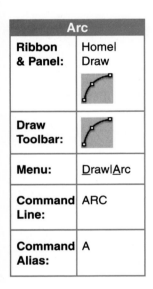 |
| **Draw Toolbar:** | |
| **Menu:** | Draw\|Arc |
| **Command Line:** | ARC |
| **Command Alias:** | A |

### The ARC Command

Arcs are created with the **ARC** command.

### 3 Point Arc

By default, AutoCAD prompts you to pick three points: a start point, a second point along the arc, and the endpoint of the arc. From these three points, AutoCAD will calculate the center point and radius of the arc as well as the starting and ending angles. AutoCAD draws an arc segment through the three points you specify. Direction is not important when picking points for a 3 point arc. AutoCAD will draw the arc through the three points in the order they are specified (see Figure 4-22).

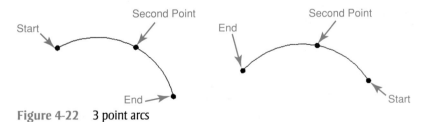

**Figure 4-22**   3 point arcs

You may find that while easy to use, the 3 point method of drawing an arc is not always practical. You may not know the exact location of a second point on the arc, or even the start or endpoint of the arc. You might know the radius of the arc, the center point, the included angle, or some combination of these properties.

### Arc Options

AutoCAD provides a number of options for constructing arcs. These options can be used in various combinations, depending on what information you know. The options are described below.

| Start | The start option defines the start point of the arc. |
|---|---|
| End | The end option defines the endpoint of the arc. |
| Center | The center option defines the center point of the arc. |
| Radius | The radius option defines the radius of the arc. This option can only be used after the start points and endpoints of the arc are defined. |
| Angle | The angle option defines the included angle of the arc. This is the difference between the starting angle and the ending angle. The angle option is available only after the start point and either the endpoint or the center points have been picked. |
| Length | The length option defines the length of the chord between the start point and endpoint of the arc (see Figure 4-23). |
| Direction | The direction option defines the direction of a line tangent to the starting point of the arc (see Figure 4-23). The direction option can only be used after the start and endpoints of the arc have been defined. |
| Continue | This is not technically an option, but a behavior of the **ARC** command. When you start the **ARC** command, if you press <**Enter** ↵> at the first prompt, AutoCAD will start drawing an arc segment tangent to the previous line or arc segment drawn. AutoCAD uses the last specified point as the start point and determines the tangent direction from the previous line or arc segment. AutoCAD then prompts you for the endpoint of the arc (see Figure 4-23). |

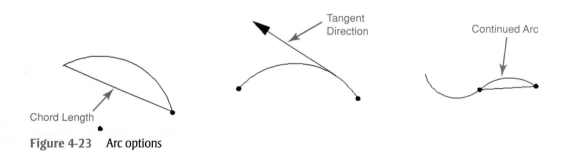

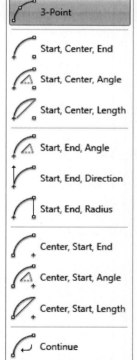

Figure 4-23    Arc options

Figure 4-24    The Home|Draw Arc menu

## Using the ARC Command

When you start the **ARC** command, AutoCAD will prompt you to *Specify start point of arc or* ↓. You can specify the start point, choose the **Center** option, or press <**Enter** ↵> to create an arc tangent to the previous line or arc segment. Depending on the options you choose, AutoCAD will present you with other options. There are ten different combinations of options for drawing an arc.

When accessing the **ARC** command from the **Draw** panel, you'll see the ten different combinations of options used to draw arcs (see Figure 4-24). When using these menu options, Auto-CAD will automatically type the options for you after each point selection.

Before drawing an arc, take a moment to consider what information you know about the arc. This will help you decide which **ARC** command options to use.

Let's look at some examples of drawing arcs.

### Exercise 4-13: Drawing Arcs

1. Continue from Exercise 4-12.
2. Choose **Start, End, Radius** from the **Draw** panel. AutoCAD prompts you to *Specify start point of arc or* ↓.
3. Type **8,7<Enter ↵>** to start the arc at the top right corner of the upper right box. A rubber-band line stretches from the point. AutoCAD prompts you to *Specify end point of arc:*. Notice that AutoCAD has specified the **End** option for you.
4. Type **6,7<Enter ↵>** to specify the upper left corner or the square. A preview image of the arc appears, and a rubber-band line stretches from the end of the arc. AutoCAD has also specified the **Radius** option for you. AutoCAD prompts you to *Specify radius of arc:*.
5. Type **1<Enter ↵>** to specify a radius of 1. AutoCAD draws the arc. Your drawing should look like Figure 4-25.

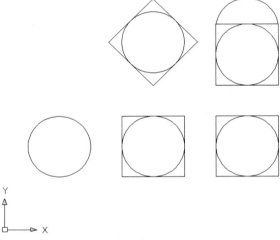

**Figure 4-25**    Start End Radius arc

6. Choose **Start, End, Angle** from the **Draw** panel. AutoCAD prompts you to *Specify start point of arc or* ↓.
7. Type **0,3<Enter ↵>** to start the arc at the left quadrant of the circle on the left of your drawing. A rubber-band line stretches from the point. AutoCAD prompts you to *Specify end point of arc:*.
8. Type **1,3<Enter ↵>** to specify the center of the circle. A preview image of the arc appears, and a rubber-band line stretches from the start of the arc. AutoCAD prompts you to *Specify included angle:*.
9. Drag the cursor up and type **180<Enter ↵>**. AutoCAD draws an arc with an 180° included angle from the start point to the end point in a counterclockwise direction. Your drawing should look like Figure 4-26.
10. Press **<Enter ↵>** to repeat the **ARC** command. AutoCAD prompts you to *Specify start point of arc or* ↓.
11. Press **<Enter ↵>** to continue an arc from the end of the last arc. AutoCAD stretches a tangent arc from the end of the last arc and prompts you to *Specify end point of arc:*.
12. Drag the cursor to the right and type **1<Enter ↵>** to specify the right quadrant of the circle. AutoCAD places the arc tangent to the first arc. Your drawing should look like Figure 4-27.
13. Save your drawing as **EX4-13**.

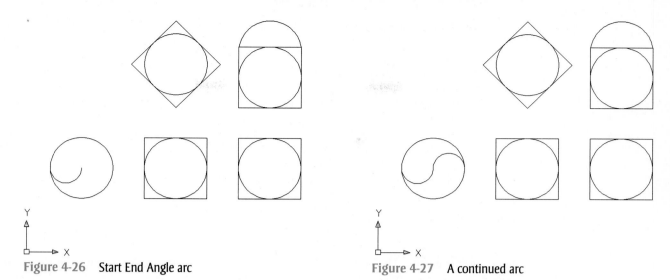

**Figure 4-26**    Start End Angle arc                    **Figure 4-27**    A continued arc

# DRAWING ELLIPSES

An ellipse (or oval) is similar in definition to a circle except that it has both a major and minor radius (see Figure 4-28).

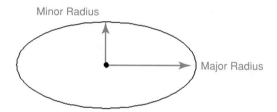

Minor Radius

Major Radius

**Figure 4-28**    An ellipse

| Ellipse | |
|---|---|
| **Ribbon & Panel:** | Homel Draw |
| **Draw Toolbar:** | |
| **Menu:** | Drawl Ellipse |
| **Command Line:** | ELLIPSE |
| **Command Alias:** | EL |

An ellipse is created with the **ELLIPSE** command.

You can construct an ellipse by either specifying the center point and points on the major and minor radii or by picking points on the major and minor axes.

Let's draw an ellipse.

## Exercise 4-14: Drawing an Ellipse

1. Start a new drawing using the acad.dwt drawing template.
2. Toggle the **Ortho Mode** setting to on and start the **ELLIPSE** command. AutoCAD prompts you to *Specify axis endpoint of ellipse or ↓*.
3. Pick a point on the screen to select the first axis endpoint. AutoCAD drags a rubber-band line from the point. AutoCAD prompts you to *Specify other endpoint of axis:*.
4. Pick a point to the right of the first point. AutoCAD will calculate the midpoint of that line and use it as the center of the ellipse. A rubber-band line stretches from this center point. AutoCAD prompts you to *Specify distance to other axis or ↓*.
5. Drag the mouse around to see how the shape of the ellipse changes as you move it. Pick a point above the center point to create the ellipse. Your drawing should look something like Figure 4-29.
6. Save your drawing as **EX4-14**.

When drawing an ellipse, once you specify the major axis (by picking either a center and major radius or two points on the major axis), you'll have a **Rotation** option available. The **Rotation** option allows you to draw the ellipse as though it is a circle being viewed from an angle. Imagine holding a hula hoop directly in front of you so it looks like a circle. Now imagine tilting the hula

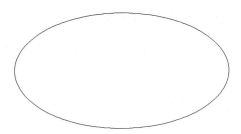

**Figure 4-29**    An ellipse

hoop away from you. The outline of the tilted circle is now an ellipse. When using the **Rotation** option, you are specifying that tilt angle. A tilt angle of 0 will draw a circular ellipse (the major and minor axes are equal). You can specify a maximum tilt angle of 89.4°. Figure 4-30 shows the results of different rotation angles.

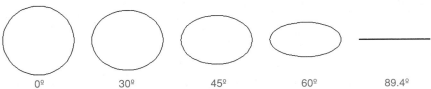

| 0° | 30° | 45° | 60° | 89.4° |

**Figure 4-30**    The Rotation option values of the ELLIPSE command

## Elliptical Arcs

Unlike circular arcs, elliptical arcs are drawn with the **ELLIPSE** command. In fact, AutoCAD considers an ellipse and an elliptical arc as the same type of object. An ellipse has an included angle of 360, while an elliptical arc has an included angle less than 360.

To create an elliptical arc, start the **ELLIPSE** command and select the **Arc** option or choose the **Ellipse Arc** tool from the **Draw** panel. Once you have defined the ellipse, you are prompted for the start angle and end angle. Like circular arcs, AutoCAD draws the elliptical arcs from the start angle to the end angle in a counterclockwise direction.

### Exercise 4-15: Drawing an Elliptical Arc

1. Start a new drawing using the acad.dwt template.
2. Toggle the **Ortho Mode** setting to on and choose the **ELLIPSE Arc** tool from the **Draw** panel. AutoCAD prompts you to *Specify axis endpoint of ellipse or* ↓.
3. Pick a point on the screen to select the first axis endpoint. AutoCAD drags a rubber-band line from the point. AutoCAD prompts you to *Specify other endpoint of axis:.*
4. Pick a point to the right of the first point. AutoCAD will calculate the midpoint of that line and use it for the center of the ellipse. A rubber-band line stretches from this center point. AutoCAD prompts you to *Specify distance to other axis or* ↓.
5. Pick a point above the center point to create the ellipse. AutoCAD prompts you to *Specify start angle or* ↓.
6. Toggle the **Ortho** setting off and pick a point along the ellipse to specify the start angle. AutoCAD prompts you to *Specify end angle or* ↓.
7. Pick a second point along the ellipse to specify the end angle. The elliptical arc is created between the start and end angles. Your drawing should look something like Figure 4-31.
8. Save your drawing as **EX4-15**.

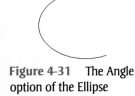

**Figure 4-31**    The Angle option of the Ellipse command

*The Parameter Option.*   When drawing elliptical arcs, the **Parameter** option is available when specifying the start and end angles of the elliptical arc. The **Parameter** option uses the same input as start angle but creates the elliptical arc using the parametric vector equation:

$$p(u) = c + a* \cos(u) + b* \sin(u)$$

Where $c$ is the center of the ellipse and $a$ and $b$ are its major and minor axes, respectively.

> **point:** A one-dimensional object that is defined as a single coordinate in space. Points have no length or width, only a coordinate location.

| FOR MORE DETAILS | See the AutoCAD **Help** file for more detailed information on using the **Parameter** option. |

# POINTS

Another basic drawing object is the *point*. To draw a point, AutoCAD simply prompts you to specify a point.

### Exercise 4-16: Drawing a Point

1. Start a new drawing using the acad.dwt template.
2. Start the **POINT** command. AutoCAD prompts you to *Specify a point:*.
3. Pick a point on the screen. AutoCAD will place a point object.

Points can be difficult to see. By default, points appear as dots with no real size or shape. When you zoom in on a point, it does not get larger. If you place a point directly on top of another object, you might not see it at all. However, you can change the appearance of points to make them easier to spot.

### Point Styles

When you start the **POINT** command, AutoCAD shows you the current value of the **PDMODE** and **PDSIZE** system variables in the **Command** window.

```
Current point modes: PDMODE=0
PDSIZE=0.0000
```

These variables control the look (style) and size of points in your drawing. The **DDPTYPE** command allows you to set the **PDMODE** and **PDSIZE** system variables.

When you start the **DDPTYPE** command, the **Point Style** dialog box appears (see Figure 4-32).

You can choose the desired point style as well as specify a display size for the points. Point size can be entered as an absolute size (for example, 0.1") or as a relative size (a percentage of the display height). When using a relative point size, AutoCAD will recalculate the point size every time the drawing regenerates.

> **Note:** Keep in mind that the point style and the point size are global settings, meaning that all the points in the drawing are affected by these settings. You cannot have one point displayed using one point style and another point with a different style.

> **Note:** You can choose a point style that will make all points invisible (PDMODE=1). When this point style is selected, points in your drawing will not be displayed on your screen but can still be moved, copied, erased, etc.

### Exercise 4-17: Changing the Point Style

1. Continue from Exercise 4-16.
2. Choose **Format, Point Style...** from the Menu browser. The **Point Style** dialog box is displayed.

| Point | |
|---|---|
| **Ribbon & Panel:** | Homel Draw □ |
| **Draw Toolbar:** | □ |
| **Menu:** | Drawl Point |
| **Command Line:** | POINT |
| **Command Alias:** | PO |

| Point Style | |
|---|---|
| **Ribbon & Panel:** | None |
| **Toolbar:** | None |
| **Menu:** | Formatl Point Style... |
| **Command Line:** | DDPTYPE |
| **Command Alias:** | None |

**Figure 4-32**   The Point Style dialog box

**Figure 4-33** Choosing a point style

3. Choose the point type shown in Figure 4-33 and choose **OK** to close the dialog box.
4. Type **REGEN<Enter ↲>** to regenerate your drawing. AutoCAD updates the point display.

The values for **PDMODE** and their associated shapes are shown in Figure 4-34.

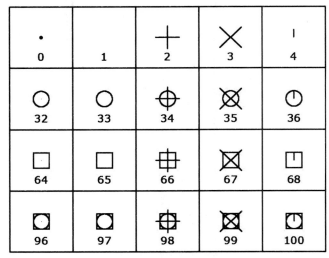

**Figure 4-34** PDMODE values and their associated point styles

When using the **POINT** command, the values shown for **PDSIZE** will be either positive numbers or negative numbers. Positive numbers indicate an absolute size, and negative numbers indicate a percentage of the viewport height. For example, a **PDSIZE** value of −10.0 would make points 10% of the current display area. A value of (+) 10 would create points that were 10 units tall. A **PDSIZE** value of 0.0 will default the point size to 5% of the current display height. The **PDSIZE** variable has no effect when **PDMODE** is set to 0 (a dot) or 1 (blank).

Points can be used for a number of things, including simple markers, and AutoCAD uses them when dimensioning. Points are also used as measurement indicators in the **DIVIDE** and **MEASURE** commands.

### Divide and Measure

The **DIVIDE** and **MEASURE** commands are used to automatically place point objects at regular intervals along an existing object. The **MEASURE** command places points at a specified distance along an object, while the **DIVIDE** command places points so that the object is divided into a specified number of segments.

*MEASURE.* The **MEASURE** command will prompt you to select an object and then ask you to specify a length. AutoCAD will then place points along the object at the specified interval, starting at the end closest to where you selected the object. For example, in Figure 4-35, if you selected the arc near point 1, AutoCAD would measure the distances from endpoint 1. If you selected the arc near point 2, AutoCAD would measure the distances starting at endpoint 2.

| Divide | |
|---|---|
| **Ribbon & Panel:** | Home\|Draw 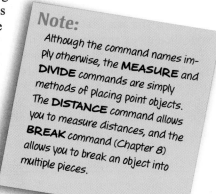 |
| **Toolbar:** | None |
| **Menu:** | Draw\|Point\|Divide |
| **Command Line:** | DIVIDE |
| **Command Alias:** | DIV |

| Measure | |
|---|---|
| **Ribbon & Panel:** | Home\|Draw |
| **Toolbar:** | None |
| **Menu:** | Draw\|Point\|Measure |
| **Command Line:** | Measure |
| **Command Alias:** | ME |

**Note:**
Although the command names imply otherwise, the **MEASURE** and **DIVIDE** commands are simply methods of placing point objects. The **DISTANCE** command allows you to measure distances, and the **BREAK** command (Chapter 8) allows you to break an object into multiple pieces.

Figure 4-35    Selecting the object to be measured

Points are not placed on the endpoints of objects and points are placed until the remaining distance is less than the specified distance.

## Exercise 4-18: Measuring with Points

1. Start a new drawing using the acad.dwt template.
2. Draw a line and an arc in your drawing similar to what is shown in Figure 4-36. Do not draw the dimension.
3. Choose **Format**, **Point Style...** from the Menu browser. Select the point style that corresponds to **PDMODE 3** (see Figure 4-34) and choose **OK**.
4. Start the **MEASURE** command. AutoCAD prompts you to *Select object to measure:*
5. Select the arc near the left endpoint. AutoCAD prompts you to *Specify length of segment or ↓.*
6. Type **.5<Enter ↵>**. AutoCAD places points every .5 unit along the arc starting at the end closest to where you picked. Your drawing should look similar to Figure 4-36.
7. Save your drawing as **EX4-18**.

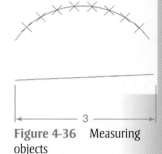

Figure 4-36    Measuring objects

*DIVIDE.*    The **DIVIDE** command prompts you to select an object and then asks for the number of segments. The number must be an integer between 2 and 32767; decimals or fractions are not allowed. AutoCAD will then place points along the object at equal intervals that divide the object into the specified number of segments.

## Exercise 4-19: Dividing Objects with Points

1. Continue from Exercise 4-18.
2. Start the **DIVIDE** command. AutoCAD prompts you to *Select object to divide:*.
3. Pick anywhere along the line object. AutoCAD prompts you to *Enter the number of segments or ↓.*
4. Type **5<Enter ↵>**. AutoCAD places 4 points along the line that divide the line into 5 equal pieces. The line object has not been changed or broken. Points have just been placed on top of the line. Your drawing should now look like Figure 4-37.
5. Save your drawing as **EX4-19**.

Figure 4-37    Placing points with DIVIDE

Like the **MEASURE** command, the **DIVIDE** command does not place points at the endpoints of objects. It will always place one point less than the number of segments you specify (for example, specifying 5 segments creates 4 points, 10 segments will create 9 points, etc.).

Both the **MEASURE** and **DIVIDE** commands have a **Block** option. This option allows you to substitute a block reference for the point objects.

| FOR MORE DETAILS | See Chapter 16 for more detailed information about blocks and how to use them with the **DIVIDE** and **MEASURE** commands. |

## SUMMARY

You have now covered some of the basic drawing objects in AutoCAD. Lines, circles, and arcs are the building blocks of all drawings. The majority of AutoCAD drawing objects are variations of these basic objects. Learning how to create and modify these objects effectively is key to becoming proficient with AutoCAD.

# CHAPTER TEST QUESTIONS

## Multiple Choice

1. The @ symbol is used to denote:
   a. Relative coordinate entry
   b. Polar coordinate systems
   c. Cartesian coordinate systems
   d. Absolute coordinate entry

2. Drawing templates have the file extension:
   a. DWF
   b. DWT
   c. DXF
   d. DWG

3. Which drawing units are specifically based on Imperial (feet-inches) units?
   a. Decimal and Engineering
   b. Engineering and Architectural
   c. Architectural and Fractional
   d. Fractional and Scientific

4. Which of the following is an example of polar coordinate entry?
   a. 3,0
   b. 3>90
   c. 3<90
   d. 90<3

5. Which of the following is an example of relative coordinate entry?
   a. 3<4
   b. 3<90
   c. 3d90
   d. @3,4

6. By default, which direction are positive angles measured in AutoCAD?
   a. 90°
   b. Clockwise
   c. Counterclockwise
   d. Depends on where you pick

7. Which of the following is NOT a valid method of drawing a circle?
   a. Center Radius
   b. 2 Points on the Diameter
   c. Tangent Tangent Radius
   d. Center Circumference

8. Which of the following is NOT a valid method for constructing an arc?
   a. Start, End, Length
   b. Start, End, Radius
   c. Start, Center, Length
   d. 3 Points on the Arc

9. Drawing templates:
   a. Cannot be created in AutoCAD.
   b. Cannot contain geometry; only drawing settings are stored.
   c. Can contain both geometry and drawing settings.
   d. Can be stored only in a specific folder on your computer.

10. Points:
    a. Do not plot.
    b. Cannot be erased or modified.
    c. Cannot change their appearance.
    d. Are stored as a single coordinate in space.

## Matching

**Column A**

a. Drawing template
b. Cartesian coordinate system
c. Scientific unit display
d. **DIVIDE**
e. Circle
f. **MEASURE**
g. Point objects
h. Architectural units

**Column B**

1. A system of locating points using an X- and Y-axis
2. N32d8'26"E
3. Command used to place points at a specified interval along an object
4. The active drawing area. In layout space, it determines the size of your paper.
5. A drawing object defined by a center point and a radius length
6. A drawing file used as a starting point when creating new drawings
7. 1.4200E+01
8. Command used to place points at equal distances along an object

i. Drawing limits

j. Surveyor units

9. 4′ 8 3/16″

10. A system of locating points using distance and direction

## True or False

1.  True or False: The **UNITS** command controls how precisely coordinates are stored in the drawing.

2.  True or False: The **Length** option in the **ARC** command determines the actual arc length.

3.  True or False: An ellipse must have different major and minor axis lengths.

4.  True or False: Architectural units are based on Imperial (feet-inch) units.

5.  True or False: A circle can be drawn tangent to three objects.

6.  True or False: Point objects do not plot.

7.  True or False: The **MEASURE** command is used to measure the distance between two points.

8.  True or False: The **DIVIDE** command will break an object into equal length pieces.

9.  True or False: Drawings can only use Imperial or Metric units.

10. True or False: Point styles can be set separately for each point.

## CHAPTER PROJECTS

### Project 4-1: Lines, Circle, and Arcs

1. Start a new drawing using the acad.dwt template.
2. Draw the lines, circle, and arcs shown in Figure P4-1 to the best of your ability. **Do not** draw dimensions. *Hint:* Use the **Tan**, **Tan**, **Tan** circle option to place the corner circles.
3. Save the drawing as **P4-1**.

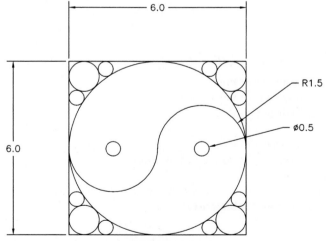

Figure P4-1

### Project 4-2: '32 Ford Special

1. Start a new drawing using the acad.dwt template.
2. Draw the car shown in Figure P4-2 to the best of your ability using the **LINE**, **CIRCLE**, and **ARC** commands.
3. Save the drawing as **P4-2**.

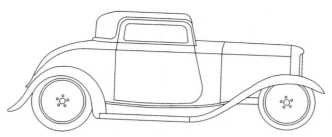

Figure P4-2

## Project 4-3: B-Size Mechanical Border

1. Start a new drawing using the acad.dwt template.
2. Set the **LIMITS** for a 17″ × 11″ drawing area.
3. Draw the border as shown in Figure P4-3 to the best of your ability. **Do not** draw the dimensions.
4. Zoom to the drawing extents.
5. Save the drawing to a template file as **Mechanical B-Size.DWT**.

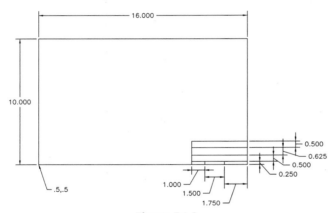

Figure P4-3

## Project 4-4: Architectural D-Size Border (36 × 24)

1. Start a new drawing using the acad.dwt template.
2. Set linear **UNITS** to **Architectural** with precision set to **1/16″**.
3. Set angular **UNITS** to **Deg/Min/Sec** with precision set to **0d00′00″**.
4. Set **LIMITS** to 36″ × 24″ for a D-size drawing.
5. Draw the border as shown in Figure P4-4 to the best of your ability. **Do not** draw the dimensions.
6. Zoom to the drawing extents.
7. Save the drawing to a template file as **Architectural D-Size.DWT**.

## Project 4-5: Electrical Schematic

1. Start a new drawing using the acad.dwt template.
2. Draw the electrical symbols shown in Figure P4-5 to the best of your ability at the sizes shown using the **LINE**, **CIRCLE**, and **ARC** commands. *Hint:* Each grid square is equal to 1/8″.
3. Save the drawing as **P4-5**.

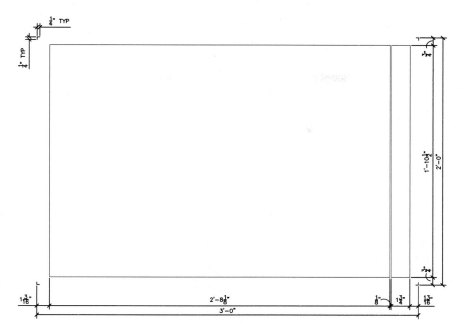

**Figure P4-4**

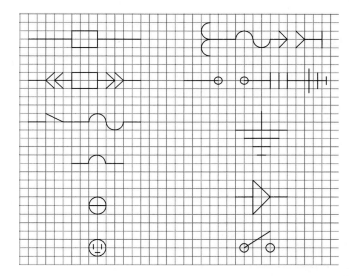

**Figure P4-5**

## Project 4-6: Piping Symbols

1. Start a new drawing using the acad.dwt template.
2. Draw the piping symbols shown in Figure P4-6 to the best of your ability at the sizes shown using the **LINE**, **CIRCLE**, and **ARC** commands. *Hint:* Each grid square is equal to 1/8″.
3. Save the drawing as **P4-6**.

## Project 4-7: Residential Architectural Plan

1. Start a new drawing using the acad.dwt template.
2. Set linear **UNITS** to **Architectural** with precision set to **1/16″**.
3. Draw the building outline as shown in Figure P4-7 to the best of your ability. Place the corner of the building at 0,0 as shown. Draw the North arrow to the best of your abilities. **Do not** include dimensions. *Hint:* The North arrow is pointing at an angle of 247°.
4. Save the drawing as **P4-7**.

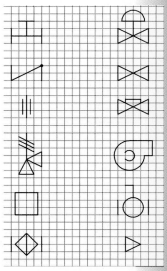

**Figure P4-6**

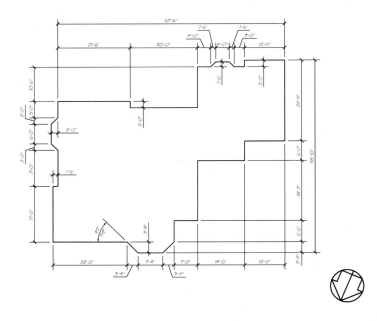

Figure P4-7

## Project 4-8: Joist Foundation Detail

1. Start a new drawing using the acad.dwt template.
2. Set linear **UNITS** to **Architectural** with precision set to **1/16″**.
3. Draw the footer outlines as shown in Figure P4-8 to the best of your ability. **Do not** include dimensions.
4. Save the drawing as **P4-8**.

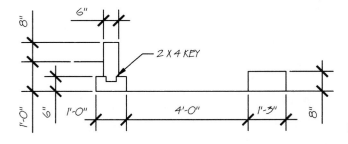

Figure P4-8

## Project 4-9: Support Plate—English Units

1. Start a new drawing using the acad.dwt template.
2. Create the geometry shown in Figure P4-9. **Do not** include dimensions.
3. Save the drawing as **P4-9**.

## Project 4-10: Gasket—Metric

1. Start a new drawing using the acadiso.dwt template.
2. Draw the gasket as shown in Figure P4-10 to the best of your ability. **Do not** include dimensions.
3. Save the drawing as **P4-10**.

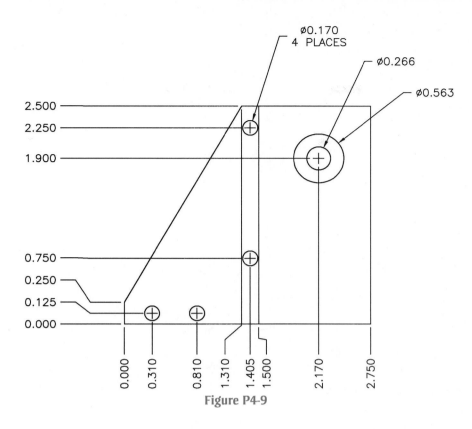

ø0.170
4 PLACES

ø0.266

ø0.563

Figure P4-9

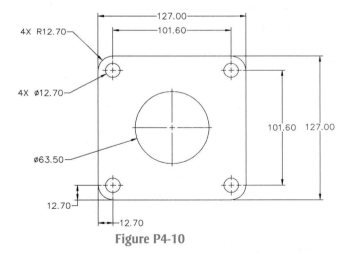

Figure P4-10

## Project 4-11: Civil Site Plan

1. Start a new drawing using the acad.dwt template. Set the linear drawing units to **Architectural** with **1/16″** precision. Set the angular units to **Surveyor** with a precision of **N0d00′00″E**.
2. Draw the site outline, elevation lines, and building site as shown in Figure P4-11 to the best of your ability. Place the corner of the site at 0,0 as shown. Draw the elevation lines approximately where shown. **Do not** include dimensions or text.
3. Save the drawing as **P4-11**.

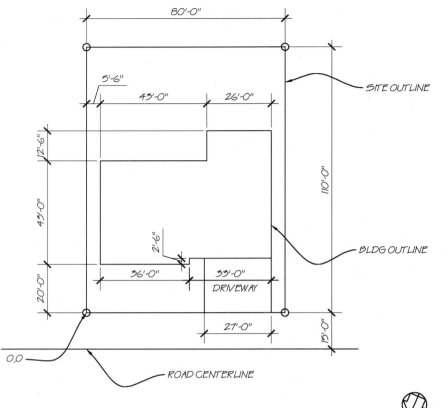

**Figure P4-11**

## Project 4-12: Manhole Construction Detail

1. Start a new drawing using the acad.dwt template.
2. Set linear **UNITS** to **Architectural** with precision set to **1/16″**.
3. Draw the plan view of the manhole as shown in Figure P4-12 to the best of your ability. **Do not** include text or dimensions.
4. Save the drawing as **P4-12**.

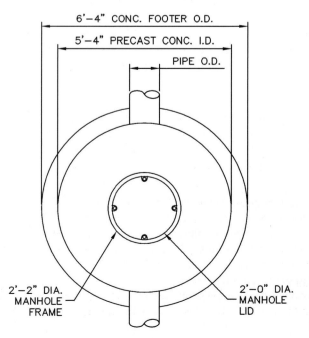

**Figure P4-12**

# Drawing Tools and Drafting Settings

**5**

## Chapter Objectives

- Use the **Grid Display** and **Snap Mode** drawing tools to locate points quickly and precisely
- Draw orthogonally using the **Ortho Mode** drawing tool
- Draw at angles using the **Polar Tracking** drawing tool
- Use basic **Object Snaps** to locate points precisely relative to existing objects
- Defer **Object Snaps** to locate complex points
- Use advanced **Object Snaps** to locate points using acquired points and alignment paths
- Locate points relative to multiple objects by using the **Object Snap Tracking** feature to display multiple intersecting alignment path tracking vectors
- Control **Dynamic Input** settings
- Use Construction Lines to increase productivity and precision when creating multiple view drawings

## INTRODUCTION

Remember from Chapter 1 that two of the most important benefits of using CAD to create technical drawings are increased productivity and improved precision.

These benefits are achieved in AutoCAD primarily through the use of the drawing tools and drafting settings explained in this chapter.

Drawing tools are toggles that can be turned on and off as needed by clicking on the appropriate Status Bar buttons located at the bottom of the AutoCAD display window shown in Figure 5-1.

Drawing Aid Buttons

**Figure 5-1**  AutoCAD Status Bar

Right-clicking with your mouse over a drawing tool button allows you to switch the Status Bar button display from icons to the traditional text-only label display by unchecking the **Use Icons** menu item as shown in Figure 5-2.

Additional button-specific menu items are also included on each button's right-click shortcut menu so that you can quickly access the selected drawing tool's settings and features. The shortcut menu for the **Snap Mode** tool is shown in Figure 5-2.

Drawing tools can also be turned on and off using the function keys at the top of your keyboard, or they can be typed in at the AutoCAD command line. Each method is listed with the corresponding drawing tool throughout this chapter.

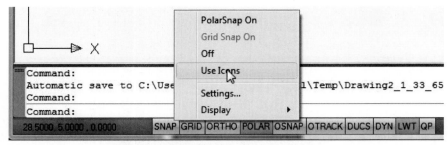

Figure 5-2    Status Bar with traditional text-buttons displayed

**FOR MORE DETAILS** See the section "Keyboard Commands" in Chapter 1 for a complete list of function keys.

**Note:**

Any of the drawing tool buttons discussed in this chapter can be removed from the Status Bar via the **Status Bar** menu. To display the **Status Bar** menu, click on the down arrow at the far right of the Status Bar.

Most of the drawing tools work in conjunction with different drafting settings. For instance, the **Grid Display** button turns a Grid display on and off, whereas the grid spacing (X and Y distance between grid dots) is controlled via the drafting settings. The grid spacing and other drafting settings are managed using the **Drafting Settings** dialog box shown in Figure 5-3.

| Drafting Settings | |
|---|---|
| **Menu:** | Tools\|Drafting Settings... |
| **Command Line:** | DSETTINGS |
| **Command Alias:** | DS or SE |

**FOR MORE DETAILS** See the "Status Bars" section in Chapter 1 for more information about turning Status Bar features on and off.

Figure 5-3    Drafting Settings dialog box

The **Drafting Settings** dialog box can be displayed by selecting **Drafting Settings...** from the **Tools** menu or typing **DSETTINGS**. Even easier, you can right-click on any of the drawing tool buttons on the Status Bar to display a shortcut menu like the one shown in Figure 5-4 and select the **Settings...** menu item.

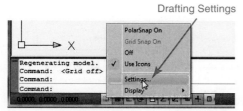

**Figure 5-4**    Drawing aids right-click shortcut menu

**TIP**    All the drawing tools and drafting settings can be accessed when a command is active. This means that you can turn drawing tools on or off or change your drafting settings in the middle of most commands on an as-needed basis.

## GRID DISPLAY

The **Grid Display** is a rectangular pattern of evenly spaced dots you can turn on in your drawing to help you visually locate points. It is similar to using a sheet of graph paper when drawing with pencil and paper, except that you can control the distance between the dots and can change them at any time using the **Drafting Settings** dialog box. The **Grid Display** does not plot and is provided strictly as a visual aid. *The Grid Display does not affect the cursor movement—* this feature is controlled by the **Snap Mode** explained in the next section.

By default, the rectangular **Grid Display** area is determined by the current drawing limits setting. The drawing limits for the default acad.dwt template are set to a rectangular area defined by the lower left coordinate value of (0.0,0.0) and an upper right corner coordinate value of (12.0,9.0).

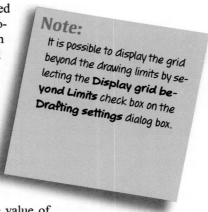

**Note:** It is possible to display the grid beyond the drawing limits by selecting the **Display grid beyond Limits** check box on the **Drafting settings** dialog box.

| Grid Display | |
|---|---|
| **Status Bar:** | ▦ or GRID |
| **Function Key:** | F7 |
| **Command Line:** | GRID |
| **Keyboard Combo:** | Ctrl+G |

**FOR MORE DETAILS**    See Chapter 4 for information about changing the drawing limits.

Figure 5-5 shows a drawing with the **Grid Display** turned on with the default spacing of 0.50″ between the dots in both the horizontal and vertical axes.

### Setting the Grid Spacing

The horizontal and vertical spacing between the grid dots is controlled on the **Snap and Grid** tab of the **Drafting Settings** dialog box shown in Figure 5-6. You can change the distance between

Grid Dots

Grid Settings

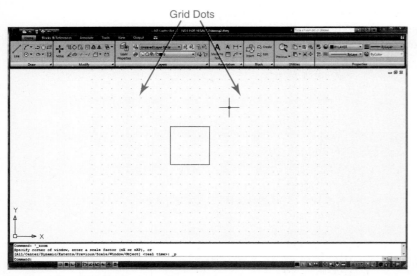

**Figure 5-5**   Grid display turned on

**Figure 5-6**   Grid display settings

the dots by specifying the **Grid X spacing** for the horizontal distance and the **Grid Y spacing** for the vertical distance. The X and Y distances are typically set to an equal value. In fact, when you try to change one distance, the other distance is updated automatically.

The **Major line every** setting specifies the frequency of major grid lines compared to minor grid lines when the visual style is set to anything other than 2D Wireframe. The other 3D visual styles display grid lines rather than grid dots. Primarily a 3D tool, the current visual style is controlled by the **VSCURRENT** command.

When the visual style is set to 2D Wireframe and the **Adaptive grid** setting is turned on in the **Grid behavior** section (explained below), the **Major line every** setting controls the grid dot display when you zoom out. If the grid spacing is too dense to display, the minor grid dots are turned off.

### Controlling Grid Display Behavior

The settings in the **Grid behavior** section of the **Drafting Settings** dialog box are primarily used to control the appearance of the grid lines that are displayed when the current visual style is set to any visual style except 2D Wireframe.

The **Adaptive grid** setting limits the density of the grid when the drawing is zoomed out using the **Major line every** setting introduced earlier to turn minor grid lines/dots off.

The **Allow subdivision below grid spacing** setting generates additional, more closely spaced grid lines/dots when zoomed in. The spacing and frequency of these minor grid lines/dots is determined by the frequency of the major grid lines.

The **Display grid beyond Limits** setting allows you to display the grid beyond the area specified by the **LIMITS** command as mentioned earlier.

The **Follow Dynamic UCS** setting is a 3D tool that allows you to automatically update the grid plane to follow the XY plane of the dynamic UCS.

## SNAP MODE

The **Snap Mode** drawing tool controls the movement of your cursor so that you can select points in your drawing only at specific X and Y increments. It is typically used in conjunction with the **Grid Display** explained in the previous section. The **Grid Display** provides the visual reference, whereas the **Snap Mode** forces your pick points to be located precisely at specific coordinate locations.

By default, the X and Y spacing for both tools are set the same so that your cursor "snaps" directly to the **Grid Display** dots when both drawing tools are turned on at the same time. It is possible to set the X and Y spacing for **Grid** and **Snap** to different values, although it is recommended that they relate to each other to avoid confusion.

## Setting the Snap Spacing

The horizontal and vertical spacing between the snap points is controlled on the **Snap and Grid** tab of the **Drafting Settings** dialog box shown in Figure 5-7. You can change the distance between the snap points by specifying the **Snap X spacing** for the horizontal distance and the **Snap Y spacing** for the vertical distance. The X and Y distances are typically set to an equal value. By default, when you try to change one distance the other distance is updated automatically. You must uncheck the **Equal X and Y spacing** check box shown in Figure 5-7 before setting values that are not the same.

As mentioned, it is possible to set the **Snap** X and Y spacing to different values than the **Grid** X and Y spacing, but it is suggested that one is an increment of the other. For instance, you might set the **Snap** X and Y spacing to 0.25″, while the **Grid** X and Y spacing remains at 0.50″. With these settings, your cursor will still snap to each grid and between each grid dot.

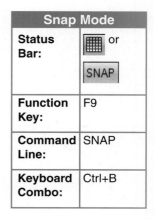

| Snap Mode | |
|---|---|
| **Status Bar:** | ⊞ or SNAP |
| **Function Key:** | F9 |
| **Command Line:** | SNAP |
| **Keyboard Combo:** | Ctrl+B |

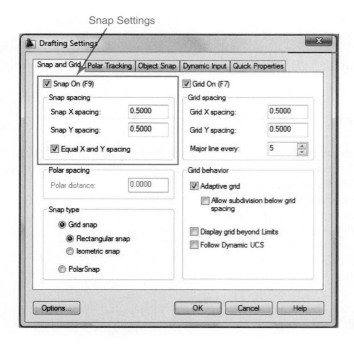

**Figure 5-7**    Snap Mode settings

## Setting the Snap Type and Style

There are two major types of **Snap Modes: Grid Snap** and **Polar Snap**. You can switch between the different types using the option buttons in the **Snap type** section of the **Drafting Settings** dialog box shown in Figure 5-7. The default mode is **Grid snap**, which has two different styles:

- **Rectangular snap (default)**    Traditional orthogonal snap pattern with rows and columns of snap points at the specified X and Y spacing

- **Isometric snap**    Angled snap pattern where snap points are aligned at 30°, 90°, and 150° angles at the specified spacing so you can create isometric drawings.

**Polar Snap** mode is used with the **Polar Tracking** drawing tool so that you can snap to points along **Polar Tracking** vectors at the specified spacing. **Polar Tracking** and the **Polar Snap** mode are explained later in this chapter.

**Exercise 5-1:** Creating a Drawing Using Snap Mode and Grid Display

1. Start a new drawing using the acad.dwt drawing template.
2. Turn off all the drawing tool buttons on the Status Bar.
3. Turn on the **Grid Display** button on the Status Bar.
4. Select the **Zoom Extents** tool to zoom to the limits of the drawing. You should now be able to see the whole grid on the drawing display.
5. Start the **LINE** command.
6. Draw a rectangle by picking points in the drawing.
7. Exit the **LINE** command.
8. Turn on the **Snap Mode** button on the Status Bar.
9. Start the **LINE** command.
10. Draw another rectangle similar to the first by picking points in the drawing. The cursor now snaps to the grid dots on the screen.
11. Exit the **LINE** command.
12. Right-click on the **Snap Mode** button on the Status Bar and select **Settings...** from the shortcut menu. The **Snap and Grid** tab of the **Drafting Settings** dialog box is displayed. See Figure 5-6.
13. Change the **Snap X spacing** to 0.25. The **Snap Y spacing** will change to match. Exit the **Drafting Settings** dialog box by selecting **OK**.
14. Start the **LINE** command.
15. Draw another rectangle by picking points in the drawing. The cursor now snaps both to the grid dots and to points halfway between the grid marks.
16. Exit the **LINE** command.
17. Save your drawing as **EX5-1**.

## ORTHO MODE

| Ortho Mode | |
|---|---|
| **Status Bar:** | 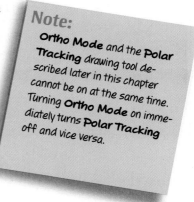 or ORTHO |
| **Function Key:** | F8 |
| **Command Line:** | ORTHO |
| **Keyboard Combo:** | Ctrl+L |

The **Ortho Mode** drawing tool restricts your cursor movement to the horizontal (*X*) and vertical (*Y*) axes so you can quickly draw horizontal and vertical lines at right angles (90°) to each other. This right-angle approach to drafting is often referred to as drawing "orthogonally," hence the term *Ortho*. Drawing with **Ortho Mode** turned on allows you to draw rectangular objects quickly and be assured that all the angles are square.

When **Ortho Mode** is turned off, the rubber-band line that indicates the cursor movement points at any angle you move your cursor, as shown in Figure 5-8A. When **Ortho Mode** is turned on, the rubber-band line that indicates the cursor direction follows the horizontal or vertical axis, depending on which axis is nearer to the cursor at the time, as shown in Figure 5-8B.

**Note:**
Ortho Mode and the Polar Tracking drawing tool described later in this chapter cannot be on at the same time. Turning Ortho Mode on immediately turns Polar Tracking off and vice versa.

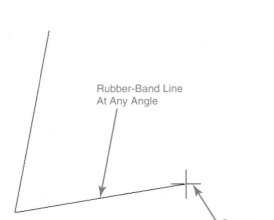
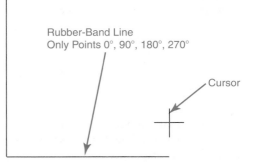

Rubber-Band Line At Any Angle

Rubber-Band Line Only Points 0°, 90°, 180°, 270°

Cursor

Cursor

**Figure 5-8A** Ortho mode turned off **B** Ortho mode turned on

AutoCAD overrides **Ortho Mode** when you enter coordinates on the command line or use any of the **Object Snaps** explained later in this chapter.

**Exercise 5-2:** Creating a Drawing Using Ortho Mode

1. Start a new drawing using the acad.dwt drawing template.
2. Turn off all the drawing tool buttons on the Status Bar.
3. Select the **Zoom Extents** tool to zoom to the limits of the drawing.
4. Turn the **Ortho Mode** button on.
5. Start the **LINE** command.
6. Type **2,2<Enter ↵>** to specify the first point.
7. Drag the cursor to the right. The **Ortho Mode** setting will lock the cursor movement to the 0° direction.
8. Type **2<Enter ↵>**. AutoCAD draws a line 2 units to the right (angle of 0°).
9. Drag the cursor up (90°) and type **2<Enter ↵>**. AutoCAD draws a line 2 units up (angle of 90°).
10. Drag the cursor to the left (180°) and type **2<Enter ↵>**. AutoCAD draws a line 2 units to the left (angle of 180°).
11. Type **C<Enter ↵>.** AutoCAD closes the square and exits the **LINE** command.
12. Save your drawing as **EX5-2**. Your drawing should look like Figure 5-9.

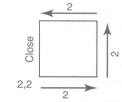

**Figure 5-9**    Drawing using Ortho Mode

# POLAR TRACKING

AutoCAD provides a feature called *AutoTracking*™ that helps you to draw objects at specific angles using dashed lines known as *alignment paths*.

The **Polar Tracking** drawing tool utilizes **AutoTracking** so you can quickly draw and modify objects using preset polar angles. **Polar Tracking** works by displaying a dashed alignment path and a **Polar Tracking** tooltip as you move your cursor around in a drawing that temporarily restricts your cursor movement to preset angle increments.

By default, the increment angle is set at 90° so that an alignment path is displayed at every 90° (0°, 90°, 180°, 270°, and 360°) when the **Polar Tracking** button is turned on. This provides the same basic functionality of the **Ortho Mode** drawing tool explained earlier in the chapter. As noted earlier, when you turn the **Polar Tracking** button on, the **Ortho Mode** button gets turned off automatically and vice versa. Both drawing tools cannot be on at the same time. Figure 5-10 shows an alignment path displayed at 0°.

AutoTracking: AutoCAD feature that helps you to draw objects at specific angles or in specific relationships to other objects.

| Polar Tracking | |
|---|---|
| **Status Bar:** | ⟋ or POLAR |
| **Function Key:** | F10 |
| **Command Line:** | None |
| **Keyboard Combo:** | None |

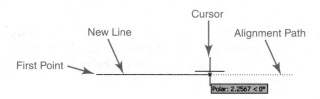

**Figure 5-10**    Polar Tracking alignment path

If you pick a point when an alignment path is displayed, the point is located at the distance and angle displayed in the **Polar Tracking** tooltip. Even better, it is possible to use the direct distance coordinate entry method explained in Chapter 4 to locate a point at a specified distance along an alignment path. Any time an alignment path is displayed, you can enter a distance, and AutoCAD will follow the alignment path the distance specified. For example, if you enter **2** in response to the *Specify next point or [Undo]:* prompt while the 0° alignment path is displayed as shown in Figure 5-10, a horizontal line segment 2 units long is created. Combining **Polar Tracking** with direct distance coordinate entry is one of the fastest and easiest ways to locate points in your drawings.

**TIP**    **Polar Tracking** is not just for drawing objects. It also works with AutoCAD's modify tools. For example, using **Polar Tracking**, you can move objects at a specific angle and distance.

**FOR MORE DETAILS**  Using the AutoCAD **MOVE** command is explained in Chapter 7.

## Setting the Polar Tracking Angle and Measurement Method

The **Polar Tracking** settings are controlled on the **Polar Tracking** tab of the **Drafting Settings** dialog box shown in Figure 5-11.

**Figure 5-11**    Polar Tracking settings

The **Polar Tracking** angle is set in the **Polar Angle Settings** area on the **Polar Tracking** tab. There are two **Polar Angle** settings:

- **Increment angle**    A list of default preset angles ranging from 5° through 90° that controls the increment angle that **Polar Tracking** alignment paths are displayed. In Figure 5-11, a default increment angle of 45° has been selected so that a **Polar Tracking** alignment path will be displayed at every increment of 45° (0°, 45°, 90°, 135°, 180°, 225°, 270°, and 315°).

- **Additional angles**    Additional angles that can be added using the **New** button. *These angles are not incremental.* **Polar Tracking** alignment paths will be displayed only at each additional angle specified.

The **Polar Tracking** measurement method is set in the **Polar Angle measurement** area on the right side of the **Polar Tracking** tab. There are two **Polar Angle measurement** options:

- **Absolute**    All **Polar Tracking** angles are measured from the current AutoCAD base angle setting. The default base angle setting is 0° due east or to the right.

- **Relative to last segment**    **Polar Tracking** angles are measured relative to the last segment, and the absolute angle is ignored.

Figures 5-12A through D show a square that is rotated at 45° being drawn with **Polar Tracking** turned on with an increment angle setting of 45° using the absolute method of angle measurement.

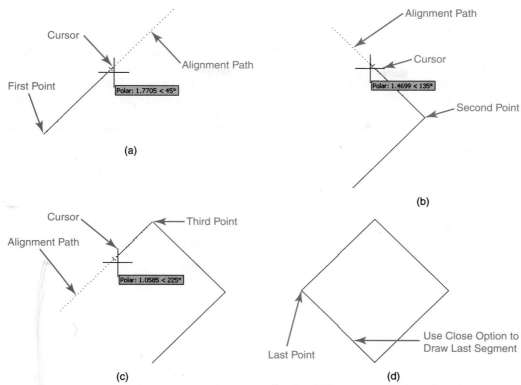

Figure 5-12    (A) Polar Tracking alignment path at 45° (B) Polar Tracking alignment path at 135°
(C) Polar Tracking alignment path at 225° (D) Completed 45° square

**TIP**    The **AutoTrack** settings are controlled via the **Drafting** tab in the **Options** dialog box. You can toggle on and off the following features: **Polar Tracking** alignment vectors, **AutoTrack** tooltips, and Full-screen tracking vectors.

## Exercise 5-3: Creating a Drawing Using Polar Tracking

1. Continue from Exercise 5-2.
2. Turn off all the drawing tool buttons on the Status Bar.
3. Right-click on the **Polar Tracking** button on the Status Bar and select **Settings...** from the shortcut menu. The **Polar Tracking** tab of the **Drafting Settings** dialog box is displayed. See Figure 5-11.
4. Change the **Increment Angle** list box setting to 45°. Make sure that the **Polar Angle measurement** setting is set to **Absolute**. Exit the **Drafting Settings** dialog box by selecting **OK**.
5. Turn the **Polar Tracking** button on.
6. Start the **LINE** command.
7. Type **3,5.5<Enter ⏎>** to specify the first point.
8. Drag the cursor up to the right until a **Polar Tracking** alignment path is displayed at 45°.
9. Type **2<Enter ⏎>** while the alignment path is displayed. AutoCAD draws a line 2 units at the angle of 45°.
10. Drag the cursor up to the left until a **Polar Tracking** alignment path is displayed at 135°.
11. Type **2<Enter ⏎>** while the alignment path is displayed. AutoCAD draws a line 2 units at the angle of 135°.
12. Drag the cursor down to the left until **Polar Tracking** alignment path is displayed at 225°.
13. Type **2<Enter ⏎>** while the alignment path is displayed. AutoCAD draws a line 2 units at the angle of 225°.
14. Type **C<Enter ⏎>**. AutoCAD closes the square and exits the command.
15. Save your drawing as **EX5-3**. Your drawing should look like Figure 5-13.

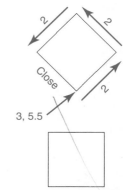

Figure 5-13    Drawing using Polar Tracking

## OBJECT SNAPS

Object Snaps, or OSNAPS as they are sometimes called, are among the most essential features available in AutoCAD. Object snaps allow your cursor to snap to exact locations relative to existing objects in your drawing so that you can locate points precisely when you are drawing or editing. Using Object Snaps, you can snap to the endpoint of a line (Figure 5-14A), the center point of a circle (Figure 5-14B), or if a line and circle overlap, their point of intersection (Figure 5-14C), just to name a few. There are more than 15 different types of Object Snaps ranging from the basic to the advanced.

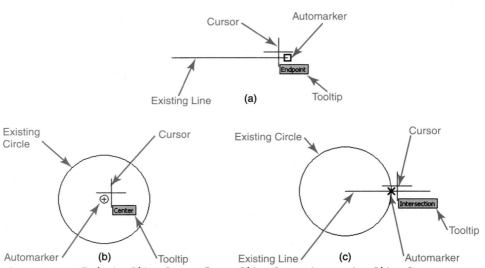

**Figure 5-14A** Endpoint Object Snap **B** Center Object Snap **C** Intersection Object Snap

In order to help you use Object Snaps most effectively, a visual aid called **AutoSnap** is provided. **AutoSnap** provides the following features, most of which are on by default:

- **Marker**   Displays the object snap type and location when the cursor moves over or near an object
- **Tooltip**   Text description of the type of object snap you are snapping to in a small box at the cursor location
- **Magnet**   Feature that attracts and locks the cursor onto the object snap point when your cursor gets near an AutoSnap marker
- **Aperture box**   Boxed area that defines how close you need to be to an object in order to snap to an object snap point. The aperture box can be resized and turned on or off.

All these settings, and a few others explained later, can be controlled on the **Drafting** tab of the **Options** dialog box shown in Figure 5-15.

Object Snaps work only when you are prompted for a point. If you try to use an Object Snap alone when no command is active, the error message *Unknown command* is displayed.

### Object Snap Modes

There are two different ways you can utilize Object Snaps:

- They can be used individually in response to each prompt for point coordinate information.
- You can turn on one or more Object Snaps on the **Object Snap** tab of the **Drafting Settings** dialog box so that they are automatically active each time you are prompted to select a point.

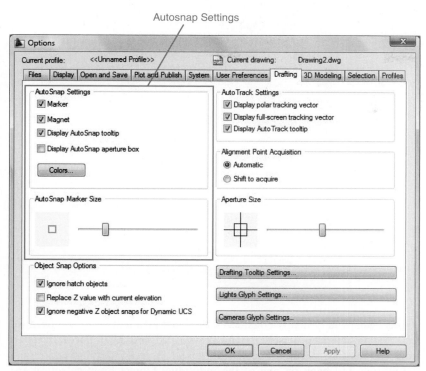

Figure 5-15   AutoSnap settings on Drafting tab of the Options dialog box

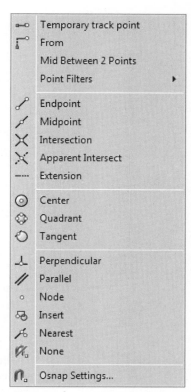

**Figure 5-16**   Right-click Object Snap shortcut menu

Entering an Object Snap individually in response to a request for point information makes the Object Snap active for only one cursor pick point. *Each time AutoCAD prompts for a point you must respond with another Object Snap.* There are a couple of ways to enter an Object Snap using this approach:

- Select the Object Snap from the **Object Snap** right-click shortcut menu (see Figure 5-16). The **Object Snap** shortcut menu is displayed by holding down the **<Shift>** key on your keyboard while right-clicking with your mouse.

- Type the desired Object Snap at the command line in response to a point request. The following is an example of activating the **Endpoint** Object Snap by typing **end** at the command line in response to a prompt for a point:

```
Specify first point: end
```

Most Object Snaps can be specified by entering the first three or four characters of the Object Snap name. In fact, if you observe the command line while selecting an Object Snap using the right-click shortcut menu, you can glean what is being entered at the command line so you can type it in the next time.

The second approach to using Object Snaps is to turn on a select number of Object Snaps via the **Object Snap** tab of the **Drafting Settings** dialog box (see Figure 5-17) so that they are automatically activated each time you are prompted for a point location.

This technique is typically referred to as *setting running Object Snaps* because the selected Object Snaps are always running in the background as you draw.

When your cursor gets close to any running Object Snap feature when you are selecting points in your drawing, an **AutoSnap** marker is automatically displayed so you can quickly snap to the corresponding feature.

You can also set running Object Snaps by right-clicking on the **Object Snap** button and selecting the desired Object Snap from the shortcut menu.

**Figure 5-17**    Setting running Object Snaps

Using running Object Snaps is typically considered the most efficient approach because it allows you to quickly locate objects precisely in your drawing without having to activate an Object Snap each time you need it. If you do need a particular Object Snap that is not currently active, you can always fall back on one of the individual Object Snap selection approaches explained earlier:

- Use the **<Shift>** key and the right-click shortcut menu.
- Type the Object Snap name at the command line.

When you activate an individual Object Snap this way, it is considered an override because you are temporarily suppressing any active running Object Snaps for a single point selection using the currently selected Object Snap. After a point is selected, all the running Object Snaps are active again until another Object Snap override is selected or Object Snaps are turned off using the **Object Snap** button on the Status Bar.

Sometimes when using running Object Snaps, you might need to select a point in your drawing without using any of the active running Object Snaps. The easiest thing to do is to disable running Object Snaps by turning off the **Object Snap** button on the Status Bar. It is also possible to activate the **None** Object Snap using one of the individual override methods. The **None** object snap turns Object Snaps off temporarily.

> As you will discover in this chapter, there are many different Object Snaps that provide a wide array of features and functionality. You will want to be judicious as you start exploring and turning on different running Object Snaps. You definitely don't want to turn them all on at the same time. This will create confusion as you try to select points in your drawing. Select a few you use most often as running Object Snaps and then select others on an as-needed basis using the override approach.

**deferred point:** Object Snap feature that allows you to "build" the Object Snap point using multiple point selection input by deferring the first point selected.

## Basic Object Snaps

The following Object Snaps are basic in nature and require minimal user interaction. Most involve a single point selection near the feature you want to snap to—end of a line, center of a circle, intersecting objects, and so on. Some of the Object Snaps in this section provide an additional feature, known as a **_deferred point_**.

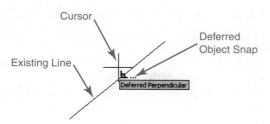

**Figure 5-18**    Deferred Object Snap

Deferred Object Snaps allow you to "build" the Object Snap point by selecting additional points and/or objects. When an Object Snap is deferred, there is an ellipsis (…) displayed after the Object Snap AutoSnap Marker, indicating that there are more selections required (see Figure 5-18).

*Endpoint.*    **Endpoint** is easily the most used Object Snap. The **Endpoint** Object Snap snaps to the closest endpoint of an arc, elliptical arc, line, multiline, polyline, spline, region, or ray. The **Endpoint** Object Snap will also snap to the closest corner of a trace, solid, or 3D face. Figures 5-19A and B show how to snap to the endpoint of a line using the **Endpoint** Object Snap when drawing a line.

**Figure 5-19A**  Using the Endpoint Object Snap—Step 1 **B** Using the Endpoint Object Snap — Step 2

*Midpoint.*    The **Midpoint** Object Snap snaps to the midway point of an arc, ellipse, elliptical arc, line, multiline, polyline, region, solid, spline, or xline. The selected object is bisected exactly at the halfway point. Figures 5-20A and B show how to snap to the midpoint of a line using the **Midpoint** Object Snap when drawing a line.

**Figure 5-20A**  Using the Midpoint Object Snap—Step 1 **B**  Using the Midpoint Object Snap—Step 2

*Intersection.*    The **Intersection** Object Snap snaps to the intersection of two objects. The two objects can be any combination of the following: arc, circle, ellipse, elliptical arc, line, multiline, polyline, ray, region, spline, or xline. Figures 5-21A and B show how to snap to the intersection of two lines using the **Intersection** Object Snap when drawing a line.

**Figure 5-21A**  Using the Intersection Object Snap—Step 1 **B** Using the Intersection Object Snap—Step 2

It is also possible to snap to the intersection of two objects that do not physically cross in your drawing but would intersect if either of them, or both, were extended. The **Extended Intersection** Object Snap snaps to the implied intersection of two objects. The extension mode occurs automatically through the deferred pick point process explained earlier. If you do not pick close to the physical intersection of two objects when using the **Intersection** Object Snap, AutoCAD automatically puts you in **Extended Intersection** mode and displays the **Extended Intersection** AutoSnap Marker (Figure 5-22A).

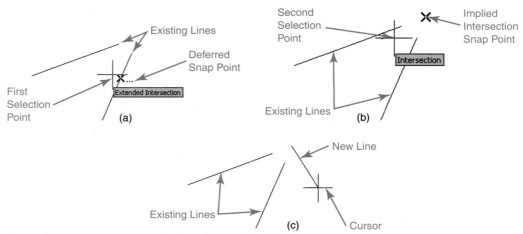

**Figure 5-22A** Using the Extended Intersection Object Snap—Step 1 **B** Using the Extended Intersection Object Snap—Step 2 **C** Using the Extended Intersection Object Snap—Step 3

Remember that any time you see the ellipsis (...) next to an AutoSnap Marker it means AutoCAD is waiting for more input. If you move your cursor over the other object that would intersect if it were extended, the typical **Intersection** AutoSnap Marker is displayed (Figure 5-22B).

As soon as the **Intersection** AutoSnap Marker is displayed, you can pick a point, and it will snap to the implied intersection (Figure 5-22C).

TIP     Extended Intersection is not available as a running Object Snap.

**Exercise 5-4:** Using the Endpoint, Midpoint, and Intersection Object Snaps

1. Continue from Exercise 5-3.
2. Turn off all the drawing tool buttons on the Status Bar.
3. Right-click on the **Object Snap** button on the Status Bar and select **Settings...** from the shortcut menu. The **Object Snap** tab of the **Drafting Settings** dialog box is displayed. See Figure 5-17.
4. Select the **Clear All** button to clear any running Object Snaps. Turn on the **Endpoint**, **Midpoint**, and **Intersection** Object Snaps. Exit the **Drafting Settings** dialog box by selecting **OK**.
5. Turn on the **Object Snap** button on the Status Bar.
6. Start the **LINE** command.
7. Place your cursor over the bottom corner of the rotated square on the top of the drawing and wait until the **Endpoint AutoSnap** Marker and tooltip are displayed. Pick a point while the **AutoSnap** Marker is displayed. See Figure 5-23.

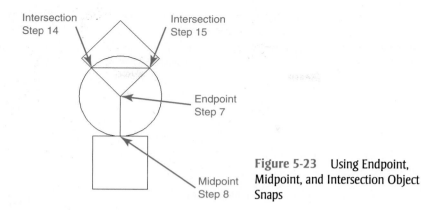

**Figure 5-23** Using Endpoint, Midpoint, and Intersection Object Snaps

8. Place your cursor over the middle of the top line of the square on the bottom of the drawing and wait until the **Midpoint** AutoSnap Marker and tooltip are displayed. Pick a point while the AutoSnap Marker is displayed. See Figure 5-23.
9. Press **<Enter ↵>** to end the **LINE** command.
10. Start the **CIRCLE** command.
11. Choose the same point selected in Step 7 to locate the circle center point.
12. Choose the same point selected in Step 8 to indicate the circle radius.
13. Start the **LINE** command.
14. Place your cursor over the intersection on the left side of the circle and bottom left angled line of the rotated square and wait until the **Intersection** AutoSnap Marker and tooltip are displayed. Pick a point while the AutoSnap Marker is displayed. See Figure 5-23.
15. Place your cursor over the intersection on the right side of the circle and bottom right angled line of the rotated square and wait until the **Intersection** AutoSnap Marker and tooltip are displayed. Pick a point while the AutoSnap Marker is displayed. See Figure 5-23.
16. Hit **<Enter ↵>** to end the **LINE** command.
17. Save your drawing as **EX5-4**. Your drawing should look like Figure 5-23.

*Apparent Intersection.* The **Apparent Intersection** Object Snap snaps to the visual intersection of two objects that are not in the same plane in 3D space so they don't physically intersect but appear to intersect when viewed from certain angles. Its use is reserved for working in 3D drawings.

*Center.* The **Center** Object Snap snaps to the center of an arc, circle, ellipse, or elliptical arc. Figures 5-24A and B show how to snap to the center of a circle using the **Center** Object Snap when drawing a line.

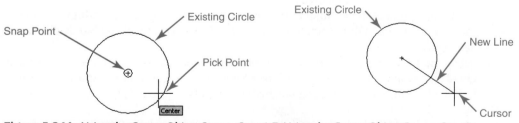

**Figure 5-24A** Using the Center Object Snap—Step 1 **B** Using the Center Object Snap—Step 2

*Quadrant.* The **Quadrant** Object Snap snaps to one of the four quadrant points (0°, 90°, 180°, or 270°) of an arc, circle, ellipse, or elliptical arc. The quadrant point selected is the one closest to where you select the object. Figures 5-25A and B show how to snap to the 0° quadrant point of a circle using the **Quadrant** Object Snap when drawing a line.

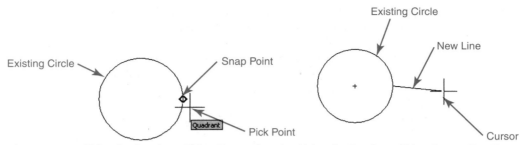

**Figure 5-25A** Using the Quadrant Object Snap—Step 1 **B** Using the Quadrant Object Snap—Step 2

**Exercise 5-5:** Using the Center and Quadrant Object Snaps

1. Start a new drawing using the acad.dwt drawing template.
2. Select **Zoom Extents** to zoom to the limits of the drawing.
3. Start the **CIRCLE** command. AutoCAD prompts you to *Specify center point for circle or ↓*.
4. Type **2,2<Enter ↵>**. AutoCAD prompts you to *Specify radius of circle or ↓*.
5. Type **1<Enter ↵>** to specify a radius of 1″.
6. Repeat Steps 4 and 5 to create two more 1″-radius circles at the coordinate locations of **(4,5)** and **(6,2)**. See Figure 5-26.

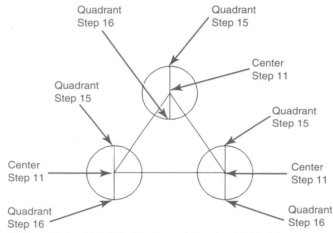

**Figure 5-26**    Using the Center and Quadrant Object Snaps

7. Turn *off* all the drawing tool buttons on the Status Bar.
8. Right-click on the **Object Snap** button on the Status Bar and select **Settings...** from the shortcut menu. The **Object Snap** tab of the **Drafting Settings** dialog box is displayed. See Figure 5-17.
9. Select the **Clear All** button to clear any running Object Snaps. Turn on the **Center** and **Quadrant** Object Snaps. Turn the **Object Snaps** check box on in the upper left corner. Exit the **Drafting Settings** dialog box by selecting **OK**.
10. Start the **LINE** command.
11. Place your cursor over the center of the circle on the bottom left of the drawing and wait until the **Center** AutoSnap Marker and tooltip are displayed. Pick a point while the AutoSnap Marker is displayed. See Figure 5-26.
12. Repeat Step 11 for the other two circles and draw 3 lines to create a triangle. See Figure 5-26.
13. Type **C<Enter ↵>**. AutoCAD closes the triangle and exits the **LINE** command.
14. Start the **LINE** command.
15. Place your cursor over the top quadrant point (90°) of the circle on the bottom left of the drawing and wait until the **Quadrant** AutoSnap Marker and tooltip are displayed. Pick a point while the AutoSnap Marker is displayed. See Figure 5-26.

16. Place your cursor over the bottom quadrant point (270°) of the circle on the bottom left of the drawing and wait until the **Quadrant** AutoSnap Marker and tooltip are displayed. Pick a point while the AutoSnap Marker is displayed. See Figure 5-26.

17. Repeat Steps 14 though 16 to create vertical lines from quadrant to quadrant on the other two circles.

18. Save your drawing as **EX5-5**. Your drawing should look like Figure 5-26.

*Tangent.*    The **Tangent** Object Snap snaps to the tangent of an arc, circle, ellipse, elliptical arc, or spline. Figures 5-27A and B show how to snap to the tangent of a circle using the **Tangent** Object Snap when drawing a line.

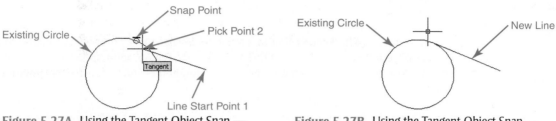

**Figure 5-27A**  Using the Tangent Object Snap — Step 1

**Figure 5-27B**  Using the Tangent Object Snap— Step 2

It is possible to defer a tangent point by first selecting the object you want to be tangent to before picking any other points. Picking a circle first displays the **Deferred Tangent** AutoSnap Marker (Figure 5-28A).

Again, the ellipsis (...) next to an AutoSnap Marker means AutoCAD is waiting for more input. Pick another point to locate the end of the line (Figure 5-28B).

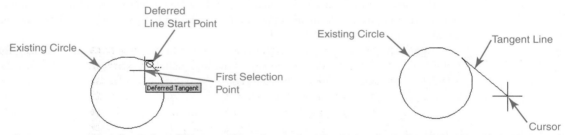

**Figure 5-28A**  Using the Deferred Tangent Object Snap—Step 1 **B** Using the Deferred Tangent Object Snap— Step 2

## Exercise 5-6: Using the Tangent Object Snap

1. Continue from Exercise 5-5.
2. Start the **LINE** command.
3. Hold down the **<Shift>** key on your keyboard while right-clicking with your mouse to display the **Object Snap** shortcut menu. See Figure 5-16.
4. Select the **Tangent** Object Snap from the menu.
5. Place your cursor over the left side of the circle on the bottom left of the drawing and wait until the **Deferred Tangent** AutoSnap Marker and tooltip are displayed. Pick a point while the AutoSnap Marker is displayed. See Figure 5-29.
6. Repeat Steps 3 and 4 to select the **Tangent** Object Snap again.
7. Place your cursor over the left side of the circle on the top middle of the drawing and wait until the **Deferred Tangent** AutoSnap Marker and tooltip are displayed. Pick a point while the AutoSnap Marker is displayed. See Figure 5-29.
8. There should now be a line segment tangent to both circles.
9. Repeat Steps 2 through 7 and create two more line segments tangent to the other two circles. See Figure 5-29.
10. Save your drawing as **EX5-6**. Your drawing should look like Figure 5-29.

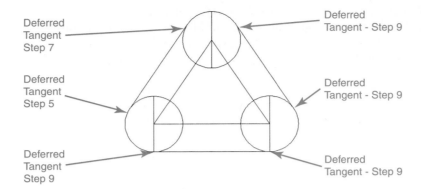

**Figure 5-29**  Using the Tangent Object Snap

*Perpendicular.*  The **Perpendicular** Object Snap snaps to a point perpendicular to an arc, circle, ellipse, elliptical arc, line, multiline, polyline, ray, region, solid, spline, or xline. Figures 5-30A and B show how to draw a line perpendicular to another line using the **Perpendicular** Object Snap.

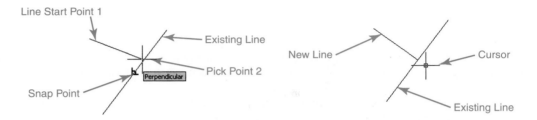

**Figure 5-30**  **(A)** Using the Perpendicular Object Snap—Step 1 **(B)** Using the Perpendicular Object Snap—Step 2

It is possible to defer a perpendicular point by first selecting the object you want to be perpendicular to before picking any other points. Picking a line first displays the **Deferred Perpendicular** AutoSnap Marker (Figure 5-31A).

Again, the ellipsis (...) next to an AutoSnap Marker means AutoCAD is waiting for more input. Pick another point to locate the end of the line, which in turn determines where the new line attaches to the existing line (Figure 5-31B).

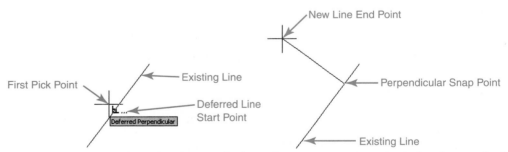

**Figure 5-31A**  Using the Deferred Perpendicular Object Snap—Step 1       **Figure 5-31B**  Using the Deferred Perpendicular Object Snap—Step 2

**Exercise 5-7:** Using the Perpendicular Object Snap

1. Continue from Exercise 5-6.
2. Turn off all the drawing tool buttons on the Status Bar.
3. Right-click on the **Object Snap** button on the Status Bar and select **Settings...** from the shortcut menu. The **Object Snap** tab of the **Drafting Settings** dialog box is displayed. See Figure 5-17.
4. Select the **Clear All** button to clear any running Object Snaps. Turn on the **Perpendicular** Object Snap. Turn Object Snaps on in the upper left corner. Exit the **Drafting Settings** dialog box by selecting **OK**.

5. Start the **LINE** command. AutoCAD prompts you to *Specify first point:.*
6. Type **8,6<Enter ↵>**. AutoCAD prompts you to *Specify next point or* ↓.
7. Place your cursor over the angled line on the right side of the triangle and wait until the **Perpendicular** AutoSnap Marker and tooltip are displayed. Pick a point while the AutoSnap Marker is displayed. See Figure 5-32.

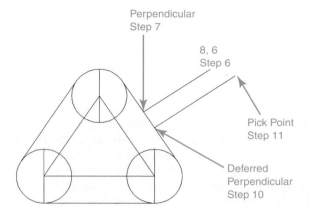

**Figure 5-32    Using the Perpendicular Object Snap**

8. Type **<Enter ↵>** to end the **LINE** command.
9. Start the **LINE** command again.
10. Place your cursor over the angled line on the right side of the triangle and wait until the **Deferred Perpendicular** AutoSnap Marker and tooltip are displayed. Pick a point while the AutoSnap Marker is displayed. See Figure 5-32.
11. Move your cursor up to the right and pick another point to create a perpendicular line segment. See Figure 5-32.
12. Type **<Enter ↵>** to end the **LINE** command.
13. Save your drawing as **EX5-7**. Your drawing should look like Figure 5-32.

*Insert.*    The **Insert** Object Snap snaps to the insertion point of an attribute, block, shape, or text. Figure 5-33 shows how to snap to the insertion point of a text object using the **Insert** Object Snap.

**Figure 5-33    Using the Insert Object Snap**

*Node.*    The **Node** Object Snap snaps to a point object, dimension definition point, or dimension text origin. Figures 5-34A and B show how to snap to a point created using the **DIVIDE** or **MEASURE** command and the **Node** Object Snap when drawing a line.

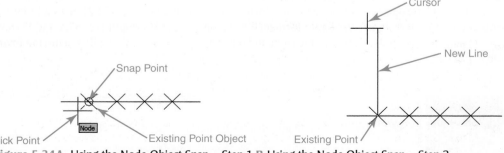

**Figure 5-34A** Using the Node Object Snap—Step 1 **B** Using the Node Object Snap—Step 2

*Nearest.*     The **Nearest** Object Snap snaps to the nearest point on an arc, circle, ellipse, elliptical arc, line, multiline, point, polyline, ray, spline, or xline. This allows you to pick a point near an object and be assured that it snaps directly on the object. Figures 5-35A and B show how to snap to a point exactly on a line using the **Nearest** Object Snap when drawing a line.

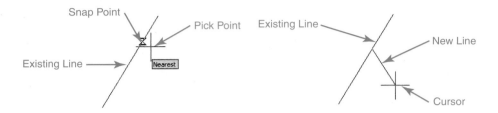

**Figure 5-35A** Using the Nearest Object Snap—Step 1 **B** Using the Nearest Object Snap—Step 2

*None.*     The **None** Object Snap allows you to snap to nothing... literally. The **None** Object Snap temporarily disables any running Object Snaps set on the **Object Snaps** tab of the **Drafting Settings** dialog box for the next picked point. This makes it possible to pick a point in your drawing that doesn't snap to any objects that might be nearby, particularly when you are working in close quarters. You can always turn the **Object Snap** button off on the Status Bar at any time as well, but then you have to turn it back on when you need Object Snaps enabled again.

### Advanced Object Snap Modes

The following Object Snaps are more advanced than those introduced in the previous section. The Object Snaps in this section require additional information to build the snap point based on the geometry of an existing object, or even objects. This can range from entering an offset distance to acquiring points that are used to display alignment paths (see Figure 5-36).

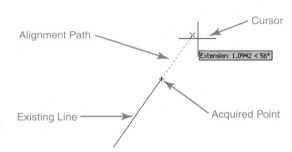

**Figure 5-36**     Acquired point and alignment path

**acquired point:** Object tracking feature used to locate a point as an intermediate location in order to locate temporary alignment paths

Some *acquired points* are selected automatically by simply moving your cursor over an object, whereas others require that you explicitly pick a point in the drawing.

The difference between the two methods of acquiring points is highlighted in the following sections to help reduce any confusion.

*From.*     The **From** Object Snap allows you to specify a relative distance from a selected point and is typically used in conjunction with other Object Snaps. The distance can be entered either as a relative Cartesian coordinate using the format @X,Y (for example, @2,2) or as a polar coordinate using the distance and angle format (for example, @2<45). Figures 5-37A and B show how to snap to a point that is 0.5″ to the right and 0.5″ above the endpoint of a line using the **From** Object Snap.

---

**FOR MORE DETAILS**     See Chapter 4 for more information about relative coordinate entry.

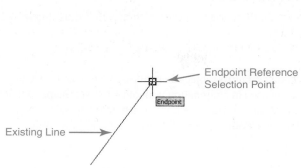

**Figure 5-37A**    Using The From Object Snap—Step 1

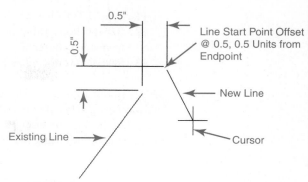

**Figure 5-37B**    Using the From Object Snap—Step 2

## Exercise 5-8: Using the From Object Snap

1. Open drawing EX5-2.dwg.
2. Turn off all the drawing tool buttons on the Status Bar.
3. Right-click on the **Object Snap** button on the Status Bar and select **Settings...** from the shortcut menu. The **Object Snap** tab of the **Drafting Settings** dialog box is displayed. See Figure 5-17.
4. Select the **Clear All** button to clear any running Object Snaps. Turn on the **Endpoint** Object Snap. Turn Object Snaps on in the upper left corner. Exit the **Drafting Settings** dialog box by selecting **OK**.
5. Start the **CIRCLE** command. AutoCAD prompts you to *Specify center point for circle or ↓*.
6. Hold down the **<Shift>** key on your keyboard while right-clicking with your mouse to display the **Object Snap** shortcut menu. See Figure 5-16.
7. Select the **From** Object Snap from the menu. AutoCAD prompts you for a base point:

   `Base point:`

8. Place your cursor over the endpoints on the bottom left corner of the square and wait until the **Endpoint** AutoSnap Marker and tooltip are displayed. Pick a point while the AutoSnap Marker is displayed. See Figure 5-38.

*Note:*
Specifying an absolute coordinate without the symbol will simply locate the point at the coordinate specified.

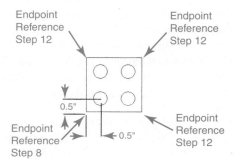

**Figure 5-38**    Using the From Object Snap

9. AutoCAD then prompts you for an offset distance:

   `<Offset>:`

10. Type **@.5,.5<Enter ↵>**. AutoCAD locates the center point of the circle and prompts you for a radius:

    `Specify radius of circle or ↓.`

11. Type **.25<Enter ↵>**.
12. Repeat Steps 5 through 11 to locate three more circles with a 0.25 radius a half inch in from each corner. See Figure 5-38.
13. Save your drawing as **EX5-8**. Your drawing should look like Figure 5-38.

*Mid Between 2 Points.*     The **Mid Between 2 Points** Object Snap allows you to locate a snap point midway between two points and is typically used in conjunction with other Object Snaps so that you can locate the point precisely. Figures 5-39A through C show how to snap midway between the endpoints of two lines using the **Mid Between 2 Points** Object Snap when drawing a circle.

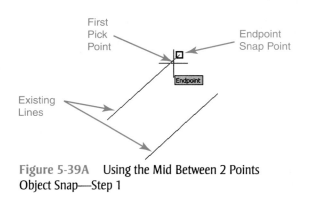

**Figure 5-39A**   Using the Mid Between 2 Points Object Snap—Step 1

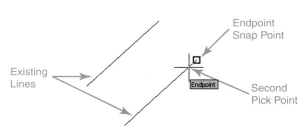

**Figure 5-39B**   Using the Mid Between 2 Points Object Snap— Step 2

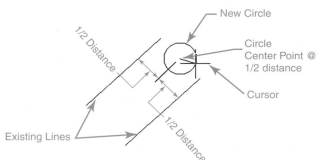

**Figure 5-39C**   Using the Mid Between 2 Points Object Snap— Step 3

*Extension.*     The **Extension** Object Snap allows you to display an alignment path along the extension of an arc, elliptical arc, line, multiline, polyline, region, or ray by acquiring an endpoint on one or more objects.

A point is acquired by simply moving your cursor over an endpoint of a valid object type. You *do not* need to pick a point to acquire it when using the **Extension** Object Snap. A small cross is displayed after a point is acquired. You can deselect an acquired point by moving your cursor back over the acquired point so the cross disappears.

After a point is acquired, you display an alignment path by moving your cursor in the object's extension direction. Once the alignment path is displayed, you can locate a point by picking a point on the path or by using direct distance entry to specify a distance to travel along the vector. Figures 5-40A and B show how to locate a line start point on the extension alignment path of a line using the **Extension** Object Snap.

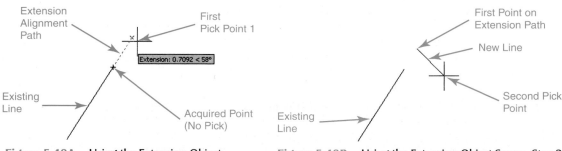

**Figure 5-40A**   Using the Extension Object Snap—Step 1

**Figure 5-40B**   Using the Extension Object Snap—Step 2

**Exercise 5-9:** Using the Extension Object Snap

1. Continue from Exercise 5-8.
2. Turn on the **Ortho Mode** button on the Status Bar.
3. Right-click on the **Object Snap** button on the Status Bar and select **Settings...** from the shortcut menu. The **Object Snap** tab of the **Drafting Settings** dialog box is displayed. See Figure 5-17.
4. Select the **Clear All** button to clear any running Object Snaps. Turn on the **Extension** Object Snap. Turn Object Snaps ON in the upper left corner. Exit the **Drafting Settings** dialog box by selecting **OK**.
5. Start the **LINE** command.
6. Place your cursor over the endpoints on the bottom left corner of the square to acquire a point. See Figure 5-41.

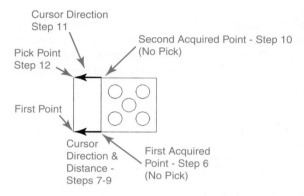

**Figure 5-41    Using the Extension Object Snap**

7. Move your cursor to the left of the corner to display a horizontal alignment path and tooltip indicating you are pointing at 180°. See Figure 5-41.
8. Type **1<Enter ↵>**.
9. AutoCAD uses direct distance entry to place a point 1 unit from the lower left corner along the 180° horizontal extension alignment path. See Figure 5-41.
10. Place your cursor over the endpoints on the top left corner of the square to acquire another point. See Figure 5-41.
11. Move your cursor to the left to display a horizontal alignment path and tooltip indicating you are pointing at 180°. See Figure 5-41.
12. Use **Ortho Mode** to pick a point on the alignment path 90° from the first point. See Figure 5-41.
13. Save your drawing as **EX5-9**. Your drawing should look like Figure 5-41.

*Parallel.*    The **Parallel** Object Snap allows you to draw a parallel line using a parallel alignment path. The alignment path is displayed by acquiring a point on the line segment to which you want to draw a parallel line when AutoCAD prompts you for the second point of a line.

A **Parallel** Object Snap point is acquired by moving your cursor over the desired line segment. You *do not* need to pick a point to acquire it when using the **Parallel** Object Snap. When you move your cursor over a line segment after selecting the **Parallel** Object Snap, the **Parallel** AutoSnap Marker is displayed, and a point is acquired showing a small cross. You can deselect an acquired point by moving your cursor back over the acquired point so the cross disappears.

After a point is acquired, you display a parallel alignment path by moving your cursor in the parallel direction. Once the alignment path is displayed, you can locate a point by picking a point on the path or by using direct distance entry to specify a distance to travel along the vector. Figures 5-42A and B show how to draw a line parallel to another line using the **Parallel** Object Snap when drawing a line.

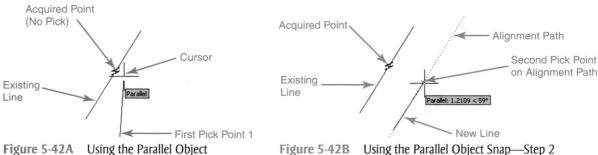

**Figure 5-42A**  Using the Parallel Object Snap—Step 1

**Figure 5-42B**  Using the Parallel Object Snap—Step 2

## OBJECT SNAP TRACKING

**Object Snap Tracking** relies on the **AutoTracking** feature (explained earlier in the "Polar Tracking" section) to display alignment paths at orthogonal or polar angle settings using points you select in your drawing using Object Snaps. The angle settings used, polar or orthogonal, are controlled in the **Object Snap Tracking Settings** section on the **Polar Tracking** tab of the **Drafting Settings** dialog box shown in Figure 5-43.

**Figure 5-43**  Object Snap Tracking Settings

By default, **Object Snap Tracking** is set to track orthogonally at horizontal and vertical angles. There are two types of **Object Snap Tracking**:

- Temporary Tracking
- **Object Snap Tracking** Mode

**Temporary Tracking** works like an Object Snap override to display tracking alignment paths on an as-needed basis at picked points. The **Object Snap Tracking** mode works with running Object Snaps so that when it is turned on, tracking alignment paths are automatically displayed at all the currently running Object Snap points. Both types of tracking are explained in detail in the following sections.

## Temporary Tracking

**Temporary Tracking** is used on an as-needed basis to display **AutoTracking** alignment paths at acquired points and is typically used in conjunction with Object Snaps.

You must pick a point in your drawing to acquire a point when using **Temporary Tracking**. A small cross is displayed after a point is acquired. You can deselect an acquired point by moving your cursor back over the acquired point so the cross disappears.

After a point is acquired, **AutoTracking** alignment paths are displayed at the angles specified on the **Polar Tracking** tab of the **Drafting Settings** dialog box. Once the alignment path is displayed, you can locate a point by picking a point on the path or by using direct distance entry to specify a distance to travel along the alignment vector. Figures 5-44A through C show how to locate the center point of a circle by tracking horizontally from the midpoint of a vertical line.

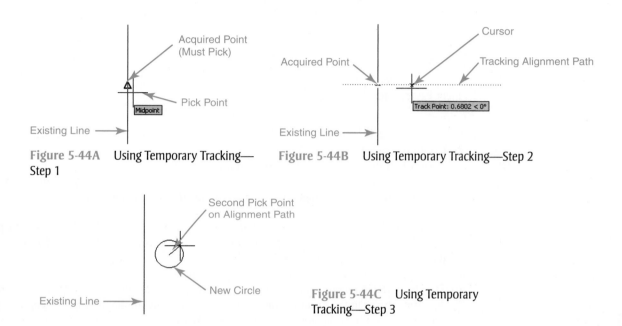

**Figure 5-44A**    Using Temporary Tracking—Step 1

**Figure 5-44B**    Using Temporary Tracking—Step 2

**Figure 5-44C**    Using Temporary Tracking—Step 3

## Object Snap Tracking

The **Object Snap Tracking** drawing tool works with running Object Snaps so that when **OTRACK** mode is turned on AutoTracking alignment paths can be displayed by acquiring a point at any currently running Object Snap point.

Unlike **Temporary Tracking**, when **Object Snap Tracking** mode is on, you *do not* have to pick a point to acquire it. You just move your cursor over an Object Snap point, and a small cross (+) is displayed, indicating the point is acquired. You can deselect an acquired point by moving your cursor back over the acquired point so the cross disappears.

After a point is acquired, **AutoTracking** alignment paths are displayed at the angle specified on the **Polar Tracking** tab of the **Drafting Settings** dialog box. Once the alignment path is displayed, you can locate a point by picking a point on the path or by using direct distance entry to specify a distance to travel along the alignment vector.

### Intersecting Alignment Paths

Both **Temporary Tracking** and **Object Snap Tracking** allow you to display multiple **AutoTracking** alignment paths so that you can locate points relative to multiple objects in your drawing. When you use **AutoTracking**, each point you snap to displays its own alignment path. If multiple alignment paths cross, it is possible to snap to their point of intersection by putting your cursor over the intersection until a small cross appears that looks similar to an acquired point and then picking a point. Figures 5-45A through C show how to locate the center of a circle using the intersection point of vertical and horizontal **AutoTracking** alignment paths.

| Object Snap Tracking | |
|---|---|
| **Status Bar:** | ∠ or OTRACK |
| **Function Key:** | F11 |
| **Command Line:** | None |
| **Keyboard Combo:** | None |

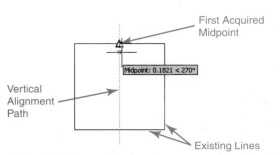

Figure 5-45A    Intersecting Alignment Paths—Step 1

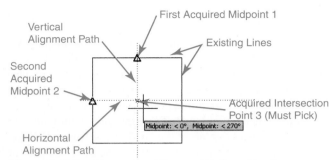

Figure 5-45B    Intersecting Alignment Paths—Step 2

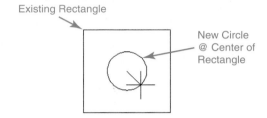

Figure 5-45C    Intersecting
Alignment Paths—Step 3

### Exercise 5-10: Using Object Snap Tracking

1. Continue from Exercise 5-9.
2. Turn off all the drawing tool buttons on the Status Bar.
3. Right-click on the **Object Snap** button on the Status Bar and select **Settings...** from the shortcut menu. The **Object Snap** tab of the **Drafting Settings** dialog box is displayed. See Figure 5-17.
4. Select the **Clear All** button to clear any running Object Snaps. Turn ON the **Midpoint** Object Snap. Turn **Object Snaps** on in the upper left corner. Exit the **Drafting Settings** dialog box by selecting the **OK** button.
5. Turn on the **Object Snap Tracking** button on the Status Bar.
6. Start the **CIRCLE** command. AutoCAD prompts you to *Specify center point for circle or ↓*.
7. Acquire a point at the middle point of the horizontal line on the top of the square by placing your cursor over the horizontal line so the **Midpoint** AutoSnap Marker and tooltip are displayed. *Do not* pick a point. See Figure 5-46.

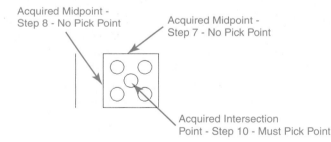

Figure 5-46    Using
Object Snap Tracking

8. Acquire a point at the middle point of the vertical line on the left of the square by placing your cursor over the vertical line so the **Midpoint** AutoSnap Marker and tooltip are displayed. *Do not* pick a point. See Figure 5-46.
9. Move your cursor to the middle of the rectangle to display both a horizontal alignment path with tooltip and a vertical alignment path with tooltip.
10. Pick a point when the two alignment paths cross and the small acquired intersection point marker (x) is displayed. See Figure 5-46.
11. AutoCAD locates the center point of the circle at the center of the rectangle and prompts you for a radius:

    `Specify radius of circle or ↓.`

12. Type **.25<Enter ↵>**.
13. Save your drawing as **EX5-10.** Your drawing should look like Figure 5-46.

# DYNAMIC INPUT

As mentioned in Chapter 1, **Dynamic Input** is a set of related input and display features that allow you to enter information near the mouse cursor so you can focus on your drawing instead of constantly switching focus to the command line for command prompts and data entry.

The **Dynamic Input** interface consists of three different components:

- **Pointer Input**
- **Dimension Input**
- **Dynamic Prompts**

Each of these different components is explained in the following sections.

| Dynamic Input | |
|---|---|
| **Status Bar:** | ⊞ or DYN |
| **Function Key:** | F12 |
| **Command Line:** | None |
| **Keyboard Combo:** | None |

## Pointer Input

When **Pointer Input** is on, the coordinate location of the mouse crosshairs is displayed as $X$ and $Y$ values in a tooltip near the cursor. As you move your mouse the coordinate values are dynamically updated to reflect the cursor's new location. The **Pointer Input** for the first point of a line is shown in Figure 5-47.

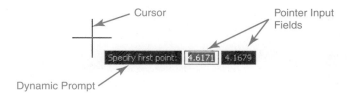

Cursor          Pointer Input Fields

Specify first point: 4.6171  4.1679

Dynamic Prompt

**Figure 5-47**    Using Pointer Input

The **Pointer Input** tooltip consists of $X$ and $Y$ input fields that you can update with a coordinate value of your choice via the keyboard using the same comma-delimited format used for entering coordinates at the command line by typing **X,Y<Enter ↵>.** Entering the comma after the $X$ value locks the input field for $X$ and shifts focus to the $Y$ input field. Entering the desired $Y$ value and hitting **<Enter ↵>** accepts the coordinate value.

**TIP**    It is also possible to use the **<Tab>** key to switch between the $X$ and $Y$ coordinate input fields.

## Dimension Input

When **Dimension Input** is on, distance and angle values are displayed in multiple tooltips near the cursor when a command prompts for a second point. The values in the dimension tooltips change as you move the cursor. The **Dimension Input** for the second point of line is shown in Figure 5-48.

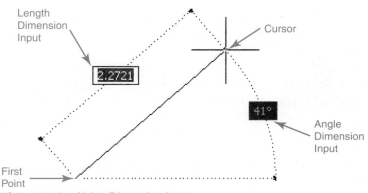

Length Dimension Input          Cursor

2.2721

41°

Angle Dimension Input

First Point

**Figure 5-48**    Using Dimension Input

You can use the <Tab> key to switch between the different length and angle **Dimension Input** fields. When you use the <Tab> key, focus switches to another **Dimension Input** field while locking the previous field. Using this feature, you can input a length for a line and then press the <Tab> key to switch to the angle field to specify the angle. Any angle you input will create a line at that angle with the length previously entered in the length field. This process also works in reverse so that you can press the <Tab> key to enter the angle first and then press the <Tab> key again to enter the length. Now a line will be created at the preset input angle at any length specified.

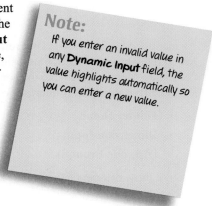

*Note:*
*If you enter an invalid value in any **Dynamic Input** field, the value highlights automatically so you can enter a new value.*

## Dynamic Prompts

When **Dynamic Prompts** are on, command prompts and options are displayed in a tooltip near the cursor. You can type a response in the **Dynamic Prompt** input field instead of on the command line. The **Dynamic Prompt** for the **POLYGON** command is shown in Figure 5-49.

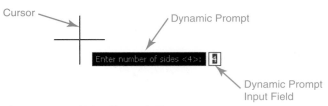

**Figure 5-49     Using Dynamic Prompts**

**Dynamic Prompts** also allow you to select command options near the cursor using the arrow keys on your keyboard. If a command has options, a down arrow is displayed in the **Dynamic Prompt** tooltip. Pressing the down arrow key displays the command options in a shortcut menu near the cursor. The **ZOOM** command options are shown in Figure 5-50.

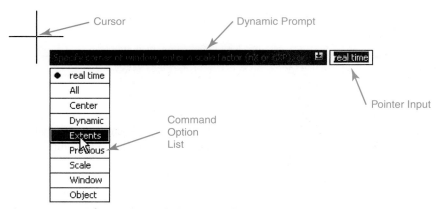

**Figure 5-50     Selecting Dynamic Prompt options**

You can use your up and down arrow keys to navigate to the desired option and hit <**Enter** ↵>, or you can select an option with your mouse pointer.

## Dynamic Input Settings

The **Dynamic Input** settings are managed in the **Dynamic Input** tab in the **Drafting Settings** dialog box shown in Figure 5-51.

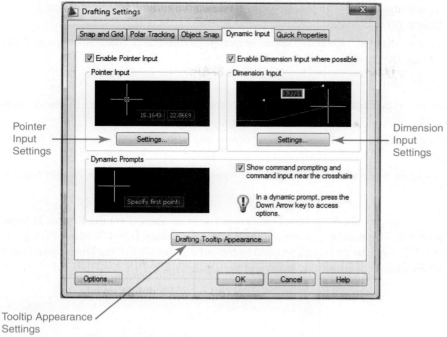

Pointer
Input
Settings

Dimension
Input
Settings

Tooltip Appearance
Settings

**Figure 5-51**    Dynamic Input Settings

The following sections explain the different dynamic input settings.

*Pointer Input Settings.*    You can turn **Pointer Input** on and off via the **Enable Pointer Input** check box. The **Settings...** button displays the **Pointer Input Settings** dialog box shown in Figure 5-52. This dialog box allows you to control the format and visibility of the **Pointer Input** coordinate tooltips.

The different format settings are as follows:

- **Polar format**    Enter the second or next point in polar coordinate format. Enter a comma (,) to change to Cartesian format.

- **Cartesian format**    Enter the second or next point in Cartesian coordinate format. You can enter an angle symbol (<) to change to polar format.

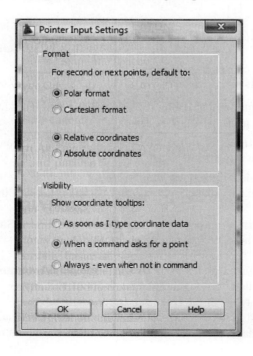

**Figure 5-52**    Pointer Input
Settings dialog box

- **Relative coordinates**   Enter the second or next point in relative coordinate format. Enter a pound sign (**#**) to change to absolute format.
- **Absolute coordinates**   Enter the second or next point in absolute coordinate format. Enter an at sign (**@**) to change to polar format.

The different visibility settings are as follows:

- **As soon as I type coordinate data**   Displays tooltips only when you start to enter coordinate data.
- **When a command asks for a point**   Displays tooltips whenever a command prompts for a point.
- **Always—even when not in command**   Always displays tooltips when Pointer Input is turned on.

*Dimension Input Settings.*   You can turn **Dimension Input** on and off via the **Enable Dimension Input** check box. The **Settings...** button displays the **Dimension Input Settings** dialog box shown in Figure 5-53. This dialog box allows you to control the visibility of the **Dimension Input** coordinate tooltips when you are editing using grips.

**Figure 5-53**   Dimension Input Settings dialog box

The different visibility settings are as follows:

- **Show only 1 dimension input field at a time**   Displays only the distance Dimension Input tooltip when you are using grips.
- **Show 2 dimension input fields at a time**   Displays the distance and angle Dimension Input tooltips when you are using grips.
- **Show the following dimension input fields simultaneously**   Displays the selected Dimension Input tooltips when you are using grips. You can select one or more of the check boxes.

*Dynamic Prompts.*   You can turn **Dynamic Prompts** on and off via the **Show command prompting and command input near the crosshairs** check box (see Figure 5-51).

*Controlling the Drafting Tooltip Appearance.*   The **Drafting Tooltip Appearance...** button displays the **Tooltip Appearance** dialog box shown in Figure 5-54. This dialog box allows you to control the color, size, and transparency of the **Dynamic Input** tooltips.

To change the color of the tooltip in model space, select the **Model Color** button. To change the color of the tooltip in paper space, select the **Layout color** button. Both buttons display the

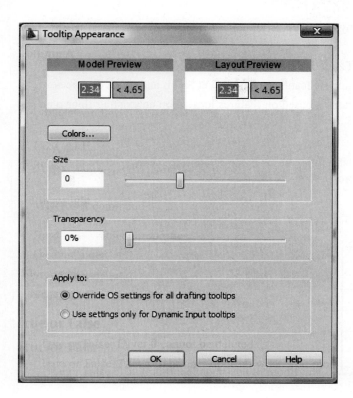

Figure 5-54    Tooltip Appearance
dialog box

AutoCAD **Select Color** dialog box where you can specify a color for the tooltips in the space you selected.

To change the size of tooltips, you can either move the slider to the right to make tooltips bigger or move it to the left to make tooltips smaller. The default size is 0.

To change the transparency of tooltips, you can either move the slider to the right to make the tooltip more transparent or move it to the left to make it less transparent. A value of 0 makes the tooltip opaque.

You can choose to apply your changes using the following:

- **Override OS settings for all drafting tooltips**    Applies the settings to all tooltips, overriding the settings in the operating system.

- **Use settings only for Dynamic Input tooltips**    Applies the settings only to the drafting tooltips used in Dynamic Input.

## USING CONSTRUCTION LINES

Construction lines are temporary lines that are used to help you lay out, or construct, a drawing. Using construction lines to create drawings is a technique that has been around since the early days of drafting. On the board, construction lines were typically drawn with very light lines that could be erased after the final drawing was created. Using AutoCAD, construction lines are typically created on a separate layer so you can control their visibility by turning them on and off.

| FOR MORE DETAILS | See Chapter 6 for detailed information on using layers to separate drawing information to control the visibility of objects. |
| --- | --- |

Construction lines serve many purposes. Some of the more common uses of construction lines are:

orthographic projection:
The two-dimensional graphic representation of an object formed by the perpendicular intersections of lines drawn from points on the object to a plane of projection.

- Creating multiple views of a mechanical drawing using **orthographic projection**
- Temporary locating of geometric features using Object Snaps and offset distances
- Creating architectural elevations based on features located on an existing floor plan and vice versa
- Bisecting an angle

One of the classic uses of construction lines is in the creation of multiple views of a mechanical drawing using orthographic projection. See Figure 5-55.

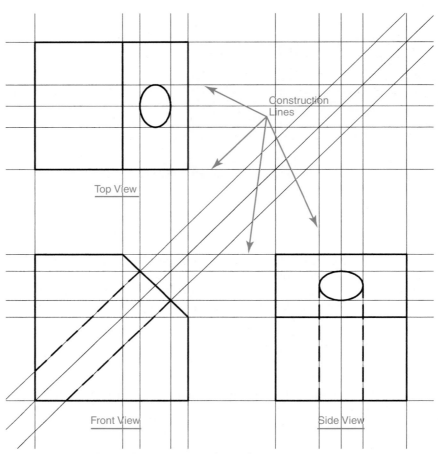

**Figure 5-55**     Multiview drawing using orthographic projection

Using construction lines, you can create one view of a part (i.e., Front, Top, Side) and then locate horizontal and vertical (orthographic) construction lines on key points of the part using the Object Snaps explained earlier in the chapter to project the points as construction lines in other views. You can then create the other views by drawing directly over the top of the construction lines using the **Intersection** Object Snap introduced earlier. Once you complete all the necessary views to describe the part, you can erase or turn off the construction line layer, and you have a finished drawing.

Using the construction line approach, you only have to measure distances once when you create the first view of the part. Most, if not all, of the other views can then be created by projecting construction lines from the original view, which you know is accurate. Theoretically, if you draw the part correctly in the first view, all the other views that are based on it should also be correct. Using construction lines is a great timesaving technique that increases production and promotes precision.

## The XLINE Command

In AutoCAD, construction lines are referred to as *Xlines* and extend infinitely in both directions. This infinite property allows you to zoom or pan as far as necessary and always have the construction lines visible so you can reference them. Construction lines are created using the **XLINE** command.

There are a number of different ways to create construction lines using the **XLINE** command:

- Using two pick points
- Horizontally
- Vertically
- Offset from an existing line
- Specified angle
- Bisected angle

The **XLINE** command options are explained in the following sections.

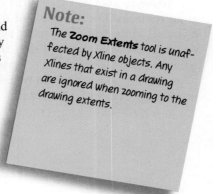

**Note:**
The **Zoom Extents** tool is unaffected by Xline objects. Any Xlines that exist in a drawing are ignored when zooming to the drawing extents.

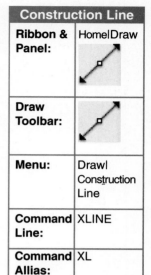

| Construction Line | |
| --- | --- |
| **Ribbon & Panel:** | Home|Draw |
| **Draw Toolbar:** | |
| **Menu:** | Draw| Construction Line |
| **Command Line:** | XLINE |
| **Command Allias:** | XL |

---

**FOR MORE DETAILS**  See Chapter 3 for more information about using the **Zoom Extents** tool.

---

*Drawing a Construction Line Using Two Points.*    This is the default option for creating construction lines. To create an Xline using two points, select the **XLINE** command and pick two points. The first point locates the Xline, and the second point determines its angle. Typically you select points using the Object Snaps explained earlier in the chapter when creating construction lines so that the construction line is drawn relative to an existing object. See Figure 5-56.

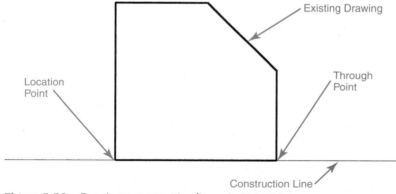

**Figure 5-56**    Drawing a construction line using two points

**TIP**    The first point you select to create a construction line using two points becomes the midpoint of the construction line so that you can snap to it using the **Midpoint** Object Snap later.

---

*Drawing Horizontal and Vertical Construction Lines.*    Horizontal and vertical construction lines are the two most popular **XLINE** command options because they help facilitate the creation of multiview drawings using orthographic projection.

To create a horizontal construction line, select the **XLINE** command and type **H<Enter ↵>** at the command line or select **Hor** from the list of **Dynamic Input** command options. To create a vertical construction line, select the **XLINE** command and type **V<Enter ↵>** at the command line or select **Ver** from the list of **Dynamic Input** command options. You then select a single point to locate the horizontal or vertical construction line in your drawing. AutoCAD continues to prompt for points until you type **<Enter ↵>** so you can create as many construction lines as needed. See Figures 5-57A and B.

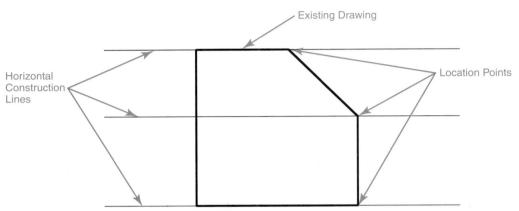

**Figure 5-57A**    Drawing horizontal construction lines

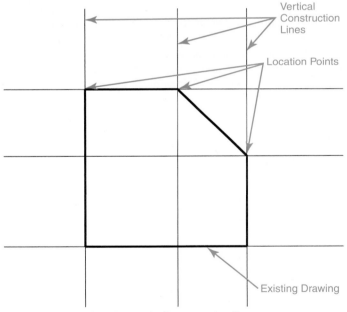

**Figure 5-57B**    Drawing vertical construction lines

**Exercise 5-11:** Drawing Horizontal and Vertical Construction Lines

1. Start a new drawing using the acad.dwt drawing template.
2. Create the drawing shown in Figure 5-58.
3. Turn off all the drawing tool buttons on the Status Bar.
4. Right-click on the **Object Snap** button on the Status Bar and select **Settings...** from the shortcut menu. The **Object Snap** tab of the **Drafting Settings** dialog box is displayed. See Figure 5-17.

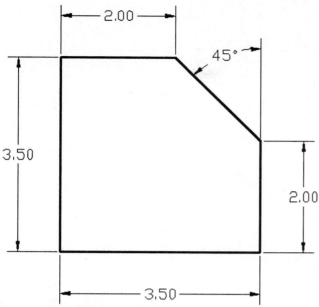

**Figure 5-58**    Front view of part

5. Select the **Clear All** button to clear any running Object Snaps. Turn on the **Endpoint, Midpoint,** and **Intersection** Object Snaps. Exit the **Drafting Settings** dialog box by selecting **OK**.
6. Turn on the **Object Snap** button on the Status Bar.
7. Start the **XLINE** command.
8. Type **H<Enter ⏎>** or select **Hor** from the **Dynamic Input** command options. AutoCAD prompts you for a through point:

   `Specify through point:`

9. Create three horizontal construction lines by snapping to the three endpoints using the **Endpoint** Object Snap as shown in Figure 5-57A.
10. Type **<Enter ⏎>** to end the **XLINE** command.
11. Start the **XLINE** command again.
12. Type **V<Enter ⏎>** or select **Ver** from the **Dynamic Input** command options. AutoCAD prompts you for a through point:

    `Specify through point:`

13. Create three vertical construction lines by snapping to the three endpoints using the **Endpoint** Object Snap as shown in Figure 5-57B.
14. Type **<Enter ⏎>** to end the **XLINE** command.
15. Save your drawing as **EX5-11**. Your drawing should look like Figure 5-59.

*Offsetting Objects with Construction Lines.*    To further facilitate the layout and construction of a drawing, you can offset an existing line object (Line, Polyline, etc.) with a parallel construction line by either specifying a distance or picking a through point.

To offset an object, select the **XLINE** command and type **O<Enter ⏎>** at the command line or select **Offset** from the list of **Dynamic Input** command options. The offset distance can either be entered via the keyboard, or it can be indicated by selecting the point in the drawing you want to offset through. The default is to enter the distance at the keyboard.

Both options require that you select the line object you want to offset (see Figure 5-60A) and then pick a point on either side of the selected line object to indicate the direction you want to

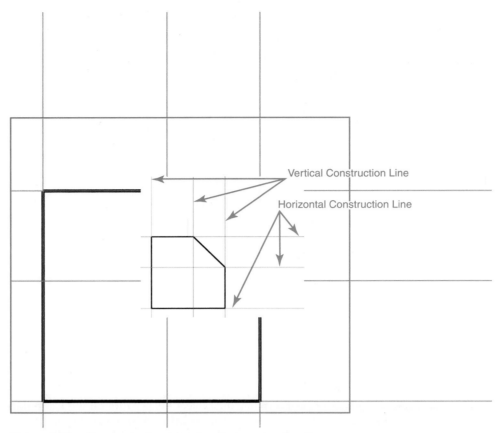

**Figure 5-59**    Drawing horizontal and vertical construction lines

offset (see Figure 5-60B). If you are using the **Through** option, the pick point is also used to locate the line.

AutoCAD will continue to prompt you to select objects to offset until you press **<Enter ↵>**
so that it is possible to offset multiple objects at a time.

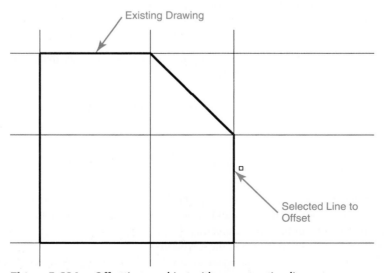

**Figure 5-60A**    Offsetting an object with a construction line

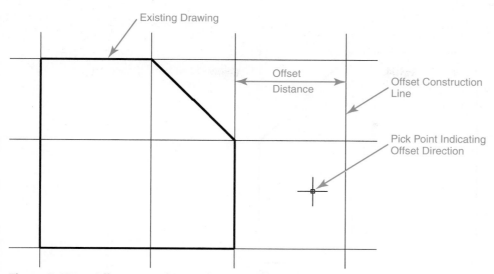

**Figure 5-60B**    Offsetting an object with a construction line

## Exercise 5-12: Offsetting Objects with Construction Lines

1. Continue from Exercise 5-11.
2. Select the **XLINE** command from the **Draw** panel.
3. Type **O<Enter ↵>** or select **Offset** from the **Dynamic Input** command options.
4. AutoCAD prompts you for an offset distance or through point:

   `Specify offset distance or ↓.`

5. Type **2<Enter ↵>**. AutoCAD prompts you to select the object you want to offset:

   `Select a line object:`

6. Select the vertical line as shown in Figure 5-60A. AutoCAD then prompts you for the side you wish to offset:

   `Specify side to offset:`

7. Pick a point on the right side of the object as shown in Figure 5-60B to indicate that you want to create a vertical construction line offset on the right-hand side of the line.
8. AutoCAD continues to prompt you to select line objects.
9. Repeat Steps 6 and 7 to create a horizontal construction line offset 2 units up from the horizontal line on top of the part as shown in Figure 5-61.
10. Type **<Enter ↵>** to end the **XLINE** command.
11. Repeat Steps 2 through 9 to create vertical and horizontal construction lines offset 3 units from the construction lines you just created so your drawing looks like Figure 5-61.
12. Save your drawing as **EX5-12**.

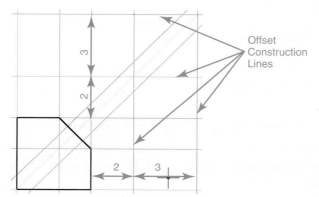

**Figure 5-61**    Offsetting objects with construction lines

**Figure 5-62** Drawing a construction line at an angle

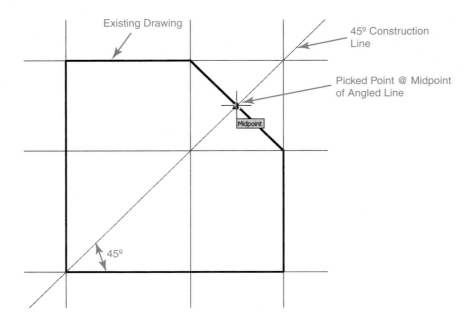

*Drawing Angular Construction Lines.* Construction lines can be created at an angle by either specifying an angle from the horizontal axis 0° or referencing an angle from an existing line.

To create a construction line at an angle, select the **XLINE** command and type **A<Enter ↵>** at the command line or select **Angle** from the list of **Dynamic Input** command options. By default, AutoCAD prompts you for an angle. Enter the desired angle and locate the construction line by selecting a point. Figure 5-62 shows a 45° construction line located at the **Midpoint** Object Snap of an angled line.

Using the **Reference** option allows you to select a line object and use its existing angle as a base angle. You can then enter the angle relative to the selected line object. For instance, to create the 45° construction line shown in Figure 5-62 using the **Reference** option, you would first select the existing angled line and then input the desired angle relative to the selected line. Inputting 90° creates a construction line perpendicular to the angled line, which just so happens to also be 45° from the *X*-axis.

### Exercise 5-13: Drawing Angular Construction Lines

1. Continue from Exercise 5-12.
2. Start the **XLINE** command.
3. Type **A<Enter ↵>** or select **Angle** from the **Dynamic Input** command options.
4. AutoCAD prompts you to enter an angle:

   `Enter angle of xline (0) or ↓.`

5. Type **45<Enter ↵>**. AutoCAD prompts you for a through point:

   `Specify through point:`

6. Select the **Midpoint** Object Snap of the angled line as shown in Figure 5-62.
7. Type **<Enter ↵>** to end the **XLINE** command.
8. Start the **XLINE** command again.
9. Type **O<Enter ↵>** or select **Offset** from the **Dynamic Input** command options.
10. AutoCAD prompts you to specify an offset distance:

    `Specify offset distance or ↓.`

11. Type **.5<Enter ↵>**. AutoCAD prompts you to select the object you want to offset:

    `Select a line object:`

12. Select the angled construction line you just created. AutoCAD then prompts you for the side you wish to offset:

    `Specify side to offset:`

13. Pick a point on the bottom right side of the angled construction line.
14. Select the angled construction line again. AutoCAD then prompts you for the side you wish to offset:

    `Specify side to offset:`

15. Pick a point on the top left side of the angled construction line.
16. Type **<Enter ↵>** to end the **XLINE** command.
17. Save your drawing as **EX5-13**. Your drawing should look like Figure 5-63.

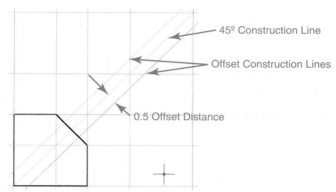

**Figure 5-63**    Drawing angular construction lines

*Bisecting an Angle with a Construction Line.*    You can split an angle into two equal parts by creating a construction line at the bisector of an existing angle using the **XLINE** command's **Bisect** option.

To create a construction line at the bisector of an angle, select the **XLINE** command and type **B<Enter ↵>** at the command line or select **Bisect** from the list of **Dynamic Input** command options. AutoCAD prompts you to select a vertex point, an angle start point, and an angle endpoint as shown in Figure 5-64.

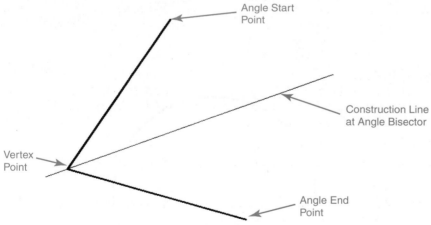

**Figure 5-64**    Drawing a construction line at an angle

AutoCAD will continue to prompt you to select angle endpoints until you press **<Enter ↵>** so that it is possible to bisect multiple related angles at the same time.

**Exercise 5-14:** Creating the Final Drawing Using Construction Lines

1. Continue from Exercise 5-13.
2. Create the remaining horizontal and vertical construction lines shown in Figure 5-65.
3. Use the **Intersection** Object Snap with the **LINE** and **ELLIPSE** commands to create the final drawing shown in Figure 5-65. Hidden lines are not required.

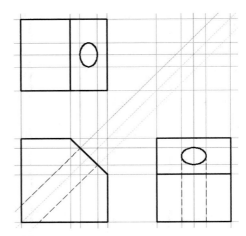

**Figure 5-65** Creating the final drawing using construction lines

4. Erase all the construction lines using the **ERASE** command.
5. Save your drawing as **EX5-14.**

## The RAY Command

| Ray | |
|---|---|
| **Ribbon & Panel:** | HomeIDraw |
| **Toolbar**: | None |
| **Menu:** | DrawIRay |
| **Command Line:** | RAY |
| **Command Allias:** | None |

It is also possible to create a special construction line known as a *ray* that is like an Xline except that, unlike an Xline, it only extends to infinity in one direction. Rays are created using the **RAY** command.

After selecting the **RAY** command, AutoCAD prompts you to pick a start point and a through point to indicate the direction and angle of the ray as shown in Figure 5-66.

AutoCAD will continue to prompt you for through points until you press **<Enter ↵>** so that it is possible to create multiple rays that share the same start point.

**Note:**
Similar to Xlines, the **Zoom Extents** tool is unaffected by ray objects. Any rays that exist in a drawing are ignored when zooming to the drawing extents.

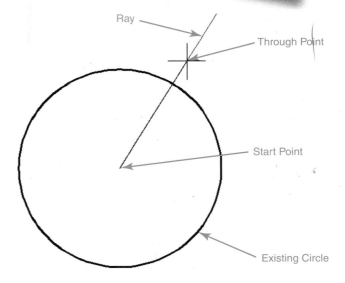

**Figure 5-66** Drawing a ray

| **FOR MORE DETAILS** | See Chapter 3 for more information about using the **Zoom Extents** tool. |
|---|---|

**TIP**

It is possible to trim and break Xlines and rays using the advanced editing commands introduced in Chapter 9 so that they can be converted into regular AutoCAD lines. When you trim or break the infinite end of a ray, it changes into a line with two endpoints. You must trim or break both infinite ends of an Xline to change it into a line. Using this approach, you can convert your construction lines directly into the final drawing geometry, thus reducing the time it takes to create a drawing.

## SUMMARY

Mastering the drawing aids and drafting settings explained in this chapter will increase your drafting productivity exponentially. Being able to locate points quickly and accurately is one of the main keys to being productive. Knowing that a point is located exactly where you intend it makes you a more confident, assured drafter. It's these qualities that help you to succeed in creating quality CAD drawings.

## CHAPTER TEST QUESTIONS

### Multiple Choice

1. Most of AutoCAD's drawing tools can be toggled on and off by:
   a. Selecting the buttons on the Status Bar
   b. Using keyboard function keys
   c. Typing them at the command line
   d. All of the above

2. The **Drafting Settings** dialog box can be displayed by:
   a. Typing **DS** at the command line
   b. Right-clicking with your mouse on a drawing tool button
   c. Selecting **Drafting Settings...** from the **Tools** menu
   d. All of the above

3. The rectangular Grid display area is determined by the:
   a. Units setting
   b. Drawing limits
   c. Zoom scale factor
   d. Size of your computer monitor

4. The two major different Snap styles are:
   a. Rectangular and polar
   b. Rotated and isometric
   c. Horizontal and vertical
   d. Rows and columns

5. The **Ortho Mode** drawing tool restricts your cursor movement to:
   a. 45° angles
   b. 90° angles
   c. Horizontal axis
   d. Vertical axis

6. **Polar Tracking** works by displaying a dashed line referred to as:
   a. Construction line
   b. Vector path
   c. Alignment path
   d. Tracking path

7. Object Snaps can be selected by:
   a. Right-clicking on the **Object Snap** button on the Status Bar
   b. Using the right-click shortcut menu
   c. Typing them at the command line
   d. All of the above

8. Turning an Object Snap on via the **Object Snap** tab of the **Drafting Settings** dialog box is referred to as:
   a. Making an Object Snap permanent
   b. Setting a running Object Snap
   c. Creating an Object Snap override
   d. Setting the default Object Snap

9. An ellipsis (...) next to an Object Snap AutoSnap Marker indicates the Object Snap is:
   a. Implied
   b. Delayed
   c. Waiting for AutoCAD to regen
   d. Deferred

10. The correct format for entering the offset distance when using the **From** Object Snap is:
    a. @2<45
    b. @2,2
    c. All of the above
    d. None of the above

11. **Object Snap Tracking** can display alignment paths:
    a. At all polar increment angles
    b. Horizontally
    c. Vertically
    d. Horizontally and vertically

12. Construction lines are used for:
    a. Laying out your drawing
    b. Creating different views using orthographic projection
    c. Bisecting angles
    d. All of the above

13. The special construction line type that extends infinitely in only one direction is:
    a. Xline
    b. Leader
    c. Ray
    d. Mline

## Matching

**Column A**

a. **Grid Display**

b. **Snap Mode**

c. **Ortho Mode**

d. **Polar Tracking**

e. Running Object Snap

f. Object Snap Override

g. Acquired Point

h. Alignment Path

i. **Object Snap Tracking**

j. Construction Line

**Column B**

1. Displays dashed alignment paths that temporarily restrict cursor to preset angle increments

2. Object Snap tracking vector used to locate a point

3. Temporary Object Snap that can be used for one pick point

4. Rectangular pattern of evenly spaced dots displayed on the screen

5. Controls movement of cursor to specific $X$ and $Y$ increments

6. Restricts cursor movement to the horizontal ($X$) and vertical ($Y$) axes

7. Displays dashed alignment paths at Object Snap points

8. Temporary lines used to lay out a drawing

9. Object Snaps that are on continuously

10. Selected point used to create complex Object Snaps

## True or False

1. True or False: It is possible to temporarily remove drawing tools buttons from the Status Bar.

2. True or False: Drawing tools can be toggled on and off when a command is active.

3. True or False: The **Grid Display** controls the cursor movement.

4. True or False: The **Snap** and **Grid** spacing must always be the same.

5. True or False: It is possible to use **Ortho Mode** and **Polar Tracking** at the same time.

6. True or False: **Polar Tracking** angles are always measured from the AutoCAD base angle (0°).

7. True or False: Object Snaps work only when you are prompted for a point at the command line.

8. True or False: It is possible to snap to the intersection of two lines even if they don't visually cross but would if they were extended.

9. True or False: You must always pick an acquired point when using Object Snaps.

10. True or False: Construction lines extend to your drawing limits.

## CHAPTER PROJECTS

### Project 5-1: Calculator

1. Start a new drawing using the acad.dwt template.
2. Draw the figure shown using the appropriate grid and snap settings. Toggle the **Object Snap** button **ON** and **OFF** as needed. The borders around the perimeter and around the screen area are 1/16″. The spacing between the buttons is 1/8″. **Do not** draw the dimensions.
3. Save the drawing as **P5-1**.

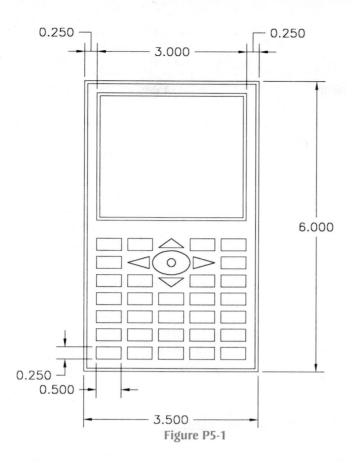

Figure P5-1

## Project 5-2: '32 Ford Special—Continued from Chapter 4

1. Open drawing **P4-2** from Chapter 4.
2. Draw the front view of the car shown in Figure P5-2 using construction lines and object snaps to project points from the side view created in P4-2. *Hint:* You can use the **DIVIDE** command to lay out the vertical radiator grill lines.
3. Save the drawing as **P5-2**.

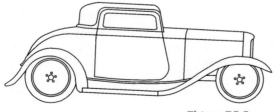

Figure P5-2

## Project 5-3: B-Size Mechanical Border—Continued from Chapter 4

1. Open drawing **Mechanical B-Size.DWT** from Chapter 4.
2. Add the line work shown in Figure P5-3. **Do not** include dimensions.
3. Save the drawing to a template file as **Mechanical B-Size.DWT.**

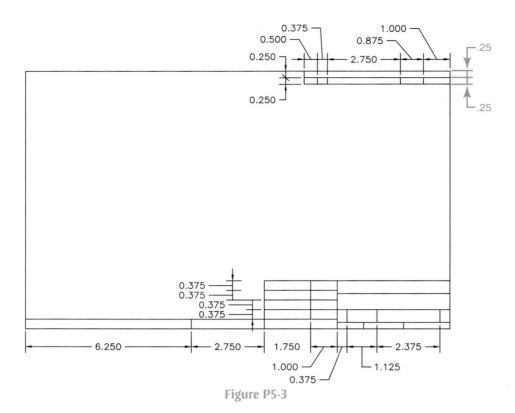

Figure P5-3

## Project 5-4: Architectural D-Size Border—Continued from Chapter 4

1. Open the template file **Architectural D-Size.DWT**.
2. Add the line work as shown to the border as shown in Figure P5-4 using construction lines and object snaps to your advantage. *Hint:* You can use the **DIVIDE** command to lay out the equally spaced title block lines.
3. Save the drawing to a template file as **Architectural D-Size.DWT**.

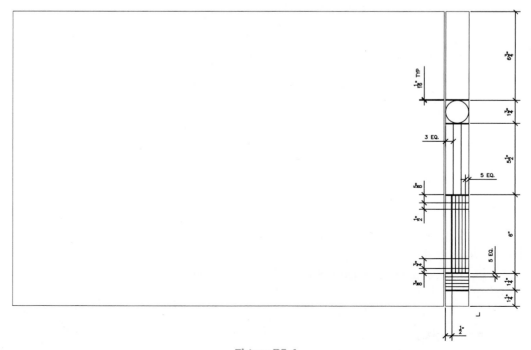

## Project 5-5: Electrical Schematic—Continued from Chapter 4

1. Open drawing **P4-5** from Chapter 4.
2. Set the **Grid Display** and **Snap Mode** drawing tools to 0.125.
3. Draw the electrical schematic shown in Figure P5-5. *Hint:* Use **Grid Display** and **Snap Mode** to draw the lines and object snaps to locate the electrical symbols.
4. Save the drawing as **P5-5**.

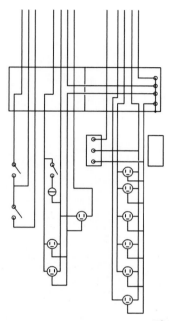

Figure P5-5

## Project 5-6: Hot Water Piping Schematic—Continued from Chapter 4

1. Open drawing **P4-6** from Chapter 4.
2. Set the **Grid Display** and **Snap Mode** drawing tools to 0.125.
3. Draw the piping schematic shown in Figure P5-6. *Hint:* Use **Grid Display** and **Snap Mode** to draw the pipe lines and object snaps to locate the piping symbols.
4. Save the drawing as **P5-6**.

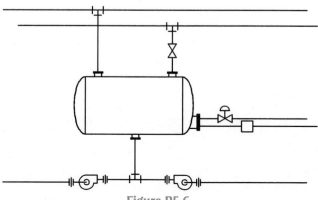

Figure P5-6

## Project 5-7: Residential Architectural Plan—Continued from Chapter 4

1. Open drawing **P4-7** from Chapter 4.
2. Draw the interior and exterior walls as shown in Figure P5-7. The exterior walls are 6″ thick; interior walls are 4″ thick. Use the appropriate Object Snap, **Ortho**, and **Polar Tracking** settings to ensure there are no gaps in the geometry and the walls are at the correct angle and location. **Do not** draw dimensions or text. *Hint:* Use the **Offset** option of the **XLINE** command to locate walls.
3. Save the drawing as **P5-7**.

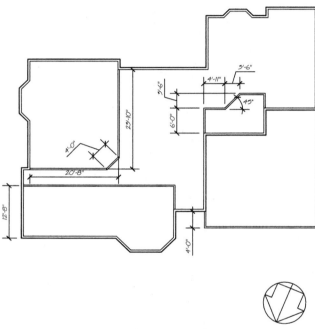

Figure P5-7

## Project 5-8: Joist Foundation Detail—Continued from Chapter 4

1. Open drawing **P4-8** from Chapter 4.
2. Draw the wood structural members with the sizes shown in Figure P5-8. **Do not** include notes. *Hint:* Use construction lines and the **Offset** option to lay out structural members. You can then create finished line work using object snaps.
3. **Do not** draw text or dimensions.
4. Save the drawing as **P5-8**.

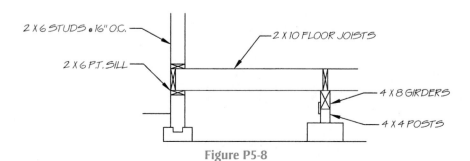

Figure P5-8

## Project 5-9: Support Plate—English Units—Continued from Chapter 4

1. Open the drawing **P4-9** from Chapter 4.
2. Create the projected front and right views as shown in Figure P5-9. **Do not** draw dimensions.
3. Save the drawing as **P5-9.**

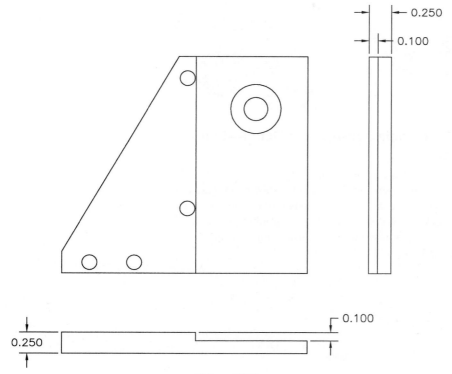

Figure P5-9

## Project 5-10: Widget—Metric

1. Start a new drawing using the acadiso.dwt template.
2. Draw the front and right side views of the part shown in Figure P5-10. **Do not** include dimensions. *Hint:* Draw the front view on the left first and then use construction lines and object snaps to draw the right side view using orthographic projection.
3. Save the drawing as **P5-10**.

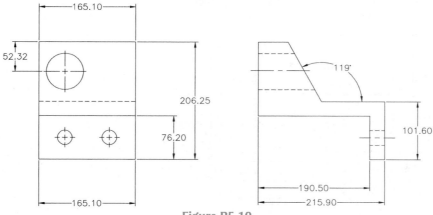

Figure P5-10

## Project 5-11: Civil Site Plan—Continued from Chapter 4

1. Open the drawing **P4-11** from Chapter 4.
2. Draw the plant symbols shown in Figure P5-11 to the best of your ability. Use object snaps where appropriate. The scale and grid lines are for reference only; **do not** draw the dimensions or reference lines.
3. Save the drawing as **P5-11**.

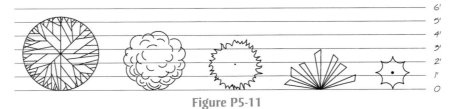

Figure P5-11

## Project 5-12: Manhole Construction Detail—Continued from Chapter 4

1. Open drawing **P4-12** from Chapter 4.
2. Draw the section view of the manhole as shown in Figure P5-12. **Do not** include notes or dimensions. *Hint:* Use construction lines to create the section using orthographic projection. You can then create finished line work using object snaps.
3. Save the drawing as **P5-12**.

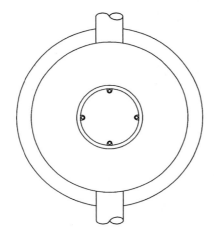

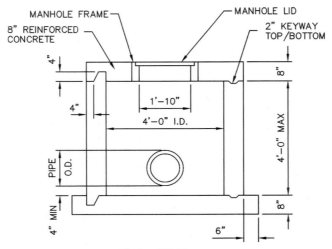

Figure P5-12

# Managing Object Properties

# 6

## Chapter Objectives

- Create layers
- Set layer properties
- Load linetypes
- Modify the properties of drawing objects
- Use DesignCenter to import layers from other drawings
- Create layer filters and groups

## INTRODUCTION

Precise, accurate, and clear drawings are a primary goal of any drafter. However, equally important in CAD is creating a well-organized drawing. Chapter 2 gave you a brief overview of object properties and layering. In this chapter, we'll take a closer look at object properties, how to effectively use layers to organize your drawing, and how to control the look and final output of your drawing.

## COMMON OBJECT PROPERTIES

Every object in AutoCAD has four primary properties associated with it: Color, Linetype, Lineweight, and Layer. These properties control how objects are displayed in your drawing and also control how objects are plotted. Color controls the color of an object and can also be used to control the plotted lineweight of an object, Linetype controls the line pattern (dashed, dotted, etc.) used to display objects, and Lineweight (or pen width) controls the width of objects when plotted.

A *layer* is a collection of color, linetype, and lineweight properties that can be used to organize the objects in your drawing. Layers are the primary way in which drawing information is organized.

**layer:** A collection of object properties and display settings that are applied to objects.

The concept of layering goes back to the days of manual drafting in which transparent overlays were used to control the content of a blueprint. For example, an architect might create an architectural base print showing the location of walls, doors, windows, and so on. An electrical engineer might then create a transparent overlay showing the location of the electrical equipment, outlets, and such. To create the electrical plan blueprint, you would take the architectural base print, place the electrical overlay on top of it, and run the stack of drawings through the blueprint machine. The resulting print would show the electrical drawing layer over the top of the architectural base drawing.

Layering in AutoCAD works in a similar way. By assigning a layer to an AutoCAD object, you are, in effect, putting those objects on a transparent overlay. You can then turn these layers on and off and control which objects are shown in the drawing.

## LAYERS

When you create a layer, you provide a name for that layer and then assign it a color, linetype, and lineweight. Any objects placed on that layer will then, by default, take on the color, linetype, and lineweight associated with that layer.

AutoCAD comes with a predefined layer, called layer **0**. By default, everything on layer 0 is drawn with color 7 (white/black), has a continuous linetype, and uses the default lineweight (.25 mm or .01 inch) for plotting. You can change the color, linetype, and lineweight settings for layer 0, but you cannot delete or rename layer **0**.

Layers are created with the **LAYER** command.

### The LAYER Command

| Layer | |
|---|---|
| **Ribbon & Panel:** | Homel Layers 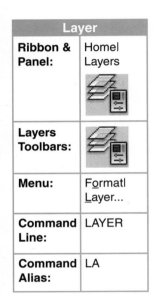 |
| **Layers Toolbars:** | |
| **Menu:** | Formatl Layer... |
| **Command Line:** | LAYER |
| **Command Alias:** | LA |

When you start the **LAYER** command, AutoCAD displays the **Layer Properties Manager** palette (see Figure 6-1). The **Layer Properties Manager** palette works like all other palettes. It can be docked, hidden, or closed as needed.

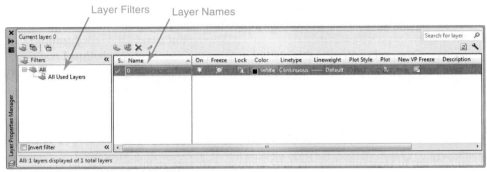

Figure 6-1     The Layer Properties Manager palette

The **Layer Properties Manager** palette allows you to create and control all aspects of your layers. The palette is divided into two main areas; the layer filters are listed on the left, and the list of layers is shown on the right.

Layer filters allow you to show only layers that match a certain criteria—for example, all the layers that start with the letter "E" or all the layers that are red. The list of layers shows the layers currently defined in your drawing along with their current settings.

### Layer Settings

The list of layers is divided into columns with each column representing a layer setting. The column headings can be resized by dragging the divider bar between each column. You can also sort the layers by any of the columns by clicking on the column heading. To change a setting for a layer, simply click on the setting. To change the settings for multiple layers, first select the layers by holding down either the **<Shift>** or **<Ctrl>** key and selecting the layers, then click on the setting you want to change. The change will be applied to all the selected layers.

*Layer Names.*     The layer name is the primary means of identifying a layer. Layer names can have up to 255 characters and can include letters and numbers as well as other special characters, including spaces. Layer names should convey the contents of that layer. Layer names can be based on part numbers, project names, design discipline (civil, architectural, etc.), or any other agreed-upon standard.

*Layer Naming Standards.*    Many companies create layering standards based on their own experience and practices, or they may adopt or adapt a national or industry CAD standard. A good standard will be well documented, showing the appropriate settings and the type of drawing content that belongs on each layer.

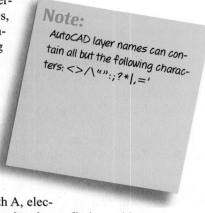

**Note:**
AutoCAD layer names can contain all but the following characters: `<>/\"":;?*|,='`

The American Institute of Architects (AIA) has published the CAD Layer Guidelines for the building industry that has been adopted by the National CAD Standards organization (*http://nationalcadstandard. org*). This layering standard describes a method of organizing layers based on a series of prefixes and descriptors that are easy to understand. Each discipline has a prefix; for example, all architectural layers start with A, electrical layers start with E, civil layers start with C, etc. Following the prefix is an abbreviation for the content of that layer, such as A-WALL for architectural walls or E-DEMO for electrical demolition.

The CD included with this book contains standard drawings for both Architectural and Mechanical Design disciplines. The drawings contain layers set up in accordance with common industry standards.

*Creating New Layers.*    To create a new layer, choose the **New Layer** button in the **Layer Properties Manager** palette. AutoCAD will create a new layer and automatically call it **Layer1**. The layer name is highlighted, so to rename the layer, simply type in the new name and press **<Enter ↵>**. You can press **<Enter ↵>** again to create another new layer.

**TIP**    You can also create multiple layers by typing the layer names separated by a comma. When you press the comma key, AutoCAD will end the first layer and create a new layer. This method allows you to create multiple layers easily.

## Exercise 6-1: Creating Layers

1. Start a new drawing using the acad.dwt drawing template.
2. Start the **LAYER** command to display the **Layer Properties Manager** palette.
3. Choose the **New Layer** button. AutoCAD will create a layer called **Layer1**.
4. Type **Object<Enter ↵>** to rename the new layer.
5. Press **<Enter ↵>** to create another new layer.
6. Type **Hidden<Enter ↵>** to rename the new layer.
7. Press **<Enter ↵>** to create another new layer.
8. Type **Center,Dim,Title<Enter ↵>** to create three new layers. Notice how every time you type the comma key, AutoCAD creates a new layer. You should now have a total of six layers (including layer **0**) in your drawing.
9. Close the **Layer Properties Manager** palette.
10. Save your drawing as **EX6-1**.

**Note:**
Layers are not actually created in the drawing until you choose **Apply** or **OK** in the **Layer Properties Manager** palette. Choosing **Cancel** or the **X** in the upper right corner of the palette will get rid of any layers created while that palette was open.

*Setting the Current Layer.*     To set a layer current, select the layer and choose the **Set Current** button (or press **<Alt> C**). The current layer is the default layer for new drawing objects. Any new object will be placed on the current layer.

*On/Off.*     The On/Off settings control the visibility of the layers in the drawing. Layers that are turned on are displayed, and those that are turned off do not display. However, when a layer is turned off, AutoCAD simply hides the layer from view. Objects can still be selected, modified, and even deleted when their layer is turned off.

*Freeze/Thaw.*     The Freeze/Thaw settings are similar to On/Off. When a layer is frozen, Auto-CAD ignores the objects on that layer and does not display them on screen. When a layer is frozen, AutoCAD will completely ignore the objects on that layer until that layer is thawed and the drawing regenerates. Objects on frozen layers cannot be modified until that layer is thawed. For this reason, freezing a layer is generally preferred to turning a layer off.

### Exercise 6-2: Freeze and Thaw Versus On and Off

1. Continue from Exercise 6-1.
2. Draw a line anywhere on the screen. Since layer **0** is current, the new line is drawn on layer **0**.
3. Start the **LAYER** command.
4. Select the **Object** layer and choose the **Set Current** button. The **Object** layer is now the current layer.
5. Select layer **0** and choose the sun icon in the **Freeze** column. The sun icon will change to a snowflake, indicating that the layer is frozen. Close or hide the **Layer Properties Manager** palette. The line will disappear because layer **0** is frozen.
6. Choose the **Erase** tool from the **Modify** panel. AutoCAD prompts you to *Select Objects:*.
7. Type **All<Enter ↵>**. This tells AutoCAD to select all the objects in the drawing. In the command window, AutoCAD responds 0 found. This tells you that AutoCAD ignored the line on the frozen layer **0**. Press **<Esc>** to end the **ERASE** command.
8. Start the **LAYER** command again and thaw layer **0** by selecting the snowflake in the layer **0 Freeze** column. Select the light bulb in the **On** column to turn off layer **0**. Close or hide the **Layer Properties Manager** palette.
9. Choose the **Erase** tool again from the **Modify** panel and type **All<Enter ↵>** at the *Select Objects:* prompt. In the command window, AutoCAD responds 1 found. This tells you that AutoCAD has selected the line on layer **0**, even though the layer is turned off. Press **<Enter ↵>** to finish the **ERASE** command. AutoCAD will erase the line.
10. Start the **LAYER** command and select the lightbulb to turn layer **0** on. Close the palette to verify that the line was erased.

    You can see that although the On/Off and Freeze/Thaw settings are similar, AutoCAD treats them very differently.

*Lock/Unlock.*     The Lock/Unlock setting controls whether objects on a layer can be modified. Objects on a locked layer can be seen but not modified. To lock a layer, choose the icon in the **Lock** column for the layer you wish to lock.

*Color.*     The color property is the default display color for objects on a layer. To assign a color to a layer, pick the color swatch for the layer you wish to change. AutoCAD will display the **Select Color** dialog box (Figure 6-2). The **Select Color** dialog box has three tabs, **Index Color, True Color,** and **Color Books**. The three tabs provide different ways to specify colors.

***The AutoCAD Color Index (ACI).***     The **Index Color** tab shows the **AutoCAD Color Index** (ACI), which is the primary way colors are assigned in AutoCAD. The ACI consists of 255 colors (numbered 1–255). Colors 1–9 are called the ***standard colors*** and are shown below the main color palette. Grayscale colors are shown below the standard colors.

**standard colors:** Colors 1–9 of the AutoCAD Color Index.

Colors 1–7 have names assigned to them. The names are shown in the following table:

| ACI Number | Color |
|:---:|:---|
| 1 | Red |
| 2 | Yellow |
| 3 | Green |
| 4 | Cyan |
| 5 | Blue |
| 6 | Magenta |
| 7 | White |

The remaining colors are shown in the large color palette (see Figure 6-2). As you drag your cursor over the various color patches, AutoCAD will display the color number as well as the red, green, and blue components of each color. To select a color, simply click on a color patch. AutoCAD will display the color name or number in the **Color** box. AutoCAD will also show you a preview of the selected color. If you know the color name or number you wish to use, you can simply type it into the **Color** text area.

**Note:**
Color 7 shows up as black on a white background and white on a black background.

***True Colors.***    The **True Color** tab allows you to select colors based on either the RGB (Red, Green, Blue) or HSL (Hue, Saturation, Luminance) color models (see Figure 6-3). You can select the color model you wish to use from the **Color model:** drop-down list.

The HSL color model allows you to control color properties in three ways. The Hue setting refers to a color in the visible spectrum, from 0 to 360. On the color chart, a Hue setting goes from 0 on the left of the chart to 360 on the right.

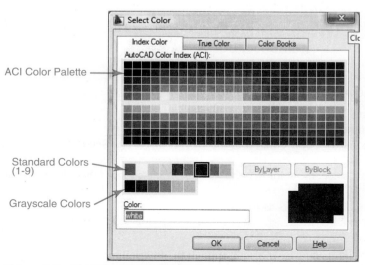

**Figure 6-2**    The Select Color dialog box

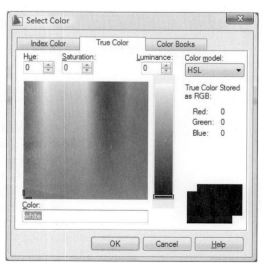

**Figure 6-3**    The HSL color model

The Saturation setting refers to the purity of that color on a scale of 0 to 100 percent. On the color chart, saturation values go from 0 (gray) at the bottom of the chart to 100 (the pure color) at the top of the chart.

The Luminance setting represents the brightness of the color on a scale of 0 to 100 percent. The Luminance setting is represented in the bar to the right of the color chart. A luminance value of 0 (the bottom of the bar) gives you black, a value of 100 (the top of the bar) gives you white, and a setting of 50 represents the brightest value of the color.

When you select a color on the chart, its color is displayed in the preview area, and its RGB color values are displayed in both the color box and below the **Color Model**: drop-down list.

The RGB color model (see Figure 6-4) allows you to mix colors based on the red, green, and blue components. An RGB number is a set of three numbers representing the red, green, and blue color components, respectively. Each component can have a value from 0 to 255 with 0 representing black, or no color, and 255 representing the pure color component. For example, a color setting of 255,0,0 represents red, 0,255,0 represents green, and 0,0,255 represents blue. White has an RGB value of 255,255,255, and black has an RGB value of 0,0,0.

When you select the RGB color model, AutoCAD gives you three sliders to control the RGB components. You can either type in a value, pick a point on each slider, or drag the indicator to a location on the slider to specify the value for each component.

***Color Books.***    The **Color Books** tab allows you to select colors based on various color matching standards, such as Pantone, DIC, or RAL. When you select the **Color Books** tab, AutoCAD provides you with a list of available color books and a list of colors in each book (see Figure 6-5). Once you select a color, AutoCAD displays its RGB color value on the right side of the dialog box and shows the color in the preview area.

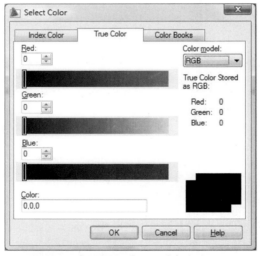

**Figure 6-4**    The RGB color model

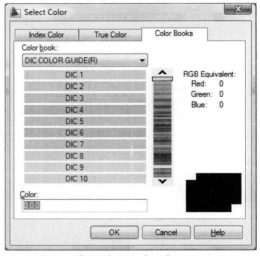

**Figure 6-5**    The Color Books tab

**Exercise 6-3:** Setting Layer Colors

1. Continue from Exercise 6-2.
2. Start the **LAYER** command.
3. Choose the color box in the **Color** column of the **Object** layer. The **Select Color** dialog box will appear.
4. In the **Index Color** tab, select the color red (color index 1) and choose **OK** to close the dialog box.
5. Continue setting colors for the layers as follows:
   Center—Blue (color 5)
   Dim—Color 8
   Hidden—Green (color 3)
   Title—White (color 7)

6. Close the **Layer Properties Manager** palette.
7. Save your drawing as **EX6-3**.

*Linetypes.*    *Linetype* refers to the pattern (continuous, dashed, dotted, etc.) of a line. Linetypes are generally a series of lines, spaces, dots, and symbols (circles, squares, text, etc.) at preset intervals. Linetypes are used to designate a particular type of object (fence line, railroad tracks, hot water line, etc.) or a feature of an object (the hidden edge of an object, centerline of a circle or arc, etc.).

To assign a linetype to a layer, choose the **Linetype** setting for the layer you want to change. The **Select Linetype** dialog box will appear (see Figure 6-6). The **Select Linetype** dialog box shows all the currently available linetypes in your drawing. Before you can use a linetype, it must first be loaded into your drawing.

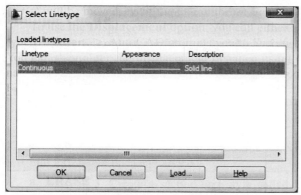

**Figure 6-6**    The Select Linetype dialog box

***Standard Linetypes.***    AutoCAD comes with a large selection of standard linetypes. These linetype definitions are stored in linetype files. AutoCAD comes with two standard linetype files, ACAD.LIN and ACADISO.LIN. The standard AutoCAD linetypes are shown in the following table. You can also create and modify linetypes to meet your needs.

| Linetype | Description |
|---|---|
| ACAD_ISO02W100 | ISO dash __ __ __ __ __ __ __ __ __ __ __ __ __ __ |
| ACAD_ISO03W100 | ISO dash space __ __ __ __ __ __ |
| ACAD_ISO04W100 | ISO long-dash dot ____ . ____ . ____ . ____ . _ |
| ACAD_ISO05W100 | ISO long-dash double-dot ____ .. ____ .. ____ . |
| ACAD_ISO06W100 | ISO long-dash triple-dot ____ ... ____ ... ____ |
| ACAD_ISO07W100 | ISO dot . . . . . . . . . . . . . . . . . . . |
| ACAD_ISO08W100 | ISO long-dash short-dash ____ __ ____ __ ____ _ |
| ACAD_ISO09W100 | ISO long-dash double-short-dash ____ __ __ ____ |
| ACAD_ISO10W100 | ISO dash dot __ . __ . __ . __ . __ . __ . |
| ACAD_ISO11W100 | ISO double-dash dot __ __ . __ __ . __ __ . __ __ |
| ACAD_ISO12W100 | ISO dash double-dot __ .. __ .. __ .. __ .. |

*(continued)*

| | |
|---|---|
| ACAD_ISO13W100 | ISO double-dash double-dot __ __ . . __ __ __ . . _ |
| ACAD_ISO14W100 | ISO dash triple-dot __ . . . __ . . . __ . . . _ |
| ACAD_ISO15W100 | ISO double-dash triple-dot __ __ . . . __ __ . . |
| BATTING | Batting SSSSSSSSSSSSSSSSSSSSSSSSSSSSSSSSSSSSSS |
| BORDER | Border __ __ . __ __ . __ __ . __ __ . __ . |
| BORDER2 | Border (.5x) __._.__._.__._.__._.__._.__._. |
| BORDERX2 | Border (2x) ____ ____ . ____ ____ . __ |
| DASHDOT | Dash dot __ . __ . __ . __ . __ . __ . __ |
| DASHDOT2 | Dash dot (.5x) _._._._._._._._._._._. |
| DASHDOTX2 | Dash dot (2x) ____ . ____ . ____ . ___ |
| DIVIDE | Divide ____ . . ____ . . ____ . . ____ . . ____ |
| DIVIDE2 | Divide (.5x) __._.__._.__._.__._.__._. |
| DIVIDEX2 | Divide (2x) _____ . . _____ . . _ |
| FENCELINE1 | Fenceline circle ----0-----0----0-----0----0-----0-- |
| FENCELINE2 | Fenceline square ----[]-----[]----[]-----[]----[]-- |
| GAS_LINE | Gas line ----GAS----GAS----GAS----GAS----GAS----GAS-- |
| HIDDEN | Hidden __ __ __ __ __ __ __ __ __ __ __ __ __ __ __ |
| HIDDEN2 | Hidden (.5x) _ _ _ _ _ _ _ _ _ _ _ _ _ _ _ |
| HIDDENX2 | Hidden (2x) ____ ____ ____ ____ ____ ____ ____ |
| HOT_WATER_SUPPLY | Hot water supply ---- HW ---- HW ---- HW ---- |
| TRACKS | Tracks -I-I-I-I-I-I-I-I-I-I-I-I-I-I-I-I-I-I-I-I-I- |
| ZIGZAG | Zigzag /\/\/\/\/\/\/\/\/\/\/\/\/\/\ |

AutoCAD's linetype files, along with the ability to create your own linetypes, means there are a potentially unlimited number of linetypes available. In any given drawing, you will only use a limited number of these linetypes so linetypes are loaded into your drawing on an as-needed basis. To load linetypes into your drawing, choose the **Load...** button in the **Select Linetype** dialog box. This will display the **Load or Reload Linetypes** dialog box (see Figure 6-7).

The **Load or Reload Linetypes** dialog box shows you the current linetype file and displays all the linetypes defined within that file. You can specify a different file by choosing the **File...** button and selecting the linetype file you wish to use.

*Note:*

The ACADISO.LIN file contains all the linetypes included in the ACAD.LIN file but also contains linetypes that support the Japanese Industrial Standard (JIS Z 8312).

To load a linetype, select a linetype from the list of available linetypes and choose **OK**. You can select multiple linetypes by holding down either the **<Shift>** or **<Ctrl>** key while selecting linetypes. Once you choose **OK**, you are returned to the **Select Linetype** dialog box.

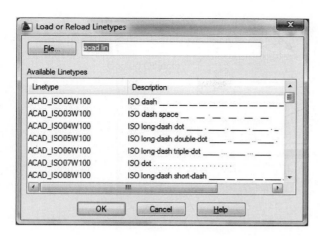

**Figure 6-7**   The Load or Reload Linetypes dialog box

Once the linetypes are loaded into your drawing, you can assign a linetype to a layer by selecting a linetype in the **Select Linetype** dialog box and choosing **OK**. The selected linetype will be assigned to the layer.

### Exercise 6-4: Setting the Layer Linetype

1. Continue from Exercise 6-3.
2. Start the **LAYER** command.
3. Choose **Continuous** in the **Linetype** column of layer Center. This displays the **Select Linetypes** dialog box.
4. Choose the **Load...** button. This displays the **Load or Reload Linetypes** dialog box.
5. Hold down the **<Ctrl>** key and select the **CENTER** and **HIDDEN** linetypes. Choose **OK** to return to the **Select Linetypes** dialog box. The linetypes have now been loaded into your drawing.
6. Choose the **CENTER** linetype and choose **OK** to assign the linetype to layer Center.
7. Choose **Continuous** in the **Linetype** column of layer Hidden. This displays the **Select Linetypes** dialog box.
8. Choose the **HIDDEN** linetype and choose **OK** to assign the linetype to layer Hidden.
9. Choose **OK** to close the **Layer Properties Manager** dialog box.
10. Save your drawing as **EX6-4**.

***Lineweights.*** *Lineweight* refers to the printed width of a line. The ANSI (American National Standards Institute) standard Y14.2 recommends using two lineweights (thick and thin) to differentiate contrasting lines. The actual values you use will depend on your particular CAD standards. AutoCAD's default lineweight is .25 mm (.010″).

**Note:**
Some linetypes have multiple versions of each linetype defined in the .LIN file. Generally, these linetypes have lines and spaces that are either half or twice the size of the original. For example, in addition to the CENTER linetype, there are also CENTER2 and CENTERX2 linetypes. The CENTER2 linetype has lines and spaces that are half (.5X) the size of the CENTER linetype. The CENTERX2 linetype has lines and spaces that are twice (2X) the size of the CENTER linetype.

**Note:**
Before the lineweight setting was introduced in AutoCAD, pen tables were used to map AutoCAD colors to plotted lineweights. For example, all red objects are plotted with a .35 mm pen, yellow objects with a .15 mm pen, etc. AutoCAD still supports pen tables and gives you a number of options for creating and managing pen tables.

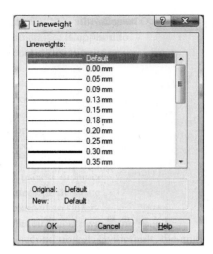

**Figure 6-8**    The Lineweight dialog box

| FOR MORE DETAILS | See Chapter 15 for more on plotting and the use of pen tables. |
| --- | --- |

To assign a lineweight to a layer, choose the value in the **Lineweight** column for that layer. This will bring up the **Lineweight** dialog box (see Figure 6-8). Select the lineweight you wish to use and choose **OK** to assign the lineweight to the layer.

**Exercise 6-5:** Setting the Layer Lineweight

1. Continue from Exercise 6-4 and start the **LAYER** command.
2. Choose **Default** in the **Lineweight** column of layer **Object**. This displays the **Lineweight** dialog box.
3. Choose **0.60 mm** from the list and choose **OK**. This sets the lineweight for layer **Object**.
4. Hold down the **<Ctrl>** key and select the Center, Hidden, and Dim layer names. The layers will highlight.
5. Choose the **Default** icon in the **Lineweight** column of the **Center** layer, and choose **0.30 mm** from the lineweight list. Choose **OK** to set the lineweight for all the selected layers.
6. Choose **OK** to close the **Layer Properties Manager** dialog box.
7. Save your drawing as **EX6-5**.

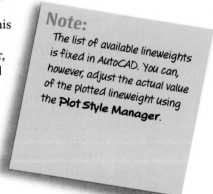

*Note:*
The list of available lineweights is fixed in AutoCAD. You can, however, adjust the actual value of the plotted lineweight using the **Plot Style Manager**.

**TIP**    You can choose whether or not to display lineweights in your drawing by toggling the **Show/Hide Lineweight** button in the AutoCAD Status Bar.

*Plot Style.*    The **Plot Style** setting is used when a drawing is set up to use color-dependent plot styles. This is a drawing setting that allows you to use AutoCAD object colors to control the plotted pen weight. Chapter 15 describes how to set up and manage color-dependent drawings.

| FOR MORE DETAILS | See Chapter 15 for more on plotting and the Plot Style Manager. |

*Plot/Noplot.*    The **Plot/Noplot** setting controls whether the contents of a layer will appear on a print of the drawing. This setting allows you to create objects in AutoCAD that will appear only in the drawing file, but not on any of the printed output of the drawing. For example, you may wish to create layers for construction lines, internal design notes, or drafting markups. To toggle the **Plot/Noplot** setting, choose the **Plot** setting for that layer. Plotting layers will show a printer icon, and nonplotting layers will have a red line through the printer icon.

*New VP Freeze.*    The **New VP Freeze** setting freezes the selected layer in any new viewports that are subsequently created in a paper space layout. It is possible to control layer visibility per individual viewport in paper space so that you can set up multiple views in one or more layouts that each show different drawing information.

In fact, if you are in a paper space layout and start the **LAYER** command to display the **Layers Properties Manager** palette, four columns are added to the right of the **New VP Freeze** column so that you can control all aspects of a layer's appearance per viewport using the following Viewport Overrides:

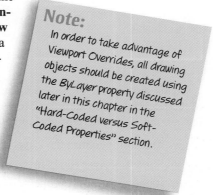

**Note:**
In order to take advantage of Viewport Overrides, all drawing objects should be created using the ByLayer property discussed later in this chapter in the "Hard-Coded versus Soft-Coded Properties" section.

- **VP Color**    Control the layer color per viewport
- **VP Linetype**    Control the layer linetype per viewport
- **VP Lineweight**    Control the layer lineweight per viewport
- **VP Plot Status**    Control if layer plots or not

| FOR MORE DETAILS | See Chapter 14 for more information on controlling layer properties per paper space viewport using Viewport Overrides. |

*Description.*    The **Description** setting allows you to add a brief description of the layer. For example, a layer named **A-Wall** might have a description of "Architectural walls." To change the description of a layer, select the layer and then single-click inside the **Description** field. A flashing text cursor will appear, allowing you to change the layer description.

*Controlling the Column Display.*    Clicking on a column heading at the top of the layer list in the **Layer Properties Manager** will toggle the display order of the layers in ascending or descending order using the information in the column header you click on.

You can resize a column by dragging the vertical bar between columns with your mouse, as well as rearrange the display order of the columns by dragging and dropping the column headings to different locations.

Right-clicking on a column heading displays a shortcut menu that allows you to turn different property columns on and off, maximize column widths, or reset everything back to the default. You can also display the **Customize Layer Columns** dialog box to turn multiple columns off simultaneously and rearrange the column order via the **Customize...** menu item.

*Layer List Right-Click Shortcut Menu.*    Right-clicking anywhere in the layer list in the **Layer Properties Manager** displays the shortcut menu shown in Figure 6-9.

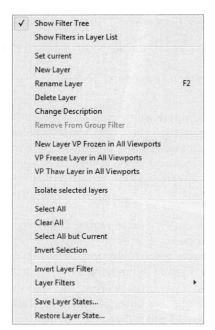

**Figure 6-9**    Layer list right-click shortcut menu

This shortcut menu provides a number of handy, timesaving features and capabilities. Many of the features and capabilities can be found elsewhere in the **Layer Properties Manager**, but a few are unique to the right-click menu. Some of the things you can do include:

- The ability to turn the **Layer Filter** pane on the left off and on
- Show any layer filters in the main layer list on the right so you can manage them as a unit
- Remove Viewport property overrides
- Select all/deselect all layers for mass property updates

You can also create and restore layer states which allow you to manage different saved layer settings. Layer states are discussed in detail later in this chapter.

### Deleting a Layer

To delete a layer from your drawing, select the layer(s) from the layer list and choose the **Delete Layer** button (or choose **<Alt>D**). A layer can only be deleted if it is not used in the drawing or if it is not the current layer. If the layer is not used and is not the current layer, AutoCAD will delete the layer. You can use **Undo** in the **Quick Access** toolbar to bring back a deleted layer.

    If the layer is used in the drawing, or if it is the current layer, AutoCAD will display an error message (see Figure 6-10).

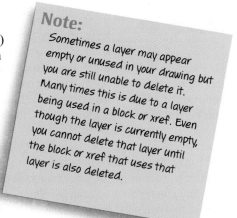

**Note:**
Sometimes a layer may appear empty or unused in your drawing but you are still unable to delete it. Many times this is due to a layer being used in a block or xref. Even though the layer is currently empty, you cannot delete that layer until the block or xref that uses that layer is also deleted.

**FOR MORE DETAILS**    See Chapter 16 for more on deleting block and xrefs from your drawing.

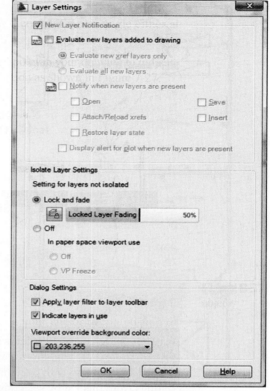

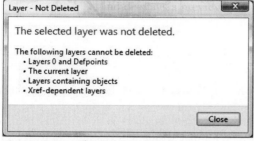

Figure 6-10    The Delete Layer error message

Figure 6-11    Layer Settings dialog box

## Layer Settings

Selecting the **Layer Settings...** button in the **Layer Properties Manager** displays the dialog box shown in Figure 6-11.

The **Layer Settings** dialog box allows you to control the **New Layer Notification** feature, apply a layer filter to the **Layer** toolbar so only filtered layers are displayed, and change the background color for Viewport Overrides, introduced earlier in the chapter.

The **New Layer Notification** feature prevents new layers from being added to your drawing without your knowledge by creating a list of what are referred to as *reconciled* layers, using all the existing layer names the first time you save or plot a drawing.

When the **Evaluate new layers added to drawing** check box is turned on, a **Notification** icon is displayed in the Status Tray at the bottom right of the AutoCAD window when a new layer is added to your drawing that does not match the reconciled layer list. Clicking on the **Notification** icon will display a list of unreconciled layers in the **Layer Properties Manager**.

**TIP**    A layer filter of unreconciled layers is automatically created in the **Layer Properties Manager** so that you can review them. You can select and reconcile layers in the **Layer Properties Manager** using the **Reconcile** option from the right-click menu explained earlier.

You can choose to evaluate only new layers that are added when an external refererence (xref) drawing is attached or to evaluate all new layers that are added to your drawing, regardless of the source.

> **FOR MORE DETAILS** See Chapter 14 for more information on controlling layer properties per paper space viewport using Viewport Overrides.

You can control when layer evaluation and notification is performed when the **Notify when new layers are present** check box is selected. Layer evaluation can be performed when the **OPEN, SAVE, ATTACH/RELOAD XREFS, INSERT,** or **RESTORE LAYER STATE** commands are activated.

The **Display alert for plot when new layers are present** check box allows you to control separately whether layer evaluation and notification is performed when a plot is created.

The **Isolate Layer Settings** area allows you to control how layers are isolated using the **LAYISO** command. The **LAYISO** command allows you to work only on a selected group of layers. Nonselected layers are either locked and faded or turned off. The **Isolate Layer Settings** area of the **Layer Settings** dialog box allows you to select which method to use as well as set the amount of fading that occurs.

## USING LAYERS

In AutoCAD, the current layer is shown in the **Layer Control** drop-down list in the **Layers** panel (see Figure 6-12). This drop-down list shows you the current settings for your layers. You can change the active layer by selecting a new layer from the drop-down list. You can also toggle layer settings from this list by selecting the icon for that setting. For example, to freeze a layer, choose the drop-down list and select the **FREEZE/THAW** icon next to the layer you wish to freeze. The icon will change from a sun to a snowflake, indicating the layer has been frozen. You can use this list to toggle the **ON/OFF**, **FREEZE/THAW**, and **LOCK/UNLOCK** settings.

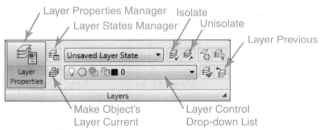

**Figure 6-12**   The Layers panel

The **Layers** panel has some additional buttons. The **Make Object's Layer Current** button allows you to select an object in your drawing and have that object's layer become the current drawing layer.

The **Layer Previous** button will switch the current layer back to its previous setting. For example, if you were to change the current layer from Object to Hidden, the **Layer Previous** button would reset the current layer to Object.

Selecting the **Layer Previous** button undoes the most recent change, or set of changes, made using either the **Layer Properties Manager** or the **Layers Control** drop-down list on the **Layers** toolbar. Every change you make to the layer settings is tracked and can be undone with **Layer Previous** with the following special exceptions:

- Deleted layers   **Layer Previous** does not restore deleted and/or purged layers
- New layers   **Layer Previous** does not remove any newly added layers
- Renamed   layers **Layer Previous** does not restore the original layer name

The **Layer States Manager** button displays the **Layer States Manager** dialog box discussed later in this chapter.

The **Isolate** button hides or locks all the objects in the drawing except for the ones you select. This allows you to work on a selected layer without worrying about accidentally modifying objects. The **Isolate Layer Settings** discussed above allows you to control how objects are isolated and displayed.

The **Unisolate** button simply undoes the **Isolate** tool. Selecting this button reverts all layers to their state prior to using the **Isolate** tool.

### Exercise 6-6: Using the Layers Panel

1. Continue from Exercise 6-5.
2. In the **Layer Control** drop-down list, choose **Hidden** to set that layer current.
3. Draw a line anywhere on the screen. The line will have the color and linetype of layer **Hidden**.
4. In the **Layer Control** drop-down list, set the layer **Object** current. Draw a line anywhere in the drawing. The line will have the color and linetype of the **Object** layer.
5. In the status bar, toggle the **Show/Hide Lineweight** button on. The line on the **Object** layer should now show the .60 mm lineweight.
6. Set the **Center** layer current and draw a circle anywhere on the drawing. The line will have the color and linetype of the **Center** layer. Your drawing should resemble Figure 6-13.
7. Save your drawing as **EX6-6**.

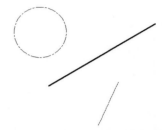

**Figure 6-13**    Drawing with layers

## LINETYPE SCALE

The linetypes displayed in the drawing are defined by the linetype definitions that were loaded from the .lin file. The linetype is defined by the length of the dashes and spaces in the line and uses the drawing units to define those lengths. For example, say a linetype is defined as a line segment .5 unit long followed by a space of .25 unit and then repeated. When drawn in a metric drawing using mm as the base unit, that linetype would be a series of .5 mm lines and .25 mm spaces.

The **LTSCALE** command allows you to set a global scaling factor for all linetypes. The **LTSCALE** command prompts you for a new linetype scale factor. The linetypes of all objects are multiplied by this scaling factor. For example, an LTSCALE setting of 2 would make each line segment and space twice its defined size. An LTSCALE of .5 would make each linetype half its defined size.

| Linetype Scale | |
|---|---|
| **Layers Toolbar:** | None |
| **Menu:** | None |
| **Command Line:** | LTSCALE |
| **Command Alias:** | LTS |
| **Properties Palette:** | Linetype Scale |

### Exercise 6-7: Setting the LTSCALE

1. Continue from Exercise 6-6.
2. Type **LTSCALE<Enter ↵>**. AutoCAD prompts you to *Enter new linetype scale factor <1.0000>:*.
3. Type **.5<Enter ↵>** to set the linetype scale. The linetype pattern of the objects on the **Hidden** and **Center** layers will scale down by 50%.
4. Save your drawing as **EX6-7**.

## HARD-CODED VERSUS SOFT-CODED PROPERTIES

> **Note:**
> The MSLTSCALE system variable allows you to scale linetype definitions by the current **Annotation Scale.** Setting MSLTSCALE to 1 turns on automatic linetype scaling. It is on by default.

By default, when an object is created in a drawing, it takes on the color, linetype, and lineweight settings of the current layer. When this happens, its properties are defined as *Bylayer*. This means that the color, linetype, and lineweight of an object are defined by the layer on which the object resides. For example, say your drawing has a layer called **Object**, which is red, and has a continuous linetype and a lineweight of .6 mm. If you draw a line on that layer, by default it would show up as a red, continuous, .6 mm-wide line. This line is considered to have soft-coded properties in that its properties are defined indirectly by the layer on which it resides. If you were to change the layer color to blue, the object would update to reflect the changes to its layer.

It is possible to override these soft-coded properties and define the color, linetype, and lineweight directly. These are called *hard-coded* properties because the properties are assigned directly to the object, regardless of which layer it resides on.

### Setting the Default Object Properties

The current settings for the Color, Linetype, and Lineweight properties are shown in the **Properties** panel (see Figure 6-14). AutoCAD applies these current property settings to all new objects. By default, these are all set to **ByLayer**.

To change the current setting, select the setting from its respective pull-down list. Any new objects you create will take on these properties.

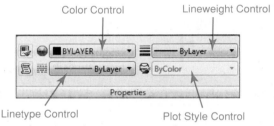

Figure 6-14    The Properties panel

### Color Property Override

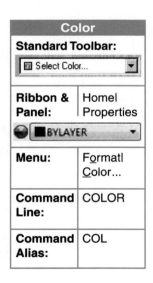
In the **Color Control** drop-down list, you see a list consisting of **ByLayer, ByBlock,** color numbers 1–7, and a **Select Color...** item (see Figure 6-15). The **Select Color...** item starts the **COLOR** command and displays the **Select Color** dialog box (see Figure 6-16). This is the same dialog box used to select colors within the **LAYER** command. To set the current drawing color, select the color from the **Color Control** drop-down list or choose the **Select Color...** item and select the color from the **Select Color** dialog box.

Figure 6-15    The Color Control drop-down list

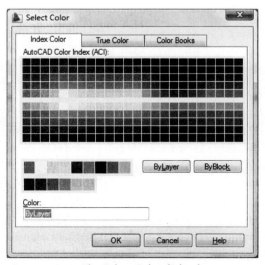

Figure 6-16    The Select Color dialog box

| **FOR MORE DETAILS** | See Chapter 16 for more on blocks and the **ByBlock** setting. |

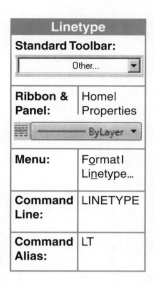

| Linetype | |
|---|---|
| **Standard Toolbar:** | |
| Other... | |
| **Ribbon & Panel:** | Homel Properties |
| 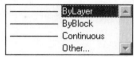 | |
| **Menu:** | Formatl Linetype... |
| **Command Line:** | LINETYPE |
| **Command Alias:** | LT |

## Linetype Property Override

In the **Linetype Control** drop-down list (see Figure 6-17), you are shown a list of all the currently loaded linetypes in the drawing as well as the **ByLayer** and **ByBlock** settings and an **Other...** item. The **Other...** item starts the **LINETYPE** command, which displays the **Linetype Manager** dialog box (see Figure 6-18).

The **Linetype Manager** dialog box is similar to the **Select Linetype** dialog box within the **LAYER** command (see Figure 6-6) but with a few added features. The **Linetype Manager** dialog box shows you all the currently loaded linetypes but also includes a filter that allows you to show all the linetypes loaded into the drawing, only the linetypes currently in use, or all that are used in any xref files. You can also invert the filter to show you only linetypes that are *not* in use or *not* used in xref files.

**Note:**
In the **LAYER** command, the **Select Color** dialog box has the **ByLayer** and **ByBlock** buttons disabled. In the **COLOR** command, these buttons are enabled. These choices are also available in the **Color Control** drop-down list in the **Standard** toolbar. The **ByLayer** setting resets the color to its layer-defined, soft-coded color property. The **ByBlock** setting creates everything using color 7 until the objects are grouped into a block.

**Figure 6-17**   The Linetype Control drop-down list

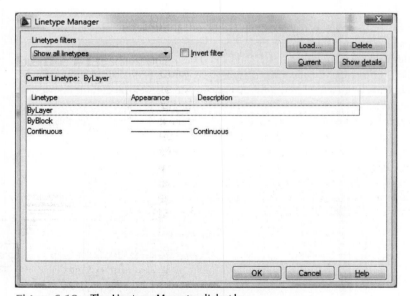

**Figure 6-18**   The Linetype Manager dialog box

| **FOR MORE DETAILS** | *Xref* stands for Externally Referenced Files. Xrefs allow you to display the contents of other drawing files overlaid onto your current drawing. Chapter 17 describes how to use and manage xrefs. |

The **Load...** button displays the **Load or Reload Linetypes** dialog box. This is the same dialog box used within the **LAYER** command and allows you to load linetypes from .LIN files.

The **Delete** button allows you to delete unused linetypes from the drawing. Only linetypes that are not currently used can be deleted.

The **Show details** button displays an additional area of the dialog box that shows additional information about each linetype and also allows you to set the linetype scale for all objects (the **Global scale factor**) or newly created objects (the **Current object scale**) (see Figure 6-19).

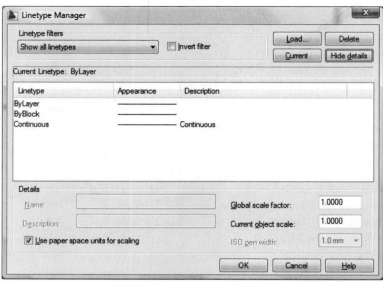

**Figure 6-19**    The Linetype Manager Details

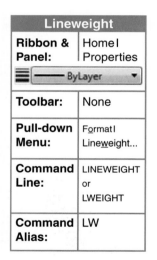

| Lineweight | |
|---|---|
| **Ribbon & Panel:** | Home l Properties |
| | ——— ByLayer ▼ |
| **Toolbar:** | None |
| **Pull-down Menu:** | Format l Lineweight... |
| **Command Line:** | LINEWEIGHT or LWEIGHT |
| **Command Alias:** | LW |

## Lineweight Property Override

The **Lineweight Control** drop-down list shows you a list of all available lineweights. These lineweights are shown as millimeter (mm) units by default. You can change these units and control other aspects of lineweight setting with the **LINEWEIGHT** command.

The **LINEWEIGHT** command displays the **Lineweight Settings** dialog box (see Figure 6-20), which includes controls to turn the lineweight display on and off, set the default lineweight, and switch the units from millimeters to inches. The **Adjust Display Scale** slider allows you to control the relative thickness of the lineweight display on your screen. It does not affect the plotted width of the lineweight.

**Figure 6-20**    The Lineweight Settings dialog box

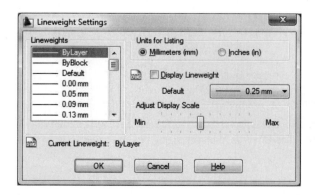

## Exercise 6-8: Setting Hard-Coded Properties

1. Continue from Exercise 6-7.
2. From the **Layer Control** drop-down list, set the **Object** layer current.
3. From the **Color Control** drop-down list, set the current color to **Magenta** (color 6).
4. From the **Linetype Control** drop-down list, choose **Other...** to display the **Linetype Manager** dialog box.

5. Load the **ZIGZAG** linetype from the acad.lin linetype file and set it to be the current line-type. Choose **OK** to close the **Linetype Manager** dialog box.
6. From the **Lineweight Control** drop-down list, set the current lineweight to **0.80 mm**.
7. Draw a line anywhere on the screen. The new line will have the current color, linetype, and lineweight settings even though the **Object** layer has different properties. Your drawing should resemble Figure 6-21.
8. Save your drawing as **EX6-8**.

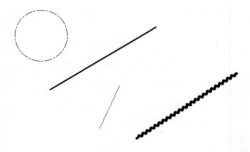

Figure 6-21    Hard-coded object properties

Hard-coded object properties can be useful in certain situations but can lead to confusion as your drawing complexity grows. In general, objects are identified by the color and linetype associated with their layer. For this reason, soft-coded, **ByLayer** properties are generally preferred.

TIP

The **SETBYLAYER** command allows you to quickly update the color, linetype, and lineweight of objects to the **ByLayer** property.

## Changing the Properties of Objects

There are a number of ways to change the properties of existing objects. In Chapter 2, you were introduced to the **Properties** palette, which provides an easy way to change the properties of any object. The **Properties** palette is accessed through the **PROPERTIES** command.

### The Properties Palette

As stated at the beginning of the chapter, there are four properties that are common to all objects, layer, color, linetype, and lineweight. These are shown in the **General** area of the **Properties** palette (see Figure 6-22). You can change any of the properties by selecting the value from the palette and choosing a new value.

The **Linetype scale** option in the **Properties** palette allows you to change the linetype scale of individual objects. This object linetype scale factor is applied in addition to the global linetype scale set by the **LTSCALE** command. For example, a line created with an object linetype of 2 in a drawing with LTSCALE set to 0.5 would appear the same as a line created with an object linetype of 1 in a drawing with a LTSCALE set to 1.

The **Hyperlink** property allows you to assign an Internet URL or email address to an object.

**Note:**
The **Thickness** property shown in the **Properties** palette is used to assign a three-dimensional "thickness" to AutoCAD objects. While it is a common property of all objects, it is rarely used in 2D drawings and is beyond the scope of this book.

| Properties | |
|---|---|
| **Ribbon & Panel:** | View\| Palettes |
| **Standard Toolbar:** | |
| **Menu:** | Modify\| Properties |
| **Command Line:** | PROPERTIES |
| **Command Alias:** | PR |

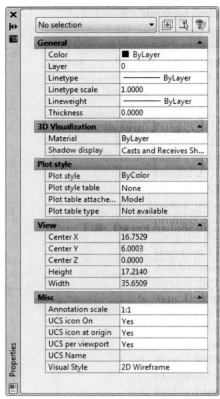

Figure 6-22    The Properties palette

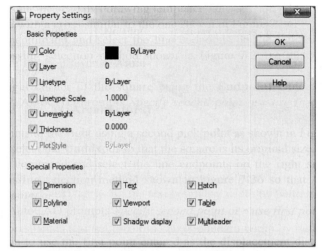

Figure 6-23    The Properties Settings dialog box

> **FOR MORE DETAILS**    See the online AutoCAD documentation for more on using the Thickness setting.

*The Properties Panel.*    Another way to change object properties is through the **Properties** pull-down menus. To change an object's property, select the object and then choose the property you wish to change from its pull-down menu.

*Copying Properties Between Objects.*    AutoCAD gives you a way to copy the properties from one object to another. This is done through the **MATCHPROP** or **PAINTER** command.

The **MATCHPROP** command prompts you to select a source object and a destination object. The properties from the source object are then applied to the destination object. There is a **Settings** option that allows you to control which object properties are applied to the destination object. When you choose the **Settings** option, AutoCAD shows you the **Property Settings** dialog box (see Figure 6-23). This shows you the properties of the source object and allows you to specify which property settings to apply to the destination object.

In the following exercise, you'll examine some of the different ways of changing object properties.

> **Note:**
> The **MATCHPROP** and **PAINTER** commands are identical. AutoCAD simply has two names for the same command.

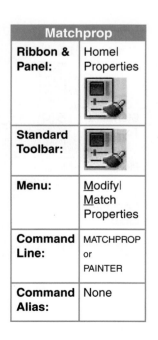

| Matchprop | |
|---|---|
| **Ribbon & Panel:** | Homel Properties |
| **Standard Toolbar:** | |
| **Menu:** | Modifyl Match Properties |
| **Command Line:** | MATCHPROP or PAINTER |
| **Command Alias:** | None |

### Exercise 6-9: Changing Object Properties

1. Continue from Exercise 6-8. Set the **Object** layer current.
2. Select the circle in your drawing. Notice that values in the **Layer, Color, Linetype, and Lineweight Control** drop-down list all change to show you the property settings for the selected circle.

3. Open the **Properties** palette.

4. Change the **Linetype scale** value to **2**. The linetype scale of the circle will double. Press <**Esc**> to clear the circle selection and close the **Properties** palette.

5. Select the line on layer Hidden. Again, the **Properties** drop-down lists show the values of the selected object.

6. Select the **Object** layer in the **Layer Control** drop-down list. The line is changed to the **Object** layer. Since the linetype, color, and lineweight properties of the line were all set to **ByLayer**, those properties were updated as well. Press <**Esc**> to clear line selection.

7. Start the **MATCHPROP** command. AutoCAD prompts you to *Select source object:*. Select one of the lines on the **Object** layer.

8. AutoCAD prompts you to *Select destination objects(s) or* ▽. Select the zigzag line. All the properties of the zigzag line are changed to match the properties of the **Object** line. Press <**Enter** ↵> or <**Esc**> to end the **MATCHPROP** command.

9. Save your drawing as **EX6-9**.

## USING DESIGNCENTER TO IMPORT LAYERS

In many cases, drawing information such as layers, linetypes, symbols, text styles, and dimension settings are common across multiple drawings. The layers you use in one drawing might be part of a company or project standard that are used over and over. AutoCAD's DesignCenter is a tool that allows you to share common information and settings between multiple drawings.

The **DesignCenter** palette (see Figure 6-24) is arranged in tabs that show drawings you currently have open, drawings in other local or network folders, drawings you've recently accessed, and DC online content, which gives you access to drawing symbols available online.

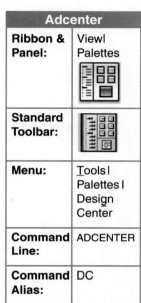

| Adcenter | |
|---|---|
| **Ribbon & Panel:** | View\| Palettes |
| **Standard Toolbar:** | |
| **Menu:** | Tools\| Palettes\| Design Center |
| **Command Line:** | ADCENTER |
| **Command Alias:** | DC |

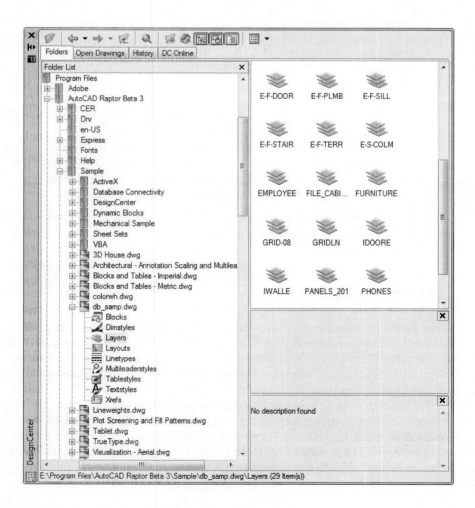

**Figure 6-24**  The Design-Center palette

**FOR MORE DETAILS** See Chapter 16 for more on the DC online content.

The **Folders** tab shows you a directory tree similar to what you might see in Windows Explorer. With the **Folders** tab, you can navigate to drawing files in any accessible local or network folder. The **Open Drawings** and **History** tabs show you a list of currently or recently open drawing files.

When you select a drawing file in DesignCenter, AutoCAD shows you a list of drawing information contained in that drawing. The drawing information is divided into categories (Blocks, Dimstyles, Layers, Layouts, Linetypes, Tablestyles, Textstyles, and Xrefs), and within each category are the specific objects and settings contained within that drawing. These objects and settings can be copied into your current drawing by selecting them from the list on the right and then dragging them into the drawing area of your current drawing. The settings and objects are then copied into your drawing.

> **Note:**
> When drawing objects such as blocks and xrefs are placed in the drawing, the objects are placed on the current layer. For settings, such as layer definitions, dimension styles, and other nongraphical information, only the settings are loaded into the drawing. If an object or setting with the same name already exists in your drawing, DesignCenter will simply ignore duplicate items and not import them.

### Exercise 6-10: Using DesignCenter to Import Layers

1. Start a new drawing using the acad.dwt drawing template.
2. Choose the **DesignCenter** button from the Palettes panel on the View ribbon. This opens the **DesignCenter** palette. Position the palette on your screen anywhere you like.
3. In the **Folders** tab, navigate to the **\AutoCAD 2009\Samples\** folder and select the + box next to the **db_samp.dwg** file. This will show the object and settings available in this drawing.
4. Select the **Layers** item in the list. A list of available layers will appear in the right-hand pane.
5. Select the **E-B-CORE** layer, hold down the **<Shift>** key, and select the **E-S-COLM** layer. AutoCAD will select all the layers between these two layers.
6. Press and hold your mouse button on one of the selected layers and drag the layers into your drawing area. When you release the mouse button, the layers will be copied into your new drawing. In the **Command** window, AutoCAD will respond with

    `Layer(s) added. Duplicate definitions will be ignored.`

7. Start the **LAYER** command to verify that the layers have been imported into your drawing.
8. Close or hide the **DesignCenter** palette.
9. Save the drawing as **EX6-10.**

## LAYER FILTERS

When working in drawings that have a large number of layers, managing layer settings in a long list of layers can prove difficult. To help manage this, AutoCAD allows you to filter the list of layers. This allows you to display only the layers you are interested in or will be using. The **Layer Filters** area of the **Layer Properties Manager** palette allows you to create and manage these filters (see Figure 6-25).

The filter tree shows you a hierarchy of layers, starting with all layers. Clicking on the **All** level will list all the layers in the drawing in the layer list area. Below the **All** filter is the **All Used Layers** filter. Selecting this will filter the layer list to show only the layers that are currently in use in the drawing. The **All** and **All Used Layers** filters are predefined filters that cannot be renamed or deleted. You can create your own custom layer filters.

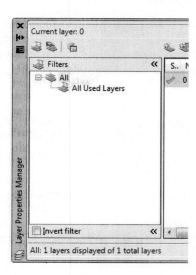

**Figure 6-25**    The Layer Filters area of the Layer Properties Manager palette

## The Filter Tree

To activate a layer filter, simply select it from the filter tree. The filter tree is hierarchical, which means that the filter is applied to the layers on the level above it in the tree.

Below the filter tree are two boxes: **Invert filter** and **Indicate layers in use**. Putting a check in the **Invert filter** box will reverse the effects of the filter. For example, if you choose the **All Used Layers** filter, putting a check in the **Invert filter** box will show you all the unused layers.

Checking the **Indicate layers in use** option will indicate which layers have drawing information on them by making the icon in the **Status** column darker for referenced layers and lighter for layers that do not have anything on them. This is a good way to determine which layers can be deleted and which layers cannot.

## Property Filters

Property filters will filter your layer list based upon certain matching criteria. For example, you might create a filter that shows you only layers that start with characters "C-," or a filter that only shows thawed layers, or only locked layers. You can also combine criteria. For example, you can create a filter that shows all layers that are both frozen and locked and contain the letter X in their name.

To create a property filter, choose the **New Property Filter** button. The **Layer Filter Properties** dialog box will appear (see Figure 6-26).

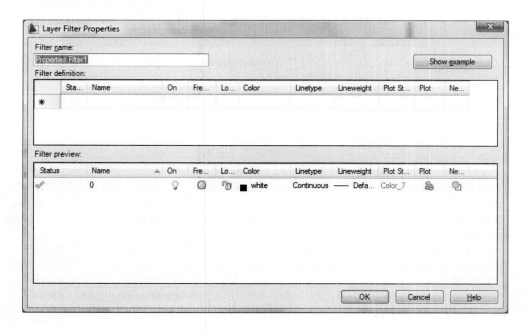

**Figure 6-26**    The Layer Filter Properties dialog box

The **Filter name** area allows you to change the name of your filter. You create a filter by selecting criteria in the **Filter definition** area. You can select multiple criteria on a single row. As you specify filter criteria, the **Filter preview** area shows you all the layers that match your filter. The various filter criteria are defined in the following table:

| | |
|---|---|
| Status | Shows only layers that are used in the drawing or only layers that are not used in the drawing. |
| Name | Shows only layer names that match the criteria. You can specify a full layer name or a partial name with wildcards. For example, **W\*** will show only layers that start with the letter W. A name filter of **\*C\*** will show you all the layer names containing the letter C. The layer name filter is not case sensitive. |
| On | Shows only layers that are turned on or only layers that are turned off. |
| Freeze | Shows only layers that are frozen or only layers that are thawed. |
| Lock | Shows only layers that are locked or only layers that are unlocked. |
| Color | Shows only layers that match the color specified. You can either specify a color name or number or choose the **...** box to select from the **Select Color** dialog box. Like the layer name, you can specify a partial color number with wildcards. For example, specifying **4\*** for the color will show color 4 and colors 40–49. |
| Linetype | Shows only layers that match the specified linetype. You can type in the linetype name or choose **...** to select the linetype from the **Select Linetype** dialog box. Partial names with wildcards are allowed. |
| Plot Style | Shows only layers that match a specific plot style. This option is available only in drawings where named plot styles are used. Partial names with wildcards are allowed. |
| Plot | Shows only layers that are set to either Plot or Noplot. |
| New VP Freeze | Shows only layers that are either frozen in new viewports or thawed in new viewports. This option is available only when accessed from a drawing layout (paper space). |

All the criteria you specify in a row are applied to the layer list. For example, a filter row with the name criteria of "A-" and "Frozen" will show only layers that both start with "A-" *and* are frozen.

Once you specify some criteria, a new row is added to the **Filter Definition** list. Each row is applied separately to the filter. For example, if you have one row that has a name criteria of "E-" and another row that has a name criteria of "Wall," all layers that start with "E-" will be shown *and* all the layers that contain the word "WALL" will also be shown.

**Note:**
Criteria within a single row are the equivalent of an AND search query. AutoCAD will show all the layers that meet all the criteria in that row (the first criteria AND the second criteria, etc.).

Criteria listed on separate rows are the equivalent of an OR search query. AutoCAD will show all the layers that match the criteria of any row (the first row OR the second row, etc.).

Exercise 6-11: Creating a Layer Property Filter

1. Continue from Exercise 6-10.
2. Start the **LAYER** command and choose the **New Property Filter** button. The **Layer Filter Properties** dialog box will appear (see Figure 6-27).
3. Change the **Filter name** to **E-B** and click inside the **Name** criteria column. An asterisk (*) will appear in the **Name** column and all the layers will appear in the **Filter preview** area.
4. Type **E-B*** in the **Name** column. The **Filter preview** area will update to show you only layer names that start with E-B.
5. Choose **OK** to save the filter and close the dialog box. The E-B filter will now appear in the **Layer Filter** area. The filter is applied to the layer list so only the E-B layers are shown.
6. Select the **Invert filter** box. The filter is reversed and all layers except the E-B layers are shown.
7. Remove the check from the **Invert filter** box. Choose **OK** to end the **LAYER** command.
8. Select the **Layer Control** drop-down list. Notice that only layers that match the E-B filter are shown.
9. Save the drawing as **EX6-11**.

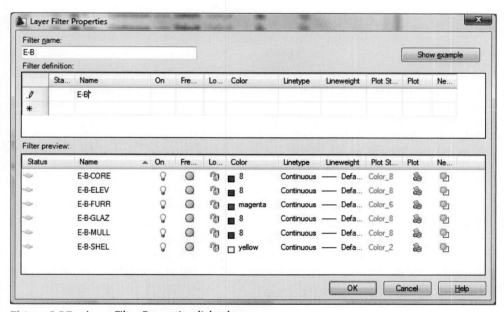

Figure 6-27    Layer Filter Properties dialog box

## Group Filters

A group filter allows you to filter your layer list to show only layers you select. The layers do not need to match any particular criteria; you simply select the layers you want to include in your filter. To create a group filter, choose the **New Group Filter** button in the **Layer Properties Manager** palette. AutoCAD will create a new group filter called **Group Filter1** and highlight the name. You can then type a new name for the filter. To add layers to the filter, select the layers from the layer list on the right side and drag them onto the group filter name on the left side.

Exercise 6-12: Creating a Group Filter

1. Continue from Exercise 6-11.
2. Start the **LAYER** command and choose the **New Group Filter** button. AutoCAD creates a new group filter called **Group Filter1** and highlights the name. Type **Misc** for the group filter name. The layer list is now empty since the new group filter is active and has no layers in it.

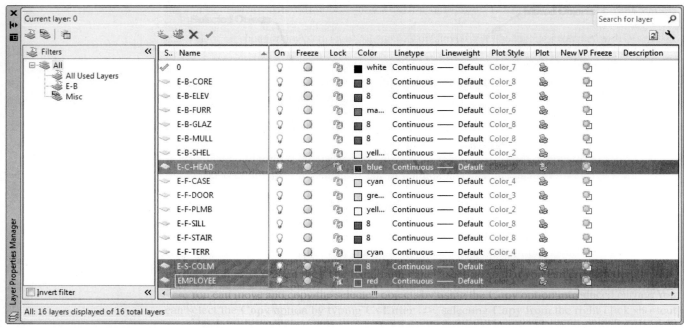

Figure 6-28 Creating a group filter

3. Select **All** in the **Layer Filter** area to show all the layers. Hold down the **<Ctrl>** key and select the **E-C-HEAD, E-S-COLM,** and **EMPLOYEE** layers from the layer list. Click and drag the layers onto the **E-B** group filter and release the mouse button (see Figure 6-28). The selected layers are added to the group filter.
4. Select the **All** filter and choose **OK** to end the **LAYER** command.
5. Save the drawing as **EX6-12**.

### Search Filter

In the top right corner of the **Layer Properties Manager** palette is a box that says **Search for layer**. This is a layer search filter that allows you to do a temporary name filter on the current list of layers. You can type in a layer name (including wildcards) to show a list of layers that match that name. The search filter cannot be saved; it only works while the dialog box is open or until you select another filter. The search filter only applies to the list of layers shown in the layer list at the time the search is done.

### LAYER STATES MANAGER

| Layer States Manager | |
|---|---|
| **Ribbon & Panel:** | Home\| Layers |
| **Standard Toolbar:** | |
| **Menu:** | Format\| Layer States Manager |
| **Command Line:** | LAYERSTATE |
| **Command Alias:** | LAS |

There may be times when you have a set of layer settings that you use or need to restore at certain times. For example, you might want to freeze a set of layers before you plot, or you might want to lock certain layers before you share them with others. The **Layer States Manager** will save a snapshot of layer settings that you can then recall at any time. To create a layer state, set the layers to the setting you want to save, and then start the **LAYERSTATE** command to display the **Layer States Manager** dialog box (see Figure 6-29).

Choose the **New...** button to create a new layer state. The **New Layer State to Save** dialog box appears (see Figure 6-30), and you are asked for a layer state name. You can also provide an optional description for the layer state. Once you've supplied a name, choose **OK**, and you'll be returned to the **Layer States Manager** dialog box.

It is possible to edit a layer state directly by selecting the **Edit** button so that the layer state does not need to be deleted and recreated. Selecting the **Edit** button displays the **Edit Layer State** dialog box so that you can update any of the standard layer properties, add new layers, or delete existing layers from the currently selected layer state.

Figure 6-29    The Layer States Manager dialog box

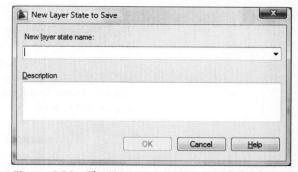

Figure 6-30    The New Layer State to Save dialog box

Selecting the **More Restore Options** arrow button on the bottom right of the dialog box displays the **Layer properties to restore** options on the right of the dialog box so you can control which layer properties you wish to save and restore. Simply select which properties you wish to maintain.

Layer states can be exported to a file. This allows you to create standard layer settings that can be shared among multiple drawings in a project or used within a company standard. Use the **Export** and **Import** buttons in the **Layer States Manager** dialog box to export a layer state setting or to import an existing layer state file with an LAS extension. It is also possible to import layer states directly from DWG, DWT, or DWS files.

To restore a layer state, choose the **Layer States Manager** button, select the layer state you wish to restore, and then choose the **Restore** button. All the settings for that layer state will be restored.

### Exercise 6-13: Creating and Restoring Layer States

1. Continue from Exercise 6-12.
2. Start the **LAYER** command and select the **All** filter from the filter tree.
3. Choose the **Layer States Manager** button to display the **Layer States Manager** dialog box.
4. Choose the **New** button to display the **New Layer State to Save** dialog box. Type **Default** in the **New layer state name** area and choose **OK** to close the dialog box. You are returned to the **Layer States Manager** palette.
5. Choose the **Select All** button and put a check in the **Turn off layers not found in layer state** box. Choose **Restore** to save the layer state and close the dialog box. You are now returned to the **Layer Properties Manager** palette.
6. Select the **E-B** filter to filter the layer list. Select all the layers in the list and select the sun icon in the **Freeze** column to freeze all the layers.
7. Select the **Misc** group filter to refilter the layer list. Select all the layers and set the color to white (color 7). Choose the **All** filter to see all layers. Notice the changes you made to the layer settings.
8. Select the **Layer States Manager** button. The **Default** layer state is highlighted. Choose **Restore** to restore the layer settings. The layer settings should now be restored to their previous state.
9. Save the drawing as **EX6-13**.

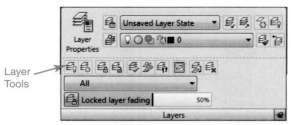

**Figure 6-31**    The Layer panel

## Layer Tools

The popular Express **Layer Tools** commands and utilities have been integrated into AutoCAD so that you can now access them via the **Layer** panel shown in Figure 6-31 and the **Layer tools** cascade menu found on the **Format** menu shown in Figure 6-32 or via the **Layers II** toolbar shown in Figure 6-33.

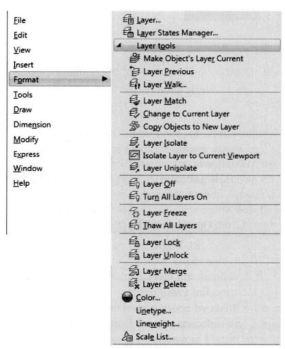

**Figure 6-32**    The Layer tools cascade menu

**Figure 6-33**    The Layers II toolbar menu

Express Tools are add-on productivity tools, developed by users and unsupported by Autodesk, which extend the power of AutoCAD's basic commands. When installed, they are typically accessed through a separate menu named **Express**.

**FOR MORE DETAILS**    See Appendix E for detailed information about the AutoCAD Express Tools.

The layer tools and their usages are listed in the following table.

| | Layer Tools | | |
|---|---|---|---|
| | **Layer Tool** | **Command** | **Description** |
| | **Make Object's Layer Current** | **LAYMCUR** | Changes the current layer to match the selected object. |
| | **Layer Previous** | **LAYERP** | Undoes the last change or set of changes made to layer settings |
| | **Layer Walk** | **LAYWALK** | Dynamically displays objects on selected layers. |
| | **Layer Match** | **LAYMCH** or **-LAYMCH** | Changes the layer(s) of selected objects to match the layer of a selected destination object. |
| | **Change to Current Layer** | **LAYCUR** | Moves selected objects to the current layer. |
| | **Copy Objects to New Layer** | **COPYTOLAYER** or **-COPYTOLAYER** | Copies selected objects to another layer, leaving the original objects intact. |
| | **Layer Isolate** | **LAYISO** | Isolates the layer of the selected object(s) so that all other layers are turned off. |
| | **Isolate Layer to Current Viewport** | **LAYVPI** | Isolates an object's layer to the current viewport. |
| | **Layer Unisolate** | **LAYUNISO** | Turns on layers that were turned off with the LAYISO command. |
| | **Layer Off** | **LAYOFF** | Turns off the layer of the selected object(s). |
| | **Turn All Layers On** | **LAYON** | Turns on all layers. |
| | **Layer Freeze** | **LAYFRZ** | Freezes the layer of selected objects. |
| | **Thaw All Layers** | **LAYTHW** | Thaws all layers. |
| | **Layer Lock** | **LAYLCK** | Locks the layer of a selected object. |

*(continued)*

| | Layer Unlock | LAYULK | Unlocks the layer of a selected object. |
|---|---|---|---|
| | Layer Merge | LAYMRG or -LAYMRG | Moves all objects from the first selected layer to the second selected layer and deletes the first layer. |
| | Layer Delete | LAYDEL or -LAYDEL | Deletes all objects from the specified layer and purges the layer from the drawing. |

# SUMMARY

A well-organized drawing is something to which every CAD user should strive. Clear and concise CAD standards and drawing objects placed on their proper layers can make the difference between a drawing that is easy to read and understand and one that is confusing. Good layer management practices are critical in group settings in which multiple people will be accessing and editing your drawings. This chapter has given you an in-depth look at how to use layers effectively to organize your drawing.

# CHAPTER TEST QUESTIONS

## Multiple Choice

1. A layer is:
   a. A separate drawing that you merge into your drawing.
   b. The only way to control the color of drawing objects.
   c. A collection of color, linetype, lineweight, and other display settings.
   d. A 3D setting.

2. Turning a layer off:
   a. Prevents objects on that layer from being seen.
   b. Prevents objects on that layer from being edited.
   c. Deletes all the objects on a layer.
   d. Is the same as freezing a layer.

3. The color blue is AutoCAD Color Index number:
   a. 3
   b. 4
   c. 5
   d. 6

4. An RGB color number of 0,255,0 is what color?
   a. red
   b. green
   c. blue
   d. black
   e. white

5. AutoCAD linetypes:
   a. Consist only of lines and spaces.
   b. Are loaded automatically when you assign them to a layer.
   c. Cannot be modified.
   d. Must be loaded into the drawing before they can be used.

6. Deleting a layer:
   a. Deletes the layer and all the objects on the layer.
   b. Deletes all the objects on a layer but keeps the layer name in the drawing.
   c. Can only be done when a layer is unused.
   d. Can be done at any time regardless of whether the layer is used or not.

7. The LTSCALE setting:
   a. Is a global scale factor applied to all objects' linetypes.
   b. Affects the lineweight of all objects.
   c. Affects the plot scale of layout viewports.
   d. Does not affect objects that have an individual object linetype scale.

8. An object with a color of ByLayer:
   a. Gets its color setting from its layer.
   b. Is white.
   c. Is white until a hard-coded color is assigned to it.
   d. Is always the same color regardless of its layer color setting.

9. Property filters:
   a. Are case sensitive.
   b. Can only filter layers based on a single criteria.
   c. Can use wildcards.
   d. Are not based on any specific criteria.

10. Group filters:
    a. Are case sensitive.
    b. Can only filter layers based on a single criteria.
    c. Can use wildcards.
    d. Are not based on any specific criteria.

## Matching

### Column A

a. Layer

b. Property filter

c. Linetype

d. LTSCALE

e. RGB

f. Lineweight

g. Hard-coded object properties

h. DesignCenter

i. Group layer filter

j. Layer state

### Column B

1. A layer filter based on user-selected layer names

2. The pattern of a line

3. A color model based on red, green, and blue color components

4. Object properties set independently of an object's layer

5. A collection of color, linetype, lineweight, and display settings

6. A tool used to share design information between Auto-CAD drawings

7. The printed width of a line

8. A saved collection of layer settings

9. A global scale factor applied to all linetypes

10. A layer filter based on matching criteria

## True or False

1. True or False: Layer **0** cannot be deleted.

2. True or False: Lineweight only appears when you plot a drawing.

3. True or False: Linetypes can be modified and new linetypes can be created.

4. True or False: A layer can be deleted only if it is unused in the drawing.

5. True or False: The **Layer Control** drop-down list always shows all the layers in a drawing.

6. True or False: Layers can be imported from other drawing files.

7. True or False: The **MATCHPROP** and **PAINTER** command do the same thing.

8. True or False: A search filter only takes effect while the **LAYER** command is active.

9. True or False: Layer states can be exported and shared between multiple drawings.

10. True or False: **DesignCenter** is used only to insert blocks from other drawings.

## CHAPTER PROJECTS

### Project 6-1: Classroom Plan

1. Start a new drawing using the acad.dwt template. Set the **UNITS** to **Architectural** with **1/16″** precision. Set the **LTSCALE** to **6**.

2. Create the following layers:

| Name | Color | Linetype | Lineweight | Description |
|---|---|---|---|---|
| A-Anno-Note | 7 | Continuous | Default | Notes |
| A-Door | 4 | Continuous | Default | Doors |
| A-Eqpm | 6 | Continuous | Default | Equipment |
| A-Furn | 7 | Continuous | Default | Furniture |
| A-Furn-Char | 7 | Continuous | Default | Chairs |
| A-Glaz | 4 | Continuous | Default | Windows |
| A-Wall | 7 | Continuous | Default | Walls |

3. Draw the desk, monitor, computer tower, mouse, chair, and keyboard shown in Figure P6-1. Draw the desk on the **A-Furn** layer. Place all other objects on the **A-Eqpm** layer. Assign the **HIDDEN** linetype to the computer as a hard-coded linetype.
4. **Do not** draw dimensions or text.
5. Save the drawing as **P6-1**.

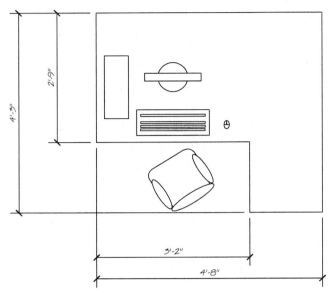

Figure P6-1

## Project 6-2: Motorcycle

1. Start a new drawing using the acad.dwt template.
2. Create the following layers:

| Name | Color | Linetype | Lineweight |
|---|---|---|---|
| Engine | 7 | Continuous | Default |
| Exhaust | 7 | Continuous | Default |
| Fender | 1 | Continuous | 0.35mm |
| Forks | 7 | Continuous | Default |
| Frame | 5 | Continuous | Default |
| Handlebars | 7 | Continuous | Default |
| Hatch_Black | 7 | Continuous | Default |
| Hatch_Gray | 9 | Continuous | Default |
| Headlight | 7 | Continuous | Default |
| Seat | 5 | Continuous | Default |
| Tank | 1 | Continuous | 0.35 mm |
| Wheels | 9 | Continuous | Default |

3. Draw the 18″ diameter rear motorcycle wheel on the **Wheels** layer using the **ARC** and **CIRCLE** commands.
4. Save the drawing as **P6-2**.

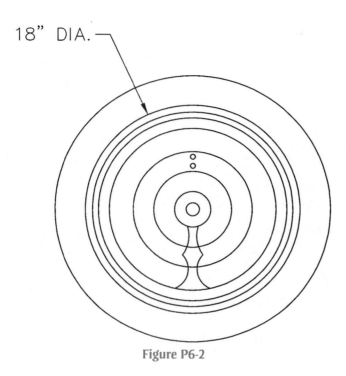

18" DIA.

Figure P6-2

## Project 6-3: B-Size Mechanical Border—Continued from Chapter 5

1. Open drawing **Mechanical B-Size.DWT** from Chapter 5.
2. Create the following layers:

| Name | Color | Linetype | Lineweight | Plot/Noplot | Description |
|------|-------|----------|------------|-------------|-------------|
| Title | 7 | Continuous | Default | Plot | Title border and text |
| Logo | 7 | Continuous | Default | Plot | Logo |
| Notes | 7 | Continuous | Default | Plot | Notes |
| Viewport | 9 | Continuous | Default | Noplot | Viewports |

3. Place the existing geometry on layer **Title**.
4. Add the line work shown in Figure P6-3 to the drawing. Use the **Title** layer for all geometry. **Do not** draw dimensions.
5. Save the drawing to a template file as **Mechanical B-Size.DWT**.

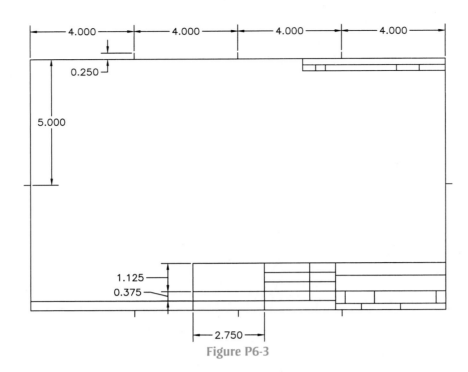

Figure P6-3

## Project 6-4: Architectural D-Size Border—Continued from Chapter 5

1. Open the template file **Architectural D-Size.DWT** from Chapter 5.
2. Create the following layers:

| Name | Color | Linetype | Lineweight | Plot/Noplot | Description |
|---|---|---|---|---|---|
| A-Anno-Ttlb | 7 | Continuous | Default | Plot | Title block/ border lines |
| A-Anno-Ttlb-Text | 1 | Continuous | Default | Plot | Title block text |
| A-Anno-Ttlb-Logo | 3 | Continuous | Default | Plot | Logo |
| A-Anno-Vprt | 7 | Continuous | Default | No Plot | Viewport lines |

3. Put all the existing line work on layer **A-Anno-Ttlb.**
4. Save the drawing to a template file as **Architectural D-Size.DWT.**

## Project 6-5: Electrical Schematic—Continued from Chapter 5

1. Open drawing **P5-5** from Chapter 5.
2. Create the following layers:

| Name | Color | Linetype | Lineweight | Description |
|------|-------|----------|------------|-------------|
| E-Anno | 7 | Continuous | Default | Title border and text |
| E-Risr | 7 | Continuous | Default | Schematic lines |

3. Add the geometry shown to the schematic using the **E-RISR** layer. Use the hard-coded **HIDDEN** linetype as needed. **Do not** draw dimensions.
4. Save the drawing as **P6-5**.

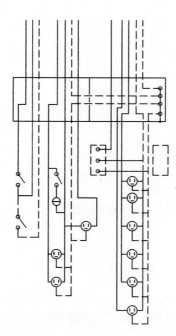

Figure P6-5

## Project 6-6: Water Heater Schematic

1. Start a new drawing using the acad.dwt template.
2. Set the **GRID** and **SNAP** drawing aids to 0.125.
3. Create the following layers:

| Name | Color | Linetype | Lineweight | Description |
|------|-------|----------|------------|-------------|
| P-Detl-P1 | 7 | Continuous | Default | Plumbing details and schematics |
| P-Detl-Hidden | 1 | Hidden | Default | Hidden lines |
| P-Anno-Note | 7 | Continuous | Default | Note text |
| P-Anno-Title | 7 | Continuous | Default | Title text |

4. Draw the piping schematic lines, symbols, and water heater shown in Figure P6-6 on layer **P-Detl-P1**.
5. Draw hidden lines on layer **P-Detl-Hidden**.
6. Save the drawing as **P6-6**.

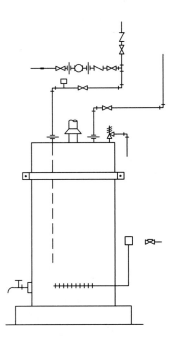

Figure P6-6

## Project 6-7: Residential Architectural Plan—Continued from Chapter 5

1. Open drawing **P5-7** from Chapter 5.
2. Create the following layers:

| Name | Color | Linetype | Description |
|---|---|---|---|
| A-Anno-Symb | 7 | Continuous | Misc. symbols, north arrow |
| A-Flor-Ovhd | 3 | Dashed | Overhead skylights and overhangs |
| A-Door | 5 | Continuous | Doors |
| A-Glaz | 5 | Continuous | Windows |
| A-Wall | 7 | Continuous | Walls |
| A-Wall-Pat | 7 | Continuous | Wall hatch patterns and fills |

3. Set the **LTSCALE** to 6.
4. Place all existing walls on the **A-Wall** layer and the north arrow on the **A-Anno-Symb** layer.
5. Draw the geometry shown in Figure P6-7 on the appropriate layer.
6. Save the drawing as **P6-7**.

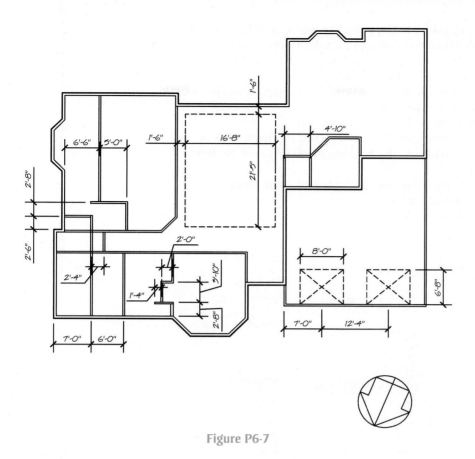

Figure P6-7

## Project 6-8: Joist Foundation Detail—Continued from Chapter 5

1. Open drawing **P5-8** from Chapter 5.
2. Create the following layers:

| Name | Color | Linetype | Lineweight | Description |
| --- | --- | --- | --- | --- |
| A-Detl-Mbnd | 1 | Continuous | Default | Detail lines that represent material in the background |
| A-Detl-Mcut | 3 | Continuous | 0.35 mm | Detail lines that represent material cut in section |
| A-Detl-P1 | 2 | Continuous | Default | Secondary (light) lines |
| A-Detl-Batt | 1 | Batting | Default | Batt insulation |
| A-Anno-Note | 3 | Continuous | Default | Note text |
| A-Anno-Title | 3 | Continuous | Default | Title text |
| A-Anno-Dims | 1 | Continuous | Default | Dimensions |

3. Put all line work that appears beyond the section cut on layer **A-Detl-Mbnd** (vertical wall lines, horizontal joist lines).

4. Put all line work that is cut by the section on layer **A-Detl-Mcut** (footers, lumber in section).

5. Draw the X's that represent lumber in section as shown in Figure P6-8 on layer **A-Detl-P1**.

6. Set the **LTSCALE** system variable to 6.

7. Draw the batt insulation lines shown in Figure P6-8 on the layer **A-Detl-Batt**, which should be set up to use the **Batting** linetype.

8. Draw all remaining lines on the layer **A-Detl-Mcut**.

9. **Do not** include notes.

10.   Save the drawing as **P6-8**.

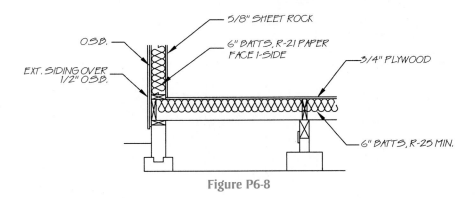

Figure P6-8

## Project 6-9: Support Plate—English Units—Continued from Chapter 5

1. Open drawing **P5-9** from Chapter 5.
2. Create the following layers:

| Name | Color | Linetype | Lineweight | Description |
|------|-------|----------|------------|-------------|
| Object | 7 | Continuous | 0.35 mm | Object lines |
| Hidden | 7 | Hidden | Default | Hidden lines |
| Center | 7 | Center | Default | Centerlines |

3. Set the **LTSCALE** to **.25**.

4. Place the existing geometry on the **Object** layer. Project the hidden lines and draw the centerlines on all views as shown in Figure P6-9.
5. Save the drawing as **P6-9**.

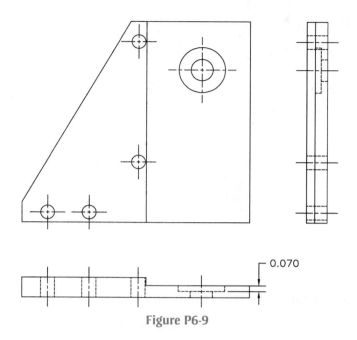

0.070

**Figure P6-9**

## Project 6-10: Hex Head Bolts and Nuts—Metric

1. Start a new drawing using the acadiso.dwt template.
2. Create the following layers:

| Name | Color | Linetype | Lineweight | Description |
| --- | --- | --- | --- | --- |
| Object | 7 | Continuous | 0.35 mm | Object lines |
| Hidden | 7 | Hidden | Default | Hidden lines |
| Center | 7 | Center | Default | Centerlines |

3. Draw object lines as shown in Figure P6-10 on layer **Object**.
4. Draw hidden lines as shown in Figure P6-10 on layer **Hidden**.
5. Draw centerlines as shown in Figure P6-10 on layer **Center**.
6. Adjust the **LTSCALE** system variable so linetypes appear properly.
7. **Do not** include text or dimensions.
8. Save the drawing as **P6-10**.

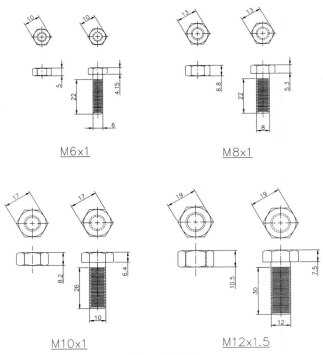

M6x1          M8x1

M10x1          M12x1.5

Figure P6-10

## Project 6-11: Civil Site Plan—Continued from Chapter 5

1. Open the drawing **P5-11** from Chapter 5.
2. Create the following layers:

| Name | Color | Linetype | Description |
|---|---|---|---|
| C-Anno-Note | 7 | Continuous | Notes |
| C-Road-Cntr | 4 | Center | Road centerlines |
| C-Topo | 6 | Hidden | Proposed contour lines and elevations |
| C-Bldg | 7 | Continuous | Building footprints |
| C-Prop | 7 | Phantom | Property lines and survey benchmarks |
| C-Watr | 4 | Continuous | Domestic water |
| C-Sswr | 5 | Dashed | Sanitary sewer |
| C-Ngas-Undr | 6 | Gas_Line | Natural gas underground |
| L-Plnt | 3 | Continuous | Plant and landscape materials |
| L-Walk | 7 | Continuous | Driveway, walks, and steps |
| L-Site-Fenc | 7 | Fenceline1 | Fencing |

3. Place the existing geometry on the appropriate layers. Draw the cut and fill lines on the **C-Topo** layer, approximately where shown in Figure P6-11. Add the water, sewer, and gas utility lines where shown. **Do not** draw text.

4. Save the drawing as **P6-11**.

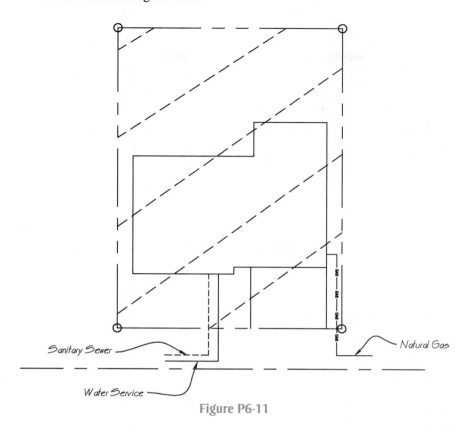

Sanitary Sewer

Water Service

Natural Gas

Figure P6-11

## Project 6-12: Manhole Construction Detail—Continued from Chapter 5

1. Open drawing **P5-12** from Chapter 5.
2. Create the following layers:

| Name | Color | Linetype | Lineweight | Description |
|------|-------|----------|-----------|-------------|
| C-Detl-P1 | 1 | Continuous | Default | Secondary lines (thin) |
| C-Detl-P2 | 3 | Continuous | 0.35 mm | Object lines (thick) |
| C-Detl-Hidden | 1 | Hidden | Default | Hidden lines |
| C-Detl-Center | 1 | Center | Default | Centerlines |

3. Put all line work from P4-12 (plan view) on layer **C-Detl-P1**.
4. Put all line work from P5-12 (section view) on layer **C-Detl-P2**.
5. Draw the rebar on the plan view on top as shown in Figure P6-12 on layer **C-Detl-Hidden**.
6. Draw the vertical rebar on the section view on the bottom as shown in Figure P6-12 on layer **C-Detl-P2**.
7. Draw the centerlines as shown in Figure P6-12 on layer **C-Detl-Center**.

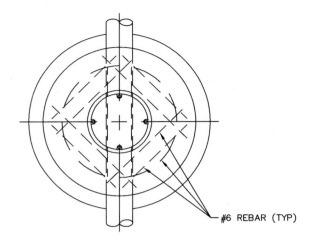

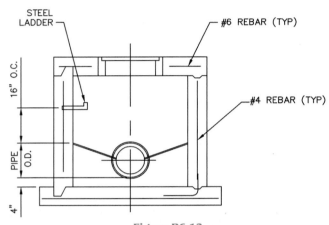

**Figure P6-12**

8. Set the **LTSCALE** system variable to 10.
9. Draw all remaining line work shown in Figure P6-12 on layer **C-Detl-P1**.
10. **Do not** include notes or dimensions.
11. Save the drawing as **P6-12**.

# Basic Editing Techniques

## Chapter Objectives

- Understand the difference between editing objects using the verb/noun technique and editing objects using the noun/verb technique
- Use the **ERASE** command to remove objects from a drawing
- Learn different ways to select one or more objects so that they can be modified
- Move objects
- Copy objects
- Mirror objects
- Rotate objects
- Scale objects
- Stretch objects
- Use grips to modify objects

## INTRODUCTION

The ability to edit and modify objects quickly and with minimum effort is one of the keys to increasing your productivity when using AutoCAD. On the board, if a line is drawn in the wrong location, you must erase it and then redraw it in the correct location. In fact, most on-the-board changes require this same process—erase and redraw, erase and redraw, erase and redraw. . . . Using AutoCAD, a drawing can be edited and revised countless times without worry of burning a hole in your drawing with an electric eraser.

In AutoCAD you simply edit the existing drawing information. If a line is in the wrong location, you can just move it. You do not need to erase it and draw it again, although you can if you want. Most of the time, you will want to take advantage of the edit and modify tools provided by AutoCAD. Most of the basic editing tools can be found on the **Modify** menu or the **Modify** panel on the **Home** ribbon. See Figure 7-1.

In this chapter, you'll learn how to modify an object, or a group of objects, using two different approaches:

- Activating a modify command and then selecting the object(s) you want to modify (verb/noun)
- Selecting the object(s) to modify and then activating a modify command (noun/verb)

The noun/verb terminology might seem a little confusing at first, but if you consider that nouns represent objects (lines, circles, text, etc.) and that verbs represent actions (move, copy, rotate, etc.) it makes sense:

- Noun = Drawing object
- Verb = AutoCAD command

The traditional approach to editing in AutoCAD is verb/noun—activate the command first and then select the object(s). The alternate noun/verb approach to editing can actually be disabled—it is

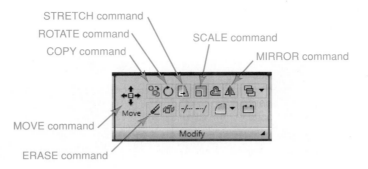

STRETCH command
ROTATE command
COPY command
SCALE command
MIRROR command
MOVE command
ERASE command

**Figure 7-1** The Modify panel

on by default. The noun/verb selection mode and other object selection features are controlled on the **Selection** tab in the **Options** dialog box shown in Figure 7-2.

Many of the settings located on the **Selection Mode** tab are explained throughout this chapter. For now, make sure that your **Selection Mode** settings match those shown in Figure 7-2. Failure to do so can cause some of the examples and exercises in this chapter to behave differently than anticipated.

> **Note:**
> You can display the **Options** dialog box using the following techniques:
> - Select **Options** from the bottom of the Menu Browser list.
> - Select **Options...** from the **Tools** menu.
> - Right-click with your mouse in the **Command Line** window and select **Options...** from the **Command Line** shortcut menu.
> - Right-click with your mouse when nothing is selected in the drawing window and select **Options...** from the **Default** shortcut menu.
> - Type **OP** or **Options**.

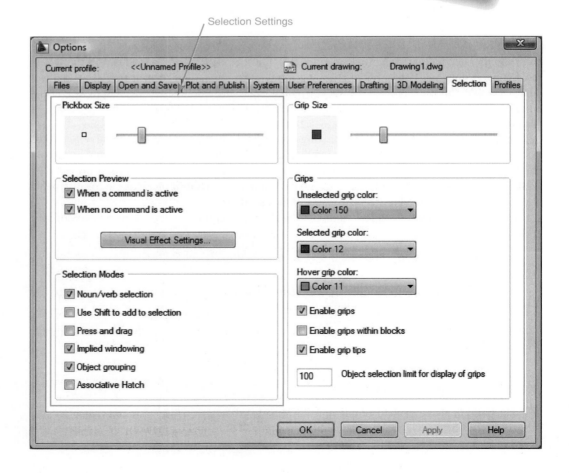

Selection Settings

**Figure 7-2** Selection settings on the Selection tab in the Options dialog box

# THE ERASE COMMAND

In order to explain the different ways to select objects using either the verb/noun approach or the noun/verb approach, we first need a verb, or command. The **ERASE** command is a good candidate, considering it is probably the most used of all the modify commands. The **ERASE** command removes, or erases, the selected objects from a drawing.

| Erase | |
|---|---|
| **Ribbon & Panel:** | Homel Modify  |
| **Modify Toolbar:** | |
| **Menu:** | Modifyl Erase |
| **Command Line:** | ERASE |
| **Command Alias:** | E |

>
> **TIP** If you erase something by accident, remember that you can always use the **UNDO** command to bring it back. You can either select the **Undo** tool from the **Quick Access** toolbar or simply type **U<Enter ↵>** at the AutoCAD command line. Entering **U** repeatedly at the command line will undo commands one at a time until you reach the beginning of your drawing session.

# SELECTING OBJECTS FOR EDITING

As described in the introduction, there are two ways to edit information in AutoCAD—verb/noun and noun/verb. The beginning of this chapter concentrates on the traditional verb/noun approach of activating the command first and then selecting the object(s). Once we understand this approach, we can explore the noun/verb way of doing things. The basics of the modify commands remain the same.

All modify commands work by modifying objects contained in what is referred to as a *selection set* in AutoCAD.

A selection set is simply the object, or objects, that you select to be modified. Anytime you activate an AutoCAD modify command, and no objects are already selected, AutoCAD prompts you to create a selection set as follows:

> **selection set:** One or more selected objects that are treated as one unit by an AutoCAD command

```
Select objects:
```

This is your cue to start selecting the object(s) in your drawing that you want to modify. Auto-CAD repeats the *Select objects:* prompt until you "accept" the selection set by pressing **<Enter ↵>** without selecting anything. This approach allows you to build a selection set using multiple selection techniques ranging from picking objects individually with your mouse to selecting multiple objects using the different selection set options explained in this chapter.

## Selecting Objects Individually

Selecting objects individually is the default selection mode. Anytime AutoCAD prompts you to *Select objects:* to create a selection set, the cursor crosshairs change to what is referred to as the *pickbox*.

The size of the pickbox is used to determine how close you need to be to an object in order to select it. To select an object, it must be within or touching the pickbox. By default, objects that are within the pickbox are previewed by highlighting the objects so that they become dashed *and* thicker. (See Figure 7-3.) This **Selection Preview** feature provides you feedback regarding what object will be selected before you pick with your mouse so that you don't pick the wrong object unintentionally.

> **pickbox:** Square box that replaces the cursor crosshairs whenever AutoCAD prompts you to *Select objects:*. It is used to pick objects in a drawing to create a selection set.

> **TIP** You can control the size of the pickbox and turn the **Selection Preview** feature on and off via the **Selection** tab of the **Options** dialog box shown in Figure 7-2. Other **Selection Preview** features are controlled via the **Visual Effect Settings** dialog box, which can be displayed by selecting the **Visual Effect Settings...** button in the **Selection Preview** area.

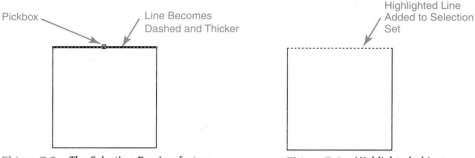

Pickbox

Line Becomes
Dashed and Thicker

Highlighted Line
Added to Selection
Set

Figure 7-3     The Selection Preview feature          Figure 7-4     Highlighted object

Picking an object adds it to the current selection set and highlights it so it is dashed. See Figure 7-4.

You also get feedback at the command line informing you that one object was found:

```
Select objects: 1 found
Select objects:
```

AutoCAD stays in the selection mode until you press the **<Enter ↵>** key without selecting anything to accept the selection set. This allows you to continue to add to the selection set by selecting more objects. As objects are selected, AutoCAD prompts you if the object was found and keeps a running tally of how many total objects are part of the current selection set:

```
Select objects: 1 found, 2 total
Select objects:
```

You can enter **U<Enter ↵>** in response to the *Select objects:* prompt to undo, or deselect, the last object selected. If you have more than one object selected, you can enter **U<Enter ↵>** repeatedly to deselect multiple objects in the order they were selected.

TIP     You can also remove selected objects from the selection set by holding down the **<Shift>** key and selecting the object you want to remove.

**implied windowing:** Feature that allows you to create a **Window** or a **Crossing** selection automatically by picking an empty space in a drawing to define the first corner point

If you try to select an object and you miss because the object isn't within the pickbox, you may automatically be put in what is known as ***implied windowing*** mode, depending if it is turned on or not.

Implied windowing is turned on and off on the **Selection** tab of the **Options** dialog box shown in Figure 7-2. If implied windowing mode is on, AutoCAD automatically initiates the **Window** selection option. The **Window** selection option is discussed in detail a little later in this section. For the time being, you can hit the **<Esc>** key to exit out of the **Window** selection mode and return to selecting objects individually.

***Toggling Between Adding and Removing Objects from a Selection Set.***   It is possible to toggle between adding and removing objects from a selection set using the **A** (Add) and **R** (Remove) selection set options. If you type **R<Enter ↵>** in response to the *Select objects:* prompt, AutoCAD enters the **Remove** object mode and the prompt changes to *Remove objects:*. Objects you then select are removed from the selection set so that they are no longer highlighted. AutoCAD stays in the **Remove** object mode until you enter **A<Enter ↵>** in response to the *Remove objects:* prompt to switch back to **Add** mode.

**Note:**
The **Add** and **Remove** toggle also works with all the multiple object selection modes described later in this chapter.

Switching to **Add** mode changes the prompt back to the familiar *Select objects:* prompt.

*Using the <Shift> Key to Add to a Selection Set.*    When selecting objects individually, it is possible to change the selection mode so that you must use the **<Shift>** key when adding objects to the current selection set. If you select the **Use Shift to add to selection** check box in the **Selection Modes** area of the **Selection** tab on the **Options** dialog box (see Figure 7-2) so that it is turned on, you must hold down the **<Shift>** key when selecting more than one object. When the **Use Shift to add to selection** mode is on and you try to select more than one object *without* using the **<Shift>** key, the first object is deselected so it is no longer highlighted. By default, the **Use Shift to add to selection** mode is off.

*Selecting Stacked and Overlaid Objects Using <Shift> + Spacebar.*    You can select objects that are overlaid on top of each other by holding down **<Shift>** + **spacebar** on your keyboard before you pick an object in response to a *Select objects:* prompt. After you select one object, you release **<Shift>** + **spacebar** and enter into a cycle mode that allows you to pick repeatedly in the same spot to cycle through the different objects that are overlaid on top of each other, highlighting each one individually. See Figures 7-5A through C. While you are in cycle mode, AutoCAD prompts you at the command line as follows:

> **Note:**
> The **LEGACYCTRL PICK** system variable controls whether the legacy **<Ctrl>** key method of selecting stacked options is used instead of **<Shift> + spacebar.**

```
Select objects: <Cycle on>
```

When the object you want to select is highlighted, press **<Enter ↵>** to exit out of the cycle mode. AutoCAD prompts you as follows:

```
Select objects: <Cycle off>
```

This puts you back in the regular selection mode so that you must press **<Enter ↵>** one additional time to accept the selection set.

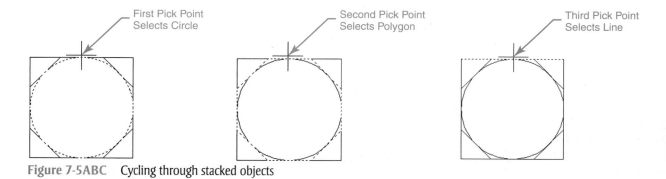

**Figure 7-5ABC**    Cycling through stacked objects

---

**Exercise 7-1:** Selecting Objects Individually
_____

1. Start a new drawing using the acad.dwt drawing template.
2. Make sure that your **Selection Modes** settings on the **Selection** tab of the **Options** dialog box match those shown in Figure 7-2.
3. Draw a rectangle similar to one shown in Figure 7-3 using the **LINE** command so that the rectangle consists of four separate line segments. *Do not use the **RECTANGLE** command!*
4. Start the **ERASE** command.
5. Select the top line as shown in Figure 7-4 and press **<Enter ↵>**. The line is erased.
6. Type **U<Enter ↵>** or select the **Undo** tool so that the line is undeleted.
7. Start the **ERASE** command again.
8. Select the top line as shown in Figure 7-4.
9. Select the other three lines in a clockwise direction using your cursor so that all the rectangle lines are highlighted.

10. Type **U<Enter ↵>** three times so that only the top line is highlighted as shown in Figure 7-4.
11. Select the other three lines again in a clockwise direction using your cursor so that all the rectangle lines are highlighted.
12. Hold down the **<Shift>** key and select the vertical line on the left side of the rectangle so it is no longer highlighted.
13. Type **R<Enter ↵>**.
14. Select the remaining three highlighted lines so that all the rectangle lines are no longer highlighted.
15. Type **A<Enter ↵>**.
16. Select all four lines so that the entire rectangle is highlighted again and press **<Enter ↵>** so that the rectangle is erased.
17. Type **U<Enter ↵>** or select the **Undo** tool so that the rectangle is undeleted.
18. Save the drawing as **EX7-1**.

## Selecting Multiple Objects

Oftentimes, you need to select more than one object when modifying a drawing. Suppose you need to erase a large portion of your drawing—you don't want to have to pick each object individually. Doing so would be very time-consuming. Fortunately, AutoCAD provides a number of selection set options that expedite the process of selecting multiple objects. All these options are entered via the keyboard in response to the *Select objects:* prompt. The following sections explain each of these selection set options.

*W—Window Option.*    To use the **Window** option, type **W<Enter ↵>** in response to the *Select objects:* prompt. The **Window** option allows you to define a rectangular window selection area by prompting you to pick two corner points as shown in Figure 7-6.

By default, the windowed area is shaded a semitransparent blue color to make it obvious which objects will be selected before the second corner point is picked. This **Selection Preview** feature helps you to avoid the unintentional selection of objects.

Using the **Window** option, only objects that are *completely within* the window boundary area are selected. Objects that cross the window boundary are ignored. See Figure 7-7.

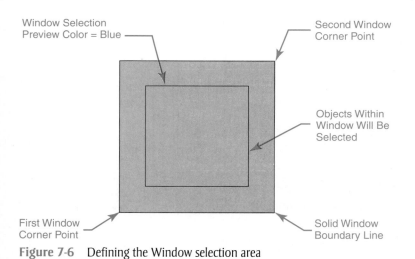

**Figure 7-6**  Defining the Window selection area

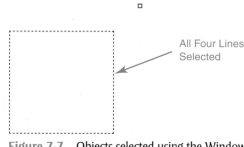

**Figure 7-7**  Objects selected using the Window option

**TIP**  Remember from Chapter 6 that objects on frozen or locked layers are not affected by any of the selection methods explained in the chapter. You can use this to your advantage when selecting multiple objects so that you can select a large group of objects but filter out the objects you don't want to be part of the selection set.

**Exercise 7-2:** Selecting Multiple Objects with the Window Option

1. Continue from Exercise 7-1.
2. Start the **ERASE** command.
3. Type **W<Enter ↵>**
4. Create a **Window** selection similar to the one shown in Figure 7-6 and press **<Enter ↵>** twice. The four lines of the rectangle are erased.
5. Type **U<Enter ↵>** or select the **Undo** tool so that the rectangle is undeleted.
6. Save the drawing as **EX7-2**.

*C—Crossing Option.*    To use the **Crossing** option, type **C<Enter ↵>** in response to the *Select objects:* prompt. The **Crossing** option allows you to define a rectangular window selection area by picking two corner points similar to the **Window** option as shown in Figure 7-8.

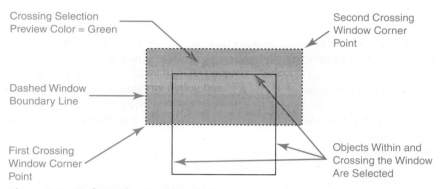

Crossing Selection Preview Color = Green

Second Crossing Window Corner Point

Dashed Window Boundary Line

First Crossing Window Corner Point

Objects Within and Crossing the Window Are Selected

**Figure 7-8**    Defining the Crossing selection area

In order to distinguish between the **Window** option and the **Crossing** option, the **Crossing** option window boundary is dashed (see Figure 7-8), whereas the **Window** option window boundary is solid (see Figure 7-6). In addition, the **Crossing** option windowed area is, by default, shaded a semitransparent green color (see Figure 7-8) instead of the default blue color used with the **Window** option (see Figure 7-6).

The major difference between the **Crossing** option and the **Window** option is that the **Crossing** option will select objects that *cross over* the rectangular window boundary in addition to the objects that lie completely within the window boundary area. See Figure 7-9.

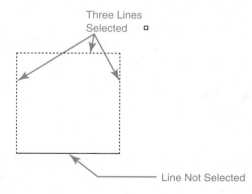

Three Lines Selected

Line Not Selected

**Figure 7-9**    Objects selected using the Crossing option

TIP    You can control the window selection shading features via the **Visual Effect Settings** dialog box, which can be displayed by selecting the **Visual Effect Settings...** button in the **Selection Preview** settings area on the **Selection** tab of the **Options** dialog box shown in Figure 7-2.

**Exercise 7-3:** Selecting Multiple Objects with the Crossing Option

1. Continue from Exercise 7-2.
2. Start the **ERASE** command.
3. Type **C<Enter ↵>**.
4. Create a **Crossing** selection similar to the one shown in Figure 7-8 and press **<Enter ↵>** twice. The top horizontal line and the two vertical lines of the rectangle are erased. The bottom horizontal line remains in the drawing.
5. Type **U<Enter ↵>** or select the **Undo** tool so that the three lines are undeleted.
6. Save the drawing as **EX7-3**.

*Press and Drag Window Mode.*    It is possible to change the window selection mode so that you can define the window area for both the **Window** and **Crossing** options by picking the first window corner point and then, instead of picking the opposite corner point, simply drag your mouse to the opposite corner location and release the button—eliminating the need to pick a second point. This semiautomated window creation mode is enabled by selecting the **Press and drag** check box in the **Selection Modes** area of the **Selection** tab on the **Options** dialog box (see Figure 7-2). By default, the **Press and drag** window selection mode is turned off.

*Implied Windowing.*    As mentioned earlier in the section "Selecting Objects Individually," it is possible to initiate the **Window** *or* the **Crossing** option automatically by relying on a feature called **Implied windowing. Implied windowing** can be turned on and off on the **Selection** tab of the **Options** dialog box shown in Figure 7-2.

When **Implied windowing** is on, you can initiate either the **Window** or **Crossing** option by picking an empty space in your drawing so that no objects fall within your pickbox in response to the *Select objects:* prompt. When you pick and no objects are found, AutoCAD interprets the pick point as the first corner point of a rectangular window area and prompts you to select the second corner point as follows:

```
Specify opposite corner:
```

This is where it gets interesting. If you move your cursor to the *right* of the first pick point, you initiate the **Window** option—the window boundary outline is solid, and the default shade color is blue (see Figure 7-6).

If you move your cursor to the *left* of the first pick point, you initiate the **Crossing** option— the window boundary outline is dashed, and the default shade color is green (see Figure 7-8).

The **Implied windowing** option can be a real timesaving device when selecting objects. Its use basically eliminates the need to enter either the **W** or **C** option at the keyboard. The key is placing the first point in the correct location in response to the *Select objects:* prompt. If you know you want to use the **Crossing** option, place the first point to the right of the objects you want to select and move your cursor to the left to pick the second point. If it's the **Window** option you desire, pick to the left and move your cursor to the right.

**Exercise 7-4:** Selecting Multiple Objects with an Implied Window

1. Continue from Exercise 7-3.
2. Start the **ERASE** command.
3. Pick a point to the lower left of the rectangle so that no objects are within your pickbox and pick a point.
4. Drag your cursor up to the right of the rectangle so that an implied window similar to the **Window** selection shown in Figure 7-6 is created.
5. Press **<Enter ↵>**. The four lines of the rectangle are erased.
6. Type **U<Enter ↵>** or select the **Undo** tool so that the four lines are undeleted.
7. Start the **ERASE** command again.
8. Pick a point to the upper right of the rectangle so that no objects are within your pickbox and pick a point.
9. Drag your cursor down and to the left of the rectangle so that an implied window similar to the **Crossing** selection shown in Figure 7-8 is created.

10. Press **<Enter ↵>**. The top horizontal line and the two vertical lines of the rectangle are erased. The bottom horizontal line remains in the drawing.
11. Type **U<Enter ↵>** or select the **Undo** tool so that the three lines are undeleted.
12. Save the drawing as **EX7-4**.

*WP—Window Polygon Option.*    To use the **Window Polygon** option, type **WP<Enter ↵>** in response to the *Select objects:* prompt. The **Window Polygon** option allows you to define a polygonal window area using multiple pick points so that you can select multiple objects in a complex drawing that you might not be able to select using a simple rectangular window. When you enter the **WP** option, AutoCAD prompts you for the first polygon point and then prompts you for line endpoints until you press **<Enter ↵>** as shown in Figure 7-10.

Similar to the **Window** option, the **Window Polygon** option selects only objects that are completely within the window boundary area. Objects that cross the window boundary are ignored. See Figure 7-11.

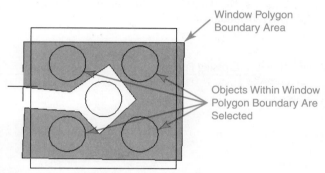

**Figure 7-10**    Defining the Window Polygon selection area

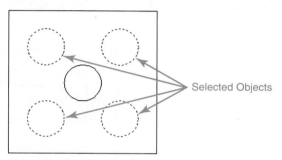

**Figure 7-11**    Objects selected using the Window Polygon option

**TIP**    All the multiple selection options that rely on more than two pick points have an **Undo** option that allows you to "unpick" points you have already selected so that you can relocate an errant pick point without canceling and starting over. To use the **Undo** option, type **U<Enter ↵>** in response to a prompt for the next point, and the last point will be erased.

**Exercise 7-5:** Selecting Multiple Objects with a Window Polygon

1. Continue from Exercise 7-4.
2. Add five circles so your drawing looks as shown in Figure 7-10.
3. Start the **ERASE** command.
4. Type **WP<Enter ↵>**.
5. Create a **Window Polygon** selection similar to the one shown in Figure 7-10 and press **<Enter ↵>** twice. The four circles at the corners of the rectangle are erased.
6. Type **U<Enter ↵>** or select the **Undo** tool so that the four circles are undeleted.
7. Save the drawing as **EX7-5**.

*CP—Crossing Polygon Option.*    To use the **Crossing Polygon** option, type **CP<Enter ↵>** in response to the *Select objects:* prompt. The **Crossing Polygon** option works similarly to the **Window Polygon** option. It also allows you to define a polygonal window area using multiple pick points except that, like the **Crossing** option, objects that cross the polygon window are also selected. When you enter the **CP** option, AutoCAD prompts you for the first polygon point and then prompts you for line endpoints until you press **<Enter ↵>** as shown in Figure 7-12.

As noted, the **Crossing Polygon** option selects objects that *cross over* the polygon window boundary in addition to the objects that lie completely within the window boundary area. See Figure 7-13.

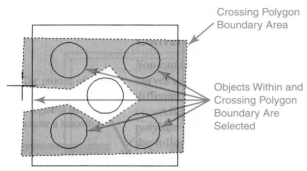

**Figure 7-12**   Defining the Crossing Polygon selection area

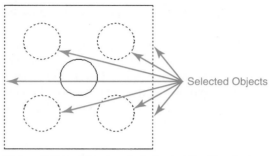

**Figure 7-13**   Objects selected using the Crossing Polygon option

---

**Exercise 7-6:** Selecting Multiple Objects with a Crossing Polygon

1. Continue from Exercise 7-5.
2. Start the **ERASE** command.
3. Type **CP<Enter ↵>**.
4. Create a **Crossing Polygon** selection similar to the one shown in Figure 7-12 and press **<Enter ↵>** twice. The four circles at the corners and the two vertical lines of the rectangle are erased.
5. Type **U<Enter ↵>** or select the **Undo** tool so that the four circles and two lines are undeleted.
6. Save the drawing as **EX7-6**.

> **Note:**
> Both the **Window Polygon** and **Crossing Polygon** options interact the same as their **Window** and **Crossing** counterparts so that a solid window boundary is used for the **Window Polygon** option and a dashed window boundary is used for the **Window Crossing** option. The window selection shading feature settings are also shared between the corresponding options.

*F—Fence Option.* To use the **Fence** option, type **F<Enter ↵>** in response to the *Select objects:* prompt. The **Fence** option allows you to define a multisegmented fence line that selects everything it crosses similar to the **Crossing** option. When you enter the **F** option, AutoCAD prompts you for the first fence point and then prompts you for additional fence endpoints until you press **<Enter ↵>** as shown in Figure 7-14.

The **Fence** option selects all objects that the fence line crosses over or touches. See Figure 7-15.

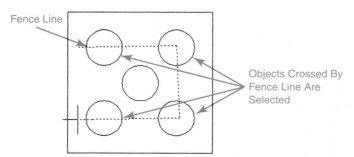

**Figure 7-14**   Defining the Fence selection line

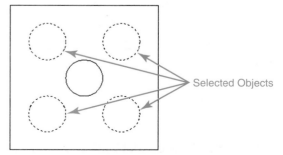

**Figure 7-15**   Objects selected using the Fence option

**Exercise 7-7:** Selecting Multiple Objects with a Fence

1. Continue from Exercise 7-6.
2. Start the **ERASE** command.
3. Type **F<Enter ↵>**.
4. Create a **Fence** selection similar to the one shown in Figure 7-14 and press **<Enter ↵>** twice. The four circles at the corners of the rectangle are erased.
5. Type **U<Enter ↵>** or select the **Undo** tool so that the four circles are undeleted.
6. Save the drawing as **EX7-7**.

## Advanced Selection Techniques

The following selection set options provide additional ways to select objects without having to pick any points in your drawing.

*All—All Option.*    To use the **All** option, type **All<Enter ↵>** in response to the *Select objects:* prompt. The **All** option selects *all* the objects in a drawing—even those objects that lie outside of the visible drawing window! Because of this, care should be taken when using it. When used properly, it can be a handy way to modify everything in a drawing.

 **TIP**    Objects that are on frozen or locked layers are protected when using the **All** option so that they are not selected.

*L—Last Option.*    To use the **Last** option, type **L<Enter ↵>** in response to the *Select objects:* prompt. The **Last** option selects the last object created in a drawing. For instance, if you draw a line in a drawing and then enter the **ERASE** command, entering **L** in response to the *Select objects:* prompt highlights and selects the line you just drew.

*P—Previous Option.*    To use the **Previous** option, type **P<Enter ↵>** in response to the *Select objects:* prompt. The **Previous** option recalls the last selection set created so that you can modify the same objects again. If no previous selection set exists, AutoCAD displays the following at the command line:

```
No previous selection set.
```

**Exercise 7-8:** Using Advanced Selection Techniques

1. Continue from Exercise 7-7.
2. Start the **ERASE** command.
3. Type **All<Enter ↵>**.
4. Press **<Enter ↵>** again. All the drawing objects are erased.
5. Type **U<Enter ↵>** or select the **Undo** tool so that everything is undeleted.
6. Start the **ERASE** command again.
7. Type **L<Enter ↵>**.
8. Press **<Enter ↵>** again. The last object added to the drawing is erased.
9. Type **U<Enter ↵>** or select the **Undo** tool so that the object is undeleted.
10. Save the drawing as **EX7-8**.

## MOVING OBJECTS

Now that you are familiar with all the different ways to select objects, it's time for some action. The **MOVE** command moves objects a user-supplied distance and angle.

| Move | |
|---|---|
| **Ribbon & Panel:** | Home \| Modify |
| | Move |
| **Modify Toolbar:** | |
| **Menu:** | Modify \| Move |
| **Command Line:** | MOVE |
| **Command Alias:** | M |

When you start the **MOVE** command, AutoCAD prompts you to *Select objects:*. Select the object(s) you want to move and press **<Enter ↵ >** to accept the selection set. AutoCAD then prompts you to *Specify base point or ↓*. You have three options:

1. Specify a base point.
2. Select the **Displacement** option using either your arrow keys or by typing **D<Enter ↵>**.
3. Enter a displacement distance using Cartesian coordinates.

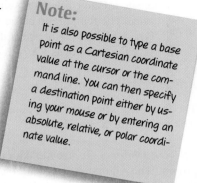

**Note:**
It is also possible to type a base point as a Cartesian coordinate value at the cursor or the command line. You can then specify a destination point either by using your mouse or by entering an absolute, relative, or polar coordinate value.

Using the first option, you typically pick a base (*from*) point by snapping to a key object feature using an Object Snap. AutoCAD then prompts you to *Specify second point or <use first point as displacement>:*. You can then pick a destination (*to*) point, and the selected objects are moved to the new location. See Figure 7-16.

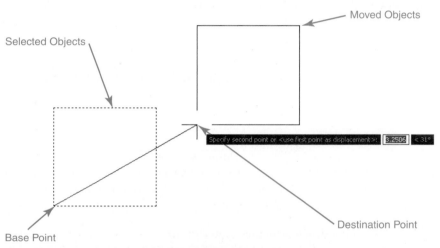

**Figure 7-16**    Moving objects using mouse pick points

You can also use direct distance entry to locate the second point. Using direct distance, you simply point the direction you want to move the selected object(s) and type in the distance you want to travel. See Figure 7-17.

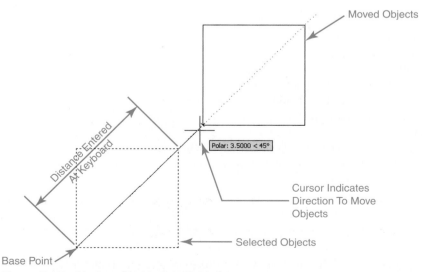

**Figure 7-17**    Moving objects using direct distance

Remember that the best way to utilize direct distance entry is to use it in conjunction with either **Polar Tracking** or **Ortho Mode**. Using either of these drawing tools allows you to lock in an angle and enter a distance for precise movement.

**FOR MORE DETAILS**    See Chapter 6 for detailed information about using the **Polar Tracking** and **Ortho Mode** drawing tools.

The **Displacement** option allows you to specify a displacement distance using rectangular or polar coordinates. The coordinate value you enter is *always* the relative distance the selected object(s) will be moved, even if you omit the @ sign.

To use the **Displacement** option, you can either select the option using your arrow keys or type **D<Enter ↵>**. AutoCAD prompts you to *Specify displacement <2.0000, 2.0000, 0.0000>:*. You can then enter the displacement distance using either rectangular (*X,Y*) or polar coordinates (@Distance<Angle). Entering **3,3<Enter ↵>** results in the move operation shown in Figure 7-18.

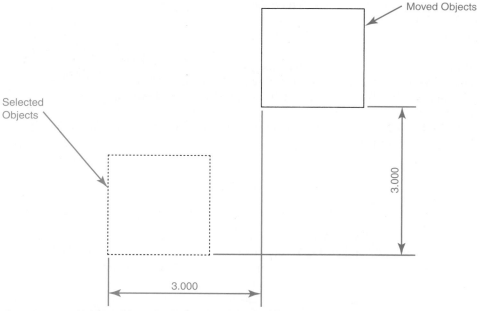

**Figure 7-18**    Moving objects using the Displacement option

AutoCAD remembers the displacement distance entered so that it is now the default distance. The next time you use the **MOVE** command, you can just press **<Enter ↵>** to move the same distance again.

The third option is basically a shortcut to the **Displacement** option explained above. It is possible to enter a Cartesian coordinate displacement distance directly in response to the first *Specify base point or ↓* prompt explained earlier. Entering an *X,Y* distance and pressing **<Enter ↵>** displays the standard prompt *Specify second point or <use first point as displacement>:*. Hitting **<Enter ↵>** selects the default **<use first point as displacement>** option so that the *X,Y* distance entered is used as the displacement distance.

**Exercise 7-9:** Moving Objects

1. Start a new drawing using the acad.dwt drawing template.
2. Draw a 2″ × 2″ square similar to one shown in Figure 7-16.
3. Start the **MOVE** command and select the square using your preferred selection method so that AutoCAD prompts *Specify base point or* ↓.
4. Snap to the lower left corner of the square using the **Endpoint** Object Snap as shown in Figure 7-16.
5. Move the square using a second pick point as shown in Figure 7-16.
6. Type **U<Enter** ↵**>** or select the **Undo** tool so that the square is in its original location.
7. Start the **MOVE** command again and select the square using your preferred selection method so that AutoCAD prompts *Specify base point or* ↓.
8. Snap to the lower left corner of the square using the **Endpoint** Object Snap as shown in Figure 7-17.
9. Move your cursor so the rubber-band line points to the right as shown in Figure 7-17 and type **3<Enter** ↵**>**. The square moves 3 units along the rubber-band line.
10. Type **U<Enter** ↵**>** or select the **Undo** tool so that the square is at its original location.
11. Start the **MOVE** command again and select the square using your preferred selection method so that AutoCAD prompts *Specify base point or* ↓.
12. Type **3,3<Enter↵>**. AutoCAD prompts *Specify second point or <use first point as displacement>:*.
13. Press **<Enter** ↵**>** again to use the first point entered as the displacement distance. The square moves +3 units on the *X*-axis and +3 units on the *Y*-axis as shown in Figure 7-18.
14. Type **U<Enter** ↵**>** or select the **Undo** tool so that the square is at its original location.
15. Save the drawing as **EX7-9**.

> **Note:**
> It is possible, and quite common, to use Object Snaps when modifying objects, especially when selecting a base point.

## COPYING OBJECTS

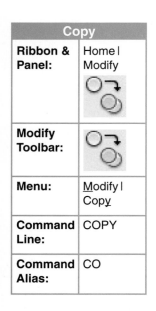

| Copy | |
|---|---|
| **Ribbon & Panel:** | Home \| Modify |
| **Modify Toolbar:** | |
| **Menu:** | Modify \| Copy |
| **Command Line:** | COPY |
| **Command Alias:** | CO |

The **COPY** command copies objects a user-supplied distance and angle. Its usage is similar to the **MOVE** command except that the **COPY** command maintains the selected objects in their original location. It is possible to make multiple copies if you specify a base point.

When you start the **COPY** command, AutoCAD prompts you to *Select objects:*. Select the object(s) you want to copy and press **<Enter** ↵**>** to accept the selection set. AutoCAD then prompts you to *Specify base point or* ↓. Similar to the **MOVE** command, you have three options:

1. Specify a base point.
2. Select the **Displacement** option either by using your arrow keys or by typing **D<Enter** ↵**>**.
3. Enter a displacement distance using Cartesian coordinates.

Using the first option, you typically pick a base (*from*) point by snapping to a key object feature using an Object Snap. AutoCAD then prompts you to *Specify second point or <use first point as displacement>:*. You can then pick a destination (*to*) point, and the selected objects are copied to the new location as shown in Figure 7-19.

Just like the **MOVE** command, you can also rely on direct distance entry to locate the second point. Using direct distance, you simply point the direction you want to copy the selected object(s) and type in the distance you want to travel.

If you use the first option and specify a base point, AutoCAD remains in the **COPY** command after the first copy is created so that it is possible to make multiple copies by specifying

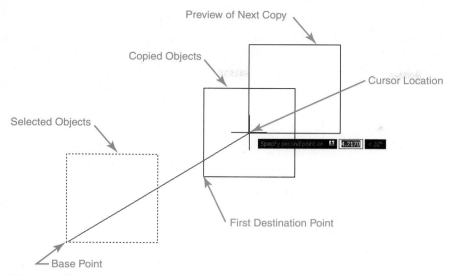

**Figure 7-19**    Copying objects using mouse pick points

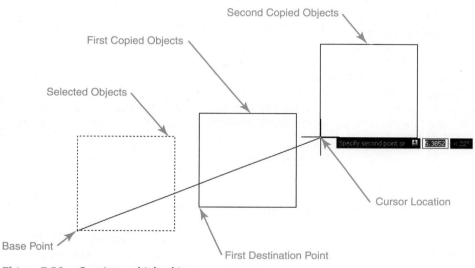

**Figure 7-20**    Copying multiple objects

multiple destination points. After making the first copy, AutoCAD repeatedly prompts you to *Specify second point or* ↓ until you select the **Exit** option or type **E<Enter ↵>** to end the command as shown in Figure 7-20.

> The **COPY** command has an **Undo** option when you are making multiple copies so that you can undo a copy operation if it is the wrong location. To use the **Undo** option, you can either select the option using your arrow keys or type **U<Enter ↵>**.

    The **Displacement** option allows you to specify a displacement distance using rectangular or polar coordinates. The coordinate value you enter is *always* the relative distance the selected object(s) will be copied, even if you omit the @ sign.

    To use the **Displacement** option, you can either select the option using your arrow keys or type **D<Enter ↵>**. AutoCAD prompts you to *Specify displacement <3.0000, 3.0000, 0.0000>:*. You can then enter the displacement distance using either rectangular (*X,Y*) or polar coordinates (@Distance<Angle). Entering **3,3<Enter ↵>** results in the copy operation shown in Figure 7-21.

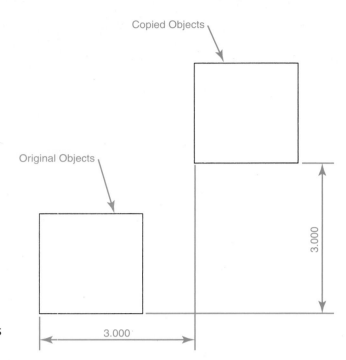

**Figure 7-21**  Copying objects using the Displacement option

**TIP**

AutoCAD remembers the displacement distance entered so that it is now the default distance. The next time you use the **COPY** command, you can just press **<Enter ↵>** to copy the same distance again.

The third option is a shortcut to the **Displacement** option explained above, similar to the **MOVE** command. It is possible to enter a Cartesian coordinate displacement distance directly in response to the first *Specify base point or ↓* prompt explained earlier. Entering an *X,Y* distance and pressing **<Enter ↵>** displays the standard prompt *Specify second point or <use first point as displacement>:*. Hitting **<Enter ↵>** selects the default **<use first point as displacement>** option so that the *X,Y* distance entered is used as the displacement distance.

### Exercise 7-10: Copying Objects

1. Continue from Exercise 7-9.
2. Start the **COPY** command and select the square using your preferred selection method so that AutoCAD prompts *Specify base point or ↓*.
3. Snap to the lower left corner of the square using the **Endpoint** Object Snap as shown in Figure 7-19. AutoCAD prompts *Specify second point or <use first point as displacement>:*.
4. Copy the square using a second pick point as shown in Figure 7-19. AutoCAD repeatedly prompts *Specify second point or ↓*.
5. Continue to pick points to make multiple copies as shown in Figure 7-20.
6. Press **<Enter ↵>**, select the **Exit** option, or type **E<Enter ↵>** to end the **COPY** command.
7. Type **U<Enter ↵>** or select the **Undo** tool so that only one square is left at its original location.
8. Start the **COPY** command and select the square using your preferred selection method so that AutoCAD prompts *Specify second point or ↓*.
9. Type **3,3<Enter ↵>**. AutoCAD prompts *Specify second point or <use first point as displacement>:*.

10. Press **<Enter ↵>** again to use the first point entered as the displacement distance. The square is copied +3 units on the *X*-axis and +3 units on the *Y*-axis as shown in Figure 7-21.
11. Type **U<Enter ↵>** or select the **Undo** tool so that only one square is left at its original location.
12. Save the drawing as **EX7-10**.

## Mirroring Objects

The **MIRROR** command creates a mirror image of objects about a mirror axis line defined by two user-supplied line endpoints.

   When you start the **MIRROR** command, AutoCAD prompts you to *Select objects:*. Select the object(s) you want to mirror and press **<Enter ↵>** to accept the selection set. AutoCAD then prompts you to specify the two endpoints of a line about which to mirror the selected objects as shown in Figure 7-22, while maintaining a ghost image of the original objects and displaying a preview of the mirrored objects.

| Mirror | |
|---|---|
| **Ribbon & Panel:** | Home\|Modify  |
| **Modify Toolbar:** | |
| **Menu:** | <u>M</u>odify\|Mirror |
| **Command Line:** | MIRROR |
| **Command Alias:** | MI |

 You can use either the **Ortho Mode** or **Polar Tracking** drawing tools to create either a horizontal or vertical mirror axis line quickly by simply picking two points.

**FOR MORE DETAILS** See Chapter 6 for more information about using the **Ortho Mode** and **Polar Tracking** drawing aids.

   After selecting the second point, AutoCAD prompts you to *Erase source objects? ↓*. You have the option of either erasing the originally selected objects, so only the mirrored copies remain, or leaving them in the drawing. The default is *not* to erase the original objects so that you can just press **<Enter ↵>**. Of course, you can also select the **No** option using your arrow keys. Either response to the *Erase source objects? ↓* prompt results with the mirrored object *and* the original as shown in Figure 7-23.

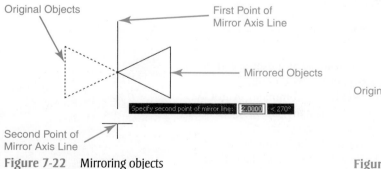

**Figure 7-22** Mirroring objects

**Figure 7-23** Mirrored objects with original objects maintained

   To erase the original objects, you can either select the **Yes** option using your arrow keys or type **Y<Enter ↵>** in response to the *Erase source objects? ↓* prompt. The result of erasing the original objects is shown in Figure 7-24.

**Figure 7-24** Mirrored objects with original objects erased

## Mirroring Text

Usually, when you mirror text you want it to retain its original left-to-right orientation so that the text isn't reversed as shown in Figure 7-25.

    The AutoCAD **MIRRTEXT** system variable controls whether or not text is reversed when it is mirrored. Setting **MIRRTEXT** to **1** (on) will cause text to be reversed when it is mirrored as shown in Figure 7-25. Setting **MIRRTEXT** to **0** (off) retains the text's original orientation as shown in Figure 7-26.

    By default, the **MIRRTEXT** system variable is set to **0** (off).

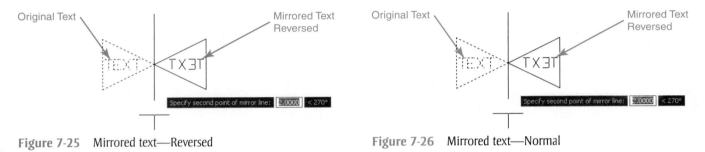

**Figure 7-25** Mirrored text—Reversed          **Figure 7-26** Mirrored text—Normal

### Exercise 7-11: Mirroring Objects

1. Start a new drawing using the acad.dwt drawing template.
2. Draw a triangle similar to the one shown in Figure 7-22.
3. Start the **MIRROR** command and select the triangle using your preferred selection method so that AutoCAD prompts *Specify first point of mirror line:*.
4. Pick a point above the right side vertex as shown in Figure 7-22. AutoCAD prompts you to *Specify second point of mirror line:*.
5. Turn on the **Ortho Mode** drawing tool if it is not already on.
6. Pick a point directly below the first point at 270° using the **Ortho Mode** drawing tool as shown in Figure 7-22. AutoCAD mirrors the triangle and prompts *Erase source objects?* ↓.
7. Press **<Enter ↓>** to accept the default and retain the original triangle so that the drawing looks similar to Figure 7-23.
8. Save the drawing as **EX7-11**.

| Rotate | |
|---|---|
| **Ribbon & Panel:** | Home I Modify |
| **Modify Toolbar:** | |
| **Menu:** | Modify I Rotate |
| **Command Line:** | ROTATE |
| **Command Alias:** | RO |

## ROTATING OBJECTS

The **ROTATE** command rotates objects a user-specified rotation angle around a user-specified base point.

    When you start the **ROTATE** command, AutoCAD prompts you to *Select objects:*. Select the object(s) you want to rotate and press **<Enter ↓>** to accept the selection set. AutoCAD then prompts you to *Specify base point:*. The base point is the axis of rotation about which the selected object(s) are rotated. Typically you pick a base point by snapping to a key object feature using an Object Snap.

    After specifying the base point, AutoCAD then prompts you to *Specify rotation angle or* ↓. You have three different ways you can enter the rotation angle:

1. Pick a point with your mouse that defines the rotation angle using the base point as the vertex.

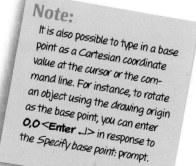

**Note:**
It is also possible to type in a base point as a Cartesian coordinate value at the cursor or the command line. For instance, to rotate an object using the drawing origin as the base point, you can enter **0,0 <Enter ↓>** in response to the *Specify base point:* prompt.

2. Enter the angle at the keyboard.

3. Use the **Reference** option to reference a start angle and then enter a new angle either at the keyboard or by picking points.

Using the first option, you simply move your cursor and pick a point in your drawing to indicate the desired rotation angle. AutoCAD provides a preview of the rotation as shown in Figure 7-27.

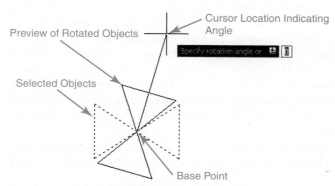

**Figure 7-27**   Rotating objects using your mouse

**TIP**   You can use either the **Ortho Mode** or **Polar Tracking** drawing aids to quickly rotate object(s) at predefined angles.

**FOR MORE DETAILS**   See Chapter 6 for more information about using the **Ortho Mode** and **Polar Tracking** drawing aids.

The second option is to enter the rotation angle at the keyboard. Angles are measured using the current base angle and direction. The default base angle is 0°=East with angles measured counterclockwise. The current direction and base angle are displayed at the command line when you use the **ROTATE** command for an easy reference as follows:

`Current positive angle in UCS: ANGDIR=clockwise ANGBASE=0`

Entering **45<Enter ↵>** with the settings above rotates the selected objects as shown in Figures 7-28A and B.

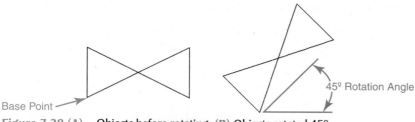

**Figure 7-28 (A)**   Objects before rotating. **(B)** Objects rotated 45°

**TIP**   It is also possible to enter a negative angle and rotate objects in the opposite direction of the current angle direction setting. For example, entering −45° is equal to entering 315°.

**FOR MORE DETAILS**   See Chapter 4 for more information about setting the base angle and direction.

The **Reference** option allows you to rotate object(s) by specifying a reference, or start angle, and then specifying a new, absolute angle to rotate to. AutoCAD determines the necessary rotation angle by calculating the difference from the reference angle to the new angle.

To use the **Reference** option, you can either select the option using your arrow keys or type **R<Enter ↵>** at the command line. AutoCAD prompts you to *Specify the reference angle <0>:*. You can either type in an angle via the keyboard, or you can select two points in your drawing that define the reference angle. The **Reference** option is invaluable if you don't know the angle of an existing object. Using Object Snaps, you can snap to two points on the object(s) that define its current angle as shown in Figure 7-29.

AutoCAD then prompts you to *Specify the new angle or ↓*. You can either type in an angle via the keyboard, or you can use the **Points** option to select two points in the drawing to define the new angle as shown in Figure 7-30.

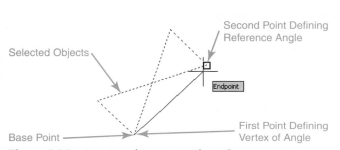

**Figure 7-29**   Rotating objects using the Reference option— Start angle

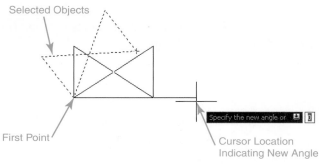

**Figure 7-30**   Rotating objects using the Reference option— New angle

### Rotating and Copying Objects

It is possible to rotate and copy objects using the **Copy** option. To use the **Copy** option, you can either select the option using your arrow keys or type **C<Enter ↵>** at the command line when AutoCAD prompts you to *Specify rotation angle or ↕*. When you select the **Copy** option, AutoCAD displays the following at the command line:

    Rotating a copy of the selected objects.

You can use any of the methods explained earlier to specify a rotation angle. Figure 7-31 shows the results of using the **Copy** option and rotating the objects shown in Figure 7-28 90° from horizontal.

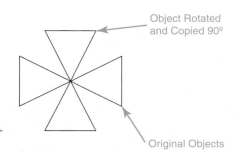

**Figure 7-31**   Rotating and copying objects

**TIP**

AutoCAD remembers the angle entered using any of the **ROTATE** command options so that it is now the default angle. The next time you use the **ROTATE** command, you can press **<Enter ↵>** to rotate the same angle again.

### Exercise 7-12: Rotating Objects

1. Continue from Exercise 7-11.
2. Start the **ROTATE** command and select both triangles using your preferred selection method so that AutoCAD prompts *Specify base point or ↓*.
3. Snap to the intersection of both triangles using the **Intersection** Object Snap as shown in Figure 7-27. AutoCAD prompts *Specify rotation angle or ↓*.
4. Rotate the triangles to any angle using a cursor pick point as shown in Figure 7-27.
5. Type **U<Enter ↵>** or select the **Undo** tool so that the triangles are oriented horizontally again as shown in Figure 7-28A.
6. Start the **ROTATE** command again and select the triangles using your preferred selection method so that AutoCAD prompts *Specify base point or ↓*.
7. Snap to the intersection of both triangles using the **Intersection** Object Snap as shown in Figure 7-27. AutoCAD prompts *Specify rotation angle or ↓*.
8. Type **45<Enter ↵>**. The triangles are rotated 45° as shown in Figure 7-28B.
9. Type **U<Enter ↵>** or select the **Undo** tool so that the triangles are oriented horizontally again as shown in Figure 7-28A.
10. Start the **ROTATE** command again and select the triangles using your preferred selection method so that AutoCAD prompts *Specify base point or ↓*.
11. Snap to the intersection of both triangles using the **Intersection** Object Snap as shown in Figure 7-27. AutoCAD prompts *Specify rotation angle or ↓*.
12. Select the **Copy** option by either selecting the option using your arrow keys or by typing **C<Enter ↵>** at the command line.
13. Type **90<Enter ↵>**. The triangles are copied and rotated 90° as shown in Figure 7-31.
14. Type **U<Enter ↵>** or select the **Undo** tool so that only two triangles are left at their original horizontal orientation.
15. Save the drawing as **EX7-12**.

## SCALING OBJECTS

The **SCALE** command scales objects a user-specified scale factor about a user-specified base point.

When you start the **SCALE** command, AutoCAD prompts you to *Select objects:*. Select the object(s) you want to scale and press **<Enter ↵>** to accept the selection set. AutoCAD then prompts you to *Specify base point:*. The base point is the point about which the selected object(s) are scaled. Typically you pick a base point by snapping to a key object feature using an Object Snap.

After specifying the base point, AutoCAD then prompts you to *Specify scale factor or ↓*. You have three different ways you can enter the scale factor:

1. Pick a point with your mouse that defines the scale factor.
2. Enter the scale factor at the keyboard.
3. Use the **Reference** option to reference a starting size/length and then enter a new size/length either at the keyboard or by picking points.

Using the first option you simply move your cursor and pick a point in your drawing to indicate the desired scale factor. AutoCAD provides a preview of the scaling process as shown in Figure 7-32.

**Note:**
It is also possible to type in a base point as a Cartesian coordinate value at the cursor or the command line. For instance, to scale an object using the drawing origin as the base point, you can enter **0,0 <Enter ↵>** in response to the *Specify base point:* prompt.

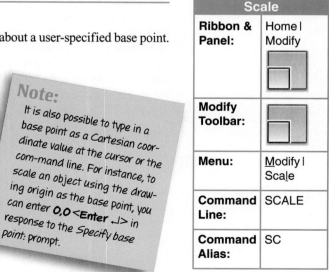

| Scale | |
|---|---|
| **Ribbon & Panel:** | Home I Modify |
| **Modify Toolbar:** | |
| **Menu:** | Modify I Scale |
| **Command Line:** | SCALE |
| **Command Alias:** | SC |

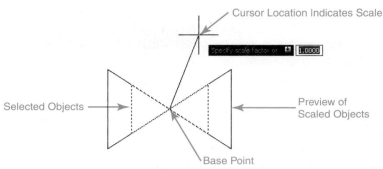

Cursor Location Indicates Scale

Selected Objects

Preview of
Scaled Objects

Base Point

**Figure 7-32**    Scaling objects using your mouse

The second option is to enter the scale factor at the keyboard. A scale factor greater than 1 makes objects larger, and a scale factor less than 1 makes objects smaller. Scale factors must always be greater than zero. Entering **2<Enter ↵>** in response to the *Specify scale factor or ↓* prompt scales the selected objects up by a factor of 2 so that they are twice as large as shown in Figures 7-33A and B.

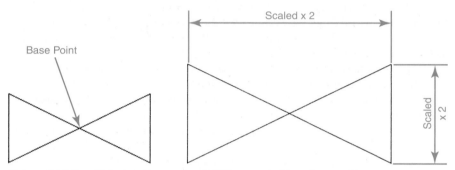

Base Point

Scaled x 2

Scaled x 2

**Figure 7-33A**    Objects before scaling **B** Objects scaled by a factor of 2

The **Reference** option allows you to scale objects by specifying a reference, or start length, and then a new, absolute length to scale to. AutoCAD determines the necessary scale factor by calculating the difference between the reference length and the new length.

To use the **Reference** option, you can either select the option using your arrow keys or type **R<Enter ↵>**. AutoCAD prompts you to *Specify reference length <1.0000>:*. You can either type in a length via the keyboard, or you can select two points in your drawing that define the reference length. The **Reference** option is invaluable if you don't know the length of an existing object but you do know the length it needs to be. Using Object Snaps, you can snap to two points on the object(s) that define its current length as shown in Figure 7-34.

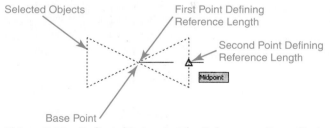

Selected Objects

First Point Defining
Reference Length

Second Point Defining
Reference Length

Midpoint

Base Point

**Figure 7-34**    Scaling objects using the Reference option—Start length

AutoCAD then prompts you to *Specify new length or ↓*. You can either type in a length via the keyboard, or you can use the **Points** option to select two points in the drawing to define the new length as shown in Figure 7-35.

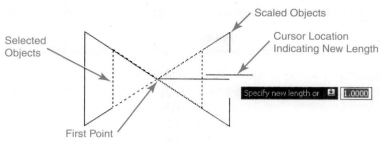

**Figure 7-35**    Scaling objects using the Reference option—New length

## Scaling and Copying Objects

It is possible to scale and copy object(s) using the **Copy** option. To use the **Copy** option, you can either select the option using your arrow keys or type **C<Enter ↵>** when AutoCAD prompts you to *Specify scale factor or ↓*. Using the **Copy** option, AutoCAD displays the following at the command line:

```
Scaling a copy of the selected objects.
```

You can use any of the methods explained earlier to specify a scale factor.

> **TIP**
>
> AutoCAD remembers the scale factor entered using any of the **SCALE** command options so that it is now the default scale factor. The next time you use the **SCALE** command, you can press **<Enter ↵>** and scale by the same factor again.

### Exercise 7-13: Scaling Objects

1. Continue from Exercise 7-12.
2. Start the **SCALE** command and select both triangles using your preferred selection method so that AutoCAD prompts *Specify base point or ↓*.
3. Snap to the intersection of both triangles using the **Intersection** Object Snap as shown in Figure 7-32. AutoCAD prompts *Specify scale factor or ↓*.
4. Scale the triangles to any scale using a cursor pick point as shown in Figure 7-32.
5. Type **U<Enter ↵>** or select the **Undo** tool so that the triangles are scaled to their original size again as shown in Figure 7-33A.
6. Start the **SCALE** command again and select the triangles using your preferred selection method so that AutoCAD prompts *Specify base point or ↓*.
7. Snap to the intersection of both triangles using the **Intersection** Object Snap as shown in Figure 7-32. AutoCAD prompts *Specify scale factor or ↓*.
8. Type **2<Enter ↵>**. The triangles are scaled up by a factor of 2 as shown in Figure 7-33B.
9. Type **U<Enter ↵>** or select the **Undo** tool so that the triangles are scaled to their original size again as shown in Figure 7-33A.
10. Save the drawing as **EX7-13**.

| Stretch | |
|---|---|
| **Ribbon & Panel:** | Home\| Modify |
| **Modify Toolbar:** | |
| **Menu:** | Modify\| Stretch |
| **Command Line:** | STRETCH |
| **Command Alias:** | S |

## STRETCHING OBJECTS

The **STRETCH** command moves or stretches objects a user-supplied distance and angle using the **Crossing Window** or **Crossing Polygon** selection option. The key to the **STRETCH** command is that it moves only endpoints and vertices that lie inside the crossing selection, leaving those outside unchanged.

When you start the **STRETCH** command, AutoCAD displays the following at the command line:

```
Select objects to stretch by crossing-window or crossing-polygon...
```

AutoCAD also prompts you to *Select objects:*. You *must* select the object(s) you want to stretch using either the **Crossing** or **Crossing Polygon** selection option and press **<Enter ↵>** to accept the selection set as shown in Figure 7-36.

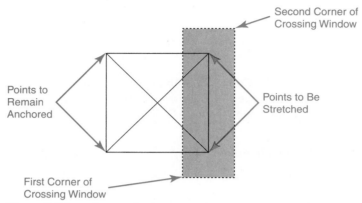

**Figure 7-36**    Selecting objects to stretch using a Crossing selection

AutoCAD then prompts you to *Specify base point or ↓*. You have three options:

1. Specify a base point.
2. Select the **Displacement** option using either your arrow keys or typing **D<Enter ↵>**.
3. Enter a displacement distance using Cartesian coordinates.

**TIP**    You can use standard object selection methods such as picking on the object, and Auto-CAD automatically treats those objects with a **MOVE** operation. You can also apply multiple crossing selections within a single **STRETCH** operation to stretch multiple object selections simultaneously.

Using the first option, you typically pick a base (*from*) point by snapping to a key object feature using an Object Snap. AutoCAD then prompts you to *Specify second point or <use first point as displacement>:*. You can then pick a destination (*to*) point, and the selected objects are stretched or moved to the new location as shown in Figure 7-37.

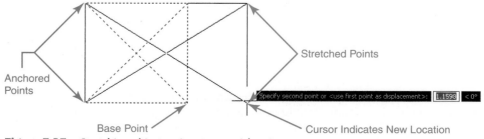

**Figure 7-37**    Stretching objects using mouse pick points

Notice in Figure 7-37 that the **STRETCH** command leaves any points or vertices outside of the crossing selection anchored in place so that they are unaffected by the move. This is useful when you need to move or stretch part of a drawing but leave other portions of the drawing intact.

In the example above, you can also rely on direct distance entry to locate the second point. Using direct distance you simply point the direction you want to stretch the selected object(s) and type in the distance you want to travel.

**Note:**

It is also possible to type a base point as a Cartesian coordinate value at the cursor or the command line. You can then specify a destination point either by using your mouse or by entering an absolute, relative, or polar coordinate value.

**TIP**    Remember that the best way to utilize direct distance entry is to use it in conjunction with either *Polar Tracking* or **Ortho Mode**. Using either of these drawing tools allows you to lock in an angle and enter a distance for precise movement.

**FOR MORE DETAILS**    See Chapter 6 for detailed information about using the **Polar Tracking** and **Ortho Mode** drawing tools.

The **Displacement** option allows you to specify a displacement distance using rectangular or polar coordinates. The coordinate value you enter is *always* the relative distance the selected object(s) will be stretched, even if you omit the @ sign.

To use the **Displacement** option, you can either select the option using your arrow keys or type **D<Enter ↵>**. AutoCAD prompts you to *Specify displacement <2.0000, 2.0000, 0.0000>:*. You can then enter the displacement distance using either rectangular (*X,Y*) or polar coordinates (@Distance<Angle). Entering **2,0<Enter ↵>** results in the stretch operation shown in Figure 7-38.

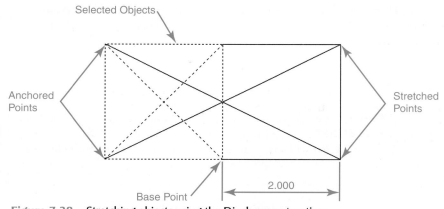

**Figure 7-38**    Stretching objects using the Displacement option

**TIP**    AutoCAD remembers the displacement distance entered so that it is now the default distance. The next time you use the **STRETCH** command, you can just press **<Enter ↵>** to stretch the same distance again.

The third option is a shortcut to the **Displacement** option explained above. It is possible to enter a Cartesian coordinate displacement distance directly in response to the first *Specify base point or* ↓ prompt explained earlier. Entering an *X,Y* distance and pressing **<Enter ⏎>** displays the standard prompt *Specify second point or <use first point as displacement>:*. Pressing **<Enter ⏎>** selects the default **<use first point as displacement>** option so that the *X,Y* distance entered is used as the displacement distance.

### Exercise 7-14: Stretching Objects

1. Start a new drawing using the acad.dwt drawing template.
2. Draw a 2″ × 2″ square with a cross similar to the one shown in Figure 7-36.
3. Start the **STRETCH** command and select the line endpoints on the right side of the square using the **Crossing** selection method shown in Figure 7-36 so that AutoCAD prompts *Specify base point or* ↓.
4. Snap to the lower right corner of the square using the **Endpoint** Object Snap as shown in Figure 7-37. AutoCAD prompts *Specify second point or <use first point as displacement>:*.
5. Stretch the line endpoints to the right using a second pick point as shown in Figure 7-37.
6. Type **U<Enter ⏎>** or select the **Undo** tool so that the square is its original size.
7. Start the **STRETCH** command and select the line endpoints on the right side of the square using the **Crossing** selection method shown in Figure 7-36 so that AutoCAD prompts *Specify base point or* ↓.
8. Type **2,0<Enter ⏎>**. AutoCAD prompts *Specify second point or <use first point as displacement>:*.
9. Press **<Enter ⏎>** again to use the first point entered as the displacement distance. The square is stretched +2 units on the *X*-axis as shown in Figure 7-38.
10. Type **U<Enter ⏎>** or select the **Undo** tool so that only one square is left at its original location.
11. Save the drawing as **EX7-14**.

## SELECTING OBJECTS FIRST

Now that you have seen how to modify objects using the traditional verb/noun approach of selecting a modify command and then the objects to modify, let's look at the noun/verb approach of selecting objects first and *then* selecting a modify command. First, make sure that the **Noun/verb selection** check box is selected on the **Selection** tab of the **Options** dialog box as shown in Figure 7-2. It is on by default.

**TIP** The **PICKFIRST** system variable can also be used to control the noun/verb selection setting. Setting **PICKFIRST** to **1** (on) is the same as selecting the **Noun/verb selection** check box. Setting **PICKFIRST** to **0** (off) turns off the **Noun/verb selection** check box.

Using noun/verb selection, you can select objects either by using your cursor or by using implied windowing to create a **Window** or **Crossing** selection. Selected objects are highlighted, and if grips are enabled, their grips are turned on as shown later in Figure 7-39. Grips are explained in detail in the next section. If you now select any of the modify commands introduced in this chapter, the selected objects become the default selection set for the modify command, and you are *not* prompted to select any objects. You can then use the command and any command options by applying the same techniques explained in the previous sections.

**Exercise 7-15:** Selecting Objects First for Editing

1. Continue from Exercise 7-14.
2. Select all the objects in the drawing either by selecting objects individually with your mouse or by using implied windowing.
3. Select the **ERASE** command. All the objects are erased.
4. Type **U<Enter ↵>** or select the **Undo** tool so that all the objects are undeleted.
5. Save the drawing as **EX7-15**.

# Using Grips to Edit

Grips are the small colored squares (default=blue) that appear at key object definition points when an object is selected as shown in Figure 7-39.

Grips act as object handles and when selected provide quick, easy access to the five basic modify commands explained earlier in this chapter so that you can maintain your focus on your drawing. The five grip commands, or modes, are as follows:

1. **Stretch**
2. **Move**
3. **Rotate**
4. **Scale**
5. **Mirror**

Selecting grips and using the different grip modes is explained in detail a little later in this section. First we need to make sure grips are enabled, as well as look at some of the different grip settings such as size and color.

## Controlling Grips

Grips are controlled on the **Selection** tab of the **Options** dialog box shown in Figure 7-40.

The different grip features and their settings are as follows:

- **Grip Size**   Controls the display size of grips
- **Unselected grip color**   Determines the color of an unselected grip
- **Selected grip color**   Determines the color of a selected grip

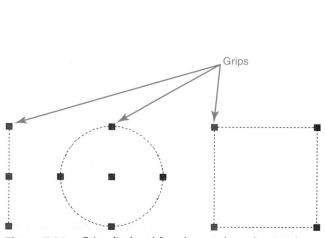

**Figure 7-39**   Grips displayed for a line, circle, and rectangle

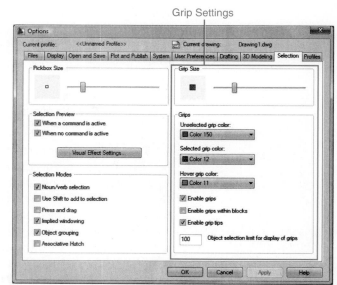

**Figure 7-40**   Grip settings on the Selection tab in the Options dialog box

- **Hover grip color**  Determines the color a grip displays when the cursor hovers over the grip
- **Enable grips**  Displays grips on an object when it is selected
- **Enable grips within blocks**  Controls how grips are displayed on a block after you select it. If this option is selected, AutoCAD displays all grips for each object in the block. If this option is cleared, AutoCAD displays one grip located at the insertion point of the block
- **Enable grip tips**  Displays grip-specific tips when the cursor hovers over a grip on a custom object that supports grip tips. This option has no effect on standard AutoCAD objects
- **Object selection limit for display of grips**  Suppresses the display of grips when the initial selection set includes more than the specified number of objects. The valid range is 1 to 32,767. The default setting is 100.

| **FOR MORE DETAILS** | See Chapter 16 for more information about blocks. |
|---|---|

For the best results, make sure that your Grip settings closely match those shown in Figure 7-40. Failure to do so can cause some of the examples and exercises in the following sections to behave differently than anticipated.

## Selecting Grips

To select a grip, you must place your cursor within the grip box and pick with your mouse. When a grip is selected, it changes color (default=red), and you are placed in grid edit mode as shown in Figure 7-41.

It is possible to select multiple grips by holding down the **<Shift>** key before selecting the first grip. You can continue to select grips until you release the **<Shift>** key. In Figure 7-42, two grips have been selected.

**Figure 7-41**  One grip selected          **Figure 7-42**  Two grips selected

To "unselect" all grips that have been selected (default=red) as shown in Figure 7-41, press the **<Esc>** key once. This changes the grips to the unselected mode (default=blue) as shown in Figure 7-41. To turn off all the grips that are unselected (default=blue), you must press the **<Esc>** key again. This will result in the object(s) being simply highlighted (dashed) with no grips displayed.

TIP    You can remove objects from the selection set by holding down the **<Shift>** key and selecting the object you want to remove.

## Grip Modes

After at least one grip is selected (default = red) and you are in grip edit mode as shown in Figure 7-42, the desired grip mode can be selected either at the command line or via the right-click **Grip** shortcut menu.

The command line approach allows you to cycle through the five different grip modes starting with **Stretch** mode by pressing the space bar or the **<Enter ↵>** key as follows:

```
** STRETCH **
Specify stretch point or [Base point/Copy/Undo/eXit]:
** MOVE **
Specify move point or [Base point/Copy/Undo/eXit]:
** ROTATE **
Specify rotation angle or [Base point/Copy/Undo/Reference/eXit]:
** SCALE **
Specify scale factor or [Base point/Copy/Undo/Reference/eXit]:
** MIRROR **
Specify second point or [Base point/Copy/Undo/eXit]:
```

Each time you press the spacebar or **<Enter ↵>**, AutoCAD cycles to the next grip mode in the order shown above, repeating the modes again when it gets back to **Stretch** mode.

**TIP** You can also type keyboard shortcuts to go directly to the desired grip mode option at the command line. The shortcuts are **ST** for **Stretch**, **MO** for **Move**, **RO** for **Rotate**, **SC** for **Scale**, and **MI** for **Mirror**.

The other option is to right-click with your mouse to display the **Grip** shortcut menu shown in Figure 7-43.

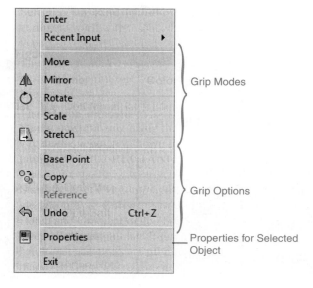

**Figure 7-43**    Grip shortcut menu

This approach allows you to go directly to the desired grip mode option without having to hit your spacebar or the **<Enter ↵>** key multiple times.

> **TIP** The **Grip** shortcut menu provides a quick way to edit the properties of the selected object using the **Properties** palette by selecting the **Properties** menu item.

Using either approach, the different grip modes work similarly to their traditional modify command counterparts explained earlier in the chapter and share most of the same options. Each grip mode shares the following options:

- **Base Point**  Allows you to specify a new base point to use with current grip mode. By default, the base point is set to the selected grip
- **Copy**  Allows you to create a copy of the selected object(s) to use with the current grip mode
- **Undo**  Undoes the last grip mode operation
- **Exit**  Exits the current grip mode and leaves grips on but unselected

In addition, the **Rotate** and **Scale** modes also have a **Reference** option that works exactly the same as described earlier in the **ROTATE** and **SCALE** modify command sections.

After selecting the desired grip mode either at the command line or via the **Grip** shortcut menu, the different grip mode options can be selected by either typing the first letter of the option at the command line, selecting the option from the right-click shortcut menu, or by using your arrow keys if you are using dynamic input.

*Stretch Mode.*  **Stretch** mode stretches the selected grip(s) while leaving unselected grips anchored in their current location. **Stretch** mode is the default mode. Figure 7-44 shows the corner point of a square being stretched using grips.

Remember that you can select multiple grip points by holding down the **<Shift>** key before selecting the first grip. Figure 7-45 shows two corner points being stretched using grips.

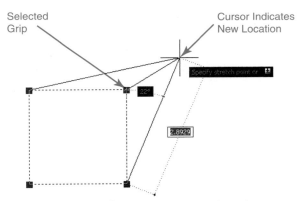

**Figure 7-44**  Stretching a corner point using grips

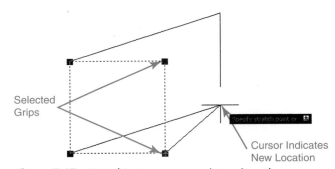

**Figure 7-45**  Stretching two corner points using grips

> **TIP** You can rely on any of the coordinate entry methods explained earlier to relocate grip points, including absolute coordinates (*X*,*Y*), relative coordinates (@*X*,*Y*), polar coordinates (@Distance<Angle), and even direct distance using the **Ortho Mode** and **Polar Tracking** drawing tools. It is also possible to tab between the different **Dimension Input** fields if **Dynamic Input** is on so that you can enter lengths and/or angles for any input field.

If you stretch a line using grips when **Dynamic Input** is on, the default dimension input field is a "delta," or change distance as shown in Figure 7-46.

Remember that you can switch between the different dimension input fields using the **<Tab>** key so that you can also enter the overall length dimension and/or the angle.

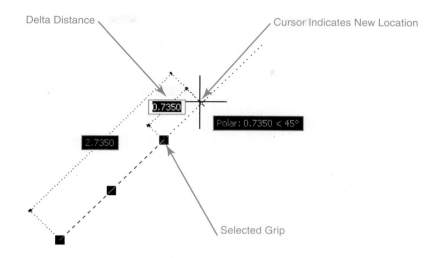

Delta Distance

Cursor Indicates New Location

0.7350

Polar: 0.7350 < 45°

2.7350

Selected Grip

**Figure 7-46**   Stretching a line segment using the delta dimension input field

**TIP**

You can change the angle and lock it in by tabbing to the angle input field, entering a new angle value, and tabbing back to the overall dimension or the delta distance dimension. Any distance you input will stretch the line using the locked-in angle.

## Exercise 7-16: Stretching Objects Using Grips

1. Start a new drawing using the acad.dwt drawing template.
2. Make sure that your **Grip** settings on the **Selection** tab of the **Options** dialog box match those shown in Figure 7-40.
3. Draw a 2″×2″ square similar to the one shown in Figure 7-44 using the **LINE** command.
4. Select all four lines by either selecting them with your mouse or by using implied windowing so that grips are displayed.
5. Select the grip at the upper right corner and stretch the objects as shown in Figure 7-44.
6. Press **<Esc>** to turn grips off.
7. Type **U<Enter ↵>** or select the **Undo** tool so that the square is returned to its original size.
8. Select all four lines again either by selecting them with your mouse or by using implied windowing so that the grips are displayed.
9. Select both grips on the right side of the square using the **<Shift>** key and stretch the objects as shown in Figure 7-45.
10. Press **<Esc>** to turn grips off.
11. Type **U<Enter ↵>** or select the **Undo** tool so that the square is returned to its original size.
12. Save the drawing as **EX7-16**.

*Move Mode.*   **Move** mode moves the selected objects a user-supplied distance and angle. By default, you can use the selected grip as the base point, or you can select a new base point via the **Base point** option introduced earlier. Figure 7-47 shows a square being moved using grips.

**TIP**

Picking a grip at a midpoint or a center point automatically puts you in **Move** mode.

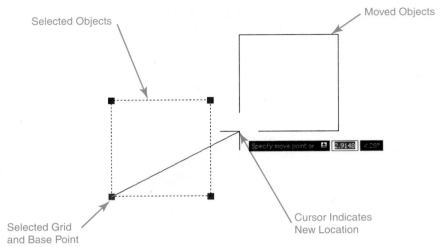

**Figure 7-47**    Moving objects using grips

You can move and copy the selected objects by using the **Copy** option introduced earlier. You can select the **Copy** option by typing **C<Enter ↵>**, selecting **Copy** from the right-click shortcut menu, or by using the arrow keys with **Dynamic Input** when AutoCAD prompts you to *Specify move point or ↓*. Figure 7-48 shows a square being copied using grips.

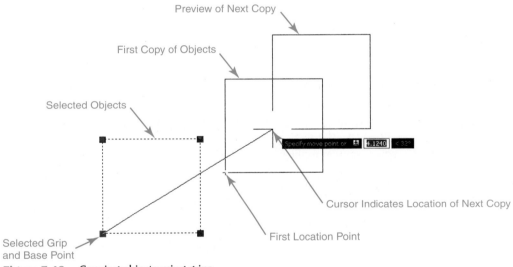

**Figure 7-48**    Copying objects using grips

## Exercise 7-17: Moving Objects Using Grips

1. Continue from Exercise 7-16.
2. Select all four lines either by using your mouse or by using implied windowing so that the grips are displayed.
3. Select the grip at the lower left corner as shown in Figure 7-47.
4. Select the **Move** grip mode by right-clicking and selecting **Move** from the **Grip** shortcut menu or by pressing the spacebar once.
5. Move the objects as shown in Figure 7-47.
6. Press **<Esc>** to turn grips off.
7. Type **U<Enter ↵>** or select the **Undo** tool so that the square is returned to its original location.
8. Select all four lines again by either selecting them with your mouse or by using implied windowing so that the grips are displayed.

9. Select the grip at the lower left corner as shown in Figure 7-48.
10. Select the **Move** grip mode by right-clicking and selecting **Move** from the **Grip** shortcut menu or by pressing the spacebar once.
11. Select the **Copy** option by right-clicking and selecting **Copy** from the **Grip** shortcut menu or by typing **C<Enter ↵>**.
12. Move and copy the objects multiple times as shown in Figure 7-48.
13. Press **<Esc>** to turn grips off.
14. Type **U<Enter ↵>** or select the **Undo** tool so that all copies of the square are undone.
15. Save the drawing as **EX7-17**.

*Rotate Mode.*     The **Rotate** mode rotates the selected objects a user-specified rotation angle around a user-specified base point. By default, you can use the selected grip as the base point, or you can select a new base point via the **Base point** option introduced earlier. Figure 7-49 shows a square being rotated using grips.

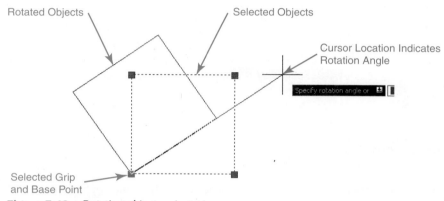

**Figure 7-49**     Rotating objects using grips

You can specify a reference, or start angle, by selecting the **Reference** option introduced earlier. The **Reference** option allows you to rotate object(s) by specifying a reference, or start angle, and then specifying a new, absolute angle to rotate to. You can select the **Reference** option by typing **R<Enter ↵>**, selecting **Reference** from the right-click shortcut menu, or by using the arrow keys with **Dynamic Input** when AutoCAD prompts you to *Specify rotation angle or ↓*.

You can rotate and copy the selected objects using the **Copy** option introduced earlier. You can select the **Copy** option by typing **C<Enter ↵>**, selecting **Copy** from the right-click shortcut menu, or by using the arrow keys with **Dynamic Input** when AutoCAD prompts you to *Specify rotation angle or ↓*.

You can rotate and copy multiple objects by entering successive angle measurements or by picking points with your mouse. Note that each angle is measured from the 0° base angle so that angle measurements must be cumulative. For example, to rotate and copy at 45° increments, you need to enter 45°, 90°, 135°, and so on.

**Exercise 7-18:** Rotating Objects Using Grips

1. Continue from Exercise 7-17.
2. Select all four lines by either selecting them with your mouse or by using implied windowing so that the grips are displayed.
3. Select the grip at the lower left corner as shown in Figure 7-49.

4. Select the **Rotate** grip mode by right-clicking and selecting **Rotate** from the **Grip** shortcut menu or by pressing the spacebar twice.
5. Rotate the objects as shown in Figure 7-49.
6. Press **<Esc>** to turn grips off.
7. Type **U<Enter ↵>** or select the **Undo** tool so that the square is rotated back to 0°.
8. Save the drawing as **EX7-18**.

*Scale Mode.*     The **Scale** mode scales the selected objects a user-specified scale factor using a user-specified base point. By default, you can use the selected grip as the base point, or you can select a new base point via the **Base point** option introduced earlier. Figure 7-50 shows a square being scaled using grips.

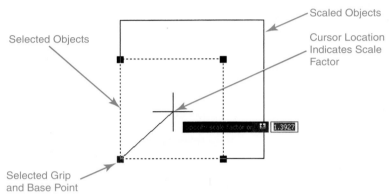

Scaled Objects

Selected Objects

Cursor Location Indicates Scale Factor

Selected Grip and Base Point

**Figure 7-50**     Scaling objects using grips

You can specify a reference, or start length, by selecting the **Reference** option introduced earlier. The **Reference** option allows you to scale object(s) by specifying a reference, or start length, and then specifying a new, absolute length to scale to. You can select the **Reference** option by typing **R<Enter ↵>**, selecting **Reference** from the right-click shortcut menu, or by using the arrow keys with dynamic input when AutoCAD prompts you to *Specify scale factor or ↓*.

**Exercise 7-19:** Scaling Objects Using Grips

1. Continue from Exercise 7-18.
2. Select all four lines by either selecting them with your mouse or by using implied windowing so that the grips are displayed.
3. Select the grip at the lower left corner as shown in Figure 7-50.
4. Select the **Scale** grip mode by right-clicking and selecting **Scale** from the **Grip** shortcut menu or by pressing the spacebar three times.
5. Scale the objects as shown in Figure 7-50.
6. Press **<Esc>** to turn grips off.
7. Type **U<Enter ↵>** or select the **Undo** tool so that the square is returned to its original size.
8. Save the drawing as **EX7-19**.

*Mirror Mode.*     The **Mirror** mode creates a mirror image of the selected objects about a mirror axis line defined by two user-supplied line endpoints. By default, you can use the selected grip as the first point of the mirror axis line, or you can select a different axis line location via the **Base point** option introduced earlier. Figure 7-51 shows a triangle being mirrored vertically by picking a point 90° above the base point in response to the *Specify second point or ↓* prompt.

TIP

Remember that you can use the **Ortho Mode** or the **Polar Tracking** drawing tool to create horizontal and vertical mirror axis lines quickly.

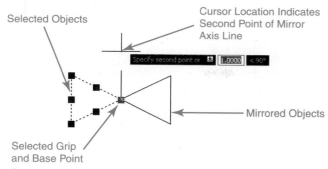

Selected Objects

Cursor Location Indicates
Second Point of Mirror
Axis Line

Specify second point or    1.0000   < 90°

Mirrored Objects

Selected Grip
and Base Point

**Figure 7-51**    Mirroring objects using grips

Unlike the **MIRROR** command explained earlier, when you use grips to mirror objects, the original objects are erased by default. To maintain the original objects, you must use the **Copy** option introduced earlier. You can select the **Copy** option by typing **C<Enter ↵>**, selecting **Copy** from the right-click shortcut menu, or by using the arrow keys with **Dynamic Input** when AutoCAD prompts you to *Specify second point or ↓*.

### Exercise 7-20: Mirroring Objects Using Grips

1. Start a new drawing using the acad.dwt drawing template.
2. Draw a triangle similar to the one shown in Figure 7-51.
3. Select all three lines by either selecting them with your mouse or by using implied windowing so that the grips are displayed.
4. Select the grip at the vertex of the triangle on the right as shown in Figure 7-51.
5. Select the **Mirror** grip mode by right-clicking and selecting **Mirror** from the **Grip** shortcut menu or by pressing the spacebar four times.
6. Turn on the **Ortho Mode** drawing tool if it is not already on.
7. Mirror the objects by picking a point 90° above the selected grip as shown in Figure 7-51.
8. Press **<Esc>** to turn grips off.
9. Type **U<Enter ↵>** or select the **Undo** tool so that the triangle is mirrored back to the original location and orientation.
10. Select all three lines again either by selecting them with your mouse or by using implied windowing so that the grips are displayed.
11. Select the grip at the vertex of the triangle on the right as shown in Figure 7-51.
12. Select the **Mirror** grip mode by right-clicking and selecting **Mirror** from the **Grip** shortcut menu or by pressing the spacebar once.
13. Select the **Copy** option by right-clicking and selecting **Copy** from the **Grip** shortcut menu or by typing **C<Enter ↵>**.
14. Mirror and copy the objects by picking a point 90° above the selected grip as shown in Figure 7-51.
15. Press **<Esc>** to turn grips off.
15. Save the drawing as **EX7-20**.

## SUMMARY

This chapter presents the basics of selecting and modifying objects in an AutoCAD drawing. The different object selection techniques explored in this chapter can be applied throughout the rest of the textbook. As you can see, there are many different ways to go about creating and modifying a selection set. Practice using, and even combining, the different selection and editing techniques and try to think "outside of the box." Sometimes you may want to pick objects first and then select a modify command; other times it makes sense to pick the command first and *then* the object(s) to modify. Find which approach to editing your drawings you are most comfortable with, but don't be afraid to experiment!

# CHAPTER TEST QUESTIONS

## Multiple Choice

1. Selecting objects first and then selecting a modify command is referred to as what type of editing process?
   a. Noun/verb
   b. Verb/noun
   c. Grip mode
   d. Cut and paste

2. A selection set is:
   a. Set of commands used to select objects
   b. All currently selected objects
   c. Group of similar objects
   d. None of the above

3. The box that appears at the mouse crosshairs when you are prompted to select objects is called:
   a. Grip
   b. Aperture
   c. Pickbox
   d. Window area

4. When you are creating a selection set, you can remove objects by:
   a. Typing **U<Enter ↵>**
   b. Holding down the **<Shift>** key while selecting objects
   c. Entering **Remove Objects** mode by typing **R<Enter ↵>**
   d. All of the above

5. The special keyboard key that allows you to select objects that are overlaid on top of each other when creating a selection set is:
   a. The **<Shift>** key
   b. The **<Esc>** key
   c. The **<Alt>** key
   d. The **<Ctrl>** key

6. The difference between the **Window** selection method and the **Crossing** selection method is:
   a. A **Window** boundary is a solid line, and a **Crossing** boundary is a dashed line.
   b. The **Window** method selects only objects inside the boundary, and the **Crossing** method selects objects inside *and* objects that cross the boundary.
   c. By default, the **Window** area preview is blue, and the **Crossing** area preview is green.
   d. All of the above

7. Implied windowing allows you to:
   a. Automatically create a **Window** or **Crossing** selection
   b. Turn off **Window** and **Crossing** selection options
   c. Pick one corner point to define a window and drag your mouse and release to create the other corner point
   d. Select objects with your mind

8. The selection set option that allows you to select the last object created in a drawing is:
   a. **Previous**
   b. **All**
   c. **Last**
   d. All of the above

9. The proper format for entering a displacement distance for the **MOVE**, **COPY**, and **STRETCH** command is:
   a. Absolute coordinates (ex. 2,2)
   b. Relative coordinates (ex. @2,2)
   c. Polar coordinates (ex. @2<45)
   d. All of the above

10. The system variable that controls whether text is reversed when it is mirrored is:
    a. **MIRRORTEXT**
    b. **MIRRTEXT**
    c. **TEXTMIRROR**
    d. **MTEXT**

11. The **ROTATE** command option that allows to you specify a start angle and then an absolute, new angle to rotate to is:
    a. **Base point**
    b. **Reference**
    c. **Copy**
    d. **Displacement**

12. The system variable that allows you to select objects first and *then* a modify command is:
    a. **FIRSTPICK**
    b. **PICKFIRST**
    c. **SELFIRST**
    d. **PICKAUTO**

13. To select multiple grips, you must hold down what key when picking the first grip?
    a. **<Ctrl>**
    b. **<Shift>**
    c. **<Esc>**
    d. Spacebar

14. Grip modes can be selected via:
    a. Command line
    b. Right-click shortcut menu
    c. Keyboard shortcuts
    d. All of the above

15. The keyboard key that turns off (deselects) grips is:
    a. **<Ctrl>**
    b. **<Enter ↵>**
    c. **<Esc>**
    d. **<Alt>**

## Matching

| Column A | Column B |
|---|---|
| a. **ERASE** command | 1. Automated **Window** and **Crossing** selection option |
| b. Selection set | 2. Moves objects a user-supplied distance and angle |
| c. Implied window | 3. Creates a mirror image of objects about a mirror axis line |
| d. Grips | 4. Small squares that appear when an object is selected |
| e. **MOVE** command | 5. Removes objects from a drawing |
| f. **COPY** command | 6. Rotates objects a user-specified rotation angle around a user-specified base point |
| g. **MIRROR** command | 7. Moves or stretches objects a user-supplied distance and angle |
| h. **ROTATE** command | 8. Scales objects a user-specified scale factor about a user-specified base point |
| i. **SCALE** command | 9. Copies objects a user-supplied distance and angle |
| j. **STRETCH** command | 10. Group of one or more objects selected in a drawing |

## True or False

1. True or False: The traditional approach to modifying objects in AutoCAD is to select the command first and then select the objects to modify.

2. True or False: The traditional approach to modifying mentioned in Question 1 is referred to as the *noun/verb approach*.

3. True or False: Once you erase something, you can never get it back.

4. True or False: Holding down the **<Shift>** key allows you to select overlapping objects.

5. True or False: It is possible to remove objects from a selection set using three different methods.

6. True or False: The **Window** and **Crossing** selection options can be initiated automatically.

7. True or False: It is possible to create a **Window** or **Crossing** selection using only one pick point.

8. True or False: The **Previous** selection option will select the previous object that was added to a drawing.

9. True or False: The displacement distance for the **MOVE**, **COPY**, and **STRETCH** commands is always relative.

10. True or False: Text is always mirrored when you use the **MIRROR** command.

11. True or False: It is possible to enter a negative rotation angle when using the **ROTATE** command.

12. True or False: Picking a grip at a midpoint or a center point automatically puts you in **Move** mode.

## CHAPTER PROJECTS

### Project 7-1: Classroom Plan—Continued from Chapter 6

1. Open drawing **P6-1**.
2. Draw the floor plan shown in Figure P7-1 using the **A-Door** and **A-Wall** layers for the doors and walls. Place the heater on the **A-Eqpm** layer. The wall next to the heater is 8″ thick; all other walls are 4″ thick. The doors are each 3′-0″ wide and the heater is 1′-0″ wide. **Do not** draw dimensions or text.
3. Use the **MOVE, COPY,** and **MIRROR** commands to place the desks in the configuration shown. Use object snaps and the **Polar Tracking** and/or **Ortho Mode** settings to ensure the desks are aligned.
4. Save the drawing as **P7-1**.

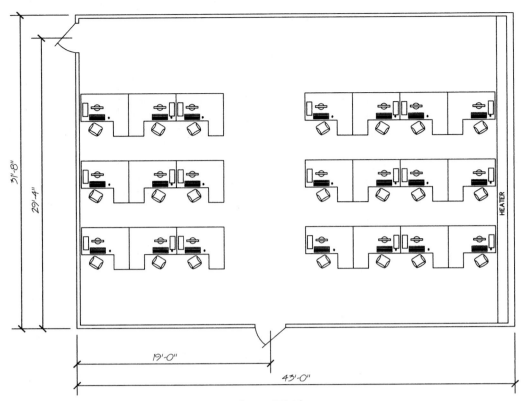

Figure P7-1

## Project 7-2: Motorcycle—Continued from Chapter 6

1. Open drawing **P6-2**.
2. Copy the wheel drawn in P6-2 as shown in Figure P7-2 so it can be used as the front wheel.
3. Draw the motorcycle frame geometry on the **Frame** layer.
4. Draw the front forks on the **Forks** layer.
5. Draw all the engine parts on the **Engine** layer. *Hint:* Draw one engine cylinder first and then mirror it using the **MIRROR** command.
6. Draw the headlight on the **Headlight** layer.
7. Draw the handlebars on the **Handlebar** layer.
8. **Do not** trim or break any line work at this time.
9. Save the drawing as **P7-2**.

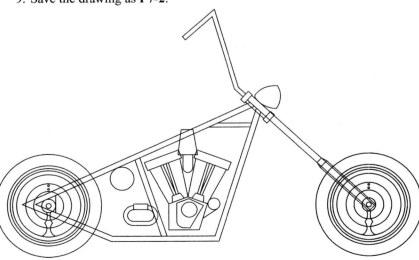

Figure P7-2

## Project 7-3: C-Size Mechanical Border

1. Start a new drawing using the acad.dwt template.
2. Set the **LIMITS** for a 22.0×17.0 drawing area.
3. Create the following layers:

| Name | Color | Linetype | Lineweight | Plot/Noplot | Description |
|------|-------|----------|------------|-------------|-------------|
| Title | 7 | Continuous | Default | Plot | Title border and text |
| Logo | 7 | Continuous | Default | Plot | Logo |
| Notes | 7 | Continuous | Default | Plot | Notes |
| Viewport | 9 | Continuous | Default | Noplot | Viewports |

4. Draw the C-size title block as shown in Figure P7-3. Use the **Title** layer for all geometry. Use appropriate **Grid**, **Snap** and, **Object Snap** settings. **Do not** draw dimensions.
5. Save the drawing to a template file as **Mechanical C-Size.DWT**.

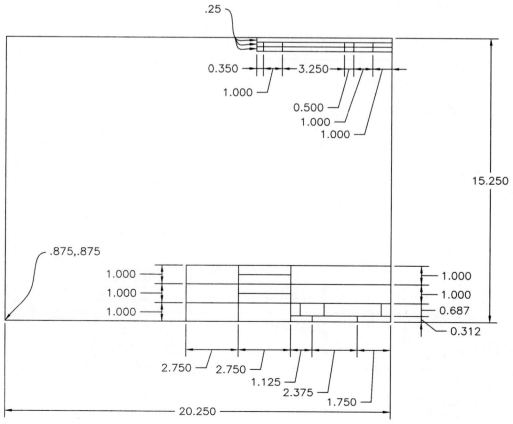

**Figure P7-3**

## Project 7-4: Architectural B-Size Border (17 × 11)

1. Start a new drawing using the acad.dwt template.
2. Set linear **UNITS** to **Architectural** with precision set to **1/16″**.
3. Set angular **UNITS** to **Deg/Min/Sec** with precision set to **0d00′00″**.
4. Set the drawing LIMITS to 17″ × 11″ for a B-size drawing.
5. Create the following layers:

| Name | Color | Linetype | Lineweight | Plot/Noplot | Description |
| --- | --- | --- | --- | --- | --- |
| A-Anno-Ttlb | 7 | Continuous | Default | Plot | Title block/ border lines |
| A-Anno-Ttlb-Text | 1 | Continuous | Default | Plot | Title block text |
| A-Anno-Ttlb-Logo | 3 | Continuous | Default | Plot | Logo |
| A-Anno-Vprt | 7 | Continuous | Default | No Plot | Viewport lines |

6. Draw the border as shown in Figure P7-4 on layer **A-Anno-Ttlb**. **Do not** include dimensions.
7. Zoom to the drawing extents.
8. Save the drawing to a template file as **Architectural B-Size.DWT**.

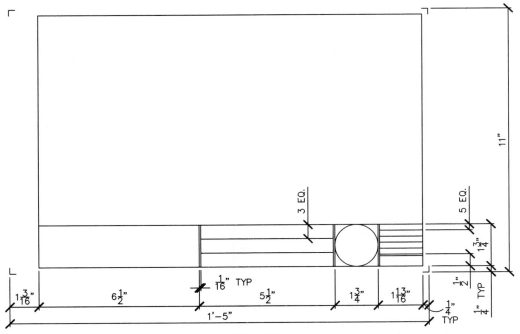

Figure P7-4

## Project 7-5: Electrical Distribution Panel

1. Start a new drawing using the acad.dwt template.
2. Create the following layer:

| Name | Color | Linetype | Lineweight | Plot/Noplot | Description |
|------|-------|----------|------------|-------------|-------------|
| E-Powr-Panl | 7 | Continuous | Default | Plot | Electrical power panels |

Figure P7-5

3. Set the **GRID** to **.5** and the **SNAP** to **.25** and draw the electrical distribution panel shown in Figure P7-5. **Do not draw text or dimensions.** *Hint:* The gridlines shown are spaced at .5 intervals.
4. Save the drawing as **P7-5**.

## Project 7-6: Compressed Air Schematic

1. Start a new drawing using the acad.dwt template.
2. Set the **GRID** and **SNAP** drawing tools to 0.125.
3. Create the following layers:

| Name | Color | Linetype | Lineweight | Description |
|------|-------|----------|------------|-------------|
| P-Detl-P1 | 7 | Continuous | Default | Plumbing details and schematics |
| P-Detl-Hidden | 1 | Hidden | Default | Hidden lines |
| P-Anno-Note | 7 | Continuous | Default | Note text |
| P-Anno-Title | 7 | Continuous | Default | Title text |

4. Draw the piping schematic lines, symbols, air tanks, and air compressor as shown in Figure P7-6 on layer **P-Detl-P1**. *Hint:* Use the **COPY**, **ROTATE**, and **MIRROR** commands to your advantage so similar symbols need to be drawn only once.
5. Save the drawing as **P7-6**.

## Project 7-7: Residential Architectural Plan—Continued from Chapter 6

1. Open drawing **P6-7** from Chapter 6.
2. Draw the door and window symbols shown in Figure P7-7A using the **A-Door** and **A-Glaz** layers.

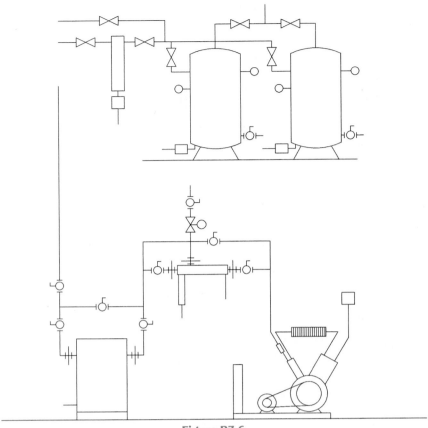

**Figure P7-6**

| WINDOW SCHEDULE | | | |
|---|---|---|---|
| SYM. | SIZE | TYPE | QTY. |
| A | 3'-0" X 3'-6" | S.H. | 10 |
| B | 2'-0" X 3'-6" | S.H./FROSTED | 1 |
| C | 2'-0" X 3'-0" | S.H. | 4 |
| D | 3'-0" X 3'-0" | PCT. | 2 |
| E | 5'-0" X 5'-0" | TEMP. PCT. | 3 |
| F | 1'-0" X 3'-0" | S.H. | 2 |
| G | 2'-0" X 6'-0" | GLASS SKY. | 2 |

| DOOR SCHEDULE | | | |
|---|---|---|---|
| SYM. | SIZE | TYPE | QTY. |
| 1 | 3'-0" X 6'-8" | M.I./R.P. | 1 |
| 2 | 2'-8" X 6'-8" | M.I./S.C. | 2 |
| 3 | 2'-8" X 6'-8" | H.C. | 8 |
| 4 | 2'-6" X 6'-8" | POCKET/H.C. | 2 |
| 5 | 2'-6" X 6'-8" | H.C./BI-FOLD | 2 |
| 6 | 6'-0" X 6'-8" | TEMP. SLIDER | 2 |
| 7 | 8'-0" X 6'-8" | GARAGE | 2 |

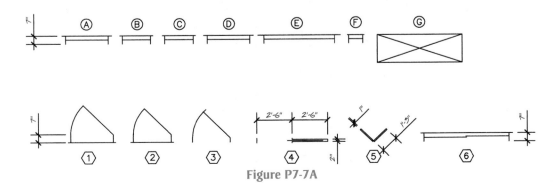

**Figure P7-7A**

3. Add the walls and place the doors and windows as shown in Figure P7-7B according to the schedules. Use appropriate **Object Snaps** to ensure the proper placement of the symbols. Doors and windows that are not dimensioned are either centered on the interior wall or located 3″ from the nearest wall. *Hint:* Use the **Offset** option of the **XLINE** command to locate the door and window symbols.

4. **Do not** draw the door schedule or identifier symbols. **Do not** draw dimensions or text.

5. Save the drawing as **P7-7**.

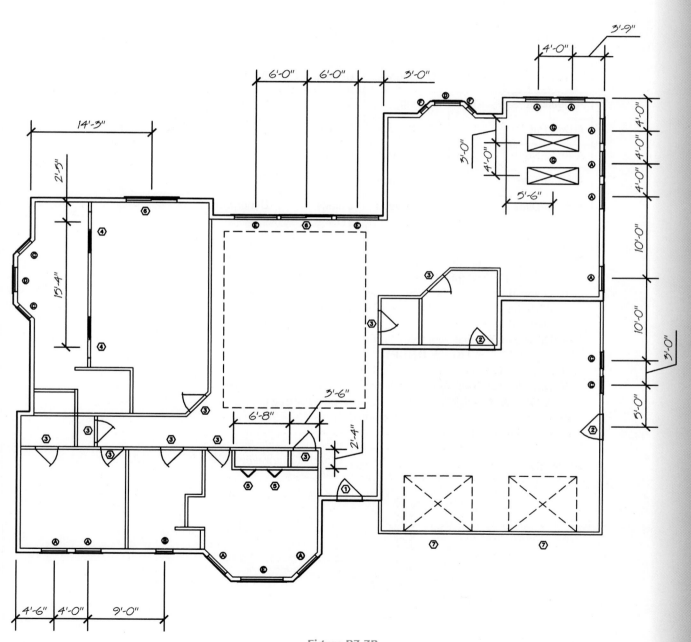

Figure P7-7B

## Project 7-8: Interior Floor Change Detail

1. Start a new drawing using the acad.dwt template.
2. Set linear **UNITS** to **Architectural** with precision set to **1/16″**.
3. Set angular **UNITS** to **Deg/Min/Sec** with precision set to **0d00′00″**.
4. Create the following layers:

| Name | Color | Linetype | Lineweight | Description |
|------|-------|----------|------------|-------------|
| A-Detl-Mbnd | 1 | Continuous | Default | Detail lines that represent material in the background |
| A-Detl-Mcut | 3 | Continuous | 0.35 mm | Detail lines that represent material cut in section |
| A-Detl-P1 | 2 | Continuous | Default | Secondary (light) lines |
| A-Detl-Batt | 1 | Batting | Default | Batt insulation |
| A-Detl-Pat | 1 | Continuous | Default | Hatch patterns and fills |
| A-Anno-Note | 3 | Continuous | Default | Note text |
| A-Anno-Title | 3 | Continuous | Default | Title text |
| A-Anno-Dims | 1 | Continuous | Default | Dimensions |

5. Draw all line work that appears beyond the section cut as shown in Figure P7-8 on layer **A-Detl-Mbnd** (vertical wall lines, horizontal joist lines, 4 × 4 posts).
6. Draw all line work that is cut by the section as shown in Figure P7-8 on layer **A-Detl-Mcut** (footers, lumber in section, plywood/gyp. board).
7. Draw the X's that represent lumber in section as shown in Figure P7-8 on layer **A-Detl-P1**.
8. Set the **LTSCALE** system variable to 6.
9. Draw the batt insulation lines shown in Figure P7-8 on the layer **A-Detl-Batt**, which should be set up to use the **Batting** linetype.
10. Do not include notes or dimensions.
11. Save the drawing as **P7-8**.

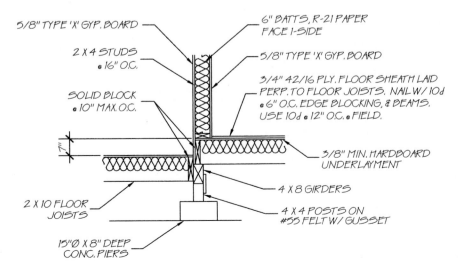

5/8″ TYPE 'X' GYP. BOARD

2 X 4 STUDS @ 16″ O.C.

SOLID BLOCK @ 10″ MAX. O.C.

2 X 10 FLOOR JOISTS

15″Ø X 8″ DEEP CONC. PIERS

6″ BATTS, R-21 PAPER FACE 1-SIDE

5/8″ TYPE 'X' GYP. BOARD

3/4″ 42/16 PLY. FLOOR SHEATH LAID PERP. TO FLOOR JOISTS. NAIL W/ 10d @ 6″ O.C. EDGE BLOCKING, & BEAMS. USE 10d @ 12″ O.C. @ FIELD.

3/8″ MIN. HARDBOARD UNDERLAYMENT

4 X 8 GIRDERS

4 X 4 POSTS ON #55 FELT W/ GUSSET

Figure P7-8

## Project 7-9: Hex Head Cap Screws—English Units

1. Start a new drawing using the acad.dwt template.
2. Create the two socket head cap screws described in the table shown in Figure P7-9. **Do not** draw dimensions or table.
3. Save the drawing as **P7-9**.

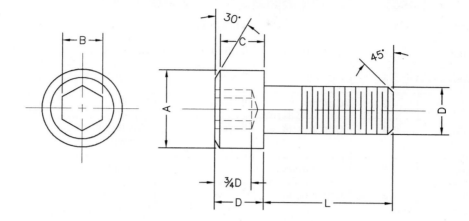

| Socket Head Cap Screw | | | | | |
|---|---|---|---|---|---|
| Nominal Size (D) | Thread/In | A | B | C | L |
| 10 (.190) | 24 | .312 | 5/32 | .171 | .500 |
| ¼ (.250) | 20 | .375 | 3/16 | .225 | .750 |

**Figure P7-9**

## Project 7-10: Motorcycle Head Gasket—Metric

1. Start a new drawing using the acadiso.dwt template.
2. Create the following layers:

| Name | Color | Linetype | Lineweight | Description |
|------|-------|----------|------------|-------------|
| Object | 7 | Continuous | 0.35 mm | Object lines |
| Hidden | 1 | Hidden | Default | Hidden lines |
| Center | 2 | Center | Default | Centerlines |
| Hatch | 4 | Continuous | Default | Hatch patterns and fills |
| Notes | 3 | Continuous | Default | Text and notes |
| Dims | 2 | Continuous | Default | Dimensions |

3. Draw object lines as shown in Figure P7-10 on layer **Object**.
4. Draw hidden lines as shown in Figure P7-10 on layer **Hidden**.
5. Draw centerlines as shown in Figure P7-10 on layer **Center**.
6. Adjust the **LTSCALE** system so linetypes appear properly.
7. **Do not** include dimensions.
8. Save the drawing as **P7-10**.

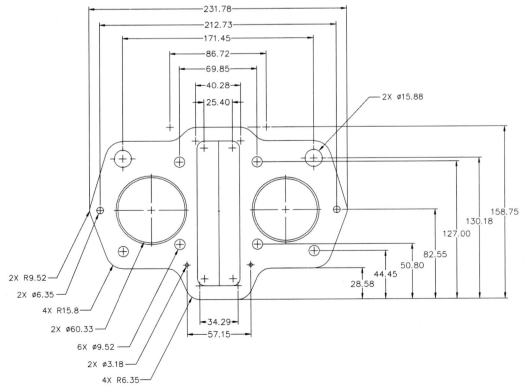

**Figure P7-10**

## Project 7-11: Civil Site Plan—Continued from Chapter 6

1. Open drawing **P6-11** from Chapter 6.
2. Move the house forward 5′. Add the swimming pool and shed shown in Figure P7-11.

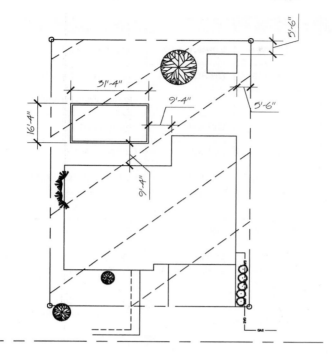

Figure P7-11

3. Use the **MOVE** and **COPY** commands to place the landscaping as shown.
4. Save the drawing as **P7-11**.

## Project 7-12: Manhole Cover

1. Start a new drawing using the acad.dwt template.
2. Set linear **UNITS** to **Architectural** with precision set to **1/16″**.
3. Create the following layers:

| Name | Color | Linetype | Lineweight | Description |
|------|-------|----------|------------|-------------|
| C-Detl-P1 | 1 | Continuous | Default | Secondary lines (thin) |
| C-Detl-P2 | 3 | Continuous | 0.35 mm | Object lines (thick) |
| C-Detl-Hidden | 1 | Hidden | Default | Hidden lines |
| C-Detl-Center | 1 | Center | Default | Center lines |
| C-Detl-Pat | 1 | Continuous | Default | Hatch patterns and fills |
| C-Anno-Dims | 1 | Continuous | Default | Dimensions |
| C-Anno-Note | 3 | Continuous | Default | Note text |
| C-Anno-Title | 3 | Continuous | Default | Title text |

4. Draw all line work for the top view shown in Figure P7-12 on layer **C-Detl-P1**.
5. Draw all line work for the section view shown in Figure P7-12 on layer **C-Detl-P2**.
6. Draw all centerlines shown in Figure P7-12 on layer **C-Detl-Center**.
7. **Do not** include notes or dimensions.
8. Save the drawing as **P7-12**.

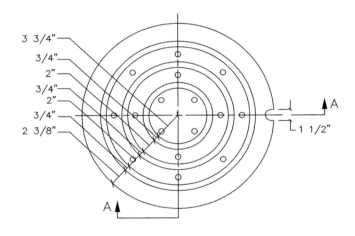

TOP VIEW

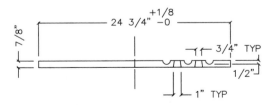

SECTION A–A

**Figure P7-12**

# Advanced Editing Techniques

# 8

## Chapter Objectives

- Offset objects through a specified distance
- Create rectangular and polar arrays
- Trim and extend objects
- Use the **FILLET** and **CHAMFER** commands to modify intersecting objects
- Break single objects into multiple objects
- Join separate objects into a single object
- Use the **LENGTHEN** command to modify the length of an object

## INTRODUCTION

As you've seen, there is usually more than one way to accomplish a given task in AutoCAD. For example, to create multiple line segments, you could simply draw multiple lines using the **LINE** command, or you could create a single line segment and copy it using grips or the **COPY** command. There are multiple ways to create arcs and circles as well as different methods for creating layers and changing object properties.

In Chapter 7, you used basic editing commands such as **MOVE**, **COPY**, and **ROTATE** to modify objects. In this chapter, you'll examine some editing tools that provide additional functionality.

**offset:** To create a parallel copy of an object

## OFFSETTING OBJECTS

To *offset* an object is to make a copy of an object parallel to the original. This is similar to the **COPY** command but allows you to make parallel copies at a specified distance from the original. This can be used to make concentric arcs and circles as well as parallel lines (such as roads, walls, etc.). Offsetting is done with the **OFFSET** command.

The **OFFSET** command works by copying an object a specified distance away from the original or source object. When using the **OFFSET** command, you specify a distance, select an object to offset, and tell AutoCAD on which side of the original object you want to place the new object. To provide the offset distance, you can either specify the distance or pick a point that the new object will pass through. The **OFFSET** command has three options: **Through**, **Erase**, and **Layer**.

| Offset | |
|---|---|
| **Ribbon & Panel:** | Homel Modify |
| **Modify Toolbar:** | |
| **Menu:** | Modifyl Offset |
| **Command Line:** | OFFSET |
| **Command Alias:** | O |

| Through | Allows you to pick a point that the new object will pass through. AutoCAD measures the distance from the point to the source object. |
| --- | --- |
| Erase | Controls whether the source object is kept or deleted after the offset is complete. You can answer **Yes** (erase the source object) or **No** (keep the source object). |
| Layer | Allows you to control the layer of the new object. You can choose to have the new object take on the current layer setting or retain the layer setting of the source object. |

### Offsetting an Object a Specified Distance

Specifying a distance is the default method and the most commonly used. When specifying a distance, you can simply type in the distance or pick two points. If you pick two points, AutoCAD will measure the distance between the two points and use that as the offset distance.

TIP    Whenever AutoCAD asks you to provide a numeric value such as a length or distance, you can usually pick two points and have AutoCAD measure the distance.

### Offsetting Through a Point

It is also possible to offset objects through a point that you pick in the drawing using the **Through** option. Typically, this is done in conjunction with Object Snaps so that you can snap to specific key features in your drawing. The easiest way to specify the **Through** options is to press <**Enter** ↵> when AutoCAD prompts you to *Select object to offset or ↓*.

### Offset Options

By default, the **OFFSET** command will copy the selected object on the same layer as the original, or source, object. The **Layer** option allows you to offset an object on the current layer. The **Erase** option allows you to erase the original object. The current settings are displayed in the Command window each time you select the **OFFSET** command.

TIP    The **OFFSET** command continues to prompt you to *Select object to offset or ↓* until you press <**Enter** ↵> so that is possible to offset multiple objects without exiting the command. Even better, after you select an object to offset, the **Multiple** option is available so that you can make multiple copies the same distance apart by continuing to click with your mouse.

### Exercise 8-1: Offsetting Objects

1. Start a new drawing using the acad.dwt drawing template.
2. Create two layers with the following settings:
   **C-ROAD**, Continuous, Color 7 (White)
   **C-ROAD-CNTR**, Center, Color 5 (Blue)
   Set layer **C-ROAD-CNTR** as the current layer.
3. Set the **LTSCALE** system variable to 12.
4. Draw a line from the coordinates 100,100 to 100,250. Zoom out until the line is somewhat centered in the screen.
5. Set the **C-ROAD** layer current and draw a circle centered at 100,250 with a radius of 35.

6. Start the **OFFSET** command. AutoCAD prompts you to *Specify offset distance or ↓*.

7. Press **<Enter ↵>** to select the **Through** option. AutoCAD prompts you to *Select object to offset or ↓*.

8. Select the centerline. AutoCAD prompts you to *Specify point on side to offset or ↓*.

9. Type **QUA<Enter ↵>** to activate the **Quadrant** Object Snap.

10. Move your cursor to the right side quadrant point on the circle and pick a point when the **Quadrant** Object Snap AutoSnap Marker is displayed. The centerline is offset through the circle quadrant point on the same layer and linetype as the original centerline.

11. Type **U<Enter ↵>** to undo the offset line and press **<Enter ↵>** to exit the **OFFSET** command.

12. Press **<Enter ↵>** to run the **OFFSET** command again. AutoCAD prompts you to *Select object to offset or ↓*.

13. Choose the **Layer** option and choose **Current**. The new objects will be placed on the current drawing layer. AutoCAD again prompts you to *Specify offset distance or ↓*.

14. Type **25<Enter ↵>** to set the offset distance. AutoCAD prompts you to *Select object to offset or ↓*.

15. Select the centerline. AutoCAD prompts you to *Specify point on side to offset or ↓*. Pick anywhere off to the left of the centerline. AutoCAD will create a new line 25 units to the left of the centerline. AutoCAD again prompts you to *Select object to offset or ↓*.

16. Select the centerline again and pick anywhere off to the right of the line. AutoCAD places a new line 25 units to the right of the original. Both of the new lines are on the current layer (**C-ROAD**).

17. Press **<Enter ↵>** or **<Esc>** to exit the **OFFSET** command.

18. Save your drawing as **EX8-1**. Your drawing should resemble Figure 8-1.

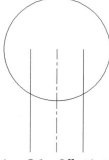

**Figure 8-1**  Offsetting objects

## ARRAYING OBJECTS

An *array* of objects is multiple objects copied in a regular pattern. In AutoCAD there are two types of arrays: rectangular and polar. A rectangular array is a pattern of rows and columns at predefined distances. A polar array is a circular pattern of objects copied around a center point. Arrays are created with the **ARRAY** command. The **ARRAY** command displays the **Array** dialog box (see Figure 8-2).

*array:* A circular or rectangular pattern of objects

| Array | |
|---|---|
| **Ribbon & Panel:** | Homel Modify |
| **Modify Toolbar:** | |
| **Menu:** | Modifyl Array... |
| **Command Line:** | ARRAY |
| **Command Alias:** | AR |

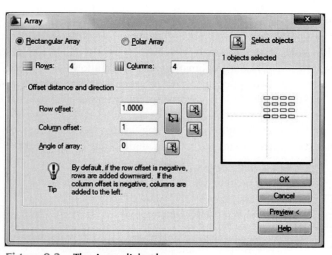

**Figure 8-2**   The Array dialog box

The **Array** dialog box is divided into two sections. The left side allows you to choose either a rectangular or polar array and allows you to control the settings for each type of array. The right-hand side allows you to select objects and displays a preview of what the array will look like.

## Creating a Rectangular Array

To create a rectangular array, choose the **Rectangular Array** button at the top of the **Array** dialog box (see Figure 8-2). A rectangular array consists of rows and columns, a distance between the rows and columns, and a rotation angle. The **Rows** and **Columns** controls allow you to specify the number of rows and columns. As you change the number of rows and columns, the preview image will update.

*Selecting Objects to Array.*   The **Select objects** button will temporarily hide the **Array** dialog box and allow you to select the objects you wish to array. You can select objects using any of the normal object selection methods.

| FOR MORE DETAILS | See Chapter 7 for more on building selections sets. |
|---|---|

*Specifying Distance Between Rows and Columns.*   The **Row offset** controls the distance between the rows (the vertical pitch of the objects). A positive offset distance will create rows in the positive $Y$ direction (up). A negative offset distance creates rows in the negative $Y$ direction (down). The **Column offset** controls the distance between the columns (the horizontal pitch of the objects). A positive offset distance creates columns to the right (positive $X$ direction). A negative value creates columns to the left (negative $X$ direction). (See Figure 8-3.)

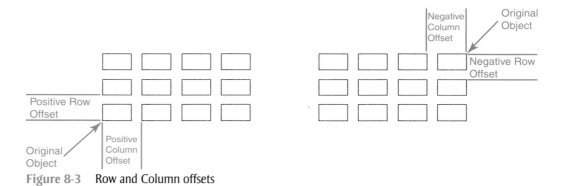

**Figure 8-3**   Row and Column offsets

You can specify the row and column offsets independently either by typing the values into the boxes or by choosing the cursor buttons. There is also a combination button that allows you to pick both the row and column offsets by specifying two opposite corners of a rectangle. The length ($X$) of the rectangle is the column offset and the width ($Y$) is the row offset (see Figure 8-4).

*Arraying at an Angle.*   You can control the overall angle of the rectangular array (see Figure 8-5) by changing the **Angle of array**. This setting determines the rotation angle of the first row of the

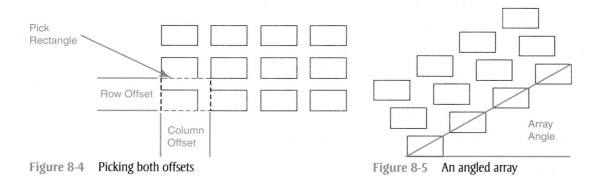

**Figure 8-4**   Picking both offsets

**Figure 8-5**   An angled array

array. You can either specify an angle or choose the cursor button to pick points in your drawing. When you choose the cursor button, you are asked to specify two points. AutoCAD will measure the angle of the line between these two points and use it for the angular measurement. By default, the angle is measured from 0 degrees (Figure 8-5).

**TIP**   Like distance measurements, whenever AutoCAD requires you to provide an angular measurement, you can typically either type in the angular value or pick points to have AutoCAD measure the angle for you.

*Previewing the Array.*   As you change each of these values, the preview image will update to show you a representation of what the final array will look like. The preview image uses boxes to represent your actual objects. To see what your final array will look like, choose the **Preview** button. AutoCAD will temporarily hide the **Array** dialog box and show you a preview of what the actual array will look like using the objects you selected. The **Preview** button will only be available after you've selected objects. Press **<Esc>** or pick anywhere on the screen to end the preview and return to the dialog box.

**Exercise 8-2:** Creating a Rectangular Array

1. Start a new drawing using the acad.dwt drawing template.
2. Use the **LINE** command to draw the geometry shown in Figure 8-6.
3. Start the **ARRAY** command. AutoCAD displays the **Array** dialog box.
4. Select **Rectangular Array** and then choose the **Select objects** button. AutoCAD hides the dialog box and prompts you to *Select objects*. Select the circle and press **<Enter ↵>** to return to the **Array** dialog box.
5. Set the **Rows** to 3 and **Columns** to 3. Set the **Row offset** to **5.25** and the **Column offset** to **3.25**.
6. Choose the **Preview** button. AutoCAD will show you a preview of the array.
7. Right-click anywhere to accept the array and end the command.
8. Use the **ERASE** command to delete the hole in the center of the part.
9. Save your drawing as **EX8-2**. Your drawing should look like Figure 8-7.

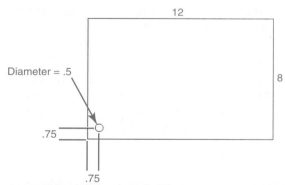

**Figure 8-6**   A rectangle and circle

**Figure 8-7**   A rectangular array

## Creating a Polar Array

To create a polar array, choose the **Polar Array** button at the top of the **Array** dialog box (see Figure 8-8). When creating a polar array, AutoCAD will copy objects in a circular pattern. You must specify the center point of that circle, as well as the number of items you want to create and the angle between the objects.

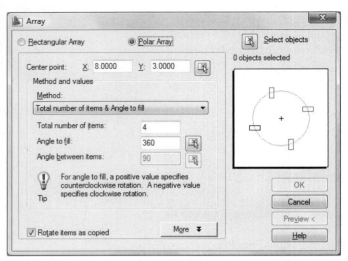

Figure 8-8     The Polar Array settings

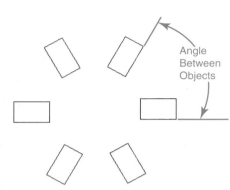

Figure 8-9     Polar Array methods

*Specifying Center Point of Polar Array.*     To specify the **Center point**, you can either type the **X** and **Y** values into the boxes or pick the cursor button to temporarily hide the dialog box and select the center point in the drawing.

*Choosing a Polar Array Method.*     AutoCAD can determine the total number of objects using one of three methods. AutoCAD is looking for three values: the total number of items to create, the total angle to fill with the polar array, and the angle between each item in the array (see Figure 8-9). You can specify any two of those values, and AutoCAD will calculate the third. The **Method** drop-down list allows you to choose which two values you are going to provide.

   ***Total Number of Items and Angle to Fill.***     Using this method, AutoCAD will take the **Angle to fill** value, divide it by the **Total number of items**, and calculate the angle between each of the items. When you select this method, the **Total number of items** box and the **Angle to fill** box are enabled, and the **Angle between items** box is disabled. To specify the **Angle to fill**, you can either type in a value or choose the cursor button to temporarily hide the dialog box and pick the angle from the drawing.

   ***Total Number of Items and Angle Between Items.***     Using this method, AutoCAD will take the **Total number of items** and multiply it by the **Angle between items** to calculate the **Total angle to fill**. When you select this method, the **Angle to fill** box is disabled. As before, you can either type in an angle or choose the cursor button to specify an angle within the drawing.

   ***Angle to Fill and Angle Between Items.***     Using this method, you provide both the angle to fill and the angle between items, and AutoCAD will calculate the total number of items to create. When you choose this method, the **Total number of items** box is disabled.

**TIP**     When specifying either the angle to fill or the angle between items, a positive value will copy items in a counterclockwise direction, and a negative value will copy items in a clockwise direction.

*Rotating Objects as They Are Arrayed.*     At the bottom of the **Polar Array** settings is a check box that allows you to control whether individual objects are rotated as they are arrayed. Removing the check from this box will keep objects at their original angle, and placing a check in this box will rotate each item around its base point as it is arrayed around the circle.

Selecting the **More** button will display additional options for controlling how various objects are rotated as they are arrayed. By default, objects are rotated based on the type of object they are. Linear objects (lines, polylines, rays, etc.) are rotated about their start point. Circles, arcs, and ellipses are rotated about their center points. Blocks and text are rotated about their insertion point, and construction lines are rotated about their midpoint. You can override these defaults by removing the check from the **Set to objects default** box, and specifying a rotation base point.

> **Note:**
> If you are unsure of the effect of any of these settings, the best approach is to simply modify the settings and keep an eye on the preview image.

### Exercise 8-3: Creating a Polar Array

1. Start a new drawing using the acad.dwt drawing template.
2. Use the **LINE** command to draw the geometry shown in Figure 8-10.
3. Start the **ARRAY** command. AutoCAD displays the **Array** dialog box.
4. Select **Polar Array** and then choose the **Select objects** button. AutoCAD hides the dialog box and prompts you to *Select objects:*. Select the two angled lines and press **<Enter ↵>** to return to the **Array** dialog box.
5. Choose the **Center point** button and select the bottom endpoint of the middle line for the center of the array.
6. In the **Method** pull-down list, choose **Total number of items and Angle to fill**. Set the **Total number of items** to **16** and the **Angle to fill** to **360**.
7. Choose the **Preview** button. AutoCAD will show you a preview of the array. Right-click anywhere to accept the array and end the command.
8. Save your drawing as **EX8-3**. Your drawing should look like Figure 8-11.

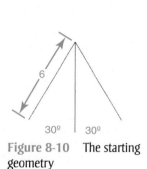

**Figure 8-10**   The starting geometry

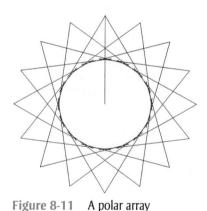

**Figure 8-11**   A polar array

## TRIMMING AND EXTENDING OBJECTS

Trimming and extending is the process of lengthening or shortening objects using AutoCAD objects as the boundaries. When you trim or extend, you use existing AutoCAD objects as the boundary edges, and AutoCAD either lengthens or shortens your objects to touch those edges.

### Trimming Objects

Objects are trimmed using the **TRIM** command. When you start the **TRIM** command, AutoCAD prompts you to select your cutting edges. These cutting edges determine the stopping boundaries of the trimmed objects. Select the cutting edges using AutoCAD's standard selection methods. Once you've selected the cutting edges, press **<Enter ↵>**, and AutoCAD will prompt you to

| Trim | |
|---|---|
| **Ribbon & Panel:** | Homel Modify |
| **Modify Toolbar:** | |
| **Menu:** | Modifyl Trim |
| **Command Line:** | TRIM |
| **Command Alias:** | TR |

select the object to trim. As you pick each object, AutoCAD will trim the object back to the cutting edge. The portion of the object you select is the part that is deleted. In order for an object to be trimmed, it must cross one of the cutting edges. If AutoCAD cannot detect an intersection between the cutting edges and the object to be trimmed, it displays a message: OBJECT DOES NOT INTERSECT AN EDGE.

*Selecting Cutting Edges.*    In some cases, the cutting edges and the objects to be trimmed may be the same objects. AutoCAD does not distinguish between the cutting edges and the objects to be trimmed. You can select a cutting edge as an object to be trimmed.

> **TIP** Sometimes determining the cutting edges can be a difficult task. If there's ever any doubt if an object should be chosen as a cutting edge, your best bet is to go ahead and select it. If you select an extra cutting edge, you may end up "nibbling away" at the object, but that is better than having to start over and reselect cutting edges.

AutoCAD will allow you to select all the drawing objects as cutting edges. To do this, simply press <**Enter ↵**> when prompted to select the cutting edges. When you do this, AutoCAD will use all the objects in the drawing as cutting edges and simply trim an object to the closest intersecting edge.

*Trim Options.*    After you select the cutting edges, the **TRIM** command has a number of options. They are listed in the following table.

| | |
|---|---|
| **Fence** | This option allows you to select multiple objects to trim by drawing a fence line. Anything that touches the fence line will be trimmed back to the nearest cutting edge. |
| **Crossing** | Like the **Fence** option, this allows you to select multiple objects to trim by drawing a crossing box. Anything that touches the edge of the crossing box is trimmed to its nearest cutting edge. |
| **Project** | This option is for objects located in different three-dimensional planes. It allows you to trim objects that appear to intersect even though they are in different 3D planes. |
| **Edge** | The **Edge** option allows you to trim objects based on an implied intersection with a cutting edge. When this option is selected, you can set the edge mode to **Extend** or **No extend**. In **No extend** mode, an object must actually intersect with a cutting edge in order to be trimmed. With **Extend** mode, an object will be trimmed as if the cutting edge extended out to infinity (see Figure 8-12). **No extend** mode is the default setting. |
| **Erase** | The **Erase** option allows you to erase objects instead of trimming them. You may find that once you start trimming an object, you simply want to trim it all away. The **Erase** option allows you to do that within the **TRIM** command instead of exiting the command and starting the **ERASE** command. |
| **Undo** | **Undo** will undo the last trim action. If you selected a single object to trim, the **Undo** option will undo that trim. If you used either the **Fence** or **Crossing** option to select multiple objects, AutoCAD will undo all the trims done with that selection. |

Some closed objects such as circles or ellipses require that the object intersect a cutting edge in at least two places. This is because these objects have no endpoints and must therefore be trimmed between two edges. If you attempt to trim one of these objects with only one cutting edge, AutoCAD will display the message: OBJECT MUST INTERSECT TWICE. Some objects cannot be trimmed, such as text and blocks.

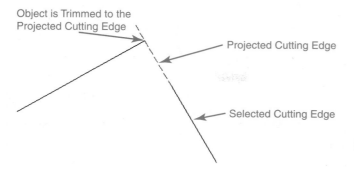

Object is Trimmed to the
Projected Cutting Edge

Projected Cutting Edge

Selected Cutting Edge

**Figure 8-12**   Extend mode settings

## Exercise 8-4: Trimming

1. Start a new drawing using the acad.dwt drawing template.
2. Draw a circle with a radius of **5.** Draw 3 lines that are **6** units long, starting at the center of the circle at an angle of **80°**, **90°**, and **100°**, respectively. Use the **OFFSET** command and offset each line .5 unit as shown in Figure 8-13.
3. Start the **TRIM** command. AutoCAD prompts you to *Select objects or <select all>:*.
4. Press **<Enter ↵>** to select all the objects as cutting edges. AutoCAD prompts you: *Select object to trim or shift-select to extend or* ↑↓ .
5. Pick the points shown in Figure 8-13 to trim the objects so that all overlapping lines at the corners are cleaned up. AutoCAD continues to prompt you: *Select object to trim or shift-select to extend or* ↑↓ .
6. Select the **eRase** option. AutoCAD prompts you to *Select objects to erase:*. Select the three vertical lines, the 80° line and the 100° line that start at the circle center point as shown in Figure 8-13. Press **<Enter ↵>** to erase the selected objects. Your drawing should look like Figure 8-14.

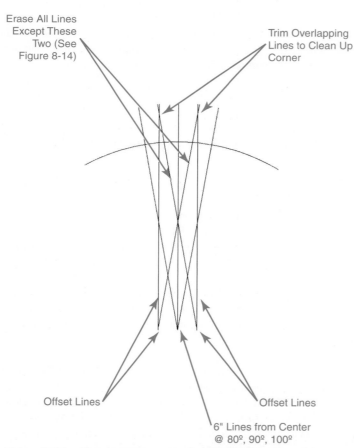

Erase All Lines
Except These
Two (See
Figure 8-14)

Trim Overlapping
Lines to Clean Up
Corner

Offset Lines

Offset Lines

6" Lines from Center
@ 80°, 90°, 100°

**Figure 8-13**   Cleaning up corners using the TRIM command

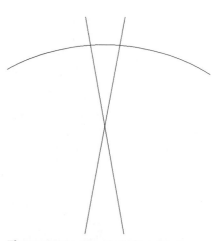

**Figure 8-14**   Drawing after objects trimmed and erased

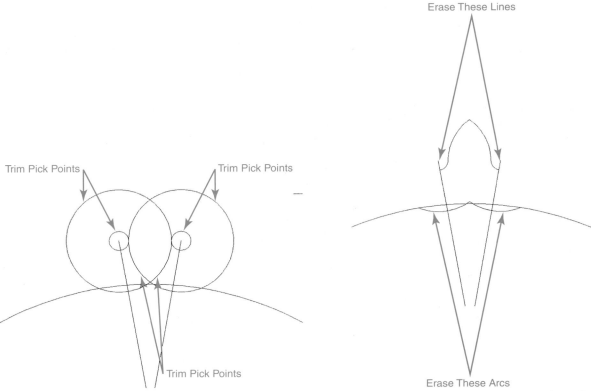

**Figure 8-15**    Offsetting and trimming the circles

**Figure 8-16**    Erasing the remaining objects

7. AutoCAD again prompts you to: *Select object to trim or shift-select to extend or* ↑↓ . Press **<Enter ↵>** or **<Esc>** to exit the **TRIM** command.

8. Draw two circles with a diameter of **0.3125** by snapping to the endpoints of the angled lines as shown in Figure 8-15. Start the **OFFSET** command and offset each of these circles **0.6875** towards the outside of each circle as shown in Figure 8-15.

9. Zoom in to the two circles at the top of the drawing. Start the **TRIM** command and press **<Enter ↵>** to select all the objects as cutting edges, then select the six trim points shown in Figure 8-15.

10. Choose the **eRase** option and select the objects shown in Figure 8-16 to erase. Press **<Enter ↵>** to erase the objects. Press **<Enter ↵>** again to end the **TRIM** command.

11. Save your drawing as **EX8-4**.

## Extending Objects

Extending objects is similar to trimming them; the objects simply get longer instead of shorter. The **EXTEND** command has options similar to the **TRIM** command except you are prompted to select boundary edges instead of cutting edges. Whether they are called boundary or cutting edges, the concept is the same; the edge determines the edge where the object is extended.

*Extend Options.*    The options for the **EXTEND** command are identical to those for the **TRIM** command with the exception of the **Erase** option. Since extending is an additive process (you are adding length to objects) and the **Erase** option is a subtractive process, this option is omitted from the **EXTEND** command.

*Using the <Shift> Key to Switch Between Trim and Extend.*    Since the **EXTEND** and **TRIM** commands are so similar, AutoCAD provides an easy way to switch back and forth between them. You may have noticed that in the **TRIM** command, after you select the cutting edges, AutoCAD prompts you to *Select object to trim or shift-select to extend or* ↓ . By holding down the **<Shift>** key while selecting the objects to extend, you can use the **TRIM** command to trim objects. The same is true for the **EXTEND** command. After you select the boundary edges, AutoCAD prompts you to *Select object to extend or shift-select to trim or ↓*. While the **<Shift>** key is depressed, the **EXTEND** command will trim objects, using the boundary edges as the cutting edges.

### Exercise 8-5: Extending Objects

1. Continue from Exercise 8-4.
2. Start the **OFFSET** command and offset the large circle **3.5** units towards the center of the circle. Repeat the **OFFSET** command and offset the new circle **.5** unit towards the center.
3. Draw two lines, each 8 units long, from the center of the circle at an angle of 85° and 95°, respectively.
4. Draw two more short lines, each 3 units long, from the center of the circle at an angle of 60° and 120°, respectively.
5. Start the **OFFSET** command, set the **Erase** option to **Yes** so the original lines are erased, and set the offset distance to **.25**. Offset the two short lines. Offset the left-hand line to the right, and the right-hand line to the left. Your drawing should look like Figure 8-17.
6. Zoom in to the top of the drawing and start the **EXTEND** command. AutoCAD prompts you to *Select objects or <select all>:*. Select the two 8″ long angled lines and press **<Enter ↵>** to make them the boundary edges.
7. AutoCAD prompts you to *Select object to extend or shift-select to trim or ↑↓*. Pick the two small arc segments nearest to the angled lines selected in step 6 as shown in Figure 8-18 so that the arcs extend out to meet the boundary edges.

| Extend | |
|---|---|
| **Ribbon & Panel:** | Homel Modify |
| **Modify Toolbar:** | |
| **Menu:** | Modifyl Extend |
| **Command Line:** | EXTEND |
| **Command Alias:** | EX |

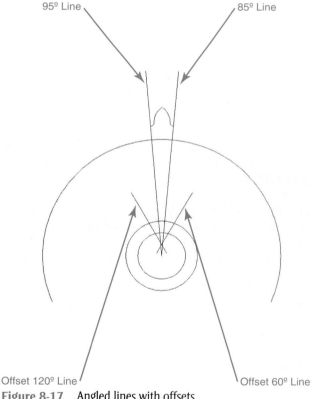

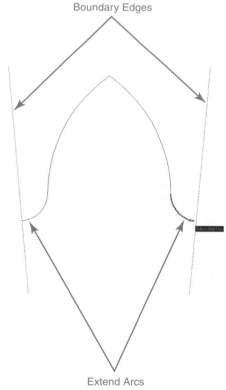

**Figure 8-17**   Angled lines with offsets                    **Figure 8-18**   Extending the arcs

8. Select the **ERASE** command and delete the two 8 ↑↓ angled lines used as boundary edges in step 7.
9. Zoom out to see the entire drawing and select the **EXTEND** command again. Select the two outer circles and the two angled lines as boundary edges as shown in Figure 8-19 and press **<Enter ↵>**.
10. Pick near the ends of the two angled lines using the pick points shown in Figure 8-19 to extend the lines to meet the outer circle.

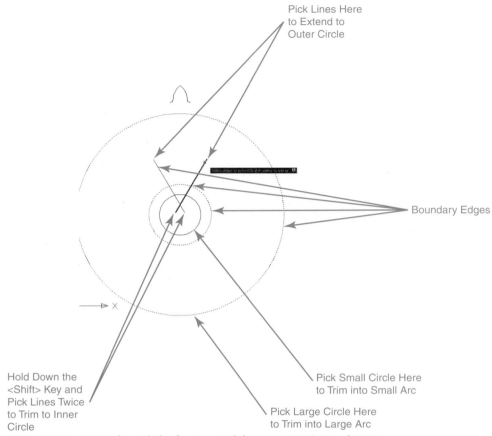

Figure 8-19     Using the <Shift> key to switch between EXTEND and TRIM

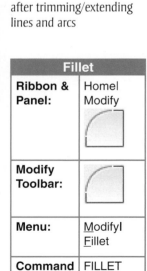

Figure 8-20     Drawing after trimming/extending lines and arcs

| Fillet | |
|---|---|
| **Ribbon & Panel:** | Home\| Modify |
| **Modify Toolbar:** | |
| **Menu:** | Modify\| Fillet |
| **Command Line:** | FILLET |
| **Command Alias:** | F |

11. Hold down the **<Shift>** key to enter **Trim** mode. Select the inner circle using the pick points shown in Figure 8-19 and trim it into the small arc segment shown in Figure 8-20.
12. Hold down the **<Shift>** key to enter **Trim** mode. Select the two angled lines using the pick points shown in Figure 8-19 and trim them to meet the small arc segment created in step 11 as shown in Figure 8-20.
13. Press **<Enter ↵>** to end the **EXTEND** command.
14. Start the **TRIM** command and select the two angled lines as cutting edges as shown in Figure 8-19 and press **<Enter ↵>**.
15. Pick the outer circle near the bottom as shown in Figure 8-19 to trim it into the large arc segment shown at the top in Figure 8-20.
16. Press **<Enter ↵>** to end the **TRIM** command.
17. Save your drawing as **EX8-5**. Your drawing should look like Figure 8-20.

## CREATING FILLETS AND CHAMFERS

Fillets and chamfers are rounded and angled corners, respectively. To create a fillet or a chamfer using basic drawing and editing commands would be a difficult task. The process of rounding a simple right-angle corner would involve shortening each leg by the radius of the round, and then creating an arc segment between the two shortened ends. Using **TRIM** and **EXTEND** might make the process easier, but you would still need to draw an arc or circle and use a combination of **TRIM** and/or **EXTEND** to clean up the intersections. Creating a chamfered or angled corner might prove easier but would still involve drawing new objects and cleaning up their intersections. The **FILLET** and **CHAMFER** commands allow you easily to add rounds and angled lines to intersecting objects.

## Creating Fillets

To create a fillet, you specify a fillet radius and select two objects. AutoCAD will place an arc between the two objects and trim and extend the objects as needed. The point where you select the objects determines where the arc is placed. AutoCAD will place the fillet so that the selected portions will remain (see Figure 8-21).

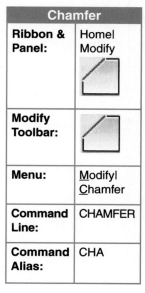

| Chamfer | |
|---|---|
| **Ribbon & Panel:** | Home\|Modify |
| **Modify Toolbar:** | |
| **Menu:** | Modify\|<u>C</u>hamfer |
| **Command Line:** | CHAMFER |
| **Command Alias:** | CHA |

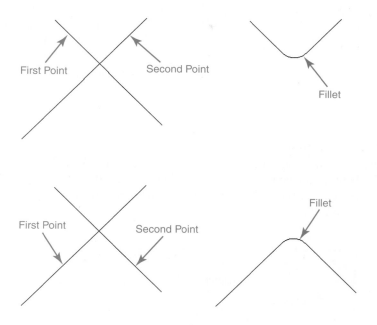

**Figure 8-21**    Fillet selections

*Radius Option.*    When you start the **FILLET** command, the current radius setting is listed in the command window. The **Radius** option allows you to set fillet radius. The fillet radius is stored in the **FILLETRAD** system variable and once set, AutoCAD will retain the setting until you change it. Setting the **Radius** option to **0** will result in AutoCAD squaring off a corner.

You can create a fillet between open objects (lines, arcs, and elliptical arcs) as well as closed objects (circles and ellipses). When you select a closed object, AutoCAD doesn't actually trim the closed object but simply draws the fillet arc. (See Figure 8-22.)

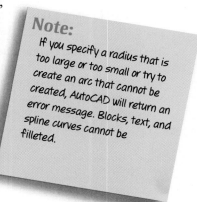

**Note:**
If you specify a radius that is too large or too small or try to create an arc that cannot be created, AutoCAD will return an error message. Blocks, text, and spline curves cannot be filleted.

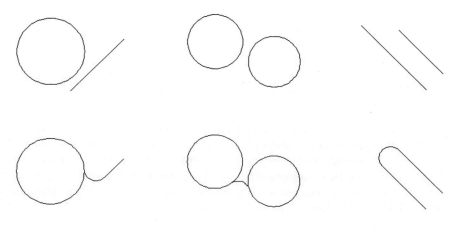

**Figure 8-22**    Some sample fillets

*Multiple Mode.*    The **Multiple** option puts you into **Multiple** mode and allows you to create multiple fillets in a single command. In **Multiple** mode, the **FILLET** command simply repeats until you press **<Enter ↵>** or **<Esc>**. The **Undo** option allows you to undo the last fillet while in **Multiple** mode. The **Undo** option only works while in **Multiple** mode.

*Trim Mode.*    The **Trim** option allows you to turn **Trim** mode on and off. With **Trim** mode turned on, objects are trimmed or extended to the fillet arc. With **Trim** mode turned off, Auto-CAD creates the fillet arc but leaves the source objects unchanged. Like the **Radius** option, the **Trim** setting is retained after the **FILLET** command is complete until you change it.

*The Polyline Option.*    The **Polyline** option allows you to add a fillet radius to all the intersections in a polyline object.

### Capping Two Parallel Lines Using the Fillet Tool

If you fillet two parallel lines, AutoCAD will create a rounded end cap between the two lines. In this case, AutoCAD will ignore the **Radius** setting and create a 180° arc using half the distance between the lines as the radius. If the lines are different length, the first object you select will determine the start point of the arc. The other line will be trimmed or extended to match the first selected object (see Figure 8-22).

| FOR MORE DETAILS | See Chapter 9 for more on creating and editing polylines. |
| --- | --- |

**Exercise 8-6:** Creating a Fillet

1. Continue from Exercise 8-5.
2. Start the **FILLET** command. AutoCAD prompts you to *Select first object or ↓*.
3. Choose the **Multiple** option to turn on **Multiple** mode.
4. Choose the **Radius** option and type **.5<Enter ↵>** to set the fillet radius.
5. Pick the lines and arc shown in Figure 8-23 to round the outer corners. AutoCAD will round the corners and continue prompting you to select objects.

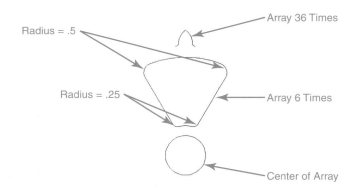

**Figure 8-23**    Creating a fillet

6. Choose the **Radius** option and type **.25<Enter ↵>** to set the fillet radius.
7. Pick the lines and arc shown in Figure 8-23 to round the inner corners. When you've finished rounding the four corners, press **<Esc>** to end the **FILLET** command.
8. Start the **ARRAY** command and create a polar array of the pointed geometry at the top of the drawing. Center the array about the center of the circle and create **36** items through **360°**, rotating the objects as they are copied.

9. Repeat the **ARRAY** command and create a polar array of the rounded wedge. Center the array about the center of the circle and create **6** items through **360°**, rotating the objects as they are copied. Your drawing should look like Figure 8-24.

10. Save your drawing as **EX8-6**.

**Figure 8-24**   The finished drawing

## Creating Chamfers

The **CHAMFER** command is used to create angled corners between two intersecting objects. Drawing a chamfer between intersecting objects is similar to drawing a fillet. However, instead of a fillet radius, you need to provide two distances from the intersection along each object, or a distance and an angle for the chamfer (see Figure 8-25).

The **CHAMFER** command has two methods for creating chamfers: distance and angle. The **mEthod** option allows you to select which chamfer method to use.

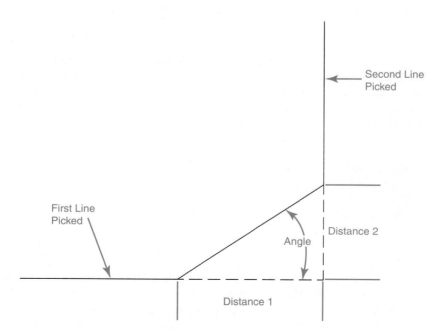

**Figure 8-25**   Creating a chamfer

*Distance Method.*   With the distance method, you specify the distance from the intersection along each line. From the intersection, AutoCAD subtracts the first chamfer distance from the first object and the second chamfer distance from the second object and then draws a line between these two points. The **Distance** option allows you to set the chamfer distances. The first distance is applied to the first object you select, and the second distance is applied to the second object.

If the chamfer distances are equal, a 45° chamfer is drawn. When you set the first distance, AutoCAD sets the default value of the second distance to the first distance. To accept this default, just press **<Enter ↵>** when prompted for the second chamfer distance.

> **Note:**
> While the **FILLET** command allows you to create arcs between both straight and curved objects, the **CHAMFER** command works only on straight, linear objects (lines, straight polylines segments, xlines, and rays).

*Angle Method.*    The angle method uses a distance and angle to determine the chamfer line. The distance is subtracted from the first object selected to determine the starting point and the chamfer line is drawn at the specified angle until it intersects with the second object. By default, the angle is measured in a counterclockwise direction from the first object (see Figure 8-26).

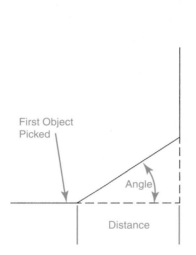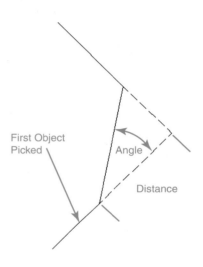

**Figure 8-26**    The angle chamfer method

*The Polyline Option.*    The **Undo, Polyline, Trim,** and **Multiple** options work the same way as the **FILLET** command. When chamfering a polyline with the **Polyline** option, the first and second objects are determined by the order in which the polyline was drawn. When in doubt, or if you are not getting the results you're expecting, your best bet may be to not use the **Polyline** option and just chamfer the polyline segments individually.

| **FOR MORE DETAILS** | See Chapter 9 for more on creating and editing polylines. |
| --- | --- |

**Exercise 8-7:** Creating a Chamfer

1. Continue from Exercise 8-2. If you've closed the drawing, open the drawing **EX8-2**.
2. Start the **CHAMFER** command and select the **Angle** option. AutoCAD prompts you to *Specify chamfer length on the first line:*. Type **.75<Enter ↵>** to set the length.
3. AutoCAD prompts you to *Specify chamfer angle from the first line:*. Type **60<Enter ↵>** to set the chamfer angle.
4. AutoCAD prompts you to *Select first line or ↓*. Pick the objects shown in Figure 8-27. AutoCAD chamfers the corner. Note that the .75 distance is taken off of the first line you selected.

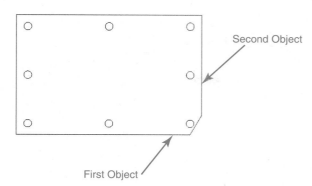

Second Object

First Object

**Figure 8-27**   Using the angle method

5. Because this chamfer comes very close to the hole, type **U<Enter ↵>** to undo the last chamfer.
6. Restart the **CHAMFER** command and select the **Distance** option. Set the first distance to .5. AutoCAD sets the default value of the second distance to match the first. Press **<Enter ↵>** to accept the default. AutoCAD prompts you to *Select first line or* ↓.
7. Select the **Multiple** option and chamfer the four corners of the part. Your drawing should look like Figure 8-28.
8. Save your drawing as **EX8-7**.

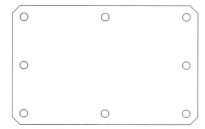

**Figure 8-28**   Creating chamfers

# Breaking an Object

The **BREAK** command allows you to remove portions of an object or to break a single object into two separate objects. The **BREAK** command requires you to select an object and then select two points on the object. The portion of the object between the two points is then removed.

## Creating a Gap in an Object

When you start the **BREAK** command, AutoCAD prompts you to select an object. By default, when you select the object, the point you pick on the object becomes the first break point, and AutoCAD will prompt you to select the second break point. If the point you select is not the point you want, you can use the **First** option to repick the first break point on the selected object.

Once you specify the first break point, AutoCAD prompts you for the second break point and breaks the object between the two points.

## Breaking an Object Exactly at a Point

There may be times when you want to break the object in two without creating a physical gap. To break an object without creating an opening, simply use the @ symbol to specify the second point. When you use the @ symbol, AutoCAD will place the second point at the same coordinate as the first point. The end result is the object is broken in two without creating a gap.

| Break | |
|---|---|
| **Ribbon & Panel:** | Home| Modify |
| **Modify Toolbar:** | |
| **Menu:** | Modify| Break |
| **Command Line:** | BREAK |
| **Command Alias:** | BR |

### Breaking Circles, Xlines, and Rays

Depending on the type of object you select, the **BREAK** command will create new objects. When you break a line, AutoCAD simply creates two lines. However, when you break a circle, xline, or ray, AutoCAD will create different types of objects.

**Note:**
Circles and ellipses must be broken in two distinct locations. Using @ when specifying the second break point is not allowed.

*Circle.*    When you break a circle, AutoCAD converts the circle to an arc. The order in which you select the points will determine which portion of the circle is kept. AutoCAD will remove the portion of the circle starting at the first in a counterclockwise direction. Figure 8-29 shows the results of selecting different points along a circle.

*Xlines and Rays.*    When you break an xline, AutoCAD will create two rays with the starting points of the rays located at the first and second break points. Breaking a ray will result in a line and a ray.

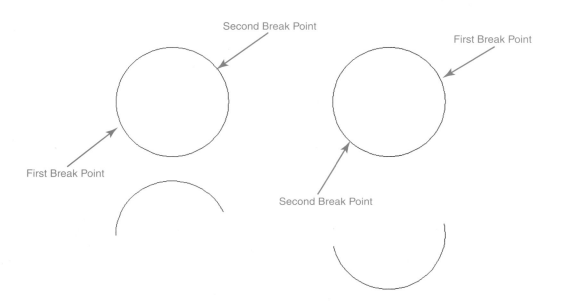

**Figure 8-29**    Breaking a circle

### Selecting the Second Points

When you select the break second point, there are a couple of things to keep in mind. First, if you select the second point somewhere away from the object, AutoCAD will project a break point along a line perpendicular to the object passing through the selected point. Second, if the second break point lies past the end of the object, AutoCAD will simply remove everything between the first point and the end of the object. Figure 8-30 shows examples of these.

### Exercise 8-8: Breaking Objects

1. Continue from Exercise 8-1. If you've closed the drawing, open the drawing **EX8-1**.
2. Start the **BREAK** command and select the circle near the bottom quadrant, between the two vertical lines. AutoCAD prompts you to *Specify second break point or ↓*. Pick anywhere near the arc to break the circle into an arc segment. Don't worry about the final length of the arc segment.
3. Restart the **BREAK** command. AutoCAD prompts you to *Select object:*. Hold down the **<Shift>** key and right-click to bring up the object snap menu. Choose **Midpoint** and select the centerline. This selects the line and places the first break point at the midpoint of the line. AutoCAD prompts you to *Specify second break point or ↓*.

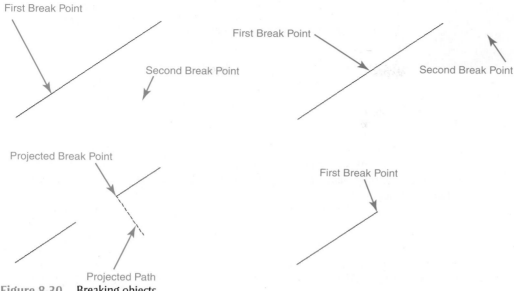

Figure 8-30    Breaking objects

Figure 8-31    Breaking objects

4. Type **@<Enter ↵>** to break the line at the midpoint. Drag your cursor over a portion of the centerline. AutoCAD will highlight half of the centerline.
5. Start the **FILLET** command and set the radius to **25**. Turn on **Multiple** mode and add fillets between the arc and line segments. Your drawing should look like Figure 8-31.
6. Save your drawing as **EX8-8**.

## JOINING MULTIPLE OBJECTS

The **JOIN** command does the opposite of the **BREAK** command by closing the gap between objects and converting multiple objects into a single object. The **JOIN** command starts by asking you to select a source object and then prompts you to select the objects to join to the source. The objects you want to join must match the source object and have different rules depending on the type of source object you choose.

*Lines.* When joining lines, all the lines must lie in the same plane and must be collinear. The line segments can overlap or there can be gaps between the line segments, but the end result must be a single, continuous line. Joining multiple line segments results in a single line object.

*Arcs.* Arcs must lie in the same circular path, meaning they must have the same center point and radius. Like lines, the arcs can overlap or have gaps between them. The end result should be a single continuous arc segment. If the arcs overlap to form a complete circle, AutoCAD will ask you if you want to convert the arcs into a circle.

You can also use the **JOIN** command to convert an arc into a circle. When you select an arc as the source object, AutoCAD provides a **cLose** option. Choosing this option will close the arc and convert it to a circle.

*Elliptical Arcs.* Elliptical arcs behave the same as circular arcs. The elliptical arcs must lie on the same elliptical path. Gaps and overlaps are allowed, and the **cLose** option is available to convert an elliptical arc into an ellipse.

*Polylines.* The objects must be lines, arcs, or open polylines. Gaps and overlapping are not allowed when joining polylines. All the segments must lie end-to-end in the same plane.

*Spline Curves.* Spline curves behave similar to polylines. All the objects must be spline curves that lie in the same plane. Gaps and overlapping are not allowed; all the segments must lie end-to-end.

| Join | |
|------|------|
| **Ribbon & Panel:** | Home\| Modify |
| **Modify Toolbar:** | |
| **Menu:** | Modify\| Join |
| **Command Line:** | JOIN |
| **Command Alias:** | J |

> **FOR MORE DETAILS**  See Chapter 9 for more on creating polylines and editing polylines and spline curves.

<u>Exercise 8-9:</u> Joining Objects

1. Continue from Exercise 8-8.
2. Start the **JOIN** command. AutoCAD prompts you to *Select source object:*.
3. Select one portion of the centerline. AutoCAD prompts you to *Select lines to join to source:*. Pick the other half of the centerline and press <**Enter** ↵>. AutoCAD joins the two lines together.
4. Drag your cursor over the centerline to verify it is a single object. Save your drawing as **EX8-9**.

| Lengthen | |
|---|---|
| **Ribbon & Panel:** | Home\| Modify  |
| **Toolbar:** | None |
| **Menu:** | Modify\| Lengthen |
| **Command Line:** | LENGTHEN |
| **Command Alias:** | LEN |

## LENGTHENING AN OBJECT

The **LENGTHEN** command allows you to lengthen or shorten drawing objects as well as get information about the length of selected objects. When you start the **LENGTHEN** command, you are asked to select an object and are given four options, **DElta**, **Percent**, **Total**, and **DYnamic**. When you select an object, the **LENGTHEN** command displays the length of the object in the **Command Line** window. If the object is an arc, the included angle of the arc is also displayed.

 **TIP**   The length information for most objects is displayed in the **Properties** palette. However, for some objects such as spline curves, ellipses, and elliptical arcs, the **Properties** palette doesn't display total length information. The **LENGTHEN** command is an easy way to display this information for these complex curves.

### The LENGTHEN Command Options

When lengthening an object, AutoCAD must know how much length to add or subtract from the object. Once it knows what changes to make, the **LENGTHEN** command will prompt you to select an object to lengthen. You can either select a single object or use the Fence selection method to drag a fence crossing line across the items you wish to lengthen. AutoCAD will keep prompting you to select objects, allowing you to lengthen multiple objects within a single command.

The **LENGTHEN** command options provide four different methods for altering the length of an object.

*DElta Option.*    The **DElta** option allows you to specify a discreet length to add or subtract from the object. When you choose the **DElta** option, AutoCAD asks you to enter a delta length and then prompts you to select an object. The length you specify is then added to the object at the end closest to where you select. A positive delta value will increase the length, and a negative delta will shorten the object.

The **DElta** option also includes an **Angle** option. This allows you to modify the included angle of an arc. By default, positive angles add length in the counterclockwise direction, and negative angles subtract length in the clockwise direction.

*Percent Option.*    The **Percent** option allows you to scale the line by a percentage value. A percent value of 200 will make an object twice as long. A value of 50 will make it half as long. A value of 110 will add 10 percent to the length of the object. A value of 100 will leave the object unchanged.

*Total Option.*    The **Total** option allows you to set the total length of an object. If the value is greater than the current length of the object, the object will increase in length. If the value is smaller, the object will shorten.

*DYnamic Option.*    The **DYnamic** option allows you to specify the length on an object by dragging it around the screen. When you use this option, you are asked to select an object. AutoCAD will then ask you to specify a new end point for the object. You can then drag your cursor around the drawing and dynamically see the length change. To set the length, simply pick a point.

## Invalid Objects

When using the **LENGTHEN** command, it's possible to ask AutoCAD to create objects that can't exist or to lengthen objects that cannot be lengthened. For example, althaugh AutoCAD will tell you the length of a closed object like a circle or an ellipse, you can't add length to a closed object. Another example would be to try to increase the included angle of a line, or to increase the included angle of an arc beyond 360°. In cases like these, AutoCAD will simply display a message stating that it cannot lengthen the object, and it will ignore the selected object.

### Exercise 8-10: Lengthening an Object

1. Continue from Exercise 8-9.
2. Start the **LENGTHEN** command and select the centerline. AutoCAD replies *Current length: 100.0000* and prompts you to *Select an object or ↓*.
3. Select the **DElta** option and enter a value of 25. AutoCAD prompts you to *Select an object to change or ↓*. Select the bottom portion of each of the vertical lines. Each line is lengthened by 25 units. AutoCAD continues to prompt you to *Select an object to change or ↓*.
4. Type **F<Enter ↵>** to specify a fence selection. Draw a fence through the three bottom lines (see Figure 8-32) and press **<Enter ↵>** to end the selection process. AutoCAD will lengthen the three lines by another 25 units.
5. Save your drawing as **EX8-10**. Your drawing should resemble Figure 8-33.

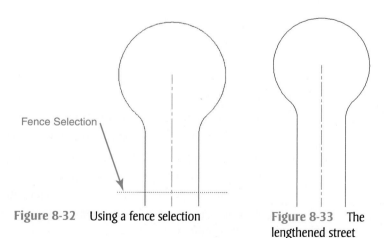

Fence Selection

Figure 8-32    Using a fence selection          Figure 8-33    The lengthened street

## SUMMARY

In this chapter you've explored some additional methods of editing geometry. The editing techniques covered here add to the basic editing commands and provide additional methods of accomplishing some potentially tedious tasks.

# CHAPTER TEST QUESTIONS

## Multiple Choice

1. Copying an object parallel to an existing object is called:
   a. Filleting
   b. Chamfering
   c. Offsetting
   d. Extending

2. In a rectangular array, the row offset represents:
   a. The horizontal (X) spacing of the arrayed objects
   b. The vertical (Y) spacing of the arrayed objects
   c. The number of rows in the array
   d. None of the above

3. In the **TRIM** command, when selecting objects to trim, holding down the **<Shift>** key:
   a. Allows you to remove objects from the selection set
   b. Puts a 0 radius corner at the intersection of the two objects
   c. Allows you to select additional cutting edges
   d. Allows you to extend objects to the cutting edges

4. In the **FILLET** command, when selecting the objects to fillet, holding down the **<Shift>** key:
   a. Allows you to remove objects from the selection set
   b. Puts a 0 radius corner at the intersection of the two objects
   c. Allows you to select additional cutting edges
   d. Allows you to extend objects to the cutting edges

5. In the **TRIM** command, when asked to select cutting edges, pressing **<Enter ↵>**:
   a. Ends the **TRIM** command
   b. Switches between **EXTEND** and **TRIM**
   c. Selects all the objects in the drawing as cutting edges
   d. None of the above

6. While creating a rectangular array, the array angle:
   a. Rotates the array
   b. Changes your rectangular array to a polar array
   c. Sets the polar array fill angle
   d. None of the above

7. When creating a polar array, entering a negative angle to fill:
   a. Will copy objects in a clockwise direction
   b. Will copy objects in the counterclockwise direction
   c. Is not allowed
   d. None of the above

8. The **BREAK** command:
   a. Will work on lines and arcs
   b. Will work on closed objects
   c. Can have the same first and second break point
   d. All of the above

9. To convert an arc to a circle:
   a. Use the **FILLET** command with a 0 radius
   b. Use the **EXTEND** command
   c. Use the **LENGTHEN** command
   d. Use the **JOIN** command

10. Breaking an xline:
    a. Creates a line and a ray
    b. Creates two rays
    c. Converts the xline to polyline
    d. Is not allowed

## Matching

| Column A | Column B |
|---|---|
| a. **ARRAY** command | 1. Items copied in a circular pattern |
| b. Polar array | 2. Moves objects a user-supplied distance and angle |
| c. Fillet radius | 3. Can convert an arc into a full circle |
| d. Rectangular array | 4. The radius of a rounded intersection |
| e. **JOIN** command | 5. Copies objects in rectangular or circular patterns |
| f. **BREAK** command | 6. Can convert a circle into an arc and turn a single object into multiple objects |
| g. **LENGTHEN** command | 7. A mode of the **OFFSET** command that deletes the source object after it is offset |
| h. **Extend** mode | 8. Items copied in a rectangular pattern of rows and columns |
| i. **Erase** mode | 9. A mode of the **TRIM** and **EXTEND** commands that allows you to trim or extend to implied intersections |
| j. **CHAMFER** command | 10. Allows you to display and modify the length of objects |

## True or False

1. True or False: The **OFFSET** command cannot be used on closed objects.

2. True or False: Objects must actually touch each other for the **TRIM** command to work.

3. True or False: The **EXTEND** command can be used to trim objects.

4. True or False: A fillet radius can be drawn between two parallel objects.

5. True or False: The **JOIN** command requires that line segments must lie end-to-end with no gaps or overlaps.

6. True or False: The **LENGTHEN** command doesn't work with arcs.

7. True or False: Holding down the <Shift> key during the **CHAMFER** command allows it to draw fillet curves.

8. True or False: The **Erase** option of the **TRIM** and **EXTEND** commands will undo any changes made during the command.

9. True or False: The **BREAK** command requires two separate points when breaking a circle.

10. True or False: The **BREAK** command converts rays into xlines.

## CHAPTER PROJECTS

### Project 8-1: Classroom Plan—Continued from Chapter 7

1. Open drawing **P7-1**.
2. Draw the remaining equipment and windows shown in Figure P8-1A using the appropriate layers. The windows are all 4′-6″ wide. **Do not** draw dimensions or text.
3. Locate the chairs and windows as shown in Figure P8-1B. Trim the walls as necessary to allow for the window openings. Change the layout of the desks to reflect the updated plan.
4. Save your drawing as **P8-1**.

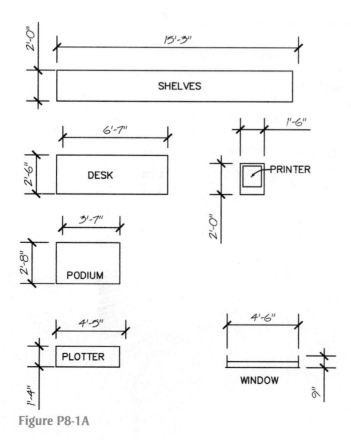

**Figure P8-1A**

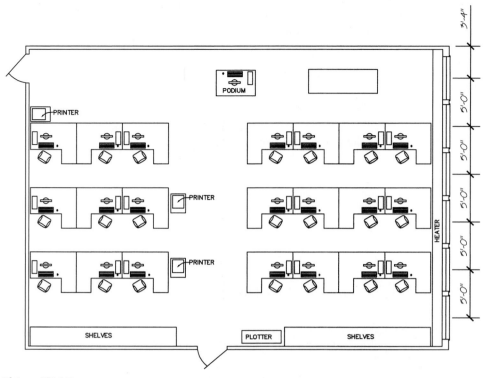

Figure P8-1B

## Project 8-2: Motorcycle—Continued from Chapter 7

1. Open drawing **P7-2**.
2. Use the **ARRAY** command to create five spokes on each wheel.
3. Use the **ARRAY** command to create $30 \times 2$ holes on the front and rear brake disks.
4. Use the **TRIM** and **BREAK** commands to trim all overlapping line work.
5. Use the **FILLET** command to fillet the bottom/front frame, bottom/front engine case, and handlebars.
6. Use the **CHAMFER** command to bevel the bottom of the front forks.
7. Use the **OFFSET** command to create the handlebar grip.
8. Save the drawing as **P8-2**.

Figure P8-2

## Project 8-3: A-Size Portrait Mechanical Border

1. Start a new drawing using the acad.dwt template.
2. Set the **LIMITS** for an 8.5 × 11.0 drawing area.
3. Create the following layers:

| Name | Color | Linetype | Lineweight | Plot/Noplot | Description |
|------|-------|----------|------------|-------------|-------------|
| Title | 7 | Continuous | Default | Plot | Title border and text |
| Logo | 7 | Continuous | Default | Plot | Logo |
| Notes | 7 | Continuous | Default | Plot | Notes |
| Viewport | 9 | Continuous | Default | Noplot | Viewports |

4. Draw the A-size title block as shown in Figure P8-3. Use the **Title** layer for all geometry. **Do not** draw dimensions.
5. Save the drawing to a template file as **Mechanical A-Size-Portrait.DWT**.

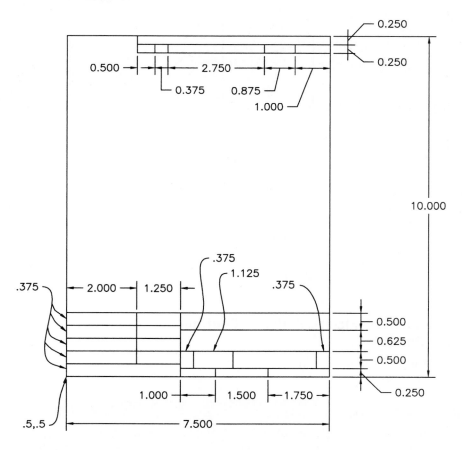

Figure P8-3

## Project 8-4: Architectural A-Size Border (8½ × 11)

1. Start a new drawing using the acad.dwt template.
2. Set linear **UNITS** to **Architectural** with precision set to **1/16″**.
3. Set angular **UNITS** to **Deg/Min/Sec** with precision set to **0d00′00″**.
4. Set the drawing **LIMITS** to **8½″ × 11″** for an A-size drawing.

5. Create the following layers:

| Name | Color | Linetype | Lineweight | Plot/Noplot | Description |
|---|---|---|---|---|---|
| A-Anno-Ttlb | 7 | Continuous | Default | Plot | Title block/border lines |
| A-Anno-Ttlb-Text | 1 | Continuous | Default | Plot | Title block text |
| A-Anno-Ttlb-Logo | 3 | Continuous | Default | Plot | Logo |
| A-Anno-Vprt | 7 | Continuous | Default | No Plot | Viewport lines |

6. Draw the border as shown in Figure P8-4 on layer **A-Anno-Ttlb**. **Do not** include dimensions.
7. Zoom to the drawing extents.
8. Save the drawing to a template file as **Architectural A-Size.DWT**.

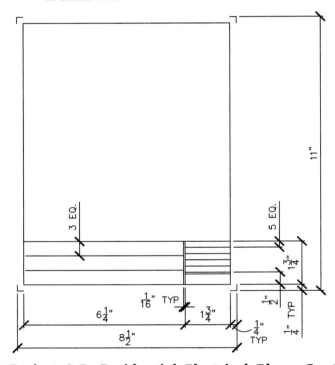

Figure P8-4

## Project 8-5: Residential Electrical Plan—Continued from Chapter 7, Problem 7

1. Open the drawing **P7-7** from Chapter 7.
2. Add the following layers:

| Name | Color | Linetype | Lineweight | Plot/Noplot | Description |
|---|---|---|---|---|---|
| E-Lite | 7 | Continuous | Default | Plot | Lighting |
| E-Lite-Circ | 7 | Continuous | Default | Plot | Lighting circuiting |
| E-Powr | 7 | Continuous | Default | Plot | Power |
| E-Powr-Circ | 9 | Continuous | Default | Plot | Power circuiting |
| E-Anno | 7 | Continuous | Default | Plot | Electrical annotation |

3. Create the symbols shown in Figure P8-5A. Place the symbols
   on the floor plan as shown in Figure P8-5B.
4. Save the drawing as **P8-5**.

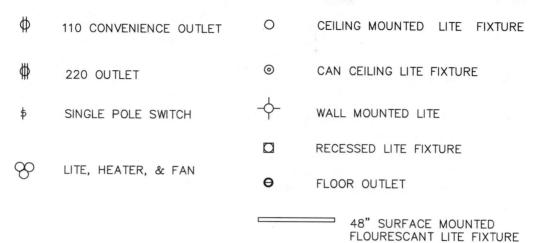

| | | | |
|---|---|---|---|
| ⌀ | 110 CONVENIENCE OUTLET | ○ | CEILING MOUNTED  LITE  FIXTURE |
| ⌀ | 220 OUTLET | ⊙ | CAN CEILING LITE FIXTURE |
| $ | SINGLE POLE SWITCH | ✛ | WALL MOUNTED LITE |
| | | ▣ | RECESSED LITE FIXTURE |
| ⊗ | LITE, HEATER, & FAN | ⊖ | FLOOR OUTLET |
| | | | 48" SURFACE MOUNTED FLOURESCANT LITE FIXTURE |

**Figure P8-5A**

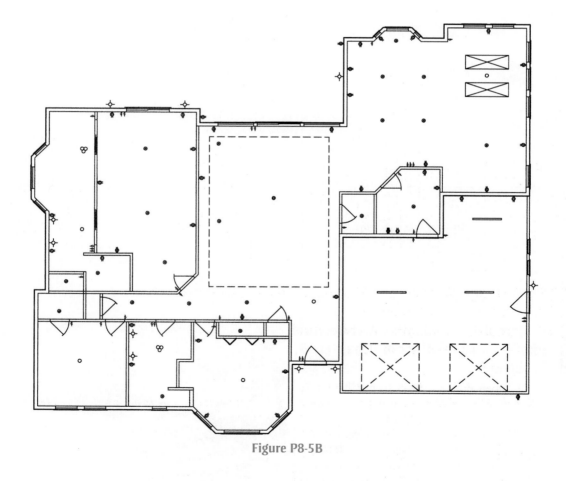

**Figure P8-5B**

## Project 8-6: Unit Heater Connections

1. Start a new drawing using the acad.dwt template.
2. Set the **GRID** and **SNAP** drawing aids to 0.125.

3. Create the following layers:

| Name | Color | Linetype | Lineweight | Description |
|------|-------|----------|------------|-------------|
| P-Detl-P1 | 7 | Continuous | Default | Plumbing details and schematics |
| P-Detl-Hidden | 1 | Hidden | Default | Hidden lines |
| P-Anno-Note | 7 | Continuous | Default | Note text |
| P-Anno-Title | 7 | Continuous | Default | Title text |

4. Draw the piping schematic lines, symbols, and unit heaters as shown in Figure P8-6 on layer **P-Detl-P1**.
5. Draw hidden lines on layer **P-Detl-Hidden**.
6. Save the drawing as **P8-6**.

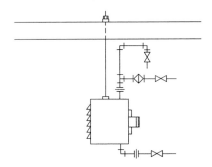

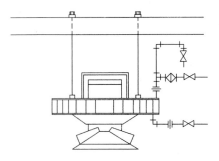

Figure P8-6

## Project 8-7: Residential Architectural Plan—Continued from Chapter 8, Problem 5

1. Open drawing **P8-5** from Chapter 8, Problem 5. If you are not completing Problem 5, open **P7-7** from Chapter 7.
2. Modify the floor plan as shown in Figure P8-7. Use the **TRIM**, **EXTEND**, and **FILLET** commands to clean up wall intersections and door/window openings. **Do not** draw dimensions or text.
3. Save your drawing as **P8-7**.

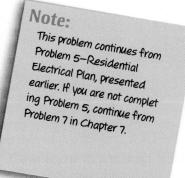

Note:
This problem continues from Problem 5—Residential Electrical Plan, presented earlier. If you are not completing Problem 5, continue from Problem 7 in Chapter 7.

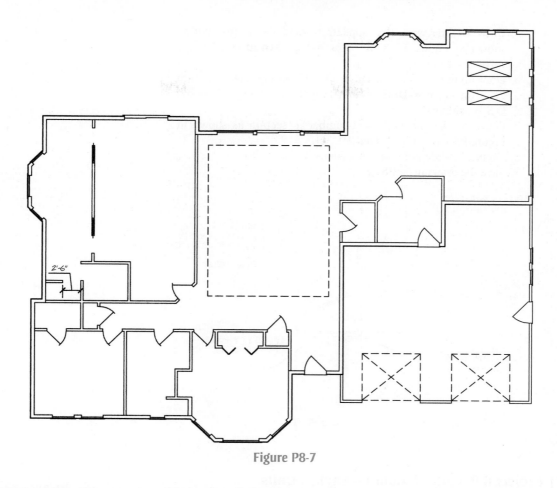

Figure P8-7

## Project 8-8: Truss with Soffited Eave Detail

1. Start a new drawing using the acad.dwt template.
2. Set linear **UNITS** to **Architectural** with precision set to **1/16″**.
3. Set angular **UNITS** to **Deg/Min/Sec** with precision set to **0d00′00″**.
4. Create the following layers:

| Name | Color | Linetype | Lineweight | Description |
|------|-------|----------|------------|-------------|
| A-Detl-Mbnd | 1 | Continuous | Default | Detail lines that represent material in the background |
| A-Detl-Mcut | 3 | Continuous | 0.35mm | Detail lines that represent material cut in section |
| A-Detl-P1 | 2 | Continuous | Default | Secondary (light) lines |
| A-Detl-Batt | 1 | Batting | Default | Batt insulation |
| A-Detl-Pat | 1 | Continuous | Default | Hatch patterns and fills |
| A-Anno-Note | 3 | Continuous | Default | Note text |
| A-Anno-Title | 3 | Continuous | Default | Title text |
| A-Anno-Dims | 1 | Continuous | Default | Dimensions |

5. Draw all line work that appears beyond the section cut as shown in Figure P8-8 on layer **A-Detl-Mbnd** (roof truss, vertical wall lines).

6. Draw all line work that is cut by the section as shown in Figure P8-8 on layer **A-Detl-Mcut** (lumber in section, plywood, O.S.B., siding).

7. Draw the X's that represent lumber in section as shown in Figure P8-8 on layer **A-Detl-P1**.

8. **Do not** include notes or dimensions.

9. Save the drawing as **P8-8**.

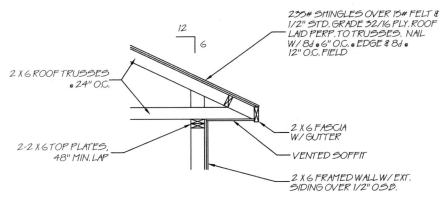

**Figure P8-8**

### Project 8-9: Optical Mount—English Units

1. Start a new drawing using the acad.dwt template.
2. Create the following layers:

| Name | Color | Linetype | Lineweight | Description |
|------|-------|----------|------------|-------------|
| Object | 7 | Continuous | 0.35 mm | Object lines |
| Hidden | 1 | Hidden | Default | Hidden lines |
| Center | 2 | Center | Default | Centerlines |
| Hatch | 4 | Continuous | Default | Hatch patterns and fills |
| Notes | 3 | Continuous | Default | Text and notes |
| Dims | 2 | Continuous | Default | Dimensions |

3. Create the three-view drawing as shown in Figure P8-9. *Hint:* Use the **FILLET** command to create the round ends of the slots.

4. Adjust the **LTSCALE** system so linetypes appear properly.

5. **Do not** include notes or dimensions.

6. Save your drawing as **P8-9**.

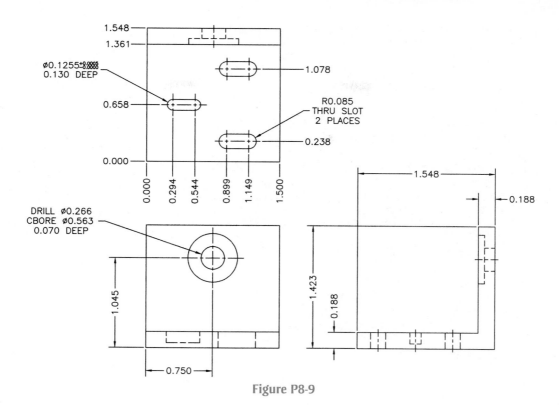

Figure P8-9

## Project 8-10: 68-Tooth Rear Sprocket—Metric

1. Start a new drawing using the acadiso.dwt template.
2. Create the following layers:

| Name | Color | Linetype | Lineweight | Description |
|------|-------|----------|------------|-------------|
| Object | 7 | Continuous | 0.35 mm | Object lines |
| Hidden | 1 | Hidden | Default | Hidden lines |
| Center | 2 | Center | Default | Centerlines |
| Hatch | 4 | Continuous | Default | Hatch patterns and fills |
| Notes | 3 | Continuous | Default | Text and notes |
| 0 Dims | 2 | Continuous | Default | Dimensions |

3. Draw object lines as shown in Figure P8-10 on layer **Object**.
4. Draw centerlines as shown in Figure P8-10 on layer **Center**.
   *Hint:* Draw one sprocket tooth as indicated in Detail A and array it using the **ARRAY** command with the **Polar** option. You can use the same technique to create the holes.
5. Adjust the **LTSCALE** system so linetypes appear properly.
6. **Do not** include notes or dimensions.
7. Save the drawing as **P8-10**.

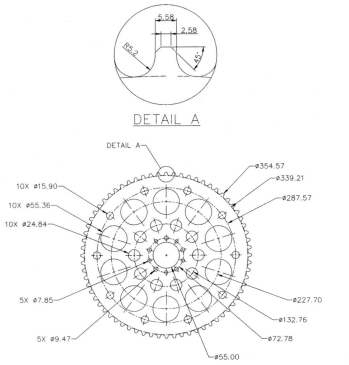

Figure P8-10

## Project 8-11: Civil Site Plan—Continued from Chapter 7

1. Open the drawing **P7-11**.
2. Round the corners of the pool as shown in Figure P8-11. Add the garden beds and plants as shown.
3. Save the drawing as **P8-11**.

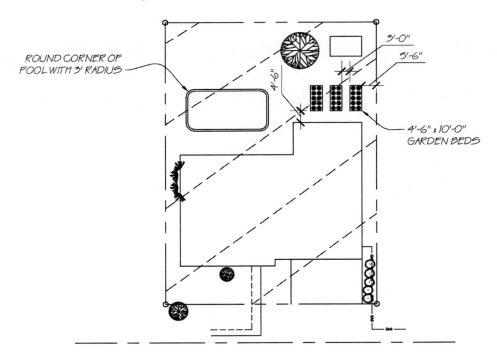

Figure P8-11

## Project 8-12: Manhole Cover—Continued from Chapter 7

1. Open drawing **P7-12**.
2. Draw the remaining line work for the section view shown in Figure P8-12 on layer **C-Detl-P2**.
3. Draw all line work for the bottom view shown in Figure P8-12 on layer **C-Detl-P1**. *Hint:* Use construction lines to create the bottom view based on the section view using orthographic projection. You can then create finished linework using object snaps.
4. Draw all centerlines shown in Figure P8-12 on layer **C-Detl-Center**.
5. **Do not** include text or dimensions.
6. Save the drawing as **P8-12**.

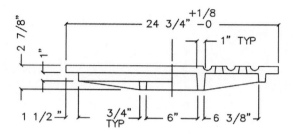

SECTION  A—A

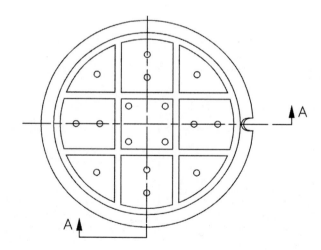

BOTTOM  VIEW

Figure P8-12

# Drawing and Editing Complex Objects

# 9

## Chapter Objectives

- Draw polylines with straight line segments
- Draw polyline arcs
- Create rectangles using two points
- Make multisided polygons
- Create solid and hollow donuts
- Draw revision clouds
- Edit polylines as a unit
- Explode complex objects

## INTRODUCTION

AutoCAD provides a number of complex line objects that consist of multiple segments but are treated as a single line with multiple points:

- Polyline
- Rectangle
- Polygon
- Donut
- Revision cloud

**contour line:** A line on a map that joins points of equal elevation

Complex line objects serve many different purposes and needs. Polylines allow you to define a closed boundary that can be used to calculate an enclosed area. Polylines are also used extensively to create *contour lines* on civil engineering maps.

In fact, AutoCAD uses polylines to create the rectangles, polygons, donuts, and revision clouds described in this chapter. This chapter explores the commands used to create and edit these different complex line objects. Also covered is the ability to break complex line objects down into their individual line and arc segments using the **EXPLODE** command.

| Polyline | |
|---|---|
| **Ribbon & Panel:** | Homel Draw |
| **Draw Toolbar:** | |
| **Menu:** | Drawl Polyline |
| **Command Line:** | PLINE |
| **Command Alias:** | PL |

## DRAWING POLYLINES

A polyline is a complex line object made up of one or more connected line segments and/or arcs that are treated as a single line. See Figure 9-1.

Polylines are created using the **PLINE** command.

When you start the **PLINE** command, AutoCAD prompts you to *Specify start point:*. You can either type in a coordinate value or pick a point in your drawing similar to the **LINE** command. After you specify the first point, AutoCAD will continue to prompt you to *Specify next point or ↓* until you press **<Enter ↵>** without specifying a point as shown in Figure 9-2.

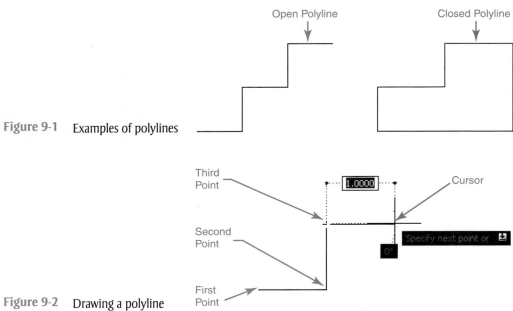

**Figure 9-1**    Examples of polylines

**Figure 9-2**    Drawing a polyline

You can specify points when drawing a polyline using absolute, relative, or polar coordinate entry methods. It is also possible to use direct distance entry with either the **Ortho Mode** or **Polar Tracking** drawing tools.

You can create a closed polyline line using the **Close** option just like the **LINE** command, except that the closed polyline creates a true closed polygon, unlike the **LINE** command, which creates individual line segments. The **Close** option will draw a line segment from the last point back to the start point. Figure 9-3 shows the result of selecting the **Close** option after drawing two line segments.

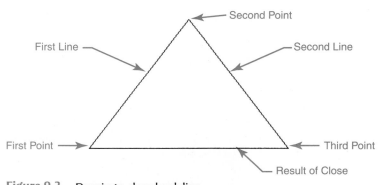

**Figure 9-3**    Drawing a closed polyline

It is possible to get the area and perimeter of a closed polyline using the **LIST** command. To use the **LIST** command type **LIST** or **LI**, select the polyline, and press **<Enter ↵>**. AutoCAD switches to the full text window and lists the area, perimeter, vertex point information, and a few other properties. You can also retrieve the same information using the **Properties** palette.

The **PLINE** command also has a built-in **Undo** option that allows you to undo points as you draw. Using the **Undo** option repeatedly will undo all the polyline points back to the first point.

> **Note:**
> By default, AutoCAD creates what's referred to as an optimized polyline that has the object name LWPOLY-LINE. The *LW* stands for lightweight because the method in which polylines store vertex point information has been optimized. The old unoptimized polyline format still exists for legacy reasons and is referred to simply as a POLY-LINE object.

**TIP**  You can control the type of polyline used via the **PLINETYPE** system variable. **PLINETYPE** controls both the creation of new polylines and the conversion of existing polylines in drawings from previous releases of AutoCAD. **PLINETYPE** has three settings.

**0**  Polylines in older drawings are not converted when opened; **PLINE** command creates old-format polylines.

**1**  Polylines in older drawings are not converted when opened; **PLINE** command creates optimized polylines.

**2**  Polylines in AutoCAD Release 14 or older drawings are converted when opened; **PLINE** creates optimized polylines.

The default setting is 2.

---

**Exercise 9-1:** Drawing a Polyline

1. Start a new drawing using the acad.dwt drawing template.
2. Create the drawing shown in Figure 9-4 using the **PLINE** command. **Do not** draw dimensions.
3. The polyline should be closed using the **Close** option.
4. Save the drawing as **EX9-1.**

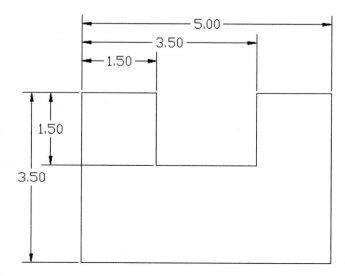

Figure 9-4    Drawing a polyline

## Drawing Polyline Arcs

It is possible to switch from drawing line segments to drawing arcs when creating a polyline using the **Arc** option. After selecting the **Arc** option, AutoCAD prompts you to *Specify endpoint of arc or* ↓. By default, specifying an arc endpoint creates an arc that is tangent to the last line or arc segment as shown in Figure 9-5.

The direction of the arc is determined by where the arc endpoint is located relative to the current polyline point. If you continue to specify points in response to the *Specify endpoint of arc or* ↓ prompt, AutoCAD will create multiple tangent arc segments as shown in Figure 9-6.

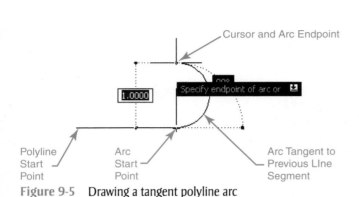

**Figure 9-5**   Drawing a tangent polyline arc

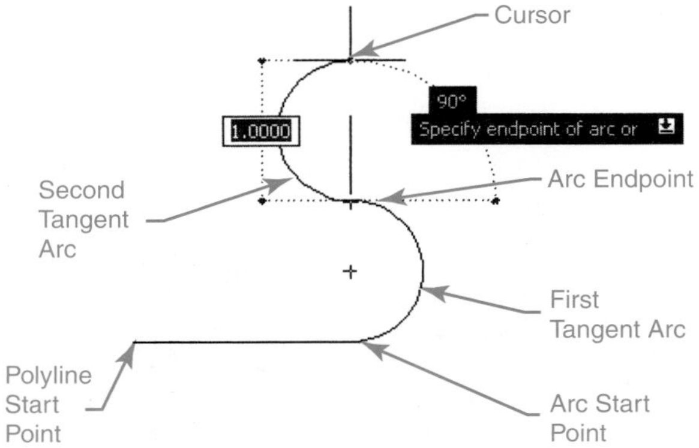

**Figure 9-6**   Drawing multiple tangent polyline arcs

You can switch back to drawing straight line segments using the **Line** option by either typing **L<Enter ↵>** or using the arrow keys if you're using **Dynamic Input** in response to the *Specify endpoint of arc or* ↓ prompt as shown in Figure 9-7.

There are a number of other options for creating polyline arcs, which are explained in the following sections.

**Exercise 9-2:** Drawing Tangent Polyline Arcs

1. Start a new drawing using the acad.dwt drawing template.
2. Create the drawing shown in Figure 9-8 using the **PLINE** command and the default tangent **Arc** option.
3. Save the drawing as **EX9-2.**

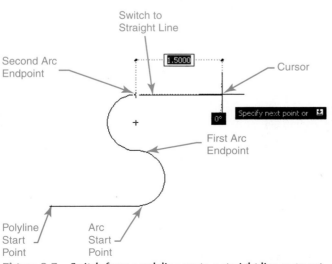

**Figure 9-7**   Switch from a polyline arc to a straight line segment

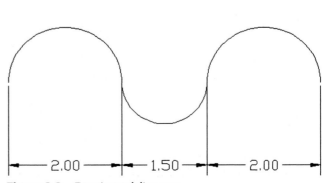

**Figure 9-8**   Drawing polyline arcs

*Angle Option.*    The **Angle** option allows you to specify the included angle of the arc segment from the start point. After you select the **Angle** option, AutoCAD prompts you to *Specify included angle:*. Enter the desired angle and press **<Enter ↵>**.

After you enter the angle, AutoCAD prompts you to *Specify endpoint of arc or* ↓. You can specify an endpoint or enter one of the following options:

> **CEnter**    Allows you to specify the center of the arc segment
>
> **Radius**    Allows you to specify the radius of the arc segment. After you enter the radius, AutoCAD prompts you to *Specify direction of chord for arc <45>:*. You can pick a point to indicate the direction or enter an angle at the keyboard.

Figure 9-9 shows the results of drawing a polyline arc using the **Angle** option.

> **Note:**
> Entering a positive number creates counterclockwise arc segments. Entering a negative number creates clockwise arc segments.

*CEnter Option.*    The **CEnter** option allows you to specify the center of the arc segment. After you select the **CEnter** option, AutoCAD prompts you to *Specify center point of arc:*. You can pick a point or enter a coordinate value at the keyboard.

After you enter the point, AutoCAD prompts you to *Specify endpoint of arc or* ↓. You can specify an endpoint or enter one of the following options:

> **Angle** Allows you to enter the included angle of the arc segment from the start point
>
> **Length** Allows you to specify the chord length of the arc segment

Figure 9-10 shows the results of drawing a polyline arc using the **CEnter** option.

> **Note:**
> AutoCAD draws the new arc segment tangent to the previous arc segment if the previous segment is an arc.

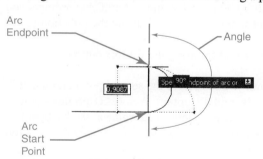

**Figure 9-9**   Drawing a polyline arc using the Angle option

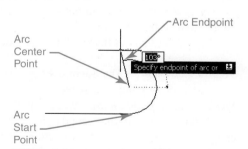

**Figure 9-10**   Drawing a polyline arc using the CEnter option

*Close Option.*    The **Close** option allows you to close a polyline with an arc segment.

*Direction Option.*    The **Direction** option allows you to indicate the starting direction for the arc segment. After you select the **Direction** option, AutoCAD prompts you to *Specify the tangent direction from the start point of arc:*. You can pick a point or enter a coordinate value at the keyboard.

After you enter the angle, AutoCAD prompts you to *Specify endpoint of arc:*. You can pick a point or enter a coordinate value at the keyboard.

Figure 9-11 shows the results of drawing a polyline arc using the **Direction** option.

> **Note:**
> The ending half-width becomes the uniform half-width for all new segments until you change the half-width again.

*Halfwidth Option.*     The **Halfwidth** option allows you to specify the width from the center of a wide polyline segment to one of its edges. After you select the **Halfwidth** option, AutoCAD prompts you to *Specify starting half-width <current>:*. Enter a value or press **<Enter ↲>** to use the current half-width. AutoCAD then prompts you to *Specify ending half-width <starting width>:*. You can either enter a different half-width value to create a tapered arc or press **<Enter ↲>** for a uniform width.

Figure 9-12 shows the results of drawing a polyline arc using the **Halfwidth** option.

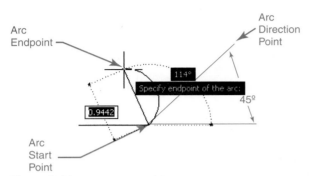

**Figure 9-11**    Drawing a polyline arc using the Direction option

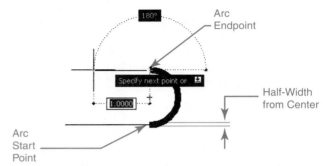

**Figure 9-12**    Drawing a polyline arc using the Halfwidth option

*Line Option.*     The **Line** option exits the **Arc** option and returns to the initial **PLINE** command prompt so you can draw straight line segments. Input at the *Specify endpoint of arc or ↲* prompt.

*Radius Option.*     The **Radius** option allows you to specify the radius of the arc segment. After you select the **Radius** option, AutoCAD prompts you to *Specify radius of arc:*. Enter the desired radius and press **<Enter ↲>**.

After you enter the radius, AutoCAD prompts you to *Specify endpoint of arc or ↓*. You can specify an endpoint or select the **Angle** option. The **Angle** option allows you to enter the included angle of the arc segment from the start point. After you enter the angle, AutoCAD prompts you to *Specify direction of chord for arc <45>:*. You can pick a point to indicate the direction or enter an angle at the keyboard.

Figure 9-13 shows the results of drawing a polyline arc using the **Radius** option.

*Second Pt Option.*     The **Second Pt** option allows you to specify the second point and the endpoint of a three-point arc. After you select the **Second Pt** option, AutoCAD prompts you to *Specify second point on arc:*. You can pick a point or enter a coordinate value at the keyboard.

After you specify the second point, AutoCAD prompts you to *Specify endpoint of arc ↓*. You can pick a point or enter a coordinate value at the keyboard.

Figure 9-14 shows the results of drawing a polyline arc using the **Second Pt** option.

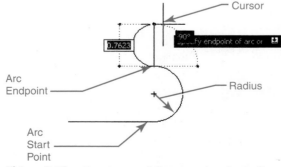

**Figure 9-13**    Drawing a polyline arc using the Radius option

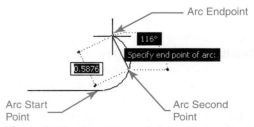

**Figure 9-14**    Drawing a polyline arc using the Second Pt option

*Undo Option.* The **Undo** option allows you to undo the most recent arc segment added to the polyline.

*Width Option.* The **Width** option allows you to change the width of the next arc segment. After you select the **Width** option, AutoCAD prompts you to *Specify starting width <current>:.* Enter a value or press **<Enter ↵>** to use the current width. AutoCAD then prompts you to *Specify ending width <starting width>:.* You can either enter a different width value to create a tapered arc or press **<Enter ↵>** for a uniform width.

> **Note:**
> The ending width becomes the uniform width for all new segments until you change the width again.

Figure 9-15 shows the results of drawing a polyline arc using the **Width** option.

---

**Exercise 9-3:** Drawing Complex Polyline Arcs

1. Start a new drawing using the acad.dwt drawing template.
2. Create the drawing shown in Figure 9-16 using the **PLINE** command and the **Arc** options covered in this section. **Do not** draw dimensions.
3. Close the polyline using the **PLINE** command's **Close** option.
4. Save the drawing as **EX9-3.**

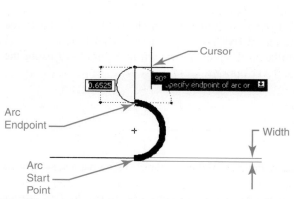

**Figure 9-15**    Drawing a polyline arc using the Width option

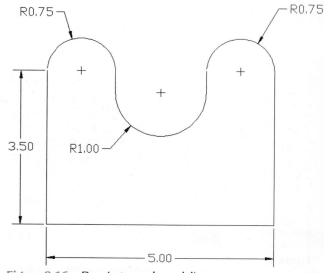

**Figure 9-16**    Drawing complex polyline arcs

## Drawing Polylines with a Width

It is possible to assign a physical width to a polyline using the **Width** option. In fact, it is possible to vary a polyline's width between vertex points using the **Width** option so that a polyline segment can be tapered.

After you select the **Width** option, AutoCAD prompts you for a starting width and an ending width. This allows you to vary the width from point to point. To apply a width to all the line segments of a polyline, you simply specify an equal starting and ending width. For instance, to draw a polyline with a constant width of 0.100″, you type **.1<Enter ↵>** when AutoCAD prompts you to *Specify starting width <0.0000>:.* AutoCAD then prompts you for the ending width of the polyline segment using the

> **Note:**
> Polyline width is not related to the lineweight property discussed in Chapter 6. Polyline width is a unique property that is assigned directly to the polyline. Because it is unrelated to the lineweight property, it is not affected by the **LWT** lineweight toggle on the Status Bar.

starting width as the default by prompting *Specify ending width <0.1000>:*. This allows you to simply press the **<Enter ↵>** key to create a constant width. Figure 9-17 shows a polyline drawn with a constant width of 0.100″.

Varying a polyline width provides many unique possibilities. For instance, you can use a polyline with varying widths to create an arrow by specifying a starting width of 0.000″ to create the point, or tip, and then specifying an ending width greater than zero for the next point so the line is tapered. For instance, to create an arrow that tapers from a point to a base width of 0.25″, you would type **0<Enter ↵>** when AutoCAD prompts *Specify starting width <0.0000>:* to create the arrow point and then type **.25<Enter ↵>** when AutoCAD prompts *Specify ending width <0.1000>:* to indicate the base width as shown in Figure 9-18.

You can even combine these varying width techniques with polyline arcs to create curved arrows that can be used for signage on parking lot plans and roadways as shown in Figure 9-19.

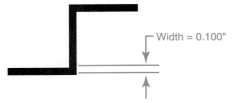 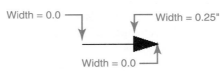 

**Figure 9-17**   A polyline drawn with a constant width of 0.100″

**Figure 9-18**   A polyline arrow created by varying the polyline width

**Figure 9-19**   A curved polyline arrow created using polyline arcs

---

**Exercise 9-4:** Drawing Polylines with a Width

1. Start a new drawing using the acad.dwt drawing template.
2. Create a polyline with a uniform width of 0.100″ similar to the polyline shown in Figure 9-17 using the **PLINE** command and the **Width** option.
3. Create a polyline arrow that tapers from a point to a base width of 0.25″ similar to the polyline shown in Figure 9-18 using the **PLINE** command and the **Width** option.
4. Create a curved polyline arrow similar to the polyline shown in Figure 9-19 using the **PLINE** command and the **Width** and **Arc** options.
5. Save the drawing as **EX9-4.**

## DRAWING RECTANGLES

| Rectangle | |
|---|---|
| **Ribbon & Panel:** | Home| Draw 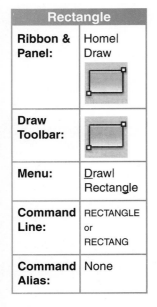 |
| **Draw Toolbar:** | |
| **Menu:** | Draw| Rectangle |
| **Command Line:** | RECTANGLE or RECTANG |
| **Command Alias:** | None |

The **RECTANGLE** or **RECTANG** command draws a polyline rectangle using two user-supplied corner points.

When you start the **RECTANG** command, AutoCAD prompts you to *Specify first corner point or ↓*. You can either type in a coordinate value, or you can pick a point in your drawing. After you specify the first point, AutoCAD prompts you to *Specify other corner point or ↓* so you can locate the other corner point as shown in Figure 9-20.

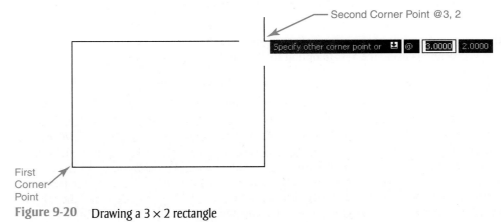

**Figure 9-20**   Drawing a 3 × 2 rectangle

Remember that it always possible to enter a coordinate value anytime AutoCAD prompts you for a point. In fact, if you know the length and width of the rectangle, you can enter a relative coordinate where *X* is the length and *Y* is the width. For instance, to draw a 3.000″ × 2.000″ rectangle, you can type **@3,2<Enter ↵>** when AutoCAD prompts you to *Specify other corner point or ↓*.

> If you are using **Dynamic Input**, you do not need to use the @ prefix. The second pick point is relative by default.

*Entering the Length and Width.*    The **Dimensions** option allows you to draw a rectangle by entering the length and width in response to AutoCAD prompts. To use the **Dimensions** option, you must pick the first corner point. After you select the **Dimensions** option, AutoCAD prompts you to *Specify length for rectangles <3.0000>:*. Enter the desired length and press **<Enter ↵>**. AutoCAD then prompts you to *Specify width for rectangles <2.0000>:* so you can enter the width. After you enter a length and width, AutoCAD prompts you for a direction point by prompting *Specify other corner point or ↓*. The point you pick determines the rectangle's orientation as shown in Figure 9-21.

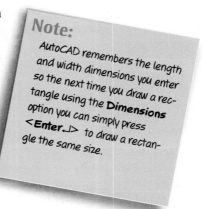

**Note:**
AutoCAD remembers the length and width dimensions you enter so the next time you draw a rectangle using the **Dimensions** option you can simply press **<Enter ↵>** to draw a rectangle the same size.

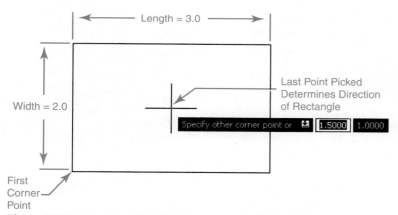

**Figure 9-21**    Drawing a rectangle by entering the length and width

*Drawing a Rectangle at an Angle.*    The **Rotation** option allows you to draw a rectangle at a user-specified angle. To use the **Rotation** option, you must pick the first corner point. After you select the **Rotation** option, AutoCAD prompts you to *Specify rotation angle or ↓*. You have three possible ways to input the rotation angle:

- Type the angle at the keyboard.
- Pick a point to define the angle using the first corner point as the base point.
- Use the **Points** option to pick two separate points to define the angle.

The first option requires that you enter the angle by typing it at the keyboard. For instance, to create a rectangle that is rotated 45°, you enter **45<Enter ↵>**. After you enter the angle, the rectangle preview changes to the input angle, and AutoCAD again prompts you to *Specify other corner point or ↓*. You can locate the second corner point using any of the techniques explained in this section, including using the **Dimensions** and **Area** options as shown in Figure 9-22.

You can also pick a point to define the angle using the first corner point as the base point, or vertex. When picking a point to define the angle, it is usually beneficial to use either the **Ortho Mode** or **Polar Tracking** drawing tool.

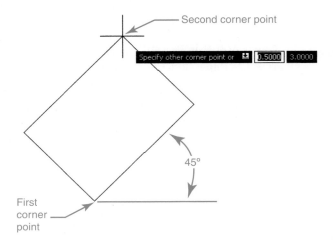

**Figure 9-22**  Drawing a rectangle
at a 45° angle

> **FOR MORE DETAILS**  See Chapter 5 for more information about using the **Ortho Mode** and **Polar Tracking** drawing tools.

The **Pick points** option gives you the ability to define the rotation angle using two *separate* points instead of using the first corner point as the default base point. After you select the **Pick points** option, AutoCAD prompts you for two pick points. After you pick the two points, the rectangle preview changes to the input angle, and AutoCAD again prompts you to *Specify other corner point or ↓*. You can locate the second corner point using any of the techniques explained in this section.

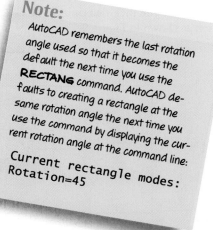

*Drawing a Rectangle by Specifying the Area.*
The **Area** option allows you to draw a rectangle by specifying its area and either the length or the width. To use the **Area** option, you must pick the first corner point. After you select the **Area** option, AutoCAD prompts you to *Enter area of rectangle in current units <100.0000>:*. Enter the desired area and press **<Enter ↓>**. AutoCAD then asks you if you want to specify the length or width by prompting *Calculate rectangle dimensions based on [Length/Width]*. AutoCAD will prompt you for the length or width accordingly. After you enter the distance, AutoCAD draws the rectangle automatically at the first corner point location as shown in Figure 9-23.

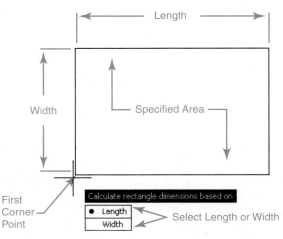

**Figure 9-23**  Drawing a rectangle
by specifying the area

**Exercise 9-5:** Drawing Rectangles

1. Start a new drawing using the acad.dwt drawing template.
2. Create a 3.000″ × 2.000″ rectangle similar to the rectangle shown in Figure 9-20 using the **RECTANG** command and relative coordinate entry.
3. Create a 3.000″ × 2.000″ rectangle similar to the rectangle shown in Figure 9-21 in another location using the **RECTANG** command and the **Dimensions** option to input the length and width.
4. Create a 3.000″ × 2.000″ rectangle at a 45° angle similar to the rectangle shown in Figure 9-22 in another location using the **RECTANG** command and the **Angle** option to input the 45° angle.
5. Save the drawing as **EX9-5**.

*Chamfering Corners.* The **Chamfer** option allows you to draw a rectangle with four beveled, or *chamfered*, corners using the specified distance from the corner point to the beginning of each chamfer.

After you select the **Chamfer** option, AutoCAD prompts you to *Specify first chamfer distance for rectangles <0.0000>:*. Enter the distance for the first leg of the chamfer and press **<Enter ↲>**. AutoCAD then prompts you to *Specify second chamfer distance for rectangles <0.2500>:* using the first distance as the default. Typically, you want to simply press **<Enter ↲>** to accept the default and create a rectangle with 45° chamfers, although you can specify a different distance. After entering the chamfer distances, you can create a rectangle with chamfered corners using any of the techniques already explained. Figure 9-24 shows a 3.000″ × 2.000″ rectangle drawn with 0.250″ × 0.250″ chamfered corners.

*Rounding Corners.* The **Fillet** option allows you to draw a rectangle with four rounded, or *filleted,* corners using the specified radius from the corner point.

After you select the **Fillet** option, AutoCAD prompts you to *Specify fillet radius for rectangles <0.2500>:*. Enter the radius and press **<Enter ↲>**. After entering the radius, you can create a rectangle using any of the techniques explained above. Figure 9-25 shows a 3.000″ × 2.000″ rectangle drawn with 0.250″ filleted corners.

> **Note:**
> AutoCAD remembers the last chamfer distances used so that they become the default the next time you use the **RECTANG** command. AutoCAD defaults to creating a rectangle with chamfered corners the next time you use the command by displaying the current chamfer distances at the command line:
>
> ```
> Current rectangle modes:
> Chamfer=0.2500 x 0.2500
> ```

> **Note:**
> AutoCAD remembers the last radius used so that it becomes the default the next time you use the **RECTANG** command. AutoCAD defaults to creating a rectangle with filleted corners the next time you use the command by displaying the current fillet radius at the command line:
>
> ```
> Current rectangle modes:
> Fillet=0.2500
> ```

**chamfer:** To cut off a corner with a slight angle or bevel

**fillet:** To round off an inside or outside corner at a specific radius

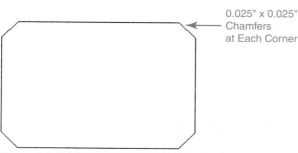

**Figure 9-24** Drawing a rectangle with chamfered corners

0.025" x 0.025" Chamfers at Each Corner

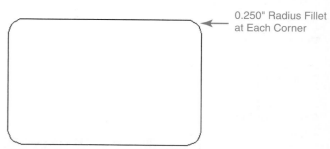

**Figure 9-25** Drawing a rectangle with filleted corners

0.250" Radius Fillet at Each Corner

*Creating Rectangles with a Width.* The **Width** option allows you to draw a rectangle with a user-specified polyline width as explained earlier in the section "Drawing Polylines with a Width."

After you select the **Width** option, AutoCAD prompts you to *Specify line width for rectangles <0.0000>:*. Enter the line width and press **<Enter ↵>**. After entering the width, you can create a rectangle using any of the techniques explained above. Figure 9-26 shows a 3.000″ × 2.000″ rectangle drawn with a 0.100″ uniform line width.

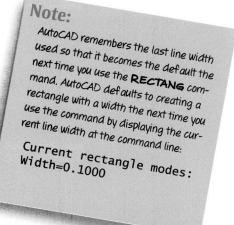

**Note:**

AutoCAD remembers the last line width used so that it becomes the default the next time you use the **RECTANG** command. AutoCAD defaults to creating a rectangle with a width the next time you use the command by displaying the current line width at the command line:

Current rectangle modes:
Width=0.1000

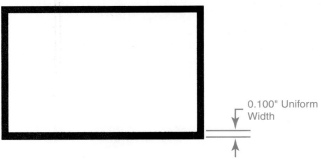

0.100″ Uniform Width

**Figure 9-26**    Drawing a rectangle with a uniform line width

---

**Exercise 9-6:** Drawing Rectangles with Chamfered and Rounded Corners

1. Start a new drawing using the acad.dwt drawing template.
2. Draw a 3.000″ × 2.000″ rectangle with 0.250″ × 0.250″ chamfered corners similar to the rectangle shown in Figure 9-24 using the **RECTANG** command and the **Chamfer** option.
3. Draw a 3.000″ × 2.000″ rectangle in another location with 0.250″ rounded corners similar to the rectangle shown in Figure 9-25 using the **RECTANG** command and the **Fillet** option.
4. Draw a 3.000″ × 2.000″ rectangle with a 0.100″ uniform width similar to the rectangle shown in Figure 9-26 using the **RECTANG** command and the **Width** option.
5. Save the drawing as **EX9-6.**

| Polygon | |
|---|---|
| **Ribbon & Panel:** | Home\| Draw |
| **Draw Toolbar:** | |
| **Menu:** | Draw\| Polygon |
| **Command Line:** | POLYGON |
| **Command Alias:** | POL |

# DRAWING POLYGONS

The **POLYGON** command draws a polyline polygon with a user-supplied number of sides. See Figure 9-27.

Diamond        Hexagon        Octagon

**Figure 9-27**    Examples of polygons

When you start the **POLYGON** command, AutoCAD prompts you to *Enter number of sides <4>:*. You can enter a number between 3 and 1024. The length of the sides is determined either by specifying a center point and a radius or by indicating the length of a typical side, called the *edge*. The default is to specify a center point and radius; the radius indicates a circle that either inscribes or circumscribes the polygon, and the length of the sides is generated automatically.

After you specify the number of sides, AutoCAD prompts you to *Specify center of polygon or ↓*. The default is to locate a center point by either picking a point or by typing in a coordinate value. AutoCAD then asks you if you want to create the polygon inscribed inside a circle (see Figure 9-28A) with the specified radius or circumscribed on the outside of the circle (see Figure 9-28B) by prompting *Enter an option ↓*. You can either type **I<Enter ↓>** for inscribed or **C<Enter ↓>** for circumscribed or use the arrow keys to select either option if you are using Dynamic Input. AutoCAD then prompts you to *Specify radius of circle:*. You can either type a radius at the keyboard or pick a point as shown in Figures 9-28A and B.

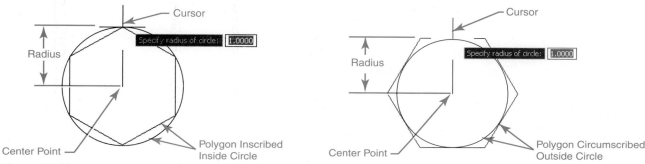

**Figure 9-28A** Polygon with six sides inscribed in a circle **B** Polygon with six sides circumscribed outside of a circle

*Specifying the Length of a Side.* The **Edge** option allows you to create a polygon by specifying the location and length of a side. AutoCAD uses the input length to automatically create the remaining specified number of sides.

After you select the **Edge** option, AutoCAD prompts you to *Specify first endpoint of edge:*. You can either pick a point or type in a coordinate value to locate the starting point of one of the sides. AutoCAD then prompts *Specify second endpoint of edge:*. The second point determines the length for all the sides specified *and* the rotation angle of the finished polygon as shown in Figure 9-29.

**Note:**
AutoCAD remembers the number of sides you enter so the next time you draw a polygon you can simply press **<Enter.↓>** to draw a polygon with the same number of sides.

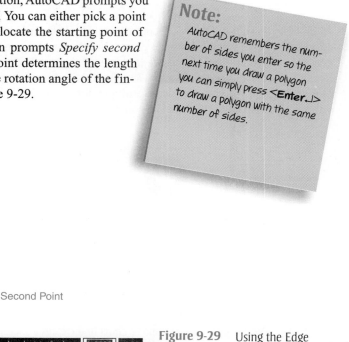

**Figure 9-29** Using the Edge option to draw a polygon

**TIP**
You can specify the second edge point using absolute, relative, or polar coordinate entry methods. It is also possible to use direct distance entry with either the **Ortho Mode** or **Polar Tracking** drawing tools.

**Exercise 9-7:** Drawing Polygons

1. Start a new drawing using the acad.dwt drawing template.
2. Draw a six-sided polygon *inscribed inside* a circle with a radius of 1.000″ similar to the polygon shown in Figure 9-28A using the **POLYGON** command.
3. Next to the polygon created in step 2, draw a six-sided polygon *circumscribed outside* a circle with a radius of 1.000″ similar to the polygon shown in Figure 9-28B using the **POLYGON** command.
4. Next to the polygon created in step 3, draw a six-sided polygon with an edge length of 0.500″ similar to the polygon shown in Figure 9-29 using the **POLYGON** command and the **Edge** option.
5. Save the drawing as **EX9-7.**

## DRAWING DONUTS

| Donut | |
|---|---|
| **Ribbon & Panel:** | Homel Draw |
| **Toolbar:** | None |
| **Menu:** | Drawl Donut |
| **Command Line:** | DONUT |
| **Command Alias:** | DO |

The **DONUT** command draws a ring, or donut, with a user-specified inside diameter and outside diameter. The ring thickness equals the outside diameter minus the inside diameter. See Figure 9-30.

**Figure 9-30**    Examples of donuts

When you start the **DONUT** command, AutoCAD prompts you to *Specify inside diameter of donut <0.5000>:*. Enter a diameter greater than or equal to zero and press **<Enter ↵>**. AutoCAD then prompts you to *Specify outside diameter of donut <1.0000>:*. Enter a value greater than the inside diameter and press **<Enter ↵>**. AutoCAD repeatedly prompts you to *Specify center of donut or <exit>:* so you can locate multiple donuts as shown in Figure 9-31. Press **<Enter ↵>** without inputting a point to exit the command.

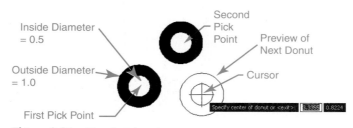

**Figure 9-31**    Drawing donuts

**TIP**
Specifying an inside diameter equal to 0 creates a solid filled circle with the specified outside diameter.

### Exercise 9-8: Drawing Donuts

1. Start a new drawing using the acad.dwt drawing template.
2. Create some donuts with an inside diameter of 0.500″ and an outside diameter of 1.000″ using the **DONUT** command.
3. Create some *solid* donuts with an inside diameter of 0.000″ and an outside diameter of 1.000″ using the **DONUT** command.
4. Save the drawing as **EX9-8.**

## DRAWING REVISION CLOUDS

The **REVCLOUD** command draws a polyline of sequential arcs to form a cloud shape that can be used as a *revision cloud* on a drawing to highlight markups and changes. See Figure 9-32.

revision cloud: Continuous line made from arcs to resemble a cloud that is used to highlight markups and changes

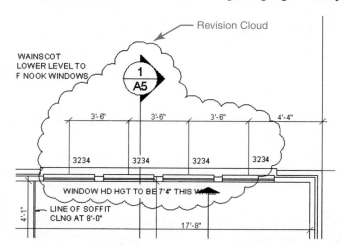

**Figure 9-32**   Example of revision cloud

There are two different styles for a revision cloud: Normal or Calligraphy. The default style, Normal, draws the revision cloud using regular polyline arcs with no thickness. The Calligraphy style tapers the polyline arc thickness so the revision cloud looks as if it were drawn with a calligraphy pen.

When you start the **REVCLOUD** command, AutoCAD displays the default settings at the command line as follows:

```
Minimum arc length: 0.5000   Maximum arc length: 0.5000
Style: Normal
```

To create a revision cloud using the default settings, pick a point with your mouse and guide your mouse along the desired revision cloud path when AutoCAD prompts you to *Specify start point or ↓*. You *do not* need to hold the mouse button down. Simply drag the mouse to create the clouded area. When your cursor position returns to the beginning point of the first arc, the revision cloud is closed automatically as shown in Figure 9-33.

| Revision Cloud | |
|---|---|
| **Ribbon & Panel:** | Home\| Draw |
| **Draw Toolbar:** | |
| **Menu:** | Draw\| Revision Cloud |
| **Command Line:** | REVCLOUD |
| **Command Alias:** | None |

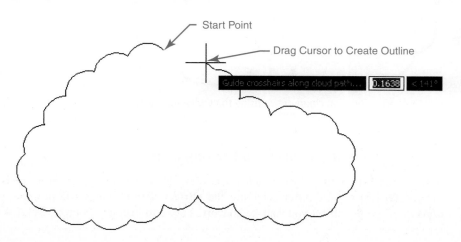

**Figure 9-33**   Drawing a revision cloud

AutoCAD interactively flips the arc direction based on the direction you drag your mouse after specifying the start point so that the arc bulge faces the proper way.

### Changing the Arc Length

The **Arc length** option allows you to change the minimum and maximum arc length used to create the polyline arcs when the revision cloud is being drawn so that you can make them bigger or smaller.

After you select the **Arc length** option, AutoCAD prompts you to *Specify minimum length of arc <0.5000>:*. Enter the desired minimum length and press **<Enter ↵>**. AutoCAD prompts you to *Specify maximum length of arc <0.5000>:*. Enter the desired maximum length and press **<Enter ↵>**. The values become the default the next time you use the **REVCLOUD** command.

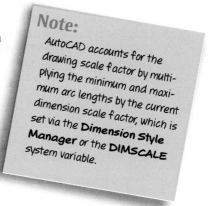

**Note:**
AutoCAD accounts for the drawing scale factor by multiplying the minimum and maximum arc lengths by the current dimension scale factor, which is set via the **Dimension Style Manager** or the **DIMSCALE** system variable.

| **FOR MORE DETAILS** | See Chapter 13 for more information about setting the dimension scale factor. See Chapter 1 for more information about the drawing scale factor. |
| --- | --- |

### Switching Styles

The **Style** option allows you to switch between the Normal style and the Calligraphy style. After you select the **Style** option, AutoCAD prompts you to *Select arc style ↓*. You can type **C<Enter ↵>** for the Calligraphy style or **N<Enter ↵>** for the Normal style or use the arrow keys to select the desired style if you're using Dynamic Input. Figure 9-34 shows a revision cloud drawn using the Calligraphy style.

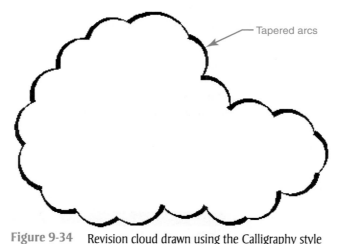

Tapered arcs

**Figure 9-34**     Revision cloud drawn using the Calligraphy style

### Creating Revision Clouds from Existing Objects

You can convert existing objects such as a circles, ellipses, and polylines into a revision cloud using the **Object** option. After selecting the **Object** option, AutoCAD prompts you to *Select object:*. Select the object you want to convert. After converting the object, AutoCAD allows you to change the direction of the arcs so they face in or out by prompting you if you want to *Reverse direction* ↓.

**TIP** You can control whether the existing object is deleted after it is converted into a revision cloud via the **DELOBJ** system variable. Setting **DELOBJ** to **1** deletes the original object and setting **DELOBJ** to **0** maintains the original object.

### Exercise 9-9: Drawing Revision Clouds

1. Start a new drawing using the acad.dwt drawing template.
2. Create a revision cloud using the Calligraphy style similar to the one shown in Figure 9-34 using the **REVCLOUD** command and the **Style** option.
3. Create a circle using the **CIRCLE** command.
4. Convert the circle to a revision cloud using the **REVCLOUD** command and the **Object** option.
5. Save the drawing as **EX9-9**.

## EDITING POLYLINES

You can edit polylines after they are created using the **PEDIT** command. The **PEDIT** command allows you to:

* Convert lines and arcs to polylines
* Close and open polylines
* Join multiple polylines together
* Change a polyline's width
* Edit polyline vertices so that you can move, add, and remove points
* Curve fit a polyline
* Control a polyline's linetype generation

When you start the **PEDIT** command, AutoCAD prompts you to *Select polyline or* ↓. You can then select a polyline, a line, or an arc. If you select an object that is not a polyline, AutoCAD displays the following at the command line so you can convert it:

```
Object selected is not a polyline
```

AutoCAD allows you to convert the object by prompting *Do you want to turn it into one?* ↓. The default is **Yes** so you can simply press **<Enter ↵>** to convert the selected line or arc.

| Edit Polyline | |
|---|---|
| **Ribbon & Panel:** | Home\| Draw |
| **Modify II Toolbar:** | |
| **Menu:** | Modify\| Object\| Polyline |
| **Command Line:** | PEDIT |
| **Command Alias:** | PE |

**TIP** The **PEDITACCEPT** system variable allows you to suppress display of the Object selected is not a polyline prompt so that objects are automatically converted. Setting the **PEDITACCEPT** to **1** (on) suppresses the prompt. Setting **PEDITACCEPT** to **0** (off) turns the prompt back on.

You can edit multiple polylines using the **Multiple** option. To select multiple objects, either type **M<Enter ↵>** or use the arrow keys to select the option if you are using **Dynamic Input** after starting the **PEDIT** command and AutoCAD prompts you to *Select polyline or* ↓. You can then use any of the selection options to select multiple objects. If any of the objects are not polylines, AutoCAD allows you to convert them using the same approach mentioned earlier.

After a polyline is selected, or converted, AutoCAD prompts you to *Enter an option* ↓ to allow you to select an editing option. All the **PEDIT** options are explored in the following sections.

## Closing and Opening Polylines

You can close or open a polyline using either the **Close** or **Open** option. The **PEDIT** command provides one option or the other depending on the polyline's current open or closed status.

To close an open polyline so that a polyline segment is created between the first and last point, you can either type **C<Enter ↓>** or use the arrow keys if you are using Dynamic Input in response to the **PEDIT** command *Enter an option* ↓ prompt. Figure 9-35 shows the result of selecting the **Close** option.

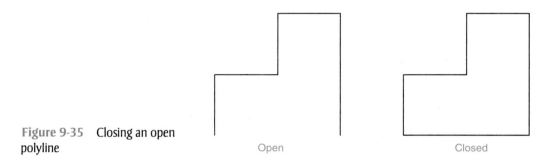

**Figure 9-35**    Closing an open polyline

Open                Closed

To open a closed polyline so that the polyline segment between the first and last point is removed, you can either type **O<Enter ↓>** or use the arrow keys if you are using Dynamic Input in response to the *Enter an option* ↓ prompt.

### Exercise 9-10: Opening and Closing a Polyline Using PEDIT

1. Open drawing **EX9-1.**
2. Open the polyline using the **PEDIT** command and the **Open** option.
3. Close the polyline using the **PEDIT** command and the **Close** option.
4. Save the drawing as **EX9-10.**

## Joining Polylines

The **Join** option allows you to join a polyline, line, or arc to one or more open polylines if their ends either connect or if they are within a specified *fuzz distance* of each other.

Applying a fuzz distance is available only when you use the **Multiple** option and is explained in detail in the following section. After you select the **Join** option, AutoCAD prompts you to *Select objects:*. You can then use any of the selection options to select one or more connected objects and press **<Enter ↓>** as shown in Figure 9-36.

**fuzz distance:** Distance used to determine if polyline endpoints that are not connected can be connected by extending them, trimming them, or connecting them with a new polyline segment

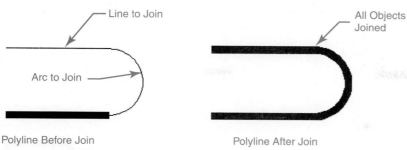

**Figure 9-36**  Joining an open polyline

AutoCAD reports the success or failure of the join attempt by displaying how many objects were added to the original polyline at the command line:

```
2 segments added to polyline
```

It is your job to determine if all the objects were joined based on how many objects you originally selected. For instance, if you selected three objects and AutoCAD says that only two segments were added, you have a problem. You then have to inspect visually the endpoints of each object that was not joined and connect any points that are not connected. This can become a very tedious process with a complex join operation that consists of many objects. Luckily, we can use the fuzz factor mentioned earlier.

***Joining Polylines That Do Not Meet.***    As mentioned earlier, you can join polylines, lines, and arcs whose endpoints are not connected but are within a specified fuzz distance of each other. AutoCAD will either extend, trim, or insert a line segment in order to create the connection. To enter a fuzz distance, you *must* use the **Multiple** option explained earlier to select the objects you want to join first. If you then select the **Join** option using the same methods explained earlier, AutoCAD prompts you to *Enter fuzz distance or* ↓ after you select the objects to join. You can then enter the distance you want to close and press <**Enter** ↓>. AutoCAD displays how many segments were added at the command line in the same fashion as a regular join operation so you can determine if all the objects were joined successfully.

You can set the method that AutoCAD uses to join polylines via the **Jointype** option. After selecting the **Jointype** option, you can choose one of the following options:

- **Extend**    Joins by extending or trimming the segments to the nearest endpoints
- **Add**    Joins by adding a straight segment between the nearest endpoints.
- **Both**    Joins by extending or trimming if possible. Otherwise joins by adding a straight segment between the nearest endpoints.

**TIP**  Joining a polyline removes the curve fitting from a curve fit polyline. Curve fitting polylines is explained later in this section.

## Exercise 9-11: Joining Polylines Using PEDIT

1. Start a new drawing using the acad.dwt drawing template.
2. Create the drawing shown in Figure 9-37 using only the **LINE** and **ARC** commands, making sure to connect all the line and arc segments.
3. Join all the line and arc segments using the **PEDIT** command and the **Join** option.
4. Save the drawing as **EX9-11.**

## Changing the Polyline Width

The **Width** option allows you to specify a new uniform width for all the polyline segments. After you select the **Width** option, AutoCAD prompts you to *Specify new width for all segments:*. Enter the new uniform width and press <**Enter** ↓> to change the width as shown in Figure 9-38.

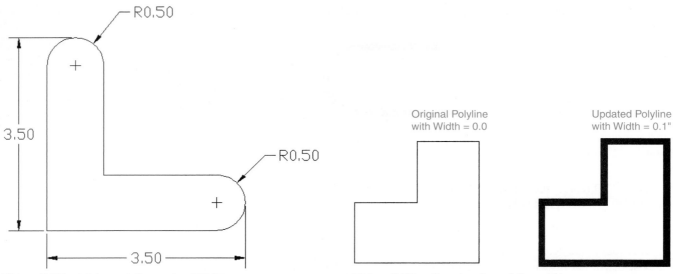

Figure 9-37    Joining polylines using PEDIT

Figure 9-38    Changing the polyline width

**TIP**    You can vary the width from point to point by either using the **Edit vertex** option explained later or, even easier yet, using the **Properties** palette. The **Properties** palette allows you to step through each vertex of a polyline and set its width property individually.

### Exercise 9-12: Changing Polyline Width Using PEDIT

1. Open drawing **EX9-11.**
2. Change the polyline width to a uniform width of 0.100″ using the **PEDIT** command and the **Width** option.
3. Save the drawing as **EX9-12.**

### Editing Polyline Vertices

The **Edit vertex** option allows you to edit a polyline's vertex points individually so you can:

- Break one or more polyline segments
- Insert a vertex point
- Move a vertex point
- Regenerate the polyline
- Straighten two more polyline segments
- Attach a tangent direction
- Change the starting and ending width of a polyline segment

**Note:**
The **X** marker stops when you get to the last polyline point. It does not skip back to the first point.

After you select the **Edit vertex** option, AutoCAD marks the first vertex of the polyline with an **X** and prompts you to *Enter a vertex editing option:*. Pressing **<Enter ↵>** will select the default **Next** or **Previous** option. These and all the other **Edit vertex** options are explained in the following sections.

*Next Option.*    The **Next** option moves the **X** marker to the next polyline vertex point. To use the **Next** option, you can either type **N<Enter ↵>** or you can use the arrow keys to select the **Next** option if you're using Dynamic Input at the *Enter a vertex editing option* prompt as shown in Figure 9-39.

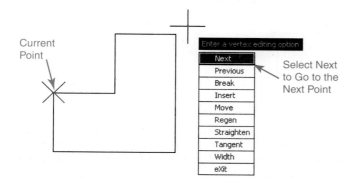

Figure 9-39    Using the Next option to move the current point

TIP    You can simply press the <**Enter ↵**> key if **Next** or **Previous** is the default option.

*Previous Option.*    The **Previous** option moves the **X** marker to the previous polyline vertex point.

*Break Option.*    The **Break** option allows you to break one or more polyline segments and create a gap from the current vertex point to the polyline vertex point you specify by stepping through the points using the **Next** and **Previous** options. After you select the **Break** option, AutoCAD prompts you to *Enter an option* ↓. You can press <**Enter ↵**> to select the default option or choose one of the following:

**Note:**
You cannot break a polyline at an endpoint.

**Next**    Moves the **X** marker to the next point

**Previous**    Moves the **X** marker to the previous point

**Go**    Deletes any segments and vertices between the two points you specify and returns to **Edit Vertex** mode

**Exit**    Exits **Break** mode and returns to **Edit Vertex** mode

The key to breaking a polyline is to start the break by selecting the **Break** option when the **X** marker is at the desired start point and then use the **Next** and **Previous** options to indicate where you want the break to end. When the **X** marker is on the desired endpoint, select the **Go** option by typing **G**<**Enter ↵**> or select the **Go** option using the arrow keys if you are using Dynamic Input to break the polyline as shown in Figure 9-40.

TIP    You can break a polyline at a point by simply using the **Go** option without using the **Next** or **Previous** option to move the **X** marker.

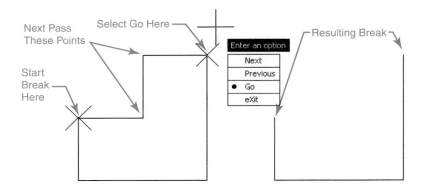

**Figure 9-40** Using the Break option to break a polyline

*Insert Option.*     The **Insert** option adds a new vertex point to a polyline after the current point with the **X** marker. After you select the **Insert** option, AutoCAD prompts you to *Specify location for new vertex:*. You can either pick a point or enter a coordinate value at the keyboard and press **<Enter ↵>** as shown in Figure 9-41.

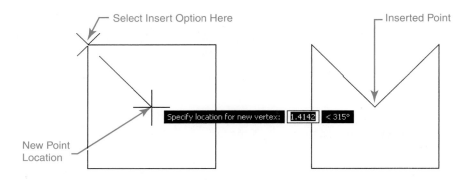

**Figure 9-41** Using the Insert option to insert a polyline vertex point

*Move Option.*     The **Move** option moves the marked vertex. After you select the **Move** option, AutoCAD prompts you to *Specify new location for marked vertex:*. You can either pick a point or enter a coordinate value at the keyboard and press **<Enter ↵>** as shown in Figure 9-42.

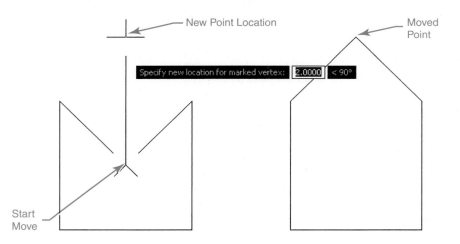

**Figure 9-42** Using the Move option to move a polyline vertex point

*Regen Option.*     The **Regen** option regenerates a polyline so any jagged curved segments are smoothed out.

*Straighten Option.*     The **Straighten** option allows you to remove one or more polyline vertex points and create a straight polyline segment from the current vertex point to the polyline vertex point you specify by stepping through the points using the **Next** and **Previous** options. After you select the **Straighten** option, AutoCAD prompts you to *Enter an option* ↓. You can press **<Enter↓>** to select the default option or choose one of the following:

**Next**   Moves the **X** marker to the next point

**Previous**   Moves the **X** marker to the previous point

**Go**   Deletes any polyline segments and vertices between the two points you specify, replaces them with a single straight line segment, and returns to **Edit Vertex** mode

**Exit**   Exits **Straighten** mode and returns to **Edit Vertex** mode

The **Straighten** option works similarly to the **Break** option. Select the **Straighten** option when the **X** marker is at the desired start point and then use the **Next** and **Previous** options to indicate where you want the straight segment to end. When the **X** marker is on the desired endpoint, select the **Go** option by typing **G<Enter ↓>** or select the **Go** option using the arrow keys if you are using Dynamic Input to delete any vertices and create a straight polyline segment as shown in Figure 9-43.

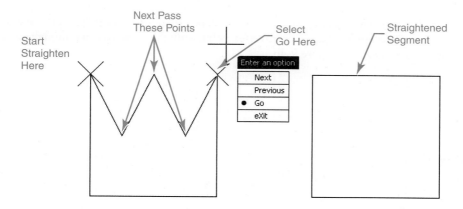

**Figure 9-43**   Using the Straighten option to straighten a polyline

*Tangent Option.*   The **Tangent** option attaches a tangent direction to the current vertex point for use in curve fitting. Curve fitting is explained in detail in the next section. After you select the **Tangent** option, AutoCAD prompts you to *Specify direction of vertex tangent:*. You can either pick a point or enter a tangent angle at the keyboard and press **<Enter ↓>**.

*Width Option.*   The **Width** option changes the starting and ending widths for the segment that immediately follows the marked vertex. Press **<Enter ↓>** to use the current width. AutoCAD then prompts you to *Specify ending width <starting width>:*. You can enter a different width value to create a tapered polyline segment as shown in Figure 9-44.

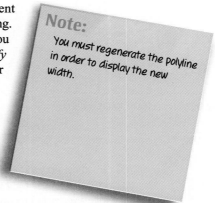

**Note:**
You must regenerate the polyline in order to display the new width.

*eXit.*   The **eXit** option exits **Edit Vertex** mode. AutoCAD returns you to the **PEDIT** command *Enter an option* ↓ prompt.

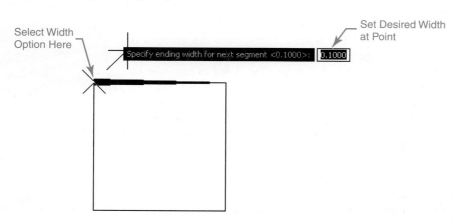

**Figure 9-44**   Using the Width option to change a polyline segment width

**Exercise 9-13:** Editing Polyline Vertices Using PEDIT

1. Open drawing **EX9-11.**
2. Change the polyline to look like the polyline shown in Figure 9-45 using the **PEDIT** command and the **Edit vertex** options.
3. Save the drawing as **EX9-13.**

## Converting Polylines into Smooth Curves

*curve fit: The process of adding vertex points to a straight line segment polyline in order to create a smooth curve*

You can transform a polyline that is made up of straight line segments into a polyline with smooth curves using the **Fit** and **Spline** options. Both options allow you to *curve fit* a polyline with very different results.

After a polyline is curve fit using either option, it is possible to convert it back to straight polyline segments using the **Decurve** option. All the curve fit options are explained in detail in the following sections.

*Fit Option.*     The **Fit** option creates an arc fit polyline. An arc fit polyline is a smooth curve consisting of arcs joining each pair of vertex points with the curve passing through all vertices of the polyline as shown in Figure 9-46.

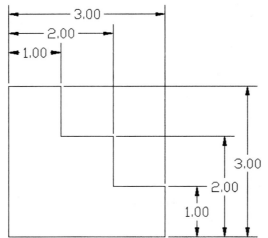

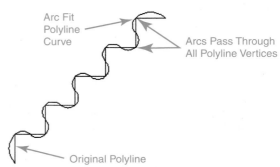

**Figure 9-45**     Editing polyline vertices using PEDIT

**Figure 9-46**     Arc fit polyline created using the Fit option

**TIP**     You can adjust how the arcs are fit by editing the tangency direction of the polyline vertex points *before* you use the **Fit** option. See the preceding section for information about how to change a vertex point's tangency direction using the **PEDIT** command's **Tangent** option.

*Spline Option.*     The **Spline** option uses the vertices of the selected polyline as the control points to create a curve approximating a *B-spline* but is not as accurate as a true spline.

*B-spline: An approximate spline curve also referred to as a nonuniform rational B-spline, or NURBS, curve*

A spline fit polyline passes through the first and last polyline vertex points unless the original polyline was closed. The curve is pulled toward the other vertex points but does not pass through them as shown in Figure 9-47. The more control points you specify, the more pull they exert on the curve.

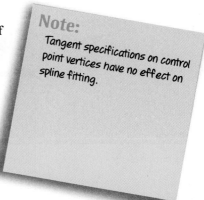

*Note:*
Tangent specifications on control point vertices have no effect on spline fitting.

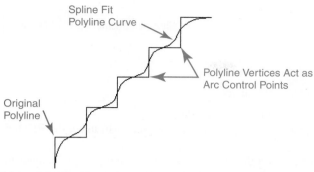

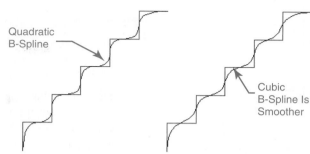

**Figure 9-47**    Spline fit polyline created using the Spline option

**Figure 9-48**    Quadratic and cubic B-splines compared

> Setting the **SPLFRAME** system variable to **1** (on) turns on the spline curve control point frame the next time the drawing is regenerated. AutoCAD draws both the frame and the spline curve. Set **SPLFRAME** to **0** (off) to turn the spline curve control frame off.

AutoCAD can generate either quadratic or cubic spline fit polylines. A cubic B-spline is very smooth, much smoother than a quadratic B-spline as shown in Figure 9-48.

The default spline curve type is the smoother cubic B-spline. The **SPLINETYPE** system variable controls the type of spline curve created. Setting **SPLINETYPE** to **5** creates a quadratic B-spline. Setting **SPLINETYPE** to **6** creates a cubic B-spline.

> You can also control the smoothness of a spline approximation via the **Segments in a polyline curve** setting in the **Display Resolution** area on the **Display** tab of the **Options** dialog box. This setting controls the number of line segments generated for each polyline curve. Setting this value higher means a greater number of line segments are drawn to create a more precise spline curve. The default value is 8. The maximum setting is 32767.

*Decurve Option.*    The **Decurve** option removes extra points inserted by an arc fit or spline fit curve and straightens all the polyline segments back to their original straight line segments as shown in Figure 9-49.

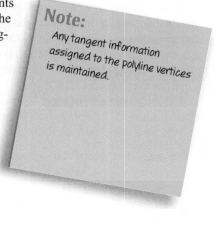

**Note:** Any tangent information assigned to the polyline vertices is maintained.

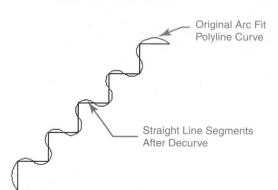

**Figure 9-49**    Curve fit polyline decurved using the Decurve option

**TIP**     You cannot use the **Decurve** option after you edit a spline fit polyline with either the **BREAK** or **TRIM** command.

**Exercise 9-14:** Converting Polylines into Smooth Curves

1. Start a new drawing using the acad.dwt drawing template.
2. Create an arc fit polyline similar to the polyline shown in Figure 9-46 using the **PEDIT** command and the **Fit** option.
3. Create a cubic spline fit polyline in another location similar to the polyline shown in Figure 9-48 using the **PEDIT** command and the **Spline** option.
4. Convert both curve fit polylines created in steps 2 and 3 back into straight line segments similar to those shown in Figure 9-49 using the **PEDIT** command and the **Decurve** option.
5. Save the drawing as **EX9-14.**

## Controlling Polyline Linetype Generation

The **Ltype gen** option allows you to generate the polyline's linetype definition in a continuous pattern through all the vertices of the polyline. When polyline linetype generation is turned off, the linetype definition is applied to each individual polyline segment so dashes, gaps, etc. are sometimes not displayed. Figure 9-50 shows a polyline with a CENTER linetype with linetype generation turned on and off.

**Note:**
The **Ltype gen** option does not apply to polylines with tapered segments.

Linetype                                                      Linetype
Generation Off —                                      ╴ Generation On

**Figure 9-50** Polyline linetype generation turned on and turned off

## EXPLODING COMPLEX OBJECTS

| Explode | |
|---------|---|
| **Ribbon & Panel:** | Homel Modify |
| **Modify Toolbar:** | |
| **Pull-down Menu:** | Modifyl Explode |
| **Command Line:** | EXPLODE |
| **Command Alias:** | X |

You can explode any of the complex line objects discussed in this chapter and convert them into multiple individual line and arc segments using the **EXPLODE** command.

When you start the **EXPLODE** command, AutoCAD prompts you to *Select objects:* so that you can select one or more complex objects.

If you select one or more objects that cannot be exploded, AutoCAD displays how many objects could not be exploded at the command line:

    1 was not able to be exploded.

**Note:**
When you explode a polyline with a width, all the associated width information is discarded, and the resulting lines and arcs follow the polyline's centerline.

**TIP**     You can also explode other complex AutoCAD objects such as hatch objects, multiline text, dimensions, and blocks into their individual subobjects. These and other complex objects are discussed later in the textbook.

# SUMMARY

This chapter showed you how to create and edit the different complex polyline objects in AutoCAD. Remember that rectangles, polygons, donuts, and revision clouds are all constructed with polylines. This means that you can use the **PEDIT** command to edit any of these objects so you can add and remove points, add or change the width, and so on.

The **EXPLODE** command can be used to explode any of the complex object types introduced in this chapter into individual line and arc segments. This can have a negative effect because it adds more information to your drawing. The complex line objects store point information in the most efficient manner. Because of this, you should use the **EXPLODE** command only when absolutely necessary.

# CHAPTER TEST QUESTIONS

## Multiple Choice

1. Complex line objects can be used for which of the following purposes?
   a. Drawing contour lines
   b. Calculating areas
   c. Drawing roadways
   d. All of the above

2. The command that breaks a complex line object down into individual lines and arcs is:
   a. **ERASE**
   b. **EXPLODE**
   c. **EXTEND**
   d. None of the above

3. The default polyline type that is created by the **PLINE** command is called a:
   a. POLYLINE
   b. LWPOLYLINE
   c. LIGHTPOLYLINE
   d. POLYLINELW

4. The system variable that controls whether an old format polyline is created or a new optimized polyline is created when you use the **PLINE** command is named:
   a. **PLTYPE**
   b. **PLINEWID**
   c. **PLINETYPE**
   d. **PTYPE**

5. By default, the polyline arcs created using the **PLINE** command's **Arc** option are:
   a. Created using three points
   b. Created using two points
   c. Tangent
   d. b and c

6. To create a clockwise polyline arc using the **Angle** option, you can:
   a. Enter an angle greater than 360°
   b. Enter an angle less than 0°
   c. Pick a point
   d. Change the base angle

7. You can use polyline widths to create:
   a. Arrowheads
   b. Road signs
   c. Border lines
   d. All of the above

8. You can draw a polyline rectangle with the **RECTANG** command by:
   a. Picking points
   b. Entering a length and width
   c. Specifying the total area and one side length
   d. All of the above

9. A polygon can have up to how many sides?
   a. 100
   b. 1024
   c. 2048
   d. None of the above

10. To draw a solid donut when using the **DONUT** command, specify an inside diameter:
    a. Greater than the outside diameter
    b. That is negative
    c. Of 0.000″
    d. Of 1.000″

11. The system variable that allows you to suppress the `Object selected is not a polyline` prompt when converting an arc or line into a polyline using the **PEDIT** command is named:
    a. **PEDITACCEPT**      c. **PLINEDIT**
    b. **ACCEPTPEDIT**      d. **APEDIT**

12. The maximum gap size that objects can be apart and still be joined using the **PEDIT** command's **Join** option is called:
    a. Join distance      c. Max gap
    b. Fuzz distance      d. Join gap

13. The system variable that allows you to control the type of spline fit polyline that is created is named:
    a. **SPLINEFIT**
    b. **SPLINESEGS**
    c. **SPLINETYPE**
    d. **SPLFRAME**

## Matching

| Column A | Column B |
|---|---|
| a. Polyline | 1. Multisided polyline object created by inputting the number of sides |
| b. Rectangle | 2. Smooth polyline curve that uses the vertices of the selected polyline as the control points to create an approximate B-spline |
| c. Polygon | 3. Polyline object with four sides that can be created with two points |
| d. Donut | 4. Smooth polyline curve consisting of arcs joining each pair of vertex points with the curve passing through all vertices |
| e. Revision cloud | 5. Complex line object made up of one or more connected line segments |
| f. Arc fit polyline | 6. Smoother of the B-spline curves |
| g. Spline fit polyline | 7. Continuous line made of arcs that resembles a cloud, used to highlight markups and changes |
| h. Quadratic B-spline | 8. Rougher of the B-spline curves |
| i. Cubic B-Spline | 9. Round polyline object that can be a ring or a solid circle |

## True or False

1. True or False: Polylines can be used to calculate an enclosed area.
2. True or False: A polyline can consist of one line segment.
3. True or False: There are two different types of polylines.
4. True or False: Entering a negative angle when using the polyline arc **Angle** option creates a counterclockwise arc.
5. True or False: It is possible to create polylines that have a varying width from vertex point to vertex point.
6. True or False: Turning off the **LWT** button on the AutoCAD status bar turns off all polyline widths.
7. True or False: It is possible to draw a rectangle by specifying its total area.
8. True or False: The **RECTANG** command's fillet option creates a rectangle with beveled corners.
9. True or False: A polygon can either be drawn inscribed inside a circle or circumscribed outside a circle of a specified radius.
10. True or False: You must specify a negative inside diameter to draw a solid (filled) donut using the **DONUT** command.
11. True or False: It is possible to join multiple objects together into one continuous polyline even when all the objects are not connected.
12. True or False: The **PEDIT** command's **Spline** option can be used to create a true B-spline.
13. True or False: It is possible to convert a curve fitted polyline back into its original straight line segments.

## CHAPTER PROJECTS

### Project 9-1: Circuit Board

1. Start a new drawing using the acad.dwt template. Set the **GRID** spacing to **.1**, the **SNAP** spacing to **.025**, and turn both **Grid Display** and **Snap Mode** on.
2. Create the following layers:

| Name | Color | Linetype | Lineweight | Description |
|------|-------|----------|------------|-------------|
| Fab | 7 | Continuous | Default | Fabrication drawing |
| Top | 5 | Continuous | Default | Top layer of metal |
| Bottom | 6 | Continuous | Default | Bottom layer of metal |
| Drill | 7 | Continuous | Default | Via drill locations |
| Smask | 3 | Continuous | Default | Top layer solder mask |
| Silkscreen | 7 | Continuous | Default | Top layer silkscreen |

3. With **Snap Mode** turned on, draw the parts shown in Figure P9-1A. Each round pad consists of a 0.060″-diameter circle on the **Top** layer, a 0.020″-diameter circle on the **Drill** layer, and another 0.060″-diameter circle on the **Bottom** layer. The center of each pad should be placed on a grid point.
4. Create the board outline and move and copy the parts to arrange them as shown in Figure P9-1B.
5. Using polylines, draw the wiring on the **TOP** layer as shown in Figure P9-1C. Use a polyline width of 0.006″. All points should be placed on snap coordinates.
6. **Do not** draw text or dimensions.
7. Save your drawing as **P9-1.**

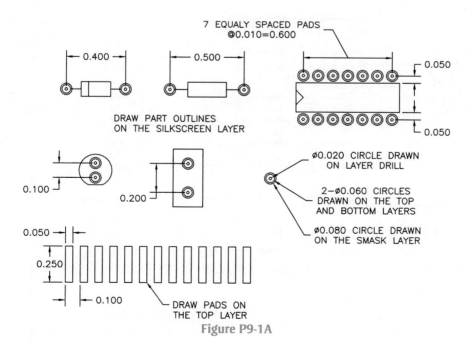

Figure P9-1A

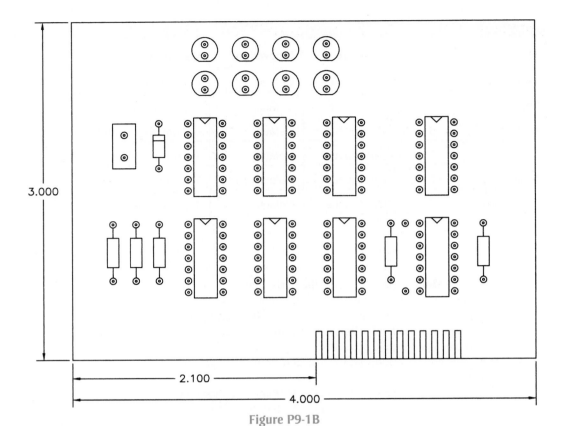

3.000

2.100

4.000

Figure P9-1B

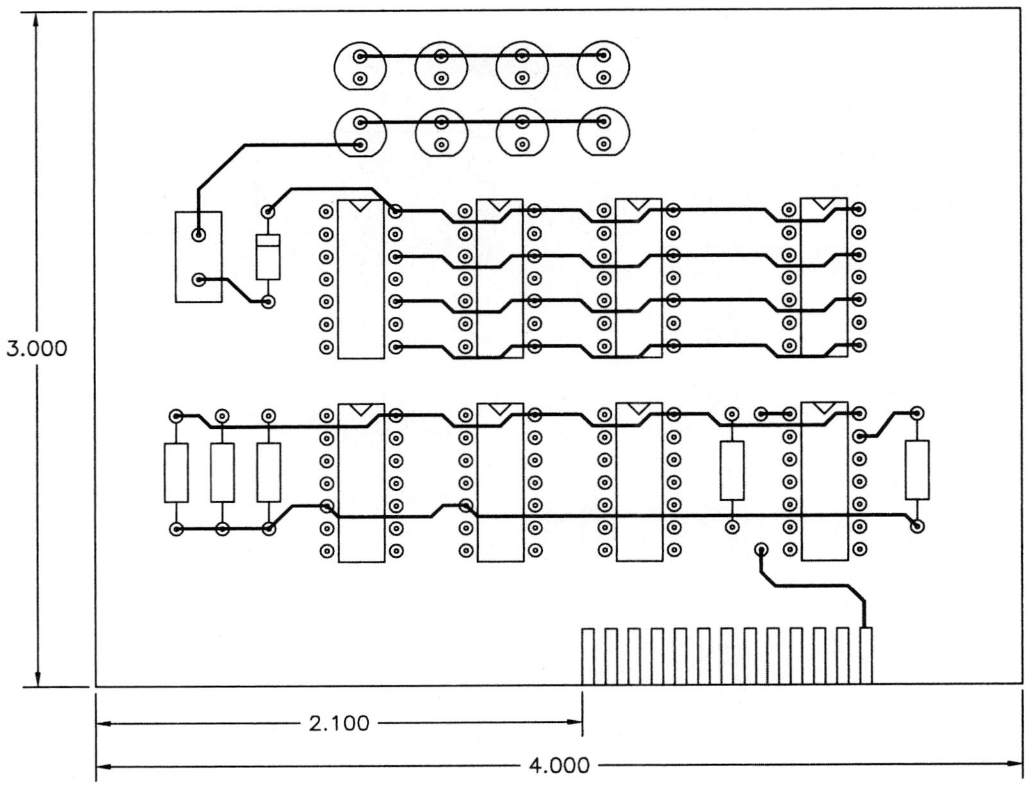

3.000

2.100

4.000

Figure P9-1C

## Project 9-2: Motorcycle—Continued from Chapter 8

1. Open drawing **P8-2.**
2. Add the rear fender, seat, exhaust pipes, and gas tank using polylines. *Hint:* It is possible to use regular lines and arcs and join them together using the **PEDIT** command.
3. Draw the cable on the handlebars using a curve fit polyline with a width.
4. Save the drawing as **P9-2.**

Figure P9-2

## Project 9-3: Logo

1. Start a new drawing using the acad.dwt template.
2. Create the logo shown in Figure P9-3 using polyline objects. **Do not** draw dimensions.
3. Save your drawing as **P9-3.**

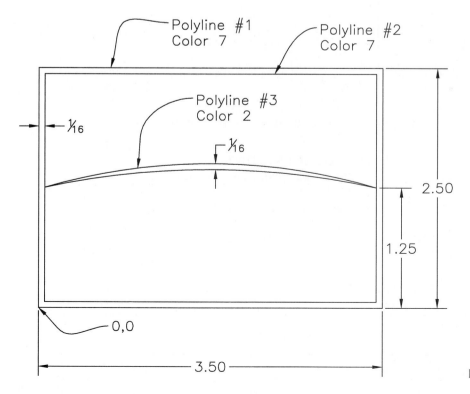

Figure P9-3

## Project 9-4a: Architectural D-Size Border—Continued from Chapter 6

1. Open the template file **Architectural D-Size.DWT**.
2. Create the logo outline and graphic scale outlines as shown in Figure P9-4A using polylines and a circle on the layer **A-Anno-Ttlb-Logo. Do not** draw dimensions.
3. Save the drawing to a template file as **Architectural D-Size.DWT.**

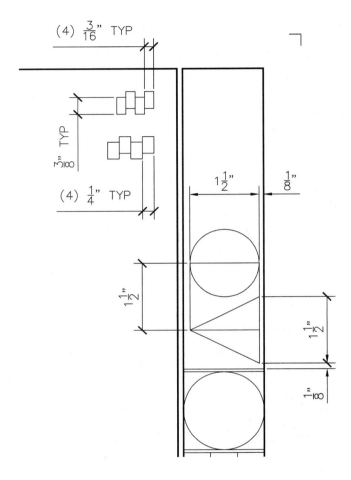

Figure P9-4A

## Project 9-4b: Architectural B-Size Border—Continued from Chapter 7

1. Open the template file **Architectural B-Size.DWT**.
2. Create the logo outline with the same dimensions shown in Figure P9-4A on the left side of the title block on the bottom of the border using polylines and a circle on the layer **A-Anno-Ttlb-Logo.**
3. Save the drawing to a template file as **Architectural B-Size.DWT.**

## Project 9-5: Residential Electrical Plan—Continued from Chapter 8, Problem 7

1. Open drawing **P8-7** from Chapter 8.
2. Modify the drawing to match Figure P9-5. Draw the wiring using polyline objects.
3. Save the drawing as **P9-5.**

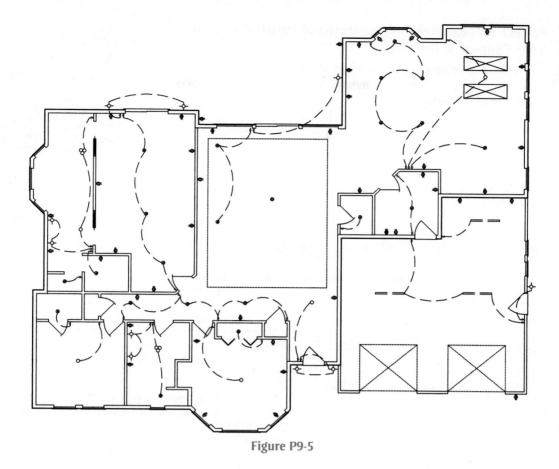

**Figure P9-5**

## Project 9-6: Pipe/Wall Penetration Detail

1. Start a new drawing using the acad.dwt template.
2. Set linear **UNITS** to **Architectural** with precision set to **1/16″**.
3. Set the **LTSCALE** system variable to **2**.
4. Create the line work for the Wall Penetration detail as shown in Figure P9-6. **Do not** draw dimensions.
5. Draw the lines representing the vertical wall section on layer **P-Detl-P2**.
6. Draw the lines representing the horizontal pipe on layer **P-Detl-P1**. *Hint:* Draw the curved end caps using a polyline; then use the **PEDIT** command to apply a **Spline** fit curve.
7. Draw the break lines using polylines on layer **P-Detl-Note**.
8. Draw hidden lines on layer **P-Detl-Hidden**.
9. Save the drawing as **P9-6**.

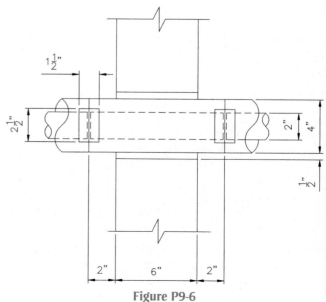

**Figure P9-6**

## Project 9-7: Residential Architectural Plan—Continued from Chapter 9, Problem 5

1. Open drawing **P9-5** from Chapter 9, Problem 5. If you are not completing Problem 5, open **P8-7** from Chapter 8.
2. Create the following layers:

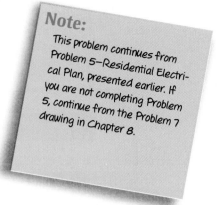

**Note:**
This problem continues from Problem 5—Residential Electrical Plan, presented earlier. If you are not completing Problem 5, continue from the Problem 7 drawing in Chapter 8.

| Name | Color | Linetype | Lineweight | Plot/Noplot | Description |
|------|-------|----------|-----------|-------------|-------------|
| A-Eqpm-Fixd | White | Continuous | Default | Plot | Fixed equipment (fireplaces) |
| L-Walk | 8 | Continuous | Default | Plot | Driveway, patio, walkways, and steps |
| L-Walk-Pat | 8 | Continuous | Default | Plot | Cross-hatch patterns for driveway, patio, walkways, and steps |

3. Draw the fireplace, patio, and driveway as shown in Figure P9-7. Use spline fit polylines to create the driveway and patio lines. **Do not** draw dimensions or text. Use appropriate layers for all objects.
4. Save your drawing as **P9-7.**

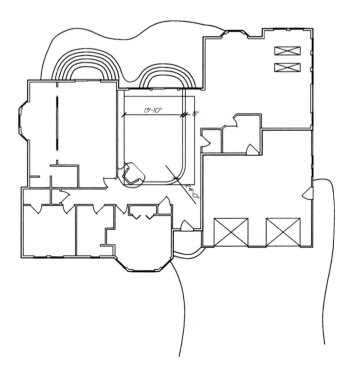

**Figure P9-7**

## Project 9-8a: Joist Foundation Detail—Continued from Chapter 6

1. Open drawing **P6-8** from Chapter 6.
2. Draw the vapor barrier shown in Figure P9-8A using a curve fit polyline on layer **A-Detl-Mcut.**
3. Draw the break lines shown in Figure P9-8A using polylines on layer **A-Detl-Note.**
4. Draw the polyline on the left side of the footing shown in Figure P9-8A that will be used later for hatching the **Earth** pattern in Problem P10-8A on layer **A-Detl-Pat.**
5. Draw the sill anchor bolt shown in Figure P9-8A on layer **A-Detl-Mbnd.**
6. Draw the footing rebar shown in Figure P9-8A using the **DONUT** command on layer **A-Detl-Mcut.**
7. **Do not** include notes.
8. Save the drawing as **P9-8A.**

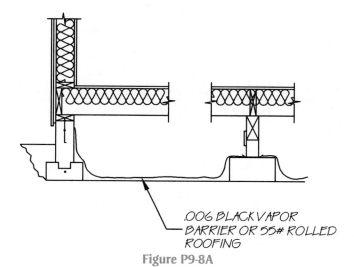

.006 BLACK VAPOR
BARRIER OR 55# ROLLED
ROOFING

**Figure P9-8A**

## Project 9-8b: Interior Floor Change Detail—Continued from Chapter 7

1. Open drawing **P7-8** from Chapter 7.
2. Draw the vapor barrier shown in Figure P9-8B using a curve fitting polyline on layer **A-Detl-Mcut.**
3. Draw the break lines shown in Figure P9-8B using polylines on layer **A-Detl-Note.**
4. Draw the polyline under the footing shown in Figure P9-8B that will be used for hatching the **Earth** pattern in Problem P10-8B on layer **A-Detl-Pat.**
5. **Do not** include notes.
6. Save the drawing as **P9-8B.**

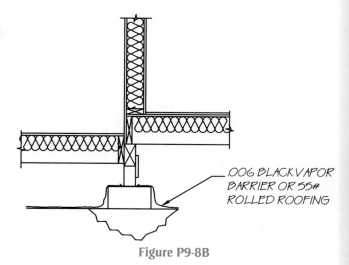

.006 BLACK VAPOR
BARRIER OR 55#
ROLLED ROOFING

**Figure P9-8B**

## Project 9-8c: Truss with Soffited Eave Detail—Continued from Chapter 8

1. Open drawing **P8-8** from Chapter 8.
2. Draw the break lines shown in Figure P9-8C using polylines on layer **A-Detl-Note**.
3. Draw the 3 × 3 and 3 × 6 plates shown in Figure P9-8C using the **RECTANG** command on layer **A-Detl-Mbnd**.
4. **Do not** include notes.
5. Save the drawing as **P9-8C**.

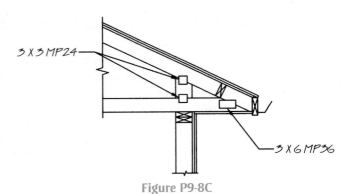

Figure P9-8C

## Project 9-9: Bearing—English Units

1. Start a new drawing using the acad.dwt template.
2. Create the following layers:

| Name | Color | Linetype | Lineweight | Description |
|------|-------|----------|------------|-------------|
| Object | 7 | Continuous | 0.60 mm | Object lines |
| Hidden | 1 | Hidden | Default | Hidden lines |
| Center | 2 | Center | Default | Centerlines |
| Hatch | 4 | Continuous | Default | Hatch patterns and fills |
| Notes | 3 | Continuous | Default | Text and notes |
| Dims | 2 | Continuous | Default | Dimensions |

3. Create the front and section views shown. Use appropriate layers for all objects. Create the section line as a single polyline. **Do not** draw dimensions or text. *Hint:* Use polyline segments with different starting and ending widths for the arrowhead.
4. Save the drawing as **P9-9**.

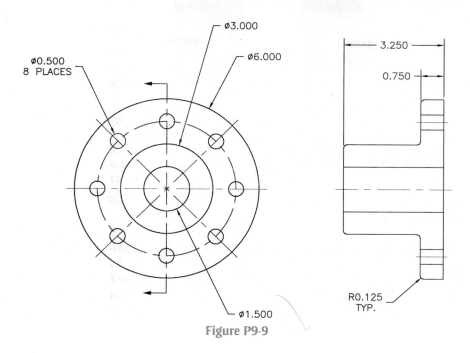

Figure P9-9

## Project 9-10: Window Extrusion—Metric

1. Start a new drawing using the acadiso.dwt template.
2. Create the following layers:

| Name | Color | Linetype | Lineweight | Description |
| --- | --- | --- | --- | --- |
| Object | 7 | Continuous | 0.60 mm | Object lines |
| Hidden | 1 | Hidden | Default | Hidden lines |
| Center | 2 | Center | Default | Centerlines |
| Hatch | 4 | Continuous | Default | Hatch patterns and fills |
| Notes | 3 | Continuous | Default | Text and notes |
| Dims | 2 | Continuous | Default | Dimensions |

3. Draw the window extrusion as shown in Figure P9-10 using a single polyline on layer **Object.**
4. Draw the 150 mm-diameter aluminum billet so that the window extrusion is contained completely within as shown in Figure P9-10.
5. **Do not** draw Detail A.
6. **Do not** include notes or dimensions.
7. Save the drawing as **P9-10.**

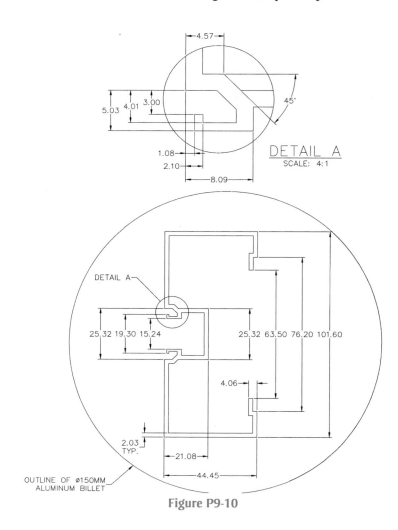

**Figure P9-10**

## Project 9-11: Civil Site Plan—Continued from Chapter 8

1. Open drawing **P8-11** from Chapter 8.
2. Use the **PEDIT** command to join the property boundary into a single closed polyline. Join the house outline into a single closed polyline as well.
3. Add the patio around the swimming pool and modify the driveway as shown. Join the patio lines into a single closed polyline as well as the modified driveway.
4. Save the drawing as **P9-11.**

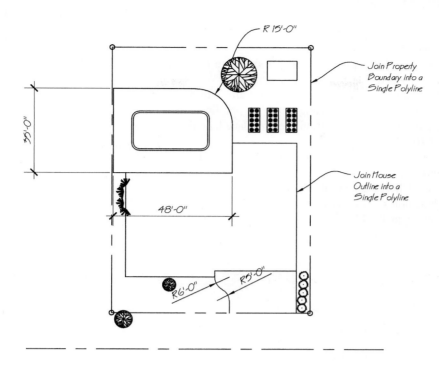

Figure P9-11

## Project 9-12: Standard Service Connection

1. Start a new drawing using the acad.dwt template.
2. Set linear **UNITS** to **Architectural** with precision set to **1/16″**.
3. Create the following layers:

| Name | Color | Linetype | Lineweight | Description |
|------|-------|----------|------------|-------------|
| C-Detl-P1 | 1 | Continuous | Default | Secondary lines (thin) |
| C-Detl-P2 | 3 | Continuous | 0.60 mm | Object lines (thick) |
| C-Detl-Hidden | 1 | Hidden | Default | Hidden lines |
| C-Detl-Center | 1 | Center | Default | Centerlines |
| C-Detl-Pat | 1 | Continuous | Default | Hatch patterns and fills |
| C-Anno-Dims | 1 | Continuous | Default | Dimensions |
| C-Anno-Note | 3 | Continuous | Default | Note text |
| C-Anno-Title | 3 | Continuous | Default | Title text |

4. Draw the 12″-diameter pipe shown in section in Figure P9-12 on layer **C-Detl-P2.**

5. Draw all the remaining pipe lines and arcs shown in Figure P9-12 on layer **C-Detl-P1.**

6. Draw the lines representing the section through earth and gravel shown in Figure P9-12 using curve fit polylines on layer **C-Detl-P1.** These lines will be used to place hatching in Problem P10-12C.

7. Draw the centerlines as shown in Figure P9-12 on layer **C-Detl-Center.**

8. Set the **LTSCALE** system variable to 10.

9. **Do not** include notes or dimensions.

10. Save the drawing as **P9-12**

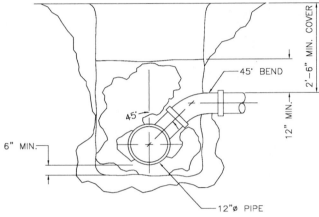

Figure P9-12

# Pattern Fills and Hatching   10

## Chapter Objectives

- Select a hatch boundary area
- Select and create hatch objects
- Modify hatched areas
- Match the settings of existing hatched areas
- Create solid and gradient fills
- Edit hatched areas
- Use DesignCenter to create hatch objects

## INTRODUCTION

*Hatching* is the process of filling in a closed area with a pattern. This is typically used in cross-section or elevation drawings to denote different material usage. Hatch patterns can consist of lines and dots as well as solid colors and gradient fill patterns. Hatching must be placed within a closed area, which means that the edges of the hatch area cannot contain any gaps or openings. AutoCAD provides a couple of different ways to create and select hatch boundaries. In this chapter, you'll look at how hatch patterns are created, controlled, and modified.

**hatching:** The process of filling in a closed area with a pattern

## HATCHING

Figure 10-1 shows some different hatched areas. The *hatch boundary* defines the area of the hatch. *Hatch islands* are closed areas inside the outer hatch boundary. When you hatch an area, you can control how island areas are dealt with. The *hatch pattern* is the pattern used to fill in the boundary. The hatch pattern has a scale, rotation angle, and origin associated with it as well.

The **HATCH** command is used to place hatch patterns. When you start the **HATCH** command, AutoCAD displays the **Hatch and Gradient** dialog box (Figure 10-2).

The **Hatch and Gradient** dialog box is divided into three general sections. The **Hatch** and **Gradient** tabs on the left side of the dialog box allow you to control how the hatch looks. The **Boundaries** area in the center of the dialog box allows you to select or create a hatch area and controls how the hatch will behave. The right side of the dialog box allows you to control how hatch boundaries are created and how island areas are treated.

**hatch boundary:** The edges of a hatched area

**hatch islands:** Closed areas within a hatch boundary

**hatch pattern:** The pattern used to fill a hatch boundary

> **Note:**
> If your **Hatch and Gradient** dialog box doesn't show all the options, select the arrow in the lower right corner of the dialog box. This will expand the dialog box to show all the options for the **HATCH** command.

| Hatch | |
|---|---|
| **Ribbon & Panel:** | Homel Draw |
| **Draw Toolbar:** | |
| **Menu:** | Drawl Hatch… |
| **Command Line:** | HATCH / BHATCH |
| **Command Alias:** | H |

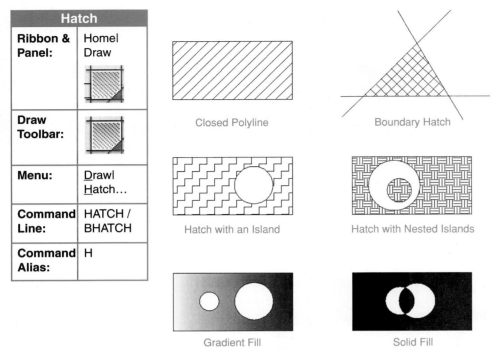

Closed Polyline

Boundary Hatch

Hatch with an Island

Hatch with Nested Islands

Gradient Fill

Solid Fill

**Figure 10-1**     Hatch and gradient fill examples

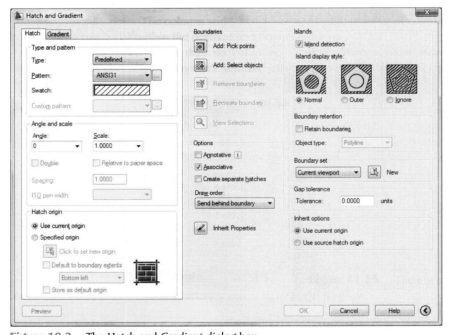

**Figure 10-2**     The Hatch and Gradient dialog box

Before you can create a hatch, you must specify the boundaries of the hatch area. This is done with the **Boundaries** area of the **Hatch and Gradient** dialog box.

## Selecting a Hatch Area

There are two ways to select hatch boundaries. One is to select objects to use as boundaries; the other is to pick points inside closed areas of your drawing.

*Selecting Objects.*     If you select closed areas (such as circles or closed polylines) AutoCAD will simply hatch inside those closed areas. If you select open objects (such as lines, arcs, and open polylines), AutoCAD will attempt to calculate a hatch area. If the open objects are placed end to end and clearly define a closed area, then the results are predictable. However, if you choose over-lapping objects, or if the objects don't clearly define a closed area, then your hatch area may not turn out the way you intend. Figure 10-3 shows some examples of selecting open and closed objects for hatch boundaries.

*Previewing the Pattern.*    Once you have defined the boundaries, you can preview how the hatch will look by choosing the **Preview** button. When you select the **Preview** button, AutoCAD will close the **Hatch and Gradient** dialog box and temporarily hatch the selected boundaries. If you're happy with the results, you can right-click or press **<Enter ↵>** to accept the hatch or press **<Esc>** to cancel the preview and return to the **Hatch and Gradient** dialog box. From there, you can modify the hatch settings and redefine the boundaries.

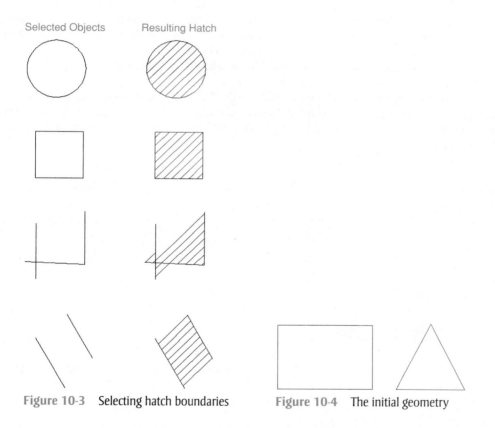

**Figure 10-3**    Selecting hatch boundaries            **Figure 10-4**    The initial geometry

## Exercise 10-1: Selecting Hatch Boundaries

1. Start a new drawing using the acad.dwt drawing template.
2. Create the geometry shown in Figure 10-4. Dimensions are not important; create the rectangle using the **RECTANGLE** command, and the triangle with the **LINE** command. Make sure the lines are touching end to end.
3. Start the **HATCH** command and pick the **Add: Select objects** button. Select the rectangle and press **<Enter ↵>** to end the selection process. AutoCAD will return you to the Hatch and Gradient dialog box.
4. Keep all the default hatch settings and choose the **Preview** button to see a preview of the hatch pattern. Press **<Enter ↵>** to accept the hatch pattern and end the **HATCH** command. Because the rectangle was a single, closed polyline, the hatch boundary was completely defined. Your drawing should look like Figure 10-5.
5. Restart the **HATCH** command and pick the Add: Select objects button. Select the bottom and right legs of the triangle and press **<Enter ↵>** to end the selection process. AutoCAD will return you to the **Hatch and Gradient** dialog box.

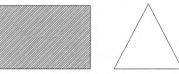

Figure 10-5     Hatching the rectangle

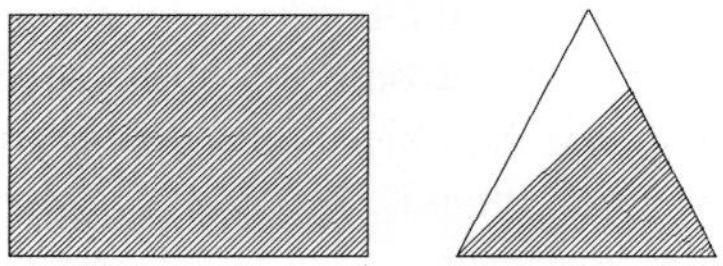

Figure 10-6     An open boundary selection

6. Choose the **Preview** button to see a preview of the hatch pattern (see Figure 10-6). Because the two lines you selected don't fully define a closed area, AutoCAD creates a pattern that doesn't extend beyond the endpoint of either boundary object. Press <**Esc**> to cancel the preview and return to the dialog box.
7. Choose the **Add: Select objects** button and select the left leg of the triangle. Press <**Enter** ↵> to end the selection process. This object is added to the previously selected lines.
8. Choose the **Preview** button to see a preview of the hatch pattern. Because the triangle boundary is fully defined, the hatch pattern completely fills the hatch area. Press <**Enter** ↵> to accept the hatch pattern and end the **HATCH command**.
9. Save your drawing as **EX10-1**. Your drawing should resemble Figure 10-7.

*Picking Points.*     When you pick points, AutoCAD will search out from the point you pick and attempt to trace a closed area around the point you selected. If it's successful, AutoCAD will highlight the closed area and allow you to select additional points. This is a quick and easy way to create hatch areas.

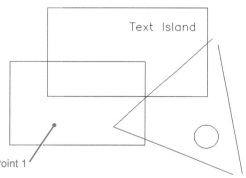

Figure 10-7     The closed boundary selection

Figure 10-8     Picking boundary points

**Exercise 10-2:** Picking Boundary Points

1. Open drawing **EX10-2** from the Student CD.
2. Start the **HATCH** command and choose the **Add: Pick points** button. Pick point 1 shown in Figure 10-8. AutoCAD will detect the boundary and highlight the boundary area. Press <**Enter** ↵> to end the boundary detection process.
3. Choose the **Preview** button to see a preview of the hatch pattern. Press <**Enter** ↵> to accept the hatch pattern and end the **HATCH** command.
4. Save the drawing as **EX10-2**. Your drawing should look like Figure 10-9.

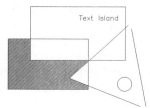

Figure 10-9     The hatched area

*Advanced Options.*    When picking points, AutoCAD provides different options that control the generation of the hatch boundaries. These advanced options allow you to control island detection, retain the hatch boundaries, and heal or ignore gaps in the boundary edge.

*Island Detection.*    The **Islands** area of the **Hatch and Gradient** dialog box allows you to turn island detection on and off and tells AutoCAD how to deal with island areas when placing the hatch. The **Island Detection** box allows you to turn island detection on and off. When turned off, AutoCAD will ignore any island areas and create a single boundary around the point you pick.

> **Note:**
> Text objects (text, mtext, and dimension text) are treated as though a closed box were drawn around the text. Selecting text inside a closed shape will result in the text being treated as an island within the boundary.

The **Island display style** area controls how island areas are treated when the hatch pattern is applied. The **Normal** setting applies the hatch pattern to every other nesting level starting with the outer boundary. The **Outer** setting applies the hatch pattern between the outer boundary and the first nesting level. All further nesting levels are ignored. The **Ignore** setting simply ignores all internal islands and fills the entire outer boundary with the hatch pattern. Figure 10-10 shows the effect of the different **Island display style** settings.

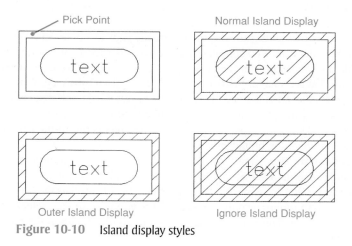

**Figure 10-10**    Island display styles

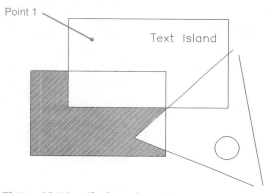

**Figure 10-11**    The boundary pick point

## Exercise 10-3: Island Detection

1. Continue from Exercise 10-2.
2. Start the **HATCH** command and make sure the **Island detection** is enabled and the **Island display style** is set to **Normal**. **Choose** the **Add: Pick points** button and pick point 1 shown in Figure 10-11. AutoCAD will detect the boundary along with the text island. Press **<Enter ↵>** to end the boundary detection process.
3. Choose the Preview button to see a preview of the hatch pattern. The hatch pattern will fill around the text island. Press **<Esc>** to cancel the preview and return to the dialog box.
4. Set the Island display style to Ignore and choose **Preview** to see a preview of the hatch pattern. The hatch pattern should now fill over the top of the text island. Press <Esc> to cancel the preview and return to the dialog box.
5. Set the **Island display style** back to **Normal** and choose **OK** to create the hatch pattern and end the **HATCH** command.
6. Save your drawing as **EX10-3**. Your drawing should resemble Figure 10-12.

*Retaining the Boundary.*    When you create a boundary hatch, you have the option of keeping the boundary as either a polyline or a region. When the **Retain boundaries** option is selected, AutoCAD will create the boundary as a polyline by default. The polyline is created on the same layer as the hatch pattern.

If your drawing has a lot of hatching or contains complex boundaries, you may wish to retain your hatch boundaries and place the boundaries and hatch patterns on a separate layer. This allows you to make changes easily to the hatch patterns and boundaries and also allows you to turn off complex patterns that can sometimes get in the way when editing your drawing.

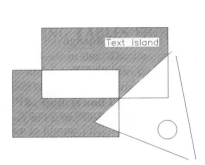

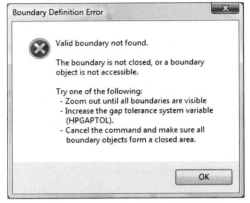

Figure 10-12     The completed hatch          Figure 10-13     Open Boundary Warning box

*Gap Tolerance.*     The **Gap tolerance** setting allows you to heal any gaps in a boundary. When the gap tolerance is set to 0, the boundary must be completely closed in order for a valid boundary to be created. When the gap tolerance is set greater than 0, AutoCAD will attempt to determine a boundary and will ignore any gaps that are smaller than or equal to the specified tolerance. When it finds a valid boundary with gaps smaller than the specified tolerance, AutoCAD will display the **Open Boundary Warning** box (see Figure 10-13) asking if you'd like to proceed with the hatch.

When AutoCAD detects a boundary with gaps, it will project the objects out to their intersection and use this point as the corner of the boundary.

*Boundary Set.*     The **Boundary set** area allows you to control which objects are used when detecting a boundary. The boundary set is a set of objects used to determine boundaries when picking points. By default, everything that is visible in the current viewport is used as the boundary set. If there are objects you wish to ignore or only certain objects you wish to use, select the **New** button to create a new boundary set. The boundary set is reset to all objects upon the completion of the **HATCH** command.

With large drawings, AutoCAD can sometimes take a while to calculate boundary areas. If this is the case, you may want to create a new boundary set or consider turning off or freezing layers to reduce the number of calculations needed to determine the boundary.

*Adding and Removing Boundaries.*     Once you have selected a hatch area, you can add additional boundaries by either selecting objects or picking additional points. You can also remove boundaries using the **Remove boundaries** button. When you choose this button, AutoCAD hides the dialog box and highlights the existing boundary edges. You can simply select an edge to remove the boundary from the selection.

*Creating Separate Hatches.*     When you select or create more than one boundary, you have the option of creating a single hatch object that spans all the boundaries, or you can create separate hatch objects in each hatch area. The **Create separate hatches** option

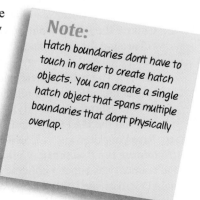

**Note:**
Hatch boundaries don't have to touch in order to create hatch objects. You can create a single hatch object that spans multiple boundaries that don't physically overlap.

allows you to control this. Placing a check in the **Create separate hatches** box will create one hatch object for each closed boundary.

Boundary Gaps

1. Continue from Exercise 10-3.
2. Start the **HATCH** command and make sure the **Island detection** is enabled and the **Island display style** is set to **Normal**. Set the **Gap Tolerance** to **2.00** and choose the **Add: Pick points** button and pick point 1 shown in Figure 10-14. AutoCAD will display the **Open Boundary Warning** box. Choose **OK** to close the warning box. AutoCAD will create a closed boundary along with the circle island. Press **<Enter ↵>** to end the boundary detection process.
3. Choose the **Preview** button to see a preview of the hatch pattern. Press **<Enter ↵>** to accept the pattern and end the **HATCH** command.
4. Save your drawing as **EX10-4**. Your drawing should resemble Figure 10-15.

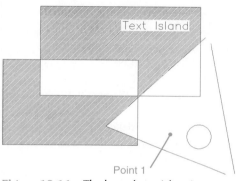

Figure 10-14    The boundary pick point

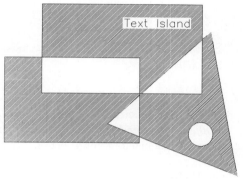

Figure 10-15    The completed hatch

## Hatch Patterns

In addition to defining the boundary of the hatch area, you need to specify how the hatch pattern should look. This includes specifying the particular pattern you wish to use as well as the size or scale of the pattern, the angle of the pattern, and the hatch origin.

**Note:**
The acadiso.pat file contains all the pattern definitions as acad.pat but also includes support for the JIS A 0150 standard.

*Specifying a Pattern.* AutoCAD hatch patterns are similar to AutoCAD linetypes. Hatch patterns are stored in external .pat files that can be modified. You can also create your own custom .pat files.

*Predefined Patterns.* AutoCAD comes with a set of predefined hatch patterns (acad.pat and acadiso.pat) that contain a number of different hatch pattern definitions. To select a predefined hatch pattern, select the **Hatch** tab in the **Hatch and Gradient** dialog box and set the **Type** to **Predefined**. A list of all predefined hatch patterns will appear in the **Pattern** drop-down list. When you select a pattern from the list, the **Swatch** setting will display a small preview of the pattern.

Next to the **Pattern** drop-down list is a **...** button. When you select this button, AutoCAD displays the **Hatch Pattern Palette** dialog box, which allows you to see a small preview of each pattern. The patterns are divided into four tabs: **ANSI, ISO, Other Predefined,** and **Custom** (see Figure 10-16). Simply click on the pattern you wish to use and choose **OK** (or double-click a pattern) to select it.

*ANSI Patterns.* Figure 10-16 shows the **ANSI** hatch patterns. These patterns are generally used to denote materials in mechanical drawings.

*ISO Patterns.* AutoCAD's 14 **ISO** patterns are designed to comply with the ISO/DIS 12011 linetype specification. When you select an ISO pattern, the **ISO pen width** drop-down list

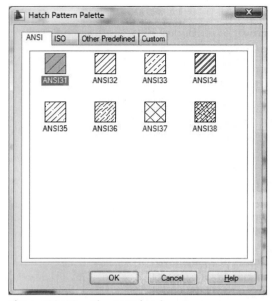

Figure 10-16    The ANSI hatch patterns

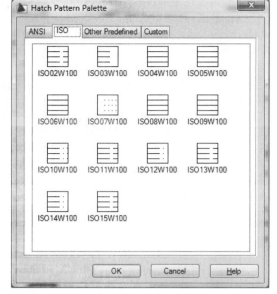

Figure 10-17    The ISO hatch patterns

is enabled and allows you to specify a pen width for the hatch pattern. Figure 10-17 shows the predefined ISO patterns.

*Other Predefined Patterns.*    The **Other Predefined** patterns are designed for a variety of applications. Included in this selection of hatch patterns are a number of patterns that start with AR-. These patterns are architectural in nature and are larger in scale than the other patterns. Figure 10-18 shows the **Other Predefined** patterns.

*Specifying an Angle and Scale.*    Like linetypes, .pat files describe the length, spacing, and angles of the lines within the pattern. For example, the ANSI31 pattern is defined as a continuous line segment, rotated 45° with 0.125 unit between each parallel line. The **Angle and scale**

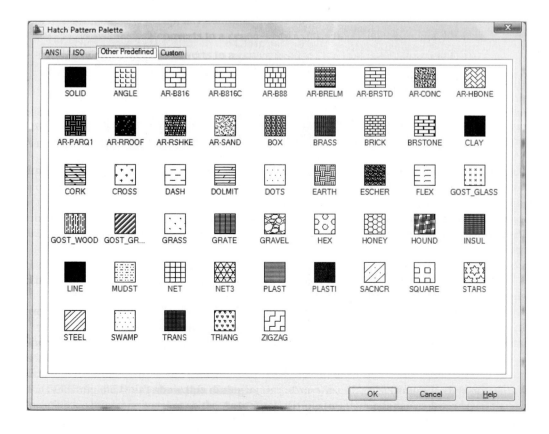

Figure 10-18    Other predefined hatch patterns

area of the **Hatch and Gradient** dialog box allows you to add additional rotation and a scaling factor to your hatch pattern. The **Angle** drop-down list contains a number of common rotation angle values. You can select a value from the list or simply type in the rotation angle.

The **Scale** drop-down list contains a list of commonly used scales. Like the **Angle** list, you can select one of the listed scales or simply type in a scale factor. The **Angle** and **Scale** values are applied to the defined scale of the selected pattern. For example, using the ANSI31 pattern already described, specifying a scale factor of **2** and a rotation angle of **45°** would result in a pattern of 90° lines (45° + 45°) with a spacing of 0.25 unit (0.125 × 2).

When working in paper space, you can also choose the **Relative to paper space** option. This will add an additional scale factor to the hatch that will adjust the hatch pattern scale according to the viewport scale factor.

*Annotative Scale.*    As mentioned in Chapter 1, you can automatically scale annotation objects such as text, dimension, and hatching using the AutoCAD **Annotation Scale** feature on the right side of the Status Bar at the bottom of the AutoCAD window. To enable the **Annotation Scale** feature, select the **Annotative** option in the **Options** area of the **Hatch and Gradient** dialog box. The hatch pattern will now scale automatically based on the current **Annotation Scale** when it is created.

---

**FOR MORE DETAILS**    See Chapter 14 for more on setting viewport scale factors and controlling the **Annotation Scale.**

---

*Associative Hatching.*    In AutoCAD, associativity means a link between one drawing object and another. In Chapter 2, you saw an example of associative dimensioning. When you placed a dimension object, it was associated with the points on the objects you dimensioned. If those points moved, the dimension object moved along with it.

Associativity can also occur between a hatch object and its boundary. If the boundary edge is modified, its associated hatch objects will update and fill in the changed boundary. The **Associative** option in the **Hatch and Gradient** dialog box turns associativity on and off.

**Note:**

Hatch pattern associativity can be a fleeting thing. Associativity can be lost if the boundary edges change significantly. For example, if two overlapping objects were used to create a hatch boundary, modifying the objects so that they no longer overlap will cause the hatch associativity to be lost. This can also happen when a boundary edge is trimmed, exploded, or filleted. When hatch associativity is lost, AutoCAD will display a message in the **Command Line** window: Hatch boundary associativity removed.

### Exercise 10-5: Hatch Patterns

1. Open drawing **EX10-5** from the Student CD.
2. Start the **HATCH** command and make sure the **Island detection** is enabled and the **Island display style** is set to **Normal**. Set the **Gap Tolerance** to **0.00**. Choose the **Add: Pick points** button and pick points 1 and 2 shown in Figure 10-19. Press **<Enter ↵>** to end the boundary selection.
3. In the **Type and pattern** area, set the **Type** to **Predefined** and select **EARTH** from the Pattern list.
4. In the **Angle and scale** area, set the **Angle** to **0.00** and the **Scale** to **0.50**.
5. Make sure the **Associative** and **Create separate hatches** options are checked and choose the **Preview** button to see a preview of the hatch pattern. Press **<Enter ↵>** to accept the **pattern** and end the **HATCH** command.
6. Zoom into the hatch boundary around the **EARTH** hatch you just created. Select the diagonal edge to activate the grips and experiment with moving the vertices of the polyline boundary around. The hatch pattern will update each time you move a vertex. When you are satisfied with the boundary changes, use the **ERASE** command to delete the diagonal **EARTH** hatch boundary lines. In the **Command Window**, AutoCAD displays the message: Hatch boundary associativity removed. Your drawing should look similar to Figure 10-20.

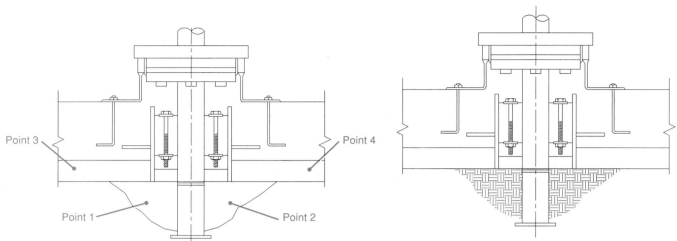

**Figure 10-19**    The boundary pick point

**Figure 10-20**    The EARTH hatch pattern

7. Restart the **HATCH** command. Choose the **Add: Pick points** button and pick points 3 and 4 shown in Figure 10-19. Press **<Enter ↵>** to end the boundary selection.

8. Select the **AR-CONC** pattern and set the **Scale** to **0.10**. Choose the **Preview** button to see a preview of the hatch pattern.

9. The pattern is a little large for the area so press **<Esc>** to cancel the preview and change the **Scale** to **0.05**. Choose the **Preview** button to see a preview of the hatch pattern and then press **<Enter ↵>** to accept the pattern and end the **HATCH** command.

10. Save your drawing as **EX10-5**. Your drawing should resemble Figure 10-21.

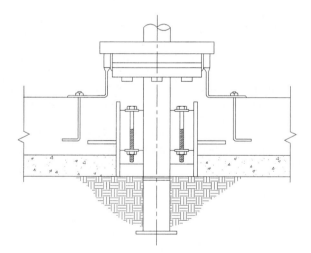

**Figure 10-21**    The completed hatch

*Solid Pattern.*    Included in the **Other Predefined** patterns is a **Solid** pattern. This is not a pattern, but rather a fill color. When you specify a **Solid** pattern, the **Swatch** display changes to a color selection list that allows you to set the color for the solid fill. Choosing **Select Color...** from the drop-down list will display AutoCAD's **Select Color** dialog box, which allows you to choose colors using the ACI, True Colors, or Color Book color definitions. The **Angle** and **Scale** options are also disabled because these settings are irrelevant with a solid fill.

*User-Defined Patterns.*    A user-defined pattern allows you to define a hatch pattern consisting of straight lines at a defined angle and spacing. The user pattern can have either a single set of parallel lines or a double set of perpendicular lines. The current linetype is used to draw the hatch pattern.

When specifying a user-defined hatch pattern, only the **Angle** and **Spacing** options are enabled. The **Angle** represents the angle of the lines (a setting of 0 would produce horizontal lines, 90 would produce vertical lines). The **Spacing** is the spacing between the parallel lines. When the

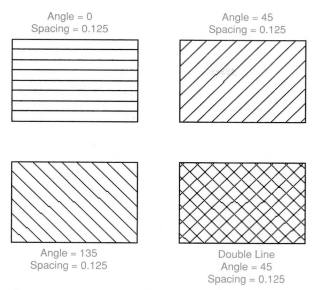

Figure 10-22    User-defined hatch patterns

**Double** option is checked, an additional set of lines will be drawn perpendicular to the first set of hatch lines. The perpendicular hatch lines will have the same spacing as the parallel hatch lines. Figure 10-22 shows some examples of user-defined patterns.

*Custom Patterns.*    When you create a custom .pat file, AutoCAD makes those patterns available in the **Custom** tab of the **Hatch Pattern Palette** dialog box. These custom patterns can be used along with all the other predefined hatch patterns.

*Setting the Hatch Origin.*    The **Hatch origin** area allows you to control the starting point of the hatch pattern. By default, all hatch patterns are drawn using 0,0 as a base point. This means that AutoCAD calculates where the hatch pattern will be drawn based on the hatch pattern definition starting at the 0,0 coordinate. Typically that is what you want; however, there may be times when you want the hatch pattern to start at a specific coordinate. For example, if you are using a brick or tile pattern, you may want the pattern to start with a full brick or tile in the corner of the boundary. To do this, you select the hatch origin to be the corner of the hatch boundary. Figure 10-23 shows some examples of setting the hatch origin.

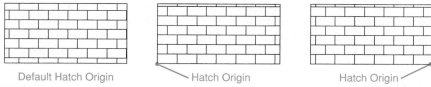

Figure 10-23    Selecting a hatch origin

The **Hatch origin** area has two options. The **Use current origin** option simply uses the default hatch origin. By default this origin is 0,0 until you change it. The **Specified origin** option allows you to either select an origin point in your drawing or use a predefined point along the boundary edge. Once you specify a new origin, placing a check in the **Store as default origin** box will retain that point at the new default hatch origin.

## Exercise 10-6: Creating a Solid Fill

1. Open drawing **EX10-6** from the student CD.
2. Start the **HATCH** command and make sure the **Island detection** is enabled and the **Island display style** is set to **Normal**. Set the **Gap Tolerance** to **0.00**, choose the **Add: Pick points** button, and pick the three points shown in Figure 10-24. Press **<Enter ↵>** to end the boundary selection.
3. In the **Type and pattern** area, set the **Type** to **Predefined** and select **Solid** from the **Pattern** list. Select **Blue** from the **Swatch** list.

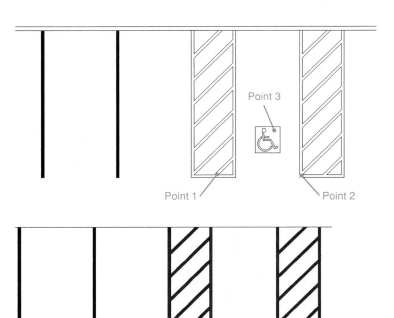

**Figure 10-24**  The boundary pick points

**Figure 10-25**  Solid fills

4. Choose the **Preview** button to see a preview of the hatch pattern. Press **<Enter ↵>** to accept the pattern and end the **HATCH** command.
5. Save your drawing as **EX10-6a**. Your drawing should look like Figure 10-25.

## Matching Existing Hatch Patterns

If you have an existing hatch pattern in your drawing, AutoCAD can read the properties of the hatch pattern and use those settings to create a new hatch pattern. The **Inherit Properties** button in the **Hatch and Gradient** dialog box allows you to select an existing hatch pattern from your drawing and will use the properties of the selected hatch as the default values in the dialog box.

*Inherit Hatch Origin.*    When you inherit hatch pattern properties, you have the option of inheriting the hatch origin of the selected hatch pattern or using the currently defined hatch origin. The **Inherit options** area of the **Hatch and Gradient** dialog box allows you to choose which origin to use. The **Use source hatch origin** option will use the hatch origin of the selected hatch pattern.

**Exercise 10-7:** Inheriting Hatch Patterns

1. Open drawing **EX10-7** from the Student CD. Set the layer **Fence** current.
2. Start the **HATCH** command and choose the **Inherit Properties** button. AutoCAD hides the **Hatch and Gradient** dialog box and prompts you to *Select hatch object:*.
3. Pick the brick wall pattern on the left side of the drawing. AutoCAD now prompts you to *Pick internal point or ↑↓*. Pick the two points shown in Figure 10-26 and press **<Enter ↵>** to return to the **Hatch and Gradient** dialog box. All the settings for the selected hatch are now the default options for your new hatch.
4. Choose the **Preview** button to see a preview of the hatch pattern. Press **<Enter ↵>** to accept the pattern and end the **HATCH** command.
5. Save your drawing as **EX10-7a**. Your drawing should look like Figure 10-27.

## Draw Order

The **Draw order** setting in the **Hatch and Gradient** dialog box allows you to control the order in which the hatch pattern is drawn with respect to the boundary. The default option is to send the hatch pattern behind the boundary, which means that the boundary will be drawn on top of the

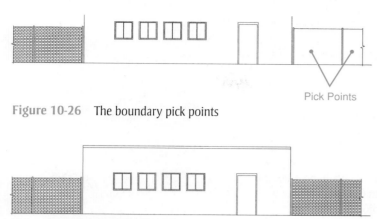

Figure 10-26    The boundary pick points

Figure 10-27    Inheriting hatch properties

hatch pattern. In most cases, the draw order doesn't matter; however, in cases where the boundary is on a different layer or is a different color from the hatch pattern, the draw order can affect the look of your drawing.

**TIP**    The draw order can also affect the ability to select easily either the hatch or the boundary, especially with solid fill or gradient patterns. The object drawn on top will be selected first when you pick along a common edge.

*The DRAWORDER Command.*    The **Draw order** setting in the **Hatch and Gradient** dialog box affects hatch patterns only at the time it is created. Subsequent editing of the boundary edges can result in the display order being changed. In this case, you can reassign the draw order with the **DRAWORDER** command.

The **DRAWORDER** command allows you to take a selection set and either draw it on top (in front) of other objects or draw it below (behind) other objects. When you start the **DRAWORDER** command, you are prompted to build a selection set. Once you've selected the objects, you have four options: **Above objects**, **Under objects**, **Front**, or **Back**. The **Front** and **Back** options send the selected objects to either the top or the bottom of the drawing order. Objects in the front are drawn last and are therefore drawn on top of other objects. Objects in the back are drawn first and are therefore drawn behind other objects.

The **Above objects** and **Under objects** options prompt you to select a second set of objects. With the **Above objects** option, the objects in the first selection set are drawn in front of or above the objects in the second selection set. With the **Under objects** option, objects in the first selection set are drawn in back of or under the objects in the second selection set.

The drawing order affects how overlapping objects are selected. Objects on top or in front are selected before objects in back of or under other objects. This can also affect the order in which things are plotted.

# GRADIENT FILLS

In addition to solid fills and hatch patterns, AutoCAD can also create gradient fills. Gradient fills create a smooth color transformation from either one color to light (or dark) or between two selected colors. Gradient fills can be created with the **Gradient** tab of the **HATCH** command or with the **GRADIENT** command.

The **GRADIENT** command displays the **Gradient** tab of the **Hatch and Gradient** dialog box. The **Gradient** options are similar to a solid hatch fill with two noticeable differences: the number of colors and the gradient pattern.

| Draw Order | |
|---|---|
| **Ribbon & Panel:** | Home\| Modify |
| **Draw Order Toolbar:** | |
| **Menu:** | Tools\| Draw Order |
| **Command Line:** | DRAWORDER |
| **Command Alias:** | DR |

| Gradient | |
|---|---|
| **Ribbon & Panel:** | Home\| Draw |
| **Draw Toolbar:** | |
| **Menu:** | Draw\| Gradient... |
| **Command Line:** | GRADIENT |
| **Command Alias:** | None |

## One-Color Gradient

A one-color gradient fill creates a smooth color transition from a selected color to another shade of that color. You can select the base color you wish to use with the **...** button located under the **One color** radio button. Selecting this button brings up AutoCAD's standard **Select Color** dialog box.

Next to the color patch is a **Shade/Tint** slider bar. This slider bar controls the shade of the transition color. With the slider at the left-hand side, the transition color is black. With the slider all the way to the right, the transition color is white.

**Note:** The **GRADIENT** command is actually the same command as the **HATCH** command. The only difference is that the **HATCH** command displays the **Hatch** tab by default, while the **GRADIENT** command displays the **Gradient** tab. Access the command by whichever name and method works best for you.

## Two-Color Gradient

A two-color gradient fill transitions between two selected colors. When the **Two color** option is selected, the **Shade/Tint** slider bar is replaced with a second color patch. You can select the second transition color by picking the **...** button and selecting a color from the **Select Color** dialog box.

## Gradient Pattern

There are nine predefined gradient fill patterns to choose from. You choose the pattern you want and then optionally choose a rotation angle. You can also choose to have the fill centered within the boundary or generated from the edge of the boundary. With the **Centered** option turned off, you can use the **Angle** setting to control which side the pattern generated from. Figure 10-28 shows some combinations of gradient patterns and rotation angles.

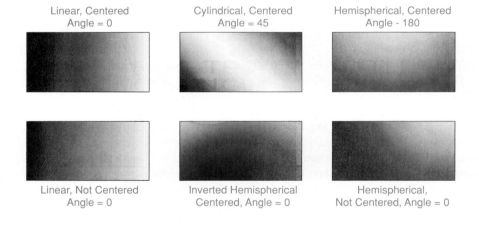

**Figure 10-28** Gradient fill patterns

Linear, Centered
Angle = 0

Cylindrical, Centered
Angle = 45

Hemispherical, Centered
Angle - 180

Linear, Not Centered
Angle = 0

Inverted Hemispherical
Centered, Angle = 0

Hemispherical,
Not Centered, Angle = 0

### Exercise 10-8: Creating a Gradient Fill

1. Continue from Exercise 10-7 and set layer **Window** current.
2. Start the **GRADIENT** command (or start the **HATCH** command and choose the **Gradient** tab). Choose **Add: Pick Points** and pick the points inside the eight windowpanes shown in Figure 10-29. Press **<Enter ↵>** to return to the **Hatch and Gradient** dialog box.

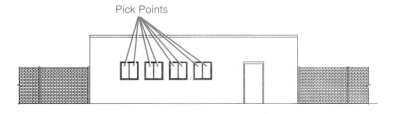

Pick Points

**Figure 10-29** The boundary pick points

3. In the Gradient tab, select the **One color** option. Select the **...** button next to the color swatch and specify **ACI color 142** as the base color for the gradient fill. Choose **OK** to close the **Select Color** dialog box.

4. In the **Shade/Tint** slider, move the slider so it is almost to the right end of the bar, near the **Tint** end.

5. Select the linear pattern (the first pattern in the upper left corner) and set the **Angle** to **270**.

6. Choose the **Preview** button to see a preview of the hatch pattern and press **<Enter ↵>** to accept the pattern and end the **HATCH** command.

7. Save your drawing as **EX10-8**. Your drawing should look like Figure 10-30.

**Figure 10-30**    A gradient fill

# EDITING HATCH PATTERNS

Once a hatch object is created, there are a number of ways to modify it. You can change the hatch pattern along with any of the hatch options. You can even change a hatch pattern to a solid or gradient fill. This is done with the **HATCHEDIT** command.

## The HATCHEDIT Command

The **HATCHEDIT** command allows you to modify any aspect of a hatch pattern. When you start the **HATCHEDIT** command, you are asked to select a hatch pattern. Once you select a hatch pattern (or a solid or gradient fill), AutoCAD displays the **Hatch Edit** dialog box (see Figure 10-31).

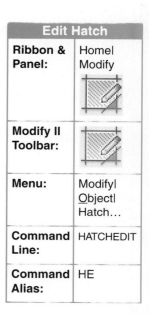

| Edit Hatch | |
|---|---|
| **Ribbon & Panel:** | Homel Modify |
| **Modify II Toolbar:** | |
| **Menu:** | Modifyl Objectl Hatch... |
| **Command Line:** | HATCHEDIT |
| **Command Alias:** | HE |

**Figure 10-31**    The Hatch Edit dialog box

**TIP**    You can double-click on a hatch object to access the **HATCHEDIT** command quickly.

This dialog box is identical to the **Hatch and Gradient** dialog box used to create hatch objects. When you select a hatch object, all of that object's settings are shown as the default values in the **Hatch Edit** dialog box. From this dialog box, you can change any aspect of the hatch object.

One option that is available in the **Hatch Edit** dialog box that is not available in the **HATCH** command is the **Recreate boundary** button. When you select this button, AutoCAD will create a new boundary for the hatch. If the hatch is associative, you have the option of keeping the association with the original boundary or reassociating the hatch with the new boundary. The **Recreate boundary** button always retains the new boundary as a new drawing object.

### Exercise 10-9: Using HATCHEDIT

1. Continue from Exercise 10-8.
2. Double-click the fence hatch pattern on the left side of the building to start the **HATCHEDIT** command. AutoCAD displays the **Hatch Edit** dialog box with the setting for the fence hatch loaded as defaults.
3. Select the **ANSI37** pattern from the **Pattern** list and set the **Scale** to **30**. Choose **Preview** to see a preview of the hatch pattern and press **<Enter ↵>** to accept the pattern and end the **HATCH** command.
4. Double-click the brick pattern on the right side of the drawing to start the **HATCHEDIT** command. Choose the **Inherit Properties** button and select the **ANSI37** pattern you just created. AutoCAD returns to the **Hatch Edit** dialog box with the setting for the **ANSI37** pattern loaded.
5. Choose the **Preview** button to see a preview of the hatch pattern and press **<Enter ↵>** to accept the pattern and end the **HATCH** command.
6. Save your drawing as **EX10-9**. Your drawing should look like Figure 10-32.

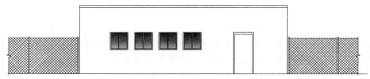

**Figure 10-32**    The modified hatch patterns

### Using the Properties Palette

The **Properties** palette is another easy way to make changes to hatch objects. Although, you can't make changes to the hatch boundaries, you can change the hatch pattern, scale, rotation angle, and hatch origin. You can also turn off the associativity and change the island detection method.

### Trimming Hatches

When using the **TRIM** and **EXTEND** commands, you can select hatch objects as cutting/ boundary edges. The edges of the individual hatch pattern lines will be used as stopping points. Only hatch patterns can be used in this manner; gradient and solid fill patterns will be ignored.

When using the **TRIM** command, you can trim hatch patterns back to selected cutting edges. When trimmed, the boundary edge of the hatch is trimmed back to the cutting edge, and the boundary is recalculated and reassociated if necessary. You cannot extend a hatch pattern out to a boundary edge.

### Exercise 10-10: Trimming Hatch Patterns

1. Continue from Exercise 10-9 and thaw layer **Fence2**. Two new fence posts are displayed on the left and right sides of the drawing.
2. Zoom into the fence post on the left side and start the **TRIM** command. Select the new fence post as the cutting edge and press **<Enter ↵>** to end the edge selection.
3. Pick the fence pattern in the middle of the post to trim the hatch pattern back to the new post. You can also select the boundary line near the top of the fence post to clean up the fence post. Repeat this process on the right-hand fence post.
4. Save your drawing as **EX10-10**. Your drawing should resemble Figure 10-33.

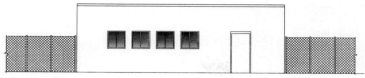

**Figure 10-33**    Trimming hatch objects

## Exploding Hatches

There may be times when you need to modify the individual lines within a hatch pattern. To do this, you can use the **EXPLODE** command on hatch patterns. The **EXPLODE** command will convert hatch patterns to individual line segments.

> You must take care when deciding to explode a hatch pattern. Exploding a hatch pattern can create a large number of individual objects and can greatly increase the size of your drawing. You may also have a hard time finding and cleaning up all the little line objects that the **EXPLODE** command creates.

# USING DESIGNCENTER WITH HATCH PATTERNS

AutoCAD's DesignCenter can also be used to create hatch patterns. When using DesignCenter, you can find and select .pat files on your hard drive or any accessible network drive. When you select a .pat file, DesignCenter will read the file and display a list of all hatch patterns defined within that file.

To create a hatch object with **DesignCenter**, you can simply drag and drop the desired hatch pattern into any closed area on your drawing. AutoCAD will create a simple boundary hatch using the default hatch settings. You can then double-click the hatch pattern to access the **HATCHEDIT** command and make any desired changes.

> **FOR MORE DETAILS**    See Chapter 16 for more information about DesignCenter.

**Exercise 10-11:** Hatching with DesignCenter

1. Continue from Exercise 10-10 and set layer **Elevation** current.
2. Start the **ADCENTER** command to display the **DesignCenter** palette. Position the **DesignCenter** palette at a convenient location on your screen.
3. In **DesignCenter**, choose the **Folders** palette and navigate to the **C:\Program Files\AutoCAD 2009\User Data Cache\Support** folder. Double-click on the acad.pat hatch pattern file. After a few moments, **DesignCenter** will show a list of all the hatch patterns defined in this file.
4. Scroll down the list and select **AR-BRELM** pattern. Drag this hatch pattern onto your drawing and release it within the boundary of the building wall. AutoCAD will fill the building wall with this pattern. Close or hide the **DesignCenter** palette.
5. Double-click the pattern you just created to start the **HATCHEDIT** command. Change the **Scale** to **2.0** and set the **Island display style** to **Outer**.
6. Choose the **Preview** button to see a preview of the hatch pattern and press **<Enter ↵>** to accept the pattern and end the **HATCH** command.
7. Save your drawing as **EX10-11**. Your drawing should resemble Figure 10-34.

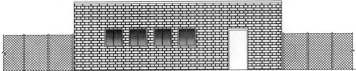

Figure 10-34   Hatching
with DesignCenter

# Summary

Hatching is an integral part of drafting and design. What was once a tedious process in manual drafting is easily accomplished in AutoCAD. AutoCAD's boundary detection and creation makes defining a hatch area a very simple process.

In this chapter you've seen how to select hatch boundary areas, specify hatch patterns and creation options, and how to preview, create, and modify hatch and fill patterns.

# Chapter Test Questions

## Multiple Choice

1.  Which of the following is *not* a way to specify hatch boundaries in the **HATCH** command?

    a.  Choose the **Add: Draw boundary** button and draw a closed shape
    b.  Choose the **Add: Select objects** button and select existing drawing objects
    c.  Choose the **Add: Pick points** button and pick points within closed areas of the drawing
    d.  Choose the **Remove Boundaries** button and select existing boundary edges to delete

2.  A hatch boundary:

    a.  Must consist of drawing objects connected end to end
    b.  Cannot contain any islands
    c.  Can only consist of straight line segments; curved boundaries are not allowed
    d.  None of the above

3.  The Island Display style setting:

    a.  Controls how island areas are hatched
    b.  Allows you to ignore all island areas
    c.  Allows you to hatch every other nested island area
    d.  All of the above

4.  A solid fill pattern:

    a.  Can only use ACI color numbers
    b.  Does not work with Color Book defined colors
    c.  Can use any valid AutoCAD color
    d.  Can only use RGB or HLS defined colors

5.  The boundary set is:

    a.  The set of objects used when detecting boundary edges
    b.  The boundary edge of a hatched area

    c.  Created when associative hatching is turned on
    d.  None of the above

6.  The **HATCHEDIT** command:

    a.  Is used to explode hatch objects
    b.  Is used to modify hatch patterns
    c.  Does not work on gradient fills
    d.  All of the above

7.  If a predefined hatch pattern is defined as a set of parallel lines .5 unit apart at a 45° angle, applying a hatch scale of 2 and a hatch angle of 180° will result in an area hatch consisting of lines:

    a.  2 units apart at an angle of 45°
    b.  1 unit apart at an angle of 225°
    c.  .5 unit apart at an angle of 180°
    d.  2 units apart at an angle of 180°

8.  The **DRAWORDER** command allows you to move objects:

    a.  To the back of all other objects
    b.  To the front of all other objects
    c.  To the back of selected objects
    d.  All of the above

9.  A one-color gradient fill transitions only between:

    a.  Black and white
    b.  A selected color and white
    c.  A selected color and black
    d.  None of the above

10. Hatch patterns can be:

    a.  Exploded
    b.  Used as edges in the **TRIM** and **EXTEND** commands
    c.  Modified with the **TRIM** command
    d.  All of the above

## Matching

**Column A**

a. Hatching

b. Gradient fill

**Column B**

1.  A file that contains hatch pattern definitions

2.  A link between two drawing objects so that when one changes, the other updates

c. Hatch boundary

d. Associativity

e. Hatch islands

f. Gap tolerance

g. Boundary set

h. Hatch pattern

i. ACAD.PAT

3. Used to place overlapping objects on top of one another

4. A solid pattern with a smooth transition from one color to another

5. The allowable open area allowed when detecting boundary edges

6. Closed areas within a hatch boundary

7. The process of filling in a closed area with a pattern

8. The set of objects used when detecting boundary edges

9. The edges of a hatched area

j. DRAWORDER

**True or False**

1. True or False: Hatch objects cannot be modified. You must delete and recreate them.

2. True or False: **DesignCenter** can be used to create hatch objects.

3. True or False: Objects must touch end to end to be used as hatch boundaries.

4. True or False: User-defined hatch patterns are always drawn with a continuous linetype.

10. The pattern used to fill a hatched area

5. True or False: Text objects are treated as closed objects when determining a boundary.

6. True or False: You can only create one hatch pattern at a time with the **HATCH** command.

7. True or False: Hatch patterns are defined in .pat files.

8. True or False: You cannot modify hatch pattern definitions.

9. True or False: Modifying hatch boundary objects can result in losing associativity with their hatch patterns.

10. True or False: AutoCAD can create one-, two-, and three-color gradient fills.

# CHAPTER PROJECTS

## Project 10-1a: **Calculator—Continued from Chapter 5**

1. Open the drawing **P5-1** from Chapter 5.
2. Create the solid and gradient fill areas shown in Figure P10-1A. Experiment with different gradient settings to achieve the desired effect.
3. Save your drawing as **P10-1A**.

Figure P10-1A

## Project 10-1b: Circuit Board—Continued from Chapter 9

1. Open the drawing **P9-1** from Chapter 9.
2. Using polylines, draw the wiring shown in Figure P10-1B on the **Bottom** layer.
3. Create the solid fill areas shown in Figure P10-1C on the **Smask** layer. Use the **ANSI31** pattern with a scale of **.25**. *Hint:* Draw the outer boundary and then freeze the **Silkscreen, Top**, and **Bottom** layers before hatching.
4. Save your drawing as **P10-1B**.

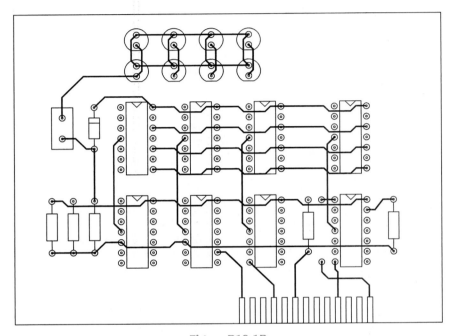

Figure P10-1B

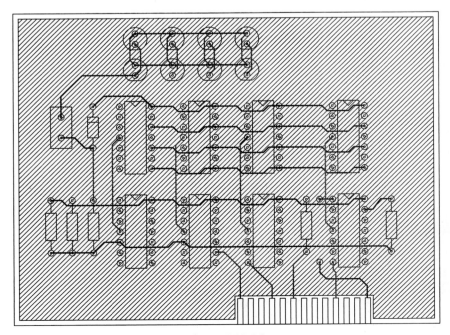

Figure P10-1C

## Project 10-2: **Motorcycle—Continued from Chapter 9**

1. Open drawing **P9-2** from Chapter 9.
2. Hatch the areas shown as black in Figure **P10-2** with the **Solid** hatch pattern on the **Hatch_Black** layer using the **BHATCH** command.
3. Hatch the areas shown as gray in Figure P10-2 with the **Solid** hatch pattern on the **Hatch_Gray** layer using the **BHATCH** command.
4. Save the drawing as **P10-2**.

Figure P10-2

## Project 10-3: **Logo—Continued from Chapter 9**

1. Open the drawing **P9-3**.
2. Create the solid fill areas shown in Figure P10-3.
3. Save your drawing as **P10-3**.

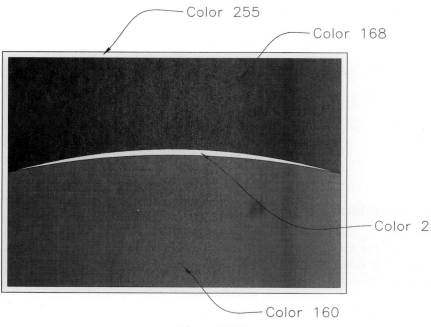

Figure P10-3

**Project 10-4a:** **Architectural D-Size Border—Continued from Chapter 9**

1. Open the template file **Architectural D-Size.DWT**.
2. Hatch the logo outline as shown in Figure P10-4A using a two-color gradient hatch on the layer **A-Anno-Ttlb-Logo**.
3. Hatch the graphic scale outline as shown in Figure P10-4A using a the **Solid** hatch on the layer **A-Anno-Ttlb-Text**.
4. Save the drawing to a template file as **Architectural D-Size.DWT**.

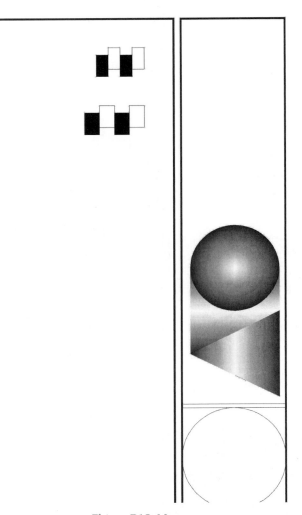

Figure P10-4A

**Project 10-4b:** **Architectural B-Size Border—Continued from Chapter 9**

1. Open the template file **Architectural B-Size.DWT**.
2. Hatch the logo outline similar to what is shown in Figure P10-4A using a two-color gradient hatch on the layer **A-Anno-Ttlb-Logo**.
3. Save the drawing to a template file as **Architectural B-Size.DWT**.

## Project 10-5: **Electrical Distribution Panel—Continued from Chapter 7**

1. Open drawing **P7-5** from Chapter 7.
2. Add the hatching shown in Figure P10-5. Make sure the hatching is placed in back of the outlines.
3. Save your drawing as **P10-5**.

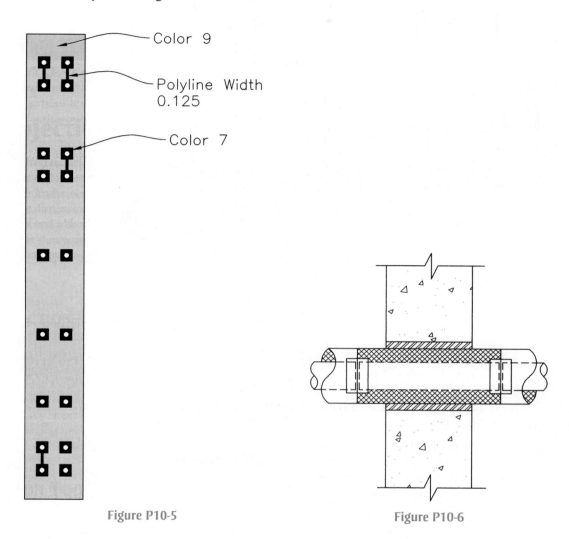

Figure P10-5                    Figure P10-6

## Project 10-6: **Pipe/Wall Penetration Detail—Continued from Chapter 9**

1. Open drawing **P9-6** from Chapter 9.
2. Add the hatching to the Wall Penetration detail as shown in Figure P10-6 on layer **P-Detl-Pat**.
3. Save the drawing as **P10-6**.

## Project 10-7: **Residential Architectural Plan— Continued from Chapter 9**

1. Open the drawing **P9-7** from Chapter 9.
2. Hatch the patio and driveway as shown in Figure P10-7. Use the **GRAVEL** hatch pattern. Experiment with the scale and rotation angle to achieve the desired stone pattern.
3. Create the solid fill areas in the walls and the north arrow.

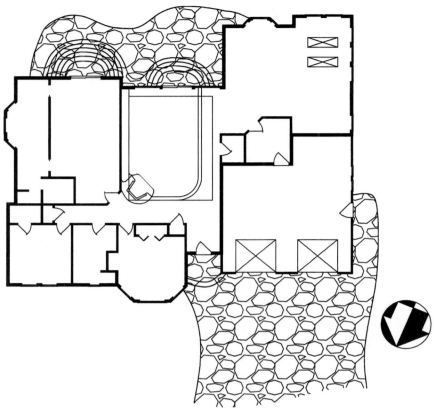

Figure P10-7

4. Use appropriate layers for all objects.
5. Save your drawing as **P10-7**.

**Project 10-8a: Joist Foundation Detail—Continued from Chapter 9**

1. Open drawing **P9-8A** from Chapter 9.
2. Add the hatching to the Joist Foundation detail as shown in Figure P10-8A on layer **A-Detl-Pa**t.
3. Save the drawing as **P10-8A**.

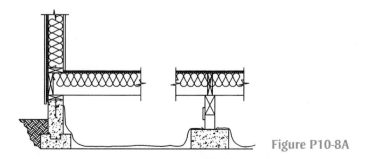

Figure P10-8A

**Project 10-8b: Interior Floor Change Detail—Continued from Chapter 9**

1. Open drawing **P9-8B** from Chapter 9.
2. Add the hatching to the Interior Floor Change detail as shown in Figure P10-8B on layer **A-Detl-Pat**.
3. Save the drawing as **P10-8B**.

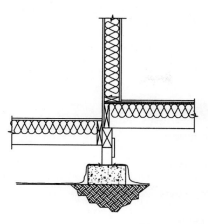

Figure P10-8B

## Project 10-8c: Truss with Soffited Eave Detail—Continued from Chapter 9

1. Open drawing **P9-8C** from Chapter 9.
2. Add the hatching to the Truss W/Soffited Eave detail as shown in Figure P10-8C on layer **A-Detl-Pat**.
3. Save the drawing as **P10-8C**.

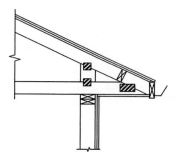

Figure P10-8C

## Project 10-9: Bearing—English Units—Continued from Chapter 9

1. Open the drawing **P9-9** from Chapter 9.
2. Create the hatch pattern on the **HATCH** layer as shown in Figure P10-9.
3. Save the drawing as **P10-9**.

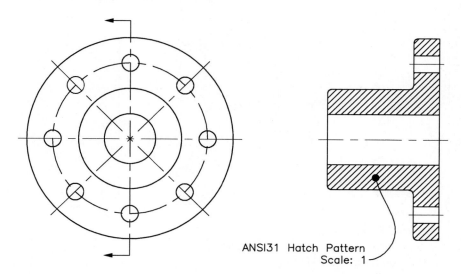

ANSI31  Hatch  Pattern
Scale:  1

Figure P10-9

## Project 10-10a: **Hub—Metric**

1. Start a new drawing using the acadiso.dwt template.
2. Create the following layers:

| Name | Color | Linetype | Lineweight | Description |
|------|-------|----------|------------|-------------|
| Object | 7 | Continuous | 0.35 mm | Object lines |
| Hidden | 1 | Hidden | Default | Hidden lines |
| Center | 2 | Center | Default | Centerlines |
| Hatch terns | 4 | Continuous | Default | Hatch pat- and fills |
| Notes notes | 3 | Continuous | Default | Text and |
| Dims | 2 | Continuous | Default | Dimensions |

3. Draw the front view and section view of the hub shown in Figure P10-10A.
4. Draw object lines as shown in Figure P10-10A on layer **Object**.
5. Draw hidden lines as shown in Figure P10-10A on layer **Hidden**.
6. Draw centerlines as shown in Figure P10-10A on layer **Center**.
7. Adjust the **LTSCALE** system so linetypes appear properly.
8. Hatch the section view as shown in Figure P10-10A on layer **Hatch**.
9. **Do not** include text or dimensions.
10. Save the drawing as **P10-10A**.

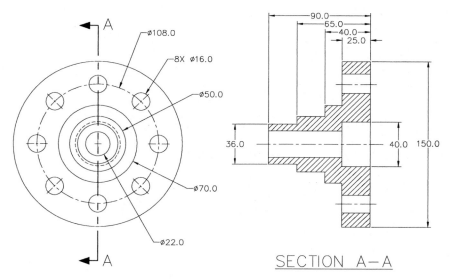

SECTION A—A

**Figure P10-10A**

## Project 10-10b: **Window Extrusion—Continued from Chapter 9**

1. Open drawing **P9-10**.
2. Add the hatching to the Window Extrusion as shown in Figure P10-10B on layer **Pattern**.
3. Save the drawing as **P10-10B**.

## Project 10-11: **Civil Site Plan—Continued from Chapter 9**

1. Open drawing **P9-11** from Chapter 9.
2. Draw the site outline, elevation lines, and building site as shown in Figure P10-11. Place the corner of the site at 0,0 as shown. Draw the elevation lines approximately where shown. **Do not** include dimensions or text.
3. Save the drawing as **P10-11**.

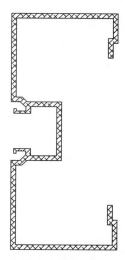

**Figure P10-10B**

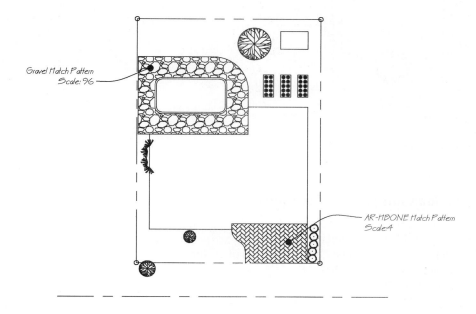

Gravel Hatch Pattern
Scale: 96

AR-HBONE Hatch Pattern
Scale:4

**Figure P10-11**

## Project 10-12a: **Manhole Construction Detail—Continued from Chapter 6**

1. Open drawing **P6-12** from Chapter 6.
2. Add the horizontal rebar using the **DONUT** command as shown in Figure P10-12A on layer **C-Detl-P2**.
3. Add the hatching to the Manhole Construction detail as shown in Figure P10-12A on layer **C-Detl-Pat**.
4. **Do no**t include notes.
5. Save the drawing as **P10-12A**.

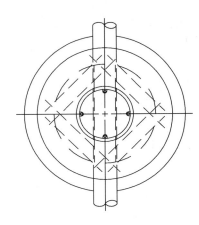

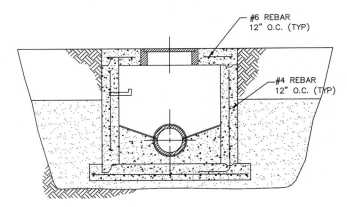

Figure P10-12A

## Project 10-12b: Manhole Cover—Continued from Chapter 8

1. Open drawing **P8-12** from Chapter 8.
2. Add the hatching to the Manhole Construction detail as shown in Figure P10-12B on layer **C-Detl-Pat**.
3. Save the drawing as **P10-12B**.

## Project 10-12c: Standard Service Connection—Continued from Chapter 9

1. Open drawing **P9-12** from Chapter 9.
2. Add the hatching to the Standard Service Connection drawing as shown in Figure P10-12C on layer **C-Detl-Pat**.
3. Save the drawing as **P10-12C**.

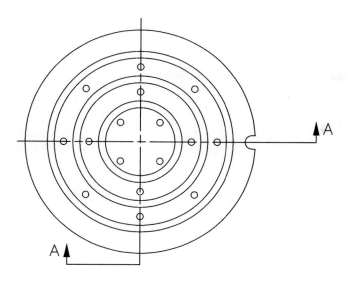

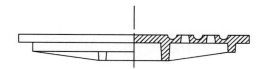

TOP VIEW

SECTION A—A

Figure P10-12B

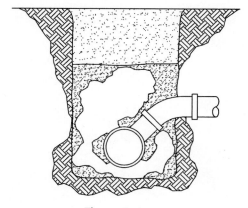

Figure P10-12C

# Adding Text

# 11

## Chapter Objectives

- Control the appearance of text using text styles and fonts
- Understand the difference between TrueType fonts and AutoCAD SHX fonts
- Create and edit multiline text
- Create and automate horizontal, diagonal, and tolerance type stacked text
- Create and edit single-line text
- Insert intelligent text fields
- Find and replace text in a drawing
- Check text spelling for a whole drawing

## INTRODUCTION

They say a picture is worth a thousand words, and while the lines, arcs, and circles on a drawing can convey a great deal of design information, at the end of the day you will need to ***annotate*** your drawings in order to completely communicate your design.

Text on a drawing comes in many different shapes, sizes, and forms. It is used in a drawing's title block to tell the reader who created the drawing and when. Title block text might also provide information about who checked the drawing or at what revision of a design you are viewing—both very important pieces of information. Of course, there is also the text that is created directly on a drawing in the form of notes, labels, and callouts with specific design instructions, references to other drawings, part numbers, and specifications, to name but a few. Figure 11-1 shows a few examples of different types of drawing annotation.

Manually annotating a drawing on the drafting board, originally referred to as *lettering,* was a tedious and time-consuming task. In fact, some considered it an art form because of the skill and dexterity needed to annotate a drawing properly.

Those days are long gone. AutoCAD provides a number of tools that allow you to annotate your drawings, in a fashion that meets or exceeds industry drafting standards quickly, and with minimum effort. You can add multiple lines of text by simply defining a boundary area that the text should fill so that as you type, AutoCAD automatically formats the text to fit. It is also possible to add text, known as a *field,* which can automatically update itself with the current date, the name of drawing file, or the properties of an object in a drawing!

In this chapter, we look at the tools AutoCAD provides for annotating your drawing. We also examine the tools used to *edit* annotation features. Once again, AutoCAD makes it quick and easy to change information once it is created in a drawing so that updating text is as simple as double-clicking with your mouse.

**annotate:** To add text, notes, and dimensions to a drawing

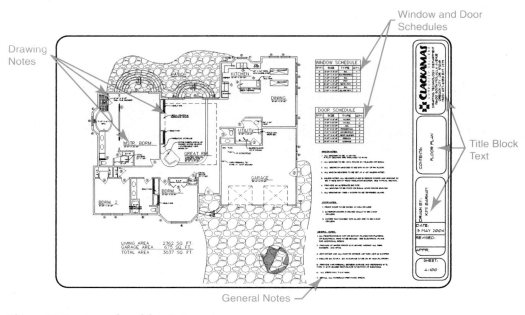

Drawing
Notes

Title Block
Text

General Notes

**Figure 11-1    Examples of drawing annotation**

> **TIP**
>
> Text and other annotation features should be placed on a unique layer so that you can control their visibility. Text can be one of the most resource-intensive objects in a drawing. A drawing with a lot of text can become significantly bogged down. Being able to freeze text on its layer can significantly increase drawing performance.

## CONTROLLING THE APPEARANCE OF TEXT

The appearance of text on a drawing is very important. Text should be created as legibly as possible so that it can be easily read and understood with minimum effort. Because of this, different standards have been established to control everything from the text font and height to how text should be located and oriented in a drawing.

> **FOR MORE DETAILS**    See Appendix A for detailed information about drafting industry text standards.

### Fonts

typeface: The style or design
of a font

These days most people are familiar with text fonts. The font is what determines how text looks by defining its *typeface*.

Some of the more popular TrueType® fonts are shown in Figure 11-2.

> **TIP**
>
> A drawing named TrueType.DWG, located in the AutoCAD Sample folder, shows the character map for many of the TrueType fonts.

Arial, **Arial Black**, Arial Narrow

*City Blueprint, Country Blueprint,* Stylus BT

Courier New, Times New Roman

**Swis721 BT**, Swiss721 Lt BT

**Impact,** Comic Sans MS, **Vineta BT**

SansSerif, Trebuchet MS, Verdana

Wingdings ✆✌✋♨☜⌘■⅛♦☺

**Figure 11-2**    Examples of TrueType fonts

| TXT | – | AaBbCcDdEe123456790 |
| MONOTXT | – | AaBbCcDdEe123456790 |
| SIMPLEX | – | AaBbCcDdEe123456790 |
| ROMANS | – | AaBbCcDdEe123456790 |
| ROMANC | – | AaBbCcDdEe123456790 |
| ROMAND | – | AaBbCcDdEe123456790 |
| ROMANT | – | AaBbCcDdEe123456790 |
| BOLD | – | **AaBbCcDdEe123456790** |
| COMPLEX | – | AaBbCcDdEe123456790 |

**Figure 11-3**    Examples of AutoCAD fonts

*TrueType Fonts Versus AutoCAD Fonts.*    The fonts shown in Figure 11-2 are known as TrueType fonts. TrueType fonts are the standard font type provided as part of Microsoft® Windows. TrueType is actually a specification developed by Apple Computer and later adopted by Microsoft that allows for scaleable text, meaning the same font can be displayed at any size and resolution. A TrueType font typically has a three-letter TTF filename extension.

In addition to TrueType fonts, AutoCAD comes with its own set of fonts referred to as *SHX fonts* because of their three-letter SHX filename extension. Some of the standard AutoCAD SHX fonts are shown in Figure 11-3.

As you can see from Figure 11-3, the AutoCAD fonts range from simple to complex. The most basic AutoCAD font is TXT.SHX, text can be one of the most demanding factors on your computer system resources. Text with a complex font consumes more memory than text with a simple font. If you have a drawing with a lot of text, a complex double- or triple-line font takes much longer to regenerate than a simple font such as TXT.SHX.

> **Note:**
> The **TEXTFILL** system variable controls the filling of TrueType fonts while plotting and rendering. Setting **TEXTFILL=0** turns off the solid fill. Setting **TEXTFILL=1** turns the solid fill on.

**TIP**    A good balance of performance versus legibility is provided by both the ROMANS.SHX and SIMPLEX.SHX AutoCAD fonts.

Fonts are typically assigned to text styles because this provides the most control over the appearance of text in your drawing. It is possible to assign fonts directly to text objects using multiline text, but this approach is typically avoided because of the increased management needs. Text styles and multiline text are both discussed later in this chapter.

**TIP**    The **FONTALT** system variable specifies an alternate font to be used when a particular font file cannot be located on your system. By default, the **FONTALT** system variable is set to the AutoCAD SIMPLEX.SHX font.

## Text Height

The height of text in a drawing is very important, and as mentioned earlier, is also determined by industry drafting standards. Text that is used for notes on a drawing is typically 0.100″ to 0.125″ (2 mm to 3 mm) tall while text for titles is typically 0.188″ to 0.25″ (5 mm to 6 mm) tall. These are the standard heights that text should be on the final plotted or printed drawing, but they are not always the heights used when text is added to a drawing. Remember from Chapter 1, that if the final printed drawing is not at a scale of 1:1, you must scale annotation features up or down so that they plot at the correct size. This is accomplished by multiplying the desired printed text height by the reciprocal of the plot or viewport scale. This multiplier is referred to as the *drawing scale factor*.

| **FOR MORE DETAILS** | See Chapter 1 for more details about calculating the drawing scale factor manually. |
|---|---|

## Annotation Scale

Instead of calculating the scale factor manually as just described, it is possible to automate the process of scaling text so that it is created at the correct height for the final plotted drawing scale using the AutoCAD **Annotation Scale** feature located on the right side of the Status Bar.

| **FOR MORE DETAILS** | See Chapter 1 for a detailed description of the **Annotation Scale** feature. |
|---|---|

When text with its **Annotative** property enabled is added to the drawing, it automatically scales up or down by the current **Annotation Scale** so that it is the correct height.

Taking it a step further, it is even possible to add additional different **Annotation Scales** to text automatically so that it can be viewed at different heights for different scale factors. Using this feature, each time the **Annotation Scale** is changed, all the text that has its **Annotative** property enabled is resized accordingly.

> **Note:**
> Remember that even though text with multiple **Annotation Scales** can be viewed at multiple scales, it is in reality represented by only one text object. AutoCAD does not make multiple copies for each scale representation. In fact, the **Annotation Scale** feature was developed to eliminate the need to create new text for each scale and to have to rely on layers to turn different scales off and on.

| **FOR MORE DETAILS** | See Chapter 14 for an example of applying the **Annotation Scale** features using paper space layouts and viewports. |
|---|---|

The best way to take advantage of the **Annotation Scale** feature when you are working with text is to enable the **Annotative** feature in the current text style. Text styles are explained in detail in the next section.

## Text Styles

The font, height, and other characteristics that affect the appearance of text are typically managed using text styles. All text in a drawing has a text style associated with it. When you add text to a drawing, it is created using the current text style settings. The current text style can be set by selecting it from the text style list on the **Annotation** panel on the **Home** ribbon or the **Text** panel on the **Annotate** ribbon shown in Figure 11-4, selecting it from the text style list in the multiline text editor explained later, or typed in if you are creating single-line text.

The default text style is named STANDARD, which is assigned the Arial True Type font with a text height of 0.000″.

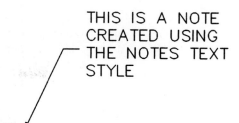

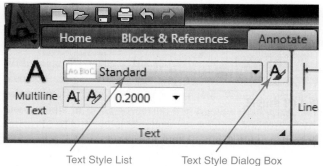

Figure 11-4    Text panel on the Annotate ribbon

Text Style List          Text Style Dialog Box

Figure 11-5    Examples of different text styles.

TIP

The **Annotate** ribbon provides quick and easy access to the most commonly used annotation tools. For this reason, you should select the **Annotate** tab to display the **Annotate** ribbon whenever you are adding text.

It is possible to modify the STANDARD text style or create one or more new text styles with user-defined names that can have different fonts, heights, or other properties.

Different text styles should be used to manage the different text types in a drawing. You might create a font named NOTES that is assigned the SIMPLEX.SHX font with a height set to 0.125″ that can be used for all note-type text in a drawing. You can then create another style named TITLES that is assigned the bold ARIAL True-Type font and a height of 0.25″ that can be used for all the title type text in a drawing. See Figure 11-5.

Using text styles to control the appearance of the different text types in a drawing provides a number of advantages. First, text styles make it easier to change the appearance of text if required. For instance, if the font specification changes for a certain type of text, you need to update only the corresponding text style. Otherwise, you must find every instance of text in a drawing that uses the old font and change it manually.

Using text styles to control the appearance of text also helps promote the use of drafting standards by providing the ability to have text look consistent for an entire project or organization.

**Note:**
Text height can be controlled either by the text style height setting, or it can be specified when the text is created. If the text height is set to 0.000″ in the text style, you must specify the text height when text is added to a drawing. If the text style height is set to any value greater than 0.000″, the text height is set automatically when text is added to a drawing.

**Note:**
Text style names can be up to 255 characters long and can consist of letters, numbers, and a few other special characters such as underscores, hyphens, and even spaces. The default style name created by AutoCAD is "Style" followed by an integer value (i.e., Style1, Style2, etc.).

TIP    Use AutoCAD template files to your advantage by creating all your standard default text styles in a template file that can be used when you start a new drawing. You can also use DesignCenter to copy text styles from another drawing using drag-and-drop techniques.

**FOR MORE DETAILS**    See Chapter 16 for more details about how to use DesignCenter.

### The Text Style Dialog Box

The **Text Style** dialog box allows you to control and manage text styles in a drawing by allowing you to do the following:

- Set a text style current
- Add or delete a text style
- Rename a text style
- Assign or change the text style font
- Set the text height
- Apply different text effects that make text read upside down, backwards, or even vertically
- Change the text width so it is wider or narrower
- Slant text at a specified angle so it leans forward or backwards

The **Text Style** dialog box can be displayed by selecting the **Text Style** button on the **Text** panel shown in Figure 11-4, selecting **Text Style...** from the **Format** menu, or by typing **STYLE** or **ST**.

The **Text Style** dialog box is shown in Figure 11-6. The following sections explain the different text style settings and features.

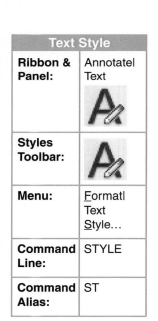

| Text Style | |
|---|---|
| **Ribbon & Panel:** | Annotatel Text |
| **Styles Toolbar:** | |
| **Menu:** | Formatl Text Style... |
| **Command Line:** | STYLE |
| **Command Alias:** | ST |

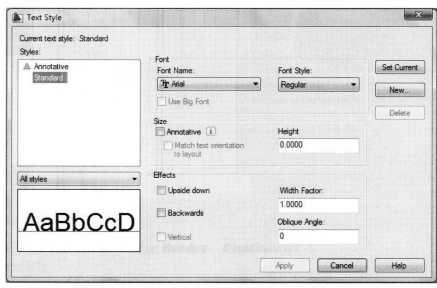

**Figure 11-6**    The Text Style dialog box

*Styles List.*    **Styles:** is where you can select a text style to be current, rename a text style, or delete an existing text style. The text style list contains all the text styles in the drawing and displays the current text style. To change the current style, you can double-click on it, right-click and select **Set Current**, or select the **Set Current** button.

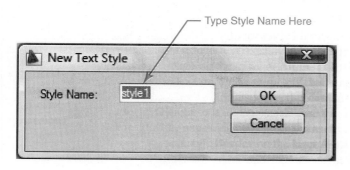

Type Style Name Here

Figure 11-7    The New Text Style
dialog box.

To create a new text style, select the **New...** button.

The **New...** button displays the **New Text Style** dialog box shown in Figure 11-7.

The default style name is "Style" followed by a sequenced number (i.e., Style1, Style2, Style3, etc.). Typically you want to supply your own style name. One common approach is to name the style the same name as its associated font. For instance, if you are going to assign the SIMPLEX.SHX font, you would name the text style "Simplex." This way when you go to make a text style current, you can immediately tell what font will be used based on its name.

The **Delete** button deletes the selected text style.

> **Note:**
> Only unreferenced text styles can be deleted. There can be no text in the drawing that uses the text style you wish to delete. In fact, the **Delete** button is disabled if the selected text style is referenced anywhere in the drawing.

*Font Area.*    The **Font** area of the **Text Style** dialog box allows you to change the style's font name and style.

The **Font Name:** drop-down list contains a list of all the registered TrueType fonts *and* the AutoCAD SHX compiled shape fonts. The TrueType fonts are preceded with the "TT" icon, and the AutoCAD fonts are preceded with an icon that looks like a compass.

The **Font Style:** list box specifies font character formatting such as italic, bold, or regular for TrueType fonts. The **Font Style:** list is disabled when an AutoCAD SHX type font is selected. When the **Use Big Font** check box is selected, this option changes to **Big Font Name** and is used to select a Big Font file name.

> **Note:**
> Changing a text style's font will automatically update all the text in the drawing that uses the selected text style with the new font. In fact, that is a good reason to use text styles to manage your fonts—you have centralized control over the text appearance.

The **Use Big Font** check box is used to specify an Asian-language Big Font file. Big Font files provide an extended character set needed for many Asian languages with large alphabets. The **Use Big Font** check box is only enabled when an AutoCAD SHX font file is selected. TrueType fonts do not have this capability.

**TIP**    It is possible to define several text styles that use the same font.

*Size Area.*    The **Size** area of the **Text Style** dialog box allows you to control the height of text based on the text style.

The **Height:** text box is where you enter the desired text height for all the text created using the selected text style. Remember earlier it was explained that if you use the default height of 0.00", AutoCAD requires you to specify a text height each time you add text and the selected text style is current. Specifying a height greater than 0.00" sets the text height for this style so that you do not need to specify a height every time you add text. Some TrueType fonts may be displayed at a smaller height than AutoCAD SHX fonts with the same height setting.

Selecting the **Annotative** check box enables the automated **Annotation Scale** feature discussed earlier for all text that is created using the current text style. When the **Annotative** check box is selected, the **Height:** text box is relabeled the **Paper Text Height** text box, and the **Match text orientation to layout** check box is enabled.

The **Paper Text Height** text box reflects what you want the final plotted text height to be. AutoCAD, in turn, will automatically scale the **Annotative** text up or down to match this height based on the current **Annotation Scale**.

Selecting the **Match text orientation to layout** check box automatically sets the orientation of the text in paper space viewports to match the orientation of the current layout.

**Note:**
Unlike changing the font, changing the height does not affect any existing text in the drawing that was created using the selected style. The new text height **will** be used by any new text that is created. Changing the height of existing text is discussed later in this chapter.

**FOR MORE DETAILS**    See Chapter 14 for more information about using the **Annotation Scale** feature with paper space layouts and viewports.

**TIP**    It is another common convention to name a text style to reflect the text height if it is set to anything other than 0.00″. For instance, a text style assigned the SIMPLEX.SHX font and a height set to 0.125″ might be named **Romans .125** or **Romans_125.** This way you know the font *and* the height when you set a text style current.

*Effects Area.*    The **Effects** area of the **Text Style** dialog box allows you to apply different font effects such as whether text is displayed upside down, backwards, or stacked vertically. You can also change the text width factor so that text can be made wider or narrower, as well as set at an oblique angle that will slant the text forward or backwards the specified angle—a technique that can be used to create italicized text.

The **Upside Down** setting displays text upside down when it is selected. The **Backwards** setting displays text backwards. The **Vertical** setting displays text stacked vertically. See Figure 11-8. The **Vertical** setting is available only if the selected font supports dual orientation.

The **Width Factor:** setting controls horizontal text spacing. The default width is 1.0. Specifying a value greater than 1.0

**Note:**
The **Upside Down** setting affects single-line text only. New and existing multiline text are not affected by the **Upside Down** setting.

**Note:**
The **Backwards** setting affects single-line text only. New and existing multiline text are not affected by the **Backwards** setting.

BACKWARDS

UPSIDE DOWN

V
E
R
T
I
C
A
L

Figure 11-8    The Backwards, Upside Down, and Vertical effects

WIDTH FACTOR = 0.5
WIDTH FACTOR = 1.0
WIDTH   FACTOR   =   2.0
**Figure 11-9**    Examples of Width Factor effects

*OBLIQUE ANGLE = +30*
*OBLIQUE ANGLE = -30*
**Figure 11-10**    Examples of Oblique Angle effects.

expands the text so that it is wider. Specifying a value less than 1.0 condenses the text so it is narrower. See Figure 11-9.

The **Oblique Angle:** setting controls the oblique angle, or slant, of the text. The angle entered is measured from 90° vertical so that a positive angle slants text forward and a negative angle slants text backwards. It is possible to enter a value between −85° and 85°. See Figure 11-10.

*Applying Changes to a Text Style.*    The **Apply** button applies any changes made in the **Text Style** dialog box to any text in the drawing that uses the selected style.

The **Cancel** button will discard any changes and exit the **Text Style** dialog box. The **Cancel** button changes to a **Close** button whenever you click on the **Apply** button. Creating, renaming, or deleting a text style are all actions that cannot be canceled.

> **Note:**
> The **Vertical** setting only affects text styles that are assigned an SHX type font. TrueType fonts cannot be displayed vertically.

> **Note:**
> Some TrueType fonts using the effects described in this section might appear bold in your drawing. Don't be too concerned because their appearance has no effect on the plotted output.

### Exercise 11-1: Creating and Modifying Text Styles

1. Start a new drawing using the acad.dwt drawing template.
2. Update the STANDARD text style so that its font is set to the SIMPLEX.SHX AutoCAD font.
3. Create a text style named NOTES with the following settings:
   a. Font = Simplex.shx
   b. Height = 0.125″
4. Create a text style named TITLES with the following settings:
   a. Font = Arial
   b. Height = 0.25″
5. Create a text style named ARCHITECTURAL with the following settings:
   a. Font = CityBlueprint
   b. Height = 0.125″
6. Create a text style named MECHANICAL with the following settings:
   a. Font = GDT.shx
   b. Height = 0.100″
7. Save the drawing as **EX11-1**.

## CREATING MULTILINE TEXT

Multiline text is a complex text object that can consist of multiple lines of text that you enter in paragraph form using an in-place text editor that resembles a simple word processing program. The text is automatically formatted to fit a rectangular boundary area that you define using two corner points before the text editor is displayed. AutoCAD automatically determines the horizontal length of the line of text by inserting soft returns similar to a word processor. The vertical height of the multiline text object depends on the amount of text, not the vertical height of the bounding box. See Figure 11-11.

MULTILINE TEXT IS A COMPLEX
TEXT OBJECT THAT CAN CONSIST
OF MULTIPLE LINES OF TEXT
THAT YOU ENTER IN PARAGRAPH
FORM. THE TEXT IS
AUTOMATICALLY FORMATTED TO
FIT A RECTANGULAR BOUNDARY
AREA THAT YOU DEFINE USING
TWO POINTS BEFORE THE TEXT
EDITOR IS DISPLAYED. AUTOCAD
AUTOMATICALLY DETERMINES THE
HORIZONTAL LENGTH OF THE LINE
OF TEXT BY INSERTING SOFT
RETURNS SIMILAR TO A WORD
PROCESSOR.

Rectangular
Text Boundary
Area

**Figure 11-11**    Multiline text

The in-place text editor creates and edits the text in its current location and is transparent so you can see the drawing linework below to locate text accordingly. Some of the features and benefits of multiline text include:

- Setting tabs and indents
- Automated field insertion
- Importing external text files in ASCII or RTF format
- Enhanced symbol and special character insertion
- Bulleted and numbered list creation
- Creating stacked fractions and geometric tolerances
- Resizing the text boundary area using grips, and reformatting the text line length automatically
- The ability to switch selected text between uppercase and lowercase with the click of a mouse
- The ability to create multiple columns of text

The **MTEXT** command is used to create multiline text using the in-place text editor. Editing multiline text using the in-place editor is explained later in this chapter.

When you start the **MTEXT** command, AutoCAD displays the current text style and height at the command line as follows:

```
Current text style: "Standard" Text height: 0.2000
```

AutoCAD prompts you to *Specify first corner:* and the text "abc" is displayed on the cursor crosshairs as shown in Figure 11-12.

Because the size of the text is the *actual size* that the text will be created based on the current text height setting, it is affected by zooming in and out of your drawing. Select the first corner of the rectangular area that you want to use to create the text. AutoCAD prompts you to

| Multiline Text | |
|---|---|
| **Ribbon & Panel:** | Home\| Annotation ![A Multiline Text icon] |
| **Draw Toolbar:** | ![A icon] |
| **Menu:** | Draw\|Text\| Multiline Text... |
| **Command Line:** | MTEXT |
| **Command Alias:** | T or MT |

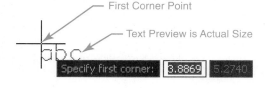

First Corner Point

Text Preview is Actual Size

**Figure 11-12**    First corner of the multiline text boundary area

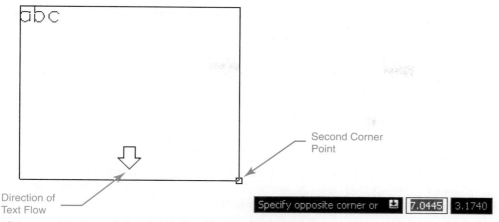

Specify opposite corner or ☑ 7.0445  3.1740

Second Corner
Point

Direction of
Text Flow

**Figure 11-13**   Second corner of the multiline text boundary area

*Specify opposite corner or ↓* and displays a preview of the
rectangular area as shown in Figure 11-13.

The arrow at the bottom of the rectangle indicates that
the text flow is top to bottom. This is because the default justification for multiline text is the top left corner. It is possible to change the justification by selecting the **Justify** option when AutoCAD prompts you to *Specify opposite
corner or ↓* by typing **J<Enter ↵>** or by using your arrow keys if you are using **Dynamic Input**. The different
multiline justification options are shown in Figure 11-14.

Notice how the arrows change to indicate how the
justification affects the text flow.

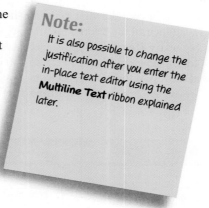

**Note:**
It is also possible to change the
justification after you enter the
in-place text editor using the
**Multiline Text** ribbon explained
later.

TL - Top Left   TC - Top Center   TR - Top Right

ML - Middle Left   MC - Middle Center   MR - Middle Right

BL - Bottom Left   BC - Bottom Center   BR - Bottom Right

**Figure 11-14**   Multiline text justification options

The other options that are available before you select the second text boundary corner point are as follows:

- Height
- Line spacing
- Rotation
- Style
- Width
- Columns

Most options can also be set in the in-place text editor *after* selecting the second corner point, whereas the rotation angle must be indicated *before* selecting the second corner point.

The **Rotation** option allows you to specify the angle for the complete multiline text object so that the whole paragraph of text is rotated at the angle you specify. To change the multiline text rotation angle, type **R<Enter ⏎>** or use the arrow keys if you're using **Dynamic Input**. Auto-CAD prompts you to *Specify rotation angle <0>:*. You can enter an angle via the keyboard or pick a point in your drawing to define the angle using the first corner point as the base point.

Once all the desired multiline options are set, select the second point to define the initial text boundary area. After you select the second point, AutoCAD displays the in-place multiline text editor shown in Figure 11-15 so you can start entering text. At the same time, the current ribbon at the top of the AutoCAD window switches to the **Multiline Text** ribbon shown in Figure 11-15 so you can access the **Multiline Text** tools and formatting options.

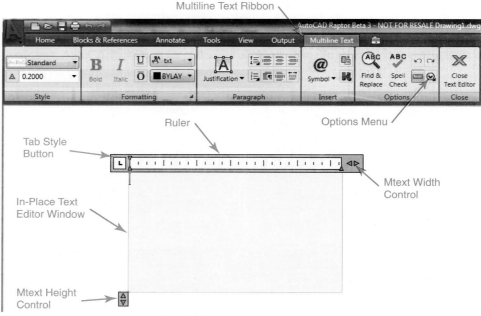

**Figure 11-15**     The in-place multiline text editor

## The In-Place Multiline Text Editor

The in-place multiline text editor consists of the following components and features:

- In-place text editor window
- Ruler
- **Multiline Text** ribbon
- Options menu
- Right-click shortcut menu

The in-place text editor window is where you enter the text. As mentioned, it works like most text editors and word processor software. As you type and the text reaches the end of the text editor window, AutoCAD automatically enters what is commonly referred to as a "soft" return to break the line. You can also enter your own "hard" returns if you wish by pressing the **<Enter ↵>** key. All the other common text editor keyboard controls are available to help you navigate, select, copy, paste, delete, and edit text as you type:

| Multiline Text Editor Keyboard Controls | |
|---|---|
| **Key or Key Combination** | **Description** |
| Home | Moves cursor to the beginning of the current line |
| End | Moves the cursor to the end of the current line |
| Ctrl + Home | Moves cursor to the first column of the first line |
| Ctrl + End | Moves cursor to the end of the last line |
| Delete | Deletes character to the right of cursor |
| Ctrl + Delete | Deletes complete word to the right of cursor |
| Page Up | Moves cursor to beginning of paragraph |
| Page Down | Moves cursor to end of paragraph |
| Arrow Keys | Moves cursor one position the direction of the arrow |
| Shift + Arrow Keys | Selects and highlights text under cursor as it moves |
| Backspace | Deletes character to the left of cursor |
| Ctrl + Backspace | Deletes word to the left of cursor |
| Ctrl + Shift + Space | Inserts a nonbreaking space |
| Ctrl + A | Selects all text |
| Ctrl + C | Copies selected text to the Windows clipboard |
| Ctrl + V | Pastes text from Windows clipboard at current cursor position |
| Ctrl + X | Cuts selected text so that the text is not copied to the Windows clipboard |
| Ctrl + Z | Undoes last operation |
| Ctrl + Shift + U | Changes selected text to all uppercase |
| Ctrl + Shift + L | Changes selected text to all lowercase |

**TIP** You can use the Windows Clipboard to copy and paste text between other Windows applications and AutoCAD.

When you are finished entering text, you have three ways to exit the multiline text editor and create the text in the drawing:

- Select the **Close Text Editor** button on the **Multiline Text** ribbon.
- Click anywhere outside of the text editor with your mouse.
- Hold down the **<Ctrl>** key and press **<Enter ↵>**.

To close the text editor without saving the text or any changes press the **<Esc>** key.

**Exercise 11-2:** Creating Multiline Text

1. Continue from Exercise 11-1.
2. Set the NOTES text style current.
3. Create the following paragraph of multiline text within an area that is 3″ wide and 3″ tall:

```
The in-place text editor window is where you enter text. As men-
tioned, it works similarly to most text editors and word processor
software you might be familiar with. As you type and the text reaches
the end of the text editor window, AutoCAD automatically enters what
is commonly referred to as a "soft" return to break the line.
```

4. Save the drawing as **EX11-2**.

*The Ruler.*   The ruler indicates the width of the text using the current units setting. The double horizontal arrow at the right end of the toolbar can be used to adjust the width of the multiline text boundary box by clicking and dragging with your mouse.

The arrow on the top left side of the ruler can be used to set the indent for the first line of a paragraph by clicking on it and dragging it to the desired position with your mouse as shown in Figure 11-16.

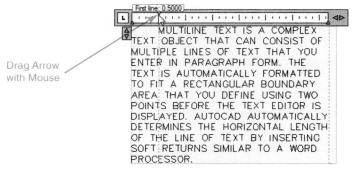

**Figure 11-16**   Setting the first line paragraph indent distance.

The arrow on the bottom left side of the ruler can be used to set the indent for the whole paragraph by clicking on it and dragging it to the desired position with your mouse as shown in Figure 11-17.

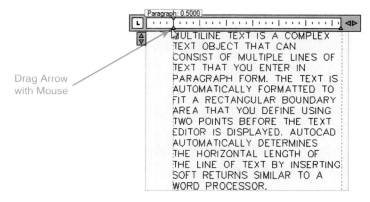

**Figure 11-17**   Setting the entire paragraph indent distance

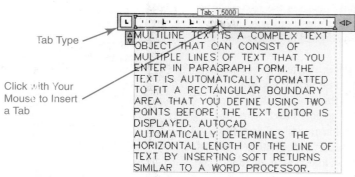

Tab Type

Click with Your
Mouse to Insert
a Tab

Figure 11-18    Setting tab stops

You can create one or more tab stops by clicking with your mouse in the ruler where you want to locate the tab stop as shown in Figure 11-18.

The button on the far left sets the tab type. Clicking on it goes through the left, center, right, and decimal tab types.

Once a tab stop is created, you can move it by placing your cursor over the top of it and dragging it when the cursor changes to a double horizontal arrow. To remove a tab stop, simply click on it with your cursor and drag it off the toolbar.

> **Note:**
> You can turn the ruler off using the **Multiline Text** ribbon explained in the next section. The ruler stays off the next time you use the multiline text editor.

### Exercise 11-3: Using Tabs

1. Continue from Exercise 11-2.
2. Set the NOTES text style current.
3. Create the following table of multiline text within an area that is 4″ wide and 4″ tall with tab stops at every 1″:

| 1 | 2 | 3 | 4 |
|---|---|---|---|
| 5 | 6 | 7 | 8 |
| 9 | 10 | 11 | 12 |

4. Save the drawing as **EX11-3**.

## The Multiline Text Ribbon

The **Multiline Text** ribbon is used to control all aspects of the text's appearance ranging from the text style and font to the text height and justification. The various settings can be applied to new text or existing text that has already been selected (highlighted). **Multiline Text** ribbon panels are explained in the following sections.

**TIP**

Remember that it is common to control most of the different format settings using text styles as explained earlier in this chapter because it provides central control over the text appearance, making text formatting easier to update. Applying different format options to text directly in the multiline text editor is considered a text style override. Using overrides is typically avoided if possible.

*The Style Panel.*    The **Style** list specifies the text style to use for new text or changes the text style of any selected text. Text styles and their usage were discussed in detail at the beginning of this chapter.

The **Annotative** button toggles the text **Annotative** property on and off for automatic text height scaling.

The **Text Height** list box sets the character height for new text or changes the height of selected text. A multi-line text object can contain characters of various heights. If the height you wish to use is not listed, you must click in the **Text Height** box and type it. It then becomes part of the list so you can select it from the list box the next time.

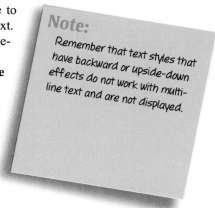

**Note:**
Remember that text styles that have backward or upside-down effects do not work with multiline text and are not displayed.

**TIP**    If the current text style height is set to 0.0, you can change the default multiline text height displayed in the **Text Height** list box by setting the **TEXTSIZE** system variable. The default text height is 0.20.

*The Formatting Panel.*    The **Bold** button turns bold formatting on and off for new or selected text. This option is available only for characters using TrueType fonts.

The **Italic** button turns italic formatting on and off for new or selected text. This option is available only for characters using TrueType fonts.

The **Underline** button turns underlining on and off for new or selected text.

The **Overline** button places a line over selected text.

The **Font** list specifies the font to use for new text or changes the font of any selected text. Both TrueType and the AutoCAD SHX fonts are listed. It is possible to mix different fonts within the same paragraph of multiline text.

The **Color** button specifies a color for new text or changes the color of selected text. You can also select one of the colors in the color list or select the **Select Colors** option to display the **Select Color** dialog box.

The **Oblique Angle** box controls the oblique angle, or slant, of new or selected text. The angle entered is measured from 90° vertical so that a positive angle slants text forward and a negative angle slants text backward. It is possible to enter a value between −85° and 85°. You can either type a value in the box or select the up and down arrows on the right to increase or decrease the value by 1. See Figure 11-10 for examples of text that has been obliqued.

The **Tracking** box decreases or increases the space between characters for new or selected text. You can either type a value in the box or select the up and down arrows on the right to increase or decrease the value by 0.1.

The **Width Factor** box controls the text character width. The default width is 1.0. Specifying a value greater than 1.0 expands the text so that it is wider. Specifying a value less than 1.0 condenses the text. You can either type a value in the box or select the up and down arrows on the right to increase or decrease the value by 0.1. See Figure 11-9 for examples of **Width Factor** settings.

*The Paragraph Panel.*    The **Justification** button displays a menu with the same two-letter multiline text justification options shown earlier in Figure 11-14 (**Top Left TL**, **Middle Left ML**, etc.) when using the **Justify** option when you first start the **MTEXT** command. The **Justification** menu allows you to change the text justification within the multiline text editor.

The **Line Spacing** button displays a menu that allows you to set the text line spacing for the multiline text object. Line spacing for multiline text is the distance between the bottom of one line of text and the bottom of the next line of text where single spacing is 1.66 times the text height. You can set the spacing increment to a multiple of single-line spacing using the following predefined scale factors:

- **1.0x**    Single-line spacing
- **1.5x**    One-and-a-half-line spacing
- **2.0x**    Double-line spacing
- **2.5x**    Two-and-a-half-line spacing

Selecting **More...** from the **Line Spacing** menu displays the **Paragraph** dialog box so you can make additional adjustments. The **Paragraph** dialog box explained in detail later in this section.

The **Numbering** button displays the menu shown in Figure 11-19 with the three different list formats (**Lettered, Numbered,** and **Bulleted**) along with various options:

- **Off**    Removes letters, numbers, and bullets from the selected text without changing the indentation.
- **Numbered**    Creates a numbered list using numbers with periods for each list item.
- **Lettered** cascade menu    Allows you to switch between uppercase and lowercase letters with periods for each list item. Double letters are used if the list has more items than the alphabet.
- **Bulleted**    Creates a bulleted list using round filled circles for each list item.
- **Start**    Starts a new numbering or lettering sequence.
- **Continue**    Adds selected text to the list above and continues the numbering or lettering sequence.
- Allow **Auto-list**    Toggles the **Auto-list** feature on and off. **Auto-list** creates a list when you enter a letter or number followed by a period "." or closing parenthesis ")", press the spacebar or **<Tab>** key, and enter at least one character of text followed by **<Enter ↵>**.
- **Use Tab Delimiter Only**    Will only use the **<Tab>** key for automatic list creation.
- **Allow Bullets and Lists**    Disables the **Numbering** button on the **Options** toolbar. **Bullets and Lists** are still enabled on the **Options** menu discussed later.

**Figure 11-19**    The Bullets and Lists menu

The **Paragraph** button displays the **Paragraph** dialog box shown in Figure 11-20 so that you can do the following:

- Add and remove tab stops
- Set left and right indents

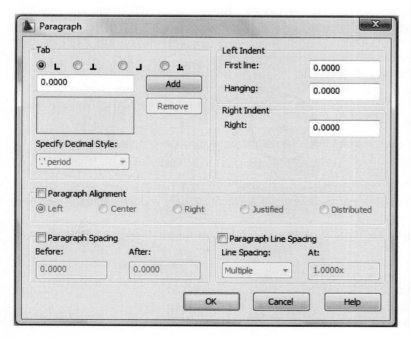

**Figure 11-20**    The paragraph dialog box

- Set the horizontal paragraph justification
- Set the spacing between paragraphs
- Set the line spacing for the paragraph

The **Tab** area allows you to add and remove left, center, right, and decimal tab stops. To add a tab, enter the tab distance and select the **Add** button. To delete a tab, select it from the list and select the **Remove** button.

The **Left Indent** area allows you to set the first line and hanging indent distance.

The **Right Indent** area allows you to set the right side indent distance.

The **Paragraph Alignment** area allows you to control the horizontal paragraph justification, text flow, and spacing using one of the following methods:

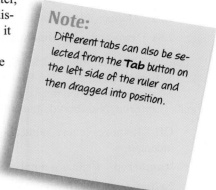

Note:
Different tabs can also be selected from the **Tab** button on the left side of the ruler and then dragged into position.

- The **Left** option aligns text on the left-hand margin so text flows right.
- The **Center** option centers text on the centerline of the text boundary and flows both directions.
- The **Right** option aligns text on the right-hand margin so text flows left.
- The **Justified** option spreads text out to fill the text boundary width by putting space between words.
- The **Distributed** option spreads text out to fill the text boundary width by putting space between letters.

The **Paragraph Spacing** area controls the spacing between paragraphs. Selecting the **Paragraph Spacing** check box enables the **Before:** and **After:** text boxes so that it is possible to set different spacing before and after a paragraph.

The **Paragraph Line Spacing** area sets the spacing between individual lines in the current or selected paragraphs using the **Exactly, At least,** and **Multiple** options. **Multiple** is the default.

The **Paragraph Line Spacing** controls the multiline line spacing. Line spacing for multiline text is the distance between the bottom of one line of text and the bottom of the next line. The default for single line spacing is 1.66 times the height of the text. The default spacing is **Multiple,** which is basically a multiplier that is applied to the preceding formula. The default setting is 1X, or one time. For double-line spacing, you would set **Multiple** to 2X and so on. The **Exactly** option maintains a consistent spacing using the absolute distance you specify. Using the **Exactly** option, it is possible to overlap rows. The **At least** line spacing option automatically increases line spacing to accommodate characters that are too large to fit.

Select **OK** in the **Paragraph** dialog box to exit and save your changes.

The five buttons to the right of the **Paragraph** button on the **Paragraph** panel control the horizontal justification and text spacing using the same **Paragraph Alignment** options provided in the **Paragraph** dialog box:

- The **Left** button aligns text on the left-hand margin so text flows right.
- The **Center** button centers text on the centerline of the text boundary and flows both directions.
- The **Right** button aligns text on the right-hand margin so text flows left.
- The **Justified** button spreads text out to fill the text boundary width by putting space between words.
- The **Distributed** button spreads text out to fill the text boundary width by putting space between letters.

**Exercise 11-4:** Formatting Multiline Text

1. Continue from Exercise 11-3.
2. Start the **MTEXT** command.

3. Define a text boundary area 3″ wide by 2″ tall.
4. Using the **Multiline Text** ribbon, do the following:
   a. Set the style to TITLES.
   b. Set the text height to 0.125″.
   c. Turn on the **Italic** option.
   d. Set the **Justification** to **Middle Center.**
5. Type the following paragraph:

```
The in-place text editor window is where you enter text. As men-
tioned, it works similarly to most text editors and word processor
software you might be familiar with. As you type and the text reaches
the end of the text editor window, AutoCAD automatically enters what
is commonly referred to as a "soft" return to break the line.
```

6. Save the drawing as **EX11-4.**

*The Insert Panel.*     The **Symbol** button displays a menu that allows you to insert a symbol or a nonbreaking space at the current cursor position. Some of the more commonly used symbols are listed on the menu with either their AutoCAD %% control code or Unicode string as shown in Figure 11-21.

Selecting the **Other...** menu item at the bottom of the menu displays the **Character Map** dialog box shown in Figure 11-22 so you can insert symbols that are not included on the menu. This dialog contains the entire character set for every available font. To insert a symbol from the **Character Map** dialog box, you must first select a symbol and then click the **Select** button to place it in the **Characters to copy** box. To insert the symbol, you must select the **Copy** button to copy the symbol to the Windows clipboard. You can then switch back to the multiline editor in AutoCAD and paste the selected symbol in the desired location.

**Note:**
The **Character Map** dialog box is actually a separate program that shows up on the Windows taskbar when you display it. It must be closed and exited manually. If you do not close the dialog box, you might find yourself running multiple copies of the program if you repeatedly display it.

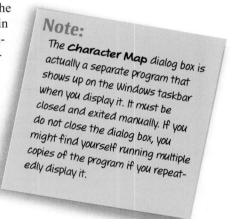

| Degrees | %%d |
| Plus/Minus | %%p |
| Diameter | %%c |
| Almost Equal | \U+2248 |
| Angle | \U+2220 |
| Boundary Line | \U+E100 |
| Center Line | \U+2104 |
| Delta | \U+0394 |
| Electrical Phase | \U+0278 |
| Flow Line | \U+E101 |
| Identity | \U+2261 |
| Initial Length | \U+E200 |
| Monument Line | \U+E102 |
| Not Equal | \U+2260 |
| Ohm | \U+2126 |
| Omega | \U+03A9 |
| Property Line | \U+214A |
| Subscript 2 | \U+2082 |
| Squared | \U+00B2 |
| Cubed | \U+00B3 |
| Non-breaking Space | Ctrl+Shift+Space |
| Other... | |

**Figure 11-21**    The Symbols menu

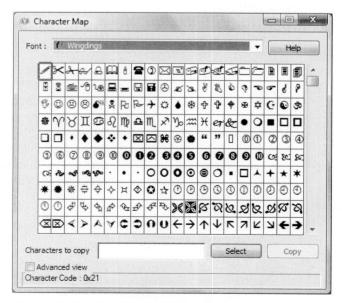

**Figure 11-22**    The Character Map dialog box

**Figure 11-23**    Columns menu

The **Insert Field** button allows you to insert a field using the **Field** dialog box. Fields and the **Field** dialog box are explained in detail later in this chapter.

The **Columns** button displays the menu shown in Figure 11-23 that allows you to format multiline text into multiple columns. You can use either a static approach in which you specify the number of columns explicitly or a dynamic approach that creates new columns automatically as you type. Both methods allow you to specify the width and height of each column, as well as the gutter width. Special grips allow you to edit the column width and height quickly after the text is added to the drawing.

To use dynamic columns, you must select either **Auto height** or **Manual height** from the **Dynamic Columns** cascade menu. Both approaches use the current width of the multiline text boundary box that you defined for the initial column width. The difference is that the **Auto height** method uses the current height of the boundary box as the column height so that when text gets to the bottom of the boundary area it automatically jumps to the next column and starts at the top. When you select **Manual height**, the text boundary box height collapses to a single row with a double arrow size control at the bottom that you must click and drag to set the column height.

TIP     It is possible to ignore the column height and simply start entering text. The text will flow down in the same column using the current column width. You can then press <**Alt**> + <**Enter ↵**> to jump to another column, and it will be created using the same width and height as the first column.

To use static columns, you must select the number of desired columns (2–6) from the **Static Columns** cascade menu. The column width is determined by the number of columns and the gutter width that can be fit within the defined text boundary area.

If you need to specify more than six columns, select the **More...** menu item on the **Static Columns** cascade menu to display the **Column Settings** dialog box shown in Figure 11-24.

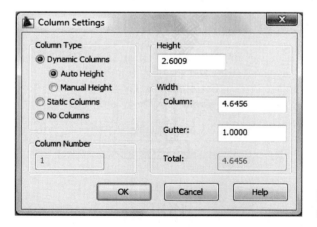

**Figure 11-24**    The Columns Setting dialog box

As you can see, the **Column Settings** dialog box controls all the other main column settings such as the number of columns, column width, height, and gutter width. This is also where you can turn existing columns off by selecting **No Columns** in the **Column Type** area on the top left. The easiest way to display the **Column Settings** dialog box is to select **Column Settings** from the main **Column** menu.

**Exercise 11-5:** Creating Lists and Inserting Symbols

1. Continue from Exercise 11-4.
2. Set the NOTES text style current.
3. Create the following bulleted list of multiline text within an area that is 4″ wide and 4″ tall:
   - This is a degree symbol °
   - This is a plus/minus symbol ±
   - This is a diameter symbol Ø

- This is a boundary line symbol ℞
- This is a centerline symbol ℭ
- This is a delta symbol Δ
- This is a property line symbol ℞

4. Change the bulleted list to a lettered list.
5. Change the lettered list to a numbered list.
6. Save the drawing as **EX11-5.**

*The Options Panel.*    The **Find & Replace** tool displays the **Find and Replace** dialog box shown in Figure 11-25 so you can search for a specific string of text and replace it with a new string of text.

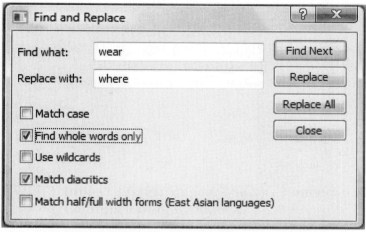

**Figure 11-25**    Find and Replace dialog box

- The **Find what:** text box is where you enter the text you want to search for.
- The **Replace with:** text box is where you enter the replacement text for the text entered in the **Find what:** text box.
- Selecting the **Match case** check box allows you to search for text that matches the uppercase and/or lowercase of the text entered in the **Find what:** text box exactly.
- Selecting the **Find whole words only** check box allows you to search only for text as a complete word with a space before and after; otherwise, the search will also find text that is part of a word.
- The **Use wildcards** check box allows the use of wild-card characters in searches. For more information on wild-card searches, see the "Finding and Replacing Text" section later in this chapter.
- The **Match diacritics** check box allows you to match diacritical marks, or accents, in search results.
- The **Match half/full width forms (East Asian languages)** check box matches half- and full-width Asian characters in search results.

The **Spell Check** button turns on and off the **Check Spelling As You Type** feature that allows you to check spelling as you enter text in the multiline text editor. Any word you enter is checked for spelling errors when it is completed so that any misspelled word is underlined in red. Spelling suggestions display when you right-click the underlined word.

The **Undo** tool undoes actions in the multiline text editor, including changes to either text content or text formatting.

The **Redo** tool redoes actions in the multiline text editor, including changes to either text content or text formatting.

The **Ruler** tool toggles the ruler on and off. Once the ruler is turned off, it remains off the next time you display the in-place multiline text editor. See the previous section for detailed information about the ruler feature.

The **Options** tool displays a menu with additional multiline text options and features, as well as access to some of the same features found on the formatting toolbar discussed in the following sections. The options and features located on the **Options** menu are explained later in the next section, "The Options and the Right-Click Menus."

After all the search criteria are entered you can choose one of three options:

* Select the **Find Next** button to search for and highlight the next occurrence of the search text.

* Select the **Replace** button to replace the highlighted text in the multiline text editor to update the text with the text entered in the **Replace with:** text box.

* Select the **Replace All** button to search and replace all the text in the multiline text editor that matches the search criteria with the text entered in the **Replace with:** text box. A message box is displayed indicating how many occurrences were replaced so that you know if, and how many, text strings were replaced.

***The Options and the Right-Click Menus.***        The **Options** menu and the right-click shortcut menu shown in Figure 11-26 provide additional multiline text options and features, as well as access to some of the same features found on the **Multiline Text** ribbon explained in the previous section.

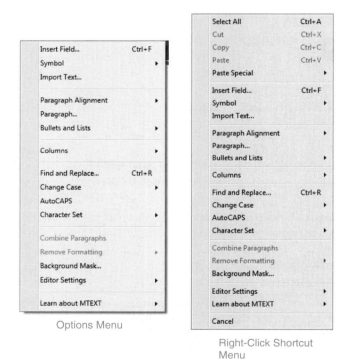

Figure 11-26        The Options and the right-click shortcut menus

The **Options** menu can be displayed by selecting the **Options** tool on the **Options** panel on the **Multiline Text** tab shown in Figure 11-15. The right-click shortcut menu can be displayed by right-clicking with your mouse anywhere in the multiline text editor window. The menus share most of the same tools and features except that the right-click shortcut menu provides a few text editing specific commands:

* **Select All**        Selects all the text in the text editor
* **Cut**        Deletes text and places it on the Windows clipboard so you can paste it later
* **Copy**        Copies text to the Windows clipboard so you can paste it later
* **Paste**        Inserts text that is currently on the Windows clipboard

- **Paste Special**   Displays a cascade menu that allows you to perform the following special paste operations:
  - **Paste without Character Formatting**   Pastes and ignores any character-based formatting such as font, text height, etc. while maintaining any paragraph-based formatting such as justification, line spacing, etc.
  - **Paste without Paragraph Formatting**   Pastes and ignores any paragraph-based formatting such as justification, line spacing, etc. while maintaining any character-based formatting such as font, text height, etc.
  - **Paste without Any Formatting**   Ignores all original formatting and uses the current formatting.

The **Insert Field** menu item allows you to insert a field using the **Field** dialog box. Fields and the **Field** dialog box are explained in detail later in this chapter.

The **Symbol** menu item displays a cascade menu that allows you to insert a symbol or a non-breaking space at the current cursor position. The **Symbol** cascade menu is the same as the **Symbol** menu displayed when you select the **Symbol** button on the **Insert** panel on the **Multiline Text** tab. See the preceding section "The Insert Panel" for complete information about using the **Symbol** menu.

The **Import Text...** menu item allows you to import an ASCII (American Standard Code for Information Interchange) text file or an RTF (Rich Text Format) text file into the multiline text editor. Selecting the **Import Text...** button displays the **Select File** dialog box shown in Figure 11-27 so you can navigate your computer or network and find the text file to import.

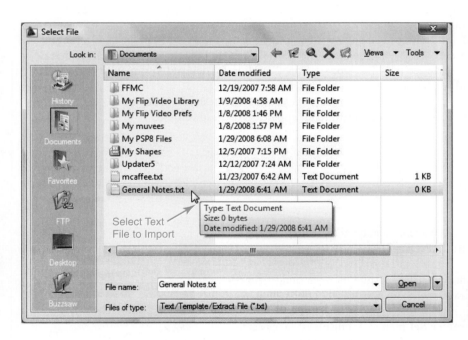

Figure 11-27   Importing a text file into the multiline text editor

Once you locate the file, select it so it is highlighted and select the **Open** button to import the text. You can then edit the text if necessary using the standard methods explained in this chapter.

The **Paragraph Alignment** menu item displays a cascade menu with the same horizontal paragraph justification, text flow, and spacing options found in the **Paragraph Alignment**

TIP   You can store text that is used in multiple drawings in an external text file so that you don't have to type the text in every drawing. For instance, you might store general notes in a file named General Notes.txt. If you locate the file on a network, all team members can then import the same text file. This approach both provides consistency and increases production.

area in the **Paragraph** dialog box shown earlier in Figure 11-20 in the "The Paragraph Panel" section:

- The **Left** option aligns text on the left-hand margin so text flows right.
- The **Center** option centers text on the centerline of the text boundary and flows both directions.
- The **Right** option aligns text on the right-hand margin so text flows left.
- The **Justified** option spreads text out to fill the text boundary width by putting space between words.
- The **Distributed** option spreads text out to fill the text boundary width by putting space between letters.

The **Paragraph...** menu item displays the same **Paragraph** dialog box shown earlier in Figure 11-20 in the "The Paragraph Panel" section so that you can control tabs, indents, paragraph alignment, and other paragraph features and settings. Please see the "The Paragraph Panel" section for detailed information regarding the **Paragraph** dialog box.

The **Bullets and Lists** menu item displays the same **Bullets and Lists** cascade menu shown earlier in Figure 11-20 in the "The Paragraph Panel" section so that you can create lettered, numbered, or bulleted lists. Please see the "The Paragraph Panel" section for detailed information regarding the **Bullets and Lists** menu.

The **Columns** menu item displays the same **Columns** cascade menu shown earlier in Figure 11-23 in the "The Insert Panel" section so that you can create dynamic and static columns. Please see the "The Insert Panel" section for detailed information regarding the **Columns** menu.

The **Find and Replace...** menu item displays the same **Find and Replace** dialog box shown earlier in Figure 11-25 so you can search for a specific string of text and replace it with a new string of text. Please see the "The Options Panel" section for detailed information regarding the **Find and Replace** dialog box.

The **Change Case** menu item displays the cascade menu shown in Figure 11-28. This menu can be used to change the selected text to all uppercase or all lowercase.

| UPPERCASE | Ctrl+Shift+U |
| lowercase | Ctrl+Shift+L |

**Figure 11-28**    Change Case cascade menu

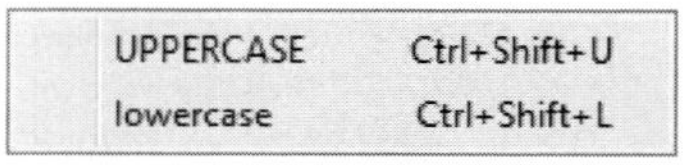

**Figure 11-29**    Character Set cascade menu

| Central Europe |
| Cyrillic |
| Hebrew |
| Arabic |
| Baltic |
| Greek |
| Turkish |
| Vietnamese |
| Japanese |
| Korean |
| CHINESE_GB2312 |
| CHINESE_BIG5 |
| ✓ Western |
| Thai |

**character set:** The set of numeric codes used by a computer system to represent the characters (letters, numbers, punctuation, etc.) of a particular country or place

The **AutoCAPS** menu item turns the **AutoCAPS** feature on and off. **AutoCAPS** can be used to lock your keyboard so only uppercase letters can be entered similar to the <Caps Lock> key. This is a handy feature in the drafting field because most drawing notes are uppercase according to industry standards.

The **Character Set** menu item displays the cascade menu shown in Figure 11-29. The **Character Set** menu item can be used to change the *character set* used so that text in other languages appears properly.

The **Combine Paragraphs** menu item will combine multiple paragraphs of selected text together, removing any line feeds so that the selected text becomes one paragraph. The original text properties are retained.

The **Remove Formatting** menu item displays a cascade menu that provides different options for removing the formatting overrides for selected text so that those overrides revert back to the text's assigned text style:

- **Remove Character Formatting**    Removes any character-based formatting such as font, text height, etc. while maintaining any paragraph-based formatting such as justification, line spacing, etc.

*Note:* The **AutoCAPS** feature overrides the **Caps Lock** key so that it cannot be used to toggle uppercase on and off. You must turn **AutoCAPS** off in order to type lowercase.

- **Remove Paragraph Formatting**   Removes any paragraph-based formatting such as justification, line spacing, etc. while maintaining any character-based formatting such as font, text height, etc.

- **Remove All Formatting**   Removes all formatting

The **Background Mask...** menu item displays the **Background Mask** dialog box shown in Figure 11-30. This dialog box allows you to make the background of the finished multiline text boundary box opaque, as well as set its color. The **Use background mask** check box turns the background on and off. The **Border offset factor:** setting allows you to extend the background area beyond the original multiline text boundary area.

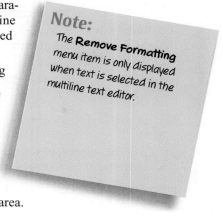

Note:
The **Remove Formatting** menu item is only displayed when text is selected in the multiline text editor.

Figure 11-30    Background Mask dialog box

You can either apply a fill color to the background area via the color list in the **Fill Color** area at the bottom of the dialog box, or you can elect to use the drawing background color by selecting the **Use drawing background color** check box. Using the drawing background color allows you to block out linework underneath the multiline text boundary box so you can't see it.

The **Editor Settings** menu item displays a cascade menu that allows you to control the following multiline text editor display features:

- **Always Display as WYS/WYG**
- **Show Toolbar**   Turns the **Text Formatting** toolbar on and off
- **Show Options**   Turns the bottom portion of the **Text Formatting** toolbar on and off
- **Show Ruler**   Turns the **Ruler** on and off
- **Opaque Background**   Allows you to make the background of the editor opaque. By default, the editor is transparent
- **Check Spelling**   Turns the **Check Spelling As You Type** feature on and off. This option is on by default
- **Check Spelling Settings...**   Displays the **Check Spelling Settings** dialog box so you can specify text options that will be checked for spelling errors within your drawing
- **Dictionaries...**   Displays the **Dictionaries** dialog box so you can control the dictionary that is checked against any found misspelled words
- **Text Highlight Color...**   Allows you to change the color used to highlight text

The **Learn about MTEXT** menu item displays a cascade menu that allows you to get help and information about using multiline text:

- **New Features Workshop**   The **New Features Workshop** introduces you to what's new in AutoCAD using a series of slides and/or animations.
- **Help**   Displays the multiline text help topic.

Exercise 11-6: Using the Options and Right-Click Menus

1. Continue from Exercise 11-5.
2. Using Windows Notepad, create a text file that contains the following text:

   This is text that is in an external file named Notes.txt that I am going to import into the multiline text editor and reformat.

> **TIP** The Notepad program can typically be started by selecting the Windows **Start** button and navigating to the Accessories folder.

3. Save the file as Notes.txt in a location where you can find it and exit out of the Notepad program.
4. Switch back to AutoCAD and start the **MTEXT** command.
5. Define a text boundary area 2″ wide by 2″ tall.
6. Using the **Options** or right-click menu, do the following:
   a. Import the Notes.txt text file.
   b. Set the background mask to red.
   c. Set the paragraph alignment to Center.
   d. Find all occurrences of the word "text" and replace it with "test."
   e. Make all the text uppercase.
7. Save the drawing as **EX11-6.**

## Creating Stacked Text

As mentioned earlier, it is possible to format text representing a fraction or tolerance so that the left character is placed on top of the right character as a horizontal fraction, diagonal fraction, or tolerance based on the following special stack characters:

- ^    Caret converts to left-justified tolerance values.
- /    Forward slash converts to a center-justified fraction with a horizontal bar.
- \    Backward slash converts to a center-justified fraction with a horizontal bar.
- #    Pound sign converts to a fraction with a diagonal bar the height of the two text strings.

This can be done manually using the **Stack** menu item located on the **Options** and **right-click** shortcut menus, or even better, it can be automated using the **AutoStack** feature in the multiline text editor so that the desired fraction type is created automatically as you type. The **AutoStack** feature and properties are explained in the following section.

*AutoStack Properties Dialog Box.*    The first time you type in a fraction or tolerance using the special characters listed in the previous section, AutoCAD displays the **AutoStack Properties** dialog box shown in Figure 11-31. This dialog box allows you to define specific text stacking properties that can be applied automatically as you type when a number is entered followed by any of the special stacking characters.

The **Enable AutoStacking** check box allows you to turn **AutoStacking** on and off. If checked, text is automatically stacked when a number is typed in followed by any of the special characters.

The **Remove leading blank:** check box allows you to remove automatically any space between the whole number and the fraction if it is checked.

You can control whether a forward slash converts to a horizontal or diagonal fraction via the **Specify how "x/y" should stack:** radio buttons. If the **Convert it to a diagonal fraction** button is selected, diagonal fractions are created. If the **Convert it to a horizontal fraction** button is selected, horizontal fractions are created.

Selecting the **Don't show this dialog again; always use these settings** check box makes the AutoStack settings permanent so the **AutoStack Properties** dialog box is not displayed the next time you type a number followed by one of the special characters. The AutoStack properties are automatically applied as you type.

If you select the **Don't show this dialog again; always use these settings** check box, the only way to display the **AutoStack Properties** dialog box again is select an existing fraction in the multiline text editor, right-click with your mouse, and select **Stack Properties** from the shortcut menu to display the **Stack Properties** dialog box. You can then select the **AutoStack...** button from the **Stack Properties** dialog box, explained in the next section.

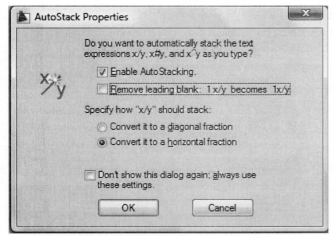

**Figure 11-31**    AutoStack Properties dialog box

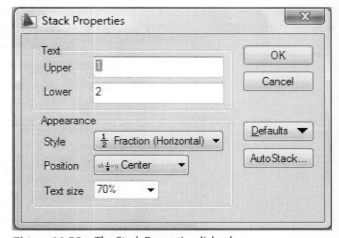

**Figure 11-32**    The Stack Properties dialog box

*Stack Properties Dialog Box.*    The **Stack Properties** dialog box shown in Figure 11-32 allows you to edit the text content, stack type, alignment, and size of stacked text. To display the dialog box, you must first select existing stacked text, right-click with your mouse, and select **Stack Properties** from the shortcut menu. The following options are available:

- The **Upper** and **Lower** text boxes in the **Text** section allow you to change the upper and lower numbers of a stacked fraction.

- The **Appearance** section allows you to edit the style, position, or text size of a stacked fraction.

- The **Style** list allows you to switch between the horizontal fraction, diagonal fraction, and tolerance stacking styles.

- The **Position** list allows you to switch between the following text alignments:
  - **Top**    Aligns the top of the fraction with the top of the previous text
  - **Center**    Centers the fraction vertically at the center of the previous text
  - **Bottom**    Aligns the bottom of the fraction with the previous text

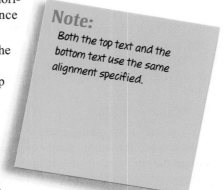

*Note:*

*Both the top text and the bottom text use the same alignment specified.*

- The **Text size** list controls the size of the stacked text as a percentage relative to the size of the whole number text height. Valid values are between 25% and 125%. The default text size is 70%.

- The **Defaults** button allows you to either restore the default stacked text properties or save the current stacked text properties as the new default.
- The **AutoStack...** button displays the **AutoStack Properties** dialog box so you can either modify or turn off **AutoStack** properties.

**Exercise 11-7:** Creating Stacked Text
_____

1. Continue from Exercise 11-6.
2. Start the **MTEXT** command.
3. Define a text boundary area 3″ wide by 3″ tall.
4. Enter the following line of text in the multiline text editor and press **<Enter ↵>**:

    THIS IS A HORIZONTAL STACKED FRACTION 1/2

5. The **AutoStack Properties** dialog box shown in Figure 11-31 is displayed.
6. Enable Autostacking so that "x/y" changes to a horizontal fraction.
7. Select the **Don't show this dialog again** check box.
8. Select **OK** to exit the **AutoStack Properties** dialog box.
9. Enter the following line of text in the multiline text editor and press **<Enter ↵>**:

    THIS IS A DIAGONAL STACKED FRACTION 1#2

10. Enter the following line of text in the multiline text editor and press **<Enter ↵>**:

    THIS IS A TOLERANCE VALUE 001^002

11. Save the drawing as **EX11-7.**

## CREATING SINGLE-LINE TEXT

In addition to multiline text, you can also create what is referred to as *single-line text* to create one or more lines of text. Single-line text is the original text type in AutoCAD that preceded the more complex and feature-rich multiline text explored in the last section. With single-line text, each line of text is an independent object that can be modified. Multiple lines of single-line text *can be* entered at the same time in paragraph form with consistent vertical spacing between each line—it's just that you must break each line at the end using the **<Enter ↵>** key. See Figure 11-33.

Each Line of Text is a
Separate Object

Press <Enter ↵> to
End Line

MULTIPLE LINES OF SINGLE LINE TEXT
CAN BE ENTERED BY PRESSING THE
<ENTER> KEY AT THE END OF EACH
LINE.

**Figure 11-33**        Single-line text

| Single-Line Text | |
|---|---|
| **Ribon & Panel:** | Home\| Annotation |
| **Text Toolbar:** | |
| **Menu:** | Draw\|Text\| Single Line Text |
| **Command Line:** | TEXT or TEXT |
| **Command Alias:** | DT |

The **TEXT** command or the **DTEXT** command can be used to create single-line text.

When you start either command, AutoCAD displays the current text style and height at the command line as follows:

    Current text style: "Standard" Text
    height: 0.2000

The text styles used for single-line text are the same as those used for multiline text, explained earlier. You can change the styles via the **Style** option explained below, although using the **Text Style** list box on the **Text** panel on the **Annotate** ribbon shown in Figure 11-4 is much easier as you will see. The text height can also be changed after you select the starting point for the text.

**Note:**
Remember from the beginning of the chapter that if you set the current text style height to anything other than 0.00″ you will not be prompted for a text height when creating single-line text.

After starting either command, AutoCAD prompts you to *Specify start point of text or* ↓. Select a starting point for the text by either picking a point in your drawing or by entering a coordinate location via the keyboard.

After locating the text start point, AutoCAD prompts you to *Specify height <0.2000>:*. Enter the desired text height and press **<Enter ↵>**. The height entered becomes the default the next time you create single-line text.

After entering the height, AutoCAD prompts you to *Specify rotation angle of text <0>:*. Enter the desired text angle or press **<Enter ↵>** to use the default.

**Note:**
By default, single-line text is left justified. This means that text that you type will flow to the right of the text start point. You can change the default justification using the **Justification** option explained in one of the next sections.

You can also use your cursor to input the angle by selecting a point in response to the *Specify rotation angle of text <0>:* prompt. The text start point is used as the base point of the angle with the second point defining the angle. You can even utilize object snaps to align the text by snapping to points on existing objects.

After you enter the desired text angle, AutoCAD displays the no frills in-place single-line text editor, which is basically a dynamically sized box that grows longer as you type as shown in Figure 11-34.

Edit Box Grows Longer as You Type

THE NO FRILLS SINGLE LINE TEXT EDITOR ]

**Figure 11-34**    Entering single-line text

As mentioned, it is possible to create multiple lines of text using single-line text; however, you must input the line breaks manually by pressing **<Enter ↵>** at the end of the line. Pressing **<Enter ↵>** places the cursor on the next line in the in-place single-line text editor so you can continue typing as shown in Figure 11-35.

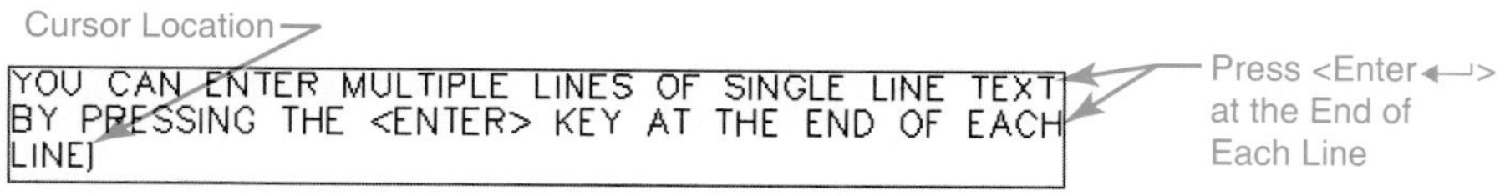

Cursor Location

YOU CAN ENTER MULTIPLE LINES OF SINGLE LINE TEXT
BY PRESSING THE <ENTER> KEY AT THE END OF EACH
LINE]

Press <Enter ↵> at the End of Each Line

**Figure 11-35**    Entering multiple lines of single-line text

You can continue to add lines of text until you press the **<Enter ↵>** key twice—meaning that you press **<Enter ↵>** without entering any text on the current line. You can also pick a point outside the edit box with your mouse to end the command. Remember that each line of text is still a separate object even though it was all entered at the same time as shown in Figure 11-36.

**Note:**
The line spacing used for single-line text is 1.5 times the text height from the bottom of one line of text to the bottom of the next line.

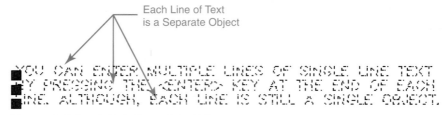

Each Line of Text
is a Separate Object

YOU CAN ENTER MULTIPLE LINES OF SINGLE LINE TEXT
BY PRESSING THE <ENTER> KEY AT THE END OF EACH
LINE. ALTHOUGH, EACH LINE IS STILL A SINGLE OBJECT.

**Figure 11-36**   Multiple lines of single-line text

> **TIP**   If **TEXT** or **DTEXT** was the last command entered, when you create additional new single-line text you can simply press <**Enter ↵**> at the *Specify start point of text or ↓* prompt and skip the prompts for a text height and rotation angle. AutoCAD automatically displays the in-place single-line text editor directly below the last line of text created in the drawing using the same height, rotation angle, and justification so you can just start typing!

## The Right-Click Menu

The single-line text editor also has the right-click menu shown in Figure 11-37, which provides additional functionality. The menu shares some of the same tools and features found on the right-click menu in the multiline text editor explained earlier:

- **Undo/Redo**   Allows you to undo/redo one or more actions in the text editor
- **Cut**   Deletes text and places it on the Windows clipboard so you can paste it later
- **Copy**   Copies text to the Windows clipboard so you can paste it later
- **Paste**   Inserts text that is currently on the Windows clipboard
- **Editor Settings**   Cascade menu with the same editor options found in **Multiline Text** editor
- **Insert Field...**   Allows you to insert a field using the **Field** dialog box. Fields and the **Field** dialog box are explained in detail later in this chapter.
- **Find and Replace...**   Displays the **Find and Replace** dialog box so you can search for and replace text
- **Select All**   Selects all the text in the single-line text editor

| | |
|---|---|
| Undo | Ctrl+Z |
| Redo | Ctrl+Y |
| Cut | Ctrl+X |
| Copy | Ctrl+C |
| Paste | Ctrl+V |
| Editor Settings | ▶ |
| Insert Field... | Ctrl+F |
| Find and Replace... | Ctrl+R |
| Select All | Ctrl+A |
| Change Case | ▶ |
| Help | F1 |
| Cancel | |

**Figure 11-37**   Single-line text editor right-click menu

- **Change Case**    Cascade menu that allows you to change the case of text
  - **UPPERCASE**    Changes text to uppercase
  - **lowercase**    Changes text to lowercase

- **Help**    Displays the single-line text help topic
- **Cancel**    Exits the single-line text editor

## Single-Line Text Justification

Single-line text has a justification property similar to multiline text that determines how the text is aligned relative to the insertion point, although unlike multiline text, single-line justification only affects one line of text, not the complete paragraph. The different justification options are shown in Figure 11-38.

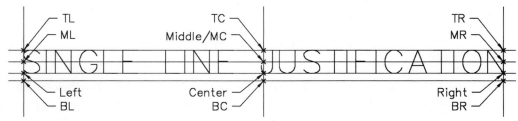

**Figure 11-38**    Single-line text justification options

The single-line text **Justification** option can be used to specify any of the justifications shown in Figure 11-37. To change the text justification, start the **TEXT** or **DTEXT** command and either type **J<Enter ↵>** or select the **Justification** option using your arrow keys if you are using Dynamic Input. AutoCAD prompts you to *Enter an option:*. After you select a justification, you specify a start point, height, and rotation angle using the methods explained earlier. The in-place single-line text editor is then displayed, and you can begin typing.

The text flow as you type is determined by the **Justification** option. Specifying **Right** justification makes text flow from the right to the left, whereas the **Center** justification option makes text spill out in both directions from the start point (see Figure 11-39).

Except for the first two options, **Align** and **Fit**, most of the justification options are fairly self-explanatory. The **Align** and **Fit** justification options both allow you to locate text using two points to define the width and angle of the text. Both options force the text to fit between the two points specified—although with different methods. The **Align** option changes the height of the text (shorter or taller) to make the text fit, and the **Fit** option changes the text's width scale factor (narrower or wider) to make the text fit.

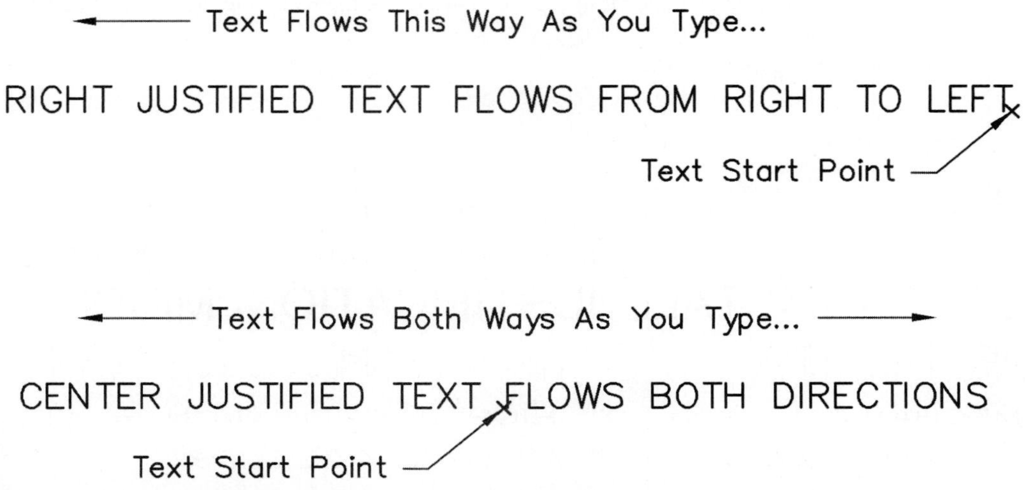

◄──────── Text Flows This Way As You Type...

RIGHT JUSTIFIED TEXT FLOWS FROM RIGHT TO LEFT×

Text Start Point ──╱

◄──────── Text Flows Both Ways As You Type... ──────►

CENTER JUSTIFIED TEXT FLOWS BOTH DIRECTIONS

Text Start Point ──╱

**Figure 11-39**    Using the Right and Center justification options

To use the **Align** option, start the **TEXT** or **DTEXT** command and select the **Justification** option using the methods explained above. AutoCAD prompts you to *Specify first endpoint of text baseline:*. Select the starting point for the text. AutoCAD then prompts you to *Specify second endpoint of text baseline:*. This point determines both the angle and final overall width of the text. Remember that the **Align** option changes the height of the text in order to make it fit between the two points. Because of this, the in-place single-line text editor box starts out tall and gets shorter as you type as shown in Figure 11-40.

**Figure 11-40**  Using the Align justification option

To use the **Fit** option, start the **TEXT** or **DTEXT** command and select the **Justification** option using the methods explained above. AutoCAD prompts you to *Specify first endpoint of text baseline:*. Select the starting point for the text. AutoCAD then prompts you to *Specify second endpoint of text baseline:*. This point determines both the angle and final overall width of the text. The **Fit** option changes the width scale factor of the text in order to make it fit between the two points. Because of this, AutoCAD prompts you to *Specify height <0.1000>:*. After you enter the desired height, the in-place single-line text editor box is displayed and you can begin typing. The text is either expanded or compressed to fit between the two points as you type but the height is maintained as shown in Figure 11-41.

**Figure 11-41**  Using the Fit justification option

**Exercise 11-8:** Creating Single-Line Text

1. Open drawing **EX11-1.**
2. Create the single-line text shown in Figure 11-42 using the text style, height, and justification indicated.
3. Save the drawing as **EX11-8.**

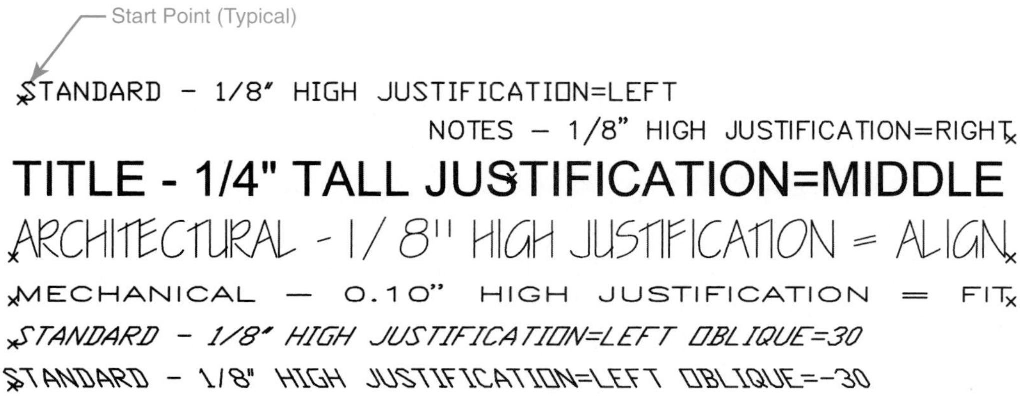

    Start Point (Typical)

STANDARD – 1/8″ HIGH JUSTIFICATION=LEFT

NOTES – 1/8″ HIGH JUSTIFICATION=RIGHT

# TITLE - 1/4" TALL JUSTIFICATION=MIDDLE

ARCHITECTURAL - 1/8″ HIGH JUSTIFICATION = ALIGN

MECHANICAL — 0.10″ HIGH JUSTIFICATION = FIT

STANDARD – 1/8′ HIGH JUSTIFICATION=LEFT OBLIQUE=30

STANDARD – 1/8″ HIGH JUSTIFICATION=LEFT OBLIQUE=-30

**Figure 11-42**  Creating single-line text

## INSERTING SPECIAL SYMBOLS IN SINGLE-LINE TEXT

You can insert a number of the same special symbols using the single-line text editor that you can insert using the multiline text editor, but your options are somewhat limited. There is no access to the **Character Map** dialog box, and the symbols you can use must be typed in using either their corresponding AutoCAD "%%" control code or their "\U+" Unicode string. The available Auto-CAD control codes are as follows:

- %%C    Draws circle diameter dimensioning symbol (Ø).
- %%D    Draws degrees symbol (°).
- %%P    Draws plus/minus tolerance symbol (±).
- %%O    Toggles overscoring on and off.
- %%U    Toggles underscoring on and off.
- %%%    Draws a single percent sign (%).

The control codes are immediately converted into their corresponding symbol as you type. For instance, entering **%%D** in the single-line text editor inserts the degree symbol shown in Figure 11-43.

TO CREATE A DEGREE SYMBOL ˚ — ENTER %%D
**Figure 11-43**    Using the %%D control code to insert a degree symbol

The underscore (%%U) and overscore (%%O) control codes are toggles that can be turned on and off as shown in Figure 11-44.

TO O̅V̅E̅R̅S̅C̅O̅R̅E̅ A WORD — ENTER %%O
TO U̲N̲D̲E̲R̲S̲C̲O̲R̲E̲ A WORD — ENTER %%U
**Figure 11-44**    Using the %%U and %%O control codes to underscore and overscore text

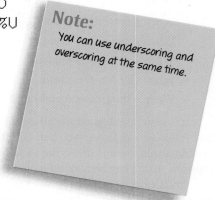
**Note:**
You can use underscoring and overscoring at the same time.

**TIP**    You can also insert the Euro symbol. If your keyboard does not have a Euro symbol key, you hold down the **<Alt>** key and enter **0128** via the numeric keypad.

Exercise 11-9: Inserting Symbols in Single-Line Text

1. Open drawing **EX11-1.**
2. Set the **STANDARD** text style current.
3. Create the single-line text shown in Figure 11-45 at 0.125″ high, 0° rotation angle, and justification set to Left.
4. Save the drawing as **EX11-9.**

THIS IS A DIAMETER SYMBOL ø
THIS IS A DEGREE SYMBOL ˚
THIS IS A PLUS/MINUS SYMBOL ±
THIS TEXT IS O̅V̅E̅R̅S̅C̅O̅R̅E̅D̅ AND U̲N̲D̲E̲R̲S̲C̲O̲R̲E̲D̲
THIS IS A SINGLE PERCENT SIGN %
**Figure 11-45**    Inserting symbols in single-line text

# Text Fields

A field is intelligent text you can insert in your drawing that dynamically updates according to the data it is based on and/or represents. A classic example is the **Date** field. You can create a **Date** field in a drawing that automatically updates to reflect the current date, and even time, using a variety of different formats:

- 2/5/2009
- Saturday, February 05, 2009
- 2009-02-05
- 5-Feb-09
- …

Fields can be created by themselves, so they stand alone, or they can be inserted in any kind of text, attribute, or attribute definition. A field uses the same text style as the text object in which it is inserted and is displayed with a light gray background that is not plotted.

| FOR MORE DETAILS | See Chapter 16 for more details about blocks and block attributes. |
|---|---|

When a field is updated, the latest data is displayed. Fields can be set to update automatically via one or all of the following events and actions:

- When a drawing is opened
- When a drawing is saved
- When a drawing is plotted
- When you use eTransmit
- When a drawing is regenerated

It is also possible to turn off all the automatic update features so you must manually update any fields in a drawing. You can control how fields are updated, and then turn the field background display on and off, in the **Fields** area on the bottom left of the **User Preferences** tab in the **Options** dialog box shown in Figure 11-46.

Unchecking the **Display background of fields** check box turns off the light gray background. Selecting the **Field Update Settings…** button displays the **Field Update Settings** dialog box shown in Figure 11-47.

This dialog box allows you to indicate what actions or events will automatically update fields. By default, they are all on. If you uncheck all the check boxes, you must update fields manually.

> **Note:**
> A field that currently has no value displays all hyphens (—). For instance, the **PlotDate** field is not set to anything until a drawing is plotted. An invalid field displays all pound signs (# # # #).

## Inserting Text Fields

There are several different ways to insert a field. To create a single stand-alone field, you use the **FIELD** command.

To insert a field into multiline text, you can either select **Insert Field…** from the multiline editor right-click menu (see Figure 11-26), or you can use the **Insert Field** button on the **Multiline Text** ribbon explained earlier (see Figure 11-15). To insert a field into single-line text, you must select **Insert Field…** from the single-line editor right-click menu explained earlier. Any of these methods displays the **Field** dialog box shown in Figure 11-48.

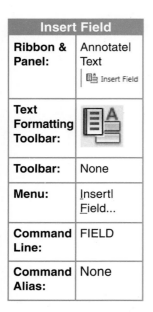

| Insert Field | |
|---|---|
| **Ribbon & Panel:** | Annotate\| Text<br>📑 Insert Field |
| **Text Formatting Toolbar:** | 📑A |
| **Toolbar:** | None |
| **Menu:** | Insert\| Field… |
| **Command Line:** | FIELD |
| **Command Alias:** | None |

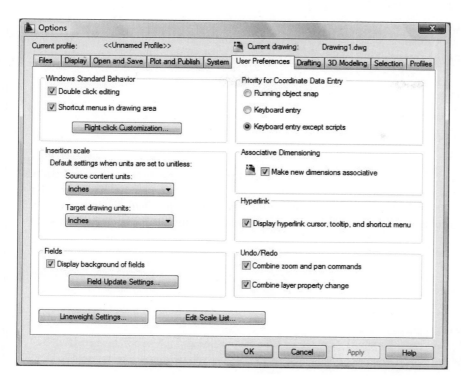

Figure 11-46   Fields settings on the User Preferences tab in the Options dialog box

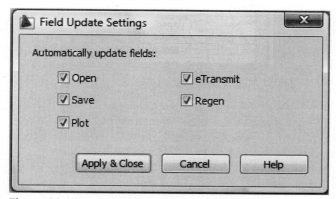

Figure 11-47   Field Update Settings dialog box

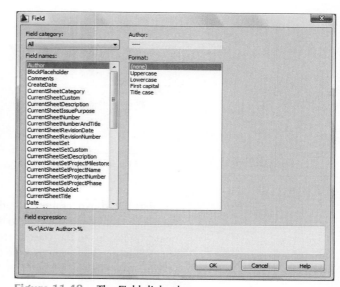

Figure 11-48   The Field dialog box

The **Field category:** list box lists the different types of fields available broken down into the following categories:

- **All**   All fields
- **Date & Time**   Date/time–related fields (created, saved, plotted)
- **Document**   Drawing file–related fields (file name, size, saved by)
- **Linked**   Hyperlink information
- **Objects**   Object information (formulas, block names, drawing object properties)
- **Other**   Miscellaneous information (diesel expressions, system variable values)
- **Plot**   Plot information (plot device, paper size, scale)
- **Sheetset**   Sheet set information

The **Field names:** list box changes based on the category selected. All the other options in the **Field** dialog box change based on the field category and field name that are selected. For instance, selecting the **Date & Time** field category displays a list of the following date-related field names:

- CreateDate
- Date
- PlotDate
- SaveDate

All the date fields allow you to specify a date format in the **Date format:** box and control how the date appears in the drawing. You can either enter your own format via the keyboard using the control codes shown in the **Hints** area on the right side of the **Field** dialog box or, even easier, select a predefined format from the **Examples:** list in the middle of the dialog box shown in Figure 11-49.

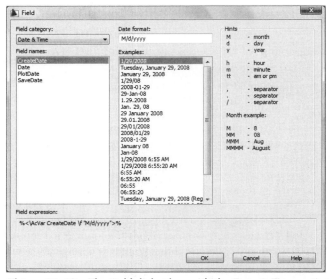

**Figure 11-49**    The Field dialog box with the Date & Time options

The **Field expression:** box displays the actual field expression that underlies the field and cannot be edited. It is possible to use the field expression as a guide so that you can construct your own expressions in the **Date format:** text box.

When you have selected the desired field name and all its formatting options, you can select **OK** to insert the field. Figure 11-50 shows a **Date** field inserted in a multiline text object.

**Figure 11-50**    A Date field inserted into a paragraph of multiline text

### Editing Text Fields

Text fields are part of either a multiline or single-line text object. If you insert a stand-alone field as described earlier, it is created as multiline text. Because of this, you must use the same tools to edit a field as you do to edit multiline and single-line text. When a field is selected, the **Edit Field** option is available on the shortcut menu, or you can double-click the field to display the **Field** dialog box. Any changes are applied to all text in the field.

**TIP** If you no longer want to update a field, you can preserve the value that is currently displayed by converting the field to text.

---

**Exercise 11-10:** Inserting Text Fields

1. Open drawing **EX11-1.**
2. Set the NOTES text style current.
3. Start the **TEXT** or **DTEXT** command to create single-line text.
4. Pick a start point for the text anywhere in your drawing.
5. Enter a rotation angle of **0°** when AutoCAD prompts you to *Specify rotation angle of text <0>:.*
6. Enter the following text followed by a space but *do not* press the **<Enter ⏎>** key:

   ```
   Drawing plotted on:
   ```

7. Right-click with your mouse while still in the single-line text editor and select **Insert Field…** from the shortcut menu (see Figure 11-37) to display the **Field** dialog box (see Figure 11-48).
8. Select **Date & Time** from the **Field category:** list box to display the **Date & Time** field names.
9. Select **PlotDate** from the **Field names:** list box.
10. Select **OK** to insert the field.
11. Press **<Enter ⏎>** twice to exit the **TEXT** command.
12. The text should read as follows:

    ```
    Drawing plotted on: - - - -
    ```

13. Plot your drawing to any plotting device or file.
14. Text is updated so that it looks similar to the following, only with today's date:

    ```
    Drawing plotted on: 2/9/2009
    ```

15. Save the drawing as **EX11-10.**

## EDITING TEXT

Both multiline and single-line text can be modified using any of the modify commands introduced earlier in the book. You can move, copy, rotate, scale, and array text just like any other drawing object. Multiline text can even be broken down into individual single-line text objects using the **EXPLODE** command.

You can also use grips to modify text. Both single-line text and multiline text can be moved using the grip located at the text insertion point. Multiline text has grips at the four corner points of the text boundary that can be used to resize the boundary area using the **Stretch** option as shown in Figure 11-51.

### Editing Text Content

The easiest way to edit the text content is to simply double-click on the text you want to edit. If you double-click on multiline text, the same in-place multiline text editor used to create the text is displayed with the selected text as shown in Figure 11-52. You can then update the text and any of its properties using the same methods and techniques introduced earlier.

Double-clicking on single-line text displays the in-place single line text editor shown in Figure 11-53.

You can also use the **DDEDIT** or **ED** command to edit text content. After starting the **DDEDIT** command, AutoCAD prompts you to *Select an annotation object or ⏎* Select the text to edit and press **<Enter ⏎>**. AutoCAD displays either the in-place multiline or single-line text editor depending on the type of text selected. You can then update the text using the methods and techniques explained earlier.

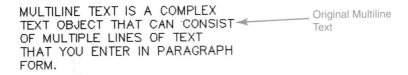

Original Multiline
Text

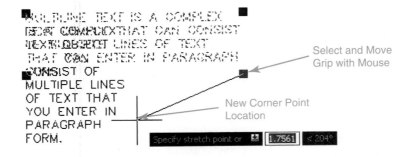

Select and Move
Grip with Mouse

New Corner Point
Location

Specify stretch point or     1.7561    < 204°

MULTILINE TEXT
IS A COMPLEX
TEXT OBJECT
THAT CAN
CONSIST OF
MULTIPLE LINES
OF TEXT THAT
YOU ENTER IN
PARAGRAPH
FORM.

Multiline
Text Automatically
Resized

**Figure 11-51**     Using grips to resize the multiline text boundary

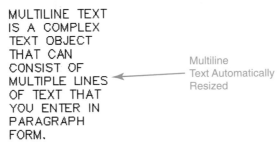

**Figure 11-52**     Editing text using the multiline text editor

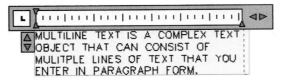

**Figure 11-53**     Editing text using the
single-line text editor

## Editing Text Using the Properties Palette

The **Properties** palette allows you to change all facets of a text object, including text content, text style, height, justification, and rotation, to name but a few. Plus, using the **Properties** palette, you can also change the text's general properties, such as layer, color, and so on. It's the Swiss army knife of text-editing tools. The properties of a multiline text object are shown in Figure 11-54.

Selecting the button to the right of the **Contents** property displays the appropriate text editor so you can update the text contents as explained earlier.

| Edit Text | |
|---|---|
| **Ribbon & Panel:** | Annotate\|Text |
| **Text Toolbar:** | |
| **Menu:** | Modify\|Object Text\|Edit |
| **Command Line:** | DDEDIT |
| **Command Alias:** | ED |

**TIP**     You can update multiple text objects using the **Properties** palette. For instance, you can use the **Properties** palette to update the text height for all text in a drawing. In fact, you can even update the text height for both single-line and multiline text at the same time.

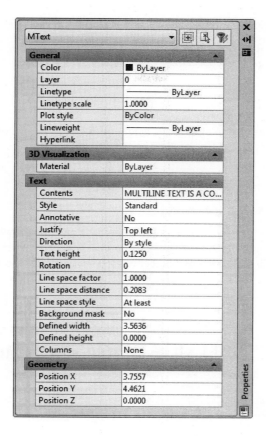

**Figure 11-54**    Properties of a multiline object

## Exercise 11-11: Editing Text

1. Open drawing **EX11-2.**
2. Select the multiline text object so grips are displayed.
3. Select the bottom right corner grip and stretch the text boundary corner to the right (see Figure 11-51).
4. Press the **<Esc>** key to turn off grips.
5. Double-click on the multiline text object to display the in-place multiline text editor.
6. Resize the text width to 3″ using the arrows on the right-hand side of the ruler (see Figure 11-15).
7. Press **<Ctrl>+A** to select all the text in the editor.
8. Use the **Multiline Text** ribbon toolbar to change the following:
   a. Set the style for all text to ARCHITECTURAL.
   b. Make all text uppercase.
   c. Deselect all text so nothing is highlighted by clicking anywhere in the text editor window with your cursor.
   d. Select the text "in-place editor" on the first line so it is highlighted.
   e. Change the selected text to bold and italic.
   f. Set the first line indent to 1″ and the paragraph indent to 0.5″ using the ruler.
9. Select **OK** or click outside the multiline text editor to exit and save your changes.
10. Save the drawing as **EX11-11A.**
11. Open drawing **EX11-8.**
12. Double-click on any of the single-line text objects to display the in-place single-line text editor.
13. Type the following over the highlighted text:

    THIS IS SOME NEW TEXT!

14. Press **<Enter ↵>** to exit the editor.
15. Hit **<Esc>** to exit the **DDEDIT** command.
16. Select all the text in the drawing and open the **Properties** palette (see Figure 11-54).

17. Change the **Height** property to 0.1″ to update the text height for all the selected text.
18. Change the **Justification** property to **Right** for all the selected text.
19. Press **<Esc>** to deselect all the text.
20. Save the drawing as **EX11-11B**.

| Scale Text | |
|---|---|
| **Ribbon & Panel:** | Annotate\|Text <br> 🅰 Scale |
| **Text Toolbar:** | 🅰 |
| **Menu:** | <u>M</u>odify\| <u>O</u>bject\| <u>T</u>ext\|<u>S</u>cale |
| **Command Line:** | SCALE TEXT |
| **Command Alias:** | NONE |

## Scaling Text

The **SCALETEXT** command allows you to change the height of one or more text objects using the following methods using a base point that you specify:

* Specifying a new height
* Specifying a scale factor
* Matching the height of an existing text object

You can elect to use each text object's insertion point as the base point about which the text is scaled, or you can select one of the different justification options explained earlier in the chapter. AutoCAD uses the base point to scale each text object but it *doesn't change* the justification point for each object as shown in Figure 11-55.

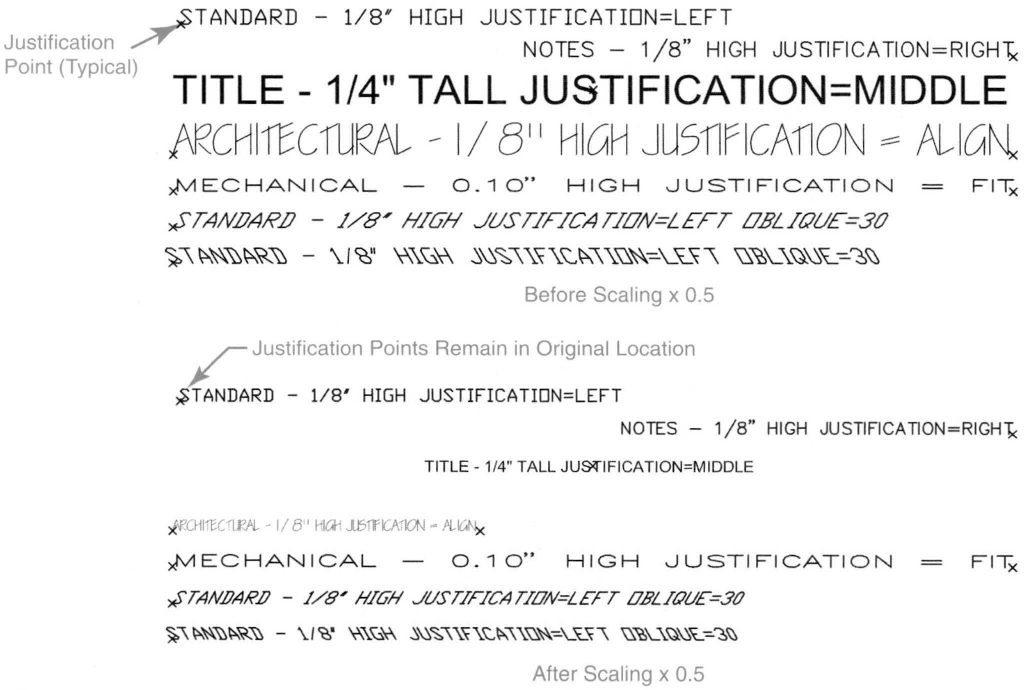

**Figure 11-55** Changing text height using the SCALETEXT command

When you start the **SCALETEXT** command, AutoCAD prompts you to *Select objects:*. Select the text you want to update using any of the selection methods and press **<Enter ↵>**. AutoCAD prompts you to *Enter a base point option for scaling:*. You can press **<Enter ↵>** to use the existing text insertion points as base points, or you can select one of the different justification options. Remember that the justification point entered is only used as a temporary base point for each text object.

After you have selected a base point option, AutoCAD prompts you to *Specify new height or* ↵. You have three options: you can enter a new height, you can specify a scale factor to multiply each text height by, or you can match the height of an existing text object in the drawing. The default is to enter a new height.

## Exercise 11-12: Scaling Text

1. Open drawing **EX11-8.**
2. Start the **SCALETEXT** command.

3. Type **ALL** and press **<Enter ↵>** twice when AutoCAD prompts you to *Select objects:* to select everything in the drawing.
4. AutoCAD prompts you to *Enter a base point option for scaling ↓*.
5. Type **E<Enter ↵>** or select the **Existing** option using your arrow keys.
6. AutoCAD prompts you to *Specify new height or ↓*.
7. Type **.1<Enter ↵>**.
8. All the text is resized to 0.1″ tall using its current insertion point.
9. Save the drawing as **EX11-12.**

## Changing Text Justification

The **JUSTIFYTEXT** command allows you to change the justification property of one or more text objects without changing their location in the drawing. Typically, when you change the justification property of text using the **Properties** palette, the text is relocated about the new justification point as shown in Figure 11-56.

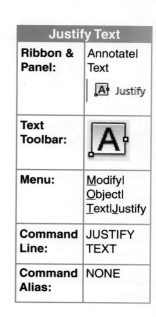

| Justify Text | |
|---|---|
| **Ribbon & Panel:** | Annotatel Text<br>📝 Justify |
| **Text Toolbar:** | ⬛ |
| **Menu:** | Modifyl Objectl TextlJustify |
| **Command Line:** | JUSTIFY TEXT |
| **Command Alias:** | NONE |

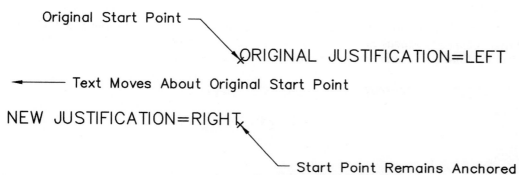

**Figure 11-56**   Changing text justification using the Properties palette

The **JUSTIFYTEXT** command provides a way around this problem. When you start the **JUSTIFYTEXT** command, AutoCAD prompts you to *Select objects:*. Select the text you want to update using any of the selection methods and press **<Enter ↵>**. AutoCAD prompts you to *Enter a justification option:*. You can select one of the different justification options either via the keyboard or by using your arrow keys if you are using Dynamic Input. The insertion points for all the selected text objects are changed to the justification point specified, but they remain in their original locations as shown in Figure 11-57.

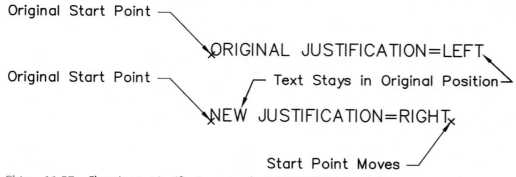

**Figure 11-57**   Changing text justification using the JUSTIFYTEXT command

## Exercise 11-13: Changing Text Justification

1. Open drawing **EX11-8.**
2. Start the **JUSTIFYTEXT** command.
3. Type **ALL** and press **<Enter ↵>** twice when AutoCAD prompts you to *Select objects:* to select everything in the drawing.

4. AutoCAD prompts you to *Enter a justification option* ↓.
5. Type **R<Enter ↵>** or select the **Right** justification option using your arrow keys.
6. All the text justification points are changed to **Right,** but the text remains in its original location.
7. Save the drawing as **EX11-13.**

## Finding and Replacing Text

The **FIND** command allows you to find and replace text that you specify. AutoCAD searches through *all* the different text types in a drawing including:

- Single-line and multiline text
- Block attributes
- Dimensions
- Tables
- Hyperlinks

It is possible to limit what type of text to search for so you can refine your search via the **FIND** command's options explained later. When you start the **FIND** command, AutoCAD displays the **Find and Replace** dialog box shown in Figure 11-58.

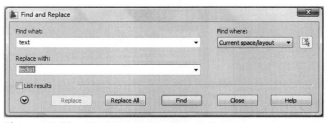

**Figure 11-58** The Find and Replace dialog box

The **Find what:** combo box is where you type in the text string for which you want to search. You can enter a text string or choose one of the recently used strings from the list. It is also possible to use the following wildcard characters to enhance your search possibilities.

> **TIP** You can enter text directly via the expanded text panel on the **Annotate** ribbon. Selecting the **Find Text** button automatically starts the search for the first match.

The **Replace with:** combo box is where you type in the text string you want to replace for any found text. You can enter a text string or choose one of the recently used strings from the list.

The **Find where:** list box allows you to specify where to search. You can search the current space/layout, the entire drawing, or selected objects. If one or more objects is already selected, the **Current selection** option is the default value; otherwise the **Current space/layout** option is the default.

The **Select objects** button to the right of the **Search in:** list box closes the dialog box temporarily so that you can select objects in your drawing. Accepting the selection set by pressing **<Enter ↵>** returns to the dialog box.

The **More Options** button on the lower left expands the dialog box as shown in Figure 11-59 so you can view and modify the search options and text types to search.

The **Replace** button replaces the found text with the text that you enter in the **Replace with:** combo box.

The **Replace All** button finds *all* occurrences of the text entered in the **Find what:** combo box and replaces them with the text entered in the **Replace with:** combo box. AutoCAD reports the success or failure of the replacement attempt in a separate dialog box by indicating how many objects have been changed.

| Find Text | |
|---|---|
| **Ribbon & Panel:** | Annotate\|Text |
| **Text Toolbar:** | |
| **Toolbar:** | None |
| **Menu:** | Edit\|Find... |
| **Command Line:** | FIND |
| **Command Alias:** | None |

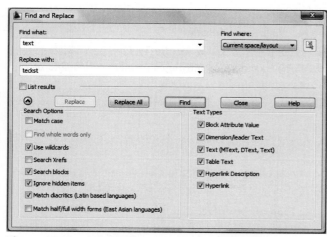

**Figure 11-59**    The Find and Replace Options dialog box

The **Find Next** button in the **Find and Replace** dialog box searches for the text that you enter in the **Find what:** combo box. Any text that is found is automatically zoomed into so you can see it in context. After finding the first occurrence of the text, the **Find** button becomes the **Find Next** button to allow you to search for the next text occurrence.

Selecting the **List results** check box displays a table with the text location (model or paper space), object type, and text string where the text was found showing it in context. Clicking on a column header in the table sorts the information based on the content in that column.

Selecting the **More Options** arrow button expands the dialog box so you can specify different search options and text types to search.

The different **Search Options** include:

- **Match case**    Includes the case of the text in **Find what.** as part of the search criteria
- **Find whole words only**    Finds only whole words that match the text in **Find what.** For example, if you select **Find whole words only** and search for "is," **Find and Replace** does not locate the text string "this"
- **Use wildcards**    Allows the use of the following wildcard characters in searches:

| Find and Replace Wildcard Characters | |
| --- | --- |
| **Wildcard Character** | **Description** |
| *(Asterisk) | Matches any text string |
| @ (At) | Matches any letter *only* |
| # (Pound) | Matches any number *only* |
| ? (Question mark) | Matches any single character (letters and numbers) |
| . (Period) | Matches any nonalphanumeric character |
| ~ (Tilde) | Matches anything *but* the pattern |
| [ ] (Square brackets) | Matches any of the characters enclosed in the brackets |
| [~] (Tilde) | Matches any character not enclosed in the brackets |
| [-] (Hyphen and brackets) | Specifies a range for a single letter |
| ' (Reverse quote) | Reads the next character literally |

- **Search Xrefs**   Include text in externally referenced files in search results
- **Search blocks**   Includes text in blocks in search results
- **Ignore hidden items**   Ignores hidden items in search results. Hidden items include text on layers that are frozen or turned off, text in block attributes created in invisible mode, and text in visibility states within dynamic blocks
- **Match diacritics** (Latin-based languages)   Matches diacritical marks, or accents, in search results
- **Match half/full width forms** (East Asian Languages)   Matches half- and full-width characters in search results
- **Text Types**   Specifies the type of text objects you want to include in the search. By default, all options are selected

The **Close** button closes and exits the **Find and Replace** dialog box.

TIP   The **FIND** command can also be found near the bottom of many of the right-click menus for easy access.

**Exercise 11-14:** Finding and Replacing Text

1. Open drawing **EX11-8.**
2. Type the word "Text" in the **Find Text** box on the expanded text panel on the **Annotate** ribbon.
3. Select the **Find Text** button on the right to display the **Find and Replace** dialog box shown in Figure 11-58.
4. Type the word "Teckst" in the **Replace with:** list box.
5. Select the **Replace** button to replace the current text.
6. Select the **Find Next** button to find the next occurrence.
7. Select the **Replace All** button to replace all the text in the drawing.
8. Note how many matches were found and how many objects were changed and select the **OK** button.
9. Select the **Close** button to exit the dialog box.
10. Save the drawing as **EX11-14.**

| Check Spelling | |
|---|---|
| **Ribbon & Panel:** | Annotate\| Text |
| | ᴬᴮᶜ✓ Check Spelling |
| **Text Toolbar:** | **ABC** ✓ |
| **Menu:** | Tools\| Spelling... |
| **Command Line:** | SPELL |
| **Command Alias:** | SP |

## The Spell Checker

The **SPELL** command allows you to check and correct the spelling for the following text object types:

- Single-line and multiline text
- Dimensions
- Block attribute values
- External references

Entering the **SPELL** command displays the **Check Spelling** dialog box shown in Figure 11-60.

The **Where to check:** drop-down list allows you to limit where and what text AutoCAD checks for spelling errors. You have the following three options:

- Entire drawing
- Current space/layout
- Selected objects

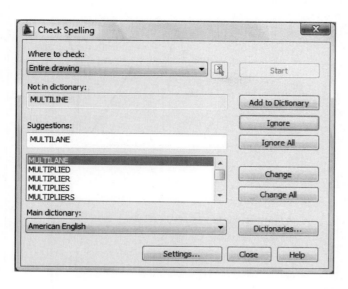

**Figure 11-60**    The Check Spelling dialog box

By default, AutoCAD checks the entire drawing for spelling errors. If you select **Selected objects,** you must select some text objects in the drawing by selecting the **Select text objects** button to the right of the **Where to check:** drop-down list. Otherwise, the **Start** button will be disabled.

Select the **Start** button to begin the spell-checking process. If no misspelled words are found, AutoCAD displays a message box indicating that the *Spelling Check is complete.* Otherwise, AutoCAD will automatically zoom to the first misspelled word in the drawing and highlight the offending text.

The **Not in dictionary:** area displays the highlighted word that is spelled incorrectly or was not found in the current dictionary. This is the text that will be updated if you select the **Change** or **Change All** buttons.

The **Suggestions:** box displays a list of suggested replacement words from the current dictionary. You can either select a replacement word from the list or type in a replacement word in the box.

The **Add to Dictionary** button adds the current word to the current custom dictionary. A different custom dictionary can be selected using the **Dictionaries...** button explained below.

The **Ignore** button skips the current word and begins searching for the next misspelled word.

The **Ignore All** button skips all the remaining occurrences of the misspelled word that match the current word.

The **Change** button replaces the current word with the word in the **Suggestions:** text box.

The **Change All** button replaces all occurrences of the misspelled word in the drawing based on the current **Where to check:** selection.

The **Dictionaries...** button displays the **Dictionaries** dialog box shown in Figure 11-61.

The **Dictionary** dialog box allows you to switch dictionaries so you can check spelling in other languages. The default main dictionary is American English. To change to another language dictionary, select it from the **Current main dictionary:** list box at the top.

To add one or more words to the dictionary, enter it in the **Content:** text box and select the **Add** button. Any words that you add using the **Add** button in the main **Check Spelling** dialog box or the **Dictionary** dialog box are stored in the custom dictionary. By default, the custom dictionary is named sample.cus and is located in your AutoCAD Support folder.

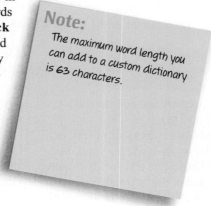

Note:
The maximum word length you can add to a custom dictionary is 63 characters.

You can manage custom dictionaries by selecting **Manage custom dictionaries...** from the **Current custom dictionary:** drop-down list to display the **Manage Custom Dictionaries** dialog box. The **Manage Custom Dictionaries** dialog box allows you to add dictionaries to check, create new dictionaries from scratch, and remove existing dictionaries.

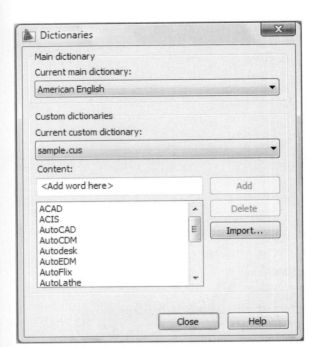

Figure 11-61    The Dictionaries dialog box

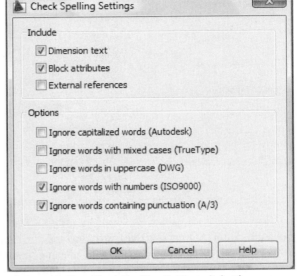

Figure 11-62    Check Spelling Settings dialog box

The **Settings** button displays the **Check Spelling Settings** dialog box shown in Figure 11-62, which allows you to control various aspects of the spell-checking behavior.

At the top of the **Check Spelling Settings** dialog box in the **Include** area, you can choose whether to check dimension text, block attributes, and external references.

At the bottom of the dialog box in the **Options** area, you can choose to ignore certain types of words commonly found in technical drawings such as words with numbers and words containing punctuation.

### Exercise 11-15: Using the Spell Checker

1. Open drawing **EX11-14.**
2. Start the **SPELL** command.
3. The **Check Spelling** dialog box is displayed.
4. Select the **Start** button.
5. AutoCAD zooms to the word "Teckst" in your drawing while also displaying it in the **Not in dictionary:** text box.
6. **Suggestions:** is set to "Text".
7. Select the **Change** button to update the current text.
8. The next occurrence of "Teckst" is found.
9. Select the **Change All** button to update all occurrences of the misspelled word.
10. The "Spelling check complete" message box is displayed.
11. Select **OK.**
12. Save the drawing as **EX11-15.**

## SUMMARY

This chapter showed you how to create and edit the different annotation features found in AutoCAD.

Remember that there are two different kinds of text: multiline and single-line. Each serves its own purpose. Many times you will want to rely on single-line text for short notes, titles, and labels in a drawing. Other times you may want the benefits of multiline text, which allows you to do things like easily insert special symbols from a menu, and create bulleted, numbered, and lettered lists.

Think about how you might incorporate text fields in your drawings. There are many fields that are well suited for title blocks. You could incorporate fields to automatically update the date, filename, and even your name!

**FOR MORE DETAILS**    See Chapter 16 for more information about extracting block attributes.

## CHAPTER TEST QUESTIONS

### Multiple Choice

1. A font determines how text looks by defining its:
   a. Boldness
   b. Typeface
   c. Language
   d. All of the above

2. AutoCAD fonts have what three-letter file extension?
   a. SHP
   b. FNT
   c. TTF
   d. SHX

3. The system variable that controls the font substituted for a font not found on your system is named:
   a. **ALTFONT**
   b. **FONTSUB**
   c. **SUBFONT**
   d. **FONTALT**

4. A common approach to naming text styles is to create the name by combining the:
   a. Font name and height
   b. Text type and height
   c. Font name and width
   d. Text height and oblique angle

5. The end of a line of multiline text is created using:
   a. A hard return
   b. A soft return
   c. **<Ctrl> + <Enter ↵>**
   d. a and b

6. The text height displayed in the in-place multiline editor is:
   a. The specified text height
   b. Real size
   c. Font size
   d. Text style height

7. To exit the in-place multiline text editor and save your text and any changes, you:
   a. Select **Close Text Editor** on the **Multiline Text** ribbon
   b. Press **<Ctrl> + <Enter ↵>**
   c. Click outside the editor window with your mouse
   d. All of the above

8. The system variable that controls the default text height displayed in the multiline text editor **Text height:** list box is:
   a. **TEXTHEIGHT**
   b. **SIZETEXT**
   c. **TXTHEIGHT**
   d. **TEXTSIZE**

9. What file type can be imported into the multiline text editor?
   a. Rich Text Format file
   b. Microsoft Word document
   c. ASCII text file
   d. a and c

10. The name of the feature in the multiline text editor that locks your keyboard so only uppercase letters can be typed is:
    a. CaseLock
    b. CapLocks
    c. AutoCAPS
    d. CapAuto

11. The AutoStack feature automatically stacks numeric text when what character is placed between two numbers?
    a. /
    b. #
    c. ^
    d. All of the above

12. What single-line justification option allows you to squeeze text between two points without changing the text height?
    a. Align
    b. Fit
    c. Center
    d. None of the above

13. The prefix used to insert special symbols into single-line text is:
    a. @
    b. %%
    c. \U++
    d. b and c

14. A text field that currently has no value assigned displays:
    a. # # # #
    b. Nothing
    c. - - - -
    d. Empty

15. To edit existing text, you can:
    a. Double-click on the text
    b. Use the **Properties** palette
    c. Use the **DDEDIT** command
    d. All of the above

16. To change the justification point of text without moving it in the drawing, use:
    a. The **JUSTIFYTEXT** command
    b. The **SCALETEXT** command
    c. The **Properties** palette
    d. a and c

## Matching

**Column A**

a. Annotate

b. Typeface

c. TEXTFILL

d. FONTALT

e. Text style

f. Multiline text

g. AutoCAPS

h. Character set

i. AutoStack

j. Field

**Column B**

1. System variable that controls the filling of TrueType fonts while plotting and rendering

2. Locks your keyboard so only uppercase letters can be entered, similar to the **<Caps Lock>** key

3. The set of numeric codes used to represent the characters of a particular country or place

4. Controls the font, height, and other characteristics that affect the appearance of text

5. Creates different formats of stacked text as you type

6. To add text, notes, and dimensions to a drawing

7. Intelligent text that dynamically updates according to the data it is based on and/or represents

8. System variable that specifies an alternate font to be used when a particular font file cannot be located on your system

9. Complex text object that can consist of multiple lines of text that you enter in paragraph form

10. The style or design of a font

## True or False

1. True or False: The text font determines the height of the text in a drawing.

2. True or False: You can use both TrueType fonts and AutoCAD SHX fonts in a drawing at the same time.

3. True or False: You should always try to use text styles to control text fonts.

4. True or False: The default font assigned to the STANDARD text style is the AutoCAD font Simplex.shx.

5. True or False: If you change a text style text height, all text of that style in a drawing is updated.

6. True or False: It is possible to resize a multiline text boundary size using grips.

7. True or False: You can copy text to and from the multiline text editor using the Windows clipboard.

8. True or False: It is possible to create a numbered list automatically in the multiline editor by entering a number followed by a period (.).

9. True or False: The **Import Text...** option in the multiline editor allows you to import a Microsoft Word document.

10. True or False: The AutoCAPS feature in the multiline editor can be turned off using your **<Caps Lock>** key.

11. True or False: If the current text style has a height assigned in the style that is greater than 0.0, you will be prompted for a text height when creating single-line text.

12. True or False: The single-line **Align** text justification option will change the text height in order to make the text entered fit between two selected points.

13. True or False: A field that currently has no value displays all pound signs (# # # #).

14. True or False: Fields can be inserted in multiline text only.

## CHAPTER PROJECTS

### Project 11-1a: Calculator—Continued from Chapter 10

1. Open drawing **P10-1A** from Chapter 10.
2. Modify the **Standard** text style to use the **ROMANS.SHX** font file. Add the text shown in Figure P11-1A.
3. Save your drawing as **P11-1A.**

Figure P11-1A

### Project 11-1b: Classroom Plan—Continued from Chapter 8

1. Open drawing **P8-1** from Chapter 8.
2. Add the text shown in Figure P11-1B. Create a text style called **ARCH** using the **CountryBlueprint.SHX** font.
3. Save your drawing as **P11-1B.**

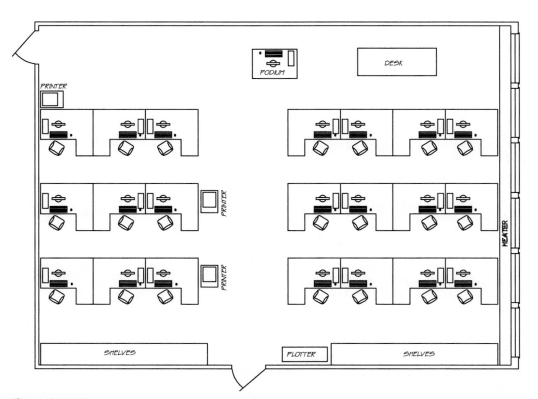

Figure P11-1B

## Project 11-1c: Circuit Board—Continued from Chapter 10

1. Open drawing **P10-1B** from Chapter 10.
2. Modify the **Standard** text style to use the **ROMANS.SHX** font file. Add the text shown in Figure P11-1C.
3. Save your drawing as **P11-1C.**

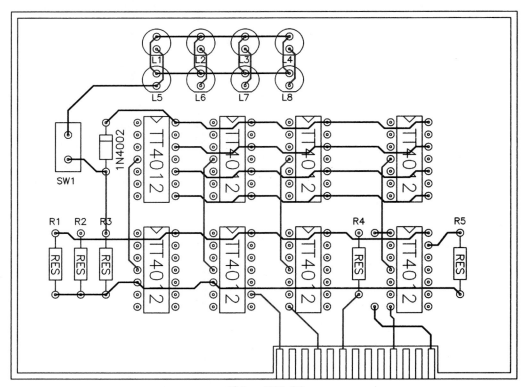

Figure P11-1C

## Project 11-2: Tachometer

1. Start a new drawing using the acad.dwt template.
2. Create the following layers:

| Name | Color | Linetype | Lineweight |
| --- | --- | --- | --- |
| Object | 7 | Continuous | Default |
| Text | 7 | Continuous | Default |
| Hatch1 | 1 | Continuous | Default |
| Hatch5 | 5 | Continuous | Default |
| Ticks | 8 | Continuous | Default |

3. Draw the front and side views of the 5″-diameter tachometer shown in Figure P11-2 using the layers in the preceding table.
4. Be sure to include all text and hatching.
5. Save the drawing as **P11-2.**

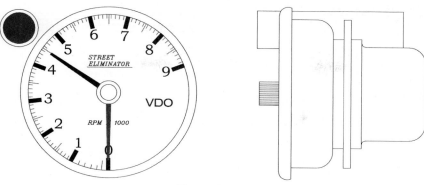

Figure P11-2

## Project 11-3a: B-Size Mechanical Border—Continued from Chapter 6

1. Open the drawing template **Mechanical B-Size.DWT**.
2. Modify the **Standard** text style to use the **ROMANS.SHX** font file.
3. Set the **Snap Mode** setting to **1/16″** and add the text shown in Figure P11-3A. Large text is **1/8″** tall, and smaller text is **1/16″**. Use multiline text for the tolerance note and single-line text for all other text. Use text fields for the drawing name, plot date, and user name.
4. Save your drawing as **Mechanical B-Size.DWT**.

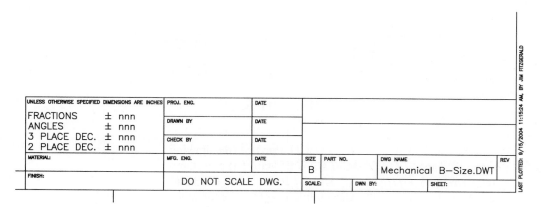

Figure P11-3A

## Project 11-3b: C-Size Mechanical Border—Continued from Chapter 7

1. Open the drawing **Mechanical C-Size.DWT**.
2. Modify the **Standard** text style to use the **ROMANS.SHX** font file.
3. Set the **Snap Mode** setting to **1/16″**. Add the zone division lines and text as shown in Figure P11-3B. All text is 1/4″ tall.

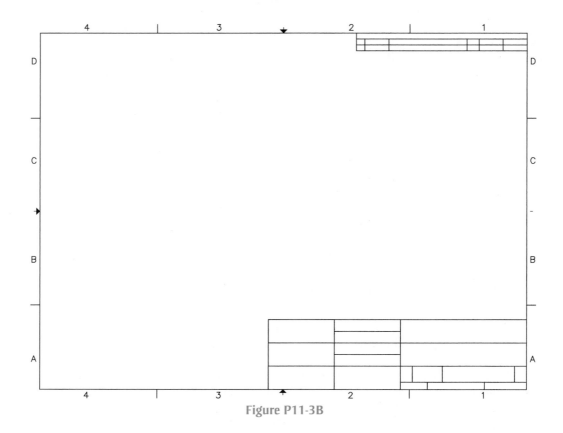

Figure P11-3B

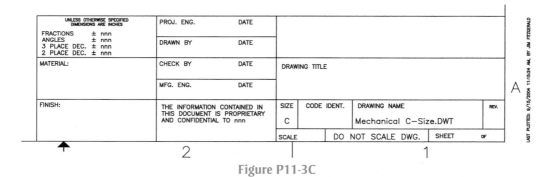

Figure P11-3C

4. Add the text shown in Figure P11-3C. Large text (the drawing name, "*C*," and "*DO NOT SCALE*") is **1/8″** tall. The plot stamp and "*UNLESS OTHERWISE SPECIFIED...*" text are **1/16″** tall. All other text is **3/32″**. Use multiline text for the tolerance note and single-line text for all other text. Use text fields for the drawing name, plot date, and user name.

5. Save your drawing as **Mechanical C-Size.DWT.**

## Project 11-3c: A-Size Portrait Mechanical Border— Continued from Chapter 8

1. Open the drawing **Mechanical A-Size-Portrait.DWT.**

2. Modify the **Standard** text style to use the **ROMANS.SHX** font file.

3. Set the **Snap Mode** setting to **1/16″** and add the text shown in Figure P11-3D. Large text is **1/8″** tall, and smaller text is **1/16″**.

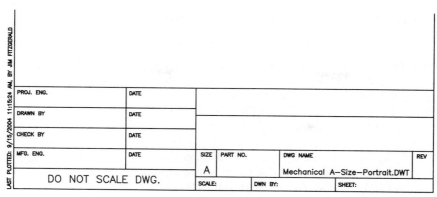

Figure P11-3D

Use text fields for the drawing name, plot date, and user name. *Hint:* Use aligned text for the drawing name field to ensure the file name fits in the allotted space.

4. Save your drawing as **Mechanical A-Size-Portrait.DWT.**

## Project 11-3d: Logo—Continued from Chapter 10

1. Open drawing **P10-3.**
2. Create a new text style called **PEARSON** using the **Lucinda Sans.TTF** TrueType font. Assign a width factor of 1.10 to the text style.
3. Create a second text style called **PH** using the **Times New Roman.TTF** TrueType font.
4. Add the text shown in Figure P11-3E. All text is **0.375** high. Assign the color **255** as a hard-coded color to all text. *Hint:* Use the **DRAWORDER** command to send the solid fill areas to the back of the borders and text.
5. Save your drawing as **P11-1D.**

Figure P11-3E

## Project 11-4a: Architectural D-Size Border—Continued from Chapter 10

1. Open template file **Architectural D-Size.DWT.**
2. Create a text style named **Border** assigned the text font **Simplex.shx.**

3. Create a text style named **Logo** assigned the text font **Century Gothic.ttf.**

4. Create a text style named **Arch** assigned the text font **CountryBlueprint.ttf.**

5. Create all text in the following steps at the approximate heights shown. Try to use standard heights when possible.

6. Create all the logo text as shown in Figure P11-4A using the text style **Logo** on the layer **A-Anno-Ttlb-Logo.**

7. Create the text on the bottom right that says "Last plotted on MM/DD/YYYY" by inserting the date as a field using the **PlotDate** field so it updates each time the drawing is plotted.

8. Create all the remaining title border text as shown in Figure P11-4A using the text style **Border** on the layer **A-Anno-Ttlb-Text.**

9. Save the drawing to a template file as **Architectural D-Size.DWT.**

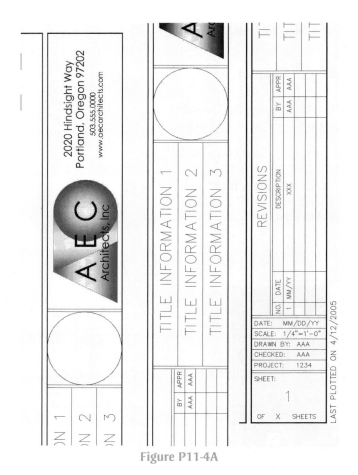

Figure P11-4A

## Project 11-4b: Architectural B-Size Border—Continued from Chapter 10

1. Open the template file **Architectural B-Size.DWT.**

2. Create a text style named **Border** assigned the text font **Simplex.shx.**

3. Create a text style named **Logo** assigned the text font **Century Gothic.ttf.**

4. Create a text style named **Arch** assigned the text font **CountryBlueprint.ttf.**

5. Create all text in the following steps at the approximate heights shown. Try to use standard heights when possible.
6. Create all the logo text as shown in Figure P11-4B using the text style **Logo** on the layer **A-Anno-Ttlb-Logo.**
7. Create the text on the bottom left that says "Last plotted on MM/DD/YYYY" by inserting the date as a field using the **PlotDate** field so it updates each time the drawing is plotted.
8. Create all the remaining title border text as shown in Figure P11-4B using the text style **Border** on the layer **A-Anno-Ttlb-Text.**
9. Save the drawing to a template file as **Architectural B-Size.DWT.**

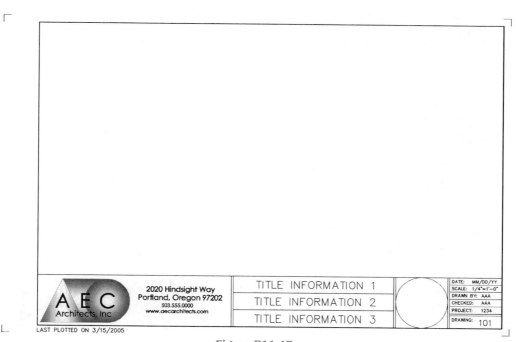

**Figure P11-4B**

## Project 11-4c: Architectural A-Size Border— Continued from Chapter 8

1. Open template file **Architectural A-Size.DWT**.
2. Create a text style named **Border** assigned the text font **Simplex.shx.**
3. Create a text style named **Arch** assigned the text font **CountryBlueprint.ttf.**
4. Create all text in the following steps at the approximate heights shown. Try to use standard heights when possible.
5. Create the text on the bottom left that says "Last plotted on MM/DD/YYYY" by inserting the date as a field using the **PlotDate** field so it updates each time the drawing is plotted.
6. Create all the remaining title border text as shown in Figure P11-4C using the text style **Border** on the layer **A-Anno-Ttlb-Text.**
7. Save the drawing to a template file as **Architectural A-Size.DWT.**

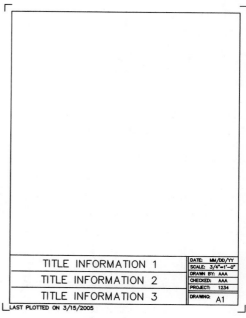

**Figure P11-4C**

## Project 11-5a: Electrical Plan—Continued from Chapter 10, Problem 7

1. Open drawing **P10-7.**
2. Create a text style called **E-Symbol** using the **ROMANS.SHX** font.
3. Add/modify the existing symbols and create the electrical symbols as shown in Figure P11-5A. Use **4″** text for all annotation within the symbols. Use **6″** text for the symbol description. Use the **E-Lite** or **E-Powr** layer to place the symbol annotation. Place all description annotation on the **E-Anno** layer.
4. Add/modify the symbols and wiring as shown in Figure P11-5B.
5. Save your drawing as **P11-5A.**

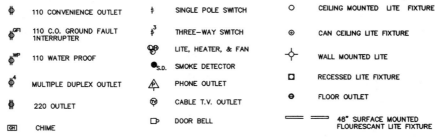

Figure P11-5A

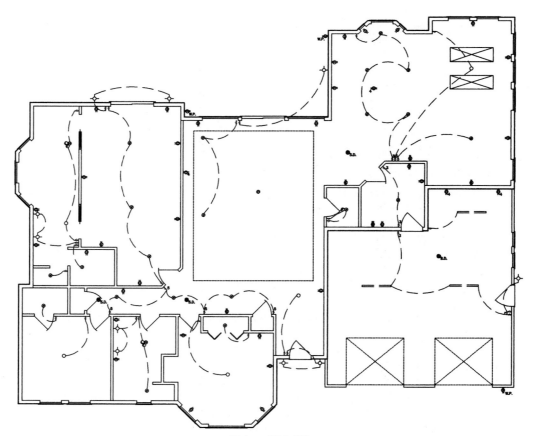

Figure P11-5B

## Project 11-5b: Electrical Distribution Panel—
## Continued from Chapter 10

1. Open drawing **P10-5** from Chapter 10.
2. Add the electrical annotation shown in Figure P11-5C. Place all annotation on the **E-Anno** layer.
3. Save your drawing as **P11-5B.**

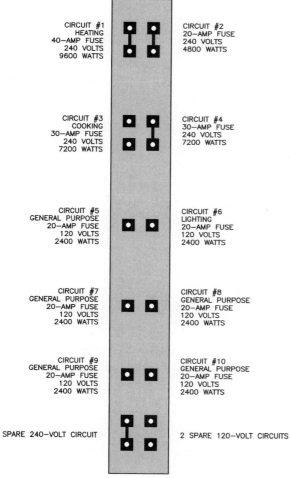

CIRCUIT #1
HEATING
40—AMP FUSE
240 VOLTS
9600 WATTS

CIRCUIT #2
20—AMP FUSE
240 VOLTS
4800 WATTS

CIRCUIT #3
COOKING
30—AMP FUSE
240 VOLTS
7200 WATTS

CIRCUIT #4
30—AMP FUSE
240 VOLTS
7200 WATTS

CIRCUIT #5
GENERAL PURPOSE
20—AMP FUSE
120 VOLTS
2400 WATTS

CIRCUIT #6
LIGHTING
20—AMP FUSE
120 VOLTS
2400 WATTS

CIRCUIT #7
GENERAL PURPOSE
20—AMP FUSE
120 VOLTS
2400 WATTS

CIRCUIT #8
GENERAL PURPOSE
20—AMP FUSE
120 VOLTS
2400 WATTS

CIRCUIT #9
GENERAL PURPOSE
20—AMP FUSE
120 VOLTS
2400 WATTS

CIRCUIT #10
GENERAL PURPOSE
20—AMP FUSE
120 VOLTS
2400 WATTS

SPARE 240—VOLT CIRCUIT

2 SPARE 120—VOLT CIRCUITS

**Figure P11-5C**

## Project 11-6a: Hot Water Piping Schematic—
## Continued from Chapter 5

1. Open drawing **P5-6** from Chapter 5.
2. Create a text style named **Notes** assigned the text font **Simplex.shx** with a height of **1/8".**
3. Create a text style named **Title** assigned the text font **Arial.ttf** with a height of **1/4".**
4. Add the notes shown in Figure P11-6A using the text style **Notes** on layer **P-Anno-Note.**
5. Add the underlined title text shown in Figure P11-6A using the text style **Title** on layer **P-Anno-Title.**
6. Add the curved line terminators shown in Figure P11-6A using curve fit polylines on layer **P-Anno-Note.**
7. Save the drawing as **P11-6A.**

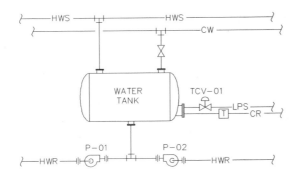

HOT WATER PIPING SCHEMATIC

NOT TO SCALE

**Figure P11-6A**

## Project 11-6b: Water Heater Schematic—Continued from Chapter 6

1. Open drawing **P6-6** from Chapter 6.
2. Create a text style named **Notes** assigned the text font **Simplex.shx** with a height of **1/8″**.
3. Create a text style named **Title** assigned the text font **Arial.ttf** with a height of **1/4″**.
4. Add the general note and scale shown in Figure P11-6B using the text style **Notes** on layer **P-Anno-Note**.
5. Add the underlined title text shown in Figure P11-6B using the text style **Title** on layer **P-Anno-Title**.
6. Add the curved line terminators shown in Figure P11-6B using curve fit polylines on layer **P-Anno-Note**.
7. Add the flow arrows shown in Figure P11-6B using tapered polylines on layer **P-Detl-P1**. *Hint:* Draw one polyline flow arrow and copy/rotate it as needed.
8. Add the squiggly lines shown in Figure P11-6B using curve fit polylines on layer **P-Detl-P1**.
9. Save the drawing as **P11-6B**.

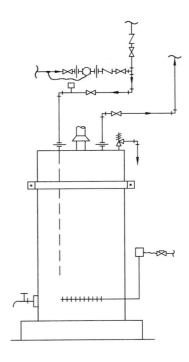

GAS WATER HEATER

NOT TO SCALE

NOTE:
N.S.P.C. 10.16.7 REQUIRES THAT WHEN A HOT WATER HEATER IS LOCATED AT AN ELEVATION ABOVE THE FIXTURE OUTLETS IN THE SYSTEM THA A VACUUM RELIEF VALVE SHALL BE INSTALLED ON THE STORAGE TANK.

**Figure P11-6B**

## Project 11-6c: Compressed Air Schematic—Continued from Chapter 7

1. Open drawing **P7-6** from Chapter 7.
2. Create a text style named **Notes** assigned the text font **Simplex.shx** with a height of **1/8″**.
3. Create a text style named **Title** assigned the text font **Arial.ttf** with a height of **1/4″**.
4. Add the in-line text, gauge text, and scale shown in Figure P11-6C using the text style **Notes** on layer **P-Anno-Note**.
5. Add the underlined title text shown in Figure P11-6C using the text style **Title** on layer **P-Anno-Title**.
6. Add the curved line terminators shown in Figure P11-6C using curve fit polylines on layer **P-Anno-Note**.
7. Save the drawing as **P11-6C**.

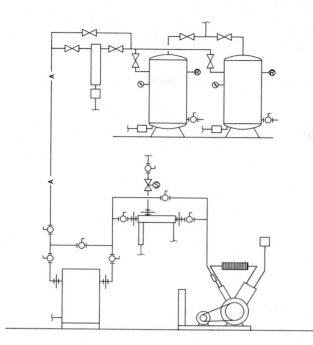

COMPRESSED AIR SYSTEM
NOT TO SCALE
**Figure P11-6C**

## Project 11-6d: Unit Heater Connections—Continued from Chapter 8

1. Open drawing **P8-6** from Chapter 8.
2. Create a text style named **Notes** assigned the text font **Simplex.shx** with a height of **1/8″**.
3. Create a text style named **Title** assigned the text font **Arial.ttf** with a height of **1/4″**.
4. Add the in-line text, general note, and scale shown in Figure P11-6D using the text style **Notes** on layer **P-Anno-Note**.
5. Add the underlined title text shown in Figure P11-6D using the text style **Title** on layer **P-Anno-Title**.
6. Add the curved line terminators shown in Figure P11-6D using curve fit polylines on layer **P-Anno-Note**.
7. Add the break lines shown in Figure P11-6D using polylines on layer **P-Anno-Note**.
8. Fillet the corners on each heater unit as shown in Figure P11-6D. *Hint:* Set layer **P-Detl-P1** current before running the **FILLET** command so arcs are created on the correct layer.
9. Save the drawing as **P11-6D**.

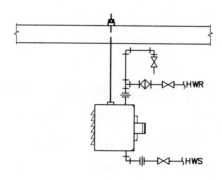

UNIDIRECTIONAL TYPE

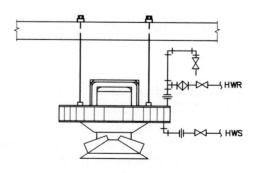

4—WAY TYPE

TYPICAL UNIT HEATER CONNECTIONS
NOT TO SCALE

NOTE:
TERMINATE MANUAL AIR VENT AT WALL 7'-0" AFF
WITH GLOBE VALVE WHEN HEATER IS GREATER THAN
OR EUQAL TO 12"-0" AFF.

**Figure P11-6D**

## Project 11-6e: Pipe/Wall Penetration Detail—Continued from Chapter 9

1. Open drawing **P9-6** from Chapter 9.
2. Create a text style named **Notes** assigned the text font **Simplex.shx** with a height of 1/2″.
3. Create a text style named **Title** assigned the text font **Arial.ttf** with a height of 1″.
4. Add the general note and scale shown in Figure P11-6E using the text style **Notes** on layer **P-Anno-Note**.
5. Add the underlined title text shown in Figure P11-6E using the text style **Title** on layer **P-Anno-Title**.
6. Save the drawing as **P11-6E**.

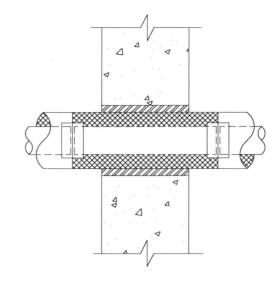

## TYPICAL WALL PENETRATION
SCALE: 3″=1′-0″

NOTE:
SIZE PIPE SLEEVE SO THAT THERE IS AT LEAST $\frac{1}{4}$″ CLEARANCE ALL AROUND

**Figure P11-6E**

## Project 11-7: Residential Architectural Plan—Continued from Chapter 11

1. Open drawing **P11-5A** from Chapter 11, Project 5. I f you are not completing Project 5, open drawing **P10-7** from Chapter 10.
2. Create the following layers:

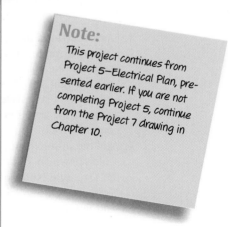

*Note:*

This project continues from Project 5—Electrical Plan, presented earlier. If you are not completing Project 5, continue from the Project 7 drawing in Chapter 10.

| Name | Color | Linetype | Description |
|------|-------|----------|-------------|
| A-Door-Iden | White | Continuous | Door tags |
| A-Glaz-Iden | White | Continuous | Window tags |
| A-Area-Iden | White | Continuous | Room numbers, room identification, and area calculations |
| A-Anno-Legn | White | Continuous | Door and window schedules |
| A-Anno-Note | White | Continuous | General notes |
| A-Anno-Dims | White | Continuous | Dimensioning |

3. Create a text style called **A-SYMBOL** using the **ROMANS. SHX** font and set it current.
4. Create the door and window schedules and tags as shown in Figure P11-7A using lines and text. Use a text height of **6″** for the door and window tags and the small text in the schedule. Use a text height of **8″** for the column heads in the table and a text height of **12″** for the schedule titles.
5. Place the door and window tags and add the room labels as shown in Figure P11-7B. Place all objects on their appropriate layer.
6. Save your drawing as **P11-7**.

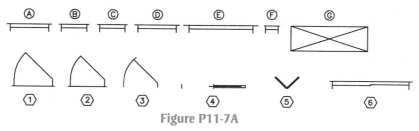

| WINDOW SCHEDULE | | | | DOOR SCHEDULE | | | |
|---|---|---|---|---|---|---|---|
| SYM. | SIZE | TYPE | QTY. | SYM. | SIZE | TYPE | QTY. |
| A | 3'-0" X 3'-6" | S.H. | 10 | 1 | 3'-0" X 6'-8" | M.I./R.P. | 1 |
| B | 2'-0" X 3'-6" | S.H./FROSTED | 1 | 2 | 2'-8" X 6'-8" | M.I./S.C. | 2 |
| C | 2'-0" X 3'-0" | S.H. | 4 | 3 | 2'-8" X 6'-8" | H.C. | 8 |
| D | 3'-0" X 3'-0" | PCT. | 2 | 4 | 2'-6" X 6'-8" | POCKET/H.C. | 2 |
| E | 5'-0" X 5"-0" | TEMP. PCT. | 3 | 5 | 2'-6" X 6'-8" | H.C./BI-FOLD | 2 |
| F | 1'-0" X 3'-0" | S.H. | 2 | 6 | 6'-0" X 6'-8" | TEMP. SLIDER | 2 |
| G | 2'-0" X 6'-0" | GLASS SKY. | 2 | 7 | 8'-0" X 6'-8" | GARAGE | 2 |

**Figure P11-7A**

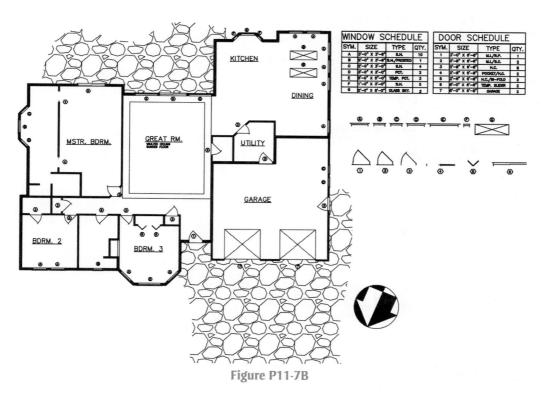

**Figure P11-7B**

## Project 11-8a: Joist Foundation Detail—Continued from Chapter 10

1. Open drawing **P10-8A** from Chapter 10.
2. Create a text style named **Notes** assigned the TrueType text font **CountryBlueprint.ttf** with a height of **3″**.
3. Create a text style named **Title** assigned the TrueType text font **CountryBlueprint.ttf** with a height of **6″**.
4. Draw the 12″-diameter title bubble and horizontal line shown in Figure P11-8A on layer **A-Detl-Note**.
5. Add the general note, scale, and title bubble text (#/###) shown in Figure P11-8A using the text style **Notes** on layer **A-Detl-Note**.

6. Add the title text shown in Figure P11-8A using the text style **Title** on layer **A-Anno-Title.**

7. Save the drawing as **P11-8A.**

### Project 11-8b: Interior Floor Change Detail—Continued from Chapter 10

1. Open drawing **P10-8B** from Chapter 10.

2. Create a text style named **Notes** assigned the TrueType text font **CountryBlueprint.ttf** with a height of **3".**

3. Create a text style named **Title** assigned the TrueType text font **CountryBlueprint.ttf** with a height of **6".**

4. Draw the 12"-diameter title bubble and horizontal line shown in Figure P11-8B on layer **A-Detl-Note.**

5. Add the scale and title bubble text (#/# # #) shown in Figure P11-8B using the text style **Notes** on layer **A-Detl-Note.**

6. Add the title text shown in Figure P11-8B using the text style **Title** on layer **A-Anno-Title.**

7. Save the drawing as **P11-8B.**

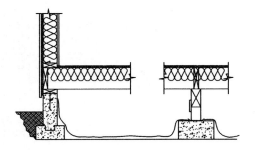

JOIST FOUNDATION
SCALE: 1/2"=1'-0"

NOTE:
PROVIDE (1) #4 UP & DN

**Figure P11-8A**

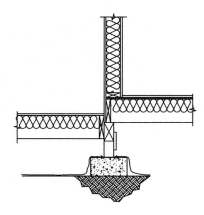

INTERIOR FLOOR CHANGE
SCALE: 1/2"=1'-0"

**Figure P11-8B**

### Project 11-8c: Truss with Soffited Eave Detail—Continued from Chapter 10

1. Open drawing **P10-8C** from Chapter 10.

2. Create a text style named **Notes** assigned the TrueType text font **CountryBlueprint.ttf** with a height of **3".**

3. Create a text style named **Title** assigned the TrueType text font **CountryBlueprint.ttf** with a height of **6".**

4. Draw the 12"-diameter title bubble and horizontal line shown in Figure P11-8C on layer **A-Detl-Note.**

5. Add the scale and title bubble text (#/# # #) shown in Figure P11-8C using the text style **Notes** on layer **A-Detl-Note.**

6. Add the title text shown in Figure P11-8C using the text style **Title** on layer **A-Anno-Title.**

7. Draw the rise/run symbol shown in Figure P11-8C on layer **A-Detl-Note.**

8. Add the rise/run text shown in Figure P11-8C using the text style **Notes** on layer **A-Detl-Note.**
9. Save the drawing as **P11-8C.**

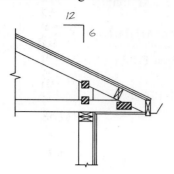

TRUSS W/ SOFFITED EAVE

SCALE: 1/2"=1'-0"

Figure P11-8C

## Project 11-9: Socket Head Cap Screws—English Units—Continued from Chapter 7

1. Open drawing **P7-9** from Chapter 7.
2. Modify the **Standard** text style to use the **ROMANS.SHX** font.
3. Create the table shown in Figure P11-9 using lines and text on the **NOTES** layer. Use a text height of **.125** for the table text and **.250** for the table title. Set the height of the top row to **.5** and the row height of all other rows to **.25.**
4. Save the drawing as **P11-9.**

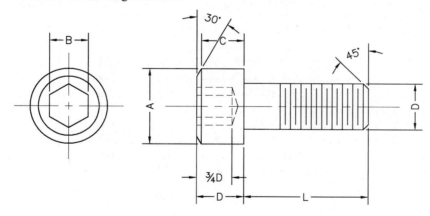

| Socket Head Cap Screw | | | | | |
|---|---|---|---|---|---|
| Nominal Size (D) | Thread/In | A | B | C | L |
| 4 (.112) | 40 | .183 | 3/32 | .103 | 1.00 |
| 5 (.125) | 40 | .205 | 3/32 | .113 | 1.00 |
| 6 (.138) | 32 | .226 | 7/64 | .125 | 1.25 |
| 8 (.164) | 32 | .270 | 9/64 | .150 | 1.25 |
| 10 (.190) | 24 | .312 | 5/32 | .171 | 1.50 |
| ¼ (.250) | 20 | .375 | 3/16 | .225 | 1.50 |

Figure P11-9

## Project 11-10a: Gasket—Continued from Chapter 4

1. Open drawing **P4-10** from Chapter 4.
2. Create a text style named **Notes** assigned the text font **Simplex.shx** with a height of **5 mm.**
3. Create a text style named **Title** assigned the text font **Arial.ttf** with a height of **10 mm.**
4. Add the scale shown in Figure P11-10A using the text style **Notes** on layer **Text**.
5. Add the underlined title text shown in Figure P11-10A using the text style **Title** on layer **Text**.
6. Save the drawing as **P11-10A.**

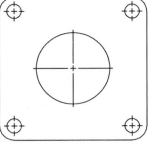

GASKET
SCALE: 1:2

**Figure P11-10A**

## Project 11-10b: Widget—Continued from Chapter 5

1. Open drawing **P5-10** from Chapter 5.
2. Create a text style named **Notes** assigned the text font **Simplex.shx** with a height of **10 mm.**
3. Create a text style named **Title** assigned the text font **Arial.ttf** with a height of **20 mm.**
4. Add the scales shown in Figure P11-10B using the text style **Notes** on layer **Text**.
5. Add the underlined title text shown in Figure P11-10B using the text style **Title** on layer **Text**.
6. Save the drawing as **P11-10B.**

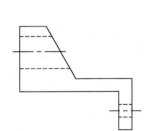

FRONT VIEW
SCALE: 1:4

RIGHT—SIDE VIEW
SCALE: 1:4

**Figure P11-10B**

## Project 11-10c: Hex Head Bolts and Nuts—Continued from Chapter 6

1. Open drawing **P6-10** from Chapter 6.
2. Create a text style named **Title** assigned the text font **Arial.ttf** with a height of **5 mm.**
3. Add the underlined title text shown in Figure P11-10C using the text style **Title** on layer **Text**.
4. Save the drawing as **P11-10C.**

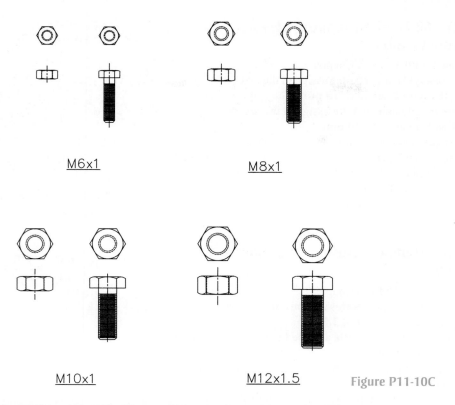

M6x1                              M8x1

M10x1                          M12x1.5      Figure P11-10C

### Project 11-10d: Motorcycle Head Gasket—Continued from Chapter 7

1. Open drawing **P7-10** from Chapter 7.
2. Create a text style named **Notes** assigned the text font **Simplex.shx** with a height of **5 mm.**
3. Create a text style named **Title** assigned the text font **Arial.ttf** with a height of **10 mm.**
4. Add the scale and general note shown in Figure P11-10D using the text style **Notes** on layer **Text.**
5. Add the underlined title text shown in Figure P11-10D using the text style **Title** on layer **Text.**
6. Save the drawing as **P11-10D.**

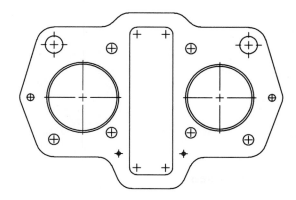

NOTE:
ALL FILLETS R12.7 UNLESS OTHERWISE NOTED

HEAD GASKET
SCALE: 1:2

Figure P11-10D

## Project 11-10e: 68-Tooth Rear Sprocket—Continued from Chapter 8

1. Open drawing **P8-10** from Chapter 8.
2. Create a text style named **Notes** assigned the text font **Simplex.shx** with a height of **10 mm.**
3. Create a text style named **Title** assigned the text font **Arial.ttf** with a height of **20 mm.**
4. Add the scale shown in Figure P11-10E using the text style **Notes** on layer **Text.**
5. Add the underlined title text shown in Figure P11-10E using the text style **Title** on layer **Text.**
6. Save the drawing as **P11-10E.**

68 TOOTH REAR SPROCKET
SCALE: 4:1
Figure P11-10E

## Project 11-10f: Window Extrusion—Continued from Chapter 9

1. Open drawing **P9-10** from Chapter 9.
2. Create a text style named **Notes** assigned the text font **Simplex.shx** with a height of **2.5 mm.**
3. Create a text style named **Title** assigned the text font **Arial.ttf** with a height of **5 mm.**
4. Add the scale shown in Figure P11-10F using the text style **Notes** on layer **Text.**
5. Add the underlined title text shown in Figure P11-10F using the text style **Title** on layer **Text.**
6. Save the drawing as **P11-10F.**

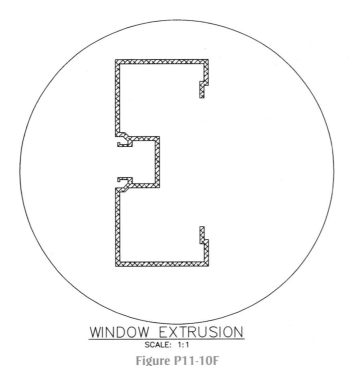

WINDOW EXTRUSION
SCALE: 1:1
Figure P11-10F

## Project 11-10g: Hub—Continued from Chapter 10

1. Open drawing **P10-10A** from Chapter 10.
2. Create a text style named **Notes** assigned the text font **Simplex.shx** with a height of **5 mm.**

3. Create a text style named **Title** assigned the text font **Arial.ttf** with a height of **10 mm.**

4. Add the scale shown in Figure P11-10G using the text style **Notes** on layer **Text.**

5. Add the underlined title text shown in Figure P11-10G using the text style **Title** on layer **Text.**

6. Save the drawing as **P11-10G.**

## Project 11-11: Civil Site Plan—Continued from Chapter 10

1. Open drawing **P10-11.**

2. Create a text style called **C-NOTE** using the **ROMANS.SHX** font and set it current.

3. Place the notes and spot elevations as shown in Figure P11-11. Use the appropriate layers for each object. *Hint:* Select **Symbol> Centerline** from the right-click menu within the **MTEXT** command to create the centerline symbol ().

4. Use the **HATCHEDIT** to modify the hatch patterns so the text is not obscured.

5. Save the drawing as **P11-11.**

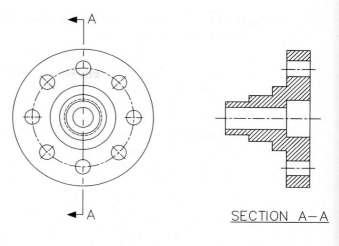

HUB
SCALE: 1:2

SECTION A—A

**Figure P11-10G**

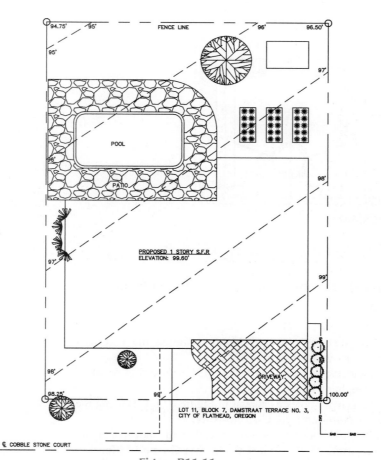

**Figure P11-11**

## Project 11-12a: Manhole Construction Detail—Continued from Chapter 10

1. Open drawing **P10-12A** from Chapter 10.
2. Create a text style named **Notes** assigned the text font **Simplex.shx** with a height of **2″**.
3. Create a text style named **Title** assigned the text font **Arial.ttf** with a height of **4″**.
4. Add the title text shown in Figure P11-12A using the text style **Title** on layer **C-Anno-Title**.
5. Save the drawing as **P11-12A**.

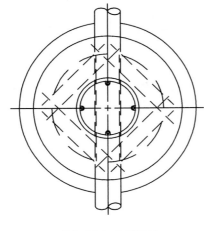

PLAN VIEW

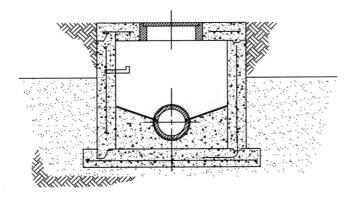

VERTICAL SECTION

Figure P11-12A

## Project 11-12b: Manhole Cover—Continued from Chapter 10

1. Open drawing **P10-12B** from Chapter 10.
2. Create a text style named **Notes** assigned the text font **Simplex.shx** with a height of **1/2″**.
3. Create a text style named **Title** assigned the text font **Arial.ttf** with a height of **1″**.
4. Add the general notes as shown in Figure P11-12B using the text style **Notes** on layer **C-Anno-Note**.
5. Add the title text and the "A" section callouts as shown in Figure P11-12B using the text style **Title** on layer **C-Anno-Title**.
6. Save the drawing as **P11-12B**.

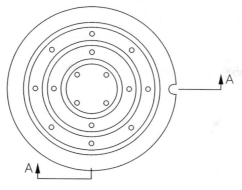

NOTE:
MATERIAL TO BE GRAY
CAST IRON    ASTM A48
CLASS 30

TOP VIEW

NOTE:
MACHINE TO A
TRUE BEARING
ALL AROUND

SECTION A—A

**Figure P11-12B**

## Project 11-12c: Standard Service Connection—
## Continued from Chapter 10

1. Open drawing **P10-12C** from Chapter 10.
2. Create a text style named **Notes** assigned the text font **Simplex.shx** with a height of **2″**.
3. Create a text style named **Title** assigned the text font **Arial.ttf** with a height of **4″**.
4. Add the "FINISH GRADE" note as shown in Figure P11-12C using the text style **Notes** on layer **C-Anno-Note.**
5. Add the title text as shown in Figure P11-12C using the text style **Title** on layer **C-Anno-Title.**
6. SAVE THE DRAWING AS **P11-12C. annotate:** To add text, notes, and dimensions to a drawing**Figure 11-1** Examples of drawing annotation

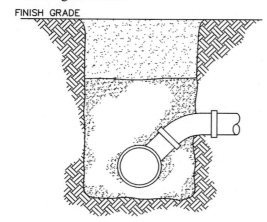

FINISH GRADE

STANDARD SERVICE CONNECTION　**Figure P11-12C**

# Working with Tables

**12**

## Chapter Objectives

- Creating tables from scratch by entering the data manually
- Creating tables by linking with a Microsoft® Excel spreadsheet
- Managing data links using the Data Link Manager
- Controlling the appearance of tables using table styles
- Modifying tables using grips
- Inserting formulas in a table

## INTRODUCTION

A table is an AutoCAD annotation object type that consists of data in rows and columns similar to an accounting spreadsheet. Many of the common spreadsheet features you may be familiar with work exactly the same in AutoCAD tables. It is even possible to paste a Microsoft Excel spreadsheet so that it converts directly into a static AutoCAD table with the desired formatting and fonts. Even better, you can link a dynamic AutoCAD table directly to an external Excel spreadsheet so that it updates automatically if the spreadsheet changes. Figure 12-1 shows an example of a table being used for an Architectural door schedule.

You can create a table based on three different types of data:

- **Static data**   Manually enter data into a table created from scratch or from pasting Excel data using the Windows clipboard

- **Externally linked data**   Create a dynamic AutoCAD table by linking to an existing Excel spreadsheet

- **Object data**   Create an AutoCAD table from object data in the drawing using the **Data Extraction** wizard which allows you to extract different object properties, including blocks and block attributes.

| FOR MORE DETAILS | See Chapter 16 for detailed information about using the **Data Extraction** wizard. |
|---|---|

**cell:** The box at the intersection of a table row and column that contains the table data or a formula. A cell is typically referenced using its column letter and row number separated with a colon. For example, the cell in column A and row 1 is referenced as A:1.

Using table styles, you can control all aspects of a table including the *cell* data format, the text and border properties, table direction, and other formatting options.

After the table has been created, the complete table, or individual rows and columns, can be resized using grips. Additional modifications can be made using the right-click shortcut menus or the **Tables** toolbar explained later in the section on modifying tables.

| WINDOW SCHEDULE | | | | | |
|---|---|---|---|---|---|
| TAG | TYPE | MANUFACTURER | HEIGHT | WIDTH | COUNT |
| A | Fixed | ACME Glass Co. | 4'-0" | 4'-0" | 20 |
| B | Fixed | ACME Glass Co. | 4'-0" | 3'-6" | 4 |
| C | Fixed | ACME Glass Co. | 3'-0" | 2'-6" | 4 |
| D | Casement | Glassarama, Inc. | 3'-0" | 2'-0" | 3 |
| E | Sidelite | Season All Windows | 4'-0" | 1'-0" | 1 |

Figure 12-1     Table used for an Architectural window schedule

## CREATING TABLES FROM SCRATCH

| Table | |
|---|---|
| **Ribbon & Panel:** | Homel Annotation |
| **Draw Toolbar:** | |
| **Menu:** | Drawl Table... |
| **Command Line:** | TABLE |
| **Command Alias:** | TB |

The **TABLE** command creates a table object by inserting an empty table in the drawing at a specified point or defined window area using the table style, number of rows, columns, and sizes you specify.

When you start the **TABLE** command, AutoCAD displays the **Insert Table** dialog box shown in Figure 12-2.

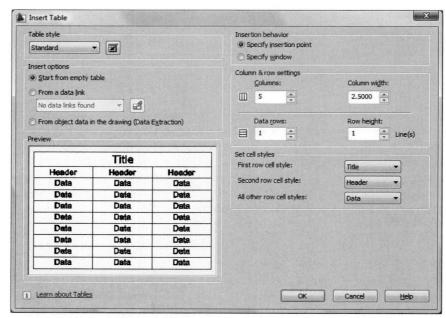

Figure 12-2     The Insert Table dialog box

The **Table Style** area on the top left side of the dialog box is used to control the appearance of the table.

The drop-down list allows you to select an existing table style and make it current. The default style is Standard. Selecting the button to the right displays the **Table Style** dialog box so that you can update the current style or add a new table style. Table styles are discussed later in this chapter.

Below the **Table Style** area is the **Insert Options** area where you select one of the three ways to insert a table. The default method is **Start from empty table**. If you select any of the other table insert options, most of the other options on the right will be disabled.

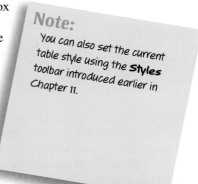

*Note:*
You can also set the current table style using the **Styles** toolbar introduced earlier in Chapter 11.

The table **Preview** provides an example of what the current table style looks like.

The **Insertion Behavior** section allows you to select how you want to locate the table. You can use an insertion point or specify a window boundary area.

The **Specify insertion point** option allows you to specify the location of the upper left corner of the table. You can either select a point with your mouse, or you can specify absolute coordinates via the keyboard.

The **Specify window** option allows you to locate and size the table by defining a rectangular window area using either your mouse or by specifying absolute coordinates via the keyboard. The specified column width and the final number of rows depend on the size of the boundary area.

The table is sized using the number and size of the rows and columns specified in the **Column & Row Settings** area on the right side of the dialog box.

The **Columns:** box is used to specify the number of columns. You can enter a value directly, or you can increase and decrease the current values using the up and down arrows on the right.

The **Column width:** box is used to specify the width of the columns. You can enter a value directly, or you can increase and decrease the current values using the up and down arrows on the right.

The **Data Rows:** box is used to specify the number of rows. You can enter a value directly, or you can increase and decrease the current values using the up and down arrows on the right. A table style with a title row and a header row has a minimum of three rows.

The **Row Height:** box is used to specify the row height in lines. The height of a line is based on the current text height and the cell margin settings in the current table style. Table styles are explored later in this section. You can enter a value directly, or you can increase and decrease the current values using the up and down arrows on the right. The minimum row height is one line.

It is possible to create and apply different cell styles per row so that you can create different formatting for titles, headers, and data, if desired. The **Set cell styles** area allows you to assign the different styles independent of the current Table style.

The **First row cell style** list box controls the cell style for the first row in the table. The **Title** cell style is used by default.

The **Second row cell style** list box controls the cell style for the second row in the table. The **Header** cell style is used by default.

The **All other row cell styles** list box controls the cell style for all other rows in the table. The **Data** cell style is used by default.

Selecting **OK** closes the dialog box, and AutoCAD prompts you to *Specify insertion point:*. You can pick a point using your mouse, or you can enter an absolute coordinate using the keyboard. The table is inserted, and you are placed in **Edit** mode. The **Text Formatting** toolbar explained in Chapter 11 is displayed, and your cursor is in the first data cell ready for data entry. Adding and modifying table data is explained in the following section.

**Note:**
If the table direction is set to UP in the current table style, the insertion point locates the lower left corner of the table.

**Note:**
When the **Specify window** option is used to locate the table and indicate its overall width, you can either specify the number of columns so that the column widths are set automatically, or you can specify the column width so that the number of columns is calculated automatically.

**Note:**
When the **Specify window** option is used to locate the table and indicate its overall height, you can either specify the number of rows so that the row height is set automatically, or you can specify the row height so that the number of rows is calculated automatically.

If you already have data in an Excel spreadsheet, you can copy and paste the Excel data as **AutoCAD Entities** using **Edit|Paste Special…** with the **Paste** option selected. Pasting Excel data as **AutoCAD Entities** automatically creates a new table with the static values already entered.

## ENTERING TABLE DATA

When a table is inserted, you are placed in **Edit** mode so that the **Multiline Text** ribbon is displayed and the first data cell is highlighted so that you can begin entering data. To move to an adjacent cell in the same row, you can use the left and right arrow keys or press the **<Tab>** key to go to the cell on the right. To move to an adjacent cell in the same column, you can use the up and down arrow keys or press **<Enter >** to go to the cell directly below in the next row.

Table cells can contain text, fields, blocks, and even formulas. Inserting formulas is explored later in the section "Inserting Formulas."

You can use any of the text formatting features and options explained earlier in the "Creating Multiline Text" section in Chapter 11 to format the text in each cell. When you are editing text, the arrow keys move the text cursor and do not take you to another cell.

When you are finished adding data to the table, you can use the same methods used for multiline text to close out of **Edit** mode and accept any additions and changes:

> **Note:**
> The row height of a cell increases to accommodate multiple lines of text if the specified row height is exceeded.

- Select **Close Text Editor** in the **Close** panel of the **Multiline Text** ribbon
- Click anywhere outside of the text editor with your mouse
- Hold down the **<Ctrl>** key and press **<Enter>**

By default, the in-place text editor displays column letters and row numbers when a table cell is selected for editing. Use the **TABLEINDICATOR** system variable to turn this display on and off. To set a new background color, select a table and click **Table Indicator Color** on the shortcut menu. The text color, size, style, and line color are controlled by the settings for column heads in the current table style.

## CREATING TABLES BY INSERTING A DATA LINK

The second way to insert a table is to link it to an existing Microsoft Excel spreadsheet using the **From a data link** method in the **Insert options** area of the **Insert Table** dialog box shown in Figure 12-2. Using data links, you can display tabular data from a spreadsheet as an AutoCAD table. This allows you to take advantage of AutoCAD fonts, colors, text styles, and all of the other

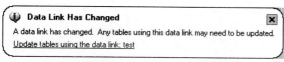

**Figure 12-3**    The Data Link Notification balloon

table formatting options while still maintaining a link to the original Excel data. If the Excel spreadsheet is updated, a notification balloon like the one shown in Figure 12-3 is displayed in the status tray on the right side of the Status Bar. It contains a link that lets you quickly update the table in the drawing so that it matches the Excel spreadsheet.

## The Data Link Manager

When a new data link is created, you must give it a name, usually related to the type of data, and select the external file to which it links (XLS or CSV) using the **Data Link Manager** shown in Figure 12-4.

After entering a name and choosing a file, AutoCAD displays the **New Excel Data Link** dialog box shown in Figure 12-5. There you can choose which sheet in the file you want to link and whether you want to link to the entire sheet or just a specific range of cells.

Once the link has been established, select **OK** to close the **Data Link Manager** and return to the **Insert Table** dialog box. A preview of the linked table is shown at the bottom of the dialog box.

Selecting **OK** closes the dialog box, and AutoCAD prompts you to *Specify insertion point:*. You can pick a point using your mouse, or you can enter an absolute coordinate using

| Data Link Manager | |
|---|---|
| **Ribbon & Panel:** | Blocks & References\|Linking & Extraction |
| **Toolbar:** | |
| **Menu:** | Tools\|Data Links\|Data Link Manager... |
| **Command** | DATALINK |
| **Command Alias:** | DL |

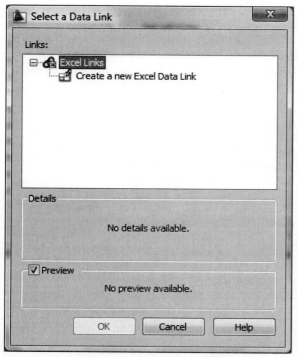

**Figure 12-4**    The Data Link Manager dialog box

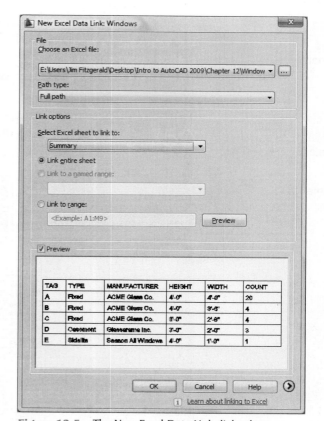

**Figure 12-5**    The New Excel Data Link dialog box

the keyboard. The table is inserted without putting you in **Edit** mode because the data is already created. It is possible to modify the table after it is inserted using the methods explained in the next section. Be careful, though, because changes made in the table do not automatically update the linked Excel spreadsheet.

**Note:**

To guard against linked data getting out of sync, the range of linked cells is indicated by green corner brackets, and the linked cells are locked to prevent editing from within AutoCAD. If you select a linked cell, its status is indicated by the locked and linked icons as well as by information in a tooltip. It is possible to unlock a cell so that it can be updated via the **Locking** cascade menu on the right-click menu or the **Table** toolbar explained in the following section.

**TIP**

If you already have data in an Excel spreadsheet, you can copy and link the Excel data as **AutoCAD Entities** using **Edit|Paste Special...** with the **Paste** option selected. Pasting Excel data as **AutoCAD Entities** automatically creates a new table with the dynamic values already entered.

| Table Style | |
|---|---|
| **Ribbon & Panel:** | Homel Annotation  |
| **Styles Toolbar:** | |
| **Menu:** | Formatl Table Style... |
| **Command Line:** | TABLESTYLE |
| **Command Alias:** | TS |

## MANAGING TABLE STYLES

Table styles are used to control the appearance of tables by allowing you to:

- Set the cell text style, height, data type, and alignment
- Control the cell border properties so you can set the border line thickness and color and turn border lines on and off
- Set the table text flow direction from top to bottom or bottom to top
- Set the horizontal and vertical cell margin distance

You can modify the default Standard table style, or you can create a new style. The **TABLESTYLE** command allows you to modify an existing table style or create a new one.

When you start the **TABLE** command, AutoCAD displays the **Table Style** dialog box shown in Figure 12-6.

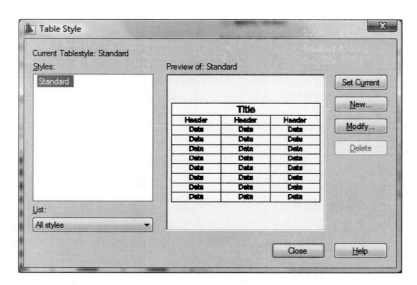

**Figure 12-6**   The Table Style dialog box

To create a new table style, select the **New...** button and enter the new table style name in the **Create New Table Style** dialog box. You can select an existing table style as a starting point by selecting it from the **Start With:** list. Selecting the **Continue...** button displays the **New Table Style** dialog box shown in Figure 12-7.

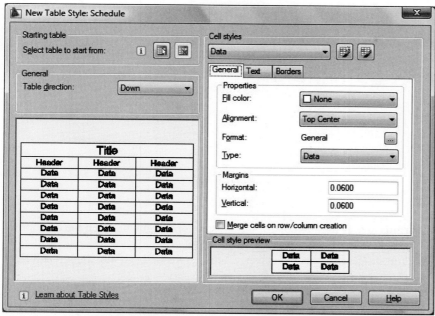

**Figure 12-7**    The New Table Style dialog box

The options in the **Modify Table Style** dialog box displayed when you select the **Modify...** button on the **Table Style** dialog are exactly the same as the **New Table Style** dialog box.

You can select a table in your drawing to use as a starting point for the new table style in the **Starting table** area on the top left of the dialog box.

The **Table direction:** list box controls the direction of the text flow for the table.

- **Down**   Text reads from top to bottom (Default)

- **Up**   Text reads from bottom to top. The title row and column heads row are located at the bottom of the table.

On the right side of the dialog box, there are three tabs that control the properties for the three default cell types in the **Cell styles** list box at the top:

- **Data**

- **Header**

- **Title**

You can set up and apply these different cell types to any row when you insert a table. You can also create your own cell styles via the **Manage Cell Styles** dialog box accessible by selecting the button to the right of the **Cell styles** list box.

The **General** tab controls general formatting and data type settings:

- The **Fill color:** list box controls the background color of the cell. The **Select color...** list item displays the AutoCAD **Select Color** dialog box.

- The **Alignment:** list box controls justification and alignment for text in a cell. The same justification options are available as used for multiline text explained earlier in the chapter.

- The **Format:** setting controls the data type and display for the text in the cell. Selecting the **...** button to the right of the current **Format:** setting displays the **Table Cell Format** dialog box shown in Figure 12-8.

Figure 12-8    The Table Cell Format dialog box

- The **Cell margins** area is used to control the spacing, or margin, between the cell border and the cell content. The default margin setting is 0.06″.
  - The **Horizontal:** text box sets the distance between the cell text and the left and right cell borders.
  - The **Vertical:** text box sets the distance between the cell text and the top and bottom cell borders.

The **Text** tab controls different text formatting settings:

- The **Text style:** list box lists all of the text styles in the drawing. The **...** button to the right displays the **Text Style** dialog box so you can create a new text style.
- The **Text height:** box sets the text height. The default text height for data and column head cells is 0.1800. The default text height for the table title is 0.25.
- The **Text color:** list box controls the text color. The **Select color...** list item displays the AutoCAD **Select Color** dialog box.

The **Borders** tab allows you to control the lineweight, linetype, and color of all four cell borders:

- The **Lineweight:** list box controls the lineweight for the borders you specify by selecting a border button below.
- The **Linetype:** list box controls the linetype for the borders you specify by selecting a border button below.
- The **Color:** list box controls the color for the borders you specify by selecting a border button below. The **Select color...** list item displays the AutoCAD **Select Color** dialog box.
- Checking the **Double line** check box will draw a double line border using the spacing specified below.

The buttons across the bottom determine to which border lines the properties above are applied.

- The **All Borders** button applies the border property settings to all four cell borders.
- The **Outside Border** button applies the border property settings to just the outside border of all cells.
- The **Inside Border** button applies the border property settings to the inside border of all cells. This option does not apply to title row cells.
- The **Bottom Border** button applies the border property settings to the bottom borders of all cells.
- The **Left Border** button applies the border property settings to the left borders of all cells.
- The **Top Border** button applies the border property settings to the top borders of all cells.

- The **Right Border** button applies the border property settings to the right borders of all cells.
- The **No Border** button hides borders for all cells.

**Exercise 12-1:** Creating a Table from Scratch
_____

1. Start a new drawing using the acad.dwt drawing template.
2. Create a text style named Notes with the following settings:
   a.   Font = Simplex.shx AutoCAD font
   b.   Height = 0.125″
3. Create a text style named Titles with the following settings:
   a.   Font = Arial TrueType font
   b.   Height = 0.25″
4. Create a text style named Architectural with the following settings:
   a.   Font = CityBlueprint TrueType font
   b.   Height = 0.125″
5. Create a new table style named Schedule with the following settings:
   a.   Set the Data rows text style to Notes
   b.   Set the Title row text style to Titles
   c.   Set the Header row text style to Architectural
   d.   Set the text alignment to Middle Center for all rows
   e.   Set all border line lineweights to 0.50mm for all rows
6. Create the window schedule shown in Figure 12-9 using the **TABLE** command with the Schedule table style you just created.
7. Save the drawing as **EX12-1.**

| WINDOW SCHEDULE | | | | | |
|---|---|---|---|---|---|
| TAG | TYPE | MANUFACTURER | HEIGHT | WIDTH | COUNT |
| A | Fixed | ACME Glass Co. | 4'-0" | 4'-0" | 20 |
| B | Fixed | ACME Glass Co. | 4'-0" | 3'-6" | 4 |
| C | Fixed | ACME Glass Co. | 3'-0" | 2'-6" | 4 |
| D | Casement | Glassarama, Inc. | 3'-0" | 2'-0" | 3 |
| E | Sidelite | Season All Windows | 4'-0" | 1'-0" | 1 |

**Figure 12-9**    Window schedule

## MODIFYING TABLES

There are two levels of modifying and editing an existing table: table level and cell level. Both methods rely on using grips.

> **FOR MORE DETAILS**    See Chapter 7 for more details about using grips.

You select a table by clicking directly on a table line so that the table level grips are displayed as shown in Figure 12-10.

You can use the table grips to resize the table by stretching any corner except the insertion corner point. The insertion grip point moves the table. When you change the height or width of a table using grips, the rows and columns change proportionally.

You can change column widths by selecting a grip at the top of a column line and stretching it to another location. To also change the table width, press **<Ctrl>** while selecting the column grip.

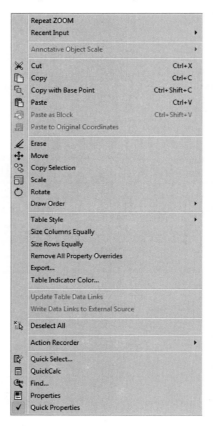

**Figure 12-10**   Selecting a table for editing using grips

The light blue triangle grip at the bottom center of the table is the table-breaking grip. A table with a large amount of data can be broken into primary and secondary table fragments. You can use the table-breaking grips found at the bottom of a table to make a table span multiple columns in your drawing or to manipulate the different table parts that have already been created.

## The Right-Click Menu

All the other table level editing options are provided via the right-click menu shown in Figure 12-11.

**Figure 12-11**   The table editing right-click menu

The **Table Style** menu item displays a cascade menu with the available table styles in the current drawing so you can change styles.

The **Size Columns Equally** menu item resizes all columns equally.

The **Size Rows Equally** menu item resizes all rows equally.

The **Remove All Property Overrides** menu item will reset the table back to its default format.

The **Export...** menu item allows you to export the table to a comma-delimited file via the **Export Data** file dialog box.

**Note:**
You can also use the **TABLEEXPORT** command to export a table to a comma-delimited file.

The **Table Indicator Color...** menu item allows you to change the color of the row/column indicators in the table editor using the standard AutoCAD **Select Color** dialog box.

The **Update Table Data Links** menu item updates the table with any changes in linked data if applicable.

The **Write Data Links to External Source** menu item writes any table data changes back to any linked source files.

## MODIFYING TABLE CELLS

To modify a table cell, you must click inside the cell with your mouse so the four cell grips display at the midpoints of each cell border line as shown in Figure 12-12.

| | A | B | C | D | E | F |
|---|---|---|---|---|---|---|
| 1 | WINDOW SCHEDULE | | | | | |
| 2 | TAG | TYPE | MANUFACTURER | HEIGHT | WIDTH | COUNT |
| 3 | A | Fixed | ACME Glass Co. | 4'–0" | 4'–0" | 20 |
| 4 | B | Fixed | ACME Glass Co. | 4'–0" | 3'–6" | 4 |
| 5 | C | Fixed | ACME Glass Co. | 3'–0" | 2'–6" | 4 |
| 6 | D | Casement | Glassarama, Inc. | 3'–0" | 2'–0" | 3 |
| 7 | E | Sidelite | Season All Windows | 4'–0" | 1'–0" | 1 |

**Figure 12-12**    Selecting a table cell for editing using grips

You can select multiple cells by clicking and dragging your cursor to create a crossing window over multiple cells. You can also select a range of cells by selecting the first cell and holding down the **<Shift>** key to select the last cell and all the cells in between.

The four cell grips can be used to resize a row or column by selecting the appropriate grip and dragging it to a new location.

The blue diamond in the bottom right corner can be dragged to copy and increment data automatically.

### The Table Ribbon

When you click inside a table cell, the **Table** ribbon shown in Figure 12-13 is displayed.

**Figure 12-13**    The Table ribbon

Using the **Table** ribbon, you can do the following:

- Edit rows and columns
- Merge and unmerge cells
- Alter the appearance of cell borders
- Edit data formatting and alignment
- Lock and unlock cells from editing
- Insert blocks, fields, and formulas
- Create and edit cell styles
- Link the table to external data

## The Right-Click Menu

With a cell selected, you can also right-click and use the options on the shortcut menu shown in Figure 12-14.

The **Cell Style** cascade menu allows you to change the cell style.

The **Alignment** cascade menu allows you to change the cell's text justification using one of the standard multiline text justification options.

The **Borders...** menu item displays the **Cell Border Properties** dialog box shown in Figure 12-15 so you can change the lineweight and/or color of one or more of the cell border lines.

Figure 12-14    The cell editing right-click menu

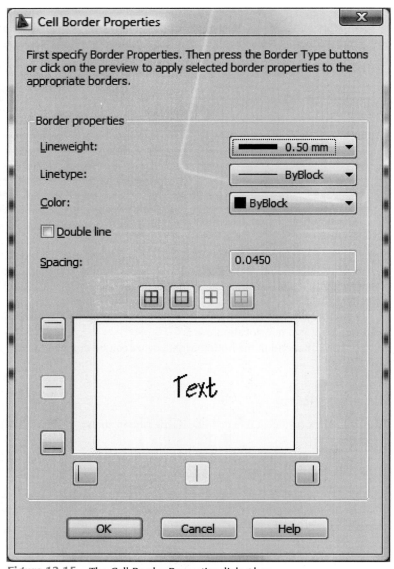

Figure 12-15    The Cell Border Properties dialog box

The **Locking** cascade menu allows you to lock and unlock data cell content and/or data cell formatting. Tables created using data linking or data extraction are automatically locked to prevent inadvertent changes and preserve data integrity.

The **Data Format...** menu item displays the **Table Cell Format** dialog box so that you can change the data type and format for a cell.

The **Match Cell** menu item allows you to copy the selected cell properties to one or more additional cells.

The **Remove All Property Overrides** will remove all property overrides and revert back to the original table style.

The **Data Link...** menu item allows you to create or edit data links using the **Data Link Manager**.

The **Insert** cascade menu allows you to insert the following items into a cell:

- The **Insert Block...** menu item displays the **Insert a Block in a Table Cell** dialog box so you can insert a block in a cell.

- The **Insert Field...** menu item displays the **Field** dialog box so you can insert an automated text field. See the "Text Fields" section in Chapter 11 for complete information about inserting and using fields.

- The **Insert Formula** cascade menu allows you to insert a formula that does calculations using values in other table cells. Inserting formulas is discussed in detail in the next section.

The **Edit Text** menu item displays the table editor and **Multiline Text** ribbon so you can edit the cell text.

The **Delete All Contents** menu item deletes the cell contents.

The **Columns** cascade menu allows you to insert a new column to the left or right of the current cell, delete columns, or size multiple columns equally.

The **Rows** cascade menu allows you to insert a new row above or below the current cell, delete rows, or size multiple rows equally.

The **Merge** cascade menu item allows you to merge two or more cells into one block, row, or column.

The **Unmerge** menu item turns merged cells back into individual cells.

The **Properties** menu item displays the **Properties** palette with the cell properties displayed as shown in Figure 12-16 so you can make any formatting or content changes.

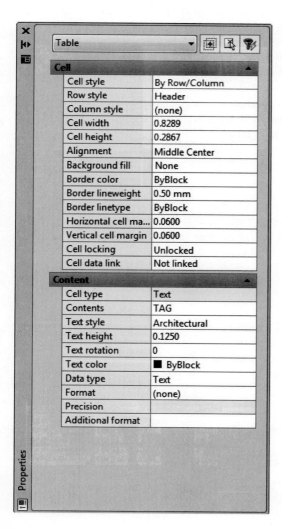

**Figure 12-16**   The Properties palette with a table cell selected

TIP     The **Properties** palette provides you most of the editing features you might need, including access to many of the right-click shortcut menu items above.

## INSERTING FORMULAS

Table cells can contain formulas similar to an accounting spreadsheet program. AutoCAD provides the following spreadsheet type functions:

- **=Sum(A1:A10)**   Sums the values in the first 10 rows in column A
- **=Average(A10:E10)**   Calculates the average of the values in the first five columns in row 10
- **=Count(A1:D100)**   Displays the total number of cells in columns A through D in rows 1 through 100
- **=A1+D1**   Adds the values in A1 and D1
- **=A1−D1**   Subtracts the value in D1 from the value in A1
- **=A1*D1**   Multiplies the values in A1 and D1
- **=A1/D1**   Divides the values in A1 by the value D1
- **=A1^2**   Squares the value in A1. The number after ^ is the exponent.

All formulas must start with an equal sign (=). Formulas perform calculations using the values in other specified table cells by referencing their column letter and row number and/or constant values. The top left cell in a table is referenced using A1. A cell range is referenced using the first and last cells separated by a colon. For example, the range A1:D10 references the cells in rows one through 10 and columns A through D. Merged cells use the letter and number of the top left cell.

When you copy a formula from one cell to another, the range changes to reflect the new location. For example, if the formula in A11 sums A1 through A10, when you copy it to B11, the range changes so that the formula sums B1 through B10.

TIP     You can create an absolute cell address that doesn't change when it is copied by preceding the row and column with a dollar sign ($). For example, if you specify $A$1, the column and row will always stay the same.

You can insert a formula via the cell edit right-click menu shown in Figure 12-14 that was introduced in the last section, select it from the cascade menu shown in Figure 12-17, or you can enter it in manually using the in-place text editor.

### Exercise 12-2: Modifying a Table

1. Continue from Exercise 12-1.
2. Modify the window schedule as shown in Figure 12-18.
3. Save the drawing as **EX12-2.**

**Note:**
The Sum, Average, and Count formulas ignore empty cells and cells that do not contain a numeric value. The other mathematical formulas display pound signs (# # # #) when a formula references empty or nonnumeric data.

| Sum |
| Average |
| Count |
| Cell |
| Equation |

**Figure 12-17**   The Insert Formula cascade menu

| WINDOW SCHEDULE | | | | | | |
|---|---|---|---|---|---|---|
| TAG | TYPE | MANUFACTURER | HEIGHT | WIDTH | SCREEN | COUNT |
| A | Fixed | ACME Glass Co. | 4'–0" | 4'–0" | No | 20 |
| B | Fixed | ACME Glass Co. | 4'–0" | 3'–6" | No | 4 |
| C | Fixed | ACME Glass Co. | 3'–0" | 2'–6" | No | 4 |
| D | Casement | Glassarama, Inc. | 3'–0" | 2'–0" | Yes | 3 |
| E | Sidelite | Season All Windows | 4'–0" | 1'–0" | No | 1 |
| F | Slider | Alumicore | 7'–0" | 8'–0" | Yes | 1 |
| G | Double Hung | Season All Windows | 4'–0" | 3'–0" | Yes | 2 |
| | | | | | TOTAL UNITS | 33 |

**Figure 12-18**   Updated Window schedule

## SUMMARY

Tables can be used for many different purposes ranging from parts lists to door and window schedules. Using AutoCAD, your tables can come alive rather than remain static. You can insert intelligent fields and blocks directly into table cells. Live data can be linked from an Excel spreadsheet. It is even possible to mix and match data types so that some data is static and some is dynamically linked. In Chapter 16, we take it a step further by extracting and linking object data such as block attributes directly to a table. Stay tuned for more!

## CHAPTER TEST QUESTIONS

### Multiple Choice

1. Tables in AutoCAD are created using what type of data:
   a. Object
   b. Static
   c. Linked
   d. All of the above

2. The box at the intersection of a row and column is referred to as:
   a. Field
   b. Square
   c. Cell
   d. A:1

3. The best way to modify a table after it is inserted is by using:
   a. Properties
   b. **Table** ribbon
   c. Grips
   d. All of the above

4. A table's appearance and formatting is typically controlled using:
   a. Text styles
   b. Table styles
   c. Dimension styles
   d. All of the above

5. The current table style can be set using:
   a. **Annotation** panel
   b. **Insert Table** dialog box
   c. **Format** menu
   d. a and b

6. The default table insertion behavior is:
   a. Specifying a window boundary
   b. Picking a point
   c. Entering an absolute coordinate value
   d. b and c

7. To insert data from an Excel spreadsheet and convert it into an AutoCAD table, you can:
   a. Use the **PASTESPEC** command.
   b. Drag-and-drop an XLS file from Windows Explorer
   c. Select **Paste Special...** from the **Edit** pull-down menu
   d. a and c

8. Table cells can contain what type of data:
   a. Text
   b. Fields
   c. Blocks
   d. All of the above

9. The system variable that controls whether the in-place text editor displays column letters and row numbers is:
   a. **TABLECOLS**
   b. **TABLEROWS**
   c. **TABLEDISPLAY**
   d. **TABLEINDICATOR**

10. The **Data Link Manager** allows you to link to what file type:
    a. XLS
    b. CSV
    c. MDB
    d. a and b

11. The different options for starting a new table style include:
    a. Copying an existing table style
    b. Starting from scratch
    c. Picking an existing table in the drawing
    d. a and c

12. The best method to modify and update an existing table in a drawing is to:
    a. Use grips
    b. Rely on right-click menus
    c. Turn on the **Table** ribbon
    d. All of the above

13. All table formulas start with:
    a. Equal sign (=)
    b. Parentheses
    c. F
    d. None of the above

## Matching

**Column A**

a. Table

b. Cell

c. Table styles

d. Cell style

e. **Paste Special**

f. **TABLEINDICATOR**

g. **Data Link Manager**

h. **TABLEEXPORT**

i. **Table** ribbon

**Column B**

1. Controls individual cell characteristics that affect the appearance of cell text and borders

2. System variable that controls the display of column letters and row numbers in the table editor

3. Ribbon used to modify tables

4. Command used to export a table to a comma-delimited file

5. Creates, edits, and manages data links

6. Command used to paste or link Excel data as an AutoCAD table

7. Controls the cell data format, the text and border properties, table direction, and other table formatting options

8. AutoCAD annotation object type that consists of data in rows and columns similar to an accounting spreadsheet

9. The box at the intersection of a table row and column that contains the table data or a formula

## True or False

1. True or False: It is possible to paste a Microsoft Excel spreadsheet into an AutoCAD drawing and automatically convert it into an AutoCAD table that can be either static or dynamic.

2. True or False: You can extract the lengths of all lines on a specified layer to an AutoCAD table that will update when a line changes length.

3. True or False: The best way to resize a table is by using grips.

4. True or False: It is possible to create and apply different cell styles per row so that you can create different formatting for titles, headers, and data.

5. True or False: You can create your own cell style if you want.

6. True or False: Selecting **Paste as Microsoft Excel Worksheet** in the **Paste Special** dialog box will convert the spreadsheet data to an AutoCAD table when inserted.

7. True or False: AutoCAD automatically updates an Excel spreadsheet that was pasted into your AutoCAD drawing.

8. True or False: Linked data cells are indicated by blue corner brackets.

9. True or False: The light blue triangle grip at the bottom center of a table that has grips on will copy data to adjacent cells when you drag it.

10. True or False: It is not possible to unlock and update data that is linked externally in a table.

11. True or False: All formulas must start with an open parenthesis.

12. True or False: The pound (#) symbol will create an absolute cell address.

# CHAPTER PROJECTS

## Project 12-1: Parts List

1. Start a new drawing using the acad.dwt template.
2. Create a table style named **Parts List** with the following settings:
   a. Text font—**Simplex.shx**
   b. Title row text height— **0.25**
   c. Header row text height— **0.125**
   d. Data row text height— **0.125**
   e. Border lineweight = **0.60mm**
3. Create the Parts List table shown in Figure P12-1 using the **TABLE** command.
4. Save the drawing as **P12-1.**

| PARTS LIST | | | |
|---|---|---|---|
| ITEM | PART NUMBER | DESCRIPTION | QUANTITY |
| 1 | 3VD−14602−01−00 | EXHAUST PIPE COMP | 1 |
| 2 | 92906−06600−00 | WASHER | 2 |
| 3 | 90101−06576−00 | BOLT | 2 |
| 4 | 3VD−14613−00−00 | GASKET, EXHAUST PIPE | 2 |
| 5 | 90179−08345−00 | NUT, SPECIAL SHAPE | 4 |
| 6 | 3VD−14710−03−00 | MUFFLER ASSEMBLY | 1 |
| 7 | 3VD−14755−00−00 | GASKET, SILENCER | 1 |
| 8 | 99999−01790−00 | BOLT, FLANGE | 1 |
| 9 | 90201−081H4−00 | WASHER, PLATE | 2 |
| 10 | 91316−08110−00 | BOLT, HEXAGON | 2 |

Figure P12-1

## Project 12-2: Bill of Materials

1. Start a new drawing using the acad.dwt template.
2. Create a table style named **BOM** with the following settings:
   a. Text font—**Romans.shx**
   b. Title row text height—**0.25**
   c. Header row text height—**0.125**
   d. Data row text height—**0.125**
   e. Border lineweight = **0.60mm**
3. Create the Bill of Materials table shown in Figure P12-2 using the **TABLE** command.
4. Save the drawing as **P12-2.**

| BILL OF MATERIALS | | | | | |
|---|---|---|---|---|---|
| PART NUMBER | PART NAME | QUANTITY | DESCRIPTION | MATERIAL | PRICE |
| 30431 | TOP | 1 | 6" X 9" SHEET METAL | STEEL | $3.00 |
| 34572 | BODY | 1 | 12" X 23 SHEET METAL | STEEL | $6.00 |
| 90321 | HANDLES | 2 | C−TYPE | ALUMINUM | $12.00 |
| 36780 | LATCHES | 4 | FRENCH MEDIUM | BRASS | $11.00 |
| 68857 | FEET | 4 | ONE−INCH DIAMETER | RUBBER | $2.00 |
| 25410 | SHELVES | 5 | 5" X 11" SHEET METAL | STEEL | $6.00 |
| 20983 | DIVIDERS | 4 | 3" X 6" SHEET METAL | STEEL | $3.00 |
| 65382 | HINGES | 2 | 2" X 2" | BRASS | $2.00 |
| 76379 | PADDING | 5 | 5" X 11" | RUBBER | $6.00 |
| 98776 | SCREWS | 16 | SHEET METAL SCREWS | STEEL | $2.00 |
| TOTAL NUMBER OF ITEMS | | 44 | | TOTAL COST | $53.00 |

Figure P12-2

## Project 12-3: Residential Architectural Plan—Continued from Chapter 11

1. Open the drawing **P11-7.**
2. Create a table style named **Schedule** with the following settings:
   a. Text font—Romans.shx
   b. Title row text height—12
   c. Header row text height—8
   d. Data row text height—6
   e. Border lineweight = 0.60mm
3. Recreate the door and window schedules created for drawing P11-7 using the **TABLE** command.
4. Save your drawing as **P12-3.**

## Project 12-4: Socket Head Cap Screws—Continued from Chapter 11

1. Open the drawing **P11-9.**
2. Create a table style named **Screws** with the following settings:
   a. Text font—Romans.shx
   b. Title row text height—0.25
   c. Header row text height—0.125
   d. Data row text height—0.125
   e. Border lineweight = 0.60mm
3. Recreate the screw table created for drawing P11-9 using the TABLE command.
4. Save your drawing as **P12-4.12**

# Dimensioning Drawings

## 13

## *Chapter* Objectives

- Control dimension associativity
- Create different types of dimension objects
- Create leader notes
- Create dimensions that match industry standards
- Create and manage dimension styles
- Update dimensions
- Match the settings of an existing dimension style

## INTRODUCTION

Dimensioning drawings can be one of the more challenging aspects of using AutoCAD. Although creating dimension objects is fairly straightforward, controlling their look and behavior can be tricky. This is due to the many different types of dimension objects and the large number of variables that control how they look and behave. How you use dimensions and how they look and behave can also vary greatly depending on your industry (mechanical design, AEC, electronics, etc.). In this chapter, you'll examine how to place dimension objects as well as how to use dimension styles to control their look and behavior.

## DIMENSION TOOLS

The most common dimension tools are located on the dimension flyout menu on the **Annotation** panel on the **Home** ribbon for easy access (see Figure 13-1). These same tools and most of the other dimension tools are located on the **Dimensions** panel on the **Annotate** ribbon (see Figure 13-2).

## TYPES OF DIMENSIONS

There are many types of dimension objects available in AutoCAD. Figure 13-3 shows some examples of the different types of dimension objects as well as some of the features found in a dimension object. The linear, radius, diameter, and angular dimensions are commonly used, but the type of dimensions you create will vary greatly based on your industry and discipline.

## DIMENSION ASSOCIATIVITY

In Chapter 2, you saw briefly how associativity works with dimensioning. Dimension objects are linked to the geometry and update automatically when the geometry changes.

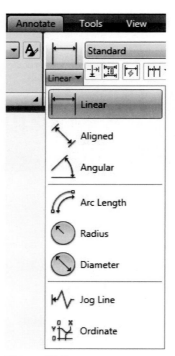

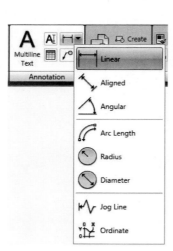

**Figure 13-1**    The Annotation panel on the Home ribbon

**Figure 13-2**    The Dimensions panel on the Annotate ribbon

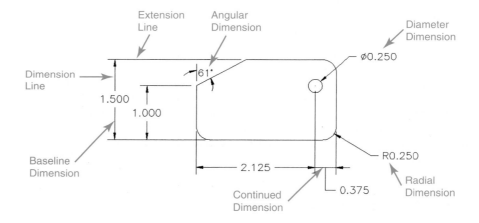

**Figure 13-3**    Types of dimension objects

## Defpoints

When you place dimension objects, you first choose the type of dimension you want to create, and then either pick points or select an object to define the placement of the dimension object. Using either method, AutoCAD automatically creates point objects that define the distance. These defining points are called *defpoints*. AutoCAD measures the distance between these defpoints and uses that distance as the default dimension text. For example, to dimension a line, you create a linear dimension. AutoCAD places defpoints at each end of the line and measures the distance between those defpoints. You then choose a location for the placement of the dimension text.

defpoint: Points created when placing dimensions that define the measurement value of the dimension

**Note:**

The **Defpoints** layer is created when you start a dimensioning command. The **Defpoints** layer is unique in that it doesn't plot, regardless of its plot/noplot layer setting. Also, once created, the **Defpoints** layer cannot be deleted with either the **PURGE** command or the **Delete Layer** button in the **LAYER** command. You can rename the **Defpoints** layer, but AutoCAD will simply create a new **Defpoints** layer when you either create a new dimension object or modify an existing one.

When you create dimensions, AutoCAD automatically creates a layer called **Defpoints**. All defpoints are placed on the **Defpoints** layer.

If your drawing has a **Defpoints** layer, but no dimension objects, and you wish to get rid of the **Defpoints** layer, you can simply rename the layer. Once it is renamed, it will behave like any other layer and can be deleted or purged as needed.

Because it doesn't plot, the **Defpoints** layer is sometimes used to draw objects you don't want to show up on plots. For example, markup notes, viewport boundaries, and notes to other users of the drawing are sometimes placed on the **Defpoints** layer.

There are actually three levels of associativity for a dimension object. The **DIMASSOC** system variable controls which level of dimension associativity AutoCAD uses.

## DIMASSOC System Variable

The **DIMASSOC** system variable can be set to a value of **0, 1,** or **2.** When set to **2** (the default setting), dimension defpoints are associated with objects in the drawing. For example, if you dimension between the two endpoints of a line, AutoCAD will create defpoints at the endpoints of the line, and these defpoints will be associated with the line object. If the line moves, the dimension will move along with it. If an endpoint of the line is moved (stretched, trimmed, extended, etc.), the defpoint associated with that endpoint will move, and the dimension will update.

When **DIMASSOC** is set to **1**, AutoCAD still creates associative dimensions, but the defpoints are not associated with any particular geometry. To update a dimension, you must modify (move or stretch) the defpoints associated with the dimension explicitly. For example, if you dimension a line with **DIMASSOC** set to **1**, AutoCAD will create defpoints at the ends of the line. But if you move the line, the dimension will not follow it. You would have to select and move the dimension along with the line to keep them together. If you move the end of the line (by stretching, trimming, extending, etc.), you will need to move the defpoint located at the end of the line as well in order for the dimension to update.

When **DIMASSOC** is set to **0,** AutoCAD creates exploded dimensions with no associativity. No defpoints are created, and each part of the dimension is created as a separate object (lines and text).

While it's possible to create exploded dimensions, it's considered bad practice in most CAD work environments. Exploded dimensions are difficult to manage and update and can lead to sloppy and inaccurate drawings.

You can toggle the **DIMASSOC** variable with the **Associative Dimensioning** check box in the **User Preferences** tab of the **OPTIONS** command (see Figure 13-4). When this box is checked, **DIMASSOC** is set to **2.** With the check removed, **DIMASSOC** is set to **1.**

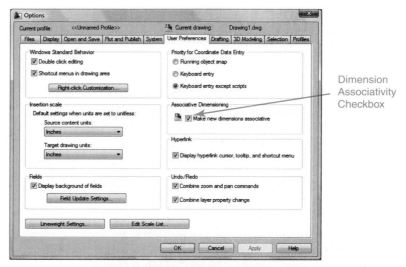

Figure 13-4    The Dimension Associativity check box

| Linear | |
|---|---|
| **Ribbon & Panel:** | Homel Annotation |
| 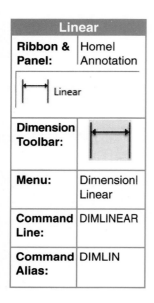 | Linear |
| **Dimension Toolbar:** | |
| **Menu:** | Dimensionl Linear |
| **Command Line:** | DIMLINEAR |
| **Command Alias:** | DIMLIN |

## CREATING HORIZONTAL AND VERTICAL DIMENSIONS

Vertical and horizontal dimensions are created with a single command, **DIMLINEAR.** The **DIMLINEAR** command measures the vertical or horizontal dimension between two definition points and allows you to pick the location of the dimension line.

### Selecting Definition Points

There are two ways to create a linear dimension: pick points or select an object. Using the pick point method, you select any two points in your drawing and then select the location of the dimension text. Where you place the dimension text determines whether a vertical or horizontal dimension is created. If you place the dimension text above or below the points, AutoCAD will create a horizontal dimension. Selecting to the left or right of the selected points will create a vertical dimension (see Figure 13-5).

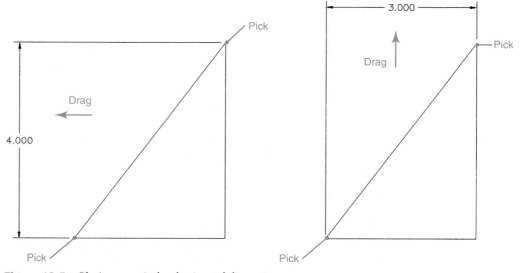

Figure 13-5    Placing a vertical or horizontal dimension

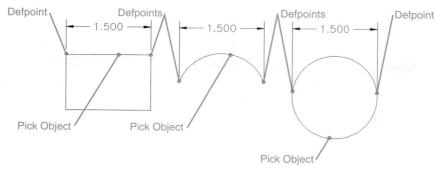

**Figure 13-6**   Linear dimensions on selected objects

## Selecting an Object

You can also create a linear dimension by selecting a line, arc, or circle. When you start the **DIMLINEAR** command, AutoCAD prompts you to *Specify first extension line origin or <select object>:*. Press **<Enter ↵>** to select a line, arc, or circle. When you select an object, AutoCAD will select the two points at the ends of the object as the definition points. Figure 13-6 shows the results of selecting different objects.

## The DIMLINEAR Options

After you select the definition points, AutoCAD provides a number of options for creating and placing the dimensions. These options are listed below.

> **Note:**
> When selecting an object, you can select only line, arc, or circle objects. Ellipses, text points, or spline curves are not allowed. When you select a polyline object, AutoCAD will dimension the line or arc segment of the polyline at the point you selected.

| | |
|---|---|
| **Mtext** | This option allows you to change the default dimension text using the MTEXT text editor. |
| **Text** | The **Text** option allows you to modify the default dimension text at the command prompt. This is similar to the **Mtext** option, except you can place only a single line of text. |
| **Angle** | The **Angle** option allows you to specify the angle of the dimension text. The dimension text will be rotated to the specified angle. |
| **Horizontal** | By default, a horizontal or vertical dimension is placed depending on where you drag your cursor. This option allows you to override the cursor location and explicitly tell AutoCAD to place a horizontal dimension. |
| **Vertical** | This is like the **Horizontal** option, except you explicitly tell AutoCAD to place a vertical dimension. |
| **Rotated** | The **Rotated** option allows you to change the measurement angle of the dimension. For example, specifying an angle of 30 will cause AutoCAD to measure the distance between the two definition points along a 30° angled line (see Figure 13-7). |

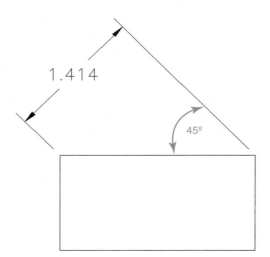

Figure 13-7     Rotated dimension text

### Exercise 13-1: Creating Linear Dimensions

1. Open the drawing **EX13-1** from the Student CD. Make sure Object Snaps are turned on and set to detect **Endpoint** and **Center.**
2. Start the **DIMLINEAR** command. AutoCAD prompts you to *Specify first extension line origin or <select object>:.*
3. Pick the endpoint P1 shown in Figure 13-8. AutoCAD prompts you to *Specify second extension line origin:.*
4. Pick the endpoint P2 shown in Figure 13-8. AutoCAD prompts you to *Specify dimension line location or* ↓ and starts dragging the dimension line.
5. Place the dimension line as shown in Figure 13-9. AutoCAD places the dimension and ends the **DIMLINEAR** command.

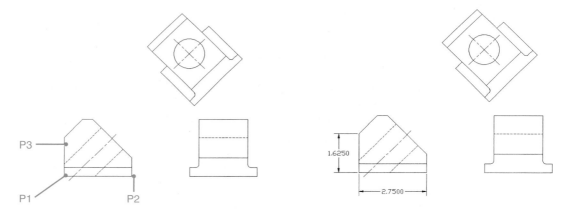

Figure 13-8     Selecting the definition points                    Figure 13-9     Linear dimensions

6. Restart the **DIMLINEAR** command. AutoCAD prompts you to *Specify first extension line origin or <select object>:.*
7. Press **<Enter ↵>**. AutoCAD prompts you to *Select object to dimension.*
8. Pick the line at P3 shown in Figure 13-8. AutoCAD places the defpoints at the ends of the line and prompts you to *Specify dimension line location or* ↓.
9. Place the dimension line as shown in Figure 13-9. AutoCAD places the dimension and ends the **DIMLINEAR** command.
10. Save your drawing as **EX13-1a.** Your drawing should look like Figure 13-9.

*Overriding Dimension Text.*    The **DIMLINEAR** command has two text options: **Mtext** and **Text.** These options allow you to override the default text associated with the dimension. By default, AutoCAD places the numerical distance between the two definition points as the dimension text. By using the **Mtext** and **Text** options, you can modify or even override the measured distance. For example, you may want to include a note or other additional text along with the default dimension, or you may want to type in a specific dimension instead of using the measured dimension value.

*The <> Brackets.*    When you use the **Mtext** option, AutoCAD displays the multiline text editor with the default dimension text highlighted (see Figure 13-10). The default dimension text is the measured distance between the definition points. You can type any text before or after the default dimension text or you can delete it, but you cannot modify the value of the highlighted text. If you remove the default text, AutoCAD will ignore the measured distance and display only the text you specify.

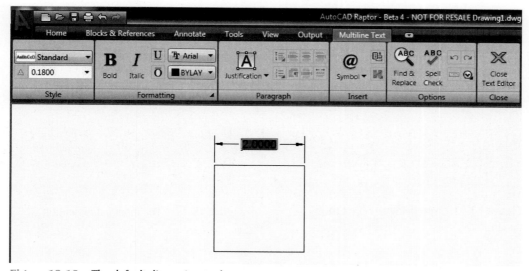

Figure 13-10    The default dimension tool

If you delete the default dimension text, you can re-create it by typing <>. When AutoCAD sees the <> brackets, it will replace it with the measured distance between the definition points.

You can use the <> brackets with the **Text** option as well. When using the **Text** option, AutoCAD will display the measured dimension as a default and allow you to type a single line of text. You can type whatever text you want, using the <> brackets as a placeholder for the measured distance between the definition points.

You can also use the **DDEDIT** command to edit dimension text.

**Exercise 13-2:** Modifying Dimension Text

1. Continue from Exercise 13-1.
2. Start the **DIMLINEAR** command. AutoCAD prompts you to *Specify first extension line origin or <select object>:.*
3. Press **<Enter ↵>**. AutoCAD prompts you to *Select object to dimension.*
4. Pick the line at **P1** shown in Figure 13-11. AutoCAD places the defpoints at the ends of the line and prompts you to *Specify dimension line location or* ↓ .

5. Choose the **Mtext** option. AutoCAD displays the multiline text editor with the default dimension text highlighted. Delete the default dimension text and type **1.00** in the mtext editor. Close the mtext editor. AutoCAD shows the dimension as 1.00.

6. Select the line you just dimensioned to activate its grips. Select the grip at one endpoint and drag it to a new location. Pick anywhere on the screen to place the end of the line. AutoCAD stretches the line and the dimension moves along with it, but the value of the dimension text does not update.

7. Start the **DDEDIT** command and select the 1.00 dimension text. Delete the 1.00 text and type <>. AutoCAD replaces the <> brackets with the measured length of the line.

8. Select the line to activate its grips and return the endpoint to its original location. AutoCAD stretches the line, and the dimension moves with it. The dimension text updates to show the change.

9. Save your drawing as **EX13-2.** Your drawing should look like Figure 13-12.

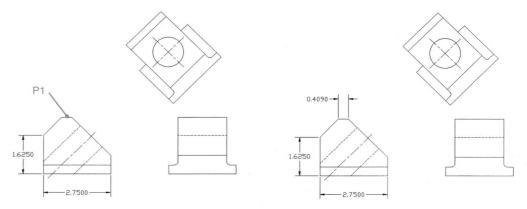

**Figure 13-11**   Specifying an object to dimension

**Figure 13-12**   The modified dimension

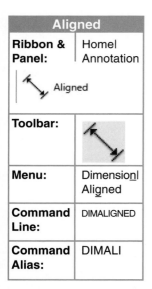

| Aligned | |
|---|---|
| **Ribbon & Panel:** | Home| Annotation |
| Aligned | |
| **Toolbar:** | |
| **Menu:** | Dimension| Aligned |
| **Command Line:** | DIMALIGNED |
| **Command Alias:** | DIMALI |

## CREATING ALIGNED DIMENSIONS

An aligned dimension is another type of linear dimension. However, while horizontal and vertical dimensions measure distances along either the *X*- or *Y*-axis, respectively, an aligned dimension measures the true distance between any two points. The dimension text is placed parallel to a line between the two points (see Figure 13-13). Aligned dimensions are created with the **DIMALIGNED** command.

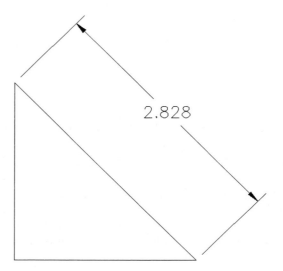

**Figure 13-13**   An aligned dimension

When using the **DIMALIGNED** command, you can select the two definition points, or you can select a line, arc, or circle. Once you specify the definition points, the **Mtext, Text,** and **Angle** options are available. These options are identical to the **Mtext, Text,** and **Angle** options in the **DIMLINEAR** command.

## Exercise 13-3: Creating Aligned Dimensions

1. Continue from Exercise 13-2.
2. Start the **DIMALIGNED** command. AutoCAD prompts you to *Specify first extension line origin or <select object>:*.
3. Press **<Enter ↵>**. AutoCAD prompts you to *Select object to dimension*.
4. Pick the line at P1 shown in Figure 13-14. AutoCAD places the defpoints at the ends of the line and prompts you to *Specify dimension line location or ↓*.
5. Place the dimension line as shown in Figure 13-14.
6. Save your drawing as **EX13-3.** Your drawing should look like Figure 13-14.

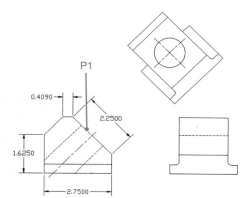

**Figure 13-14**    An aligned dimension

**TIP** You can also select the extension line origin points to define the angle of the aligned dimension. Typically. you would rely on Object Snaps to snap to endpoints or intersections.

## DIMENSIONING CIRCLES AND ARCS

When dimensioning circles and arcs, you will typically be calling out either radius or diameter dimensions, or in the case of arcs, the length of an arc segment. AutoCAD provides a dimensioning command for each of these types of dimensions.

### Radius Dimension

Radius dimensions are placed with the **DIMRADIUS** command. When you select this command, AutoCAD will prompt you to select an arc or circle. You can select circles, arcs, and polyline arc segments. Once you select an arc or circle, AutoCAD measures the radius of the arc and prompts you for the location of the text. You can place the text inside or outside the arc. AutoCAD will place a leader line perpendicular to the arc through the specified point on the arc and put a center mark in the center of the circle or arc. When you place the text, AutoCAD will automatically place an **R** prefix before the measured radius (see Figure 13-15). Like the **DIMLINEAR** and **DIMALIGNED** commands, you have the **Mtext, Text,** and **Angle** options for modifying the dimension text.

| Radius | |
|---|---|
| **Ribbon & Panel:** | Home\| Annotation |
| | Radius |
| **Dimension Toolbar:** | |
| **Menu:** | Dimension\| Radius |
| **Command Line:** | DIMRADIUS |
| **Command Alias:** | DIMRAD |

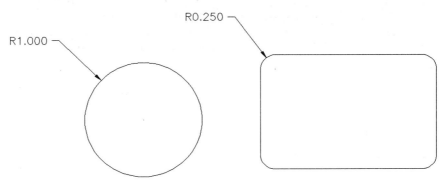

Figure 13-15    The radius prefix

| Jogged | |
|---|---|
| **Ribbon & Panel:** | None |
| **Dimension Toolbar:** | 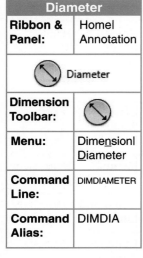 |
| **Menu:** | Dime<u>n</u>sionl <u>J</u>ogged |
| **Command Line:** | DIMJOGGED |
| **Command Alias:** | JOG |

## Creating a Jogged Radius Dimension

With the **DIMRADIUS** command, the leader line will always point perpendicular to the circle or arc segment. The start point of the leader will always be in line with the center point of the arc (see Figure 13-16). A jogged radius dimension is similar to a regular radius dimension except the leader line has an offset jog built into it. This allows you to specify a different center point for the leader. This can be useful when dimensioning large radii in which the center point lies outside of your drawing area. Jogged radius dimensions are created with the **DIMJOGGED** command.

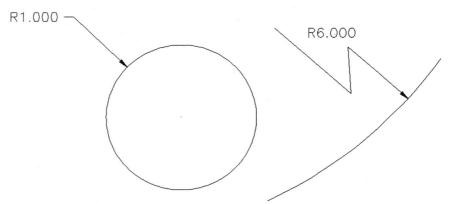

Figure 13-16    A radial and jogged dimension

When you start the **DIMJOGGED** command, you are prompted to select a circle or arc. Once you select an object, AutoCAD prompts you to *Specify center location override:*. This is the location of the starting point (nonarrow end) of the leader line. The leader line is drawn from this point to a point on the circle or arc segment. You are then prompted for the location of the dimension text. Once you place the text, you can adjust the location of the jogged segment (see Figure 13-17).

## Diameter Dimension

Diameter dimensions are placed with the **DIMDIAMETER** command. The **DIMDIAMETER** command behaves just like the **DIMRADIUS** command. The only difference is that text shown is the diameter of the arc or circle, and AutoCAD places the diameter symbol Ø in front of the text.

| Diameter | |
|---|---|
| **Ribbon & Panel:** | Homel Annotation |
| | Diameter |
| **Dimension Toolbar:** | Diameter |
| **Menu:** | Dime<u>n</u>sionl <u>D</u>iameter |
| **Command Line:** | DIMDIAMETER |
| **Command Alias:** | DIMDIA |

**TIP**    It is possible to dimension an arc beyond its endpoints. AutoCAD automatically creates an arc extension line.

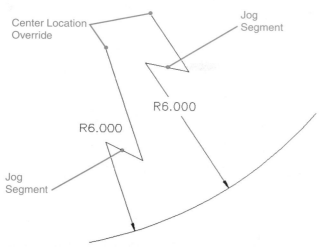

**Figure 13-17**   The jogged segment

**Figure 13-18**   Radial and diameter dimensions

## Exercise 13-4: Creating Radius and Diameter Dimensions

1. Continue from Exercise 13-3.
2. Start the **DIMRADIUS** command. AutoCAD prompts you to *Select arc or circle:*.
3. Pick the arc at P1 shown in Figure 13-18. AutoCAD places the defpoints at the center of the arc and at the point you selected on the arc. You are then prompted to *Specify dimension line location or ↓*.
4. Choose the **Mtext** option and type **TYP.** after the default dimension text. Close the mtext editor.
5. Place the dimension line as shown in Figure 13-18.
6. Start the **DIMDIAMETER** command. AutoCAD prompts you to *Select arc or circle:*.
7. Pick the circle at P2 shown in Figure 13-18. AutoCAD places the defpoints at the center of the arc and at the point you selected on the circle. You are then prompted to *Specify dimension line location or ↓*.
8. Place the dimension line as shown in Figure 13-18.
9. Save your drawing as **EX13-4.** Your drawing should look like Figure 13-18.

## Dimensioning the Length of an Arc

Similar to a linear dimension, AutoCAD can dimension the length of an arc using the **DIMARC** command. When using the **DIMARC** command, you select an arc segment, and AutoCAD measures the distance along the arc. By default, AutoCAD will dimension the entire length of the arc from endpoint to endpoint, but you can also opt to dimension a portion of the arc length. In addition to the **Mtext, Text,** and **Angle** options, the **Partial** option allows you to pick a start and end point along the arc segment and dimension only the portion of the arc between the two points.

When you place an arc length dimension, AutoCAD automatically places the arc symbol ∩ in front of the dimension value (see Figure 13-19).

| Arc Length | |
|---|---|
| **Ribbon & Panel:** | Homel Annotation <br> Arc Length |
| **Dimension Toolbar:** | |
| **Menu:** | Dimensionl Arc Length |
| **Command Line:** | DIMARC |
| **Command Alias:** | None |

## Exercise 13-5: Creating an Arc Length Dimension

1. Open the drawing EX13-5 from the Student CD.
2. Start the **DIMARC** command. AutoCAD prompts you to *Select arc or polyline arc segment:*.
3. Pick the arc at P1 shown in Figure 13-20. AutoCAD places the defpoints at the center of the arc and at the point you selected on the arc. You are then prompted to *Specify dimension line location or ↓*.
4. Place the dimension line as shown in Figure 13-20.
5. Start the **DIMRADIUS** command. AutoCAD prompts you to *Select arc or circle:*.
6. Pick the arc at P2 shown in Figure 13-18. You are prompted to *Specify arc length dimension location or ↓*.

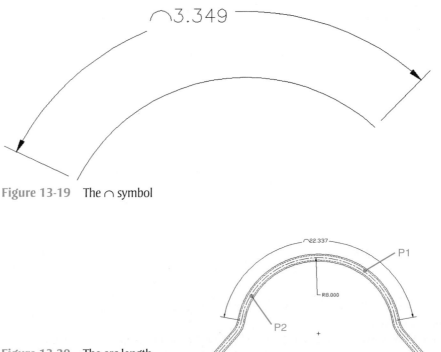

**Figure 13-19** The ∩ symbol

**Figure 13-20** The arc length dimension

7. Place the dimension line as shown in Figure 13-20.
8. Save your drawing as **EX13-5.** Your drawing should look like Figure 13-20.

## Creating Center Marks

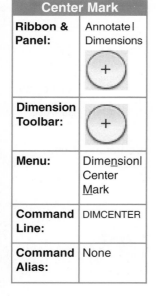

| Center Mark | |
|---|---|
| **Ribbon & Panel:** | Annotate\| Dimensions ⊕ |
| **Dimension Toolbar:** | ⊕ |
| **Menu:** | Dimension\| Center Mark |
| **Command Line:** | DIMCENTER |
| **Command Alias:** | None |

When dimensioning arcs and circles, AutoCAD places marks at the center of the dimensions (see Figure 13-21). You may have a need to place center marks on arcs and circles that are not dimensioned. AutoCAD has a number of ways to create center marks. One option is to simply draw center marks using either the **LINE** or **PLINE** commands. Another way is to use the **DIMCENTER** command.

The **DIMCENTER** command places orthogonal line segments at the center of a circle or arc segment. When you start the **DIMCENTER** command, AutoCAD prompts you to select a circle or an arc segment and then places center mark line segments.

> **Note:**
> When using the **DIMCENTER** command, the resulting lines are not dimension objects but simply line segments.

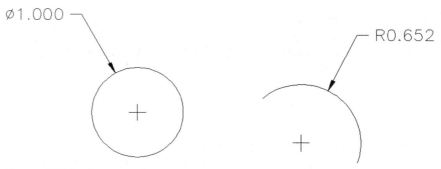

**Figure 13-21** Center marks

| FOR MORE DETAILS | The **DIMCEN** system variable controls the size of center marks. Dimension variables are typically controlled through dimension styles, which are covered later in this chapter. For more information on the **DIMCEN** system variable, see Appendix D. |
|---|---|

## ANGULAR DIMENSIONS

With linear dimensions, AutoCAD needs to have two definition points in order to calculate the dimension value. With radius and diameter dimensions, AutoCAD can calculate the dimension value directly from the arcs and circles. When dimensioning angles, AutoCAD needs to know three points in order to define the angular dimension: a center vertex and two endpoints (see Figure 13-22). Angular dimensions are placed with the **DIMANGULAR** command. When using this command, you have three options for defining angular dimension: selecting an arc or circle, selecting two intersecting lines, or picking three points to define the vertex and the two endpoints.

| Angular | |
|---|---|
| **Ribbon & Panel:** | Home\| Annotation \| Angular |
| **Dimension Toolbar:** | |
| **Pull-down Menu:** | Dimension\| Angular |
| **Command Line:** | DIMANGULAR |
| **Command Alias:** | DIMANG |

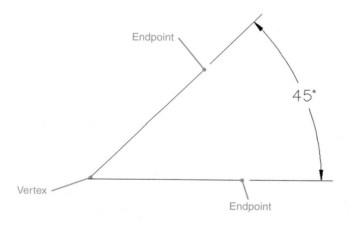

**Figure 13-22**    Angular dimension defpoints

### Selecting Objects

When you start the **DIMANGULAR** command, AutoCAD prompts you to *Select arc, circle, line, or <specify vertex>*. If you select an arc, AutoCAD uses the center and ends of the arc to determine the angular dimensions.

If you select a circle, AutoCAD uses the selection point as one endpoint of the angle and the center of the circle as the vertex. AutoCAD then prompts you for a second endpoint and allows you to place the dimension text.

If you select a line segment, AutoCAD will ask you to select another line segment and will dimension the angle between endpoints of the first and second lines. AutoCAD will use the endpoints closest to the selection point of the line. Figure 13-23 shows the results of selecting two lines at various points.

### Selecting Vertex and Angle Endpoints

To specify the vertex and angle endpoints, press **<Enter ↵>** when AutoCAD prompts you to *Select arc, circle, line, or <specify vertex>*. AutoCAD will prompt you for a vertex point and then prompt you for two endpoints.

### The Quadrant Option

The **Quadrant** option allows you to place dimension text outside of the angle being measured. The only way to access the **Quadrant** option is from the right-click menu after selecting the angle to measure when AutoCAD prompts you: *Specify dimension arc line location or ↓*.

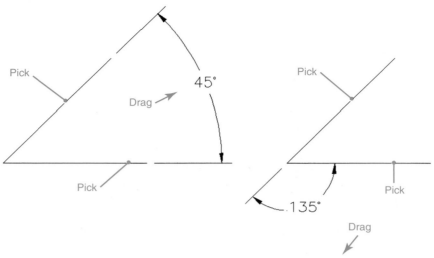

**Figure 13-23**    Specifying angular defpoints

The **Quadrant** option prompts you to specify the quadrant that you want to dimension separate from specifying the dimension arc line location. If the dimension arc line is outside of the quadrant that is being measured, AutoCAD automatically creates an arc extension line using the current extension line settings.

**Exercise 13-6:** Creating an Angular Dimension

1. Continue from Exercise 13-5.
2. Start the **DIMANGULAR** command. AutoCAD prompts you to *Select arc, circle, line, or <specify vertex>*.
3. Pick the line at P1 shown in Figure 13-24. AutoCAD prompts you to *Select second line:*.
4. Pick the line at P2 shown in Figure 13-24. AutoCAD prompts you to *Specify dimension arc line location or ↓*.
5. Place the dimension line as shown in Figure 13-24. Notice that the angle that is dimensioned varies with your cursor location.
6. Save your drawing as **EX13-6**. Your drawing should look like Figure 13-24.

> **Note:**
> If you select two parallel lines, AutoCAD will show you the message "Lines are parallel" in the **Command Window** and end the command. If you select anything but a line segment for the second line, AutoCAD will display the message "Object selected is not a line" in the **Command Window** and prompt you to "Select second line."

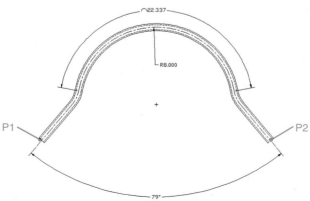

**Figure 13-24**    An angled dimension

# CREATING DATUM AND CHAIN DIMENSIONS

Datum and chain dimensioning refers to linear dimensions that share common extension lines. A datum dimension is also known as a baseline dimension, in which multiple features are measured from a common feature. Chain dimensions are also known as continued dimensions, in which linear dimensions continue end-to-end. Figure 13-25 shows examples of baseline and continued dimensions.

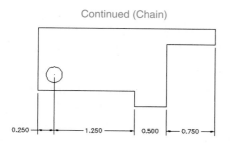 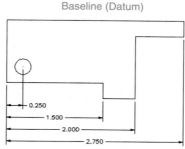

**Figure 13-25**    Continued and baseline dimensions

## Continued Dimension

A continued dimension is similar to a baseline dimension. It requires an existing linear or angular dimension, and it allows you to place multiple dimension lines in a single command. The only difference is that while baseline dimensions measure dimensions from a common extension line, continued dimensions measure from the last placed dimension line. The result is a chain of dimensions, each one measured from the last. Continued (or chain) dimensions are created with the **DIMCONTINUE** command.

When you start the **DIMCONTINUE** command, AutoCAD will place the dimension line at the second extension line of the last linear or angular dimension placed in the drawing. If you want to continue the dimension from dimension, you can press <**Enter ↵**> to select a different extension line. Like the **DIMBASELINE** command, the **DIMCONTINUE** command will repeat until you end the command. You also have the **Undo** and **Select** options to undo the last continued dimension or to select a different extension line to continue from.

## Baseline Dimension

Baseline dimensions are measured from an extension line of an existing linear or angular dimension. When you place a baseline dimension, each dimension is measured from this extension line, and the dimension lines are spaced at a predefined distance. Baseline dimensions are created with the **DIMBASELINE** command.

| | Continue | |
|---|---|---|
| **Ribbon & Panel:** | Annotate \| Dimensions | |
| | Continue | |
| **Dimension Toolbar:** | | |
| **Menu:** | Dimension \| Continue | |
| **Command Line:** | DIMCONTINUE | |
| **Command Alias:** | DIMCONT | |

| | Baseline | |
|---|---|---|
| **Ribbon & Panel:** | Annotate \| Dimensions | |
| | Baseline | |
| **Dimension Toolbar:** | | |
| **Menu:** | Dimension \| Baseline | |
| **Command Line:** | DIMBASELINE | |
| **Command Alias:** | DIMBASE | |

**FOR MORE DETAILS** The **DIMDLI** system variable controls the spacing of the baseline dimension lines. Dimension variables are typically controlled through dimension styles, which are covered later in this chapter. For more information on the **DIMDLI** system variable, see Appendix D.

The **DIMBASELINE** command requires an existing linear or angular dimension. By default, AutoCAD will use the first extension line of the last linear or angular dimension as the baseline. If you want to use a different extension line, you can press <**Enter ↵**> to select a different extension line. If AutoCAD cannot locate or determine where the last dimension line is, it will prompt you to select an extension line to use for the baseline.

Once you've specified the extension line to use as the baseline, AutoCAD prompts you to pick a definition point for the next extension line. The **DIMBASELINE** command will continue to place baseline dimensions until you end the command. While placing baseline dimensions, you can use the **Undo** option to undo a dimension line placement or press **<Enter ↵>** to select a different extension baseline.

**Exercise 13-7:** Creating Chain and Baseline Dimensions

1. Open the drawing **EX13-7** from the Student CD.
2. Start the **DIMLINEAR** command and place the horizontal dimension between P1 and P2 as shown in Figure 13-26.
3. Start the **DIMCONTINUE** command. AutoCAD starts dragging a dimension from the previous dimension. You are prompted to *Specify a second extension line origin or ↓*.
4. Place the dimensions P3 and P4 as shown in Figure 13-26. Press **<Esc>** to exit the **DIMCONTINUE** command.
5. Start the **DIMBASELINE** command. AutoCAD starts dragging a dimension from the previous dimension. You are prompted to *Specify a second extension line origin or ↓*.
6. Press **<Enter ↵>** to choose the **Select** option. AutoCAD prompts you to *Select base dimension:*.
7. Choose the extension line at P1 shown in Figure 13-27. AutoCAD prompts you to *Specify a second extension line origin or ↓*.
8. Select the end of the line shown at point P2 shown in Figure 13-27. AutoCAD automatically spaces the dimension above the selected dimension.
9. Save your drawing as **EX13-7a**. Your drawing should look like Figure 13-27.

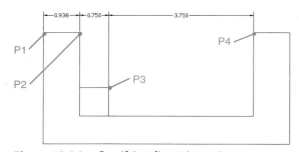

**Figure 13-26**    Specifying dimension points

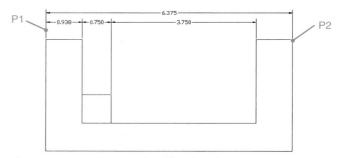

**Figure 13-27**    Continued and baseline dimensions

| Adjust Space | |
|---|---|
| **Ribbon & Panel:** | AnnotateI Dimensions |
| **Dimension Toolbar:** | |
| **Menu:** | DimensionI Dimension Space |
| **Command Line:** | DIMSPACE |
| **Command Alias:** | None |

## DIMENSION TOOLS

AutoCAD provides a few handy dimension tools that allow you to automate tasks that used to be much more time-consuming. There are tools to evenly space stacked dimensions and to break dimension lines and extension lines that cross other dimensions, as well as the ability to create jog lines in linear dimensions when a distance is too long to fit on the specified sheet size.

### The Adjust Space Tool

The **Adjust Space** tool allows you to evenly space selected dimensions as shown in Figure 13-28. You can specify the spacing distance between dimension lines or let AutoCAD automatically determine a minimum spacing distance.

When you select the **Adjust Space** tool, AutoCAD prompts you to *Select the base dimension:* so that you can select the first dimension in the stack. After selecting a base dimension, AutoCAD then prompts you to *Select dimensions to space:*. Select the dimensions you want to space and either enter a distance or press **<Enter ↵>** to select the **Auto** option. The **Auto** option automatically spaces the dimensions based on the current dimension text height.

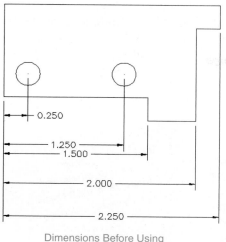 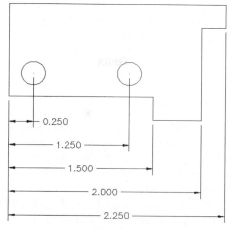

Dimensions Before Using
Adjust Space Tool

Dimensions After Using
Adjust Space Tool

**Figure 13-28**    The Adjust Space tool

## The Break Tool

The **Break** tool allows you to break dimension or extension lines where they intersect other dimensions or objects in your drawing as shown in Figure 13-29.

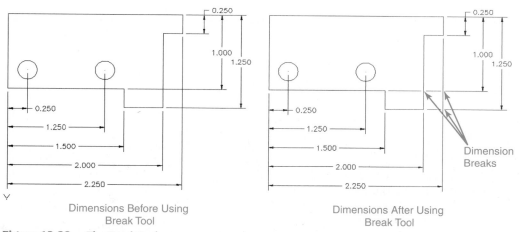

Dimensions Before Using
Break Tool

Dimensions After Using
Break Tool

Dimension
Breaks

**Figure 13-29**    The Break tool

| Break | |
|---|---|
| **Ribbon & Panel:** | Annotate\| Dimensions |
| **Dimension Toolbar:** | |
| **Menu:** | Dimension\| Dimension Break |
| **Command Line:** | DIMBREAK |
| **Command Alias:** | None |

When you select the **Break** tool, AutoCAD prompts you to *Select dimension to add/remove break or* ↓ so that you can select the dimension. After selecting the dimension, you have four options:

- Select intersecting objects to use as cutting edges for the break. AutoCAD prompts for objects until you press <**Enter** ↵>.
- Use the **Auto** option to automatically trim around all intersecting objects
- Use the **Manual** option so that you have to manually pick break points
- Use the **Remove** option to remove all the breaks from selected dimensions or leaders

**Note:**
When you break a dimension by either selecting objects or by using the **Auto** option, the breaks will automatically update when the intersection point moves. If the objects are moved so that they no longer intersect, the break will disappear; if they are moved back, the break will automatically return to the original location.

**TIP**    You can break more than one dimension at a time by selecting the **Multiple** option after the **Break** tool.

| Jog Line | |
|---|---|
| **Ribbon & Panel:** | Home\|Annotation |
| | ⩘  Jog Line |
| **Dimension Toolbar:** | ⩘ |
| **Menu:** | Dimension\|Jogged Linear |
| **Command Line:** | DIMJOGLINE |
| **Command Alias:** | None |

### The Jog Line Tool

The **Jog Line** tool allows you to add a jog, or breakline, to linear dimensions to represent measurements whose values are not the same length as the dimension line. Jogged dimension lines are typically used when a sheet is too small to display the true length of a dimension line as shown in Figure 13-30.

When you select the **Jog Line** tool, AutoCAD prompts you to *Select dimension to add jog or* ↓ so that you can select the dimension to add the jog. After selecting a dimension, AutoCAD then prompts you to *Specify jog location (or press Enter):*. You can either pick the location on the dimension line to locate the jog line or press **<Enter ↵>** to place the jog line automatically based on the direction of the dimension definition points. The jog line is created closest to the first dimension definition point.

**Note:** The linear jog size can be specified on the **Symbols and Arrows** tab of the **Dimension Style** dialog box explained later.

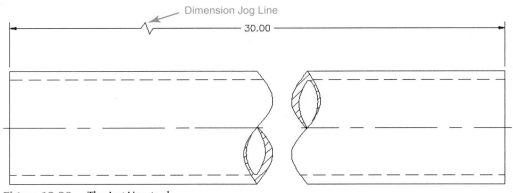

Dimension Jog Line — 30.00

**Figure 13-30**    The Jog Line tool

| Quick Dimension | |
|---|---|
| **Ribbon & Panel:** | Annotate\|Dimensions |
| | ⤴ |
| **Dimension Toolbar:** | ⤴ |
| **Menu:** | Dimension\|Quick Dimension |
| **Command Line:** | QDIM |
| **Command Alias:** | None |

**TIP**    You can change the jog location using grips. You can turn off a jog line or edit its height using the **Properties** palette.

## QUICK DIMENSIONING

When creating dimension objects, you may find that placing dimensions can be a somewhat tedious, repetitive process. Many times you may wish to simply place some dimensions on the drawing and then go back and adjust their placement and orientation to suit your drawing. AutoCAD helps automate the process of placing dimensions by allowing you to create multiple dimensions at once. The **QDIM** command (quick dimension) allows you to select multiple objects and then select a type of dimension to place. AutoCAD will then automatically detect definition points and place the specified dimensions based on those points.

## Quick Dimension

When you start the **QDIM** command, AutoCAD will prompt you to *Select geometry to dimension:*. Once you have built your selection set of objects, press **<Enter ↵>**, and AutoCAD will provide a number of options. These options are described below.

*Continuous.*    The **Continuous** option places continuous dimensions from the outermost points of the selected geometry. When you select this option, AutoCAD will place the dimension objects and allow you to select a placement point for the dimensions. The dimensions will either be vertical or horizontal based on where you drag your cursor.

*Staggered.*    The **Staggered** option places a series of staggered or nested linear dimensions, starting from the innermost pair of definition points. From there, it will place a linear dimension on the next outer level of points and continue outward until the geometry is dimensioned. Figure 13-31 shows some examples of staggered dimensions placed with the **QDIM** command.

*datumPoint.*    The **datumPoint** option sets a base point for the **Baseline** and **Ordinate** dimension options. By default, when you use the **Baseline** option, it places the datum or base point of the dimensions on the definition point nearest to 0,0. The **datumPoint** option allows you to override this and place the datum point at any point in the drawing.

*Baseline.*    The **Baseline** option creates a series of baseline dimensions starting at either 0,0, or at the point specified with the **datumPoint** option. Figure 13-32 shows you some examples of baseline dimensions.

*Ordinate.*    Ordinate dimensioning displays *X*- and *Y*-datum coordinates based on an origin, or datum point. The datum point is typically located at a key point on the geometry such as the corner of a part. The **Ordinate** option of the **QDIM** command creates a set of ordinate dimensions with the origin being either 0,0 or a point specified with the **datumPoint** option.

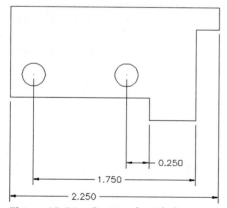

**Figure 13-31**    Staggered quick dimensions

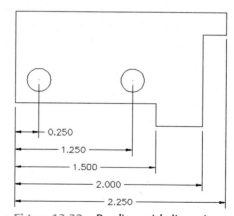

**Figure 13-32**    Baseline quick dimensions

Ordinate dimensions can also be created with the **DIMORDINATE** command. However, the **DIMORDINATE** command does not allow you to set a 0,0 datum point. To use the **DIMORDINATE** command, you must first establish a User Coordinate System (UCS) with its origin located at your desired datum point, which is beyond the scope of this book. Using the **QDIM** command with the **datumPoint** and **Ordinate** options is a much quicker way of creating ordinate dimensions.

*Radius.*   The **Radius** option will search through your selection of objects and find any circles or arcs. You are then prompted for a location for the leaders. The leaders are placed in the same relative position on each arc or circle. Figure 13-33 shows an example of using the **Radius** option.

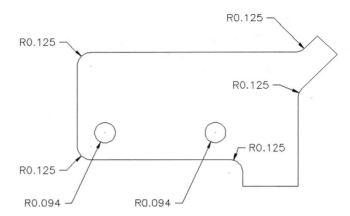

**Figure 13-33**   Radius quick dimensions

*Diameter.*   The **Diameter** option works the same way as the **Radius** option. AutoCAD places diameter dimensions at the same relative points on each arc or circle.

*Edit.*   The **Edit** option allows you to edit the definition points within the selection set. When you choose this option, AutoCAD will show you all the definition points found in the selection set. You can add or delete definition points prior to placing your dimensions.

*seTtings.*   The **seTtings** option allows you to set the preference for determining definition points. By default, AutoCAD will look for endpoints of objects. You can set it to **Intersection** or **Endpoint.**

### Exercise 13-8: Creating Quick Dimensions

1. Open the drawing **EX13-8** from the Student CD.
2. Start the **QDIM** command. AutoCAD prompts you to *Select geometry to dimension:*.
3. Type **ALL<Enter ↵>** to select all the geometry in the drawing. AutoCAD prompts you to *Specify dimension line position or ↓.*
4. Choose the **datumPoint** option and pick the endpoint P1 shown in Figure 13-34. AutoCAD prompts you to *Specify dimension line position or ↓.*

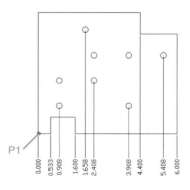

**Figure 13-34**   Selecting a datum point

5. Choose the **Ordinate** option. AutoCAD prompts you to *Specify dimension line position, or ↓.*
6. Place the *X*-datum dimensions as shown in Figure 13-35. AutoCAD prompts you to *Specify dimension line position, or ↓.*

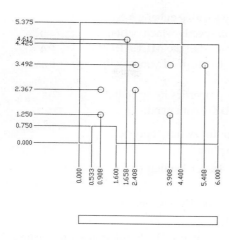

**Figure 13-35**    Ordinate quick dimensions

7. Restart the **QDIM** command. AutoCAD defaults to the **Ordinate** option. Place the *Y*-datum dimensions shown in Figure 13-35.
8. Save your drawing as **EX13-8a**. Your drawing should look like Figure 13-35.

# CREATING LEADERS

Leaders are used for a variety of items when annotating a drawing, such as manufacturing notes, detail bubbles, etc. In general, a leader consists of an end symbol (arrow head, dot, circle, etc.), a leader line (either curved or straight), and a callout (mtext, block, tolerance, etc.). Figure 13-36 shows some different examples of leaders. Leaders are created with the **MLEADER** command.

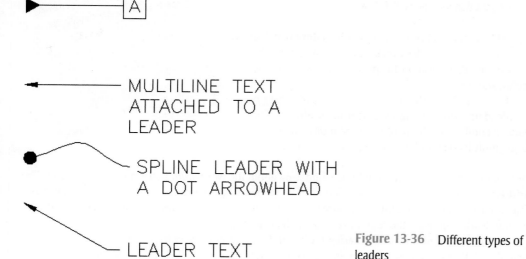

**Figure 13-36**    Different types of leaders

| Multileader | |
|---|---|
| **Ribbon & Panel:** | Homel Annotation |
| | ⊙ Multileader |
| **Multileader Toolbar:** | ⊙ |
| **Menu:** | Dimensionl Multileader |
| **Command Line:** | MLEADERA |
| **Command Alias:** | MLA |

## The Multileader Tool

By default, when you start the **MLEADER** command, AutoCAD prompts you to *Specify leader arrowhead location or* ↓ so that you first select the arrowhead location. AutoCAD then prompts you to *Specify leader landing location or* ↓. Picking a point creates the landing, or tail of the leader, and puts you in the multiline text editor so you can begin adding text.

It is possible to create a leader by locating either the arrow-head, the landing, or text first. You can specify which option to use via the command options when you start the **MLEADER** command or via a right-click menu. The method you specify remains in effect for subsequent leaders.

You can change the multileader properties by selecting **Options** when you start the **MLEADER** command:

- **Leader type**   Allows you to switch between straight line segments and a spline.
- **Leader landing**   Turns the leader landing (tail) on or off.
- **Content type**   Allows you to specify whether to use text, a block, or nothing.
- **Maxpoints**   The maximum number of pick points used to create a leader. Default value is two points.
- **First angle**   Allows you to constrain the angle of the first line to a specific angle increment.
- **Second angle**   Allows you to constrain the angle of the second line to a specific angle increment.

You must use the **Exit** option to exit the **Options** settings and begin drawing leaders.

**Note:** AutoCAD's **MLEADER** command replaces the **QLEADER** command, which created Auto-CAD quick leaders. It is still possible to create quick leaders by entering **QLEADER** or **LE** at the keyboard.

| FOR MORE DETAILS | See the next section in this chapter for more on creating geometric dimension and tolerance callouts. See Chapter 16 for more on creating and using blocks. |
|---|---|

After you create a leader, the easiest way to edit it is by using grips. Grips can be used to relocate the arrowhead location and resize a leader tail by selecting special arrow grips. Leaders are associative just like dimensions; that is, if you move the text, the leader line will follow.

**Note:** The **MLEADEREDIT** command can also be used to add and remove leader lines. The command alias is **MLE**.

*The Multileaders Panel.*   The **Mulitleaders** panel shown in Figure 13-37 provides quick access to all the commands and options discussed so far plus some additional useful multileader tools.

Using the **Multileaders** panel, you can create new multileaders, add and remove leader lines, align multiple leaders, combine multiple block–type multileaders into a single multileader, and manage multileader styles.

*The Add Leader Tool.*   You might be wondering about the word *multi* in the multileader name. The **Add Leader** tool allows you to add one or more leaders and arrowheads to an existing multileader object so that it points to multiple features. All the additional leader lines remain associated with the original leader so that if the text moves, so do the leader lines.

When you select the **Add Leader** tool, AutoCAD prompts you to *Specify leader arrowhead location:* so that you can select as many arrowhead locations as needed. You must press <**Enter ↵**> to end command.

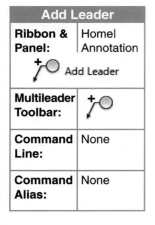

| Add Leader | |
|---|---|
| **Ribbon & Panel:** | Home\| Annotation\| Add Leader |
| **Multileader Toolbar:** | |
| **Command Line:** | None |
| **Command Alias:** | None |

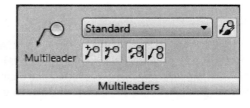

**Figure 13-37**   The Multileaders panel

*The Remove Leader Tool.*    The **Remove Leader** tool allows you to remove one or more leaders from an existing multileader.

When you select the **Remove Leader** tool, AutoCAD prompts you to *Select a multileader:* so you can select the multileader to update. AutoCAD then prompt you to *Specify leaders to remove:* so that you can continue to remove leaders until you press <**Enter** ↵> to end the command.

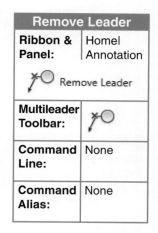

| Remove Leader | |
|---|---|
| **Ribbon & Panel:** | Homel Annotation |
| | Remove Leader |
| **Multileader Toolbar:** | |
| **Command Line:** | None |
| **Command Alias:** | None |

 It is also possible to add and remove multileaders by selecting the multileader and right-clicking to display the shortcut menu in Figure 13-38.

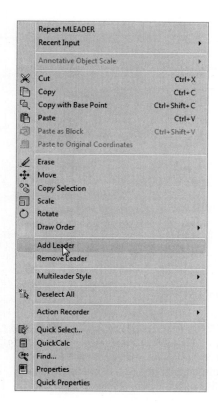

| Repeat MLEADER |
|---|
| Recent Input ▸ |
| Annotative Object Scale ▸ |
| Cut                Ctrl+X |
| Copy               Ctrl+C |
| Copy with Base Point    Ctrl+Shift+C |
| Paste              Ctrl+V |
| Paste as Block     Ctrl+Shift+V |
| Paste to Original Coordinates |
| Erase |
| Move |
| Copy Selection |
| Scale |
| Rotate |
| Draw Order ▸ |
| Add Leader |
| Remove Leader |
| Multileader Style ▸ |
| Deselect All |
| Action Recorder ▸ |
| Quick Select... |
| QuickCalc |
| Find... |
| Properties |
| Quick Properties |

**Figure 13-38**    The Multileader right-click menu

*The Multileader Align Tool.*    The **Multileader Align** tool allows you to quickly align a group of leaders along a line that you specify as shown in Figure 13-39.

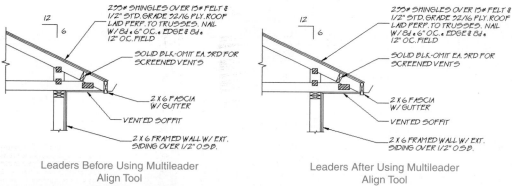

Leaders Before Using Multileader Align Tool

Leaders After Using Multileader Align Tool

**Figure 13-39**    The Multileader Align tool

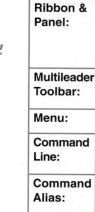

| Align | |
|---|---|
| **Ribbon & Panel:** | Homel Annotation |
| | Align |
| **Multileader Toolbar:** | |
| **Menu:** | None |
| **Command Line:** | MLEADERALIGN |
| **Command Alias:** | MLA |

You can control the leader spacing by selecting **Options** when you start the **Multileader Align** tool:

- **Distribute**    Distributes leaders evenly (default)
- **Make leader segments Parallel**    Makes angle portion of leader lines parallel
- **Specify Spacing**    Allows you to specify the spacing distance
- Use current spacing

***The Multileader Collect Tool.***    The **Multileader Collect** tool allows you to collect and combine multiple blocks so that they are attached to one landing line as shown in Figure 13-40.

Using the **Multileader Collect** tool, blocks can be collected horizontally, vertically, or within a user-defined area.

| Collect | |
|---|---|
| **Ribbon & Panel:** | Homel Annotation  Collect |
| **Multileader Toolbar:** | |
| **Menu:** | None |
| **Command Line:** | MLEADERCOLLECT |
| **Command Alias:** | MLC |

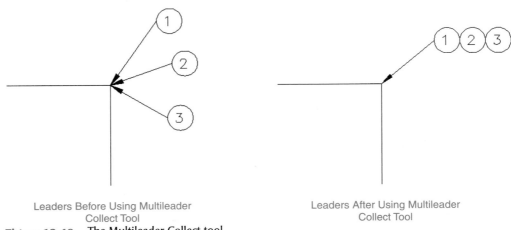

Leaders Before Using Multileader Collect Tool

Leaders After Using Multileader Collect Tool

**Figure 13-40**    The Multileader Collect tool

**FOR MORE DETAILS**    See Chapter 16 for more on creating and using blocks.

***Multileader Style.***    The **Multileader Style Manager** shown in Figure 13-41 allows you to control the multileader format and display options using a multileader style in a similar fashion to text styles, table styles, and dimension styles which are explained later in this chapter.

The **Leader Format** tab allows you to specify the type of leader line to use (straight or spline), control general properties (color, linetype, and lineweight), as well as specify the arrowhead type and size. The **Leader break** setting determines the break size for the selected multileader when the **DIMBREAK** command is used.

| Multileader Style | |
|---|---|
| **Ribbon & Panel:** | Homel Annotation |
| **Multileader Toolbar:** | |
| **Menu:** | None |
| **Command Line:** | MLEADERSTYLES |
| **Command Alias:** | MLS |

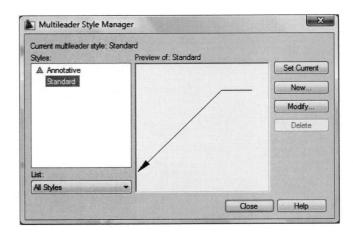

**Figure 13-41**    The Multileader Style Manager

The **Leader Structure** tab allows you to control constraints such as the maximum number of points and the first and second segment angles. You can also turn the landing (tail) on and off, as well as specify its length. The **Scale** area allows you to take advantage of **Annotative** scaling, use the layout viewport scale, or specify the scale explicitly so text and arrows are created the correct size.

The **Content** tab allows you to indicate whether to use text, blocks, or nothing when creating leaders using the **Multileader type** drop-down list. If you are using text, the **Text options** and **Leader connection** areas are enabled so that you can control default text, text style, angle, color, and height. The **Leader connection** area allows you to control where the text is attached vertically and specify the gap distance between the end of the landing and the beginning of the text.

> **Note:**
> AutoCAD provides a number of predefined annotation blocks that allow you to quickly create detail callouts, circles, boxes, and other standard items that include attribute information. See Chapter 16 for more information about blocks and attributes.

If you specify a block as the **Multileader type,** the **Text options** and **Leader connection** areas change to **Block options** so that you can specify a block name, where the block will be attached and its color.

When possible, you should try to use multileader styles to control the appearance of multiline leaders in your drawings.

**TIP**    The **Properties** palette also provides access to all the multileader settings discussed in this section for easy updating after a multileader is created.

**Exercise 13-9:** Creating a Leader

1. Continue from Exercise 13-8.
2. Display the **Multileader Style Manager** dialog box. Select the **Modify** button and on the **Leader Format** tab, set the **Arrowhead** to **Dot.** Choose **OK** to save the change and close the **Multiline Style Manager** dialog box by selecting **Close.**
3. Start the **MLEADER** command. AutoCAD prompts you to *Specify leader arrowhead location or ↓*.
4. Pick the points P1 and P2 shown in Figure 13-42 and press <**Enter ↵**> to end the point placement. AutoCAD starts the multiline text editor.
5. Type **SEE NOTE 1** and select **OK** or click anywhere outside the multiline text editor to end the **MLEADER** command.
6. Save your drawing as **EX13-9.** Your drawing should look like Figure 13-42.

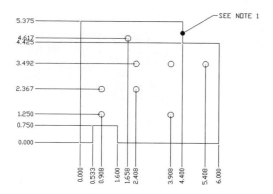

**Figure 13-42**    Creating a leader

## CREATING GEOMETRIC DIMENSION AND TOLERANCE SYMBOLS (GD&T)

Geometric dimensioning and tolerancing (GD&T) is a method of specifying geometry requirements in mechanical engineering drawings. GD&T callouts use a series of symbols and numbers to convey specifications for mechanical parts and assemblies. Figure 13-43 shows an example of a GD&T callout (also called a *feature control frame*). GD&T is used primarily in mechanical design environments such as automotive, aerospace, electronic, and other manufacturing industries.

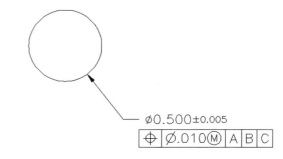

Figure 13-43    A feature control frame

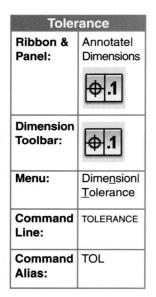

| Tolerance | |
|---|---|
| **Ribbon & Panel:** | Annotate‖ Dimensions |
| **Dimension Toolbar:** | |
| **Menu:** | Dimension‖ Tolerance |
| **Command Line:** | TOLERANCE |
| **Command Alias:** | TOL |

GD&T symbols denote acceptable variations in form, profile, orientation, location, and runout of a feature. You add GD&T callout symbols in feature control frames. These frames contain all the tolerance information for a single dimension. In AutoCAD, GD&T control feature frames are created with either the **LEADER** or **TOLERANCE** command. The **LEADER** command creates GD&T callouts with a leader attached to them, while the **TOLERANCE** command creates callouts without leaders.

> **FOR MORE DETAILS**    Geometric tolerancing is covered by ASME Y14.5M—1994, which supercedes ANSI Y14.5M—1982. See Appendix A for more on drafting standards.

When you create a GD&T callout, AutoCAD displays the **Geometric Tolerance** dialog box (see Figure 13-44). With this dialog box, you can construct GD&T callouts. To construct a callout, work from left to right to specify the symbols and tolerance values that apply to the feature you are dimensioning. When you select the **Sym** box, AutoCAD displays the **Symbol** dialog box (see Figure 13-45).

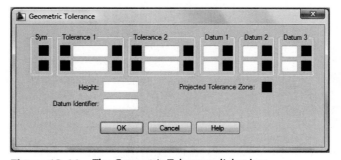

Figure 13-44    The Geometric Tolerance dialog box

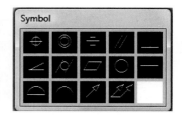

Figure 13-45    The Symbol dialog box

### GDT Font

The GDT font used in the **TOLERANCE** command, as well as other mechanical callout symbols, can be found in the GDT.SHX font file. The GDT.SHX font uses geometric symbols for the lowercase letters a–z, and the capital roman simplex letters for the uppercase letters A–Z. The symbols used in the GDT.SHX font are shown in Figure 13-46 along with their corresponding keystroke.

| GDT.SHX Characters | |
|---|---|
| a | ∠ |
| b | ⊥ |
| c | ▱ |
| d | ⌒ |
| e | ◯ |
| f | ∥ |
| g | ⌀ |
| h | ↗ |
| i | ⩶ |
| j | ⊕ |
| k | ⌓ |
| l | Ⓛ |
| m | Ⓜ |
| n | ⌀ |
| o | ▢ |
| p | Ⓟ |
| q | ₵ |
| r | ◎ |
| s | Ⓢ |
| t | ⟋⟋ |
| u | — |
| v | ⊔ |
| w | ⌄ |
| x | ⏉ |
| y | ▷ |
| z | ◁ |
| ' | ± |

**Figure 13-46**   The GDT.SHX font characters

## INSPECTION DIMENSIONS

Inspection dimensions allow you to communicate how often manufactured parts should be checked to ensure that the tolerances of a part stay within the range specified in the dimension value. This is done using an inspection label, dimension value, and inspection rate as shown in Figure 13-47.

The dimension value is the value of the dimension before the inspection dimension is added. It can contain tolerances, text, and the measured value. The label and inspection rate fields are added using the **Inspection** tool explained below.

The **DIMINSPECT** command allows you to add or remove inspection dimensions and control their appearance including the shape, label, and inspection rate via the **Inspection Dimension** dialog box shown in Figure 13-48.

The **Shape** area allows you to control the type of inspection dimension shape used. You can switch between angular, round, or none.

**Note:**
You can add inspection dimensions to any type of dimension.

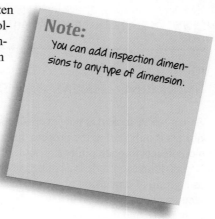

| Inspect | |
|---|---|
| **Ribbon & Panel:** | Annotate\|Dimensions |
| **Dimension Toolbar:** | |
| **Menu:** | Dimension\|Inspection |
| **Command Line:** | DIMINSPECT |
| **Command Alias:** | None |

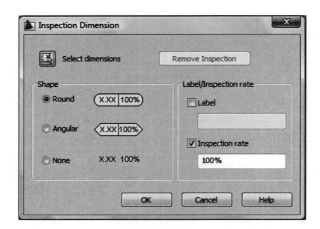

**Figure 13-47**     Inspection
dimension

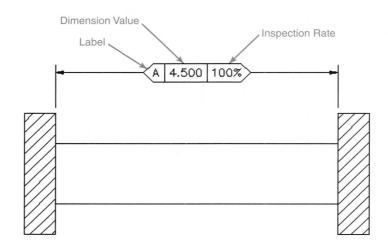

**Figure 13-48**     Inspection
dimension dialog Box

The **Label** check box allows you to add a text label to the inspection dimensions. The label is located on the far left of the inspection dimension as shown in Figure 13-47.

The **Inspection Rate** check box allows you to indicate the frequency that the dimension should be inspected and is typically expressed as a percentage. The inspection rate is located on the far right of the inspection dimension as shown in Figure 13-47.

| Dimension Style | |
|---|---|
| **Ribbon & Panel:** | Home\| Annotation |
| **Dimension Toolbar:** | |
| **Menu:** | Dimension\| Dimension Style… |
| **Command Line:** | DIMSTYLE |
| **Command Alias:** | DDIM |

TIP    You can change the shape, label, and inspection rate of an inspection dimension after it is created using the **Properties** palette under the **Miscellaneous** category.

## MANAGING DIMENSION STYLES

So far, we've looked at how to create and place dimension objects. Creating and placing dimension objects is only part of the process. In this section, you'll examine how to control the look of dimension objects through dimension styles.

A dimension style is a collection of dimension settings that are assigned a name and are applied as a group to dimension objects. Dimension styles control the look and behavior of dimension objects, such as the type of arrowhead used, the text style used in the dimensions, tolerance values and formatting, and the overall scale of the dimension.

Dimension styles work similarly to text styles or layers: you set a dimension style current and then any new objects are created using the settings contained within that style. Dimension styles are managed with the **DIMSTYLE** command.

When you start the **DIMSTYLE** command, AutoCAD displays the **Dimension Style Manager** dialog box (see Figure 13-49). From this dialog box, you can create dimension styles, modify dimension styles, compare dimension styles, and set a dimension style current. The **Styles** list shows dimension styles defined in your drawing. The **List** options allow you to control which dimension styles are shown in the **Styles** list. You can choose to show all dimension styles or only the ones currently used in the drawing. You can also choose to show or hide dimension styles contained in referenced drawings.

---

**FOR MORE DETAILS**   See Chapter 17 for more on referencing drawings.

---

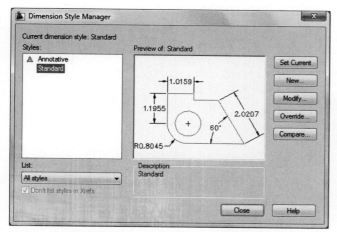

**Figure 13-49**   The Dimension Style Manager dialog box

**Figure 13-50**   Create New Dimension Style dialog box

The **Preview** area shows a preview image of the current dimension style and tells you which dimension style is current. The buttons along the right-hand side of the dialog box allow you to create, modify, override, and compare dimension styles.

## Creating a Dimension Style

AutoCAD comes with two predefined dimension styles: **Annotative** and **Standard. Standard** is AutoCAD's default dimension style. Both can be modified, renamed, or even deleted if one is not the current style. The settings for the dimension styles are defined in the template file used to create the drawing. To create a new dimension style, choose the **New...** button. AutoCAD will display the **Create New Dimension Style** dialog box (see Figure 13-50).

When you create a new dimension style, AutoCAD will create a copy of an existing dimension style as the starting point. In the **Create New Dimension Style** dialog box, you specify the name for the new dimension style and tell AutoCAD which style to copy as the starting point. You can also create a dimension style that applies only to a certain type of dimension. For example, you might want all your dimension text to align with the dimension line, except for radial and diameter dimensions, where you might want the text to be horizontal. These styles are known as *child dimension styles* and appear as a substyle of the parent dimension style.

**TIP**   When you select a child dimension style in the **Dimension Style Manager** dialog box, the **Preview** area shows you only the dimension settings that are different from the parent style, and the **Description** area lists the differences between the parent and child dimension styles.

**Exercise 13-10:** Creating a New Dimension Style

1. Continue from Exercise 13-9.
2. Start the **DIMSTYLE** command. AutoCAD displays the **Dimension Style Manager** dialog box. Choose **New...** to display the **Create New Dimension Style** dialog box.
3. Type **Mech** in the **New Style Name** box and make sure the **Start With** box is set to **Standard** and the **Use for** box is set to **All Dimensions**. Choose **Continue** to create the new dimension style. AutoCAD displays **New Dimension Style** dialog box.
4. Choose **OK** to accept the dimension style settings. AutoCAD returns you to the **Dimension Style Manager** dialog box. The new dimension style is listed in the **Styles** list. Choose the **Close** button to end the **DIMSTYLE** command.
5. Start the **DIMLINEAR** command and place the dimension shown at P1 in Figure 13-51.
6. Save your drawing as **EX13-10**.

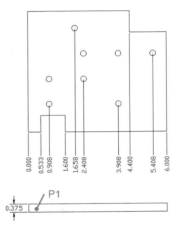

**Figure 13-51**    Creating a new dimension style

## Modifying an Existing Dimension Style

To modify a dimension style, select the style name from the **Dimension Style Manager** and choose the **Modify** button. This will display the **Modify Dimension Style** dialog box (see Figure 13-52). This dialog box is divided into seven different tabs that contain the settings for various aspects of your dimensions. These tabs are described in the following sections.

*Lines Settings.*    The **Lines** tab (see Figure 13-52) controls the dimension and extension lines within a dimension object. Figure 13-53 shows how these various settings map to dimension objects. The **Dimension Lines** area allows you to set the **Color, Linetype,** and **Lineweight** of the dimension lines as well as the spacing between dimension lines when creating baseline dimensions. The **Extend beyond ticks** setting is available only when certain types of arrowheads are specified. For example, when an architectural tick is used, the **Extend beyond ticks** setting controls how far past the tick to extend the dimension line. You can suppress the dimension line on either side of the text. This comes in handy when dimensioning in tight areas where the dimension lines tend to obscure dimension text.

The **Extension lines** area has similar controls for extension lines. You can set the **Color, Linetype,** and **Lineweight** of the extension lines as well as control the length of the extension line and the gap between the extension line and the object you are dimensioning.

Checking the **Fixed Length** check box will create extension lines that are all the same length specified in the **Length:** box regardless of their origin point locations. The fixed length is calculated using the distance from the second extension line origin point (second pick point) to the dimension line location point (third pick point) minus the distance specified in the **Offset from origin:** box.

*Symbols and Arrows.*    The **Symbols and Arrows** tab (see Figure 13-54) allows you to set the size and type of arrowheads used in dimensions. You can set different arrowheads for the first and second dimension lines as well as a separate arrowhead for leaders. The **Center marks** area

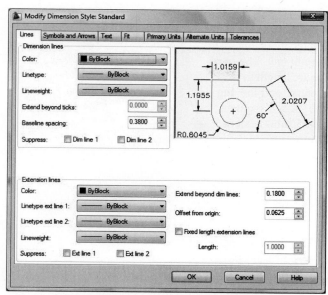

Figure 13-52    Modify Dimension Style dialog box

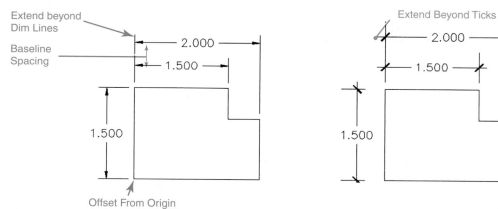

Figure 13-53    Dimension line settings

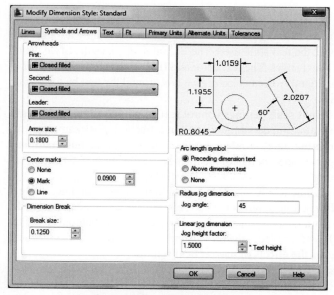

Figure 13-54    The Symbols and Arrows tab

allows you to set the size and type of center marks. This affects how center marks are shown in radial and diameter dimensions and also controls how center mark lines are created with the **DIMCENTER** command. The **Arc length symbol** area controls where the arc length symbol is displayed with the **DIMARC** command, and the **Jog angle** setting controls the angle of the jogged segment in the **DIMJOG** command. Figure 13-55 shows examples of settings in the **Symbols and Arrows** tab.

The **Jog height factor** setting controls the height of the jog created by the **Jogged Linear** tool explained earlier.

**Note:**
The **Leader:** arrowhead setting is used only by the old style **QLEADER** command. Use the **Multileader Style Manager** introduced earlier to control the arrowhead for the default leader type.

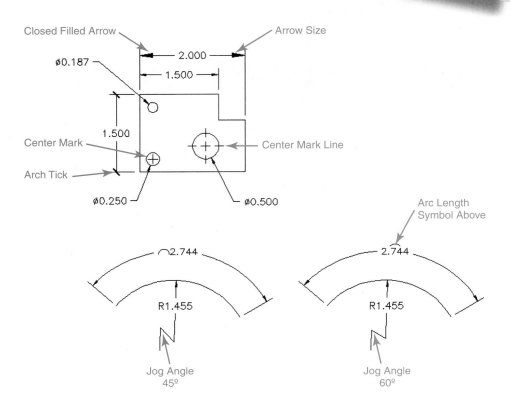

**Figure 13-55**  Symbols and Arrows settings

*Text Settings.*    The **Text** tab (see Figure 13-56) controls how text is placed and how it looks. The **Text appearance** area allows you to set the text style used. The **...** button displays the **Style** dialog box to allow you to create and modify text styles. The text color and fill buttons control the color of the text and the color of the text background. You can also draw a box around the text by turning on the **Draw frame around text** option.

The **Text height** and **Fraction height scale** settings control text height. The **Fraction height scale** is a scale factor applied to numerator and denominator text in a fraction. For example, if the **Text height** is set to .125 and the **Fraction height scale** is set to .5, the size of the numerator and denominator would be .0625, making the overall height of the fraction .125. Figure 13-57 shows examples of the **Text appearance** settings.

The **Text placement** area controls how text is placed in regard to the dimension lines and extension lines. The **Offset from dim line** setting controls the gap between the dimension line and the dimension text. The **Vertical** setting allows you to place the text above, below, or centered on the dimension line. You can also choose **JIS**, which places the dimension text to conform to the Japanese Industrial Standard. Figure 13-58 shows the effects of the **Vertical** setting.

The **Horizontal** setting controls where the text is placed in reference to the extension lines. You can place the text near the first or second extension line, or have the text drawn over the first or second extension line. Figure 13-59 shows the effects of the **Horizontal** setting.

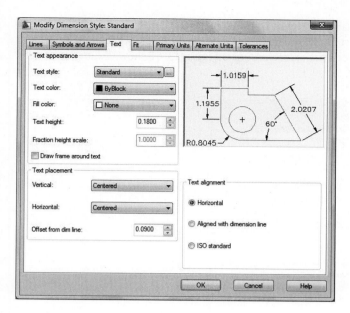

**Figure 13-56**    The Text tab

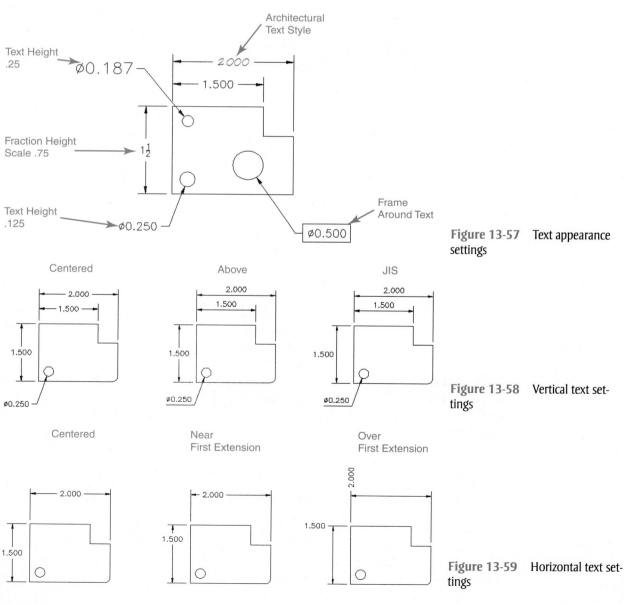

**Figure 13-57**    Text appearance settings

**Figure 13-58**    Vertical text settings

**Figure 13-59**    Horizontal text settings

*Fit and Scale Settings.*          The **Fit** tab (see Figure 13-60) controls the behavior and scale of dimension objects. The **Fit** options control how dimensions behave when AutoCAD cannot place both the dimension lines and text between the extension lines. Figure 13-61 shows examples of each of these settings.

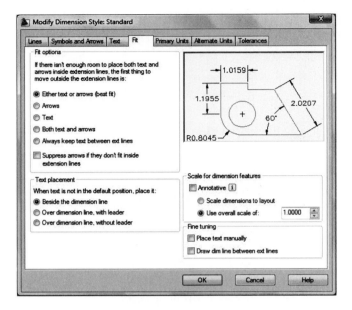

**Figure 13-60**    The Fit tab

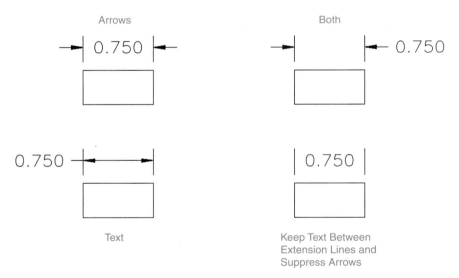

**Figure 13-61**    Fit settings

The **Text placement** area controls where text is placed when it is not in its default position. You can choose to have AutoCAD move the text beside the dimension line (outside the extension line), over the dimension line with a leader line running between the text and the dimension line, or over the dimension line without a leader. Figure 13-62 shows the effect of each of these options.

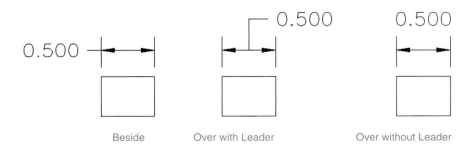

**Figure 13-62**    Text placement settings

Chapter 1 discussed annotation scale factors. For example, if you have a drawing plotted at a scale of 1/8″ = 1-0″, you need to scale all of your model space annotation by a factor of 96. This ensures that as the drawing is scaled down for plotting, the annotation appears at the correct size. The **Scale for dimension features** area controls the overall annotation scale of dimension objects.

The **Annotative** scale setting utilizes the AutoCAD **Annotation Scale** feature located on the right side of the Status Bar so that dimension features are scaled automatically when dimensions are added to your drawing. This setting will also add different scaled dimension features if you are using the **Annotation Scale** feature that automatically adds annotative scale objects.

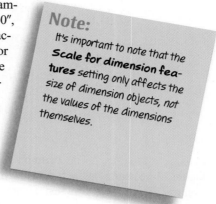

**Note:**
It's important to note that the **Scale for dimension features** setting only affects the size of dimension objects, not the values of the dimensions themselves.

> **FOR MORE DETAILS**  See Chapter 1 for a detailed description of the **Annotation Scale** feature.

The **Scale dimensions to layout** setting will automatically scale all your dimension features to match the scale of the layout viewport. This feature requires that you add dimensions through the paper space viewport so that AutoCAD knows what scale you are currently using.

> **FOR MORE DETAILS**  See Chapter 14 for a detailed description of using paper space layouts and the different scale options for annotation features.

The **Use overall scale of** setting is a manual scale factor that is applied to all dimension features. For example, if your text and arrowheads are set to a height of **.125** and the overall scale is set to **2**, AutoCAD will draw your text and arrowheads at a size of **.25**. Figure 13-63 shows an example of setting the overall dimension scale factor.

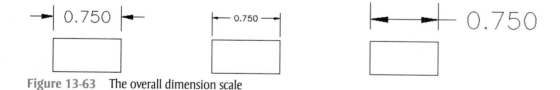

**Figure 13-63**    The overall dimension scale

> **FOR MORE DETAILS**  See Chapter 14 for more on how to place and scale dimensions in paper space.

The **Fine tuning** area gives you some additional options for controlling the look of your dimension. When turned on, the **Place text manually** box adds an additional prompt when creating dimensions, which allows you to specify a location for the dimension text after you locate the dimension line.

The **Draw dim line between ext lines** option will force a dimension line to be placed between the extension lines, regardless of the location of the dimension text. Figure 13-64 shows some examples of turning on this option.

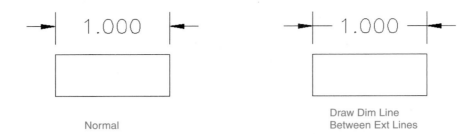

**Figure 13-64**   Draw dim line between ext lines options

Normal

Draw Dim Line
Between Ext Lines

*Primary Units Tab.*   The **Primary Units** tab (see Figure 13-65) controls the formatting of the dimension text. The **Linear dimensions** area allows you to control how units are displayed; the **Angular dimensions** area controls the display of angular dimensions. The options are listed next.

*Unit Format.*   This option sets the units format for all dimension types except Angular. This is typically set to match the units of your drawing. In addition to the standard AutoCAD unit settings, you can also choose the **Windows Desktop** units, which use the settings contained in the **Regional and Language Options** in the Windows **Control Panel** (see Figure 13-66).

In the **Angular dimensions** area, the **Units format** list allows you to control how angular dimensions are displayed. You can choose from **Decimal Degrees, Degrees Minutes Seconds, Gradians**, or **Radian** units.

**Note:**
Dimensions can be placed in either model space or layout (paper) space in AutoCAD. The decision of where to place dimensions (model or paper space) can be a hotly debated topic in the AutoCAD world. Regardless of how dimensioning is handled, the important thing is to maintain consistency among drawings for any given project. Your company's CAD standards should provide clear guidelines for how dimensioning should be handled and where dimensions should be placed.

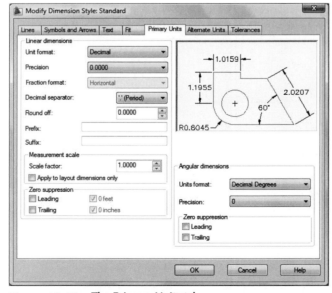

**Figure 13-65**   The Primary Units tab

**Figure 13-66**   Windows Regional and Language Options dialog box

*Precision.*   This option controls the number of decimal places in the dimension text. This setting controls only how the dimension text is displayed; it does not change the drawing geometry or affect the actual measured value of the dimension. There are two settings: one for linear dimensions and one for angular dimensions. Figure 13-67 shows some examples of this setting.

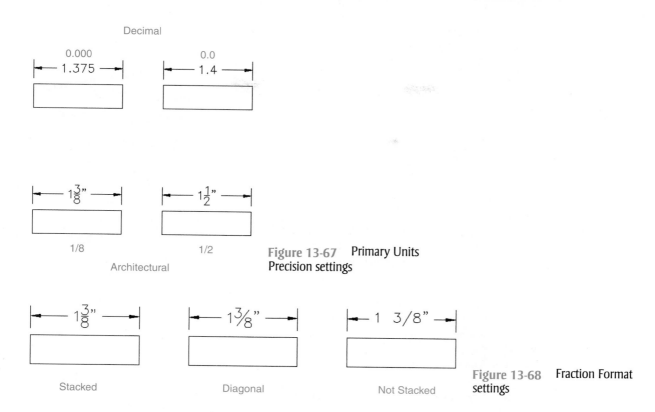

**Figure 13-67**  Primary Units Precision settings

**Figure 13-68**  Fraction Format settings

***Fraction Format.***  This controls how fractions are displayed. This option is available only when the **Unit Format** is set to either **Architectural** or **Fractional**. This format is used in conjunction with the **Fractional height scale** in the **Text** tab. Figure 13-68 shows examples of these settings.

***Decimal Separator.***  When the **Unit format** is set to **Decimal**, this option sets the character used for the decimal separator.

***Round Off.***  This option sets the rounding rules for all dimension types except Angular. If you enter a value of **0.25,** all distances are rounded to the nearest 0.25 unit. If you enter a value of **1.0,** all dimension distances are rounded to the nearest integer. The number of digits displayed after the decimal point depends on the **Precision** setting. Like the **Precision** setting, this setting affects only how dimensions are displayed; it does not change the geometry or the actual measured value of the dimension.

***Prefix.***  The **Prefix** option allows you to set a prefix in the dimension text. The specified text is placed in front of the default dimension text. You can enter any text you want or use control codes to display special symbols. For example, entering the control code **%%c** displays the diameter symbol.

***Suffix.***  The **Suffix** option works the same as the **Prefix** option except the specified text is placed after the default dimension text. For example, specifying the inch character (") would place a " mark after each dimension.

**Note:**
Although it is common to set the dimension units of a dimension style the same as the display units used in the drawing, it is not required. As an example, you might have Decimal display units set in the drawing and Architectural units set in a dimension style. The separate unit settings also make it possible to create additional dimension styles with distinct dimension unit settings so that you can use different dimension standards in the same drawing.

**Note:**
When you enter a prefix, it replaces any default prefixes such as those used in diameter and radius dimensioning. If you specify tolerance values, the prefix is also added to the tolerance text as well as to the regular dimension text.

***Measurement Scale.*** The **Measurement Scale** area allows you to define a scale factor for the default dimension text values. The **Scale factor** option sets a scale factor for linear dimension measurements. The value of any linear dimension is multiplied by this scale factor, and the resulting value is used as the default dimension text. For example, if you set a measurement scale factor of **2**, the dimension text for a 1-inch line is displayed as two inches. The value does not apply to angular dimensions and is not applied to rounding values or to plus or minus tolerance values.

When the **Apply to layout dimensions only** is turned on, AutoCAD will apply the measurement scale value only to dimensions created in layout (paper space) viewports.

**Note:** Do not confuse the **Measurement Scale** with the **Use overall scale of:** setting located on the **Fit** tab discussed earlier. The **Measurement Scale** factor changes the numerical value of a dimension so that it no longer represents the actual length in the drawing. The **Use overall scale of:** setting, or dimension scale, affects only the appearance of dimension features like arrowheads and text size. The numerical dimension value always reflects its true length.

**FOR MORE DETAILS**   See Chapter 14 for more on dimensioning in layout (paper) space.

***Zero Suppression.*** These options control the display of leading and trailing zeros in dimension text. For example, when set to decimal units, turning on the **Leading** option means that a dimension value of 0.5000 would be shown as .5000. With the **Trailing** option turned on, a dimension of 12.5000 would be displayed as 12.5. There are separate settings for both linear dimensions and angular dimensions.

The **0 feet** and **0 inches** options control the display of zeros in feet and inches dimensions. For example, when the **0 feet** option is turned on, 0′-8″ would be displayed as 8″. With **0 inches** turned on, 12′-0″ would be displayed as 12′.

*Alternate Units Tab.* The **Alternate Units** tab (see Figure 13-69) allows you to show dimensions in two different formats. A typical example of this is to show both inch and millimeter dimensions such as **2.00 [50.8mm]**. The **Alternate Units** tab contains settings that are similar to the **Primary Units** tab. To enable alternate units, select the **Display alternate units** box. Once this is selected, the remaining options are enabled.

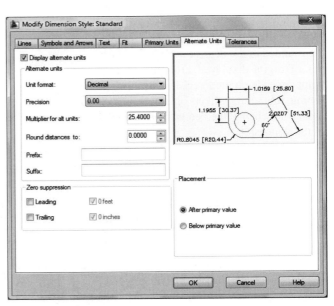

**Figure 13-69**   The Alternate Units tab

The **Unit format** and **Precision** work the same as the **Primary Units** tab settings. When using fractional unit formats (Architectural and Fractional), you can choose between stacked or unstacked fractions.

***Multiplier for Alternate Units and Round Distances To.***    The **Multiplier for alt units:** setting specifies the conversion factor between the primary units and the alternate units. For example, to convert inches to millimeters, specify a multiplier of 25.4. The value has no effect on angula dimensions. The **Round distances to:** setting allows you to apply a rounding value to the alternate dimensions. This rounding value is independent of the primary units round-off value.

***Prefix and Suffix and Zero Supression.***    The **Prefix:** and **Suffix:** values work the same as the primary units. To place a mm notation after the alternate dimensions, set the suffix to **mm**. The **Zero suppression** settings also work the same as the primary units.

***Placement.***    This controls where the alternate units are displayed. You can choose between **After Primary Value** and **Below Primary Value.**

*The Tolerances Tab.*    The **Tolerances** tab allows you to control the display and values of tolerances for both primary and alternate units. The **Zero suppression** and **Precision** settings work the same way as the primary and alternate units settings but control only the tolerance values. The **Upper** and **Lower** values control the upper and lower limits of the tolerance settings.

***Method.***    The Method setting controls how the tolerances are displayed. These settings are described below. Figure 13-70 shows an example of each setting.

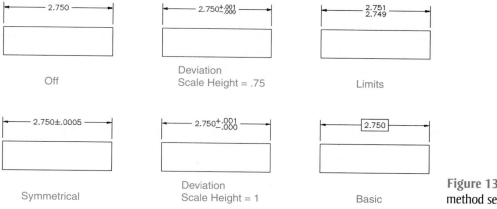

**Figure 13-70**   The tolerance method settings

| None | This setting turns off the tolerance display. |
|---|---|
| Symmetrical | This setting adds a plus/minus tolerance to the dimension measurement. A plus or minus sign appears before the tolerance. The Symmetrical setting uses the upper tolerance value. For example, when using the Symmetrical setting, if the upper tolerance value is set to **.001**, a **1″** dimension would be displayed as 1.0060.001. |
| Deviation | This is similar to symmetrical but allows you to display separate upper (+) and lower (−) tolerance values. The values appear stacked after the primary dimension. |
| Limits | The Limits setting replaces the primary dimension value with two stacked values. The upper value represents the sum of the primary dimension and the upper tolerance value. The lower value represents the primary dimension minus the lower tolerance value. |
| Basic | This setting creates a basic dimension, which displays a box around the full extents of the dimension. |

*Scaling for Height.* The **Scaling for height** setting controls the relative size of the tolerance text. The value is a scale factor, which is multiplied by the primary unit text height. For example, if you set a **Scaling for height** value of **.5,** the tolerance text would be half the size of the primary units. This is primarily used with the Deviation and Limits methods.

*Vertical Position.* This option controls the vertical location of the primary dimension text in relation to the tolerance text. You can choose either **Top, Middle,** or **Bottom.** Figure 13-71 shows examples of the **Vertical position** setting.

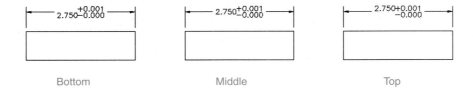

**Figure 13-71** Vertical position settings

Bottom     Middle     Top

**Exercise 13-11:** Modifying an Existing Dimension Style

1. Continue from Exercise 13-10. Start the **DIMSTYLE** command to display the **Dimension Style Manager** dialog box.
2. Choose the **Mech** dimension style and choose the **Modify...** button. This will display the **Modify Dimension Style** dialog box.
3. In the **Symbols and Arrows** tab, set the **Arrow size** to **.125.**
4. In the **Text** tab, choose the **...** button next to the **Text style** list. This displays the **Text Style** dialog box. Choose **New** and create a text style named **DIM** using the romans.shx font. Choose **Apply** and then **Close** to close the **Text Style** dialog box. AutoCAD returns you to the **Text** tab of the **Modify Dimension Style** dialog box.
5. Choose the **Dim** text style you just created in the **Text style** list and set the **Text height** to **.125.**
6. Choose **OK** to save the dimension style changes and return to the **Dimension Style Manager** dialog box. Select the **Mech** dimension style and choose **Set Current** to set the dimension style current. Choose the **Close** button to end the **DIMSTYLE** command. Any dimensions that have this style are updated.
7. Save your drawing as **EX13-11**. Your drawing should resemble Figure 13-72.

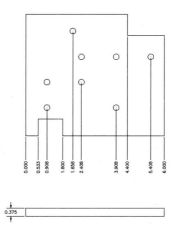

**Figure 13-72** The modified dimension style

## Modifying Dimension Styles Versus Overriding Dimension Styles

When modifying dimensions, any changes made to the dimension style will affect all the dimensions that use that style. There may be times when you want to change the settings for a single dimension without making changes to the dimensions style. In this case, a dimension override is what you need.

A dimension override allows you to make changes to dimension settings without applying them to the dimension style. Once you make a dimension override, any new dimensions will be placed with the settings of the dimension override until that override is changed or deleted. The dimension objects created with the override will retain the override setting until the dimension style is reapplied to the dimension.

> **Note:**
> A dimension override is similar to hard-coding object properties. For example, Chapter 6 showed how an object can have color, linetype, and lineweight settings that are different from the layer setting.

*Overriding a Dimension Style.*   To create a dimension override, choose the **Override** button from the **Dimension Style Manager** dialog box. When you choose this button, AutoCAD displays the **Override Current Style** dialog box (see Figure 13-73). This dialog box is the same as the **Modify Dimension Style** dialog box and allows you to make changes to the current dimension style settings. The difference is that the changes are not applied to the dimension style, but stored in a **<style overrides>** setting that appears as a child style of the parent dimension (see Figure 13-74).

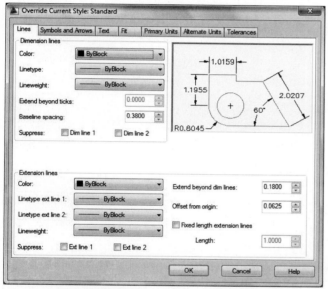

**Figure 13-73**   The Override Current Style dialog box

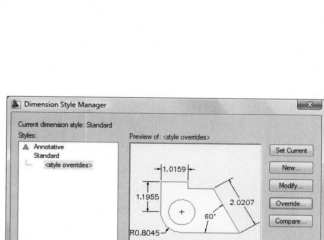

**Figure 13-74**   A dimension style override

Once you create an override, the override settings are set current and are applied to all new dimensions.

*Dimension Variables.*   Another way to create a dimension override is to change the dimension variables directly. The dimension variables are system variables that control the dimension settings. When you make changes to the dimension style, its corresponding dimension variable is also set accordingly. A dimension style is basically a collection of these dimension variable settings. AutoCAD's dimension variables are listed in Appendix D. To change a dimension variable, just type the variable name and set the value. When you change a dimension variable, AutoCAD creates a dimension style override.

> **Note:**
> When you save a style override to a new dimension style, any dimensions created with the style overrides keep their original dimension style and the override settings. They are not changed to the new dimension style.

*Saving an Override to a Style.*   If you decide you want to keep the override setting, you can save the setting to the current dimension style, making the changes permanent. To make the dimension overrides permanent, right-click on the **<style over-rides>** in the **Dimension Style Manager** dialog box in the **DIMSTYLE** command and choose **Save to current style** in the menu. Doing this will apply the dimension override settings to all the dimensions that use the current style.

You can also save the dimension override settings to a new dimension style. To do this, right-click on the **<style overrides>** in the **Dimension Style Manager** dialog box in the **DIMSTYLE** command and choose **Rename.** You can then type in a name for the new dimension style. When you press **<Enter ↵>,** AutoCAD will save the dimension style overrides to a new dimension style and move that style to the top level in the style list.

***Deleting an Override.*** There are two ways to delete a style override. One way is to set another dimension style current. AutoCAD will display an **Alert box** stating that the overrides will be deleted (see Figure 13-75). Choose **Yes** to delete the current style override.

Another way to delete an override is to select the override name in the **Dimension Style Manager** dialog box and press the **<Delete>** key on your keyboard. You can also right-click on the override name and choose **Delete** from the menu. AutoCAD will ask if you're sure you want to delete the override. Choose **OK** to delete the override.

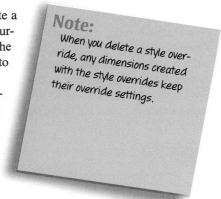

**Note:**
When you delete a style override, any dimensions created with the style overrides keep their override settings.

**Figure 13-75** Delete overrides Alert box

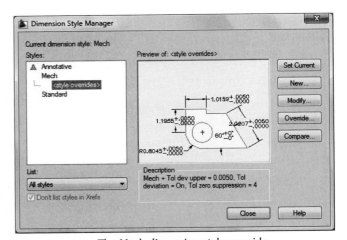

**Figure 13-76** The Mech dimension style override

---

**Exercise 13-12:** Overriding a Dimension Style

1. Continue from Exercise 13-11.
2. Start the **DIMSTYLE** command. AutoCAD displays the **Dimension Style Manager** dialog box. Select the **Mech** dimension style and choose the **Override...** button. AutoCAD displays the **Override Current Style** dialog box.
3. In the **Tolerances** tab, set the **Method** to **Deviation.** Set the **Upper Value** to **.005** and the **Lower Value** to **0.** Set the **Scaling for height** to **.5** and turn on the **Leading** zero suppression. Choose **OK** to finish creating the overrides. AutoCAD returns you to the **Dimension Style Manager** dialog box. You should see the override listed as a child style of the **Mech** dimension style (see Figure 13-76). Choose **Close** to end the **DIMSTYLE** command.
4. Start the **DIMDIAMETER** command and select the circle shown at P1 in Figure 13-77. Place the dimension as shown. The new dimension has the settings of the override while the existing dimensions remain unchanged.
5. Save your drawing as **EX13-12.** Your drawing should look like Figure 13-77.

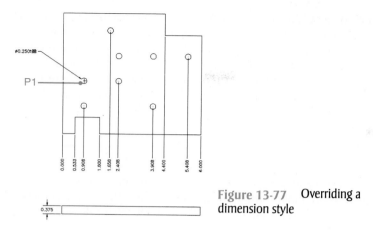

Figure 13-77    Overriding a
dimension style

## Comparing Dimension Styles

If you have a dimension style override or more than one dimension style, it is often helpful to know
the differences between these styles. AutoCAD can compare two dimension styles and tell you which
settings are different. When you select a dimension style in the **Dimension Style Manager** dialog
box, AutoCAD will give you a description of the dimension style. If that style was based on an existing dimension style, AutoCAD will list the changes in the **Description** area (see Figure 13-78).

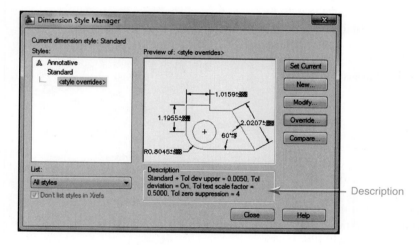

Figure 13-78    The Description
area of the Dimension Style Manager dialog box

Another way to compare dimensions is to choose the **Compare** button in the **Dimension
Style Manager** dialog box. When you choose this button, AutoCAD will display the **Compare
Dimension Styles** dialog box (see Figure 13-79).

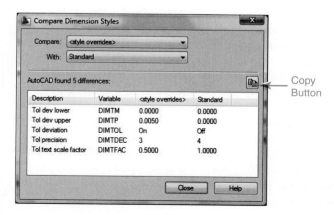

Figure 13-79    The Compare
Dimension Styles dialog box

To compare two dimension styles, select one dimension style in the **Compare** list and one style in the **With** list. AutoCAD will display the differences in the bottom portion of the dialog box. To see a listing of all the settings for a given dimension style, select the style in the **Compare** list and choose **<none>** in the **With** list. AutoCAD will list all the dimensions settings for that style. You can copy the list of results to the Windows clipboard by choosing the **Copy** button (see Figure 13-79). The list is copied as tab-separated text, which can then be pasted into another Windows application.

## MODIFYING DIMENSIONS

When you use associative dimensions and make changes to your geometry, the dimensions will change right along with it. However, you may need to modify dimension objects for a number of other reasons: to relocate the dimension text, to flip the arrowheads to the other side of the dimension line, or to modify the dimension text. In this section, you'll look at some ways to make changes to dimension objects.

Dimensions are objects, just as lines, arcs, circles, and text are objects. As such, they can be moved, copied, rotated, and so on just like other objects. However, unlike other objects, dimensions contain multiple parts (text, dimension lines, extension lines, etc.), and each part can be modified. In the next sections, you'll take a look at some different methods of modifying dimensions.

### Grip Editing Dimensions

Grip editing is one way to modify dimensions. When you select a dimension object, AutoCAD will display grip edit points at the definition points, the ends of the dimension lines, and the insertion point of the dimension text. By selecting and moving these grips, you can quickly and easily modify dimension objects.

### Right-Click Shortcut Menu

AutoCAD's right-click context menu provides some unique editing abilities with dimensions. To activate the right-click menu, first select the dimension object(s) to activate its grips and then right-click anywhere on the drawing to display the menu. When dimensions are selected, the right-click menu will display the menu options shown in Figure 13-80. These are described in the following sections.

> **Note:**
> Take care when you use grip editing on dimension definition points. If you have associate dimensioning turned on (**DIMASSOC** set to 2), modifying the definition points of a dimension will drop the association between the dimension and its object. When this happens, AutoCAD will display a message in the **Command Line** window stating: Dimension extension disassociated. This occurs only when modifying the definition points; modifying the dimension line or text grips has no effect on associativity.

*Dim Text Position.*     The **Dim Text position** item allows you to modify the placement of the dimension text. You can place the dimension text above the dimension line, centered on the dimension line, or you can move it back to its default position. When you select one of these options, AutoCAD moves the text immediately to the selected position.

You can also move the dimension text by dragging only the text, the text along with a leader, or both the text and dimension line. When you select one of these options, you are returned to the drawing and can place the dimension text by dragging your cursor and selecting a new position for the dimension text.

**TIP**     The **Move text alone** menu item found on the **Dim Text position** cascade menu is the only way to break text free from a dimension so that you can move it alone without affecting the dimension line appearance and configuration.

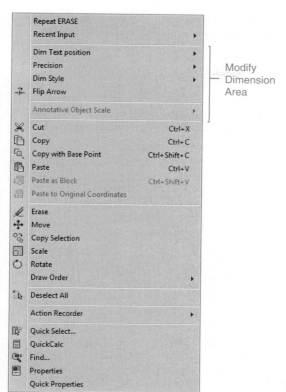

**Figure 13-80**    The right-click
dimension editing menu

*Precision.*    This option allows you to modify the precision setting of the dimension text. The options for this menu change depending on the units set in the objects dimension style.

*Dim Style.*    This option allows you to apply a different dimension style to the selected dimensions. When you choose this option, you can select from a list of currently defined dimension styles. If you've made changes to the dimension and want to save those changes to a new style, choose the **Save as New Style** option. AutoCAD will display the **Save as New Dimension Style** dialog box, where you can type a new dimension style name or choose an existing dimension style name to overwrite.

*Flip Arrow.*    You can flip dimension arrowheads to the opposite side of the extension line by selecting the **Flip arrow** option. The arrowhead closest to the selection point will flip to the opposite side of the extension line. This option is available only when a single dimension object is selected.

*Annotative Object Scale.*    This option is only enabled if you are using the **Annotation Scale** feature for dimensions. When enabled, this option displays a cascade menu with options to add or remove annotation scales so the same dimension can be used for multiple scale drawings. It is also possible to align multiple scale representations so they are in the same location using the **Synchronize Multiple-scale Positions** option.

> **FOR MORE DETAILS**    See Chapter 1 for a detailed description of the **Annotation Scale** feature.

## Exercise 13-13: Relocating Dimension Text

1. Open the drawing **EX13-13** from the Student CD. This drawing has a number of overlapping dimensions.
2. Select the dimension shown at **P1** in Figure 13-81. Right-click the dimension and choose **Dim Text position|Move with leader**. AutoCAD will start dragging the dimension text. Place the dimension text as shown in Figure 13-82.

3. Select the arrowhead shown at **P2** in Figure 13-81. Right-click the arrowhead and choose **Flip Arrow**. The arrowhead flips to the other side of the extension line.

4. Save your drawing as **EX13-13a**.

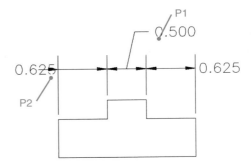

**Figure 13-81**  Relocating dimension text

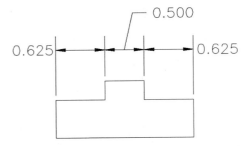

**Figure 13-82**  The modified dimensions

## Modifying Dimension Text and Extension Lines

Sometimes it is necessary to modify dimension text and extension lines after a dimension has been created. The following sections provide an overview of some of the available tools and methods to replace, relocate, and modify dimension text, as well as change the angle of dimension extension lines in order to create oblique dimensions.

*The DDEDIT Command.*    The **DDEDIT** command works on dimension objects as well as regular **Text** and **Mtext** objects. Simply select the dimension object when you are prompted to *Select annotation object*. AutoCAD will display the dimension text in the multiline text editor. AutoCAD's default dimension text will appear highlighted. You can place additional text before or after the default text, or replace it altogether.

If you delete the default dimension text, you can restore it by typing <> brackets in the mtext editor. AutoCAD will replace the <> brackets with the measured distance between the definition points.

| Oblique | |
|---|---|
| **Ribbon & Panel:** | Annotate\| Dimensions 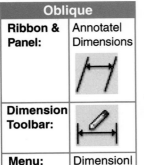 |
| **Dimension Toolbar:** |  |
| **Menu:** | Dimension\| Oblique |
| **Command Line:** | DIMEDIT |
| **Command Alias:** | DIMED |

If alternate dimensions are turned off, you can show the alternate dimension text by placing the square brackets [] along with the default brackets text <>. This works only if the default dimension text is present.

*The Oblique Tool.*    The **Oblique** tool allows you to adjust the angle of the extension lines for linear dimensions using the **Oblique** option of the **DIMEDIT** command. The **Oblique** tool is useful when extension lines conflict with other features of the drawing or you need to dimension an isometric drawing.

When you start the **Oblique** tool, AutoCAD prompts you to *Select objects:* so you can select one or more dimensions and press <**Enter** ↵>. AutoCAD then prompts you to *Enter obliquing angle (press Enter for none):* so you can enter the desired oblique angle.

*Align Text Tools.*     The **Align Text** tools allow you to relocate or rotate dimension text using any of the **DIMTEDIT** command options described in the following table.

| Home | This moves the dimension text back to its default position. |
|---|---|
| Angle | This changes the angle of the dimension text. Entering an angle of **0** degrees puts the text in its default orientation. |
| Left | This left-justifies the dimension text along the dimension line. This option works only with linear, radial, and diameter dimensions. |
| Center | This centers the dimension text on the dimension line. |
| Right | This right-justifies the dimension text along the dimension line. This option works only with linear, radial, and diameter dimensions. |

| Align Text | |
|---|---|
| **Ribbon & Panel:** | Annotatel Dimensions |
| **Dimension Toolbar:** |  |
| **Menu:** | Dimensionl Align Text |
| **Command Line:** | DIMTEDIT |
| **Command Alias:** | DIMTED |

### Exercise 13-14: Editing Dimension Text and Extension Lines

1. Open the drawing **EX13-14** from the Student CD.
2. Select the **Oblique** tool from the expanded **Dimensions** panel on the **Annotate** ribbon.
3. Select the dimensions shown at P1 and P2 in Figure 13-83 and press **<Enter ↵>**. AutoCAD prompts you to *Enter obliquing angle (press ENTER for none):*.
4. Type **30** and press **<Enter ↵>**. AutoCAD adjusts the angle of the extension lines.
5. Select the **Oblique** tool again. Select the dimension shown at P3 in Figure 13-83 and press **<Enter ↵>**.

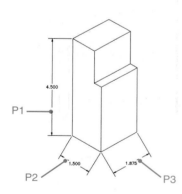

**Figure 13-83**    Selecting dimension text

6. Set the oblique angle to **150.** AutoCAD adjusts the extension line angle.
7. Select the **Text Angle** tool from the expanded **Dimension** panel on the **Annotate** ribbon. AutoCAD prompts you to *Select dimension:*. Select the dimension text shown at P1 in Figure 13-83.
8. AutoCAD prompts you to *Specify angle for dimension text:*. Enter **−30** for the dimension text angle. AutoCAD rotates the dimension text.
9. Restart the **Text Angle** tool and select the dimension shown at P2 in Figure 13-83. Enter **30** for the dimension text angle. AutoCAD rotates the dimension text.
10. Restart the **Text Angle** tool and select the dimension shown at P3 in Figure 13-83. Enter **30** for the dimension text angle. AutoCAD rotates the dimension text.
11. Start the **DDEDIT** command and select the dimension text P1. AutoCAD displays the multiline text editor with the default dimension text shown. Highlight the dimension text and set the oblique angle to **30**. Choose **OK** to close the text editor.
12. Repeat step 11 with the text at points P2 and P3. Set the oblique angle to **30** and **−30, respectively.**
13. Save your drawing as **EX13-14a**. Your drawing should resemble Figure 13-84.

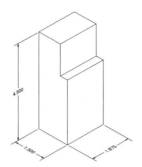

**Figure 13-84** The modified dimension text

## Reassociating Dimensions

| Reassociate | |
|---|---|
| **Ribbon & Panel:** | Annotate\|Dimensions<br>⟶⊠<br>⊤⋮⋮ |
| **Menu:** | Dimension\|Reassociate Dimensions |
| **Command Line:** | DIMREASSOCIATE |
| **Command Alias:** | None |

The association between a dimension object and other drawing objects can be somewhat precarious. There are times when, in the course of editing object geometry, the original drawing objects may be redefined or modified in such a way that the objects' association with a dimension object is lost. This may happen when polylines are exploded, when objects are trimmed or broken, or when multiple objects are joined. You may want to change the association to have the dimension be associated with another drawing object. AutoCAD provides a way to change dimension associativity with the **DIMREASSOCIATE** command.

When you start the **DIMREASSOCIATE** command, AutoCAD asks you to select a dimension object. When you select a dimension object, AutoCAD places an X at the first definition point and asks you to specify a new location for it. You can simply pick a new location for the definition point or skip to the next definition point by pressing <**Enter** ↵>. Depending on the type of dimension, AutoCAD will continue to prompt you for a new location for each definition point until the dimension is completely defined.

If you want to reassociate the dimension with a new object, use the **Select** option and select a new object to associate with your dimension. The type of object you select will depend on the type of dimension you select.

**Note:**
The **DIMREASSOCIATE** command works only with dimension objects. If a dimension is exploded or created when the **DIMASSOC** system variable is set to **0**, the dimension text, lines, and arrows are no longer dimension objects and cannot be reassociated.

### Exercise 13-15: Reassociating a Dimension

1. Continue from Exercise 13-14.
2. Select the dimension shown at P1 in Figure 13-85. The grips for the dimension appear.
3. Select the definition point grip shown at P1 and drag it off the object. AutoCAD displays the message *Dimension extension disassociated* in the **Command Line** window. The dimension is no longer associated with the geometry.
4. Start the **DIMREASSOCIATE** command. Select the dimension you just modified and press <**Enter** ↵>. AutoCAD places an X at the first defpoint and prompts you to *Specify first extension line origin or* ↓.
5. Choose the **Select object** option and select the line shown at P2 in Figure 13-85. AutoCAD reassociates the dimension with the selected line.
6. Save your drawing as **EX13-15.**

## Applying Dimension Styles

When working with multiple dimension styles, you may need to apply the settings on one style to an existing dimension. AutoCAD provides a number of ways to do this.

*The Dimension Style Lists.* One of the simplest ways to control the dimension styles in a drawing is via the **Dimension Style** list on the expanded **Annotation** panel on the **Home** ribbon. See Figure 13-86.

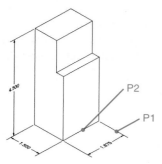

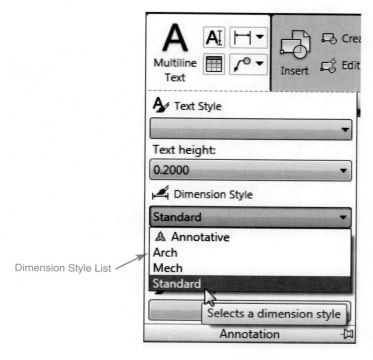

**Figure 13-85**    The reassociated dimension

**Figure 13-86**    Using the Dimension Style list on the Annotation panel

Selecting a dimension style from the dimension style drop-down list when no objects are selected will set the dimension style current so that any new dimensions will be created using that style. If one or more dimensions are selected so that their grips are displayed, selecting a different dimension style from the list will change the object's associated dimension styles to the new dimension style.

You can also control dimension styles via the **Dimension Style** list on the **Dimensions panel** on the **Annotate** ribbon. See Figure 13-87.

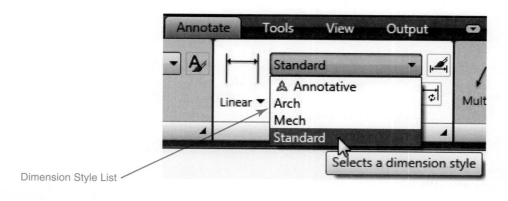

**Figure 13-87**
Dimension Style list on the Dimensions panel

*Properties Palette.*     A dimension style is simply an object property that applies only to dimension objects. Like other object properties, the **Properties** palette allows you to change the style of any selected dimension objects (see Figure 13-88). In addition to changing the style, you can also change the value of any style settings within the selected dimensions. This effectively creates dimension overrides for these dimension objects.

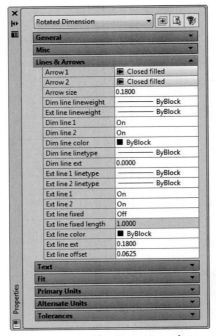

**Figure 13-88**     The Properties palette

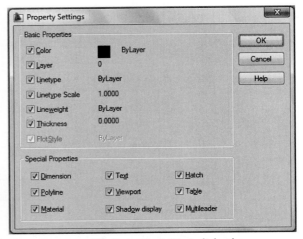

**Figure 13-89**     The Property Settings dialog box

*Match Properties.*     Because dimension styles are just a property of dimension objects, the **MATCHPROP** command can be used to match the dimension style properties of an existing dimension object. When you start the **MATCHPROP** command, you are prompted to select a source object and then destination object(s). The properties of the source object are applied to the destination objects.

When you use the **MATCHPROP**, by default, all valid properties of the source object are applied to the destination objects, including layer, color, linetype, etc. To control which properties are applied, choose the **Settings** option of the **MATCHPROP** command. This will display the **Property Settings** dialog box (see Figure 13-89). This allows you to select which properties you want to apply to the destination objects. To apply only the dimension style properties, place a check in the **Dimension** box and remove the checks from all other boxes. Selecting only the **Dimension** option will filter the properties so that only the dimension style properties of the source object are applied to the destination objects.

**TIP**     It is possible to use the **MATCHPROP** command between drawings so you can select the source object in a drawing other than the destination object(s). This is a handy way to copy dimension style settings from one drawing to another without recreating it from scratch or using DesignCenter.

**Exercise 13-16:** Using Match Properties to Update Dimension Styles

1. Open the drawing **EX13-16** from the Student CD.
2. Start the **MATCHPROP** command. AutoCAD prompts you to *Select source object:*.
3. Select the leader shown at P1 in Figure 13-90. This dimension has a dimension style override for the arrowhead. AutoCAD prompts you to *Select destination object(s) or* ↓.
4. Choose the **Settings** option. AutoCAD displays the **Property Settings** dialog box. In the **Special Properties** area, remove the check from all the settings except **Dimension**. Press **OK** to close the dialog box. AutoCAD prompts you to *Select destination object(s) or* ↓.
5. Select the leader shown at P2 in Figure 13-90. AutoCAD updates the leader to match the source object and prompts you to *Select destination object(s) or* ↓. Press <**Enter** ↵> to end the **MATCHPROP** command.
6. Save your drawing as **EX13-16**.

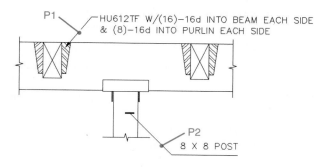

**Figure 13-90**  Matching dimension properties

*The Dimension Update Tool.* If you've created dimension style overrides and want to apply those overrides to an existing dimension, AutoCAD provides a tool for applying dimension styles (including overrides) to existing dimension objects.

When you choose this tool, AutoCAD lists the current dimension style, along with any overrides, in the **Command Window** (see Figure 13-91) and prompts you to *Select objects:*. Once you select the dimension object, AutoCAD applies the current dimension style settings, including overrides, to the selected dimensions.

**Note:** The Dimension Update tool is not technically a command. It is actually the **Apply** option of the **-DIMSTYLE** command, which is the **Command Window** version of the **DIMSTYLE** command. When you select this tool, AutoCAD starts the **-DIMSTYLE** command and automatically selects the **Apply** option.

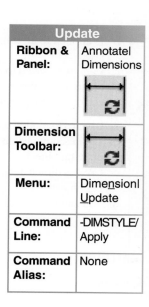

| Update | |
|---|---|
| **Ribbon & Panel:** | Annotatel Dimensions |
| **Dimension Toolbar:** | |
| **Menu:** | Dimensionl Update |
| **Command Line:** | -DIMSTYLE/ Apply |
| **Command Alias:** | None |

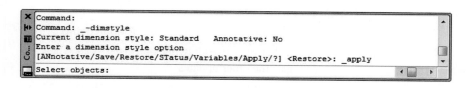

```
Command:
Command: _-dimstyle
Current dimension style: Standard    Annotative: No
Enter a dimension style option
[ANnotative/Save/Restore/STatus/Variables/Apply/?] <Restore>: _apply
Select objects:
```

**Figure 13-91**  Updating dimensions

## SUMMARY

Dimensioning can be one of the more difficult aspects of AutoCAD. Managing all the various settings can be daunting at times. However, AutoCAD provides a wide variety of tools to create, modify, and update dimension objects. The effective use of dimension styles and the ability to make changes to the dimension settings is key to being successful with AutoCAD.

## CHAPTER TEST QUESTIONS

### Multiple Choice

1. When using the **DIMLINEAR** command, which of the following is not a valid selection object?
   a. Line
   b. Arc
   c. Ellipse
   d. Circle

2. An arc length dimension:
   a. Is a linear dimension between the endpoints of an arc
   b. Measures the true distance along an arc segment
   c. Cannot be used on circles
   d. None of the above

3. To create a dimension with angled (oblique) extension lines you would:
   a. Use the **DIMOBLIQUE** command
   b. Use the **DIMEDIT** command and select the **Oblique** option
   c. Use grips to drag the extension lines to the desired angle
   d. None of the above; you cannot create angled extension lines.

4. A dimension style override:
   a. Allows you to make temporary changes to a dimension style
   b. Is applied to all dimensions with the current dimension style
   c. Cannot be saved to a dimension style
   d. None of the above

5. Setting the **DIMASSOC** system variable to **1**:
   a. Creates exploded dimensions
   b. Creates dimensions that are not associated with other drawing objects
   c. Creates dimensions that are associated with other drawing objects
   d. You cannot set **DIMASSOC** to **1**.

6. In the **Fit** tab of the **Modify Dimension Style** dialog box, the **Use overall scale of** setting:
   a. Controls the overall size of all elements of a dimension object
   b. Controls the value of dimension text
   c. Does not apply to dimensions placed in model space
   d. All of the above

7. The **Angle** option of the **DIMLINEAR** command:
   a. Creates an angular dimension instead of linear dimension
   b. Creates extension lines at the specified angle
   c. Controls the angle of the dimension line
   d. Controls the angle of the dimension text

8. To flip a dimension arrowhead:
   a. Select the arrowhead and choose **Flip arrow** from the right-click menu
   b. Delete the dimension and re-create it picking different defpoints
   c. Use the **MIRROR** command
   d. You cannot flip dimension arrowheads once they are placed.

9. A baseline dimension:
   a. Creates dimensions that are aligned end to end
   b. Creates dimensions that are referenced from a common extension line
   c. Must be placed first before any other linear dimensions are created.
   d. None of the above

10. Diameter dimensions:
    a. Automatically have the Ø symbol placed in front of the dimension text
    b. Can be used with either arcs or circles
    c. Cannot be used on an ellipse
    d. All of the above

### Matching

**Column A**
a. Linear dimension
b. Angular dimension
c. **Defpoints** layer
d. Associativity
e. Aligned dimension
f. Radius dimension
g. Dimension style override

**Column B**
1. Layer automatically created for definition points
2. A link between two drawing objects so that when one changes, the other updates
3. A linear dimension between two points along an angled line
4. A dimension of an angle
5. A dimension from the center to the edge of an arc or circle
6. The system variable that controls dimension associativity
7. A link between dimension definition points and other drawing geometry

h. Diameter dimension

i. Arc length dimension

j. **DIMASSOC**

8. A dimension between two opposite points on a circle or arc

9. A temporary change to dimension style settings

10. A dimension of the true length of an arc segment

## True or False

1. True or False: The **Defpoints** layer will never plot.

2. True or False: Dimensions cannot be exploded.

3. True or False: Dimension arrowheads can be flipped around the extension line.

4. True or False: The color and linetype of dimension lines are always BYLAYER.

5. True or False: You can override the default dimension text.

6. True or False: Centerline marks are created only with radius and diameter dimensions.

7. True or False: The **QDIM** command creates only linear dimensions.

8. True or False: Dimension style overrides are automatically applied to all existing dimension objects.

9. True or False: The **DDEDIT** command can be used to modify dimension objects.

10. True or False: The **DIMRADIUS** command can be used to dimension an ellipse.

## CHAPTER PROJECTS

### Project 13-1: Classroom Plan—Continued from Chapter 11

1. Open drawing **P11-1B** from Chapter 11.
2. Create a dimension style called **ARCH**. Use the settings shown in Figures P13-4A–E.
3. Add the dimensions shown in Figure P13-1.
4. Save your drawing as **P13-1.**

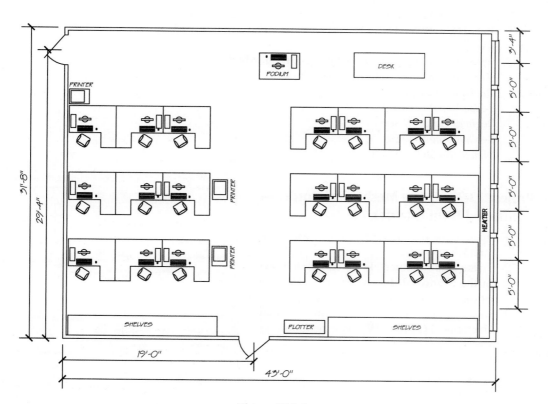

Figure P13-1

## Project 13-2: Motorcycle—Continued from Chapter 10

1. Open drawing **P10-2** from Chapter 10.
2. Add the dimensions and notes as shown in Figure P13-2.
3. Save the drawing as **P13-2.**

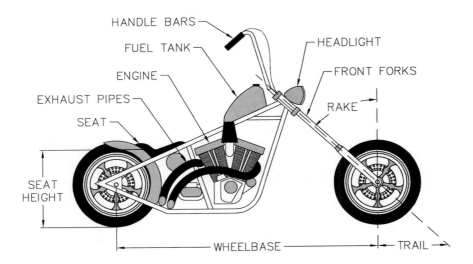

# CUSTOM CHOPPER

**Figure P13-2**

## Project 13-3a: B-Size Mechanical Border—Continued from Chapter 11.

1. Open drawing **Mechanical B-Size.DWT** from Chapter 11.
2. Create a dimension style called **Mech** based on the **Standard** dimension style. Use the settings shown in Figures P13-3A–E.
3. Save the drawing as a template called **Mechanical B-Size.DWT** with the following description:
   *Mechanical Drawing Template:*
   *B-Size - 17.0 × 11.0*
   *Decimal Units - 0.000*
   *Decimal Angles - 0.0*
   *Dimension Style - Mech*

## Project 13-3b: C-Size Mechanical Border—Continued from Chapter 11

1. Open drawing **Mechanical C-Size.DWT** from Chapter 11.
2. Create a dimension style called **Mech** based on the **Standard** dimension style. Use the settings shown in Figures P13-3A–E.
3. Save the drawing as a template called **Mechanical C-Size.DWT** with the following description:
   *Mechanical Drawing Template:*
   *C-Size - 22.0 × 17.0*
   *Decimal Units - 0.000*
   *Decimal Angles - 0.0*
   *Dimension Style - Mech*

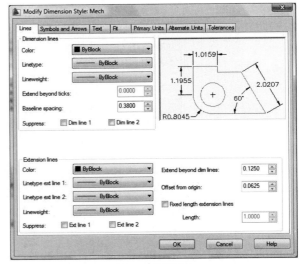

**Figure P13-3A**

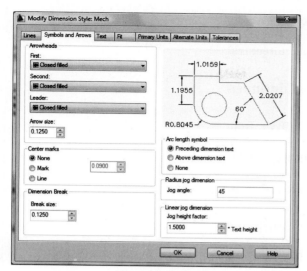

Figure P13-3B

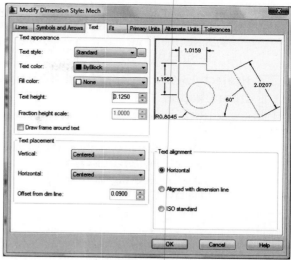

Figure P13-3C

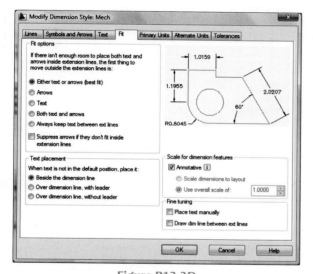

Figure P13-3D

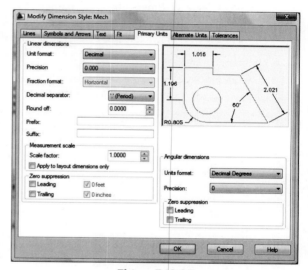

Figure P13-3E

## Project 13-3c: A-Size Portrait Mechanical Border—Continued from Chapter 11

1. Open drawing **Mechanical A-Size-Portrait.DWT** from Chapter 11.
2. Create a dimension style called **Mech** based on the **Standard** dimension style. Use the settings shown in Figures P13-3A–E.
3. Save the drawing as a template called **Mechanical A-Size-Portrait.DWT** with the following description:
   *Mechanical Drawing Template:*
   *A-Size Portrait - 8.50 × 11.0*
   *Decimal Units - 0.000*
   *Decimal Angles - 0.0*
   *Dimension Style - Mech*

## Project 13-4a: Architectural D-Size Border—Continued from Chapter 11

1. Open the template file **Architectural D-Size.DWT** from Chapter 11.
2. Create a dimension style named **ARCH** with the settings shown in Figures P13-4A–E.

3. Dimension the graphic scales as shown in Figure P13-4F using the dimension style Standard on the layer **A-Anno-Dims.**

4. Save the drawing to a template file as **Architectural D-Size.DWT.**

## Project 13-4b: Architectural B-Size Border—Continued from Chapter 11

1. Open the template file **Architectural B-Size.DWT** from Chapter 11.

2. Create a dimension style named **ARCH** with the settings shown in Figures P13-4A–E.

3. Save the drawing to a template file as **Architectural B-Size.DWT.**

## Project 13-4c: Architectural A-Size Border—Continued from Chapter 11

1. Open the template file **Architectural A-Size.DWT** from Chapter 11.

2. Create a dimension style named **ARCH** with the settings shown in Figures P13-4A–E.

3. Save the drawing to a template file as **Architectural A-Size.DWT.**

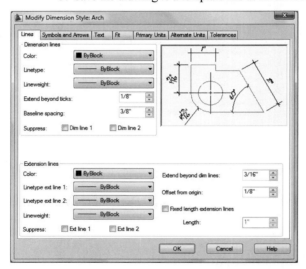

Figure P13-4A

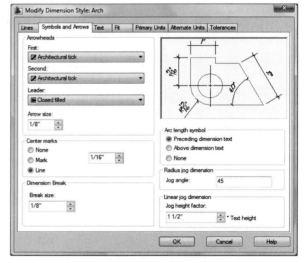

Figure P13-4B

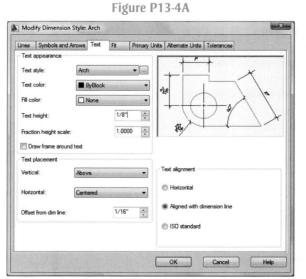

Figure P13-4C

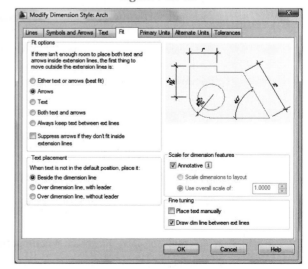

Figure P13-4D

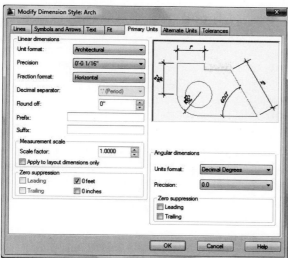

Figure P13-4E

Figure P13-4F

## Project 13-5: Electrical Distribution Panel

1. Create a new drawing using the acad.dwt template.
2. Create a dimension style called **Mech** based on the **Standard** dimension style. Use the settings shown in Figures P13-3A–E. *Hint:* You can use DesignCenter to drag-and-drop the dimension style from the mechanical drawing templates.
3. Draw the electrical panel drawing shown in Figure P13-5. Include all dimensions and text.
4. Save your drawing as **P13-5.**

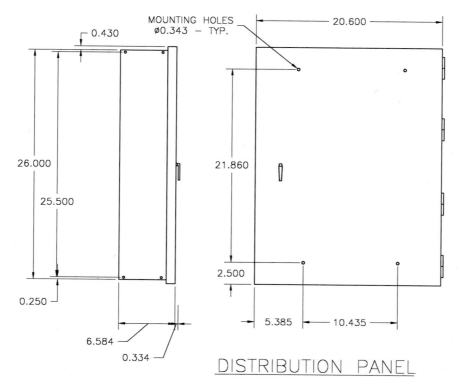

DISTRIBUTION PANEL

Figure P13-5

## Project 13-6a: Hot Water Piping Schematic—Continued from Chapter 11

1. Open drawing **P11-6A** from Chapter 11.
2. Update the Standard dimension style so that the text style is set to Notes and the arrow size is 1/8″.
3. Use the **MLEADER** command to add the notes shown in Figure P13-6A using the **Standard** multileader style on layer **P-Anno-Note**.
4. Save the drawing as **P13-6A**.

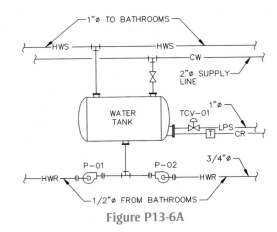

**Figure P13-6A**

## Project 13-6b: Water Heater Schematic—Continued from Chapter 11

1. Open drawing **P11-6B** from Chapter 11.
2. Update the Standard dimension style so that the text style is set to Notes and the arrow size is **1/8″**.
3. Use the **MLEADER** command to add the notes shown in Figure P13-6B using the **Standard** multileader style on layer **P-Anno-Note**.
4. Save the drawing as **P13-6B**.

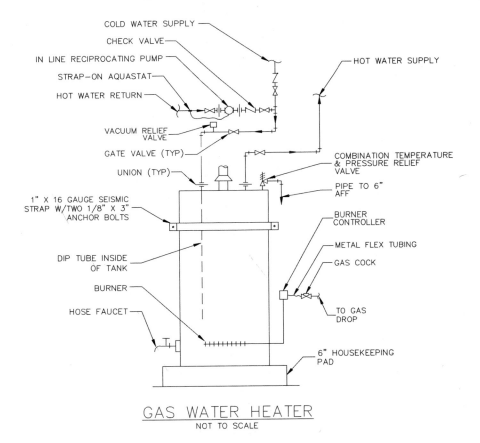

**Figure P13-6B**

## Project 13-6c: Compressed Air Schematic—Continued from Chapter 11

1. Open drawing **P11-6C** from Chapter 11.
2. Update the **Standard** dimension style so that the text style is set to **Notes** and the arrow size is **1/8″.**
3. Use the MLEADER command to add the notes shown in Figure P13-6C using the **Standard** multileader style on layer **P-Anno-Note.**
4. Save the drawing as **P13-6C.**

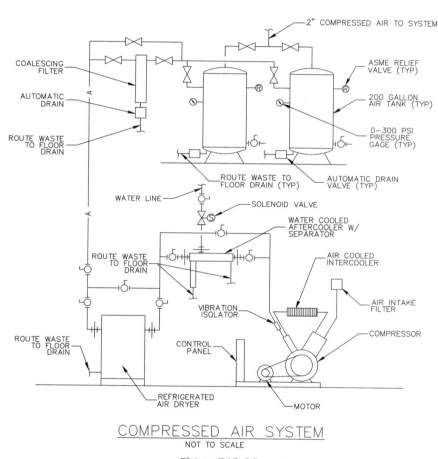

## COMPRESSED AIR SYSTEM
NOT TO SCALE

**Figure P13-6C**

## Project 13-6d: Unit Heater Connections—Continued from Chapter 11

1. Open drawing **P11-6D** from Chapter 11.
2. Update the **Standard** dimension style so that the text style is set to **Notes** and the arrow size is **1/8″.**
3. Use the **MLEADER** command to add the notes shown in Figure P13-6D using the **Standard** multileader style on layer **P-Anno-Note.**
4. Save the drawing as **P13-6D.**

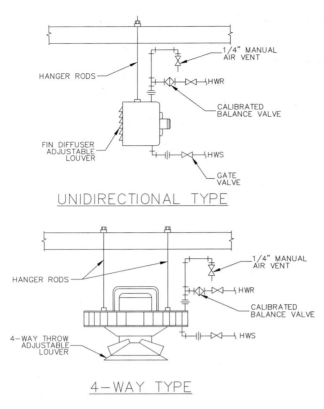

UNIDIRECTIONAL TYPE

4–WAY TYPE

TYPICAL UNIT HEATER CONNECTIONS

NOT TO SCALE

NOTE:
TERMINATE MANUAL AIR VENT AT WALL 7'-0" AFF
WITH GLOBE VALVE WHEN HEATER IS GREATER THAN
OR EUQAL TO 12"-0" AFF.

**Figure P13-6D**

## Project 13-6e: Pipe/Wall Penetration Detail—Continued from Chapter 11

1. Open drawing **P11-6E** from Chapter 11.
2. Update the **Standard** dimension style so that the text style is set to Notes, the arrow size is **1/8″,** and the dimension scale factor is set to 4. *Hint:* You can set the dimension scale factor as an override by updating the **DIMSCALE** system variable.
3. Use the **MLEADER** command to add the notes shown in Figure P13-6E using the **Standard** multileader style on layer **P-Anno-Note.**
4. Save the drawing as **P13-6E.**

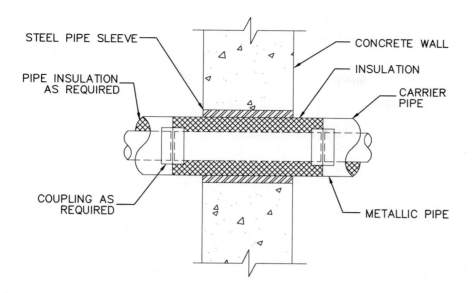

<u>TYPICAL WALL PENETRATION</u>
SCALE:  3"=1'-0"

<u>NOTE:</u>
SIZE PIPE SLEEVE SO THAT THERE IS AT LEAST $\frac{1}{4}$"
CLEARANCE ALL AROUND
**Figure P13-6E**

**Project 13-7: Residential Architectural Plan—Continued from Chapter 11**

1. Open the drawing **P11-7** from Chapter 11.
2. Create the following layer:

| Name | Color | Linetype | Lineweight | Description |
|------|-------|----------|------------|-------------|
| C-Anno-Dims | 7 | Continuous | Default | Dimensioning |

3. Create a dimension style called **ARCH.** Use the settings shown in Figures P13-4A–E. *Hint:* You can use DesignCenter to drag-and-drop the dimension style from the architectural drawing templates.
4. Add the dimensions shown in Figure P13-7.
5. Save your drawing as **P13-7.**

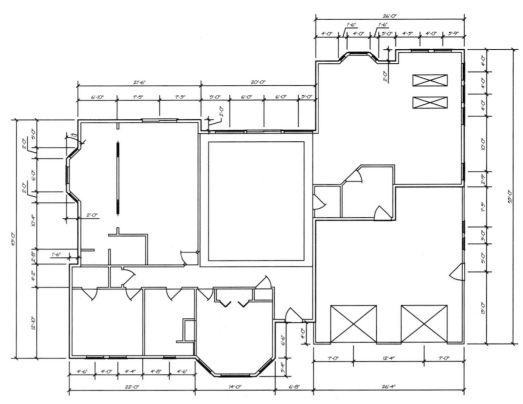

**Figure P13-7**

## Project 13-8a: Joist Foundation Detail—Continued from Chapter 11

1. Open drawing **P11-8A** from Chapter 11.
2. Create a text style named **Arch** assigned the TrueType text font **CountryBlueprint.ttf** with a height of 0″. This text style will be used with the **Arch** dimension style below.
3. Update the **Standard** dimension style so that the text style is set to **Arch,** the arrow size is **1/8″,** and the dimension scale factor is set to 24. *Hint:* You can set the dimension scale factor as an override by updating the **DIMSCALE** system variable.
4. Use the **MLEADER** command to add the notes shown in Figure P13-8A using the **Standard** multileader style on layer **A-Anno-Note.**
5. Create a dimension style named **Arch** with the settings shown in Figures P13-4A–E from Project 13-4A and set it current.
6. Make sure the dimension scale factor is set to **24.**
7. Add the dimensions shown in Figure P13-8A using the **Arch** dimension style on layer **A-Anno-Dims.**
8. Save the drawing as **P13-8A.**

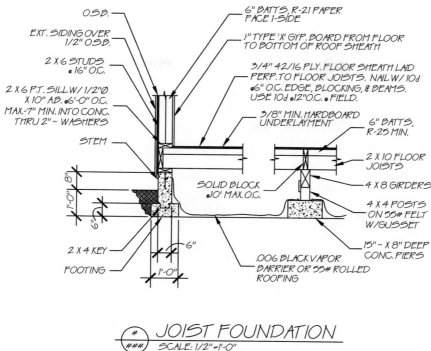

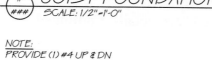

NOTE:
PROVIDE (1) #4 UP & DN

**Figure P13-8A**

## Project 13-8b: Interior Floor Change Detail—Continued from Chapter 11

1. Open drawing **P11-8B** from Chapter 11.
2. Create a text style named **Arch** assigned the TrueType text font **CountryBlueprint.ttf** with a height of **0″**. This text style will be used with the **Arch** dimension style below.
3. Update the **Standard** dimension style so that the text style is set to **Arch,** the arrow size is **1/8″,** and the dimension scale factor is set to 24. *Hint:* You can set the dimension scale factor as an override by updating the **DIMSCALE** system variable.
4. Use the **MLEADER** command to add the notes shown in Figure P13-8B using the **Standard** multileader style on layer **A-Anno-Note.**
5. Create a dimension style named **Arch** with the settings shown in Figures P13-4A–E from Project 13-4A and set it current.
6. Make sure the dimension scale factor is set to **24.**
7. Add the dimensions shown in Figure P13-8B using the **Arch** dimension style on layer **A-Anno-Dims.**
8. Save the drawing as **P13-8B.**

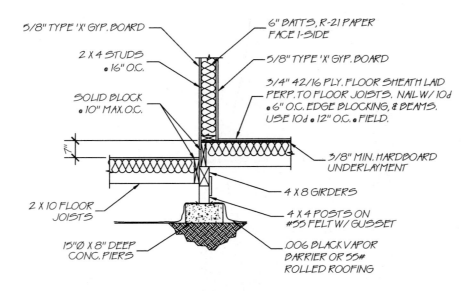

5/8" TYPE 'X' GYP. BOARD

6" BATTS, R-21 PAPER FACE 1-SIDE

2 X 4 STUDS ● 16" O.C.

5/8" TYPE 'X' GYP. BOARD

SOLID BLOCK ● 10" MAX. O.C.

3/4" 42/16 PLY. FLOOR SHEATH LAID PERP. TO FLOOR JOISTS. NAIL W/ 10d ● 6" O.C. EDGE BLOCKING, & BEAMS. USE 10d ● 12" O.C. ● FIELD.

7"

3/8" MIN. HARDBOARD UNDERLAYMENT

4 X 8 GIRDERS

2 X 10 FLOOR JOISTS

4 X 4 POSTS ON #55 FELT W/ GUSSET

15"Ø X 8" DEEP CONC. PIERS

.006 BLACK VAPOR BARRIER OR 55# ROLLED ROOFING

INTERIOR FLOOR CHANGE

SCALE: 1/2"=1'-0"

**Figure P13-8B**

 architectural

## Project 13-8c: Truss with Soffited Eave Detail—Continued from Chapter 11

1. Open drawing **P11-8C** from Chapter 11.
2. Create a text style named **Arch** assigned the TrueType text font **CountryBlueprint.ttf** with a height of 0″. This text style will be used with the **Arch** dimension style below.
3. Update the **Standard** dimension style so that the text style is set to **Arch,** the arrow size is **1/8″,** and the dimension scale factor is set to 24. *Hint:* You can set the dimension scale factor as an override by updating the DIMSCALE system variable.
4. Use the **MLEADER** command to add the notes shown in Figure P13-8C using the **Standard** multileader style on layer **A-Anno-Note.**
5. Create a dimension style named **Arch** with the settings shown in Figures P13-4A–E from Project 13-4A and set it current.
6. Make sure the dimension scale factor is set to **24.**
7. Add the dimensions shown in Figure P13-8C using the **Arch** dimension style on layer **A-Anno-Dims.**
8. Save the drawing as **P13-8C.**

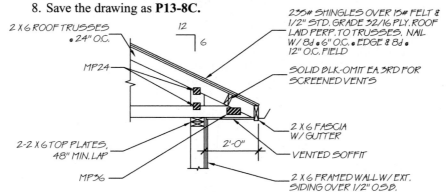

2 X 6 ROOF TRUSSES ● 24" O.C.

12

6

235# SHINGLES OVER 15# FELT & 1/2" STD. GRADE 32/16 PLY. ROOF LAID PERP. TO TRUSSES, NAIL W/ 8d ● 6" O.C. ● EDGE & 8d ● 12" O.C. FIELD

MP24

SOLID BLK.-OMIT EA. 3RD FOR SCREENED VENTS

2-2 X 6 TOP PLATES, 48" MIN. LAP

2'-0"

2 X 6 FASCIA W/ GUTTER

VENTED SOFFIT

MP36

2 X 6 FRAMED WALL W/ EXT. SIDING OVER 1/2" O.S.B.

TRUSS W/ SOFFITED EAVE

SCALE: 1/2"=1'-0"

**Figure P13-8C**

## Project 13-9: Optical Mount—English Units—Continued from Chapter 8

1. Open the drawing **P8-9** from Chapter 8.
2. Create a dimension style called **Mech** based on the **Standard** dimension style. Use the settings shown in Figures P13-3A–E. *Hint:* You can use DesignCenter to drag-and-drop the dimension style from the mechanical drawing templates.
3. Add the dimensioning shown in Figure P13-9. *Hint:* Use the **QDIM** command to create ordinate dimensioning.
4. Save the drawing as **P13-9.**

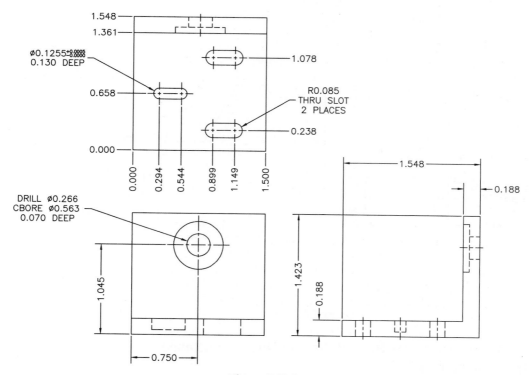

Figure P13-9

## Project 13-10a: Gasket—Continued from Chapter 11

1. Open drawing **P11-10A** from Chapter 11.
2. Update the **Standard** text style so that it is assigned the text font **Simplex.shx** with a height of **0.0mm.**
3. Update the **ISO-25** dimension style so that decimal separator is set to a period (.) instead of the default comma (,) and the dimension scale factor is set to 2. *Hint:* You can set the dimension scale factor as an override by updating the **DIMSCALE** system variable.
4. Add the dimensions shown in Figure P13-10A using the **ISO-25** dimension style on layer **Dimensions.**
5. Save the drawing as **P13-10A.**

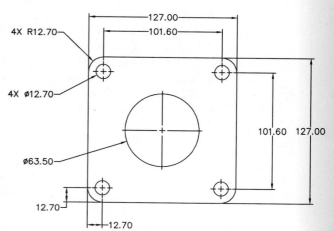

GASKET
SCALE: 1:2

Figure P13-10A

## Project 13-10b: Widget—Continued from Chapter 11

1. Open drawing **P11-10B** from Chapter 11.
2. Update the **Standard** text style so that it is assigned the text font **Simplex.shx** with a height of **0.0mm.**
3. Update the **ISO-25** dimension style so that decimal separator is set to a period (.) instead of the default comma (,) and the dimension scale factor is set to **4.** *Hint:* You can set the dimension scale factor as an override by updating the **DIMSCALE** system variable.
4. Add the dimensions shown in Figure P13-10B using the **ISO-25** dimension style on layer **Dimensions.**
5. Save the drawing as **P13-10B.**

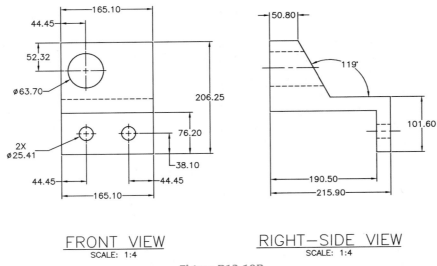

Figure P13-10B

## Project 13-10c: Hex Head Bolts and Nuts—Continued from Chapter 11

1. Open drawing **P11-10C** from Chapter 11.
2. Update the **Standard** text style so that it is assigned the text font **Simplex.shx** with a height of **0.0mm.**
3. Update the **ISO-25** dimension style so that decimal separator is set to a period (.) instead of the default comma (,).
4. Add the dimensions shown in Figure P13-10C using the **ISO-25** dimension style on layer **Dimensions.**
5. Save the drawing as **P13-10C.**

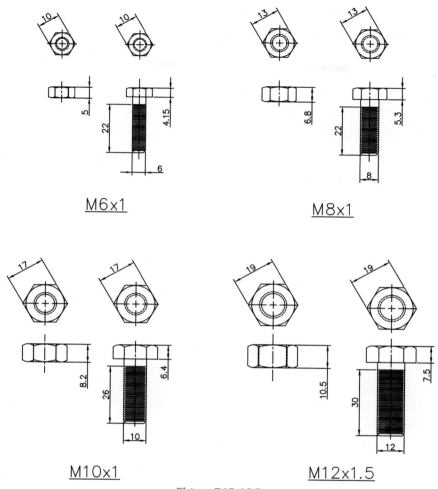

Figure P13-10C

## Project 13-10d: Motorcycle Head Gasket—Continued from Chapter 11

1. Open drawing **P11-10D** from Chapter 11.
2. Update the **Standard** text style so that it is assigned the text font Simplex.shx with a height of 0.0mm.
3. Update the **ISO-25** dimension style so that decimal separator is set to a period (.) instead of the default comma (,) and the dimension scale factor is set to 2. *Hint:* You can set the dimension scale factor as an override by updating the **DIMSCALE** system variable.
4. Add the dimensions shown in Figure P13-10D using the **ISO-25** dimension style on layer **Dimensions.**
5. Save the drawing as **P13-10D.**

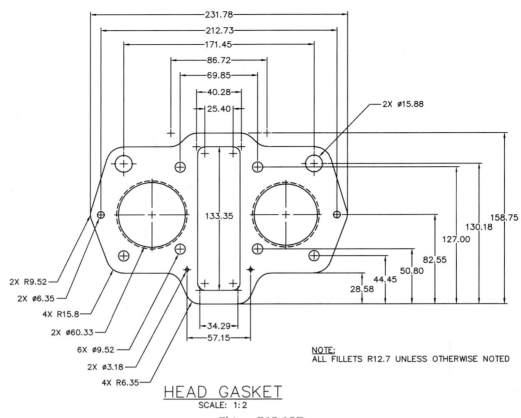

### Project 13-10e: 68-Tooth Rear Sprocket—Continued from Chapter 11

1. Open drawing **P11-10E** from Chapter 11.
2. Update the Standard text style so that it is assigned the text font **Simplex.shx** with a height of **0.0mm.**
3. Update the **ISO-25** dimension style so that decimal separator is set to a period (.) instead of the default comma (,) and the dimension scale factor is set to **4.** *Hint:* You can set the dimension scale factor as an override by updating the **DIMSCALE** system variable.
4. Add the dimensions shown in Figure P13-10E using the **ISO-25** dimension style on layer **Dimensions.**
5. Save the drawing as **P13-10E.**

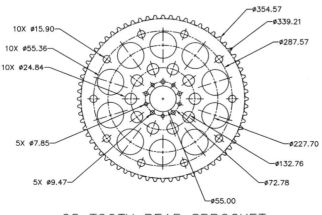

68 TOOTH REAR SPROCKET

Figure P13-10E

## Project 13-10f: Window Extrusion—Continued from Chapter 11

1. Open drawing **P11-10F** from Chapter 11.
2. Update the **Standard** text style so that it is assigned the text font **Simplex.shx** with a height of **0.0mm.**
3. Update the **ISO-25** dimension style so that decimal separator is set to a period (.) instead of the default comma (,).
4. Add the dimensions and leader shown in Figure P13-10F using the **ISO-25** dimension style on layer **Dimensions.**
5. Save the drawing as **P13-10F.**

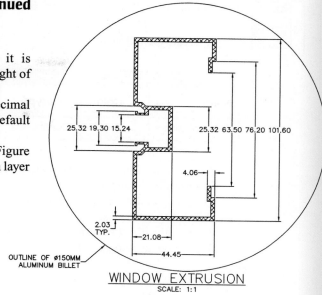

WINDOW EXTRUSION
SCALE: 1:1

**Figure P13-10F**

## Project 13-10g: Hub—Continued from Chapter 11

1. Open drawing **P11-10G** from Chapter 11.
2. Update the **Standard** text style so that it is assigned the text font **Simplex.shx** with a height of **0.0mm.**
3. Update the **ISO-25** dimension style so that decimal separator is set to a period (.) instead of the default comma (,) and the dimension scale factor is set to 2. *Hint:* You can set the dimension scale factor as an override by updating the **DIMSCALE** system variable.
4. Add the dimensions shown in Figure P13-10G using the **ISO-25** dimension style on layer Dimensions.
5. Save the drawing as **P13-10G.**

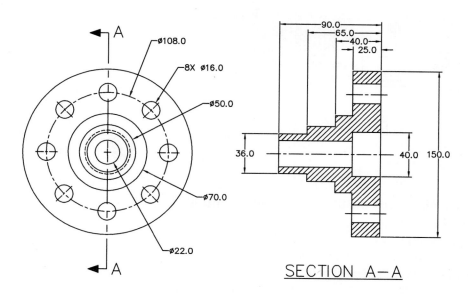

HUB
SCALE: 1:2

SECTION A—A

**Figure P13-10G**

## Project 13-11: Civil Site Plan—Continued from Chapter 11

1. Open the drawing **P11-11** from Chapter 11.
2. Create the following layer:

| Name | Color | Linetype | Lineweight | Description |
|---|---|---|---|---|
| A-Anno-Dims | 7 | Continuous | Default | Dimensioning |

3. Create a dimension style called **ARCH.** Use the settings shown in Figures P13-4A–E. *Hint:* You can use DesignCenter to drag-and-drop the dimension style from the architectural drawing templates.
4. Place the dimensions as shown in Figure P13-11.
5. Save the drawing as **P13-11.**

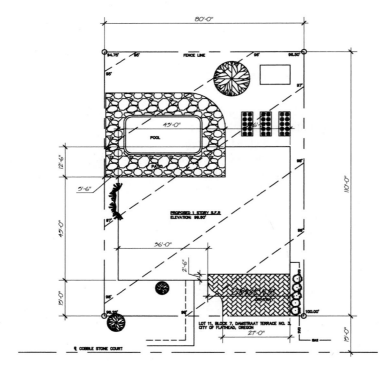

Figure P13-11

## Project 13-12a: Manhole Construction Detail—Continued from Chapter 11

1. Open drawing **P11-12A** from Chapter 11.
2. Update the **Standard** text style so that it is assigned the text font **Simplex.shx** with a height of **0″.**
3. Update the **Standard** dimension style so that the arrow size is **1/80,** the primary units are **Architectural,** and the dimension scale factor is set to **20.** *Hint:* You can set the dimension scale factor as an override by updating the **DIMSCALE** system variable.

4. Add the dimensions shown in Figure P13-12A using the **Standard** dimension style on layer **C-Anno-Dims.**

5. Use the **MLEADER** command to add the notes shown in Figure P13-12A using the **Standard** multileader style on layer **C-Anno-Note.**

6. Save the drawing as **P13-12A.**

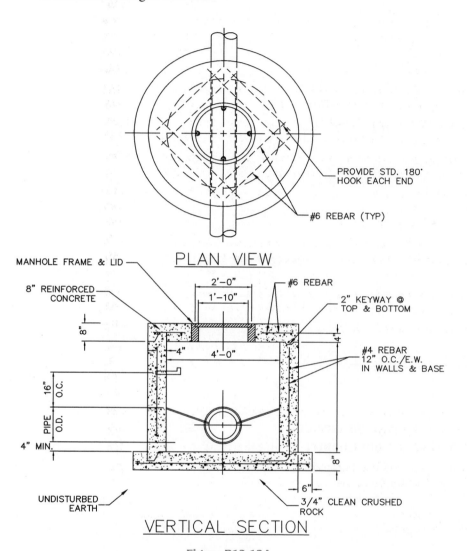

Figure P13-12A

## Project 13-12b: Manhole Cover—Continued from Chapter 11

1. Open drawing **P11-12B** from Chapter 11.

2. Update the **Standard** text style so that it is assigned the text font **Simplex.shx** with a height of **0″.**

3. Update the **Standard** dimension style so the arrow type is **Oblique,** the primary units are **Architectural,** and the dimension scale factor is set to 5. *Hint:* You can set the dimension scale factor as an override by updating the **DIMSCALE** system variable.

4. Add the dimensions shown in Figure P13-12B using the **Standard** dimension style on layer **C-Anno-Dims.**

5. Save the drawing as **P13-12B.**

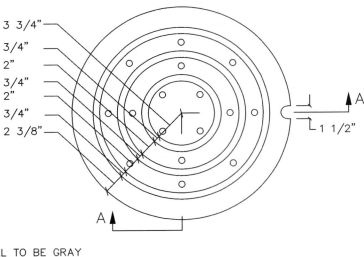

3 3/4"
3/4"
2"
3/4"
2"
3/4"
2 3/8"

1 1/2"

A

NOTE:
MATERIAL TO BE GRAY
CAST IRON ASTM A48
CLASS 30

TOP VIEW

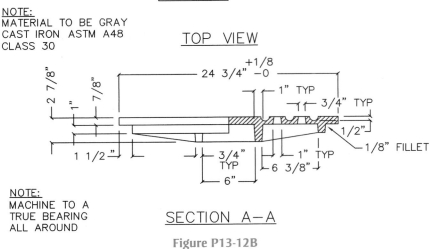

2 7/8"

7/8"

1"

24 3/4" $^{+1/8}_{-0}$

1" TYP

3/4" TYP

1/2"

1/8" FILLET

1 1/2"

3/4"
TYP

1" TYP

6 3/8"

6"

NOTE:
MACHINE TO A
TRUE BEARING
ALL AROUND

SECTION A—A

Figure P13-12B

### Project 13-12c: Standard Service Connection—Continued from Chapter 11

1. Open drawing **P11-12C** from Chapter 11.
2. Update the **Standard** text style so that it is assigned the text font **Simplex.shx** with a height of 0″.
3. Update the **Standard** dimension style so that the arrow size is **1/8″**, the primary units are **Architectural,** and the dimension scale factor is set to **20.** *Hint:* You can set the dimension scale factor as an override by updating the **DIMSCALE** system variable.
4. Add the dimensions shown in Figure P13-12C using the **Standard** dimension style on layer **C-Anno-Dims.**
5. Use the **MLEADER** command to add the notes shown in Figure P13-12C using the **Standard** multileader style on layer **C-Anno-Note.**
6. Save the drawing as **P13-12C.**

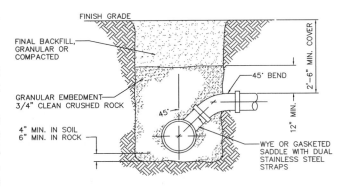

FINISH GRADE

FINAL BACKFILL,
GRANULAR OR
COMPACTED

GRANULAR EMBEDMENT
3/4" CLEAN CRUSHED ROCK

4" MIN. IN SOIL
6" MIN. IN ROCK

45° BEND

45°

2'-6" MIN. COVER

12" MIN.

WYE OR GASKETED
SADDLE WITH DUAL
STAINLESS STEEL
STRAPS

STANDARD SERVICE CONNECTION

Figure P13-12B

## 14

## Chapter Objectives

- Understand how and why paper space layouts are used
- Associate a printer/plotter with a layout
- Set the page size of a layout
- Create and import page setups
- Create layout viewports
- Set the viewport display scale
- Lock the viewport display
- Control layer visibility per viewport
- Modify viewports
- Create and manage layouts
- Use advanced paper space scaling features
- Create dimensions in paper space instead of model space

> **Note:**
> When model space is the active drawing environment, the UCS icon in the lower left-hand corner of the drawing window defaults to the icon shown in Figure 14-2.

## INTRODUCTION

In Chapter 1, we explained how AutoCAD has two distinct drawing environments: model space and paper space.

Remember that model space is the theoretically infinite 3D drawing environment where you locate most of the linework and annotation features that make up a drawing. To draw in model space, you select the **Model** button on the right side of the Status Bar as shown in Figure 14-1 to make it current.

> **TIP** You can turn the UCS icon on/off and control its other properties via the **UCS Icon** cascade menu on the **Display** cascade menu located on the **View** menu.

To reiterate, paper space is the 2D environment where you lay out the drawing information created in model space for plotting/printing on the desired size of paper and at a specified scale factor. In effect, a layout represents what the drawing will look like when it is printed.

> **TIP** It is common to locate the title border information in a layout. Locating the border and title text in paper space allows them to be drawn at a scale of 1:1 because the plot scale in paper space is typically 1:1. Many of the default AutoCAD template files have the title border located in paper space.

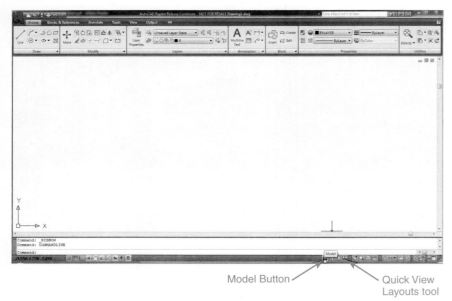

Model Button                                    Quick View
                                                Layouts tool

**Figure 14-1**    Switching between model space and paper space layouts

**Figure 14-2**    The model space UCS icon

It is possible to have multiple layouts in a drawing, each one a different paper size and scale. A new AutoCAD drawing that is based on the default template file (Acad.dwt) contains two generic layouts named **Layout1** and **Layout2.**

The quickest and easiest way to switch between model space and the paper space layouts is by using the Quick View Layouts tool located on the right side of the Status Bar. See Figure 14-1.

**Note:**
When paper space is the active drawing environment, the UCS icon in the lower left-hand corner of the drawing window defaults to the icon shown in Figure 14-4.

## QUICK VIEW LAYOUTS

NEW to AutoCAD 2009

The **Quick View Layouts** tool displays a horizontal row of layout preview images at the bottom of the AutoCAD window so you can quickly switch between model space and all the layouts contained in a drawing. See Figure 14-3.

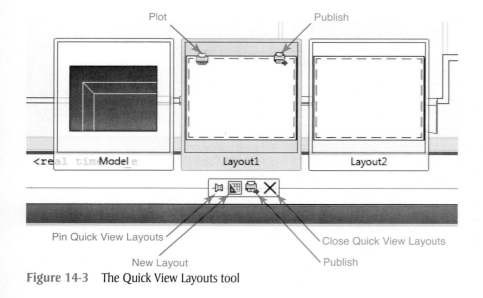

Plot                          Publish

Model                Layout1                Layout2

Pin Quick View Layouts                      Close Quick View Layouts

New Layout                      Publish

**Figure 14-3**    The Quick View Layouts tool

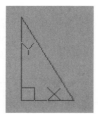

**Figure 14-4**
The paper space UCS icon

In addition, moving your cursor over a layout preview displays **Plot** and **Publish** buttons in the upper corners of the image so that you can print directly from the **Quick View Layouts** tool.

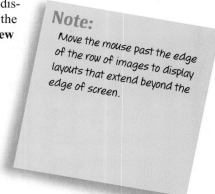

**Note:**
Move the mouse past the edge of the row of images to display layouts that extend beyond the edge of screen.

**TIP**   You can increase or decrease the layout preview image size by holding down the <**Ctrl**> key while rolling the mouse wheel in and out.

Using the accompanying control panel displayed below the preview images you can select the **Pin Quick View Layouts** button to keep the **Quick View Layouts** tool open so the previews are visible while you work. You can then select the **Close Quick View Layouts** button to turn off previews when you no longer want them displayed.

The **New Layout** button instantly creates a new generic layout in the drawing and displays its preview at the end of the current row of preview images. Creating and managing layouts is explained in detail later in this chapter.

The **Publish** button displays the **Publish** tool so you can quickly plot all the currently open drawings and layouts.

**FOR MORE DETAILS**   See Chapter 15 for more detailed information about using the **Publish** tool for quickly plotting multiple drawings and layouts.

## LAYOUT PAPER SIZE

The paper size used by an AutoCAD layout is controlled via its *page setup,* similar to setting the paper size of a document in a word processing program.

The difference is that, using AutoCAD, the available paper sizes are determined by the limits of the layout's associated plotting/printing hardware device. For instance, if you are printing on a printer whose maximum paper size capability is $8\frac{1}{2}'' \times 11''$ (A-size/letter), then an $8\frac{1}{2}'' \times 11''$ paper size is the maximum size you can specify for the layout. Applying this logic, a large format plotter that is capable of printing up to a $36'' \times 24''$ drawing (D-size) has many more paper size settings available than the average $8\frac{1}{2}'' \times 11''$ office printer. Associating a printer/plotter with a layout and selecting the desired paper size are both controlled using the **Page Setup Manager** explained later in this chapter.

### Layout Viewport Scale

The scale of a drawing is controlled via one or more *layout viewports* created in a layout.

In Chapter 1 we used the analogy that an AutoCAD paper space layout can be thought of as a 2D sheet of paper that hovers over your 3D model space drawing information. Views of the model space information are created by cutting one or more holes referred to as layout viewports in the paper so that you can see the drawing model below. You scale the model space information displayed in the viewport by zooming in and out at a specific scale factor. It is even possible to create multiple viewports and specify a different scale factor for each individual viewport, as shown in Figure 14-5, allowing you to easily create multiscaled drawings.

**layout viewport:** The user-defined window created in a paper space layout that allows you to view drawing information that resides in model space

**Figure 14-5** Paper space
layout with multiple scaled
viewports

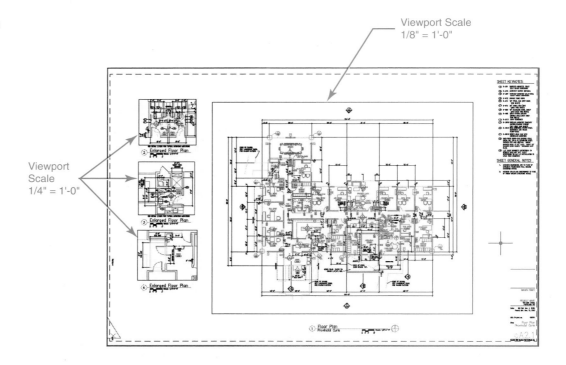

**Figure 14-5** Paper space
layout with multiple scaled
viewports

Viewport Scale
1/8" = 1'-0"

Viewport
Scale
1/4" = 1'-0"

**TIP**

AutoCAD provides a list of all of the standard viewport scales on the Status Bar and also on the **Viewports** toolbar so that you can quickly set a viewport scale without having to calculate the zoom scale factor each time. Both methods are described later in this chapter.

Being able to create plots with differently scaled viewports is one of the primary benefits of using paper space layouts. This is something you simply can't do in model space unless you scale the actual drawing information—which should be avoided at all costs. Remember that in Auto-CAD, the key is to draw everything exactly as it exists in the real world.

### Controlling Layers per Layout Viewport

Another very useful capability of layout viewports is that you can freeze and thaw layers per viewport using the viewport layer freeze option introduced in Chapter 6. This allows you to create multiple viewports on one or more layouts that each displays different model space drawing information.

You can also control the layer color, linetype, lineweight, and plot style properties per viewport using viewport layer overrides. Viewport layer overrides allow you to change the layer color, linetype, lineweight, and plot style properties in each viewport while retaining the original layer properties in model space and in the other layout viewports. Viewport layer overrides are discussed in detail later in this chapter.

**FOR MORE DETAILS**    See Chapter 6 for more information about using layers to organize drawing information.

### SETTING UP A LAYOUT

Once you are ready to lay out a drawing for plotting from paper space, select one of the default layouts (**Layout1** or **Layout2**).

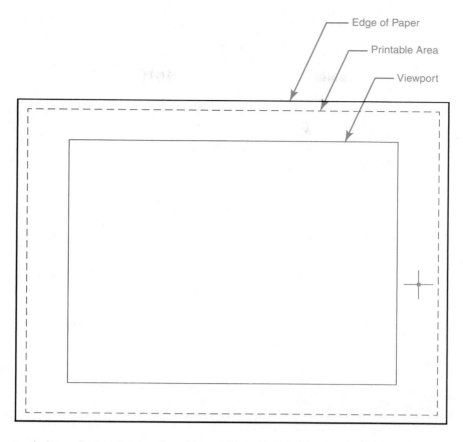

Figure 14-6    Switching to a layout the first time

When you switch to a layout for the first time, a single layout viewport is displayed on the page with a dashed line indicating the ***printable area*** as shown in Figure 14-6.

The first thing you need to do when you are setting up a layout is to specify the desired printer/plotter output device. Once you specify an output device, *then* you can select a paper size. Remember that the two are intimately related because the available paper sizes are determined by the capabilities of the currently associated printer/plotter. The printer/plotter, paper size, and most of the other plot settings are controlled via the page setup associated with the layout.

To modify the settings for the page setup, you use the **Page Setup Manager** explained in the next section.

printable area: The actual physical area that can be printed for the currently specified plotting device and paper size

## The Page Setup Manager

The Page Setup Manager allows you to do the following:

- Display details of the current page setup
- Set another page setup current
- Create a new page setup
- Modify an existing page setup
- Import a page setup from another drawing

The **Page Setup Manager** dialog box is shown in Figure 14-7.

**Current page setup:** displays the page setup that is applied to the current layout. By default it is set to **<None>**.

The **Page setups** box lists the page setups that can be modified or applied to the current layout.

By default, a page setup is automatically applied to each layout with the same name as the layout with an asterisk (*) added to the beginning and end of the layout name. For instance, the default page setups for the **Layout1** and **Layout2** layouts are **\*Layout1\*** and **\*Layout2\***, respectively.

Any new or imported page setups are automatically added to the **Page setups** list. You can make a page setup current by double-clicking on it in the list or by highlighting the page setup and selecting the **Set Current** button.

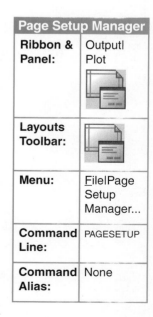

| Page Setup Manager | |
|---|---|
| **Ribbon & Panel:** | Output\| Plot |
| **Layouts Toolbar:** | |
| **Menu:** | File\|Page Setup Manager... |
| **Command Line:** | PAGESETUP |
| **Command Alias:** | None |

**Figure 14-7** The Page Setup
Manager dialog box

If you right-click in the **Page setups** list box, a shortcut menu is displayed that allows you
to set current, delete, or rename a page setup.

The **Selected page setup details** area at the bottom of the
dialog box displays the following information about the currently selected page setup:

- **Device name**   Name of the plot device specified in
  the currently selected page setup.
- **Plotter**   Type of plot device specified in the currently selected page setup.
- **Plot size**   Plot size and orientation specified in
  the currently selected page setup.
- **Where**   Physical location of the output device
  specified in the currently selected page setup.
- **Description**   Description of the output device specified in the currently selected page setup.

**Note:**
It is not possible to set current,
rename, or delete any of the
default page setups that begin
and end with an asterisk.

The **Display when creating a new layout** check box allows you to control whether the **Page
Setup Manager** is displayed when a new layout tab is selected or a new layout is created.

You can also control whether the **Page Setup Manager** is displayed for new layouts via the
**Show Page Setup Manager for new layouts** option on the **Display** tab of the **Options**
dialog box.

*Modifying a Page Setup.*   You can modify the settings of a page setup at any time. In order to
modify any default page setup, the layout the page setup is associated with must first be set current. Selecting the **Modify...** button in the **Page Setup Manager** displays the **Page Setup** dialog
box shown in Figure 14-8.

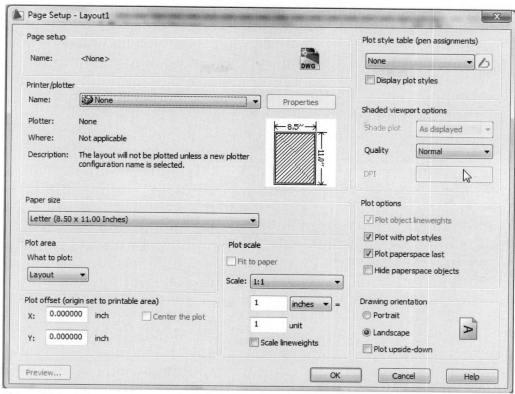

**Figure 14-8**    The Page Setup dialog box

The **Page Setup** dialog box is almost exactly the same as the **Plot** dialog box shown in Figure 14-9. In fact, the two dialog boxes control the same settings. The only differences between the two are:

- Changes made in the **Page Setup** dialog box are saved with the layout. Changes made in the **Plot** dialog box are *not* saved, unless you select the **Apply to Layout** button.

- You can plot from the **Plot** dialog box. You *cannot* plot from the **Page Setup** dialog box.

- The **Plot** dialog box can be toggled to display more plot options using the **More Options** arrow button on the bottom right of the dialog box as shown in Figure 14-9, or it can be set to display a limited number of options.

In this chapter, the main concern is controlling the paper size of the layout so that you can properly set up a drawing for plotting (discussed in Chapter 15). For this reason, most of the other plot-related page setup settings are mentioned only briefly. The following sections explain primarily how to associate an output device so that you can select the desired layout paper size.

***Selecting a Printer/Plotter Device.***    The **Printer/Plotter** area of the **Page Setup** dialog box allows you to specify a printer/plotter by selecting it from the **Name:** list box shown in Figure 14-10.

The **Name:** list box provides a list of the available printers/plotters you can associate with a layout. The list includes both *.PC3 files* and system printers that are prefixed with different icons—a plotter icon for a .PC3 file and a printer icon for a system printer.

The **Properties** button displays the **Plotter Configuration Editor** so you can view or modify the current plotter configuration.

**.PC3 file:** Plotter configuration file used to store and manage printer/plotter settings

| FOR MORE DETAILS | See Chapter 15 for more on using the **Plotter Configuration Editor** to manage .PC3 files. |
|---|---|

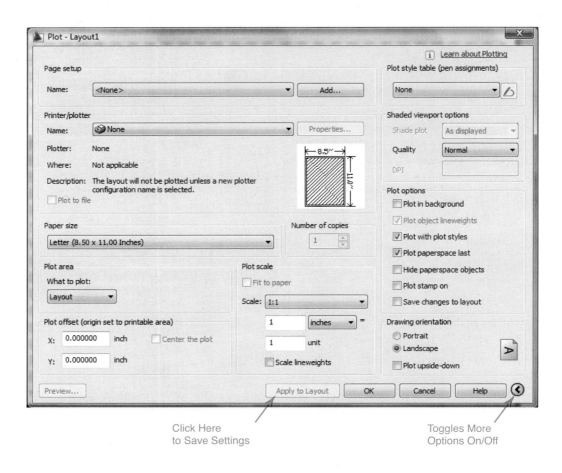

**Figure 14-9** The Plot dialog box

Click Here
to Save Settings

Toggles More
Options On/Off

Select Desired Output
Device from List

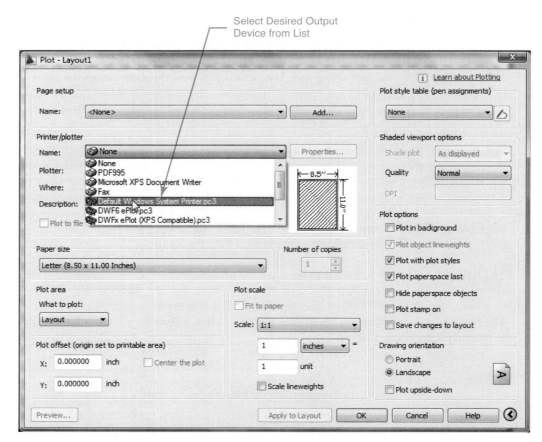

**Figure 14-10** Selecting a printer/plotter from the Name: list box

Other information provided about the currently selected printer/plotter includes the following:

- **Plotter**   Displays the current name
- **Where**   Displays the physical location or port
- **Description**   Displays a description if available

The **Preview** window displays the plot area relative to the paper size and the printable area.

**TIP**   If you place your mouse pointer over the preview, a tooltip is displayed with the paper size and the printable area.

---

**FOR MORE DETAILS**   See Chapter 15 for more on using the **Add-A-Plotter wizard.**

---

***Selecting a Paper Size.***   The **Paper size** list box displays the standard paper sizes that are available for the associated printer/plotter. Every time a different printer/plotter is selected, the **Paper size** list is updated with the paper sizes supported by that device. If no plotter is selected so that the **Name:** list box is set to <**None**>, a list of all the standard paper sizes is provided.

If you are plotting a raster image, such as a BMP or TIFF file, the size of the plot is specified in pixels, not in inches or millimeters.

> **Note:**
> If the printer/plotter you wish to use is not listed, you can add it using the **Plotter Manager's Add-A-Plotter wizard.**

**TIP**   If you are unsure what printer/plotter to specify, you can set the plotter to <**None**> so that it is still possible to select the desired paper size.

***Other Page Setup Settings.***   The following is a brief overview of a few of the other page setup settings.

The **Plot area** settings determine the area of the drawing to plot. The **What to plot:** list box provides five different options:

- **Display**   The current screen display
- **Extents**   The extents of the drawing
- **Layout**   The current layout
- **View**   A named view (must have at least one named view to be enabled)
- **Window**   User-specified window area

> **Note:**
> If the selected printer/plotter doesn't support the current paper size, the warning shown in Figure 14-11 is displayed. If you select **OK**, the paper size is changed to the default paper size for the new printer/plotter. If you select **Cancel**, the printer/plotter is changed to <**None**>, and the paper size is not changed.

The **Plot area** is typically set to **Layout** for a paper space layout. The other **Plot area** settings are more commonly used when plotting in model space.

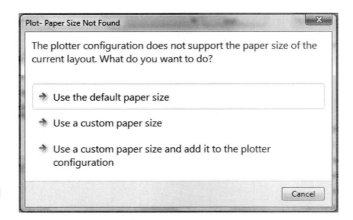

**Figure 14-11** Unsupported paper size warning

The **Plot offset** area allows you to offset the plot area relative to the lower-left corner of the printable area or the edge of the paper.

**FOR MORE DETAILS**    See Chapter 15 for more detailed information about controlling the other plot settings and plotting your drawing.

The **Plot scale** area controls the ratio of the plotted units to the drawing units. Most of the standard drafting scales are listed in the **Scale:** list box. The default scale is 1:1 when plotting a layout. In fact, if the **Layout** option is selected as **What to plot:** in the **Plot area,** AutoCAD ignores the scale selected in the **Scale:** list box and prints the layout at 1:1.

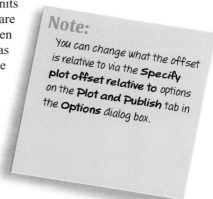

Note:
You can change what the offset is relative to via the **Specify plot offset relative to** options on the **Plot and Publish** tab in the **Options** dialog box.

*Creating a New Page Setup.*    If you think that you might use the same page setup settings in another layout in the current drawing or even in a layout in another drawing, you can create a named page setup. Named page setups are saved in the drawing file so that they can be applied to other layouts or imported into other drawing files. Importing page setups is explained in the next section.

Using named page setups also allows you to plot the same layout more than one way. You can apply different named page setups to the same layout so that there are different output results each time. For example, you might create different named page setups to plot to printers/plotters that are in different locations.

To create a new named page setup, select the **New...** button in the **Page Setup Manager.** The **New Page Setup** dialog box shown in Figure 14-12 is displayed.

Enter the name for the new page setup in the **New page setup name:** text box. The default name is **Setup** followed by an integer representing a sequential number (i.e., **Setup1, Setup2,** etc.). You should enter a descriptive name indicating the page setup's purpose.

The **Start with:** list allows you to select a page setup to use as a starting point for the new page setup:

- **<None>**    No page setup is used as a starting point.
- **<Default output device>**    The default output device specified on the **Plot and Publish** tab in the **Options** dialog box is set as the printer in the new page setup.
- **<Previous plot>**    The new page setup uses the settings specified in the last plot.

When you select the **OK** button at the bottom of the **New Page Setup** dialog box, the **Page Setup** dialog box shown earlier in Figure 14-8 is displayed using the settings saved with the

**Figure 14-12**   The New Page Setup dialog box

selected starting point page setup. You can then modify any settings if necessary. When you exit the **Page Setup** box, the new named page setup is displayed in the list of page setups in the **Page Setup Manager** as shown in Figure 14-13.

**Figure 14-13**   Page Setup Manager with new page setup

*Importing a Page Setup from Another Drawing.*    A named page setup can be imported from another drawing file (DWG), drawing template file (DWT), or drawing exchange format file (DXF). To import a named page setup, select the **Import...** button in the **Page Setup Manager** shown in Figure 14-7. The **Select Page Setup from File** dialog box is displayed so that you can select the source file from which you want to import. After you locate the file and select the **Open** button, the **Import Page Setups** dialog box shown in Figure 14-14 is displayed so you can select one or more page setups.

Select Page Setup to Import

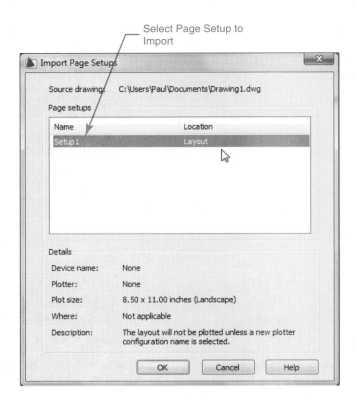

**Figure 14-14**   The Import Page Setups dialog box

The **Page setups** list box lists the page setups that can be imported from the selected drawing and whether they are located in model space or paper space. The **Name** column lists the name of the page setup, and the **Location** column lists the page setup location (model or layout).

The **Details** area at the bottom of the dialog box displays information about the selected page setup.

> **Note:**
> If a page setup with the name selected already exists in the drawing, a warning is displayed asking you if you want to redefine it. Selecting **OK** overwrites the page setup with the new page setup settings.

- **Device name**   The name of the plot device specified in the currently selected page setup

- **Plotter**   The type of plot device specified in the currently selected page setup

- **Plot size**   The plot size and orientation specified in the currently selected page setup

- **Where**   Physical location of the output device specified in the currently selected page setup

- **Description**   Description of the output device specified in the currently selected page setup

Select **OK** to import the selected page setup.

*Setting a Page Setup Current.*   The **Set Current** button sets the selected page setup current for the active layout so that all the page setup settings are updated to match the selected page setup.

**Exercise 14-1:** Using the Page Setup Manager

1. Open the building floor plan drawing named **EX14-1** from the Student CD to display the building floor plan shown in Figure 14-15.
2. Select the **Layout1** button on the Status Bar so that paper space is active and **Layout1** is the current layout.
3. Use the **Page Setup Manager** to set the associated plotter to <**None**> and the paper size to **ARCH D (36.00 × 24.00 Inches).**
4. Select the **Quick View Layouts** button and switch to the **Layout2** layout.

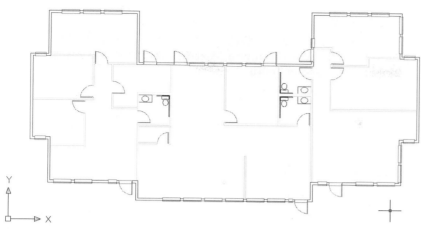

**Figure 14-15**    Building floor plan

5. Use the **Page Setup Manager** to set the associated plotter to **<None>** and the paper size to **ANSI B (17.00 × 11.00 Inches)**.
6. Save the drawing as **EX14-1**.

## Creating Layout Viewports

Layout viewports are the windows that you create in paper space that allow you to view the drawing information in model space at a specified scale (refer to Figure 14-5). Just like the windows in a building, layout viewports can be many different shapes and sizes. A layout viewport can be rectangular, polygonal, or even circular! You can create a single viewport that fits the paper size of the layout, or you can create multiple viewports. Each viewport is controlled independently so that different model space information can be displayed in each viewport, even at different scales if necessary.

> **Note:**
> Do not attempt to create one layout viewport completely within the borders of another layout viewport because unpredictable results can occur. It is possible, though, to overlap viewports.

A layout viewport is treated just like other basic Auto-CAD drawing objects such as lines, circles, and arcs. Similar to drawing other AutoCAD objects, a new viewport assumes the current object properties such as layer, color, and linetype when it is created.

After a viewport is created, you can modify it using any of the standard modify commands (**ERASE, MOVE, COPY, SCALE,** etc.). You can even use grips to resize a viewport quickly using the **STRETCH** option.

> **TIP**
> Typically, you do not want viewports to be displayed on the final plotted drawing. Because of this, layout viewports should be created on a unique layer so that you can control their visibility. The best approach is to create layout viewports on a layer whose **Plot** property is set to **No plot** so that you can see the viewports in the AutoCAD drawing window, but they do not plot.

You can create one or more layout viewports using the **MVIEW, -VPORTS,** or **VPORTS** command. Creating layout viewports using each of these commands is explained in the following sections.

*Creating a Single Rectangular Viewport.*    The most common type of layout viewport is a single rectangular viewport. A single rectangular viewport is created by selecting two corner points. It is the default viewport option when you use either the **MVIEW** or **-VPORTS** command.

| Single Viewport | |
|---|---|
| **Ribbon & Panel:** | None |
| **Viewports Toolbar:** | |
| **Menu:** | Views\| Viewports\|1 Viewport |
| **Command Line:** | MVIEW, VPORTS |
| **Command Alias:** | MV |

Do not forget to create a unique viewport layer set to **No plot** and make it current before you create a viewport using the **MVIEW** or **-VPORTS** command. Some typical layer names used include **Viewport** or **Vport.**

When you start either command, AutoCAD prompts you to *Specify corner of viewport or* ↓ as shown in Figure 14-16.

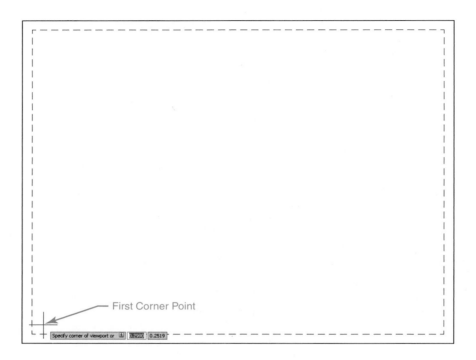

**Figure 14-16**   Locating the first corner point of a layout viewport

Select the first corner of the viewport or enter a coordinate value at the keyboard. AutoCAD then prompts you to *Specify opposite corner:* as shown in Figure 14-17 so you can specify the second point.

**Figure 14-17**   Locating the opposite corner point of a layout viewport

New Viewport with Display
Zoomed to Extents

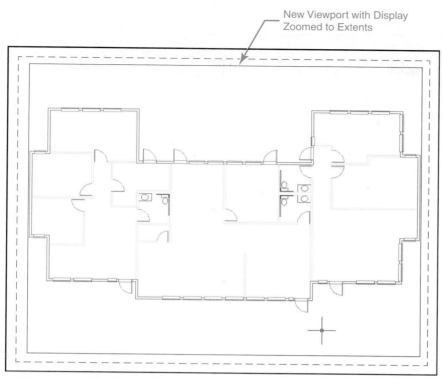

**Figure 14-18**   New layout viewport defaults to zoom extents

The viewport is immediately zoomed to the extents of the model space drawing information as shown in Figure 14-18.

At this point, the viewport is not set at any standard scale. You must manually set the viewport scale factor using the techniques explained later in this chapter.

> You can create a rectangular viewport that is the exact size of the layout's printable area using the **Fit** option. **Fit** is the default option so that you can simply press the **<Enter ↵>** key when you run either the **MVIEW** or **-VPORTS** command before specifying the first viewport corner point.

*Creating a Polygonal Viewport.*   You can create an irregular shaped viewport with three or more sides using the **Polygonal** option of the **MVIEW** or **-VPORTS** command. A polygonal viewport is created by selecting multiple points.

To create a polygonal viewport, start the **MVIEW** or **-VPORTS** command and either type **P<Enter ↵>** or select the **Polygonal** option using your arrow keys if you are using Dynamic Input. AutoCAD prompts you to *Specify start point:*. After selecting the first point, AutoCAD prompts you to *Specify next point or ↓* so you can start selecting points and define the viewport polygon as shown in Figure 14-19.

To finish the polygon viewport, you close it by either typing **C<Enter ↵>** or by selecting the **Close** option using your arrow keys. The **Close** option draws a viewport segment from the last current point to the start point and exits the command. Similar to a rectangular viewport, a polygonal viewport is immediately zoomed to the extents of the model space drawing information as shown in Figure 14-20.

| Polygonal Viewport | |
|---|---|
| **Ribbon & Panel:** | View\| Viewports |
| **Viewports Toolbar:** | |
| **Menu:** | Views\| Viewports\| Polygonal Viewport |
| **Command Line:** | MVIEW, VPORTS |
| **Command Alias:** | MV |

> You can also press **<Enter ↵>** to close a polygonal viewport after three or more viewport points have been defined.

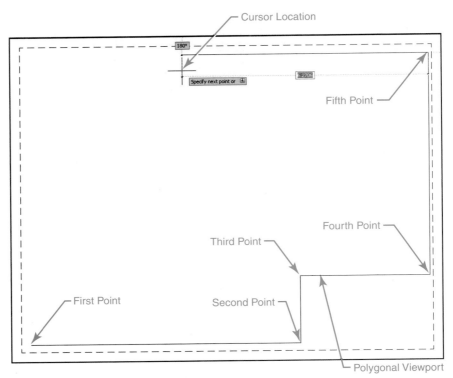

**Figure 14-19**    Creating a polygonal viewport

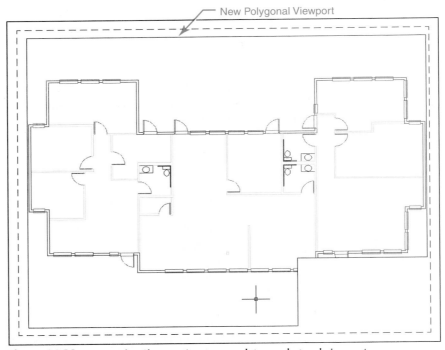

**Figure 14-20**    Using the Close option to complete a polygonal viewport

The **Arc** option allows you to create arc segments when you are defining a polygonal viewport. You can pick a second point to define the arc, or you can select from a number of arc suboptions. The arc creation suboptions are the same as those used with the **PLINE** command.

**FOR MORE DETAILS**  See Chapter 9 for more detailed information about using the **PLINE** command **Arc** options.

The **Length** option creates a viewport segment a specified length at the same angle as the previous segment. If the previous viewport segment is an arc, the new segment is drawn tangent to that arc segment.

The **Undo** option will undo the most recent viewport segment.

*Converting an Object into a Viewport.*    You can convert any of the following objects into a layout viewport:

- Polyline
- Circle
- Ellipse
- Region
- Spline

To convert an object into a layout viewport, start the **MVIEW** or **-VPORTS** command and either type **O<Enter ↵>** or select the **Object** option using your arrow keys if you are using Dynamic Input. AutoCAD prompts you to *Select object to clip viewport:* so you can pick the object to convert. A circle is shown converted to a viewport in Figure 14-21.

**Note:** In order to convert a polyline into a viewport, the polyline must be closed, and it must have more than three vertices.

| Object | |
|---|---|
| **Ribbon & Panel:** | Viewl Viewports |
| **Viewports Toolbar:** | |
| **Menu:** | Viewsl Viewportsl Object |
| **Command Line:** | MVIEW, VPORTS |
| **Command Alias:** | MV |

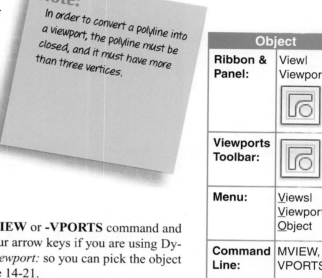

Circle Converted to Viewport

**Figure 14-21**    Converting a circle to a viewport

| New Viewport | |
|---|---|
| **Ribbon & Panel:** | Viewl Viewports  New |
| **Viewports Toolbar:** | |
| **Menu:** | Viewsl Viewportsl New Viewports... |
| **Command Line:** | VPORTS |
| **Command Alias:** | None |

*Using the Viewports Dialog Box.*    You can automatically create one or more rectangular viewports using the **Viewports** dialog box. The **VPORTS** command displays the **Viewports** dialog box shown in Figure 14-22.

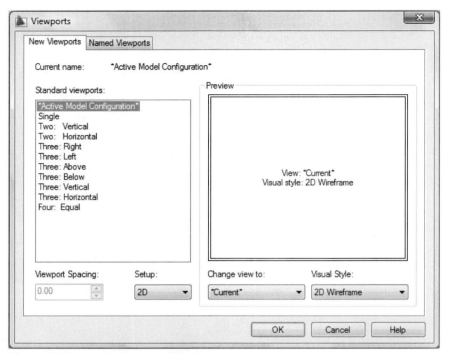

**Figure 14-22**    The Viewports dialog box

The **Standard Viewports** box on the left displays a list of standard viewport configurations that you can select. The **Preview** window displays a preview of the selected viewport configuration.

The **Viewport Spacing** box allows you to specify the spacing you want to apply between the viewports for the selected configuration. The **Preview** window is updated to show the results of the spacing indicated.

The **Setup** list box allows you to switch between a 2D and a 3D viewport setup. When you select 3D, standard orthogonal 3D views are applied to the selected viewport configuration. The **Change view to:** list box replaces the view in the selected viewport with the view you select from the list.

Select **OK** after you have specified the desired configuration and spacing to exit the **Viewports** dialog box. After the dialog box is closed, AutoCAD asks you to specify the rectangular area within which to fit the viewport configuration by prompting you to pick two corner points.

You can use the **Fit** option to make the viewport configuration fill the layout's printable area by pressing the <**Enter ↵**> key when AutoCAD prompts for the first corner point.

**Exercise 14-2:** Creating Layout Viewports

1. Continue from Exercise 14-1.
2. Select the **Layout 1** button on the Status Bar so that paper space is active and **Layout1** is the current layout.
3. Create a new layer named **Viewport,** set its **Plot** property to **No plot,** and make it the current layer.
4. Create a rectangular viewport using the **MVIEW** or **-VPORTS** command that is the same size as the printable area. *Hint:* The **Fit** option creates a viewport the same size as the printable area.
5. Select the **Quick View Layouts** button and switch to the **Layout2** layout.

6. Create a rectangular viewport using the **MVIEW** or **-VPORTS** command that is the same size as the printable area.

7. Save the drawing as **EX14-2.**

## Making a Viewport Current

There are two ways to make a layout viewport current:

* Enter the **MSPACE** or **MS** command.

* Double-click with your mouse inside a viewport.

The first method works best when you are working with a single layout viewport. If you have more than one viewport, you must double-click with your mouse inside the viewport you want to make current. When a viewport is current, its borderline becomes bold, and your mouse pointer changes to the cursor crosshair mode as shown in Figure 14-23.

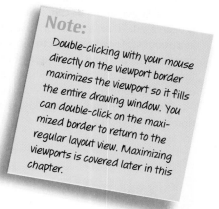

**Note:**
Double-clicking with your mouse directly on the viewport border maximizes the viewport so it fills the entire drawing window. You can double-click on the maximized border to return to the regular layout view. Maximizing viewports is covered later in this chapter.

Cursor Crosshairs

Bold Outline Indicates
Current Viewport

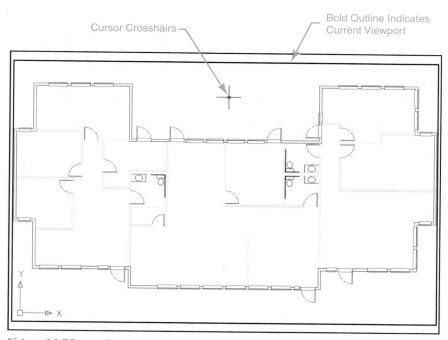

**Figure 14-23**   Making a layout viewport current

When a viewport is current, you can work on the model space drawing just like you are in model space—although it can be somewhat cumbersome working "through" the viewport. The ability to maximize viewports, which is discussed later in the chapter, makes this process much more user-friendly.

*Switching Back to Paper Space.*    There are two ways to switch back to paper space so that no viewports are current:

* Enter the **PSPACE** or **PS** command.

* Double-click with your mouse outside of all viewports.

All information that is created when paper space is active and no viewports are current is added to paper space exclusively (**TILEMODE**=0). In this mode, it is possible to add information (such as titles and drawing scales) directly above a viewport. This approach allows you to add information to your drawing that is displayed on the plotted drawing but does not need to be part of the model space design.

## Setting the Viewport Scale

As explained in the introduction to the chapter, the scale of the drawing information displayed in a layout viewport is controlled by zooming in and out of the active viewport. If you zoom in, the drawing gets larger, and the scale is increased. If you zoom out, the drawing gets smaller, and the scale is decreased. To set a viewport to a standard drafting scale, you must zoom in or out in the viewport at a zoom scale factor equal to the scale you want the drawing information to plot. For instance, if you want the drawing information in a viewport to plot at a scale of 2:1, you must zoom in by a scale factor of 2 in the viewport so that everything appears twice as large as actual size. To plot at a scale of 1:2, you zoom out by a scale factor of 1/2 so that everything is half of its actual size.

Zooming in and out in a layout viewport to a specific scale factor is done using the **XP** option of the **ZOOM** command.

---

| **FOR MORE DETAILS** | See Chapter 3 for more details about using the **ZOOM** command. |
|---|---|

---

The **X** in the **XP** option represents a multiplication sign, and the **P** stands for paper space. The number preceding the **XP** is the value the view is scaled relative to the paper space scale, which is 1:1. For example, to create a viewport that is scaled at 2:1 you enter **2XP** in response to the **ZOOM** command. In order to create a view that is scaled 1:2, you would enter **1/2XP** or **.5XP.**

Using the **ZOOM** command with the **XP** option to set the viewport scale is fine when you are working with simple scales such as 2:1 or 1:2. Converting standard drafting scales such as $\frac{1}{4}'' = 1'-0''$ or $1\frac{1}{2}'' = 1'-0''$ to their equivalent scale factors takes a little more time and effort. Luckily, AutoCAD provides some easier ways to set a viewport's scale, which are explained in the following sections.

*Setting the VP Scale on the Status Bar.*  The easiest way to set the viewport scale is via the **Viewport Scale** button on the right side of the AutoCAD Status Bar. The arrow to the right of the **Viewport Scale** button displays a list of standard drafting scales that you can use to set the zoom scale factor of the current viewport as shown in Figure 14-24.

The **Viewport Scale** is only displayed on the Status Bar when a viewport is current. You can make a viewport current by double clicking in the viewport with your mouse. Select the desired scale factor from the list, and the viewport is zoomed in or out by the pre-established scale factor.

**TIP**  After the viewport scale is set, zooming in and out using any zoom tools should be avoided. Any incremental zoom is enough to change the zoom scale factor so that it is no longer correct. Panning the display is not a problem because the zoom factor remains the same. The easiest way to prevent inadvertent zooms is to lock the viewport by selecting the **Lock/Unlock Viewport** button to the left of the **Viewport Scale** button on the Status Bar when the viewport is current and toggling it so the **Lock** icon is closed.

*Using the Viewports Toolbar to Set the Viewport Scale.*  The **Viewports** toolbar provides a list box with standard drafting scales that you can use to set the zoom scale factor of the current layout viewport. See Figure 14-25.

To set the viewport scale, you must first make the viewport current by double-clicking in the viewport with your mouse.

You can then pan the view as necessary using the **PAN** command to get it centered correctly in the viewport. *Do not* use any other **ZOOM** command. Zooming in or out even the tiniest amount will change the viewport's scale factor. To help prevent this from

**Note:**
The standard scales list box is only displayed when the **Viewports** toolbar is oriented horizontally. If you dock the toolbar on the left or right side of the drawing window the scale list box does not appear in the toolbar.

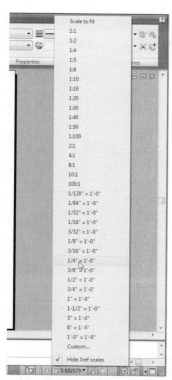

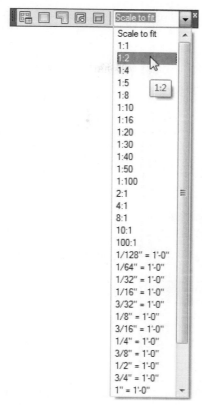

**Figure 14-24**   Setting the Viewport
Scale

**Figure 14-25**   Scale list box on the
Viewports toolbar

happening accidentally you can lock a viewport so it is impossible to zoom in or out. Viewport
locking is explained in the next section.

*Using the Properties Palette to Set the Viewport Scale.*   You can also control the viewport scale
factor via the **Properties** palette. Setting the viewport scale is a little different than using the
**Viewports** toolbar because using the **Properties** palette requires that you are in paper space in
order to select the viewport object. Selecting a viewport displays the properties shown in
Figure 14-26 so that you can select a standard scale from the list.

TIP

> You can also set a custom scale using the **Properties** palette if the scale you need is not in
> the standard scale list. To specify a custom scale, enter the desired scale factor in the
> **Custom Scale** property text field.

## Locking the Viewport Display

You can protect the viewport scale from being accidentally changed by locking the viewport display
so it is impossible to zoom or pan inside the viewport when it is current. When a viewport is locked,
any attempt to zoom or pan affects the entire paper space layout similarly to if you were working in
paper space. The current viewport remains active; it is just temporarily disabled during the zoom or
pan process. The easiest way to lock a viewport is to select the **Lock/Unlock Viewport** button on
the Status Bar as shown in Figure 14-27. In addition, you can also use the following methods:

- Select viewport and right-click to display the shortcut menu and set the **Display locked**
  menu item to **Yes.**

- Set the **Display locked** property to **Yes** via the **Properties** palette.

- Use the **MVIEW** command's **Lock** option and select the viewport.

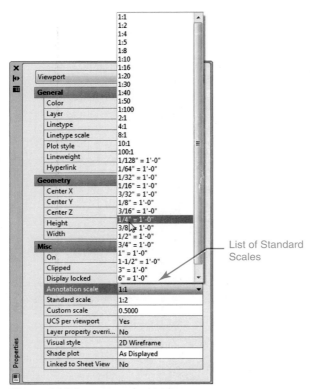

List of Standard Scales

**Figure 14-26**   Setting the Viewport scale via the Properties palette

Lock/Unlock Viewport

**Figure 14-27**   The Lock/Unlock Viewport button

To unlock a viewport, select the **Lock/Unlock Viewport** button or use any of the options listed above and set the **Locked** property to **Off** or **No.**

*Adding and Editing Scales in the Standard Scale List.*   The **SCALELISTEDIT** command allows you to add new scales or edit existing scales that appear in the scale list box used by the **Viewports** toolbar, the **Page Setup** dialog box, and the **Plot** dialog box. You can either type in the command, or you can select **Custom...** from the bottom of the scale list. The **Edit Scale List** dialog box shown in Figure 14-28 is displayed.

The **Scale List** on the left displays the list of currently defined scales. Selecting a scale from the list displays the ratio of paper units to drawing units at the bottom of the scale list.

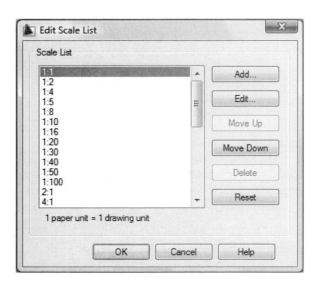

**Figure 14-28**   The Edit Scale List dialog box

The **Add** button allows you to add a custom scale to the list via the **Add Scale** dialog box shown in Figure 14-29. In this dialog box:

- The **Scale name** area is where you enter the descriptive or numeric name as you want it to appear in the list in the **Name appearing in scale list:** text box.
- The **Scale properties** area is where you set the ratio of paper units to drawing units by entering the numeric values in the **Paper units:** and **Drawing units:** text boxes.

The **Edit** button in the **Edit Scale List** dialog box allows you to edit an existing scale via the **Edit Scale** dialog box shown in Figure 14-30. In this dialog box:

- The **Scale name** area is where you update the descriptive or numeric name as you want it to appear in the list in the **Name appearing in scale list:** text box.
- The **Scale properties** area is where you change the ratio of paper units to drawing units by entering new numeric values in the **Paper units:** and **Drawing units:** text boxes.

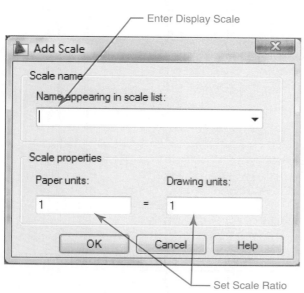

**Figure 14-29**   The Add Scale dialog box

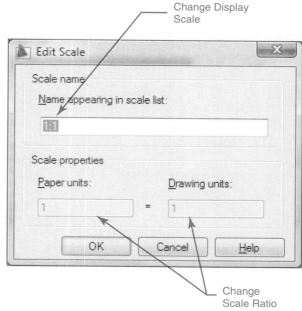

**Figure 14-30**   The Edit Scale dialog box

The **Move Up** button in the **Edit Scale List** dialog box moves the currently selected scale in the scale list up one position so that it appears in that position in all scale list boxes. The **Move Down** button moves the currently selected scale in the scale list down one position so that it appears in that position in all scale list boxes.

The **Delete** button permanently removes the currently selected scale from the scale list. The **Reset** button deletes any custom scales that were added and restores the default list of standard AutoCAD scales.

### Exercise 14-3: Setting the Viewport Scale

1. Continue from Exercise 14-2.
2. Select the **Layout1** button on the Status Bar so that paper space is active and **Layout1** is the current layout.
3. Make the viewport created in Exercise 14-2 the active viewport and **Zoom Extents** so that the entire floor plan fills the viewport.
4. Set the viewport scale to 1/4″ = 1′-0″ by selecting it from the **Viewport Scale** list on the right side of the Status Bar.
5. Select the **Lock/Unlock Viewport** button to the left of the **Viewport Scale** list to lock the viewport.

6. Make paper space the active drawing environment by double-clicking outside the viewport.
7. **Layout1** should now look similar to Figure 14-31.
8. Select the **Quick View Layouts** button and switch to the **Layout2** layout.
9. Make the viewport created in Exercise 14-2 the active viewport and **Zoom Extents** so that the entire floor plan fills the viewport.
10. Set the viewport scale to 1/8″ = 1′-0″ by selecting it from the **Viewport Scale** list on the right side of the Status Bar.
11. Select the **Lock/Unlock Viewport** button to the left of the **Viewport Scale** list to lock the viewport.
12. **Layout2** should now look similar to Figure 14-32.
13. Make paper space the active drawing environment by double-clicking outside the viewport.
14. Save the drawing as **EX14-3.**

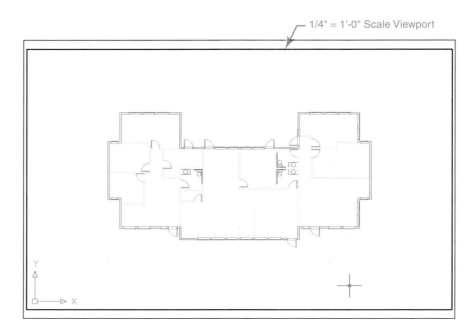

1/4" = 1'-0" Scale Viewport

**Figure 14-31**   Layout1 with 1/4″ = 1′-0″ scale viewport

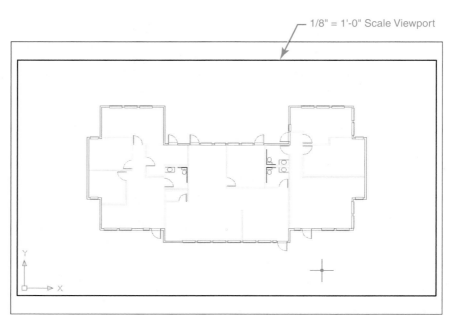

1/8" = 1'-0" Scale Viewport

**Figure 14-32**   Layout2 with 1/8″ = 1′-0″ scale viewport

## Controlling Layers per Layout Viewport

As mentioned earlier, it is possible to control layers per layout viewport so that you can display different model space drawing information in each individual viewport while not affecting the information in model space. You can freeze and thaw layers in individual viewports, as well as control the color, linetype, and lineweight used. These individual viewport specific layer settings are referred to as *viewport layer overrides*.

The most popular viewport layer override is the ability to freeze a layer in an individual viewport. This allows you to leave all of the layers on (thawed) in model space but then freeze different layers in each viewport to create multiple views of the same model space information and create different drawings. For example, one layout could be used to display the electrical plan information, and another layout might only display the HVAC plan information. The possibilities are endless, especially when combined the with concept of external reference drawings.

 **FOR MORE DETAILS**    See Chapter 17 for more information about using external reference drawings (xrefs).

There are two different ways to freeze layers per viewport: in the current viewport or in any new viewports. Freezing layers in the **New VP Freeze** column means that any information on the selected layers will not be displayed when you create any new layout viewports in the future.

Freezing layers in the current viewport is most common. Obviously, to freeze layers in the current viewport, you must first make the viewport current. After the viewport is current, start the **LAYER** command to display the **Layer Properties Manager.**

The viewport layer override columns are displayed at the right before the **Description** column as shown in Figure 14-33.

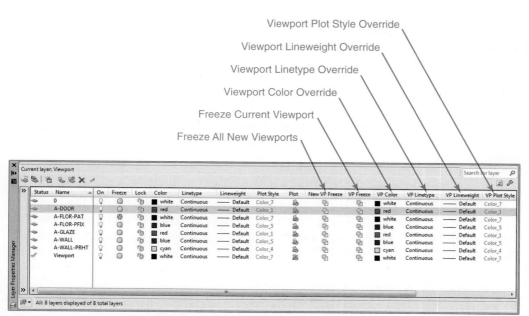

**Figure 14-33**   The Layer Properties Manager in paper space

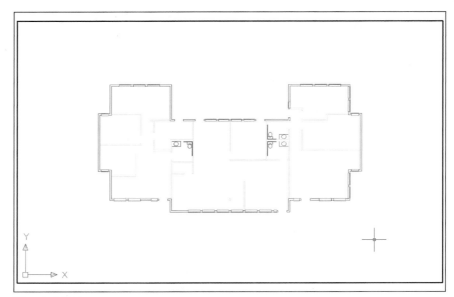

**Figure 14-34**    Freezing layers per viewport

To freeze a layer in the current viewport, click on the sun icon in the **VP Freeze** column and change it to a snowflake icon, just like the regular **Freeze** option. The selected layer is frozen in the current viewport as shown in Figure 14-34.

The same technique can be used to override the other layer settings (color, linetype, and lineweight). Simply make the viewport current and select the desired overrides.

You can remove viewport layer overrides using the right-click menu in the **Layer** list in the **Layers Properties** dialog box. The **VPLAYEROVERRIDESMODE** system variable allows you to temporarily turn off all viewport layer overrides.

**Note:**
When any viewport layer override is applied, a different background color is used in the **Layer Properties Manager**.

**TIP**    When a viewport contains layer overrides, a **Viewport Overrides** property filter is automatically created so that you can select the **Viewport Overrides** filter and view only the layers that contain overrides.

**FOR MORE DETAILS**    See Chapter 6 for more detailed information about layers and controlling the different layer properties using the **Layer Properties Manager.**

## Modifying Layout Viewports

Because they are treated just like most other AutoCAD objects, layout viewports can be modified using most of the same modify commands you are already familiar with. You can move or copy viewports using the **MOVE** and **COPY** commands, just as you can scale and stretch viewports via the **SCALE** and **STRETCH** commands. Probably the most important is the ability to delete viewports using the **ERASE** command.

*Resizing Viewports Using Grips.*    One of the most common ways to resize a viewport is to simply rely on grips. Using a viewport's grips and the **STRETCH** option allows you to modify a viewport quickly and make it the size needed as shown in Figure 14-35.

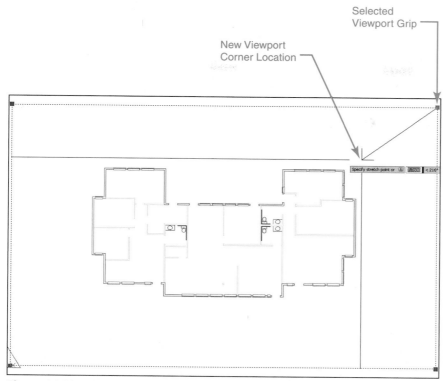

**Figure 14-35**    Using grips to resize a viewport

| | |
|---|---|
| **FOR MORE DETAILS** | See Chapter 7 for detailed information about using grips. |

*Clipping Viewports.*    You can change the shape of a viewport using the **VPCLIP** command.

Using the **VPCLIP** command you can either select a different object to convert into a viewport, or you can redefine the viewport using a new polygon viewport.

When you start the **VPCLIP** command and a viewport is not already selected, AutoCAD prompts you to *Select viewport to clip:* so you can select a viewport. Once a viewport is selected, AutoCAD prompts you to *Select clipping object or ↓*. You can either select an object to convert into a viewport, or you can define a new polygon window by typing **P<Enter ↵>** or selecting the **Polygon** option using your arrow keys. The options for creating a polygon viewport are the same as explained earlier in the chapter. The new viewport that is created to replace the existing viewport is referred to as a *clipping boundary,* as shown in Figure 14-36.

The **Delete** option deletes the clipping boundary of a selected viewport. The **Delete** option is available only if the selected viewport has already been clipped once using the **VPCLIP** command.

**Note:**
It is possible to convert circles, closed polylines, ellipses, closed splines, and regions into a layout viewport.

| Viewport Clip | |
|---|---|
| **Ribbon & Panel:** | View\| Viewports |
| **Viewports Toolbar:** | |
| **Pull-down Menu:** | None |
| **Command Line:** | VPCLIP |
| **Command Alias:** | None |

You can determine if a viewport has been clipped using the **VPCLIP** command by checking the viewport's **Clipped** property via the **Properties** palette. If it is set to **Yes,** the viewport has been clipped.

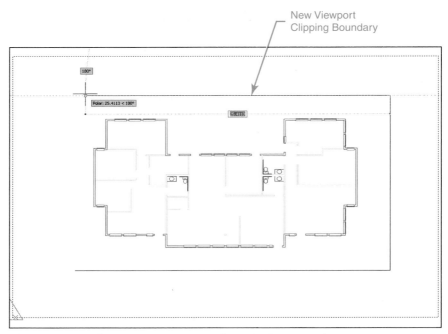

New Viewport
Clipping Boundary

**Figure 14-36**    Clipping a viewport using the VPCLIP command

## Turning Viewport Display Off and On

You can turn the viewport display on and off temporarily so that the model space objects displayed in the viewport are no longer visible. This can be used to speed up drawing regeneration time or control what drawing information is plotted. There are three ways to turn a viewport off:

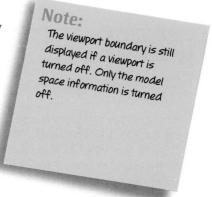

**Note:**
The viewport boundary is still displayed if a viewport is turned off. Only the model space information is turned off.

- Select the viewport, right-click to display the shortcut menu, and set the **Display Viewport Objects** menu item to **No.**
- Set the viewport's **On** property to **No** via the **Properties** palette.
- Use the **MVIEW** command's **Off** option and select the viewport.

A viewport that has been turned off is considered inactive. You can only have up to 64 viewports active at one time.

To make a viewport active again, use any of the options listed above to toggle the viewport's **Display** property to **On** or **Yes.**

TIP

The maximum number of active viewports is controlled using the **MAXACTVP** system variable. The maximum value is 64.

## Maximizing a Viewport

You can maximize a layout viewport so that it fills the entire drawing window area which makes it is easier to work on your model space design without switching entirely from paper space to model space. This feature was introduced to get around the complications of working "through" a layout viewport to get to the model space drawing information while you were still in paper space. There are four ways to maximize a layout viewport:

- Select the **Maximize Viewport** button on the right side of the Status Bar.
- Double-click on the viewport.
- Select the viewport, right-click to display the shortcut menu, and select the **Maximize Viewport** menu item.
- Type **VPMAX<Enter ↵>**.

Either method enlarges the viewport to fit the drawing window display area and changes the border to a thick red hashed line (see Figure 14-37).

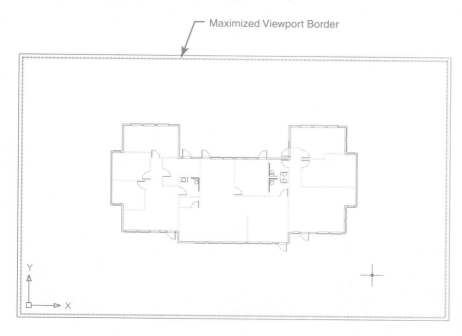

Maximized Viewport Border

**Figure 14-37**  Drawing display with a layout viewport maximized

To pan and zoom when a viewport is maximized and not change the original viewport display when you switch back to the viewport, use the **Minimize Viewport** commands listed below. When a viewport is maximized, it is almost as if you were working in model space on the **Model** tab.

There are four ways to restore the maximized layout viewport back to its original size and display:

- Select the **Minimize Viewport** button on the right side of the Status Bar.
- Double-click on the maximized viewport.
- Select the viewport, right-click to display the shortcut menu, and select the **Minimize Viewport** menu item.
- Type **VPMIN<Enter ↵>**.

## Exercise 14-4: Working with Multiple Annotation Scales

1. Continue from Exercise 14-3.
2. Create a text style named **Notes** with the following settings:
   a. Font = Simplex.shx AutoCAD font
   b. **Annotative** should be checked
   c. Paper Text Height = 0.125″
3. Create the following layer:

| Name | Color | Linetype | Lineweight | Description |
|------|-------|----------|------------|-------------|
| A-Anno-Note | 3 | Continuous | Default | Drawing note text |

4. Double-click inside the viewport so that model space is active.
5. Set the **Notes** text style current on the **Styles** toolbar.
6. Set the **A-Anno-Note** layer current in the **Layer** list box.
7. Set the **Viewport Scale** to 1/8″ = 1′-0″ by selecting it from the **Viewport Scale** list on the right side of the Status Bar.
8. Create the text shown in Figure 14-38 using the **Center** justification option.

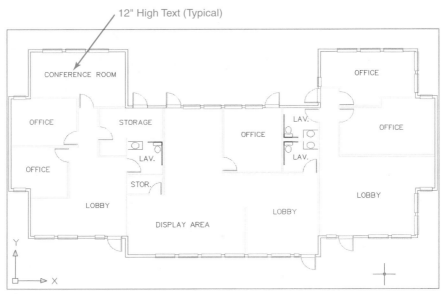

**Figure 14-38**   1/8″ = 1′-0″ scale view with text

9. Select the **Automatically add scales to annotative objects when the annotation scale changes** icon on the far right of the **Viewport Scale** button on the Status Bar so it is on.
10. Set the **Viewport Scale** to 1/4″ = 1′-0″ by selecting it from the list on the right side of the Status Bar. All text in the drawing should scale down by 1/2.
11. Center the 1/4″ = 1′-0″ text in each room by using the upper left grip to move each piece of text individually of its 1/8″ = 1′-0″ scale representation as shown in Figure 14-39.

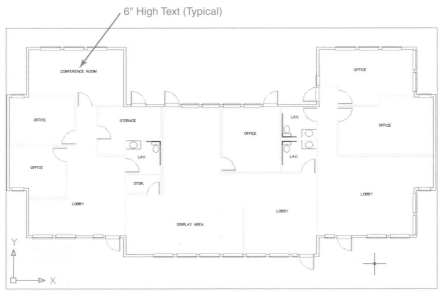

**Figure 14-39**   1/4″ = 1′-0″ scale view with text

12. Select the **Layout1** button on the Status Bar so that paper space is active and **Layout1** is the current layout. Only the 1/4″ = 1′-0″ text is visible.
13. Select the **Quick View Layouts** button and switch to the **Layout2** layout. Only the 1/8″ = 1′-0″ text is visible.
14. Make paper space the active drawing environment by double-clicking outside the viewport.
15. Save the drawing as **EX14-4.**

## MANAGING LAYOUTS

The following sections describe how to manage layouts so that you can do the following:

- Create a new layout
- Rename a layout
- Move or copy a layout
- Delete a layout

One of the easiest ways to accomplish any of these tasks is to rely on the layout's right-click shortcut menu in the **Quick View Layouts** display. Right-clicking with your mouse on any Layout preview in **Quick View Layouts** displays the shortcut menu shown in Figure 14-40.

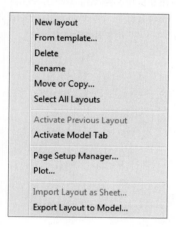

New layout
From template...
Delete
Rename
Move or Copy...
Select All Layouts

Activate Previous Layout
Activate Model Tab

Page Setup Manager...
Plot...

Import Layout as Sheet...
Export Layout to Model...

**Figure 14-40**   The Layout right-click shortcut menu

**TIP**   The **Select All Layouts** menu item on the **Layout** right-click menu provides a quick way to perform a task on all the layouts at one time.

The **LAYOUT** command also provides most of the same functionality, but as you might expect, it's not quite as user-friendly. Emphasis is placed on using the right-click menu where appropriate in the following sections.

### Creating a New Layout

There are four ways to create a new layout:

- Add a new generic Layout tab with the default settings so that the settings must be updated via the **Page Setup Manager.**
- Import a layout from an existing drawing file (DWG), drawing template file (DWT), or drawing exchange format file (DXF).
- Use the **Create Layout Wizard** that steps you through the layout setup.
- Copy an existing Layout tab in the current drawing file and rename it.

| New Layout | |
|---|---|
| **Ribbon & Panel:** | None |
| **Layouts Toolbar:** | |
| **Menu:** | Insert\| Layout\| New Layout |
| **Command Line:** | LAYOUT |
| **Command Alias:** | LO |

| Layout from Template | |
|---|---|
| **Ribbon & Panel:** | None |
| **Layouts Toolbar:** |  |
| **Menu:** | Insert\|Layout\|Layout from Template |
| **Command Line:** | LAYOUT |
| **Command Alias:** | LO |

The first three methods are described in the following sections. Copying a layout is covered a little later.

*Adding a Generic Layout with Default Settings.*     You can quickly add a generic layout with default page setup settings. You must then use the **Page Setup Manager** described earlier in this chapter to set up the layout as required.

You can add a generic layout by either selecting **New Layout** from the **Layout** cascade menu on the **Insert** menu, right-clicking and selecting **New Layout** from the shortcut menu, or by using the **New** option of the **LAYOUT** command.

AutoCAD prompts you to *Enter new Layout name <Layout3>:* if you add a new layout via the **Insert** pull-down menu or the **LAYOUT** command. The default layout name is "Layout" followed by an integer representing the layout number in the sequence.

When you use select **New Layout** from the right-click shortcut menu, a layout is added with the default name, and you must rename it. Renaming layouts is covered later in this chapter.

*Importing a Layout from a Drawing Template.*     To save time and effort, you can import a layout that is already set up with the correct paper size and plot settings from an existing drawing file (DWG), drawing template file (DWT), or drawing exchange format file (DXF).

You can import a layout by either selecting **Layout from Template...** from the **Layout** cascade menu on the **Insert** menu, right-clicking and selecting **From template...** from the shortcut menu, or using the **Template** option of the **LAYOUT** command.

AutoCAD displays the **Select Template From File** standard file dialog box so you can select the file from which you want to import the layout. Selecting the **Open** button gets a list of the layouts in the selected file and displays them in the **Insert Layout(s)** dialog box shown in Figure 14-41.

Select Layout to Import

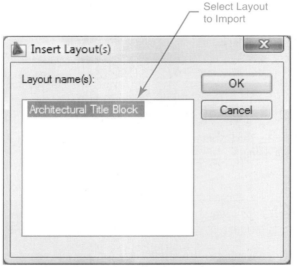

*Note:*
If a layout with the same name already exists in the current drawing during the import process, the layout is still added, but it is renamed by prefixing the layout name with a default layout name and a dash (-).

**Figure 14-41**     The Insert Layout(s) dialog box

| Create Layout Wizard | |
|---|---|
| **Ribbon & Panel:** | None |
| **Layouts Toolbar:** | None |
| **Menu:** | Insert\|Layout\|Create Layout Wizard |
| **Command Line:** | LAYOUTWIZARD |
| **Command Alias:** | None |

Select one or more layouts you want to import in the **Layout name(s):** list box and select **OK.** The selected layout(s) are imported with all their settings and drawing information and added to the right end of the Layout tabs on the bottom of the drawing window.

*Creating a New Layout Using the Layout Wizard.*     The **Create Layout Wizard** automates the process of creating, *and setting up,* a new layout by prompting you for information about the different layout settings in a series of preprogrammed steps.

You can start the **Create Layout Wizard** by selecting **Create Layout Wizard** from the **Layout** cascade menu on the **Insert** menu or by using the **LAYOUTWIZARD** command. The **Create Layout** dialog is displayed with the **Begin** step displayed as shown in Figure 14-42.

The steps that the wizard will take you through are listed on the left in sequence from top to bottom with the arrow to the left indicating the current step. Select the **Next** button to

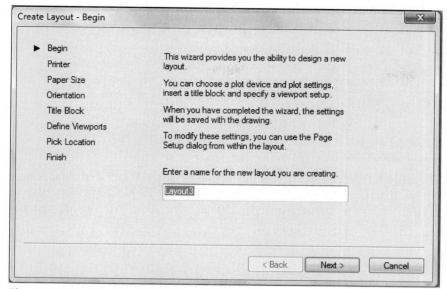

**Figure 14-42**    The Create Layout—Begin step

continue to the next step and the **Back** button to return to a previous step if you want to verify or change anything. The setup steps and options are as follows:

- **Begin**    Allows you to enter the desired name for the new layout
- **Printer**    Allows you to select a system printer/plotter output device
- **Paper Size**    Allows you to specify a paper size based on the printer selected in the previous step and switch drawing units between millimeters and inches
- **Orientation**    Allows you to switch between the portrait and landscape paper orientation modes
- **Title Block**    Allows you to insert a predefined title block in the layout as a block or an xref. The title block drawings listed are located in the default AutoCAD template folder.

> **FOR MORE DETAILS**    See Chapter 16 for more information about blocks. See Chapter 17 for more information about external references (xrefs).

- **Define Viewports**    Allows you to select a layout viewport configuration and set the viewport scale from a list of predefined standard scales
- **Pick Location**    Allows you to define the area to fill with the viewport configuration selected in the previous step by picking two corner points. If no location is selected, AutoCAD uses the layout's printable area.
- **Finish**    Exits the **Layout Wizard** and creates the new layout with the selected settings

> **Note:**
> You can always change the information entered in the **Create Layout Wizard** later by selecting the layout and using the **Page Setup Manager** explained earlier in the chapter.

## Renaming a Layout

The easiest way to rename a layout is to right-click on the layout in **Quick View Layouts** and select **Rename** from the shortcut menu. You can then update the layout name directly on the Layout preview as shown in Figure 14-43.

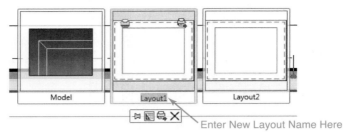

**Figure 14-43**   Renaming a layout

You can also rename a layout using the **Rename** option of the **LAYOUT** command. Using the **LAYOUT** command requires that you enter the layout to change in response to *Enter layout to rename <Layout1>:* where the current layout is the default name. AutoCAD then prompts you to *Enter new layout name:* so you can enter the new name.

## Moving and Copying a Layout

The easiest way to move or copy a layout is to right-click on the layout in **Quick View Layouts** and select **Move or Copy...** from the shortcut menu to display the **Move or Copy** dialog box shown in Figure 14-44.

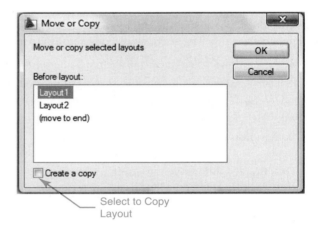

**Figure 14-44**   The Move or Copy dialog box

Select the layout from the list in the **Before layout:** list box that you want to locate the current layout *before*. When you select **OK,** the layout will be moved or copied so it appears as the Layout tab directly preceding, or to the left of, the selected tab.

If you want to make a copy of a layout and move it at the same time, select the **Create a copy** check box on the bottom of the dialog box. AutoCAD creates a copy of the layout with the same name as the current layout with a numerical suffix representing the sequence appended in parentheses. For instance, **Layout1** becomes **Layout1(2).**

## Deleting a Layout

The easiest way to delete a layout is to right-click on the Layout in **Quick View Layouts** and select **Delete** from the shortcut menu. AutoCAD displays a warning before deleting the layout so you can cancel the operation or select **OK** to continue.

You can also delete a layout using the **Delete** option of the **LAYOUT** command. Using the **LAYOUT** command requires that you enter the layout to delete in response to *Enter name of layout to delete <Layout1>:* where the current layout is the default name.

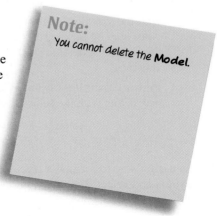

*Note:*
You cannot delete the **Model.**

## Displaying the Model and Layout Tabs

You can turn on the old style **Model** and **Layout** tabs at the bottom of the drawing window as shown in Figure 14-45 by right-clicking with your mouse while it is over the **Model** or current **Layout** button on the Status Bar and selecting **Display Layout and Model Tabs** from the shortcut menu.

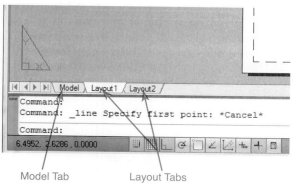

Model Tab                    Layout Tabs

**Figure 14-45**    Displaying the Model and Layout tabs

| Export Layout to Model | |
|---|---|
| **Ribbon & Panel:** | Output\| Send  Export Layout to Model |
| **Toolbar:** | None |
| **Pull-down Menu:** | File\| Export Layout to Mo<u>d</u>el |
| **Command Line:** | EXPORTLAYOUT |
| **Command Alias:** | None |

To turn the tabs off, right-click over any of the tabs displayed and select **Hide Layout and Model Tabs** from the shortcut menu.

## Exporting Layout Geometry

You can convert drawing information that resides in a paper space layout into a drawing where everything is in model space with the **Export Layout to Model** tool. When you select the tool the **Export Layout to Model Space Drawing** dialog box is displayed so you can specify a file name and location.

### Exercise 14-5: Managing Layouts

1. Continue from Exercise 14-4.
2. Select the **From template…** menu item on the right-click menu in **Quick View Layouts** in order to insert a new **Architectural D-Size** layout from an existing AutoCAD drawing template file.
3. Select the **Architectural, D-Size.dwt** template file on the Student CD in the **Select Template From File** dialog box and the **Open** button to display the **Insert Layout(s)** dialog box.
4. Select the **Architectural Title Block** layout and select the **OK** button.
5. Select the **Quick View Layouts** button and switch to the **Architectural Title Block** layout.
6. Set the viewport scale to 1/4″ = 1′-0″ using the techniques learned in Exercise 14-3 and center the floor plan in the viewport so it looks similar to Figure 14-46.
7. Rename the **Architectural Title Block** layout to **ANSI D Title Block** by right-clicking with your mouse on the **Architectural Title Block** layout in **Quick View Layouts** and selecting **Rename** from the shortcut menu.
8. Rename the **Layout2** layout to **ANSI B Title Block** by right-clicking with your mouse on the **Layout2** layout in **Quick View Layouts** and selecting **Rename** from the shortcut menu.
9. Delete the **Layout1** layout by right-clicking with your mouse on the **Layout1** layout in **Quick View Layouts** and selecting **Delete** from the shortcut menu.
10. Save the drawing as **EX14-5.**

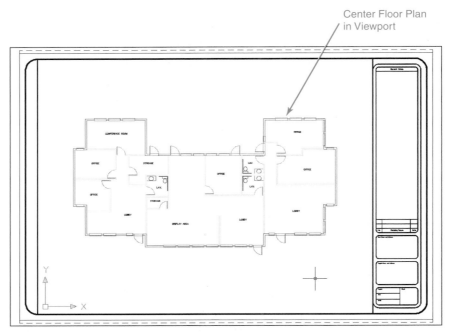

Center Floor Plan in Viewport

**Figure 14-46** The Architectural Title Block layout with 1/4″ = 1′-0″ viewport

## ADVANCED PAPER SPACE SCALING FEATURES

AutoCAD provides advanced paper space scaling options that allow you to control the scale of linetype definitions and hatch patterns based on the layout viewport scale. Basically, AutoCAD scales these features using a multiplier that is the inverse of the current viewport scale. For instance, for a viewport with a scale set to 1/4″ = 1′-0″, the zoom factor scale is 1/48XP. To make linetype definitions and hatch patterns display correctly, they must be scaled up by 48, the inverse of 1/48.

**Note:**
In order to use any of these features, you must be in paper space working through a layout viewport in model space (**TILEMODE**=0). It is possible to use the **Viewport Maximize** feature discussed earlier but do not zoom in or out because the viewport scale is affected.

### Paper Space Linetype Scale

The **PSLTSCALE** system variable allows you to scale line-type definitions based on the viewport scale so that linetype definitions will display the same in multiple viewports that have different scale factors. Without paper space line-type scaling, the same linetype definition will appear at different scales in each viewport as shown in Figure 14-47.

Setting **PSLTSCALE** to **1** (on) tells AutoCAD to scale the linetype definitions of all the objects displayed in a viewport by the inverse of the viewport scale factor as shown in Figure 14-48.

Be aware that the global linetype scale controlled using the **LTSCALE** system variable is still in effect when paper space linetype scale is turned on and can have some unintended effects. Typically, the **LTSCALE** system variable is set to 1 when paper space linetype scale is being used (**PSLTSCALE**=1).

| FOR MORE DETAILS | See Chapter 6 for more information about linetype definitions and the **LTSCALE** system variable. |

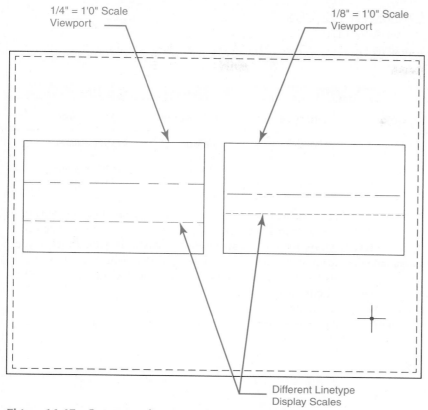

**Figure 14-47**   Paper space linetype scaling not turned on

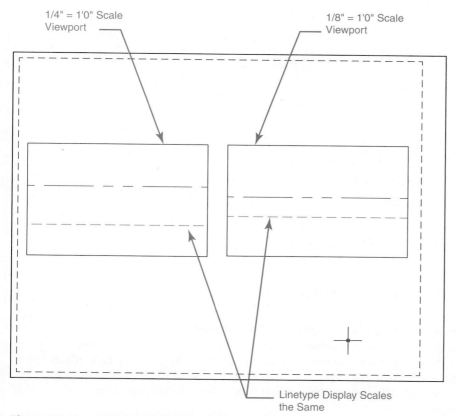

**Figure 14-48**   Paper space linetype scaling not turned on

## Exercise 14-6: Paper Space Linetype Scaling

1. Continue from Exercise 14-5.
2. Create the following layers:

| Name | Color | Linetype | Lineweight | Description |
|------|-------|----------|------------|-------------|
| A-Roof-Otln | 1 | Hidden | Default | Roof outline |
| A-Site-Prop | 5 | Phantom | Default | Property line |

3. Set the **PSLTSCALE** system variable to **1** so paper space linetype scaling is turned on.
4. Set the **LTSCALE** system variable to **1** to so that global linetype scaling is turned off.
5. Select the **Quick View Layouts** button and switch to the **ANSI D Title Block** layout. Double-click outside the viewport so paper space is the active drawing environment.
6. Maximize the viewport using the **Maximize Viewport** button on the right side of the Status Bar so you can work in model space.
7. Set the **A-Roof-Otln** layer current in the **Layer** list box.
8. Create the roof outline as shown in Figure 14-49. *Do not* draw dimensions.

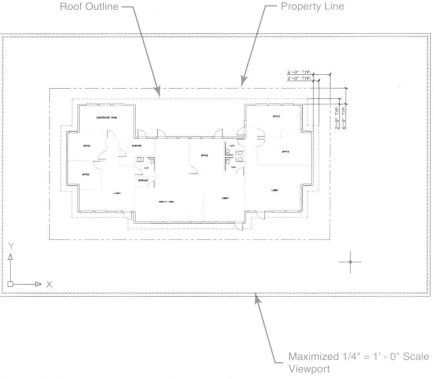

**Figure 14-49**    Using paper space linetype scaling

9. Set the **A-Site-Prop** layer current in the **Layer** list box.
10. Create the property line as shown in Figure 14-49. *Do not* draw dimensions.
11. Select the **Quick View Layouts** button and switch to the **ANSI B Title Block** layout. Double-click outside the viewport so paper space is the active drawing environment.
12. The roof line and property line should appear scaled correctly in the 1/8″ = 1′-0″ viewport.
13. Save the drawing as **EX14-6.**

## Paper Space Hatch Pattern Scale

You can create a boundary hatch that is automatically scaled relative to the layout viewport scale when using the **BHATCH** command so that you do not have to manually calculate the hatch scale factor. The hatch scale is set to the inverse of the current layout viewport scale.

To calculate the hatch scale automatically, select the **Relative to paper space** check box in the **Angle and scale** area of the **Hatch and Gradient** dialog box as shown in Figure 14-50.

Be aware that AutoCAD multiplies the viewport scale factor by the scale factor specified in the **Scale:** list box to come up with the final calculated scale factor. For this reason, the hatch scale factor specified in the **Scale:** list box is also typically set to 1 if you are going to use the **Relative to paper space** option.

**Note:** Hatch pattern scales must be updated manually using the **HATCHEDIT** command if the viewport scale is changed by zooming in or out.

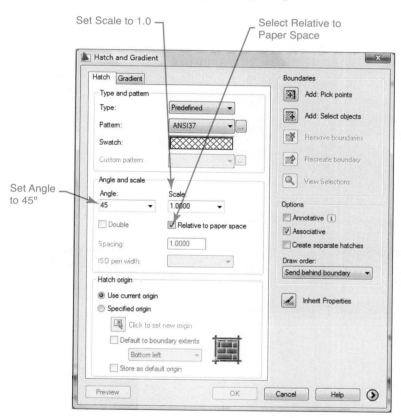

Figure 14-50    Setting the hatch scale factor relative to paper space

The **Annotative** option allows you to take this concept a step further by using the **Annotation Scale** setting to control the hatch scale. This approach is superior when you have multiple scaled views because each scaled hatch pattern is displayed separately similar to the **Annotative** text styles discussed in Chapter 11.

---

**FOR MORE DETAILS**   See Chapter 10 for more information about the **BHATCH** and **HATCHEDIT** commands.

---

## Exercise 14-7: Annotative Hatch Pattern Scaling

1. Continue from Exercise 14-6.
2. Select the **Model** button on the Status Bar so that model space is active.

3. Thaw the **A-Flor-Pat** layer in the **Layer** list box so the floor tile hatch outlines are displayed on the building floor plan and make it the current layer.
4. Set the **Annotation Scale** to 1/8″ = 1′-0″ by selecting it from the **Viewport Scale** list on the right side of the Status Bar.
5. Start the **BHATCH** command to display the **Hatch and Gradient** dialog box.
6. Set the **Pattern:** list box to the **AR-HBONE** hatch pattern, the **Scale:** list box to **2,** and select the **Annotative** check box as shown in Figure 14-50.
7. Select the **Add: Pick points** button and pick 3 points on the building floor plan to add the hatch patterns to as shown in Figure 14-51.

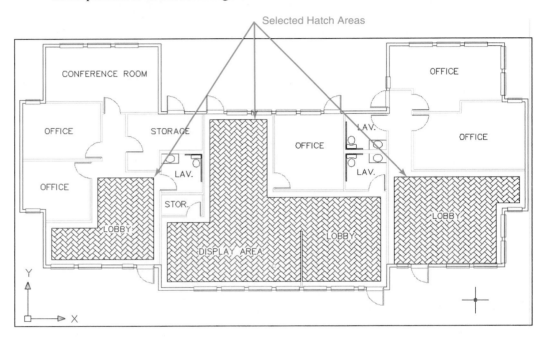

**Figure 14-51** Adding hatching to the 1/8″ = 1′-0″ scale view of a floor plan

8. Set the **Annotation Scale** to 1/4″ = 1′-0″ by selecting it from the **Viewport Scale** list on the right side of the Status Bar. All hatching in the drawing should scale down by 1/2 as shown in Figure 14-52.

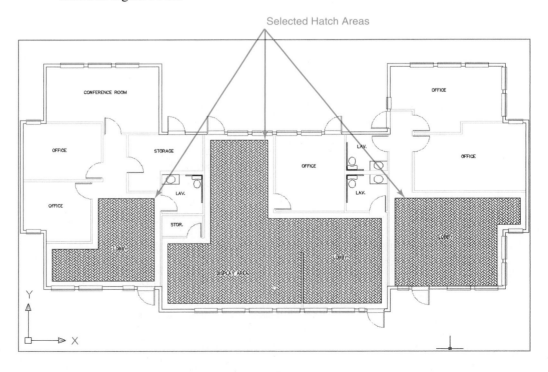

**Figure 14-52** 1/4″ = 1′-0″ scale view with hatching

9. Select the **Quick View Layouts** button and switch to the **ANSI B Title Block** layout. Only the 1/8″ = 1′-0″ hatching is visible.
10. Select the **Quick View Layouts** button and switch to the **ANSI D Title Block** layout. Only the 1/4″ = 1′-0″ text is visible.
11. Double-click outside the viewport so paper space is the active drawing environment.
12. Save the drawing as **EX14-7.**

## PAPER SPACE AND DIMENSIONING

There are two different ways that paper space can influence how, *and where,* you dimension a drawing. Both approaches are explained in the following sections.

### Scaling Dimension Features Using the Viewport Scale

Rather than providing a dimension scale factor (**DIMSCALE**) to control the size of dimension features such as text height and arrow sizes, you can rely on the viewport scale to control dimension feature sizes automatically. The only requirement is that, just like the other paper space scaling features described earlier, you must dimension the drawing while in paper space working through the layout viewport—yet another good reason to utilize the **Maximize Viewport** feature.

To scale dimension features using the viewport scale, select the **Scale dimensions to layout** button on the **Fit** tab in the **Modify Dimension Style** dialog box shown in Figure 14-53.

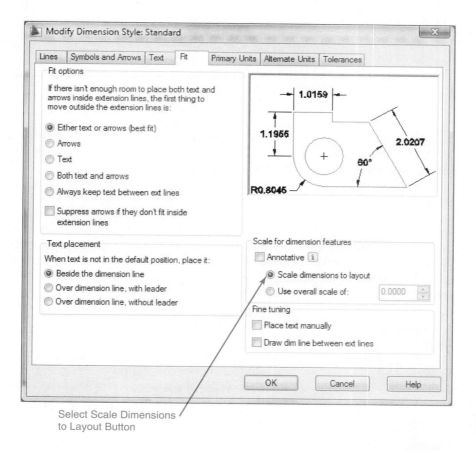

Select Scale Dimensions
to Layout Button

**Figure 14-53** Setting dimension features to scale using the viewport scale

**TIP**    You can also set the system variable **DIMSCALE** to **0** to turn on the **Scale dimensions to layout** feature.

When the **Scale dimensions to layout** feature is on, or **DIMSCALE** is set to 0, dimension features are automatically scaled by the inverse of the current viewport scale as shown in Figure 14-54.

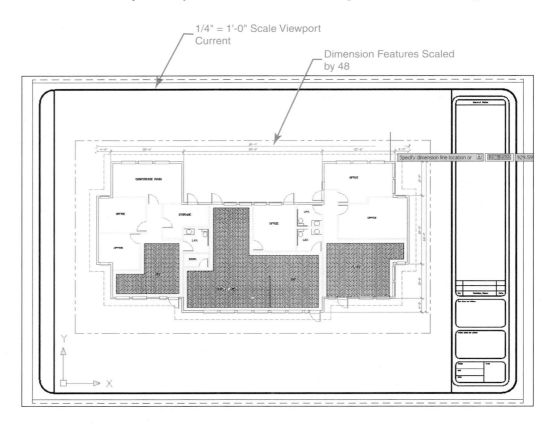

**Figure 14-54** Scaling dimension features using the viewport scale

If the viewport scale changes by zooming in or zooming out, dimension features *are not* automatically rescaled even if the **Scale dimensions to layout** feature is currently on. You must update the dimensions by selecting either **Update** from the **Dimension** pull-down menu or the **Dimension Update** button on the **Dimension** toolbar.

As mentioned in Chapter 13, the **Annotative** scale setting utilizes the AutoCAD **Annotation Scale** feature located on the right side of the Status Bar so that dimension features are scaled automatically when dimensions are added to your drawing. Once again, this setting is superior when you have multiple scale viewports because it will also add different scaled dimension features if the **Automatically add scales to annotative objects when the annotation scale changes** button to the right of the **Annotation Scale** setting is on. The best part is that each scale representation is displayed separately depending on the current **Annotation Scale** so that you no longer need to create duplicate information on separate layers!

| **FOR MORE DETAILS** | See Chapter 1 for a detailed description of the **Annotation Scale** feature. |
|---|---|

| **FOR MORE DETAILS** | See Chapter 13 for more details about scaling and updating dimension features. |
|---|---|

**Exercise 14-8:** Scaling Dimension Features Using the Annotation Scale

1. Continue from Exercise 14-7.
2. Create the following layers:

| Name | Color | Linetype | Lineweight | Description |
|------|-------|----------|------------|-------------|
| A-Anno-Dims-Ms | 1 | Continuous | Default | Dimensions located in model space |
| A-Anno-Dims-Ps | 1 | Continuous | Default | Dimensions located in paper space |

3. Select the **Model** button on the Status Bar so that model space is active.
4. Set the **Annotation Scale** to 1/4″ = 1′-0″ by selecting it from the **Viewport Scale** list on the right side of the Status Bar.
5. Set the **A-Anno-Dims-Ms** layer current in the **Layer** list box.
6. Add the dimensions as shown in Figure 14-55.
7. Save the drawing as **EX14-8.**

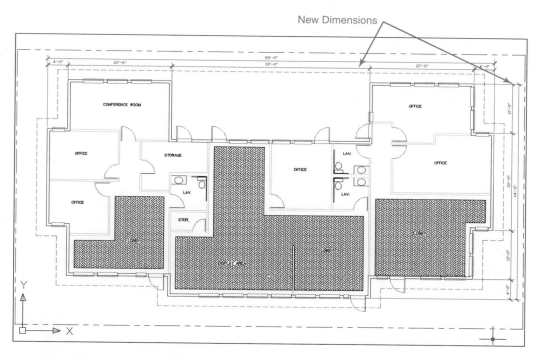

**Figure 14-55** Scaling dimension features using the Annotation Scale

## Dimensioning in Paper Space

Historically in AutoCAD, it has been the practice to locate all dimensions in model space with the drawing model information. Doing so made it possible to take advantage of dimension associativity so that when the drawing model changed, the dimensions updated automatically.

| FOR MORE DETAILS | See Chapter 13 for more details about the benefits of associated dimensioning. |
|---|---|

It is now possible in AutoCAD to locate associated dimensions in paper space that update automatically when the drawing model changes—even though the drawing information is in model space and the dimensions are located in paper space. It is even possible to switch completely to model space, change the drawing model, and have the associated dimensions update in paper space so that the dimensions are correct when you switch to the layout.

One of the main advantages of locating dimensions in the paper space layout is that you do not have to worry about scaling dimension features such as text height and arrow sizes as you do when you locate dimensions in model space. This is particularly advantageous on drawings with multiple scaled viewports. This is because everything in paper space is drawn at the size it will plot because the final plotted scale is typically 1:1.

Except for the scaling part, dimensioning in paper space is almost the same as dimensioning in model space. All that is required is that you create dimensions in paper space when no viewport is current. You can either use object snaps to snap to dimension definition points on the objects in model space, or you can select the objects and dimension them automatically—even though you are still in paper space as shown in Figure 14-56.

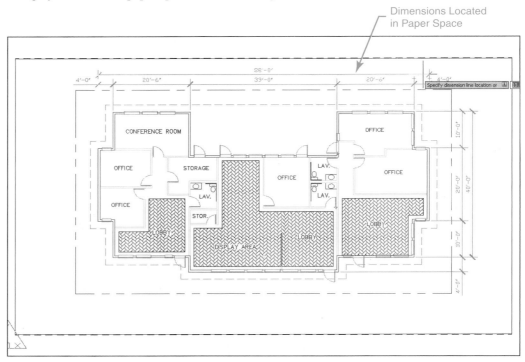

Dimensions Located in Paper Space

**Figure 14-56** Dimensioning in paper space

The one caveat to locating dimensions in paper space is that if the viewport display changes because you are panning or zooming inside the viewport, the paper space dimensions become temporarily detached from the model space drawing. Don't fret though; the **DIMREGEN** command can be used to "reattach" the paper space dimensions to their model space counterparts. Unfortunately, the **DIMREGEN** command is not found on any menu or toolbar, so you must type **DIMREGEN<Enter ↵>**. All paper space dimensions are automatically reassociated with the appropriate model space drawing information.

**Note:**

Dimension features for dimensions located in paper space are still affected by the current dimension scale (**DIMSCALE**) setting on the **Fit** tab in the **Dimension Style** dialog box. Typically, **DIMSCALE** is set to 1 when locating dimensions in paper space because there is no need to scale the dimension features.

**Exercise 14-9:** Placing Dimensions in Paper Space

1. Continue from Exercise 14-8.
2. Select the **Quick View Layouts** button and switch to the **ANSI B Title Block** layout.
3. Double-click inside the viewport to make the viewport active.
4. Freeze the **A-Anno-Dims-Ms** layer in the current viewport by changing the **Freeze or thaw in current viewport** column (third from left) to the snowflake in the **Layer** list box.
5. Toggle the **Model** button on the right side of the Status Bar to **Paper** so that paper space is the current environment.
6. Set the **A-Anno-Dims-Ps** layer current in the **Layer** list box.
7. Set the **DIMSCALE** system variable to **1** so that dimension features are not scaled and add the dimensions as shown in Figure 14-57 in paper space.
8. Save the drawing as **EX14-9**.

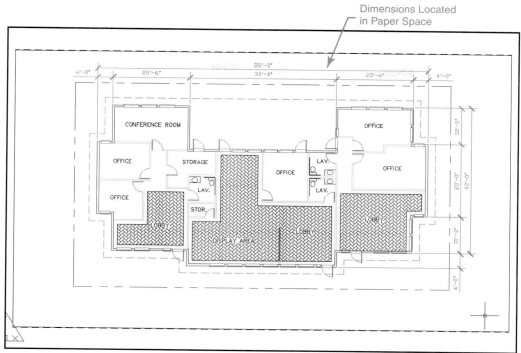

**Figure 14-57**    Placing dimensions in paper space

## SUMMARY

In this chapter, we explained the different ways to set up and lay out a drawing using paper space techniques so that it is ready for output to the associated printer, plotter, or other output device.

> **FOR MORE DETAILS**    See Chapter 15 for detailed information about plotting to different output devices.

As you found out in this chapter, using paper space to lay out a drawing is the industry standard for good reason. Using the techniques and methods you learned in this chapter will enable you to take take advantage of benefits that include:

- Creating multiple layouts that are different sheet sizes
- Associating multiple printer/plotter devices to create different output results
- Setting up layouts with multiple scale views
- Controlling layer visibility individually per layout viewport

In addition to setting up a drawing for output, we also introduced some advanced paper space scaling techniques that allow you to rely on the scale of the current layout viewport to save time and increase productivity.

Finally, locating dimensions in the paper space layout instead of the traditional method of locating dimensions in model space was explored. While creating dimensions in paper space has some distinct advantages, it is still common to locate dimensions in model space. Both approaches have advantages and disadvantages. For this reason, no real consensus exists as to which approach should be used.

> **FOR MORE DETAILS**    See Chapter 13 for detailed information about dimensioning.

## CHAPTER TEST QUESTIONS

### Multiple Choice

1. Most of a drawing's linework and annotation features are drawn in:
   a. Paper space
   b. Model space
   c. Drawing space
   d. None of the above

2. The system variable that controls whether model space or paper space is active is named:
   a. **DRAWMODE**     c. **TILEMODE**
   b. **SPACEMODE**     d. **MODETILE**

3. The paper size of a layout is controlled via its:
   a. Drawing limits
   b. Associated plotting device
   c. b and d
   d. Page setup

4. The user-defined window created in a paper space layout that allows you to view and scale information in model space is referred to as a:
   a. Layout portal     c. Layout window
   b. Layout viewport     d. Layout aperture

5. The printable area of a layout is represented by:
   a. Shadow
   b. Edge of the layout
   c. Dashed line
   d. Drawing limits

6. The command used to create a layout viewport is:
   a. **MVIEW**     c. **-VPORTS**
   b. **VPORTS**     d. All of the above

7. The layout viewport creation option that creates a viewport the same size as a layout's printable area is:
   a. Polygonal     c. Fit
   b. Object     d. Restore

8. To make a layout viewport current:
   a. Double-click with the mouse inside the viewport.
   b. Type **MS<Enter ↵>**
   c. Type **PS<Enter ↵>**
   d. a and b

9. Layout viewport scale is controlled by:
   a. **SCALE** command
   b. Zooming in and out of a viewport
   c. Panning the display in the viewport
   d. **VPSCALE** system variable

10. The scale of a layout viewport can be set using:
    a. The **Viewport Scale** list on the Status Bar
    b. The **ZOOM** command to specify a zoom scale factor
    c. The **Properties** palette
    d. All of the above

11. To prevent a viewport scale from changing accidentally, it is best to:
    a. Turn the viewport off
    b. Work only in model space
    c. Freeze the viewport layer
    d. Lock the viewport display

12. The command that allows you to change the shape of a viewport is:
    a. **SCALE**     c. **MOVE**
    b. **VPORTCLIP**     d. **VPCLIP**

13. The **LAYOUT** command allows you to:
    a. Rename a layout
    b. Delete a layout
    c. Create a new layout
    d. All of the above

14. The system variable used to control whether paper space linetype scaling is on or off is:
    a. **PSLTSCALE**
    b. **LTSCALE**
    c. **PAPERSCALE**
    d. All of the above

15. To make dimension features scale according to the viewport scale, you can set the **DIMSCALE** system variable to:
    a. 1
    b. Inverse of the plot scale
    c. 0
    d. None of the above

### Matching

**Column A**
a. **TILEMODE**

b. Page setup

c. Layout viewport

d. Printable area

**Column B**
1. Displays details of the current page setup, creates new page setups, and modifies existing page setups
2. System variable that controls whether paper space linetype scaling is on or off
3. Command used to create one or more layout viewports
4. Plotter configuration file used to store and manage printer/plotter settings

e. Page Setup Manager

f. .PC3 file

g. **MVIEW** command

h. **-VPORTS** command

i. **VCLIP** command

j. **PSLTSCALE**

5. Command used to create one or more layout viewports

6. System variable that controls whether you are working in model space or paper space

7. User-defined window created in a paper space layout that allows you to view drawing information in model space

8. Controls the settings that affect the appearance of a plotted drawing

9. Actual physical area that can be printed for the currently specified plotting device and paper size

10. Command used to change the shape of a viewport

## True or False

1. True or False: Most drawing linework and annotation features are drawn in model space.

2. True or False: You cannot locate any drawing information in a paper space layout.

3. True or False: The associated printer/plotter device determines what paper sizes are available.

4. True or False: Layout viewport scale is controlled by zooming in and out in a viewport.

5. True or False: It is possible to print to the edges of the paper in layout.

6. True or False: Setting the associated plot device to <**None**> allows you select any standard paper size.

7. True or False: A layout viewport is treated like most other AutoCAD drawing objects (lines, circles, etc.).

8. True or False: It is not possible to create circular viewports.

9. True or False: The **Properties** palette can be used to set the viewport scale.

10. True or False: It is possible to add your own custom scales to the AutoCAD standard scale list.

11. True or False: It is possible to freeze and thaw layer information in each individual viewport.

12. True or False: The shape of a viewport cannot be changed; it must be deleted, and then recreated in the new shape.

13. True or False: To take full advantage of the advanced paper space scaling features, you must work in model space through the paper space viewport.

14. True or False: You must set the **LTSCALE** system variable to 0 in order to use paper space linetype scaling.

15. True or False: You must set the **DIMSCALE** system variable to 0 in order to scale dimension features using the current viewport scale.

## CHAPTER PROJECTS

### Project 14-1: Classroom Plan—Continued from Chapter 13

1. Open drawing **P13-1**.

2. Select the **Quick View Layouts** button, right-click on layout, and select **From template...** on the shortcut menu to import a layout.

3. Open the **Architectural D-Size.dwt** drawing template on the student CD and import the **Architectural Title Block** layout from the template.

4. Select the **Architectural Title Block** layout in **Quick View Layouts** to set it current. There is a single viewport in this layout. Make the viewport current by double-clicking inside of the viewport boundary.

5. Zoom extents so the drawing fills the viewport and set the viewport scale to **1/2″ = 1′-0″**. Position the drawing within the viewport so it matches Figure P14-1.

6. Start the **DIMSTYLE** command and modify the **Arch** dimension style. In the **Fit** tab, set the **Scale for dimension features** to **Scale dimensions to layout.**

7. Switch back to paper space by double-clicking outside the viewport.

8. Delete the **Layout1** and **Layout2** layouts.

9. Save the drawing as **P14-1.**

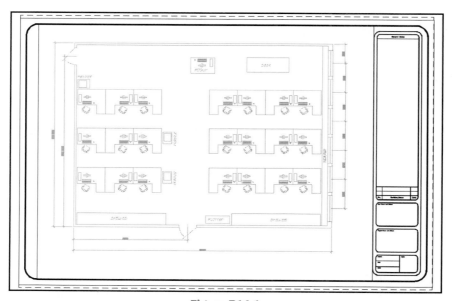

**Figure P14-1**

## Project 14-2: Motorcycle—Continued from Chapter 13

1. Open drawing **P13-2.**

2. Select the **Layout1** button on the Status Bar to switch to paper space.

3. Select the viewport boundary and change its layer to the **Defpoints** layer. *Hint:* The **Defpoints** layer is added to the drawing when you create dimensions and is used to locate dimension definition points so that they do not plot.

4. Make the viewport current by double-clicking inside of the viewport boundary.

5. Zoom extents so the drawing fills the viewport as shown in Figure P14-2.

6. Switch back to paper space by double-clicking outside the viewport.

7. Save the drawing as **P14-2.**

## Project 14-3A: B-Size Mechanical Border—Continued from Chapter 13

1. Open drawing **Mechanical B-Size.DWT** from Chapter 13.

2. Select **Select All** from the **Edit** pull-down menu or press the **<Ctrl>+A** keyboard combination to select everything in the drawing.

3. Select **Copy with Base Point** from the **Utilities** panel on the **Home** ribbon or press the **<Ctrl+Shift>+C** keyboard combination and specify **0,0** as the base point.

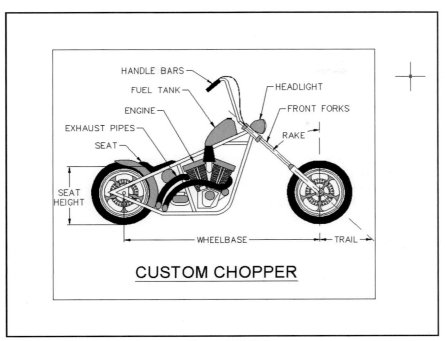

**Figure P14-2**

4. Press the **<Delete>** key or use the **ERASE** command to delete all the selected objects.
5. Select the **Layout1** button on the Status Bar to switch to paper space.
6. Erase the existing default viewport.
7. Use the **Page Setup Manager** to set the associated plotter to **None** and the paper size to **ANSI B (17.00 × 11.00 Inches).**
8. Select **Paste** from the **Utilities** panel on the **Home** ribbon or press the **<Ctrl>+V** keyboard combination and enter **-.25,-.75** when AutoCAD prompts you to *Specify insertion point:* to paste the title border in paper space.
9. Create a polygonal viewport on layer **Viewport** at the insider border edges as shown in Figure P14-3A.

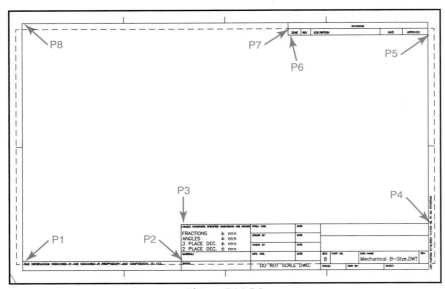

**Figure P14-3A**

10. Rename the **Layout1** layout to **Mechanical B-Size** and delete the **Layout2** layout.

11. Select the **Quick View Layouts** button.

12. Right-click on the **Mechanical B-Size** layout and choose **Move or Copy...** Choose **(move to end)** and check the **Create a copy** box and choose **OK**. Rename the layout **Metric Mechanical B-Size**.

13. Use the **Page Setup Manager** and set the **Plot scale** to **1 inches = 25.4 units**.

14. Start the **SCALE** command and select all the geometry in the **Metric Mechanical B-Size** layout. Use a base point of **0,0** and a scale factor of **25.4**.

15. Save the drawing as a template file named **Mechanical B-Size.DWT**.

## Project 14-3B: C-Size Mechanical Border—Continued from Chapter 13

1. Open drawing **Mechanical C-Size.DWT** from Chapter 13.

2. Select **Select All** from the **Utilities** panel on the **Home** ribbon or press the **<Ctrl>+A** keyboard combination to select everything in the drawing.

3. Select **Copy with Base Point** from the **Utilities** panel on the **Home** ribbon or press the **<Ctrl+Shift>+C** keyboard combination and specify **0,0** as the base point.

4. Press the **<Delete>** key or use the **ERASE** command to delete all the selected objects.

5. Select the **Layout1** button on the Status Bar to switch to paper space.

6. Erase the existing default viewport.

7. Use the **Page Setup Manager** to set the associated plotter to **None** and the paper size to **ANSI C (22.00 × 17.00 Inches)**.

8. Select **Paste** from the **Utilities** panel on the **Home** ribbon or press the **<Ctrl>+V** keyboard combination and enter **-.25,-.75** when AutoCAD prompts you to *Specify insertion point:* to paste the title border in paper space.

9. Create a polygonal viewport on layer **Viewport** at the inside border edges as shown in Figure P14-3B.

10. Rename the **Layout1** layout to **Mechanical C-Size** and delete the **Layout2** layout.

11. Make sure that paper space is the current drawing environment by double-clicking outside the viewport.

12. Save the drawing as a template file named **Mechanical C-Size.DWT**.

## Project 14-3C: A-Size Portrait Mechanical Border—Continued from Chapter 13

1. Open drawing **Mechanical A-Size-Portrait.DWT** from Chapter 13.

2. Select **Select All** from the **Utilities** panel on the **Home** ribbon or press the **<Ctrl>+A** keyboard combination to select everything in the drawing.

3. Select **Copy with Base Point** from the **Utilities** panel on the **Home** ribbon or press the **<Ctrl+Shift>+C** keyboard combination and specify **0,0** as the base point.

4. Press the **<Delete>** key or use the **ERASE** command to delete all the selected objects.

5. Select the **Layout1** button on the Status Bar to switch to paper space.

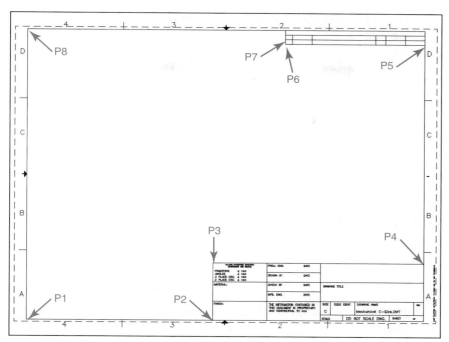

**Figure P14-3B**

6. Erase the existing default viewport.
7. Use the **Page Setup Manager** to set the associated plotter to **None** and the paper size to **Letter (8.50 × 11.00 Inches).**
8. Select **Paste** from the **Utilities** panel on the **Home** ribbon or press the **<Ctrl>+V** keyboard combination and enter **-.25,-.25** when AutoCAD prompts you to *Specify insertion point:* to paste the title border in paper space.
9. Create a polygonal viewport on layer **Viewport** at the inside border edges as shown in Figure P14-3C.

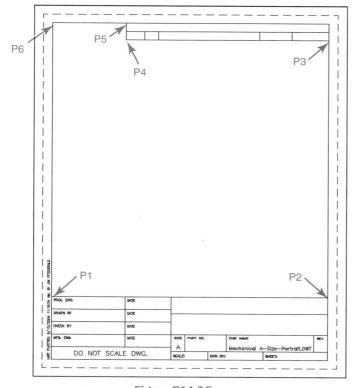

**Figure P14-3C**

10. Rename the **Layout1** layout to **Mechanical A-Size-Portrait** and delete the **Layout2** layout.

11. Make sure that paper space is the current drawing environment by double-clicking outside the viewport.

12. Save the drawing as a template file named **Mechanical A-Size-Portrait.DWT.**

## Project 14-4A: Architectural D-Size Border—Continued from Chapter 13

1. Open the template file **Architectural D-Size.DWT** from Chapter 13.

2. Select **Select All** from the **Utilities** panel on the **Home** ribbon or press the **<Ctrl>+A** keyboard combination to select everything in the drawing.

3. Select **Copy with Base Point** from the **Utilities** panel on the **Home** ribbon or press the **<Ctrl+Shift>+C** keyboard combination and select the bottom left corner of the border corner tick marks using the **Endpoint** object snap.

4. Press the **<Delete>** key or use the **ERASE** command to delete all the selected objects.

5. Select the **Layout1** button on the Status Bar to switch to paper space.

6. Erase the existing default viewport.

7. Use the **Page Setup Manager** to set the associated plotter to **None** and the paper size to **ARCH D (36.00 × 24.00 Inches).**

8. Select **Paste** from the **Utilities** panel on the **Home** ribbon or press the **<Ctrl>+V** keyboard combination and enter **-.25,-.75** when AutoCAD prompts you to *Specify insertion point:* to paste the title border in paper space.

9. Create a rectangular viewport on layer **A-Anno-Vprt** at the insider border edges as shown in Figure P14-4A.

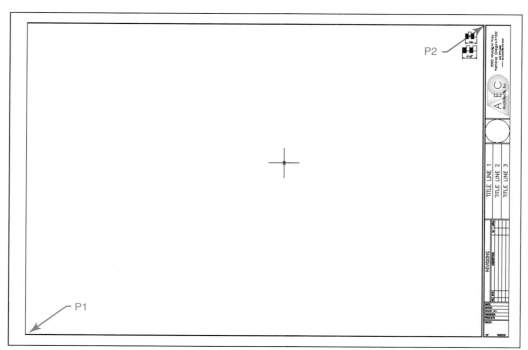

**Figure P14-4A**

10. Rename the **Layout1** layout to **Architectural D-Size** and delete the **Layout2** layout.

11. Make sure that paper space is the current drawing environment by double-clicking outside the viewport.

12. Save the drawing to a template file as **Architectural D-Size.DWT**.

## Project 14-4B: Architectural B-Size Border—Continued from Chapter 13

1. Open the template file **Architectural B-Size.DWT**.

2. Select **Select All** from the **Utilities** panel on the **Home** ribbon or press the **<Ctrl>+A** keyboard combination to select everything in the drawing.

3. Select **Copy with Base Point** from the **Utilities** panel on the **Home** ribbon or press the **<Ctrl+Shift>+C** keyboard combination and select the bottom left corner of the border corner tick marks using the **Endpoint** object snap.

4. Press the **<Delete>** key or use the **ERASE** command to delete all the selected objects.

5. Select the **Layout1** button on the Status Bar to switch to paper space.

6. Erase the existing default viewport.

7. Use the **Page Setup Manager** to set the associated plotter to **None** and the paper size to **ANSI B (17.00 × 11.00 Inches)**.

8. Select **Paste** from the **Utilities** panel on the **Home** ribbon or press the **<Ctrl>+V** keyboard combination and enter **-.25,-.75** when AutoCAD prompts you to *Specify insertion point:* to paste the title border in paper space.

9. Create a rectangular viewport on layer **A-Anno-Vprt** at the inside border edges as shown in Figure P14-4B.

10. Rename the **Layout1** layout to **Architectural B-Size** and delete the **Layout2** layout.

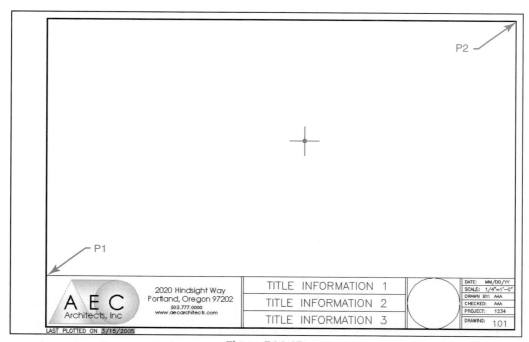

**Figure P14-4B**

11. Make sure that paper space is the current drawing environment by double-clicking outside the viewport.

12. Save the drawing to a template file as **Architectural B-Size.DWT.**

## Project 14-4C: Architectural A-Size Border—Continued from Chapter 13

1. Open the template file **Architectural A-Size.DWT.**

2. Select **Select All** from the **Edit** pull-down menu or press the **<Ctrl>+A** keyboard combination to select everything in the drawing.

3. Select **Copy with Base Point** from the **Utilities** panel on the **Home** ribbon or press the **<Ctrl+Shift>+C** keyboard combination and select the bottom left corner of the border corner tick marks using the **Endpoint** object snap.

4. Press the **<Delete>** key or use the **ERASE** command to delete all the selected objects.

5. Select the **Layout1** button on the Status Bar to switch to paper space.

6. Erase the existing default viewport.

7. Use the **Page Setup Manager** to set the associated plotter to **None** and the paper size to **ANSI A (8.50 × 11.00 Inches).**

8. Select **Paste** from the **Utilities** panel on the **Home** ribbon or press the **<Ctrl>+V** keyboard combination and enter **-.25,-.75** when AutoCAD prompts you to *Specify insertion point:* to paste the title border in paper space.

9. Create a rectangular viewport on layer **A-Anno-Vprt** at the inside border edges as shown in Figure P14-4C.

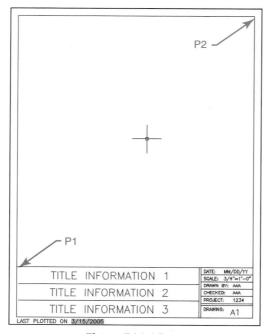

**Figure P14-4C**

10. Rename the **Layout1** layout to **Architectural A-Size** and delete the **Layout2** layout.

11. Make sure that paper space is the current drawing environment by double-clicking outside the viewport.
12. Save the drawing to a template file as **Architectural A-Size.DWT.**

## Project 14-5: Electrical Schematic—Continued from Chapter 13

1. Open drawing **P13-5**.
2. Select **Layout from Template...** from the **Layout** cascade menu on the **Insert** menu to import a layout.
3. Import the **Architectural D-Size** layout and border from the **Architectural D-Size.dwt** template file created in Problem 14-4C.
4. Select the **Architectural D-Size** layout to make it current.
5. Set the viewport scale to **1:2** and center the view as shown in Figure P14-5.
6. Lock the viewport display so the view scale doesn't change.
7. Start the **DIMSTYLE** command and modify the **Arch** dimension style. In the **Fit** tab, set the **Scale for dimension features** to **Scale dimensions to layout.**
8. Delete the **Layout1** and **Layout2** layouts.
9. Save the drawing as **P14-5.**

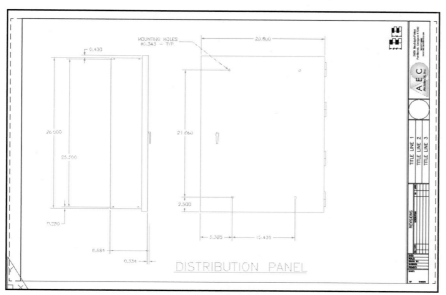

**Figure P14-5**

## Project 14-6A: Hot Water Piping Schematic—Continued from Chapter 13

1. Open drawing **P13-6A**.
2. Select **Layout from Template...** from the **Layout** cascade menu on the **Insert** menu to import a layout.
3. Insert the **Architectural A-Size** layout and border from the **Architectural A-Size.dwt** template file created in Problem 14-4C.
4. Select the **Architectural A-Size** layout to make it current.

5. Set the viewport scale to **1:1** and center the view as shown in Figure P14-6A.
6. Lock the viewport display so the view scale doesn't change.
7. Delete the **Layout1** and **Layout2** layouts.
8. Save the drawing as **P14-6A**.

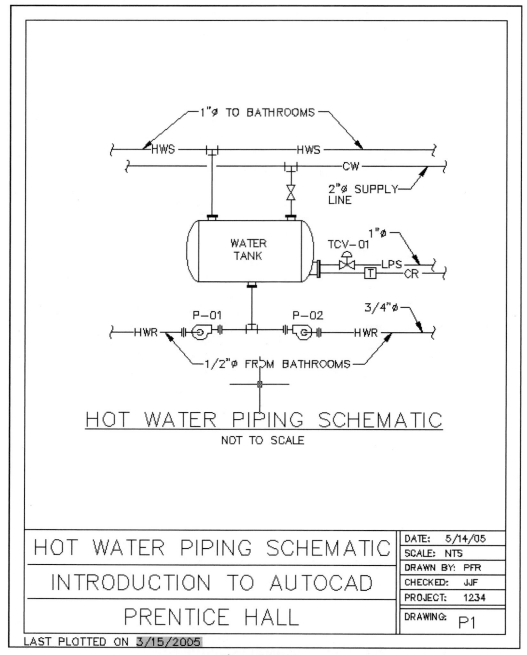

**Figure P14-6A**

### Project 14-6B: Water Heater Schematic—Continued from Chapter 13

1. Open drawing **P13-6B**.
2. Select **Layout from Template...** from the **Layout** cascade menu on the **Insert** menu to import a layout.

3. Insert the **Architectural A-Size** layout and border from the **Architectural A-Size.dwt** template file created in Problem 14-4C.
4. Select the **Architectural A-Size** layout to make it current.
5. Set the viewport scale to **Scale to fit** and center the view as shown in Figure P14-6B.
6. Lock the viewport display so the view scale doesn't change.
7. Delete the **Layout1** and **Layout2** layouts.
8. Save the drawing as **P14-6B**.

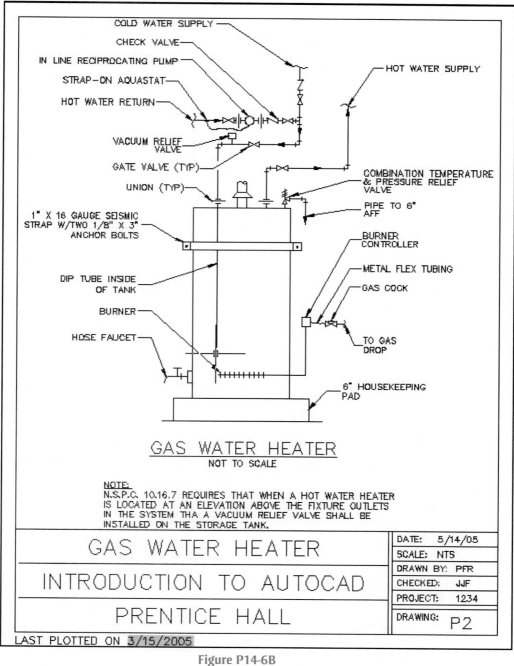

**Figure P14-6B**

## Project 14-6C: Compressed Air Schematic—Continued from Chapter 13

1. Open drawing **P13-6C.**
2. Select **Layout from Template...** from the **Layout** cascade menu on the **Insert** menu to import a layout.
3. Insert the **Architectural A-Size** layout and border from the **Architectural A-Size.dwt** template file created in Problem 14-4C.
4. Select the **Architectural A-Size** layout to make it current.
5. Set the viewport scale to **Scale to fit** and center the view as shown in Figure P14-6C.
6. Lock the viewport display so the view scale doesn't change.
7. Delete the **Layout1** and **Layout2** layouts.
8. Save the drawing as **P14-6C.**

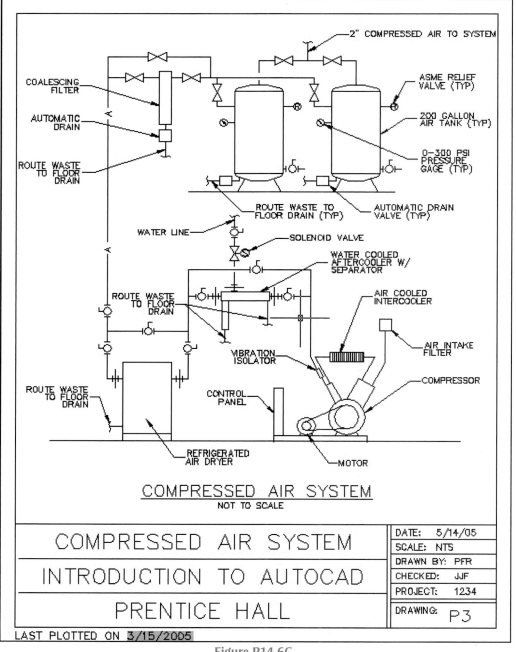

**Figure P14-6C**

## Project 14-6D: Unit Heater Connections—Continued from Chapter 13

1. Open drawing **P13-6D.**
2. Select **Layout from Template...** from the **Layout** cascade menu on the **Insert** menu to import a layout.
3. Insert the **Architectural A-Size** layout and border from the **Architectural A-Size.dwt** template file created in Problem 14-4C.
4. Select the **Architectural A-Size** layout to make it current.
5. Set the viewport scale to **Scale to fit** and center the view as shown in Figure P14-6D.
6. Lock the viewport display so the view scale doesn't change.
7. Delete the **Layout1** and **Layout2** layouts.
8. Save the drawing as **P14-6D.**

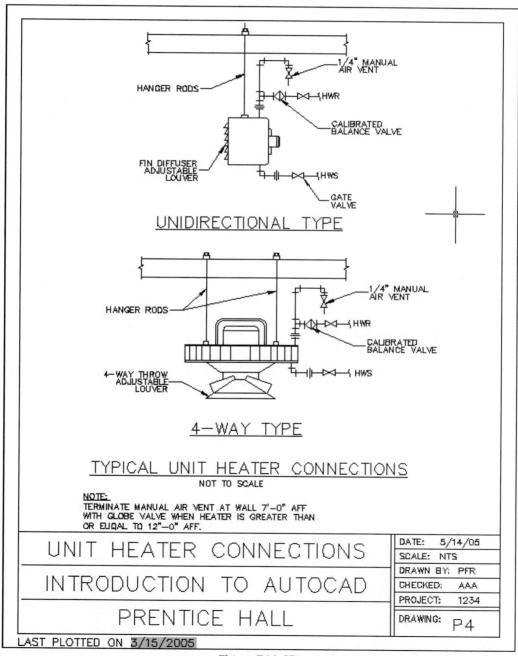

Figure P14-6D

## Project 14-6E: Pipe/Wall Penetration Detail—Continued from Chapter 11

1. Open drawing **P11-6E.**
2. Select **Layout from Template...** from the **Layout** cascade menu on the **Insert** menu to import a layout.
3. Insert the **Architectural A-Size** layout and border from the **Architectural A-Size.dwt** template file created in Problem 14-4C.
4. Select the **Architectural A-Size** layout to make it current.
5. Set the viewport scale to **3″ = 1′-0″** and center the view as shown in Figure P14-6E.
6. Lock the viewport display so the view scale doesn't change.
7. Delete the **Layout1** and **Layout2** layouts.
8. Save the drawing as **P14-6E.**

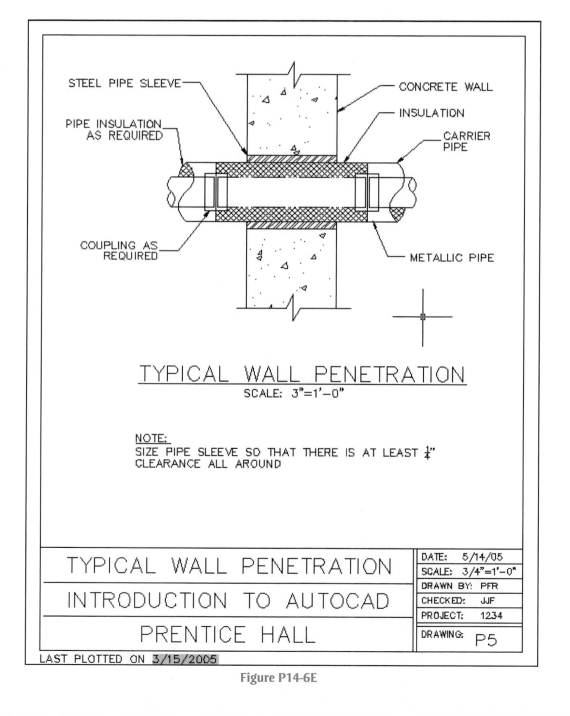

**Figure P14-6E**

## Project 14-7: Architectural Plan—Continued from Chapter 13

1. Open drawing **P13-7.**
2. Select **Layout from Template...** from the **Layout** cascade menu on the **Insert** menu to import a layout.
3. Import the **Architectural D-Size** layout and border from the **Architectural D-Size.dwt** template file created in Problem 14-4A.
4. Select the **Architectural D-Size** layout to make it current.
5. Set the viewport scale to **1/4″ = 1′-0″** and center the view as shown in Figure P14-7.
6. Lock the viewport display so the view scale doesn't change.
7. Delete the **Layout1** and **Layout2** layouts.
8. Save the drawing as **P14-7.**

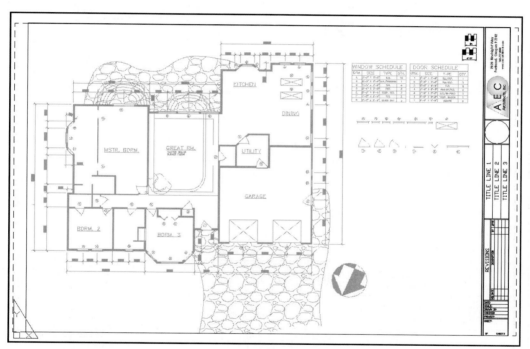

Figure P14-7

## Project 14-8A: Joist Foundation Detail—Continued from Chapter 13

1. Open drawing **P13-8A.**
2. Select **Layout from Template...** from the **Layout** cascade menu on the **Insert** menu to import a layout.
3. Insert the **Architectural A-Size** layout and border from the **Architectural A-Size.dwt** template file created in Problem 14-4C.
4. Select the **Architectural A-Size** layout to make it current.
5. Set the viewport scale to **1/2″ = 1′-0″** and center the view as shown in Figure P14-8A.
6. Lock the viewport display so the view scale doesn't change.
7. Delete the **Layout1** and **Layout2** layouts.
8. Save the drawing as **P14-8A.**

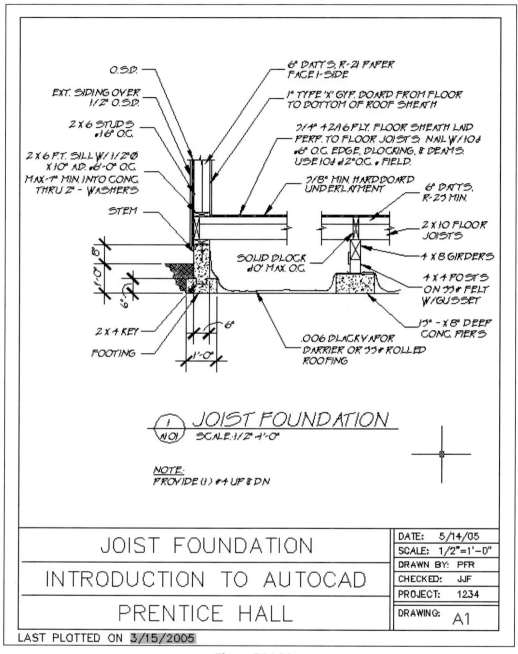

Figure P14-8A

## Project 14-8B: Interior Floor Change Detail—Continued from Chapter 13

1. Open drawing **P13-8B.**
2. Select **Layout from Template...** from the **Layout** cascade menu on the **Insert** menu to import a layout.
3. Insert the **Architectural A-Size** layout and border from the **Architectural A-Size.dwt** template file created in Problem 14-4C.
4. Select the **Architectural A-Size** layout to make it current.
5. Set the viewport scale to **1/2″ = 1′-0″** and center the view as shown in Figure P14-8B.

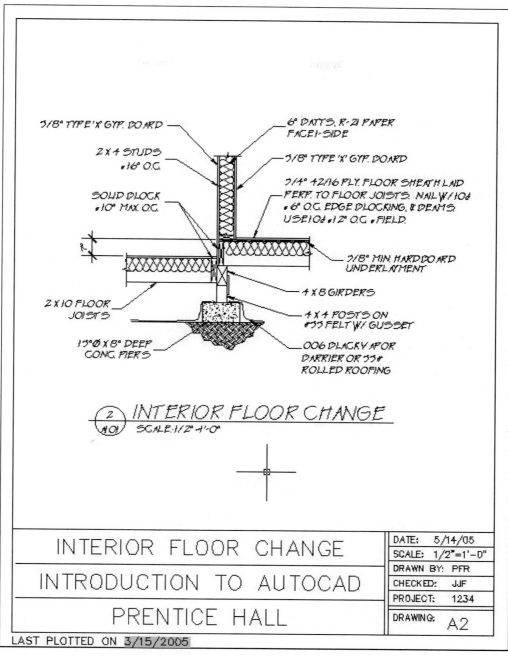

6. Lock the viewport display so the view scale doesn't change.
7. Delete the **Layout1** and **Layout2** layouts.
8. Save the drawing as **P14-8B.**

## Project 14-8C: Truss with Soffited Eave Detail—Continued from Chapter 13

1. Open drawing **P13-8C.**
2. Select **Layout from Template...** from the **Layout** cascade menu on the **Insert** menu to import a layout.
3. Insert the **Architectural A-Size** layout and border from the **Architectural A-Size.dwt** template file created in Problem 14-4C.

4. Select the **Architectural A-Size** layout to make it current.
5. Set the viewport scale to **1/2″ = 1′-0″** and center the view as shown in Figure P14-8C.
6. Lock the viewport display so the view scale doesn't change.
7. Delete the **Layout1** and **Layout2** layouts.
8. Save the drawing as **P14-8C**.

### Project 14-9: Optical Mount—English Units—Continued from Chapter 13

1. Open drawing **P13-9**.
2. Select **Layout from Template…** from the **Layout** cascade menu on the **Insert** menu to import a layout.

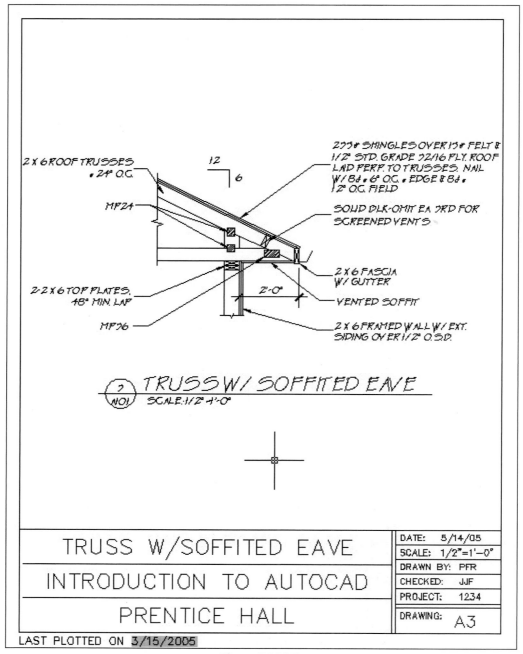

**Figure P14-8C**

3. Import the **Mechanical B-Size** layout and border from the **Mechanical B-Size.dwt** template file created in Problem 14-3A.
4. Select the **Mechanical B-Size** layout to make it current.
5. Set the viewport scale to **2:1** and center the view as shown in Figure P14-9.
6. Lock the viewport display so the view scale doesn't change.
7. Delete the **Layout1** and **Layout2** layouts.
8. Save the drawing as **P14-9.**

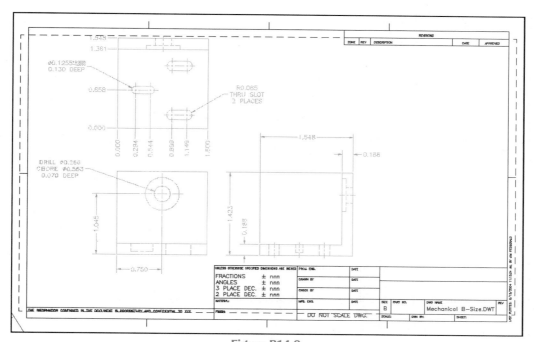

Figure P14-9

## Project 14-10A: Gasket—Continued from Chapter 13

1. Open drawing **P13-10A.**
2. Select **Layout from Template...** from the **Layout** cascade menu on the **Insert** menu to import a layout.
3. Insert the **Metric Mechanical B-Size** layout and border from the **Mechanical B-Size.dwt** template file created in Problem P14-3A.
4. Select the **Metric Mechanical B-Size** layout to make it current.
5. Set the viewport scale to **1:2** and center the view as shown in Figure P14-10A.
6. Lock the viewport display so the view scale doesn't change.
7. Delete the **Layout1** and **Layout2** layouts.
8. Save the drawing as **P14-10A.**

## Project 14-10B: Widget—Continued from Chapter 13

1. Open drawing **P13-10B.**
2. Select **Layout from Template...** from the **Layout** cascade menu on the **Insert** menu to import a layout.
3. Insert the **Metric Mechanical B-Size** layout and border from the **Mechanical B-Size.dwt** template file created in Problem 14-3A.

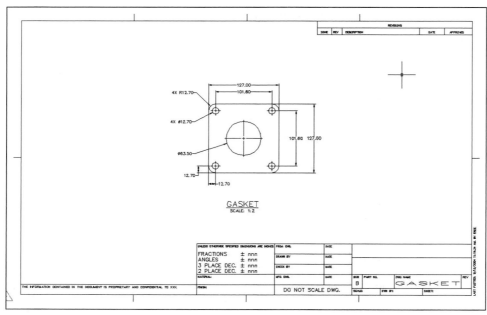

Figure P14-10A

4. Select the **Metric Mechanical B-Size** layout to make it current.
5. Set the viewport scale to **1:4** and center the view as shown in Figure P14-10B.
6. Lock the viewport display so the view scale doesn't change.
7. Delete the **Layout1** and **Layout2** layouts.
8. Save the drawing as **P14-10B.**

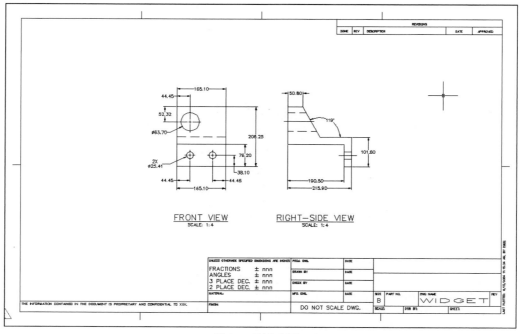

Figure P14-10B

## Project 14-10C: Hex Head Bolts and Nuts—Continued from Chapter 13

1. Open drawing **P13-10C.**
2. Select **Layout from Template...** from the **Layout** cascade menu on the **Insert** menu to import a layout.
3. Insert the **Metric Mechanical B-Size** layout and border from the **Mechanical B-Size.dwt** template file created in Problem 14-3A.
4. Select the **Metric Mechanical B-Size** layout to make it current.
5. Set the viewport scale to **1:1** and center the view as shown in Figure P14-10C.
6. Relocate bolts and nuts as necessary to fit in viewport.
7. Lock the viewport display so the view scale doesn't change.
8. Delete the **Layout1** and **Layout2** layouts.
9. Save the drawing as **P14-10C.**

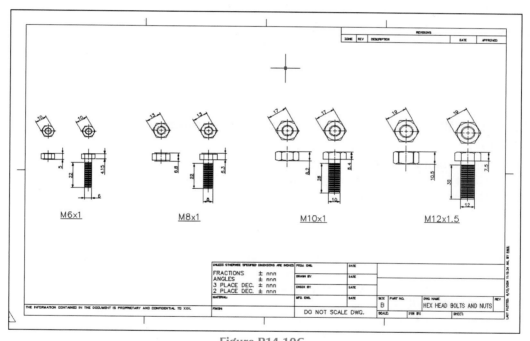

**Figure P14-10C**

## Project 14-10D: Motorcycle Head Gasket—Continued from Chapter 13

1. Open drawing **P13-10D.**
2. Select **Layout from Template...** from the **Layout** cascade menu on the **Insert** menu to import a layout.
3. Insert the **Metric Mechanical B-Size** layout and border from the **Mechanical B-Size.dwt** template file created in Problem 14-3A.
4. Select the **Metric Mechanical B-Size** layout to make it current.
5. Set the viewport scale to **1:2** and center the view as shown in Figure P14-10D.
6. Lock the viewport display so the view scale doesn't change.
7. Delete the **Layout1** and **Layout2** layouts.
8. Save the drawing as **P14-10D.**

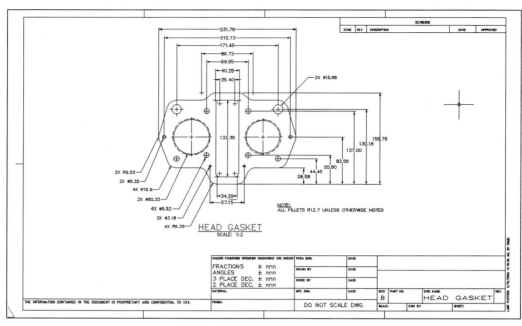

**Figure P14-10D**

## Project 14-10E: 68-Tooth Motorcycle Sprocket—Continued from Chapter 13

1. Open drawing **P13-10E.**
2. Select **Layout from Template...** from the **Layout** cascade menu on the **Insert** menu to import a layout.
3. Insert the **Metric Mechanical B-Size** layout and border from the **Mechanical B-Size.dwt** template file created in Problem 14-3A.
4. Select the **Metric Mechanical B-Size** layout to make it current.
5. Set the viewport scale to **1:4** and center the view as shown in Figure P14-10E.
6. Lock the viewport display so the view scale doesn't change.
7. Delete the **Layout1** and **Layout2** layouts.
8. Save the drawing as **P14-10E.**

## Project 14-10F: Window Extrusion—Continued from Chapter 13

1. Open drawing **P13-10F.**
2. Select **Layout from Template...** from the **Layout** cascade menu on the **Insert** menu to import a layout.
3. Insert the **Metric Mechanical B-Size** layout and border from the **Mechanical B-Size.dwt** template file created in Problem 14-3A.
4. Select the **Metric Mechanical B-Size** layout to make it current.
5. Set the viewport scale to **1:1** and center the view as shown in Figure P14-10F.
6. Lock the viewport display so the view scale doesn't change.
7. Delete the **Layout1** and **Layout2** layouts.
8. Save the drawing as **P14-10F.**

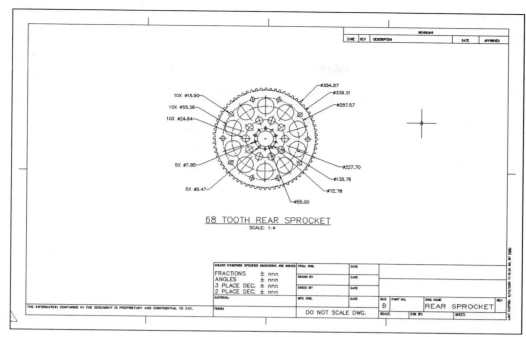

**Figure P14-10E**

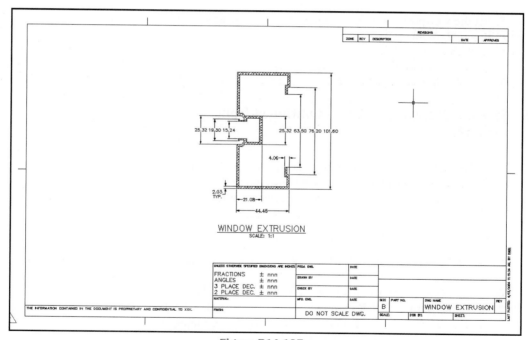

**Figure P14-10F**

## Project 14-10G: Hub—Continued from Chapter 13

1. Open drawing **P13-10G.**
2. Select **Layout from Template...** from the **Layout** cascade menu on the **Insert** menu to import a layout.
3. Insert the **Metric Mechanical B-Size** layout and border from the **Mechanical B-Size.dwt** template file created in Problem 14-3A.
4. Select the **Metric Mechanical B-Size** layout to make it current.

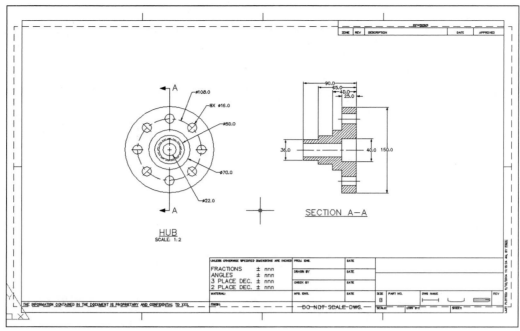

Figure P14-10G

5. Set the viewport scale to **1:2** and center the view as shown in Figure P14-10G.
6. Lock the viewport display so the view scale doesn't change.
7. Delete the **Layout1** and **Layout2** layouts.
8. Save the drawing as **P14-10G.**

## Project 14-11: Civil Site Plan—Continued from Chapter 13

1. Open drawing **P13-11.**
2. Select **Layout from Template…** from the **Layout** cascade menu on the **Insert** menu to import a layout.
3. Import the **Architectural D-Size** layout and border from the **Architectural D-Size.dwt** template file created in Problem 14-4A.
4. Select the **Architectural D-Size** layout to make it current.
5. Set the viewport scale to **1/8″ = 1′-0″** and center the view as shown in Figure P14-11.
6. Lock the viewport display so the view scale doesn't change.
7. Start the **DIMSTYLE** command and modify the **Arch** dimension style. In the **Fit** tab, set the **Scale for dimension features** to **Scale dimensions to layout**.
8. Delete the **Layout1** and **Layout2** layouts.
9. Save the drawing as **P14-11.**

## Project 14-12A: Manhole Construction Detail—Continued from Chapter 13

1. Open drawing **P13-12A.**
2. Select **Layout from Template…** from the **Layout** cascade menu on the **Insert** menu to import a layout.
3. Insert the **Architectural A-Size** layout and border from the **Architectural A-Size.dwt** template file created in Problem 14-4C above.

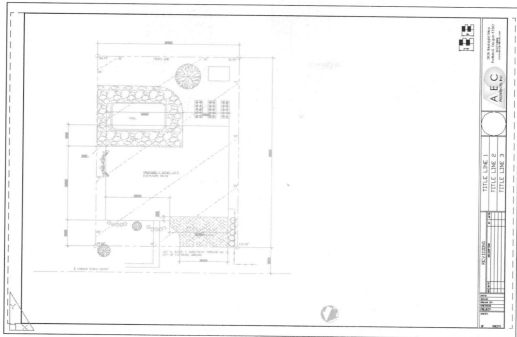

**Figure P14-11**

4. Select the **Architectural A-Size** layout to make it current.
5. Set the viewport scale to **1:20** and center the view as shown in Figure P14-12A.
6. Lock the viewport display so the view scale doesn't change.
7. Delete the **Layout1** and **Layout2** layouts.
8. Save the drawing as **P14-12A.**

## Project 14-12B: Manhole Cover—Continued from Chapter 13

1. Open drawing **P13-12B.**
2. Select **Layout from Template...** from the **Layout** cascade menu on the **Insert** menu to import a layout.
3. Insert the **Architectural A-Size** layout and border from the **Architectural A-Size.dwt** template file created in Problem 14-4C.
4. Select the **Architectural A-Size** layout to make it current.
5. Set the viewport scale to **1:5** and center the view as shown in Figure P14-12B.
6. Lock the viewport display so the view scale doesn't change.
7. Delete the **Layout1** and **Layout2** layouts.
8. Save the drawing as **P14-12B.**

## Project 14-12C: Standard Service Connection—Continued from Chapter 13

1. Open drawing **P13-12C.**
2. Select **Layout from Template...** from the **Layout** cascade menu on the **Insert** menu to import a layout.
3. Insert the **Architectural A-Size** layout and border from the **Architectural A-Size.dwt** template file created in Problem 14-4C.

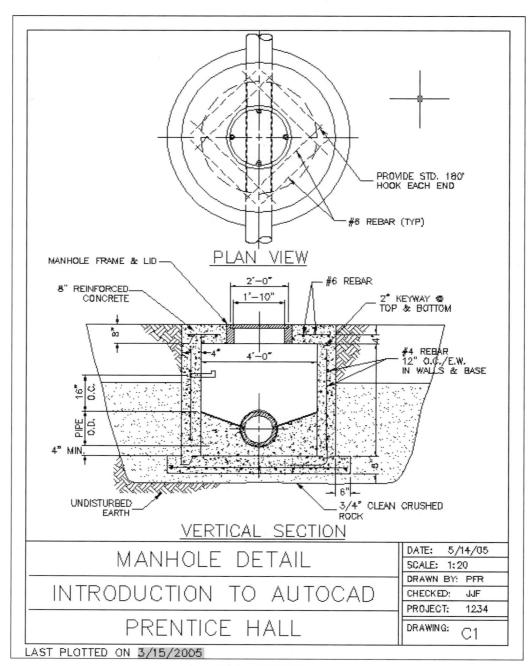

**Figure P14-12A**

4. Select the **Architectural A-Size** layout to make it current.
5. Set the viewport scale to **1:20** and center the view as shown in Figure P14-12C.
6. Lock the viewport display so the view scale doesn't change.
7. Delete the **Layout1** and **Layout2** layouts.
8. Save the drawing as **P14-12C.**

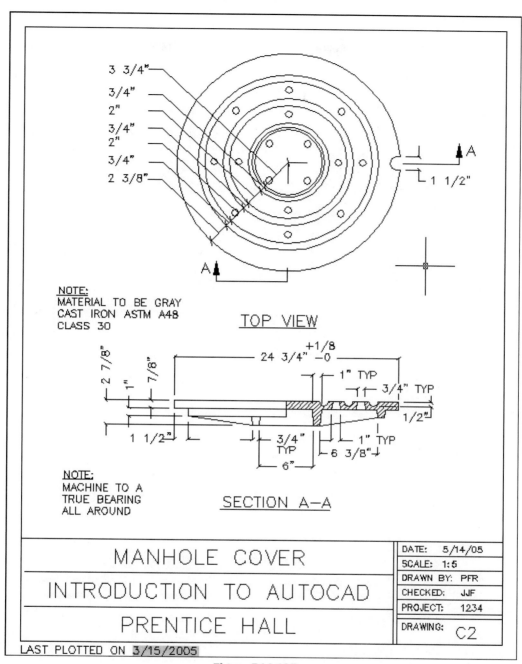

Figure P14-12B

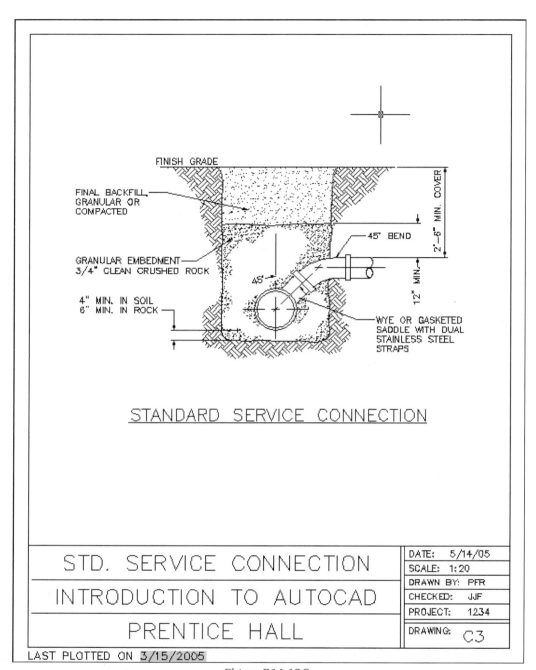

STANDARD SERVICE CONNECTION

| STD. SERVICE CONNECTION | DATE: 5/14/05 |
| | SCALE: 1:20 |
| INTRODUCTION TO AUTOCAD | DRAWN BY: PFR |
| | CHECKED: JJF |
| | PROJECT: 1234 |
| PRENTICE HALL | DRAWING: C3 |

LAST PLOTTED ON 3/15/2005

**Figure P14-12C**

# Plotting and Publishing

## *Chapter* Objectives

- Plot from both model space and layout space
- Control the final look of a plotted sheet
- Create, import, and manage page setups with the **PLOT** command
- Select, add, and configure various plotting devices
- Create electronic plot files including DWF and various raster file formats
- View DWF files in the DWF Viewer application

## INTRODUCTION

In most cases, the purpose of creating AutoCAD drawings is to create a set of printed hard-copy drawings. In AutoCAD, this process is called *plotting*. In Chapter 14, we looked at how to create and manage paper space layouts, which (among other things) allow you to define the default settings for a plot. In this chapter, we examine various ways of outputting drawings, including how to plot from model space and how to plot to various file formats.

**plotting:** The process of printing a drawing in AutoCAD

## PAGE SETUPS AND PLOTTING

In Chapter 14, we looked at how to create a page setup using the **PAGESETUP** command. Page setups are simply collections of plot settings that have a name assigned to them. When creating a page setup, you specify the default printer/plotter, the default paper size, and other default output options. Each drawing space (model space and each paper space layout) has a default page setup assigned to it that contains all the default plot settings for that drawing space.

**Note:**
In the early days of AutoCAD, drawings were typically output to pen plotters, which would create hard-copy prints by physically grabbing a pen and moving it around a piece of paper or Mylar. While these types of plotters are rarely used today, the terminology has remained. Today, the terms print and plot are synonymous in AutoCAD.

**FOR MORE DETAILS**   See Chapter 14 for more on creating and managing page setups.

Plotting is done with the **PLOT** command. When you start the **PLOT** command, AutoCAD looks at the current page setup and displays those settings in the **Plot** dialog box (see Figure 15-1).

**Figure 15-1    The Plot dialog box**

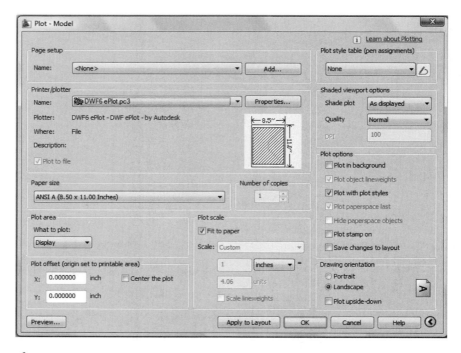

| Plot | |
|---|---|
| **Ribbon & Panel:** | Output\|Plot |
| **Standard Toolbar:** | |
| **Menu:** | File\|Plot... |
| **Command Line:** | PLOT/ PRINT |
| **Command Alias:** | CTRL+P |

**TIP**    The quickest way to start the **PLOT** command is by selecting the **Plot...** button on the **Quick Access** toolbar, which is always displayed on the top left of the AutoCAD window.

The **Plot** dialog box has the same settings as the **Page Setup** dialog box and allows you to make any final adjustments to your plot settings before outputting your drawing. The **Plot** dialog box also has additional controls, which allow you to create and modify page setups.

To create a plot using the default page setup values, you can simply start the **PLOT** command and choose **OK.** However, before you commit your drawing to paper, it's a good idea to check over your default settings and preview your plot.

> **Note:** Page setups can be created for both paper space layouts and for model space; however, page setups cannot be shared between paper space and model space. Page setups created for a paper space layout cannot be used in model space, and page setups created for model space cannot be used in a paper space layout.

### Previewing Your Plot

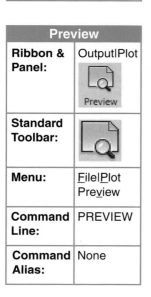

| Preview | |
|---|---|
| **Ribbon & Panel:** | Output\|Plot |
| **Standard Toolbar:** | |
| **Menu:** | File\|Plot Preview |
| **Command Line:** | PREVIEW |
| **Command Alias:** | None |

The **Preview...** button in the **Plot** dialog box allows you to see a preview of the final output before you commit it to paper. When you choose the **Preview...** button, AutoCAD switches to plot preview mode (see Figure 15-2). In preview mode, the AutoCAD toolbars and pull-down menus are replaced with the **Preview** toolbar. These tools allow you to zoom and pan around the drawing to inspect it before you send it to the printer. If you are satisfied with the preview, you can choose the **Plot** button to send the drawing to the printer. Otherwise, you can choose **Cancel** to return to the **Plot** dialog box. The tools available in the **Preview** toolbar are also available in the right-click menu (see Figure 15-3).

*The PREVIEW Command.*    If you're confident in your plot settings, you can go directly to a plot preview with the **PREVIEW** command. The **PREVIEW** command bypasses the **PLOT** command and goes directly to plot preview mode. If you're satisfied with the plot preview, you can choose the **Plot** button and output your drawing. However, if you need to make changes, choosing **Cancel** will return you to your drawing. You then have to use the **PLOT** or **PAGESETUP** command to make changes to your default plot settings.

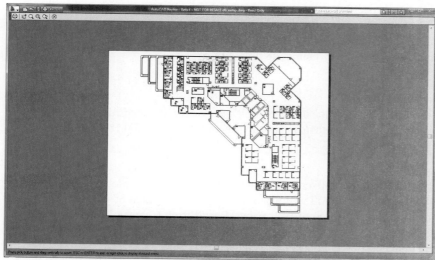

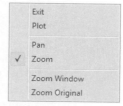

Figure 15-3   The
preview mode right-
click menu

Figure 15-2    Plot preview mode

## Plotting from Model Space

The process of plotting is the same whether you plot from model space or paper space. However, there are some things to keep in mind when plotting from model space, particularly with regard to plot scale.

*Specifying the Plot Area.*    When plotting a layout space, you will typically plot the entire layout. Selecting the **Layout** option in the **What to plot** list tells AutoCAD to plot the area defined in the paper space layout. When plotting from model space, the **Layout** option is not available, and you must choose a specific area to plot. The **What to plot** drop-down list allows you to specify a number of different plot areas. The options are described below.

| | |
|---|---|
| **Display** | Plots the objects currently displayed on the screen. |
| **Extents** | Plots all the objects currently visible in the drawing. Does not include objects on frozen layers but does include objects on layers that are turned off. |
| **Limits** | Plots objects located within the drawing limits. |
| **View** | Plots named views saved with the **VIEW** command. When selected, a list of named views is enabled, allowing you to select the view you wish to plot. |
| **Window** | Allows you to select a plot area by picking a window area. When selected, a **Window** button is enabled. Picking the **Window** button temporarily hides the dialog box and allows you to pick a window area to plot. |

*Setting the Plot Scale.*    Because a paper space layout represents an actual piece of paper, the plot scale of a paper space layout is typically 1:1. The plot scale of your model is set within each viewport.

However, model space represents the actual full-size version of your design. When you plot from model space, you typically need to adjust the plot scale so that the full-size version of your design will fit on a piece of paper.

The **Plot scale** area of the **Plot** dialog box allows you to set the drawing scale. When selected, the **Fit to paper** check box will examine the specified plot area and scale it to fit the specified paper size. The calculated scale will appear grayed out in the **Scale** area.

To plot at a specific scale, remove the check from the **Fit to paper** box to enable the **Scale** area. Once enabled, you can specify a plot scale by selecting it from the **Scale** list or by selecting

**Custom** from the list and specifying a custom scale. Custom scales are entered as plotted (paper) units in either inches or millimeters (mm) and their equivalent drawing units. For example, to specify a scale of 1/4″ = 1′ −0″, you could either choose it from the **Scale** list or choose **Custom** and specify .25 inch = 12 units, or 1 inch = 48 units.

You can add and modify the list of available plot scales with the **SCALELISTEDIT** command. See Chapter 14 for more information about the **SCALELISTEDIT** command.

*Setting the Plot Offset.*    The **Plot** offset area allows you to position your plot area on your paper. When set to **X: 0** and **Y: 0,** AutoCAD will place the specified plot area of your drawing at the lower left corner of the printable area of your paper. Recall from Chapter 14 that the printable area is the actual physical area that can be printed for a specified plotting device and paper size. This area varies with the printer and paper size you select.

By changing the X and Y offset values, you can reposition the drawing plot area on the paper. If your plot area goes outside the printable area, AutoCAD will warn you by showing a red line in the preview area of the **Plot** dialog box (see Figure 15-4).

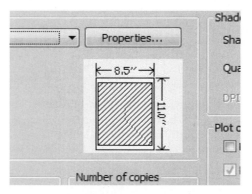

Figure 15-4    The preview area of the Plot dialog box

The **Center** check box will compare the printable area of your paper to the plot area of your drawing and calculate the appropriate X and Y offset values to center the plot area in the printable area of your paper.

**Exercise 15-1:** Plotting from Model Space

1. Open the drawing **db_samp** from the AutoCAD **Sample** folder.
2. Start the **PLOT** command to display the **Plot** dialog box.
3. Select the **DWF6 ePlot.pc3** printer and then select the **ARCH D (36.00 × 24.00 Inches)** paper size.
4. Select **Extents** from the **What to plot** list.
5. Remove the check from the **Fit to paper** box and choose **3/32″ = 1′-0″** from the **Scale** list.
6. Choose **Center the plot** option in the **Plot offset** area and choose **Preview....**
7. AutoCAD will display the plot preview shown earlier in Figure 15-2. You can zoom and pan to examine the plot preview. When done, choose the **Close Preview Window** button to return to the **Plot** dialog box.
8. In the **What to plot** list, choose **Window**. AutoCAD will close the dialog box and prompt you to *Specify first corner:*.
9. Draw a window around the upper right corner of the building as shown in Figure 15-5. After drawing the window, AutoCAD returns you to the **Plot** dialog box.
10. Choose **1/4″ = 1′-0″** from the **Scale** list and choose **Preview....** AutoCAD displays the plot preview as shown in Figure 15-6.
11. Choose the **Close Preview Window** button to close the plot preview and choose **Cancel** to close the **Plot** dialog box. *Do not* save the drawing.

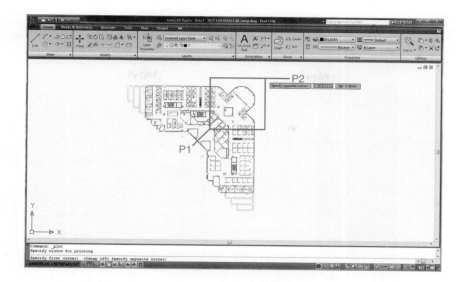

Figure 15-5    Selecting a plot window

**Figure 15-5**    Selecting a plot window

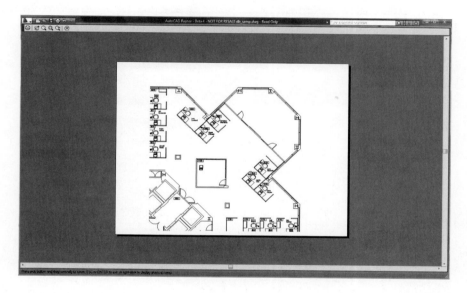

**Figure 15-6**    The plot preview of the selected area

## Plotting a Page Layout

Plotting a page layout is in many aspects simpler than plotting from model space. In setting up the page layout, you will typically define many or all of the plotting defaults. However, when you plot, you will still want to double-check your plot settings and do a plot preview before sending it to the printer. This also gives you the opportunity to temporarily override plot settings for any given plot.

### Exercise 15-2: Plotting a Page Layout

1. Open the drawing **Welding Fixture-1** from the Student CD.
2. Select the **Mounting Bar Casting Support** page layout tab.
3. Start the **PLOT** command to display the **Plot** dialog box and choose **Preview** to display the plot preview. Notice that the viewports are displayed on the plot preview (see Figure 15-7). This is because the viewports are currently on a plotting layer.
4. Choose the **Close Preview Window** button to exit the plot preview and choose **Cancel** to close the **Plot** dialog box.
5. Select the two viewports and choose **Viewport** from the layer drop-down list. This places the viewports on the nonplotting **Viewport** layer.
6. Restart the **PLOT** command. Notice that the plot preview area shows a red bar on the right-hand side of the page. This is due to the **Plot offset X** value being set to **0.010**.

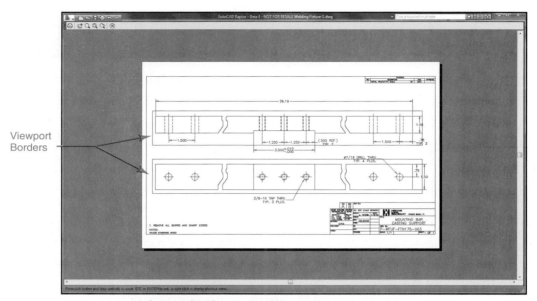

Viewport
Borders

**Figure 15-7**    Viewport outlines in the plot preview

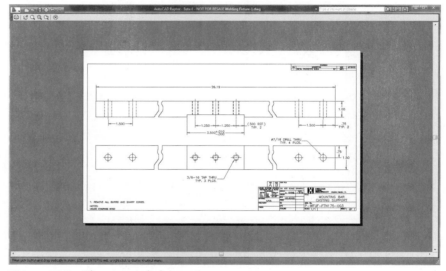

**Figure 15-8**    The corrected plot preview

7. Set the **X** value in the **Plot offset** to **0.00** and choose **Preview.** This displays the plot preview. The plot preview now looks correct, and the drawing is ready to plot (see Figure 15-8).
8. Choose the **Close Preview Window** button to exit the plot preview and choose **Cancel** to close the **Plot** dialog box. *Do not* save the drawing file.

## Default Plot Settings and Page Setups

Keep in mind that each drawing environment (model space and each layout) has a set of default plot settings associated with it. A page setup is a collection of default plot settings that are assigned a name and saved in the drawing. Once a page setup is created, its settings can be applied to a given drawing space. Model space page setups can be applied to the model space environment, and layout page setups can be applied to layout (paper) spaces.

*Selecting a Page Setup.*    In the **Plot** dialog box, the **Page setup** area allows you to apply the settings stored in a page setup to the current plot. When you start the **Plot** command, AutoCAD displays the name of the current page setup in the **Name** drop-down list. When you select the **Name** drop-down list, you'll see a list of page setups stored in the drawing. Selecting one of these page setups will apply the settings stored in the page setup to the current plot.

In addition to page setups, there are three additional items in the **Name** list: **<None>, <Previous plot>,** and **Import....** The **<None>** setting tells you that the current plot settings do not match any stored page setups. If you are using a page setup and make any changes to the setting in the **Plot** dialog box, the **Name** setting will change to **<None>,** noting that the current plot settings no longer match the settings stored in the page setup.

The **<Previous plot>** setting will reuse the settings from the last successful **PLOT** command.

*Importing a Page Setup.*    Selecting **Import...** from the **Name** list allows you to import a page setup from another drawing. When you select **Import...,** AutoCAD displays the **Select Page Setup From File** dialog box (see Figure 15-9), which allows you to select a drawing file. Once you select a drawing file, AutoCAD will display the **Import Page Setups** dialog box (see Figure 15-10), which displays all the saved page setups within a drawing. Select a page setup from the dialog box and choose **OK** to import the page setup into your current drawing. The imported page setup will now be listed in the **Name** drop-down list.

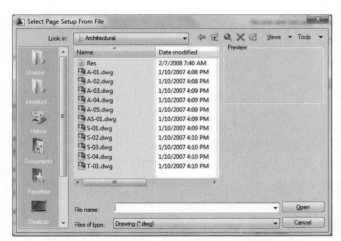

**Figure 15-9**    The Select Page Setup From File dialog box

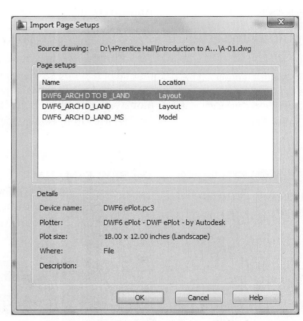

**Figure 15-10**    The Import Page Setups dialog box

*Creating a Page Setup.*    AutoCAD also allows you to save your current plot settings to a page setup. Once you have your plot settings to your liking, choose the **Add...** button in the **Page setup** area. AutoCAD will display the **Add Page Setup** dialog box (see Figure 15-11). Simply type a name and choose **OK** to save the current plot settings to the new page setup.

You can update an existing page setup by entering the existing page setup name into the **Add Page Setup** dialog box. AutoCAD will display a **Question** dialog box (see Figure 15-12) telling

**Figure 15-11**    The Add Page Setup dialog box

**Figure 15-12**    The Add Page Setup Question dialog box

you the page setup already exists and asking if you'd like to redefine it. Choose **Yes** to update the existing page setup with the current plot settings.

*Applying Plot Settings to the Current Layout.*    As we mentioned earlier, each drawing space has a set of default plot settings. The **Apply to Layout** button allows you to take the settings displayed in the **Plot** dialog box and apply them to the current layout. These settings then become the default plot settings for that layout or model space.

## PLOT STYLES AND LINEWEIGHTS

As noted earlier in the chapter, in the early days of AutoCAD, pen plotters were commonly used. These plotters typically had a pen carousel in which you loaded pens. You would load pens with different pen widths or different colors in each position in the carousel. You would also have a pen table that would tell AutoCAD which pen to use for each AutoCAD color. For example, use pen 4 for color 1, pen 2 for colors 2 and 3, etc. Modern printers no longer use physical pens, but AutoCAD still allows you to use pen tables to control the final look of your plot. Today, AutoCAD refers to these pen tables as *plot styles*.

A plot style is a table of settings that allow you to control all aspects of your plotted output. For example, you may have a plot table that converts AutoCAD colors to grayscale colors or a plot table that allows you to screen back certain colors.

There are two types of plot styles, ***named plot styles*** and ***color-dependent plot styles***. Named plot styles are stored in .STB files. Color-dependent plot styles are stored in .CTB files. A drawing can use either color-dependent plot styles or named plot styles, but not both.

**named plot style:** Plot style that is organized by a user-defined name. Named plot styles are stored in .STB files.

**color-dependent plot style:** Plot style that is organized by the AutoCAD Color Index (ACI) number. Color-dependent plot styles are stored in .CTB files.

### Plot Style Manager

The **STYLESMANAGER** command will open the folder where the plot style table files are stored (see Figure 15-13). From this folder, double-clicking on a .CTB or an .STB file will start the **Plot Style Table Editor** application (see Figure 15-14). This is a stand-alone Windows program that runs outside of AutoCAD. This program allows you to create and modify AutoCAD

| Plot Style Manager | |
|---|---|
| **Ribbon & Panel:** | Output\|Plot |
| **Toolbar:** | None |
| **Menu:** | File\|Plot Style Manager... |
| **Command Line:** | STYLESMANAGER |
| **Command Alias:** | None |

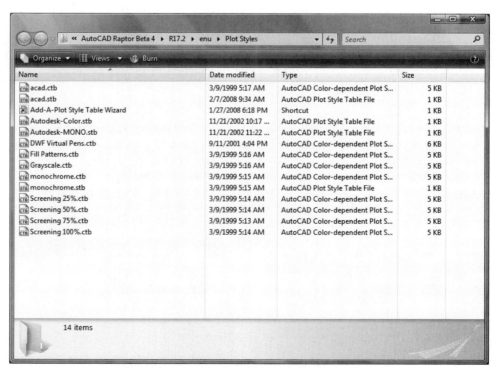

**Figure 15-13**    Plot styles folder

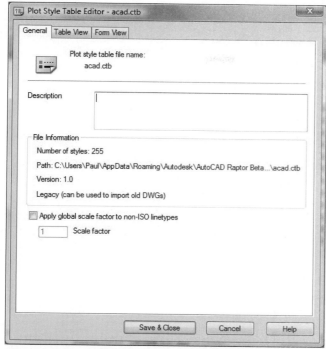

**Figure 15-14**   Plot Style Table Editor

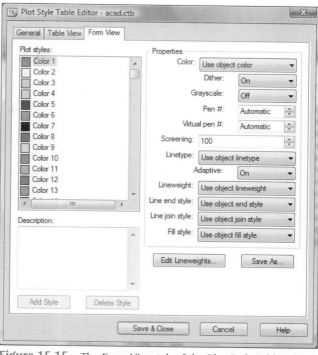

**Figure 15-15**   The Form View tab of the Plot Style Table Editor

plot style tables. The **General** tab displays information about the plot style. The **Table View** and **Form View** tabs display the table settings in different formats. The **Form View** tab (see Figure 15-15) is useful for setting the properties of multiple colors at once. In this view, you can select multiple pens and apply settings to them in a single step.

## Color-Dependent Plot Styles

Color-dependent plot styles map AutoCAD colors within your drawing to specific plotter settings. When you use color-dependent plot styles, all objects with the same color are plotted with the same plotter settings.

## Named Plot Styles

Named plot styles allow you to assign plotter settings directly to AutoCAD objects or AutoCAD layers. Within each .STB file, plotter settings are assigned to plot style names (see Figure 15-16). These plot styles are then assigned to each drawing layer and therefore to each object in the drawing. When named plot styles are used in a drawing, the **Plot Style** column is enabled in the **Layer Properties Manager** dialog box (see Figure 15-17). This allows you to assign a named plot style to a layer.

When using named plot styles, AutoCAD creates a plot style called **Normal.** This is AutoCAD's default named plot style name and is included in each .STB file. This is similar to the **0** layer name and the **Continuous** linetype. It cannot be deleted and is always available.

**Note:**
The specifics of each of these settings are beyond the scope of this book. For detailed information on these settings, choose the **Help** button on the **Plot Style Table Editor** application. Keep in mind that some settings (such as pen numbers and virtual pen numbers) may not be supported by your specific printer. Refer to your printer documentation to see which features are supported.

**Note:**
When using named plot styles, the plot style name behaves like other object properties. By default, plot styles are assigned by layer, but you can hard-code a plot style for any specific object.

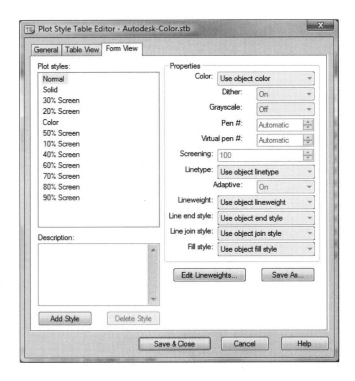

**Figure 15-16**    Named plot styles

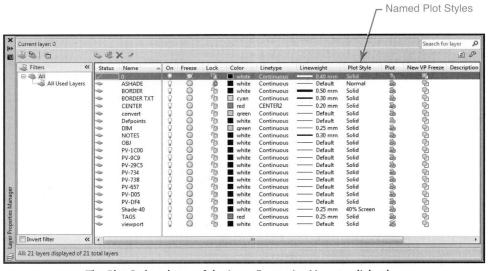

**Figure 15-17**    The Plot Style column of the Layer Properties Manager dialog box

## Using Plot Styles

As mentioned earlier, an AutoCAD drawing can use either color-dependent plot styles or named plot styles but not both. When you create a new drawing file, the drawing template typically determines whether AutoCAD uses color-dependent plot styles or named plot styles as well as the default plot style file (see Figure 15-18).

TIP    You can use the **CONVERTPSTYLES** command to convert a named plot style drawing to a color-dependent plot style drawing or vice versa.

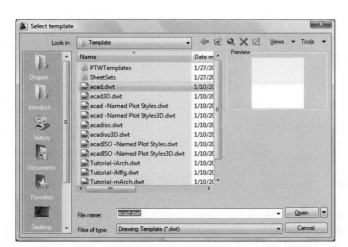


Figure 15-18    Drawing templates with various plot styles

Figure 15-19    Select Plot Style dialog box

Once a drawing has been created and the type of plot styles has been set, the **Plot style table** area in the **Plot** dialog box will show either .STB or .CTB files. From this list, you can tell AutoCAD which plot style table to use for your plot.

When working with named plot styles, it is possible to assign a plot style table that does not include plot styles that are used in your drawing. For example, say you create a drawing and assign the plot style named **40% Screen** that's defined in the **Autodesk-MONO.STB** file. If you then select the **ACAD.STB** plot style table, the **40% Screen** style is not defined in that .STB file. When this happens, AutoCAD will display the **Select Plot Style** dialog box (see Figure 15-19) and ask you to select a different plot style for that layer.

When you select a plot style table, the **Edit...** button is enabled (see Figure 15-20), which starts the **Plot Style Table Editor** application (see Figure 15-14). This allows you to view and/or modify the selected plot style table.

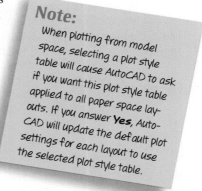

**Note:**
When plotting from model space, selecting a plot style table will cause AutoCAD to ask if you want this plot style table applied to all paper space layouts. If you answer **Yes**, AutoCAD will update the default plot settings for each layout to use the selected plot style table.

## Plot Options

The **Plot options** area of the **Plot** dialog box allows you to specify options for plotting lineweights, plot styles, shaded plots, and the order in which objects are plotted.

*Plot in Background.*    This option specifies that the plot is processed in the background. Typically, when you plot, AutoCAD stops all other activity while the drawing is plotting and will show you a plotting progress bar (see Figure 15-21).

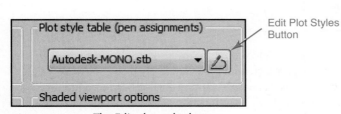

Figure 15-20    The Edit plot styles button

Figure 15-21    The Plot Job Progress bar

When the **Plot in background** option is turned on, AutoCAD will return you to the drawing environment and process the plot in the background. This allows you to work while the plot is being generated, but may also increase the time it takes to plot the drawing.

*Plot Object Lineweights.*    This option specifies whether lineweights assigned to objects and layers are plotted. When turned on, any lineweight information assigned in your drawing will be applied to the plot. When turned off, a lineweight of 0 will be applied to all objects in the plot, which results in all objects being plotted with a very thin lineweight.

*Plot with Plot Styles.*    This option specifies whether plot styles applied to objects and layers are plotted. This means that the plot style settings contained in the specified .CTB or .STB file will be applied to the plot. When you select this option, the **Plot Object Lineweights** option is automatically enabled.

*Plot Paperspace Last.*    This option allows you to control which space is plotted first. Generally, paper space geometry is usually plotted before model space geometry. Turning this option ON will force AutoCAD to plot the model space geometry first.

*Hide Paperspace Objects.*    This option typically affects only 3D drawings and is available only when plotting from a paper space layout. When plotting a 3D object, you may want to have AutoCAD do a hidden line removal, which eliminates any lines appearing behind a 3D object. This option tells AutoCAD whether the hidden line removal process applies to objects in the paper space as well as objects in model space.

*Plot Stamp On.*    Turning this option ON places a plot stamp on a specified corner of each drawing and/or logs it to a file.

Plot stamp settings are specified in the **Plot Stamp** dialog box (see Figure 15-22), which allows you to control the information that you want to appear in the plot stamp, such as drawing name, date and time, plot scale, and so on. To open the **Plot Stamp** dialog box, turn on the **Plot Stamp** option and then click the **Plot Stamp Settings** button.

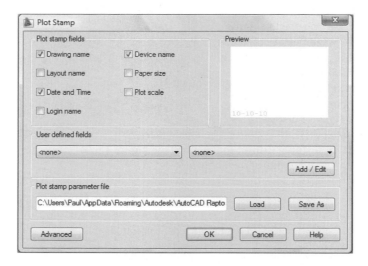

**Figure 15-22** The Plot Stamp dialog box

You can also open the **Plot Stamp** dialog box by clicking the **Plot Stamp Settings** button on the **Plot and Publish** tab of the **Options** dialog box.

From the **Plot Stamp** dialog box, you can select what information you want to display, and you also can create user-defined text to display a custom plot stamp.

Selecting the **Advanced** button displays the **Advanced Options** dialog box (see Figure 15-23), which allows you to control the placement and orientation of the plot stamp as well as the font and height of the plot stamp text.

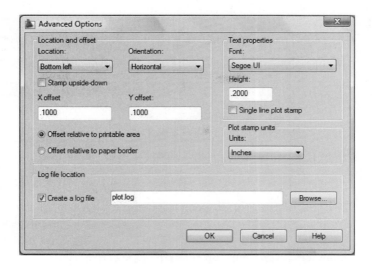

Figure 15-23   The Advanced Options dialog box

# PLOTTER SETUP

The **Printer/plotter** area of the **Plot** dialog box lists all the printers available when plotting a drawing. To select a printer, simply select it from the **Name** list. Once selected, AutoCAD will display information about the printer beneath the name, including the name of the printer driver, the printer port, and any description about the printer. The list of printers is divided into two types: Windows-configured printers and AutoCAD-configured printers.

## Windows System Printers

The Windows printers are printers that are configured with the **Printers** applet in the Windows **Control Panel** (see Figure 15-24). These are printers that are available to all Windows applications. Any printer configured for Windows will be listed in the **Name** list.

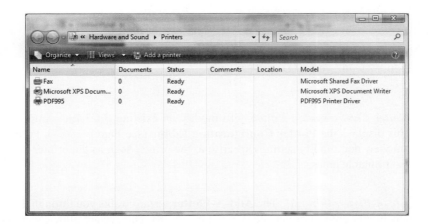

Figure 15-24   The Printers control window

## AutoCAD Printers

AutoCAD printers are configured and controlled by AutoCAD directly. They bypass the Windows printing system and allow AutoCAD to print directly to the printer. AutoCAD-configured printers may also have features available that are not available in a Windows printer. There are also AutoCAD printer drivers that allow you to convert AutoCAD drawings to various raster and vector file formats, such as JPG, BMP, or HPGL.

*PC3 and PMP Files.*    AutoCAD-configured printers are stored in plotter configuration files (.PC3 files). These files are also listed in the **Name** list (see Figure 15-25).

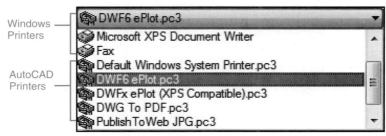

Windows Printers

AutoCAD Printers

Figure 15-25     The Printer/plotter Name list

In addition to .PC3 files, AutoCAD also uses plot model parameter (.PMP) files to store custom plotter calibration settings as well as user-defined custom paper sizes.

| Plotter Manager | |
|---|---|
| **Ribbon & Panel:** | Output\|Plot |
| **Toolbar:** | None |
| **Menu:** | File\|Plotter Manager... |
| **Command Line:** | PLOTTERMANAGER |
| **Command Alias:** | None |

*Plotter Manager.*     The **PLOTTERMANAGER** command displays the folder containing AutoCAD .PC3 files (see Figure 15-26). From this folder, you can create new plotter configurations and modify existing ones.

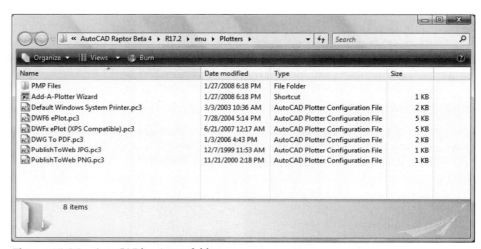

Figure 15-26     AutoCAD's printers folder

*Plotter Configuration Editor.*     To modify an existing .PC3 file, simply double-click the file. This displays the **Plotter Configuration Editor** (see Figure 15-27). From this dialog box, you can view and modify settings specific to the printer such as the printer port, custom page sizes, and printable areas.

*Add-A-Plotter Wizard.*     The **Add-A-Plotter** wizard walks you through the process of creating a new plotter configuration file (see Figure 15-28). This wizard allows you to create a new plotter configuration using either AutoCAD-supplied print drivers, drivers supplied by the printer manufacturer, or by importing a plotter configuration file from an earlier version of AutoCAD (.PCP or .PC2 files).

*Overriding a .PC3 File.*     When you select a printer from the **Name** list, the **Properties** button is enabled. When you select this button, AutoCAD displays the **Plotter Configuration Editor** (see Figure 15-27). This allows you to make changes to the plotter configuration within the **PLOT** command. When you make changes to the plotter configuration from within the **PLOT** command, AutoCAD will ask you if you want to save the changes to the .PC3 file or make the changes only for the current plot (see Figure 15-29).

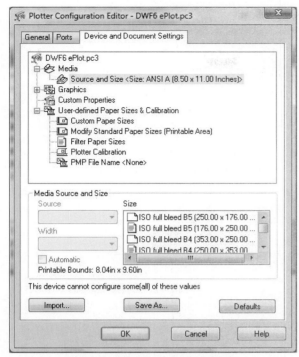

Figure 15-27    The Plotter Configuration Editor

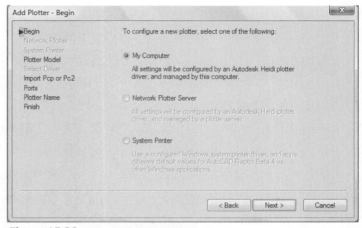

Figure 15-28    The Add-A-Plotter wizard

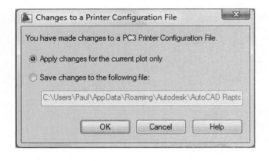

Figure 15-29    The Changes to a Printer Configuration File dialog box

## Exercise 15-3: Adding a New Plotter

1. Open the drawing **db_samp** from the AutoCAD **Sample** folder.
2. Start the **PLOTTERMANAGER** command to display the **Plotters** folder.
3. Double-click the **Add-A-Plotter** wizard. AutoCAD displays the **Add Plotter** dialog box. Choose **Next** to begin the wizard.
4. Choose **My Computer** to tell AutoCAD that the printer will be controlled locally from your computer (see Figure 15-28). Choose **Next** to continue to the **Plotter Model** step.
5. Choose **Hewlett-Packard** in the **Manufacturers** list and **Draftpro (7570A)** from the **Models** list (see Figure 15-30). Choose **Next** to continue to the **Import Pcp or Pc2** step.
6. You are given the opportunity to import a .PCP or .PC2 file from an older version of AutoCAD. Choose **Next** to continue to the **Ports** step.
7. Because this plotter is not actually hooked up to your computer, select the **Plot to File** option (see Figure 15-31). This will redirect the printer output to a file. Choose **Next** to continue to the **Plotter Name** step.
8. Accept the default name of **DraftPro (7570A).** Choose **Next** to continue to the **Finish** step.
9. At this point, you can modify the plotter defaults by choosing the **Edit Plotter Configuration...** button (see Figure 15-32). The **Calibrate Plotter...** button allows you to verify the accuracy of the plotter output by creating a sample plot, measuring the output, and inputting the measured results back into the plotter calibration. Choose **Finish** to complete the plotter configuration.

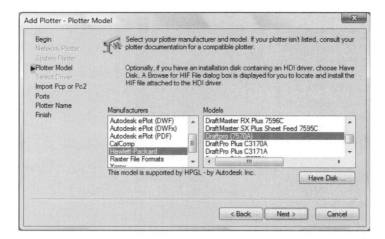

**Figure 15-30**   Selecting a plotter

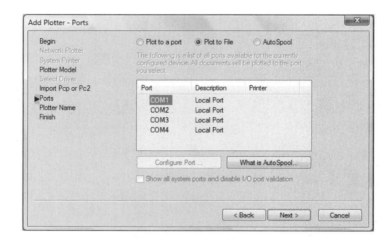

**Figure 15-31**   Specifying a port

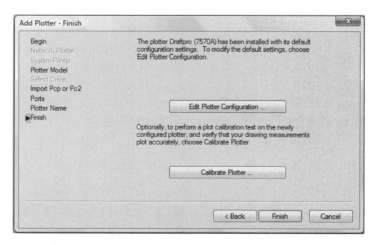

**Figure 15-32**   The configured plotter

10.  From AutoCAD, start the **PLOT** command. The **Draftpro (7570A).PC3** file is now listed in the **Printer/plotter Name** list.

11.  Choose **Cancel** to close the **Plot** dialog box. *Do not* save the drawing.

### Plotting to a File

As mentioned earlier, when you select a plotter in the **Plot** dialog box, AutoCAD will display information about the printer, including the port. The port describes where the plot output will be directed—for example, a USB port, an LPT port, or a network printer location. The output port for any particular printer is defined within the plotter configuration (.PC3) file for the printer.

*Plot File—PLT.*    The **Plot to file** box in the **Plot** dialog box allows you to redirect the output from the specified port to a plot file. Plot files can be used in various ways. Some office environments use plot management software that may require plot files. Some plot files can be used in other programs. The Hewlett-Packard Graphics Language (HPGL or HPGL/2) is a plot file format used in many Hewlett-Packard plotters. Some graphics programs support HPGL files instead of AutoCAD files. If you have a need to create a plot file, select the **Plot to file** option in the **Plot** dialog box. When you plot, AutoCAD will ask you for the name and location of the plot file. Plot files typically use a .PLT file extension.

*Design Web Format File—DWF/DWFx.*    The Design Web Format (DWF) is a file format developed by Autodesk that allows you to publish your drawing on the World Wide Web or an intranet network. DWF files can contain one or more drawing sheets (layouts) and also support real-time panning and zooming as well as control over the display of layers and named views. DWF files cannot be opened in AutoCAD.

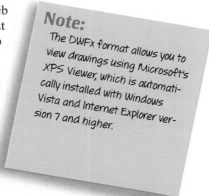

**Note:**
The DWFx format allows you to view drawings using Microsoft's XPS Viewer, which is automatically installed with Windows Vista and Internet Explorer version 7 and higher.

DWF files can be reviewed, marked up, and plotted using the free Autodesk® Design Review software. DWF files can also be viewed and shared using Autodesk's free web service named Freewheel at http://freewheel. autodesk.com.

To plot to a DWF file, select either the **DWF6 ePlot.pc3** or the **DWFx ePlot (XPS compatible) .pc3** plot configuration in the **Printer/plotter Name** list. To change the DWF preferences, choose the **Properties** button in the **Plot** dialog box and choose the **Custom Properties** in the **Device and Documentation Settings** tab of the **Plotter Configuration Editor** dialog box (see Figure 15-33). The **DWF6 ePlot Properties** dialog box is shown Figure 15-34.

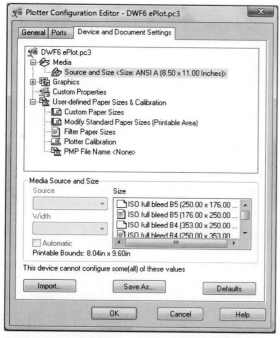

**Figure 15-33**    Device and Documentation Settings tab

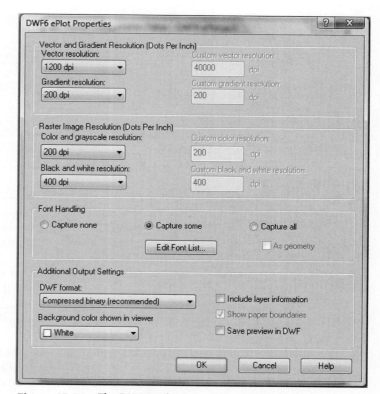

**Figure 15-34**    The DWF6 ePlot Properties dialog box

In this dialog box, you can set the resolution of the raster and vector components of the DWF file, control which fonts are embedded in the DWF file, set the background color, and control whether layer control is included in the DWF file.

*Adobe® Portable Document Format—PDF.*   PDF files are the industry standard for sharing graphical information. Using PDF files, you can share drawings with almost anyone because the Adobe Reader® is already installed on most computers. If the Adobe Reader is not installed, it can be easily downloaded and installed for free from the Internet, most of the time, automatically.

To plot to a PDF file, select the **DWG to PDF.PC3** plot configuration in the **Printer/Plotter Name** list. When you plot, the standard Windows file dialog box is displayed so that you can specify a file name and location to save the PDF file.

*Raster Image File—BMP/CALS/JPEG/PNG/TIFF.*   AutoCAD comes with a number of plot drivers that allow you to plot to various raster file formats. When you plot a drawing to a raster file, AutoCAD objects are converted to a series of pixels. When plotting to a raster image file, sheet size is measured in pixels instead of inches or millimeters. The resolution and color depth of the raster file determines the quality of the final output and also affects the size of the final file.

To configure AutoCAD to plot to a raster image file, run the **Add-A-Plotter** wizard, select **My Computer, Next,** and choose **Raster File Formats** in the **Manufacturers** list (see Figure 15-35). AutoCAD provides support for a number of raster file formats.

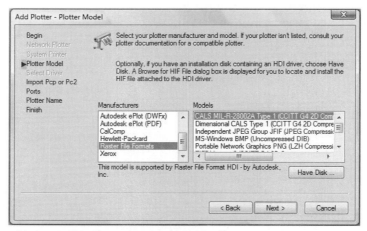

**Figure 15-35**   Plotting to a raster image file

**Exercise 15-4:** Plotting to a File

1. Continue from Exercise 15-3.
2. Start the **PLOT** command to display the **Plot** dialog box.
3. Select the **DWF6 ePlot.pc3** printer and then select the **ARCH D (36.00 × 24.00 Inches)** paper size.
4. Select **Extents** from the **What to plot** list.
5. Remove the check from the **Fit to paper** box and choose **3/32″ = 1′-0″** from the **Scale** list.
6. Choose the **Center the plot** option in the **Plot offset** area (see Figure 15-36) and choose **Preview…**.
7. AutoCAD will display the plot preview. You can zoom and pan to examine the plot preview. When done, choose the **Plot** button to create the plot.
8. AutoCAD prompts you for the name and location of the plot file. Save the plot as **EX15-4.DWF** and choose **Save** to create the DWF file. AutoCAD plots the drawing and ends the **PLOT** command.

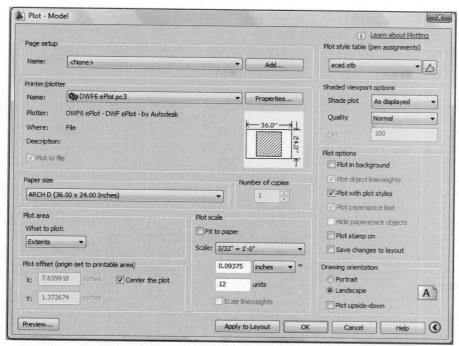

**Figure 15-36**   The Plot dialog box

## PLOTTING A SET OF DRAWINGS

Although the **PLOT** command allows you to create a single plot, there are many times when you need to create a set of drawings. This might include multiple layouts within a single drawing or include layouts from other drawing files. You may even need to mix model space plots with paper space layout plots. AutoCAD's **PUBLISH** command allows you to create multiple plots and to save the settings so the plot set can be recreated.

### Publish Utility

When you start the **PUBLISH** command, AutoCAD displays the **Publish** dialog box (see Figure 15-37).

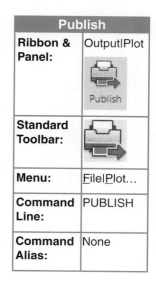

| Publish | |
|---------|--|
| **Ribbon & Panel:** | Output\|Plot<br>Publish |
| **Standard Toolbar:** | |
| **Menu:** | File\|Plot... |
| **Command Line:** | PUBLISH |
| **Command Alias:** | None |

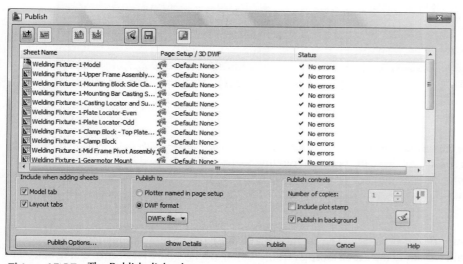

**Figure 15-37**   The Publish dialog box

When the **PUBLISH** command starts, AutoCAD automatically imports all the drawing tabs currently defined in the drawing and shows them in the list. The drawings are listed by their file name and drawing tab name and also show the current page setup and the status of the last plot. You can change the page setup used for a plot sheet by selecting the page setup and selecting an available page setup from the drop-down list. You can also import page setups from other drawings to use in your plot sheet set.

*Creating a Plot File Drawing Set.*     The **Add Sheets** and **Remove Sheets** buttons allow you to make changes to the list of plot sheets. To remove a plot sheet from the list, simply select the plot sheet(s) and choose the **Remove Sheets** button.

To add plot sheets to the list, choose the **Add Sheets** button. AutoCAD will show you the **Select Drawings** dialog box (see Figure 15-38), which allows you to select a drawing file. Once you select a drawing, AutoCAD will add a plot sheet for each drawing tab in the selected drawing. You can control whether AutoCAD imports model space and/or layout tabs by checking the **Model tab** and **Layout tabs** options in the **Include when adding sheets** area.

The **Move Sheet Up** and **Move Sheet Down** buttons allow you to control the order of the plot sheets in the list. AutoCAD will plot the sheets in the order listed in the plot sheet list. The **Reverse Order** button will plot the drawing in the reverse order when selected.

Once you have created the plot sheet list and have the order and plot stamp setting selected, the **Save Sheet List...** button allows you to save the list and settings to a file that can be loaded and reused later.

When you're ready to publish your plot sheet list, the **Preview** button allows you to see a plot preview of each plot sheet. The **PUBLISH** command preview mode works exactly like the single sheet plot preview but includes forward and back arrows (see Figure 15-39) that allow you to move through the plot sheet previews.

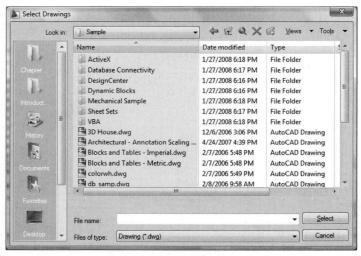

**Figure 15-38**   The Select Drawings dialog box

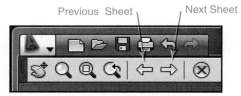

**Figure 15-39**   The Publish preview controls

*Creating an Electronic Drawing Set Using the Design Web Format (DWF).*     When you publish a set of plot sheets, you have the option of plotting to the printer defined in the layout or overriding that printer and printing to a DWF file. When you select the DWF file option in the **Publish to** area, AutoCAD will ignore the printer set in the page layout and instead create a DWF or a DWFx file.

*Publish Controls and Options.*     The **Include Plot Stamp** option allows you to turn plot stamping on and off. Selecting the **Plot Stamp Settings** button displays the **Plot Stamp** dialog box (see Figure 15-40), which allows you to change the plot stamp options.

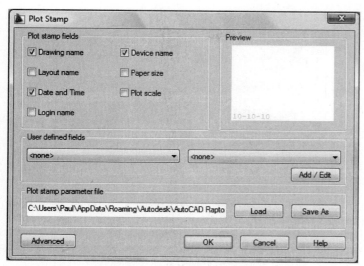

Figure 15-40    The Plot Stamp dialog box

The **Publish is background** option allows you to process the list of drawings and layouts in the background so that you can continue to work in AutoCAD. A notification balloon is displayed in the AutoCAD status tray on the right side of the Status Bar when plotting is complete.

The **Show Details** button expands the **Publish** dialog box (see Figure 15-41) and shows details for each of the plot sheets. The **Publish Options...** button displays the **Publish Options** dialog box shown in Figure 15-42 and enables you to view and modify settings for the DWF output.

Because DWF files support multiple sheets, you have the option of printing each sheet to a separate DWF file or plotting all the sheets to a single, multisheet DWF file. You also have the option of including layer and block information and enabling password protection for the DWF file.

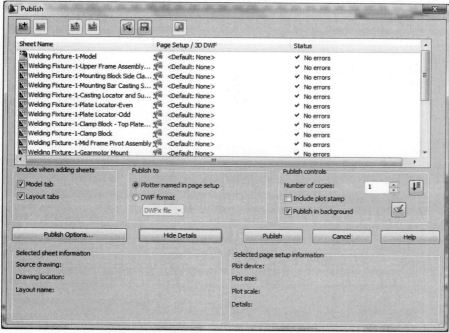

Figure 15-41    Plot sheet Publish details

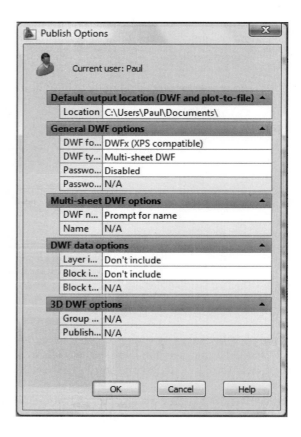

**Figure 15-42**    Publish Options dialog box

**Exercise 15-5:** Publishing an Electronic Drawing Set

1. Open the drawing **Welding Fixture-1** from the Student CD. This drawing contains multiple paper space layouts for a welding fixture.
2. Start the **PUBLISH** command to display the **Publish** dialog box (see Figure 15-43).

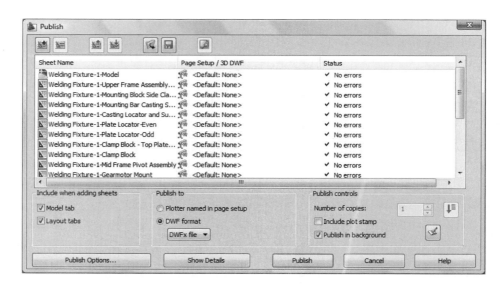

**Figure 15-43**    The Publish dialog box

3. Because we're only interested in plotting the paper space layouts, select the **Welding Fixture-1-Model** sheet from the list of sheet names. Choose the **Remove Sheets** button to remove this sheet from the list.
4. Select the **DWF format** option in the **Publish to** area to direct the results to a DWF file.
5. Choose the **Publish Options...** button to display the **Publish Options** dialog box (see Figure 15-44).

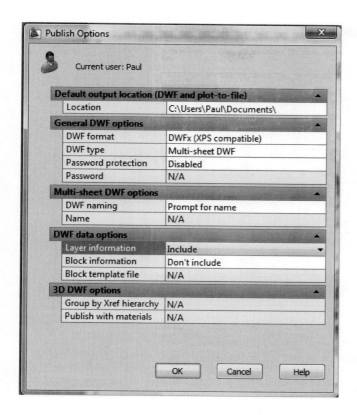

**Figure 15-44**    Publish options

6. Verify that the DWF type is set to **Multi-sheet DWF** and that **Password protection** is **Disabled.** Choose **Include** in the **Layer information** list and choose **OK** to close the dialog box.

7. Choose the **Preview** button to switch to preview mode. Examine the plot sheets to make sure they look correct. Choose the **Close Preview** button to end the preview.

8. Choose **Publish** to create the DWF file. AutoCAD will prompt you for the name of the DWF file. Specify **EX15-5.DWF** and choose **Select** to create the DWF file.

9. AutoCAD will publish the DWF files and ask if you'd like to save the plot sheet list. Choose **No** to return to the drawing. *Do not* save the drawing file.

## WORKING WITH DWF FILES

Once you've created a DWF file, you have a couple of options for viewing and sharing them. Autodesk Design Review is installed when AutoCAD is installed and is also available as a free download from the Autodesk Website for those who do not have AutoCAD.

### Autodesk Design Review

Autodesk Design Review allows you to view, mark up, and print DWF files. To run Autodesk Design Review from Windows, choose **Start>Autodesk>Autodesk.** This displays the **Autodesk Design Review** application (see Figure 15-45).

In the **Navigation** pane on the left, you're shown all the plot sheets included in the DWF file. Selecting a sheet displays it in the main viewing window. You can view these as a list of sheet names or as thumbnail images. If any bookmarks or markups are included in the DWF file, you can view those from the **Navigation** pane as well.

Along the top of the application, you have tools for opening, printing, copying, and navigating through the

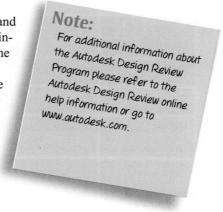

Note:
For additional information about the Autodesk Design Review Program please refer to the Autodesk Design Review online help information or go to www.autodesk.com.

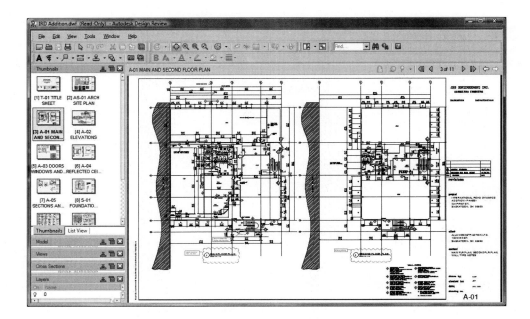

**Figure 15-45**   Autodesk
Design Review

plot sheets. The zoom tools work the same way as in AutoCAD. You can dynamically zoom and pan around the drawing using either the dynamic zoom and pan button or the wheel mouse.

### Exercise 15-6: Viewing a DWF File

1. Continue from Exercise 15-5.
2. In Windows, choose **Start>Autodesk>Autodesk Design Review** to start the program.
3. Open the file **EX15-5.DWF** you created in the previous exercise. AutoCAD loads the DWF file (see Figure 15-46).
4. Navigate around the DWF file and examine the multiple plot sheets.

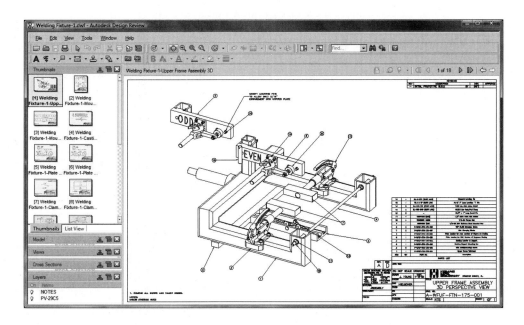

**Figure 15-46**   The published DWF file

### Autodesk DWF Writer

The Autodesk DWF Writer is a Windows system printer driver that allows you to publish DWF files by simply selecting **Autodesk DWF Writer** from your standard **Printer Name** drop-down list in any Windows application. The DWF Writer allows you to create DWF files from any application that does not offer built-in DWF publishing. The DWF Writer is available as a free download from the Autodesk website (www.autodesk.com).

# SUMMARY

Whether you do quick check plots to check your work, create drawing sets to send to contractors, create full-color presentation drawings, or create electronic plots to share and collaborate with others over the Internet, plotting is an integral part of using AutoCAD.

AutoCAD provides a large number of options to precisely control the look and format of your output. This chapter gave you an overview of AutoCAD's plotting capabilities and some of the options available to controlling the output.

# CHAPTER TEST QUESTIONS

## Multiple Choice

1. A page setup is:
   a. A paper space layout
   b. A set of default plot settings
   c. A way to assign lineweights to AutoCAD objects
   d. A print driver

2. Which of the following model space plot scales will result in a drawing scaled to $1/2'' = 1'\text{-}0''$?
   a. .5 = 1
   b. 1 = 24
   c. 24 = 1
   d. 1 = .5

3. Named plot style tables are stored in:
   a. .CTB files
   b. .PC3 Files
   c. .DWF files
   d. .STB Files

4. Plotter configurations are stored in:
   a. .CTB files
   b. .PC3 files
   c. .DWF files
   d. .STB files

5. To plot everything visible in the drawing, you would set the plot area to:
   a. Limits
   b. Extents
   c. Layout
   d. Display

6. A DWF file:
   a. Is a Design Web Format file
   b. Can be viewed only electronically; it cannot be printed
   c. Can be opened in AutoCAD
   d. Does not show layer information

7. Which of the following AutoCAD commands does not print drawings?
   a. **PREVIEW**
   b. **PLOT**
   c. **SAVEAS**
   d. **PUBLISH**

8. Color-dependent plot style tables are stored in:
   a. .CTB files
   b. .PC3 files
   c. .DWF files
   d. .STB files

9. Plot stamps:
   a. Can contain only specific preset information
   b. Always appear in the lower left corner of the plot
   c. Use only the TXT.SHX text font
   d. None of the above

10. Raster files:
    a. Contain only pixels, no actual AutoCAD objects
    b. Are not supported in AutoCAD
    c. Must not exceed 640 × 480 resolution
    d. None of the above

## Matching

| Column A | Column B |
|----------|----------|
| a. .PC3 | 1. Plotter configuration file |
| b. DWF | 2. Text added to a drawing at plot time |
| c. Page setup | 3. Command used to print multiple plot sheets |
| d. .STB | 4. Color-dependent style table file |
| e. .CTB | 5. Command used to print a single plot sheet |
| f. **PLOT** | 6. An electronic plot file format |
| g. **PUBLISH** | 7. A group of default plot settings |
| h. Plot Stamp | 8. A type of raster file |
| i. PLT | 9. Named plot style table file |
| j. BMP | 10. An AutoCAD plot file |

## True or False

1. True or False: Page setups are used only in layout space.

2. True or False: You can use both color-dependent plot styles and **Named** plot styles within a single drawing.

3. True or False: Page setups can be created with the **PLOT** command.

4. True or False: DWF files cannot be opened in AutoCAD.

5. True or False: DWF files can contain only a single plot sheet.

6. True or False: DWF files do not support AutoCAD layers.

7. True or False: .PC3 files cannot be modified.

8. True or False: Objects in paper space are always plotted first.

9. True or False: You can publish layouts from multiple drawings files.

10. True or False: Color-dependent plot styles are assigned by layer name.

## CHAPTER PROJECTS

### Project 15-1: Classroom Plan—Continued from Chapter 14

1. Open the drawing **P14-1.**
2. Start the **PLOT** command so that the **Plot** dialog box is displayed.
3. Set the **Printer/plotter** name to a large format plotter capable of printing on 36″ × 24″ paper (D-size). If you do not have access to a large format plotter, set the **Printer/plotter** name to **DWF6 ePlot.pc3** to create a Drawing Web Format (DWF) file.
4. Make sure the **Paper size** is correct.
5. Make sure that the **Plot area** is set to **Layout.**
6. Make sure that the **Plot scale** is set to **1:1.**
7. Select the **More Options** arrow button on the bottom right of the dialog box to display the additional plotting options.
8. Turn off the **Plot with plot styles** option in the **Plot options** area and turn on the **Plot object lineweights** option.
9. Select the **Preview** button on the bottom left of the dialog box to preview the plot and make sure that everything is OK.
10. Select the **Apply to Layout** button on the bottom of the dialog box to save the changes with the layout.
11. Select **OK** to plot the drawing.
12. Save the drawing as **P15-1.**

### Project 15-2: Motorcycle—Continued from Chapter 14

1. Open drawing **P14-2.**
2. Start the **PLOT** command so that the **Plot** dialog box is displayed.
3. Set the **Printer/plotter** name to **Default Windows System Printer.pc3.** If you do not have access to a printer/plotter, set the **Printer/plotter** name to **DWF6 ePlot.pc3** to create a Drawing Web Format (DWF) file.
4. Make sure the **Paper size** is correct.
5. Make sure that the **Plot area** is set to **Layout.**
6. Make sure that the **Plot scale** is set to **1:1.**
7. Select the **More Options** arrow button on the bottom right of the dialog box to display the additional plotting options.
8. Turn off the **Plot with plot styles** option in the **Plot options** area and turn on the **Plot object lineweights** option.
9. Select the **Preview** button on the bottom left of the dialog box to preview the plot and make sure that everything is OK.

10. Select the **Apply to Layout** button on the bottom of the dialog box to save the changes with the layout.
11. Select **OK** to plot the drawing.
12. Save the drawing as **P15-2.**

## Project 15-3A: B-Size Mechanical Border—Continued from Chapter 14

1. Open template file **Mechanical B-Size.DWT.**
2. Start the **PLOT** command so that the **Plot** dialog box is displayed.
3. Set the **Printer/plotter** name to a printer or plotter capable of printing on 11″ × 17″ paper (B-size). If you do not have access to a printer/plotter that can print 11″ × 17″, set the **Printer/plotter** name to **DWF6 ePlot.pc3** to create a Drawing Web Format (DWF) file.
4. Make sure the **Paper size** is correct.
5. Make sure that the **Plot area** is set to **Layout.**
6. Make sure that the **Plot scale** is set to **1:1.**
7. Select the **More Options** arrow button on the bottom right of the dialog box to display the additional plotting options.
8. Turn off the **Plot with plot styles** option in the **Plot options** area and turn on the **Plot object lineweights** option.
9. Select the **Preview** button on the bottom left of the dialog box to preview the plot and make sure that everything is OK.
10. Select the **Apply to Layout** button on the bottom of the dialog box to save the changes with the layout.
11. Select **OK** to plot the drawing.
12. Save the drawing as **P15-3A.**

## Project 15-3B: C-Size Mechanical Border—Continued from Chapter 14

1. Open template file **Mechanical C-Size.DWT.**
2. Start the **PLOT** command so that the **Plot** dialog box is displayed.
3. Set the **Printer/plotter** name to a printer or plotter capable of printing on 22″ × 17″ paper (C-size). If you do not have access to a printer/plotter that can print 22″ × 17″, set the **Printer/plotter** name to **DWF6 ePlot.pc3** to create a Drawing Web Format (DWF) file.
4. Make sure the **Paper size** is correct.
5. Make sure that the **Plot area** is set to **Layout.**
6. Make sure that the **Plot scale** is set to **1:1.**
7. Select the **More Options** arrow button on the bottom right of the dialog box to display the additional plotting options.
8. Turn off the **Plot with plot styles** option in the **Plot options** area and turn on the **Plot object lineweights** option.
9. Select the **Preview** button on the bottom left of the dialog box to preview the plot and make sure that everything is OK.
10. Select the **Apply to Layout** button on the bottom of the dialog box to save the changes with the layout.
11. Select **OK** to plot the drawing.
12. Save the drawing as **P15-3B.**

## Project 15-3C: A-Size Portrait Mechanical Border—Continued from Chapter 14

1. Open template file **Mechanical A-Size-Portrait.DWT.**
2. Set the **Printer/plotter** name to **Default Windows System Printer.pc3.** If you do not have access to a printer/plotter, set the **Printer/plotter** name to **DWF6 ePlot.pc3** to create a Drawing Web Format (DWF) file.
3. Make sure the **Paper size** is correct.
4. Make sure that the **Plot area** is set to **Layout.**
5. Make sure that the **Plot scale** is set to **1:1.**
6. Select the **More Options** arrow button on the bottom right of the dialog box to display the additional plotting options.
7. Turn off the **Plot with plot styles** option in the **Plot options** area and turn on the **Plot object lineweights** option.
8. Select the **Preview** button on the bottom left of the dialog box to preview the plot and make sure that everything is OK.
9. Select the **Apply to Layout** button on the bottom of the dialog box to save the changes with the layout.
10. Select **OK** to plot the drawing.
11. Save the drawing as **P15-3C.**

## Project 15-4A: Architectural D-Size Border—Continued from Chapter 14

1. Open the template file **Architectural D-Size.DWT.**
2. Start the **PLOT** command so that the **Plot** dialog box is displayed.
3. Set the **Printer/plotter** name to a large format plotter capable of printing on 36″ × 24″ paper (D-size). If you do not have access to a large format plotter, set the **Printer/plotter** name to **DWF6 ePlot.pc3** to create a Drawing Web Format (DWF) file.
4. Make sure the **Paper size** is correct.
5. Make sure that the **Plot area** is set to **Layout.**
6. Make sure that the **Plot scale** is set to **1:1.**
7. Select the **More Options** arrow button on the bottom right of the dialog box to display the additional plotting options.
8. Turn off the **Plot with plot styles** option in the **Plot options** area and turn on the **Plot object lineweights** option.
9. Select the **Preview** button on the bottom left of the dialog box to preview the plot and make sure that everything is OK.
10. Select the **Apply to Layout** button on the bottom of the dialog box to save the changes with the layout.
11. Select **OK** to plot the drawing.
12. Save the drawing as **P15-4A.**

## Project 15-4B: Architectural B-Size Border—Continued from Chapter 14

1. Open the template file **Architectural B-Size.DWT**.
2. Start the **PLOT** command so that the **Plot** dialog box is displayed.
3. Set the **Printer/plotter** name to a printer or plotter capable of printing on 11″ × 17″ paper (B-size). If you do not have access to a printer/plotter that can print 11″ × 17″, set the **Printer/plotter** name to **DWF6 ePlot.pc3** to create a Drawing Web Format (DWF) file.

4. Make sure the **Paper size** is correct.
5. Make sure that the **Plot area** is set to **Layout.**
6. Make sure that the **Plot scale** is set to **1:1.**
7. Select the **More Options** arrow button on the bottom right of the dialog box to display the additional plotting options.
8. Turn off the **Plot with plot styles** option in the **Plot options** area and turn on the **Plot object lineweights** option.
9. Select the **Preview** button on the bottom left of the dialog box to preview the plot and make sure that everything is OK.
10. Select the **Apply to Layout** button on the bottom of the dialog box to save the changes with the layout.
11. Select **OK** to plot the drawing.
12. Save the drawing as **P15-4B.**

## Project 15-4C: Architectural A-Size Border—Continued from Chapter 14

1. Open the template file **Architectural A-Size.DWT.**
2. Start the **PLOT** command so that the **Plot** dialog box is displayed.
3. Set the **Printer/plotter** name to **Default Windows System Printer.pc3.** If you do not have access to a printer/plotter, set the **Printer/plotter** name to **DWF6 ePlot.pc3** to create a Drawing Web Format (DWF) file.
4. Make sure the **Paper size** is correct.
5. Make sure that the **Plot area** is set to **Layout.**
6. Make sure that the **Plot scale** is set to **1:1.**
7. Select the **More Options** arrow button on the bottom right of the dialog box to display the additional plotting options.
8. Turn off the **Plot with plot styles** option in the **Plot options** area and turn on the **Plot object lineweights** option.
9. Select the **Preview** button on the bottom left of the dialog box to preview the plot and make sure that everything is OK.
10. Select the **Apply to Layout** button on the bottom of the dialog box to save the changes with the layout.
11. Select **OK** to plot the drawing.
12. Save the drawing as **P15-4C.**

## Project 15-5: Electrical Schematic—Continued from Chapter 14

1. Open drawing **P14-5.**
2. Start the **PLOT** command so that the **Plot** dialog box is displayed.
3. Set the **Printer/plotter** name to a large format plotter capable of printing on 36″ × 24″ paper (D-size). If you do not have access to a large format plotter, set the **Printer/plotter** name to **DWF6 ePlot.pc3** to create a Drawing Web Format (DWF) file.
4. Make sure the **Paper size** is correct.
5. Make sure that the **Plot area** is set to **Layout.**
6. Make sure that the **Plot scale** is set to **1:1.**
7. Select the **More Options** arrow button on the bottom right of the dialog box to display the additional plotting options.
8. Turn off the **Plot with plot styles** option in the **Plot options** area and turn on the **Plot object lineweights** option.
9. Select the **Preview** button on the bottom left of the dialog box to preview the plot and make sure that everything is OK.

10. Select the **Apply to Layout** button on the bottom of the dialog box to save the changes with the layout.
11. Select **OK** to plot the drawing.
12. Save the drawing as **P15-5.**

## Project 15-6A: Hot Water Piping Schematic—Continued from Chapter 14

1. Open drawing **P14-6A.**
2. Start the **PLOT** command so that the **Plot** dialog box is displayed.
3. Set the **Printer/plotter** name to **Default Windows System Printer.pc3.** If you do not have access to a printer/plotter, set the **Printer/plotter** name to **DWF6 ePlot.pc3** to create a Drawing Web Format (DWF) file.
4. Make sure the **Paper size** is correct.
5. Make sure that the **Plot area** is set to **Layout.**
6. Make sure that the **Plot scale** is set to **1:1.**
7. Select the **More Options** arrow button on the bottom right of the dialog box to display the additional plotting options.
8. Turn off the **Plot with plot styles** option in the **Plot options** area and turn on the **Plot object lineweights** option.
9. Select the **Preview** button on the bottom left of the dialog box to preview the plot and make sure that everything is OK.
10. Select the **Apply to Layout** button on the bottom of the dialog box to save the changes with the layout.
11. Select **OK** to plot the drawing.
12. Save the drawing as **P15-6A.**

## Project 15-6B: Water Heater Schematic—Continued from Chapter 14

1. Open drawing **P14-6B.**
2. Start the **PLOT** command so that the **Plot** dialog box is displayed.
3. Set the **Printer/plotter** name to **Default Windows System Printer.pc3.** If you do not have access to a printer/plotter, set the **Printer/plotter** name to **DWF6 ePlot.pc3** to create a Drawing Web Format (DWF) file.
4. Make sure the **Paper size** is correct.
5. Make sure that the **Plot area** is set to **Layout.**
6. Make sure that the **Plot scale** is set to **1:1.**
7. Select the **More Options** arrow button on the bottom right of the dialog box to display the additional plotting options.
8. Turn off the **Plot with plot styles** option in the **Plot options** area and turn on the **Plot object lineweights** option.
9. Select the **Preview** button on the bottom left of the dialog box to preview the plot and make sure that everything is OK.
10. Select the **Apply to Layout** button on the bottom of the dialog box to save the changes with the layout.
11. Select **OK** to plot the drawing.
12. Save the drawing as **P15-6B.**

## Project 15-6C: Compressed Air Schematic—Continued from Chapter 14

1. Open drawing **P14-6C.**
2. Start the **PLOT** command so that the **Plot** dialog box is displayed.

3. Set the **Printer/plotter** name to **Default Windows System Printer.pc3.** If you do not have access to a printer/plotter, set the **Printer/plotter** name to **DWF6 ePlot.pc3** to create a Drawing Web Format (DWF) file.

4. Make sure the **Paper size** is correct.

5. Make sure that the **Plot area** is set to **Layout.**

6. Make sure that the **Plot scale** is set to **1:1.**

7. Select the **More Options** arrow button on the bottom right of the dialog box to display the additional plotting options.

8. Turn off the **Plot with plot styles** option in the **Plot options** area and turn on the **Plot object lineweights** option.

9. Select the **Preview** button on the bottom left of the dialog box to preview the plot and make sure that everything is OK.

10. Select the **Apply to Layout** button on the bottom of the dialog box to save the changes with the layout.

11. Select **OK** to plot the drawing.

12. Save the drawing as **P15-6C.**

## Project 15-6D: Unit Heater Connections—Continued from Chapter 14

1. Open drawing **P14-6D.**

2. Start the **PLOT** command so that the **Plot** dialog box is displayed.

3. Set the **Printer/plotter** name to **Default Windows System Printer.pc3.** If you do not have access to a printer/plotter, set the **Printer/plotter** name to **DWF6 ePlot.pc3** to create a Drawing Web Format (DWF) file.

4. Make sure the **Paper size** is correct.

5. Make sure that the **Plot area** is set to **Layout.**

6. Make sure that the **Plot scale** is set to **1:1.**

7. Select the **More Options** arrow button on the bottom right of the dialog box to display the additional plotting options.

8. Turn off the **Plot with plot styles** option in the **Plot options** area and turn on the **Plot object lineweights** option.

9. Select the **Preview** button on the bottom left of the dialog box to preview the plot and make sure that everything is OK.

10. Select the **Apply to Layout** button on the bottom of the dialog box to save the changes with the layout.

11. Select **OK** to plot the drawing.

12. Save the drawing as **P15-6D.**

## Project 15-6E: Pipe/Wall Penetration Detail—Continued from Chapter 14

1. Open drawing **P14-6E.**

2. Start the **PLOT** command so that the **Plot** dialog box is displayed.

3. Set the **Printer/plotter** name to **Default Windows System Printer.pc3.** If you do not have access to a printer/plotter, set the **Printer/plotter** name to **DWF6 ePlot.pc3** to create a Drawing Web Format (DWF) file.

4. Make sure the **Paper size** is correct.

5. Make sure that the **Plot area** is set to **Layout.**

6. Make sure that the **Plot scale** is set to **1:1.**

7. Select the **More Options** arrow button on the bottom right of the dialog box to display the additional plotting options.

8. Turn off the **Plot with plot styles** option in the **Plot options** area and turn on the **Plot object lineweights** option.

9. Select the **Preview** button on the bottom left of the dialog box to preview the plot and make sure that everything is OK.
10. Select the **Apply to Layout** button on the bottom of the dialog box to save the changes with the layout.
11. Select **OK** to plot the drawing.
12. Save the drawing as **P15-6E.**

## Project 15-7: Architectural Plan—Continued from Chapter 14

1. Open drawing **P14-7.**
2. Start the **PLOT** command so that the **Plot** dialog box is displayed.
3. Set the **Printer/plotter** name to a large format plotter capable of printing on 36″ × 24″ paper (D-size). If you do not have access to a large format plotter, set the **Printer/plotter** name to **DWF6 ePlot.pc3** to create a Drawing Web Format (DWF) file.
4. Make sure the **Paper size** is correct.
5. Make sure that the **Plot area** is set to **Layout.**
6. Make sure that the **Plot scale** is set to **1:1.**
7. Select the **More Options** arrow button on the bottom right of the dialog box to display the additional plotting options.
8. Turn off the **Plot with plot styles** option in the **Plot options** area and turn on the **Plot object lineweights** option.
9. Select the **Preview** button on the bottom left of the dialog box to preview the plot and make sure that everything is OK.
10. Select the **Apply to Layout** button on the bottom of the dialog box to save the changes with the layout.
11. Select **OK** to plot the drawing.
12. Save the drawing as **P15-7.**

## Project 15-8A: Joist Foundation Detail—Continued from Chapter 14

1. Open drawing **P14-8A.**
2. Start the **PLOT** command so that the **Plot** dialog box is displayed.
3. Set the **Printer/plotter** name to **Default Windows System Printer.pc3.** If you do not have access to a printer/plotter, set the **Printer/plotter** name to **DWF6 ePlot.pc3** to create a Drawing Web Format (DWF) file.
4. Make sure the **Paper size** is correct.
5. Make sure that the **Plot area** is set to **Layout.**
6. Make sure that the **Plot scale** is set to **1:1.**
7. Select the **More Options** arrow button on the bottom right of the dialog box to display the additional plotting options.
8. Turn off the **Plot with plot styles** option in the **Plot options** area and turn on the **Plot object lineweights** option.
9. Select the **Preview** button on the bottom left of the dialog box to preview the plot and make sure that everything is OK.
10. Select the **Apply to Layout** button on the bottom of the dialog box to save the changes with the layout.
11. Select **OK** to plot the drawing.
12. Save the drawing as **P15-8A.**

## Project 15-8B: Interior Floor Change Detail—Continued from Chapter 14

1. Open drawing **P14-8B.**
2. Start the **PLOT** command so that the **Plot** dialog box is displayed.
3. Set the **Printer/plotter** name to **Default Windows System Printer.pc3.** If you do not have access to a printer/plotter, set the **Printer/plotter** name to **DWF6 ePlot.pc3** to create a Drawing Web Format (DWF) file.
4. Make sure the **Paper size** is correct.
5. Make sure that the **Plot area** is set to **Layout.**
6. Make sure that the **Plot scale** is set to **1:1.**
7. Select the **More Options** arrow button on the bottom right of the dialog box to display the additional plotting options.
8. Turn off the **Plot with plot styles** option in the **Plot options** area and turn on the **Plot object lineweights** option.
9. Select the **Preview** button on the bottom left of the dialog box to preview the plot and make sure that everything is OK.
10. Select the **Apply to Layout** button on the bottom of the dialog box to save the changes with the layout.
11. Select **OK** to plot the drawing.
12. Save the drawing as **P15-8B.**

## Project 15-8C: Truss with Soffited Eave Detail—Continued from Chapter 14

1. Open drawing **P14-8C.**
2. Start the **PLOT** command so that the **Plot** dialog box is displayed.
3. Set the **Printer/plotter** name to **Default Windows System Printer.pc3.** If you do not have access to a printer/plotter, set the **Printer/plotter** name to **DWF6 ePlot.pc3** to create a Drawing Web Format (DWF) file.
4. Make sure the **Paper size** is correct.
5. Make sure that the **Plot area** is set to **Layout.**
6. Make sure that the **Plot scale** is set to **1:1.**
7. Select the **More Options** arrow button on the bottom right of the dialog box to display the additional plotting options.
8. Turn off the **Plot with plot styles** option in the **Plot options** area and turn on the **Plot object lineweights** option.
9. Select the **Preview** button on the bottom left of the dialog box to preview the plot and make sure that everything is OK.
10. Select the **Apply to Layout** button on the bottom of the dialog box to save the changes with the layout.
11. Select **OK** to plot the drawing.
12. Save the drawing as **P15-8C.**

## Project 15-9: Optical Mount—English Units—Continued from Chapter 14

1. Open drawing **P14-9.**
2. Start the **PLOT** command so that the **Plot** dialog box is displayed.
3. Set the **Printer/plotter** name to a large format plotter capable of printing on 36″ × 24″ paper (D-size). If you do not have access to a large format plotter, set the **Printer/plotter** name to **DWF6 ePlot.pc3** to create a Drawing Web Format (DWF) file.

4. Make sure the **Paper size** is correct.

5. Make sure that the **Plot area** is set to **Layout.**

6. Make sure that the **Plot scale** is set to **1:1.**

7. Select the **More Options** arrow button on the bottom right of the dialog box to display the additional plotting options.

8. Turn off the **Plot with plot styles** option in the **Plot options** area and turn on the **Plot object lineweights** option.

9. Select the **Preview** button on the bottom left of the dialog box to preview the plot and make sure that everything is OK.

10. Select the **Apply to Layout** button on the bottom of the dialog box to save the changes with the layout.

11. Select **OK** to plot the drawing.

12. Save drawing as **P15-9.**

## Project 15-10A: Gasket—Continued from Chapter 14

1. Open drawing **P14-10A.**

2. Start the **PLOT** command so that the **Plot** dialog box is displayed.

3. Set the **Printer/plotter** name to a printer or plotter capable of printing on 11″ × 17″ paper (B-size). If you do not have access to a printer/plotter that can print 11″ × 17″, set the **Printer/plotter** name to **DWF6 ePlot.pc3** to create a Drawing Web Format (DWF) file.

4. Make sure the **Paper size** is correct.

5. Make sure that the **Plot area** is set to **Layout.**

6. Make sure that the **Plot scale** is set to **1:1.**

7. Select the **More Options** arrow button on the bottom right of the dialog box to display the additional plotting options.

8. Turn off the **Plot with plot styles** option in the **Plot options** area and turn on the **Plot object lineweights** option.

9. Select the **Preview** button on the bottom left of the dialog box to preview the plot and make sure that everything is OK.

10. Select the **Apply to Layout** button on the bottom of the dialog box to save the changes with the layout.

11. Select **OK** to plot the drawing.

12. Save the drawing as **P15-10A.**

## Project 15-10B: Widget—Continued from Chapter 14

1. Open drawing **P14-10B.**

2. Start the **PLOT** command so that the **Plot** dialog box is displayed.

3. Set the **Printer/plotter** name to a printer or plotter capable of printing on 11″ × 17″ paper (B-size). If you do not have access to a printer/plotter that can print 11″ × 17″, set the **Printer/plotter** name to **DWF6 ePlot.pc3** to create a Drawing Web Format (DWF) file.

4. Make sure the **Paper size** is correct.

5. Make sure that the **Plot area** is set to **Layout.**

6. Make sure that the **Plot scale** is set to **1:1.**

7. Select the **More Options** arrow button on the bottom right of the dialog box to display the additional plotting options.

8. Turn off the **Plot with plot styles** option in the **Plot options** area and turn on the **Plot object lineweights** option.

9. Select the **Preview** button on the bottom left of the dialog box to preview the plot and make sure that everything is OK.

10. Select the **Apply to Layout** button on the bottom of the dialog box to save the changes with the layout.

11. Select **OK** to plot the drawing.
12. Save the drawing as **P15-10B.**

## Project 15-10C: Hex Head Bolts and Nuts—Continued from Chapter 14

1. Open drawing **P14-10C.**
2. Start the **PLOT** command so that the **Plot** dialog box is displayed.
3. Set the **Printer/plotter** name to a printer or plotter capable of printing on 11″ × 17″ paper (B-size). If you do not have access to a printer/plotter that can print 11″ × 17″, set the **Printer/plotter** name to **DWF6 ePlot.pc3** to create a Drawing Web Format (DWF) file.
4. Make sure the **Paper size** is correct.
5. Make sure that the **Plot area** is set to **Layout.**
6. Make sure that the **Plot scale** is set to **1:1.**
7. Select the **More Options** arrow button on the bottom right of the dialog box to display the additional plotting options.
8. Turn off the **Plot with plot styles** option in the **Plot options** area and turn on the **Plot object lineweights** option.
9. Select the **Preview** button on the bottom left of the dialog box to preview the plot and make sure that everything is OK.
10. Select the **Apply to Layout** button on the bottom of the dialog box to save the changes with the layout.
11. Select **OK** to plot the drawing.
12. Save the drawing as **P15-10C.**

## Project 15-10D: Motorcycle Head Gasket—Continued from Chapter 14

1. Open drawing **P14-10D.**
2. Start the **PLOT** command so that the **Plot** dialog box is displayed.
3. Set the **Printer/plotter** name to a printer or plotter capable of printing on 11″ × 17″ paper (B-size). If you do not have access to a printer/plotter that can print 11″ × 17″, set the **Printer/plotter** name to **DWF6 ePlot.pc3** to create a Drawing Web Format (DWF) file.
4. Make sure the **Paper size** is correct.
5. Make sure that the **Plot area** is set to **Layout.**
6. Make sure that the **Plot scale** is set to **1:1.**
7. Select the **More Options** arrow button on the bottom right of the dialog box to display the additional plotting options.
8. Turn off the **Plot with plot styles** option in the **Plot options** area and turn on the **Plot object lineweights** option.
9. Select the **Preview** button on the bottom left of the dialog box to preview the plot and make sure that everything is OK.
10. Select the **Apply to Layout** button on the bottom of the dialog box to save the changes with the layout.
11. Select **OK** to plot the drawing.
12. Save the drawing as **P15-10D.**

## Project 15-10E: 68-Tooth Motorcycle Sprocket—Continued from Chapter 14

1. Open drawing **P14-10E.**
2. Start the **PLOT** command so that the **Plot** dialog box is displayed.

3. Set the **Printer/plotter** name to a printer or plotter capable of printing on 11″ × 17″ paper (B-size). If you do not have access to a printer/plotter that can print 11″ × 17″, set the **Printer/plotter** name to **DWF6 ePlot.pc3** to create a Drawing Web Format (DWF) file.

4. Make sure the **Paper size** is correct.

5. Make sure that the **Plot area** is set to **Layout.**

6. Make sure that the **Plot scale** is set to **1:1.**

7. Select the **More Options** arrow button on the bottom right of the dialog box to display the additional plotting options.

8. Turn off the **Plot with plot styles** option in the **Plot options** area and turn on the **Plot object lineweights** option.

9. Select the **Preview** button on the bottom left of the dialog box to preview the plot and make sure that everything is OK.

10. Select the **Apply to Layout** button on the bottom of the dialog box to save the changes with the layout.

11. Select **OK** to plot the drawing.

12. Save the drawing as **P15-10E.**

## Project 15-10F: Window Extrusion—Continued from Chapter 14

1. Open drawing **P14-10F.**

2. Start the **PLOT** command so that the **Plot** dialog box is displayed.

3. Set the **Printer/plotter** name to a printer or plotter capable of printing on 11″ × 17″ paper (B-size). If you do not have access to a printer/plotter that can print 11″ × 17″, set the **Printer/plotter** name to **DWF6 ePlot.pc3** to create a Drawing Web Format (DWF) file.

4. Make sure the **Paper size** is correct.

5. Make sure that the **Plot area** is set to **Layout.**

6. Make sure that the **Plot scale** is set to **1:1.**

7. Select the **More Options** arrow button on the bottom right of the dialog box to display the additional plotting options.

8. Turn off the **Plot with plot styles** option in the **Plot options** area and turn on the **Plot object lineweights** option.

9. Select the **Preview** button on the bottom left of the dialog box to preview the plot and make sure that everything is OK.

10. Select the **Apply to Layout** button on the bottom of the dialog box to save the changes with the layout.

11. Select **OK** to plot the drawing.

12. Save the drawing as **P15-10F.**

## Project 15-10G: Hub—Continued from Chapter 14

1. Open drawing **P14-10G.**

2. Start the **PLOT**command so that the **Plot** dialog box is displayed.

3. Set the **Printer/plotter** name to a printer or plotter capable of printing on 11″ × 17″ paper (B-size). If you do not have access to a printer/plotter that can print 11″ × 17″, set the **Printer/plotter** name to **DWF6 ePlot.pc3** to create a Drawing Web Format (DWF) file.

4. Make sure the **Paper size** is correct.

5. Make sure that the **Plot area** is set to **Layout.**

6. Make sure that the **Plot scale** is set to **1:1.**

7. Select the **More Options** arrow button on the bottom right of the dialog box to display the additional plotting options.
8. Turn off the **Plot with plot styles** option in the **Plot options** area and turn on the **Plot object lineweights** option.
9. Select the **Preview** button on the bottom left of the dialog box to preview the plot and make sure that everything is OK.
10. Select the **Apply to Layout** button on the bottom of the dialog box to save the changes with the layout.
11. Select **OK** to plot the drawing.
12. Save the drawing as **P15-10G**.

## Project 15-11: Civil Site Plan—Continued from Chapter 14

1. Open drawing **P14-11**.
2. Start the **PLOT** command so that the **Plot** dialog box is displayed.
3. Set the **Printer/plotter** name to a large format plotter capable of printing on 36″ × 24″ paper (D-size). If you do not have access to a large format plotter, set the **Printer/plotter** name to **DWF6 ePlot.pc3** to create a Drawing Web Format (DWF) file.
4. Make sure the **Paper size** is correct.
5. Make sure that the **Plot area** is set to **Layout.**
6. Make sure that the **Plot scale** is set to **1:1.**
7. Select the **More Options** arrow button on the bottom right of the dialog box to display the additional plotting options.
8. Turn off the **Plot with plot styles** option in the **Plot options** area and turn on the **Plot object lineweights** option.
9. Select the **Preview** button on the bottom left of the dialog box to preview the plot and make sure that everything is OK.
10. Select the **Apply to Layout** button on the bottom of the dialog box to save the changes with the layout.
11. Select **OK** to plot the drawing.
12. Save the drawing as **P15-11**.

## Project 15-12A: Manhole Construction Detail—Continued from Chapter 14

1. Open drawing **P14-12A**.
2. Start the **PLOT** command so that the **Plot** dialog box is displayed.
3. Set the **Printer/plotter** name to **Default Windows System Printer.pc3**. If you do not have access to a printer/plotter, set the **Printer/plotter** name to **DWF6 ePlot.pc3** to create a Drawing Web Format (DWF) file.
4. Make sure the **Paper size** is correct.
5. Make sure that the **Plot area** is set to **Layout.**
6. Make sure that the **Plot scale** is set to **1:1.**
7. Select the **More Options** arrow button on the bottom right of the dialog box to display the additional plotting options.
8. Turn off the **Plot with plot styles** option in the **Plot options** area and turn on the **Plot object lineweights** option.
9. Select the **Preview** button on the bottom left of the dialog box to preview the plot and make sure that everything is OK.
10. Select the **Apply to Layout** button on the bottom of the dialog box to save the changes with the layout.
11. Select **OK** to plot the drawing.
12. Save the drawing as **P15-12A**.

## Project 15-12B: Manhole Cover—Continued from Chapter 14

1. Open drawing **P14-12B.**
2. Start the **PLOT** command so that the **Plot** dialog box is displayed.
3. Set the **Printer/plotter** name to **Default Windows System Printer.pc3.** If you do not have access to a printer/plotter, set the **Printer/plotter** name to **DWF6 ePlot.pc3** to create a Drawing Web Format (DWF) file.
4. Make sure the **Paper size** is correct.
5. Make sure that the **Plot area** is set to **Layout.**
6. Make sure that the **Plot scale** is set to **1:1.**
7. Select the **More Options** arrow button on the bottom right of the dialog box to display the additional plotting options.
8. Turn off the **Plot with plot styles** option in the **Plot options** area and turn on the **Plot object lineweights** option.
9. Select the **Preview** button on the bottom left of the dialog box to preview the plot and make sure that everything is OK.
10. Select the **Apply to Layout** button on the bottom of the dialog box to save the changes with the layout.
11. Select **OK** to plot the drawing.
12. Save the drawing as **P14-12B.**

## Project 15-12C: Standard Service Connection—Continued from Chapter 14

1. Open drawing **P14-12C.**
2. Start the **PLOT** command so that the **Plot** dialog box is displayed.
3. Set the **Printer/plotter** name to **Default Windows System Printer.pc3.** If you do not have access to a printer/plotter, set the **Printer/plotter** name to **DWF6 ePlot.pc3** to create a Drawing Web Format (DWF) file.
4. Make sure the **Paper size** is correct.
5. Make sure that the **Plot area** is set to **Layout.**
6. Make sure that the **Plot scale** is set to **1:1.**
7. Select the **More Options** arrow button on the bottom right of the dialog box to display the additional plotting options.
8. Turn off the **Plot with plot styles** option in the **Plot options** area and turn on the **Plot object lineweights** option.
9. Select the **Preview** button on the bottom left of the dialog box to preview the plot and make sure that everything is OK.
10. Select the **Apply to Layout** button on the bottom of the dialog box to save the changes with the layout.
11. Select **OK** to plot the drawing.
12. Save the drawing as **P15-12C.**

# Blocks and Block Attributes

16

## *Chapter* Objectives

- Learn how to create and insert blocks
- Understand the difference between a block definition and a block reference
- Explore the different types of blocks
- Create unit blocks that can be inserted with different *X* and *Y* scale factors
- Manage block object properties such as layer, color, linetype, and lineweight
- Understand the significance of creating blocks on layer **0**
- Insert drawing files as blocks using Windows Explorer
- Create a drawing file (DWG) out of an internal block
- Create and update block attributes
- Extract block attributes to an AutoCAD table or external file
- Use DesignCenter to insert blocks
- Use and customize tool palettes
- Introduction to dynamic blocks

## INTRODUCTION

Blocks, also referred to as *symbols*, are one of the most valuable features in AutoCAD. A block is a named collection of AutoCAD objects treated as a single complex object that can be inserted in a drawing one or more times. Blocks provide the following benefits and features:

- Provide the ability to reuse drawing information repeatedly in one or more drawings
- Increase drawing uniformity and consistency
- Promote and help maintain drafting standards
- Reduce drawing size
- Reduce amount of time and effort to update and revise drawings
- Add intelligence to drawings

Blocks can be made from practically any type of AutoCAD objects including lines, circles, text, dimensions, and even hatching. They may be as simple as a single line or as complex as a complete drawing. There are three basic types of blocks as shown in Figure 16-1:

> **Note:**
> It is possible to make a block **Annotative** so it scales up or down automatically using the current **Annotation Scale**.

- Annotation  Detail bubbles, section marks, door/window tags
- Schematic  Electrical symbols, plumbing symbols, weld symbols
- Real-Size  Furniture, doors/windows, plumbing fixtures

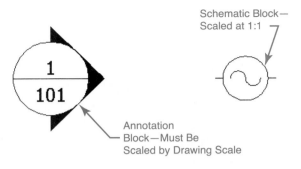

**Figure 16-1**    Examples of block types

Annotation blocks need to be scaled up or down when they are inserted to account for the drawing scale, just like text and dimensions. For instance, a detail bubble drawn with a 1/2″-diameter circle as shown in Figure 16-1 would have to be scaled up by 48 in drawing with the scale of 1/4″ = 1′-0″ in order to plot at the correct size.

Schematic blocks are created at the size they will plot so that you can create schematic drawings at a scale of 1:1. For instance, the electrical symbol in Figure 16-1 is drawn with a 1/4″ diameter so that it can easily be located in a schematic drawing created on a 1/4″ or 1/8″ grid layout.

Real-size blocks are created at the actual size that the objects exist in the real world so that they can be used to accurately lay out a drawing. For instance, a 2′-0″ wide chair is drawn 24″ wide so that when it is located on a floor plan it represents the actual furniture.

It is even possible to attach dynamic intelligent text referred to as a ***block attribute*** that can be updated when a block is inserted or at anytime later.

**block attribute:** A dynamic text-like object that can be included in a block definition to store alphanumeric data

Existing block attributes can be extracted directly to an AutoCAD table so that you can automatically create schedules, parts lists, bills of materials, and other tabular type information. In fact, block attributes can even be extracted to an external text file, spreadsheet, or database so that the attribute information can be shared with others, used to generate reports, and perform other tasks.

As you can see, blocks are very useful. The following sections explain how to exploit the power of blocks and block attributes in your AutoCAD drawings.

**Note:**
Like other complex objects, a block can be converted back into its original subobjects using the **EXPLODE** command. Using the **EXPLODE** command with blocks is examined later in this chapter.

## CREATING BLOCKS

The named group of AutoCAD objects that make up a block is referred to as a ***block definition***.

**block definition:** A user-defined collection of drawing objects assigned a base point and a name that is stored centrally in a drawing

Every time a block is inserted in a drawing it refers back to the centrally located block definition. In fact, when a block is inserted in a drawing, it is referred to as a ***block reference*** because it refers back to the block definition to determine its appearance and other properties.

**block reference:** An instance of a block definition inserted in a drawing that references the central block definition drawing data

All that is stored with the block reference is the block's insertion point, scale ($X$, $Y$, and $Z$), and rotation angle. The rest of the information is derived from the block definition. This arrangement provides a couple of advantages. One advantage is that the drawing size is reduced because the block definition is centrally stored in *one* place, regardless of how many references of the block exist in a drawing. The other advantage is that if you update a block definition, all references

**Note:**
It is possible to create blocks that are made up of other blocks. Creating a block within a block is a concept referred to as block nesting because one block is nested inside another block.

to that block definition in a drawing are automatically updated, regardless of how many references there are.

Creating a new block definition is easy. You simply draw the objects you want the block to consist of using standard drawing techniques and then start the **BLOCK** command so you can select the objects and give them a descriptive name that you can reference later.

## The BLOCK Command

The **BLOCK** command creates a block definition using the objects you select with the name specified via the **Block Definition** dialog box shown in Figure 16-2.

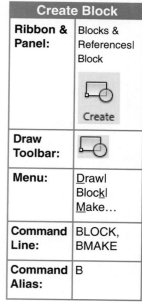

| Create Block | |
|---|---|
| **Ribbon & Panel:** | Blocks & References\| Block |
| **Draw Toolbar:** | |
| **Menu:** | Draw\| Block\| Make… |
| **Command Line:** | BLOCK, BMAKE |
| **Command Alias:** | B |

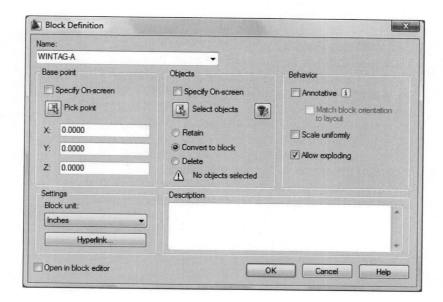

Figure 16-2    The Block Definition dialog box

The **Name:** list box is where you enter the desired block name. The name can be up to 255 characters long and can include letters, numbers, or blank spaces. Typically, you want to use a descriptive name that reflects the block's contents and/or usage.

Selecting an existing block name from the list will redefine all references to that block in the drawing if you make any changes. Redefining blocks is explained later in this chapter.

The **Base point** area allows you to specify an insertion point for the block. This point is used to locate the block in the drawing when it is inserted later. The default insertion point is 0,0,0. You can either enter the *X, Y,* and *Z* coordinate values directly in their respective text boxes or pick a point in your drawing by selecting the **Pick point** button. The **Pick point** button temporarily closes the **Block Definition** dialog box so that you can pick a point in the drawing as shown in Figure 16-3.

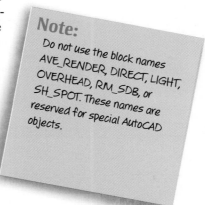

**Note:**
Do not use the block names AVE_RENDER, DIRECT, LIGHT, OVERHEAD, RM_SDB, or SH_SPOT. These names are reserved for special AutoCAD objects.

**TIP**    Typically, you should rely on object snaps to snap to a key point on the objects that comprise the block. For instance, you might select the center point if you are creating a detail bubble block or the endpoint at a corner of a desk block.

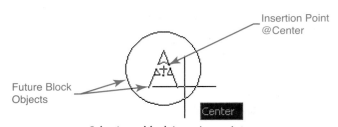

**Figure 16-3**   Selecting a block insertion point

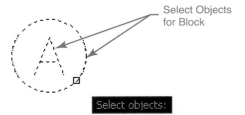

**Figure 16-4**   Selecting objects that will
make up the block

The **Objects** area allows you to select the objects to include in the new block definition if there are none already selected in the drawing, as well as to indicate what to do with the selected objects after the block definition is created.

The **Select objects** button closes the **Block Definition** dialog box temporarily so you can select objects in the drawing as shown in Figure 16-4.

You can use any standard selection process. When you finish selecting objects, press **<Enter ↵>** to redisplay the **Block Definition** dialog box and continue defining the block. Pressing the **<Esc>** key when selecting objects will deselect the objects so that nothing is selected and redisplay the **Block Definition** dialog box.

The **QuickSelect** button closes the **Block Definition** dialog box temporarily and displays the **Quick Select** dialog box shown in Figure 16-5 so you can select objects by filtering on one or more object properties.

**Note:**
If no objects are selected, the warning shown in Figure 16-2 is displayed at the bottom of the **Objects** area. Otherwise, the number of objects that are currently selected is displayed.

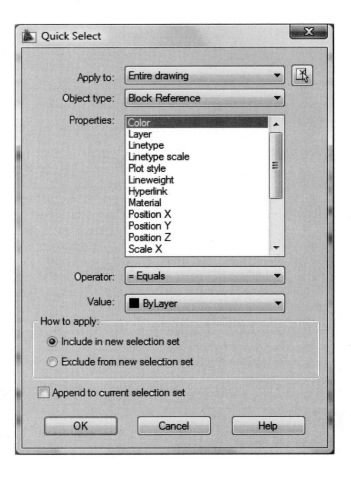

**Figure 16-5**   The Quick Select
dialog box

The other three options in the **Objects** area directly below the **Select objects** button determine what happens to the selected objects after the block is created:

- **Retain**   Retains the original selected objects in the drawing without doing anything
- **Convert to block (default)**   Converts the selected objects to a block reference "in-place"
- **Delete**   Deletes all the selected objects after the block is created so that they no longer exist

**TIP**   If you use the **Delete** option by accident, you can use the **OOPS** command to undelete the block subobjects. Type **OOPS <Enter ↵>** immediately after the block is created in order to return the original block subobjects to your drawing.

The **Settings** area at the bottom is where you specify different settings for the block.

The **Block unit:** list box lists the different possible insertion units for the block. If you insert a block that is created with different block drawing units than the insertion scale units currently set for the drawing, the block is automatically scaled up or down according to scale factor equivalent of the ratio between the different unit systems.

**Note:** The insertion scale units are set via the **Drawing Units** dialog box, which can be displayed by selecting **Units...** from the **Format** pull-down menu or using the **UNITS** command.

The **Hyperlink ...** button displays the **Insert Hyperlink** dialog box so that you can associate a hyperlink with the block definition. Hyperlinks can be attached to almost any AutoCAD object so that it is possible to link objects to Websites and even other documents.

The **Behavior** area at the top right is where you control what happens after a block is inserted.

The **Annotative** check box indicates if the block can be scaled up and down automatically using the current **Annotation Scale.**

The **Scale uniformly** check box indicates whether or not the block reference can be nonuniformly scaled when it is inserted so that the $X$, $Y$, and $Z$ scales are not all equal.

The **Allow exploding** check box indicates whether or not the block reference can be exploded when it is inserted or afterwards.

The **Description:** text box allows you to input a text description for the block that appears in the **DesignCenter** block drawing content management tool discussed later in this chapter.

**Note:** The block definition is created in the current drawing **only**. To use the block in any other drawing, you must first export it to a separate drawing file using the **WBLOCK** command explained later in this chapter.

The **Open in block editor** check box opens the current block definition in the **Block Editor** after you select **OK**. The **Block Editor** is described briefly later in this chapter.

After you have entered a name for the block, selected one or more objects, and specified the desired settings described above, select **OK** to close the dialog box and create the block.

## Block Object Properties

When you insert a block, the block reference assumes the current object properties (layer, color, linetype, lineweight) just like other AutoCAD objects. Be aware that the current properties are assigned to the overall complex block reference *only*. The object properties of the subobjects that make up the block are determined by how the objects were originally created before they were made into a block.

There are three different techniques for controlling the properties of a block's subobjects that result in the following effects when the block is inserted:

- Create subobjects on layer **0** with the color, linetype, and lineweight set to ByLayer.
- Create subobjects on any layer other than **0**.
- Create subobjects using the ByBlock property set for color, linetype, or lineweight.

*Creating Blocks on Layer 0.*    Creating block subobjects on layer **0** with object properties set to ByLayer is the most popular approach to creating blocks because it provides the most flexibility. Blocks with subobjects created on layer **0** have the special ability to assume the current object properties when they are inserted. This allows you to create one block that can be used in multiple scenarios based on the layer that is current when the block is inserted.

*Hard-Coding a Block's Object Properties.*    Creating block subobjects on any layer other than **0** locks the subobjects on the layer on which they were created so that the subobjects always maintain their original properties regardless of what layer or other properties are current when the block is inserted. This approach provides the least amount of flexibility because the block's subobjects are always located on the layer on which they were created regardless of the current layer and object properties in the drawing when the block is inserted. However, this hard-coded approach can have its uses, especially if standards dictate that a particular layer should be maintained for the life of a drawing.

*Using the ByBlock Object Property.*    The ByBlock property allows you to create block sub- objects that will assume the current color, linetype, or lineweight property when the block is inserted. Normally, a block and its subobjects ignore the color, linetype, and lineweight properties when the block is inserted. If you create a block subobject with any of these properties set to ByBlock, the subobject will assume the current setting for the property during the insertion process. For instance, setting a line's color property to ByBlock and including it in a block definition forces the line to assume the current color when the block is inserted. If the current color setting is red, then the line subobject is red. The same logic applies to the linetype and lineweight properties.

### Exercise 16-1: Creating Blocks

1. Start a new drawing using the acad.dwt drawing template.
2. Create the following layers:

| Name | Color | Linetype | Lineweight | Description |
|---|---|---|---|---|
| WINTAG-B | 1 | Continuous | Default | Layer used for all WINTAG-B block subobjects |
| A-Glaze-Iden | 3 | Continuous | Default | Window tag layer |

3. Create the "A" window tag shown in Figure 16-6 on layer **0**.
4. Create the "B" window tag shown in Figure 16-6 on layer **WINTAG-B**.
5. Create the "C" window tag drawing shown in Figure 16-6 on layer **0** with the color, linetype, and lineweight properties all set to ByBlock.
6. Start the **BLOCK** command to display the **Block Definition** dialog box.
7. Enter the name **WINTAG-A** in the **Name:** list box.
8. Select the **Pick point** button in the **Base point** area.
9. Select the center point of the "A" window tag circle using the **Center** object snap.
10. Select the **Select objects** button in the **Objects** area.
11. Select the "A" window tag circle and text and press <**Enter ↵**> to return to the **Block Definition** dialog box.
12. Make sure that the **Convert to block** button is selected.
13. Select the **Annotative** check box in the **Behavior** area.
14. Select **OK** to create the block.

**Figure 16-6** Window tag blocks

15. Repeat steps 6 through 13 to create blocks named WINTAG-B and WINTAG-C for the "B" window tag and the "C" window tag, respectively.
16. Save the drawing as EX16-1.

# INSERTING BLOCKS

As mentioned earlier, when you insert a block, it creates a block reference. Remember that the information about the objects that make up the block and what the block looks like is determined by the block definition explained in the previous section. All that you need to specify when inserting a block is the following:

- Block name
- Insertion point
- *X, Y,* and *Z* scale
- Rotation angle

In fact, besides the standard object properties such as layer, color, and linetype discussed later, this constitutes the majority of the information that is stored with the block reference. This is evident when you list a block reference using the AutoCAD **LIST** command:

```
BLOCK REFERENCE Layer: "0"
Space: Model space
Handle = a4
Block Name: "WINTAG-A"
at point, X=   0.0000   Y=  0.0000   Z=  0.0000
X scale factor: 1.0000
Y scale factor: 1.0000
rotation angle: 0
Z scale factor: 1.0000
InsUnits: Inches
Unit conversion: 1.0000
Scale uniformly: No
Allow exploding: Yes
```

Remember that a block reference assumes the object properties that are current when the block is inserted just like any other AutoCAD object. However, how the object properties affect the appearance of the block reference is dependent on how the block was created as explained earlier in the section, "Creating Blocks."

## The INSERT Command

The **INSERT** command allows you to insert a block reference by specifying the block name, insertion point, scale, and rotation angle via the **Insert** dialog box shown in Figure 16-7.

The **Name:** list box lists the names of all the blocks defined in a drawing that can be inserted.

The **Browse ...** button displays the standard **Select Drawing File** dialog box so you can select a block or drawing file to insert.

The **Path**: label specifies the path to the block if you select an external drawing file using the **Browse ...** button above.

The **Preview** window displays a preview of the specified block to insert. A lightning bolt icon in the lower-right corner of the preview indicates that the block is dynamic.

The **Insertion point** area allows you to specify the insertion point for the block. You can either pick a point in the drawing after you select **OK** (default), or you can specify the coordinate

| Insert Block | |
|---|---|
| **Ribbon & Panel:** | Blocks & References\| Block |
| **Draw Toolbar:** | |
| **Menu:** | Insert\| Block... |
| **Command Line:** | INSERT |
| **Command Alias:** | I |

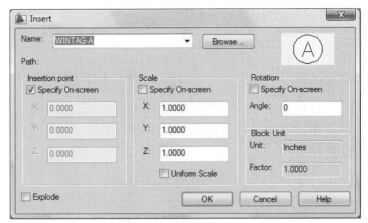

**Figure 16-7**    The Insert dialog box

position in the **X:, Y:,** and **Z:** text boxes. The **Specify On-screen** check box toggles between the two methods.

The **Scale** area allows you to specify the *X*, *Y*, and *Z* scale factors for the inserted block. You can either enter the scale factors in the **X:, Y:,** and **Z:** text boxes (default), or you can enter the scale factors after you select **OK**. The **Specify On-screen** check box toggles between the two methods.

The **Uniform Scale** check box forces a single scale value for the *X, Y,* and *Z* axes. When the **Uniform Scale** check box is selected, the *Y* and *Z* scales default to the value specified for *X*.

The **Rotation** area allows you to specify the rotation angle for the inserted block in the current UCS. You can either enter the rotation angle in the **Angle:** text box (default), or you can enter the rotation angle after you select **OK**. The **Specify On-screen** check box toggles between the two methods.

> **Note:**
> It is possible to insert an external drawing file (DWG) file from anywhere on your computer or network. Inserting external drawing files is explained in detail later in this chapter.

The **Block Unit** area displays information about the block units. The **Unit:** label indicates the insert units for the block. The **Factor:** displays the unit scale factor, which is calculated based on the insert units of the block and the drawing units. Neither of these settings can be changed in the **Insert** dialog box.

The **Explode** check box explodes the block immediately after it is inserted. It is only possible to specify a uniform scale factor when the **Explode** check box is selected.

After all the desired settings have been specified, select **OK** to insert the block as shown in Figure 16-8.

Figure 16-8 shows a block being inserted using the default settings, which prompt you to *Specify insertion point or ↓* on-screen during the insertion process.

If the **Specify On-screen** check box is selected for the **Scale** settings, AutoCAD prompts you to *Enter X scale factor, specify opposite corner, or ↓* so that you can either enter the desired scale for the *X* axis at the keyboard or pick a corner point in your drawing that dynamically defines both the *X* and *Y* scale. The default scale factor is always 1.

If you enter an *X* scale and press **<Enter ↵>**, AutoCAD then prompts you to *Enter Y scale factor <use X scale factor>: ↓*. You can either press **<Enter ↵>** so that the *X* and *Y* scales are equal, or you can enter a different scale factor to create a nonuniformly scaled block. Nonuniformly scaled blocks are discussed in the next section.

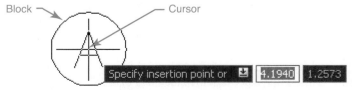

**Figure 16-8**    Inserting a block

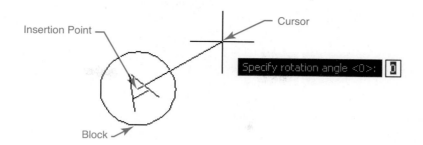

Specify rotation angle <0>:

Insertion Point

Cursor

Block

Figure 16-9    Inserting a
block and specifying the rotation angle on-screen

If the **Specify On-screen** check box is selected for the **Rotation** settings, AutoCAD prompts you to *Specify rotation angle <0>:* so that you can either enter the desired rotation angle at the keyboard or pick a point in your drawing that dynamically defines the angle using the insertion point as the angle base point as shown in Figure 16-9.

## Exercise 16-2: Inserting Blocks

1. Continue from Exercise 16-1.
2. Set the current layer to **A-Glaze-Iden** via the **Layers** drop-down list.
3. Set the current color to **Blue** via the **Properties** panel on the **Home** ribbon.
4. Use the **INSERT** command to insert the WINTAG-A, WINTAG-B, and WINTAG-C blocks anywhere in the drawing so that you can see all three block references in the drawing window.
5. Compare how the object properties are different for each block reference.
6. Turn on the **Automatically add scales to annotative objects when the annotation scale changes** button on the right side of the Status Bar.
7. Change the **Annotation Scale** to **12**.
8. Insert one of the WINTAG blocks.
9. Change the **Annotation Scale** to **2:1**.
10. Insert another WINTAG block.
11. Save the drawing as **EX16-2**.

## Nonuniformly Scaled Unit Blocks

If the **Scale uniformly** check box was not selected when the block was created, you can specify different *X, Y,* and *Z* scale factors when a block is inserted so that the block can be scaled along a single axis. In fact, this is a technique that is used to create what are known as ***unit blocks***.

Unit blocks can be scaled along one axis so that one block definition can serve multiple purposes. A classic example is a structural lumber section, which is typically represented by a nominally sized rectangle with a cross through it. See Figure 16-10. Creating the lumber section as a unit block allows you to specify different *X* and *Y* scales when the block is inserted so that different lumber sizes can be created as shown in Figure 16-10.

**unit block:** A block or symbol drawn within a 1 × 1 unit square that is inserted in the drawing with different *X* and *Y* scales to achieve different final sizes

## Exercise 16-3: Nonuniformly Scaled Unit Blocks

1. Start a new drawing using the **acad.dwt** drawing template.
2. Create the unit block drawing shown in Figure 16-11.
3. Use the **BLOCK** command to create a block named STUD that consists of the linework created in step 2 with a base point at the lower left-hand corner.
4. Start the **INSERT** command to display the **Insert** dialog box.
5. Select STUD from the **Name:** list box.
6. Make sure the **Specify On-screen** check box is unselected in the Scale: area.
7. Set the **X:** scale to 2.0.
8. Set the **Y:** scale to 4.0.
9. Select **OK** to insert the 2 × 4 stud anywhere in your drawing.
10. Start the **INSERT** command to display the Insert dialog box.
11. Select STUD from the **Name:** list box if not selected.
12. Set the **X:** scale to **2.0**.

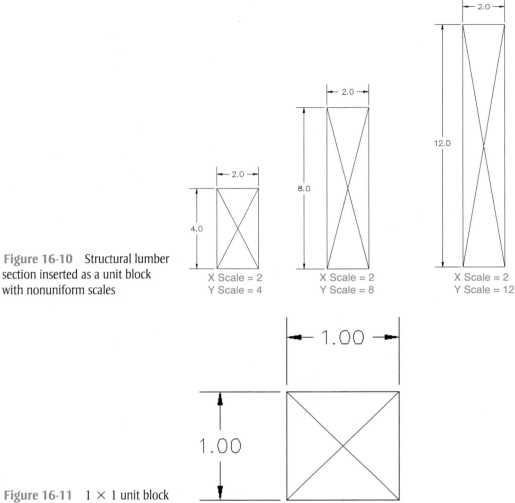

**Figure 16-10**    Structural lumber section inserted as a unit block with nonuniform scales

| X Scale = 2 | X Scale = 2 | X Scale = 2 |
| Y Scale = 4 | Y Scale = 8 | Y Scale = 12 |

**Figure 16-11**    1 × 1 unit block

13. Set the **Y**: scale to 8.0.
14. Select **OK** to insert the 2 × 8 stud anywhere in your drawing.
15. Start the **INSERT** command to display the **Insert** dialog box.
16. Select STUD from the **Name**: list box if not selected.
17. Set the **X**: scale to **2.0**.
18. Set the **Y**: scale to **12.0**.
19. Select **OK** to insert the 2 × 12 stud anywhere in your drawing.
20. Your drawing should look like Figure 16-10.
21. Save the drawing as **EX16-3**.

## Exploding Blocks

As mentioned earlier in the Introduction, a block reference is considered a complex object just like a polyline, boundary hatch, or dimension. If the **Allow exploding** check box was selected when the block was created, you can explode a block back into its original individual subobjects either after it is inserted using the **EXPLODE** command or when it is inserted by selecting the **Explode** check box in the **Insert** dialog box shown in Figure 16-7.

**TIP**    Typically, you do not want to explode blocks because you lose all the advantages of using them in the first place. Not only can you no longer automatically update an exploded block using the techniques explained later in this chapter, but you also increase the size of the drawing because each subobject is added as a new object and is no longer simply a reference.

## Inserting a Drawing File as a Block

It is possible, and actually quite common, to insert an entire drawing file (DWG) as a block. When you insert a drawing file, a block definition with the same name as the file is automatically created using all the information in the drawing file.

There are a couple of ways to insert a drawing file as a block. To insert a drawing file via the **Insert** dialog box explained earlier, select the **Browse . . .** button shown in Figure 16-7 to display the **Select Drawing File** dialog box shown in Figure 16-12.

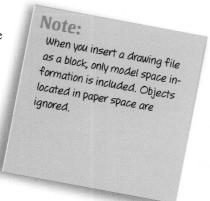

**Note:**
When you insert a drawing file as a block, only model space information is included. Objects located in paper space are ignored.

Select File to Insert

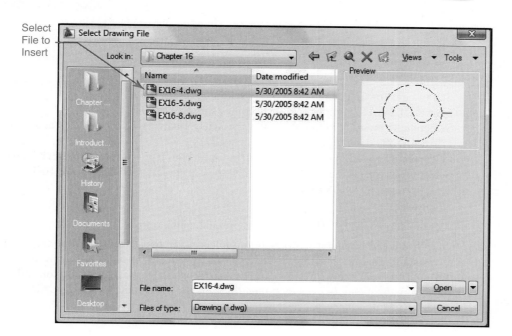

**Figure 16-12** Selecting a drawing file to insert as a block

Find the file you want to insert and select the **Open** button. A block definition with the same name as the drawing file is added to the **Name:** list box, and it becomes the current block to insert as shown in Figure 16-13.

Once a drawing has been selected and it has been made a block definition, the exact same settings can be specified. You can select **OK** to insert the block.

**Note:**
When you insert a drawing file, all the nongraphical named information defined in the drawing such as layers, linetypes, text styles, dimension styles, etc. comes along for the ride so that any named information defined in the original drawing becomes part of the current drawing.

TIP

By default, the insertion base point for a drawing file inserted as a block is the coordinate location 0,0,0 in the original drawing file. You can change the insertion base point by opening the drawing file and using the **BASE** command to set it to another location. Don't forget to save the drawing.

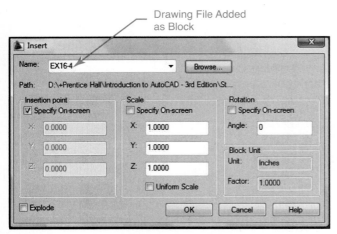

Drawing File Added
as Block

Figure 16-13    New block definition added to list

Figure 16-14    Inserting drawing files as blocks

### Exercise 16-4: Inserting a Drawing File as a Block

1. Start a new drawing using the **acad.dwt** drawing template.
2. Start the **INSERT** command to display the **Insert** dialog box.
3. Select the **Browse . . .** button to display the **Select Drawing File** dialog box and locate the EX16-4.DWG drawing file on the Student CD.
4. Select the EX16-4.DWG file and select the **Open** button to return to the **Insert** dialog box.
5. Select **OK** to insert the block anywhere in the drawing as shown in Figure 16-14.
6. Save the drawing as **EX16-4**.

## Using Windows Explorer to Insert a Drawing File

You can use Windows® Explorer to drag-and-drop a drawing file directly into the current drawing. You can start Windows Explorer a number of ways including double-clicking on the **My Computer** icon on the Windows desktop, right-clicking on the Windows **Start** button and selecting **Explore** from the menu, or even by typing the **EXPLORE** command in AutoCAD.

In order to use drag-and-drop techniques, you must be able to have both AutoCAD and Explorer visible on your computer at the same time, as shown in Figure 16-15.

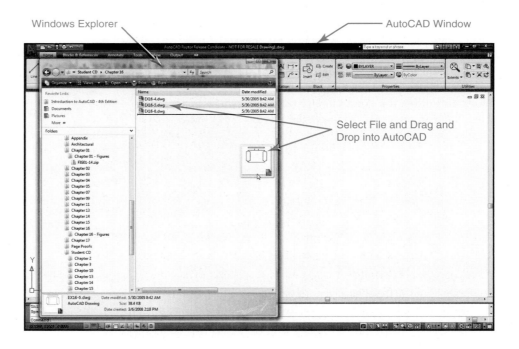

Figure 16-15    Using Windows Explorer to insert files

If you select a file with the *left* mouse button and drag-and-drop it into your drawing, the same insertion point, scale factor, and rotation angle command prompts are displayed as if the **Specify On-screen** check boxes were selected in the **Insert** dialog box described earlier.

If you select a file with the *right* mouse button and drag-and-drop it into your drawing, the shortcut menu shown in Figure 16-16 is displayed.

Using the shortcut menu, you can elect to do one of the following:

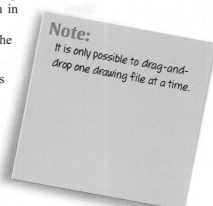

**Note:**
It is only possible to drag-and-drop one drawing file at a time.

**Figure 16-16**    Right-click drag-and-drop shortcut menu

- **Insert Here**    Inserts the file as a block the same as above

- **Open**    Opens the drawing file in a new window

- **Create Xref**    Attaches the drawing as an xref

- **Create Hyperlink Here**    Creates a hyperlink to the drawing on the object you select

- **Cancel**    Cancels drag-and-drop operation

| FOR MORE DETAILS | See Chapter 17 for more details about using xrefs (external references). |
|---|---|

**Exercise 16-5:** Using Windows Explorer to Insert a Drawing File

1. Start a new drawing using the **acad.dwt** drawing template.
2. Start Windows Explorer using one of the techniques explained above.
3. Set up your computer display so that both the AutoCAD drawing window and Windows Explorer window are both visible, similar to the display shown in Figure 16-15.
4. In Windows Explorer, locate the EX16-5.DWG drawing file on the Student CD.
5. Select the EX16-5.DWG drawing file with your *left* mouse button and drag-and-drop it into the current drawing.
6. Select the EX16-5.DWG drawing file with your *right* mouse button and drag and drop it into the current drawing.
7. Select **Insert Here** from the shortcut menu.
8. Select an insertion point in the drawing and press **<Enter ↵>** three times to accept the defaults for the *X* scale (1), *Y* scale (1), and rotation angle (0).
9. Save the drawing as **EX16-5**.

## EXPORTING BLOCKS

As mentioned earlier in the "Creating Blocks" section, by default, a block definition is stored *only* in the drawing it is created. In order to use the block in another drawing, you must first export it to a drawing file (DWG). You can then insert it using the techniques explained above.

### The WBLOCK Command

The **WBLOCK** command, short for "write block," writes a block definition to an external drawing file (DWG) with the file name and location you specify using any of the following methods:

- Write an existing block definition that is already defined internally in a drawing
- Create a new block definition *and* write the block to an external drawing file
- Create a new block definition using *all* the information in the drawing and write the block to an external drawing file

Starting the **WBLOCK** command displays the **Write Block** dialog box shown in Figure 16-17. The **Source** area is the main area of the dialog box used to specify how to create the block.

| Write Block | |
|---|---|
| Ribbon & Panel: | None |
| Toolbar: | None |
| Menu: | None |
| Command Line: | WBLOCK |
| Command Alias: | W |

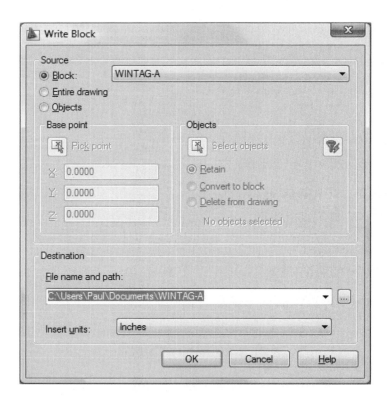

Figure 16-17    The Write
Block dialog box

The **Block** option allows you to select a block that has already been defined in the drawing from the list on the right. This option and the list are disabled if there are no blocks defined in the drawing. The **Entire drawing** option creates a block out of the entire drawing and writes it out to a file.

> Using **WBLOCK** to create a block out of the entire drawing and write it to a file is an old trick used to quickly purge a drawing of all its unreferenced drawing information such as layers, linetypes, text styles, dimension styles, other blocks and so on, so that the file size is reduced.

The **Objects** option allows you to create a new block on the fly and write it out to an external file using the exact same techniques as the **BLOCK** command explained earlier in the chapter. See the earlier section, "Creating Blocks," for complete, detailed information about creating a block from scratch.

The **Base Point** area allows you to specify a base point for the block. The default value is 0,0,0.

The **Select objects** button closes the **Block Definition** dialog box temporarily so you can select objects in the drawing as shown earlier in Figure 16-4. The **QuickSelect** button closes the **Block Definition** dialog box temporarily and displays the **Quick Select** dialog box shown earlier in Figure 16-5 so you can select objects by filtering on one or more object properties.

The other three options in the **Objects** area directly below the **Select objects** buttons determine what happens to the selected objects after the block is created:

- **Retain** (default)   Retains the original selected objects in the drawing without doing anything

- **Convert to block**   Converts the selected objects to a block reference "in-place"

- **Delete from drawing**   Deletes all the selected objects after the block is created so that they no longer exist

The **Destination** area is where you specify the file name and location and the units of measurement to be used when the block is inserted.

The **File name and path**: text box allows you to enter the file name and path where the block will be saved.

Selecting the **[…]** button displays the standard **Browse for Drawing File** dialog box so you can select a file or specify another drive and folder location. The selected file and location is displayed in the **File name and path**: text box above when you exit the dialog box by selecting the **Save** button.

The **Insert units**: list box lists the different possible insertion units for the block. If you insert a block that is created with different block drawing units from the insertion scale units currently set for the drawing, the block is automatically scaled up or down according to the scale factor equivalent of the ratio between the different unit systems.

### Exercise 16-6: Using the WBLOCK Command to Export a Block

1. Continue from Exercise 16-1.
2. Start the **WBLOCK** command to display the **Write Block** dialog box.
3. Select the **Block** option in the **Source** area at the top of the dialog box.
4. Select the **WINTAG-A** block from the block list box.
5. Set the **File name and path**: setting in the **Destination** area to a folder location of your choice using the WINTAG-A.DWG file name and select **OK** to export the block.
6. Draw a "D" window tag similar to the others with the same circle diameter and text height somewhere in the drawing.
7. Start the **WBLOCK** command to display the **Write Block** dialog box again.
8. Select the **Objects** option in the **Source** area at the top of the dialog box.
9. Select the **Pick poin**t button in the **Base point** area.
10. Select the center point of the "D" window tag circle you just created using the **Center** object snap.
11. Select the **Select objects** button in the **Objects** area.
12. Select the "D" window tag circle and text and press **<Enter ↵>** to return to the **Write Block** dialog box.
13. Set the **File name and path**: setting in the **Destination** area to a folder location of your choice with the file name WINTAG-D.DWG and select **OK** to export the block.
14. Save the drawing as **EX16-6**.

## BLOCK ATTRIBUTES

As explained in the Introduction, an attribute is a text-like object included in a block definition that is used to store alphanumeric information. It can either be updated dynamically when a block is inserted or updated manually after the block is inserted later by selecting the block. Updated attribute data can then be used to automatically create tables or exported to external files using the **Data Extraction** wizard explained later in this chapter.

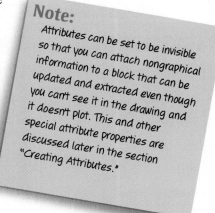

**Note:** Attributes can be set to be invisible so that you can attach nongraphical information to a block that can be updated and extracted even though you can't see it in the drawing and it doesn't plot. This and other special attribute properties are discussed later in the section "Creating Attributes."

The key to an attribute is its tag, which is used to store and retrieve the attribute data. A tag is an attribute's unique identifier, similar to a field in a database or a row/column in a spreadsheet. The tag allows you to specify which attributes to extract when you use the **Data Extraction** wizard. Tags are always all uppercase and cannot include any spaces or special characters. They are typically given a descriptive name indicating the type of data they are storing. For example, the attribute tags for a window tag block that contains information about the window type, width, height and manufacturer might be defined as shown in Figure 16-18.

Figure 16-18 shows what the window tag block looks like prior to being defined. Attributes that are defined to be invisible are not turned off until the block is defined and inserted as a block reference in the drawing as shown later in Figure 16-21.

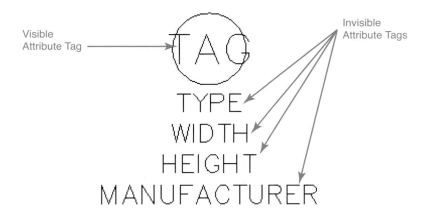

Visible
Attribute Tag

Invisible
Attribute Tags

Figure 16-18   Window
tag block with attribute
tags—before block
definition

The other key parts of an attribute definition are its prompt and default value. The prompt is what you see when you insert the block so you know what type of information to enter. The default value is what the attribute is automatically set to if no information is entered. The attribute tag, prompt, and default value for the window tag block's manufacturer attribute are shown in Figure 16-19.

After the block is defined and you insert it, you are automatically prompted to enter the attribute values either individually at the command prompt or en masse via the **Edit Attributes** dialog box shown in Figure 16-20.

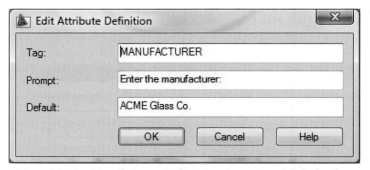

Figure 16-19   Manufacturer attribute tag, prompt, and default value

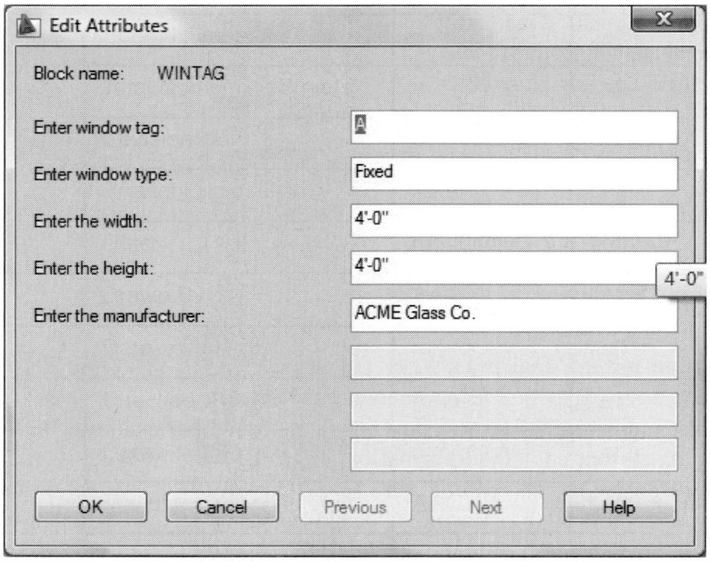

Figure 16-20   The Edit Attributes dialog box

After the attribute values have been entered either via the **Edit Attributes** dialog box or at the command prompt, a block reference is created as shown in Figure 16-21.

Notice that the attributes that were defined as invisible are now no longer displayed, although it is possible to turn them on if necessary.

It is possible to update the attributes after the block is inserted using a number of different approaches, all of which are explained later in the section, "Updating and Editing Attributes." First, though, we need to create a block with some attributes.

> **Note:**
> Attribute display is controlled via the **Attribute Display** cascade menu on the **Display** cascade menu located on the **View** menu. The **On** option turns all invisible attributes on, and the **Off** option turns off all attributes. The **Normal** option displays attributes as they were originally defined. You can also use the **ATTDISP** command to control the same settings.

**Figure 16-21** The inserted block reference with attributes

## CREATING ATTRIBUTES

When working with attributes, you follow the same steps you would for creating a standard block. First you draw any line work and/or text that will make up the block, and then you can define the attributes. Attributes share many of the same properties as text, including the ability to assign text styles and fonts. When you add an attribute, you must also specify a justification and insertion point, similar to the manner in which you add single-line text.

| FOR MORE DETAILS | See Chapter 11 for more details about the different text properties and effects. |
|---|---|

Just like other AutoCAD objects, attributes also assume the current object properties such as layer, color, and linetype. Some organizations create attributes on their own individual layer so you can further control their visibility and appearance.

| FOR MORE DETAILS | See Chapter 6 for more details about managing object properties. |
|---|---|

### Attribute Definition

The **ATTDEF** command creates an attribute definition via the **Attribute Definition** dialog box shown in Figure 16-22.

The **Mode** area is where you control the visibility and other attribute options that are set when you insert the block. There are four different options:

- **Invisible**   Specifies that attribute values are not displayed or printed when you insert the block

- **Constant**   Makes attribute a constant value so that it cannot be updated either when it is inserted or anytime later

- **Verify**   Has you verify that the attribute value is correct when you insert the block by prompting you for the attribute information twice

- **Preset**   Sets the attribute to its default value and does not prompt you for the attribute information although it is possible to still update the attribute after it is inserted using the techniques explained in the following section

- **Lock Position**   Locks the position of the attribute definition in the block so that it cannot be moved after the block is inserted using grips

| Define Attributes | |
|---|---|
| **Ribbon & Panel:** | Blocks & References\| Attributes<br><br>Define Attributes |
| **Toolbar:** | None |
| **Menu:** | Draw\| Block\| Define Attributes… |
| **Command Line:** | ATTDEF |
| **Command Alias:** | ATT |

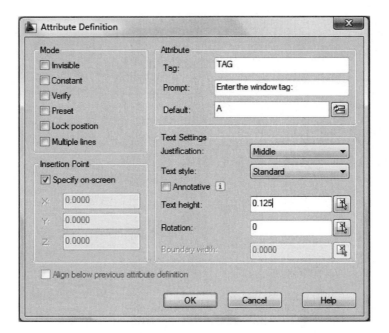

**Figure 16-22** The Attribute Definition dialog box

- **Multiple Lines** Allows you to create multiple line attributes by selecting the [...] button next to the **Default** value to display a stripped-down version of the Multiline text editor introduced in Chapter 11 and add multiple lines of text

The **Attribute** area is where you define the attribute tag, prompt, and default value:

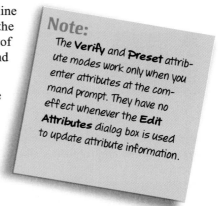

Note: The **Verify** and **Preset** attribute modes work only when you enter attributes at the command prompt. They have no effect whenever the **Edit Attributes** dialog box is used to update attribute information.

- **Tag** The unique alphanumeric key used to identify the attribute. Enter a descriptive name using any combination of characters except spaces. Lowercase letters are automatically changed to uppercase. Attribute tags can contain up to 256 characters.
- **Prompt** The prompt that is displayed either in the **Edit Attributes** dialog box or at the command prompt when you insert the block. If the prompt field is left blank, the attribute tag is used as a prompt. The **Prompt** option is disabled if you are defining an attribute with the **Constant** mode selected.
- **Value** Specifies the default attribute value used

The **Insert Field** button displays the **Field** dialog box so you can insert a field into the attribute value.

**FOR MORE DETAILS**     See Chapter 11 for more details about using about text fields.

The **Insertion Point** area specifies the location for the attribute in the drawing. You can enter coordinate values via the keyboard, or if you select the **Specify On-screen** check box, you can pick a point in your drawing after you select **OK** and the dialog box closes.

The **Text Options** area sets the justification, text style, height, and rotation of the attribute text:

- **Justification** Allows you to set the attribute justification from a list of standard single-line text justification options

- **Text Style**   Allows you to assign a text style from a list of text styles defined in the current drawing
- **Annotative**   Allows you to make the attribute Annotative so that it scales up and down automaticaly based on the current **Annotation Scale**
- **Height**   Allows you to specify the height of the attribute text. You can enter a height value via the keyboard, or select the **Height<** button to define the height by picking points with your mouse. The **Height** option is disabled if a text style with a height greater than 0.0 is selected or if the justification is set to **Align**.
- **Rotation**   Allows you to specify the rotation angle of the attribute text. You can enter a value via that keyboard or select the **Rotation<** button to define the rotation angle by picking points with your mouse. The **Rotation** option is disabled if the justification is set to **Align** or **Fit**.

| **FOR MORE DETAILS** | See Chapter 11 for more details about the different text options |
|---|---|

The **Align below previous attribute definition** check box allows you to automatically locate an attribute tag directly below the previously defined attribute using all of the same text options. If selected, both the **Insertion Point** and **Text Options** areas of the dialog box are disabled. This option is disabled if you have not previously created an attribute definition.

Selecting **OK** closes the dialog box, and AutoCAD prompts you to *Specify start point:* so you can locate the attribute in the drawing. If the **Align below previous attribute definition** check box is selected, the attribute is automatically located directly below the last attribute that was defined.

**TIP**   Although you can change the prompt order of the attributes after a block is defined, it is best to select the attributes individually in the order you want to be prompted. If you select all the attributes using any of the window selection methods, the ordering of the attributes can be random.

## Exercise 16-7: Creating a Block with Attributes

1. Start a new drawing using the acad.dwt drawing template.
2. Create the window tag drawing shown in Figure 16-23 on layer **0** at 0,0,0 with the following attributes and settings:

| Tag | Prompt | Default | Mode |
|---|---|---|---|
| TAG | Enter window tag: | A | Visible |
| TYPE | Enter window type: | Fixed | Invisible |
| WIDTH | Enter window width: | 4'-0" | Invisible/Verify |
| HEIGHT | Enter window height: | 4'-0" | Invisible/Verify |
| MANUFACTURER | Enter window manufacturer: | ACME Glass Co. | Invisible/Preset |

3. Save the drawing as **EX16-7**.

**Figure 16-23**   Window tag block definition with attributes

## UPDATING AND EDITING ATTRIBUTES

By default, when you insert a block with attributes, you automatically get prompted to update the attribute values individually at the command prompt in the order in which the attributes were created. The alternate **Edit Attributes** dialog box can be displayed during the insertion process by setting the **ATTDIA** system variable to **1** (on). Setting **ATTDIA** to **0** (off) turns the **Edit Attributes** dialog box off.

**TIP**   It is possible to turn attribute prompts off temporarily when you are inserting a block by setting the **ATTREQ** system variable to **0** (off). When **ATTREQ=0**, an attributed block is inserted as though there are no attributes attached. The attributes can still be updated after the block is inserted using the techniques explained below. Set **ATTREQ** to **1** (on) to turn attribute prompts back on.

The easiest way to update attributes after they are inserted is to simply double-click on the attributed block. Double-clicking on a block with attributes displays the **Enhanced Attribute Editor** dialog box discussed in the next section so that you can update attribute values, as well as change attribute text options and attribute object properties.

The **Block Attribute Manager** discussed a little later in this section allows you to edit block attribute definitions on a global scale so that you can change the attribute modes, the attribute prompt order, and even remove attributes, so that *all* existing and future block references in the drawing are updated.

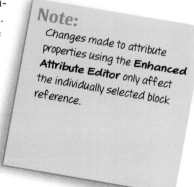

**Note:**
Changes made to attribute properties using the **Enhanced Attribute Editor** only affect the individually selected block reference.

**TIP**   It is possible to use grips to modify attributes so that you can perform basic editing tasks such as moving, rotating, and scaling attributes. Any changes affect the whole block if the **Lock position** check box was selected when the block was created.

**FOR MORE DETAILS**   See Chapter 7 for more details about using grips.

## Editing Attributes Individually

The **EATTEDIT** command allows you to update attributes via the **Enhanced Attribute Editor** dialog box so that you can do the following:

- Update attribute values
- Control attribute text options (text style, height, etc.)
- Manage attribute object properties (layer, color, linetype, etc.)

After starting the **EATTEDIT** command, AutoCAD prompts you to *Select a block:*. Select the block to update and press **<Enter ↵>** to display the **Enhanced Attribute Editor** dialog box shown in Figure 16-24.

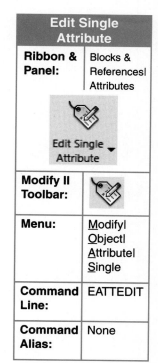

| Edit Single Attribute | |
|---|---|
| **Ribbon & Panel:** | Blocks & References\| Attributes |
| **Modify II Toolbar:** | |
| **Menu:** | Modify\| Object\| Attribute\| Single |
| **Command Line:** | EATTEDIT |
| **Command Alias:** | None |

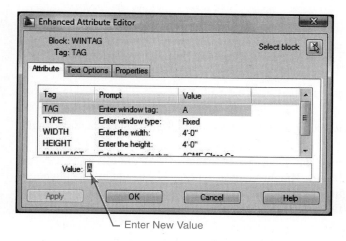

— Enter New Value

**Figure 16-24**   The Enhanced Attribute Editor dialog box— Attribute tab

The name of the selected block along with the current attribute tag is displayed at the top left of the dialog box. The **Select block** button on the right temporarily closes the dialog box so you can select another block to update.

The **Attribute** tab is the default tab shown in Figure 16-24 that allows you to update attribute values. All the block's attribute tags and their corresponding prompts and values are displayed in a tabulated list that you can navigate by selecting an attribute with your mouse or by pressing **<Enter ↵>** while the **Value** text box below is selected. Pressing **<Enter ↵>** while the **Value:** text box is current cycles through all the block attributes in the list.

**Note:**
If you modify a block and then select another block before saving the changes, you are prompted to save the changes first. To save changes and update the selected block, select the **Apply** button on the bottom of the dialog box.

The **Value:** text box displays the current value assigned to the attribute highlighted in the list box above. Enter a new value and press **<Enter ↵>** to update the attribute and proceed to the next attribute in the list.

You can insert a field in a value by right-clicking and selecting **Insert Field...** on the shortcut menu to display the **Field** dialog box.

If a multiline attribute is selected, the **[...]** button is displayed to the right of the **Value:** text box so you can select it to display the stripped-down multiline text editor and edit multiline attribute values.

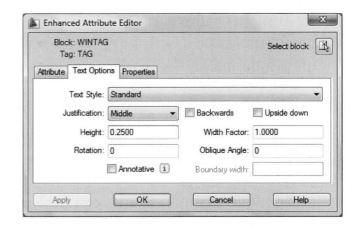

**Figure 16-25**   The Enhanced Attribute Editor dialog box—Text options tab

The **Text Options** tab shown in Figure 16-25 allows you to control the text properties of the currently selected attribute:

- **Text Style**   Allows you to assign a text style from a list of text styles defined in the current drawing
- **Justification**   Allows you to set the attribute justification from a list of standard single-line text justification options
- **Height**   Allows you to specify the height of the attribute text. You can enter a height value via the keyboard or select the **Height<** button to define the height by picking points with your mouse. The **Height** option is disabled if a text style with a height greater than 0.0 is selected or if the justification is set to **Align**.
- **Rotation**   Allows you to specify the rotation angle of the attribute text. You can enter a value via the keyboard or select the **Rotation<** button to define the rotation angle by picking points with your mouse. The **Rotation** option is disabled if the justification is set to **Align** or **Fit**.
- **Backwards**   Specifies whether or not the attribute text is displayed backwards
- **Upside down**   Specifies whether or not the attribute text is displayed upside down
- **Width Factor**   Sets the character spacing for the attribute text. Entering a value less than 1.0 condenses the text. Entering a value greater than 1.0 expands it.
- **Oblique Angle**   Specifies the angle that the attribute text is slanted
- **Annotative**   Specifies if annotation scaling is on or off

**FOR MORE DETAILS**   See Chapter 11 for more details about the different text properties and effects.

The **Properties** tab shown in Figure 16-26 allows you to control the general object properties of the currently selected attribute:

- **Layer**   Specifies the attribute layer
- **Linetype**   Specifies the attribute linetype
- **Color**   Specifies the attribute color
- **Lineweight**   Specifies the attribute lineweight
- **Plot style**   Specifies the attribute plot style

**Note:**
If the current drawing uses color-dependent plot styles, the **Plot style** list is disabled.

When you are done making changes or updates, you can either select **OK** to exit the dialog box and update the block, or you can select **Apply** to update the block and keep the **Enhanced Attribute Editor** open so you can make more changes.

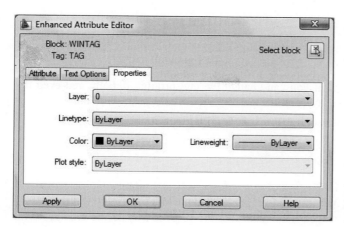

**Figure 16-26**   The Enhanced Attribute Editor dialog box—Properties tab

## Editing Attributes Globally

The **-ATTEDIT** command allows you to quickly update attribute values globally throughout an entire drawing at the same time.

The **-ATTEDIT** command is rather archaic. In fact, the **-ATTEDIT** command is actually just the old command line version of the **ATTEDIT** dialog box driven command. It may be an old, clunky command, but it is the only way to update more than one attribute at a time in a drawing so that you don't have to select and update each block individually.

After starting the **-ATTEDIT** command, AutoCAD prompts: *Edit attributes one at a time?* ↵. Enter **N** or **No <Enter ↵>** to update attributes globally. AutoCAD then prompts: *Edit only attributes visible on screen?* ↓ Typically, you should enter **No <Enter ↵>** to ensure all attributes in the drawing are updated accordingly and not just those shown in the drawing window.

AutoCAD then prompts you for the block name, attribute tag, and attribute value to be found. The default asterisk (*) value represents a wildcard, meaning that all blocks that match that category will be processed. If you know the block name, attribute tag, or attribute value for the block you want to update, you can enter the information to limit the number of blocks that are processed. Pressing **<Enter ↵>** in response to all these prompts forces AutoCAD to process all the attributed blocks in the drawing.

AutoCAD then requests the original value of the attribute text value to change by prompting *Enter string to change:* so you can enter the current attribute value. You are then prompted for a new attribute value *Enter new string:* so you can enter a new value. Immediately after you press **<Enter ↵>,** AutoCAD searches the drawing for all the attributes with a value of the text to change and updates the attribute with the new value as shown in Figure 16-27.

| Edit Attributes Globally | |
|---|---|
| **Ribbon & Panel:** | Blocks & References\| Attributes |
| | Edit Attributes ▼ |
| **Toolbar:** | None |
| **Menu:** | Modify\| Object\| Attribute\| Global |
| **Command Line:** | -ATTEDIT |
| **Command Alias:** | -ATE |

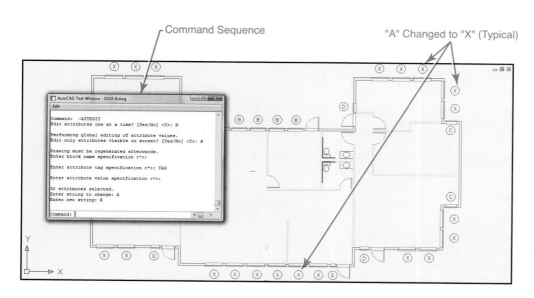

**Figure 16-27**   Updating attributes globally in a drawing

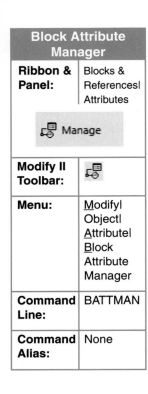

## Managing Attributes

The **BATTMAN** command allows you to update one or more block attribute definitions via the **Block Attribute Manager** dialog box so that you can do the following:

- Edit attribute definitions so that you can change the tag, prompt, default, and even the modes (invisible, constant, verify, preset)
- Control attribute definition text options (text style, height, etc.)
- Manage attribute definition object properties (layer, color, linetype, etc.)
- Change the attribute prompt order
- Remove attribute definitions

Changes made with the **Block Attribute Manager** update the block definition so that all future block insertions reflect the changes. It is also possible to synchronize the changes with blocks that have already been inserted.

Starting the **BATTMAN** command displays the **Block Attribute Manager** dialog box shown in Figure 16-28.

The **Select block** button allows you to choose a block definition to edit by selecting a corresponding block reference in the current drawing. Selecting the **Select block** button temporarily closes the **Block Attribute Manager** dialog box and prompts you to *Select a block:.* Select the block to update, and the dialog box is redisplayed.

The **Block**: list box allows you to select the block from the list of blocks currently defined in the drawing.

The tag, prompt, default, and mode properties of all the attributes defined for the selected block are displayed in the list box in the middle of the dialog box. The number of block references found in the drawing and whether or not they are located in the current layout is displayed directly below the list box.

The **Settings...** button on the bottom of the dialog box allows you to control what information is displayed in the attribute list box. Selecting the **Settings...** button displays the **Settings** dialog box shown in Figure 16-29.

**Note:**
If you modify a block and then select another block before saving the changes, you are prompted to save the changes first. To save changes and update the selected block, select the **Apply** button on the bottom of the dialog box.

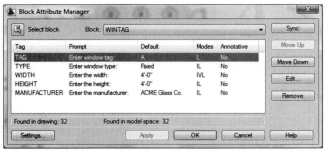

**Figure 16-28**   The Block Attribute Manager dialog box

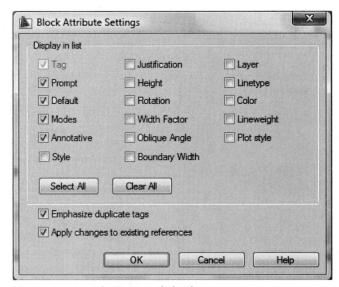

**Figure 16-29**   The Settings dialog box

The following options are available:

- The **Display in list** area is where you select which properties you want to display in the attribute list. Selected properties are displayed as an additional column in the list. The **Tag** property is always displayed.

- The **Select All** button selects all of the properties in the **Display in list** area above.

- The **Clear All** button clears all of the properties in the **Display in list** area above.

- The **Emphasize duplicate tags** check box turns duplicate tag emphasis on and off. When the **Emphasize duplicate tags** check box is selected, duplicate tag names are changed to red in the attribute list in the **Block Attribute Manager** dialog box so they can be easily identified.

- The **Apply changes to existing references** check box indicates whether or not to update all the existing block references in the drawing when any changes are made. When the **Apply changes to existing references** checkbox is selected, all existing and new block references are updated with the new attribute definitions. If it is not selected, only new block references have the new attribute definitions.

- The **OK** button accepts any setting changes, closes the **Settings** dialog box, and returns you to the **Block Attribute Manager** so you can continue to make any changes.

In the **Block Attribute Manager** dialog box, there are several more options:

- The **Sync** button updates all block references in the drawing with the currently defined attribute properties. Attribute values are not affected by any changes.

- The **Move Up** button moves the selected attribute tag up in the prompt order.

- The **Move Down** button moves the selected attribute tag down in the prompt order.

- The **Edit...** button displays the **Edit Attribute** dialog box shown in Figure 16-30.

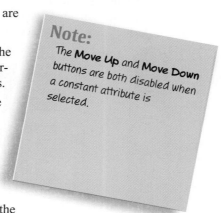

Note:
The **Move Up** and **Move Down** buttons are both disabled when a constant attribute is selected.

Using the **Edit Attribute** dialog box, you can modify the attribute definition properties.

- The name of the selected block is displayed at the top left of the dialog box.

- The **Attribute** tab is the default tab shown in Figure 16-30 that allows you to update attribute definitions.

- The **Mode** area is where you update the visibility and other attribute options that are set when you insert the block. There are five different options:
  - **Invisible**   Specifies that attribute values are not displayed or printed when you insert the block

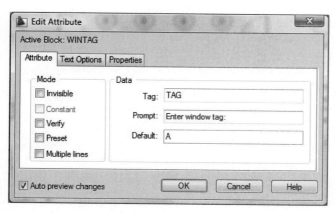

**Figure 16-30**   The Edit Attribute dialog box

- **Constant**   Makes attribute a constant value so that it cannot be updated either when it is inserted or anytime later. This option is disabled when using the **Block Attribute Manager**. The **Constant** option can only be used when an attribute is first defined.
- **Verify**   Has you verify that the attribute value is correct when you insert the block by prompting you for the attribute information twice
- **Preset**   Sets the attribute to its default value and does not prompt you for the attribute information although it is possible to still update the attribute after it is inserted using the techniques explained in the following section
- **Multiple Lines**   Allows you to use multiline attributes

- The **Data** area is where you update the attribute tag, prompt, and default value:
  - **Tag**   The unique alphanumeric key used to identify the attribute. Enter a descriptive name using any combination of characters except spaces. Lowercase letters are automatically changed to uppercase. Attribute tags can be up to 256 characters long.
  - **Prompt**   The prompt that is displayed either in the **Edit Attributes** dialog box or at the command prompt when you insert the block. If the prompt field is left blank, the attribute tag is used as a prompt. The **Prompt** option is disabled if you are defining an attribute with the **Constant** mode selected.
  - **Value**   Specifies the default attribute value used

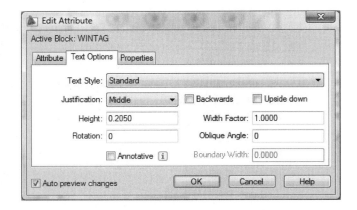

**Figure 16-31**   The Edit Attribute dialog box—Text options tab

The **Text Options** tab shown in Figure 16-31 allows you to control the text properties of the currently selected attribute definition:

- **Text Style**   Allows you to assign a text style from a list of text styles defined in the current drawing
- **Justification**   Allows you to set the attribute justification from a list of standard single-line text justification options
- **Height**   Allows you to specify the height of the attribute text. The **Height** option is disabled if a text style with a height greater that 0.0 is selected or if the justification is set to **Align**.
- **Rotation**   Allows you to specify the rotation angle of the attribute text. The **Rotation** option is disabled if the justification is set to **Align** or **Fit**.
- **Backwards**   Specifies whether or not the attribute text is displayed backwards
- **Upside down**   Specifies whether or not the attribute text is displayed upside down
- **Width Factor**   Sets the character spacing for the attribute text. Entering a value less than 1.0 condenses the text. Entering a value greater than 1.0 expands it.
- **Oblique Angle**   Specifies the angle that the attribute text is slanted
- **Annotative**   Specifies whether the attribute scales up and down using the current **Annotation Scale**

| FOR MORE DETAILS | See Chapter 11 for more details about the different text properties and effects. |

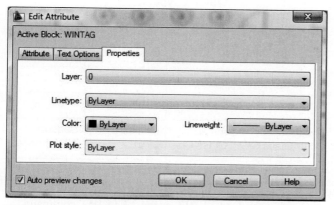

**Figure 16-32**   The Edit Attribute dialog box—Properties tab

The **Properties** tab shown in Figure 16-32 allows you to control the general object properties of the currently selected attribute definition:

- **Layer**   Specifies the attribute layer
- **Linetype**   Specifies the attribute linetype
- **Color**   Specifies the attribute color
- **Lineweight**   Specifies the attribute lineweight
- **Plot style**   Specifies the attribute plot style

The **Auto preview changes** check box allows you to immediately display any updates or changes made in the **Edit Attribute** dialog box. If the **Auto preview changes** check box is selected, any changes are immediately displayed.

The **OK** button accepts any setting changes, closes the **Edit Attribute** dialog box, and returns you to the **Block Attribute Manager** so you can continue to make any changes.

The **Remove** button removes the selected attribute from the block definition. The **Remove** button is disabled when a block has only one attribute.

The **Apply** button applies the changes you made to all block references in the drawing, but does not close the **Block Attribute Manager**.

Select **OK** to accept any updates and close the **Block Attribute Manager** dialog box.

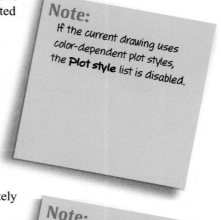

**Note:**
If the current drawing uses color-dependent plot styles, the **Plot style** list is disabled.

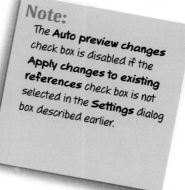

**Note:**
The **Auto preview changes** check box is disabled if the **Apply changes to existing references** check box is not selected in the **Settings** dialog box described earlier.

**Exercise 16-8:** Updating and Editing Attributes

1. Open the building floor plan drawing named **EX16-8** from the Student CD.
2. Set layer **A-Glaze-Iden** current.
3. Start the **INSERT** command.
4. Select the **Uniform Scale** check box and set the **X Scale** to 48.
5. Insert the EX16-7.DWG file created in Exercise 16-7 as a block using the **Browse...** button.

6. Locate the window tags as shown in Figure 16-33 and update them with the following attribute values:

| Attribute | Window Type | | | | |
|---|---|---|---|---|---|
| TAG | A | B | C | D | E |
| TYPE | Fixed | Fixed | Fixed | Casement | Sidelite |
| WIDTH | 4'-0" | 3'-6" | 2'-6" | 2'-0" | 1'-0" |
| HEIGHT | 4'-0" | 4'-0" | 3'-0" | 3'-0" | 4'-0" |
| MANUFACTURER | ACME Glass Co. | ACME Glass Co. | ACME Glass Co. | Glassarama, Inc. | Season All Windows |

7. Change the window manufacturer from **Glassarama, Inc.** to **SpectorLite** for all "D" type window tags in the drawing using either the **EATTEDIT** or the **ATTEDIT** command.
8. Change the attribute text color to **blue** for the TAG attribute for all blocks in the building plan drawing using the **BATTMAN** command.
9. Save the drawing as **EX16-8**.

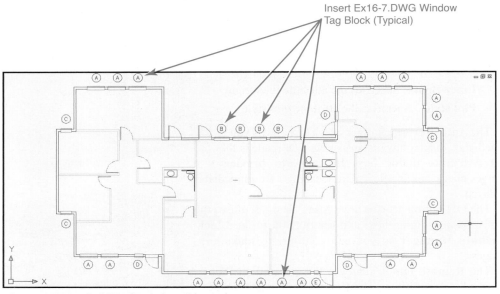

Insert Ex16-7.DWG Window Tag Block (Typical)

**Figure 16-33**  Building floor plan with window tags

## EXTRACTING ATTRIBUTES

It is possible to extract property information from objects in drawings, including blocks and their attributes, to a formatted table in the current drawing or to an external file so that you can quickly create schedules, parts lists, bills of materials, and other tabular-type information based on the current drawing, or even multiple drawings.

**TIP**  The extracted data can even be merged and linked with information in a Microsoft Excel spreadsheet so that is possible to include additional external information.

To make the extraction process as easy as possible, AutoCAD provides the **Data Extraction** wizard, which guides you through a series of preprogrammed steps so that you can provide the following information.

- Data source for information to extract
  - Current drawing
  - Multiple drawings or sheet set
  - Selected objects
- The block names and attribute tags to extract
- Whether to output the attribute information to an AutoCAD table or to output the information to one of the following external file types:
  - Comma-delimited text file (CSV)
  - Microsoft Excel® spreadsheet (XLS)
  - Microsoft Access® database (MDB)
  - Generic text file (TXT)

The **Data Extraction** wizard saves all the settings you specify in each step to an external file (DXE) so that you can use it the next time you use the **Data Extraction** wizard.

## Extracting Attribute Data

The **DATAEXTRACTION** command starts the **Data Extraction** wizard to guide you through the steps to extract attribute information.

Starting the **DATAEXTRACTION** command displays the **Data Extraction** wizard on the **Begin** page as shown in Figure 16-34.

| Data Extraction | |
|---|---|
| **Ribbon & Panel:** | Blocks & References\| Linking & Extraction |
| **Modify II Toolbar:** | |
| **Menu:** | Tools\|Data Extraction... |
| **Command Line:** | DATAEXTRACTION |
| **Command Alias:** | DX |

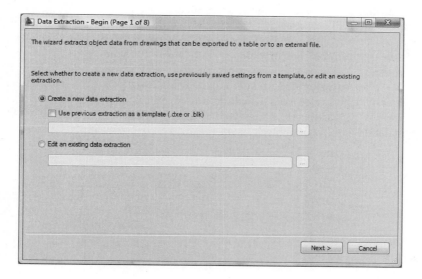

**Figure 16-34**   The Data Extraction Wizard —Begin page

The **Begin** page allows you to select whether you want to specify new extraction settings from scratch or use settings previously saved in an attribute extraction file (DXE or BLK).

If you select the **Use previous extraction as a template** option, you must select the **[...]** button on the right to select a file using the standard file selection dialog box.

The **Edit an existing data extraction** option allows you to modify an existing data extraction (DXE) file. You must select the **[...]** button on the right to select a file using the standard file selection dialog box.

Select the **Next >** button on the bottom to proceed to the **Define Data Source** page shown in Figure 16-35 or the **Cancel** button to close the wizard.

The **Define Data Source** page allows you to select one of the following data sources from which to extract the attribute information:

- **Drawings/Sheet Set**   Enables the **Add Folder...** and **Add Drawings...** buttons so you can add a folder or more drawings (DWG) or sheet sets (DST) using the standard file selection dialog box. The current drawing is included by default.

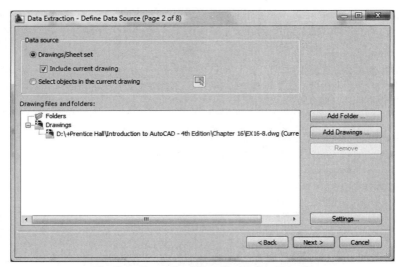

**Figure 16-35**    The Data Extraction Wizard—Define Data Source page

- **Select objects in the current drawing**    Enables the **Select objects** button so you can select one or more blocks in the current drawing.

The **Drawing files and folders** list box lists all the drawing files or sheets in the selected sheet set from which attributes will be extracted.

The **Settings...** button displays the **Data Extraction—Additional Settings** dialog box shown in Figure 16-36.

The **Additional Settings** dialog box allows you specify whether or not to include nested blocks and xrefs, as well as specify which types of blocks should be included in the overall block count.

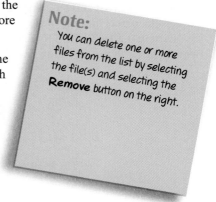

Note: You can delete one or more files from the list by selecting the file(s) and selecting the **Remove** button on the right.

**Figure 16-36**    The Data Extraction—Additional Settings dialog box

The **Extraction settings** area allows you to control which blocks are included in the attribute extraction process and whether or not to include xrefs in the block count.

- **Extract objects from blocks**    Includes blocks nested within other blocks
- **Extract objects from xrefs**    Includes blocks located in any attached xrefs
- **Include xrefs in block counts**    Includes attached xrefs as blocks in block counts.

| FOR MORE DETAILS | See Chapter 17 for more details about xrefs. |
| --- | --- |

The **Extract from** area provides options for which objects to include in the extraction process.

- **Objects in model space**   Extracts from only block references in model space and ignores any blocks located in paper space layouts
- **All objects in drawing**   Extracts from all block references in the entire drawing (model space and paper space)

The **OK** button accepts any setting changes, closes the **Additional Settings** dialog box, and returns you to the **Data Extraction** wizard so you can continue to the next step.

Select the **Next >** button on the bottom to proceed to the **Select Objects** page shown in Figure 16-37, the **Cancel** button to close the wizard, or the **< Back** button to return to the previous page.

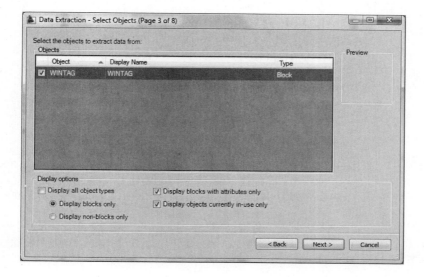

**Figure 16-37**   The Data Extraction Wizard—Select Objects page

The **Select Objects** page allows you to select the objects and drawing information to be extracted. Just about any AutoCAD object information can be extracted including blocks and non-blocks.

> It is possible to resize columns with your mouse and reverse the sort order by clicking on the column header. You can also select or unselect all objects via a right-click shortcut menu.

The **Objects** list displays each object by its name in the **Object** column. Blocks are listed by block name, and non-blocks are listed by their object name.

The **Display Name** column allows you to enter an optional alternative name for an object as it will appear in the extracted information. To change a display name, right-click in the **Display Name** column and select **Edit Display Name** from the shortcut menu.

The **Type** column indicates whether the object is a block or non-block.

The **Preview** image displays a preview image of the checked block in the **Objects** list.

You can limit the types of objects displayed in the **Objects** list in the **Display options** area at the bottom.

The **Display all object types** option displays a list of all object types (blocks and non-blocks) in the **Objects** list. It is on by default.

Turning off the **Display all object types** option allows you to toggle between the **Display blocks only** option and the **Display non-blocks only** option so you can further filter the **Objects** list.

The **Display blocks with attributes only** option displays only those blocks that have attributes in the **Objects** list.

The **Display objects currently in-use only** will limit the **Objects** list to objects that exist in the selected drawings.

Select the **Next >** button on the bottom to proceed to the **Select Properties** page shown in Figure 16-38, the **Cancel** button to close the wizard, or the **< Back** button to return to the previous page.

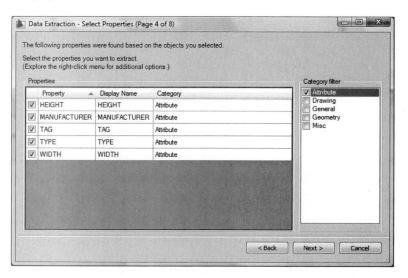

**Figure 16-38**    The Data Extraction Wizard—Select Properties page

The **Select Properties** page allows you to control the object, block, and drawing properties to extract.

Each row in the **Properties** list displays a property name, display name, and category.

**TIP**     It is possible to resize columns with your mouse and reverse the sort order by clicking on the column header. You can also select or unselect all properties via a right-click shortcut menu.

The **Property** column displays the properties of all the objects selected on the **Select Objects** page in the previous step. These are the same object properties displayed in the **Properties** palette in AutoCAD.

The **Display Name** column allows you to enter an optional alternative name for a property as it will appear in the extracted information. To change a display name, right-click in the **Display Name** column and select **Edit Display Name** from the shortcut menu.

The **Category** column displays a category for each property. For example, General designates ordinary object properties, such as color or layer. Attribute designates user-defined attributes. These are the same object categories displayed in the **Properties** palette in AutoCAD.

The **Category filter** check box list allows you to filter the list of properties shown in the **Properties** list based on the category listed in the **Category** column. Only checked categories are displayed.

Select the **Next >** button on the bottom to proceed to the **Refine Data** page shown in Figure 16-39, the **Cancel** button to close the wizard, or the **< Back** button to return to the previous page.

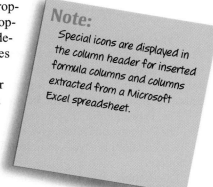

**Note:**
Special icons are displayed in the column header for inserted formula columns and columns extracted from a Microsoft Excel spreadsheet.

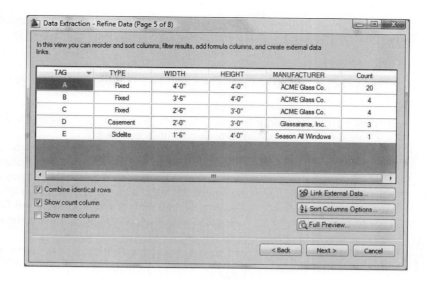

**Figure 16-39**  The Data Extraction Wizard—Refine Data page

The **Refine Data** page allows you to modify the structure of the data extraction table. You can reorder and sort columns, filter results, add formula columns and footer rows, and even create a link to data in a Microsoft Excel spreadsheet.

The grid in the middle of the dialog box displays properties that were selected in the **Select Properties** page in the previous step in a tabular format. The **Count** and **Name** columns display by default and can be turned off as explained below.

The **Combine identical rows** check box groups identical records by row in the table and updates the **Count** column with the sum total.

The **Show count column** check box toggles the **Count** column on and off in the table display.

The **Show name column** check box toggles the **Name** column on and off in the table display.

The **Link External Data...** button displays the **Link External Data** dialog box, where you can create a link between the extracted drawing data and data in an Excel spreadsheet.

The **Sort Columns Options...** button displays the **Sort Columns** dialog box, where you can sort data across multiple columns.

The **Full Preview...** button displays a full preview of the final output, including linked external data. The preview is for viewing only.

Right-clicking in a column displays the shortcut menu shown in Figure 16-40 that gives you the following options:

| Option | Description |
| --- | --- |
| **Sort Descending** | Sorts column data in a descending order |
| **Sort Ascending** | Sorts column data in an ascending order |
| **Sort Column Options** | Displays the **Sort Columns** dialog box so you can sort data across multiple columns |
| **Rename Column** | Allows in-place editing of the selected column name |
| **Hide Column** | Hides the selected column |
| **Show Hidden Columns** | Displays the hidden column. The cascade menu allows you to **Display All Hidden Columns.** |
| **Set Column Data Format** | Displays the **Set Cell Format** dialog box so you can set a data type for cells in the selected column |

| Insert Formula Column | Displays the **Insert Formula Column** dialog box so you can insert a formula into the table to the right of the selected column |
|---|---|
| Edit Formula Column | Displays the **Edit Formula Column** dialog box. Only available when a formula column is selected. |
| Remove Formula Column | Removes the selected formula column. Only available when a formula column is selected. |
| Combine Record Mode | Displays numeric data in the selected column as separate values or collapses identical property rows into one row and displays the sum of all the numeric data in the selected column. This option is available when the **Combine Identical Rows** is checked and the selected column contains numerical data. |
| Show Count Column | Displays a **Count** column that lists the quantity of each property |
| Show Name Column | Displays a **Name** column that displays the name of each property |
| Insert Totals Footer | Displays a cascade menu with options for Sum, Max, Min, and Average formulas. Creates a footer row for the selected column that is placed below all data rows and displays values based on the selected arithmetic function. Only available for columns that have a numeric data type. |
| Sum | Displays a sum of all the values in the selected column in a footer row |
| Max | Displays the maximum value in the selected column in a footer row |
| Min | Displays the minimum value in the selected column in a footer row |
| Average | Displays the average value in the selected column in a footer row |
| Remove Totals Footer | Removes the **Totals** footer. Only available when a footer row exists. |
| Filter Options | Displays the **Filter Column** dialog box so you can specify filter conditions for the selected column |
| Reset Filter | Restores the default filter for the selected column |
| Reset All Filters | Restores default filters for all columns that have filters |
| Copy to Clipboard | Copies selected data cells to the Clipboard |

Select the **Next >** button on the bottom to proceed to the **Choose Output** page shown in Figure 16-41, the **Cancel** button to close the wizard, or the **< Back** button to return to the previous page.

The **Choose Output** page allows you to select the type of output to which the data is extracted.

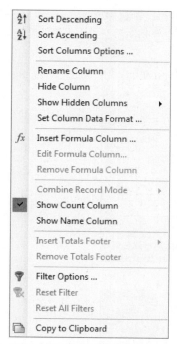

Figure 16-40   The Data Extraction Wizard—Refine Data shortcut menu

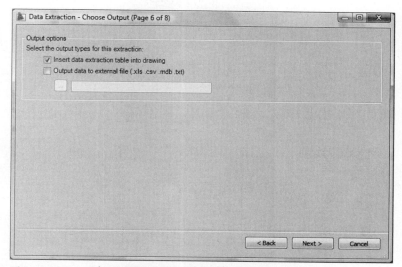

Figure 16-41   The Data Extraction Wizard—Choose Output page

The **Insert data extraction table into drawing** check box allows you to extract the attribute information to an AutoCAD table.

The **Output data to external file** check box allows you to export the attribute information to the file type and location you specify. Selecting the **[...]** button displays the standard **Save As** file dialog box so you can select the file type via the **File of type:** list box at the bottom of the dialog box and the folder location to save the file. By default, the file name is the same name as the current drawing file.

Select the **Next >** button on the bottom to proceed to either the **Table Style** page shown in Figure 16-42 or the **Finish** page shown in Figure 16-43, the **Cancel** button to close the wizard, or the **< Back** button to return to the previous page.

The **Table Style** page allows you to control the appearance of the table before it is inserted in the drawing.

The **Table style** area at the top allows you to control the table style used for the extracted data. The **Select the table style to use for the inserted table** list box allows you to select an existing table style. You can also select the **Table Style** button to the right to display the **Table Style** dialog box to modify an existing table style or create a new one.

The **Formatting and structure** area allows you to fine-tune the final table structure and format.

The **Use table in table style for label rows** option creates the data extraction table with a set of top rows that contain label cells and a bottom set of label rows that contain header and footer cells. Extracted data is inserted between the top and bottom label rows.

**Note:**
Selecting the **Insert data extraction table into drawing** check box displays the **Table Style** page when you select the **Next>** button.

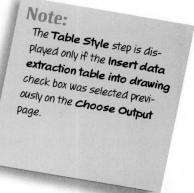

**Note:**
The **Table Style** step is displayed only if the **Insert data extraction table into drawing** check box was selected previously on the **Choose Output** page.

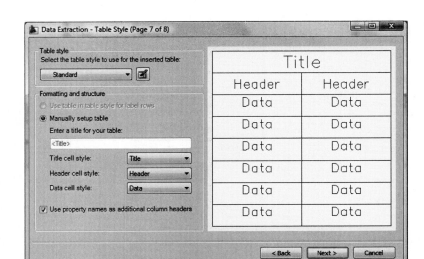

**Figure 16-42**  The Data Extraction Wizard—Table Style page

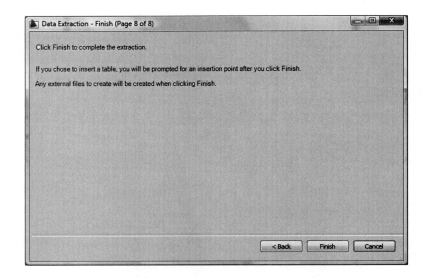

**Figure 16-43**  The Data Extraction Wizard—Finish page

The **Manually setup table** option allows you to manually enter a title and select a specific title, header, and data cell style.

The **Enter a title for your table** text box allows you to enter a title for the table. This row is not overwritten when the table is updated. If the selected table style does not include a title row, this option is not available. The default table style, Standard, includes a title row.

The **Title cell style** list allows you to select a separate style for the title cell. Select the drop-down list to select a title cell style defined in the selected table style.

The **Header cell style** allows you to select a separate style for the header row. Select the drop-down list to select a cell style defined in the selected table style.

The **Data cell style** list allows you to select a separate style for data cells. Select the drop-down list to select a cell style defined in the selected table style.

The **Use property names as additional column headers** check box includes column headers and uses the **Display Name** property as the header row.

The preview image on the right displays a preview of the table layout. If the table style does not include a title row or header row, they are not displayed.

| **FOR MORE DETAILS** | See Chapter 12 for more details about controlling table format using table styles. |

Select the **Next >** button on the bottom to proceed to the **Finish** page shown in Figure 16-43, the **Cancel** button to close the wizard, or the **< Back** button to return to the previous page.

The **Finish** page allows you to complete the process of extracting object property data that was specified in the wizard and creates the output type that was specified on the **Choose Output** page.

If you select the **Insert data extraction table into drawing** check box on the **Choose Output** page when you select the **Finish** button, a table will be attached to your mouse cursor. AutoCAD then prompts you to *Specify insertion point:* so you can locate the table as shown in Figure 16-44.

If the **Output data to external file** option was selected, the extracted data is saved to the specified file type.

> **Note:**
> If data linking and column matching to an Excel spreadsheet was defined in the **Link External Data** dialog box, the selected data in the spreadsheet is also extracted.

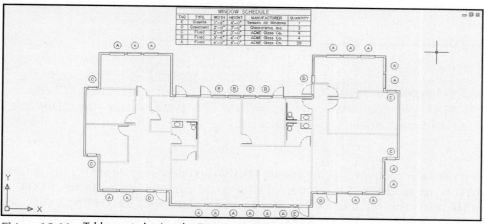

**Figure 16-44**    Table created using the Data Extraction Wizard

## Updating Data Extraction Table Data Manually

Data extraction table data is locked by default to prevent it from being updated and possibly getting out of sync with the source data (attributes). When you click on a table cell, a lock icon is displayed along with the data extraction information as shown in Figure 16-45.

**Figure 16-45**    Locked cell in a data extraction table

You can unlock a cell by selecting **Locking** from the right-click menu and checking the **Unlocked** cascade menu item. Table data that is overwritten manually will be updated when the table data is updated using the automated update data links options explained in the following section.

## Updating Data Extraction Table Data Automatically

You can update data extraction table data automatically when the extracted source data (attributes) changes.

AutoCAD locates a **Data Link** icon in the status tray on the far right of the Status Bar anytime a data extraction table is located in your drawing. You can right-click on the icon and select **Update all Data Links...** from the shortcut menu shown in Figure 16-46, and AutoCAD will read all the attributes in the drawing and update the table data with any changes.

You can select to be notified when extracted data has changed. When information in the data source has changed that affects the extracted data in a table, the **Data Extraction—Out of Date Table** dialog box is displayed so that you can update the table data automatically (see Figure 16-47).

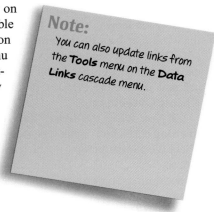

Note:
You can also update links from the **Tools** menu on the **Data Links** cascade menu.

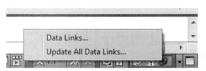

**Figure 16-46** Updating data links via the Data Link shortcut menu

**Figure 16-47** The Data Extraction—Out of Date Table dialog box

Notification is controlled by the current **DXEVAL** system variable setting. By default, **DXEVAL** is set to check if the extracted data is not current only when the **PLOT** or **PUBLISH** commands are used. It can also be set to occur with the **OPEN, SAVE,** and **ETRANSMIT** commands. The **DXEVAL** system is stored as an integer using the sum of the following values:

- **0**    No notification
- **1**    Open
- **2**    Save
- **4**    Plot
- **8**    Publish
- **16**    eTransmit/Archive
- **32**    Save with Automatic Update
- **64**    Plot with Automatic Update
- **128**    Publish with Automatic Update
- **256**    eTransmit/Archive with Automatic Update

The default value of **DXEVAL** is 12.

### Exercise 16-9: Extracting Attributes

1. Continue from Exercise 16-8.
2. Use the **Data Extraction** wizard and extract all of the CH16_EX7 block attributes to create the window schedule shown in Figure 16-44 using the AutoCAD table option.
   *Hint:* Use your mouse to reorder and sort the columns as needed in the **Refine Data** page shown in Figure 16-39. Table must be scaled by a drawing scale factor of 48 after the table is inserted if it is inserted in model space.
3. Save the drawing as **EX16-9**.

# REDEFINING BLOCKS

One of the greatest benefits of using blocks in your drawings is that it makes it possible to quickly redefine a block so that all existing and future block references are automatically updated in the drawing to match the new block definition. You may have hundreds, or even thousands, of references of a block in a drawing, and they will all be updated. Think how much time it would take to update each one manually, and it's easy to appreciate why it is such a great feature.

## Updating Blocks Created in the Current Drawing

To redefine a block in the current drawing, you simply follow the steps outlined earlier in the chapter to create the updated block information. You then use the **BLOCK** command to save the drawing information with the same block name as the existing block name to update by selecting it from the **Name:** list box at the top of the **Block Definition** dialog box, as shown in Figure 16-48.

When you select **OK** to update the block information, AutoCAD displays a message like the one shown in Figure 16-49. This informs you that the block definition already exists and asks you whether you want to update it.

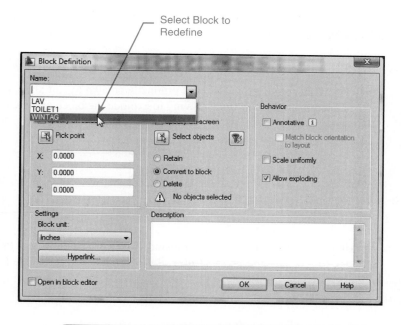

Figure 16-48    Redefining an existing block

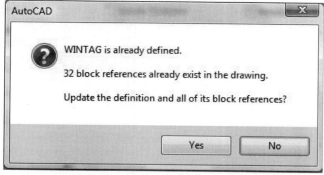

Figure 16-49    Updating a block definition

Selecting the **Yes** button replaces the existing block definition with the new one, and all the existing block references in the drawing are immediately updated to reflect the new definition. All future block insertions will also refer to the new block definition.

The easiest way to update a block is to insert the original block and explode it so that you can update its subobjects and then redefine it using the **BLOCK** command as explained above.

**TIP**

Be sure that when you insert the original block that you specify a base point that you can remember, a uniform scale of 1.0, and a rotation angle of 0.0. If the base point, scale, or rotation angle is different from the original when you redefine the block, all block references will be updated to reflect the change, causing unpredictable results.

### Updating Blocks Inserted from an External Drawing File

Block definitions created by inserting an external drawing file are not automatically updated when the original drawing file is modified. The easiest way to update a block definition created by inserting a drawing file is to simply reinsert the updated drawing file using the **INSERT** command explained earlier to display the **Insert** dialog box shown in Figure 16-7 and select the **Browse...** button to select the updated drawing file using the standard **Select Drawing File** dialog.

When you select **OK** to exit the **Insert** dialog box and insert the updated block, AutoCAD displays a message like the one shown in Figure 16-50. This informs you that the block definition already exists and asks whether you want to update it. Rather than insert another block reference by picking a point in the drawing you can press the **<Esc>** key to cancel the insertion process. All the existing block references are still updated, but you don't end up with a new unwanted block reference in your drawing.

### Editing Blocks In-Place

The **REFEDIT** command, which was originally created to edit xrefs, can be used to quickly redefine a block "in-place" without having to explode the block and recreate it using the **BLOCK** command as explained above.

**FOR MORE DETAILS**     See Chapter 17 for more details about xrefs and using the **REFEDIT** command.

After starting the **REFEDIT** command, AutoCAD prompts you to *Select reference:*. Select the block to redefine and press **<Enter ↵>** to display the **Reference Edit** dialog box shown in Figure 16-50.

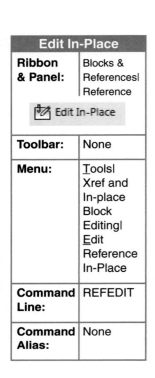

| Edit In-Place | |
|---|---|
| **Ribbon & Panel:** | Blocks & References\| Reference<br> Edit In-Place |
| **Toolbar:** | None |
| **Menu:** | Tools\| Xref and In-place Block Editing\| Edit Reference In-Place |
| **Command Line:** | REFEDIT |
| **Command Alias:** | None |

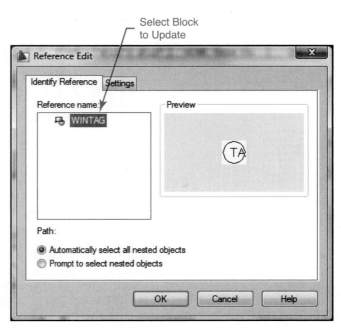

**Figure 16-50**   The Reference Edit dialog box

This dialog box provides the following options:

- The **Identity Reference** tab is used to identify and select the block definition you want to edit.

- The block name is listed on the left in the **Reference name:** box along with any blocks that might be nested within the block. If multiple blocks are displayed, you must select the block you want to modify from the list. Only one block can be edited in place at a time.

- The **Preview** window displays a preview image of the currently selected block.

- The **Automatically select all nested objects** option controls whether nested blocks are included automatically in the block editing session.

- The **Prompt to select nested objects** controls whether nested blocks must be selected individually in the block editing session.

- The **Settings** tab is used to control various block editing settings.

- The **Create unique layer, style, and block names** check box allows you to control how xref layers and other named objects are managed.

- The **Display attribute definitions for editing** check box allows you to control whether all the attribute definitions in a block reference are displayed during the block editing session.

> **Note:**
> When **Display attribute definitions for editing** is selected, attribute values are turned off, and all the block attribute definitions are displayed so that they can be edited. The updated attribute definitions affect only future block insertions—the attributes in existing block references are unchanged. Attributes defined as **Constant** cannot be updated.

Additionally, the **Lock objects not in working set** check box allows you to lock all objects not in the *working set* so that you don't inadvertently modify other objects in the drawing while in a block editing session. Locked objects behave similarly to objects on a locked layer—they can be viewed, but they cannot be selected.

**working set:** The group of objects selected for in-place editing using the **REFEDIT** command

Selecting **OK** puts you in the block editing mode where all the objects that are not part of the working set are locked *and* faded back so that the objects to edit in the working set stand out as shown in Figure 16-51.

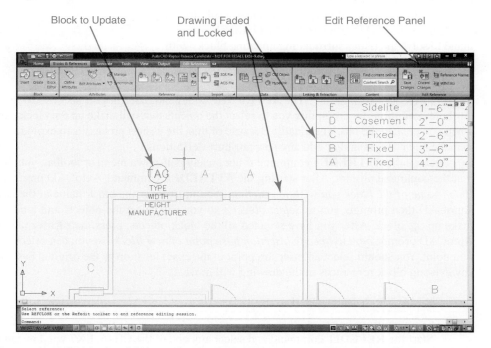

Figure 16-51    Drawing display in block editing mode

When you are in block editing mode, the **Edit Reference** panel shown in Figure 16-52 is turned on to allow you to manage the working set and save or discard any changes made to block definition.

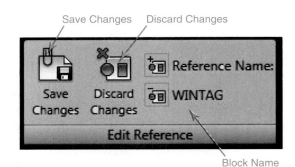

**Figure 16-52**   Edit Reference
panel

In block editing mode, you can edit the block definition using any of the standard AutoCAD drawing and editing commands. You can add information, erase information, and change object properties—almost anything you would normally do in the AutoCAD drawing editor.

When you are done updating the block definition, select the **Save Changes** button on the left side of the **Edit References** panel shown in Figure 16-52 to save the changes and exit block editing mode. You can discard any changes and exit block editing mode by selecting the **Discard Changes** button shown in Figure 16-52.

## Redefining Blocks with Attributes

It is possible to redefine block attributes using any of the standard techniques explained so far, but there are a few idiosyncrasies to be aware of. For the most part, only future block references will reflect the changes made to the attribute definition properties and modes—existing block references do not get updated.

Adding new attribute definitions is even more problematic—adding a new attribute to a block only affects future block insertions. Not even the **BATTMAN** command described earlier allows you to add new attributes. Fortunately, AutoCAD provides the **ATTREDEF** command to solve the issues surrounding updating blocks with attributes.

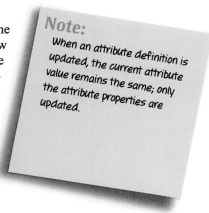

*Note:*
*When an attribute definition is updated, the current attribute value remains the same; only the attribute properties are updated.*

*The ATTREDEF Command.*   The **ATTREDEF** command redefines the specified block and its attribute definitions by prompting you to select the objects that will make up the block, similar to when you created the block originally. Because of this, the easiest process is to explode the block to make any changes and/or add any new attribute definitions.

Because the **ATTREDEF** command is not on any pull-down menu or toolbar, you must type it at the command prompt. After starting the **ATTREDEF** command, AutoCAD prompts you to *Enter name of the block you wish to redefine:*. You must enter the block name at the keyboard. AutoCAD then prompts you to *Select objects:* so you can select the objects and attributes that make up the block. After you have selected all the block objects, press the **<Enter ↵>** key, and AutoCAD prompts you to *Specify insertion base point of new Block:* so you can select the insertion point. You should select an insertion point in the exact location as the original base point, or any existing block references in the drawing will move.

### Exercise 16-10: Redefining Blocks

1. Continue from Exercise 16-9.
2. Start the **REFEDIT** command and select any one of the CH16_EX7 window tag blocks.
3. Select **OK** in the **Reference Edit** dialog box to enter block editing mode.
4. Change the window tag circle to a hexagon as shown in Figure 16-53 by erasing the circle and using the **POLYGON** command to create the hexagon.

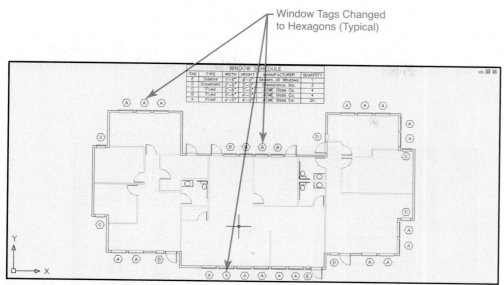

**Figure 16-53**    Redefined window tag blocks

5. Select the **Save Changes** button on the **Edit Reference** panel to save your changes. All window tags in the drawing should immediately change to hexagons.
6. Save the drawing as **EX16-10**.

## Using DesignCenter to Manage Blocks

AutoCAD's **DesignCenter** is a multipurpose tool that provides easy access to blocks, hatch patterns, layers, linetypes, text styles, dimension styles, and other named object information contained in other drawings on your computer, network location, or even on the Internet.

**DesignCenter** allows you to "open" another drawing so that you can view the drawing's named objects, referred to as *drawing content*, in list or icon form. You can then copy any of the drawing content from the source drawing to your current drawing by simply dragging-and-dropping it with your mouse. You can even select multiple objects, making it possible to copy a group of named objects as one. For instance, using this approach, you could copy all the layer definitions from one drawing to another, saving a lot of time. In addition to layers, **DesignCenter** provides access to the following drawing content:

- Blocks
- Dimension styles
- Layers
- Linetypes
- Table styles
- Text Styles
- Xrefs

For the purpose of this chapter, we are going to concentrate on using **DesignCenter** to manage and insert blocks. For more information about **DesignCenter**, please consult the online Help.

**TIP**    Using **DesignCenter**, you can create a standard drawing, or drawings, that contains all of your organization's standard layers, linetypes, text styles, and so on. Then locate it centrally on a network drive, giving your coworkers access to it so all they have to do is drag-and-drop to set up their drawings.

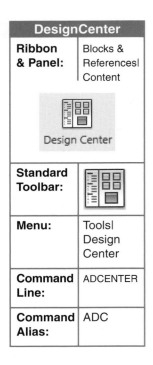

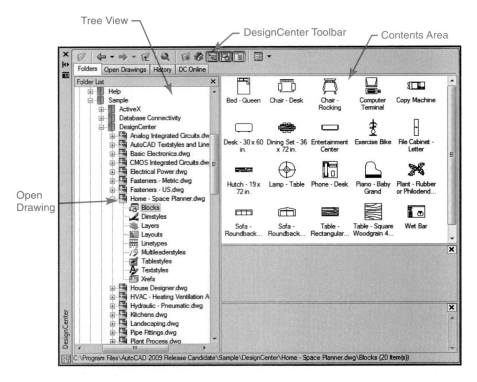

**Figure 16-54** The DesignCenter window

## The DesignCenter Window

The **ADCENTER** command displays the **DesignCenter** window so that you can locate and insert drawing content from other drawings located on your computer, network, or Internet.

Starting the **ADCENTER** command displays the **DesignCenter** window shown in Figure 16-54.

The **DesignCenter** window consists of three parts:

- **Tree view** (left pane)    Navigation tools used to locate drawing files and Web-based content
- **Contents area** (right pane)    Displays the contents of a drawing or Web content once it is located
- **Toolbar** (top)    Additional navigation and display tools

The following sections explain each of these parts as well as other **DesignCenter** features.

> **Note:**
> If the Tree view is not displayed, select the **Tree View Toggle** toolbar button on the top of the **DesignCenter** window shown in Figure 16-54.

*Tree View.*    The Tree view on the left allows you to locate a drawing file using the following methods so that you can display the drawing's contents in the Contents area on the right:

- **Folders** tab    Explorer-like interface that allows you to navigate the hierarchy of files and folders on your computer or attached network drives (see Figure 16-54)
- **Open Drawings** tab    List of all currently open drawings
- **History** tab    History of the last drawings accessed
- **DC Online** tab    Accesses the DesignCenter online Internet Web page (see Figure 16-55)

You can remove a file from the **History** tab by selecting the file, right-clicking, and selecting **Delete** from the shortcut menu.

Web Based Categories

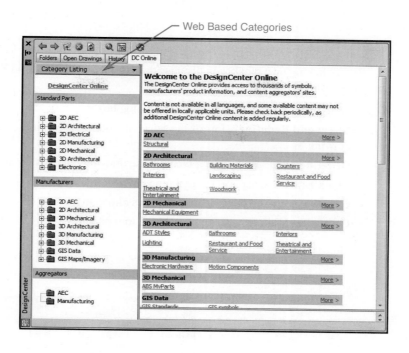

**Figure 16-55** The DesignCenter Online tab

*Contents Area.* The Contents area on the right side of the window displays the contents of the drawing, named object collection, or **DesignCenter Online** category currently selected in the Tree view on the left. When a block is selected, it is possible to display a preview and a description as shown in Figure 16-56.

The Preview window and Description window can be toggled on and off by selecting the **Preview** and **Description** buttons on the **DesignCenter** toolbar shown in Figure 16-58. It is also possible to switch how the information is viewed in the Contents pane via the **Views** flyout menu on the right side of the **DesignCenter** toolbar shown in Figure 16-58 to one of the following standard Explorer-type formats:

- Large icons
- Small icons
- List
- Details

Selected Block

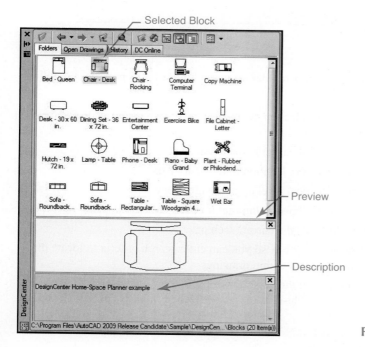

Preview

Description

**Figure 16-56** The Contents area

You can navigate in the Contents pane by double-clicking an icon with your mouse to display its contents. You can then select the Up arrow on the **DesignCenter** toolbar shown in Figure 16-58 to go back up one level in the hierarchy.

Right-clicking on a block icon displays the shortcut menu shown in Figure 16-57 so that you can do the following:

- **Insert Block...**     Displays the Insert dialog box
- **Insert and Redefine**     Inserts the selected block and redefines all block definitions in the drawing
- **Redefine only**     Redefines a block in the drawing but does not insert a copy
- **Block Editor**     Displays the dynamic block editor
- **Copy**     Copies the block to the Windows clipboard
- **Create Tool Palette**     Creates a custom tool palette

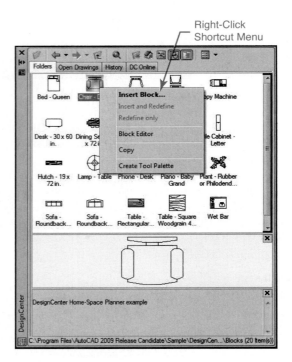

**Figure 16-57**     The Contents area shortcut menu

*DesignCenter Toolbar.*     The **DesignCenter** toolbar shown in Figure 16-58 provides the following navigation tools and display options:

- **Load**     Displays the standard file selection dialog box so you can locate a file and load its information in the Contents area
- **Back**     Returns to the most recent location in the history list
- **Forward**     Moves forward to a recent location in the history list
- **Up**     Displays the contents of the next level up in the hierarchy
- **Stop** (DC Online only)     Stops the current Internet transfer
- **Reload** (DC Online only)     Reloads the current web page
- **Search**     Displays the **Search** dialog box so you can enter search criteria to locate drawings, blocks, and other named objects within drawings
- **Favorites**     Displays the contents of the Favorites folder in the Contents area. You can add items to the Favorites folder by right-clicking and selecting Add to Favorites from the shortcut menu.

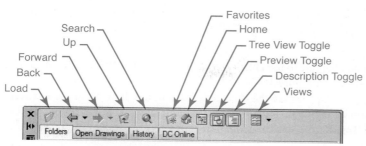

**Figure 16-58**    The DesignCenter toolbar

- **Home**    Returns **DesignCenter** to the home folder. You can change the home folder by navigating to the desired folder in the Tree view, right-clicking, and selecting Set as Home from the shortcut menu.
- **Tree View Toggle**    Displays and hides the tree view. When the tree view is hidden, you can still navigate in the Contents area using the techniques described earlier.
- **Preview**    Toggles the Preview pane on and off in the Contents area
- **Description**    Toggles the Description pane on and off in the Contents area
- **Views**    Allows you to switch between different display formats in the Contents area

*DesignCenter Properties.*    Just like other AutoCAD windows and palettes, the **DesignCenter** window can be moved, resized, and docked using your mouse. You can also control these and other features by selecting the **Properties** button on the window title bar to display the shortcut menu shown in Figure 16-59.

Using the shortcut menu, you can prevent the **DesignCenter** window from being docked. You can also toggle on and off the auto-hide feature that collapses the window, so that only the title bar is visible when the mouse pointer is not directly over the window.

**Figure 16-59**    The DesignCenter Properties shortcut menu

The <**Ctrl**>+**2** keyboard combination can be used to quickly toggle **DesignCenter** on and off.

*Inserting Blocks.*    Once you locate a block using one of the methods described above and it is visible in the Contents area, there are three ways you can insert the block into the current drawing using **DesignCenter**:

- Drag and drop the block into the current drawing using your mouse.
- Double-click on the block in the Contents area to display the **Insert** dialog box.
- Right-click on the block in the Contents area to display the shortcut menu shown earlier in Figure 16-57.

**Note:**
The following exercise requires that you install the sample **DesignCenter** drawing files that come with AutoCAD 2009. By default, the sample drawings are located in the **C:\Program Files\AutoCAD 2009\Sample\DesignCenter** folder.

Each method has its merits. Dragging-and-dropping a block is obviously the fastest method, while double-clicking on a block provides the most control because you can specify different block settings in the **Insert** dialog box. Finally, right-clicking provides the only option to redefine a block. Practice using each method so that you are prepared for any situation.

## Exercise 16-11: Using DesignCenter

1. Continue from Exercise 16-10.
2. Set layer **A-Furn** current.
3. Start **DesignCenter** and navigate to the **Home-Space Planner.dwg** file located in the DesignCenter folder as shown in Figure 16-54.
4. Select the **Blocks** icon so you can see the blocks defined in the drawing in the Contents area on the right as shown in Figure 16-56.
5. Select the **Tree View Toggle** button on the **DesignCenter** toolbar shown in Figure 16-58 to turn off the Tree view.
6. Insert blocks using the techniques explained above and furnish the floor plan in a manner similar to Figure 16-60.
7. Save the drawing as **EX16-11**.

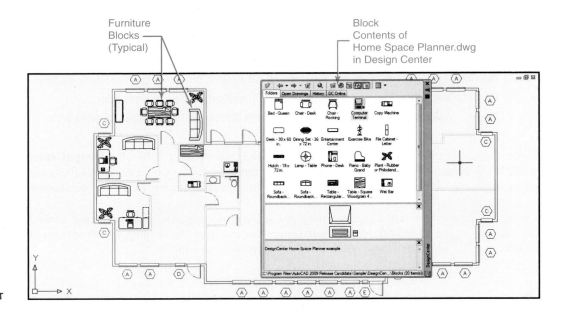

**Figure 16-60**  Building floor plan with office furniture and equipment blocks inserted using DesignCenter

| Tool Palettes | |
|---|---|
| **Ribbon & Panel:** | View\| Palettes<br><br>Tool Palettes |
| **Standard Toolbar:** | |
| **Menu:** | Tools\| Palettes\| Tool Palettes |
| **Command Line:** | TOOL PALETTES |
| **Command Alias:** | TP |

## TOOL PALETTES AND DYNAMIC BLOCKS

**Tool** palettes are highly customizable palette-type windows that allow you to group and organize blocks, hatch patterns, and even commands, using graphical icons on easily accessible palettes organized in a series of named tabs.

Dynamic blocks are multipurpose blocks that can be changed after they are inserted using special grips that allow you to display multiple block views, sizes, block behavior, and more. Using dynamic blocks, one block definition can be used for a myriad of different scenarios and situations. Dynamic blocks are covered in detail later in this section. The AutoCAD **Dynamic Blocks Tool** palettes are shown in Figure 16-61.

**Tool palette** tools can be either dragged and dropped directly into your drawing to perform the associated action or selected like a toolbar button by left-clicking on the tool's icon with your mouse. Figure 16-62 shows the **Door-Imperial** block being inserted in the drawing by dragging-and-dropping it from the sample **Architectural** palette.

**Note:** All dynamic blocks have a lightning bolt in the lower right corner of their **Tool palette** icon as shown in Figure 16-61 to indicate that they can be dynamically updated after they are inserted. Inserting and updating dynamic blocks is explained later in this section.

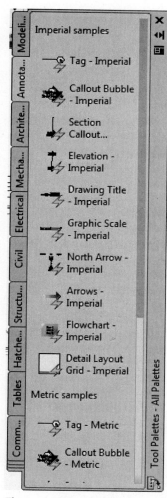

**Figure 16-61**    AutoCAD Dynamic Blocks Tool palettes

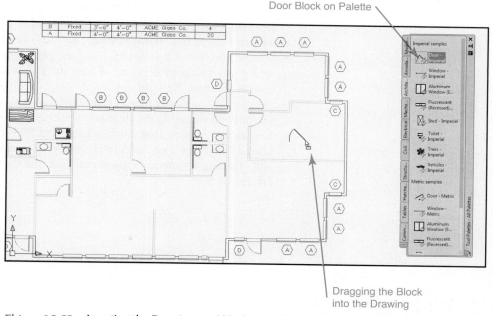

**Figure 16-62**    Inserting the Door-Imperial block from the sample Architectural palette

## Controlling Tool Palettes

Because they utilize the palette-type window, **Tool** palettes can be hidden when you are not using them via the **Auto-hide** palette feature, as well as made transparent so that you can see through them to your drawing below using the **Transparency** palette feature. These and other features can be controlled via the **Properties** shortcut menu that can be displayed by clicking on the **Properties** button on the bottom of the palette title bar. See Figure 16-61.

**TIP**  The Auto-hide feature can also be quickly turned on and off via the **Auto-hide** button located directly above the **Properties** button. See Figure 16-61.

**FOR MORE DETAILS**    See Chapter 1 for more information about controlling different palette properties such as **Auto-hide** and **Transparency**.

More options are available by right-clicking anywhere on the title bar to display the shortcut menu shown in Figure 16-63.

In addition to the **Auto-hide** and **Transparency** palette features, the **Tool** palettes title bar right-click menu allows you to do the following:

- Turn **Tool** palette docking off so that if you drag a palette to the far left or right side of your screen, the palette will remain in a floating state and not attach itself to the AutoCAD window.
- **Anchor Tool** palettes on the left or right side of the AutoCAD window. Anchored palettes are palettes that are docked but hidden using the **Auto-hide** feature so that only the title bar is visible. Placing your mouse over the palette title bar displays the entire palette, but it remains anchored.
- Create new empty **Tool** palettes and rename existing **Tool** palettes.
- Turn **Tool** palette groups off and on. Related **Tool** palettes can be grouped together in categories so you can control what palettes are displayed by category.
- Customize **Tool** palette groups. The **Customize Palettes...** menu item displays the **Customize** dialog box shown in Figure 16-64 so you can do the following:
  - Add/remove/move palettes by dragging palettes with your mouse. A palette can be added to a group by dragging it from the **Palettes:** list box on the left to the desired palette group on the right.
  - Add/remove palette groups by right-clicking on a group in the **Palette Groups:** list box on the right and using the shortcut menu.
  - Export and import **Tool** palettes using the XTP file format so that palettes can be shared with other users by right-clicking on a palette in the **Palettes:** list box on the left and selecting **Export...** or **Import...** from the shortcut menu to display the Windows file dialog box.

**Figure 16-63** Tool palette title bar right-click menu

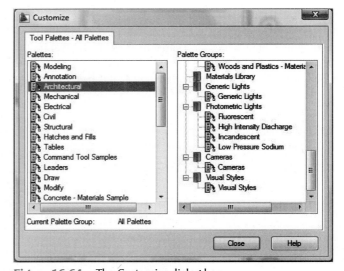

**Figure 16-64** The Customize dialog box

- Add custom commands. The **Customize commands...** menu item displays the **Customize User Interface** dialog box with a list of all the AutoCAD commands. To add a command to a **Tool palette**, you simply drag it from the **Command List:** and drop it onto the **Tool** palette of your choice.

But wait, there's more. There are a total of four different **Tool** palette right-click shortcut menus depending on where you right-click with your mouse. If you right-click on a **Tool** palette anywhere between toolbar icons on an empty space on the palette background, the shortcut menu in Figure 16-65 is displayed.

In addition to most of the commands and features already discussed, this menu also allows you to control different display options. The **View Options...** menu item displays the **View Options** dialog box so that you can switch between icon and list view, as well as control the size of the images used for the icons. The **Sort By** cascade menu allows you to automatically sort tool icons by name or type.

Right-clicking on the named tab on a **Tool** palette displays yet another shortcut menu. This menu allows you to move a palette up and down in the palette order, rename a palette, or create a new palette.

Finally, right-clicking directly over a **Tool palette** icon displays a shortcut menu that allows you cut, copy, delete, rename, and control the selected tool's properties.

## Tool Properties

The **Properties...** menu item located on the bottom of a tool's right-click shortcut menu displays the **Tool Properties** dialog box shown in Figure 16-66 so you can edit the tool's name and description, as well as control tool-specific properties like block locations, hatch pattern names,

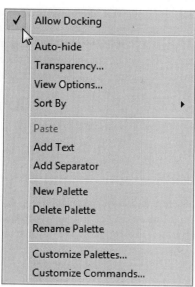

**Figure 16-65**   Tool palette background right-click menu

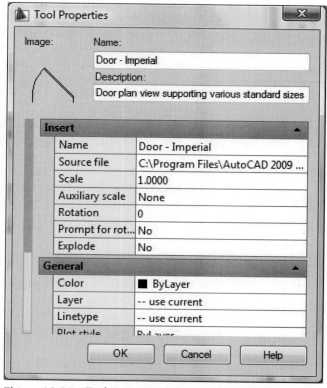

**Figure 16-66**   Tool Properties dialog box for a block

and command macros depending on the tool type selected. The properties for a block are shown in Figure 16-66.

Each tool also has general properties such as layer, color, and linetype that can be controlled via the **Tool Properties** dialog box. See Figure 16-66. These properties are applied to any object type that is created when the corresponding **Tool palette** icon is selected. For instance, setting a block's **Layer** property to any layer setting other than "—use current" will insert the block on the layer specified.

**TIP** It is possible to rearrange the order of the tools on a **Tool** palette by left-clicking a tool icon and dragging it to another location.

**Exercise 16-12:** Using Tool Palettes

1. Continue from Exercise 16-11.
2. Turn on **Tool** palettes via the **Palettes** panel on the **View** ribbon.
3. Right-click anywhere on the blue **Tool** palettes title bar and select **Annotation and Design** from the shortcut menu to turn on only the **Annotation and Design Tool** palettes shown in Figure 16-61.
4. Size and position the palettes on the screen using your mouse.
5. Turn the **Auto-hide** feature on by selecting the **Auto-hide** button on the bottom of the palette title bar directly above the **Properties** menu button.
6. Move your mouse off the palette so that the palette closes and only the palette title bar is visible.
7. Right-click anywhere on the blue **Tool** palettes title bar again and select **Anchor Right >** to anchor the **Tool** palette on the right side of the screen.
8. Put your cursor over the anchored **Tool** palette to display it and select the **Architectural** palette tab to make it active.
9. Select the **Door-Imperial** block at the top of the **Architectural** palette by clicking on it with your left mouse button. AutoCAD should prompt you to *Specify insertion point or ↓*.
10. Pick a point to locate the block anywhere on the floor plan.
11. Select the **Fluorescent (Recessed)-Imperial** block, hold your mouse button down, and drag-and-drop the light fixture block anywhere in the drawing.
12. Right-click on the **Door-Imperial** block on the **Architectural** palette and select **Properties...** from the shortcut menu to display the **Tool Properties** dialog box.
13. Change the **Layer** property under the **General** category from "—use current" to "A-DOOR" and select **OK** to close the dialog box.
14. Insert another **Door-Imperial** block. It should now always insert on the **A-DOOR** layer regardless of what layer is current.
15. Save the drawing as **EX16-12**.

## Adding Tools to Tool Palettes

One of the coolest things about **Tool** palettes is that you can add information to a palette by simply selecting an object in your drawing and dragging it onto the **Tool** palette where you want it to be located. If the object is a block, it is added to the palette as a block. If the object is a hatch pattern, the hatch pattern is added to the palette. If the object selected is not a block or hatch pattern, the command used to create the object is added to the palette. For instance, dragging a piece of multiline text from a drawing onto a **Tool** palette will add the **MTEXT** command using the default multiline text icon as shown in Figure 16-67.

There are a couple of different ways to add blocks to a palette besides dragging them from the drawing.

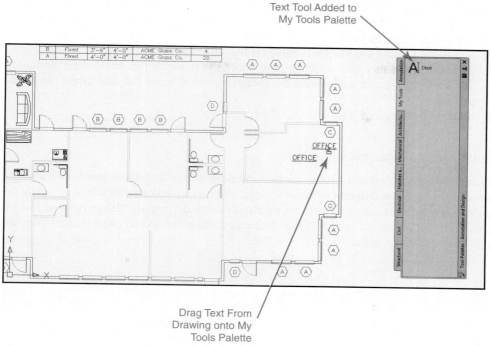

**Figure 16-67**    Adding tools by dragging-and-dropping them from the drawing

Using the **DesignCenter** palette described earlier, it is possible to automatically create a new palette that contains all the blocks in a drawing by right-clicking on a drawing on the **DesignCenter Folders** tab and selecting the **Create Tool Palette** menu item from the shortcut menu. A new palette with the same name as the drawing is added to the current palette group with blocks and tool icons generated for each block.

**DesignCenter** can also create a new palette that consists of all the drawing files located in a folder. If you right-click on a folder that contains drawing (DWG) files and select **Create Tool Palette of Blocks** from the shortcut menu, AutoCAD will create a new tool palette with the same name as the folder with blocks and icons for each drawing file in the folder.

**TIP**  Drawing (DWG) files can also be added to a **Tool** palette by dragging-and-dropping them from Windows Explorer onto the desired palette. It is even possible to add multiple drawings at the same time using the <**Ctrl**> and <**Shift**> keys to select multiple files.

**Exercise 16-13:** Adding Tools to Tool Palettes

1. Continue from Exercise 16-12.
2. Right-click anywhere on the blue **Tool** palettes title bar and select **New Palette** from the shortcut menu to create a new palette. Name the new palette **My Tools**.
3. Select any toilet block on the floor plan in the drawing so it is highlighted and add it to the **My Tools** palette by dragging-and-dropping it onto the palette from the drawing. *Be careful not to select a grip when dragging it.*
4. Select any wall line so it is highlighted and add it to the **My Tools** palette by dragging and dropping it onto the palette from the drawing. You should now have a **Line** command tool with a flyout of assorted drawing commands.

5. Select the **Line** tool and create a line.
6. Right-click on the **My Tools** tab and select **Move Up** from the shortcut menu to move the **My Tools** palette up in the palette order.
7. Repeat step 6 until the **My Tools** palette is the top-level palette.
8. Select the **Line** tool and, while holding your left mouse button down, drag the tool to the top of the palette and release the mouse button to move the tool to the top of the palette.
9. Save the drawing as **EX16-13**.

## Introduction to Dynamic Blocks

As mentioned earlier, dynamic blocks are multipurpose blocks that allow you to use a single block to represent many different variations, sizes, and typical actions that would normally require a block library consisting of numerous different block definitions. Using dynamic blocks, you typically insert a generic version of the block and then use the special grips shown in the following table to update it dynamically:

| Dynamic Block Grips | | |
|---|---|---|
| **Grip** | | **Description** |
| ▼ | **List Arrow** | Selecting grip displays a list of block options such as size, configuration, number, or views to choose from. |
| ▶ | **Stretch Arrow** | Dragging grip allows you to stretch, scale, and array a block to predefined sizes and configurations. |
| ■ | **Locater Box** | Dragging grip allows you to stretch or move a block or block subcomponent. |
| ◀ | **Flip Arrow** | Selecting grip flips a block in the direction of the arrow. |
| ⬠ | **Alignment** | Dragging grip aligns a block with existing objects in the drawing. |
| ● | **Rotate** | Selecting grip allows you to rotate a block to predefined angles using your cursor. |

For example, using dynamic block technology, one single block of an architectural-type door for a floor plan can be updated so that you can:

- Switch between different standard door opening angles
- Resize the door using standard door opening and frame widths
- Flip the door horizontally or vertically about the center of the door opening
- Automatically align the door along a wall

**FOR MORE DETAILS**    See Chapter 7 for more information about using grips to modify objects.

Using the **List Arrow** grip, the door opening angle can be set to 30°, 45°, 60°, 90°, or even appear closed as shown in Figure 16-68.

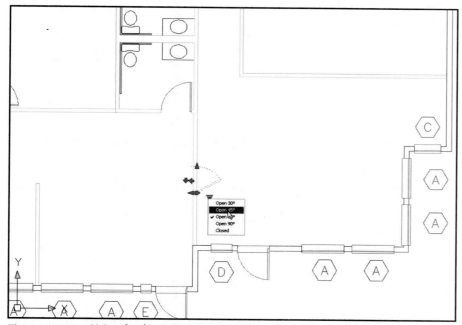

**Figure 16-68**    Using the dynamic List Arrow grip to change the door opening angle

Using the **Stretch Arrow** grip, you can resize the door to any predefined opening size (24″, 28″, 30″, 32″, 36″, 40″) as shown in Figure 16-69.

Using the **Flip Arrow** grip, you can mirror the door about the center of the opening either horizontally or vertically as shown in Figure 16-70.

With the **Alignment** grip, you can drag the door near a wall, and it will automatically align itself along the same angle as the wall as shown in Figure 16-71.

Unfortunately, covering all the dynamic block update options and features is beyond the scope of this textbook, as is the complex process involved in creating a dynamic block. Be-

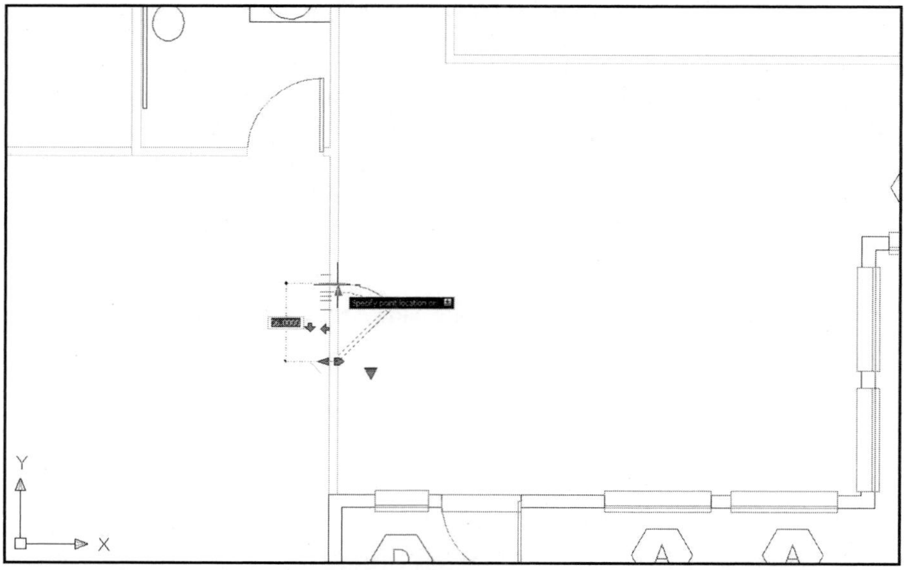

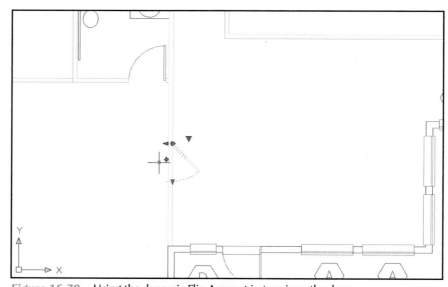

**Figure 16-69**    Using the dynamic Stretch Arrow grip to change the door opening size

**Figure 16-70**    Using the dynamic Flip Arrow grip to mirror the door

cause of their complex nature, AutoCAD includes a special "Block Editor" environment for creating and updating dynamic blocks that has its own set of "authoring" palettes where you define parameters and actions. You might have started it accidentally at some point and wondered what it was because it changes the color of the AutoCAD background as shown in Figure 16-72.

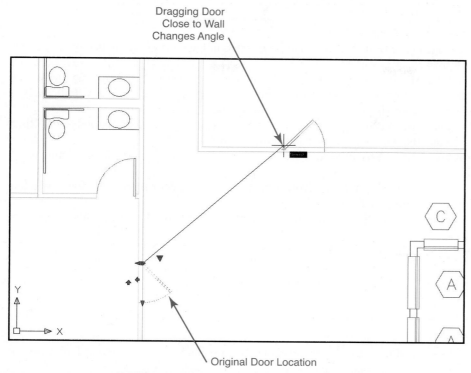

**Figure 16-71**    Using the Alignment grip to align the door with the wall

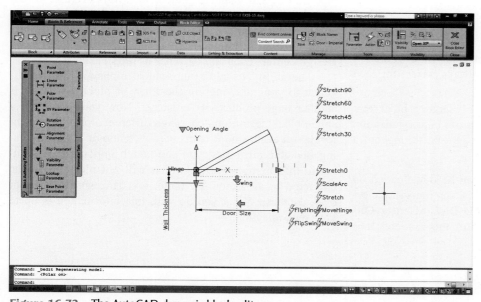

**Figure 16-72**    The AutoCAD dynamic block editor

If this happens, the best thing to do at this point is to select the **Close Block Editor** button on the toolbar at the top of the screen to exit the editor and get back to your drawing.

Fortunately, AutoCAD has many sample dynamic blocks available on the sample **Tool** palettes that come with AutoCAD (shown earlier in Figure 16-61) that you can play with and use in your drawings.

**Exercise 16-14:** Using Dynamic Blocks

1. Continue from Exercise 16-13.
2. Select one of the **Door-Imperial** blocks inserted in Exercise 16-12 so that dynamic grips are displayed.
3. Select the **Alignment** grip and align the door with the vertical wall by dragging it with your mouse close to the wall until the block rotates 90° and is aligned with the wall as shown in Figure 16-71. Select a point to locate the door on the wall.
4. Select the **List Arrow** grip to display all the door opening angle options and select **Open 45°** so that the door angle is updated as shown in Figure 16-68.
5. Select the vertical **Stretch Arrow** grip and stretch the door so that the door opening is 36″ wide as shown in Figure 16-69.
6. Select the horizontal **Stretch Arrow** grip and stretch the door so the door frame width is 4″ wide, the same as the wall thickness.
7. Select the vertical **Flip Arrow** grip and mirror the door horizontally as shown in Figure 16-70.
8. Save the drawing as **EX16-13**.

# SUMMARY

In this chapter, we learned how to create, insert, and manage blocks. Blocks have been around for a long time and are one of the primary features of most CAD software because you can draw something once and use it many times. This simple capability provides three basic but overwhelmingly important benefits:

- *Increased productivity*   Draw it once and use it over and over again.

- *Increased precision*   If you take the time to draw a block right the first time, it is always correct for each subsequent insertion.

- *Increased standards compliance*   Draw a block that you are sure meets the standards of your organization and then distribute it so that it is used throughout a project.

Many blocks already exist that can be downloaded on the Internet from various manufacturers, suppliers, trade organizations, and others. The AutoCAD **DesignCenter On-line** feature provides access to much of this content. It is even possible to download complete symbol libraries of blocks.

Take the time to consider when to make a block. If you are going to use something in a drawing more than three times, it might be a good candidate for a block. Think about creating a block library and what it might look like. You can create several separate block drawing files and organize them in folders so they can be inserted using Windows Explorer, or you might put all the blocks in a single drawing file and access them using **DesignCenter**. Each approach has its pros and cons.

The ability to add nongraphical alphanumeric intelligence to your drawings in the form of block attributes is another huge productivity enhancer. Now you can create a single block definition and assign different alphanumeric information each time it is inserted—visible or invisible! Using invisible attributes, you can attach important alphanumeric information to blocks that will not plot but can be extracted to an AutoCAD table, text file, spreadsheet, or even database. What you do with this information is up to your own imagination.

Be careful when downloading any information from the Internet. You will want to examine any blocks you download and check them for accuracy and standards compliance. Just like anything on the Internet, there is some bad information to be found—you must take the time to separate the wheat from the chaff.

# CHAPTER TEST QUESTIONS

## Multiple Choice

1. An AutoCAD block is best described as a:

   a. Hatch pattern
   b. Named collection of AutoCAD objects treated as a single complex object
   c. Title border
   d. Group of layers

2. The advantage of using blocks in a drawing is:

   a. Reduced drawing size
   b. Increased accuracy
   c. Ease of updating drawings
   d. All of the above

3. When inserting an annotation-type block, it necessary to:

   a. Put it on a text layer
   b. Scale the block by the drawing scale.
   c. Set the text style
   d. All of the above

4. A block attribute is:

   a. An object property such as layer, color, linetype, or lineweight
   b. A scale
   c. A rotation
   d. Dynamic text used to store alphanumeric data

5. The only information stored with a block reference is the:

   a. Insertion point
   b. Scale factor
   c. Rotation angle
   d. All of the above

6. Defining a block within another block is referred to as:

   a. Block assembly
   b. Impossible
   c. Block reference
   d. Block nesting

7. Block subobjects created on layer **0** with all their object properties set to ByLayer assume what current object property when the block is inserted?

   a. Color
   b. Lineweight
   c. Layer
   d. All of the above

8. Unit blocks allow you to:

   a. Maintain consistent grid and snap settings
   b. Scale a block differently in the *X* and *Y* scale for different results

   c. Transfer blocks from one unit system to another
   d. All of the above

9. Dragging-and-dropping a drawing from Windows Explorer into a drawing using the right mouse button allows you to:

   a. Open a drawing
   b. Insert a drawing as a block
   c. Attach an xref
   d. All of the above

10. By default, when you create a block using the **WBLOCK** command, it does what with the original objects selected to make the block?

    a. Converts them to a block in-place
    b. Deletes the original objects
    c. Retains them in the drawing
    d. None of the above

11. The command that allows you to turn invisible attributes on so they are displayed in the drawing is:

    a. **ATTREQ**
    b. **ATTDIA**
    c. **ATTDISP**
    d. **-ATTEDIT**

12. The command that allows you to update the value of an attribute is:

    a. **-ATTEDIT**
    b. **BATTMAN**
    c. **EATTEDIT**
    d. a and c

13. The easiest way to update a changed block definition after it has been inserted is:

    a. Explode all block references and redraw each of them in-place
    b. Explode the block and redefine it using the **BLOCK** command
    c. Use the **REFEDIT** command
    d. Freeze the layer the block is on and draw over it

14. To insert a block from **DesignCenter**, you can:

    a. Drag-and-drop the block using your mouse
    b. Double-click on the block
    c. Right-click on the block and use a shortcut menu command
    d. All of the above

## Matching

**Column A**

a. Block attribute

b. Block definition

c. Block reference

d. **BLOCK** command

e. ByBlock property

f. **INSERT** command

g. Unit block

h. **WBLOCK** command

i. **ATTDIA** system variable

j. **REFEDIT** command

**Column B**

1. Block drawn within a $1 \times 1$ unit square that is inserted in the drawing with different $X$ and $Y$ scales

2. Writes a block definition to an external drawing file (DWG)

3. Dynamic text-like object that can be included in a block definition to store alphanumeric data

4. User-defined collection of drawing objects stored centrally in a drawing

5. Controls whether the **Edit Attributes** dialog box is displayed during the insertion process

6. Creates a block definition using the objects you select with the name specified

7. Property that will assume the current color, linetype, or lineweight property when a block is inserted

8. Redefines a block "in-place" without having to explode the block

9. Inserts a block reference by specifying the block name, insertion point, scale, and rotation angle

10. Instance of a block definition inserted in a drawing that references the central block definition drawing data

## True or False

1. True or False: Using blocks substantially increases drawing sizes.

2. True or False: Blocks must always be drawn at a scale of 1:1.

3. True or False: Blocks can be defined so that they cannot be exploded.

4. True or False: It is not possible to create a block with the same name as a block already defined in a drawing.

5. True or False: A block definition cannot be inserted in another drawing until it is exported as a drawing file.

6. True or False: Using the special ByBlock object property allows you to make sure that subobjects are updated to match the current object properties when the block is inserted.

7. True or False: It is possible to *always* specify a different $X$, $Y$, and $Z$ scale when inserting a block.

8. True or False: When inserting a drawing file (DWG) as a block, both model space and paper space information are included.

9. True or False: It is possible to export all the objects in a drawing automatically using the **WBLOCK** command.

10. True or False: Attributes can be located automatically so that they align below the previous attribute.

11. True or False: Setting the **ATTDIA** system variable to **1** turns on the **Enhanced Attribute Editor** dialog box.

12. True or False: It is possible to insert an AutoCAD field in an attribute value.

13. True or False: The **-ATTEDIT** command allows you to update multiple attributes with the same value at one time.

14. True or False: A table created using the **Data Extraction Wizard** can be set to update automatically if a referenced attribute value changes.

15. True or False: You must use the **ATTREDEF** command to add attribute definitions to an existing block definition.

## CHAPTER PROJECTS

### Project 16-1: Classroom Plan—Continued from Chapter 14

1. Open the drawing **P14-1**.
2. Create separate blocks for each of the items shown in Figure P16-1 using the insertion points shown.
3. Create blocks for the left- and right-hand workstations as shown in Figure P16-1 using the insertion points shown. Use the blocks created in the previous step as components of the workstation blocks.

4. Replace the original workstations with the new workstation blocks.
5. Save your drawing as **P16-1**.

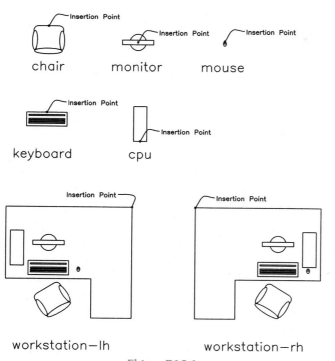

Figure P16-1

## Project 16-2: Vehicle Symbol Library

1. Start a new drawing using the **acad.dwt** template.
2. Draw the vehicle symbols shown in Figure P16-2 to the best of your ability at the sizes shown. *Hint:* Each grid square is equal to 1 decimal foot.
3. Create blocks from the vehicle symbols drawn in step 2 using the following settings:
   a. Name the blocks as indicated in Figure P16-2. Do not include the text in the block definition.
   b. Specify a base point.
   c. Select the **Convert to block** option so the block is converted in place.
   d. Select the **Allow exploding** option.
4. Save the drawing as **Vehicle Symbols** but leave the drawing open.
5. Start a new drawing using the **acad.dwt** template.
6. Start **DesignCenter** and select the **Open Drawings** tab.
7. Select the plus symbol (+) next to the **Vehicle Symbols.dwg** drawing to expand the tree.
8. Select the **Blocks** icon so that the vehicle blocks you created in step 2 are displayed in the Contents pane on the right.
9. Practice dragging-and-dropping vehicle symbols into your drawing using both the left and right mouse buttons.
10. Double-click on a block to display the **Insert** dialog box.

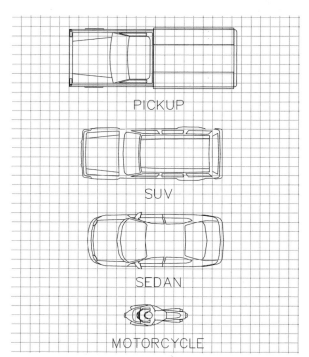

PICKUP

SUV

SEDAN

MOTORCYCLE

**Figure P16-2**

## Project 16-3A: B-Size Mechanical Border—Continued from Chapter 15

1. Open the template file **Mechanical B-Size.DWT**.
2. Create the title block attribute definitions shown in Figure P16-3A. Place the attributes on the **Title** layer. Use the definitions shown in the following table:

| Tag | Prompt | Default | Justification | Height |
| --- | --- | --- | --- | --- |
| TITLE | Drawing Title | Title | Center | 0.2 |
| DESCRIPTION | Description | Description | Center | 0.125 |
| PARTNO | Part Number | xxx | Left | 0.125 |
| SCALE | Drawing Scale | 1:1 | Left | 0.09375 |
| DWN | Drawn By | AAA | Left | 0.09375 |
| SHEET | Sheet Number | 1 of 1 | Left | 0.09375 |
| REV | Revision Number | 0 | Center | 0.125 |
| PROJ_ENG | Project Engineer | AAA | Left | 0.09375 |
| PE_DATE | Date | mm/dd/yy | Left | 0.09375 |
| DWN_BY | Drawn By | AAA | Left | 0.09375 |
| DWN_DATE | Date | mm/dd/yy | Left | 0.09375 |

| CHK_BY | Checked By | AAA | Left | 0.09375 |
|---|---|---|---|---|
| CHK_DATE | Date | mm/dd/yy | Left | 0.09375 |
| MFG_ENG | Manufacturing Engineer | AAA | Left | 0.09375 |
| ME_DATE | Date | mm/dd/yy | Left | 0.09375 |

3. Use the **WBLOCK** command to create a block/drawing named **Title Attributes Mechanical B-Size.DWG** by selecting the attributes defined above and shown in Figure P16-3B using the following settings:
   a. Set the **Base point** to 0,0,0.
   b. Set the **Objects** option to the **Delete from drawing** setting so the attributes are deleted.
   c. Set **Insert units** to **Unitless**.
4. Create the revision block geometry and attribute definitions shown in Figure P16-3A. Place the geometry and attributes on the **Title** layer. Use the definitions shown in the following table:

| Tag | Prompt | Default | Justification | Height |
|---|---|---|---|---|
| ZONE | ZONE | A1 | Left | 0.09375 |
| REV | Revision Number | 1 | Left | 0.09375 |
| DESCRIPTION | Description | xxx | Left | 0.09375 |
| REV_DATE | Revision Date | MM/DD/YY | Left | 0.09375 |
| APRVD_BY | Approval By | AAA | Left | 0.09375 |

5. Use the **WBLOCK** command to create a block/drawing named **Revision Block - Mechanical.dwg** by selecting the revision block attributes defined above and shown in Figure P16-3A using the following settings:
   a. Set the **Base point** by snapping to the lower left corner of the revision block.
   b. Set the **Objects** option to the **Delete from drawing** setting so the attributes are deleted.
   c. Set **Insert units** to **Unitless.**
6. Use the **WBLOCK** command to create a block/drawing named **Mechanical B-Size.DWG** by selecting all the remaining title border line work and static text that never changes using the following settings:
   a. Set the **Base point** to 0,0,0.
   b. Set the **Objects** option to the **Delete from drawing** setting so the attributes are deleted.
   c. Set **Insert units** to **Unitless**.

7. Close the drawing template. *Do not save changes to the drawing template.*

Insertion Point

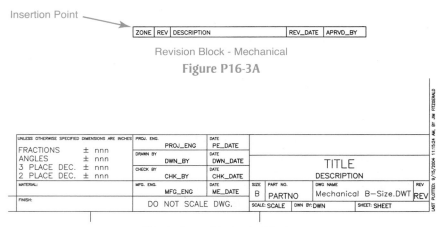

Revision Block - Mechanical

**Figure P16-3A**

Title Attributes Mechanical B-size

**Figure P16-3B**

## Project 16-3B: C-Size Mechanical Border—Continued from Chapter 15

1. Open template file **Mechanical C-Size.DWT**.
2. Create the title block attribute definitions shown in Figure P16-3C. Place the attributes on the **Title** layer. Use the definitions shown in the following table:

| Tag | Prompt | Default | Justification | Height |
|-----|--------|---------|---------------|--------|
| TITLE | Drawing Title | Title | Center | 0.2 |
| DESCRIPTION | Description | Description | Center | 0.125 |
| PARTNO | Part Number | xxx | Left | 0.125 |
| SCALE | Drawing Scale | 1:1 | Left | 0.09375 |
| SHEET | Sheet Number | n | Left | 0.09375 |
| TOT_SHT | Total Number of Sheets | n | Left | 0.09375 |
| REV | Revision Number | 0 | Center | 0.125 |
| PROJ_ENG | Project Engineer | AAA | Left | 0.09375 |
| PE_DATE | Date | mm/dd/yy | Left | 0.09375 |
| DWN_BY | Drawn By | AAA | Left | 0.09375 |
| DWN_DATE | Date | mm/dd/yy | Left | 0.09375 |
| CHK_BY | Checked By | AAA | Left | 0.09375 |
| CHK_DATE | Date | mm/dd/yy | Left | 0.09375 |
| MFG_ENG | Manufacturing Engineer | AAA | Left | 0.09375 |
| ME_DATE | Date | mm/dd/yy | Left | 0.09375 |

3. Use the **WBLOCK** command to create a block/drawing named **Title Attributes Mechanical C-Size.DWG** by selecting the attributes defined above and shown in Figure P16-3C using the following settings:

   a. Set the **Base point** to 0,0,0.

   b. Set the **Objects** option to the **Delete from drawing** setting so the attributes are deleted.

   c. Set **Insert units** to **Unitless**.

4. Use the **WBLOCK** command to create a block/drawing named **Mechanical C-Size.DWG** by selecting all the remaining title border line work and static text that never changes using the following settings:

   a. Set the **Base point** to 0,0,0.

   b. Set the **Objects** option to the **Delete from drawing** setting so the attributes are deleted.

   c. Set **Insert units** to **Unitless**.

5. Close the drawing template. *Do not save changes to the drawing template.*

**Figure P16-3C**

## Project 16-3C: A-Size Portrait Mechanical Border—Continued from Chapter 15

1. Open template file **Mechanical A-Size-Portrait.DWT**.

2. Create the title block attribute definitions shown in Figure P16-3D. Place the attributes on the **Title** layer. Use the definitions shown in the following table:

| Tag | Prompt | Default | Justification | Height |
|---|---|---|---|---|
| TITLE | Drawing Title | Title | Center | 0.2 |
| DESC | Description | Description | Center | 0.125 |
| PARTNO | Part Number | xxx | Left | 0.125 |
| SCALE | Drawing Scale | 1:1 | Left | 0.09375 |
| DWN | Drawn By | AAA | Left | 0.09375 |
| SHEET | Sheet Number | 1 of 1 | Left | 0.09375 |
| REV | Revision Number | 0 | Center | 0.125 |
| PROJ_ENG | Project Engineer | AAA | Left | 0.09375 |
| PE_Date | Date | mm/dd/yy | Left | 0.09375 |
| Dwn_By | Drawn By | AAA | Left | 0.09375 |

| Dwn_Date | Date | mm/dd/yy | Left | 0.09375 |
|---|---|---|---|---|
| CHK_BY | Checked By | AAA | Left | 0.09375 |
| Chk_Date | Date | mm/dd/yy | Left | 0.09375 |
| MFG_ENG | Manufacturing Engineer | AAA | Left | 0.09375 |
| ME_Date | Date | mm/dd/yy | Left | 0.09375 |

3. Use the **WBLOCK** command to create a block/drawing named **Title Attributes Mechanical A-Size-Portrait.DWG** by selecting the attributes defined above and shown in Figure P16-3D using the following settings:
   a. Set the **Base point** to 0,0,0.
   b. Set the **Objects** option to the **Delete from drawing** setting so the attributes are deleted.
   c. Set **Insert units** to **Unitless**.
4. Use the **WBLOCK** command to create a block/drawing named **Mechanical A-Size-Portrait.DWG** by selecting all the remaining title border line work and static text that never changes using the following settings.
   a. Set the **Base point** to 0,0,0.
   b. Set the **Objects** option to the **Delete from drawing** setting so the attributes are deleted.
   c. Set **Insert units** to **Unitless**.
5. Close the drawing template. *Do not save changes to the drawing template.*

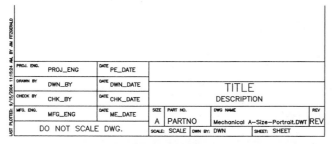

Figure P16-3D

## Project 16-4A: Architectural D-Size Border—Continued from Chapter 15

1. Open the template file **Architectural D-Size.DWT**.
2. Create a layer named **A-ANNO-TTLB-ATTS** with default properties. Set its color to **red** and make it the current layer.
3. Replace all the updateable title block text with the attribute definitions shown in Figure P16-4A and defined in the following table:

| Tag | Prompt | Default |
|---|---|---|
| DATE | Enter the date: | MM/DD/YY |
| SCALE | Enter the scale: | 1/4″ = 1′-0: |
| DRNBY | Enter drawn by initials: | AAA |

| CHKBY | Enter checked by initials: | AAA |
| PROJECT | Enter project number: | 1234 |
| SHTNO | Enter the sheet number: | 1 |
| TOTAL | Enter the total number of sheets: | 100 |
| TITLE1 | Enter the first title line: | TITLE |
| TITLE2 | Enter the second title line: | INTRODUCTION TO AUTOCAD |
| TITLE3 | Enter the third title line: | PRENTICE HALL |

4. Use the **WBLOCK** command to create a block/drawing named **Title Attributes Architectural D-Size.DWG** by selecting the attributes defined above and shown in Figure P16-4A using the following settings:
   a. Set the **Base point** to 0,0,0.
   b. Set the **Objects** option to the **Delete from drawing** setting so the attributes are deleted.
   c. Set **Insert units** to **Unitless**.
5. Replace all the updateable revision text with the attribute definitions shown in Figure P16-4A and defined in the following table:

| Tag | Prompt | Default |
|---|---|---|
| REVNO | Enter the revision number: | 1 |
| REVDATE | Enter the revision date: | MM/DD/YY |
| REVDESC | Enter the revision description: | REVISED |
| REVBY | Enter revision by initials: | AAA |
| APPBY | Enter revision approved by initials: | AAA |

6. Use the **WBLOCK** command to create a block/drawing named **Revision Block - Architectural.DWG** by selecting the revision block attributes defined above and shown in Figure P16-4A using the following settings:
   a. Set the **Base point** by snapping to the left endpoint of the line directly above the **REVNO** attribute definition as shown in Figure P16-4A.
   b. Set the **Objects** option to the **Delete from drawing** setting so the attributes are deleted.
   c. Set **Insert units** to **Unitless**.
7. Use the **WBLOCK** command to create a block/drawing named **Architectural D-Size.DWG** by selecting all the remaining title border line work and static text that never changes as shown in Figure P16-4A using the following settings.
   a. Set the **Base point** to 0,0,0.

b. Set the **Objects** option to the **Delete from drawing** setting
so the objects are deleted.

c. Set **Insert units** to **Unitless**.

*Note:* Do not include the graphic scale in the upper right-
hand corner as part of title block definition!

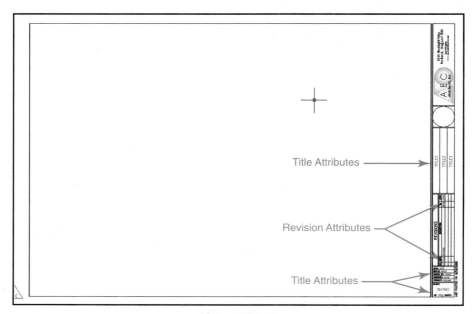

Figure P16-4A

## Project 16-4B: Architectural B-Size Border—Continued from Chapter 15

1. Open the template file **Architectural B-Size.DWT**.
2. Create a layer named **A-ANNO-TTLB-ATTS** with default properties. Set its color to **red** and make it the current layer.
3. Replace all the updateable title block text with the attribute definitions shown in Figure P16-4B and defined in the following table:

| Tag | Prompt | Default |
|---|---|---|
| DATE | Enter the date: | MM/DD/YY |
| SCALE | Enter the scale: | 1/8″ = 1′-0: |
| DRNBY | Enter drawn by initials: | AAA |
| CHKBY | Enter checked by initials: | AAA |
| PROJECT | Enter project number: | 1234 |
| DWGNO | Enter the drawing number: | 1 |
| TITLE1 | Enter the first title line: | TITLE |
| TITLE2 | Enter the second title line: | INTRODUCTION TO AUTOCAD |
| TITLE3 | Enter the third title line: | PRENTICE HALL |

4. Use the **WBLOCK** command to create a block/drawing named **Title Attributes Architectural B-Size.DWG** by selecting the attributes defined above and shown in Figure P16-4B using the following settings:
   a. Set the **Base point** to 0,0,0.
   b. Set the **Objects** option to the **Delete from drawing** setting so the attributes are deleted.
   c. Set **Insert units** to **Unitless**.
5. Use the **WBLOCK** command to create a block/drawing named **Architectural B-Size.DWG** by selecting all the remaining title border line work and static text that never changes as shown in Figure P16-4B using the following settings:
   a. Set the **Base point** to 0,0,0.
   b. Set the **Objects** option to the **Delete from drawing** setting so the attributes are deleted.
   c. Set **Insert units** to **Unitless**.

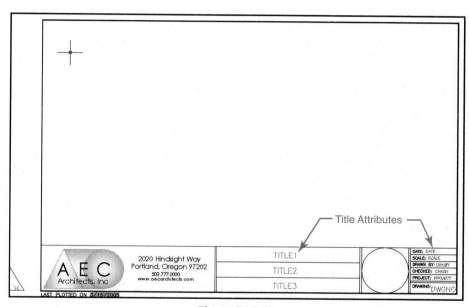

**Figure P16-4B**

## Project 16-4C: Architectural A-Size Border—Continued from Chapter 15

1. Open the template file **Architectural A-Size.DWT**.
2. Create a layer named **A-ANNO-TTLB-ATTS** with default properties. Set its color to **red** and make it the current layer.
3. Replace all the updateable title block text with the attribute definitions shown in Figure P16-4C and defined in the following table:

| Tag | Prompt | Default |
|-----|--------|---------|
| DATE | Enter the date: | MM/DD/YY |
| SCALE | Enter the scale: | 1/4″ = 1′-0: |
| DRNBY | Enter drawn by initials: | AAA |

| CHKBY | Enter checked by initials: | AAA |
|---|---|---|
| PROJECT | Enter project number: | 1234 |
| SHTNO | Enter the sheet number: | 1 |
| TITLE1 | Enter the first title line: | TITLE |
| TITLE2 | Enter the second title line: | INTRODUCTION TO AUTOCAD |
| TITLE3 | Enter the third title line: | PRENTICE HALL |

4. Use the **WBLOCK** command to create a block/drawing named **Title Attributes Architectural A-Size.DWG** by selecting the attributes defined above and shown in Figure P16-4C using the following settings:
   a. Set the **Base point** to 0,0,0.
   b. Set the **Objects** option to the **Delete from drawing** setting so the attributes are deleted.
   c. Set **Insert units** to **Unitless**.

5. Use the **WBLOCK** command to create a block/drawing named **Architectural A-Size.DWG** by selecting all the remaining title border line work and static text that never changes as shown in Figure P16-4C using the following settings:
   a. Set the **Base point** to 0,0,0.
   b. Set the **Objects** option to the **Delete from drawing** setting so the attributes are deleted.
   c. Set **Insert units** to **Unitless**.

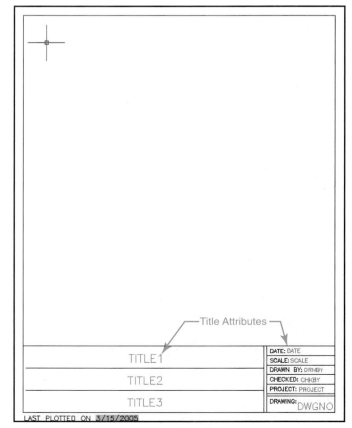

Figure P16-4C

## Project 16-5: Electrical Schematic—Continued from Chapter 14

1. Open drawing **P14-7**.
2. Create blocks for each of the electrical symbols shown in Figure P16-5. Choose appropriate names and insertion points for each block. Use the **E-Lite** or **E-Powr** layers to place the symbol annotation. Place all description annotation on the **E-Anno** layer.
3. Replace the symbols in the drawing with the new blocks you just created.
4. Freeze all layers *except* the electrical layers (layers starting with E-).
5. Use the **WBLOCK** command to create a drawing called **Electrical Plan.dwg** by selecting all the geometry on the electrical layers using the following settings:
   a. Set the **Base point** to 0,0,0.
   b. Set the **Objects** option to the **Delete from drawing** setting so geometry is deleted.
   c. Set **Insert units** to **inches**.
6. Use the **PURGE** command to remove the E- layers and all electrical blocks from the drawing.
7. Save the drawing as **P16-5**.

ELECTRICAL SYMBOLS:

**Figure P16-5**

## Project 16-6: Piping Symbol Library—Continued from Chapter 4

1. Open drawing **P4-6**.
2. Create blocks from the piping symbols created for Chapter 4 using the following settings:
   a. Name the block as indicated in Figure P16-6. Do not include the text in the block definition.
   b. Specify the base point shown with "X" in Figure P16-6.
   c. Select the **Convert to block** option so the block is converted in place.
   d. Select the **Allow exploding** option.
3. Save the drawing as **Piping Symbols** but leave the drawing open.
4. Start a new drawing using the **acad.dwt** template.
5. Start **DesignCenter** and select the **Open Drawings** tab.
6. Select the plus symbol (+) next to the **Piping Symbols.dwg** drawing to expand the tree.
7. Select the **Blocks** icon so that the piping blocks you created in step 1 are displayed in the Contents pane on the right.

8. Update the schematic drawings P4-6A, P4-6B, and P4-6C and replace all the existing piping symbols with their corresponding blocks in the **Piping Symbols** drawing.

9. Practice dragging-and-dropping piping symbols into your drawing using both the left and right mouse buttons.

10. Double-click on a block to display the **Insert** dialog box.

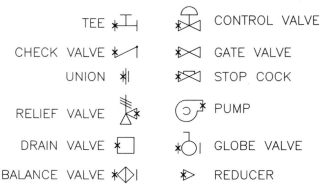

**Figure P16-6**

## Project 16-7: Architectural Plan—Continued from Exercise 16-5

1. Open drawing **P16-5**.

2. Freeze the layers **L-Walk, L-Walk-Pat, A-Area,** and **A-Area-Iden** layers.

3. Create blocks for each of the symbols shown in Figure P16-7A. Choose appropriate insertion points for each block. For the door and window callouts, create attributes with the definitions shown in the following table. Choose appropriate default values for the door and window attributes. Place all geometry on appropriate layers.

| Tag | Prompt | Invisible | Justification | Height |
|-----|--------|-----------|---------------|--------|
| SYM | Callout Symbol | N | Middle | 4 |
| SIZE | Size | Y | Middle | 4 |
| TYPE | Type | Y | Middle | 4 |

4. Replace the symbols in the drawing with the new blocks. Delete the door and window schedules from the model space environment. Place the new blocks on the appropriate layer.

5. Switch to **Architectural D-Size** layout. Select the **Extract Data** tool on the **Linking & Extraction** panel on the **Blocks & References** ribbon to start the **Data Extraction** wizard. Create a window schedule by extracting the **W-Callout** block attributes to a table. Arrange the columns in the order shown and sort the table by the **SYM** field. Create/modify table styles as needed to match the table shown in Figure P16-7B.

6. Create another table for the door schedule shown in Figure P16-7B by extracting the **D-Callout** block attributes to a table.

7. Save the drawing as **Architectural Plan.dwg.**

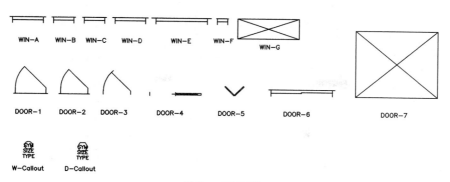

Figure P16-7A

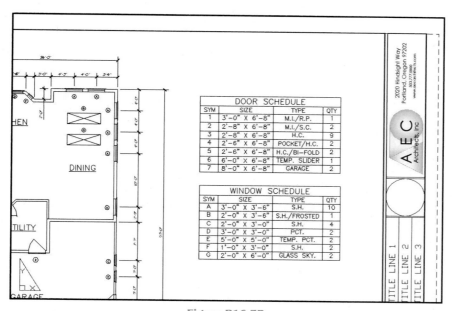

Figure P16-7B

## Project 16-8: Structural Steel Symbol Library

1. Start a new drawing using the **acad.dwt** template.
2. Draw eight wide flange shapes using the designation and dimensions in the steel table below using the wide flange profile shown in Figure P16-8.

| Designation | Depth—d | Web Thickness—w | Flange Width—f | Flange Thickness—t |
|---|---|---|---|---|
| W8x67 | 9.00 | 0.570 | 8.280 | 0.935 |
| W8x58 | 8.75 | 0.510 | 8.220 | 0.810 |

| W8x48 | 8.50 | 0.400 | 8.110 | 0.685 |
| W8x40 | 8.25 | 0.360 | 8.070 | 0.560 |
| W8x35 | 8.12 | 0.310 | 8.020 | 0.495 |
| W8x31 | 8.00 | 0.285 | 7.995 | 0.435 |
| W8x28 | 8.06 | 0.285 | 6.535 | 0.465 |
| W8x24 | 7.93 | 0.245 | 6.495 | 0.400 |

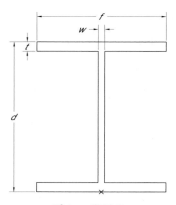

Figure P16-8

3. Create blocks from the wide flange shapes drawn in step 2 using the following settings:
   a. Name the block using its corresponding steel designation (i.e., **W8x67**). Do not include text or dimensions in the block definition.
   b. Specify the base point shown with "X" in Figure P16-8.
   c. Select the **Convert to block** option so the block is converted in place.
   d. Select the **Allow exploding** option.
4. Save the drawing as **Structural Steel Symbols** but leave the drawing open.
5. Start a new drawing using the **acad.dwt** template.
6. Start **DesignCenter** and select the **Open Drawings** tab.
7. Select the plus symbol (+) next to the **Stuctural Steel Symbols.dwg** drawing to expand the tree.
8. Select the **Blocks** icon so that the structural steel blocks you created in step 2 are displayed in the Contents pane on the right.
9. Practice dragging-and-dropping structural steel symbols into your drawing using both the left and right mouse buttons.
10. Double-click on a block to display the **Insert** dialog box.

## Project 16-9: Socket Head Cap Screws—English Units—Continued from Chapter 11

1. Open drawing **P11-9**.
2. Create blocks from the metric fasteners created for Chapter 6 using the following settings:
    a. Name the block as indicated in Figure P16-9. Do not include the text in the block definition.
    b. Specify the base point shown with "X" in Figure P16-9.
    c. Select the **Convert to block** option so the block is converted in place.
    d. Select the **Allow exploding** option.
3. Save the drawing as **Socket Head Cap Screws.dwg** but leave the drawing open.
4. Start a new drawing using the **acad.dwt** template.
5. Start **DesignCenter** and select the **Open Drawings** tab.
6. Select the plus symbol (+) next to the **Fastener Symbols.dwg** drawing to expand the tree.
7. Select the **Blocks** icon so that the fastener blocks you created in step 1 are displayed in the Contents pane on the right.
8. Practice dragging-and-dropping fastener symbols into your drawing using both the left and right mouse buttons.
9. Double-click on a block to display the **Insert** dialog box.

10−24−T          10−24−500            25−20−T          25−20−750

**Figure P16-9**

## Project 16-10: Metric Fastener Symbol Library—Continued from Chapter 6

1. Open drawing **P6-10**.
2. Create blocks from the metric fasteners created for Chapter 6 using the following settings:
    a. Name the block as indicated in Figure P16-10. Do not include the text in the block definition.
    b. Specify the base point shown with "X" in Figure P16-10.
    c. Select the **Convert to block** option so the block is converted in place.
    d. Select the **Allow exploding** option.
3. Save the drawing as **Fastener Symbols** but leave the drawing open.
4. Start a new drawing using the **acad.dwt** template.
5. Start **DesignCenter** and select the **Open Drawings** tab.
6. Select the plus symbol (+) next to the **Fastener Symbols.dwg** drawing to expand the tree.
7. Select the **Blocks** icon so that the fastener blocks you created in step 1 are displayed in the Contents pane on the right.
8. Practice dragging-and-dropping fastener symbols into your drawing using both the left and right mouse buttons.
9. Double-click on a block to display the **Insert** dialog box.

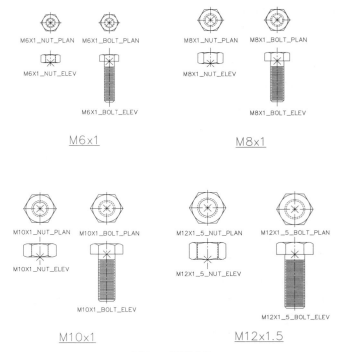

Figure P16-10

## Project 16-11: Civil Site Plan—Continued from Chapter 14

1. Open drawing **P14-11**.
2. Create blocks for the landscaping objects and north arrow as shown in Figure P16-11.
3. Replace the landscaping symbols with the blocks.
4. Save the drawing as **EX16-11**.

Figure P16-11

## Project 16-12: Civil Symbol Library

1. Start a new drawing using the **acad.dwt** template.
2. Start the **UNITS** command to display the **Drawing Units** dialog box and set the **Insertion scale** setting to **Feet**.
3. Draw the civil engineering symbols shown in Figure P16-12 to the best of your ability at the sizes shown. *Hint:* Each grid square is equal to 1 decimal foot.
4. Create blocks from the civil engineering symbols drawn in step 2 using the following settings:
   a. Name block as indicated on Figure P16-12. Do not include the text in the block definition.
   b. Select the **Convert to block** option so the block is converted in place.
   c. Select the **Allow exploding** option.
   d. Make sure the **Block unit** list box is set to **Feet**.
5. Save the drawing as **Piping Symbols** but leave the drawing open.

6. Start a new drawing using the **acad.dwt** template.
7. Start **DesignCenter** and select the **Open Drawings** tab.
8. Select the plus symbol (+) next to the **Civil Symbols.dwg** drawing to expand the tree.
9. Select the **Blocks** icon so that the civil engineering blocks you created in step 3 are displayed in the Contents pane on the right.
10. Practice dragging-and-dropping civil engineering symbols into your drawing using both the left and right mouse buttons.
11. Double-click on a block to display the **Insert** dialog box.
12. Start the **UNITS** command to display the **Drawing Units** dialog box and set the **Insertion scale** setting to **Inches**.
13. Insert the same symbols again. The symbols are now scaled up by a factor of 12.

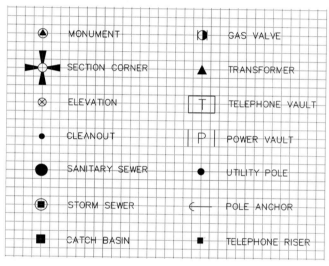

**Figure P16-12**

# Working with External References 17

## INTRODUCTION

Rapidly produced, high-quality drawings are the objective of any drafter or designer. When changes are made to a design, drawings must be updated to reflect the changes. Opening and editing each drawing affected by a change can be a time-consuming process. AutoCAD can help with this process by allowing changes in one drawing to be automatically reflected in other files. This is done through the use of externally referenced drawings, called *xrefs*.

When you create an xref, you are placing a reference to another drawing into your drawing. When changes are made to the referenced drawing, your drawing is updated to reflect the changes.

For example, consider the design of a building where multiple people are working on various aspects of the building at once. People working on the HVAC, piping, and electrical systems need to see where the walls, doors, and windows are located. In this situation, the HVAC, piping, and electrical designers could place an xref of the floor plan into their drawings. That way, when changes are made to the floor plan, the xref will update to show those changes, and they can adjust their design as needed.

AutoCAD also allows you to create similar references to raster images. Raster images can enhance your drawing by providing additional visual information to your drawing. Civil or architectural drawings can use an image as a background to locate placement points or structural positions. Satellite or aerial views can be used to trace or locate utilities or roadways. Raster images can also be used to enhance the appearance of your company name or logo. Images are similar to xrefs in that AutoCAD creates a reference to the raster image file. If and when the raster image updates, the changes are automatically reflected in your drawing.

In many design environments, design data can come from many different sources and in different formats. Often, vector drawing data may be provided in a format that you only wish to view, but not modify. To accommodate this, AutoCAD provides a way to display and view this type of CAD information, called *underlays*. An underlay is similar to both xref drawings and raster images.

AutoCAD allows you to display DWF (Design Web Format) and DGN (MicroStation Design) files as an underlay. The DWF file format is a compressed vector-based drawing file format

**xref:** A drawing that is referenced by another drawing. The drawing references are updated when the source drawing is modified.

**underlay:** A CAD file that is not directly modifiable by AutoCAD but is still displayed within a drawing and updated when the source data is changed.

developed by Autodesk that allows you to share your drawings with other individuals who do not have AutoCAD and/or who should not have access to sensitive, proprietary design information.

DWF files cannot be modified; they can only be viewed and marked up. Autodesk provides free downloadable software on its Website, called Design Review, that allows you to view, mark up, and print DWF files. Another advantage of DWF files is that DWF file sizes are significantly smaller than the original drawing files (DWG) so that they take up less room and can be transferred faster electronically via email or the Internet.

DGN files are vector-based drawing files created by MicroStation, a CAD package similar to AutoCAD. AutoCAD currently supports DGN files created by version 8 (V8) of MicroStation. DGN files cannot be modified by AutoCAD directly; however, AutoCAD can convert DGN files to the DWG file format. AutoCAD can also export drawing data to the DGN file format. See Chapter 18 for more on importing and exporting drawing data.

In this chapter, we'll examine xrefs, images, and underlays, the different ways they can be embedded in a drawing, how they are updated, and how to manage and keep track of their relationships.

## EXTERNAL REFERENCES PALETTE

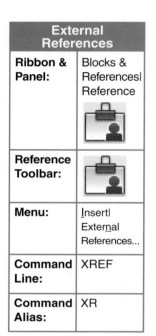

| External References | |
|---|---|
| **Ribbon & Panel:** | Blocks & References\| Reference |
| **Reference Toolbar:** | |
| **Menu:** | Insert\| External References... |
| **Command Line:** | XREF |
| **Command Alias:** | XR |

Xrefs, raster images, and underlay files are all managed using the **External References** palette shown in Figure 17-1.

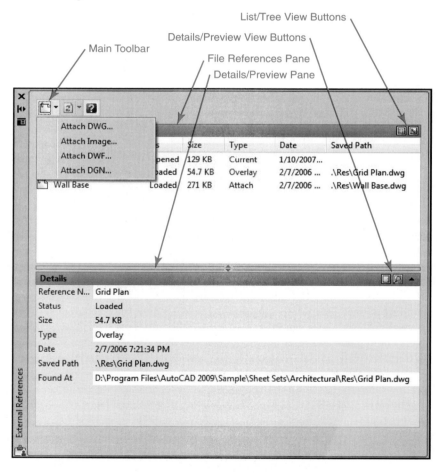

**Figure 17-1**   The External References palette

The toolbar on the top of the **External References** palette allows you to create new file references and refresh the status of existing file references. The button on the left of the toolbar displays a drop-down menu with the following reference attachment options:

- **Attach DWG...**   References another drawing file (DWG) using the **XATTACH** command
- **Attach Image...**   References a raster image file (BMP, JPG, GIF, etc.) using the **IMAGEATTACH** command

- **Attach DWF...**   References a Drawing Web Format file (DWF) using the **DWFATTACH** command
- **Attach DGN...**   References a DGN file using **DGNATTACH**

Whichever of these attachment options is selected becomes the default button displayed on the toolbar.

The **Refresh** button in the middle updates the status of reference files so that they are current, and the question mark (?) button displays the AutoCAD Help topic for External References.

The **File References** pane lists the current drawing, referred to as the *master drawing,* and any referenced drawings, raster images, or DWF files along with their current status, size, type and the date/time they were last updated. Files can be displayed in the default **List View** mode (F3) or in **Tree View** mode (F4) using the buttons on the top right of the **File References** pane or their corresponding function key. The **Tree View** mode makes it possible to view any nested references and how they are related.

**TIP**   In the **List View** mode, you can select two or more files using the standard Windows <**Shift**> and <**Ctrl**> key methods.

Right-click shortcut menus provide most of the options for working with the files in the **File References** pane. If you right-click when no files are selected, a shortcut menu with the following options is displayed:

- **Reload All References**   Reloads all referenced files
- **Select All**   Selects all file references except the current drawing
- **Attach DWG...**   References another drawing using the **XATTACH** command
- **Attach Image...**   References an image file using the **IMAGEATTACH** command
- **Attach DWF...**   References a DWF file using the **DWFATTACH** command
- **Attach DGN...**   References a DGN file using the **DGNATTACH** command
- **Tooltip Style**   Allows you to set the tooltip style shown when you hover your mouse pointer over a reference name to display either the file name of the reference, a graphical preview in one of three sizes, or a list of details as shown in Figure 17-2
- **Preview/Details Pane**   Toggles the **Preview/Details** pane at the bottom of the palette on and off

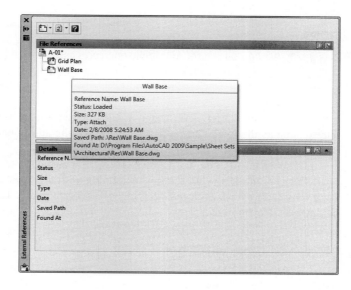

**Figure 17-2**   Tooltip Style set to Details mode

Right-clicking when one or more files are selected displays a shortcut menu with some or all of the following options, depending on the file type(s) selected:

- **Open**   Opens the selected file reference using the associated application
- **Attach...**   Displays the attach dialog box corresponding to the selected reference type
- **Unload**   Unloads the selected file reference
- **Reload**   Reloads the selected file reference
- **Detach**   Detaches the selected file reference
- **Bind...**   Displays the **Bind Xrefs** dialog box so that you can make an xref part of the current drawing (available only for referenced DWG files)

The **Details/Preview** pane on the bottom can either display properties for the selected file references or a thumbnail preview if available. Use the buttons on the top right of the **Details/Preview** pane to switch between the two different modes. The default **Details** pane displays the following properties for all reference files types:

> **Note:**
> The majority of reference file properties are read-only and cannot be edited unless otherwise noted.

- **Reference Name**   File reference name in drawing. Displays *Varies* if multiple file references are selected (Editable)
- **Status**   Displays whether file reference is loaded, unloaded, or not found (Read-only)
- **Size**   Displays the file size of selected file reference (Read-only)
- **Type**   Indicates if a DWG file reference is an attachment or overlay, the image file type or underlay (Editable for DWG files/Read-only for images, DWF, and DGN files). You can use this property to quickly switch referenced drawings between the Attach and Overlay attachment type after an xref has been attached without having to detach and reattach it again.
- **Date**   Displays last date the file reference was modified (Read-only)
- **Saved Path**   Displays the saved path of the selected file reference. This path can be different from where the file was found because of the different options available for locating reference files (Read-only).
- **Found At**   Displays full path of the selected file reference. This path is where the referenced file is actually found and might not be the same as the **Saved Path** property above. Selecting the [**...**] button to the right displays the **Select new path** dialog box where you can select a different file or file location. Valid path changes are stored to the **Saved Path** property above (Editable).

**TIP**   It is possible to specify a different reference file using the [**...**] button on the right. When you do this, AutoCAD simply references the specified file instead of the file specified in the **Reference Name**. This allows you to quickly swap one reference file for another.

If you select a referenced raster image file, additional image-specific properties are displayed such as the image size and resolution. All the additional image properties are read-only and cannot be edited.

The specifics of using the **External References** palette to reference and manage file types are detailed in the following sections beginning with the first, and arguably the most popular of the reference file types, external drawing (DWG) references. These are commonly referred to in the industry as *xrefs*.

## BLOCKS VERSUS XREFS

Xrefs are similar to blocks but with a few notable exceptions.

## Blocks

When you insert a block, you are creating a reference to a block definition that exists entirely inside the drawing file. When you insert an external drawing file with the **INSERT** command, AutoCAD converts the external drawing file into an internal block definition. Changes to the original drawing file are not reflected in the drawings containing the inserted blocks.

## Xrefs

When you attach an xref, you are directly referencing an external drawing file. Whenever changes are made to the external drawing file, all the references to that drawing are updated as well. Because xrefs point to external drawings, the location of the drawing file (the file path) is important.

## Attaching an Xref

When you attach an xref, you attach an external drawing file to your drawing. When you choose **Attach DWG…,** AutoCAD prompts you to select the drawing file. Once you've selected a drawing, AutoCAD displays the **External Reference** dialog box (see Figure 17-3).

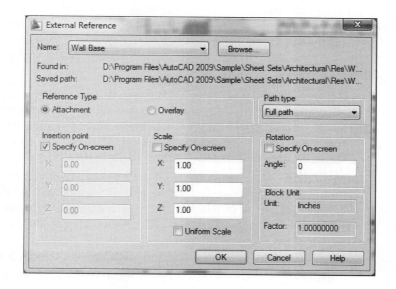

**Figure 17-3**   The External Reference dialog box

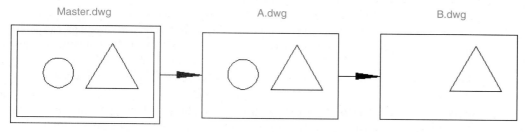

**Figure 17-4**   Nested xrefs

*Nested Xrefs.*   Any drawing can be attached as an xref to another xref, a concept known as nesting. To view nested xrefs, select the **Tree View** button on the **File References** pane on the **External References** palette.

It is possible to place a drawing that contains an xref as an xref. For example, say you have a drawing called MASTER that contains a reference to drawing A, and drawing A contains a reference to drawing B (see Figure 17-4). In this example, drawing B is referred to as a ***nested xref***.

Xref nesting can lead to some interesting or unexpected results. In the example above, when you reference drawing A, drawing B comes along as a nested xref. However, drawing B could also contain an xref

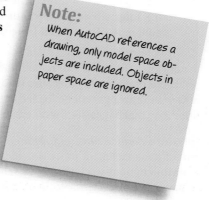

**Note:**
When AutoCAD references a drawing, only model space objects are included. Objects in paper space are ignored.

nested xref: An xref within an xref. This occurs when the drawing you are referencing contains a reference to another drawing.

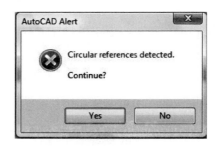

**Figure 17-5**    Circular xrefs warning

(drawing C), and drawing C might also contain an xref, and the nesting could go on and on. You can also create circular xrefs where drawings reference one another. For example, drawing A could reference drawing B, and drawing B could reference drawing A.

If AutoCAD detects circular xrefs, it will display a warning that circular references are detected (see Figure 17-5) and ask if you want to continue. If you choose Yes, AutoCAD will break the circular reference and proceed with loading the xref.

*Attach Versus Overlay.*    When you attach an xref, you can tell AutoCAD how you want that xref to behave when referenced in other drawings. The **Attach** option tells AutoCAD to load this drawing and any nested xrefs. The **Overlay** option tells AutoCAD to ignore any nested xrefs and load only the top-level drawing.

The **Attach** and **Overlay** options control only how nested xrefs behave when the drawing is referenced in another drawing.

*Setting the Path Type.*    When AutoCAD loads an xref, it must locate the drawing on your computer or network. The file path is the location of the drawing file on your system. It includes the drive letter or server name along with the list of folders and subfolders where the drawing file is located.

When you create an xref, you can tell AutoCAD how you want to store the path to the drawing file. You have the option of saving the **Full path, Relative path,** or **No path**:

- **Full path**    If the **Path type** is set to **Full path,** AutoCAD stores the entire path, including the local hard drive name or the network location and the entire list of folders and subfolders where the drawing is located. For example, *C:\Design\Projects\8013\arch\* describes the full path to a drawing file. In this example, the xref is located on the local *C:* drive, in the *Design\Projects\8013\arch* folder.

- **Relative path**    Using the **Relative path** option, AutoCAD automatically updates the xref path to assume the current path of the master, or host, drawing so that drive letters and network server names are not a factor as long as the subfolder structure stays the same. AutoCAD replaces the period (.) in the relative path with the path to the master drawing file. For example, if the relative path is set to *.\Xrefs*, the referenced drawings can be located at *C:\Design\Projects\8013\Xrefs* on one computer or at the network location *N:\Consultants\AEC Architects\Projects\8013\Xrefs* on another computer. The only requirement is that the master drawing is located in the *8013* folder on both computers so that the subfolder structure is the same.

- **No path**    Using **No path,** AutoCAD will store only the xref drawing name and no path information. When AutoCAD opens the drawing, it will look for the xref in the current drawing folder. If it doesn't find the xref there, it will then search the folders defined in the AutoCAD **Support File Search Path.** The **Support File Search Path** is defined in the **Files** tab on the **Options** dialog box. If it still doesn't find the xref, it will display a note in the **Command Line** window that the xref cannot be found.

If your drawing files remain at a single location and are never moved or sent to another site, the drawing file paths will remain the same every time you load a drawing file. However, if you send your drawings to other sites (to a contractor, client, manufacturer, etc.), you need to consider how your drawings will be loaded at these remote sites. Using the **Relative path** or **No path** options may make it easier for others to locate the xref drawings.

*Insertion Point, Scale, and Rotation.*    Once you set the reference **Type** and the **Path** type, the rest of the attachment process is identical to inserting a block. The **Insertion point, Scale,** and **Rotation** options work exactly like those in the **INSERT** command. You can specify these values in the dialog box or by selecting them in the drawing.

*Xref Notification Icon.*    When xrefs are attached to a drawing, an icon is displayed in the system tray in the lower-right corner (see Figure 17-6). Clicking on the icon displays the **External References** palette, providing a quick way to check xrefs and their status in the current drawing. If an attached xref changes, a notification balloon is displayed, indicating that the xref needs to be reloaded with a link to reload it.

**Figure 17-6**    The xref icon

### Exercise 17-1: Attaching an Xref

1. Start a new drawing using the **Architectural D-size.DWT** drawing template located on the Student CD.
2. Switch to the **Model**.
3. Create a layer named **References** and assign a **Continuous** linetype and color **7**. Set this layer **Current**.
4. Select the **Blocks & References** tab to display the **Reference** panel and select the **External References** button to display the **External References** palette.
5. Select **Attach DWG…** from the **External References** palette toolbar. Select the **Grid Plan.dwg** located in AutoCAD's **\Sample\Sheet Sets\Architectural\Res\** folder.
6. Set the **Reference Type** to **Attach**. Set the **Insertion point** to **0,0**, the **Scale** to **1**, and the **Rotation** to **0**. Choose **OK** to place the xref in your drawing. Do a **Zoom Extents** to see the entire xref.
7. Select **Attach DWG…** from the **External References** palette toolbar again. Select the **Wall Base.dwg** located in the **\Sample\Sheet Sets\Architectural\Res\** folder.
8. Set the **Reference Type** to **Attach**. Set the **Insertion point** to **0,0**, the **Scale** to **1**, and the **Rotation** to **0**. Choose **OK** to place the xref in your drawing. Do another **Zoom Extents** to see the entire xref.
9. Save the drawing as **EX17-1**. Your drawing should resemble Figure 17-7.

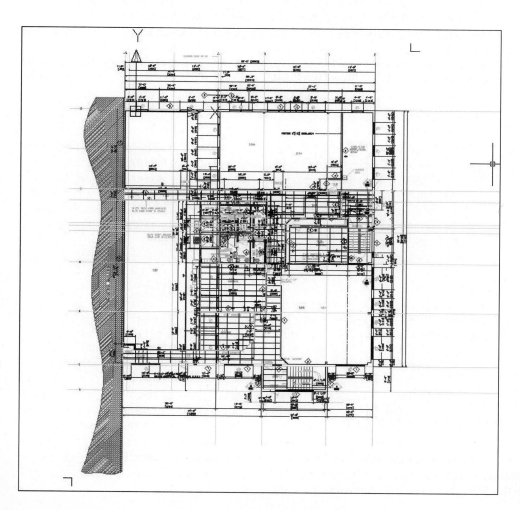

**Figure 17-7**    The attached xrefs

| DWG Reference | |
|---|---|
| Ribbon & Panel: | Blocks & References\| Reference <br><br> DWG |
| Reference Toolbar: | |
| Menu: | Insert\| DWG Reference... |
| Command Line: | XATTACH |
| Command Alias: | XA |

## The XATTACH Command

You can use the **XATTACH** command to attach a drawing reference directly via the **Select Reference File** dialog box instead of selecting **Attach DWG...** from the **External References** palette.

The **XATTACH** command displays a standard Windows file dialog box so you can navigate and locate the drawing file (DWG) file you want to attach and then displays the **External Reference** dialog box shown in Figure 17-3 so that you can specify different xref settings.

## Layers and Xrefs

When you attach an xref to a drawing, all the drawing's layers come with it. However, AutoCAD distinguishes between layers in the current drawing and layers in an xref by appending the file name along with the pipe (|) character to the layer name. For example, if you reference a drawing called **Grid**, which contains a layer called **S-Grid**, AutoCAD will display the layer name as **Grid|S-Grid** in the **Layer Manager** dialog box.

If your drawing contains multiple references to the same drawing file, AutoCAD will assign a number to each reference and append it along with the file name. For example, if you have two references to the drawing **Grid** in your drawing, AutoCAD will display the layers **Grid|1_S-Grid** and **Grid|2_S-Grid** in the **Layer Manager** dialog box. The **Layer Manager** dialog box also gives you filters for displaying the layers for any given xref.

*Changing Xref Layers.* The initial state of the xref layers will be the state in which the source drawing was saved. A layer that was frozen in a drawing will initially appear frozen when that drawing is referenced. You can make changes to xref layers, but there are some limitations on what you can do. You cannot set an xref layer as the current layer, and you cannot rename xref layers. However, you can change the color, linetype, lineweight, and visibility of xref layers. This allows you to change how xref layers are displayed and plotted within your drawing.

When you make changes to xref layers settings, AutoCAD will retain any changes to the layer settings the next time the drawing is loaded.

You can control the retention of xref layer settings with the **VISRETAIN** system variable. Setting **VISRETAIN** to **1** tells AutoCAD to retain any changes made to xref layers. Setting **VISRETAIN** to **0** tells AutoCAD to ignore changes made to xref layers and use the setting stored in the reference drawing each time the reference is loaded. This variable can also be set with the **Retain changes to Xref layers** box in the **Open and Save** tab of the **OPTIONS** command.

### Exercise 17-2: Xref Layers

1. Continue from Exercise 17-1.
2. Start the **LAYER** command. AutoCAD displays the **Layer Manager** palette.
3. Expand the **Xref** tree in the filters on the left side of the palette. You'll see the loaded xrefs listed in the tree. Choose the **Wall Base** xref to show only the layers in that xref.
4. Freeze all the layers that start with **Wall Base|1_.** Thaw all the **Wall Base|2_** layers. Freeze all the **Wall Base|2_Arch_Reflected_Ceiling_Plan_** layers. This isolates the second-floor layers for this building. Choose **OK** to close the **Layer Manager** palette.
5. Save the drawing as **EX17-2**. Your drawing should resemble Figure 17-8.

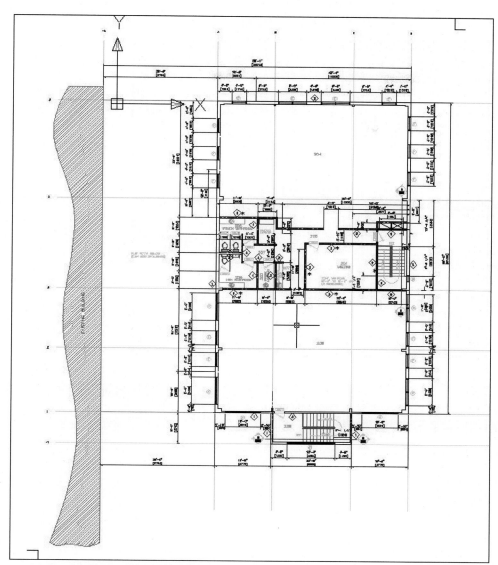

**Figure 17-8**    The modified xref layers

## Managing Xrefs

The **External References** palette discussed earlier is the main xref management tool (see Figure 17-9).

The default **List** view shows each reference along with its status (loaded or unloaded), file size, attachment type (attach or overlay), file date, and the full path to where the reference is located. The list can be sorted by any column type by selecting the column header at the top of the list as shown in Figure 17-9.

The **Tree** view shows the hierarchy of the loaded xrefs. This allows you to see nested xrefs and their relationship with other xrefs in the drawing as shown in Figure 17-10.

As mentioned earlier, most of the xref options and settings are provided via a shortcut menu that is displayed when you right-click on an xref in the **File References** pane as shown in Figure 17-11.

*Open.*    The **Open** menu item will open the selected referenced drawing(s) in a new drawing window. When you select **Open,** AutoCAD changes the status of the drawing(s) to **Opened** in the **External References** palette. This is the same as choosing **Open** from the **File** pull-down menu and opening the referenced file directly. The advantage of using **Open** from the **File References** palette is that AutoCAD will locate the drawing and open it automatically. It also allows you to open multiple drawings at the same time.

Click on Any Column Header to Sort Info

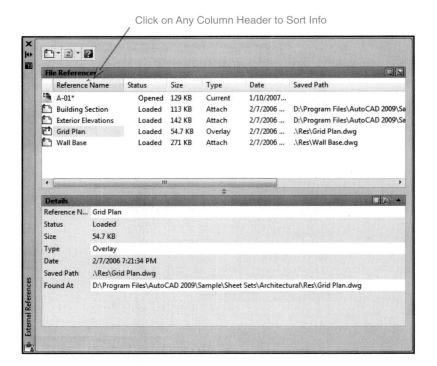

Figure 17-9   External References palette – List view

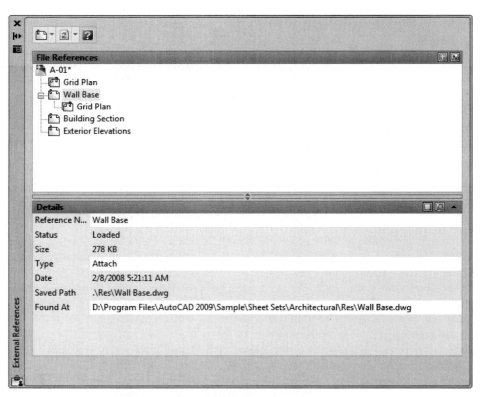

Figure 17-10   External References palette – Tree view

*Attach....*    The **Attach...** menu item will display the corresponding attach-type dialog box for the currently selected file type so you can attach another reference file of the same type. This option is unavailable when more than one file is selected.

*Unload.*    The **Unload** menu item will remove the selected xref(s) from the drawing screen but will retain the reference within the drawing. The xref layers are still retained but the drawing is not displayed.

Right-Click Shortcut Menu

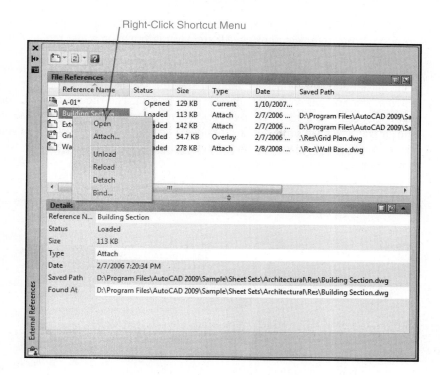

**Figure 17-11**    External References palette – right-click menu

*Reload.*    The **Reload** menu item reloads xref(s) in the current drawing. When you reload an xref, AutoCAD reopens the drawing from the location specified in the path. Reloading is necessary when changes are made to an xref while the current drawing is open. The **Reload** menu item also allows you to reload any unloaded xrefs. Once you reload an xref, the **Status** column changes to **Reloaded.** If you have an xref loaded into your drawing and changes are made to the source of the xref, AutoCAD will display a notification balloon (see Figure 17-12) telling you that changes have been made and that reloading is necessary. AutoCAD will also change the status in the **File References** palette to note that reloading is necessary (see Figure 17-13).

Xref Status Changed to Indicate it Needs Reloaded

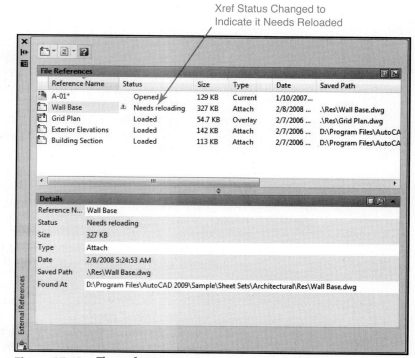

**Figure 17-12**    The xref notification balloon

**Figure 17-13**    The xref status

*Detach.*    The **Detach** menu item will remove attached xref(s). This completely removes the xref and any nested xrefs from your drawing. All xref layer information is also removed from your drawing.

*Bind.*    The **Bind...** menu item converts an externally referenced drawing to an AutoCAD block in the master drawing. When you bind an xref, the xref becomes a permanent part of the current drawing, and any link to the referenced file is broken. The file is removed from the **File References** palette and changes made to the original referenced drawing will not be updated. When you bind an xref, you have some options for how to deal with layer names. When you choose the **Bind** button, AutoCAD displays the **Bind Xrefs** dialog box (see Figure 17-14), which allows you to control how the xrefs are bound.

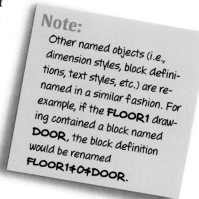

**Figure 17-14**    The Bind Xrefs
dialog box

*The Bind Option.*    The **Bind** option binds the selected xref to the current drawing. Xref layers are converted from the format *xref|layer* to the format *xref%n%*layer, where the number *n* is assigned automatically. This allows xref-dependent layers to retain their unique identity.

For example, if you have an xref named **FLOOR1** containing a layer named **WALL,** this layer would appear as **FLOOR1|WALL** while the drawing is an xref. Once you bind the xref using the **Bind** option, the layer name is converted to **FLOOR1$0$WALL.** If the layer **FLOOR1$0$WALL** already existed, the layer **FLOOR1|WALL** would be converted to **FLOOR1$1$WALL.**

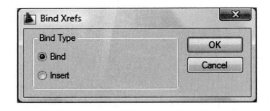

Note:
Other named objects (i.e., dimension styles, block definitions, text styles, etc.) are renamed in a similar fashion. For example, if the **FLOOR1** drawing contained a block named **DOOR,** the block definition would be renamed **FLOOR1$0$DOOR.**

**TIP**    The **BINDTYPE** system variable allows you to change how object definitions are renamed when bound. When **BINDTYPE** is set to **0** (the default), object definitions are renamed using the numbering convention. For example, **FLOOR1|WALL** is converted to **FLOOR1$0$WALL.**

When **BINDTYPE** is set to **1,** object definitions are not renamed, and the xref name is ignored. For example, **FLOOR1|WALL** is converted to **WALL.**

*The Insert Option.*    The **Insert** option binds the xref to the current drawing in a way similar to detaching and inserting the reference drawing. Rather than renaming xref layers, the layers are stripped of their xref name and no numbering occurs. If a layer already exists, the layers are simply merged into a single layer, and the layer retains the properties of the existing layer.

For example, if you have an xref named **FLOOR1** containing a layer named **WALL,** after binding it with the **Insert** option, the xref-dependent layer **FLOOR1|WALL** becomes layer **WALL.**

Exercise 17-3: Managing Xrefs

1. Continue from Exercise 17-2.
2. Display the **External References** palette if it is not already displayed.
3. Select the **Grid Plan** reference. In the **Type** property, select **Attach** and change the attachment type to **Overlay.** Repeat this for the **Wall Base** reference.

4. Select the **Wall Base** reference, right-click, and select **Unload...** from the shortcut menu. The **Status** column changes to **Unload.**
5. The **Wall Base** reference drawing is unloaded and disappears from your drawing.
6. The **Wall Base** drawing is shown as unloaded but is still referenced in the drawing (see Figure 17-15). Select the **Wall Base** drawing and choose **Reload...** from the right-click shortcut menu. The status changes to **Reload.**

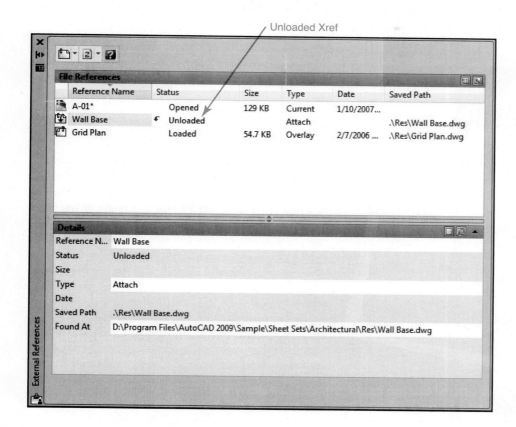

Unloaded Xref

| Reference Name | Status | Size | Type | Date | Saved Path |
|---|---|---|---|---|---|
| A-01* | Opened | 129 KB | Current | 1/10/2007... | |
| Wall Base | Unloaded | | Attach | | .\Res\Wall Base.dwg |
| Grid Plan | Loaded | 54.7 KB | Overlay | 2/7/2006 ... | .\Res\Grid Plan.dwg |

**Details**

| | |
|---|---|
| Reference N... | Wall Base |
| Status | Unloaded |
| Size | |
| Type | Attach |
| Date | |
| Saved Path | .\Res\Wall Base.dwg |
| Found At | D:\Program Files\AutoCAD 2009\Sample\Sheet Sets\Architectural\Res\Wall Base.dwg |

**Figure 17-15** The unloaded xref

7. AutoCAD reloads the reference drawing, and it is displayed in its original location.
8. Save your drawing as **EX17-3.**

## Editing Xrefs

There may be times when you want to change a referenced drawing. AutoCAD gives you a couple of ways to make changes to a referenced drawing.

*Opening Xrefs.* Of course, an easy way to make changes to an xref is to simply open the referenced drawing file with the **OPEN** command. When you make changes to the referenced drawing and save them, AutoCAD will notify you that changes have been made to the referenced drawing and allow you to update the xref.

The **Open** option in the **External References** palette also allows you to open a referenced drawing. As we discussed in the previous section, selecting one or more xrefs in the **External References** palette and choosing **Open...** from the right-click menu will cause AutoCAD to open each xref in a separate drawing window.

The **XOPEN** command also allows you to open referenced drawings. You are prompted to select the xref in your current drawing. Once you select an xref, AutoCAD will open the

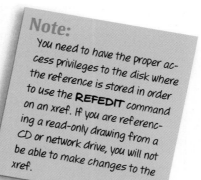

**Note:**
You need to have the proper access privileges to the disk where the reference is stored in order to use the **REFEDIT** command on an xref. If you are referencing a read-only drawing from a CD or network drive, you will not be able to make changes to the xref.

| Open Reference | |
|---|---|
| **Ribbon & Panel:** | None |
| **Toolbar:** | None |
| **Menu:** | Tools\|Xref and Block In-place Editing\| Open Reference |
| **Command Line:** | XOPEN |
| **Command Alias:** | None |

selected xref in a new drawing window. Again, you are notified if any changes are made to the referenced drawing.

*Edit in Place.*    The methods listed above are basically different methods for opening drawing files. All the drawings are opened in separate drawing windows. It is possible to edit an xref directly within the host drawing. In Chapter 16, you looked at how to use the **REFEDIT** command to modify block definitions. The **REFEDIT** command also allows you to modify an xref from within your current drawing. This is known as *edit in place*.

edit in place:  Using the **REFEDIT** command to make changes to an externally referenced drawing

---

| **FOR MORE DETAILS** | See Chapter 16 for more on using the **REFEDIT** command. |
| --- | --- |

---

When you start the **REFEDIT** command, you are asked to select a reference. If you select an external reference, AutoCAD displays the **Reference Edit** dialog box and shows the selected reference drawing along with any blocks or nested xrefs contained in the reference drawing. You can then select the reference you wish to edit and proceed with the **REFEDIT** command. If you make changes to a reference drawing, AutoCAD will automatically update the source drawing file and save the changes.

> **TIP**  To prevent others from using the REFEDIT command to edit your drawing, remove the check from the **Allow other users to Refedit current drawing** option in the **Open and Save** tab on the **Options** dialog box.

| Bind | |
| --- | --- |
| **Ribbon & Panel:** | None |
| **Reference Toolbar:** |  |
| **Menu:** | Modify\| Object\| External Reference\| Bind... |
| **Command Line:** | XBIND |
| **Command Alias:** | XB |

*Binding Parts of an Xref.*    Using the **Bind** menu item within the **External References** palette allows you to bind an entire reference file to your current drawing. This results in the entire drawing being converted to a block and inserted into your drawing. The **XBIND** command allows you to selectively bind individual named objects (layers, blocks, text styles, etc.) to your current drawing.

When you start the **XBIND** command, AutoCAD displays the **Xbind** dialog box (see Figure 17-16). The **Xrefs** area displays all the xrefs in the drawing. Clicking on an xref name will display a list of all the named objects within the xref. To bind an individual object, select the object and choose the **Add->** button to add it to the **Definitions to Bind** list. You can add and remove objects from the list. When you are satisfied with the list of object definitions, choose **OK** to bind those object definitions to your current drawing.

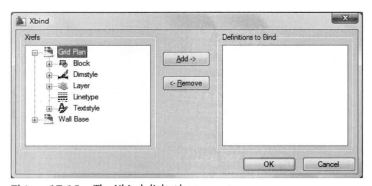

**Figure 17-16**    The Xbind dialog box

## Exercise 17-4: Editing Xrefs

1. Continue from Exercise 17-3.
2. Display the **External Reference** palette if it is not already displayed.
3. Select the **Grid Plan** reference and choose **Open...** from the right-click shortcut menu. The status changes to **Open.**
4. AutoCAD opens the **Grid Plan.dwg** file in a new window (see Figure 17-17).
5. Close the **Grid Plan** drawing. *Do not save any changes.*

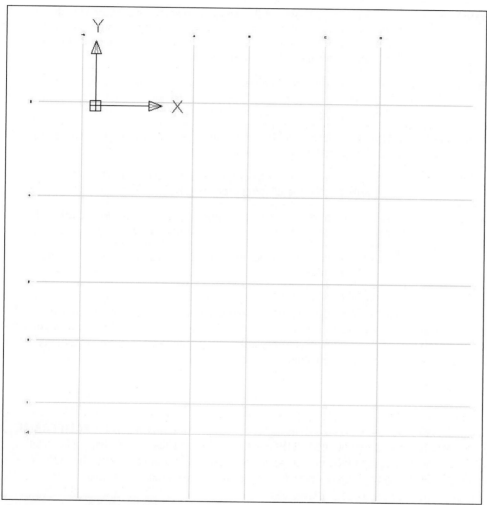

**Figure 17-17**    The opened xref

## Clipping an Xref

There may be times when you only want to view a portion of an xref. The **XCLIP** command allows you to "clip out" part of the displayed xref. The drawing or xref is not altered, but the xref is clipped to limit the display to only a portion of the xref.

 **TIP**    You can also start the **XCLIP** command by selecting an xref and choosing **Clip Xref** from the right-click menu.

When you start the **XCLIP** command, AutoCAD asks you to select an xref and then presents a number of options. These are described below:

| Clip Xref | |
|---|---|
| **Ribbon & Panel:** | Blocks & References |
| **Reference Toolbar:** | |
| **Menu:** | Modify| Clip|Xref |
| **Command Line:** | XCLIP |
| **Command Alias:** | XC |

| On / Off | Turns clipping on and off for a given xref. Turning clipping Off will cause AutoCAD to ignore any clipping boundaries assigned the xref. |
| --- | --- |
| Clip Depth | This option is used in 3D xrefs. The Clip Depth allows you to set the viewing depth of 3D models. |
| Delete | Deletes any xclip boundaries associated with an xref. |
| Generate Polyline | Draws a polyline around the edge of an xclip area. When you choose this option, AutoCAD will create a polyline along the outline of a clipped xref. Once the polyline is created, it has no association with the xref. It is simply a polyline object in the drawing. |
| New Boundary | Defines a new clipping area. If the xref has an existing clipping boundary, AutoCAD will ask you if you want to delete the old boundary. You then have three methods for defining a new clipping area. |
| Select Polyline | Uses an existing polyline to define a new clipping area. The existing polyline remains after the new clipping area is defined. |
| Polygonal | Allows you to draw a polygon to define the clip area. The polygon does not remain after the clipping area is defined. |
| Rectangular | Allows you to draw a box or rectangle to define the clipping area. The rectangle does not remain after the clipping area is defined. |
| Invert Clip | Inverts the clipping boundary. Clipped objects are shown, and shown object are hidden |

Xref clipping is similar to cropping an image in other Windows applications. When you clip an xref, you are simply selecting an area of the xref to display. Once an xref is clipped, you cannot modify the clipping area directly. To modify an xref clipping boundary, you must first delete the old clipping area and create a new one.

> You can change the visibility of an xref clipping boundary by changing the **XCLIPFRAME** system variable. Setting the **XCLIPFRAME** variable to **1** makes xref clipping boundaries visible. Setting it to **0** hides xref clipping frames. It is possible to edit the boundary of a clipped xref using grips to resize the area, as well as, invert the clipping area.

### Exercise 17-5: Clipping Xrefs

1. Continue from Exercise 17-4.
2. Start the **XCLIP** command and select both the **Grid Base** and **Wall Base** drawings and press **<Enter ↵>.**
3. Select the **New boundary** option and then choose **Rectangular** to create a rectangular clipping boundary.
4. Pick the endpoints at **P1** and **P2** as shown in Figure 17-18. AutoCAD clips the xrefs around the rectangular area.
5. Save your drawing as **EX17-5.**

### Demand Loading Xrefs

demand loading: Loading only the visible part of a referenced drawing

Demand loading is designed to help make AutoCAD run faster and more efficiently. If you have a number of xrefs loaded, or your referenced drawings are large and complex, you may notice slower system performance. To help with this, AutoCAD uses a method called ***demand loading***.

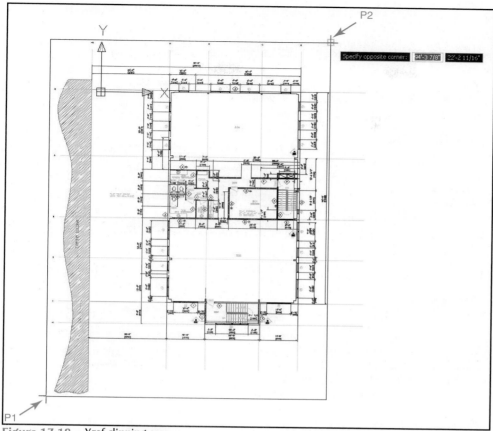

**Figure 17-18**    Xref clipping area

Demand loading works by loading only the parts of an xref that AutoCAD is actually show-ing. Layers that are turned off or frozen or any geometry hidden by a clipping boundary are not loaded into your drawing until they are needed. When a layer state or a clipping boundary changes, AutoCAD loads the geometry from the referenced drawing. AutoCAD gives you some options for controlling demand loading. These options are found in the **Open and Save** tab on the **Options** dialog box (see Figure 17-19). Demand loading can be set to **Disabled, Enabled** or **Enabled with Copy.** These options are described below:

| | |
|---|---|
| Disabled | Turns off demand loading. Each referenced drawing is completely loaded when AutoCAD loads your drawing. |
| Enabled | Turns demand loading on, making AutoCAD run faster and regenerate views quicker. However, the referenced drawings will be locked, pre-venting others from modifying the referenced drawing while your draw-ing is open. |
| Enabled with Copy | This is AutoCAD's default setting. AutoCAD will make a temporary copy of any referenced drawings and load this copy into your drawing. This enables demand loading while still allowing other users to modify the referenced drawings. |

The **Enabled with Copy** option provides the benefits of demand loading while still allowing others to work on the referenced drawings. If you use the **REFEDIT** command while the **Enabled with Copy** option is set, AutoCAD will save the changes back to the original referenced file, not the temporary copy.

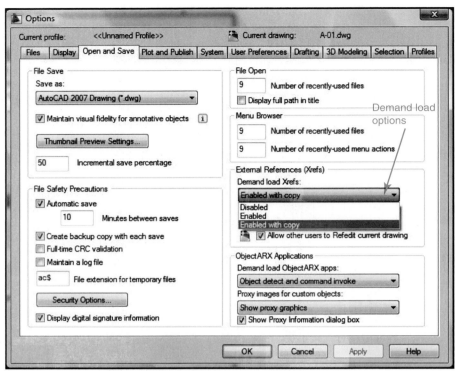

Figure 17-19     Options for demand load xrefs

## WORKING WITH RASTER IMAGES

Raster images can enhance your drawings in a number of ways. They can provide colorful backgrounds with a company logo or background images for accurately tracing shapes. Architectural and civil drawings can benefit greatly by attaching satellite or aerial images to show site locations or conditions.

These views can then serve as backgrounds to help the reader visualize locations or to help the designer to locate utility points for xrefs or inserts. An image can also help provide vital information about your drawing or the function of your part.

An image can be just about any of the popular raster image formats including .BMP, .GIF, .PNG, .TIF, and others. Much like xrefs, the images are simply linked to your drawing so they can be quickly changed, updated, or removed.

Raster images are treated and behave much the same way as xrefs but have additional controls to control image quality and transparency as well as brightness, contrast, and background fading.

### Attaching Raster Images

It is also possible to attach raster images using the **External References** palette (see Figure 17-20). Selecting **Attach Image...** displays the **Select Image File** dialog box (see Figure 17-21), which allows you to select an image file to place in your drawing. When you select an image, the **Preview** window will show you a preview of the raster image. Once you select an image and choose **Open,** AutoCAD displays the **Image** dialog box (see Figure 17-22), which allows you to set the type of path along with the **Insertion point, Scale,** and **Rotation** angle. All these functions work the same as the **XREF** command.

The **Details** button will display information about the resolution and size of the raster image (see Figure 17-23). This will tell you how AutoCAD will convert raster image resolution to physical size. For example, a raster image that has a resolution of 72 pixels per inch, and is 144 pixels by 108 pixels, will be converted to 2″ × 1.5″ in AutoCAD. The **Details** button displays information about the image resolution, AutoCAD units, and the image size in both pixels and AutoCAD units.

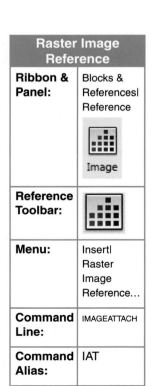

| Raster Image Reference | |
|---|---|
| **Ribbon & Panel:** | Blocks & ReferencesI Reference |
| | Image |
| **Reference Toolbar:** | |
| **Menu:** | Insertl Raster Image Reference... |
| **Command Line:** | IMAGEATTACH |
| **Command Alias:** | IAT |

Attach Image

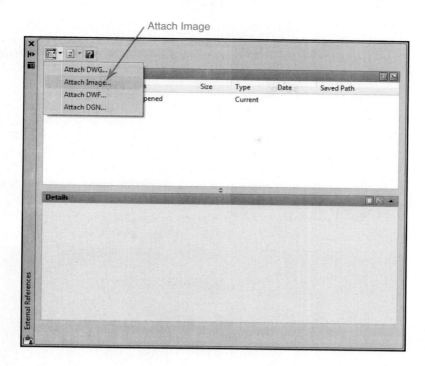

**Figure 17-20**    The External References palette

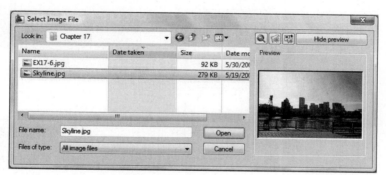

**Figure 17-21**    The Select
Image File dialog box

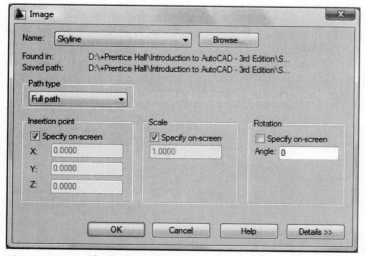

**Figure 17-22**    The Image dialog box

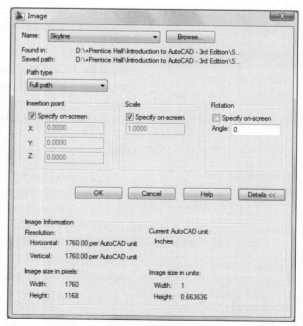

**Figure 17-23**    Raster image details

*The IMAGEATTACH Command.*    Like the **XATTACH** command, the **IMAGEATTACH** command allows you to attach a raster image directly, bypassing the **External References** palette. The dialog is the same as starting the **IMAGE** command and selecting **Attach Image...**

### Exercise 17-6: Attaching Raster Images

1. Continue from Exercise 17-5.
2. Switch to the **Architectural Title Block** layout. Use grips to move and resize the viewport as shown in Figure 17-24. Set the viewport scale to ⅛″ = 1′-0″.
3. Display the **External Reference** palette if it is not already displayed.
4. Choose **Attach Image...** and select the image **EX17-6.jpg** from the Student CD. Check the **Specify on-screen** option for the **Insertion point** and set the **Scale** at **2**. Choose **OK** and place the image as shown in Figure 17-24.
5. Save the drawing as **EX17-6.**

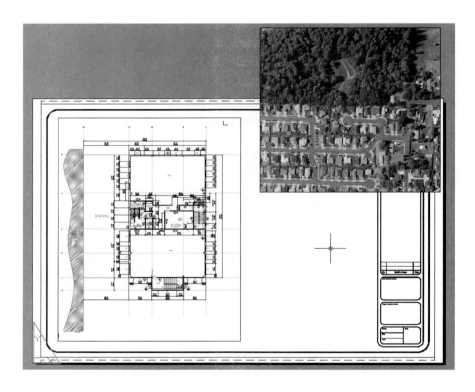

**Figure 17-24**    The attached image

| Clip Image | |
|---|---|
| **Ribbon & Panel:** | Blocks & References\| Reference |
| **Reference Toolbar:** | |
| **Menu:** | Modify\| Clip\|Image |
| **Command Line:** | IMAGECLIP |
| **Command Alias:** | ICL |

*Managing Images.*    Once you have loaded images into your drawing, AutoCAD will list the images, their status, file type, file date, and the saved path to the image file. **Detach, Reload,** and **Unload** work identically to their xref counterparts. You can also update the **Saved Path** property via the **Found at** property on the **Preview/Details** pane in the **External Reference** palette.

*Image Clipping.*    Like xrefs, you can apply clipping boundaries to images. The **IMAGECLIP** command allows you to define and control clipping boundaries associated with images. When you start the **IMAGECLIP** command, the options are identical to the **XCLIP** command.

Image clipping boundaries can be modified directly using grips. When you select a clipped image, AutoCAD displays grips at the corners of the clipping boundary. If the clipping\| boundary is rectangular, moving a grip changes the length and width of the clipping boundary. If the boundary is polygonal, moving a grip will change the shape of clipping boundary.

## Controlling Image Settings

Placing and displaying images can be a somewhat subjective process. The quality, size, and format of raster images can vary widely. AutoCAD provides some tools for controlling and managing raster images.

*Image Quality.*    The **IMAGEQUALITY** command will let you toggle between **Draft** or **High** quality mode. If the large file size of an attached image results in a substantial slowing of Auto-CAD, the **IMAGEQUALITY** command can be set to **Draft** mode. The image will still be visible but at a lower resolution and smaller file size so that performance is improved.

*Controlling Image Frames.*    The **IMAGEFRAME** system variable controls the display of the image outline. If an image is clipped, it controls the display of the clipping boundary. There are three settings for the **IMAGEFRAME** variable: **0, 1,** or **2.** These are described below:

| | |
|---|---|
| 0 | Image frames are not displayed or plotted. |
| 1 | Image frames are both displayed and plotted. |
| 2 | Image frames are displayed but not plotted. |

| Image Quality | |
|---|---|
| **Ribbon & Panel:** | None |
| **Reference Toolbar:** | 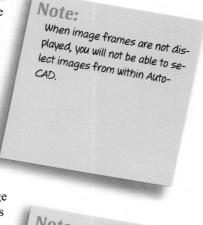 |
| **Menu:** | Modify\| Object\| Image\| Quality |
| **Command Line:** | IMAGEQUALITY |
| **Command Alias:** | None |

*Adjusting Image Brightness, Contrast, and Fade Settings.*
The **IMAGEADJUST** command allows you to set the brightness, contrast, and fade of a raster image. Starting the **IMAGEADJUST** command displays the **Image Adjust** dialog box (see Figure 17-25).

The **Brightness** adjustment changes the brightness of an image. This can range from completely black to completely white.

The **Contrast** adjustment allows you to control the relative difference between dark and light areas of the image.

The **Fade** adjustment allows you to blend the image into the background. Moving the **Fade** control towards the **Max** end will adjust the overall color of the image to match the background color. If AutoCAD's background is set to black, increasing the Fade setting causes the image to fade to black. If the background color is set to white, increasing the Fade setting causes the image to fade to white.

The **Reset** button returns all settings to their original settings.

*Transparency.*    Some image file formats (such as GIF or PNG) support transparent pixels. When using images with transparency, you can turn the transparency on and off with the **TRANSPARENCY** command. When you start the **TRANSPARENCY** command, AutoCAD will prompt you to select image(s) and then allow you to turn transparency **On** or **Off.** If your image file format supports transparency, setting it to **On** will allow objects behind the image to be seen through the transparent pixels in the image.

**Note:**
When image frames are not displayed, you will not be able to select images from within Auto-CAD.

**Note:**
Many of the image settings discussed in the section can also be controlled via the **Image** cascade menu located on the right-click menu displayed when an image is selected, as well as in the **Properties** palette.

| Image Adjust | |
|---|---|
| **Ribbon & Panel:** | None |
| **Reference Toolbar:** | |
| **Menu:** | Modify\| Object\| Image\| Adjust... |
| **Command Line:** | IMAGEADJUST |
| **Command Alias:** | IAD |

| Image Transparency | |
|---|---|
| **Ribbon & Panel:** | None |
| **Reference Toolbar:** | |
| **Menu:** | Modify\| Object\| Image\| Trans-parency |
| **Command Line:** | TRANSPARENCY |
| **Command Alias:** | IAD |

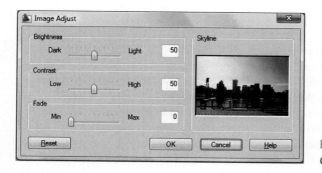

**Figure 17-25**    The Image Adjust dialog box

### Exercise 17-7: Controlling Image Settings

1. Continue from Exercise 17-6.
2. Start the **IMAGECLIP** command. Pick the raster image and select the **New Boundary** option. Select the **Rectangular** option and clip the image as shown in Figure 17-26. Position the image as necessary to match Figure 17-26.
3. Start the **IMAGEADJUST** command. Select the image and press **<Enter ↵>** to open the **Image Adjust** dialog box.
4. Adjust the **Brightness** and **Contrast** settings to your liking. Choose **OK** to close the dialog box.
5. Save your drawing as **EX17-7.**

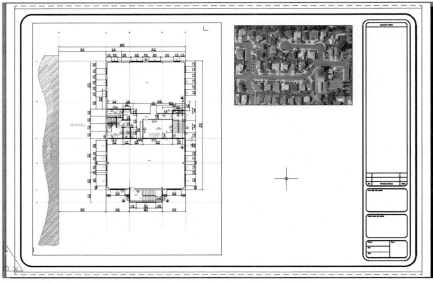

**Figure 17-26**   The clipped image

## WORKING WITH DWF UNDERLAYS

Remember from the beginning of the chapter that the DWF file format is a compressed vector-based drawing file format that allows you to share your drawings with other individuals who should not have access to sensitive, proprietary design information.

It is possible to reference DWF files in a similar fashion as xref drawings and raster images using the **DWF Underlay** feature by specifying a file path, insertion point, scale, and rotation angle.

You can modify the appearance of a DWF underlay after it is attached so that it is possible to change the DWF underlay from color-based to monochrome, adjust its fade and contrast, as well as automatically adjust the DWF colors to match the drawing background. It is also possible to define a clipping boundary to limit the visible area of the DWF underlay in a fashion similar to xrefs and images.

### Attaching DWF Underlays

You can attach a DWF underlay by selecting **Attach DWF...** from the drop-down menu in the **External References** palette explained earlier (see Figure 17-1) or you can bypass the **External References** palette and attach a DWF underlay directly using the **DWFATTACH** command.

Either method displays the **Select DWF File** dialog box shown in Figure 17-27, which allows you to select a DWF file to attach to your drawing. After you select a file and choose **Open,** AutoCAD displays the **Attach DWF Underlay** dialog box shown in Figure 17-28 where you set the type of path along with the **Insertion point, Scale,** and **Rotation** angle. These options are the same as those for the **XREF** command.

| DWF Underlay | |
|---|---|
| **Ribbon & Panel:** | Blocks & References\| Reference ⬚ DWF DWF |
| **Insert Toolbar:** | ⬚ DWF |
| **Menu:** | Insert\| DWF Underlay... |
| **Command Line:** | DWFATTACH |
| **Command Alias:** | None |

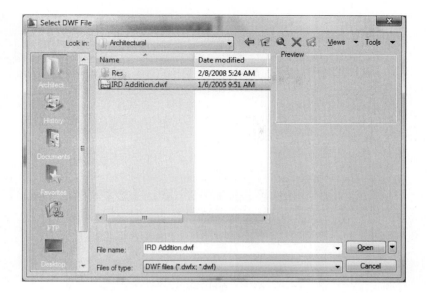

**Figure 17-27**    The Select DWF File dialog box

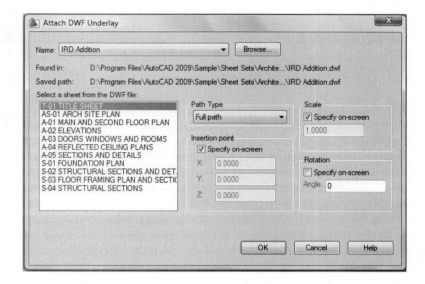

**Figure 17-28**    The Attach DWF Underlay dialog box

If the DWF file consists of multiple sheets, you must select the sheet to attach from the **Select a sheet from the DWF file:** list box on the left.

## Managing DWF Underlays

Once you attach one or more DWF underlays in your drawing, AutoCAD will list the DWF file names, their status, file type, file date, and the saved path to the DWF file in the **External References** palette as shown in Figure 17-29.

Similar to xrefs, most of the DWF underlay options and settings are provided via a right-click shortcut menu similar to the xref shortcut menu shown earlier in Figure 17-11. The DWF underlay options work the same as the xref file options, with a few subtle differences.

Selecting **Open...** from the shortcut menu will open the DWF file using the downloadable Autodesk Design Review software mentioned earlier so that you can view, *but not edit*, the DWF file.

The **Attach...** menu item displays the **Select DWF File** dialog box shown in Figure 17-27 so that you can attach another DWF File; the other DWF underlay options, **Unload, Reload,** and **Detach,** work the same as their xref counterparts.

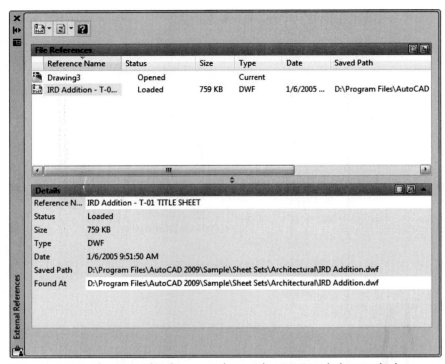

**Figure 17-29**    The External References palette with a DWF Underlay attached

When a DWF file is created, the user has the option of including layer information within the DWF file. This allows people viewing the DWF file to turn layers on and off. People viewing the DWF file cannot control the name, color, linetype, etc., of DWF layers, only the layer visibility.

When you attach a DWF underlay, if the DWF file contains layer information, AutoCAD allows you this same ability. The **DWFLAYERS** command allows you to turn on and off the layers within a DWF file. The **DWFLAYERS** command is also available by selecting a DWF underlay and choosing **DWF Layers...** from the right-click menu.

When you start the **DWFLAYERS** command, AutoCAD will prompt you to select the DWF underlay. If the DWF underlay contains layer information, AutoCAD will display the layer names in the **DWF Layers** dialog box (Figure 17-30). In this dialog box, you can turn DWF layers on and off by clicking the light bulb icon next to each layer. You can select multiple layers by pressing the <Ctrl> or <Shift> key while clicking layer names. You can also turn layers on and off by right-clicking highlighted layers and choosing **Layer(s) On** or **Layer(s) Off** from the right-click menu.

| DWF Layers | |
|---|---|
| **Ribbon & Panel:** | None |
| **Reference Toolbar:** | None |
| **Menu:** | None |
| **Command Line:** | DWFLAYERS |
| **Command Alias:** | None |

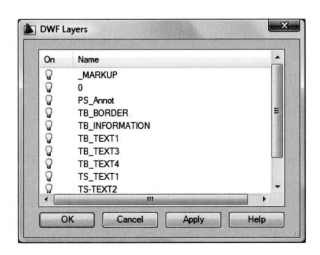

**Figure 17-30**    The DWF Layers dialog box

## DWF Underlay Clipping

Similar to both xrefs and images, you can apply clipping boundaries to DWF underlays. The **DWFCLIP** command allows you to define and control clipping boundaries associated with DWF files. When you start the **DWFCLIP** command, the options are identical to the **XCLIP** and **IMAGECLIP** commands.

| DWF Clip | |
|---|---|
| **Ribbon & Panel:** | None |
| **Toolbar:** | None |
| **Menu:** | None |
| **Command Line:** | DWFCLIP |
| **Command Alias:** | None |

# CONTROLLING DWF UNDERLAY SETTINGS

## Adjusting Fade Effect, Contrast, and Color Settings

The **DWFADJUST** command allows you to set the fade effect, contrast, and whether a DWF underlay is displayed in color or monochrome via a command line interface.

After entering the **DWFADJUST** command, AutoCAD prompts you to Select DWF underlay: so you can select the DWF underlay you want to adjust. After selecting the DWF underlay, you have the following options:

| DWF Adjust | |
|---|---|
| **Ribbon & Panel:** | None |
| **Toolbar:** | None |
| **Menu:** | None |
| **Command Line:** | DWFADJUST |
| **Command Alias:** | None |

* **Fade**   Controls the fade effect of the underlay. Valid settings, are from 0 to 80. The higher the setting, the lighter the linework in the underlay. The lower the setting, the darker the linework. (Default=25)
* **Contrast**   Controls the contrast of the underlay. Values settings are from 0 to 100. The greater the setting, the higher the contrast between dark and light colors, and vice versa. (Default=75)
* **Monochrome**   Toggles the DWF underlay between color display and monochrome display (black and white). (Default=On)

## Controlling DWF Underlay Frames

The **DWFFRAME** system variable controls the display of the DWF underlay outline. If a DWF underlay is clipped, it controls the display of the clipping boundary. There are three settings for the **DWFFRAME** variable: **0, 1,** and **2.** These are described below.

| | |
|---|---|
| **0** | DWF underlay frames are not displayed and are not plotted. |
| **1** | DWF underlay frames are both displayed and plotted. |
| **2** | DWF underlay frames are displayed but not plotted (default). |

## Adjusting Colors for the Current Background

The **Adjust Colors for Background** option controls whether the DWF underlay colors are visible against the current drawing background color. The option is only accessible via the **Properties** palette under the **Underlay Adjust** category.

The default setting of **Yes** forces AutoCAD to analyze the background colors of the DWF underlay and the drawing environment to determine if they are both light or both dark. If necessary, the colors of the DWF underlay are adjusted so the underlay is visible.

If the **Adjust Colors for Background** option is changed to **No,** the original colors of the underlay are always used regardless of the current background color. If you use this setting, the DWF underlay might not always be visible.

**TIP**   The **DWFOSNAP** system variable allows you to control whether object snapping to objects that are part of a DWF file is enabled. Setting **DWFOSNAP** = **1** (default) allows you to snap to DWF underlay objects. Setting **DWFOSNAP** = **0** turns DWF underlay object snaps off.

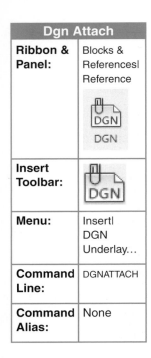

| Dgn Attach | |
|---|---|
| **Ribbon & Panel:** | Blocks & References\| Reference |
| **Insert Toolbar:** | |
| **Menu:** | Insert\| DGN Underlay… |
| **Command Line:** | DGNATTACH |
| **Command Alias:** | None |

# WORKING WITH DGN UNDERLAYS

Similar to the DWF Underlay, AutoCAD supports the referencing of MicroStation V8 DGN design files. Like a DWF underlay, a DGN underlay is a view-only version of the design data contained in the DGN file. DGN underlays are attached in the same way DWF files are, with some slight changes. You can also change the DGN underlay setting just as you do a DWF underlay. However, unlike a DWF underlay, there is currently no way to control layer visibility within a DGN underlay.

## Attaching DGN Underlays

You can attach a DWF underlay by selecting **Attach DGN...** from the drop-down menu in the **External References** palette, or you can bypass the **External References** palette and attach a DGN underlay directly using the **DGNATTACH** command.

Starting the **DGNATTACH** command displays the **Select DGN File** dialog box shown in Figure 17-31. After you select a file and choose **Open,** AutoCAD displays the **Attach DGN Underlay** dialog box shown in Figure 17-32 where you set the type of path along with the **Insertion point, Scale,** and **Rotation** angle. All of these options are the same as with the **XREF** command.

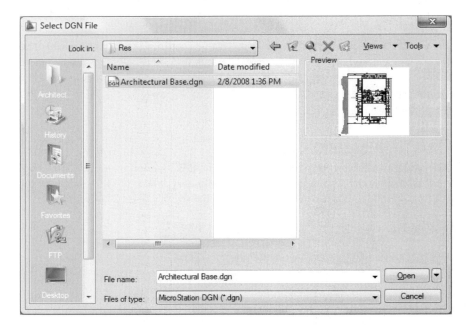

**Figure 17-31**  The Select DGN File dialog box

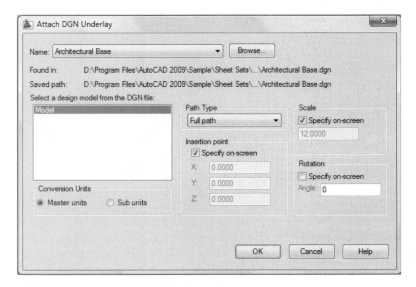

**Figure 17-32**  Attach DGN Underlay dialog box

Unlike AutoCAD, which has only one model design space, DGN files can contain multiple design models. Select the desired design model from the **Select a Design Model from the DGN File** list. Only a single design model can be displayed per underlay. Sheet models within a DGN file (similar to DWF sheets) are not listed.

The **Conversion Units** area of the dialog box allows you to control how units are converted in the DGN file. DGN files use *working units* (imperial or metric) called *master units* and *sub-units*. Some number of sub-units is equal to one master unit. Select the unit you wish to use in your AutoCAD drawing. For example, if master units are set to feet and sub-units are set to inches, then 12 sub-units would equal 1 master unit (feet). Selecting master units in the **Conversion Units** area would convert DGN master units (feet) to AutoCAD's unit of measurement.

The **Insertion Point, Scale,** and **Rotation** settings are the same as those for xrefs and DWF underlays.

*Managing DGN Underlays*    Once you attach one more DGN underlay in your drawing, Auto-CAD will list all of them along with all the other xrefs, images, and DWF underlays in the **External Reference** palette.

Like DWF underlays, the different DGN underlay options and settings are provided via a right-click shortcut menu. The DGN underlay options work exactly the same as their DWF under-lay counterparts with some slight differences.

The **Open...** option from the shortcut menu is not selectable. This is because AutoCAD does not include a DGN file viewer with AutoCAD.

The **Attach...** menu item displays the **Select DGN File** dialog box shown in Figure 17-30 so that you can attach another DGN file; all the other DGN underlay options—**Unload, Reload,** and **Detach**—work exactly the same as their xref counterparts and DWF underlay.

*DGN Underlay Clipping*    Like DWF underlays, you can apply clipping boundaries to DGN un-derlays as well as control the fade effect, contrast, and color display of the DGN underlay. The **DGNCLIP** and **DGNADJUST** commands work just like their DWF underlay counterparts.

Likewise the **DGNOSNAP** and **DGNFRAME** system variables work the same as the **DWFOSNAP** and **DWFFRAME** variables.

# TRANSMITTING DRAWINGS WITH XREFS AND IMAGES

When creating drawings that use referenced drawings or images, it's important to consider what happens to those drawings when they are given to others (clients, contractors, vendors, etc.). When you provide drawings to others, any referenced files must be supplied as well. This can be a difficult task when there are multiple references stored in different locations. The problem is compounded if nested xrefs are used.

Fortunately, AutoCAD provides the **ETRANSMIT** command to help manage these external files. The **ETRANSMIT** command helps solve the problem of sending incomplete files by com-piling all external files into a separate folder or ZIP file. You can also create an email and auto-matically attach the files to the email.

## Using eTRANSMIT

Before using the **ETRANSMIT** command, you need to save any changes to your drawing. If you start the command before you save any changes, AutoCAD will ask you to save the changes be-fore continuing (see Figure 17-33).

*Selecting Files.*    When you start the **ETRANSMIT** command, AutoCAD displays the **Create Transmittal** dialog box (see Figure 17-34). The **Files Tree** tab shows you a hierarchical tree view of your drawing and any files that are associated with it. From this view, you can see the relation-ships of the files and also which files are attached to which.

The **Files Table** tab (see Figure 17-35) shows you a flattened list of all files associated with your drawing. This view does not show file relationships but may be easier to work with because all the files are displayed in a single list.

| DGN Adjust | |
| --- | --- |
| **Ribbon & Panel:** | None |
| **Toolbar:** | None |
| **Menu:** | None |
| **Command Line:** | DGNADJUST |
| **Command Alias:** | None |

| DGN Clip | |
| --- | --- |
| **Ribbon & Panel:** | None |
| **Toolbar:** | None |
| **Menu:** | None |
| **Command Line:** | DGNCLIP |
| **Command Alias:** | None |

| eTransmit | |
| --- | --- |
| **Ribbon & Panel:** | Output\| Send eTransmit |
| **Toolbar:** | None |
| **Menu:** | File\| eTransmit... |
| **Command Line:** | ETRANSMIT |
| **Command Alias:** | None |

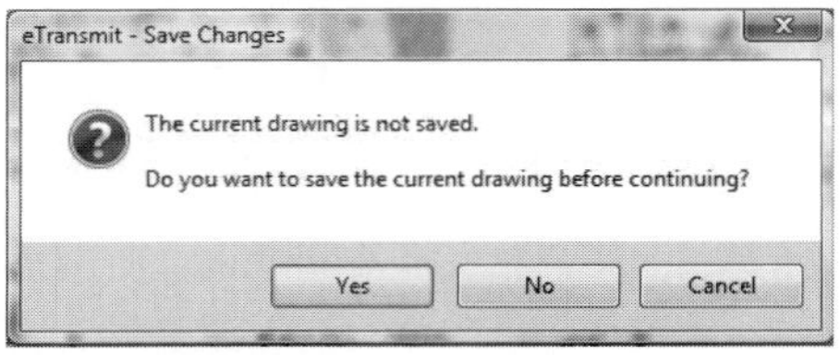

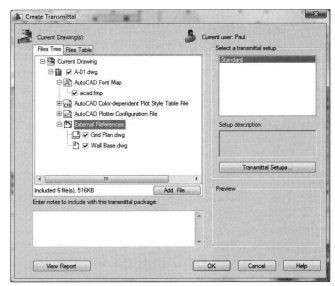

Figure 17-34    The Create Transmittal dialog box

**Figure 17-33**    The Save Changes notification

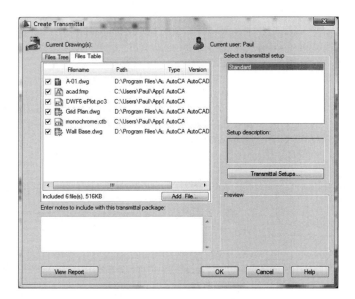

**Figure 17-35**    The Files Table tab

With either view, you can select the files you wish to include in your transmittal by checking or unchecking the box next to the file.

The **Add File...** button allows you to specify additional files you wish to include in your transmittal, such as design specifications, product data sheets, or cover letters.

*The Transmittal Report.*    When you create your transmittal, AutoCAD will create a transmittal report to include with the transmittal. The **View Report** button displays the **View Transmittal Report** dialog box, which shows you a copy of the information that will be included in this report. The **Save As...** button allows you to save this report to a text file. The **Close** button closes the **View Transmittal Report** dialog box.

> **Note:**
> The AutoCAD Font Map is a file that allows AutoCAD to locate and, if necessary, substitute standard AutoCAD fonts for nonstandard font files. If you use nonstandard AutoCAD fonts, you may want to include the Font Map file in your transmittal.

You can add additional information to this report by typing it into the text area above the **View Report** button. Any text typed here will be added to the transmittal report (see Figure 17-36).

## Configuring the Transmittal

A transmittal setup contains all the settings for the transmittal, including which files to include, how the files are organized, and how xrefs are included with the drawing. Multiple transmittal setups can be created and saved. This allows you to create different setups for different clients or needs. When you choose the **Transmittal Setups...** button, AutoCAD displays the **Transmittal Setups** dialog box (see Figure 17-37). This allows you to modify, rename, or delete an existing setup or create a new transmittal setup. Transmittal setups are similar to page setups or dimension styles in that they simply assign a name to a collection of settings.

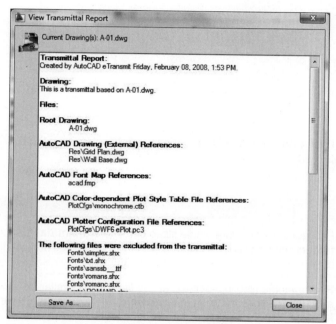

Figure 17-36    The sample transmittal report

Figure 17-37    The Transmittal Setups dialog box

To create a new setup, choose the **New...** button in the **Transmittal Setups** dialog box. This displays the **New Transmittal Setup** dialog box (see Figure 17-38) where you can assign a name to your new transmittal setup. Each new transmittal setup is created from an existing setup. The **Based on:** list allows you to choose which setup to use as a basis for your new setup.

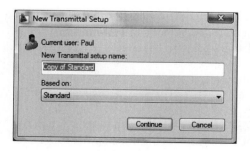

Figure 17-38    The New Transmittal Setup dialog box

Once you create a new setup or choose the **Modify...** button, AutoCAD will display the **Modify Transmittal Setup** dialog box (see Figure 17-39). This dialog box allows you to modify the setting for the transmittal.

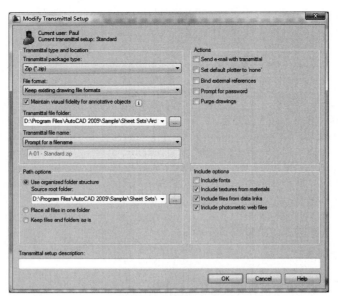

Figure 17-39    The Modify Transmittal Setup dialog box

*Transmittal Settings.*    The **Transmittal package type:** allows you to select how the files will be stored. The options are described below:

| | |
|---|---|
| Folder (Set of Files) | Packages the files in a single file folder. The **Transmittal file folder:** setting specifies the location of the folder. You may want to create a new folder to store the transmittal files. |
| Self-extracting Executable (.exe) | Packages the files in a self-extracting file. This is similar to a zip file but does not require a separate zip program to open the files. The user can simply double-click on the files to open, de-compress, and extract them. |
| Zip (*.zip) | Packages the files in compressed zip file. All files are com-pressed into a single file, which makes them easy to send electronically. Windows XP systems have built-in support for zip files. Earlier versions of Windows way require a zip program such as Winzip. |

The **File format:** option lets you convert AutoCAD 2009 drawings back to the AutoCAD 2007 and 2007 LT, AutoCAD 2004 and 2004 LT, or AutoCAD 2000 and 2000 LT release for-mats. All drawing files and xrefs are converted back to the selected file format prior to packag-ing them.

The **Transmittal file folder:** is the location for the transmitted files. The drop-down list will display the nine previous locations that have been used, or you can choose the **Browse** button to specify a new location.

The **Transmittal file name:** determines the ZIP or EXE file name and tells AutoCAD which method is used for naming. By default, AutoCAD combines the drawing file name with the transmittal setup name. For example, a drawing called **Plan.dwg** using the **Standard** trans-mittal setup with the **Zip** package option would have a transmittal file name called **Plan - Standard.zip.** You can change the default file name by typing a new name in the space below the **Transmittal file name:**. This option is disabled if the **Folder** package type is used. These options are described below:

| Prompt for a file name | This method will prompt you for a file name each time you create a transmittal. The file will be stored in the folder set in the **Transmittal file folder:** setting. |
|---|---|
| Overwrite if necessary | This option will automatically name the file. If that file already exists, AutoCAD will automatically overwrite the existing file. |
| Increment file name if necessary | This option will automatically name the file. If the file already exists, AutoCAD will create a new file name by adding a number to the end of the file name. For example, a Zip file called **Plan - Standard.zip** would be incremented to **Plan - Standard 1.zip**. |

The **Path Options** area allows you to choose how the files are organized within the package. These are described below:

| Use organized folder structure | This method duplicates the folder structure for the files being transmitted. The root folder is the top-level folder for the transmittal. For files that lie within the root folder path, a folder is created for each file's parent folder. Files that are outside the root folder path are placed in the root folder. Other folders are created as needed for fonts and plot configurations. |
|---|---|
| Place all files in one folder | This option places all files in a single folder defined in the **Transmittal file folder:** option. No subfolders are created. |
| Keep files and folders as is | This option replicates the existing folder structure of all the files included in the transmittal. This option works well when you have xrefs or images stored with full paths because it retains the complete folder structure for all files. |

The **Send e-mail with transmittal** option will cause AutoCAD to start a new email message with the transmittal files included as attachments.

The **Set default plotter to 'none'** option changes the default plotter for all model and paper space layouts to **None**. This prevents AutoCAD from trying to communicate with plotters that may not be configured on another user's system.

The **Bind external references** option causes AutoCAD to bind all xrefs in the transmittal drawing file. This means that no xref files are included with the transmittal and that all xrefs are automatically bound before packaging. This does not affect the source drawing file, only the transmittal copy. The advantage of using this option is that the person receiving the transmittal will not have to deal with xref paths or missing files. The disadvantage is that for large or complex drawings, binding xrefs may cause the file size to increase significantly.

The **Prompt for password** option is available only when packaging the transmittal as a ZIP or EXE file. When this option is selected, AutoCAD will password-protect the ZIP or EXE file. When using this option to create the transmittal package, AutoCAD will display the **Transmittal-Set Password** dialog box (see Figure 17-40) that will prompt you for a password and ask you to confirm that password. The recipient of the transmittal package will need to type in the password to gain access to the files.

The **Purge Drawings** option will do a complete purge of all the drawings in the transmittal package.

The **Include options** area allows you to specify whether to include associated fonts, textures from materials, external files referenced by a data link, and photometric web files that are associated with web lights.

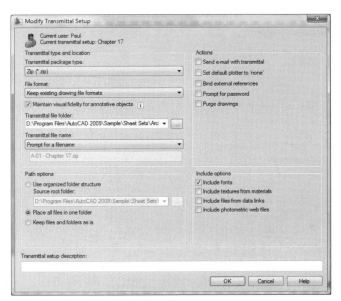

**Figure 17-40**　The Set Password dialog box

**Figure 17-41**　Transmittal settings

## Exercise 17-8: Transmitting Xrefs

1. Continue from Exercise 17-7.
2. Start the **ETRANSMIT** command. If you have any unsaved changes, AutoCAD will ask if you want to save them. Choose **OK** to save any changes.
3. Look at the **Files Tree** and **Files Table** tabs to see which files are going to be included in the transmittal.
4. Choose the **Transmittal setups...** button and choose **New** to create a new transmittal setup. Name the transmittal setup **Chapter 17** and choose **Continue** to continue setting up the transmittal.
5. Set the **Transmittal package type:** to **Zip** and **Keep existing drawing file formats.** Select a location from the **Transmittal file folder:** and choose **Prompt for a filename.**
6. Choose **Place all files in one folder** and **Include fonts**. Turn all other options off. Choose **OK** to save the transmittal setup and **Close** to return to the **Create Transmittal** dialog box. Your settings should be set to match Figure 17-41.
7. Choose **OK** to create the transmittal. Save the transmittal as **EX17-8.**

## SUMMARY

Using xrefs and images allows you to share and update information across multiple drawings with relative ease. This can greatly facilitate the sharing of information in a group environment. Planning and CAD standards are key to successfully using these features, especially in multiuser environments.

One of the challenging aspects of using referenced files is tracking and managing all the files related to a particular drawing. The **ETRANSMIT** command provides an easy way to track and assemble all files associated with a drawing into a single location.

## CHAPTER TEST QUESTIONS

### Multiple Choice

1. One advantage of using xrefs in a team environment is:
   a. The ability to share drawings with team members
   b. The ability to attach drawings to other drawings
   c. The ability to bind drawings to other drawings
   d. All of the above

2. Which of the following statements best defines an xref?
   a. A drawing that is independent of all other drawings
   b. A drawing attached to the current or host drawing with a link back to the original drawing
   c. A drawing that can bind only to the current drawing
   d. All of the above

3. Which of the following are commonly used options when attaching an xref?

   a. Attach and Bind
   b. Block and Insert
   c. Cut and Paste
   d. None of the above

4. The insertion point of an xref from the **External Reference** dialog box can be which of the following options?

   a. Fix-and-place at origin
   b. Drag-and-drop
   c. Cut-and-paste
   d. Specify on-screen or *X, Y,* and *Z* coordinate specification

5. Which of the following are options of the **Attach** option?

   a. Scale
   b. Rotation
   c. Block unit
   d. All of the above

6. Why would "Reload" be needed when using xrefs?

   a. To lock changes out of the current drawing
   b. To check updates to a current attached drawing
   c. To bind changes to a current drawing
   d. All of the above

7. Binding an attached xref drawing will:

   a. Isolate the drawing from any more updates
   b. Make the attached drawing more editable
   c. Bind it somewhat permanently to the current drawing
   d. All of the above

8. Which of the following is true when using the **Open** option in the **External References** palette?

   a. Opens a new drawing to attach to the current drawing
   b. Opens the xref drawing in a new drawing window
   c. Opens only current layers in an xref
   d. All of the above

9. Which bind-type option will bind named xref objects such as layers, linetypes, and textstyles, and not rename them with the xref name and a "$0$" prefix?

   a. Bind option
   b. Insert option
   c. Setting **BINDTYPE** system variable to **0**
   d. None of the above

10. The **XOPEN** command is used for:

    a. Opening a deleted drawing
    b. Opening a new drawing
    c. Directly opening an attached xref
    d. All of the above

11. The **XBIND** command is used for:

    a. Adding or removing individual dependent definitions from the xrefed drawing to the host drawing.
    b. Managing xref layer settings.
    c. Adding or removing layers definitions to the current host drawing.
    d. All of the above

12. Options on the **REFEDIT** toolbar include:

    a. Edit in place
    b. Add to working set
    c. Remove from working set
    d. All of the above

13. The purpose of clipping an xref would be to:

    a. Clip out unused layers
    b. Clip out part of the displayed xref
    c. Trim portions of the host drawing
    d. All of the above

14. An eTransmit report contains the following information:

    a. Date and drawing name
    b. File paths and xref file paths
    c. Any excluded files
    d. All of the above

15. eTransmit files can be which of the following?

    a. .exe (self-extracting executable files)
    b. .ZIP (zip files)
    c. Folder (set of files)
    d. All of the above

16. Why would "demand loading" be applied to xrefs?

    a. To automatically load your drawing when AutoCAD is opened
    b. To speed up AutoCAD and make it run more efficiently
    c. To block others from using your xrefs
    d. All of the above

17. Why would raster images be applied to a drawing?

    a. To provide a company logo background image
    b. To provide location points for satellite topographical drawings
    c. To trace shapes or profiles
    d. All of the above

18. Which of the following is an option when applying a raster image?

    a. Scale
    b. Rotation
    c. Insertion point
    d. All of the above

19. Reloading an image would be for what benefit?

    a. To block further changes to the drawing
    b. To restrict uploading of the image
    c. To update any changes that may have been done to the image
    d. All of the above

20. What "details" can be adjusted or included in an image?

    a. Brightness
    b. Resolution
    c. The image frame
    d. All of the above

## Matching

| Column A | Column B |
|---|---|

**Column A**

a. **External Reference**

b. **ETRANSMIT**

c. **IMAGEATTACH**

d. **XCLIP**

e. **REFEDIT**

f. **XATTACH**

g. **XBIND**

h. **IMAGEADJUST**

i. **XOPEN**

j. **IMAGEQUALITY**

**Column B**

1. Displays the **Select Image File** dialog box

2. Bypasses the **External Reference** palette and directly attaches an xref

3. A reference to a drawing file that retains a link back to the original drawing file

4. Opens an attached xref directly in your current drawing

5. Packages drawing and dependent files for file transfer

6. Binds individual named object definitions from an xref drawing

7. Toggles an image between draft and high-quality mode

8. Opens a referenced drawing in a new drawing window

9. Sets contrast, brightness, and fade on an attached image

10. Crops an external reference to a defined boundary

## True or False

1. True or False: Changes to "attached" drawings are not shown on the host drawing.

2. True or False: Changes to "bound" drawings are not shown on the host drawing.

3. True or False: Using overlay will cause the drawing to not be included if the host drawing is xrefed to another drawing or nested drawing.

4. True or False: The **Open** option, while using xrefs, allows editing of the attached drawing.

5. True or False: "Detach" removes an xref attached drawing.

6. True or False: "Binding" an xref provides an update link to the original drawing.

7. True or False: "Reloading" an xref is done to remove any changes made to the attached drawing.

8. True or False: Layers can be included in attached drawings.

9. True or False: When binding an xref, named objects such as layers, linetypes, and textstyles are always renamed by prefixing the named object with the xref file name followed by "$0$".

10. True or False: **XCLIP** can be used to "clip out" part of the displayed xref.

11. True or False: eTransmit can also provide a report and other files along with the drawing file to be transmitted.

12. True or False: Zip format drawing files cannot be sent with the eTransmit option.

13. True or False: The "FTP" protocol can be used to transfer files with eTransmit.

14. True or False: With Demand loading, "Enabled with Copy" lets others use your drawing while you continue to edit it.

15. True or False: While attaching an image onto the current drawing, you can enter only the X, Y, and Z coordinates to place the image.

16. True or False: The resolution can be adjusted on an attached image on your AutoCAD drawing.

17. True or False: Image quality cannot be adjusted on an attached image on your AutoCAD drawing.

18. True or False: The brightness of an image is adjusted with the **IMAGEADJUST** command.

19. True or False: The contrast of an image is adjusted with the **IMAGEADJUST** command.

20. True or False: The rotation of an image is adjusted with the **IMAGEADJUST** command.

## CHAPTER PROJECTS

### Project 17-1: Classroom Plan—Continued from Chapter 16

1. Open drawing **P16-1**.

2. Switch to the **Architectural Title Block** layout. Attach the drawing **Architectural D-Size.dwg** created in Chapter 16 as an overlay xref. Place the xref at the coordinates **-.75,-.5**.

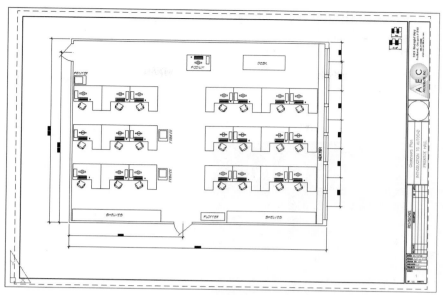

Figure P17-1

3. Insert the drawing **Title Attributes D-Size.dwg** as a block. Use an insertion point of **-.5,.25.** Fill in appropriate values for the attributes. Your drawing should resemble Figure P17-1.
4. Save your drawing as **P17-1.**

## Project 17-2: Motorcycle—Continued from Chapter 15

1. Open drawing **P14-2.**
2. Select the **Model** button to switch to model space.
3. Attach the raster image file **Skyline.jpg** from the Student CD.
4. Resize and move the image file as necessary so it looks similar to Figure P17-2.
5. Change the draw order of the image so it is behind the motorcycle.
6. Use the **Properties** palette to change the Fade property to 50%.
7. Select the **Layout1** layout to make it current.
8. Save the drawing as **P17-2.**

Figure P17-2

## Project 17-3A: Logo—Continued from Chapter 11

1. Open drawing **P11-3D.** Move the geometry so the lower left corner of the logo is located at 0,0.
2. Scale the logo so the height is **.375** as shown in Figure P17-3A.
3. Save the drawing as **PH-Logo.**

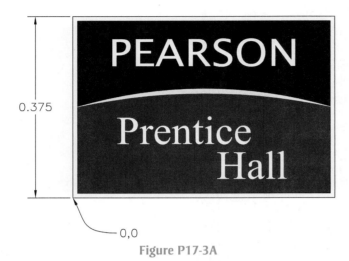

0.375

0,0

Figure P17-3A

## Project 17-3B: B-Size Mechanical Border—Continued from Chapter 16

1. Open the template file **Mechanical B-Size.DWT.**
2. Set the **Mechanical B-Size** layout current and attach the drawing **PH-Logo** as an overlay reference. Place the drawing as shown in Figure P17-3B.

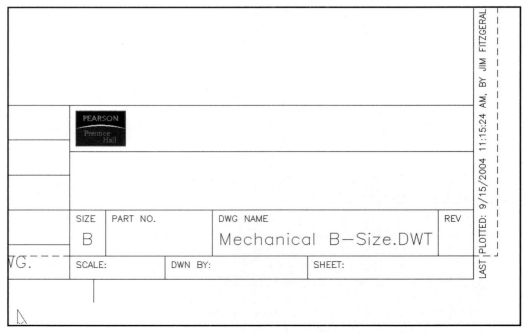

Figure P17-3B

3. Switch to the **Metric Mechanical B-Size** layout and attach the drawing **PH-Logo** as an overlay reference. Set a uniform scale of **25.4** and place the logo as shown in Figure P17-3B.
4. Save the drawing as **Mechanical B-Size.DWT.**
5. Open the **Mechanical B-Size.DWG.**
6. Attach the drawing **PH-Logo** as an overlay reference. Place the drawing as shown in Figure P17-3B.
7. Save the drawing as **Mechanical B-Size.DWG.**

## Project 17-3C: C-Size Mechanical Border—Continued from Chapter 16

1. Open the template file **Mechanical C-Size.DWT.**
2. Set the **Mechanical C-Size** layout current and attach the drawing **PH-Logo** as an overlay reference. Place the drawing as shown in Figure P17-3C. Scale as necessary.
3. Save the drawing as **Mechanical C-Size.DWT.**
4. Open the **Mechanical C-Size.DWG.**
5. Attach the drawing **PH-Logo** as an overlay reference. Place the drawing as shown in Figure P17-3C.
6. Save the drawing as **Mechanical C-Size.DWG.**

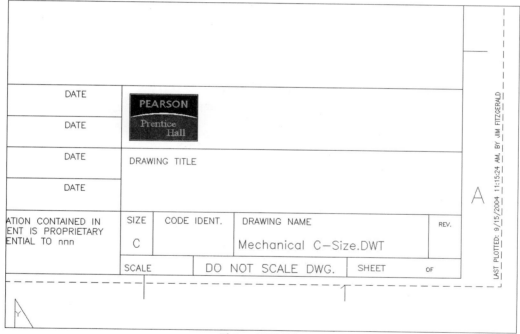

Figure P17-3C

## Project 17-3D: A-Size Portrait Mechanical Border—Continued from Chapter 16

1. Open the template file **Mechanical A-Size-Portrait.DWT.**
2. Set the **Mechanical A-Size-Portrait** layout current and attach the drawing **PH-Logo** as an overlay reference. Place the drawing as shown in Figure P17-3D.
3. Save the drawing as **Mechanical A-Size-Portrait.DWT.**
4. Open the **Mechanical A-Size-Portrait.DWG.**
5. Attach the drawing **PH-Logo** as an overlay reference. Place the drawing as shown in Figure 17-3D.
6. Save the drawing as **Mechanical A-Size-Portrait.DWG.**

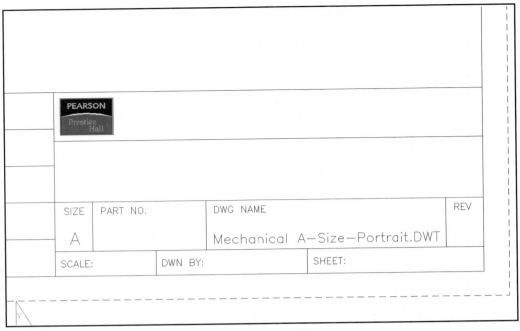

Figure P17-3D

## Project 17-4A: Architectural D-Size Border—Continued from Chapter 16

1. Start a new drawing using the **acad.dwt** template.
2. Create the architect's professional seal shown in Figure P17-4 as follows:
   a. All information should be drawn on layer **0.**
   b. Use the **DONUT** command to create a donut at 0,0 with an inside diameter of **1.70″** and an outside diameter of **1.75″.**

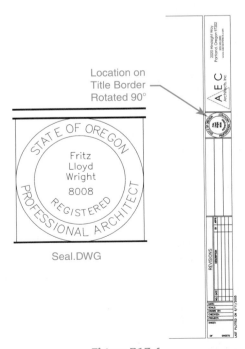

Figure P17-4

   c. Use the **CIRCLE** command to create the inside circle with
      a diameter of **1.25″**.

   d. Use the **TEXT** command to create all text as single-line
      text. Outside curved text is **0.125″** high. Inside text is
      **0.093″**.

   e. Save the drawing as **Seal.DWG**.

3. Open the template file **Architectural D-Size.DWT**.

4. Attach the architect's professional seal drawing created above
   (**Seal.DWG**) as an external reference at the center of the title
   border circle as shown in Figure P17-4 so that it is rotated **90°**.

5. Save the drawing to a template file as **Architectural
   D-Size.DWT**.

6. Open the D-size title border drawing file **Architectural
   D-Size.DWG**.

7. Attach the architect's professional seal drawing created above
   (**Seal.DWG**) as an external reference at the center of the title
   border circle as shown in Figure P17-4 so that it is rotated
   **90°**.

8. Save the **Architectural D-Size.DWG** drawing file.

## Project 17-4B: Architectural B-Size Border—Continued from Chapter 16

1. Open the template file **Architectural B-Size.DWT**.

2. Attach the architect's professional seal drawing created above
   (**Seal.DWG**) as an external reference at the center of the title
   border circle similar to that shown in Figure P17-4. Xref does
   *not* need to be rotated in this drawing.

3. Save the drawing to a template file as **Architectural
   B-Size.DWT**.

4. Open the B-size title border drawing file **Architectural
   B-Size.DWG**.

5. Attach the architect's professional seal drawing created above
   (**Seal.DWG**) as an external reference at the center of the title
   border circle similar to as shown in Figure P17-4. Xref does
   *not* need to be rotated in this drawing.

6. Save the **Architectural B-Size.DWG** drawing file.

## Project 17-5: Electrical Schematic—Continued from Chapter 16

1. Open drawing **Electrical Plan.dwg**.

2. In model space, attach the drawing **Architectural Plan.dwg**
   as an overlay xref. Place the reference at **0,0** at a scale of **1** and
   a rotation angle of **0**.

3. Set the color of the layers associated with the **Architectural
   Plan** xref to **9**.

4. Switch to the **Architectural D-Size** layout. Erase the existing
   title block geometry, leaving only the viewport.

5. Attach the drawing **Architectural D-Size.DWG** as an overlay
   xref. Place the reference at **0,0** at a scale of **1** and a rotation
   angle of **0**.

6. Insert the drawing **Title Attributes D-Size.dwg** as a block.
   Place the block at **0,0** at a scale of **1** and a rotation angle of **0**.
   Enter appropriate values for the title block attributes. Your
   drawing should look like Figure P17-5.

7. Save the drawing as **Electrical Plan.dwg**.

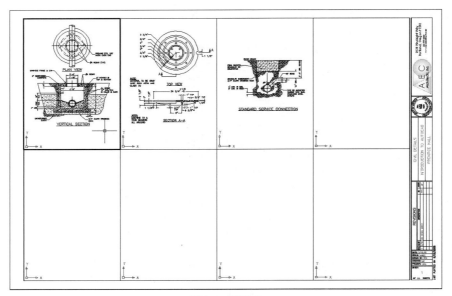

Figure P17-5

## Project 17-6: Piping Schematics Sheet

1. Start a new drawing using the **acad.dwt** template.
2. Select the **Layout1** layout to make it current.
3. Use the **Page Setup Manager** to set the associated plotter to **None** and the paper size to **ARCH D (36.00 × 24.00 Inches).**
4. Attach the **Architectural D-Size.dwg** title block drawing from Problem P17-4A as an external reference file at **0,0,0** in paper space.
5. Rename the **Layout1** tab to **Piping Schematics** and delete the **Layout2** layout.
6. Create eight equal viewports as shown in Figure P17-6.
7. Select the **Model** tab to switch to model space.
8. Attach the project drawings **P14-6A.DWG, P14-6B.DWG, P14-6C.DWG** and **P14-6D.DWG** as external reference files anywhere in model space so that you can see all four drawings.

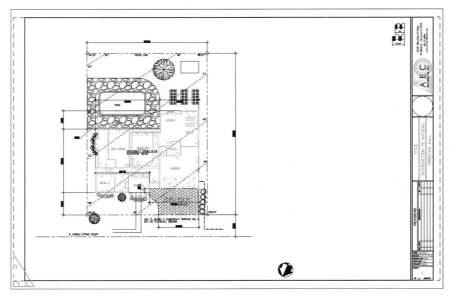

Figure P17-6

9. Select the **Piping Schematics** tab to switch back to paper space.
10. Make the top left viewport current and set its viewport scale to 1:2.
11. Pan the display so that the **HOT WATER PIPING SCHEMATIC** is centered in the view as shown in Figure P17-6.
12. Make the second top viewport current and set its viewport scale to 1:2.
13. Pan the display so that the **GAS WATER HEATER** is centered in the view as shown in Figure P17-6.
14. Make the third top viewport current and set its viewport scale to 1:2.
15. Pan the display so that the **COMPRESSED AIR SYSTEM** is centered in the view as shown in Figure P17-6.
16. Make the fourth top viewport current and set its viewport scale to 1:2.
17. Pan the display so that the **TYPICAL UNIT HEATER CONNECTIONS** is centered in the view as shown in Figure P17-6.
18. Switch back to paper space by double-clicking outside of the viewport in the layout.
19. Insert the **Title Attributes Architectural D-Size.dwg** block at **(0,0)**, set the first line of the title to "PIPING SCHEMATICS," and update all the other attributes appropriately.
20. Insert the **Revision Block - Architectural.dwg** block on the first revision line, set the revision description to "NEW SCHEMATIC SHEET," and update all of the other attributes appropriately.
21. Save the drawing as **P17-6.**

## Project 17-7: Architectural Plan—Continued from Chapter 16

1. Open drawing **Architectural Plan.dwg.**
2. Switch to the **Architectural D-Size** layout. Erase the existing title block geometry, leaving only the viewport.
3. Attach the drawing **Architectural D-Size.DWG** as an overlay xref. Place the reference at **0,0** at a scale of **1** and a rotation angle of **0.**
4. Insert the drawing **Title Attributes D-Size.dwg** as a block. Place the block at **0,0** at a scale of **1** and a rotation angle of **0.** Enter appropriate values for the title block attributes. Your drawing should look like Figure P17-7.
5. Save the drawing as **Architectural Plan.dwg.**

## Project 17-8: Architectural Detail Sheet

1. Start a new drawing using the **acad.dwt** template.
2. Select the **Layout1** layout to make it current.
3. Use the **Page Setup Manager** to set the associated plotter to **None** and the paper size to **ARCH D (36.00 × 24.00 Inches).**
4. Attach the **Architectural D-Size.dwg** title block drawing from Problem P17-4 as an external reference file at **0,0,0** in paper space.
5. Rename the **Layout1** tab to **Architectural Details** and delete the **Layout2** layout.
6. Create eight equal viewports as shown in Figure P17-8.

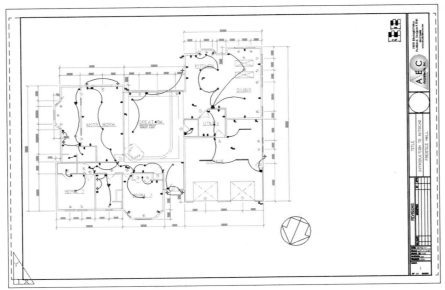

Figure P17-7

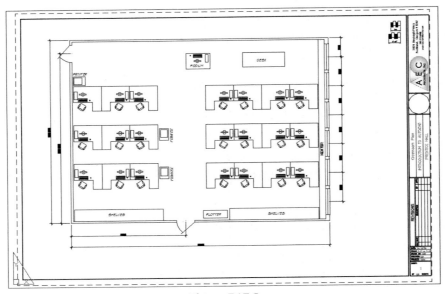

Figure P17-8

7. Select the **Model** button to switch to model space.
8. Attach the project drawings **P14-8A.DWG, P14-8B.DWG,** and **P14-8C.DWG** as external reference files anywhere in model space so that you can see all three drawings.
9. Select the **Architectural Details** tab to switch back to paper space.
10. Make the top left viewport current and set its viewport scale to ½″ = **1′ -0″**.
11. Pan the display so that the **JOIST FOUNDATION DETAIL (1/A101)** is centered in the view as shown in Figure P17-8.
12. Make the second top viewport current and set its viewport scale to ½″ = **1′ -0′**.
13. Pan the display so that the **INTERIOR FLOOR CHANGE DETAIL (2/A101)** is centered in the view as shown in Figure P17-8.

14. Make the third top viewport current and set its viewport scale to **1/2″ = 1′ −0″**.

15. Pan the display so that the **TRUSS W/SOFFITED EAVE DETAIL (3/A101)** is centered in the view as shown in Figure P17-8.

16. Switch back to paper space by double-clicking outside all the viewports in the layout.

17. Insert the **Title Attributes Architectural D-Size.dwg** block at **(0,0),** set the 1st line of the title to "ARCHITECTURAL DETAILS," and update all the other attributes appropriately.

18. Insert the **Revision Block - Architectural.dwg** block on the first revision line, set the revision description to "NEW DETAIL SHEET," and update all the other attributes appropriately.

19. Save the drawing as **P17-8.**

## Project 17-9: Optical Mount—English Units— Continued from Chapter 14

1. Open drawing **P14-9.**
2. Switch to the **Mechanical B-Size** layout. Erase the existing title block geometry, leaving only the viewport.
3. Attach the drawing **Mechanical B-Size.DWG** as an overlay xref. Place the reference at **0,0** at a scale of **1** and a rotation angle of **0.**
4. Insert the drawing **Title Attributes Mechanical B-Size.dwg** as a block. Place the block at **0,0** at a scale of **1** and a rotation angle of **0.** Enter appropriate values for the title block attributes. Your drawing should look like Figure P17-9.
5. Save the drawing as **P17-9.dwg.**

## Project 17-10A: Gasket—Continued from Chapter 14

1. Open drawing **P14-10A.**
2. Select the **Metric Mechanical B-Size** layout to make it current.
3. Erase all the title border information except the polygonal viewport.

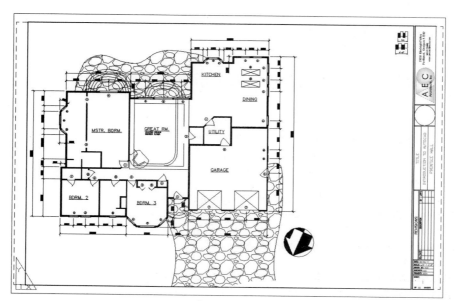

**Figure P17-9**

4. Attach the **Mechanical B-Size.DWG** title block drawing from Problem P16-3A as an external reference file at **0,0,0** in paper space. The title block should scale automatically using the insert units. If it does not scale, you must set the *X*, *Y*, and *Z* scale factors to **25.4.**

5. Insert the **Title Attributes Mechanical B-Size.dwg** block at **0,0,0** and update the attributes accordingly.

6. Save the drawing as **P17-10A.**

## Project 17-10B: Widget—Continued from Chapter 14

1. Open drawing **P14-10B.**
2. Select the **Metric Mechanical B-Size** layout to make it current.
3. Erase all the title border information except the polygonal viewport.
4. Attach the **Mechanical B-Size.DWG** title block drawing from Problem P16-3A as an external reference file at 0,0,0 in paper space. The title block should scale automatically using the insert units. If it does not scale, you must set the *X*, *Y*, and *Z* scale factors to **25.4.**
5. Insert the **Title Attributes Mechanical B-Size.dwg** block at **0,0,0** and update the attributes accordingly.
6. Save the drawing as **P17-10B.**

## Project 17-10C: Hex Head Bolts and Nuts—Continued from Chapter 14

1. Open drawing **P14-10C.**
2. Select the **Metric Mechanical B-Size** layout to make it current.
3. Erase all the title border information except the polygonal viewport.
4. Attach the **Mechanical B-Size.DWG** title block drawing from Problem P16-3A as an external reference file at **0,0,0** in paper space. The title block should scale automatically using the insert units. If it does not scale, you must set the *X*, *Y*, and *Z* scale factors to **25.4.**
5. Insert the **Title Attributes Mechanical B-Size.dwg** block at **0,0,0** and update the attributes accordingly.
6. Save the drawing as **P17-10C.**

## Project 17-10D: Motorcycle Head Gasket—Continued from Chapter 14

1. Open drawing **P14-10D.**
2. Select the **Metric Mechanical B-Size** layout to make it current.
3. Erase all the title border information except the polygonal viewport.
4. Attach the **Mechanical B-Size.DWG** title block drawing from Problem P16-3A as an external reference file at **0,0,0** in paper space. The title block should scale automatically using the insert units. If it does not scale, you must set the *X*, *Y*, and *Z* scale factors to **25.4.**
5. Insert the **Title Attributes Mechanical B-Size.dwg** block at **0,0,0** and update the attributes accordingly.
6. Save the drawing as **P17-10D.**

## Project 17-10E: 68-Tooth Motorcycle Sprocket—Continued from Chapter 14

1. Open drawing **P14-10E.**
2. Select the **Metric Mechanical B-Size** layout to make it current.
3. Erase all the title border information except the polygonal viewport.
4. Attach the **Mechanical B-Size.DWG** title block drawing from Problem P16-3A as an external reference file at **0,0,0** in paper space. The title block should scale automatically using the insert units. If it does not scale, you must set the *X, Y,* and *Z* scale factors to **25.4.**
5. Insert the **Title Attributes Mechanical B-Size.dwg** block at **0,0,0** and update the attributes accordingly.
6. Save the drawing as **P17-10E.**

## Project 17-10F: Window Extrusion—Continued from Chapter 14

1. Open drawing **P14-10F.**
2. Select the **Metric Mechanical B-Size** layout to make it current.
3. Erase all the title border information except the polygonal viewport.
4. Attach the **Mechanical B-Size.DWG** title block drawing from Problem P16-3A as an external reference file at **0,0,0** in paper space. The title block should scale automatically using the insert units. If it does not scale, you must set the *X, Y,* and *Z* scale factors to **25.4.**
5. Insert the **Title Attributes Mechanical B-Size.dwg** block at **0,0,0** and update the attributes accordingly.
6. Save the drawing as **P17-10F.**

## Project 17-10G: Hub—Continued from Chapter 14

1. Open drawing **P14-10G.**
2. Select the **Metric Mechanical B-Size** layout to make it current.
3. Erase all the title border information except the polygonal viewport.
4. Attach the **Mechanical B-Size.DWG** title block drawing from Problem P16-3A as an external reference file at **0,0,0** in paper space. The title block should scale automatically using the insert units. If it does not scale, you must set the *X, Y,* and *Z* scale factors to **25.4.**
5. Insert the **Title Attributes Mechanical B-Size.dwg** block at **0,0,0** and update the attributes accordingly.
6. Save the drawing as **P17-10G.**

## Project 17-11: Civil Site Plan—Continued from Chapter 16

1. Open drawing **EX16-11.**
2. In model space, attach the drawing **Architectural Plan.dwg** as an overlay xref. Align the reference to the building outline at a scale of **1** and a rotation angle of **E (0).**
3. Set the color of the layers associated with the **Architectural Plan** xref to **9.**

4. Switch to the **Architectural D-Size** layout. Erase the existing title block geometry, leaving only the viewport.

5. Attach the drawing **Architectural D-Size.DWG** as an overlay xref. Place the reference at **0,0** at a scale of **1** and a rotation angle of **0.**

6. Insert the drawing **Title Attributes D-Size.dwg** as a block. Place the block at **0,0** at a scale of **1** and a rotation angle of **0.** Enter appropriate values for the title block attributes. Your drawing should look like Figure P17-11.

7. Save the drawing as **Civil Plan.dwg.**

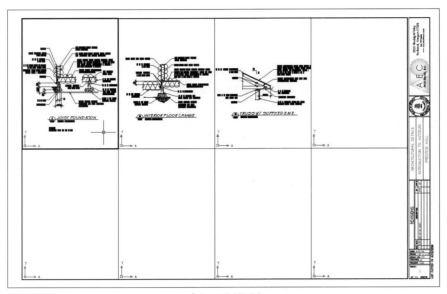

**Figure P17-11**

## Project 17-12: Civil Detail Sheet

1. Start a new drawing using the **acad.dwt** template.

2. Select the **Layout1** layout to make it current.

3. Use the **Page Setup Manager** to set the associated plotter to **None** and the paper size to **ARCH D (36.00 × 24.00 Inches).**

4. Attach the **Architectural D-Size.dwg** title block drawing from Problem P17-4A as an external reference file at **0,0,0** in paper space.

5. Rename the **Layout1** tab **Civil Details** and delete the **Layout2** layout.

6. Create eight equal viewports as shown in Figure P17-12.

7. Select the **Model** button to switch to model space.

8. Attach the project drawings **P14-12A.DWG, P14-12B.DWG,** and **P14-12C.DWG** as external reference files anywhere in model space so that you can see all three drawings.

9. Select the **Civil Details** tab to switch back to paper space.

10. Make the top left viewport current and set its viewport scale to **1:20**.

11. Pan the display so that the **MANHOLE DETAIL** is centered in the view as shown in Figure P17-12.

12. Make the second top viewport current and set its viewport scale to **1:5** using the **ZOOM** command to zoom **1/5XP.**

13. Pan the display so that the **MANHOLE COVER** is centered in the view as shown in Figure P17-12.

14. Make the third top viewport current and set its viewport scale to **1:20**.

15. Pan the display so that the **STANDARD SERVICE CONNECTION** is centered in the view as shown in Figure P17-12.

16. Switch back to paper space by double-clicking outside all the viewports in the layout.

17. Insert the **Title Attributes Architectural D-Size.dwg** block at **(0,0),** set the first line of the title to "CIVIL DETAILS," and update all the other attributes appropriately.

18. Insert the **Revision Block - Architectural.dwg** block on the first revision line, set the revision description to "NEW DETAIL SHEET," and update all the other attributes appropriately.

19. Save the drawing as **P17-12.**

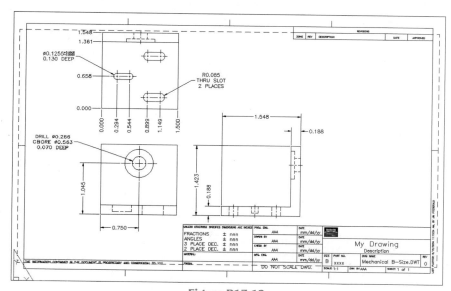

**Figure P17-12**

# File Management and Object Linking and Embedding

18

## Chapter Objectives

- Understand the backup and AutoSave settings
- Fix a corrupt drawing
- Purge a drawing
- Import and export different drawing file types
- Copy and paste information between different software applications
- Using Object Linking and Embedding objects in AutoCAD drawings

## INTRODUCTION

Successful AutoCAD file management requires thorough attention to drawing file creation, maintenance, saving, and naming conventions. File management also includes addressing corrupt drawing files, importing and exporting various CAD drawing formats as well as combining and sharing data using the Windows clipboard feature or Object Linking and Embedding (OLE). In this chapter, we will examine the AutoCAD Drawing Utilities and additional file management procedures to use when different source applications are needed to increase productivity.

## DRAWING FILE BACKUP AND RECOVERY

Anyone who has used a computer has undoubtedly experienced computer problems. Operating systems that lock up, programs that stop responding, viruses, power outages, and equipment failures are a routine part of working with computers. How do you protect your drawings which represent many hours of valuable work? For starters, safe computing practices such as regular backups, up-to-date anti-virus and anti-spyware software scans, and routine computer maintenance can greatly reduce the risk of data loss. AutoCAD offers some additional ways of backing up your design data as well as some tools to help monitor file integrity and recover lost design data.

### File Safety Precautions

The **File Safety Precautions** area of the **Open and Save** tab on the **Options** dialog box allows you to control some of these backup and file recovery options (Figure 18-1).

*Backup Files.* By default, when you save a drawing in AutoCAD, the file is saved with a DWG file extension. The previously saved version of that drawing is renamed with a BAK file extension. For example, you have a drawing called A-06.DWG. When you open that drawing, make changes to it, and then save your drawing, the previously saved file is renamed A-06.BAK, and the new changes are saved to A-06.DWG. If a BAK file already exists, it is overwritten with the new BAK file.

If you are unable to open your current drawing, or if you need to recover changes made to your drawing, you can simply rename the BAK file extension to DWG and open the backup file

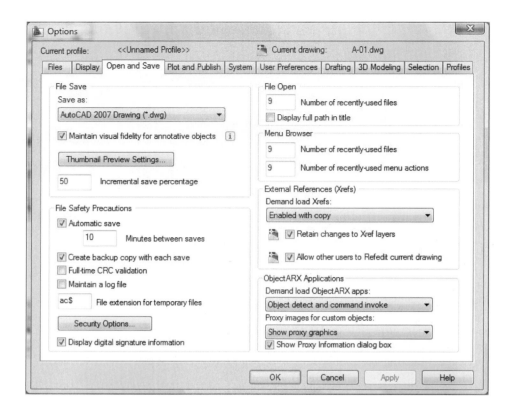

**Figure 18-1** The Open and Save tab on the Options dialog box

in AutoCAD. You may want to change the file name as well to avoid confusion. For example, you have two files: A-06.BAK and A-06.DWG. You wish to open the BAK file to recover some objects you deleted. To avoid confusing the two files, you can rename the BAK file to A-06-Backup.DWG and then open the backup file in AutoCAD.

By default, AutoCAD has backup files enabled. To disable the backup file creation, remove the check from the **Create backup copy with each save** box in the **Open and Save** tab on the **Options** dialog box (Figure 18-1).

***Autosave Files.*** Backup files (BAK) are created only when you save your drawing. For this reason, it's considered good practice to save your drawing often. However, there are times when AutoCAD, quits before you have the opportunity to save. To help recover from these instances, AutoCAD can automatically save your drawing file at regular intervals. This is known as an ***autosave***. By default, AutoCAD does this every 10 minutes.

autosave: The practice of AutoCAD automatically saving your drawing at regular intervals. The default save interval is 10 minutes.

Files created with the **Autosave** feature are considered temporary files. When AutoCAD performs an autosave, it assigns a name consisting of the file name combined with a random number and the file extension .SV$. These files are placed in the **Windows Temp** folder and are created as a failsafe to recover drawing information in the event of a program failure or power failure. If your drawing is closed normally, these temporary save files are deleted. If the drawing does not close normally, the temporary files are retained and can be renamed and opened in AutoCAD.

When you start a command, AutoCAD looks at the time since the last autosave was done. If the time is greater than the autosave interval, AutoCAD will do an autosave before it starts your command. AutoCAD displays a message when it is performing an automatic save while you are working. Following is an example:

```
Automatic save to C:\DOCUME~1\JIMFIT~1\LOCALS~1\Temp\
Drawing1_1_1_0372.sv$ ...
```

If you do not see a message from AutoCAD, you should check that the **Autosave** feature is enabled and that a reasonable save interval is set. You can set this in the **Automatic save** box in the **Open and Save** tab on the **Options** dialog box (Figure 18-1). The **Automatic Save File Location** setting in the **Files** tab on the **Options** dialog box allows you to change the location where the files are saved.

*Temporary Files.*    In addition to the autosave files, AutoCAD also creates temporary files in the **Windows Temp** folder. These temporary files are used by AutoCAD and Windows to manage data while your drawing file is open. These keep track of Undo and Redo information as well as store changes to your drawing in between saves. These files are given a random name with a .AC$ file extension.

Like the autosave files (.sv$) when a drawing is closed normally, these temporary files are deleted. However, if a drawing is not closed properly, these temporary files are retained. They can also be renamed as .DWG and opened in AutoCAD. Since these files are randomly named, finding the exact file you are looking for can be hit-and-miss. Also, there is no guarantee that the information you're seeking will be contained in these files, but it does give you some additional places to look if you lose valuable design information.

The **File extension for temporary files** box in the **Open and Save** tab on the **Options** dialog box (Figure 18-1) allows you to change the file extension of these temporary files. Also, the **Temporary Drawing File Location** setting in the **Files** tab on the **Options** dialog box allows you to change the location where these temporary files are stored (Figure 18-2).

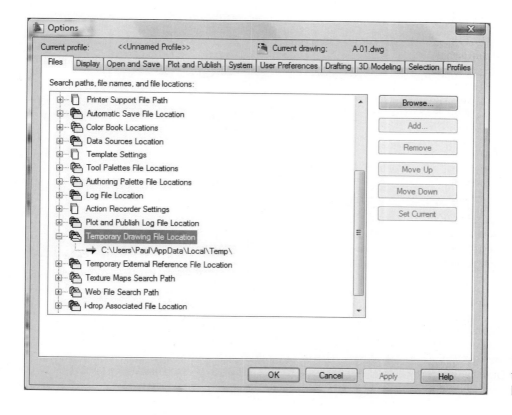

**Figure 18-2**    The Files tab on the Options dialog box

*Corrupt Drawing Objects.*    Drawing corruption can occur when a drawing object is not defined properly within the drawing file. This can happen when importing drawing information from other CAD applications, if you are using custom software applications inside AutoCAD, or if AutoCAD closes without saving your drawing.

Corrupt objects can cause a variety of problems from AutoCAD locking up to a drawing failing to load properly. When you consider that drawings can be used as xrefs and that nested references may be used, a single corrupt object can wreck havoc on a design project.

If you suspect that corrupt objects may be causing a problem, AutoCAD allows you to turn on a cyclic redundancy check (CRC) to monitor all new objects created during the drawing session. This option will check all new objects to ensure they are well defined before AutoCAD adds them to the drawing. This is set by checking the **Full-time CRC validation** box in the **Open and Save** tab on the **Options** dialog box (Figure 18-1). This checking can slow down the drawing process slightly, so this option should be turned on only as needed to help track down the source of corrupt drawing objects.

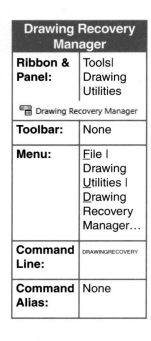

| Drawing Recovery Manager | |
|---|---|
| **Ribbon & Panel:** | Tools\| Drawing Utilities |
| 🖼 Drawing Recovery Manager | |
| **Toolbar:** | None |
| **Menu:** | File \| Drawing Utilities \| Drawing Recovery Manager… |
| **Command Line:** | DRAWINGRECOVERY |
| **Command Alias:** | None |

## Recovering Lost or Corrupt Drawings

If your AutoCAD session locks up or closes before you can save your drawing, AutoCAD provides some tools for recovering lost drawing information and fixing corrupt drawings.

***The Drawing Recovery Manager.*** If your AutoCAD session ends prematurely, the next time you start AutoCAD, it will display a message about Drawing Recovery (Figure 18-3), and the **Drawing Recovery Manager** (Figure 18-4) will start automatically. You can also start the **Drawing Recovery Manager** with the **DRAWINGRECOVERY** command.

**Note:** Although these tools can recover many damaged or corrupt drawings, they are not guaranteed to recover all lost information. Remember to save often and back up critical drawing files on a regular basis.

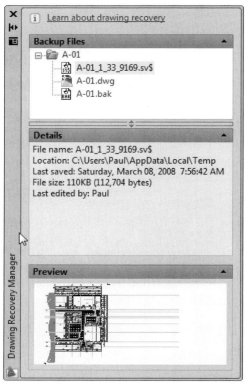

**Figure 18-4**   The Drawing Recovery Manager palette

**Figure 18-3**   The Drawing Recovery message

The **Drawing Recovery Manager** provides an easy way to examine backup and autosave files. When the **Drawing Recovery Manager** starts, it searches for backup (BAK) and autosave (SV$) files along with their associated DWG files and displays them in the **Drawing Recover Manager** palette (Figure 18-4).

The **Backup** area displays all of the backup, autosave, and drawing files associated with a given drawing. Selecting one of the listed files will display information about the file in the **Details** area and a preview of the file in the **Preview** area.

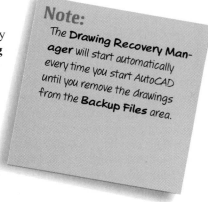

**Note:** The **Drawing Recovery Manager** will start automatically every time you start AutoCAD until you remove the drawings from the **Backup Files** area.

You can open the selected file by double-clicking it or choosing **Open** from the right-click menu. This allows you to examine in detail the various backup files. When you find the one you want to keep, save it using the file name of your choosing. You can then remove the drawing from the **Drawing Recovery Manager** by selecting the drawing file name folder in the **Backup Files** area and choosing **Remove** from the right-click menu (Figure 18-5).

| Audit | |
|---|---|
| **Ribbon & Panel:** | Tools\| Drawing Utilities <br><br> ? <br> Audit |
| **Toolbar:** | None |
| **Menu:** | File \| Drawing Utilities \| Audit |
| **Command Line:** | AUDIT |
| **Command Alias:** | None |

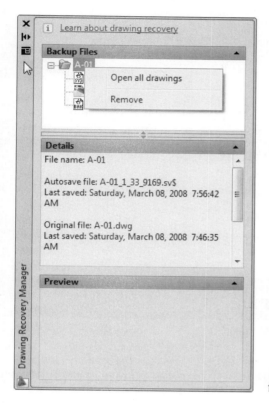

**Figure 18-5**  Removing drawings from the Drawing Recovery Manager

***Fixing Corrupt Drawings.***    If you find yourself with a corrupt drawing file, AutoCAD provides two commands to examine and repair these files: **AUDIT** and **RECOVER**.

The **AUDIT** and **RECOVER** commands will both scan a drawing for any corruption and will allow you to attempt to correct any problems they find. The **RECOVER** command allows you to select any drawing file to scan. The **AUDIT** command only scans the currently open drawing file. In addition, the **AUDIT** command gives you the option of just scanning the file without attempting to correct the problems.

The **AUDIT** and **RECOVER** commands only operate on a single drawing file. If the drawing has any xrefs, the xrefs will not be scanned for problems. If you wish to scan a drawing and all of its associated xrefs, you should use the **RECOVERALL** command. The **RECOVERALL** command scans the drawing and any xrefs attached to the drawing. The **RECOVERALL** command also displays a report at the end of the command showing the results for each drawing it scans (Figure 18-6).

## Cleaning Up Drawing Files

As you have seen, AutoCAD drawings consist of both graphical and nongraphical elements. Layer settings, block definitions, linetypes, text styles, plot styles, table styles, dimension styles, and other nongraphical elements can be stored in a drawing, even if they may not be

| Recover | |
|---|---|
| **Ribbon & Panel:** | Tools\| Drawing Utilities <br><br> Recover ▼ |
| **Toolbar:** | None |
| **Pull-down Menu:** | File \| Drawing Utilities \| Recover... |
| **Command Line:** | RECOVER |
| **Command Alias:** | None |

| Recover with Xrefs | |
|---|---|
| **Ribbon & Panel:** | Tools\| Drawing Utilities 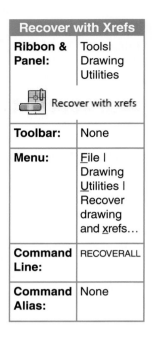 Recover with xrefs |
| **Toolbar:** | None |
| **Menu:** | File \| Drawing Utilities \| Recover drawing and xrefs… |
| **Command Line:** | RECOVERALL |
| **Command Alias:** | None |

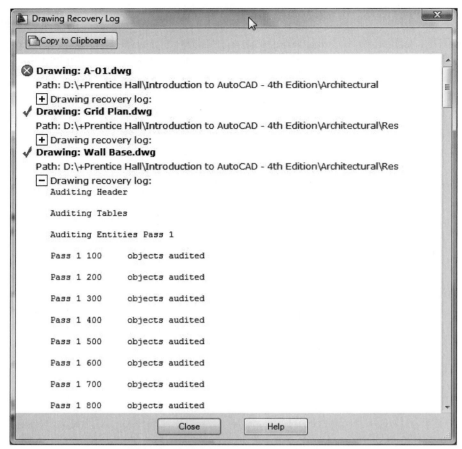

**Figure 18-6**  The RECOVERALL error report

---

| Purge | |
|---|---|
| **Ribbon & Panel:** | Tools\| Drawing Utilities |
| **Toolbar:** | None |
| **Menu:** | File\| Drawing Utilities\| Purge |
| **Command Line:** | PURGE |
| **Command Alias:** | None |

used within the drawing. It is possible to have empty layers, unused linetypes, dimension styles, etc.

Although these elements can reside in the drawing without being used, they do add to the size of the drawing file and can add complexity to a drawing. For example, a CAD layering standard may have hundreds of potential layers, but only a handful of them are used in any given drawing. Similarly, you may have a block library that consists of many symbols, but you may only use a few in any single drawing. There is no need to have all of these extra settings and block definitions stored with every drawing.

To help manage these various definitions and style settings, AutoCAD provides the **PURGE** command to view unused styles and definitions and remove them from the drawing.

*The PURGE Command.*     When you start the **PURGE** command, AutoCAD displays the **Purge** dialog box (Figure 18-7). This dialog box has a list of the various items that can be purged from a drawing. By default, AutoCAD shows you all the items that can be purged. A plus (+) symbol next to any item denotes a category that contains items that can be purged. Clicking on the + symbol expands the tree to show you the specific items. To purge an item, simply select the object from the list and choose the **Purge** button. You can select multiple items using either **<Ctrl>** or **<Shift>** while selecting items. To purge all unused objects from a drawing, choose the **Purge All** button. Placing a check in the **Confirm each item to be purged** check box will cause AutoCAD to prompt you before it purges each object.

You can also choose to display items that cannot be purged by selecting the **View items you cannot purge** button. Keep in mind that only unused objects can be purged from the drawing. When the **View items you cannot purge** button is selected, you will not be able to purge any objects. In addition, the following default AutoCAD objects cannot be purged from a drawing.

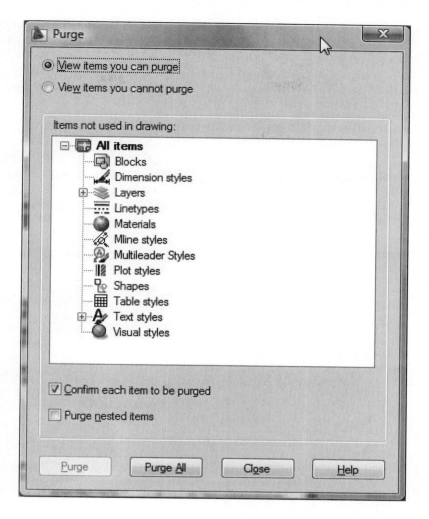

**Figure 18-7**    The Purge dialog box

| Default Objects | Name |
|---|---|
| Layers | 0, Defpoints |
| Linetypes | ByLayer, Continous, ByBlock |
| Multileader Style | Standard |
| Multiline Style | Standard |
| Dimension Style | Standard |
| Plot Style | Normal |
| Table Style | Standard |
| Text Style | Standard |

*Purging Nested Items.*    Some objects may be nested, meaning that unused objects are dependent on other unused objects. For example, you may have a block definition that contains an unused layer definition. In order for the layer definition to be purged, the block definition containing the layer definition must first be purged.

To purge nested items, you can keep selecting items and choosing **Purge,** or you can check the **Purge nested items** box. When this box is checked, all selected items and any items nested below them will also be purged.

To quickly purge all unused objects from your drawing, start the **PURGE** command, check the **Purge nested objects** box, turn off the **Confirm each item to be purged,** and choose **Purge All**.

**TIP**

Sometimes you may have a layer that appears to be unused but cannot be purged. Layers that are frozen within a layout viewport (**VP Freeze** in the **Layer** dialog box) cannot be purged until they are thawed within that viewport.

## Working with Different CAD File Formats

At some point, you may need to work with a drawing file created in another drafting program or use AutoCAD data in another software application. AutoCAD has the ability to read and write a number of different raster and vector file formats. Importing and exporting various file formats can be done in a variety of ways. The **IMPORT** and **EXPORT** commands are the most common ways of reading and writing various file formats. AutoCAD also provides a number of commands that work with specific file formats.

The following table describes the various file formats that AutoCAD supports and the commands that are available to read or write.

*Note:*
This section will cover some of the basics of importing and exporting various file formats. However, the specifics of working with each individual file type are beyond the scope of this book. If you have a specific file format you need to read or write, please consult the AutoCAD 2009 Help feature and search for your specific file format.

| File Format | Description | Import Commands | Export Commands |
|---|---|---|---|
| DXF | Drawing Exchange File. A text file used by Autodesk to exchange CAD information. The most common way of exchanging AutoCAD drawing information between various CAD packages. | OPEN, DXFIN | SAVEAS, DXFOUT |
| DGN | MicroStation Design file. A 2D/3D vector file format created by MicroStation. Currently, only the V8 version of this file format is supported. | IMPORT | EXPORT |
| DWF/ DWFx | Drawing Web Format. A read-only version of an AutoCAD drawing file. See Chapter 15 for more on the DWF file format. | | EXPORT, DWFOUT, PLOT |
| DXB | Drawing Exchange Binary file. A binary version of the DXF file. This file is typically used to flatten 3D models to 2D drawings. 3D models are plotted to a flat 2D DXB file. | DXBIN | PLOT |

| ACIS/SAT | Standard Acis Text. A 3D solid file format. Only **REGION** or **3DSOLID** objects are supported in this file format. | **IMPORT, ACISIN** | **EXPORT, ACISOUT** |
|---|---|---|---|
| STL | Stereolithography file. A 3D solid file format typically used in rapid prototyping applications.  Only **REGION** or **3DSOLID** objects are supported in this file format. | Not Supported | **STLOUT** |
| 3DS | 3D Studio file. Typically a 3D file format used primarily with rendering and animation applications. | Not Supported | **3DSOUT** |
| DXX | Attribute extract DXF file. An abbreviated type of DXF file created by the **ATTEXT** command in AutoCAD.  Only block and attribute information is included in a DXX file. | Not Supported | **EXPORT, ATTEXT** |
| EPS | Encapsulated Postscript file. Used in a variety of desktop publishing applications and maintains a high resolution print capability. | Not Supported | **EXPORT, PSOUT** |
| WMF | Windows Metafile. A combination of raster and vector formats used in Microsoft Windows and Office applications. | **IMPORT, WMFIN** | **EXPORT, WMFOUT** |
| BMP, JPG, PNG, TIF | Various raster file formats. | **IMAGE** | **BMPOUT, JPGOUT, PNGOUT, TIFOUT** |

**The EXPORT Command.**    The **EXPORT** command allows you to export AutoCAD drawing information to various file formats. When you start the **EXPORT** command, AutoCAD will display the **Export Data** dialog box (Figure 18-8) where you can specify the output file type as well as the file name.

Once you specify the file name and file type, AutoCAD will prompt you to select the objects you want to export. Once you select the objects to export, press <**Enter ↵**> to export the objects to the specified file.

**The IMPORT Command.**    The **IMPORT** command allows you to convert various file formats to AutoCAD objects. When you start the **IMPORT** command, AutoCAD will display the **Import File** dialog box (Figure 18-9) and allow you to specify the file type as well as the file name.

After you specify the file name and file type, AutoCAD imports the data and places it in the drawing. The imported objects are typically converted to a block and placed as a single object which can then be exploded.

**Note:**
The **PLOT** command also provides some additional ways to export your file to various raster and vector file formats. These file formats include JPG, BMP, PNG, CALS, TIF, TGA, PDF, PCX, and HPGL. These formats require the configuration of plotters via the **Add-A-Plotter Wizard** which can be accessed with the **Add or Configure Plotters...** button in the **Plot and Publish** tab on the **Options** dialog box.

**Note:**
Take care when exporting objects from paper space layouts. Because you are prompted to select objects, only selected objects in the current drawing space will be exported. Exporting objects from both model space and paper space is not allowed.

| Export | |
|---|---|
| **Ribbon & Panel:** | Output | Send |
| **Toolbar:** | None |
| **Menu:** | File | Export... |
| **Command Line:** | EXPORT |
| **Command Alias:** | EXP |

| Import | |
|---|---|
| **Ribbon & Panel:** | Blocks & References | Import |
| **Insert Toolbar:** | |
| **Menu:** | File | Import... |
| **Command Line:** | IMPORT |
| **Command Alias:** | IMP |

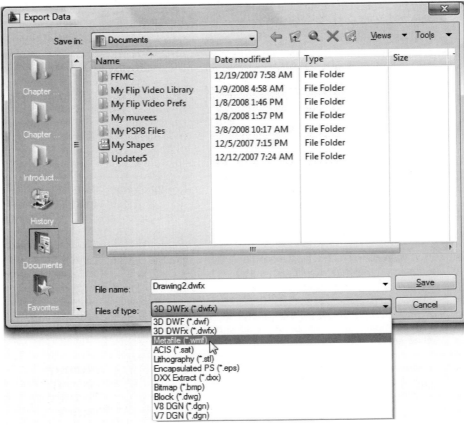

**Figure 18-8**   The Export Data dialog box

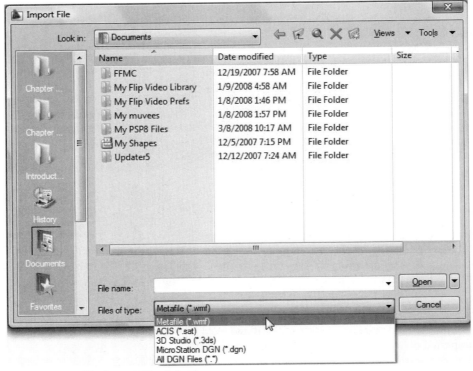

**Figure 18-9**   The Import File dialog box

*Working with DXF Files.*    DXF stands for *Drawing Exchange File* and is the primary method that AutoCAD uses for importing and exporting data between CAD applications. A DXF file can be either binary or ASCII text (most commonly used) and is widely used and supported by most CAD applications. DXF Files can be created in AutoCAD with the **SAVEAS** or **DXFOUT** commands. The **DXFOUT** command is actually a command alias for the **SAVEAS** command.

*Creating a DXF File.*    Although the **EXPORT** command only allows you to export selected objects within a drawing, a DXF file represents the entire drawing (paper space, model space, layers, blocks, etc.). Like the DWG file format, the DXF file format has changed over the various releases of AutoCAD. AutoCAD can currently create DXF files in the following formats: AutoCAD 2007, AutoCAD 2004, AutoCAD 2000, and AutoCAD R12.

When you start the **SAVEAS** command, AutoCAD displays the **Save Drawing As** dialog box (Figure 18-10). Specify the file name, location, and type of file you wish to create and choose **Save.**

**Note:**
The specifics of importing a file will vary depending on the type of file selected. See the AutoCAD 2009 Help file for the specifics of importing each type of file.

**Note:**
The DXF file format is defined in the AutoCAD Customization Guide section of the AutoCAD 2009 Help.

**Note:**
Keep in mind that some object types are not supported in earlier versions of AutoCAD and will be translated to their earlier object types. For example, ellipses and spline curves are converted to polylines in the R12 file format.

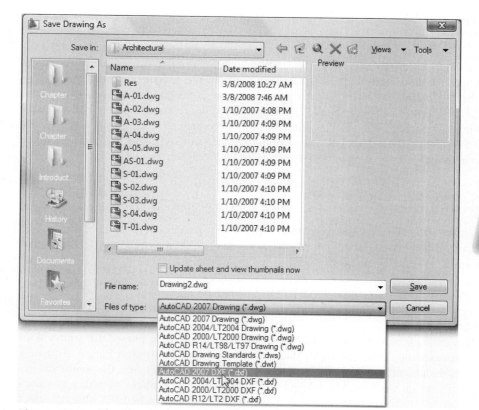

**Figure 18-10**    The Save Drawing As dialog box

# OBJECT LINKING AND EMBEDDING

Another way to share information between AutoCAD and other applications is to use Object Linking and Embedding (OLE). OLE allows you to share information between two Windows applications. To use OLE, you need both the source and the destination applications that support OLE. The source application is the program used to create the document. The destination application is the program that is going to receive the source document. For example, if you were to embed an AutoCAD drawing in a Word document, AutoCAD is the source, and Word is the destination.

> **Note:**
> Although the Windows OLE feature can use AutoCAD as either a source or a destination application, this chapter focuses primarily on placing OLE objects in AutoCAD drawings. Keep in mind that the behavior of data from other applications will vary from program to program. To link or embed AutoCAD drawings in other applications, refer to the documentation for that application for specifics on using OLE within that program.

## Object Linking Versus Object Embedding

Both the linking and embedding processes insert information from one program's document into another program's document. The difference between linking and embedding involves how the information is stored. The difference is similar to the difference between inserting a block and creating an external reference.

*Object Embedding.* When an object is embedded into a document, that object is completely stored with the destination application. For example, if you created a Word document and then embedded it into an AutoCAD drawing, you would not need to save the Word file to a separate file. That Word document would exist entirely within the AutoCAD drawing. When the AutoCAD drawing is saved, the embedded Word document is saved along with it. This is similar to the relationship between an AutoCAD drawing and a block definition. Block definitions are defined and stored entirely within the AutoCAD drawing. The block does not need to exist as a separate drawing file.

*Object Linking.* When an object is linked, Windows simply creates a link between the source file and the destination file. Any changes made to the source document will be reflected in the destination document. If the source document is deleted, the link will be broken, and the OLE object will not be updated. This is similar to the relationship between an AutoCAD drawing and an xref. The drawing file does not store the entire xref, only a link to the referenced file. When the referenced file is updated, the AutoCAD drawing containing the xref is also updated.

## Inserting OLE Objects

| Insert OLE Object | |
|---|---|
| Ribbon & Panel: | None |
| Insert Toolbar: | |
| Menu: | Insert\|OLE Object... |
| Command Line: | INSERTOBJ |
| Command Alias: | None |

There are a number of ways to create and insert OLE objects within an AutoCAD drawing. The method you use will depend primarily on whether you want to link or embed the OLE object and how you want the OLE object to be displayed within the drawing.

*The INSERTOBJ Command.* The **INSERTOBJ** command allows you to create a linked or embedded object. When the command starts, AutoCAD displays the **Insert Object** dialog box (Figure 18-11).

From this dialog box, you can choose whether you want to create a new OLE source document or use an existing file as the source document. Select the **Create New** button to create a new embedded document. Selecting this will only allow you to embed a new file. Once you select the type of file you wish to embed, Windows will launch that application with a new document for you to modify. Once you are done modifying the embedded object, select **File\|Update Drawing** in the source application, and the embedded object will appear in your

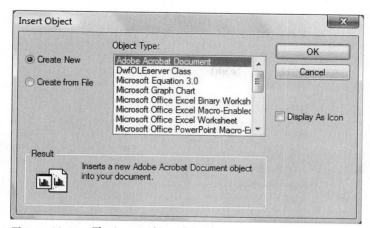

**Figure 18-11**    The Insert Object dialog box

drawing. Because the object is now embedded in the Auto-CAD drawing, you can close the source application.

If you want to use insert an existing document as on OLE object, select the **Create from File** button and then choose **Browse...** to select the source document. Once you select the source file, you can choose whether you want to link to the source file by putting a check in the **Link** box. Not checking the **Link** box will embed the source file in your drawing.

Placing a check in the **Display As Icon** box will display the OLE object as an icon within the drawing. This only affects how the OLE object is displayed in Auto-CAD and does not affect the contents of the OLE object.

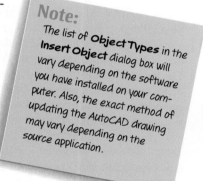

**Note:**
The list of *Object Types* in the *Insert Object* dialog box will vary depending on the software you have installed on your computer. Also, the exact method of updating the AutoCAD drawing may vary depending on the source application.

*Using the Windows Clipboard.*    The Windows Clipboard feature can also be used to link and embed data from other applications. The Windows Clipboard provides a way to store data temporarily from most Windows programs. In most Windows applications, you can select data and choose **Copy** from the **Edit** pull-down menu or press **<Ctrl+C>** within that application. Once information is copied to the Windows Clipboard, it can be pasted into other locations within the same program or into other Windows applications.

The Windows Clipboard can be used to store information from within a file or to copy entire files or multiple files and folders.

When data is stored in the Windows Clipboard, it can be placed into an AutoCAD drawing using either the **PASTECLIP** or **PASTESPEC** commands.

The **PASTECLIP** command will place the contents of the Clipboard as an embedded OLE object. When you start the **PASTECLIP** command, AutoCAD will prompt you for an insertion point. Depending on the type of data in the Clipboard, AutoCAD may display the **OLE Text Size** dialog box (Figure 18-12). This dialog box allows you to control how Windows fonts are displayed within AutoCAD and allows you to convert the Windows text point size to AutoCAD text height.

| Paste | |
|---|---|
| **Ribbon & Panel:** | Homel Utilities  Paste |
| **Standard Toolbar:** | |
| **Menu:** | Edit\|Paste |
| **Command Line:** | PASTECLIP |
| Command Alias: | Ctrl+V |

| Paste Special | |
|---|---|
| **Ribbon & Panel:** | Homel Utilities  Paste Special |
| **Toolbar:** | None |
| **Menu:** | Edit\|Paste Special... |
| **Command Line:** | PASTESPEC |
| **Command Alias:** | None |

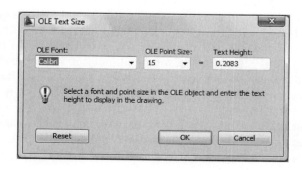

**Figure 18-12**    The OLE Text Size dialog box

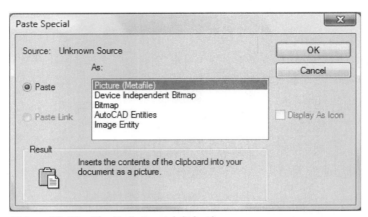

**Figure 18-13**   The Paste Special dialog box

The **PASTESPEC** command gives you a little more control over how the Clipboard data is stored in AutoCAD. When you start the **PASTESPEC** command, AutoCAD displays the **Paste Special** dialog box (Figure 18-13).

The **PASTESPEC** command allows you to place an OLE object as either a linked or embedded object. It also gives you the ability to convert the Clipboard contents to AutoCAD entities. The types of entities created depend on the type of data in the Clipboard. AutoCAD will automatically convert the Clipboard data to the most appropriate AutoCAD object. For example, Excel spreadsheet data is converted to an AutoCAD table, Word data is converted to AutoCAD text, raster image data is converted to AutoCAD image overlays, etc.

*Drag-and-Drop.*   Another feature of Windows is the ability to drag-and-drop data between Windows applications. Drag-and-drop involves selecting data in the source application and, while holding your left mouse button down, dragging the data onto your AutoCAD drawing. This can take a little practice and preplanning because both applications must be visible and accessible.

Drag-and-drop works the same as **PASTECLIP;** the only difference is that drag-and-drop bypasses the Windows Clipboard.

### Editing OLE Objects

The nature of OLE objects is that they are edited in their source application. Double-clicking an OLE object will launch the source application with the OLE data. You can make changes to the source data and then either close the source application or, in most applications, choose **Close and Return to Drawing** from the **File** menu in the source application.

*Managing Linked Objects.*   Linked objects, because they rely on the coordination of multiple files, require a little more attention than embedded objects. The location of the linked file is critical to updating and maintaining the information in the OLE object. The way in which you want the information updated and the ability to terminate a link are also part of maintaining an OLE linked object. The **OLELINKS** command allows you to manage linked OLE objects from within AutoCAD.

The **OLELINKS** command only works if you have linked OLE objects in your AutoCAD drawing. When you start the **OLELINKS** command, AutoCAD displays the **Links** dialog box (Figure 18-14). The **Update Now** button will refresh the OLE object from the source file. The **Open Source** button will open the source file and allow you to make changes. The **Change Source** button allows you to specify a different source file for the OLE object. When you change the source file, the new source file must be the same type of file as the original source file. The **Break Link** button will terminate the link between AutoCAD and the source file and turn the linked object into an embedded object.

At the bottom of the **Links** dialog box are two buttons which allow you to control how the OLE objects are updated. Choosing **Automatic** causes AutoCAD to update the OLE object

| OLE Links | |
|---|---|
| **Ribbon & Panel:** | None |
| **Toolbar:** | None |
| **Menu:** | Edit|OLE Links |
| **Command Line:** | OLELINKS |
| **Command Alias:** | None |

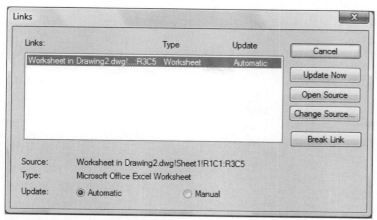

Figure 18-14    The Links dialog box

whenever the source file changes. Choosing **Manual** tells AutoCAD not to update the OLE object until you choose the **Update Now** button.

*Plot Quality.*    OLE objects are treated as raster objects when a raster plotter is used. Because large, high-resolution, color-rich rasters can be expensive to plot, you can set the **OLEQUALITY** system variable to control how each OLE object is plotted. There are four possible settings: 0 (Monochrome), 1 (Low Quality), 2 (High Quality), and 3 (Automatically Select). The default setting, Automatically Select, assigns a plot-quality level based on the type of object. The higher the plot-quality setting, the more time and memory are used to plot. The **OLEQUALITY** variable can be applied separately to each OLE object in the drawing.

*Controlling the Visibility of OLE Objects.*    While working on a drawing, you may want to suppress the display or plotting of OLE objects. The **OLEHIDE** system variable allows you to control the visibility and plotting of OLE objects in model space, paper space, or both. The default setting is **0** which displays and plots all OLE objects in both model and paper space. Setting **OLEHIDE** to 1 displays and plots OLE objects in paper space only. Setting **OLEHIDE** to **2** displays and plots OLE objects in model space only. Setting **OLEHIDE** to **3** suppresses the display and plotting of all OLE objects in both model and paper space. The **OLEHIDE** variable applies globally to all OLE objects in a drawing.

*OLEFRAME System Variable.*    When OLE objects are placed in AutoCAD, they behave like other AutoCAD objects in that they have default properties, such as layer color and linetype, associated with them. Like raster image overlays, these properties apply to the frame surrounding the OLE objects. The **OLEFRAME** system variable controls the display and plotting of the OLE object frame. Setting **OLEFRAME** to **0** turns off the OLE frame, and it will not be displayed or plotted. Setting **OLEFRAME** to **1** displays the OLE frame both on screen and in plots. Setting **OLEFRAME** to **2** displays the OLE frame in the display but suppresses it in plots. The **OLEFRAME** variable applies globally to all OLE objects in a drawing.

*OLE Properties.*    As stated earlier, OLE objects behave similarly to other objects in a drawing. They can be moved, copied, resized, etc. The **Properties** palette (Figure 18-15) displays information specific to OLE objects, such as the location and the height and width scale of the OLE object. You can also control the plot quality of the OLE object.

## Action Recorder

The **Action Recorder** tool allows you to automate repetitive tasks by recording the AutoCAD commands, inputs, and options you enter as an **Action Macro** that you, or anyone else, can replay later. If you find yourself doing the same series of steps over and over again, the **Action**

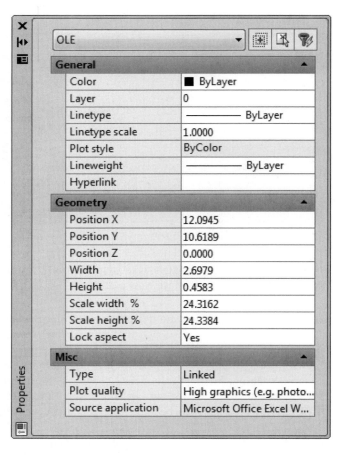

**Figure 18-15**  The Properties Palette

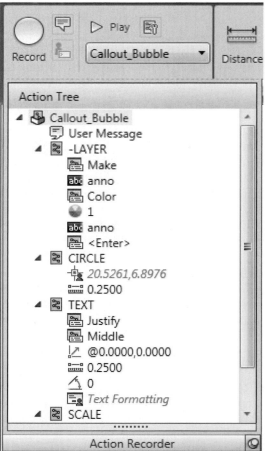

**Figure 18-16**  The Action Recorder panel

**Recorder** can help by recording them so that the next time you need to do the same thing, all you have to do is press the **Play** button. The **Play** button and all the other **Action Recorder** tools and features are located on the **Action Recorder** panel on the **Tools** ribbon shown in Figure 18-16.

> **Note:**
> There are certain actions that cannot be recorded—specifically, file operation commands such as **OPEN** and **CLOSE**, as well as any type of grip editing. While it is possible to display a dialog box, it is not possible to track and record your actions once it is displayed. Additionally, the **Quick Properties** palette is not recognized and certain tool palette commands cannot be recorded.

To use the use the **Action Recorder** you simply press the **Record** button and step through the series of commands that you would normally go through to complete a task and push the **Stop** button when you are done. The **Action Recorder** can record actions entered via the command line, ribbon panels, menus, the **Layer Properties Manager**, the **Properties** palette, tool palettes and even toolbars. While recording an **Action Macro**, a red recording circle icon is displayed near the crosshairs to indicate that the **Action Recorder** is running and any commands and input are being recorded.

**TIP**    Many commands have an alternate command line only version that can be accessed by prefixing the command with a hyphen (–) that allows you to work around the **Action Recorder's** inability to record dialog box actions. For instance, while the HATCH command displays the **Hatch & Gradiant** dialog box, which cannot be recorded, the **-HATCH** commands allows you to place hatches by entering all the command options via the keyboard so that the **Action Recorder** can record them.

When you press the **Stop** button the **Action Macro** dialog box shown in Figure 18-17 is displayed so you can enter a command name for the macro.

---

**Action Macro**

Action Macro Command Name:

ActMacro001

File Name:

ActMacro001.actm

Folder Path:

C:\Users\Paul\AppData\Roaming\Autodesk\AutoCAD 2009 Release Car

Description:

OK    Cancel    Help

**Figure 18-17**   The Action Macro dialog box

All the actions entered are saved to an **Action Macro** file with an **.ACTM** file extension. The default macro and file name provided is **ActMacro001**, where the 3-digit suffix is incremented each time. It is suggested that you enter a more descriptive name that better indicates the nature of the macro.

The best thing about **Action Macros** is that after you are done recording a macro you can go back and customize it by adding your own text messages and requests for user input by right-clicking on an action in the **Action Tree** window and using the shortcut menu shown in Figure 18-18.

**Note:**
There are a few limitations when naming an **Action Macro**. An **Action Macro** cannot have the same name as an AutoCAD command. For instance, you cannot create a macro named **LINE**. It is also not possible to use spaces or special characters. It is suggested you substitute a dash (-) or an underscore ( ) when a space is required.

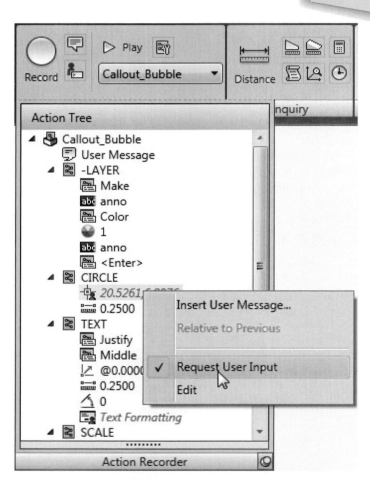

**Figure 18-18** Adding messages and requests for user input

The **Preferences** button on the **Action Recorder** panel displays the **Action Recorder Preferences** dialog box shown in Figure 18-19, which allows you to control whether the **Action Recorder** panel expands when recording or playing back an action macro, and if you are prompted to provide a command name for the **Action Macro** when you press the **Stop** button and recording is stopped.

**TIP**   By default, **Action Macro** files are stored in the folder specified in the **Actions Recording File Location** setting under **Action Recorder Settings** on the **Files** tab in the **Options** dialog box. The **Additional Actions Reading File Locations** setting allows you share **Action Macro** files in a network location so multiple people on different computers can access and run them.

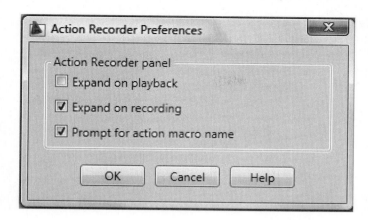

**Figure 18-19**   Action Recorder Preferences dialog box

# SUMMARY

This chapter explored additional file management techniques that include recovering and fixing corrupt files and changing settings in AutoCAD to create backup files. Remember that AutoCAD drawings can be shared with other CAD programs and viewed in other software applications. In turn, other CAD and Windows-based files can be translated into AutoCAD. Sharing data from one software application to another is cost efficient, productive, and becoming commonplace in the design industry. AutoCAD has internal tools to assist with these file translations. As with most Windows software, AutoCAD provides all the Object Linking and Embedding tools such as **Copy, Cut,** and **Paste,** as well as a Clipboard that makes sharing information even easier. Last, AutoCAD provides ways to enhance OLE objects with system variables that control display, plotting, and editing options.

# CHAPTER TEST QUESTIONS

## Multiple Choice

1. The **PURGE** command can remove unused:
   a. Layers
   b. Linetypes
   c. Blocks
   d. All of the above

2. The **EXPORT** command supports the following file type:
   a. WMF, JPG, EPS, DXX, BMP, DWG, 3DS
   b. WMF, SAT, EPS, DXX, BMP, 3DS, DWG
   c. JPG, PNG, DXX, BMP, DXX, EPS, SAT
   d. None of the above

3. The command that saves and exports an AutoCAD object into a drawing file is:
   a. **WBLOCK**
   b. **WMFOUT**
   c. **JPGOUT**
   d. **DWGOUT**

4. The Backup File extension is:
   a. AC$
   b. BAC
   c. SV$
   d. BAK

5. A DXF file can be created by:
   a. Pasting a DWG file into Word
   b. Using the **SAVE** or **SAVEAS** command
   c. Using the **XREF** command
   d. None of the above

6. A source application file:
   a. Is where an object is linked
   b. Can never be changed or edited
   c. Is the same as a destination file
   d. None of the above

7. Dragging-and-dropping objects is the same as:
   a. Embedding and linking
   b. Copying and pasting
   c. Cutting and pasting
   d. All of the above

8. An AutoCAD file with linked objects:
   a. Can be automatically updated if there are changes to the source file
   b. Tends to be smaller in file size than files with embedded objects

c. Must be updated if either the source or destination file is moved to another drive or directory

d. All of the above

9. An embedded object can be changed or edited in an AutoCAD file:

a. By right-clicking on the object and selecting **Edit**

b. By double-clicking on the object to bring up the source application

c. By deleting the object, recreating an updated version in the source file, and bringing it back into AutoCAD through the Clipboard

d. Is not allowed

10. The **OLEHIDE** system variable will display and plot OLE objects in model space if the value is:

a. Set to **0**     c. Set to **2**

b. Set to **1**     d. Set to either **0** or **2**

## Matching

**Column A**

a. BAK

b. **PASTECLIP**

c. **AUDIT**

d. Drawing Recovery Manager

e. **Options** dialog box

f. **OLELINKS**

g. **PURGE**

h. DXX

i. **IMPORT**

j. **EXPORT**

**Column B**

1. Eliminates unused lines, blocks, and layers

2. Pastes copied objects

3. Controls settings of AutoCAD software

4. AutoCAD backup file

5. Attribute extract DXF file

6. Changes other file types into an AutoCAD drawing file

7. Modifies existing OLE links

8. Changes AutoCAD drawing file types into a specific file format

9. Checks and fixes errors in a drawing file

10. Attempts to restore or retrieve open and backup drawing files

## True or False

1. True or False: The **RECOVER** command can be used on open drawings.

2. True or False: The **AUDIT** command can be used on closed drawings.

3. True or False: **The Drawing Recovery Manager** can restore an unsaved drawing file.

4. True or False: The **PURGE** command is used to erase named unused objects.

5. True or False: The **INSERTOBJ** command can be used to create a table from scratch in Word and link it into AutoCAD.

6. True or False: The **OLE Links** dialog box is used to update, change, or break a linked object in AutoCAD.

7. True or False: The **OLEFRAME** system variable when set to **2** will display a frame around an OLE object on the screen and a plot.

8. True or False: An OLE object in AutoCAD can be resized using grips or the **Properties** palette.

9. True or False: The BMP export file is a raster image.

10. True or False: OLE also means Object Linking and Editing.**File Management and Object Linking and Embedding**

# Drafting Standards Overview

## STANDARDS ORGANIZATIONS

Standards provide a basis for uniformity in engineering drawing. Many industries and governments can use these standards as a guideline to develop their documents. It is not the intent of recognized national standards organizations to prevent individual organizations from designing specific formats. The intent is to provide common engineering standards to aid the interchange of drawings between companies, government, and other users.

The following organizations are three leaders in drafting standards.

### American National Standards Institute (ANSI)

ANSI has been a leader in the voluntary standards system of the United States. This organization has provided a forum for private and public sectors to collectively work together toward the development of national standards. Efforts to coordinate national standards date back to 1911. In 1916, the following agencies were instrumental in establishing a national body to oversee the development of national standards:

1. The American Institute of Electrical Engineers (now IEEE)
2. The American Society of Mechanical Engineers (ASME)
3. The American Society of Civil Engineers (ASCE)
4. The American Institute of Mining and Metallurgical Engineers (AIMME)
5. The American Society for Testing Materials (ASTM)

These organizations along with the U.S. Departments of War, Navy, and Commerce were the founders of the American Engineering Standards Committee (AESC). This organization led to the formation of the American National Standards Institute (ANSI) in 1969. Throughout its history, ANSI has continued to coordinate national and international efforts to approve voluntary standards. Over the past 85 years, this organization has maintained its strong ties with the original founding organizations and others to become one of the most highly regarded standards systems in the world.

Specific standards are revised periodically by a committee of industrial leaders who also serve as representatives of various industrial service organizations. For example, the vice president of engineering at Xerox Corporation might serve on the board of the American Society of Mechanical Engineers (ASME). These committee members revise such standards as Drawing Sheet Size and Format, Dimensioning and Tolerancing, and Line Conventions and Lettering. The standards should be readily available in the classroom so that students can develop engineering drawings that adhere to these standards. Specific standards need to be available for each content area—mechanical, electrical, or civil. The following is an example of some commonly used mechanical engineering standards.

## American Society of Mechanical Engineers (ASME)

The American Society of Mechanical Engineers conducts one of the world's largest publishing operations to produce technical and engineering documents to establish standards. ASME documents are recognized worldwide for industrial and manufacturing codes and standards. Some of the popular documents on engineering standards include:

> **Y14.2M-1992 Line Conventions and Lettering**
>
> **Y14.5.2-2000-2001 Certification of Geometric Dimensioning and Tolerancing**
>
> **Y14.38-1999 Abbreviations and Acronyms**
>
> **Y14.1-1980 (R1987) Drawing Sheet Size and Format**
>
> **Y14.1M-1992 Metric Drawing Sheet Size and Format**
>
> **Y14.3M-1994 Multiview and Sectional View Drawings**

## International Organization for Standardization (ISO)

The International Organization for Standardization is an organized network of the national standards institutes of 148 countries. It is a nongovernmental organization, but its members are not. ISO has a unique mission in acting as a bridge between business/industry and consumers/users. ISO has published more than 13,700 International Standards ranging from engineering drawing to medical devices. ISO is also responsible for providing a framework for quality management throughout the processes of producing and delivering products and services by implementing ISO 9000.

Some of the more commonly used ISO drawing standards are:

**ISO 10135:1994**

Technical drawings—Simplified representation of molded, cast, and forged parts

**ISO 10209-1:1992**

Technical product documentation—Vocabulary—Part 1: Terms relating to technical drawings: general and types of drawings

**ISO 10209-2:1993**

Technical product documentation—Vocabulary—Part 2: Terms relating to projection methods

Many companies, such as General Electric and General Motors, develop their own standards by incorporating the use of ANSI, ASME, and ISO criteria. In this way, national standards can be incorporated with company standards to meet specific requirements.

## Text

Text can be inserted into the model space or into paper space layouts. When inserting text into a layout, the height of the text is equal to the printed or plotted size. Layouts are normally printed or plotted on a one-to-one scale. If the text height is inserted at 0.125 into the layout and printed at 1:1, the printed text height will be 0.125.

When text is entered into model space, consideration must be given to the drawing scale factor. See the following section for additional information about standard model space text heights.

## Standard Text Heights

The typical standard height for text on a drawing is ⅛″. Fractions need to be created ¼″ tall. These are general guidelines for text height. Text height should be increased or decreased based on individual situations.

To achieve these final printed and plotted text sizes, it is necessary to create the text within the AutoCAD drawing at the correct size. The following table lists examples of the relationship between plot scale, sheet size, the model space drawing area, and text height.

|  | Sheet Size | Plot Scale | Scale Factor | Model Space Drawing Area | Text Height |
|---|---|---|---|---|---|
| Architect's Scale | 12″ × 9″ | 1/8″ = 1′-0″ | 96 | 96′ × 72′ | 1′-0″ |
|  | 24″ × 18″ | 1/2″ = 1′-0″ | 24 | 48′ × 36′ | 3″ |
| Engineer's Scale (Civil) | 18″ × 12″ | 1″ = 200′ | 2400 | 3600′ × 2400′ | 25′ |
|  | 36″ × 24″ | 1″ = 50′ | 600 | 1800′ × 1200′ | 6.25′ |
| Engineer's Scale (Mech.) | 11″ × 8.5″ | 1″ = 2″ | 2 | 22″ × 17″ | .25″ |
|  | 34″ × 22″ | 1″ = 1.5″ | 1.5 | 51″ × 33″ | 3/16″ |
| Metric Scale | 279 mm × 216 mm | 1 mm = 5 mm | 5 | 1395 mm × 1080 mm | 15.875 mm |
|  | 432 mm × 279 mm | 1 mm = 20 mm | 20 | 7620 mm × 5080 mm | 63.5 mm |

## Notes and Locating Text on a Drawing

Notes and text are necessary to supplement a fully dimensioned engineering drawing. Notes should be clear and concise to avoid any misinterpretation. Notes are always lettered horizontally on the sheet and systematically organized. Do not place notes and text in crowded or busy locations on the drawing. Avoid placing notes in between orthographic views. Use only standard ANSI or ASME abbreviations with a note.

Notes are classified as General Notes or Local/Specific Notes.

## General Notes

General notes apply to the entire drawing. General notes are typically placed in the lower right-hand corner of the drawing above or to the left of the title block. Title blocks may provide general information about the drawing such as tolerance, material, or treatment. General notes may be placed below the view to which the note applies.

## Local/Specific Notes

Local notes provide specific detailed information. These notes are placed adjacent to the specific feature they describe. Local notes may be connected with a leader. The leader arrow or dot will touch the detail and end with a note.

## Leaders

Leaders should be attached at the middle front of the first word of the note or after the last word of the note. Leaders to a circle should be developed radially. The slanted line of the leader should be aimed at the center of the circle or arc. A shoulder or horizontal line of the leader is optional. Leader lines should not cross each other. Refer to the following standard for additional information:

**Y14.5.2-2000-2001 Certification of Geometric Dimensioning and Tolerancing**

## Sheet Layouts

A convenient code to identify American National Standard sheet sizes and forms suggested by the authors for title, parts or material list, and revision blocks, for use of instructors in making assignments, is shown here. All dimensions are in inches.

Three sizes of sheets are illustrated: Size A, Figure A-1, Size B, Figure A-5, and Size C, Figure A-6. Metric size sheets are not shown.

Eight forms of lettering arrangements are suggested, known as Forms 1, 2, 3, 4, 5, 6, 7, and 8, as shown below and on the next page. The total length of Forms 1, 2, 3, and 4 may be adjusted to fit Sizes A4, A3, and A2.

The term *layout* designates a sheet of certain size plus a certain arrangement of lettering. Thus Layout A–1 is a combination of Size A, Figure A-1, and Form 1, Figure A-2. Layout C–678 is a combination of Size C, Figure A-6, and Forms 6, 7, and 8, Figures A-9, A-10, and A-11. Layout A4–2 (adjusted) is a combination of Size A4 and Form 2, Figure A-3, adjusted to fit between the borders. Other combinations may be employed as assigned by the instructor.

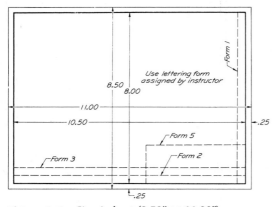

**Figure A-1**    Size A sheet (8.50″ × 11.00″)

**Figure A-2**    Form 1. Title block

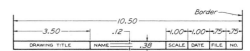

**Figure A-3**    Form 2. Title block

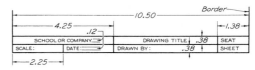

**Figure A-4**    Form 3. Title block

### Sheet Sizes

#### American National Standard

A  −  8.50″ × 11.00″
B  −  11.00″ × 17.00″
C  −  17.00″ × 22.00″
D  −  22.00″ × 34.00″
E  −  34.00″ × 44.00″

#### International Standard

A4  −  210 mm  ×  297 mm
A3  −  297 mm  ×  420 mm
A2  −  420 mm  ×  594 mm
A1  −  594 mm  ×  841 mm
A0  −  841 mm  × 1189 mm
    (25.4 mm  =  1.00″)

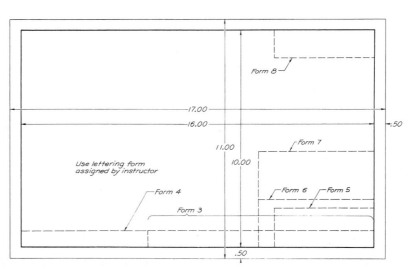

**Figure A-5**    Size B sheet (11.00″ × 17.00″)

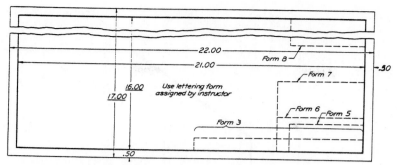

**Figure A-6**    Size C sheet (17.00″ × 22.00″)

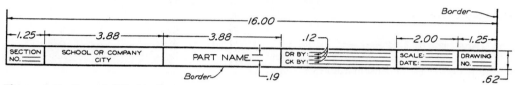

**Figure A-7**    Form 4. Title block

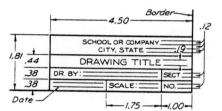

**Figure A-8**    Form 5. Title block

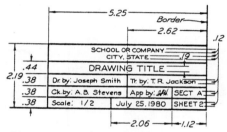

**Figure A-9**    Form 6. Title block

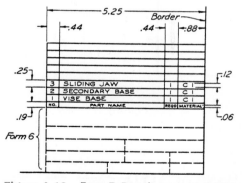

**Figure A-10**    Form 7. Parts list or material list

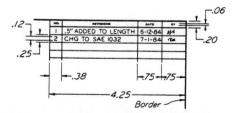

**Figure A-11**    Form 8. Revision block

# DIMENSIONS

The views of an object will describe the shape. The size of the object is described by the use of modern dimensioning techniques. It is important that an engineering drawing have accurate and functional dimensions.

## Standard Feature Sizes

Figures A-12 and A-13 illustrate some common terms and distances to consider when dimensioning standard feature sizes.

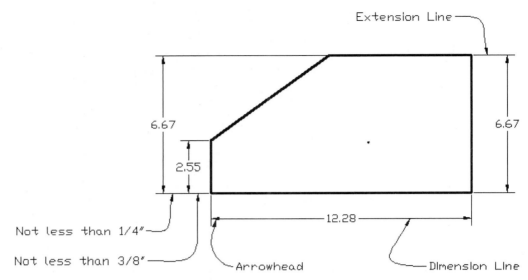

**Figure A-12**   Linear dimension features

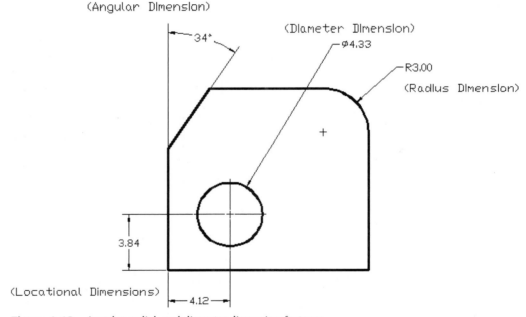

**Figure A-13**   Angular, radial, and diameter dimension features

## ARCHITECTURAL STYLE VERSUS MECHANICAL STYLE

### Architectural Style

The architectural style of dimensioning has numbers placed on top of an unbroken dimension line. The dimension line typically ends with a slash, dot, or arrowhead. The numbers normally are designated with an inch (″) and foot (′) symbol (see Figure A-14).

### Mechanical Style

The mechanical style of dimensioning has numbers centered in the middle of a broken dimension line. The dimension line typically ends with an arrow.

There are two systems of reading dimensions on a drawing, the *unidirectional system* and the *aligned system*. In the unidirectional system, all the dimension figures and notes are lettered

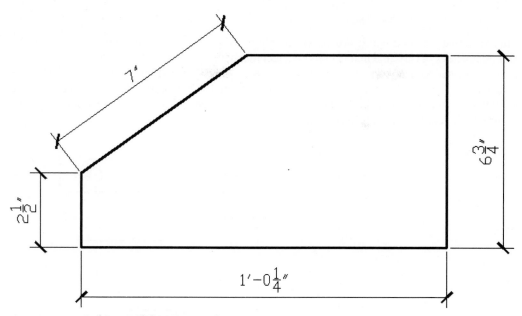

**Figure A-14**   Architectural dimension style

horizontally on the sheet. This is the preferred system of the American National StandardsInstitute. The mechanical style of dimensioning illustrates the unidirectional system. The unidirectional system is widely used because it is easy to read and interpret on large drawings. The unidirectional system is the standard default dimensioning system in AutoCAD.

The aligned system has all the dimension figures aligned with the dimension line. The architectural style of dimensioning illustrates the aligned system. Many of the dimension figures are horizontal on the sheet and some are aligned or turned. Any rotated figures are to be read from the right side of the sheet. Figures are not to be read from the right and left of the sheet. AutoCAD will dimension aligned figures after a few variables have been changed in the dimensioning environment (see Figure A-15).

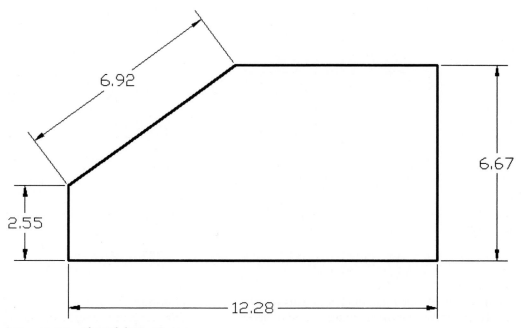

**Figure A-15**   Aligned dimensioning

## Linetypes and Thicknesses

Linetypes that are used within AutoCAD should correspond with the standard ANSI Linetypes and thicknesses. Every line that is used on a technical drawing has a specific meaning and needs to be illustrated in a certain way. The American National Standards Institute has established the Line Convention and Lettering standard ANSI Y-14.2m-1992. This standard describes the size, application, and construction of various lines that are used in creating engineering drawings. Figure A-16 details various linetypes and their applications.

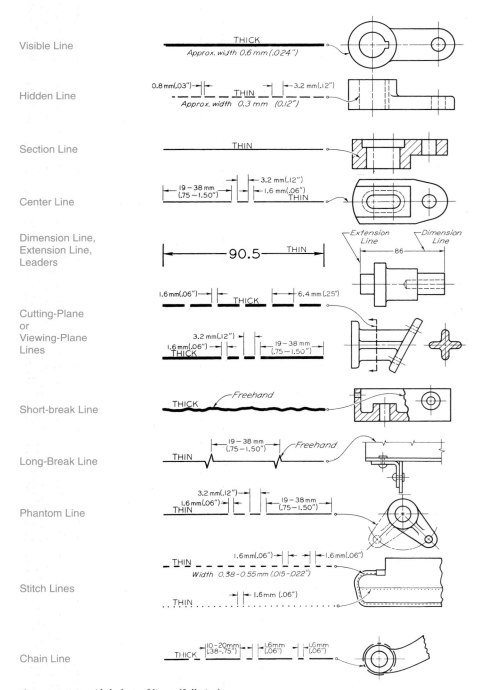

**Figure A-16**   Alphabet of lines (full-size)

It should be noted that the line widths established in this illustration are approximate and the actual width is governed by the size and style of the drawing. Large drawings will need to have wider lines, and drawings that are reduced in size will need to have smaller line widths than specified in this illustration. The ANSI Y14.2M standard and this illustration should be used as a guide to produce crisp and legible engineering drawings from AutoCAD.

Linetypes are described in an AutoCAD file called ACAD.LIN. These linetypes should be loaded into the AutoCAD drawing file and assigned correct line weights that correspond with the ANSI standards. The AutoCAD command, LTSCALE, should be used to adjust the size of the linetypes to match the size of the drawing area in AutoCAD. Figure A-17 shows examples of AutoCAD's standard linetypes, which are defined in the ACAD.LIN file.

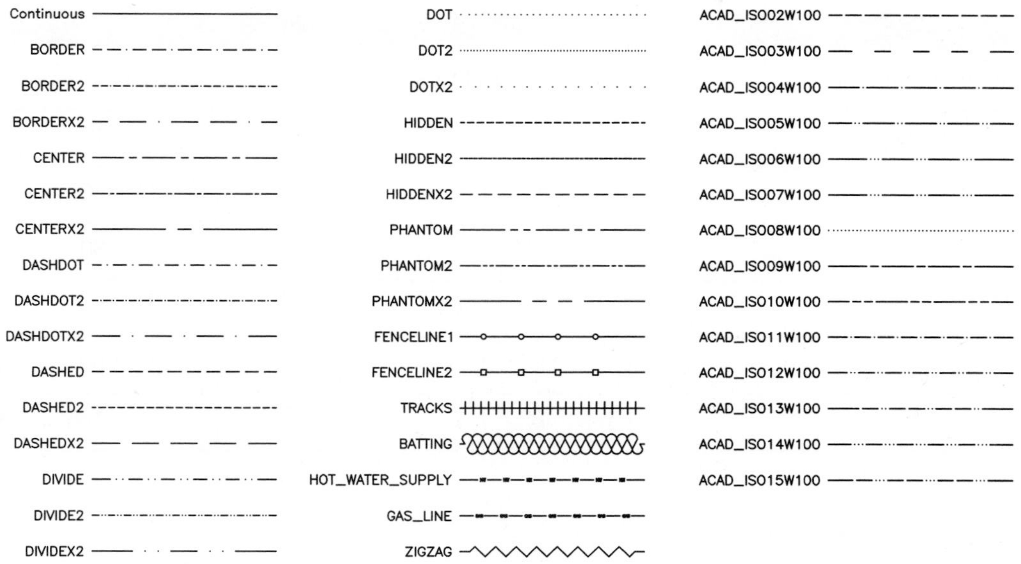

**Figure A-17**    Standard AutoCAD linetypes

## STANDARD SHEET SIZES AND SCALES

The use of standard sheet sizes and the uniform location of the title block, revision block, and bill of material provide definite advantages for engineering drawings. These advantages include readability, handling, filing, and reproduction. As drawings are shared between organizations and companies, an advantage is realized when information is located in the same location on all drawings.

Standard sheet size also provides consistency between hand-drawn and printer/plotter-created engineering drawings. Drawings that are created on printers can use standard engineering sheet sizes of 8.5″ × 11″ or 17″ × 11″. Drawings that are created with plotters that use rolls of various media need to be trimmed to final standard size such as 17″ × 22″ or 22″ × 34″. International sheet sizes based on millimeters would need to be trimmed to final standard size such as 420 mm × 594 mm or 594 mm × 841 mm. (See Figure A-18.)

| Nearest International Size[a] (millimeter) | Standard U.S. Size[a] (inch) |
|---|---|
| A4 210 × 297 | A  8.5 × 11.0 |
| A3 297 × 420 | B 11.0 × 17.0 |
| A2 420 × 594 | C 17.0 × 22.0 |
| A1 594 × 841 | D 22.0 × 34.0 |
| A0 841 × 1189 | E 34.0 × 44.0 |
| [a] ANSI Y14.1m-1992. | |

**Figure A-18**    Standard U.S. and metric paper sizes

## STANDARD PLOT SCALES

Each drafting discipline has plot scales that are commonly used within that discipline. The following table lists standard plot scales for the mechanical, architectural, and civil engineering disciplines. These are preferred plot sales; other plot scales may be used as needed. In all cases, the plot scale should be clearly indicated on the drawing.

| Mechanical Scale | Architectural Scale | Engineers' Scale |
|---|---|---|
| 1:1 | 1/8″ = 1′-0″ | 1″ = 10′ |
| 1:2 | ¼″ = 1′-0″ | 1″ = 20′ |
| 1:4 | ½″ = 1′-0″ | 1″ = 30′ |
| 2:1 | 1″ = 1′-0″ | 1″ = 50′ |
| 4:1 | 1½″ = 1′-0″ | 1″ = 60′ |
| 10:1 | 3″ = 1′-0″ | 1″ = 100′ |

### Specifying the Scale on a Drawing

For machine drawings, the scale indicates the ratio of the size of the drawn object to its actual size, irrespective of the unit of measurement used. The recommended practice is to letter full-size or 1:1; half-size or 1:2; and similarly for other reductions. Expansion or enlargement scales are given as 2:1 or 2:3; 3:1 or 3:3; 5:1 or 5:3; 10:1 or 10:3; and so on.

The various scale calibrations available on the metric scale and the engineers' scale provide almost unlimited scale ratios. The preferred metric scale ratios appear to be 1:1; 1:2; 1:5, 1:10, 1:20, 1:50, 1:100, and 1:200.

Map scales are indicated in terms of fractions, such as scale $\frac{1}{62500}$, or graphically, such as 400  0  400  800 Ft.

## STANDARD ANSI HATCH PATTERNS

### Section Lining

Section-lining symbols (Figure A-19) have been used to indicate specific materials. These symbols represent general material types only, such as cast iron, brass, and steel. Now, however, because there are so many different types of materials, and each has so many subtypes, a general name or symbol is not enough. For example, there are hundreds of different kinds of steel. Since detailed specifications of material must be lettered in the form of a note or in the title strip, the general-purpose (cast-iron) section lining may be used for all materials on detail drawings (single parts).

Section-lining symbols may be used in assembly drawings in cases where it is desirable to distinguish different materials; otherwise, the general-purpose symbol is used for all parts.

CAD programs usually include a library that allows the user to select from a variety of section-lining patterns, making it easy to indicate various types of material rather than using the generic cast-iron symbol for all sectioned parts.

ANSI has standardized many section lines that are used for sectional drawing. AutoCAD uses the **HATCH** command to insert hatch patterns that are used to illustrate these section lines. The following table lists the ANSI section line with corresponding AutoCAD hatch pattern, as seen in Figure A-19.

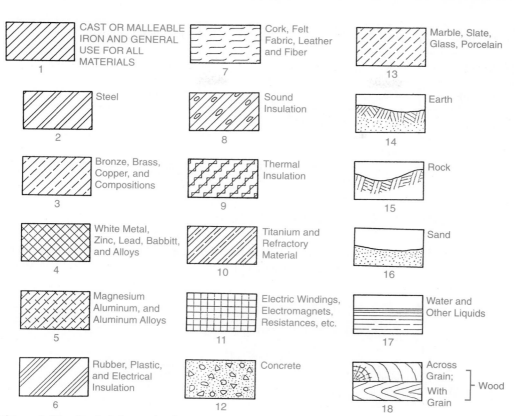

**Figure A-19**    Symbols for section lining

| Figure Number | ANSI Pattern Name | AutoCAD Hatch Pattern |
| --- | --- | --- |
| A-19 (1) | Cast/General Use | ANSI 31 |
| A-19 (2) | Steel | ANSI 32 or Steel |
| A-19 (3) | Bronze, brass, copper, etc. | ANSI 33 |
| A-19 (4) | White metal, zinc, lead, etc. | ANSI 37 |
| A-19 (5) | Magnesium, aluminum, etc. | ANSI 38 (include a material note) |
| A-19 (6) | Rubber, plastic, electrical insulation | ANSI 34 |
| A-19 (7) | Cork, felt, fabric, leather, fiber | Cork |
| A-19 (8) | Sound insulation | Insulation (include a material note) |
| A-19 (9) | Thermal insulation | Insulation (include a material note) |
| A-19 (10) | Titanium/refractory material | |
| A-19 (11) | Electric windings, electromagnets, etc. | ANSI 37 (rotate 45°) |
| A-19 (12) | Concrete | AR-CONC |
| A-19 (13) | Marble, slate, glass, porcelain | Dash (rotate 45°) |

*(continued)*

| A-19 (14) | Earth | Earth (rotate angle) |
| A-19 (15) | Rock | |
| A-19 (16) | Sand | AR-SAND |
| A-19 (17) | Water and other liquids | |
| A-19 (18) | Wood | |

## U.S. TO METRIC UNITS CONVERSIONS

AutoCAD provides some utilities for combining Metric and Imperial units within a single drawing. The following table lists standard U.S. (Imperial) units of measurements and their Metric conversions.

| Length | |
|---|---|
| **U.S. to Metric** | **Metric to U.S.** |
| 1 inch = 2.540 centimeters<br>1 foot = .305 meter<br>1 yard = .914 meter<br>1 mile = 1.609 kilometers | 1 millimeter = .039 inch<br>1 centimeter = .394 inch<br>1 meter = 3.281 feet or 1.094 yards<br>1 kilometer = .621 mile |
| **Area** | |
| 1 inch$^2$ = 6.451 centimeter$^2$<br>1 foot$^2$ = .093 meter$^2$<br>1 yard$^2$ = .836 meter$^2$<br>1 acre$^2$ = 4,046.873 meter$^2$ | 1 millimeter$^2$ = .00155 inch$^2$<br>1 centimeter$^2$ = .155 inch$^2$<br>1 meter$^2$ = 10.764 foot$^2$ or 1.196 yard$^2$<br>1 kilometer$^2$ = .386 mile$^2$ or 247.04 acre$^2$ |
| **Volume** | |
| 1 inch$^3$ = 16.387 centimeter$^3$<br>1 foot$^3$ = .028 meter$^3$<br>1 yard$^3$ = .764 meter$^3$<br>1 quart = 0.946 liter<br>1 gallon = .003785 meter$^3$ | 1 centimeter$^3$ = .061 inch$^3$<br>1 meter$^3$ = 35.314 foot$^3$ or 1.308 yard$^3$<br>1 liter = .2642 gallons<br>1 liter = 1.057 quarts<br>1 meter$^3$ = 264.02 gallons |
| **Weight** | |
| 1 ounce = 28.349 grams<br>1 pound = .454 kilogram<br>1 ton = .907 metric ton | 1 gram = .035 ounce<br>1 kilogram = 2.205 pounds<br>1 metric ton = 1.102 tons |
| **Velocity** | |
| 1 foot/second = .305 meter/second<br>1 mile/hour = .447 meter/second | 1 meter/second = 3.281 feet/second<br>1 kilometer/hour = .621 mile/second |
| **Acceleration** | |
| 1 inch/second$^2$ = .0254 meter/second$^2$<br>1 foot/second$^2$ = .305 meter/second$^2$ | 1 meter/second$^2$ = 3.278 feet/second$^2$ |
| **Force** | |
| N (newton) = basic unit of force, kg-m/s$^2$. A mass of one kilogram (1 kg) exerts a gravitational force of 9.8 N (theoretically 9.80665 N) at mean sea level. | |

# Command Reference

Use the Help feature of AutoCAD for additional information about commands and their options.

| Command | Description |
|---------|-------------|
| 3D | Creates 3D surfaced objects. |
| 3DALIGN | Aligns objects with other objects in 2D and 3D environment. |
| 3DARRAY | Copies objects in a rectangular or polar 3D array. |
| 3DCLIP | Opens the Adjust Clipping Planes window and starts the 3D Orbit view. |
| 3DCONFIG | Allows user to specify 3D graphics system configuration settings. |
| -3DCONFIG | Provides a command line interface to 3D graphics system's configuration settings. |
| 3DCORBIT | Opens the 3D Orbit view and places selected objects in continuous orbit based on mouse click and drag direction and speed. |
| 3DDISTANCE | Opens the 3D Orbit view and allows user to move camera relative to object either increasing or decreasing object's apparent size without changing perspective. |
| 3DDWF | Displays Export 3D DWF dialog box. |
| 3DFACE | Creates a three- or four-sided surface. |
| 3DFLY | Activates fly-through mode and enables you to navigate in any direction, including off *XY* plane. |
| 3DFORBIT | Controls interactive viewing of objects in 3D, using an unconstrained orbit. |
| 3DMESH | Creates a free-form polygon mesh on an M×N grid. |
| 3DMOVE | Displays move grip tool in a 3D view and moves objects a specified distance in a specified direction. |
| 3DORBIT | Allows interactive viewing of selected 3D objects by clicking and dragging the mouse. |

| Command | Description |
|---|---|
| 3DORBITCTR | Allows user selection of a center of rotation for the 3D Orbit view. |
| 3DPAN | Initiates interactive viewing of selected 3D objects and enables dragging the view. |
| 3DPOLY | Creates a polyline with 3D line segments. |
| 3DROTATE | Displays rotate grip tool in a 3D view and revolves objects around a base point. |
| 3DSIN | Starts import process for a 3D Studio file. |
| 3DSWIVEL | Initiates interactive viewing of selected 3D objects and moves the camera based on cursor movement. |
| 3DWALK | Interactively changes view of a 3D drawing so that you appear to be walking through the model. |
| 3DZOOM | Initiates interactive viewing of selected 3D objects and allows zooming in or out. |
| ABOUT | Displays information about the software such as version number and the license agreement. |
| ACISIN | Imports an SAT ACIS file into the drawing. |
| ACISOUT | Exports an AutoCAD body, solid, or region to a SAT ACIS file. |
| ACTRECORD | Starts the recording of an Action Macro. |
| ACTSTOP | Stops the recording of an Action Macro. |
| -ACTSTOP | Stops the recording of an Action Macro. |
| ACTUSERINPUT | Requests a user input during playback. |
| ACTUSERMESSAGE | Inserts a message that will be viewed during playback. |
| -ACTUSERMESSAGE | Inserts a message that will be viewed during playback. |
| ADCCLOSE | Closes DesignCenter window. |
| ADCENTER | Opens DesignCenter window. |
| ADCNAVIGATE | Loads a specified path or drawing file name into the tree view of DesignCenter. |
| ALIGN | Aligns two objects in either 2D or 3D using one, two, or three pairs of source and destination points. |
| ALLPLAY | Plays all named views in current drawing. |
| AMECONVERT | Converts Advanced Modeling Extension (AME) regions or solids to AutoCAD solid models. |
| ANIPATH | Saves an animation along a path in a 3D model. |
| ANNORESET | Resets the location of all scale representations for an annotative object to that of the current scale representation. |
| ANNOUPDATE | Updates existing annotative objects to match the current properties of their styles. |

| Command | Description |
|---|---|
| APERTURE | Specifies size of the object snap target box. |
| APPLOAD | Opens Load/Unload Applications dialog box. |
| ARC | Draws an arc based on specified points. |
| ARCHIVE | Opens the Archive Sheet Set dialog box, which packages the current sheet set files to be archived. |
| AREA | Calculates area and perimeter of specified objects or areas. |
| ARRAY | Copies selected objects in either a rectangular or polar pattern. |
| ARX | Loads and unloads ObjectARX applications. |
| ATTACHURL | Associates hyperlinks with selected objects or areas in a drawing. |
| ATTDEF | Opens the Attribute Definition dialog box. |
| ATTDISP | Controls visibility of block attributes in a drawing. |
| ATTEDIT | Opens Edit Attributes dialog box, which permits editing of attribute values for a selected block. |
| ATTEXT | Opens Attribute Extraction dialog box, which permits informational text stored in blocks to be saved to a file. |
| ATTIPEDIT | Changes the textual content of an attribute within a block. |
| ATTREDEF | Redefines an existing block and updates attribute definitions. |
| ATTSYNC | Updates all occurrences of a specified block with the current attributes. |
| AUDIT | Finds and attempts to correct errors in a drawing. |
| AUTOPUBLISH | Publishes drawings to DWF files automatically. |
| BACKGROUND | Reintroduction of Background Command. |
| BACTION | Associates an action with a parameter in a dynamic block definition. |
| BACTIONSET | Enables user to specify objects associated with an action in a dynamic block. |
| BACTIONTOOL | Adds an action to a dynamic block. |
| BASE | Sets the insertion base point coordinates of a drawing in the current UCS. |
| BASSOCIATE | Associates an action whose parameter has been removed with a new parameter in a dynamic block definition. |
| BATTMAN | Displays the Block Attribute Manager, which permits block attribute property edits. |
| BATTORDER | Controls order in which block attributes are listed when the block is inserted or edited. |

| Command | Description |
| --- | --- |
| BAUTHORPALETTE | Opens Block Authoring Palettes window. |
| BAUTHORPALETTECLOSE | Closes Block Authoring Palettes window. |
| BCLOSE | Closes the Block Editor. |
| BCYCLEORDER | Displays Insertion Cycling Order dialog box allowing user to change the cycling order of grips in a dynamic block. |
| BEDIT | Opens the Edit Block Definition dialog box. |
| BGRIPSET | Controls number and position of grips for a parameter in a dynamic block. |
| BHATCH | See HATCH. |
| BLIPMODE | Controls display of temporary marks associated with point selection. |
| BLOCK | A group of reusable objects with flexible insert options. |
| BLOCKICON | Creates preview images for blocks displayed in DesignCenter. |
| BLOOKUPTABLE | Displays Property Lookup Table dialog box. |
| BMPOUT | Creates a bitmap file from selected objects. |
| BOUNDARY | Converts an enclosed area into a region or a polyline. |
| BOX | Draws a solid 3-dimensional box. |
| BPARAMETER | Adds a parameter to a dynamic block. |
| BREAK | Splits the selected object into two parts. |
| BREP | Removes history from 3D solid primitives and composite solids. |
| BROWSER | Launches the default Web browser. |
| BSAVE | Saves changes to the current block definition and retains the same name. |
| BSAVEAS | Saves a copy of a block definition under a new name. |
| BVHIDE | Makes selected objects invisible in a visibility state. |
| BVSHOW | Controls visibility of objects in a dynamic block. |
| BVSTATE | Manages visibility states in a dynamic block. |
| CAL | Calculates mathematical and geometric expressions. |
| CAMERA | Sets position of camera and target for viewing. |
| CHAMFER | Draws an angled corner between two lines. |
| CHANGE | Changes the properties of selected objects. |
| CHECKSTANDARDS | Compares the current drawing with a standards file and notes violations. |

| Command | Description |
|---|---|
| CHPROP | Enables changing the color, layer, linetype, linetype scale factor, lineweight, and thickness of a selected object. |
| CHSPACE | Moves objects from model space to paper space, or vice versa. (former Express Tool) |
| CIRCLE | Draws a circle. |
| CLEANSCREENOFF | Restores all toolbars and dockable windows cleared by the CLEANSCREENON command. |
| CLEANSCREENON | Clears the screen of all toolbars and dockable windows. |
| CLOSE | Closes current active drawing. |
| CLOSEALL | Closes all open drawings. |
| COLOR | Specifies color for new objects. |
| COMMANDLINE | Restores the command line. |
| COMMANDLINEHIDE | Hides the command line. |
| COMPILE | Compiles PostScript font and shape files. |
| CONE | Draws a 3D solid cone with a circular or elliptical base. |
| CONVERT | Updates 2D polylines and associative hatches created in AutoCAD Release 13 or earlier. |
| CONVERTCTB | Changes a color-dependent plot style table to a named plot style table. |
| CONVERTOLDLIGHTS | Converts lights created in previous releases to lights in AutoCAD 2007 format. |
| CONVERTOLDMATERIALS | Converts materials created in previous releases to materials in AutoCAD 2007 format. |
| CONVERTPSTYLES | Changes current drawing to either a named or color-dependent plot style. |
| CONVTOSOLID | Converts polylines and circles with thickness to 3D solids. |
| CONVTOSURFACE | Converts objects to surfaces. |
| COPY | Creates copies of selected objects at a specified location. |
| COPYBASE | Copies selected objects with a user-defined base point. |
| COPYCLIP | Copies all selected objects to the Clipboard. |
| COPYHIST | Copies command line text to the Clipboard. |
| COPYLINK | Copies the current view to the Clipboard for inclusion in other OLE applications. |
| COPYTOLAYER | Copies one or more objects to another layer. (former Express Tool) |
| -COPYTOLAYER | Copies one or more objects to another layer. (command line version) |

| Command | Description |
| --- | --- |
| CUI | Allows customization of workspaces, toolbars, menus, shortcut menus, and keyboard shortcuts. |
| CUIEXPORT | Exports customized settings. |
| CUIIMPORT | Imports customized settings. |
| CUILOAD | Loads a CUI file. |
| CUIUNLOAD | Unloads a CUI file. |
| CUSTOMIZE | Allows customization of tool palettes. |
| CUTCLIP | Removes objects from the drawing and places them on the Clipboard. |
| CYLINDER | Draws a solid 3D cylinder with either a circular or elliptical cross section. |
| DASHBOARD | Opens Dashboard window. |
| DASHBOARDCLOSE | Closes Dashboard window. Routed to the RIBBONCLOSE command. |
| DATAEXTRACTION | Exports object property, block attribute, and drawing information to a data extraction table or to an external file and specifies a data link to an Excel spreadsheet. |
| DATALINK | Displays the Data Link Manager. |
| DATALINKUPDATE | Updates data to or from an established external data link. |
| DBCLOSE | Closes the dbConnect Manager and removes the dbConnect menu from the menu bar. |
| DBCONNECT | Opens dbConnect Manager and adds dbConnect menu to the menu bar, establishing an interface with external database tables. |
| DBLIST | Displays database information about drawing objects in the text window. |
| DDEDIT | Enables editing of single-line text, dimension text, attribute definitions, and feature control frames. |
| DDPTYPE | Specifies point display style and size. |
| DDVPOINT | Specification 3D viewing direction. |
| DELAY | Specifies the length of a timed pause in a script. |
| DETACHURL | Removes hyperlinks from selected objects. |
| DGNADJUST | Changes the display options of selected DGN underlays. |
| -DGNADJUST | Provides a command line interface to the DGN underlay display options. |
| DGNATTACH | Attaches a DGN underlay to the current drawing. |
| -DGNATTACH | Attaches a DGN underlay to the current drawing from the command line. |

| Command | Description |
| --- | --- |
| DGNCLIP | Defines a clipping boundary for a selected DGN underlay. |
| DGNEXPORT | Creates one or more DGN files from the current drawing. You will be able to attach DGN files with non-DGN extensions. |
| -DGNEXPORT | Creates one or more DGN files from the current drawing from the command line. |
| DGNIMPORT | Creates one or more DGN files from the current drawing. You will be able to attach DGN files with non-DGN extensions. |
| -DGNIMPORT | Creates one or more DGN files from the current drawing from the command line. |
| DGNMAPPING | Opens the DGN Mapping Setups Manager dialog. |
| DIM and DIM1 | Initiates Dimensioning mode. DIM1 allows user to execute a single dimensioning command before returning to the Command prompt. |
| DIMALIGNED | Creates a linear dimension parallel to an angled edge. |
| DIMANGULAR | Creates an angular dimension between two lines or three points. |
| DIMARC | Creates an arc length dimension. |
| DIMBASELINE | Creates a linear, angular, or ordinate dimension from a selected baseline. |
| DIMBREAK | Adds or removes a dimension break. |
| DIMCENTER | Creates center marks or centerlines of circles and arcs. |
| DIMCONTINUE | Creates a chained linear, angular, or ordinate dimension. |
| DIMDIAMETER | Creates diameter dimensions for circles and arcs, which include the diameter symbol. |
| DIMDISASSOCIATE | Removes associativity from specified dimensions. |
| DIMEDIT | Edits dimension extension lines and text. |
| DIMINSPECT | Creates or removes inspection dimensions. |
| -DIMINSPECT | Provides a command line interface to create or remove inspection dimensions. |
| DIMJOGGED | Creates a foreshortened radius dimension. |
| DIMJOGLINE | Adds or removes a jog line on a linear or aligned dimension. |
| DIMLINEAR | Creates horizontal or vertical linear dimensions. |
| DIMORDINATE | Creates ordinate dimensions based on specified $x$ and $y$ data. |
| DIMOVERRIDE | Temporarily changes a dimension system variable without changing the dimension style. |

| Command | Description |
| --- | --- |
| DIMRADIUS | Creates a radius dimension for a circle or arc, which includes a radius symbol. |
| DIMREASSOCIATE | Links selected dimensions to association points on objects. |
| DIMREGEN | Updates the locations of associative dimensions. |
| DIMSPACE | Adjusts the spacing equally between parallel linear and angular dimensions. |
| DIMSTYLE | Manages dimension styles. |
| DIMTEDIT | Permits moving and rotating dimension text. |
| DIST | Measures the distance and angle between two specified points. |
| DISTANTLIGHT | Creates a distant light. |
| DIVIDE | Divides an object into evenly spaced segments marked by points. |
| DONUT | Draws filled rings and circles. |
| DRAGMODE | Controls display of dragged objects. |
| DRAWINGRECOVERY | Displays list of files open during a system failure and offers options for recovery. |
| DRAWINGRECOVERYHIDE | Closes the Drawing Recovery Manager. |
| DRAWORDER | Changes the draw order of drawing objects. |
| DSETTINGS | Sets snap, grid, polar tracking, object snap, and dynamic input. |
| DSVIEWER | Opens Aerial View window. |
| DVIEW | Creates parallel projection or perspective views in 3D. |
| DWFADJUST | Allows adjustment of a DWF underlay from the command line. |
| DWFATTACH | Attaches a DWF underlay to current drawing. |
| DWFCLIP | Uses clipping boundaries to define a subregion of a DWF underlay. |
| DWFFORMAT | Sets the default DWF format to the selected format to DWF or DWFx for the PUBLISH, 3DDWF, and EXPORT commands. |
| DWFLAYERS | Controls the display of layers in a DWF underlay. |
| DWGPROPS | Sets and displays the properties of the current drawing. |
| DXBIN | Imports Drawing Exchange Binary format files. |
| EATTEDIT | Edits block attributes. |
| EATTEXT | Extracts block attribute data to a table or to an external file. |
| EDGE | Changes display visibility of 3D Face edges. |

| Command | Description |
|---|---|
| EDGESURF | Creates a 3D mesh conforming to four selected edges. |
| EDITSHOT | Opens the Edit View dialog box with the Shot Properties tab active. |
| ELEV | Sets elevation and extrusion thickness for new objects. |
| ELLIPSE | Draws an ellipse or an elliptical arc. |
| ERASE | Removes selected objects. |
| ETRANSMIT | Packages files for Internet transmission. |
| EXPLODE | Breaks a selected compound object into component parts. |
| EXPORT | Saves object to other file formats. |
| EXPORTLAYOUT | Exports all visible objects from current layout to the model space of a new drawing. |
| EXPORTTOAUTOCAD | Creates a new DWG file with all AEC objects expolded. |
| -EXPORTTOUTOCAD | Provides a command line interface to creating a new DWG file with all AEC objects exploded. |
| EXTEND | Extends selected object to meet a selected boundary edge. |
| EXTERNALREFERENCES | Displays External References palette. |
| EXTERNALREF-ERENCESCLOSE | Closes External References palette. |
| EXTRUDE | Creates a solid by extruding a cross-section to a specified height. |
| FIELD | Creates a multiline text object, which can be updated automatically when the field value changes. |
| FILL | Controls the display of filled areas in hatches, 2D solids, and polylines. |
| FILLET | Creates a rounded corner tangent to two objects with a specified radius. |
| FILTER | Allows creation of a list of criteria for creating a selection set. |
| FIND | Enables finding, selecting, and replacing specified text. |
| FLATSHOT | Creates a 2D representation of all 3D objects in the current view. |
| FREESPOT | Creates a free spotlight which is similar to a spotlight without a specified target. |
| FREEWEB | Creates a free web light which is similar to a web light without a specified target. |
| GEOGRAPHICLOCATION | Specifies latitude and longitude of a location. |
| GOTOURL | Opens the file or Web page associated with a hyperlink in the drawing. |
| GRADIENT | Fills a closed area with a gradient fill pattern. |

| Command | Description |
|---|---|
| GRAPHSCR | Closes the text window. |
| GRID | Displays a reference pattern of dots at user-specified spacing. |
| GROUP | Creates and manages sets of grouped objects. |
| HATCH | Creates a hatch pattern, solid fill, or gradient fill inside a closed area. |
| HATCHEDIT | Changes existing hatches or fills. |
| HELIX | Creates a 2D or 3D spiral. |
| HELP | Displays explanation of concepts, commands, and procedures. |
| HIDE | Regenerates model and suppresses hidden lines. |
| HIDEPALETTES | Hides all currently displayed palettes such as the command line, DesignCenter, and properties, keeping track of their positions. |
| HLSETTINGS | Controls hidden line display properties. |
| HYPERLINK | Attaches or modifies a hyperlink to a drawing object. |
| HYPERLINKOPTIONS | Manages display of hyperlink properties. |
| ID | Displays coordinates of selected point. |
| IMAGE | Opens Image Manager. |
| IMAGEADJUST | Controls image brightness, contrast, and fade values. |
| IMAGEATTACH | Attaches image to drawing. |
| IMAGECLIP | Creates clipping boundaries for images. |
| IMAGEFRAME | Controls image frame display and plotting. |
| IMAGEQUALITY | Controls image display quality. |
| IMPORT | Imports files from other applications. |
| IMPRESSION | Gives a CAD drawing a hand-drawn look by exporting it for rendering in Autodesk Impression. |
| IMPRINT | Imprints an edge on a 3D solid. |
| INSERT | Places drawings or blocks into drawing. |
| INSERTOBJ | Inserts a linked or embedded object. |
| INTERFERE | Determines if two solid objects overlap. |
| -INTERFERE | Highlights 3D solids that overlap. (command line version) |
| INTERSECT | Creates a new solid from the area common to two or more solids or regions. |
| ISOPLANE | Selects active isometric plane. |
| JOGSECTION | Adds a jogged segment to a section object. |

| Command | Description |
| --- | --- |
| JOIN | Combines similar objects into a single object. |
| JPGOUT | Saves selected objects to a JPEG file format. |
| JUSTIFYTEXT | Changes the justification point of text. |
| LAYCUR | Changes layer of selected objects to current layer. (former Express Tool) |
| LAYDEL | Deletes layer of a selected object and all objects on layer, and purges layer from drawing. (former Express Tool) |
| -LAYDEL | Deletes layer of a selected object and all objects on layer, and purges layer from drawing. (command line version) |
| LAYER | Manages layers. The Layer Properties Manager dialog is a modeless dialog. |
| LAYERCLOSE | Closes the Layer Properties Manager dialog from the command line. |
| LAYERP | Undoes changes to layer settings. |
| LAYERPMODE | Controls tracking of layer setting changes. |
| LAYERSTATE | Saves, restores, and manages named layer states. |
| LAYFRZ | Freezes layer of selected objects. (former Express Tool) |
| LAYISO | Isolates layer of selected objects so that all other layers are turned off. (former Express Tool) |
| LAYLCK | Locks layer of selected objects. (former Express Tool) |
| LAYMCH | Changes layer of a selected object to match destination layer. (former Express Tool) |
| -LAYMCH | Changes layer of a selected object to match destination layer. (command line version) |
| LAYMCUR | Makes layer of a selected object current. (renamed AI_MOLC) |
| LAYMRG | Merges selected layers onto a destination layer. (former Express Tool) |
| -LAYMRG | Merges selected layers onto a destination layer. (command line version) |
| LAYOFF | Turns off layer of selected object. (former Express Tool) |
| LAYON | Turns on all layers. (former Express Tool) |
| LAYOUT | Manages drawing layout tabs. |
| LAYOUTWIZARD | Starts layout wizard. |
| LAYTHW | Thaws all layers. (former Express Tool) |
| LAYTRANS | Converts drawing layers to specified standards. |
| LAYULK | Unlocks layer of a selected object. (former Express Tool) |

| Command | Description |
|---|---|
| LAYUNISO | Turns on layers that were turned off with last LAYISO command. (former Express Tool) |
| LAYVPI | Isolates an object's layer to the current viewport. (former Express Tool) |
| LAYWALK | Dynamically displays layers in a drawing. (former Express Tool) |
| LEADER | Creates leader lines for notes and dimensions. |
| LENGTHEN | Modifies object length. |
| LIGHT | Controls lights in rendered scenes. |
| LIGHTLIST | Opens Lights in Model window to add and modify lights. |
| LIGHTLISTCLOSE | Closes Lights in Model window. |
| LIMITS | Sets drawing size. |
| LINE | Draws straight line segments. |
| LINETYPE | Manages linetypes. |
| LIST | Displays database information. |
| LIVESECTION | Turns on live sectioning for a selected section object. |
| LOAD | Loads shapes for use by the SHAPE command. |
| LOFT | Creates a 3D solid or surface by lofting through a set of two or more curves. |
| LOGFILEOFF | Closes the log file. |
| LOGFILEON | Records contents of text window to a file. |
| LTSCALE | Sets drawing linetype scale. |
| LWEIGHT | Manages lineweights. |
| MACROTRACE | Evaluates DIESEL expressions. |
| MARKUP | Manages markup sets. |
| MARKUPCLOSE | Closes Markup Set Manager. |
| MASSPROP | Displays mass properties of solids and regions. |
| MATCHCELL | Copies the properties of one table cell to other selected table cells. |
| MATCHPROP | Copies the properties of one object to other selected objects. |
| MATERIALATTACH | Attaches materials to objects by layer. |
| MATERIALMAP | Displays a material mapper grip tool to adjust mapping on a face or an object. |
| MATERIALS | Manages, applies, and modifies materials. |

| Command | Description |
| --- | --- |
| MATERIALSCLOSE | Closes Materials window. |
| MEASURE | Marks segments of a specified length on an object. |
| MENU | Loads a customizable XML-based file containing menus, toolbars, tool palettes, and other interface elements. |
| MINSERT | Inserts copies of a block in a rectangular array. |
| MIRROR | Creates a mirror image about an axis. |
| MIRROR3D | Creates a mirror image about a plane. |
| MLEADER | Creates a line that connects annotation to a feature. |
| MLEADERALIGN | Organizes selected multileaders along a specified line. |
| MLEADERCOLLECT | Organizes selected multileaders containing blocks as content into a group attached to a single leader line. |
| MLEADEREDIT | Adds leader lines to, or removes leader lines from, a multileader object. |
| MLEADERSTYLE | Defines a new multileader style. |
| MLEDIT | Modifies multiline vertices, breaks, and intersections. |
| MLINE | Creates multiple parallel lines. |
| MLSTYLE | Controls multiline styles. |
| MODEL | Enters model space. |
| MOVE | Moves objects from one location to another. |
| MREDO | Reverses multiple UNDO commands. |
| MSLIDE | Makes a slide file of current model viewport or layout. |
| MSPACE | Enters model space for active viewport in layout space. |
| MTEDIT | Modifies multiline text. |
| MTEXT | Creates multiple lines of text as a single object. |
| MULTIPLE | Repeats the next command until you enter <Esc>. |
| MVIEW | Creates and manages layout viewports. |
| MVSETUP | Helps set up drawing views. |
| NAVSMOTION | Displays the ShowMotion interface. |
| NAVSMOTIONCLOSE | Closes the ShowMotion interface. |
| NAVSWHEEL | Displays the SteeringWheel. |
| NAVVCUBE | Shows/hides the ViewCube. |
| NETLOAD | Loads a .NET application. |
| NEW | Starts a new drawing. |

| Command | Description |
| --- | --- |
| NEWSHEETSET | Creates a new sheet set. |
| NEWSHOT | Opens the New View dialog box with the Shot Properties tab active. |
| OBJECTSCALE | Adds or deletes supported scales for annotative objects. |
| -OBJECTSCALE | Provides a command line interface to add or delete supported scales for annotative objects. |
| OFFSET | Draws objects parallel to a specified object. |
| OLELINKS | Manages OLE (Object Linking and Embedding) links. |
| OLESCALE | Manages OLE (Object Linking and Embedding) object properties. |
| OOPS | Restores objects removed by the last ERASE command. |
| OPEN | Opens a previously created drawing file. |
| OPENDWFMARKUP | Opens a marked up DWF file. |
| OPENSHEETSET | Opens a specified sheet set. |
| OPTIONS | Controls AutoCAD settings. |
| ORTHO | Limits cursor movement to horizontal and vertical directions while in drawing and editing commands. |
| OSNAP | Sets running object snaps. |
| PAGESETUP | Manages page layout, plotting device, paper size, and other layout settings. |
| PAN | Moves drawing on screen without changing zoom factor. |
| PARTIALOAD | Loads additional components into a partially opened drawing. |
| PARTIALOPEN | Opens selected views and layers from a drawing file. |
| PASTEASHYPERLINK | Pastes information from the Clipboard as a hyperlink. |
| PASTEBLOCK | Pastes objects from the Clipboard as a block. |
| PASTECLIP | Pastes data from the Clipboard. |
| PASTEORIG | Pastes objects from the Clipboard retaining coordinate information from original drawing. |
| PASTESPEC | Sets file formats and linking options for pasted objects. |
| PCINWIZARD | Opens wizard to import PCP and PC2 configuration file plot settings. |
| PEDIT | Modifies polylines and 3D meshes. |
| PFACE | Creates a 3D mesh by entering vertices. |
| PLAN | Creates a view looking down the current UCS Z-axis toward the origin. |

| Command | Description |
|---|---|
| PLANESURF | Creates a planar surface. |
| PLINE | Creates a connected sequence of line and arc segments as a single object. |
| PLOT | Prints a drawing to a plotter, printer, or file. |
| PLOTSTAMP | Places information on corner of drawing and creates a log file. |
| PLOTSTYLE | Manages plot styles for new or selected objects. |
| PLOTTERMANAGER | Adds or modifies a plotter configuration. |
| PNGOUT | Saves to a Portable Network Graphics format file. |
| POINT | Draws a point. |
| POINTLIGHT | Creates a point light. |
| POLYGON | Draws regular polygons with up to 1024 sides. |
| POLYSOLID | Creates a 3D polysolid. |
| PRESSPULL | Presses or pulls bounded areas. |
| PREVIEW | Shows plot appearance. |
| PROPERTIES | Used to view or change object properties. |
| PROPERTIESCLOSE | Closes Properties palette. |
| PSETUPIN | Imports a page setup. |
| PSPACE | Enters paper space. |
| PUBLISH | Creates a paper or electronic drawing set. |
| PUBLISHTOWEB | Converts drawings to HTML pages. |
| PURGE | Removes unused items from the drawing database. |
| PYRAMID | Creates a 3D solid pyramid. |
| QCCLOSE | Closes the QuickCalc calculator. |
| QDIM | Quickly creates or edits a series of dimensions. |
| QLEADER | Quickly creates leader line and text. |
| QNEW | Starts a new drawing from the default template file. |
| QSAVE | Saves the current drawing. |
| QSELECT | Quickly creates a selection set based on filtering criteria. |
| QTEXT | Controls text and attribute display and plotting. |
| QUICKCALC | Opens the QuickCalc calculator. |
| QUICKCUI | Displays the CUI editor in a collapsed state. Additional support for enhanced tooltips, quick access panel, and ribbons. |
| QUIT | Exits AutoCAD and prompts to save or discard changes. |

| Command | Description |
| --- | --- |
| QVDRAWING | Displays a two-level structure of preview images at the bottom of the application. The first level displays the images of open drawings and the second level displays the images for model space and layouts in a drawing. |
| QVDRAWINGCLOSE | Closes preview images of open drawings and layouts in a drawing. |
| RAY | Creates a line extending to infinity in one direction. |
| RECOVER | Repairs a damaged drawing. |
| RECOVERALL | Repairs a damaged drawing and xrefs. |
| RECTANG | Creates rectangles. |
| REDEFINE | Restores AutoCAD commands previously changed by the UNDEFINE command. |
| REDO | Reverses the effects of a single UNDO command. |
| REDRAW | Refreshes current viewport display. |
| REDRAWALL | Refreshes display in all viewports. |
| REFCLOSE | Saves or discards changes made during in-place editing of an xref or block. |
| REFEDIT | Selects a reference for editing. |
| REFSET | Modifies working set during in-place editing of a reference. |
| REGEN | Regenerates the entire drawing and recomputes geometry for objects in the current viewport. |
| REGENALL | Regenerates and recomputes geometry for all viewports. |
| REGENAUTO | Controls automatic regeneration of a drawing. |
| REGION | Creates a 2-dimensional area object from a closed shape or loop. |
| REINIT | Reinitializes digitizer, digitizer input/output port, and program parameters file. |
| RENAME | Changes object names. |
| RENDER | Produces a realistically shaded view of a 3D model. |
| RENDERCROP | Selects a specific region in an image for rendering. |
| RENDERENVIRONMENT | Provides visual cues for the apparent distance of objects. |
| RENDEREXPOSURE | Provides settings to interactively adjust the lighting global for the most recent rendered output. |
| RENDERPRESETS | Specifies render presets, reusable rendering parameters for rendering an image. |
| RENDERWIN | Displays Render Window without starting a render task. |
| RESETBLOCK | Restores dynamic block references to the default value. |

| Command | Description |
|---|---|
| RESUME | Restarts an interrupted script. |
| REVCLOUD | Creates a cloud-shaped polyline. |
| REVOLVE | Creates a solid by revolving a closed 2-dimensional shape around an axis. |
| REVSURF | Creates a rotated surface about an axis. |
| RIBBON | Opens the Ribbon window. |
| RIBBONCLOSE | Closes the Ribbon window. |
| ROTATE | Rotates selected objects around a specified base point. |
| ROTATE3D | Rotates an object in a 3D coordinate system. |
| RPREF | Controls rendering preferences. |
| RPREFCLOSE | Closes Advanced Render Settings palette, if it is displayed. |
| RSCRIPT | Creates a continuously running script. |
| RULESURF | Creates a polygon mesh between two curves. |
| SAVE | Saves a drawing. |
| SAVEAS | Saves current drawing with options for renaming file, changing file type, or changing file location. |
| SAVEIMG | Saves a rendered image to a BMP, TGA, or TIFF file. |
| SCALE | Proportionally enlarges or reduces objects relative to a base point. |
| SCALELISTEDIT | Manages scales available for layout viewports, page layouts, and plotting. |
| SCALETEXT | Enlarges or reduces text objects while maintaining location. |
| SCRIPT | Executes a sequence of commands from a script file. |
| SECTION | Creates a cross-section through a solid. |
| SECTIONPLANE | Creates a section object that acts as a cutting plane through a 3D object. |
| SECURITYOPTIONS | Controls drawing security settings. |
| SELECT | Places objects in the Previous selection set. |
| SEQUENCEPLAY | Plays the named views in one view category. |
| SETBYLAYER | Changes property and ByBlock settings for selected objects to ByLayer. |
| SETIDROPHANDLER | Sets i-drop content default type. |
| SETVAR | Lists or changes system variable values. |
| SHADEMODE | Controls solid model shading. |
| SHAPE | Inserts a shape into the current drawing. |

| Command | Description |
| --- | --- |
| SHEETSET | Opens the Sheet Set Manager. |
| SHEETSETHIDE | Closes the Sheet Set Manager. |
| SHELL | Allows execution of operating system commands within AutoCAD. |
| SHOWPALETTES | Restores the state of the display and position of palettes hidden by HIDEPALETTES. Press CTRL + SHIFT + H to switch between HIDEPALETTES and SHOWPALETTES. |
| SIGVALIDATE | Displays digital signature information. |
| SKETCH | Draws a freehand line composed of segments. |
| SLICE | Divides a solid along a specified plane. |
| SNAP | Limits cursor movement to specified intervals. |
| SOLDRAW | Generates visible and hidden lines for viewports created with SOLVIEW. |
| SOLID | Creates 2D filled triangles and four-sided polygons. |
| SOLIDEDIT | Edits faces and edges of 3D solid objects. |
| SOLPROF | Creates a 2D profile of a 3D solid. |
| SOLVIEW | Creates orthographic, auxiliary, and sectional views of 3D solids. |
| SPACETRANS | Converts lengths between model space units and paper space units. |
| SPELL | Checks spelling of selected objects in a drawing. |
| SPHERE | Creates a solid sphere. |
| SPLINE | Creates a smooth curve fit to a sequence of points within a specified tolerance. |
| SPLINEDIT | Modifies splines or spline-fit polylines. |
| SPOTLIGHT | Creates a spotlight. |
| STANDARDS | Associates the current drawing with a Standards file. |
| STATUS | Displays drawing statistics, modes, and extents. |
| STLOUT | Stores solid data in a STL file format for stereo lithography. |
| STRETCH | Stretches selected objects. |
| STYLE | Manages text styles. |
| STYLESMANAGER | Manages plot styles. |
| SUBTRACT | Creates composite solid or region by subtracting selected objects or regions. |
| SUNPROPERTIES | Opens Sun palette and sets properties of the sun. |
| SUNPROPERTIESCLOSE | Closes Sun Properties window. |

| Command | Description |
| --- | --- |
| SWEEP | Creates a 3D solid or surface by sweeping a 2D curve along a path. |
| SYSWINDOWS | Arranges windows and icons when the application window is shared with external applications. |
| TABLE | Creates an empty table in the drawing. |
| TABLEDIT | Edits text in a selected table cell. |
| TABLEEXPORT | Exports data from a table object in comma-separated file format. |
| TABLESTYLE | Sets the current table style. Creates, modifies, and deletes table styles. |
| TABLET | Turns on and off, calibrates, and configures an attached digitizing tablet input device. |
| TABSURF | Creates a surfaced polygon mesh by specifying a path curve and direction vector. |
| TASKBAR | Controls drawing display mode on the Windows taskbar. |
| TEXT | Creates a single line of user-entered text. |
| TEXTSCR | Opens the command line in a separate window. |
| TEXTTOFRONT | Brings text and/or dimensions in front of other drawing objects. |
| THICKEN | Creates a 3D solid by thickening a surface. |
| TIFOUT | Creates a TIFF file from selected objects. |
| TIME | Displays drawing date and time statistics. |
| TINSERT | Inserts a block in a table cell. |
| TOLERANCE | Adds geometric tolerances in feature control frames. |
| TOOLBAR | Manages toolbar display and customization. |
| TOOLPALETTES | Opens Tool Palettes window. |
| TOOLPALETTESCLOSE | Closes Tool Palettes window. |
| TORUS | Creates a donut-shaped solid. |
| TPNAVIGATE | Displays a specified tool palette or palette group. |
| TRACE | Creates solid lines. |
| TRANSPARENCY | Controls transparency of background in images. |
| TRAYSETTINGS | Controls Status Bar tray content. |
| TREESTAT | Displays information about a drawing's spatial index. |
| TRIM | Removes part of an object at a selected cutting edge. |
| U | Undo. |
| UCS | Creates and manages User Coordinate Systems. |

| Command | Description |
| --- | --- |
| UCSICON | Controls display and location of UCS icon. |
| UCSMAN | Manages defined User Coordinate Systems. |
| UNDEFINE | Allows an application-defined command to override an AutoCAD command. |
| UNDO | Reverses previous commands. |
| UNION | Adds selected regions or solids. |
| UNITS | Sets coordinate and angle display precision and formats. |
| UPDATEFIELD | Updates fields for selected items. |
| UPDATETHUMBSNOW | Updates thumbnail previews in the Sheet Set Manager. |
| VBAIDE | Edits code, forms, and references for any loaded or embedded VBA projects in the current drawing. |
| VBALOAD | Loads a VBA (Visual Basic for Applications) project into the current work session. |
| VBAMAN | Loads, unloads, saves, creates, embeds, and extracts VBA projects. |
| VBARUN | Runs a VBA macro. |
| VBASTMT | Executes a Visual Basic complete instruction in the context of the current drawing on the AutoCAD command line. |
| VBAUNLOAD | Unloads a VBA (Visual Basic for Applications) project. |
| VIEW | Saves and restores named views. |
| VIEWGO | Navigates to a named view. |
| VIEWPLAY | Plays the ShowMotion animation for the named view. |
| VIEWPLOTDETAILS | Displays information about completed plot and publish jobs. |
| VIEWRES | Sets resolution for objects in the current viewport. |
| VISUALSTYLES | Creates and modifies visual styles and applies a visual style to a viewport. |
| -VISUALSTYLES | Creates and modifies visual styles and applies a visual style to a viewport. (command line version). |
| VISUALSTYLESCLOSE | Closes Visual Styles Manager dialog box. |
| VLISP | Opens the Visual Lisp Console window to develop, test, and debug AutoLISP programs. |
| VPCLIP | Clips viewport objects and modifies viewport boundary. |
| VPLAYER | Sets layer visibility within viewports. VPLAYER can now run in Model tab with a limited set of options. |
| VPMAX | Enlarges current viewport to full screen and switches to model space for editing. |

| Command | Description |
|---|---|
| VPMIN | Restores viewport to settings prior to maximizing. |
| VPOINT | Sets 3D viewing direction. |
| VPORTS | Creates viewports in model or paper space. |
| VSCURRENT | Sets visual style in current viewport. |
| VSLIDE | Opens an image slide file for viewing in the current viewport. |
| VSSAVE | Saves a visual style. |
| VTOPTIONS | Controls view transitions. |
| WALKFLYSETTINGS | Specifies walk and fly settings. |
| WBLOCK | Saves a block to a new drawing file. |
| WEBLIGHT | Creates a web light. |
| WEDGE | Creates a 3D solid wedge. |
| WHOHAS | Displays the current user's computer name, login ID, and full name (if available) and the date and time the drawing file was opened. |
| WIPEOUT | Creates a polygonal area that covers existing objects with the current background color. |
| WMFIN | Imports a Windows metafile as a block. |
| WMFOPTS | Sets options for the WMFIN command. |
| WMFOUT | Saves selected objects to a Windows metafile format. |
| WORKSPACE | Manages workspaces. |
| WSSAVE | Saves a workspace scheme and settings. |
| WSSETTINGS | Sets workspace options. |
| XATTACH | Attaches a drawing as an external reference to the current drawing. |
| XBIND | Adds specified xref-dependent named objects to the drawing. |
| XCLIP | Defines an external reference display clipping boundary. |
| XEDGES | Creates wireframe geometry by extracting edges from a 3D solid or surface. |
| XLINE | Creates a line that is infinite in both directions. |
| XOPEN | Opens an external reference for editing in a new window. |
| XPLODE | Disassembles a block into its component objects for editing. |
| XREF | Manages external references. |
| ZOOM | Changes the magnification of objects in the current viewport. |

# Command Aliases

Command aliases are shortcuts for commands that you enter at the keyboard. *Note:* Command aliases beginning with a dash (-) suppress display of dialog box windows and force input entry from the command line.

| Command | Alias | Command | Alias |
|---------|-------|---------|-------|
| 3DARRAY | 3A | BACTION | AC |
| 3DALIGN | 3AL | BLOCK | B |
| ATTIPEDIT | ATI | -BLOCK | -B |
| 3DFACE | 3F | BCLOSE | BC |
| 3DMOVE | 3M | BEDIT | BE |
| 3DORBIT | 3DO, ORBIT | BOUNDARY | BO |
| 3DPOLY | 3P | -BOUNDARY | -BO |
| 3DROTATE | 3R | BPARAMETER | PARAM |
| 3DWALK | 3DNAVIGATE, 3DW | BREAK | BR |
| ADCENTER | ADC, DC, DCENTER | BSAVE | BS |
| ALIGN | AL | BVSTATE | VS |
| APPLOAD | AP | CAMERA | CAM |
| ARC | A | CHAMFER | CHA |
| AREA | AA | CHANGE | -CH |
| ARRAY | AR | CHECKSTANDARDS | CHK |
| -ARRAY | -AR | CIRCLE | C |
| ATTDEF | ATT | COLOR | COL, COLOUR |
| -ATTDEF | -ATT | COMMANDLINE | CLI |
| ATTEDIT | ATE | COPY | CO, CP |
| -ATTEDIT | -ATE, ATTE | CTABLESTYLE | CT |

| Command | Alias | Command | Alias |
|---|---|---|---|
| CYLINDER | CYL | DRAWORDER | DR |
| DATAEXTRACTION | DX | DSETTINGS | DS, SE |
| DATALINK | DL | DVIEW | DV |
| DATALINKUPDATE | DLU | ELLIPSE | EL |
| DBCONNECT | DBC | ERASE | E |
| DDEDIT | ED | EXPLODE | X |
| DDGRIPS | GR | EXPORT | EXP |
| DDVPOINT | VP | -EXPORTTOAUTOCAD | AECTOACAD |
| DIMALIGNED | DAL | EXTEND | EX |
| DIMANGULAR | DAN | EXTERNALREFERENCES | ER |
| DIMARC | DAR | EXTRUDE | EXT |
| DIMBASELINE | DBA | FLATSHOT | FSHOT |
| DIMCENTER | DCE | GEOGRAPHICLOCATION | GEO, NORTH, NORTHDIR |
| DIMCONTINUE | DCO | FILLET | F |
| DIMDIAMETER | DDI | FILTER | FI |
| DIMDISASSOCIATE | DDA | GRADIENT | GD |
| DIMEDIT | DED | GROUP | G |
| DIMJOGGED | DJO, JOG | -GROUP | -G |
| DIMJOGLINE | DJL | HATCH | BH, H |
| DIMLINEAR | DLI | -HATCH | -H |
| DIMORDINATE | DOR | HATCHEDIT | HE |
| DIMOVERRIDE | DOV | HIDE | HI |
| DIMRADIUS | DRA | IMAGE | IM |
| DIMREASSOCIATE | DRE | -IMAGE | -IM |
| DIMSTYLE | D, DST | IMAGEADJUST | IAD |
| DIST | DI | IMAGEATTACH | IAT |
| DIVIDE | DIV | IMAGECLIP | ICL |
| DONUT | DO | IMPORT | IMP |
| DRAWINGRECOVERY | DRM | INSERT | I |

| Command | Alias | Command | Alias |
|---|---|---|---|
| -INSERT | -I | MLINE | ML |
| INSERTOBJ | IO | MOVE | M |
| INTERFERE | INF | MSPACE | MS |
| INTERSECT | IN | MTEXT | MT, T |
| JOIN | J | -MTEXT | -T |
| LAYER | LA | MVIEW | MV |
| -LAYER | -LA | OFFSET | O |
| -LAYOUT | LO | OPTIONS | OP |
| LAYERSTATE | LAS | OSNAP | OS |
| LAYERSTATE | LMAN | -OSNAP | -OS |
| LENGTHEN | LEN | PAN | P |
| LINE | L | -PAN | -P |
| LINETYPE | LT, LTYPE | -PARTIALOPEN | PARTIALOPEN |
| -LINETYPE | -LT, -LTYPE | PASTESPEC | PA |
| LIST | LI, LS, SHOWMAT | PEDIT | PE |
| LTSCALE | LTS | PLINE | PL |
| LINEWEIGHT | LW, LWEIGHT | PLOT | PRINT |
| MARKUP | MSM | POINT | PO |
| MATCHPROP | MA | POINTLIGHT | FREEPOINT |
| MATERIALMAP | SETUV | POLYGON | POL |
| MATERIALS | FINISH, MAT, RMAT | POLYSOLID | PSOLID |
| MEASURE | ME | PREVIEW | PRE |
| MIRROR | MI | PROPERTIES | CH, MO, PR, PROPS |
| MIRROR3D | 3DMIRROR | PROPERTIESCLOSE | PRCLOSE |
| MLEADER | MLD | PSPACE | PS |
| MLEADERALIGN | MLA | PUBLISHTOWEB | PTW |
| MLEADERCOLLECT | MLC | PURGE | PU |
| MLEADEREDIT | MLE | -PURGE | -PU |
| MLEADERSTYLE | MLS | PYRAMID | PYR |

| Command | Alias | Command | Alias |
|---|---|---|---|
| QLEADER | LE | SOLID | SO |
| QUICKCALC | QC | SPELL | SP |
| QUICKCUI | QCUI | SPLINE | SPL |
| QUIT | EXIT | SPLINEDIT | SPE |
| RECTANG | REC | STANDARDS | STA |
| REDRAW | R | STRETCH | S |
| REDRAWALL | RA | STYLE | ST |
| REGEN | RE | SUBTRACT | SU |
| REGENALL | REA | TABLE | TB |
| REGION | REG | TABLESTYLE | TS |
| RENAME | REN | TABLET | TA |
| -RENAME | -REN | TEXT | DT |
| RENDER | RR | THICKNESS | TH |
| RENDERCROP | RC | TILEMODE | TI |
| RENDERENVIRONMENT | FOG | TOLERANCE | TOL |
| RENDERPRESETS | RFILEOPT, RP | TOOLBAR | TO |
| RENDERWIN | RENDSCR, RW | TOOLPALETTES | TP |
| REVOLVE | REV | TORUS | TOR |
| ROTATE | RO | TRIM | TR |
| RPREF | RPR | UCSMAN | UC |
| SCALE | SC | VISUALSTYLES | VSM |
| SCRIPT | SCR | -VISUALSTYLES | -VSM |
| SECTION | SEC | VSCURRENT | VS |
| SECTIONPLANE | SPLANE | UNION | UNI |
| SETVAR | SET | UNITS | UN |
| SHADEMODE | SHA | -UNITS | -UN |
| SHEETSET | SSM | VIEW | V |
| SLICE | SL | -VIEW | -V |
| SNAP | SN | VPOINT | -VP |

| Command | Alias | Command | Alias |
|---------|-------|---------|-------|
| WBLOCK | W | XCLIP | XC |
| -WBLOCK | -W | XLINE | XL |
| WEDGE | WE | XREF | XR |
| XATTACH | XA | -XREF | -XR |
| XBIND | XB | ZOOM | Z |
| -XBIND | -XB | | |

# System Variables

AutoCAD stores the values for its operating environment and some of its commands in system variables. System variables control how the commands work. They also set default colors, sizes, and values. They store information about the drawing and the software configuration. Some system variables can be changed by the user; others are read-only.

To see a list of all system variables and their current settings type **SETVAR** at the command line, type "**?**", and then "**\***".

Use AutoCAD's Help feature for additional information about system variables and their options.

| Name | Description | Type | Storage Location | Initial Value |
|------|-------------|------|------------------|---------------|
| 3DCONVERSIONMODE | Used to convert material and light definitions to the current product release. | Integer | Drawing | 1 |
| 3DDWFPREC | Controls the precision of 3D DWF publishing. | Integer | Drawing | 2 |
| 3DSELECTIONMODE | Controls the selection precedence of visually overlapping objects when using 3D visual styles. | Integer | User-settings | 1 |
| ACADLSPACDOC | Controls loading of acad.lsp file. | Integer | Registry | 0 |
| ACADPREFIX | Stores directory path. | String | Not-Saved | pathname |
| ACADVER | Stores AutoCAD version number. | String | Not-Saved | (Read-only) |
| ACISOUTVER | Controls ACIS version of SAT files created with ACISOUT command. | Integer | Not-Saved | 70 |
| ACTPATH | System variable that stores the paths where additional Action Scripts can be found. | String | Registry | " " |
| ACTRECORDSTATE | Specifies the current state of the Action Recorder. | Integer | Not-Saved | 0 |
| ACTRECPATH | System Variable that stores the path where the Action Scripts are saved. | String | Registry | pathname |

| Name | Description | Type | Storage Location | Initial Value |
|------|-------------|------|------------------|---------------|
| ACTUI | Controls the type and level of user UI feedback provided during the playback and recording phase. | Bitcode | Registry | 6 |
| ADCSTATE | Indicates whether DesignCenter™ is active. | Integer | Not-Saved | varies |
| AFLAGS | Sets options for attributes. | Integer | Not-Saved | 16 |
| ANGBASE | Sets base angle relative to current UCS. | Real | Drawing | 0.0000 |
| ANGDIR | Sets direction of positive angle measurement. | Integer | Drawing | 0 |
| ANNOALLVISIBLE | Hides or displays annotative objects that do not support the current annotation scale. | Integer | Drawing | 1 |
| ANNOAUTOSCALE | Updates annotative objects to support the annotation scale when the annotation scale is changed. | Integer | Registry | -4 |
| ANNOTATIVEDWG | Specifies whether or not the drawing will behave as an annotative block when inserted into another drawing. | Integer | Drawing | 0 |
| APBOX | Controls display of AutoSnap™ aperture box. | Integer | Registry | 0 |
| APERTURE | Controls display size for object snap target box in pixels (1–50). | Integer | Registry | 10 |
| AREA | Stores last area computed by AREA command. | Real | Not-Saved | (Read-only) |
| ATTDIA | Controls whether INSERT command uses dialog box. | Integer | Registry | 0 |
| ATTIPE | Controls the display of the in-place editor used to create multiline attributes. | Integer | Registry | 0 |
| ATTMODE | Controls attribute display. | Integer | Drawing | 1 |
| ATTMULTI | Controls whether multiline attributes can be created. | Integer | Registry | 1 |
| ATTREQ | Controls whether INSERT command uses default attribute settings. | Integer | Registry | 1 |
| AUDITCTL | Controls writing of audit report files. | Integer | Registry | 0 |

| Name | Description | Type | Storage Location | Initial Value |
|------|-------------|------|------------------|---------------|
| AUNITS | Sets angle units. | Integer | Drawing | 0 |
| AUPREC | Sets precision of angular units. | Integer | Drawing | 0 |
| AUTODWFPUBLISH | Controls whether the AutoPublish feature is on or off. | Bitcode | Registry | 0 |
| AUTOSNAP | Controls display of AutoSnap marker, tooltip, and magnet. Turns on and off polar and object snap tracking. Controls display of polar and object snap tracking tooltips. | Integer | Registry | 63 |
| BACKGROUNDPLOT | Controls background plotting. | Integer | Registry | 2 |
| BACTIONCOLOR | Sets text color for Block Editor actions. | String | Registry | 7 |
| BACZ | Controls location of back clipping plane. | Real | Drawing | None |
| BDEPENDENCYHIGHLIGHT | Controls highlighting of dependent objects when editing blocks. | Integer | Registry | 1 |
| BGRIPOBJCOLOR | Sets grip color in Block Editor. | String | Registry | 141 |
| BGRIPOBJSIZE | Sets custom grip size in Block Editor relative to screen display (1–256). | Integer | Registry | 8 |
| BINDTYPE | Controls naming of xrefs when binding or editing in place. | Integer | Not-Saved | 0 |
| BLIPMODE | Controls display of marker blips. | Integer | Registry | 0 |
| BLOCKEDITLOCK | Controls opening Block Editor. | Integer | Registry | 0 |
| BLOCKEDITOR | Indicates whether Block Editor is open. | Integer | Not-Saved | 0 |
| BPARAMETERCOLOR | Sets parameter color in Block Editor. | String | Registry | 7 |
| BPARAMETERFONT | Sets font for parameters and action in Block Editor. | String | Registry | Simplex.shx |
| BPARAMETERSIZE | Sets parameter and feature text size in Block Editor relative to screen display (1–256). | Integer | Registry | 12 |
| BTMARKDISPLAY | Controls display of value set markers. | Integer | Registry | 1 |
| BVMODE | Controls display of hidden objects in Block Editor. | Integer | Not-Saved | 0 |

| Name | Description | Type | Storage Location | Initial Value |
|---|---|---|---|---|
| CALCINPUT | Controls evaluation of mathematical expressions and global constants in windows and dialog boxes. | Integer | Registry | 1 |
| CAMERADISPLAY | Toggle whether camera objects are displayed in the current drawing. | Integer | Drawing | 0 |
| CAMERAHEIGHT | Stores the default height for newly created camera objects. | Integer | Drawing | 0 |
| CANNOSCALE | Sets the name of the current annotation scale for the current space. | String | Drawing | 1:1 |
| CANNOSCALEVALUE | Returns the value to the current annotation scale. | Real | Drawing | 1 |
| CAPTURETHUMBNAILS | Controls whether thumbnails are generated for the Rewind tool when a view is changed by a navigation tool except ViewCube, SteeringWheel, and ShowMotion, and when to generate this type of thumbnail. | Integer | Registry | 1 |
| CDATE | Reads calendar date and time. | Real | Not-Saved | (Read-only) |
| CECOLOR | Sets new object color. | String | Drawing | BYLAYER |
| CELTSCALE | Sets object linetype scaling factor relative to LTSCALE setting. | Real | Drawing | 1.0000 |
| CELTYPE | Sets new object linetype. | String | Drawing | BYLAYER |
| CELWEIGHT | Sets new object lineweight. | Integer | Drawing | -1 |
| CENTERMT | Controls grip stretching of horizontally centered multiline text. | Switch | User-settings | 0 |
| CHAMFERA | Sets first chamfer distance. | Real | Drawing | 0.0000 |
| CHAMFERB | Sets second chamfer distance. | Real | Drawing | 0.0000 |
| CHAMFERC | Sets chamfer length. | Real | Drawing | 0.0000 |
| CHAMFERD | Sets chamfer angle. | Real | Drawing | 0.0000 |
| CHAMMODE | Sets CHAMFER input method. | Integer | Not-Saved | 0 |
| CIRCLERAD | Sets circle radius default value. | Real | Not-Saved | 0.0000 |
| CLAYER | Sets current layer. | String | Drawing | 0 |

| Name | Description | Type | Storage Location | Initial Value |
|---|---|---|---|---|
| CLEANSCREENSTATE | Stores a value that indicates whether the clean screen state is on or off. | Integer | Not-Saved | 0 |
| CLISTATE | Controls display of command window. | Integer | Not-Saved | 1 |
| CMATERIAL | Sets the material of new objects. | String | Drawing | BYLAYER |
| CMDACTIVE | Indicates whether ordinary command, transparent command, script, or dialog box is active. | Integer | Not-Saved | None |
| CMDDIA | Controls command dialog box display. | Integer | Registry | 1 |
| CMDECHO | Controls echoing of prompts and input during scripts. | Integer | Not-Saved | 1 |
| CMDINPUTHISTORYMAX | Sets maximum number of previous input values stored in command prompt. | Integer | Registry | 20 |
| CMDNAMES | Displays names of active and transparent commands. | String | Not-Saved | None |
| CMLEADERSTYLE | Sets the name of the current multileader style. | String | Drawing | STANDARD |
| CMLJUST | Specifies multiline justification. | Integer | Drawing | 0 |
| CMLSCALE | Controls multiline overall width. | Real | Drawing | 1.0000 (Imperial) 20.0000 (metric) |
| CMLSTYLE | Sets multiline style. | String | Drawing | STANDARD |
| COMPASS | Controls display of 3D compass in current viewport. | Integer | Not-saved | 0 |
| COORDS | Controls updating of coordinates on status line. | Integer | Registry | 1 |
| COPYMODE | Controls whether the COPY command repeats automatically. | Integer | Registry | 0 |
| CPLOTSTYLE | Controls new object plot style. | String | Drawing | Varies |
| CPROFILE | Displays current profile name. | String | Registry | (Read-only) <<Unnamed Profile>> |
| CROSSINGAREACOLOR | Controls the color of the selection area during crossing selection. | Integer | Registry | 100 |
| CSHADOW | Sets the shadow display property for a 3D object. | Integer | Drawing | 0 |

| Name | Description | Type | Storage Location | Initial Value |
|------|-------------|------|------------------|---------------|
| CTAB | Stores name of current tab in drawing (model or layout). | String | Drawing | Varies |
| CTABLESTYLE | Sets current table style name. | String | Drawing | STANDARD |
| CURSORSIZE | Sets crosshair size as percentage of screen size (1–100 percent). | Integer | Registry | 5 |
| CVPORT | Sets identification number of current viewport. | Integer | Drawing | 2 |
| DASHBOARDSTATE | Determines whether the Dashboard window is active or not. | Integer | Not-Saved | Varies |
| DATALINKNOTIFY | Controls the notification for updated or missing data links. | Integer | Registry | 2 |
| DATE | Stores current date and time in Modified Julian format. | Real | Not-Saved | Varies |
| DBLCLKEDIT | Controls the double-click editing behavior in the drawing area. Double-click actions can be customized using the Customize User Interface (CUI) editor. The system variable can accept the values of On and Off in place of 1 and 0. | Integer | Registry | 1 |
| DBCSTATE | Stores status of cbConnect Manager. | Integer | Drawing | (Read-only) 0 |
| DBMOD | Indicates drawing modification status. | Integer | Not-Saved | (Read-only) 0 |
| DCTCUST | Displays path and file name of current custom spelling dictionary. | String | Registry | Pathname |
| DCTMAIN | Displays file name of current main spelling dictionary. | String | Registry | Varies by country/region |
| DEFAULTLIGHTING | Turns default lighting on and off. | Integer | Drawing | 1 |
| DEFAULTLIGHTINGTYPE | Specifies the type of default lighting. | Integer | Drawing | 1 |
| DEFLPLSTYLE | Specifies layer 0 default plot style. | String | Registry | Varies |
| DEFPLYSTYLE | Specifies new object default plot style. | String | Registry | None |
| DELOBJ | Controls whether source objects for new object creation are retained or deleted. | Integer | Registry | 1 |

| Name | Description | Type | Storage Location | Initial Value |
|---|---|---|---|---|
| DEMANDLOAD | Specifies if and when to demand load certain applications. | Integer | Registry | 3 |
| DGNFRAME | Determines whether DGN underlay frames are visible or plotted in the current drawing. | Integer | Drawing | 0 |
| DGNIMPORTMAX | Controls the maximum number of elements translated during DGNIMPORT. | Real | Registry | 10000000 |
| DGNMAPPINGPATH | Stores the location of the DGNSetups.INI file, which stores the DGN mapping setups. | String | Registry | C:\Documents and Settings\ <username>\ Application Data\Autodesk\ AutoCAD\ R17.2\enu\ Support |
| DGNOSNAP | Controls object snapping for geometry in DGN underlays. | Integer | Registry | 1 |
| DIASTAT | Specifies exit method for most recently used dialog box. | Integer | Not-Saved | None |
| DIMADEC | Controls angular dimension precision display. | Integer | Drawing | 0 |
| DIMALT | Controls display of dimension alternate units. | Switch | Drawing | OFF |
| DIMALTD | Controls precision of alternate units. | Integer | Drawing | 2 |
| DIMALTF | Controls multiplier for alternate units. | Real | Drawing | 25.4 |
| DIMALTRND | Rounds off alternate dimension units. | Real | Drawing | 0.00 |
| DIMALTTD | Sets tolerance value precision for alternate dimension units. | Integer | Drawing | 2 |
| DIMALTTZ | Controls tolerance value zero suppression. | Integer | Drawing | 0 |
| DIMALTU | Sets units format for alternate units of all secondary dimension styles except Angular. | Integer | Drawing | 2 |
| DIMALTZ | Controls alternate unit dimension value zero suppression. | Integer | Drawing | 0 |

| Name | Description | Type | Storage Location | Initial Value |
|------|-------------|------|------------------|---------------|
| DIMANNO | Indicates whether or not the current dimension style is annotative. | Integer | Drawing | Based on current style |
| DIMAPOST | Specifies text prefix or suffix for alternate dimension values, except for angular dimensions. | String | Drawing | None |
| DIMARCSYM | Controls display of the arc symbol in an arc length dimension. | Integer | Drawing | 0 |
| DIMASO | Controls dimension object associativity. Obsolete—replaced by DIMASSOC. | Switch | Drawing | On |
| DIMASSOC | Controls dimension object associativity. | Integer | Drawing | 2 |
| DIMASZ | Controls dimension line and leader line arrowhead size. | Real | Drawing | 0.1800 |
| DIMATFIT | Controls spacing of dimension text and arrows when both will not fit between extension lines. | Integer | Drawing | 3 |
| DIMAUNIT | Sets angular dimension unit format. | Integer | Drawing | 0 |
| DIMAZIN | Suppresses angular dimension zeros. | Integer | Drawing | 0 |
| DIMBLK | Controls arrowhead style. | String | Drawing | None |
| DIMBLK1 | Controls arrowhead style for first end of dimension line when DIMSAH is on. | String | Drawing | None |
| DIMBLK2 | Controls arrowhead style for second end of dimension line when DIMSAH is on. | String | Drawing | None |
| DIMCEN | Controls drawing of circle and arc center marks or centerlines. | Real | Drawing | 0.0900 |
| DIMCLRD | Controls colors of dimension lines, arrowheads and leader lines. | Integer | Drawing | 0 |
| DIMCLRE | Controls colors of dimension extension lines. | Integer | Drawing | 0 |
| DIMCLRT | Controls color of dimension text. | Integer | Drawing | 0 |
| DIMDEC | Sets precision of primary dimension units. | Integer | Drawing | 4 |

| Name | Description | Type | Storage Location | Initial Value |
|------|-------------|------|------------------|---------------|
| DIMDLE | Sets dimension line extension beyond extension line for oblique line arrowhead style. | Real | Drawing | 0.0000 |
| DIMDLI | Controls dimension line spacing for baseline dimensions. | Real | Drawing | 0.3800 |
| DIMDSEP | Specifies decimal format dimension separator. | Single-character | Drawing | Decimal point |
| DIMEXE | Specifies distance extension line extends beyond dimension line. | Real | Drawing | 0.1800 |
| DIMEXO | Specifies extension line offset distance from origin points. | Real | Drawing | 0.0625 |
| DIMFIT | Preserves script integrity. Replaced by DIMATFIT and DIMTMOVE. | Integer | Drawing | 3 |
| DIMFRAC | Sets fraction format for architectural or fractional dimensions. | Integer | Drawing | 0 |
| DIMFXL | Sets the total length of the extension lines starting from the dimension line toward the dimension origin. | Real | Drawing | 1 |
| DIMFXLON | Controls whether extension lines are set to a fixed length. | Switch | Drawing | Off |
| DIMGAP | Sets distance around dimension text when text is between dimension lines. | Real | Drawing | 0.0900 |
| DIMJOGANG | Determines the angle of the transverse segment of the dimension line in a jogged radius dimension. | Real | Drawing | 45° (90° Metric) |
| DIMJUST | Controls horizontal placement of dimension text. | Integer | Drawing | 0 |
| DIMLDRBLK | Specifies leader arrow type. | String | Drawing | None |
| DIMLFAC | Sets linear dimension measurement scale factor. | Real | Drawing | 1.0000 |
| DIMLIM | Generates dimension limits as default text. | Switch | Drawing | Off |
| DIMLTEX1 | Sets the linetype of the first extension line. | String | Drawing | " " |

| Name | Description | Type | Storage Location | Initial Value |
|---|---|---|---|---|
| DIMLTEX2 | Sets the linetype of the second extension line. | String | Drawing | " " |
| DIMLTYPE | Sets the linetype of the dimension line. | String | Drawing | " " |
| DIMLUNIT | Sets units for all dimension types, except Angular. | Integer | Drawing | 2 |
| DIMLWD | Assigns dimension line lineweight. | Enum | Drawing | -2 |
| DIMLWE | Assigns extension line lineweight. | Enum | Drawing | -2 |
| DIMPOST | Specifies text prefix or suffix for dimension measurements. | String | Drawing | None |
| DIMRND | Sets rounding increment for dimension distances. | Real | Drawing | 0.0000 |
| DIMSAH | Controls dimension line arrowhead display. | Switch | Drawing | Off |
| DIMSCALE | Sets overall dimensioning variable scale factor. | Real | Drawing | 1.0000 |
| DIMSD1 | Controls first dimension line suppression. | Switch | Drawing | Off |
| DIMSD2 | Controls second dimension line suppression. | Switch | Drawing | Off |
| DIMSE1 | Controls first extension line suppression. | Switch | Drawing | Off |
| DIMSE2 | Controls second extension line suppression. | Switch | Drawing | Off |
| DIMSHO | Preserves script integrity. | Switch | Drawing | On |
| DIMSOXD | Controls display of dimension lines outside extension lines. | Switch | Drawing | Off |
| DIMSTYLE | Stores name of current dimension style. | String | Drawing | (Read-only) STANDARD |
| DIMTAD | Controls vertical location of dimension text relative to dimension line. | Integer | Drawing | 0 |
| DIMTDEC | Sets precision of tolerance value display for primary dimension units. | Integer | Drawing | 4 |

| Name | Description | Type | Storage Location | Initial Value |
|------|-------------|------|------------------|---------------|
| DIMTFAC | Specifies scale factor for fraction and tolerance value text relative to dimension text height. | Real | Drawing | 1.0000 |
| DIMTFILL | Controls the background of dimension text. | Integer | Drawing | 0 |
| DIMTFILLCLR | Sets the color for the text background in dimensions. | Integer | Drawing | 0 |
| DIMTIH | Controls dimension text position inside extension lines, except for ordinate dimensioning. | Switch | Drawing | On |
| DIMTIX | Positions dimension text between extension lines. | Switch | Drawing | Off |
| DIMTM | Sets lower tolerance limit for dimension text when DIMTOL or DIMLIM is on. | Real | Drawing | 0.0000 |
| DIMTMOVE | Sets dimension text movement rules. | Integer | Drawing | 0 |
| DIMTOFL | Controls drawing of dimension line between extension lines. | Switch | Drawing | Off |
| DIMTOH | Controls dimension text position outside extension lines | Switch | Drawing | Off |
| DIMTOL | Adds tolerances to dimension text. | Switch | Drawing | Off |
| DIMTOLJ | Sets tolerance value vertical justification relative to nominal dimension text. | Integer | Drawing | 1 |
| DIMTP | Sets upper tolerance limit for dimension text when DIMTOL or DIMLIM is on. | Real | Drawing | 0.0000 |
| DIMTSZ | Specifies size of oblique line arrowhead style. | Real | Drawing | 0.0000 |
| DIMTVP | Controls vertical placement of dimension text relative to dimension line. | Real | Drawing | 0.0000 |
| DIMTXSTY | Specifies dimension text style. | String | Drawing | STANDARD |
| DIMTXT | Specifies dimension text height unless current text style has fixed height. | Real | Drawing | 0.1800 |

| Name | Description | Type | Storage Location | Initial Value |
|------|-------------|------|------------------|---------------|
| DIMTZIN | Controls zero suppression in tolerance values. | Integer | Drawing | 0 |
| DIMUNIT | Obsolete—replaced by DIMLUNIT and DIMFRAC. Retained to preserve script integrity. | Integer | Drawing | 2 |
| DIMUPT | Controls options for dimension user-positioned text. | Switch | Drawing | Off |
| DIMZIN | Controls zero suppression in primary dimension unit values. | Integer | Drawing | 0 |
| DISPSLIH | Controls silhouette curve display for solid objects in wireframe display mode. | Integer | Drawing | 0 |
| DISTANCE | Stores value computed by DIST command. | Real | Not-Saved | None |
| DONUTID | Sets default value for donut inside diameter. | Real | Not-Saved | 0.5000 |
| DONUTOD | Sets default value for donut outside diameter. | Real | Not-Saved | 1.0000 |
| DRAGMODE | Controls visibility of objects during dragging. | Integer | Registry | 2 |
| DRAGP1 | Sets regen-drag input sampling rate. | Integer | Registry | 10 |
| DRAGP2 | Sets fast-drag input sampling rate. | Integer | Registry | 25 |
| DRAGVS | Sets the visual style while creating 3D objects. | String | Drawing | Current visual style |
| DRAWORDERCTL | Controls draw order functionality. | Integer | Drawing | 3 |
| DRSTATE | Controls Drawing Recovery window. | Integer | Not-Saved | Varies |
| DTEXTED | Controls user interface for editing text. | Integer | Registry | 0 |
| DWFFRAME | Determines whether the DWF frame is visible and if it will plot. | Integer | Drawing | 2 |
| DWFOSNAP | Determines whether object snapping is enabled for DWF underlays. | Integer | Registry | 1 |
| DWGCHECK | Checks drawings for problems when opening. | Integer | Registry | 0 |

| Name | Description | Type | Storage Location | Initial Value |
|---|---|---|---|---|
| DWGCODEPAGE | Stores same value as SYSCODEPAGE (for compatibility reasons). | String | Drawing | (Read-only) |
| DWGNAME | Stores drawing name entered by user. | String | Not-Saved | Drawing.dwg |
| DWGPREFIX | Stores drive/directory prefix for drawing. | String | Not-Saved | (Read-only) |
| DWGTITLED | Indicates current drawing naming status. | Integer | Not-Saved | 0 |
| DXEVAL | Controls when data extraction tables are compared against the data source, and if the data is not current, displays an update notification. | Integer | Drawing | 12 |
| DYNDIGRIP | Controls dynamic dimension display during grip stretch editing. | Bitcode | Registry | 31 |
| DYNDIVIS | Controls number of dynamic dimensions displayed during grip stretch editing. | Integer | User-settings | 1 |
| DYNMODE | Turns Dynamic Input features on and off. | Integer | User-settings | 3 |
| DYNPICOORDS | Controls type of coordinate, relative or absolute, used for pointer input. | Switch | User-settings | 0 |
| DYNPIFORMAT | Controls type of coordinate, polar or Cartesian, used for pointer input. | Switch | User-settings | 0 |
| DYNPIVIS | Controls pointer input display. | Integer | User-settings | 1 |
| DYNPROMPT | Controls Dynamic Input tooltip prompt display. | Integer | User-settings | 1 |
| DYNTOOLTIPS | Controls which tooltips are impacted by tooltip appearance settings. | Switch | User-settings | 0 |
| EDGEMODE | Controls cutting and boundary edge behavior in TRIM and EXTEND commands. | Integer | Registry | 0 |
| ELEVATION | Stores current elevation of new objects relative to active UCS. | Real | Drawing | 0.0000 |
| ENTERPRISEMENU | Stores CUI file name including path. | String | Registry | (Read-only) "" |

| Name | Description | Type | Storage Location | Initial Value |
|---|---|---|---|---|
| ERRNO | Displays error code number when AutoLISP function causes error detected by AutoCAD. | Integer | Not-Saved | (Read-only) 0 |
| ERSTATE | Determines whether the External References window is inactive, active/visible, or active/auto-hidden. | Integer | Not-Saved | Varies |
| EXPERT | Controls display of selected warning prompts. | Integer | Not-Saved | 0 |
| EXPLMODE | Controls whether EXPLODE command supports nonuniformly scaled blocks. | Integer | Not-Saved | 1 |
| EXTMAX | Stores upper-right coordinates of drawing extents. | 3D-point | Drawing | Varies |
| EXTMIN | Stores lower-left coordinates of drawing extents. | 3D-point | Drawing | Varies |
| EXTNAMES | Sets named object name parameters. | Integer | Drawing | 1 |
| FACETRATIO | Controls faceting aspect ratio for cylindrical and conic ShapeManager solids. | Integer | Not-Saved | 0 |
| FACETRES | Adjusts smoothness of shaded and rendered objects and objects with hidden lines removed (0.01–10.0). | Real | Drawing | 0.5 |
| FIELDDISPLAY | Controls field background display. | Integer | Registry | 1 |
| FIELDEVAL | Controls timing of field updates. | Integer | Drawing | 31 |
| FILEDIA | Controls display of file navigation dialog boxes. | Integer | Registry | 1 |
| FILLETRAD | Stores current fillet radius. | Real | Drawing | 0.0000 |
| ILLMODE | Controls display of filled objects. | Integer | Drawing | 1 |
| FONTALT | Specifies alternate font used when specified font cannot be found. | String | Registry | simplex.shx |
| FONTMAP | Specifies font mapping file. | String | Registry | acad.fmp |
| FRONTZ | Stores back clipping plane location. | Real | Drawing | None |
| FULLOPEN | Indicates whether drawing is partially open. | Integer | Not-Saved | (Read-only) |

| Name | Description | Type | Storage Location | Initial Value |
|---|---|---|---|---|
| FULLPLOTPATH | Controls whether plot spooler is sent full path of drawing file. | Integer | Registry | 1 |
| GEOLATLONGFORMAT | Controls the format of the Latitude/Longitude representation in the drawing. | Integer | Drawing | 0 |
| GEOMARKERVISIBILITY | Controls the visibility of geographic markers. | Integer | Drawing | 1 |
| GRIDDISPLAY | Controls the display behavior and display limits of the grid. | Bitcode | Drawing | 3 |
| GRIDMAJOR | Controls the frequency of major grid lines compared to minor grid lines. | Integer | Drawing | 5 |
| GRIDMODE | Controls grid display. | Integer | Drawing | 0 |
| GRIDUNIT | Specifies the grid spacing (*X* and *Y*) for the current viewport. | 2D-point | Drawing | 0.500,0.500 (Imperial) or 10, 10 (Metric) |
| GRIPBLOCK | Controls block grip locations. | Integer | Registry | 0 |
| GRIPCOLOR | Controls the color of nonselected grips. | | Registry | 150 |
| GRIPDYNCOLOR | Controls dynamic block custom grip color. | Integer | Registry | 140 |
| GRIPHOT | Controls the color of selected grips (drawn as filled boxes). | Integer | Registry | 12 |
| GRIPHOVER | Controls the color of hoover grips (drawn as filled boxes). | Integer | Registry | 11 |
| GRIPOBJLIMIT | Sets object number limit for selection set and suppresses grip display when limit is exceeded (1–32,767). | Integer | Registry | 100 |
| GRIPS | Turns grips on and off. | Integer | Registry | 1 |
| GRIPSIZE | Sets size of grip box in pixels (1–255). | Integer | Registry | 5 |
| GRIPTIPS | Controls display of grip tips. | Integer | Registry | 1 |
| GTAUTO | Controls whether or not grip tools display automatically when selecting objects in 3D space. | Integer | Registry | 1 |

| Name | Description | Type | Storage Location | Initial Value |
|------|-------------|------|------------------|---------------|
| GTDEFAULT | Controls whether or not the 3DMOVE, 3DROTATE, and 3DSCALE commands start automatically when the MOVE, ROTATE, and SCALE commands (respectively) are started in a 3D view. | Integer | Registry | 0 |
| GTLOCATION | Sets the default location for grip tools. | Integer | Registry | 0 |
| HALOGAP | Sets size of gap to be displayed when an object is hidden by another. | Integer | Drawing | 0 |
| HANDLES | Preserves integrity of scripts. Handles are always on. | Integer | Drawing | (Read-only) ON |
| HIDEPRECISION | Controls hide and shade accuracy. | Integer | Not-Saved | 0 |
| HIDETEXT | Specifies whether text objects are included in HIDE command. | Integer | Drawing | 1 |
| HIDEXREFSCALES | Controls the display of Xref scales. 0—Xref scales are displayed, 1—Xref scales are hidden. | Integer | Registry | 1 |
| HIGHLIGHT | Controls object highlighting. | Integer | Not-saved | 1 |
| HPANG | Specifies hatch pattern angle. | Real | Not-saved | 0 |
| HPASSOC | Controls associativity of hatch patterns and gradient fills. | Integer | Registry | 1 |
| HPBOUND | Controls object type created by BHATCH and BOUNDARY commands. | Integer | Not-Saved | 1 |
| HPDOUBLE | Specifies hatch pattern doubling for user-created patterns. | Integer | Not-Saved | 0 |
| HPDRAWORDER | Controls draw order of hatches and fills. | Integer | Not-Saved | 3 |
| HPGAPTOL | Sets allowable gap in hatch boundary. | Real | Registry | 0 |
| HPINHERIT | Controls how MATCHPROP copies hatch origin from source to destination object. | Integer | Drawing | 0 |

| Name | Description | Type | Storage Location | Initial Value |
|------|-------------|------|------------------|---------------|
| HPMAXLINES | Controls the maximum number of hatch lines that will generate. Values can be set at a minimum of 100 and a maximum of 10,000,000. | Real | Registry | 1000000 |
| HPNAME | Creates default hatch pattern name. | String | Not-Saved | ANSI131 |
| HPOBJWARNING | Sets number of hatch boundary objects that can be selected before triggering a warning message. | Integer | Registry | 10000 |
| HPORIGIN | Sets hatch origin point for new hatch objects. | 2D-point | Drawing | 0,0 |
| HPORIGINMODE | Controls determination of default hatch origin point. | Integer | Registry | 0 |
| HPSCALE | Specifies hatch pattern scale factor. | Real | Not-Saved | 1.0000 |
| HPSEPARATE | Controls number of hatch objects created when HATCH operates on multiple closed boundaries. | Integer | Registry | 0 |
| HPSPACE | Specifies pattern line spacing for user-created hatch patterns. | Real | Not-saved | 1.0000 |
| HYPERLINKBASE | Specifies the path used for all relative hyperlinks in the drawing. If no value is specified, the drawing path is used for all relative hyperlinks. | String | Drawing | " " |
| IMAGEHLT | Controls highlighting of raster images. | Integer | Registry | 0 |
| IMPLIEDFACE | Controls the detection of implied faces. | Integer | Registry | 1 |
| INDEXCTL | Controls whether layer and spatial indexes are created and saved in drawing files. | Integer | Registry | 0 |
| INETLOCATION | Stores Internet location used by BROWSER command and Browse the Web dialog box. | String | Registry | http://www.autodesk.com |
| INPUTHISTORYMODE | Controls the content and location of the display of a history of user input. | Bitcode | Registry | 15 |

| Name | Description | Type | Storage Location | Initial Value |
|------|-------------|------|------------------|---------------|
| INSBASE | Stores insertion base point set by BASE. | 3D-point | Drawing | 0.0000, 0.0000 |
| INSNAME | Sets default block name for INSERT command. | String | Not-Saved | " " |
| INSUNITS | Specifies drawing units value for automatic scaling of blocks, images, or xrefs inserted or attached to a drawing. | Integer | Drawing | 1 |
| INSUNITSDEFSOURCE | Sets source content units value (0–20). | Integer | Registry | 1 |
| INSUNITSDEFTARGET | Sets target drawing units value (0–20). | Integer | Registry | 1 |
| INTELLIGENTUPDATE | Controls graphic refresh rate. | Integer | Registry | 20 |
| INTERFERECOLOR | Sets the color of interference objects. | Integer | Drawing | 1 |
| INTERFEREOBJVS | Sets the visual style for interference objects. | String | Drawing | Realistic |
| INTERFEREVPVS | Sets the visual style for the current viewport while using the INTERFERENCE command. | String | Drawing | Wireframe |
| INTERSECTIONCOLOR | Sets color of intersection polylines. | Integer | Drawing | 257 |
| INTERSECTIONDISPLAY | Controls display of intersection polylines. | Switch | Drawing | Off |
| ISAVEBAK | Controls creation of backup files (BAK). | Integer | Registry | 1 |
| ISAVEPERCENT | Sets allowable amount of wasted space in a drawing file (0–100). | Integer | Registry | 50 |
| ISOLINES | Sets number of contour lines on surfaced objects (0–2047). | Integer | Drawing | 4 |
| LASTANGLE | Stores end angle of last arc created. | Real | Not-Saved | (Read-only) 0 |
| LASTPOINT | Stores last point entered. | 3D-point | Not-Saved | 0.0000, 0.0000 |
| LASTPROMPT | Stores last string echoed to the command line. | String | Not-Saved | " " |
| LATITUDE | Specifies the latitude of the drawing model. | Real | Drawing | Varies |

| Name | Description | Type | Storage Location | Initial Value |
|------|-------------|------|------------------|---------------|
| LAYEREVAL | Controls when the Unreconciled New Layer filter list in the Layer Properties Manager is evaluated for new layers. | Integer | Drawing | 1 |
| LAYERFILTERALERT | Controls layer filters. | Integer | Registry | 2 |
| LAYERNOTIFY | Specifies when an alert displays for new layers that have not yet been reconciled. | Bitcode | Drawing | 15 |
| LAYLOCKFADECTL | Controls the dimming for objects on locked layers. | Integer | Registry | 50 |
| LAYOUTREGENCTL | Controls display list updates in model and layout tabs. | Integer | Registry | 2 |
| LEGACYCTRLPICK | Specifies the keys for selection cycling and the behavior for <Ctrl> + left-click. | Integer | Registry | 0 |
| LENSLENGTH | Stores lens length used if perspective viewing. | Real | Drawing | (Read-only) 50.0000 |
| LIGHTGLYPHDISPLAY | Controls whether light glyphs are displayed. | Integer | Drawing | 1 |
| LIGHTINGUNITS | Controls whether generic or photometric lights are used, and indicates the current lighting units. | Integer | Drawing | 0 |
| LIGHTLISTSTATE | Indicates whether the Lights in Model window is open or closed. | Integer | Not-Saved | 0 |
| LIGHTSINBLOCKS | Controls whether lights contained in blocks are used when rendering. | Integer | Drawing | 0 |
| LIMCHECK | Controls object creation outside grid limits. | Integer | Drawing | 0 |
| LIMMAX | Stores coordinates of upper-right grid limits. | 2D-point | Drawing | 12.0000, 9.0000 |
| LIMMIN | Stores coordinates of lower-left grid limits. | 2D-point | Drawing | 0.0000, 0.0000 |
| LINEARBRIGHTNESS | Controls the global brightness level of the drawing in the standard lighting workflow. | Integer | Drawing | 0 |
| LINEARCONTRAST | Controls the global contrast level of the drawing in the standard lighting workflow. | Integer | Drawing | 0 |

| Name | Description | Type | Storage Location | Initial Value |
|---|---|---|---|---|
| LOCALE | Returns code indicating current locale. | String | Not-Saved | (Read-only) " " |
| LOCALROOTPREFIX | Stores path to root folder where local customizable files installed. | String | Registry | (Read-only) "pathname" |
| LOCKUI | Locks position and size of toolbars and windows. | Bitcode | Registry | 0 |
| LOFTANG1 | Sets the draft angle through the first cross-section in a loft operation. | Real | Drawing | 90 |
| LOFTANG2 | Sets the draft angle through the last cross-section in a loft operation. | Real | Drawing | 90 |
| LOFTMAG1 | Sets the magnitude of draft angle through the first cross-section in a loft operation. | Integer | Drawing | 1 |
| LOFTMAG2 | Sets the magnitude of draft angle through the last cross-section in a loft operation. | Integer | Drawing | 1 |
| LOFTNORMALS | Controls the normals of a lofted object where it passes through cross-sections. | Integer | Drawing | 1 |
| LOFTPARAM | Controls the shape of lofted solids and surfaces. | Bitcode | Drawing | 7 |
| LOGEXPBRIGHTNESS | Controls the global brightness level of the drawing when using photometric lighting. | Real | Drawing | 65.0 |
| LOGEXPCONTRAST | Controls the global contrast level of the drawing when using photometric lighting. | Real | Drawing | 50.0 |
| LOGEXPDAYLIGHT | Controls if exterior daylight is used when using photometric lighting. | Integer | Drawing | 2 |
| LOGEXPMIDTONES | Controls the global midtones level of the drawing when using photometric lighting. | Real | Drawing | 1.0 |
| LOGFILEMODE | Controls creation of log file. | Integer | Registry | 0 |
| LOGFILENAME | Specifies path and name of log file for current drawing. | String | Drawing | (Read-only) Varies |

| Name | Description | Type | Storage Location | Initial Value |
|------|-------------|------|------------------|---------------|
| LOGFILEPATH | Specifies path for log files for all session drawings. | String | Drawing | "c:\Documents and Settings\ username\ LocalSettings\ ApplicationData\ Autodesk\ application_ name\release_ number\ locale_code" |
| LOGINNAME | Displays user's name. | String | Not-Saved | " " |
| LONGITUDE | Specifies the longitude of the drawing model. | Real | Drawing | Varies |
| LTSCALE | Sets global linetype scale factor. | Real | Drawing | 1.0000 |
| LUNITS | Sets linear unit type. | Integer | Drawing | 2 |
| LUPREC | Sets precision for all read-only linear units. | Integer | Drawing | 4 |
| LWDEFAULT | Sets default lineweight value. | Enum | Registry | 25 |
| LWDISPLAY | Controls lineweight display. | Integer | Drawing | 0 |
| LWUNITS | Sets lineweight display unit as inches or millimeters. | Integer | Registry | 1 |
| MATSTATE | Indicates whether the Materials window is open or closed. | Integer | Not-Saved | 0 |
| MAXACTVP | Sets maximum number of active layout viewports. | Integer | Drawing | 64 |
| MAXSORT | Sets maximum number of symbol or block names sorted by listing commands. | Integer | Registry | 1000 |
| MBUTTONPAN | Controls pointing device third button or wheel behavior. | Integer | Registry | 1 |
| MEASUREINIT | Sets default units, Imperial or Metric, for drawing started from scratch. | Integer | Registry | Varies by country/region |
| MEASUREMENT | Sets units, Imperial or Metric, for hatch patterns and linetype files. | Integer | Drawing | 0 |
| MENUBAR | Controls the display of the menu bar. | Integer | Registry | 0 |
| MENUCTL | Controls screen menu page switching. | Integer | Registry | 1 |

| Name | Description | Type | Storage Location | Initial Value |
|------|-------------|------|------------------|---------------|
| MENUECHO | Sets menu echo and prompt control bits. | Integer | Not-Saved | 0 |
| MENUNAME | Stores customization file name and path. | String | Registry | (Read-only) "customization _file_name" |
| MIRRTEXT | Controls text mirroring. | Integer | Drawing | 0 |
| MODEMACRO | Displays a text string on the status line. | String | Not-Saved | " " |
| MSMSTATE | Stores a value that indicates whether the Markup Set Manager is open or closed. | Integer | Not-Saved | 0 |
| MSOLESCALE | Controls scale of an OLE object pasted into model space. | Real | Drawing | 1.0 |
| MSLTSCALE | Scales linetypes displayed on the Model tab by the annotation scale. | Real | Drawing | 1 |
| MTEXTED | Defines application for editing multiline text. | String | Registry | "Internal" |
| MTEXTFIXED | Obsolete. | Integer | Registry | 0 |
| MTEXTTOOLBAR | Controls the display of the In-Place Text Editor. | Integer | User-settings | 2 |
| MTJIGSTRING | Sets content of sample text for MTEXT command. | String | Registry | "abc" |
| MYDOCUMENTSPREFIX | Stores full path to My Documents folder for current user. | String | Registry | (Read-only) "pathname" |
| NAVSWHEELMODE | Mode of the SteeringWheel. | Integer | Registry | 0 |
| NAVSWHEELOPACITYBIG | Controls the opacity of the big SteeringWheels. | Integer | Registry | 50 |
| NAVSWHEELOPACITYMINI | Controls the size of the mini SteeringWheels. | Integer | Registry | 50 |
| NAVVCUBEDISPLAY | Controls the display of the ViewCube on the canvas when the 3D graphic system is active. | Integer | Drawing | 1 |
| NAVVCUBELOCATION | Controls the display location of the ViewCube. | Integer | Registry | 0 |
| NAVVCUBEORIENT | Controls whether the ViewCube always reflects the WCS. | Integer | Registry | 1 |
| NAVVCUBESIZE | Controls the display size of the ViewCube. | Integer | Registry | 1 |

| Name | Description | Type | Storage Location | Initial Value |
|------|-------------|------|------------------|---------------|
| NAVVCUBOPACITY | Controls the opacity of ViewCube when it is inactive. | Integer | Registry | 50 |
| NEWTRANSIENTAPI | Controls which version of APIs are used for 2D and 3D objects. | Integer | Registry | 1 |
| NOMUTT | Controls message display. | Short | Not-Saved | 0 |
| NORTHDIRECTION | Specifies the angle of the Sun from north. | Real | Drawing | Varies |
| OBSCUREDCOLOR | Sets obscured line color. | Integer | Drawing | 257 |
| OBSCUREDLTYPE | Sets obscured line linetype. | Integer | Drawing | 0 |
| OFFSETDIST | Sets offset distance default value. | Real | Not-Saved | 1.0000 |
| OFFSETGAPTYPE | Controls polyline gaps when polyline is offset. | Integer | Registry | 0 |
| OLEFRAME | Controls OLE object frame display and plotting. | Integer | Drawing | 2 |
| OLEHIDE | Controls OLE object display and plotting. | Integer | Registry | 0 |
| OLEQUALITY | Sets OLE object default plot quality. | Integer | Registry | 3 |
| OLESTARTUP | Controls loading of OLE source applications. | Integer | Drawing | 0 |
| OPENPARTIAL | Controls whether visible objects in a layout display as a drawing is being opened. | Integer | Registry | 1 |
| OPMSTATE | Stores a value that indicates whether the Properties palette is open, closed, or hidden. | Integer | Not-Saved | 0 |
| ORTHOMODE | Controls Ortho mode. | Integer | Drawing | 0 |
| OSMODE | Sets running Object Snap modes using the following bitcodes. | Integer | Registry | 4133 |
| OSNAPCOORD | Controls conflicts between running object snaps and entered coordinates. | Integer | Registry | 2 |
| OSNAPNODELEGACY | Controls whether the Node object snap can be used to snap to multiline text objects. | Integer | Registry | 0 |
| OSNAPZ | Controls projection of object snaps. | Integer | Not-Saved | 0 |

| Name | Description | Type | Storage Location | Initial Value |
|---|---|---|---|---|
| OSOPTIONS | Automatically suppresses object snaps on hatch objects and when using a dynamic UCS. | Bitcode | Registry | 3 |
| PALETTEOPAQUE | Controls window transparency. | Integer | Registry | 0 |
| PAPERUPDATE | Controls print warning dialog display. | Integer | Registry | 0 |
| PDMODE | Sets point object symbol. | Integer | Drawing | 0 |
| PDSIZE | Sets point object display size. | Real | Drawing | 0.0000 |
| PEDITACCEPT | Controls display of PEDIT prompt. | Integer | Registry | 0 |
| PELLIPSE | Controls ellipse type. | Integer | Drawing | 0 |
| PERIMETER | Stores last perimeter computed by AREA or LIST command. | Real | Not-Saved | 0.0000 |
| PERSPECTIVE | Specifies whether the current viewport displays a perspective working view. | Integer | Drawing | Varies |
| PERSPECTIVECLIP | Determines the location of eyepoint clipping. The value determines where the eyepoint clipping occurs as a percentage. Values can range between 0.01 and 10.0.If you select a small value, the $z$-values of objects will be compressed at the target view and beyond. If you select a value such as 0.5%, the clipping will appear very close to the eyepoint of the view. In some extreme cases, it might be appropriate to use 0.1%, but it is recommended to change the setting to a higher value such as 5%. | Real | User-settings | 5 |
| PFACEVMAX | Sets maximum vertices per face. | Integer | Not-Saved | (Read-only) 4 |
| PICKADD | Controls object selection. | Integer | Registry | 1 |
| PICKAUTO | Controls automatic windowing for object selection. | Integer | Registry | 1 |
| PICKBOX | Sets object selection target height in pixels. | Integer | Registry | 3 |
| PICKDRAG | Controls selection window drawing method. | Integer | Registry | 0 |

| Name | Description | Type | Storage Location | Initial Value |
|------|-------------|------|------------------|---------------|
| PICKFIRST | Controls object selection order. | Integer | Registry | 1 |
| PICKSTYLE | Controls group and associative hatch selection. | Integer | Registry | 1 |
| PLATFORM | Stores name of platform in use. | String | Not-Saved | (Read-only) Varies |
| PLINEGEN | Controls polyline linetype generation around vertices. | Integer | Drawing | 0 |
| PLINETYPE | Controls type of polyline. | Integer | Registry | 2 |
| PLINEWID | Stores default polyline width. | Real | Drawing | 0.0000 |
| PLOTOFFSET | Controls location of plot offset. | Integer | Registry | 0 |
| PLOTROTMODE | Controls plot orientation. | Integer | Registry | 2 |
| PLQUIET | Controls display of plot dialog boxes and nonfatal errors. | Integer | Registry | 0 |
| POLARADDANG | Controls user-defined polar angles. | String | Registry | " " |
| POLARANG | Sets polar angle increment. | Real | Registry | 90 |
| POLARDIST | Sets polar snap increment. | Real | Registry | 0.0000 |
| POLARMODE | Controls polar and object snap tracking settings. | Integer | Registry | 0 |
| POLYSIDES | Sets POLYGON default side number (3–1024). | Integer | Not-Saved | 4 |
| POPUPS | Displays status of current display driver. | Integer | Not-Saved | (Read-only) 1 |
| PREVIEWEFFECT | Specifies display method for previewing selection of objects. | Integer | Registry | 2 |
| PREVIEWFILTER | Controls object types included in selection previewing. | Bitcode | Registry | 1 |
| PREVIEWTYPE | Controls the view to use for generating the thumbnail when the drawing is saved. | Integer | Drawing | 0 |
| PRODUCT | Returns product name. | String | Not-Saved | (Read-only) "AutoCAD" |
| PROGRAM | Returns program name. | String | Not-Saved | (Read-only) "acad" |
| PROJECTNAME | Assigns project name to current drawing. | String | Drawing | " " |

| Name | Description | Type | Storage Location | Initial Value |
|------|-------------|------|------------------|---------------|
| PROJMODE | Sets projection mode for trimming or extending. | Integer | Registry | 1 |
| PROXYGRAPHICS | Controls saving of proxy object images. | Integer | Drawing | 1 |
| PROXYNOTICE | Controls proxy warning display. | Integer | Registry | 1 |
| PROXYSHOW | Controls proxy object display. | Integer | Registry | 1 |
| PROXYWEBSEARCH | Controls checking for object enablers. | Integer | Registry | 1 |
| PSLTSCALE | Controls paper space linetype scaling. | Integer | Drawing | 1 |
| PSOLHEIGHT | Sets the default height for a swept solid object created with the POLYSOLID command. | Real | Drawing | 4 (Imperial) or 80 (Metric) |
| PSOLWIDTH | Sets the default width for a swept solid object created with the POLYSOLID command. | Real | Registry | 0.25 (Imperial) or 5 (Metric) |
| PSTYLEMODE | Controls plot style table type. | Integer | Drawing | (Read-only) 1 |
| PSTYLEPOLICY | Controls association of color with plot style. | Integer | Registry | 1 |
| PSVPSCALE | Sets view scale factor for new viewports. | Real | Drawing | 0 |
| PUBLISHALLSHEETS | Controls how the Publish dialog list is populated. | Integer | Registry | 1 |
| PUBLISHCOLLATE | Controls whether sheets are published as a single job. | Integer | User-settings | 1 |
| PUBLISHHATCH | Controls whether hatch patterns published to DWF format are treated as a single object when they are opened in Autodesk Impression. | Integer | Registry | 1 |
| PUCSBASE | Stores UCS name defining origin and orientation of orthographic UCS settings in paper space. | String | Drawing | " " |
| QCSTATE | Activates QuickCalc calculator. | Integer | Not-Saved | (Read-only) Varies |
| QPLOCATION | Sets the location mode of Quick Properties panel. | Integer | Registry | 0 |
| QPMODE | Sets the on or off state of Quick Properties panel. | Integer | Registry | 1 |

| Name | Description | Type | Storage Location | Initial Value |
|------|-------------|------|------------------|---------------|
| QTEXTMODE | Controls text display. | Integer | Drawing | 0 |
| QVDRAWINGPIN | Controls the default display state of preview images of drawings. | Integer | Registry | 0 |
| QVLAYOUTPIN | Controls the default display state of preview images of model space and layouts in a drawing. | Integer | Registry | 0 |
| RASTERDPI | Controls paper size and plot scaling when converting from dimensional to dimensionless output devices (100–32,767). | Integer | Registry | 300 |
| RASTERPREVIEW | Controls creation of BMP preview images. | Integer | Registry | 1 |
| RECOVERYMODE | Controls recording of drawing recovery information after system failure. | Integer | Registry | 2 |
| REFEDITNAME | Displays name of edited reference. | String | Not-Saved | " " |
| REGENMODE | Controls automatic drawing regeneration. | Integer | Drawing | 1 |
| RE-INIT | Reinitializes digitizer, digitizer port, and acad.pgp file. | Integer | Not-Saved | 0 |
| REMEMBERFOLDERS | Controls default path stored in standard file selection dialog boxes. | Integer | Registry | 1 |
| RENDERPREFSSTATE | Stores a value that indicates whether the Advanced Render Settings palette is open. | Integer | Not-saved | 0 |
| RENDERUSERLIGHTS | Controls whether user-lights are translated during rendering. | Integer | Drawing | 1 |
| REPORTERROR | Controls reporting of errors to Autodesk. | Integer | Registry | 1 |
| RIBBONSTATE | Determines whether the Ribbon window is active or not. | Integer | Not-saved | 1 |
| ROAMABLEROOTPREFIX | Stores path to folder where roamable customizable files are stored. | String | Registry | (Read-only) "pathname" |
| ROLLOVERTIPS | Controls the display of rollover tooltips in the application. | Integer | Registry | 1 |

| Name | Description | Type | Storage Location | Initial Value |
|------|-------------|------|------------------|---------------|
| RTDISPLAY | Controls raster image and OLE content display during Realtime ZOOM and PAN. | Integer | Registry | 1 |
| SAVEFIDELITY | Controls whether the drawing is saved with visual fidelity. | Bitcode | Registry | 1 |
| SAVEFILE | Saves name of current automatic save file. | String | Registry | (Read-only) "c:\Documents and Settings\ username\ LocalSettings\ TEMP\ Drawing1.dwg" |
| SAVEFILEPATH | Specifies path to directory for all automatic save files in current session. | String | Registry | "c:\Documents and Settings\ username\Local Settings\TEMP\" |
| SAVENAME | Stores file name and directory path for most recently saved drawing. | String | Not-Saved | (Read-only) " " |
| SAVETIME | Sets automatic save interval, in minutes. | Integer | Registry | 10 |
| SCREENBOXES | Stores number of boxes in screen menu area. | Integer | Not-Saved | (Read-only) 0 |
| SCREENMODE | Indicates display state. | Integer | Not-Saved | (Read-only) 3 |
| SCREENSIZE | Stores current viewport size in pixels. | 2D-point | Not-Saved | (Read-only) Varies |
| SELECTIONANNODISPLAY | Controls whether alternate scale representations are temporarily displayed in a dimmed state when an annotative object is selected. | Integer | Registry | 1 |
| SELECTIONAREA | Controls display effects for selection areas. | Integer | Registry | 1 |
| SELECTIONAREAOPACITY | Controls selection area opacity during window and crossing selection (0–100). | Integer | Registry | 25 |
| SELECTIONPREVIEW | Controls selection previewing display. | Bitcode | Registry | 3 |
| SETBYLAYERMODE | Controls which properties are selected for SETBYLAYER. | Integer | User-settings | 127 |
| SHADEDGE | Controls edge shading in rendering. | Integer | Drawing | 3 |

| Name | Description | Type | Storage Location | Initial Value |
|---|---|---|---|---|
| SHADEDIF | Sets ratio of diffuse reflective light to ambient light. | Integer | Drawing | 70 |
| SHADOWPLANELOCATION | Controls the location of an invisible ground plane used to display shadows. | Integer | Drawing | 0 |
| SHORTCUTMENU | Controls display of Default, Edit, and Command mode shortcut menus. | Integer | Registry | 11 |
| SHOWHIST | Controls the Show History property for solids in a drawing. | Integer | Drawing | 1 |
| SHOWLAYERUSAGE | Controls Layer Properties Manager layer icon display. | Integer | Registry | 1 |
| SHOWMOTIONPIN | Controls the default state for ShowMotion. The setting of this system variable is cross session. | Integer | Registry | 1 |
| SHPNAME | Sets default shape name. | String | Not-Saved | " " |
| SIGWARN | Controls digital signature warning. | Integer | Registry | 1 |
| SKETCHIN | Sets SKETCH command record increment. | Real | Drawing | 0.1000 |
| SKPOLY | Sets SKETCH command to create lines or polylines. | Integer | Drawing | 0 |
| SNAPANG | Sets snap and grid rotation angle for current viewport. | Real | Drawing | 0 |
| SNAPBASE | Sets snap and grid origin point for current viewport. | 2D-point | Drawing | 0.0000, 0.0000 |
| SNAPISOPAIR | Controls isometric plane for current viewport. | Integer | Drawing | 0 |
| SNAPMODE | Turns Snap on and off. | Integer | Drawing | 0 |
| SNAPSTYLE | Sets snap style for current viewport. | Integer | Drawing | 0 |
| SNAPTYPE | Sets snap type for current viewport. | Integer | Registry | 0 |
| SNAPUNIT | Sets snap spacing for current viewport. | 2D-point | Drawing | 0.5000, 0.5000 |
| SOLIDCHECK | Controls solid validation. | Integer | Not-Saved | 1 |
| SOLIDHIST | Controls the default History property setting for new and existing objects. | Integer | Drawing | 1 |

| Name | Description | Type | Storage Location | Initial Value |
|------|-------------|------|------------------|---------------|
| SPLFRAME | Controls spline and spline-fit polyline display. | Integer | Drawing | 0 |
| SPLINESEGS | Sets number of segments in each spline-fit polyline. | Integer | Drawing | 8 |
| SPLINETYPE | Sets curve type for spline-fit polylines. | Integer | Drawing | 6 |
| SSFOUND | Displays sheet set path and file name. | String | Not-Saved | (Read-only) " " |
| SSLOCATE | Controls opening of associated sheet sets when drawing is opened. | Integer | User-settings | 1 |
| SSMAUTOOPEN | Controls Sheet Set Manager display when drawing is opened. | Integer | User-settings | 1 |
| SSMPOLLTIME | Sets time interval for automatic refreshes of sheet set status data. | Integer | Registry | 60 |
| SSMSHEETSTATUS | Controls refreshing of sheet set status data. | Integer | Registry | 2 |
| SSMSTATE | Activates Sheet Set Manager. | Integer | Not-saved | (Read-only) Varies |
| STANDARDSVIOLATION | Controls standards violation notification. | Integer | Registry | 2 |
| STARTUP | Controls display of Create New Drawing dialog box. | Integer | Registry | 0 |
| STATUSBAR | Controls the display of the application and drawing status bars. | Integer | Registry | 1 |
| STEPSIZE | Specifies the step size in current units when users are in Walk mode. | Real | Drawing | 6.000 |
| STEPSPERSEC | Specifies the number of steps taken per second when users are in Walk mode. | Real | Drawing | 2 |
| SUNPROPERTIESSTATE | Indicates whether the Sun Properties window is open or closed. | Integer | Not-saved | 0 |
| SUNSTATUS | Controls whether the Sun is casting light in the viewport. | Integer | Drawing | 1 |
| SURFTAB1 | Sets tabulation number for RULESURF and TABSURF commands and M mesh density for REVSURF and EDGESURF. | Integer | Drawing | 6 |

| Name | Description | Type | Storage Location | Initial Value |
|------|-------------|------|------------------|---------------|
| SURFTAB2 | Sets N mesh density for REVSURF and EDGESURF. | Integer | Drawing | 6 |
| SURFTYPE | Controls surface type for PEDIT smooth option. | Integer | Drawing | 6 |
| SURFU | Sets M surface density for PEDIT smooth. | Integer | Drawing | 6 |
| SURFV | Sets N surface density for PEDIT smooth. | Integer | Drawing | 6 |
| SYSCODEPAGE | Returns system code page. | String | Not-Saved | (Read-only) " " |
| TABLEINDICATOR | Controls row and column label display for table cell text editor. | Integer | User-Settings | 1 |
| TABLETOOLBAR | Controls the display of the Table toolbar. | Integer | Registry | 2 |
| TABMODE | Controls tablet use. | Integer | Not-Saved | 0 |
| TARGET | Stores location of target point for current viewport. | 3D-point | Drawing | (Read-only) 0.0000, 0.0000 |
| TBCUSTOMIZE | Controls customization of toolbars. | Switch | Registry | 1 |
| TDCREATE | Stores local time and date of drawing creation. | Real | Drawing | (Read-only) Varies |
| TDINDWG | Stores total drawing editing time. | Real | Drawing | (Read-only) Varies |
| TDUCREATE | Stores universal time and date of drawing creation. | Read | Drawing | (Read-only) Varies |
| TDUPDATE | Stores local time and date of last drawing update/save. | Real | Drawing | (Read-only) Varies |
| TDUSRTIMER | Stores user-elapsed timer. | Real | Drawing | (Read-only) Varies |
| TDUUPDATE | Stores universal time and date of last drawing update/save. | Real | Drawing | (Read-only) Varies |
| TEMPOVERRIDES | Controls temporary override keys. | Integer | Registry | 1 |
| TEMPREFIX | Contains directory name for temporary file placement. | String | Not-Saved | (Read-only) "c:\Documents and Settings \username\Local Settings\Temp\" |
| TEXTEVAL | Controls evaluation of text strings entered with TEXT or -TEXT. | Integer | Not-Saved | 0 |

| Name | Description | Type | Storage Location | Initial Value |
|------|-------------|------|------------------|---------------|
| TEXTFILL | Controls TrueType font fill when plotting and rendering. | Integer | Registry | 1 |
| TEXTOUTPUTFILEFORMAT | Provides Unicode options for plot and text window log files. | Integer | Registry | 0 |
| TEXTQLTY | Sets TrueType font outline resolution tessellation fineness for plotting and rendering (0–100). | Integer | Not-Saved | 50 |
| TEXTSIZE | Sets default text height for current style. | Real | Drawing | 0.2000 |
| TEXTSTYLE | Sets name of current text style. | String | Drawing | STANDARD |
| THICKNESS | Sets current 3D thickness. | Real | Drawing | 0.0000 |
| THUMBSIZE | Controls the display of the ViewCube on the canvas when the 3D graphic system is active. | Integer | Registry | 1 |
| TILEMODE | Makes Model tab or last layout tab active. | Integer | Drawing | 1 |
| TIMEZONE | Sets the time zone for a sun study. | Enum | Drawing | -8000 |
| TOOLTIPMERGE | Combines drafting tooltips into a single tooltip. The appearance of the merged tooltip is controlled by the settings in the Tooltip Appearance dialog box. | Switch | User-settings | 0 |
| TOOLTIPS | Controls tooltip display. | Integer | Registry | 1 |
| TPSTATE | Indicates whether Tool Palettes window is active. | Integer | Not-Saved | (Read-only) Varies |
| TRACEWID | Sets default trace width. | Real | Drawing | 0.0500 |
| TRACKPATH | Controls polar and object snap tracking alignment path display. | Integer | Registry | 0 |
| TRAYICONS | Controls Status Bar tray display. | Integer | Registry | 1 |
| TRAYNOTIFY | Controls display of service notifications in Status Bar tray. | Integer | Registry | 1 |
| TRAYTIMEOUT | Controls display time for service notifications. | Integer | Registry | 5 |
| TREEDEPTH | Controls spatial index tree branches. | Integer | Drawing | 3020 |

| Name | Description | Type | Storage Location | Initial Value |
|------|-------------|------|------------------|---------------|
| TREEMAX | Controls number of nodes in spatial index. | Integer | Registry | 10000000 |
| TRIMMODE | Controls trimming of chamfers and fillets. | Integer | Registry | 1 |
| TSPACEFAC | Controls multiline line spacing expressed as a factor of text height (.25–4.0). | Real | Not-Saved | 1.0 |
| TSPACETYPE | Controls multiline line spacing type. | Integer | Registry | 1 |
| TSTACKALIGN | Controls stacked text vertical alignment. | Integer | Drawing | 1 |
| TSTACKSIZE | Controls stacked text fraction height expressed as percentage of text height (25–125). | Integer | Drawing | 70 |
| UCSAXISANG | Stores default UCS rotation angle for *X, Y, Z,* option of UCS command. | Integer | Registry | 90 |
| UCSBASE | Stores name of UCS that defines origin and orientation of orthographic UCS settings. | String | Drawing | WORLD |
| UCSDETECT | Controls whether dynamic UCS acquisition is active or not. | Integer | Drawing | 1 |
| UCSFOLLOW | Generates a plan view when UCS changes. | Integer | Drawing | 0 |
| UCSICON | Controls UCS icon display. | Integer | Drawing | 3 |
| UCSNAME | Stores name of current coordinate system for current viewport in current space. | String | Drawing | (Read-only) |
| UCSORG | Stores origin point of current coordinate system for current viewport in current space. | 3D-point | Drawing | (Read-only) |
| UCSORTHO | Determines whether related UCS is restored when an orthographic view is restored. | Integer | Registry | 1 |
| UCSVIEW | Determines whether current UCS is saved with named view. | Integer | Registry | 1 |
| UCSVP | Determines whether UCS in viewports remains fixed or changes to reflect the UCS of the current viewport. | Integer | Drawing | 1 |

| Name | Description | Type | Storage Location | Initial Value |
|------|-------------|------|------------------|---------------|
| UCSXDIR | Stores *X* direction of current UCS for current viewport in current space. | 3D-point | Drawing | (Read-only) 1.0000, 0.0000, 0.0000 |
| UCSYDIR | Stores *Y* direction of current UCS for current viewport in current space. | 3D-point | Drawing | (Read-only) 0.0000, 1.0000, 0.0000 |
| UNDOCTL | Stores state of Auto, Control, and Group options of UNDO command. | Integer | Not-Saved | (Read-only) 21 |
| UNDOMARKS | Stores number of marks set in UNDO command by Mark option. | Integer | Not-Saved | (Read-only) 0 |
| UNITMODE | Controls unit display format. | Integer | Drawing | 0 |
| UPDATETHUMBNAIL | Controls Sheet Set Manager thumbnail preview updates. | Bitcode | Drawing | 15 |
| USERI1-5 | Provides storage and retrieval of integer values. | Integer | Drawing | 0 |
| USERR1-5 | Provides storage and retrieval or real numbers. | Real | Drawing | 0.0000 |
| USERS1-5 | Provides storage and retrieval of text string data. | String | Not-Saved | " " |
| VIEWCTR | Stores current viewport center. | 3D-point | Drawing | (Read-only) Varies |
| VIEWDIR | Stores current viewport viewing direction. | 3D-vector | Drawing | (Read-only) None |
| VIEWMODE | Stores current viewport View mode. | Integer | Drawing | (Read-only) |
| VIEWSIZE | Stores current viewport view height. | Real | Drawing | (Read-only) Varies |
| VIEWTWIST | Stores current viewport twist angle. | Real | Drawing | (Read-only) 0 |
| VISRETAIN | Controls x-ref dependent layer properties. | Integer | Drawing | 1 |
| VPLAYEROVERRIDES | Indicates if there are any layers with viewport (VP) property overrides for the current layout viewport. | Integer | Drawing | 1 |
| VPLAYEROVERRIDESMODE | Controls whether layer property overrides associated with layout viewports are displayed and plotted. | Integer | Registry | 1 |

| Name | Description | Type | Storage Location | Initial Value |
|------|-------------|------|------------------|---------------|
| VPMAXIMIZEDSTATE | Indicates whether viewport is maximized. | Integer | Not-Saved | (Read-only) 0 |
| VSBACKGROUNDS | Controls whether backgrounds are displayed in the current viewport. | Integer | Drawing | 1 |
| VSEDGECOLOR | Sets the color of edges. | String | Drawing | 7 |
| VSEDGEJITTER | Controls the degree to which lines are made to appear as though sketched with a pencil. | String | Drawing | -2 |
| VSEDGEOVERHANG | Makes lines extend beyond their intersection, for a hand-drawn effect. | Integer | Drawing | -6 |
| VSEDGES | Controls the types of edges that are displayed in the viewport. | Integer | Drawing | 1 |
| VSEDGESMOOTH | Specifies the angle at which crease edges are displayed. | Integer | Drawing | 1 |
| VSFACECOLORMODE | Controls how the color of faces is calculated. | Integer | Drawing | 0 |
| VSFACEHIGHLIGHT | Controls the display of specular highlights on faces without materials in the current viewport. The range is -100 to 100. The higher the number, the larger the highlight. Objects with materials attached ignore the setting of VSFACEHIGHLIGHT when VSMATERIALMODE is on. | Integer | Drawing | -30 |
| VSFACEOPACITY | Controls the transparency of faces in the current viewport. The range is -100 to 100. At 100, the face is completely opaque. At 0, the face is completely transparent. Negative values set the transparency level but turn off the effect in the drawing. | Integer | Drawing | -60 |
| VSFACESTYLE | Controls how faces are displayed in the current viewport. | Integer | Drawing | 1 |
| VSHALOGAP | Sets the halo gap in the visual style applied to the current viewport. | Integer | Drawing | 1 |

| Name | Description | Type | Storage Location | Initial Value |
|---|---|---|---|---|
| VSHIDEPRECISION | Controls the accuracy of hides and shades in the visual style applied to the current viewport. | Integer | Not-Saved | 0 |
| VSINTERSECTIONCOLOR | Specifies the color of intersection polylines in the visual style applied to the current viewport. | Integer | Drawing | 7 |
| VSINTERSECTIONEDGES | Specifies the display of intersection edges in the visual style applied to the current viewport. | Switch | Drawing | 0 |
| VSINTERSECTIONLTYPE | Controls whether obscured lines are displayed in the current viewport and sets their linetype. | Integer | Drawing | 1 |
| VSISOONTOP | Displays isolines on top of shaded objects in the visual style applied to the current viewport. | Integer | Drawing | 0 |
| VSLIGHTINGQUALITY | Sets the lighting quality in the current viewport. | Integer | Drawing | 1 |
| VSMATERIALMODE | Controls the display of materials in the current viewport. | Integer | Drawing | 0 |
| VSMAX | Stores coordinate of upper-right corner of current viewport's virtual screen. | 3D-point | Drawing | (Read-only) Varies |
| VSMIN | Stores coordinate of lower-left corner of current viewport's virtual screen. | 3D-point | Drawing | (Read-only) Varies |
| VSMONOCOLOR | Sets the color for monochrome display of faces. | String | Drawing | 255,255,255 |
| VSOBSCUREDCOLOR | Specifies the color of obscured lines in the visual style applied to the current viewport. | String | Drawing | BYENTITY |
| VSOBSCUREDEDGES | Controls whether obscured (hidden) edges are displayed. | Integer | Drawing | 1 |
| VSOBSCUREDLTYPE | Specifies the linetype of obscured lines in the visual style applied to the current viewport. | Integer | Drawing | 1 |
| VSSHADOWS | Controls whether a visual style displays shadows. | Integer | Drawing | 0 |

| Name | Description | Type | Storage Location | Initial Value |
|------|-------------|------|------------------|---------------|
| VSSILHEDGES | Controls display of silhouette curves of solid objects in the visual style applied to the current viewport. | Integer | Drawing | 0 |
| VSSILHWIDTH | Specifies the width in pixels for display of silhouette edges in the current viewport. | Integer | Drawing | 5 |
| VSSTATE | Stores a value that indicates whether the Visual Styles window is open. | Integer | Not-Saved | 0 |
| VTDURATION | Sets smooth view transition duration (0–5000). | Integer | Registry | 750 |
| VTENABLE | Controls use of smooth view transitions. | Integer | Registry | 3 |
| VTFPS | Sets smooth view transition minimum speed (1.0–30.0). | Real | Registry | 7.0 |
| WHIPARC | Controls circle and arc display smoothness. | Integer | Registry | 0 |
| WHIPTHREAD | Controls multithreaded processing. | Integer | Registry | 1 |
| WINDOWAREACOLOR | Controls the color of the transparent selection area during window selection. The valid range is 1 to 255. SELECTIONAREA must be on. | Integer | Registry | 150 |
| WMFBKGND | Controls background display of Windows metafile objects. | Integer | Not-Saved | Off |
| WMFFORGND | Controls foreground color for Windows metafile objects. | Integer | Not-Saved | Off |
| WORLDUCS | Indicates whether UCS is same as WCS. | Integer | Not-Saved | (Read-only) 1 |
| WORLDVIEW | Determines whether input to DVIEW, VPOINT, 3DORBIT is relative to WCS or current UCS. | Integer | Drawing | 1 |
| WRITESTAT | Indicates write status of drawing file. | Integer | Not-Saved | (Read-only) 1 |
| WSCURRENT | Returns name of current workspace and sets workspace to current. | String | Not-Saved | AutoCAD Default |
| XCLIPFRAME | Controls xref clipping boundary visibility. | Integer | Drawing | 0 |

| Name | Description | Type | Storage Location | Initial Value |
|------|-------------|------|------------------|---------------|
| XEDIT | Controls availability of in-place reference editing. | Integer | Drawing | 1 |
| XFADECTL | Controls fading intensity percentage for references edited in place (0–90). | Integer | Registry | 50 |
| XLOADCTL | Controls xref demand loading. | Integer | Registry | 2 |
| XLOADPATH | Creates path for storing temporary copies of demand-loaded xref files. | String | Registry | "pathname" |
| XREFCTL | Controls creation of external reference log files. | Integer | Registry | 0 |
| XREFNOTIFY | Controls notification for updated or missing xrefs. | Integer | Registry | 2 |
| XREFTTYPE | Controls default reference type when attaching or overlaying an xref. | Integer | Registry | 0 |
| ZOOMFACTOR | Controls magnification changes when mouse wheel moves (3–100). | Integer | Registry | 60 |
| ZOOMWHEEL | Allows users to toggle the behavior of mouse wheel zoom operations. | Integer | Registry | 0 |

# Express Tools

Express Tools are additional productivity tools originally developed by users and unsupported by Autodesk, which extend the power of AutoCAD's basic commands. They cover a wide range of functions. All Express Tools can be entered at the command line; some are accessible through the Express pull-down menu and the Express toolbars.

Express tools are automatically installed with a full software installation or a custom installation with the Express Tool option selected. To activate Express Tools, enter **EXPRESSTOOLS** at the command line to load the library of tools. If the Express menu is not present, enter **EXPRESSMENU** to display the menu.

| Tool Name | Description | Command Line | Toolbar | Express Menu |
|---|---|---|---|---|
| ALIASEDIT | Creates, modifies, and deletes command aliases. | ALIASEDIT | | Tools – Command Alias Editor |
| ALIGNSPACE | Adjusts a viewport's zoom factor and position based on model space and/or paper space alignment points. | ALIGNSPACE | | Layout – Align Space |
| ARCTEXT | Aligns text with a specified arc. | ARCTEXT | Express Tools Text | Text – Arc Aligned Text |
| ATTIN | Imports block attribute values from an external file. | ATTIN | | Blocks – Import Attribute Information |
| ATTOUT | Exports block attribute values to an external file. | ATTOUT | | Blocks – Export Attribute Information |
| BCOUNT | Counts blocks. | BCOUNT | | |
| BLOCK? | Lists objects in block. | BLOCK? | | |
| BLOCKREPLACE | Replaces block with another. | BLOCKREPLACE | | Blocks – Replace block with another block |
| BLOCKTOXREF | Replaces block with xref. | BLOCKTOXREF | | Blocks – Convert block to xref |
| BREAKLINE | Draws a breakline. | BREAKLINE | Express Tools Standard | Draw – Break line Symbol |
| BSCALE | Scales blocks. | BSCALE | | Blocks – Scale blocks |

| Tool Name | Description | Command Line | Toolbar | Express Menu |
|---|---|---|---|---|
| BURST | Explodes block and converts attribute values to text. | BURST | Express Tools Block | Blocks – Explode Attributes to Text |
| CDORDER | Arranges object draw order based on color number. | CDORDER | | |
| CHURLS | Changes a URL. | CHURLS | | Web – Change URLs |
| CLIPIT | Clips xrefs or images with curves or lines. | CLIPIT | Express Tools Block | Modify – Extended Clip |
| CLOSEALL | Closes all open drawings prompting to save changes. | CLOSEALL | | File tools – Close All Drawings |
| COPYM | Copies objects with options for repeat, array, divide, and measure. | COPYM | Express Tools Standard | Modify – Multiple copy |
| DIMEX | Exports dimension style to an external file. | DIMEX | | Dimension – Dimstyle Export |
| DIMIN | Imports named dimension styles to drawing. | DIMIN | | Dimstyle – Import |
| DIMREASSOC | Restores dimension value to measured value. | DIMREASSOC | | Dimension – Reset Dim Text Value |
| DUMPSHX | Converts SHX files to SHP files. | See Express Help. This is an Operating System command. | | |
| DWGLOG | Useful in network environments; identifies user of drawing. | DWGLOG | | |
| EDITTIME | Tracks active editing time. | EDITTIME | | Tools – Dwg Editing Time |
| EXOFFSET | Enhanced offset command. | EXOFFSET | | Modify – Extended Offset |
| EXPLAN | Enhanced plan command. | EXPLAN | | Tools – Plan View |
| EXPRESS-MENU | Loads Express Tool menu and displays menu on menu bar. | EXPRESSMENU | | |
| EXPRESS-TOOLS | Loads Express Tools libraries. Adds Express directory to search path. Enables Express menu. | EXPRESSTOOLS | | |
| EXTRIM | Enhanced trim command. Extends cutting edge options. | EXTRIM | | |
| FASTSELECT | Creates selection set from objects touching selected object. | FS | Express Tools Standard | Selection – Fast Select |
| FLATTEN | Creates 2D drawing from 3D object. | FLATTEN | | |

| Tool Name | Description | Command Line | Toolbar | Express Menu |
|---|---|---|---|---|
| FULLSCREEN | Hides title and menu bars to maximize drawing area. | FULLSCREEN, FULLSCREENON, FULLSCREENOFF, FULLSCREENOP-TIONS | | Tools – Full Screen AutoCAD |
| GATTE | Globally edits attribute values for selected block. | GATTE | | |
| GETSEL | Creates temporary selection set. | GETSEL | | Selection – Get Selection Set |
| IMAGEDIT | Launches image editing program. | IMAGEDIT | | File tools – Image edit |
| JULIAN | Performs calendar conversions. | DATE | | |
| LAYOUTMERGE | Merges selected layouts into one. | LAYOUTMERGE, - LAYOUTMERGE | | Layout – Merge layout(s) |
| LSP | Displays AutoLISP commands. | LSP | | |
| LSPSURF | Displays AutoLISP file contents. | LSPSURF | | |
| MKLTYPE | Makes a linetype from selected objects. | MKLTYPE | | Tools – Make Linetype |
| MKSHAPE | Makes an AutoCAD shape from selected objects. | MKSHAPE | | Tools – Make Shape |
| MOCORO | Moves, copies, rotates, and scales with a single command. | MOCORO | Express Tools Standard | Modify – Move Copy Rotate |
| MOVEBAK | Changes storage location for BAK files. | MOVEBAK | | |
| MPEDIT | Like PEDIT but with with multiple polyline capabilities. | MPEDIT | | |
| MSTRETCH | Allows more than one crossing window or polygon selection for a stretch operation. | MSTRETCH | Express Tools Standards | Modify – Multiple Object Stretch |
| NCOPY | Copies nested objects in an xref or block. | NCOPY | Express Tools Block | Blocks – Copy Nested Objects |
| OVERKILL | Removes duplicate objects and overlapping lines and arcs. | OVERKILL, - OVERKILL | | |
| PLT2DWG | Imports HPGL files retaining colors. | PLT2DWG | | File tools – Convert PLT to DWG |
| PROPULATE | Manages Drawing Properties data. | PROPULATE | | File tools – Updates Drawing Properties data |

| Tool Name | Description | Command Line | Toolbar | Express Menu |
|---|---|---|---|---|
| PSBSCALE | Scales blocks relative to paper space. | PSBSCALE | | Blocks – Paper space block scale |
| PSTSCALE | Scales model space text to correct height in paperspace. | PSTSCALE | | Text – Paper space text height |
| QLATTACH | Attaches leader line to mtext, tolerance or a block. | QLATTACH | | Dimension - Leader Tools – Attach Leader to Annotation |
| QLATTACHSET | Attaches leader lines to AutoCAD 13 objects. | QLATTACHSET | | Dimension - Leader Tools – Global Attach Leader to Annotation |
| QLDEATACHSET | Globally detaches leaders from annotation objects. | QLDETACHSET | | Dimension - Leader Tools – Detach Leaders from Annotation |
| QQUIT | Closes all open drawings and exits AutoCAD. | QQUIT | | File tools – Quick ext |
| REDIR | Redefines file paths in xrefs, images, shapes, styles, and rtext. | REDIR | | File tools – Path Substitution |
| REDIRMODE | Sets object types or REDIR command. | REDIRMODE, -REDIRMODE | | |
| REPRULS | Find and replace function for URL addresses. | REPURLS | | Web – Replace URLs |
| REVERT | Closes and reopens current drawing saving changes. | REVERT | | File – Revert |
| RTEDIT | Edit remote text objects. | RTEDIT | | |
| RTEXT | Creates reactive text. | RTEXT | | Text – Remote Text |
| RTUCS | Rotates UCS dynamically. | RTUCS | Express Tools UCS | Tools – Realtime UCS |
| SAVEALL | Saves all open drawings keeping drawings open. | SAVEALL | | File tools – Save All Drawings |
| SHOWURLS | Displays all embedded URLs for viewing or editing. | SHOWURLS | Express Tools Standard | Web – Show URLs |
| SHP2BLK | Converts existing shape to block. | SHP2BLK | | Modify – Convert Shape to Block |
| SSX | Creates a selected set. | SSX | | |
| SUPERHATCH | Extends HATCH command to permit use of additional types of hatch patterns. | SUPERHATCH | Express Tools Standard | Draw – Super Hatch |
| SYSVDLG | Manages system variable settings. | SYSVDLG | | Tools – System Variable Editor |
| TCASE | Changes case of text. | TCASE, -TCASE | | Text – Change text case |

| Tool Name | Description | Command Line | Toolbar | Express Menu |
|---|---|---|---|---|
| TCIRCLE | Encloses selected text with a circle, slot, or rectangle. | TCIRCLE | | Text – Enclose Text with Object |
| TCOUNT | Adds numbering to text objects. | TCOUNT | | Text – Automatic Text Numbering |
| TEXTFIT | Fits text to selected start and end points. | TEXTFIT | Express Tools Text | Text – Text Fit |
| TEXTMASK | Places a mask behind selected text. | TEXTMASK | Express Tools Text | Text – Text Mask |
| TEXTUNMASK | Removes mask created by TEXTMASK. | TEXTUNMASK | | Text – Unmask Text |
| TFRAMES | Toggles frames for wipeout and image objects on and off. | TFRAMES | Express Tools Standard | |
| TJUST | Changes justification for text without moving text. | TJUST | | Text – Justify Text |
| TORIENT | Adjusts rotated block text to horizontal or right-read. | TORIENT | | Text – Orient Text |
| TREX | Combines TRIM and EXTEND commands. | TREX | | |
| TSCALE | Scales text, mtext, attributes, and attribute definitions. | TSCALE | | Text – Scale Text |
| TXT2MTXT | Converts TEXT or DTEXT objects to MTEXT. | TXT2MTXT | | Text – Convert Text to Mtext |
| TXTEXP | Explodes text into lines and arcs. | TXTEXP | Express Tools Text | Text – Explode Text |
| VPSCALE | Displays viewport scale factor. | VPSCALE | | Layout – List Viewport Scale |
| VPSYNC | Synchronizes one or more viewports with a master. | VPSYNC | | Layout – Synchronize Viewports |
| XDLIST | Lists extended object data for selected object. | XDLIST | | Tools – List Object Xdata |
| XLIST | Extends LIST command to nested objects in blocks or xrefs. | XLIST, -XLIST | Express Tools Block | Blocks – List Xref/Block Objects |
| XDATA | Attaches extended object data to an object. | XDATA | | Tools – Xdata Attachment |

# Glossary

**absolute coordinate entry:** The process of specifying a point by typing in a coordinate. The coordinate is measured from the origin or 0,0 point in the drawing.

**acquired point:** Object tracking feature used to locate a point as an intermediate location in order to locate temporary alignment paths. Acquired points show up as a small cross in the drawing. Some points are acquired by simply placing your cursor over key object definition points while other acquired points require selecting a point with your mouse.

**annotate:** To add text, notes, and dimensions to a drawing to communicate a complete design by indicating materials, locations, distances, and other key information.

**array:** A circular or rectangular pattern of objects.

**associativity:** A link between drawing objects and dimension objects. Associative dimensions will update and follow the drawing objects to which they are linked.

**autosave:** The practice of AutoCAD automatically saving your drawing at regular intervals. The default save interval is 10 minutes. Autosave files have a .5V$ file extension by default and are automatically deleted when the drawing is closed normally.

**AutoTracking:** AutoCAD feature that helps you to draw objects at specific angles or in specific relationships to other objects. When you turn on AutoTracking, temporary alignment paths help you create objects at precise positions and angles. Both orthogonal and polar tracking are available.

**block attribute:** A dynamic text-like object that can be included in a block definition to store alphanumeric data. Attribute values can be preset, specified when the block is inserted, or updated anytime during the life of a drawing. Attribute data can be automatically extracted from a drawing and output to an AutoCAD table or an external file.

**block definition:** A user-defined collection of drawing objects assigned a base point and a name that is stored centrally in a drawing. A block can be inserted in a drawing multiple times as a block reference. When a block definition is updated, all block references with the same name are automatically updated.

**block reference:** An instance of a block definition inserted in a drawing that references the central block definition drawing data. All that is stored with the block reference is an insertion point, scale, and rotation angle. All other data is derived from the block definition.

**B-spline:** An approximate spline curve also referred to as a nonuniform rational B-spline or NURBS curve.

**building a selection set:** The process of specifying the objects you wish to edit. You can add and remove objects to a selection set and reuse previous selection sets.

**cell:** The box at the intersection of a table row and column that contains the table data or a formula. A cell is typically referenced using its column letter and row number separated with a colon. For example, the cell in column A and row 1 is referenced as A:1.

**chamfer:** To cut off a corner with a slight angle or bevel.

**character set:** The set of numeric codes used by a computer system to represent the characters (letters, numbers, punctuation, etc.) of a particular country or place. The most common character set in use today is ASCII (American Standard Code for Information Interchange).

**color-dependent plot style:** Plot style that is organized by the AutoCAD Color Index (ACI) number. Color-dependent plot styles are automatically assigned by the color of the AutoCAD object. All objects with the same color are assigned the same plot style settings. Color-dependent plot styles are stored in .CTB files.

**command alias:** An abbreviated definition of a command name that enables you to enter commands more quickly at the keyboard by entering the first one or two letters of the command name. Appendix C contains a complete list of the default AutoCAD command aliases.

**contour line:** A line on a map that joins points of equal elevation. On a single contour line, all points have the same elevation. Contour lines are typically placed at designated vertical intervals to indicate elevation changes.

**coordinate entry:** The process of specifying point locations.

**crossing box:** A method of selecting objects in a selection set by specifying a rectangular area. Anything that touches the crossing box area is selected.

**curve fit:** The process of adding vertex points to a straight line segment polyline in order to create a smooth curve. Adding more points creates a smoother curve fit.

**deferred point:** Object Snap feature that allows you to "build" the Object Snap point using multiple point selection input by deferring the first point selected so that it can be used in conjunction with other point or object selections. For example, to find the intersection of two lines that don't physically intersect but that would intersect if they were extended in the same direction requires that you pick both lines. The first point selection is deferred while you pick the second line. Deferred point AutoMarkers are followed by an elllipsis (...), indicating that more information is needed.

**defpoints:** Points created when placing dimensions that define the measurement value of the dimension. AutoCAD measures the distance between the defpoints and uses the value as the default dimension text.

**demand loading:** Loading only the visible part of a referenced drawing. Others parts of the drawing are loaded only when necessary. AutoCAD uses demand loading to increase system performance when xrefs are used.

**dimension style:** A collection of dimension settings that control how dimension objects act and are displayed.

**direct distance entry:** The process of specifying a point by dragging the AutoCAD cursor to specify direction and typing in a distance.

**drawing template:** A drawing used as a starting point when creating a new drawing. Drawing templates can include title blocks, dimension styles, layer definitions, or any information found in a regular drawing. Drawing templates have a file extension of .DWT.

**edit in place:** Using the **REFEDIT** command to make changes to an externally referenced drawing. This allows you to make changes to one drawing from within another drawing.

**fillet:** To round off an inside or outside corner at a specific radius.

**floating viewport:** Paper space viewport created in a drawing layout tab that can have almost any size and shape—including circles and polygons. Paper space viewports are referred to as "floating" because they can be modified using standard AutoCAD editing commands so that they can be moved, resized, and erased. Unlike model space tiled viewports, paper space floating viewports can overlap and have space in between them.

**freeze/thaw:** Hiding or displaying the contents of a drawing layer. Objects on a frozen layer are ignored by AutoCAD, are not shown in the drawing, and cannot be edited.

**fuzz distance:** Distance used to determine if polyline endpoints that are not connected can be connected by extending them, trimming them, or connecting them with a new polyline segment.

**grips:** Editing points that appear at key locations on drawing objects. Once grips are activated, you can directly modify drawing objects by selecting their grips.

**hatch boundary:** The edges of a hatched area. These edges can be closed objects (such as a circle or closed polyline) or a combination of objects that define a closed area.

**hatch islands:** Closed areas within a hatch boundary. You have the option of telling AutoCAD how to deal with island areas when creating hatch objects.

**hatch patterns:** The pattern used to fill a hatch boundary. Hatch patterns are defined in .pat files and also include solid and gradient fill patterns.

**hatching:** The process of filling in a closed area with a pattern. Hatching can consist of solid filled areas, gradient filled areas, or areas filled with patterns of lines.

**implied windowing:** Feature that allows you to create a Window or a Crossing selection automatically by picking an empty space in a drawing to define the first corner point. The opposite corner point defines a Window selection if it is picked to the right of the first corner point and a Crossing selection if it is picked to the left.

**isometric view:** A pseudo-3D pictorial drawing in which three axes represent accurate measurements of the drawing model in order to show three sides of an object. Sometimes called 2 1/2D because three sides of an object are shown but the drawing is still only two-dimensional.

**layers:** A collection of object properties and display settings that are applied to objects.

**layout:** 2D page setups created in paper space that represents the paper size and what the drawing will look like when it is printed.

**layout viewport:** The user-defined window created in a paper space layout that allows you to view drawing information that resides in model space. Layout viewports are sometimes referred to as "floating" viewports because they can be moved, copied, and resized unlike the "tiled" viewports created in model space that are static and must abut each other.

**model:** The geometry (lines, circles, etc.) created in a drawing that defines the object or objects drawn. The graphical representation of the real-world object or part.

**named plot style:** Plot style that is organized by a user-defined name. Named plot styles can be assigned to AutoCAD layers or hard-coded to individual drawing objects. Named plot styles are stored in .STB files.

**nested xref:** An xref within an xref. This occurs when the drawing you are referencing contains a reference to another drawing. For example, you reference drawing A, and drawing A contains a reference to drawing B. Drawing B is the nested xref.

**objects:** Graphical drawing elements, such as lines, arcs, circles, polylines, and text.

**object snaps/osnaps:** Geometric points on objects such as the endpoints or midpoint of a line or the center of an arc of circle. Object snaps can be construction points on objects or calculated points such as a point of tangency, a perpendicular point, or the projected intersection of two drawing objects.

**offset:** To create a parallel copy of an object.

**orthographic:** 90° increments. When the ORTHO mode is turned on, AutoCAD locks the cursor movement to 0°, 90°, 180°, and 270° angles.

**orthographic projection:** The two-dimensional graphic representation of an object formed by the perpendicular intersections of lines drawn from points on the object to a plane of projection. Orthographic projection is a drafting technique commonly used to create multiple view drawings by creating one view, then projecting perpendicular lines from the complete view to create the other views. This approach limits the number of times you need to measure in your drawing, reducing errors and increasing productivity.

**page setup:** A collection of plot settings that are applied to a drawing layout. Page setups can be used and shared among multiple drawings.

**pan:** The process of moving your drawing from side to side in the display window so the location of the view changes without affecting the zoom scale.

**parametric:** Automated creation of a drawing based on a given set of dimensions referred to as *parameters*. These input parameters are applied against algorithms that create points, distances, and angles for the creation of drawing geometry. A simple example of creating a drawing parametrically is entering a width (*X*) and a height (*Y*) to create a rectangle.

**parsec:** A unit of astronomical length based on the distance from Earth at which stellar parallax is one second of arc and equal to 3.258 light-years, $3.086 \times 10^{13}$ kilometers, or $1.918 \times 10^{13}$ miles.

**.PC3 file:** Plotter configuration file used to store and manage printer/plotter settings. PC3 files control plot device settings such as port connections and output settings, media, graphics, physical pen configuration, custom properties, initialization strings, calibration, and user-defined paper sizes.

**pickbox:** Square box that replaces the cursor crosshairs whenever AutoCAD prompts you to *Select objects:*. It is used to pick objects in a drawing to create a selection set.

**plot style:** A collection of property settings defined in a plot style table that is applied when the drawing is plotted to control the appearance of the drawing objects on the printed drawing. Plot styles can be used to control line thickness, grayscale, screening, and other plot features.

**plotting:** The process of printing a drawing in AutoCAD. Plotting includes outputting your drawing to printers and plotters as well as various electronic file formats.

**point:** A one-dimensional object that is defined as a single coordinate in space. Points have no length or width, only a coordinate location. Points are referenced with the Node object snap.

**polar tracking:** A process where AutoCAD will lock the cursor movement to predefined angles. When the cursor gets close to one of these predefined angles, AutoCAD will lock onto that angle and display the angle measurement at the cursor.

**printable area:** The actual physical area that can be printed for the currently specified plotting device and paper size. Most printers cannot print to the very edge of the paper because of mechanical limitations.

**properties:** The settings that control how and where a drawing object is shown in the drawing. Some properties are common to all objects (layer, color, linetype, and lineweight) or specific to a particular type of drawing object (the radius of a circle or the endpoint of a line).

**revision cloud:** Continuous line made from arcs to resemble a cloud that is used to highlight markups and changes. Sometimes marked with a delta triangle indicating the revision number or letter.

**right-hand rule:** Easy-to-understand reference that can be used to determine the positive and negative direction of the *X*, *Y*, and *Z* axes. To use the right-hand rule, you clench your right hand into a fist with your palm facing towards you and extend your thumb to the right, point your pointer finger straight up, and point your middle finger towards you. If your palm is the origin at 0,0,0, then your thumb represents positive *X*, your pointer finger represents positive *Y*, and your middle fingers represent positive *Z*.

**rubber-band:** A live preview of a drawing object as it is being drawn. The rubber-band preview allows you to see objects as they are being created.

**scale factor:** Multiplier that determines the size of annotation features such as text height, dimension features, and linetype appearance when a drawing is plotted or printed. The scale factor is typically the reciprocal of the plot scale or view scale.

**selection set:** One or more selected objects that are treated as one unit by an AutoCAD command. Objects in a selection set are typically highlighted (dashed).

**sheet sets:** An organized and named collection of sheets created from multiple AutoCAD drawing files.

**Standard Colors:** Colors 1–9 of the AutoCAD Color Index.

**system variable:** A named setting maintained by AutoCAD that controls an aspect of a drawing or the drawing environment. Most system variables can be changed by entering the variable name at the command line, although some variables are read-only and cannot be changed.

**tiled viewport:** Rectangular model space viewport. Model space viewports are referred to as "tiled" because multiple viewports in model space must abut each other with no overlap or space in between them to create a tile pattern.

**transparent command:** A command that can be used without interrupting the currently active command. Most display commands can be used transparently so that you can pan and zoom in a drawing while simultaneously using the drawing and editing commands. Transparent commands are run by entering an apostrophe (') before the command name.

**typeface:** The style or design of a font. Other unique properties include size, boldness (line thickness), and obliqueness (an angle applied to the characters, not to be confused with an italic font).

**underlay:** A CAD file that is not directly modifiable by AutoCAD but is still displayed within a drawing and updated when the source data is changed. AutoCAD currently supports the display of DWF and DGN files as underlays.

**unit block:** A block or symbol drawn within a $1 \times 1$ unit square that is inserted in the drawing with different $X$ and $Y$ scales to achieve different final sizes.

**User Coordinate System (UCS):** A user-defined variation of the World Coordinate system. Variations in the coordinate system range from moving the default drawing origin (0,0,0) to another location to changing orientations for the $X$, $Y$, and $Z$ axes. It is possible to rotate the WCS on any axis to create a UCS with a different two-dimensional $XY$ plane—a technique commonly used to create multiview 3D drawings.

**viewport:** A window in the paper space environment that shows the view of the model space environment.

**working set:** The group of objects selected for in-place editing using the **REFEDIT** command. Objects can be added to and removed from the working set using the Refedit toolbar during the in-place editing process.

**World Coordinate System (WCS):** The default coordinate system in AutoCAD upon which all objects and user coordinate systems are based.

**xref:** A drawing that is referenced by another drawing. The drawing references are updated when the source drawing is modified.

**zooming:** The process of moving around the drawing. Zooming in shows you a close-up view of a drawing area. Zooming out shows you a larger viewing area.

# Index